MW01196226

Psalms

BAKER COMMENTARY *on the* OLD TESTAMENT

WISDOM AND PSALMS

Tremper Longman III, EDITOR

Volumes now available

Psalms, vol. 1, *Psalms 1–41*, John Goldingay
Psalms, vol. 2, *Psalms 42–89*, John Goldingay
Proverbs, Tremper Longman III
Song of Songs, Richard S. Hess

Psalms

Volume 2
Psalms 42–89

John Goldingay

Baker Academic
Grand Rapids, Michigan

©2007 by John Goldingay

Published by Baker Academic
a division of Baker Publishing Group
P.O. Box 6287, Grand Rapids, MI 49516–6287
www.bakeracademic.com

Printed in the United States of America

Library of Congress Cataloging-in-Publication Data
Goldingay, John.
    Psalms / John Goldingay.
        p.   cm. — (Baker commentary on the Old Testament wisdom and Psalms)
        "The first of a three-volume commentary on the book of Psalms" —ECIP data
    view.
    Includes bibliographical references and indexes.
    ISBN 10: 0-8010-2703-9 (cloth : v. 1)
    ISBN 978-0-8010-2703-1 (cloth : v. 1)

    ISBN 10: 0-8010-2704-7 (cloth : v. 2)
    ISBN 978-0-8010-2704-8 (cloth : v. 2)
    1. Bible. O.T. Psalms—Commentaries. I. Title. II. Series.

BS1430.53.G65 2006
223′.2077—dc22   2006009724

Contents

Series Preface 7
Author's Preface *11*
Abbreviations *13*

Psalms 42–43: Coping with Separation from God's Presence *19*
Psalm 44: Coping with Defeat *35*
Psalm 45: The True King and True Queen *52*
Psalm 46: Trust and Stop *64*
Psalm 47: God Has Begun to Reign *74*
Psalm 48: God Made Known in the City of God *82*
Psalm 49: Can Death Be Escaped? *95*
Psalm 50: Worship and Life *108*
Psalm 51: Sin, Cleansing, Renewal *122*
Psalm 52: Divine and Human Commitment *141*
Psalm 53: Is God There? *149*
Psalm 54: The Name That Rescues *157*
Psalm 55: How to Throw Things at Yhwh *163*
Psalm 56: Fear of Humanity, Trust in God *181*
Psalm 57: Simultaneously Expecting and Possessing *191*
Psalm 58: The Gods Must and Will Fulfill Their Responsibility *201*
Psalm 59: How to Pray in Terror *211*
Psalm 60: How to Claim God's Past Word *224*
Psalm 61: How Prayer Suspends the Distantness *235*
Psalm 62: The Heart of Old Testament Theology *243*
Psalm 63: A Threefold Dynamic for Life *254*

Psalm 64: The Power of Language and the Power of Recollection *264*

Psalm 65: Politics and Harvest, Israel and the World *272*

Psalm 66: Praise and Thanksgiving, Community and Individual, Israel and the World *285*

Psalm 67: Blessed for the Sake of the World *298*

Psalm 68: God Then and Now *305*

Psalm 69: When People Mock Zeal for Yhwh's House *335*

Psalm 70: A Plea for Haste *357*

Psalm 71: The God of Past, Present, and Future *363*

Psalm 72: A Vision for Government *379*

Psalm 72:18–20: Coda to Book II *395*

Psalm 73: Yes, God Will Restore Me *397*

Psalm 74: What Is Permanent? *420*

Psalm 75: In Your Way and in Your Time *438*

Psalm 76: Revere or Fear *448*

Psalm 77: The Pain and the Hope of Recollection *458*

Psalm 78: The Story That Needs Passing On *474*

Psalm 79: When Nations Attack Us and Scorn God *517*

Psalm 80: Praying for Joseph *531*

Psalm 81: Do Listen! *545*

Psalm 82: God Must Accept Responsibility *558*

Psalm 83: Confrontation, Shame, Death, Acknowledgment *571*

Psalm 84: The Double Good Fortune of the Trusting Person *586*

Psalm 85: God Speaks of Shalom *603*

Psalm 86: A Servant's Claim on His Master *617*

Psalm 87: The Nations as Citizens of Zion *631*

Psalm 88: Abba, Father *642*

Psalm 89: Facing Two Sets of Facts (Again) *660*

Psalm 89:52: Coda to Book III *693*

Glossary *695*

Bibliography *708*

Subject Index *713*

Author Index *720*

Index of Scripture and Other Ancient Writings *727*

Series Preface

At the end of the book of Ecclesiastes, a wise father warns his son concerning the multiplication of books: "Furthermore, of these, my son, be warned. There is no end to the making of many books!" (12:12). The Targum to this biblical book characteristically expands the thought and takes it in a different, even contradictory, direction: "My son, take care to make many books of wisdom without end."

When applied to commentaries, both statements are true. The past twenty years have seen a significant increase in the number of commentaries available on each book of the Bible. On the other hand, for those interested in grappling seriously with the meaning of the text, such proliferation should be seen as a blessing rather than a curse. No single commentary can do it all. In the first place, commentaries reflect different theological and methodological perspectives. We can learn from others who have a different understanding of the origin and nature of the Bible, but we also want commentaries that share our fundamental beliefs about the biblical text. Second, commentaries are written with different audiences in mind. Some are addressed primarily to laypeople, others to clergy, and still others to fellow scholars. A third consideration, related to the previous two, is the subdisciplines the commentator chooses to draw from to shed light on the biblical text. The possibilities are numerous, including philology, textual criticism, genre/form criticism, redaction criticism, ancient Near Eastern background, literary conventions, and more. Finally, commentaries differ in how extensively they interact with secondary literature, that is, with what others have said about a given passage.

The Baker Commentary on the Old Testament Wisdom and Psalms has a definite audience in mind. We believe the primary users of commentaries are scholars, ministers, seminary students, and Bible study leaders. Of these groups, we have most in mind clergy and future clergy, namely, seminary students. We have tried to make the commentary accessible to nonscholars by putting most of the technical discussion and interaction with secondary literature in the footnotes. We do not mean to suggest that such information is unimportant. We simply concede that, given the present state of the church, it is the rare layperson who will read such technical material with interest and profit. We hope we are wrong in this assessment, and if we are not, that the future will see a reverse in this trend. A healthy church is a church that nourishes itself with constant attention to God's words in Scripture, in all their glorious detail.

Since not all commentaries are alike, what are the features that characterize this series? The message of the biblical book is the primary focus of each commentary, and the commentators have labored to expose God's message for his people in the book they discuss. This series also distinguishes itself by restricting its coverage to one major portion of the Hebrew Scriptures, namely, the Psalms and Wisdom books (Proverbs, Job, Ecclesiastes, and Song of Songs). These biblical books provide a distinctive contribution to the canon. Although we can no longer claim that they are neglected, their unique content makes them harder to fit into the development of redemptive history and requires more effort to hear their distinctive message.

The book of Psalms is the literary sanctuary. Like the physical sanctuary structures of the Old Testament, it offers a textual holy place where humans share their joys and struggles with brutal honesty in God's presence. The book of Proverbs describes wisdom, which on one level is skill for living, the ability to navigate life's actual and potential pitfalls; but on another level, this wisdom presents a pervasive and deeply theological message: "The fear of the LORD is the beginning of knowledge" (Prov. 1:7). Proverbs also raises a disturbing issue: the sages often motivate wise behavior by linking it to reward, but in reality, bad things happen to good people, and the wise are not always rewarded as they expect. This raises the question of the justice of God. Both Job and Ecclesiastes struggle with the apparent disconnect between God's justice and our actual life experience. Finally, the Song of Songs is a passionate, sensuous love poem that reminds us that God is interested in more than just our brains and our spirits; he wants us to enjoy our bodies. It reminds us that we are not merely souls encased in bodies but whole persons made in God's image.

Limiting the series to the Psalms and Wisdom books has allowed us to tailor our work to the distinctive nature of this portion of the canon. With some few exceptions in Job and Ecclesiastes, for instance, the material in these biblical books is poetic and highly literary, and so the commentators have highlighted the significant poetic conventions employed in each book. After an introduction discussing important issues that affect the interpretation of the book (title, authorship, date, language, style, text, ancient Near Eastern background, genre, canonicity, theological message, connection to the New Testament, and structure), each commentary proceeds section by section through the biblical text. The authors provide their own translation, with explanatory notes when necessary, followed by a substantial interpretive section (titled "Interpretation") and concluding with a section titled "Theological Implications." In the interpretation section, the emphasis is on the meaning of the text in its original historical setting. In the theological implications section, connections with other parts of the canon, both Old and New Testaments, are sketched out along with the continuing relevance of each passage for us today. The latter section is motivated by the recognition that, while it is important to understand the individual contribution and emphasis of each book, these books now find their place in a larger collection of writings, the canon as a whole, and it is within this broader context that the books must ultimately be interpreted.

No two commentators in this series see things in exactly the same way, though we all share similar convictions about the Bible as God's Word and the belief that it must be appreciated not only as ancient literature but also as God's Word for today. It is our hope and prayer that these volumes will inform readers and, more importantly, stimulate reflection on and passion for these valuable books.

It has long been observed that the book of Psalms is a "microcosm" of the message of the Old Testament. Athanasius, the fourth-century theologian, called the Psalms "an epitome of the whole Scriptures." Basil, bishop of Caesarea in the same time period, regarded the Psalms as a "compendium of all theology." Martin Luther said the book is "a little Bible, and the summary of the Old Testament." The book of Psalms is theologically rich, so the readers of this commentary are privileged to be guided by John Goldingay, one of the foremost experts on biblical theology today. Our prayer is that as you read the Psalms with this commentary, you will grow in your knowledge of the God who reveals himself through the prayers of his ancient people.

Tremper Longman III
Robert H. Gundry Professor of Biblical Studies
Westmont College

Author's Preface

The Psalter is divided into five books, presumably by analogy with the Torah. That division of the Torah is somewhat artificial (notably, between Exodus and Leviticus), and the division of the Psalter is much more so. So the fact that this volume covers books II and III and thus Psalms 42–89 is convenient, but a little arbitrary.

Admittedly to make that statement is to take a position on a topic of interest in current study. For most of the twentieth century, scholarship on the Psalms focused its attention on individual psalms and largely ignored their position within this larger whole. Then, in the pendulum fashion of scholarship, near the end of that century the structure of the Psalter as a whole became a topic of interest. Indeed, the cutting edge of scholarship came to be the question of the arrangement of the psalms and the way sequences of psalms belong together and expound a theological view of their own.[1] The reader of this commentary should be aware that I am not enamored of this study. It seems to me to involve too much imagination in the connecting of too few dots. I recognize that there are often links between adjacent psalms, but I remain of the view that the main focus of psalm study needs to be the individual psalm.

An opposite subject of study is the redactional history of individual psalms. I also find this speculative, and I prefer to focus on the psalms as we have them. For these two forms of study, the reader will have to look elsewhere.

I noted in the preface to volume 1 that my starting point for the commentary is the Masoretic Text as it appears in the Leningrad Codex copied by Samuel ben Jacob in the eleventh century and published in

---

1. See, e.g., Flint and Miller, eds., *Book of Psalms*, part 3; Hossfeld and Zenger, *Psalms 2*; McCann, "Psalms"; McCann, ed., *Shape and Shaping*.

NJPS and *BHS*. I have assumed that this is a broadly reliable guide to a textual tradition going back into the pre-Christian period. In the translation, I have also included some alternative renderings based on the LXX or other ancient versions where these seem to reflect different Hebrew traditions (though I have assumed that much versional variation over matters such as suffixes cannot be assumed to indicate a different Hebrew tradition). I have assumed that variants in post-MT Hebrew MSS constitute post-MT errors or "corrections" rather than preservations of pre-MT readings, but I have occasionally referred to such variants on that understanding. I have noted some modern proposals for emending the text, though I rarely followed them, and I have also rarely followed modern proposals for understanding Hebrew words in light of Arabic or Ugaritic.

In translating the Psalms, I have often let the Hebrew's gendered language stand where, for instance, using a gender-inclusive plural would obscure the dynamic of the poetry, and in other respects I have aimed at a translation that sticks closely to the dynamics of the Hebrew, even if this sometimes means it is not as elegant as a translation for reading in church. All Bible translations are my own except where otherwise noted. References are to the versification in English Bibles; where the printed Hebrew Bible differs, its references follow in square brackets (e.g., "Ps 51:1 [3]"), except that I omit these in the case of cross references to other verses within the psalm I am commentating on. References to parts of verses such as "v. 1a" and "v. 1b" generally denote the verses as subdivided by MT, but where verses comprise more than two cola (or where I differ from MT in understanding verse divisions), I have often used references that correspond to the subdivisions in my translation. Thus, I have referred, for instance, to "v. 1c" and "v. 1d" rather than to "v. 1bα" and "v. 1bβ" and have used Greek letters only to mark subdivisions within a colon.

The introduction to the commentary appears in the first volume. I here repeat only the abbreviations, glossary, and bibliography in forms adapted to the contents of this volume. I particularly draw the reader's attention to the glossary, which comments on important words asterisked in the body of the book.

I am grateful to Micah Haney for checking biblical references and spotting other slips and to Federico Roth and Daryl Jump for their work on the indices.

Abbreviations

Bibliographic and General

*	indicates that the word appears in the glossary
abs.	absolute
acc.	accusative
adj.	adjective, adjectival
Akk.	Akkadian
ANET	James B. Pritchard, ed., *Ancient Near Eastern Texts Relating to the Old Testament*, 3rd ed. (Princeton: Princeton University Press, 1969)
Aq	Aquila's translation of the Psalms, as printed in Fridericus Field, *Origenis Hexaplorum quae supersunt*, vol. 2 (Oxford: Oxford University Press, 1874; repr., Hildesheim: Olms, 1964)
AUSS	*Andrews University Seminary Studies*
BASOR	*Bulletin of the American Schools of Oriental Research*
b.	Babylonian Talmud
BBR	*Bulletin for Biblical Research*
BCP	*The Book of Common Prayer . . . Together with the Psalter or Psalms of David* [repr. from the Great Bible of 1539] (repr., London: Collins, n.d.)
BDB	Francis Brown, S. R. Driver, and Charles A. Briggs, *A Hebrew and English Lexicon of the Old Testament* (repr., London: Oxford University Press, 1962)
BETL	Bibliotheca ephemeridum theologicarum lovaniensium
BHS	H. Bardtke, *Liber Psalmorum*, Biblical Hebraica Stuttgartensia 21 (Stuttgart: Würtembergische Bibelanstalt, 1969)
Bib	*Biblica*
BibInt	*Biblical Interpretation*
BN	*Biblische Notizen*
BSac	*Bibliotheca sacra*

BT	*The Bible Translator*
BZ	*Biblische Zeitschrift*
BZAW	Beihefte zur Zeitschrift für die alttestamentliche Wissenschaft
C	The Cairo MS of MT, as reported in *BHS*
CBQ	*Catholic Biblical Quarterly*
CBQMS	Catholic Biblical Quarterly Monograph Series
const.	construct
CP	James Barr, *Comparative Philology and the Text of the Old Testament* (Oxford: Oxford University Press, 1968)
CTJ	*Calvin Theological Journal*
DCH	D. J. A. Clines, ed., *The Dictionary of Classical Hebrew* (Sheffield: Sheffield Academic Press, 1993–)
DG	J. C. L. Gibson, *Davidson's Introductory Hebrew Grammar: Syntax*, 4th ed. (Edinburgh: T&T Clark, 1994)
dittog.	dittography
DTT	Marcus Jastrow, *A Dictionary of the Targumim, the Talmud Babli and Yerushalmi, and the Midrashic Literature* (New York: Choreb, 1926)
esp.	especially
EstBib	*Estudios b blicos*
et al.	and other(s)
ETL	*Ephemerides theologicae lovanienses*
ETR	*Etudes théologiques et religieuses*
EvT	*Evangelische Theologie*
EVV	(many) English versions
ExpT	*Expository Times*
f.	feminine
GKC	*Gesenius' Hebrew Grammar*, ed. and enlarged by E. Kautzsch, English translation by A. E. Cowley, 2nd ed. (Oxford: Oxford University Press, 1910; repr. with corrections, 1966)
HALOT	Ludwig Koehler, Walter Baumgartner, et al., *The Hebrew and Aramaic Lexicon of the Old Testament*, 2 vols. (Leiden: Brill, 2001)
hapax/es	hapax legomenon/a
HAR	*Hebrew Annual Review*
HBT	*Horizons in Biblical Theology*
HSM	Harvard Semitic Monographs
HTR	*Harvard Theological Review*
HUCA	*Hebrew Union College Annual*
IBHS	Bruce K. Waltke and Michael O'Connor, *An Introduction to Biblical Hebrew Syntax* (Winona Lake, IN: Eisenbrauns, 1990)
impv.	imperative
inf.	infinitive
Int	*Interpretation*
JANESCU	*Journal of the Ancient Near Eastern Society of Columbia University*

JBL	*Journal of Biblical Literature*
Jerome	Jerome's Latin translation of the Psalms as printed in *Biblia sacra iuxta vulgatam versionem*, 3rd ed. (Stuttgart: Deutsche Bibelgesellschaft, 1983)
JETS	*Journal of the Evangelical Theological Society*
JM	Paul Joüon, *A Grammar of Biblical Hebrew*, trans. and rev. T. Muraoka, 2 vols. (Rome: Pontifical Biblical Institute, 1991)
JNES	*Journal of Near Eastern Studies*
JNSL	*Journal of Northwest Semitic Languages*
JQR	*Jewish Quarterly Review*
JSOT	*Journal for the Study of the Old Testament*
JSOTSup	Journal for the Study of the Old Testament: Supplement Series
JSS	*Journal of Semitic Studies*
JTS	*Journal of Theological Studies*
K	Kethib, the written (consonantal) Hebrew text; contrast Q
KJV	King James Version (Authorized Version)
L	Leningrad manuscript of MT, as printed in *BHS*
lit.	literally (translated)
LXX	Septuagint translation of the Psalms, as printed in Alfred Rahlfs, ed., *Psalmi cum Odis* (repr., Göttingen: Vandenhoeck & Ruprecht, 1979)
m.	masculine
mg	margin
MS(S)	manuscript(s)
MT	Masoretic Text, as printed in *BHS*
n.d.	no date
NEB	*The New English Bible with the Apocrypha* (Oxford: Oxford University Press; Cambridge: Cambridge University Press, 1970)
NIDOTTE	Willem A. VanGemeren, ed., *New International Dictionary of Old Testament Theology and Exegesis*, 5 vols. (Grand Rapids: Zondervan, 1996; Carlisle, UK: Paternoster, 1997)
NIVI	*The Holy Bible: New International Version: Inclusive Language Edition* (London: Hodder & Stoughton, 1996)
NJPS	*JPS Hebrew-English Tanakh*, 2nd ed. (Philadelphia: Jewish Publication Society, 1999)
NovT	*Novum Testamentum*
NPNF[2]	*Nicene and Post-Nicene Fathers*, Series 2
NRSV	*The Holy Bible: New Revised Standard Version* (New York: Oxford University Press, 1989)
n.s.	new series
NT	New Testament
NTS	*New Testament Studies*
obj.	object
OBO	Orbis biblicus et orientalis
OT	Old Testament

OtSt	*Oudtestamentische Studiën*
PBH	Postbiblical Hebrew
pl.	plural
prep.	preposition
ptc.	participle
Q	Qere, the Hebrew text as read out (i.e., with the vowels); contrast K
RB	*Revue biblique*
repr.	reprinted
ResQ	*Restoration Quarterly*
RevExp	*Review and Expositor*
RevQ	*Revue de Qumran*
RHPR	*Revue d'histoire et de philosophie religieuses*
SBLDS	Society of Biblical Literature Dissertation Series
SEÅ	*Svensk exegetisk årsbok*
sg.	singular
subj.	subject
SJOT	*Scandinavian Journal of the Old Testament*
Sym	Symmachus's translation of the Psalms, as printed in Fridericus Field, *Origenis Hexaplorum quae supersunt*, vol. 2 (Oxford: Oxford University Press, 1874; repr., Hildesheim: Olms, 1964)
Syr	Syriac translation of the Psalms, as printed in *The Old Testament in Syriac according to the Peshiṭta Version*, part 2.3 (Leiden: Brill, 1980)
TDOT	G. Johannes Botterweck et al., eds., *Theological Dictionary of the Old Testament* (Grand Rapids: Eerdmans, 1974–)
Tg	The Targum to the Psalms, as printed in *Miqrā'ôt Gĕdôlôt*, vol. 10 (repr., New York: Pardes, 1951)
Th	Theodotion's translation of the Psalms, as printed in Fridericus Field, *Origenis Hexaplorum quae supersunt*, vol. 2 (Oxford: Oxford University Press, 1874; repr., Hildesheim: Olms, 1964)
ThTo	*Theology Today*
TLOT	Ernst Jenni and Claus Westermann, eds., *Theological Lexicon of the Old Testament*, 3 vols. (Peabody, MA: Hendrickson, 1997)
TNIV	*The Holy Bible: Today's New International Version* (Colorado Springs: International Bible Society, 2005)
TLZ	*Theologische Literaturzeitung*
TTH	S. R. Driver, *A Treatise on the Use of the Tenses in Hebrew and Some Other Syntactical Questions*, 3rd ed. (London: Oxford University Press, 1892)
TZ	*Theologische Zeitschrift*
UF	*Ugarit-Forschungen*
v./vv.	verse/s

Vg	The Vulgate Latin translation of the Psalms, as printed in *Biblia sacra iuxta vulgatam versionem*, 3rd ed. (Stuttgart: Deutsche Bibelgesellschaft, 1983)
Vrs	The ancient versions (LXX, Aq, Sym, Th, Vg, Jerome, Syr, Tg) or most of them
VT	*Vetus Testamentum*
VTSup	Vetus Testamentum Supplements
WBC	Word Biblical Commentary
WMANT	Wissenschaftliche Monographien zum Alten und Neuen Testament
WTJ	*Westminster Theological Journal*
ZAW	*Zeitschrift für die alttestamentliche Wissenschaft*
ZKT	*Zeitschrift für katholische Theologie*

Old Testament

Gen.	Genesis		Song	Song of Songs
Exod.	Exodus		Isa.	Isaiah
Lev.	Leviticus		Jer.	Jeremiah
Num.	Numbers		Lam.	Lamentations
Deut.	Deuteronomy		Ezek.	Ezekiel
Josh.	Joshua		Dan.	Daniel
Judg.	Judges		Hosea	Hosea
Ruth	Ruth		Joel	Joel
1–2 Sam.	1–2 Samuel		Amos	Amos
1–2 Kings	1–2 Kings		Obad.	Obadiah
1–2 Chron.	1–2 Chronicles		Jon.	Jonah
Ezra	Ezra		Mic.	Micah
Neh.	Nehemiah		Nah.	Nahum
Esther	Esther		Hab.	Habakkuk
Job	Job		Zeph.	Zephaniah
Ps(s).	Psalms		Hag.	Haggai
Prov.	Proverbs		Zech.	Zechariah
Eccles.	Ecclesiastes		Mal.	Malachi

New Testament

Matt.	Matthew		1–2 Cor.	1–2 Corinthians
Mark	Mark		Gal.	Galatians
Luke	Luke		Eph.	Ephesians
John	John		Phil.	Philippians
Acts	Acts		Col.	Colossians
Rom.	Romans		1–2 Thess.	1–2 Thessalonians

1–2 Tim.	1–2 Timothy		1–2 Pet.	1–2 Peter
Titus	Titus		1–3 John	1–3 John
Philem.	Philemon		Jude	Jude
Heb.	Hebrews		Rev.	Revelation
James	James			

Psalms 42–43

Coping with Separation from God's Presence

Translation

The leader's. Instruction. The Korahites'.

42:1 Like a deer[1] that strains
  toward streams of water,
So my whole person strains for you
  with all my longing, God.
2My whole person thirsts for God,
  for the living God;
When shall I come
  and see the face of God? [Tg]/appear before God? [MT]
3My tears have been my food
  day and night,
While people say to me all day,
  "Where is your God?"
4Of these things I shall be mindful
  as I shall pour out my feelings,

---

1. *'Ayyāl* usually refers to a male, but the verb is f. Fortunately, English "deer" likewise strictly refers to a male but can loosely apply to either gender. JM 174d reckons that *k* here has the force of *ka'ăšer*; the translation would then be "as a deer strains."

That I shall pass into the shelter;[2]
  I shall lead them in procession to God's house, [MT]
  [or, That I shall proceed into the shelter of the majestic one,
    to God's house, (cf. LXX)]
With the sound of thanksgiving resounding,[3]
  a tumult keeping festival.
[5]Why are you cast down, my soul,
  and tumultuous within me?
Wait for God, because I will yet confess him
  for the deliverance that comes from his face.[4]

[6]God, my soul is downcast within me;
  therefore I am mindful of you,
From the land of Jordan and the Hermons,
  from Little Mount.
[7]Deep is calling to deep
  at the sound of your waterfalls;[5]
All your breakers and your waves
  have passed over me.
[8]By day Yhwh will command his commitment,
  and by night his song will be with me.
A plea to my living God:
  [9]I will say to my craglike God,
Why have you put me out of mind,
  why do I go about dark?
Because of the oppression by the enemy,
  [10]because of the slaughter in my bones,
My foes have reproached me
  as they say to me all day,
  "Where is your God?"
[11]Why are you cast down, my soul,
  And why are you tumultuous within me?
Wait for God, because I will yet confess him,
  the deliverance of my face, my God.

2. *Sak* comes only here. BDB takes it to mean a throng (an interwoven mass), but LXX and Jerome more plausibly take it as a variant for *sukkâ* referring to Yhwh's shelter or tent. Ibn Ezra interprets in light of *mûsak* in 2 Kings 16:18, another hapax legomenon, which may mean "walkway" (cf. Barthélemy, *Psaumes*, 247–52).

3. Lit. "with the sound of resounding and thanksgiving," a hendiadys.

4. *Yĕšû'ôt* is pl. of abstraction (JM 136g; *IBHS* 7.4.2a). LXX, Syr assimilate the colon to 42:11; 43:5. Jerome follows MT.

5. So the ancient versions translate *ṣinnôr*, which is compatible with later usage (see *HALOT*). The only other OT instance is the difficult 2 Sam. 5:8, which might rather point to the meaning "spouts," the reference then being to the sources and conduits for Yhwh's resources of water in the heavens (cf. BDB). The general meaning of the line would not be affected.

43:1Contend for me, God,
 determine my case.
From a nation that does not keep commitment,
 from someone deceitful and wicked, rescue me.
2For you are the God who is my stronghold;
 why have you spurned me?
Why do I go about dark,
 because of the oppression of the enemy?
3Send your light and your truthfulness;
 they themselves can lead me,
They can bring me to your holy mountain,
 to your dwelling,
4So that I can come to God's altar,
 to the God of my joyful rejoicing,
And I will confess you with the lyre,
 God my God.
5Why are you cast down, my soul,
 and tumultuous within me?
Wait for God, because I will yet confess him,
 the deliverance of my face, my God.

Interpretation

Psalm 42 comprises two stanzas with similar refrains. Psalm 43 is a further similar unit with the same refrain as appears at 42:11; 43:2 also takes up words from 42:9. Psalm 43 has no heading, unlike Pss. 34–42 and 44–70 (though LXX provides a heading corresponding to the familiar "Composition. David's"). Either a single psalm has been divided into two, perhaps to facilitate liturgical use as happened to Pss. 9–10, or Ps. 43 was composed to accompany Ps. 42.

Psalms 42–43 together manifest a balance between lament, plea, and looking to the future such as often appears in prayer psalms. They speak for someone who longs to get to the temple but cannot do so. We do not know the reason. This might be illness or the conflict the psalms refer to, or simply the fact of living too far away; most Israelites would be unable to visit the temple at will. The psalm has often been read as a kind of journal of a spiritual struggle, with the suppliant striving to find faith (see the refrain) but finding it hard to do so, yet gradually working toward plea and hope.[6] But the prayer's careful composition in three stanzas (with the standard features of a prayer psalm such as lament, plea, and a looking to the future) suggests that this is an oversimplification. Like other psalms, the prayer reflects real struggles and longings, but it has taken these as the

6. E.g., Weiser, *Psalms*, 346–52.

21

raw material for a prayer composition that we can imagine being used by an ordinary individual, by a leader, or by the congregation. The rhythm is predominantly one that has only two stresses in the second colon of each line (often 3-2), the rhythm characteristic of more pensive prayers.

Psalms 42–43 include twelve occurrences of "God," unqualified by pronouns or other qualifiers. In Pss. 1–41 one would often have found the name "Yhwh" rather than "God"; in Pss. 42–43 "Yhwh" comes only once. This general preference for "God" rather than the name Yhwh continues through Pss. 42–83. This may be an instance of the varied inclination to avoid using the name Yhwh that developed as centuries passed, perhaps to avoid giving too esoteric or parochial an impression of the God whom the Israelites worshipped, perhaps to safeguard against casual use of the name.[7] One can see that in some instances parallelism between "Yhwh" and some variant on "God" such as "the living God" or "my God" would have worked (e.g., 42:2a, 11; 43:4b, 5). Perhaps these "Elohistic psalms" have been revised to remove most of the occurrences of Yhwh, or perhaps this was simply the preferred usage in some circles (for instance, in northern Israel). See further on Ps. 53.

The leader's. Instruction. The Korahites'.

Heading. See glossary.

42:1–5. The first stanza expresses a longing to come to God (vv. 1–2), articulates the grief of being cut off from God (v. 3), recalls the joy of having access to God (v. 4), and urges the self to live in expectation of deliverance (v. 5). It opens by addressing God (v. 1), moves to reflection (vv. 2–4), and ends in argument (v. 5).

> [42:1]Like a deer that strains
> toward streams of water,
> So my whole person strains for you
> with all my longing, God.

Thus the psalm begins with four lines expressing that longing. All four are more or less parallel, though each goes beyond the previous one. Thus v. 1a sets out a simile and v. 1b interprets it, v. 2a repeats v. 1b with some nuancing, and v. 2b sharpens the point with a rhetorical question. Conversely, there is no parallelism within the lines, except in v. 2a. The simile in v. 1a would be easy to identify with. Human beings, too, knew what it was like to be without water and to long to find a stream (with little possibility of doing so in the summer, when few streams still flow) or to come

---

7. For a discussion see Laura Joffe, "The Elohistic Psalter," *SJOT* 15 (2001): 142–66.

to a canyon where one might expect to find a stream and to discover it dry. The verb occurs only here and in Joel 1:20, in a similar connection; the meaning of cognates suggests it means inclining the head in a direction.[8] The second line's talk of my *person straining for you emphasizes the way the whole being, body and spirit, is straining with intensity.

> [2]My whole person thirsts for God,
>   for the living God;
> When shall I come
>   and see the face of God? [Tg]/appear before God? [MT]

The third line begins with another occurrence of *nepeš*. Here it is more significant that *nepeš* can refer specifically to desire and longing. The line restates the simile/metaphor in more everyday terms by speaking in terms of thirst and then nuances the description of God, who is "the living God." In the context we might wonder whether to make a link with the life-giving nature of water and the death-threatening nature of the suppliant's position, and one might even think of translating the expression more literally as "the God of life." But there are no such implications when the expression recurs in 84:2 [3]; what that psalm has in common with this is an orientation toward seeking to get to the temple. More likely, then, the title "the living God" is one that belongs to the temple as a source of life, and this is the first indication of such an orientation to getting to the temple. That point is then made a little more explicit in the parallel line, v. 2b. The suppliant wants to appear before God (so MT), indeed wants to see God's face (more likely the original pointing; cf. Tg).[9] In either case, the temple is where that happened. A religion that uses images could speak more literally of "seeing God"; in the religious practice that the OT approves, there were no images of God, and thus "seeing" God is a more metaphorical idea for having a sense of being in God's presence, though it also implies that seeing God's *face means having prayers answered. Evidently the suppliant cannot go to the temple to have recourse to God in the place where God had promised always to be available, though we do not know why, at least not yet.

> [3]My tears have been my food
>   day and night,

8. Cf. BDB.

9. There is no word for "before." This parallels other passages where the Hebrew reads in an odd way and seems to have been repointed to avoid the idea of seeing God, which could be misunderstood (e.g., Deut. 31:11; Isa. 1:12). So an original qal *wě'er'eh* has been repointed to niphal *wě'ērā'eh*. See discussion in Carmel McCarthy, *The Tiqqune Sopherim* (OBO 36; Göttingen: Vandenhoeck & Ruprecht, 1981), 197–202.

> While people say to me all day,
> "Where is your God?"

Two further linked lines follow. They manifest no mutual or internal parallelism, though in general terms they continue the parallelism that ran through vv. 1–2. The tears give a more literal suggestion of the depth of the suppliant's longing, albeit as a hyperbole,[10] while "day and night" underlines that. Instead of eating, all the suppliant does is cry. And the taunting questions of other people externalize the question that presses itself in the suppliant's own mind. The comment on God's location has different implications from those in vv. 1–2. By the end of v. 2 it seemed clear where God is. God is in the temple, and the problem is that the suppliant cannot get there. There was no problem about God's location; the problem lay in the suppliant's location. Here the matter is differently conceived. While God was committed to being in the temple and could always be met there, this did not mean God was confined to the temple. God could act anywhere, and did come to meet people's needs anywhere. So why was God not reaching out to wherever the suppliant was? The people who ask the question may or may not be Israelites, but either way they probably have a theory about that. It might be that God is not capable of doing so; the implication may then be that God is incurring discredit through failing to act on the suppliant's behalf. Or it might be that God has abandoned the suppliant. The foes may infer that there is good reason for God's doing so and that they may then appropriately attack the suppliant themselves, knowing they are on God's side. Although formally the suppliant is involved in reflection and is not addressing God, the suppliant knows that God will overhear this reflection, and it is meant for God's ears.

> ⁴Of these things I shall be mindful
>   as I shall pour out my feelings,
> That I shall pass into the shelter;
>   I shall lead them in procession to God's house, [MT]
> [or, That I shall proceed into the shelter of the majestic one,
>   to God's house, (cf. LXX)]
> With the sound of thanksgiving resounding,
>   a tumult keeping festival.

The suppliant returns to looking to the future and expresses a determination to be *mindful of the experience to come; the verbs in v. 4a–b are cohortative. Being so mindful is an integral aspect of pouring out

10. Watson (*Classical Hebrew Poetry*, 266) notes it is known in Akkadian and Ugaritic.

one's *nepeš* (*person). Literally, "I pour out my *nepeš* on myself": this outpouring is not something that happens inside the person but something externalized. It is as if the feelings overwhelm the person. The suppliant "went to pieces,"[11] but the person deliberately lets that happen. This verb, too, is cohortative.

Verse 4c–d identifies more explicitly what "these things" are. The EVV take the yiqtol verbs to refer to the past, but LXX more plausibly assumes that they have their more usual future reference. In keeping with the longings of vv. 1–2, the suppliant is looking forward to joining in the festal procession in the temple, God's shelter or tent (cf. 27:5–6); perhaps using the former term (*sak*) makes a link with the Feast of Sukkot. For the first time in the psalm, the second colon then seriously takes the first colon further, at least in the form suggested by MT's consonants, which speak of leading people in a slow and deliberate movement.[12] The suppliant is then not an ordinary worshipper but a worship leader.

Verse 4e–f adds anticipation of the noisy enthusiasm of such events, with the gratefulness to God this noise expresses. The second colon follows on from the first with a reference to the tumultuous, noisy crowd (*hāmôn*, from *hāmâ*) and with its talk of this crowd keeping festival (*ḥāgag*). That word comes to mean making merry or reeling about (1 Sam. 30:16; Ps. 107:27), which gives one the flavor of a festal celebration. Such is the celebratory worship that the suppliant looks forward to.

> [5]Why are you cast down, my soul,
>   and tumultuous within me?
> Wait for God, because I will yet confess him
>   for the deliverance that comes from his face.

The first stanza closes with the refrain that will recur in slightly varying forms. The first line is neatly parallel.[13] The first verb usually refers to a physical bowing down, a literal humbling or a self-lowering in connection with mourning (35:14; 38:6 [7]). The second is the verb from which the noun "tumult" comes. It thus suggests the contrast between the suppliant's former and present circumstances. Both involve turmoil,

---

11. Theodore, *Psalms 1–81*, 524–25, following Sym.

12. MT *'eddaddēm* from *dādâ* combines the consonants of hitpael *'eddaddeh*, "I used to go slowly" (Isa. 38:15, though it makes poor sense there) and the vowels of piel *'ădaddēm*, with 3rd pl. suffix, "I used to lead people slowly." The LXX's *thaumastēs* suggests that it reads *'addîr*, which implies "I would proceed to the majestic tent [or "to the tent of the majestic one"], to the house of God"—which gives good parallelism.

13. Three expressions apply to both cola, the "why" at the beginning, the invocation "my soul" [*nepeš* again; *person] at the center, and at the end "within me" (lit. "upon me"—see v. 4b). The intervening second and fourth words are parallel second-person f. yiqtol verbs.

but an unhappy inner turmoil has replaced the celebratory communal turmoiling crowd that the suppliant once led. That is reality; yet the line begins "Why?" The psalm began by addressing God, but it has apparently been addressing the self through vv. 2–4, and here it continues to do that but also begins to argue with the self. Yet the fact that the psalm began by addressing God and will be doing so again in v. 6 reminds us that this account of an internal conversation, like vv. 2–4, is also formulated for God to hear. It thus forms a variant on the statement of faith and hope that often comes in a prayer psalm and a variant form of the declaration of intent to come to *confess God for the answer to one's prayer. Further, it thus forms part of the motivation for God to answer the prayer. It says to God, "Do you see how I am battling with this experience?"

More commonly such a *Why? question in a prayer would address God, and it might receive an answer. This might take the form of a rebuke, or the form of a promise that God is acting. Here the dynamics are simultaneously similar but quite different. It is not God who encourages the suppliant to hope nor some priestly or prophetic servant of God. The suppliant has to accept responsibility for his or her own encouraging. The content of the argument is similar to what might appear in a word from God. God's *face will turn to the suppliant, God will act in *deliverance, there is reason to *wait for God, the suppliant will be able to return to make *confession of that. These motifs come not in a word from God to which the suppliant responds, but in words that the suppliant addresses to the self, which does not respond.

Jesus takes up the words of vv. 5–6 in Gethsemane (Mark 14:34; cf. John 12:27).[14]

42:6–11. The suppliant has not won the argument; the situation in vv. 6–11 is the same as that in vv. 1–5. Once again the psalm begins by addressing God (vv. 6–7), then moves to reflection (vv. 8–10), and finally comes back to argument (v. 11).

> [6]God, my soul is downcast within me;
>   therefore I am mindful of you,
> From the land of Jordan and the Hermons,
>   from Little Mount.

The turning to God in vv. 6–7 begins by expressing to God the terms of that argument in v. 5; each word in the first colon in v. 6a–b comes from there. But the suppliant now intends to take the argument fur-

---

14. More broadly, see Johannes Beutler, "Psalm 42/43 in Johannesevangelium," *NTS* 25 (1978): 33–57; Edwin D. Freed, "Psalm 42/43 in John's Gospel," *NTS* 29 (1983): 62–73; Joachim Schaper, *"Wie der Hirsch lechzt nach frischen Wasser"* (Neukirchen: Neukirchener Verlag, 2004), 92–103.

ther, and that by another act of *mindfulness (cf. v. 4), though the way this works out is a little paradoxical. Initially vv. 6c–7 offer another expression of pain that goes behind and beyond the one in vv. 1–2. We know that the suppliant is unable to go to the temple. In v. 6c–d that is apparently pictured as being as far away from there as it is possible to imagine while still being on the borders of the land, though the details are uncertain. "Hermons" is unusually plural, though that is intelligible as a way of referring to the several peaks of the mountain at Israel's far northeastern frontier. There the Jordan rises from the foothills of Mount Hermon, and "the land of Jordan" might thus also point to that area, but it might equally point to the Jordan River area more generally as Israel's natural eastern frontier. Little Mount is often transliterated as Mount Mizar, but such a mountain is otherwise unknown.[15] So we cannot be sure of the geographical references, but even if they were literal geographical notes for the psalm's author, for subsequent users of the psalm they are metaphors for being far away from Jerusalem.[16]

> [7]Deep is calling to deep
>   at the sound of your waterfalls;
> All your breakers and your waves
>   have passed over me.

A reference to Mount Hermon and the Jordan headwaters could link with the imagery in v. 7. The streams that come together to form the Jordan pass through several waterfalls and cascades of crashing waters where deep calls to deep, and breakers and waves pass over rocks and bathers. The "sound" of the worshipping crowd and the prospect of "passing" on into the temple is here replaced by the "sound" of the crashing waters that are "passing" over the suppliant.[17] The imagery of breakers and waves is independent of this particular geography (e.g., 88:7 [8]) and links more directly with the idea of death as a force that overwhelms and drowns us (e.g., 2 Sam. 22:5; Jon. 2:3 [4] uses the same phrase as here in connection with another geography). Here the point is that deathly forces are overwhelming the suppliant, but the crashing Jordan headwaters could provide an image for that. "The poet who desperately seeks water finds it, but it is not life-giving water—it is destructive. God *sends* water, overwhelming, destructive of life. God, who was to have been the life of

15. Midrash Tehillim takes the phrase to refer to Mount Zion (*Midrash on Psalms* 1:443), though this does not fit very well in the context.

16. Goulder (*Psalms of the Sons of Korah*, 23–37) argues that the suppliant is on the way to the festival at Dan that takes place near these waters; but the "from" is then odd.

17. Fokkelman, *Major Poems*, 2:155.

the psalmist, has become his death."[18] Indeed, this is the psalm's third watery image: the suppliant longs for refreshing water, weeps watery tears, and drowns in death's waters.[19] Among other peoples, the idea that such forces are overwhelming us would imply that Death in person has taken hold of us. The psalm's commitment to the fact that Yhwh is the only God means this cannot be so, or at least only metaphorically. The waves and breakers that overwhelm are Yhwh's. That is both a further distress and a comfort. There is no one else working against us who might frustrate Yhwh's purpose.

> [8a-b]By day Yhwh will command his commitment,
> and by night his song will be with me.

Verse 8a–b parallels v. 4 in indicating the content of the suppliant's mindfulness. I again follow LXX in translating the yiqtol verb with a future tense.[20] The idea of Yhwh's issuing a command or commission to *commitment anticipates the prayer in 43:3 and suggests that here, as there, this aspect of Yhwh is personalized as an agent whereby Yhwh acts in a committed way toward people. In a psalm with relatively little parallelism, v. 8a–b forms a neatly interwoven parallel line. Its point is not that daytime as opposed to night is the time when Yhwh will command commitment, and nighttime as opposed to day is the time when the suppliant will sing Yhwh's praise, but that day and night Yhwh will command commitment, and the suppliant will respond with that song. In its reference to future worship, the mindfulness thus overlaps in content as well as in form and place with v. 4.[21]

> [8c]A plea to my living God:
> [9a]I will say to my craglike God,

The MT verse division implicitly identifies "a *plea to my living God" as another way of describing that song, but the song will surely be a song of praise rather than a prayer. Thus under the influence of the verse division, some post-MT MSS have *těhillâ* (praise song) for *těpillâ*

18. Luis Alonso Schökel, "The Poetic Structure of Psalm 42–43," *JSOT* 1 (1976): 4–11 (see 7).

19. Cf. Schaefer, *Psalms*, 108.

20. NRSV and TNIV translate it as present, taking the line to indicate the suppliant's current experience, but in the context this makes for an implausible clash with the verses on either side. Jerome takes it to suggest past experience, which is a possible meaning of a yiqtol but a less usual one, and not suggested by the context—one expects some looking to the future in the stanza, as there is in each of the others.

21. Contrast H. H. Rowley ("The Structure of Psalm xlii–xliii," *Bib* 21 [1940]: 45–50), who argues that it must be taken as an affirmation in the present at the center of the psalm.

(plea). More likely v. 8c is actually the introduction to the prayer that follows in v. 9. The appeal to God as living God takes up that in v. 2 but personalizes it. Yhwh is "my living God." The prayer will appeal to the God known in the temple as the source of life and known thus to the suppliant in particular. This God surely must respond to the prayer that follows! Verse 9a then pairs with v. 8c and forms an introduction to the actual prayer. Like v. 8a–b it pairs a verbal clause with a noun clause, then parallels expressions that read literally "to the God of my life"[22] and "to the God of my crag."

> 9b–cWhy have you put me out of mind,
> why do I go about dark?

In turn the two Why? clauses that follow form a further parallel line.[23] The psalm has twice referred to being mindful of God and to the suppliant's past with God. This mindfulness contrasts with God's putting the suppliant out of mind (*ignore). *Why does God's present neglect so contrast with God's past ongoing commitment? It is as a consequence of this neglect that the suppliant goes about gloomy and/or in the garb of a mourner. So what is the reason for the action of God that caused it?

> 9dBecause of the oppression by the enemy,
> 10because of the slaughter in my bones,
> My foes have reproached me
> as they say to me all day,
> "Where is your God?"

The last phrase in v. 9 then parallels and pairs with the first phrase in v. 10. Each phrase begins with *b* followed by a segholate noun, "oppression" (*lāḥaṣ*, lit. "squeezing") then being exceeded by "slaughter." The *b* hardly indicates the *means* of the foes' reproachful reviling; one does not revile *by* oppressing and slaying. More likely it is the basis for the reviling.

We know from the first stanza that the suppliant had to face people's scornful questioning; it is repeated in the next line, a tricolon that closes off the lament before the transition to the repeated internal argument. It may be that these "foes" are different people from the "enemy"; part of the basis for their questioning will then be these attacks of a more

---

22. But this is not the phrase's actual meaning. The second noun modifies the first and the suffix applies to the whole phrase. Cf. *IBHS* 9.5.3b.

23. Both begin "Why?" then one has a second-person qatal, the other a first-person yiqtol, while the second builds on the first insofar as the obj. of the first verb is the subj. of the second.

violent kind from this other enemy. But this involves a prosaic reading of the words, and more likely the singular "enemy" and the plural "foes" are the same people. Either way, it is people's attacks that embody the crashing of the waters that v. 7 referred to (cf. Ps. 46).

> ¹¹Why are you cast down, my soul,
>   And why are you tumultuous within me?
> Wait for God, because I will yet confess him,
>   the deliverance of my face, my God.

The stanza ends by returning to the internal argument that closed off the first stanza. As is often the case with repetitions in Hebrew poetry, the refrain manifests variation and not pure identity. It thus resembles the immediately preceding repetition of the foes' words, which incorporated an extra suffix on "as they say." Here the second colon repeats the opening *Why? and the last colon keeps us alert with a quite different ending. In the first stanza, deliverance came from God's face. Here the last colon is an invocation identifying God as the one through whom deliverance comes to the suppliant's face. More literally, God just *is* that deliverance. And God is "my God." That picks up v. 8 and also confronts the repeated question about where "your God" is.

43:1–5. Psalm 42 reached no resolution, though that does not mean it was incomplete; Pss. 88 and 89 reach no resolution. Psalm 43 provides it with resolution in the sense that here the suppliant speaks with conviction as if having won the battle with the questioning inner person expressed in the refrain. Thus the psalm alternates two verses of plea (vv. 1, 3) with two verses of reasons, one based in the present (v. 2), one based in the future (v. 4). But the refrain then recurs (v. 5). Resolution in the form of deliverance has not yet come, but the suppliant can live with things better.

> ⁴³:¹Contend for me, God,
>   determine my case.
> From a nation that does not keep commitment,
>   from someone deceitful and wicked, rescue me.

There was no actual plea in Ps. 42 (despite vv. 8c–9c); here v. 1 launches straight into plea. But the plea concerns not the suppliant's longing to be able to get back to Jerusalem to see God, nor the scornful questions, nor God's own abandonment; instead, the plea concerns the enemy who makes that return both desirable and impossible, the one who reviles or provides the reason for the reviling and is the evidence of God's abandonment. Solve this problem, and all the others will be solved. The plea works with a legal framework, suggesting God seated in the court in the heavens; that is the nature of a "plea." We know from 42:9 that the suppliant feels in the right over against the "enemy."[24]

Further basis for that comes in the second line. It is a nation that does not keep *commitment; the parallel colon re-expresses it in terms of a man (the leader or the kind of person who belongs to this nation) of deceit and *wickedness. We could imagine a person such as a king leading an army against another people that had been committed to giving Israel support and alliance, presumably because there was a treaty between the two parties. Instead, this king is attacking Israel and seeking to kill its king in his capacity as commander in chief and figurehead (cf. 1 Kings 22:31; 2 Kings 23:29). Therefore, the king needs the kind of *rescue that someone such as Jehoshaphat experienced (1 Kings 22:30–33). The line thus comprises balancing *min* clauses, one referring to a people and one to an individual, and closes with the verb that applies to both cola.

> ²For you are the God who is my stronghold;
>   why have you spurned me?
> Why do I go about dark,
>   because of the oppression of the enemy?

The reasoning sums up the plaint of the first two stanzas, in cola that work abb'c. "God who is my stronghold" is literally "God of my *stronghold" and thus recalls "God of life," "God [of] my life," and "God [of] my crag" (42:2, 8, 9), particularly the last of these, though here "God" is 'ĕlōhîm, not 'ēl. "*Why have you spurned me?" recalls the charge in 42:9 but suggests that the suppliant is indeed someone bringing a plea before a court, yet finding the court unaccountably unwilling to recognize the justice of the case. "Why do I go about dark because of the oppression of the enemy?" repeats the remainder of 42:9 except that the verb is now hitpael, and the closing phrase links with that verb and not with what follows.

> ³Send your light and your truthfulness;
>   they themselves can lead me,
> They can bring me to your holy mountain,
>   to your dwelling,

The second verse of plea begins a return to the opening theme of Ps. 42.[25] First, the appeal to send out *light and *truthfulness recalls the

24. The opening line balances synonymous verbs, one accompanied by an invocation, the other by a cognate noun, with a first-person suffix on the verb in the first colon and on the noun in the second.

25. MT apparently takes v. 3 as one 4-3 line, but its length is similar to vv. 1, 2, and 4 and looks more like two lines.

recollection of God's former commanding of commitment (42:8) and also the frequent pairing of commitment and truthfulness (e.g., 25:10; 40:10–11 [11–12]). These two are further personalized qualities or acts of God, or are ethicized persons. The supplicant, that is, speaks of them the way one might ask for God to send a heavenly aide, one of the members of the court presupposed by the appeal in v. 1. But the aide is not merely someone who takes action on God's behalf but also someone who explicitly embodies God's own qualities, an inclination to shine brightly and warmly on people and an inclination to be truthful and steadfast. Indeed, the emissary thus brings God in person. The plea recalls the way Yhwh's aide in Genesis and elsewhere is hard to distinguish from Yhwh but is a way of speaking of the presence of Yhwh in person without (*per impossibile*) implying that Yhwh in all fullness is present. So the psalm asks for God truly to reach out to earth in the way Ps. 42:1 missed, but allows for God acting via these agents; that will do. "*They* [the pronoun *hēmmâ*] can lead me." While the middle two cola are parallel, so that the verse works abb'c like v. 2, the second line as a whole explains the destination of that leading. The verb simply restates its predecessor, and then two parallel phrases state that destination, taking up earlier references to appearing before God and proceeding to God's house (42:2, 4). "Dwelling" is an intensive plural, like "dwelling" and "altar" in 84:1–3 [2–4], suggesting "the special quality of this particular dwelling."[26]

> [4]So that I can come to God's altar,
> 　　to the God of my joyful rejoicing,
> And I will confess you with the lyre,
> 　　God my God.

Verse 4 makes the point even more explicit and concrete. The two lines are parallel, arranged aba'b'. The opening colon in each line speaks of the object of the journey to the temple. Coming to the altar need not imply that the supplicant is a person such as a priest; a king or an ordinary person bringing a sacrifice brings it to the altar for the priest to offer. In this case the psalm will be referring to a thank-offering for the deliverance that the plea looks for. The parallel opening colon in the second line confirms this with its reference to *confession or testimony, accompanied by the *lyre. The second colon in each line then offers a description of the God to whom the supplicant comes and who is the object of the testimony. The first of these descriptions, "God of my joyful rejoicing," again parallels descriptions in 42:8, 9; 43:2. Because God will have proved to be living God, my craglike God, my living God, and

26. Keel, *Symbolism*, 151.

God my stronghold (against present appearances but in accordance with the suppliant's faith), God can once again be God my joyful rejoicing. Likewise God can be "God, my God," "Yhwh my God."

> [5]Why are you cast down, my soul,
>   and tumultuous within me?
> Wait for God, because I will yet confess him,
>   the deliverance of my face, my God.

The refrain this time exactly repeats 42:11, but its being present at all surprises us. The plea of vv. 3–4 is just that, a plea. In the present the suppliant still has to argue with the self in order to maintain hope that the vision of the plea will be realized and to declare that argument in order to add to the pressure on God to act.

Theological Implications

When Christians speak of thirsting for God, they are inclined to refer to an essentially inward quest, a longing for an inner sense of meeting with God. Psalms 42–43 instruct us by inviting us to see contact with God as more bodily, spatial, and corporate than this understanding does. This prayer does not issue from a "dark night of the soul." God has not just "withdrawn his spiritual favors."[27] This is not to say that its darkness is not an inward matter. The prayer's own balance is symbolized by its repeated reference to the suppliant's *nepeš* (*person). The suppliant's *nepeš* strains for God and thirsts for God (42:1–2). It longs to be able to get to Jerusalem to have the satisfaction that comes from seeing God. The suppliant pours the *nepeš* out (42:4) but also asks it why it is downcast (42:5, 11; 43:5; cf. 43:1). The *nepeš* is the soul, but not a soul that can be divorced from the body. Soul and body are two aspects of the person. The soul longs for contact with God, but it knows that the whole person needs to get to the temple for that to become reality. Perhaps Israelites sometimes regretted David's initiative in asking Yhwh to let the temple be a dwelling place. Yhwh's agreement to that meant they could be sure of finding Yhwh at home there, but that was of more practical advantage to people who lived in Jerusalem than to people who lived in (say) the foothills of Mount Hermon or the Gileadites' side of the Jordan. The prayer lives with the gracious reality of Yhwh's response to David's own perhaps-unwise initiative. Thus having God's light and truthfulness come

---

27. Dahood, *Psalms*, 1:255. Robert C. Hill notes the way the Antiochene exegetes are more inclined to interpret the psalm in a liturgical context than a spiritual or mystical one ("Psalm 41 [42]," *Irish Theological Quarterly* 68 [2003]: 25–33).

out to meet the suppliant will not make it superfluous to go to the temple. It reminds Christians that there continue to be places where God has been especially manifest and active over the centuries. The premise of the movie *James' Journey to Jerusalem* was the decision of a Zulu village to send their prospective pastor on a pilgrimage to Jerusalem to prepare him for his ministry. This may have been as logical as sending him to seminary. Yet the suppliant's mindfulness and expectancy concern not a "dead" place but one where the suppliant used to know God keeping commitment, where the suppliant thus used to pray and praise. It concerns a place where the suppliant used to join with the people of God in riotous worship and where the suppliant will once again stand before such people and offer thanksgiving and testimony.

The prayer is full of questions, "When?" and "Where?" but especially "Why?" But unusually, most are not addressed to God. Some are addressed to the suppliant or to no one in particular (they are part of the suppliant's personal reflection), but most are addressed to that *nepeš*, to the self. There are other psalms in which one can perceive an inner argument (notably Ps. 22), and many others imply such an inner argument, but here it is uniquely overt. Further, a prayer such as Ps. 22 quite loses itself into the praise that is appropriate in light of the fact that Yhwh has heard the suppliant's plea, so that at the end we have forgotten that the suppliant is still oppressed by enemies and has seen no action from God. In Pss. 42–43 there is no indication that Yhwh has answered the prayer. The whole is a statement of faith and hope. While Ps. 22 is thus a remarkable statement of faith when the suppliant has heard Yhwh reply but not seen Yhwh's act, Pss. 42–43 are a remarkable statement of faith on the part of a suppliant who has not yet either heard or seen Yhwh. "But even though absent, how present God turns out to be," being mentioned twenty-two times in the two psalms, with a series of titles suggesting a personal relationship: the living God, the face of God, your God, my God, my living God, my rock, God in whom I take refuge, God my exceeding joy. "God is omnipresent in a poem that complains of his absence" and "ironically, the pain of separation is a way of feeling the presence."[28]

28. Schaefer, *Psalms*, 109.

Psalm 44

Coping with Defeat

Translation

The leader's. The Korahites'. Instruction.

¹God, we have heard with our ears,
    our ancestors have told us,
The deed you did in their days,
    in the days of old, ²you yourself with your hand.[1]
You dispossessed nations and planted them,
    you would bring trouble on countries and you spread them out.[2]
³For not through their sword did they gain possession of the land,
    nor did their arm bring deliverance to them,
But your right hand, your arm, and the light of your face,
    because you delighted in them.

⁴You yourself are my king, God:
    order deliverance for Jacob. [MT]
[or, You yourself are my king, my God,

---

1. Treating "you yourself with your hand" as the close of v. 1b rather than the beginning of v. 2 generates better balance in both lines. See (e.g.) Fokkelman, *Major Poems*, 3:64.
2. In isolation, *šālaḥ* (piel) could mean "cast out [peoples]" (cf. NJPS), but this ill fits the parallelism and the transition to v. 3; or it could mean "set free [our ancestors]" (cf. NRSV), but then it is odd that this apparent reference to the exodus comes after speaking of the conquest of the land. "Spread out" (cf. TNIV "made flourish"; and 80:8–11 [9–12]) meets both points.

one who orders deliverance for Jacob. (LXX)][3]
[5]Through you we may charge at our foes,
    through your name we may tread down our adversaries.
[6]For I do not trust in my bow;
    my sword will not deliver me.
[7]For you delivered us from our foes,
    shamed the people who were against us.
[8]We have praised God every day;
    we will confess your name forever. (Rise)

[9]Yet you have spurned and disgraced us;
    you do not go out among our armies.
[10]You turn us back from the foe,
    and the people who are against us have plundered at will.[4]
[11]You make us like sheep for food;
    you have scattered us among the nations.
[12]You sell your people for no value;
    you have not set a high price for them.
[13]You make us an object of reviling for our neighbors,
    derision and scorn for the people around us.[5]
[14]You make us a byword among the nations,
    a reason for shaking the head among the countries.[6]
[15]Every day our disgrace is before us;
    shame has covered our face,
[16]At the voice of one reproaching and taunting,
    at the face of one attacking and exacting redress.

[17]All this has come upon us, and we had not ignored you
    or been false to your covenant.
[18]Our heart had not turned aside
    or our steps deviated from your path
[19]That[7] you should have broken us up[8] into the place of jackals/the
       sea dragon[9]
    and covered over us with deathly darkness.

3. In the middle of the line MT has *ʾĕlōhîm ṣawwēh*; cf. Jerome. Most LXX MSS imply a different division of the words and a different pointing, *ʾĕlōhay mĕṣawweh*, though Barthélemy (*Psaumes*, 259–61) suggests that LXX originally read *ʾĕlōhîm mĕṣawweh*. The *hûʾ* is demonstrative and strengthens the "you" (see *IBHS* 16.3.3c).

4. Lit. "for them[selves]." Tg and Syr may imply *lānû* ([have plundered] us) or may be paraphrasing.

5. Watson (*Classical Hebrew Poetry*, 127) notes the f.-m.-m.-f. gender patterning in the nouns.

6. L's text misdivides the expression as *bal-ʾummîm*.

7. For the use of *kî*, see BDB 473a.

8. Resultative piel.

9. Syr *tnynʾ*, Jerome *draconum* may imply *tannîn* (sea dragon) for *tannîm*, and some later Hebrew MSS have this reading; NJPS understands *tannîm* itself to have this meaning.

²⁰If we had ignored our God's name
    and spread our hands to a strange god,
²¹Would God not search this out?—
    for he gets to know the secrets of the heart.
²²For because of you we have been slain every day;
    we have been regarded as sheep for slaughtering.

²³Get up, why do you sleep, my Lord?—
    wake up, do not reject forever.
²⁴Why do you hide your face,
    ignore our weakness and oppression?
²⁵For our whole being is sunk down to the dirt,
    our heart clings to the ground.
²⁶Rise up as a help for us;
    redeem us for the sake of your commitment!

Interpretation

Eventually it becomes clear that this psalm presupposes a situation in which the people have gone out in battle against their enemies and have been defeated. The fast called for in Joel 1:14 might be the kind of occasion when the psalm would be used. We do not have any clue for dating the psalm, though 2 Kings 15;[10] 2 Kings 18; and 1 Macc. 1–9[11] as well as Joel 1 illustrate the sort of context in which it might be prayed. The psalm is for the most part a "we" psalm, though "I" appears in vv. 4 and 6. It is the first "we" lament in the Psalter. The alternating of "I" and "we" might indicate that the speaker is a leader or that the psalm was a liturgy involving leader and congregation alternately, but vv. 4 and 6 could equally be used on behalf of the community as a whole, individualizing their commitment. If we begin from this individualized strand, the psalm with its focus on military defeat stands closer to Pss. 42–43 than looks at first sight. The combination of terms in the heading is distinctive to Pss. 42–43 and 44 (though the order of the terms is different), and there are a number of verbal links between them that their juxtaposition draws attention to. Psalm 44 once more talks about "deliverance" using the plural (v. 4; cf. 42:5, 11 [6, 12]; 43:5). It makes a commitment to "confess" God (v. 8; cf. 42:5, 11 [6, 12]; 43:5). It talks about God's "spurning" the people (vv. 9, 23; cf. 43:2), about being a

10. See Goulder, *Psalms of the Sons of Korah*, 90, 265.
11. Cf. R. Köbert, "Ibn aṭ-Taiyib's Erklärung von Psalm 44," *Bib* 43 (1962): 338–48; Diodore, *Psalms 1–51*, 138; Chrysostom, *Psalms*, 1:231; Theodoret, *Psalms*, 1:254; Calvin, *Psalms*, 2:148. Harold M. Parker, "Artaxerxes III Ochus and Psalm 44," *JQR* 68 (1978): 152–68, argues for a fourth-century BC context.

reproach (v. 13; cf. 42:10 [11]), about God's "ignoring" the suppliants (v. 24; cf. 42:9 [10]), and about "oppression" (v. 24; cf. 42:9 [10]; 43:2; these are the only psalms where the word comes). "Sunk down" (*šāḥâ*, v. 25) is a similar word to the root "cast down" (*šāḥaḥ*; 42:5, 6, 11 [6, 7, 12]; 43:5) and might in fact come from a by-form.

The psalm is structured particularly clearly. Verses 1–3 recall God's activity in the past, and on the basis of that vv. 4–8 declare present trust, but vv. 9–16 then make a contrast with recent experience, while vv. 17–22 assert that people had not turned their backs on God. On the basis of all that has preceded, vv. 23–26 bring the psalm to a climax in urging God therefore to arise and act on their behalf.

> The leader's. The Korahites'. Instruction.

Heading. See glossary.

44:1–3. The opening of the psalm thus recollects in five lines the way God brought the people into the land. Four of the lines are internally parallel; only the last is not, marking the end of the recollection. But the first pair of lines (v. 1–2a) belong closely together because the second provides the objects for the verbs in the first; in v. 3c–d, the second colon provides the backing for the first. In between these, vv. 2b–c and 3a–b are thus the only self-contained internally parallel lines. In light of where the psalm will eventually go, perhaps vv. 1–3 are already a polemical declaration regarding the community's integrity. They have done what the Torah told them to do (e.g., Deut. 6:20–25) in making sure that the story of God's gift of the land was proclaimed and heard from generation to generation.

> ¹God, we have heard with our ears,
> > our ancestors have told us,
> The deed you did in their days,
> > in the days of old, ²you yourself with your hand.
> You dispossessed nations and planted them,
> > you would bring trouble on countries and you spread them out.

The first word of the first line also hints at where the psalm will go, because although the contents of vv. 1–3 (and vv. 4–8) are characteristic of praise, the direct address "God" is more characteristic of protest than of praise (e.g., 38:1 [2]; 42:1 [2]; contrast 46:1 [2]; 47:1 [2]; 48:1 [2]).[12] The invocation applies to both cola and introduces a verbal recollection pairing a first-person verb and a third-person verb. Hearing with the ears would naturally suggest the recounting of Israel's story in worship or in

---

12. Cf. Gerstenberger, *Psalms*, 1:183.

other celebrations in family or community; the ancestors are presumably seen as speaking through that story.

In the middle line NRSV and NJPS have "deeds," but the word is singular and vv. 2b–3 will confirm that the psalm refers to one particular deed, the giving of the land, which recent reversals have imperiled (vv. 9–16). "In their days / in the days of old" likewise presupposes that the psalm is not referring to the history of God's acts in general but to something back at the beginning. The closing appended phrase "you yourself with your hand" leads into the emphasis running through vv. 2b–3.

Verse 2b–c itself then comprises parallel cola with verbs about bringing calamity, objects, and verbs about positive action, though the words come in abcb'a'c' order, and "brought trouble" is surprisingly yiqtol (see on 77:13–20 [14–21]).

> 3For not through their sword did they gain possession of the land,
>   nor did their arm bring deliverance to them,
> But your right hand, your arm, and the light of your face,
>   because you delighted in them.

Verse 3 spells out further the positive process whereby the ancestors found themselves planted in the land, with a contrast between its two lines (and the verbs in the first carrying over into the second). In v. 3a–b the two cola are fundamentally parallel in substance, though the first relates more to the land and the second to the people, and formally the second also varies matters by making "their arm" the subject (contrast "through their sword did *they* gain possession"). According to Josh. 1–12, often the Israelites did use their sword, though Joshua himself later declares that it was not their bow or sword that won them the land (Josh. 24:12; cf. v. 6); the psalm, too, implies that this was not the key factor in their victory. Verse 3c–d then first sets against that not only God's arm but also God's right hand and God's *face with the *light it shines. The arm suggests strength, the hand personal involvement, the face the attitude that directs those two. Its second colon purports to explain this stance, though it leaves us uncertain about how far it does so. The stance reflects God's delight in the people (*rāṣâ*), but what explains that delight? Sometimes delight implies there were qualities in the object that aroused it (e.g., 51:16–17 [18–19]; 147:10–11). But here reference to this delight seems to have no such implication, and the delight simply issues out of a relationship or restates the fact that there is a relationship (e.g., 40:13 [14]; 85:1 [2]; 149:4).

In scholarly study of the OT, there is considerable doubt regarding the idea that Israel's position in the land came about through an incursion from outside. The psalm assumes that it did and assumes that the kind

39

of story that appears in Joshua is more like fact than fiction. Its prayer would rather deconstruct if this is not so.

44:4–8. Five further lines declare the present trust and confidence that builds itself on that past event. They interweave first-person singular and first-person plural. Thus the psalm could be used by a leader such as a king speaking on the people's behalf or could be used by the whole people in such a way as to affirm their corporate stance but also to require them to make their individual affirmations. Either way, like vv. 1–3 the verses will turn out to constitute declarations of integrity indicating that there is no good reason for the divine abandonment the people have experienced.

> [4]You yourself are my king, God:
>> order deliverance for Jacob. [MT]
> [or, You yourself are my king, my God,
>> one who orders deliverance for Jacob. (LXX)]

The reference to God's delivering in the previous verse is taken up by the noun *deliverance. But the line first declares emphatically that God is "my king": not just "the king" or "the king of kings," but the king committed to Israel as God's servant. Verses 1–3 have implicitly portrayed God acting in relation to the ancestors both as king and as their king; v. 4 makes that relationship explicit for the present generation. In MT the worshipper then goes on to a sudden bidding to God, which might not seem odd if it were accompanied by further biddings, but is surprising when it stands in isolation; there will be no more biddings until vv. 23–26, and this one therefore gives an anticipatory hint of where the psalm is going. In LXX, the second colon rather continues the affirmation of the first. History establishes that God is one who commands deliverance for Jacob. The LXX's version makes vv. 1–8 more a coherent whole and/but makes vv. 9–26 more of a surprise.

> [5]Through you we may charge at our foes,
>> through your name we may tread down our adversaries.

Verse 5 moves from present affirmation to a statement of confidence for the future in closely parallel cola.[13] The way God dispossessed the nations before Israel also means that Israel can with God's help first charge like an ox and then trample on its attackers. There might seem a gap in the logic here. Is Israel really able to take on this behavior be-

---

13. They comprise two *b*-expressions of similar meaning, two first-person plural yiqtol verbs of similar meaning, and two rhyming monosyllabic words for enemies, with first-person plural suffixes (*ṣārênû, qāmênû*), though the words are arranged abca'c'b'.

cause God acted that way in the past? But we have noted that it was of course through Israel that God acted that way before. Even at Jericho, God's victims in Josh. 1–12 did not fall miraculously like Sennacherib's army (2 Kings 19:35). But Israel expects its victims to fall only because God acts. It is "through you," "through your *name."

> **6**For I do not trust in my bow;
> my sword will not deliver me.

It has to be so. Trusting in its weapons will not work. The two cola are parallel in substance though not in form. "I" as subject is balanced by "me" as object, "my sword" balances "my bow," and *trust and *deliver are correlative verbs.

> **7**For you delivered us from our foes,
> shamed the people who were against us.

The basis for this is the declaration that ran through vv. 1–3. Once again God becomes the subject of the two verbs (followed again by parallel objects) as once again the psalm refers to that initial act of *deliverance (cf. vv. 3, 4, 6). But this time it caps the reference to the victory with reference to the shame that attached to the defeat of the people who were *against us.

> **8**We have praised God every day;
> we will confess your name forever. (Rise)

The logical, theological, doxological end term of these affirmations comes in two more balancing cola.[14] *Praise suggests enthusiasm, while *confessing God's *name suggests the content of the praise and its public, testimony-like nature. The temporal terms suggest the regularity and consistency of this confessional praise and its permanent nature.

44:9–16. The lectionary of my church prescribes vv. 1–8 on their own for use on certain occasions and thus obscures their significance. They could indeed stand alone as a praise psalm, especially in their LXX form, but they do not stand alone. Like the much more extensive praise in 89:1–37 [2–38], vv. 1–8 turn out to have been setting God up. If the psalm was used at a regular festival and vv. 1–3 refer to the celebrating of God's acts on such an occasion,[15] the transition at v. 9 will be the more force-

---

14. Arranged abca'c'b', these begin with God and God's name and go on to two first-person plural verbs (one qatal, one yiqtol) and two expressions suggesting permanence.
15. So Weiser, *Psalms*, 355–56; Goulder, *Psalms of the Sons of Korah*, 92–93.

ful. The psalm turns out to be a polemical actualization of a declaration about God's activity such as appears elsewhere in the Scriptures.[16] The section alternates qatal verbs (vv. 9a, 10b, 11b, 12b, 15) and yiqtol verbs (vv. 9b, 10a, 11a, 12a, 13, 14). I have translated these as perfects and presents, both reflecting the way past events have a continuing effect. But one might translate them all as past, as in 18:3–6 [4–7], with LXX and NRSV (other translations alternate without obvious principle).[17] After the opening colon, vv. 9–12 belong together as more concrete statements of the military consequences of God's "spurning," while vv. 13–16 belong together as developing the idea of God's "disgracing" the people. In other words, vv. 9–12 are broadly parallel, as are vv. 13–16. While the first protest does refer to the action of the enemies (v. 10b) and the second closes with a variant form of a declaration regarding how the suppliants themselves feel (vv. 15–16), both protests put the emphasis on God's action (vv. 9, 10a, 11–14). This is the other side of the coin in relation to the affirmations in vv. 1–8. The fact that God is the one who gives the people victory means that God is also the one who brings about their defeat.

> [9]Yet you have spurned and disgraced us;
> you do not go out among our armies.

The "yet" (*'ap*) opening v. 9 advertises the contrast with vv. 1–8. The first colon with its own internal parallelism comprises a summary statement in terms of God's attitude, and the second colon answers the question "So how did God spurn and disgrace?" (indeed, the whole of vv. 9b–16 will do that). On one hand God has spurned the people, which is the opposite of abandoning: it involves not moving away from people but pushing them away, repudiating them or discarding them.[18] Pushing them away has left them on their own. Not surprisingly in light of the facts noted in vv. 1–8, it has thereby condemned them to defeat and thus to disgrace. The second colon indicates that spurning and abandoning are two images for the same reality. They went out on their own because God did not go with them, though apparently they perceived that only through experiencing the consequences.

> [10]You turn us back from the foe,
> and the people who are against us have plundered at will.

---

16. Cf. Walter Beyerlin, "Innerbiblische Aktualisierungsversuche: Schichte im 44. Psalm," *Zeitschrift für Theologie und Kirche* 73 (1976): 446–60.

17. Cf. JM 62a.

18. It perhaps makes little difference if with Reuven Yaron we translate *zānaḥ* as "be angry" ("The Meaning of *zanaḥ*," *VT* 13 [1963]: 237–39).

> ¹¹You make us like sheep for food;
>   you have scattered us among the nations.

The result is defeat and loss, death and scattering. Turning back corresponds to disgrace; running away is a particularly dishonorable way to lose. Becoming plunder is then a consequence of God's absence. In v. 10b alone are the people who are *against us the subject of the protest; v. 11 returns to God and paints an even gloomier picture than v. 10. This is not merely a matter of defeat and loss but of massacre and exile. Being food refers to their becoming like a sheep that has died in the open country, whose carcass is eaten by scavenging animals and birds (cf. 74:14; 79:2; Jer. 7:33; 16:4; 19:7). Obviously the same people cannot be killed in battle and scattered among the nations; perhaps the psalm combines images for the varying consequences that can follow from God's spurning.

> ¹²You sell your people for no value;
>   you have not set a high price for them.

Verse 12 heightens the sense of hurt and mystery. As the people puzzle over why events should work out in this way, they cannot even see how God gains from making them happen. Selling people is a nefarious deed, but there is a sense in which it is understandable when the seller gains significantly from it (Amos 2:6). But God has hardly gained anything from the sale. They have been put on eBay for a few cents, with no reserve. (We cannot press the image by asking who God sold the people to, and what was the small profit God did make.) God must really care nothing for them.

> ¹³You make us an object of reviling for our neighbors,
>   derision and scorn for the people around us.
> ¹⁴You make us a byword among the nations,
>   a reason for shaking the head among the countries.

There now begins the further unfolding of that other opening verb, "disgraced." As a whole the two lines are parallel, with the opening verb in v. 13 reappearing as the opening verb in v. 14.[19] The people protest

19. In each line, letting this verb also govern the second colon leaves space for a double noun expression (in each case a less familiar expression than the one in the first colon), though these take different forms. Likewise the final words of all four cola parallel each other, though *l* introduces the words for neighbors/people around us (people such as Moab and Edom), and *b* then introduces the words for nations/countries (the superpower of the day, such as Assyria or Babylon).

the way they have become an object of reviling; they are upbraided as presumed wrongdoers. The parallel nouns in v. 13b also come together in 79:4, have similar meaning, and constitute a hendiadys. In "scornful derision" people laugh at their pretension to military power when they are so easily and comprehensively defeated. The phrase suggests a contrast with 2:4; 59:8 [9]; things are not working out the way they should.

In v. 14 the people are a byword or an example (*māšāl*): they indicate what happens if you trust in a God who cannot deliver, or if you think that God is with you when that is not so, perhaps because you have done wrong. According to BDB the parallel expression "a reason for shaking the head" denotes a laughingstock, which provides a good parallel with the previous line, but elsewhere shaking the head is an expression of horror (e.g., Jer. 18:16), and that fits the parallelism with "example."

> ¹⁵Every day our disgrace is before us;
>   shame has covered our face.

The suppliants now speak more systematically about themselves and their feelings, though the point is still made abstractly. "Disgrace" explicitly recurs, now paired with the synonym "shame" (cf. 35:26; 69:19 [20]; 109:29). In other respects the cola in v. 15 are parallel in substance though different in the way they express the point. The first is a noun clause, the second a verbal clause, and their imagery contrasts: in the first colon the people's face is open to their shame, in the second it is covered over by it.

> ¹⁶At the voice of one reproaching and taunting,
>   at the face of one attacking and exacting redress.

These cola are also parallel, with the line as a whole dependent on v. 15 and "reproach" forming an inclusion with v. 13. Each colon begins with a *min* expression ("voice" and "face" then complement each other), and each double participial phrase forms a hendiadys. The second pair of participles corresponds to 8:2 [3] and raises the question why this is happening if God has stilled the attacker/punisher. The obvious answer is that it has something to do with the people's wrongdoing, but the next section will rule out that possibility.

44:17–22. "So what?" God might retort. God does so retort in Isa. 40–55: Yes, I did all that, and you quite deserved it. In a way unique among the we-laments, vv. 17–22 respond in anticipation to that possible rejoinder and claim a life of commitment to God. The opening lines could be referring either to a commitment the people showed before the calamity (which therefore made the calamity unjustified) or to a commitment that has persisted through the enduring of calamity; so Jerome.[20] Even v. 19 is ambiguous; Jerome translates the opening *kî* "because." But the last line suggests that there at least the section refers to the former commitment, and I have assumed that this is true of the whole section.

> [17]All this has come upon us, and we had not ignored you
> or been false to your covenant.

Thus, after a summary reference to the experience described in vv. 9–16, two parallel short clauses make a first affirmation that this experience could not have been punishment for unfaithfulness. The possibility of *ignoring God is a familiar one; "being false to God's covenant" is a rarer way of making the point. The notion of *falsehood usually applies to people's falsehood in their relationship with one another; applying it to people's attitude to God is rarer (cf. only Isa. 63:8 for the verb). It suggests a mismatch between words and reality. It would imply maintaining a formal commitment to God's covenant when in private people were worshipping other gods or using images in their worship. Speaking in terms of "God's covenant" makes clear that the psalm has in mind not a mutual relationship between God and people but a commitment God lays on the people (cf. 25:10).

> [18]Our heart had not turned aside
> or our steps deviated from your path

Two concrete pictures reaffirm the point. The parallel cola refer to heart and steps, the inner person and the outer activity; the people claim faithfulness throughout their being. The two verbs have similar meaning,[21] suggesting an inward or outward deviating from the way God had set before the people under the terms of the covenant.

> [19]That you should have broken us up into the place of jackals/the sea
> dragon
> and covered over us with deathly darkness.

So there is no such unfaithfulness that could have warranted what God has done. The parallel cola both end with *b*-expressions, but these

---

20. Cf. Adele Berlin, "Psalms and the Literature of Exile," in *Book of Psalms*, ed. Flint and Miller, 65–86 (see 72–73).

21. *Sûg* is usually rendered "turn back," though BDB rather gives the first meaning as "move away," and "turn aside" makes sense for all the occurrences. That fits the parallelism here.

have different meanings. A place of jackals is a total ruin, a place of desolation no longer fit for human habitation and inhabited only by such wild creatures (cf. Isa. 34:13). The place of the sea serpent would be the place where it lay after God slew it (e.g., Isa. 51:9). For "deathly darkness," see Ps. 23:4.

> ²⁰If we had ignored our God's name
>   and spread our hands to a strange god,

Verse 20 goes back to the possibility that the people might have *ig-nored their God's *name and ceased to call on God, and then makes explicit the alternative possibility. That is not that people would have stopped praying at all, which in a traditional society would hardly occur to someone. People knew that there were heavenly beings; the questions were, What is their true nature? Who are the ones we are in relationship with? It would thus be possible to "spread one's hands" toward someone else: the phrase indicates the posture of prayer (cf. 28:2). One could do that to a deity other than Yhwh, but this would be a "strange god," one with whom the people had no relationship and who had not been involved with them in the way vv. 1–3 describe (cf. Isa. 43:12). It would therefore be a strange thing to do.

> ²¹Would God not search this out?—
>   for he gets to know the secrets of the heart.

And it would not escape God's awareness. The first colon declares that God is able to find things out, which implies that God does not "auto-matically" know everything but does have infinite capacity to discover things (cf. 7:9 [10]; 11:5; 17:3). The verb (*ḥāqar*) usually refers to human investigation that discovers things by looking and exploring (e.g., Deut. 13:14 [15]; Ezek. 39:14), but it can also be applied to God (Ps. 139:1, 23). So God is able to go behind locked doors, for instance, and discover what religious practices people are undertaking in the apparent privacy of their own homes and to look into people's hearts to see where they are even more secretly appealing to strange deities. As traditionally rendered, the second colon then gives a different account of the way God knows things, implying that God does "automatically" know matters such as what people are thinking in their inner beings. It may be that we should leave in tension the two descriptions, that God discovers and that God knows. Both make significant statements (like the statement that people do see God and the statement that seeing God is impossible). The first preserves the dynamic nature of God's relationship with us; the second safeguards the supernatural nature of God's knowledge. But elsewhere in Scripture, the first of these statements (that God discovers things) is more common than any declaration that God knows everything without discovering things, so we should hardly dismiss that first statement as anthropomorphism. The translation above reconciles the two statements by seeing "searching out" as the way God "gets to know," a feasible meaning for *yāda'* (e.g., 79:10; 119:152; Jer. 38:24).

> 22For because of you we have been slain every day;
> we have been regarded as sheep for slaughtering.

The section comes to a dramatic close. Given that God would be able to know what has been going on, God knows (the psalm implies) that Israel has been guilty of no such unfaithfulness. So people are not suffering because of their own actions but because of God. The preposition is *'al*, and this can mean "for [your] sake," which facilitates Paul's application of the psalm to his ministry (Rom. 8:36). But in the psalm there is no suggestion that their enemies are attacking them because of their allegiance to God. Rather, they are being killed because of God, because of God's action (vv. 9–14) and/or because God ignores their plight (v. 24). The closing comparison takes up the image in v. 11a but tweaks it; here the sheep are not being killed by an animal but slaughtered for eating at a celebration. And it is all "because of you," not because of us and our wrongdoing.[22]

44:23–26. The previous section leads into a straight challenge to God. This final section comprises, indeed, a series of challenges to God, presupposing that God has been doing things one would not have thought God did (sleep, reject, hide the face, ignore) and thus must do things that one would not have thought God needed to do (get up, wake up, rise up). The directness of the challenges is reinforced by the parallelism in each line; the point is driven home twice each time.

> 23Get up, why do you sleep, my Lord?—
> wake up, do not reject forever.

The opening challenge, probably reverting to the first-person singular in addressing "my *Lord," is neatly but dynamically balanced.[23] The line

22. The "because of you" applies to both cola, as does "every day." The two verbal expressions are then parallel, both being first-person plural qatal passive verbs (one hophal, one niphal); the second is completed by a *k* phrase.

23. The invocation stands at the center, with a three-stress double clause on either side. Each of these comprises two verbs, an impv. (each time slightly softened by the -*â* sufformative) followed by a yiqtol. Each thus has a third element—the "why" in the first, the "forever" in the second. Formally the two yiqtols function in different ways, one in a

is as bold a confrontation as we read anywhere in the Psalms. Elijah once derided Canaanite gods as deities that were too sleepy to respond to their worshippers (1 Kings 18:27); here worshippers speak the same way to God. Psalm 121:4 indeed denies that God drops off to sleep, but that does not hinder this psalm from speaking in terms of God's having done so and asking *Why? and no weasel words about "seeming to be asleep" take the edge off the challenge. The second-century high priest Johanan, John Hyrcanus, stopped the Levites using it now that the Jewish people lived in a situation in which it had been demonstrated that their God was by no means asleep (b. Soṭah 48a). In a context when God appears to be asleep, suppliants will be quite happy if God responds by saying, "I am not asleep." They will have achieved their aim of inducing a response. And over against anyone who quotes Ps. 121 to them,[24] they can respond with a psalm that speaks of God waking up like someone asleep (78:65), other psalms that urge God to get up or wake up (e.g., 7:6 [7]; 35:23), and even a prophecy that describes God doing so (Isa. 42:13).[25]

> [24]Why do you hide your face,
>   ignore our weakness and oppression?

Compared with that first line, v. 24 is more conventional. Other psalms ask *Why? and speak of God hiding the *face and *ignoring the suppliant (e.g., 13:1 [2]; 42:9 [10]). Particular force attaches to the second verb in light of the suppliants' repeated claim not to have ignored God (vv. 17, 20). *Weakness is also a familiar idea (9:13 [14]; 25:18; 31:7 [8]), as is oppression (42:9 [10]; 43:2), yet the line gains force by virtue of the fact that the combination of these two words suggests that God is letting the people's affliction in Egypt recur (cf. Exod. 3:7, 9; Deut. 26:7). That was an occasion when God was mindful of them rather than ignoring them (zākar, the antonym of šākaḥ; Exod. 2:24; 6:5).

> [25]For our whole being is sunk down to the dirt,
>   our heart clings to the ground.

In ideas, v. 25 is also conventional, and after the "for" the cola make a neat parallelism, abca'b'c'. The verbs are less conventional. "Sunk down" (šāḥâ) comes only here, though it resembles the more common verb

---

rhetorical question, one in a negative bidding, but in substance they are similar, as the rhetorical question is also a disguised bidding.

24. E.g., Cassiodorus, *Psalms*, 1:437.

25. I take the hiphil in Isa. 42:13 as declarative, as in Ps. 35:23; qin'â is not its obj. but the first word of the subsequent colon.

"cast down" (*šāḥaḥ*; 35:14; 38:6 [7]; 42:5, 6, 11 [6, 7, 12]; 43:5). "Clings" (*dābaq*) suggests sticking close to something in such a way that the two cannot be prized apart (cf. 22:15 [16]). The use of *nepeš* illustrates how the word frequently refers to the *person as a whole rather than the soul as opposed to the body; it is the outer person that is literally sunk down to the dirt, while the inner person is metaphorically so. "Heart" (*beṭen*, lit. a person's "insides") can similarly refer to the inner person and is here a less familiar synonym for *nepeš*. The dirt and the ground are the realm of death; we are as good as dead, the line declares.[26]

> [26]Rise up as a help for us;
>   redeem us for the sake of your commitment!

The closing line begins by repeating the thrust of the first line of this section, though "rise up" (*qûmâ*) is also the bidding to God as the covenant chest sets out ahead of the Israelites marching for the promised land (Num. 10:35), a suggestive link. *Help then begins to give more specificity to what the suppliants seek from God. *Redeem us gives the point yet more precision in the second colon: selling off (v. 12) has to be replaced by buying back. The psalm closes with a significant one-word appeal to God's *commitment, which is belied by the way God has been acting. This appeal stands out from the rest of vv. 23–26 and brings the psalm to a brisk but powerful conclusion. It might have contrasting relationships with vv. 17–22. The people have been keeping their commitment to God's covenant, and it is time for God to do so. And/or it might imply a recognition that our final appeal is not to our own integrity but to God's. "Whether then we suffer in tribulations, or rejoice in prosperities, redeem Thou us, not for our merits, but for Thy name's sake."[27] In this connection the closing word recalls the reference to God's delight at the end of the first section of the psalm (v. 3).[28]

Theological Implications

Experiencing reversal for which there seems to be no religious or moral reason, the psalm implies three significant convictions. First, the people of God should be able to claim integrity in their relationship with God. It is of course regularly the case that the church lacks such integrity, and the church in Europe that has collapsed or the church in

26. While in another context the words might refer to mourning rites, this does not fit the context here so well.
27. Augustine, *Psalms*, 145.
28. Cf. Kraus, *Psalms 1–59*, 447.

the United States that is collapsing cannot claim that such collapses happen despite their faithfulness to God. But there are churches that experience persecution despite their faithfulness. As I write, the church in Sri Lanka is an example. In the same way, there were times (such as the exile) when Israel could hardly claim to be suffering despite its faithfulness. But the psalm presupposes that there are times, and should be times, when the people of God do live faithfully. It is not always called to "worm theology."

Second, God really is the sovereign Lord of our lives as the people of God and therefore bears responsibility for the tough things that happen to us. When the people experienced defeat, "the battle was staged not between 'us' and 'them' but between 'God' and 'them.' A victory would have been described in terms of praise, but a rout could be spelled out only as a *God*-lament."[29] Since it is God's delight that brings about deliverance (v. 3), it must be God's spurning that brings about defeat (v. 9). The former reflects the light of God's face (v. 3), the latter the hiding of God's face (v. 24). If it is God who shames the people's attackers when they lose (v. 7), it is God who shames the people when they lose (vv. 13–16). The psalm confronts the God who obviously knows what goes on with the God who is not behaving in accordance with such knowledge (vv. 20–22).[30] The experience of the Lord sleeping when we are in trouble continues for Christians; it is therefore good that the picture of the sleeping Lord is "acted out in the New Testament" (Mark 4:38).[31] The experience reached an apogee in the Holocaust, when the people of God were again deserted and shamed, torn to pieces, and handed over like sheep to be devoured in gas chambers, crematoria, and mass burning pits, and treated in such a way as to become a reason for the nations to shake their heads in disbelief.[32]

Third, in this psalm there is no suggestion that there is anything positive in the people's suffering "because of God," as if this could somehow bring glory to God or be used by God. While there are contexts where that is so, this is not one of them. The psalm does not point in the direction of seeing redemptive possibilities in suffering; nor would it gain deeper significance if it did so.[33] It rather gives a different testimony from that of Rom. 8:36, but just as significant a one. Punishment and martyrdom

29. Broyles, *Conflict of Faith and Experience*, 140.

30. Ibid., 143.

31. Kidner, *Psalms*, 1:170.

32. David R. Blumenthal, *Facing the Abusing God* (Louisville: Westminster/John Knox, 1993), 99–100. Abraham J. Heschel takes his epigraph from vv. 17–18, 22, 24 in dedicating *The Prophets* ([repr., New York: HarperCollins, 2001], v) to "the martyrs of 1940–45."

33. Against Mays, *Psalms*, 179–80; McCann, "Psalms," 858–59; Rogerson and McKay, *Psalms*, 1:210.

are not the only possible significances of the fact that trouble comes to the people of God. The people of God experience trouble that has no meaning. Nor is it the case that "it is only in the New Testament that the discords of the psalm are dissolved" when people know that nothing can separate them from God's love.[34] On the contrary, on the one hand the psalm begins and ends with the awareness that nothing can separate the people from God's love; on the other, after the NT and Christ's first coming people still suffer in inexplicable ways. The psalm invites us to confront God with that fact, not to accept the trouble that comes to us.

34. So Weiser, *Psalms*, 360.

Psalm 45

The True King and True Queen

Translation

The leader's. On lilies. The Korahites'. Instruction. Love song.

[1]My heart is stirring with a fine word;
 I am speaking my verses for a king,
 my tongue is the pen of an expert[1] scholar.

[2]You are the most handsome[2] of human beings;
 grace is poured on your lips;
 therefore God has blessed you forever.
[3]Fasten your sword to your side, warrior,
 [fasten] your glory and majesty, [4]and in your majesty advance.[3]
Ride for a truthful purpose and a faithful cause,[4]
 so that the awesome deeds of your right hand may point you out.[5]

1. Etymologically "quick," but Ethiopic suggests "expert" (cf. *CP* 295, 330), which makes better sense esp. in Ezra 7:6; Prov. 22:29.
2. *Yopyāpîtā* is an odd form and could be regularized; see (e.g.) *BHS*. But see JM 59d.
3. EVV translate *ṣĕlaḥ* as "triumph" or the like, but in the context "advance" makes better sense (see Barthélemy, *Psaumes*, 263–66; also discussion in *HALOT*).
4. EVV take *'ănāwâ* to mean meekness, but it is questionable whether it is logically possible to be a warrior-king and to be *'ānî*. As at 18:35 [36], I derive the word from *'ānâ* I and see it having similar meaning to *ma'ănâ* in Prov. 16:4. Cf. C. F. Whitley, "Textual and Exegetical Observations on Ps 45,4–7," *ZAW* 48 (1986): 277–82 (see 279), though he emends to provide a form of the verb *'ānâ* I.
5. Jerome translates, "so that your right hand may teach you marvels," but this makes for a less natural meaning; I follow Dahood, *Psalms*, 1:272. For the pl. noun with f. sg. verb, see GKC 145k.

⁵Your arrows are sharpened—peoples are beneath your feet—
  they fall in the heart of the king's enemies;
⁶the throne, God's, is yours forever and ever.⁶
Your royal rod is an upright rod;⁷
  ⁷you have dedicated yourself to faithfulness and thus been against
    faithlessness.
Therefore God, your God, anointed you
  with joyful oils beyond⁸ your fellows.
⁸All your garments are myrrh, aloes, and cassia;
  from your great ivory palace⁹ strings¹⁰ entertain you.
⁹The great princess stands in your jewels,
  the queen, at your right hand in gold from Ophir.

¹⁰Listen, young lady, and look, incline your ear;
  put out of mind your people and your father's household,

6. LXX and Jerome translate v. 6 more straightforwardly, "Your throne, O God, is forever and ever," but it is difficult to make sense of this in the context. If the words address the king (so Rashi, comparing Exod. 7:1), it is hard to see how they relate to the next verse, where *'ĕlōhîm* means "God" and is distinguished from the king. Further, there are no other passages in the OT where the king is addressed as *'ĕlōhîm*. Hebrews 1:8–9 is able to give a new sense to the words in light of the incarnation (cf. Allan M. Harman, "The Syntax and Interpretation of Psalm 45:7," in *The Law and the Prophets* [O. T. Allis Festschrift; ed. John H. Skilton et al.; Nutley, NJ: Presbyterian and Reformed, 1974], 337–47), and the passage subsequently became important in patristic discussions of the person of Christ; see Elisabeth Grünbeck, *Christologische Schriftargumentation und Bildersprache* (Leiden: Brill, 1994). In origin, as an invocation the word would have to address Yhwh (so Tg), but that would require implausibly unannounced transitions between vv. 6, 7, and 8. Rather, I follow Ibn Ezra in understanding the expression to denote "your throne of God." *TTH* 194 argues rather for "Your throne is God," i.e., "is divine," which makes little difference. C. R. North ("The Religious Aspects of Hebrew Kingship," *ZAW* 50 [1932]: 8–38 [see 29–30]) prefers "Your throne is [like] God's," comparing Song 1:15; 4:1—and 5:12, where the prep. *k* is present. J. R. Porter ("Psalm xlv.7," *JTS*, n.s., 12 [1961]: 51–53) questions these parallels, but J. A. Emerton ("The Syntactical Problem of Psalm xlv.7," *JSS* 13 [1968]: 58–63) defends North. See further Johannes S. M. Mulder, *Studies on Psalm 45* (Ph.D. diss., Nijmegen; Oss: Offsetdrukkerij Witsiers, 1972), 31–80; Leslie C. Allen, "Psalm 45:7–8 [6–7] in Old and New Testament Settings," in *Christ the Lord* (Donald Guthrie Festschrift; ed. Harold H. Rowdon; Leicester, UK: Inter-Varsity, 1982), 220–42. For the argument that *'ĕlōhîm* has a broad enough meaning to refer to the king, see Claus Schedl, "Neue Vorschläge zu Text und Deutung des Psalmes xlv," *VT* 14 (1964): 310–18 (see 316–17); B. Couroyer, "Dieu ou Roi," *RB* 78 (1978): 233–41; Richard D. Patterson, "A Multiplex Approach to Psalm 45," *Grace Theological Journal* 6 (1985): 29–48 (see 40).

7. The context of vv. 3–5 suggests that the *šēbeṭ* is a weapon (cf. 2:9; 23:4; so LXX) rather than a scepter, a ceremonial sign of royal authority (so Jerome; and cf. J. P. J. Olivier, "The Sceptre of Justice and Ps. 45:7b," *JNSL* 7 [1979]: 45–54).

8. Or "rather than" (Craigie, *Psalms 1–50*, 336).

9. Pl. of extension (cf. *IBHS* 7.4.1c).

10. *Minnî* is apparently an apocopated pl. (cf. GKC 87f).

[11]So that the king may desire your beauty;[11]
    since he is your lord, bow down to him.
[12]The city of Tyre will court your favor with a gift,
    the richest of the people [13]with all wealth.
To the inside,[12] the princess (with gold embroidery,
    her dress of colored materials) [14]will be led[13] to the king.
The bridesmaids behind her, her friends,
    brought to you,
[15]Will be led with joyful rejoicing;
    they will go into the king's palace.
[16]Instead of your ancestors, you will have sons;
    you will appoint them as leaders throughout the land.

[17]I will commemorate your name for all generations;
    therefore peoples will confess you forever and ever.

Interpretation

Uniquely within the Psalter, this "psalm" addresses and focuses on human beings rather than God. Its content eventually makes clear that it is a marriage song, though this does not emerge until near the end. It seems plausible to reckon that the psalm was composed for a particular royal wedding, perhaps Solomon's or Ahab's.[14] Further, vv. 10–12 suggest that the bride was foreign, as many brides would be; the object of many royal weddings was to cement relationships with other states. But the psalm does not actually tell us which wedding, and the inclusion of the psalm in the Psalter implies that it was used for many. In the postmonarchic period it came to be interpreted allegorically of the Messiah and his bride, the people of God,[15] and it may also have been used for ordinary

11. The jussive with simple *w* denotes purpose: see DG 87.

12. *Pĕnîmâ* with the suffix *-â* denoting a destination should suggest movement, and while such expressions can be used loosely, the verb of motion that follows suggests that we should take it literally.

13. Or perhaps "carried" on a sedan to the king; "carry" is the most frequent meaning of *yābal* (cf. Goulder, *Psalms of the Sons of Korah*, 136). But in v. 15 the verb also applies to the bridesmaids, who were presumably not all carried.

14. Mulder (*Studies on Psalm 45*, 81–158) emphasizes the influence of late Assyrian court style and argues for a seventh-century Judean origin, but Rendsburg (*Linguistic Evidence*, 45–50) argues on linguistic grounds for an Ephraimite origin of the psalm. Brendan McGrath ("Reflections on Psalm 45," *The Bible Today* 26 [1966]: 1837–42) reads it resolutely in connection with the marriage of Ahab and Jezebel.

15. Raymond Tournay sees this as its original meaning ("Les affinités du Ps. xlv avec le Cantique des Cantiques et leur interprétation messianique," in *Congress Volume: Bonn, 1962* [VTSup 9; Leiden: Brill, 1963], 168–212). Oswald Loretz sees this as reflected in some glosses in the text (*Das althebräische Liebeslied* [Kevelaer: Butzon, 1971], 67–70). Saur

couples who on the occasion of their wedding become king and queen for a day.[16] The prominent emphasis on the groom's warring activity contrasts with the Song of Songs, on the assumption that this language is literally meant and is not figurative, as it is in the Song.[17]

The poem's dominant rhythm is 4-4. It opens and closes (vv. 1, 17) with statements by a person who speaks in the manner of the best man (or of a prophet) who in the poem gives his compliments and advice to the groom and bride. There are eight lines for him (vv. 2–9), three for her (vv. 10–12). The remaining lines (vv. 13–16) picture the marriage itself or at least the arrival of the bride, though "it is . . . not advisable to regard the poem, which ties together in a single bunch of many-coloured flowers a variety of essential motifs and thoughts associated with the feast, as some kind of account of the course of events that took place at the celebration of the wedding; it is even less advisable to attempt to deduce from it exactly when and where the recital of the psalm took place within the framework of the feast."[18]

The leader's. On lilies. The Korahites'. Instruction. Love song.

Heading. See glossary. "Love song" comes only here. The psalm itself does not refer to love, only to marriage, though we are used to speaking of "loved ones" in a loose sense, meaning simply family members.[19] But perhaps the title relates to the use of the title for an ordinary marriage, which might be more likely to involve love.

> [1]My heart is stirring with a fine word;
>   I am speaking my verses for a king,
>   my tongue is the pen of an expert scholar.

45:1. In the opening and closing lines, the poet assumes the position of the one who will actually declaim the poem. This first line is a sonorous

---

(*Königspsalmen*, 113–31) sees it as a celebration of the king and Ms. Zion, comparing Zech. 9:9.

16. Cf. T. H. Gaster, "Psalm 45," *JBL* 74 (1955): 239–51. Robert Couffignal sees it as handling fundamental themes in the institution of marriage as embodied in this archetypal union, such as power and libido ("Les structures figuratives du Psaume 45," *ZAW* 113 [2001]: 198–208).

17. Against Gerstenberger, *Psalms*, 1:188. G. Lloyd Carr ("The Old Testament Love Songs and Their Use in the New Testament," *JETS* 24 [1981]: 97–105) emphasizes the difference between the psalm and the Song of Songs.

18. Weiser, *Psalms*, 362.

19. Goulder (*Psalms of the Sons of Korah*, 124–25) suggests that the pl. word indeed refers to the king's "loved ones," his many wives, but it seems odd for a psalm relating to the marriage of one to begin with reference to all the others.

asyndetic 4-4-4 tricolon with intricate patterns of parallelism that befit the intricate patterning the poem will soon refer to. Thus my heart, I, and my tongue form a triplet, with the middle word standing out; stirring, speaking, and the pen do likewise, with the third word standing out; "fine word" and "verses" pair, as do "king" and "expert scholar." In each of these last two cases, one of the nouns is qualified by an adjective, and the other stands alone. The subject of the entire line is the oral delivery of the poem. The poem represents the words someone speaks (the best man? or a court sage?) and his stance as he speaks them. Thus, while the poem may well have been composed orally, the heart-stirring of the first colon does not refer to the way the poet was moved in the process of composing but to the way the speaker is moved as he delivers his fine poem. The verb *rāḥaš* comes only here, but a derived noun refers to a cooking pot, showing the background of the idea of "stirring." The king who is the subject of the composition is unnamed, facilitating the poem's use at any royal wedding (or at an ordinary wedding). The third colon again makes clear that it represents the words of the person who declaims the poem, whose words are as fluent and mellifluous as words written by a scholar. For much of OT times as in modern cultures, while ordinary people might be able to read and write in a rudimentary way, they would not be used to writing poems. Literary production would be the realm of a professional group of scholars or scribes. The reader may be such a scribe or may imagine himself as such. In the latter case, his fluent reading will recall such an expert's fluent reading. They will do so with irony then, since the words will indeed have been written by a speedy scholar or an expert scholar.[20]

45:2–9. The address to the groom.

> ²You are the most handsome of human beings;
>   grace is poured on your lips;
>   therefore God has blessed you forever.

The address begins with another sonorous asyndetic tricolon. The first two lines are parallel, complimenting the king on his appearance and his own use of words. The former is a standard expectation of a king, and it is therefore not surprising that, apart from Joseph, David is the only "handsome" man in Israel's story (1 Sam. 16:12; 17:42), though the man in the Song of Songs (1:16) is also handsome. Notwithstanding God's interest in looking inside a person, God is the creator of the body, and it is natural for a person's appearance to match their personal

---

20. Thus the line has been a locus classicus for thinking about biblical inspiration: see Robert C. Hill, "Psalm 45," *Studia patristica* 25 (1993): 95–100; see, e.g., Diodore, *Psalms 1–51*, 143.

and official significance. While graciousness of speech might suggest something such as the generosity to the poor expressed in the decisions promulgated by the king (cf. Ps. 37:21, 26; Prov. 26:25; Dan. 4:27 [24]), the context of other references to gracious speech rather suggests that the king has a way with words, a facility for speaking a winning word (Prov. 22:11; Eccles. 10:12). That would also be expected of a king (cf. 1 Sam. 16:18; 17:31–47). To say that such grace is "poured" on the king's lips may suggest that it is there in abundance, or there in fixed form (the verb *yāṣaq* often refers to casting), or by metonymy that it pours from his lips. The fact that he has qualities fit for a king makes it appropriate for God to bless him in the way that David prays in 2 Sam. 7:29; the earlier parts of that chapter suggest aspects of what this blessing will look like. (There is no need to take the "therefore" to mean "That is the way we know it is the case that . . .") There and in the context of this wedding poem, we may recall the basic nature of blessing as the gift of children. A more general understanding of blessings introduces an irony. The king will know blessing through his life; the actual experience of Israel's first three kings was to know blessing in their early lives but then see their lives unravel.

> ³Fasten your sword to your side, warrior,
> 　[fasten] your glory and majesty, ⁴ᵃand in your majesty advance.

With *BHS* I take vv. 3–4a as another 4-4 line, with the verb also governing the two nouns at the beginning of the second colon. Like the president of the United States, the Israelite king is the commander in chief of the armed forces. He is challenged to set about the exercise of this power in a resolute way.

> ⁴ᵇRide for a truthful purpose and a faithful cause,
> 　so that the awesome deeds of your right hand may point you out.

MT then points to taking v. 4b–c as a 3-3 line, parallel to vv. 3–4a but nuancing its point. Over against v. 3a, v. 4b makes it clear that this exercise of power is not merely based on the principle that might is right. Israel is not entitled to make war simply in order to gain territory; the king is to put war at the service of *truthfulness and *faithfulness in relation to his people. Saul's battle against Ammon (1 Sam. 11) would be a fine example of a king(-designate) fulfilling this commission. Then the promise in v. 4c restates the point about glory and majesty in vv. 3b–4a. "Awesome deeds" are extraordinary acts that make people bow down in *reverence before God. David refers to such awe-inspiring marvels in his dealings with God (2 Sam. 7:23). Only God can do such deeds;

God's blessing will mean that the king sees God do them by means of his own deeds as he himself rides out in the cause of truthfulness and faithfulness.

> [5]Your arrows are sharpened—peoples are beneath your feet—
> they fall in the heart of the king's enemies;
> [6a]the throne, God's, is yours forever and ever.

This subsequent promise about victory (4-4-4) stands in the context of that moral and religious concern. As the king acts in the pursuit of truthfulness and faithfulness, expecting to see God doing marvels, then opponents will fall before him. On any reading the order of the cola is jerky; EVV reverse some of the phrases to make the text read more smoothly. Verse 5 is yet another pair of four-stress cola,[21] with the second clause in v. 5a forming a parenthesis; the "they" is the arrows. The declaration in v. 6a then closes off these comments on the king's power. His victories reflect the fact that he sits on God's throne (e.g., 1 Chron. 29:23), ruling Israel on God's behalf, and destined to rule the world on God's behalf (cf. Ps. 2). That in itself would make the king's throne last forever. The fact that God made a lasting commitment to the Davidic king's throne would also have that implication. It is a further reason for the king to go out confidently to impose truthfulness and faithfulness on the nations, and the fact that he does so victoriously is an indication that he indeed sits on this throne.

> [6b]Your royal rod is an upright rod;
> [7a]you have dedicated yourself to faithfulness and thus been against faithlessness.

I thus take vv. 6b–7a as a pair of parallel cola, reverting to the moral implications of that power of the king. The force he exercises on God's behalf is exercised on behalf of uprightness. The noun clause in v. 6b expresses itself as descriptive statement, though under the surface it might be another prescriptive one. In v. 7a the verbal clause pairing with the noun clause makes an affirmation of the king's commitment that accompanies the implicit exhortation, though the affirmation may be made in faith.[22] By virtue of being king, he has *dedicated himself to *faithfulness and committed himself to being *against *faithlessness. The commission in v. 4 is thus in keeping with the commitment involved in his accepting designation as king.

---

21. Against MT, which divides the verse after "fall."
22. Dahood (*Psalms*, 1:273) sees it as a precative perfect, but the succeeding "therefore" rather suggests a statement.

> 7bTherefore God, your God, anointed you
>   with joyful oils beyond your fellows.

I then take v. 7b–c as a line in its own right, its two cola belonging together as vv. 6b–7a belong together, though they constitute a sentence rather than two parallel cola. It was the king's commitment to action on behalf of faithfulness that made God anoint him. The anointing will be that referred to in (e.g.) 89:20 [21]; 1 Sam. 10:1; 2 Sam. 12:7; God is the subject of the verb, though the literal agent of the anointing is God's prophet. Although Saul had already been anointed, it was after demonstrating that he was committed to action on behalf of faithfulness and against faithlessness that he was actually made king (1 Sam. 11). God had David anointed on the basis of seeing what was inside David and not just what was outside, which I take to imply seeing he would be committed to faithfulness and against faithlessness (the kind of qualities expressed in his willingness to take on Goliath). Subsequent kings are anointed on the supposition that they affirm that commitment. The fact that they sit on God's throne, the throne of the sovereign of heaven and earth, means that their anointing has the most exotic joyfulness about it, far exceeding that of other kings.[23]

> 8All your garments are myrrh, aloes, and cassia;
>   from your great ivory palace strings entertain you.
> 9The great princess stands in your jewels,
>   the queen, at your right hand in gold from Ophir.

So far there has been no mention of a wedding, and there is no need to interpret vv. 8–9 as relating distinctively to a wedding scene. For any great ceremonial occasion, including his anointing or coronation, the king would waft myrrh, aloes, and cassia (cf. 133:2). All three are aromatic substances, derived from trees, which are used as ingredients in perfumes. Myrrh is referred to most often in the OT. This particular Hebrew word for cassia comes only here, but it is apparently related to cinnamon; myrrh and cinnamon are among the ingredients in the anointing oil prescribed by Exod. 30, though also in the perfumes that lovers would use (e.g., Prov. 7:17; Song 4:14). Again, for any great ceremonial occasion strings would play in the palace decorated with ivory (cf. 1 Kings 10:18; 22:39; Amos 3:15; 6:4). And for any such great ceremonial occasions, one would not be surprised if a queen were at the king's side. Verse 9 expresses that in two cola of neat overlapping parallelism.

23. There are no parallels in Scripture for understanding this anointing as a figure for subsequent blessing of the king.

| The great princess[24] | in your jewels[25] | stands |
| The queen | at your right hand | in gold of Ophir |

The gold of Ophir may be her crown; we do not know where Ophir was, but the expression is a standard one for fine gold. The great princess/ queen is probably not the bride but the queen mother, who will now address the bride.[26]

45:10–13a. Although not explicitly referring to a wedding, vv. 8–9 form a natural segue into material that relates more directly to that. Just three lines address the bride, and they issue no compliments on her appearance to match the compliments to the groom, only somewhat stern exhortations.

> [10]Listen, young lady, and look, incline your ear;
>   put out of mind your people and your father's household,

They begin in v. 10 with a solemn threefold bidding to the bride, whose solemnity the second colon explains. Genesis 2:18–25 speaks of a man leaving his father and mother to cleave to his wife, and that might introduce some counterbalance to the power of the man in a patriarchal society. Psalm 45 manifests no such balance. In coming to the warrior who has been addressed in vv. 2–9, she has to turn her back on her people and her family (*ignore). Since royal brides were often from other peoples, the implication would be that she needs to turn her back on her own culture, her loyalties, and her religion, like Ruth. Foreign brides such as Solomon's and Ahab's notoriously did not do so, with the apparent conniving of their Israelite husbands.

> [11]So that the king may desire your beauty;
>   since he is your lord, bow down to him.

Verse 11 offers two reasons for the forgetting, such as might further rejoice her groom and all the other men who listen but cause some grief among the women. She leaves her family in order to become an object of desire and the subject of submission. Once again it is clear that we live

---

24. Perhaps *bĕnôt* is honorific pl. (cf. *IBHS* 7.4.3), or perhaps it is a northern sg. form, of which Rendsburg finds other examples in the psalm (*Linguistic Evidence*, 45), or perhaps it is a slip for *bat*. Syr has sg. *brt*.

25. KJV has "honourable women," but the word never otherwise refers to people and usually refers to jewelry, in the expression *'eben yĕqārâ* (cf. LXX, Jerome); cf. the parallelism.

26. See Christoph Schroeder, "A Love Song," *CBQ* 58 (1996): 417–32 (see 428–29); cf. A. S. van der Woude, "Psalm 45:11–18," in *Loven en geloven* (N. H. Ridderbos Festschrift; ed. M. H. van Es et al.; Amsterdam: Ton Bolland, 1975), 111–16 (see 113).

the wrong side of Gen. 3:1–6, in a situation where "'To love and to cherish' becomes 'To desire and to dominate'" (Gen. 3:16).[27] Whereas the noun there referring to the woman's desire is *tĕšûqâ*, here the verb "desire" is *'āwâ* (hitpael), but this verb form also usually denotes a wrong form of desire, something like lust (e.g., 106:14), while the related noun *ta'ăwâ* characterized the sinful desirability of the good-and-bad-knowledge tree (Gen. 3:6). Further, in the second colon the bride's prospective husband is characterized not as her *'îš* (her man, the usual expression for husband, even in Gen. 3:16) but as her *'ādōn* (her lord and master). She has to bow down to him. That will be because he is the king, but it looks as if the patriarchal authority embodied in his kingship carries over into his marriage. She is not encouraged to expect a marriage of equals.

> [12]The city of Tyre will court your favor with a gift,
>   the richest of the people [13a]with all wealth.

Instead, she is offered people's regard and their gifts. At the center of this line stands the verb, which applies to both cola and suggests the way people could reckon that gaining the queen's favor may stand them in good stead. In each colon there is then a subject for the verb, the collective singular "city of Tyre" and the plural "the richest of the people." Tyre may be mentioned because it is a near and prosperous neighbor of Israel, as it was in Solomon's day, or a near and prosperous neighbor of Ephraim in particular, or because it epitomizes wealth and prosperity in any period (cf. Ezek. 27–28), or because it was where a famous royal bride came from (1 Kings 16:31).[28] The phrase in the second colon interprets and/or generalizes the point. In each colon there is then the means they will use to win the queen's favor, and "with a gift" is given more precision by "[with] all wealth."[29]

45:13b–16. Four lines now speak about, rather than to, the bride and begin to return to addressing the king (vv. 14b–c, 16). This perhaps alerts us to the fact that actually the king is the real addressee even in vv. 10–12. The words spoken to the princess are spoken for his benefit. Even "in vv. 11–16 the king remains the main character."[30]

---

27. Derek Kidner, *Genesis* (London: Inter-Varsity, 1967), 71.

28. NJPS indeed sees the psalm as addressing a Tyrian bride, but it is hard to find a parallel for an expression such as *bat-ṣōr* meaning "a young woman of Tyre"; such expressions regularly refer to the people of a place (e.g., 137:8).

29. The prep. *b* carries over from the parallel colon. In taking the first phrase in v. 13 with v. 12, I understand *kĕbûddâ* as the same word that appears otherwise only in Judg. 18:21, an alternative to the regular *kābôd*, rather than as the f. of the adj. *kābôd*, which appears otherwise only in Ezek. 23:41.

30. N. H. Ridderbos, "The Psalms: Style-Figures and Structure," *OtSt* 13 (1963): 43–76 (see 72).

> ¹³ᵇTo the inside, the princess (with gold embroidery,
>   her dress of colored materials) ¹⁴ᵃwill be led to the king.

In vv. 13b–14a (4–4; cf. NJPS), the opening and closing phrases speak of the bride's processing to the groom, and the middle phrases describe her appearance. The precise meaning and the interrelationship of these middle phrases (the parenthesis in the translation) are unclear. The expression for gold embroidery is one that recurs in Exod. 28 and 39 to refer to settings of gold thread or filigree for the precious stones on the high priest's garment. The word for colored materials can refer to anything of a mixture of colors but most commonly denotes material with such a variety of colors, achieved either through the way it is woven or through the way it has been embroidered.

> ¹⁴ᵇThe bridesmaids behind her, her friends,
>   brought to you,
> ¹⁵Will be led with joyful rejoicing;
>   they will go into the king's palace.

Attention passes to the bridesmaids. They, too, are brought to the king ("you"), into the royal palace.

> ¹⁶Instead of your ancestors, you will have sons;
>   you will appoint them as leaders throughout the land.

A further significance of marriage surfaces. Any man wants to have sons who will continue his line; they take forward the line that comes down to him from his own ancestors. A bride is necessary to that end. A king in particular feels the need to have sons; his marriage means he can have the sons he needs to share in his government of the country. The poem may, indeed, refer to the government of the world that is the destiny of the Israelite king.

> ¹⁷I will commemorate your name for all generations;
>   therefore peoples will confess you forever and ever.

The final line pairs with the first in expressing the poet's homage to the king's *name. Here the significance of this homage is that it will lead to the further homage of the peoples. Thus the first halves of each colon stand parallel, as then do the time references in each second half.

Theological Implications

As usual, it is important to reflect on the theological significance of the psalm's original meaning and not merely its messianic or Christian reinterpretation, which is appropriate in a commentary on Hebrews. "After prophesying grievous things in the psalm before this, the inspired word now forecasts cheerful things, encouraging the downcast and teaching that they will both conquer and persevere."[31] Like (e.g.) Ps. 2, the poem affirms the position of the king, affirms his role as warrior, and reaffirms his position as someone marked out and blessed by God. But it insists that the king fights battles that embody truthfulness and faithfulness and combat faithlessness, battles such as Saul's against Ammon. The king is not to fight (for instance) simply to create an empire or work out a grudge. Royal power must be exercised to the right ends. In turn, the queen is reminded that she must forget her past. Israel was only too familiar with queens who did not do so. The queen's example must be Ruth (see Ruth 1:16–17), not Jezebel. Perhaps her submission to the king works within this framework. The psalm would then not be making a point about submission in general but urging the opposite marital-religious dynamic to the one that obtained at Ahab's court. And likewise, her attractiveness to the king will encourage a process whereby together they generate sons to rule throughout the land or throughout the earth. To many brides and grooms in the cultural setting of the West in the third millennium AD, this might not seem much of a prospect, but for a couple who must work within that traditional cultural context, it might have its satisfactions and its rewards. Perhaps more to the point, it sets constraints around groom and bride that their people might be grateful for.

31. Theodoret, *Psalms*, 1:259.

Psalm 46

Trust and Stop

Translation

The leader's. The Korahites'. On secrets/for girls/on eternities. Song.

[1]God is for us refuge and strength,
   help in troubles, readily available.
[2]Therefore we are not afraid when earth changes
   and when mountains fall down into the midst of the seas,
[3]Its waters foam in rage,[1]
   the mountains quake when it rises up.[2] (Rise)

[4]A river—its streams gladden God's city,
   the holy dwelling of the Most High.[3]
[5]God in its midst, it does not fall down;
   God helps it as morning comes.
[6]Nations have raged, kingdoms fallen down,
   he has given voice, earth shakes.
[7]Yhwh Armies is with us,
   Jacob's God is a haven for us. (Rise)

1. In the asyndetic construction, the first verb qualifies the second. Cf. JM 177g.
2. I take the finite verbs to continue the infinitival construction (cf. GKC 114r). DG 123 rather sees them as conditional asyndetic clauses.
3. On the adj. construction and the pl. noun, see GKC 124b, 132c; *IBHS* 14.3.3; DG 42.4. It seems less likely that the adj. is superlative when the pl. noun is intensive not numerical (and cf. the similar 65:4 [5] with a sg. noun). The textual variants (cf. *BHS*) likely reflect the unusual nature of the construction.

[8]Come and see Yhwh's deeds,
   how he has wrought great desolation[4] in the earth,
[9]terminating wars to the end of the earth.
He breaks the bow and snaps the spear,
   burns shields[5] in fire.
[10]"Stop, and acknowledge that I am God;
   I will be high among the nations, I will be high in the earth."
[11]Yhwh Armies is with us,
   Jacob's God is a haven for us. (Rise)

Interpretation

This psalm of trust does not fit the regular categories of a praise psalm, of a thanksgiving/testimony, or of a prayer psalm; there are features of each that it manifests and features of each that it lacks. It lacks the commitment to praise of a thanksgiving, the summons to praise of a hymn, and the invocation of a lament. It speaks in the first-person plural about Yhwh in the manner of a community thanksgiving/testimony, but it speaks of big truths about Yhwh in the manner of a hymn (with some allusion to the Red Sea deliverance) rather than telling a concrete story like a thanksgiving/testimony. It speaks of troubles and of nations raging in the manner of a prayer psalm but again tells of no specific present crisis. As a psalm of trust it indeed overlaps with all these. Like a protest psalm it presupposes the experience of trouble and pressure, and it incorporates a word from Yhwh designed to change the attitude of people, though this word is addressed only indirectly to the people under pressure. Like a praise psalm it declares the great truths about God on which the worshippers base their confidence, and like a praise psalm it assumes that these truths need to be heeded by the nations. Like a thanksgiving/testimony psalm, it speaks of God's proven trustworthiness, and in this sense "psalm of trust" is a misnomer. It does not talk about trust (it does not use the word); the only attitude it refers to is fear, the fear that it abjures. What it talks about is God and the security God means.

The psalm contains no concrete indication of a chronological setting, though the Assyrian invasions provide a backcloth for imagining the psalm's use (e.g., 2 Kings 17–18).[6] It gives ambiguous hints of geo-

4. Intensive pl. (see GKC 124c).
5. *'Ăgālôt* usually means "carts" (cf. Jerome) but never as war transport (for which one would expect *rekeb* or *merkābâ*). LXX and Tg more plausibly translate "shields"—in Aramaic, *'ăgîlā'*; perhaps one should repoint as *'ăgilôt* (cf. *HALOT*).
6. Lloyd Neve ("The Common Use of Traditions by the Author of Psalm 46 and Isaiah," *ExpT* 86 [1974–75]: 243–46) argues that parallels with Isaiah imply that the author lived

graphical background. Cliffs and sea, a city with a river, and exposure to the nations suggest a northern location such as Dan.[7] But presumably the preservation and ongoing use of the psalm so that it came to be in the Psalter imply that it came to be a Jerusalem psalm (a "Zion song"; see on Ps. 48) even though Jerusalem is unmentioned. Either way it glories in the fact that Yhwh is present in the city in its sanctuary, so that people can be sure of finding security through Yhwh their refuge there.

The threefold *Rise marks a plausible division into three sections; the end of the second and third are also marked by a refrain. There is no basis for adding the refrain after v. 3,[8] since refrains in the Psalms do not manifest the regularity that characterizes refrains in modern verse, and it is hard to believe that a refrain at this point could have been omitted by accident. The three sections describe violence in nature, political violence, and military violence,[9] the first a figure for the second and third, the second seeking to have its way through the third. There is no suggestion of an eschatological orientation in the psalm, in the sense that it looks forward to the End (certainly not a far-off End). It thus contrasts with the orientation on the End that sometimes appears in the prophets (e.g., Isa. 2:2–4). It speaks of an event whereby the ultimate purpose of God is put into effect in the experience of the worshippers.

The conviction that God helps "as morning comes" (v. 5) puts us on the track of its links with the Red Sea story, for Exod. 14:27 uses exactly that phrase (lit. "at the turning of morning") to refer to the moment when Moses made the sea return to drown the Egyptians.[10] Moses's praise song on that occasion speaks of the deeps freezing in the midst of the sea, and the psalm speaks of the mountains tottering in the midst of the seas (v. 2; cf. Exod. 15:8).[11] Both Moses's song and the psalm speak of Yhwh as stronghold (v. 1; cf. Exod. 15:2). Moses sings of Yhwh rising up; the psalm speaks of the sea's rising up but getting nowhere (v. 3; cf. Exod. 15:1, 7). Moses sings of setting Yhwh on high; the psalm speaks of Yhwh being on high (v. 10; cf. Exod. 15:2). Moses sings of God's holy abode; the psalm speaks of God's holy dwelling (v. 4; cf. Exod. 15:13, 17). Moses's song pictures peoples panicking at what Yhwh does; the psalm urges nations to look at what Yhwh has done and to stop resisting Yhwh's

---

in Isaiah's time. Otto Eissfeldt (*Kleine Schriften* [Tübingen: Mohr, 1968], 4:8–11) argues for the time of David.

7. H. Junker, "Der Strom, dessen Arme die Stadt Gottes erfreuen (Ps 46,5)," *Bib* 43 (1962): 197–201, suggests rather a background in Babylon with its canals.

8. Against (e.g.) Gunkel, *Psalmen*, 197.

9. Peterson, *Where Your Treasure Is*, 72.

10. Otherwise the phrase comes only in Judg. 19:26, with irony, since for the woman, this was not a moment of divine or Mosaic deliverance.

11. "Midst" is *lēb*, a rare usage.

purpose. The psalm affirms that the victory over Egypt at the Red Sea is a pattern for understanding Yhwh's relationship with Israel and its attackers and invites such other peoples to recognize the fact.

> The leader's. The Korahites'. On secrets/for girls/on eternities. Song.

Heading. See glossary, and for the third expression, see Ps. 9.

46:1–3. Three opening lines declare trust in God, or rather, declare God's trustworthiness; each is internally parallel.

> ¹God is for us refuge and strength,
>   help in troubles, readily available.

A series of noun statements thus puts the emphasis on factual statements about God rather than on the human attitude of trust or faith; what matters is not whether you have faith but whether what you have faith in is trustworthy. "We" appear only in a prepositional expression. The important thing is that God is *refuge and *strength. We could take this as a hendiadys: God is a strong refuge, a refuge whose security can be trusted. The second colon sharpens the definition. As a strong refuge, Yhwh is a means of *help in times of trouble and is totally available (*māṣāʾ* niphal). Yhwh is always there. All we have to do is run into this refuge. It was a truth that Martin Luther rejoiced in and made the starting point for his hymn "A Safe Stronghold."

> ²Therefore we are not afraid when earth changes
>   and when mountains fall down into the midst of the seas,

It is those facts about Yhwh that make the decisive difference to our attitude. "Do not be afraid" is a common prophetic/pastoral exhortation confronting people afraid of situations or threats (e.g., Isa. 41:10, 13, 14), to which "We are not afraid" is an appropriate response. The other two parallel clauses in v. 2 indicate potentially frightening situations, each involving an infinitive preceded by *b*, then a subject for the infinitive, with qal complementing hiphil (declarative) and plural noun complementing singular. The earth might seem the epitome of stability and unchangingness. But what if it changes, as when a landslide changes its surface shape? The second colon sharpens the point and gives precision to it. The potentially threatening factor is not earthquake, a rare event in Israel (cf. 18:7 [8]), but the power of the sea as it assails coastal cliffs. What if the effect is to tumble the cliffs into the sea? Occasionally this does cause cliff falls. We will discover that the psalm speaks metaphorically, and it may also speak mythically of the power of the supernatural waters of disorder, but whether such events take place literally, metaphorically, or mythically, "we are not afraid" because we have that refuge.

> ³Its waters foam in rage,
>   the mountains quake when it rises up. (Rise)

Verse 3 underlines the point, slightly ungrammatically: "it" each time is the plural "seas."[12] The line makes more explicit that it is those seas that cause the cataclysm of v. 2. Describing them as foaming in rage personalizes them: when seas pound and crash with monumental energy, it is as if they are overcome by rage, with the frightening energy that rage can engender. Likewise the mountains or cliffs are personalized: it is as if they shake with fright as the seas lift themselves up and throw themselves at them. And sometimes the cliffs do fall into the sea, or the force of the waters that emerge from Hermon causes a rock fall.

46:4–7. So how does God's protection work out? How do people find it? Verses 4–7 follow directly on from the first section as they continue the water image (one can see another reason not to insert the refrain here, as this interrupts the flow).

> ⁴A river—its streams gladden God's city,
>   the holy dwelling of the Most High.

Thus the opening reference to a river does not advertise a change of subject; in 24:2 "rivers" stood in parallel with "seas" in a reference to the waters that flow around and beneath the earth (cf. 74:13–15; 80:11 [12]). But "streams" (*peleg*) does not belong in this pool of ideas, and they are a less worrisome idea (see 1:3; 65:9 [10]). It is thus not so surprising that the verb these two nouns introduce (the above English word order follows the unusual Hebrew word order) is such a positive one. Perhaps the implication is that "the waters which threatened destruction have been subdued and thus transformed into the river of life."[13] Only this line and 87:3 refer to "God's city" (but see 48:1, 8 [2, 9] for similar expressions). It is natural to infer that the psalm refers to Jerusalem, but that is not explicit (contrast those other psalms), and no river with streams gladdens Jerusalem in the way it does Dan. Counterintuitively, the imagery

12. See GKC 132h. Or do the suffixes refer to God? So Meir Weiss, "Wege der neuen Dichtungswissenschaft in ihrer Anwendung auf die Psalmenforschung (Methodologische Bemerkungen, dargelegt am Beispiel von Psalm xlvi)," *Bib* 42 (1961): 255–302 (see 276); Fokkelman, *Major Poems*, 2:158.

13. Sidney Kelly, "Psalm 46," *JBL* 89 (1970): 305–12 (see 309). David Tsumura suggests a link with the twofold capacity of wine to rage and foam but also to gladden ("Twofold Image of Wine in Psalm 46:4–5," *JQR* 71 [1981]: 167–75).

does come to be attached to Jerusalem (cf. Isa. 33:21), perhaps through such a Danite psalm's coming to be used at Jerusalem. However this happened, whereas v. 4a is literal reality at Dan, at Jerusalem it is pure metaphor. Yhwh's presence means there are metaphorical streams that refresh Jerusalem. The fact that literal water supply is often a problem in that city would add power to the metaphor. Further, talk of a river with streams reminds us of Gen. 2. The word for river is the same, though the word for streams is different. But a more significant difference is that the Eden river watered a garden. This river waters a city, and the line thus hints that God's story could make its way from the garden where it began to the city where it will end.

The parallelism in v. 4 then makes more specific the object of this gladdening. Parallel to "God" is "the *Most High" and parallel to "city" is "holy dwelling."[14] The point is not that the city is itself identified as God's dwelling; there is no parallel for that idea. It is that the presence of the dwelling, the sanctuary (cf. 26:8; 43:3), makes this God's city.

> [5]God in its midst, it does not fall down;
> God helps it as morning comes.

I take the opening noun clause as subordinate to the verbal clause that follows. The noun clause summarizes an implication of v. 4, and the verb draws an inference that begins to make explicit the link with the psalm's opening lines. It does that verbally (though *môṭ* is now niphal rather than qal) and substantially. Whereas apparently secure entities such as the earth and the mountains may turn out to be less secure than they look, the city of God does not *fall down (the suffix "its" and the verb are feminine, showing that they refer to "city" rather than "dwelling"). The second colon indicates how this is so. The city is secure not because of its natural strength or its walls but because God *helps it, "at the turning of the morning," the expression for the moment when Moses made the Red Sea return and drown the Egyptians (Exod. 14:27).[15]

> [6]Nations have raged, kingdoms fallen down,
> he has given voice, earth shakes.

The significance of this allusion becomes clear. In Israel's experience the entities that "rage" (the verb recurs from v. 3) are other nations that attack

---

14. Pl.; see 43:3.

15. I doubt whether the significance of this distinctive expression should be assimilated to that of other expressions referring to the coming of morning, studied by Joseph Ziegler, "Die Hilfe Gottes 'am Morgen,'" in *Alttestamentliche Studien* (Friedrich Nötscher Festschrift; ed. Hubert Junker and Johannes Botterweck; Bonn: Hanstein, 1950), 281–88.

Israel. Like the sea, they will not actually be angry, but they behave with the kind of aggression that sometimes emerges from anger. In the Prophets, plural "nations" often refers to the great imperial superpower (e.g., Isa. 5:26; 14:26; 30:28), and this reference would make sense here. Ephraimite and Judean royal cities such as Dan, Samaria, and Jerusalem were vulnerable to attack by powers such as Assyria. The psalm's declaration is that when that happens, these nations themselves *fall down in the way that mountains might (v. 2), but because of God's presence, God's city does not (v. 5). The nations are also characterized as kingdoms, another plural that can be used to refer to the superpower (Isa. 13:4; 47:5; Jer. 1:10, 15).

The second colon then indicates how this fall will come about. God gives voice. In 18:13 [14] the parallelism indicates that the phrase there refers to thunder,[16] and so it may be here; Ps. 29 likewise speaks much of the power of Yhwh's voice as it thunders, specifically over mighty waters (cf. also 68:33 [34]). When Yhwh thunders, the earth trembles.[17] The psalm thus mixes its metaphors, or, rather, mixes the use of its metaphor. Earlier, the seas stood for the superpower, and the earth stood for the smaller nations under its attack. That is a natural image, given the way the seas stand for dynamic energy that assails God and God's ordered world. But then the river with its streams stood for beneficent provision, and now earth seems to be a figure for nations and kingdoms and thus for the superpower. Earth has become an alternative figure to sea, but now the earth is made to collapse rather than causing collapse.

> [7]Yhwh Armies is with us,
> 　Jacob's God is a haven for us. (Rise)

And all that is so because Yhwh *Armies is "with us"; the preposition suggests God's being "with" people not merely as a presence but also as active and bringing deliverance. In the second colon "Jacob's God" parallels that earlier title, and God being our *haven parallels God being with us. "Jacob's God" appears in the context of trouble (v. 1), as in 20:1 [2], which also speaks of the name of Jacob's God putting us on high to keep us safe (*śāgab* piel, the root of the word for "haven"). Jacob's God is our "taker up" (Vg).[18] It is because God is with us that we have a haven.

---

16. I take *nātan qōl* there and *nātan bĕqôl* here as variants, with JM 125m; cf. *IBHS* 11.2.5d. GKC 119q sees the expression here as meaning "thundered with his voice," i.e., mightily, but this seems unwarranted.

17. *DCH* distinguishes two verbs *mûg*, one meaning "melt," the other "waver," though it then gives "tremble" as a meaning of the first and lists this occurrence under both. Applied to the earth, "waver" seems more appropriate than "melt," and the idea of the earth trembling links better with the idea of Yhwh thundering.

18. See Augustine's comments, *Psalms*, 158.

46:8–11. Imperatives now suddenly feature in driving home the implications of the psalm.

> ⁸Come and see Yhwh's deeds,
>   how he has wrought great desolation in the earth,
>   ⁹ᵃterminating wars to the end of the earth.

The first colon in v. 8 stands alone as an introduction to two parallel bicola: that is, the section begins with a tricolon (against MT, which makes the second line in the section a tricolon). The opening invitation to "come" is presumably an invitation to take part in worship (cf. 95:1), and "come and see" implies something to see. Since the people who speak are those who know that Yhwh is their refuge and strength and know that Yhwh is with them, presumably the people who are addressed are other peoples, as is often the case in praise psalms. The same phrase addressed to other peoples in 66:5 leads into an account of the Red Sea event, and the sequence here is similar while less specific. It may be that the worship included some symbolic reenactment of Yhwh's deeds, but we have no evidence for that beyond the ambiguous expressions in these two psalms. In 48:8 [9], talk of "seeing" rather refers to the acts of God in the people's ongoing life, and it is simpler to assume that this is also so here. These events whose results can be seen (Dan and Jerusalem stand bloody but unbowed) embody a promise of something much bigger and more final. The invitation to the nations then offers them an alternative to the destruction they are being invited symbolically to witness. At the same time the psalm might covertly address Israelites who at best half-believed the statements about God being "our" security. It thus encourages Israel to live by the affirmations of trust that characterize the psalm, which Israel often found difficult. It would then indicate the subtext of the psalm's affirmations. It says, "We are not afraid." It means, "You need not and must not be afraid." Yhwh's deeds are then first spelled out in v. 8b as involving terrible desolation.

The parallel colon (v. 9a) explains that here desolation is good news, as was the case at the Red Sea. "Terminating wars" parallels and gives specificity to "wreaking desolation," the participle pairing with the qatal. "To the end of the earth" then pairs with and goes beyond "in the earth." The earth is perhaps once again the world ruled by the superpower, while the end of the earth may reach beyond that to far-off peoples at the edge of the known world, beyond the superpower's rule (cf. the movement between "the nations" and peoples such as Tarshish, Put, and Lud in Isa. 66:18–19). To put the superpower out of action will terminate the

71

threat of war for peoples that are yet beyond the superpower's reach but may not always stay that way.

> [9b]He breaks the bow and snaps the spear,
> burns shields in fire.

Yhwh brings about this termination by destroying the weapons of war. Here the first colon refers to the disabling of the offensive weapons of the individual soldier, the weapon with which he kills from a distance and the weapon with which he kills in hand-to-hand fighting. The parallel colon refers to the soldier's means of defense, using another yiqtol but one that goes beyond breaking to burning. It means there will be no more fighting; soldiers cannot fight without shields.[19]

> [10]"Stop, and acknowledge that I am God;
> I will be high among the nations, I will be high in the earth."

Suddenly and unannounced, Yhwh then speaks. Presumably the addressee of Yhwh's exhortation is also the nations. They are to stop asserting themselves, behaving like the seas pointlessly hurling themselves against the land that they are never going to overwhelm.[20] They need to *acknowledge who it is that they are seeking to assail. Once more, the nations/the earth will signify the superpower that pretends to be high in authority and splendor (cf. 66:7). Yhwh intends to stand high in what the superpower pretends to be its sphere. At the same time, the indirect addressee may again be Israel, whom Yhwh urges not to stop fighting aggressively but to stop trying to look after its own destiny and defense. Israel, too, needs to acknowledge that God is God (and therefore that God is its refuge and stronghold, its help and its haven). It needs to see that Yhwh intends to be high in the superpower's sphere.

> [11]Yhwh Armies is with us,
> Jacob's God is a haven for us. (Rise)

The repeated declaration of trust forms a response to that challenge, the response that the psalmist and God look for from Israel.

19. Nor without carts carrying supplies, on the traditional translation. On this motif, see Robert Bach, "'. . . , Der Bogen zerbricht, Spiesse zerschlägt und Wagen mit Feuer verbrennt,'" in *Probleme biblischer Theologie* (Gerhard von Rad Festschrift; ed. Hans Walter Wolff; Munich: Kaiser, 1971), 13–26.
20. Cf. Tg, "cease from war."

Theological Implications

Violence (natural, political, military) is a prominent fact of human life, and one we cannot evade. Prayer is not designed to make it possible for us to escape from violence into peace. "Praying in the midst of violence . . . is our desperately needed corrective to the widespread malpractice of prayer as withdrawal." But neither do we confront violence. Rather, it is "dealt with indirectly: it is absorbed into the forms and ceremonies of prayer."[21] Indeed, the subject of the psalm is not violence but God.

"Be still and know that I am God" is a common invitation in Christian spirituality. This involves a reinterpretation of the psalm. Nowhere do the psalms have an ideal of silence. Their assumption is that one finds God not in silence but in noise. In noisy Western cultures, we may need to cultivate silence, and the use of the psalm to this end may be inspired by the Holy Spirit, even though it does make the words mean something that the psalmist did not say and would not have dreamed of saying. Spirit-inspired interpretation often works by making the words of Scripture mean something quite different from what they actually meant, because new situations make it necessary for God to say new things. At the same time, we have to be wary of missing what the text actually did say. Here it issues an important challenge to the superpower to stand still and recognize that God is God and that the superpower is not.

In contrast to a currently popular view (but in keeping with the last book in the NT), Yhwh reckons that violence can stop violence. Martin Klingbeil suggests that it is this declaration in Ps. 46 that shows us the way to integrate the idea that God is warrior into theological conceptions about God.[22] Further, the challenge to stop also issues an important challenge to the people of God to give up thinking that it has responsibility for its destiny or that its task is to bring in the kingdom of God, extend the kingdom of God, or further the kingdom of God. Scripture does not think in such terms. The psalm makes clear that the city of God is not a mere heavenly community (as Augustine's *City of God* might seem to imply) but an earthly reality. But in this city, it is not for us to fix things. It is for us to expect God to fix things.

21. Peterson, *Where Your Treasure Is*, 71.
22. *Yahweh Fighting from Heaven*, OBO 169 (Göttingen: Vandenhoeck & Ruprecht, 1999), 309–10.

Psalm 47

God Has Begun to Reign

Translation

The leader's. The Korahites'. Composition.

[1]All you peoples, clap hands,
    shout to God with resounding voice.
[2]For Yhwh Most High is to be revered,
    the great king over all the earth.[1]
[3]He subjected[2] peoples under us,
    countries under our feet.
[4]He chose our possession for us,
    the rising of Jacob that he loves. (Rise)
[5]God has gone up with a shout,
    Yhwh with the sound of a horn.

[6]Make music for our God,[3] make music,
    make music for our king, make music.
[7]For God is king of all the earth;
    make music with understanding.[4]

1. The copula ("is") could be placed instead or additionally in the second colon.
2. For the verb, see 18:47 [48]; on the apparent jussive, see *IBHS* 34.2.1c; GKC 109k.
3. I take the suffix and the prep. *l* in the second colon as also applying in the first (cf. LXX). In isolation, the bare Hebrew *'ĕlōhîm* could be a vocative addressed to subordinate heavenly beings, as in 29:1, but it means God in the lines on either side.
4. *Maśkîl*: the term comes in psalm headings (*instruction), but a more general meaning seems appropriate here (cf. LXX, Jerome).

[8]God has begun to reign over the nations;
   as God he has sat on his holy throne.
[9]The peoples' nobles—they have joined
   the people of the God of Abraham.
For the shields of the earth are God's;
   he has gone right up.[5]

Interpretation

The psalm follows the classic form of a praise psalm, a bidding followed by the reasons for praise or content of praise in a kî ("for") clause;[6] like other instances (e.g., Ps. 95; 100), it goes through this sequence twice, in vv. 1–5 and 6–9. Thus one can outline the psalm as follows:

v. 1	Bidding to praise	v. 6
v. 2	kî clause: Yhwh as universal king	v. 7
vv. 3–4	Yhwh has asserted power over the nations	vv. 8–9b
v. 5	Yhwh has gone up on high	vv. 9c–d

In each half, the bidding thus occupies one line, the reasons four lines: one line by way of noun clause, three lines of verbal clauses. The first bidding (v. 1) focuses on the noise of praise (clapping and shouting), the second (v. 6) emphasizes its musical nature (four occurrences of the same imperative, with another in v. 7b). The initial lines of reasons in the form of noun clauses (vv. 2, 7) are rather similar, both referring to Yhwh's universal kingship. The first set of subsequent lines in verbal clauses (vv. 3–5) concentrate on Yhwh's acts in relation to Israel, the second set (vv. 8–9) on God's relationship with the world as a whole. Unusually for this part of the Psalter, the first half of the psalm uses the name Yhwh twice, while the second half uses only the word "God." One can see the logic in this, as the "Yhwh" half relates more to acts in relation to Israel, while the "God" half relates to acts in relation to the world as a whole. But in each of these sets of reasoning, the first line refers to Yhwh's power over the nations (vv. 3, 8), while the last refers to Yhwh's going up (vv. 5, 9c–d). The *Rise after v. 4 should not mislead us into seeing a division in the psalm at that point or into seeing v. 5 as distinctively important.

5. LXX and Jerome imply na'ălû, "They have gone right up."
6. Karl Heinz Ratschow ("Epikrise zum Psalm 47," ZAW 53 [1935]: 171–80) less plausibly takes the three kî clauses to suggest a threefold structure for the psalm. Watson (Classical Hebrew Poetry, 371–73) divides the psalm into five stanzas, patterned abca'b'.

Like Ps. 46, the psalm implies a celebration of God's acts on Israel's behalf, though the focus of this celebration is more the acts recounted in the story from Joshua to David. It implies that Israel's worship recounted those acts, too, in such a way as to bring home the way they provide the clue to political events in the contemporary world. In recounting them, the psalm points to their significance both for Israel and for the nations that were put in their place in that story. Thus other nations of a later day are urged to come to recognize the truth expressed in that story and to see its implications for them, though that urging will again have more immediate significance for Israel: the exhortation formally addressed to the nations is designed to encourage Israel itself. In these respects, too, the psalm compares with the preceding one. There is also some overlap with Ps. 24, another psalm implying a worship event that celebrates Yhwh's coming to the city where Yhwh's own sanctuary already stands. The theme of Yhwh's beginning to reign reappears in Pss. 93; 96–99.

Artur Weiser speaks of historical, eschatological, and cultic interpretations of the psalm: we can seek to interpret it in light of a historical event such as a victory in war, we can refer it to the consummation of Yhwh's reign at the End, or we can link it with a celebration in worship. Weiser seeks to combine these.[7] The difficulty is that we have no means of linking the psalm with a particular event, it makes no reference to a future consummation of God's reign,[8] and we can only speculate about how to move from the liturgical references in vv. 1 and 6 to any specific liturgical event or practice. Succeeding the historical, eschatological, and cultic fashions of the past two centuries of Psalms study is the canonical fashion of present Psalms study,[9] and this points in another direction. The psalm is more directly referring not to historical events, to eschatological events, or to liturgical events, but to a story. The story no doubt refers to historical events, carries eschatological implications, and was celebrated in worship. But we have too little further information on these three to make them keys to the psalm's interpretation; that is to interpret the known by the unknown. What we do have elsewhere in the OT is a version of the story to which the psalm refers, so we can interpret it by that.

---

7. *Psalms*, 375; cf. A Caquot, "Le psaume 47 et la royauté de Yahwé," *RHPR* 39 (1959): 311–37 (see 312–14). J. J. M. Roberts ("The Religio-Political Setting of Psalm 47," *BASOR* 221 [1976]: 129–31) combines the historical and liturgical in another way. James Muilenburg ("Psalm 47," *JBL* 63 [1944]: 235–56) emphasizes its liturgical nature.

8. Craigie (*Psalms 1–50*, 350) tellingly refers to the eschatological interpretation as a "re-reading"—that is, it is not the psalm's inherent meaning. But contrast W. A. M. Beuken, "Psalm xlvii," *OtSt* 21 (1981): 38–54.

9. But J. Schaper ("Psalm 47 und sein 'Sitz im Leben,'" *ZAW* 106 [1994]: 262–75) argues for a postexilic date (and therefore that the psalm is not evidence for a celebration of Yhwh's kingship in the monarchic period).

The leader's. The Korahites'. Composition.

Heading. See glossary. This is not a David psalm. Against the background of the story of the occupation of the land and the bringing up of the covenant chest, it makes no reference to a human king, though it makes four references to God's being king or reigning. In this psalm Yhwh's power does not "consolidate and legitimate a dynasty. There is no trace of royal ideology in Psalm 47."[10]

47:1–5. The psalm begins with five six-stress lines, all internally parallel.

> ¹All you peoples, clap hands,
>> shout to God with resounding voice.

"Clap a hand" (the noun is actually singular) and "shout with a voice" complement each other in referring to noise made with body and with mouth; "*resounding" then nuances the second expression. The invocation to "all peoples" and the address "to Yhwh" each apply to both cola. The bidding indicates the important role that noise makes in worship. It parallels the noise at a football game or a rock concert.[11] Such expressions of celebration and enthusiasm often issue instinctively from inside the person, require the avoidance of constraints such as music or poetic form, and by their unrestrained gusto give maximum honor to the one they pay homage to. Significantly, clapping and shouting also belong at a coronation (1 Sam. 10:24; 2 Kings 11:12–13).

> ²For Yhwh Most High is to be revered,
>> the great king over all the earth.

In the first *kî* clause, the second colon nuances the first: it is by virtue of being the great king over all the earth that Yhwh's being the *Most High impacts other peoples and not merely Israel, so that for them too Yhwh is to be *revered. The assertion that Yhwh is the great king is a bold one, given that the Assyrian king (the king of the nations) claimed that title (cf. 2 Kings 18:19). The psalm makes a counterassertion about who exercises sovereignty in the world. What evidence is there of this, such as might convince the nations?

10. Gerstenberger, *Psalms*, 1:198. Contrast James Wharton's emphasis on the link between divine and human kingship ("Psalm 47," *Int* 47 [1993]: 163–65).

11. Cf. Chrysostom's expression of concern at the idea that such noise should feature in church (*Psalms*, 1:298–99); also Cassiodorus, *Psalms*, 1:459; less overtly, Augustine, *Psalms*, 161.

> ³He subjected peoples under us,
>   countries under our feet.

Verse 3 begins to offer an answer to this implicit question. Yhwh subjected peoples (of the kind v. 1 has called on) under us; the verb applies to both cola, but the second colon adds "countries" (the much rarer word *lĕ'ummîm*) and underlines their location. The main verbs in vv. 3–4 are yiqtol,[12] and the Midrash understands it to refer to the day when Yhwh *will* subdue the peoples, choose our possession, and overthrow the throne of the kingdoms (Hag. 2:22) so as to sit on the throne that belongs to Yhwh as the holy one.[13] But the great time of subjecting and choosing lies in the past, and v. 5 makes a transition to qatal without apparently changing the psalm's time reference. So I take the whole of vv. 3–5 to refer to the past (cf. LXX), the time Yhwh and Israel entered the land.[14]

> ⁴He chose our possession for us,
>   the rising of Jacob that he loves. (Rise)

Verse 4 then offers a rationale for that subduing of other peoples. It was a means to the end of giving Israel its land. Here the verb "chose" similarly applies to both cola, and "rising of Jacob" nuances "our possession." EVV have "pride of Jacob," but this misses one aspect of the connotations of *gā'ôn*. Psalm 46:3 spoke of the sea's "rising up" (*ga'ăwâ*) and then of its being put down: the sea lifts itself up literally, and the literal is a sign of the metaphorical. Here the rising or height of Jacob is a literal (but probably also a metaphorical) description of Israel's mountain heartland running from the Negeb to the Galilee, the special "possession" that Yhwh put Israel in control of. The parallelism further suggests that the object of God's love is then not the ancestor Jacob nor the people Jacob but those heights of Jacob (cf. LXX); that is, "loves" parallels "chose" in the first colon. In other words, "He loves that mountain country and [therefore] chose it as a possession for us, the people of Jacob."

> ⁵God has gone up with a shout,
>   Yhwh with the sound of a horn.

12. "Loves" is qatal, but *'āhēb* is a stative verb, so an English present tense is natural. Perhaps it also carries the connotation of *dedicate oneself.

13. See *Midrash on Psalms*, 1:458–59.

14. Against Goldingay, *Songs from a Strange Land*, 77–78! Compare the verbs in Ps. 18.

The qatal verb makes more explicit that vv. 3–5 as a whole are recalling the occasion when Yhwh and Israel came into possession of the promised land. As Israel visibly ascended to the heights of Jacob (as they will now become), Yhwh invisibly did so. Theologically, perhaps one should reverse that. It was Yhwh's entering into possession of this land formally controlled by Baal that meant Israel came into possession of it. Once more one verb governs two cola, with "Yhwh" balancing "God" and "the sound of a horn" balancing "a *shout." Both a shout and the sound of a horn are part of the story of Israel's original taking of Canaan and then of its establishing its capital there (see esp. Josh. 6; 2 Sam. 6:15). Taking up the ark (ʿālâ hiphil; "went up" here is ʿālâ qal) is part of the latter story (2 Sam. 6:2, 12, 15). The shout and the horn are also part of worship, and it is easy to imagine that the sounds of battle were echoed in that worship. Israel's worship thus followed the shape and sound of the events even as the story of the events echoed the nature of their liturgical celebration.[15] Like shouting, blowing a horn is also part of crowning a king (e.g., 1 Kings 1:39). The OT does not say that the chest was annually taken up to the temple, and it would be hazardous to infer this from v. 5 or v. 9b.[16]

47:6–9. The second section comprises five further bicola; only vv. 6 and 8 are internally parallel.

> [6]Make music for our God, make music,
>   make music for our king, make music.

The section begins with a very emphatic encouragement to make *music in Yhwh's name. The beauty and form of music thus complements the unformed energy of cheering and clapping (v. 1) in bringing glory to God. The fact that Yhwh is *the* great king is complemented by the fact that Yhwh is *our* king, though that hardly means the addressees must be different from v. 1; the psalm speaks to the nations about Israel's God.

> [7]For God is king of all the earth;
>   make music with understanding.

The backing for that immediately returns to the fact that Yhwh is *the* king. A fifth exhortation to make music follows, qualified by explicit reference to the rational content of this form of worship; music combines expressiveness with content.

15. Tg understands the height of Jacob to refer to the temple, whose location was the destination of the covenant chest.
16. Contrast (e.g.) Mowinckel, *Psalms in Israel's Worship*, 1:171.

> [8]God has begun to reign over the nations;
>   as God he has sat on his holy throne.

The psalm again makes a transition to talking in qatal terms, and LXX thus translates *ebasileusen*, Jerome *regnavit*. In contrast, TNIV has "reigns," and NRSV has "is king."[17] But the form of the verb in the psalm is exactly the one used when a human king begins his reign (e.g., 2 Sam. 15:10; 1 Kings 1:11).[18] Yhwh became king in Canaan when arriving there with the Israelites. God's beginning to reign (v. 8) is the event that initiates God's being king and reigning on an ongoing basis (v. 7).[19] The parallel colon restates the point. When David brought the covenant chest up to Jerusalem, this was the moment when Yhwh sat invisibly enthroned there as God. From there henceforth Yhwh reigned over Israel, and over the nations.

> [9]The peoples' nobles—they have joined
>   the people of the God of Abraham.
> For the shields of the earth are God's;
>   he has gone right up.

The fact that the nobles of the peoples were compelled to acknowledge Yhwh along with Israel is a sign of that reign. The point is spelled out in the second colon, though ambiguously. The line could imply that the nobles join in with Israel, though one would then usually expect a preposition such as *'el*. Or it could imply that they join as members of Israel. Perhaps there is little difference. Either way, their action resembles that of people such as Jethro, Rahab, the Gibeonites, or subsequent people such as Uriah the Hittite; one might see all these as joining *with* Israel in its acknowledgment of Yhwh or as *becoming* (part of) Israel.[20] Either way, this is a fulfillment of Yhwh's promise to Abraham, and it helps resolve a tension set up by the opening verses, where the peoples were exhorted to hail Yhwh with enthusiasm on the basis of Yhwh's having subdued them under Israel's feet.

17. DG 57 (remark 1) describes this as a stative qatal. JM 112a thinks the parallel *yāšab* may be stative qal: "he sits."

18. It would also be used in expressions such as "he reigned for two years," but the psalm would not be implying that Yhwh's reign has now ended.

19. See, e.g., Edward Lipiński, "*Yāhweh mâlāk*," *Bib* 44 (1963): 405–60; Leo Perdue, "'Yahweh Is King over All the Earth,'" *ResQ* 17 (1974): 85–98. On the debate over this expression, see J. J. M. Roberts, "Mowinckel's Enthronement Festival," in *Book of Psalms*, ed. Flint and Miller, 97–115 (see 105–8).

20. LXX implies *'im* (with) for *'am* (people of); *BHS* suggests haplography and that we should read both. Keith Bodner suggests taking v. 9b as vocative ("The 'Embarrassing Syntax' of Ps. 47:10," *JTS*, n.s., 54 [2003]: 570–75); one could then translate "The people's nobles have gathered, people of the God of Abraham. . . ."

Either way, it is not an expression of a humanly centered universalism of the kind that Christians approve of. The point is not that these representatives of the nations were able to share in Israel's privileged relationship with Yhwh (though that is true). It is that in the person of these people, other nations were acknowledging the sovereignty of Yhwh in the world as Yhwh has demonstrated it in events involving Israel and other peoples such as the Egyptians and the Canaanites. The psalm pushes that point further in speaking of "nobles" involved in this joining.

That point is more explicit in v. 9c–d. The nobles are now referred to as the shields, the protectors or guardians of the nations.[21] They belong to Yhwh. They are Yhwh's underlings. The final colon explains this, while also picking up the verb *ʿālâ* from v. 5, though it now uses the niphal and adds an adverb to indicate how far Yhwh has gone. In climbing to the top of the mountain ridge with the Israelites and then ascending to a throne in Jerusalem, Yhwh asserted lordship over all the nations around.

Theological Implications

It can seem odd to speak of God "beginning to reign," as if God stopped reigning. God's throne stands firm from of old (93:2). At the Red Sea the Israelites declared the conviction that Yhwh would henceforth reign forever (Exod. 15:18). Yet alongside the conviction that God is always sovereign and can never be frustrated, the OT from time to time makes the declaration that God is beginning to reign in the sense of asserting an authority in a realm or at a time when that has not been recognized. That happened at the Red Sea, it happened at the conquest of Canaan, it happened when Yhwh brought about the end of the exile (see Isa. 52:7). It happens again when Jesus comes along and declares that God's reign is here, in a situation when it had long not been a reality in the experience of the Jewish people (Mark 1:14–15). The psalm's assertion is not that God always reigns (though there is a sense in which that is so). It is that from time to time God reigns. This is really good news, because if events as we usually experience them result from God reigning, it is not much of a reign. Much of the time we live between the reigns. Other parts of Scripture (not this psalm) promise that one day God will reign. This psalm assures us that there have been occasions when God reigned. In using this psalm in worship, we remind ourselves of that and build up our conviction that it can happen again. In this sense, the psalm is indeed a statement of hope, though implicitly rather than explicitly.

---

21. I thus assume that the psalm uses "shield" as a metaphor rather than that *māgēn* is here a different word from that for "shield" (see *CP* 241–42, 251).

Psalm 48

God Made Known in the City of God

Translation

Song. Composition. The Korahites'.

[1]Yhwh is great and much praised
in the city of our God.
His holy mountain [2]is the most beautiful height,
the greatest joy in all the earth.
Mount Zion is Zaphon's heights,[1]
the town of the great king.

[3]In its citadels[2] God
has made himself known as a haven.
[4]For now: when the kings assembled,[3]
people passed over altogether.
[5]As those saw, they were stunned,
they were terrified, they panicked.
[6]Trembling seized them there,
writhing like a woman birthing.

[7]With an east wind you break up
Tarshish ships.

1. *Yārēk* and *yarkâ* can mean "thigh," "loin," or "side," but in the pl. also "the extremities" in distance, height, or depth.
2. Not "palaces" in this context, since the point is the defensive strength of these buildings.
3. I take the word order in which the subj. precedes the verb as a sign that this is a circumstantial clause (cf. *TTH* 159; JM 155nc).

⁸As we have heard, so have we seen,
    in the city of Yhwh Armies,
In the city of our God
    which God will establish forever. (Rise)

⁹We think about your commitment, God,
    within your palace.
¹⁰Like your name, God, so your praise
    reaches to the ends of the earth.
Your right hand is full of faithfulness;
    ¹¹Mount Zion rejoices.
The cities of Judah are glad[4]
    for the sake of your decisions.

¹²Go around Zion, go about it,
    count its towers,
¹³Give your mind to its rampart,[5]
    pass through its citadels,
So that you may recount to the next generation
    ¹⁴that this is God.
Our God forever and ever—
    he will drive us against death [MT]/to the end [LXX].[6]

Interpretation

Psalm 48 links with both the preceding psalms. In terms of theme, it again takes up the story of Israel's deliverance at the Red Sea and its conquest of Canaan and sees the same dynamics in Yhwh's relationship with a sanctuary in the land, here explicitly Zion. Like Ps. 47, it is in general terms a praise psalm, and while it lacks the formal structure of exhortation to praise followed by reasons for praise that appeared there, vv. 1–8 could be seen as an instance of that structure; v. 3 simply lacks a "for." But vv. 9–14 then take the psalm in new directions that give it further overlap with the stress on confidence in Yhwh in Ps. 46.[7]

It thus can be outlined as follows:

4. LXX takes the verbs in v. 11 as jussive (cf. NRSV), but the context in vv. 9–11 suggests rather that they are statements (cf. TNIV).

5. I take ḥêlâ as a slip for ḥêlāh (sg. and bearing a third-person sg. suffix).

6. MT has 'al-mût, the inf. const. (!) of mût (cf. Jerome and Syr, who may imply inf. abs. or the noun); LXX implies 'ōlāmôt. But the expression resembles ones that come in the headings to Pss. 9 and 46, and it might be a displaced element from the heading to Ps. 49 (so Gunkel, Psalmen, 208).

7. Julian Morgenstern ("Psalm 48," HUCA 16 [1941]: 1–95) sees it as resulting from the combining of two earlier psalms, vv. 4–7 and vv. 1–3, 8–14.

Declaration about Yhwh (vv. 1–2)
Basis of that declaration (vv. 3–8)
  In past events (vv. 3–6)
  In present experience (vv. 7–8)
Confession (vv. 9–11)
Commission (vv. 12–14)

Each of the four main sections refers to or hints at a point of the compass: north (*ṣāpôn*) in v. 2; east in v. 7; the right hand, a way of referring to the south, in v. 10; and "behind," a way of referring to the west, in v. 13.[8] A reader who noticed that would be reminded that Yhwh is the God of all four points of the compass. Such a declaration stands in tension with the protest of a person like Job, who cannot find God in any of the directions (Job 23:8–9). The psalm reassures Job (cf. Ps. 139:7–12); Job challenges the psalm.

The psalm is distinctive in focusing the basis for its praise so much on God's involvement with Jerusalem and specifically with the temple. In this sense it is the kind of psalm described as a "Zion song" in 137:3, like Pss. 46 and 76. These glory in the presence of Yhwh in the city and in Yhwh's victory over forces that oppose Yhwh's lordship in the world, exercised from there: each is thus "not so much a song about Zion as it is a song about the God who is manifested in Zion."[9] During the twentieth century it was conventional to reckon that these psalms relate to an annual liturgical celebration of Yhwh's commitment to Zion, and this may be right, but we would be unwise to try to infer the nature of this liturgy from the psalm. Nor do we know what historical acts of God it may relate to, but we can imagine it being used in connection with various occasions when Yhwh rescued the city from attackers. While it is not fashionable to connect the psalm historically with the city's deliverance from Assyria in the time of Hezekiah, this is the kind of event against which we may usefully imagine the psalm, as is the case with Pss. 46 and 47. But the nature of each psalm is to omit concrete reference to such events and to focus on seeing such deliverances in Israel's history in light of events at the beginning of Israel's story. The hyperbolic nature of the psalm's references to an experience of deliverance should not be reckoned to mean it is not referring to a

8. See Martin Palmer, "The Cardinal Points in Psalm 48," *Bib* 46 (1965): 357–58; Israelites orientate on the east, so that the south is on the right and the west is what lies behind us. Palmer links this point with a fourfold outline of the psalm, to which v. 8 is then central (cf. Leo Krinetzki, "Zur Poetik und Exegese von Ps 48," *BZ* 4 [1960]: 70–97).
9. Nasuti, *Tradition History and the Psalms of Asaph*, 151.

historical deliverance.[10] Psalm 48 thus encourages people who use it to praise Yhwh on the basis of the awareness that Yhwh acts in relation to Jerusalem in succeeding centuries as at the beginning.

Song. Composition. The Korahites'.

Heading. See glossary. The LXX adds "On the second day of the week"; the psalm was used on Monday in the daily service in the Second Temple.[11]

48:1–2. The psalm begins with a three-line summary of Zion's significance for the praise of Yhwh.[12] The lines comprise simply a succession of nominal expressions without verbs, making it difficult to be sure how to construe them as lines. I follow NRSV in taking the last phrase in v. 1 with the words that follow. One can then construe the lines as following a reasonably conventional rhythm (4-2, 3-2, 3-3). As usual, there is also some uncertainty about how to turn these noun expressions into English verbal sentences. Thus NJPS provides a copula only in the first, with the remaining nominal expressions hanging from it, NRSV provides a copula in the first two lines but not the third, TNIV in the first and third but not the second, while NIVI provides one in all three lines. In keeping with the common self-contained nature of poetic lines, I have followed NIVI.

> [1]Yhwh is great and much praised
>   in the city of our God.
> His holy mountain [2]is the most beautiful height,
>   the greatest joy in all the earth.
> Mount Zion is Zaphon's heights,
>   the town of the great king.

The deep structure of the opening statement about Yhwh's praiseworthiness is not so different from the opening line of a hymn of praise; it might have begun "Praise Yhwh, for he is great." But its form gives immediate prominence to Yhwh, both in the affirmation of Yhwh's greatness and in the declaration that Yhwh is to be praised or (more likely) actually is praised.[13] Yet the prepositional phrase does divert the psalm from giving prominence to Yhwh toward the agenda that will dominate

10. Cf. Robert P. Gordon, "How Did Psalm 48 Happen? in *Holy Land, Holy City* (Carlisle, UK: Paternoster, 2004), 35–45.

11. See Trudiger, *The Psalms of the Tamid Service*, 75–87.

12. See Michael L. Barré, "The Seven Epithets of Zion in Ps 48,2–3," *Bib* 69 (1988): 557–63.

13. In 18:3 [4]; 96:4; 113:3; 145:3 the context suggests that the pual ptc. *mĕhullāl* is gerundive ("to be praised"), but in Ezek. 26:17 it is descriptive ("praised"), and that fits

the psalm. The place where Yhwh is praised is "the city of our God." The phrase comes in the Psalms only here and in v. 8; simple "city of God" comes only in 46:4 [5] and 87:3. Zion is the city that belongs to Yhwh.

The second line extends the point. Because it is a city, it is on a hill, as cities often were. Because it belongs to Yhwh, it is holy. So to say it is "his holy mountain" restates the point in the first line. What characterizes the city on the mountain, however, is first that it is the most beautiful of heights[14] and then that it is the most joyous place in all the earth.[15] Geographically and aesthetically, there is nothing remarkable about Mount Zion. It is neither as high nor as attractive as the mountains around. Neither can one say that there has actually been more joy there than anywhere else on earth, though that might be so. Both descriptions are theological statements. It is the most beautiful height because Yhwh lives there and can be met there. And for the same reason it is a place where joy is more appropriate than is the case anywhere else on earth. Lamentations 2:15 will refer to (almost) these very words, with grievous irony.

The third line makes the point once more. "Mount Zion" is simply its name. But Mount Zion is also Zaphon's heights. In terms of geography, this is another strange observation.[16] Ugaritic texts indicate that the literal Zaphon is Mount Casios, Jebel el-ʾAqraʿ, Baal's mountain, the high peak at the far north of Syria-Palestine (hence ṣāpôn comes to be a term for the north). The claim that Mount Zion is Zaphon's heights is thus laughable as a comment about physical geography, but it makes another theological statement. The psalm knows that Yhwh, not Baal, is the real sovereign power in heaven and on earth. The mountain where Yhwh lives is therefore a much more important place than the mountain where Baal lives and is the real impressive mountain, the real thing of which Mount Zaphon is a shadow. Worship of Baal Zaphon had long spread south as far as Egypt and given its name to places there (cf. Exod. 14:2, 9), and at least one other

---

the present context where the psalm makes statements rather than issuing exhortations; cf. NJPS.

14. EVV take yĕpēh nôp (lit. "beautiful of height") to mean simply "beautiful height," but such adj. expressions commonly have superlative significance (see GKC 133g). That gives more point to the statement in this context and leads better into the next declaration about the mountain's significance for the whole world. Cf. Gunkel, *Psalmen*, 204; Dahood, *Psalms*, 1:289.

15. Lit. "the joy of all the earth," which sounds as if it means that Zion brings joy to the whole world. While this would be untrue as a purely factual statement, it could make a true theological comment on what could or should be so. But in any case, in the psalm the question of the whole earth *rejoicing* in Zion seems irrelevant, and this is surely another quasi-superlative statement; the genitive is partitive rather than subjective.

16. Goulder (*Psalms of the Sons of Korah*, 159) notes that it would be more applicable to Dan and suggests that a Dan psalm has again been turned into a Zion psalm.

mountain had thus come to be called Zaphon because of its association with Baal Zaphon.[17] So the idea of viewing a mountain as a kind of honorary or substitute Zaphon was not a wholly new one. To put it another way, Zaphon had become something of a generic term for a sacred mountain. Indeed, it may be that the real Mount Zaphon, Baal's heavenly dwelling, was always assumed to be a heavenly reality that could be geographically embodied at a number of locations.[18] To identify Zion as Zaphon was thus not an empty conceit but a theological assertion. Mount Zion is Zaphon because it is the Great King's town. That declaration implies another theological and political claim (see 47:2 [3]). Perhaps it is also theologically significant that Yhwh chooses to live on a small and unimpressive mountain, not a tall impressive one. And it is theologically significant that Mount Zion counts not because it is the city of David, the earthly king (who is unmentioned), but because it is the city of Yhwh, the Great King.

48:3–6. What is the basis for the statements in the first three lines? These next four lines answer that question with declarations about past events.

> [3]In its citadels God
>   has made himself known as a haven.

Verse 3 summarizes the point with a reference to the familiar notion of Yhwh being a *haven. That has been proved in experience.[19] Paradoxically, it is not the mountain or the citadels themselves that count. It is God who is the haven. Perhaps the city itself is thus "a symbol of God who is the refuge of those who trust in him," so that "the citadels represent to the eye the refuge created by the rule of the LORD."[20] But in the psalm itself the relationship between the strength of citadels and the strength of Yhwh remains rather unstated.

> [4]For now: when the kings assembled,
>   people passed over altogether.

"God made himself known" (*nôda'*) when "the kings assembled" (*nô'ădû*). The paronomasia underlines the link and the contrast between the pretense of the kings and the effective action of God.[21] The fact that

17. See *TDOT*, 12:439.
18. See A. Robinson, "Zion and *ṣāphôn* in Psalm xlviii 3," *VT* 24 [1974]: 118–23; cf. Craigie, *Psalms 1–50*, 353, and his references.
19. LXX has a present verb and some EVV follow, but what follows suggests that this verb introduces the past account.
20. Mays, *Psalms*, 190.
21. Cf. Schaefer, *Psalms*, 122.

we already know who is "the great king" (v. 2) adds to this effect.[22] The nature of the events is described in terms familiar from other contexts. It is here that the psalm begins to make reference to events from the Red Sea to the occupation of Canaan. There was one occasion when "kings assembled," at Hazor after the Israelites' initial victories in conquering Canaan; they came together to stop this dangerous horde (Josh. 11:5; cf. 9:2). But the dangerous horde that had "passed over" the Red Sea and "passed over" the Jordan also continued to "pass through" the land; the verb *'ābar* is characteristic of the story's account of Israel in these different connections (e.g., Exod. 15:16; Josh. 1:2; 3:16; 4:22; 6:8; 10:29, 31, 34; 18:9; 24:11, 17). "Altogether" (*yaḥdāw*), on the other hand, is characteristic of the threatening activity of enemies (Josh. 9:2; 11:5; Ps. 2:2).[23] So here Israel's passing over and passing through the land appropriates that threatening expression.

> [5]As those saw, they were stunned,
>   they were terrified, they panicked.

The "those" alerts us to the fact that the kings are now again the subject. The breathless asyndetic terseness of the line conveys the reality: "these saw, thus stunned, terrified, panicked."

> [6]Trembling seized them there,
>   writhing like a woman birthing.

Then v. 6 makes the point again in two parallel cola with a shared verb. In the two lines the characterization of the kings again recalls the response associated with Israel's movement from Egypt to Canaan. The looking and the reaction recalls the reaction attributed to Moab (Num. 22:2–3) and prospectively (without the reference to looking) also to Philistia, Edom, and Canaan in connection with Israel's passing over the Red Sea (Exod. 15:14–16), as well as the references to being terrified and to trembling in Ps. 2:5, 11. Like and unlike Caesar, they came, they saw—and they fled.[24]

> [7]With an east wind you break up
>   Tarshish ships.

---

22. Alter, *Art of Biblical Poetry*, 123.

23. Some MSS of the LXX and of Jerome have "kings of the earth," assimilating the text to 2:2. Psalm 48 is more "realistic" than Ps. 2 in that it has a particular group of kings in mind.

24. Cf. Calvin, *Psalms*, 2:223.

Verses 4–6 as a whole thus recall the way God was at work at the beginning of Israel's story, but that recollection was set in the context of the declaration in v. 3 about God's having been known as a haven here and now in Jerusalem. In vv. 7–8 the psalm returns to affirmations about the way God's work in the past set a pattern for the present community's ongoing experience.

Verse 7 does that with its yiqtol verb that still speaks in images as it begins by adding another Red Sea allusion, drawing attention to the decisive effect of the east wind summoned up by Yhwh (cf. Exod. 14:21; 15:10). At the same time the reference to breaking up Tarshish ships, substantial oceangoing cargo vessels perhaps named after the far-distant Phoenician colony of Tartessus in Spain,[25] recalls a more recent historical event (see 1 Kings 22:48). Yhwh has shown the ability to destroy the power of apparently strong forces exerted against Israel. That is what has happened in Yhwh's proving to be a haven in Jerusalem.

> [8]As we have heard, so have we seen,
>   in the city of Yhwh Armies,
> In the city of our God
>   which God will establish forever. (Rise)

Two further lines more directly make the point that these acts are not confined to the past. The worshippers have not merely heard about them (cf. 44:1 [2]; 78:3) but seen them for themselves. In some contexts hearing and seeing might refer to words accompanied by visual or dramatic presentations, but it is doubtful whether this would count as "making oneself known." More likely the psalm antithesizes hearing and seeing in the way already presupposed by Ps. 44. There people protested that they had heard of Yhwh's acts but not seen any (cf. 74:9); what they have seen is trouble, and what they want is for Yhwh's works to be seen (90:15–16). Psalm 48 testifies to experience working more the way it should (cf. 66:5). People have both heard and seen. Metaphorically speaking, people have seen Yhwh destroying Tarshish ships in Jerusalem. Their seeing is the same kind of seeing as that of the kings to which v. 5 referred. There might be a link with the characterizing of Zion as Zaphon, given that Zaphon lay in Phoenicia and Tartessus was a Phoenician colony.[26]

The second line once again picks up the Red Sea story. There the worshippers affirmed prospectively that Yhwh had established the sanctuary (the verb kûn polel), and added that Yhwh would reign (there?) forever

---

25. But Cyrus H. Gordon ("The Wine-Dark Sea," *JNES* 37 [1978]: 51–52) argues that *taršîš* simply means "the open sea"; it has also been identified with Tarsus and located in Sardinia.

26. So Kraus, *Psalms 1–59*, 475.

(Exod. 15:17). The psalm affirms that Yhwh will indeed establish the city forever. The event at the Red Sea, the conquest of the land, and the establishing of Jerusalem have been repeated in their experience, building up their confidence for the future.

48:9–11. The third section focuses on the human response to those present acts of Yhwh's in Jerusalem. The four lines form two pairs.

> ⁹We think about your commitment, God,
>   within your palace.

If one were to imagine Israel dramatizing Yhwh's acts in worship, the verb *dāmâ* (v. 9) might refer to that portrayal (*děmût* means likeness), as NEB implies.[27] But we have no evidence that Israel did so, and the verb elsewhere refers to the forming of images in one's mind, which makes sense here. Indeed, the line sums up what the psalm has been doing so far. In these words that belong in the context of worship in Yhwh's *palace, people have been reflecting on Yhwh's *commitment, making it a reality in their imaginations as they bring together the events that established Israel as a people and the expressions of commitment that belong more in Jerusalem's experience.

> ¹⁰ᵃ⁻ᵇLike your name, God, so your praise
>   reaches to the ends of the earth.

An implication of that reflection is the affirmation about Yhwh's *name and *praise. Again the two words recur from the Song at the Sea (Exod. 15:3, 11). The triumphs that have been the subject of reflection related to Yhwh's acts in relation to the great empires of Israel's world, Egypt and Assyria. There is thus no doubt that Yhwh's name reaches to the end of the world; Egypt in the past and Assyria in the present could not get away from Yhwh's name. And thus there is no doubt that Yhwh's praise also reaches there. The nations acknowledge the frightening awesomeness of Yhwh.

> ¹⁰ᶜYour right hand is full of faithfulness;
>   ¹¹Mount Zion rejoices.
> The cities of Judah are glad
>   for the sake of your decisions.

In the second pair of lines, the expression "your right hand is full" makes for yet another pair of links with Exod. 15. There, the enemy's appetite (they think) will have its fill of Israelites, but in fact Yhwh's

27. Cf. Johnson, *Sacral Kingship*, 79–80.

right hand, glorious in power, shatters the enemy and extends to make the earth swallow the latter (Exod. 15:6, 9, 12). Here the same words are recycled to make the point in another way. That hand of Yhwh is full of *faithfulness, divine energy exercised in doing right by Israel. As a whole the pair of lines hold together the classic pair of value terms, faithfulness and *decisions. The Red Sea deliverance was an act of decisive faithfulness, though actually the Song at the Sea does not use those words to make the point. Now the psalm does use them. The plural term "decisions," decisive acts, perhaps points to the way the act at the Red Sea and the acts in defense of Jerusalem belong together. "Rejoice" and "be glad" form another pair, as do "Mount Zion" and "the cities of Judah" (literally the daughters of Judah) that pay as great a price as the capital when invaders attack the country. The two lines thus work abcb′c′a′.

48:12–14. The last section returns to addressing Israelites; indeed, it does so more explicitly than any other part of the psalm. In substance it returns to the focus of vv. 1–2 in enthusing over the city itself. Once more the four lines form two pairs, though three of the lines are also internally parallel.

> ¹²Go around Zion, go about it,
>   count its towers,

The first comprises three exhortations, though the first two form a pair of synonyms. They make another ironic link with the story of Israel's origins, because going around and going about a city (*sābab, nāqap* hiphil) was what the Israelites did to the first city they came to in Canaan (see Josh. 6:3, 7, 11). That first walk was a procession led by priests, and so may this one be if the line refers to a literal procession, though again we have no account elsewhere in the OT of regular processions around the city as opposed to onetime events such as that in Neh. 12:27–43. Processing may thus be an act of the imagination, or the psalm may be encouraging people to think in this way as they go around the city in the course of their regular lives. As is often the case, the second colon then sharpens the point of the first by indicating the purpose of this walkabout or by beginning to do so. One can imagine that the people on that first procession counted the towers of the city of Jericho and were rather overawed by it. This time the procession is invited to be positively impressed by what it sees. The towers are on its side. Each time people walk about Jerusalem, they can have their faith built up.

> ¹³ᵃ⁻ᵇGive your mind to its rampart,
>   pass through its citadels,

The second line as a whole parallels the first as a whole. It has no resonances in Israel's story but draws unqualified attention to the actual rock of the wall and citadels that people see.

> ¹³ᶜSo that you may recount to the next generation
> ¹⁴ᵃthat this is God.

The third line states the aim of the entire tour. It presupposes a similar point to that of vv. 1–2. This is an impressive city; it therefore brings glory to the one who lives there. The psalm goes to within a whisker of glorying in earthly might and defenses rather than God, in a way prophets criticize, but in the end keeps the focus on God. The city with its unconquered towers (you can count them to make sure they are still there), its unclimbed rampart, and its unassailed citadels witnesses to the might of the one who defended it. The psalm does not say "This is Zion" but "This is God."²⁸ The point is also made by the reference to telling the next generation. There would be no need to tell them that these are Jerusalem's battlements; they can see for themselves. What they need to hear is what the battlements stand for. By going around them, the present generation reminds itself of their meaning. It is not that the battlements demonstrate the strength of the city but that the battlements demonstrate the strength of the God who kept them intact. That is the message that needs to be conveyed to future generations as they face attack, the conveying presupposed by 44:1 [2].

> ¹⁴ᵇOur God forever and ever—
> he will drive us against death [MT]/to the end [LXX].

The formulation "forever and ever" (*'ôlām wā'ed*) constitutes yet another recollection of the Song at the Sea, for this was the Israelites' declaration concerning God's reign. Yes, Yhwh will be God forever and ever. Experience has confirmed what the story declares. The last colon then makes a final ironic allusion to the Red Sea event. Yhwh caused the Egyptians to drive (*nāhag*) their chariots to death (Exod. 14:25); the Israelites saw the Egyptians "dead" on the seashore (Exod. 14:30). Later Israel itself faces similar deathly challenges, but it will always be able to expect them to have a happier outcome because of the way Yhwh drives/leads the people.

Theological Implications

The psalm is talking about God, about a city, and about the relationship between God's acts at the beginning and God's acts now. The city is one

---

28. Cf. Rogerson and McKay, *Psalms*, 1:227.

with good foundations and a strong wall (cf. Heb. 11:10; Rev. 21:14). But it is not "the Jerusalem that is above" (Gal. 4:26), "the heavenly Jerusalem" (Heb. 12:22), or "the new Jerusalem" (Rev. 3:12; 21:2, 10), and we should not assimilate it to that or turn it into a foreshadowing of that, because we then lose the distinctive significance of this Scripture. It is not speaking about a mere community such as the church but about a place, "the present Jerusalem" (Gal. 4:25), with no implication that there is anything wrong with its being that. It is the Jerusalem that Jesus confirmed was "the city of the great king" (Matt. 5:35), from which the gospel goes out and which Paul seeks to serve (e.g., Rom. 15:18–32), but which was to be long trampled by Gentiles until their times are fulfilled.

The psalm is not representing the heavenly by means of the earthly but the earthly in terms of the heavenly.[29] It does not assume that what alone truly counts is the heavenly. It knows that God cares about the earthly. But neither does it think that what alone truly counts is the earthly. It knows that God has entered into relationship with the earthly and that the earthly is never truly understood unless it is seen in light of this relationship. This city is a specific visible place on earth where God acted and came to be known in a concrete visible way. Zion is God's city, and Yhwh is God of this city.

Psalm 48 thus insists that Christians take Jerusalem seriously as a place to which God made a commitment and to which God fulfilled that commitment. The psalm witnesses to the fact that the realities associated with God's acts at the Red Sea, at the conquest of Canaan, and in the establishment of Jerusalem continued to be realities in the history of this city. In light of the history of God's involvement with it, how could we make light of the significance of the earthly Jerusalem? It is therefore wondrous that God is praised day-to-day, week-to-week, and year-to-year in this city by Jews and Christians (and Muslims?) and that, through the dispersion of Jews and Christians (and Muslims?) all over the world, the name and the praise of this God reach to the end of the earth. Its story is still designed to be an encouragement to us.

All that makes for depressing contrast with the fact that, in the week I write, the government of the State of Israel has been erecting a massive wall to divide suburbs of Jerusalem from one another and members of Jerusalem families from one another in order to attempt to avoid members of some Jerusalem families from killing members of other Jerusalem families (I do not intend by this particular sentence to take sides in the conflict). The OT suggests its own version of that contrast when Lam. 2:15 has people passing by the city in its devastated state and asking, "Is this the city that was called perfect in beauty, the source of

29. Mays, *Psalms*, 190.

joy for all the earth?" It certainly did not look like it at the time. Indeed, in a sense it never did. The claims about Jerusalem were always larger than life because they were always really claims about Yhwh. Perhaps it is theologically significant that Yhwh chose to make a commitment to such a small and insignificant city. That helped to make clear that God chooses what is weak in the world to shame the strong, what is low and despised and what barely exists, to reduce to nothing things that do exist, so that people who boast must boast in Yhwh (cf. 1 Cor. 1:27–31), as the psalm actually does. Perhaps the story of Jerusalem will still have such an ending, even though one cannot imagine how that can come about. "Cheer up, prophets of doom," Edmund Hill therefore comments on the basis of the psalm.[30]

---

30. *Prayer, Praise and Politics*, 172.

Psalm 49

Can Death Be Escaped?

Translation

The leader's. The Korahites'. Composition.

[1]Listen to this, all you peoples,
  give ear, all inhabitants of the age,
[2]Both ordinary people and people of importance,
  rich and needy alike.
[3]My mouth will speak with great insight,
  the talk of my heart with much understanding.[1]
[4]I will incline my ear to a lesson,
  resolve my question to the lyre.

[5]Why should I be afraid in times of trouble,
  when the waywardness of my assailants surrounds me,[2]
[6]People who trust in their resources,
  who exult themselves in their great wealth?
[7]Huh![3] It cannot at all redeem a person,
  give God his ransom.

---

1. I take the two abstract nouns as intensive pl., though they might be Phoenician-type sg. See Dahood, *Psalms*, 1:296–97; contrast *HALOT* on *těbûnâ*.
2. NJPS takes "the waywardness of my persecutors that surrounds me" as the obj. of the verb "be afraid," but this would be an unusual and unexpectedly elegant construction. LXX and Jerome take v. 5b as a statement attached asyndetically to v. 5a, but this would be a perhaps unexpectedly inelegant construction. More likely it is a circumstantial clause.
3. LXX and Jerome understandably take *'āḥ* as the word "brother," but in this position in the sentence it is more likely the onomatopoeic interjection *'āḥ* (cf. **BDB** 25a). But see Heinrich Gross's discussion in "Self- oder Fremderlösung," in *Wort, Lied und Gottesspruch:*

⁸The redemption price for their life would be costly,
   it would be permanently insufficient,⁴
⁹So that he should live on forever,
   not see the Abyss.

¹⁰For he can see that the insightful die,
   foolhardy and idiot perish, alike.
¹¹They leave their resources to others,
   though their inward thought is that their home will be forever, [MT]
   [or] people whose grave will be their home forever, [LXX]⁵
Their dwelling for all generations—
   people who called extensive land their own.⁶
¹²So a human being with prestige does not abide;⁷
   he is like animals that perish.

¹³This is the way of the foolhardy,⁸
   and after them those who like their talk. (Rise) [MT]
   [or] and the end of those who like their talk. (Rise) [Tg]⁹
¹⁴Like sheep they have headed¹⁰ for Sheol;
   death shepherds them.¹¹
The upright have dominion¹² over them at morning,
   and their form¹³ is for wasting by Sheol

Beiträge zu Psalmen und Propheten (Joseph Ziegler Festschrift; ed. Josef Schreiner; Würzburg: Echter, 1972), 65–70.

4. For *wĕḥādal* NJPS has "and so one ceases to be," but this requires a unique meaning for the verb and makes it hard to construe v. 9 (which NJPS turns into a question).

5. MT has *qirbām* (cf. Jerome); LXX implies *qibrām* (cf. Syr, Tg), perhaps the easier reading.

6. Lit. "who called by their name over lands." To call by name generally means to give a name or to summon by name. NJPS's "those once famous on earth" would imply a pair of very distinctive usages. Mark S. Smith ("The Invocation of Deceased Ancestors," *JBL* 112 [1993]: 105–7) sees the phrase as referring to people calling on their ancestors.

7. LXX assimilates the verb to v. 20a; Jerome follows MT.

8. More literally, "[There is] foolhardiness to them." While no doubt they are self-confident (NJPS; cf. TNIV), it is doubtful whether the words make this explicit.

9. MT has *'aḥărêhem*; Tg *wbswphwn* implies *'aḥărîtām*.

10. *Šātat*, a by-form of *šît*—cf. the occurrence in 9:20 [21]. For the translation cf. NJPS; other EVV understand "they [impersonal] appoint [them]," but *šît* can be used intransitively (cf. 3:6 [7]), and this understanding avoids hypothesizing a change of subj.

11. Or "feeds on them" (KJV), which need not require a prep. (see BDB; against C. John Collins, "'Death Will Be Their Shepherd' or 'Death Will Feed on Them,'" *BT* 46 (1995): 320–26.

12. JM 82 sees the wayyiqtol as equivalent to a prophetic perfect; *TTH* 80 sees it as continuing the present (general) reference of the preceding yiqtol.

13. Following K *wṣyrm*, implying *wĕṣîrām* rather than Q *wĕṣûrām*, which should mean "and their rock" (cf. LXX, Syr)—unless it presupposes a by-form. On this word, see Staffan Olofsson, "Death Shall Be Their Shepherd," in *The Interpretation of Scripture in Early Judaism and Christianity*, ed. Craig A. Evans (Sheffield: Sheffield Academic Press, 2000), 75–105 (see 89–92).

> instead of its having a lofty home.[14]
> [15]Yet God will redeem my life from the power of Sheol,
>   for he will take me. (Rise)
>
> [16]Do not be afraid when someone becomes rich,
>   when the honor of his house increases,
> [17]For at his death he cannot take it all;
>   his honor does not go down after him.
> [18]When[15] he blesses himself while he is alive,
>   and they praise you when you do well for yourself,[16]
> [19]He goes[17] to the company of his ancestors,
>   who to the end will not see light.
> [20]A human being is with prestige but does not understand;
>   he is like animals that perish.

Interpretation

Like Pss. 1 and 37, this psalm is a piece of teaching or a homily rather than a piece of prayer or praise, and as a homily about wealth it could have appeared in Proverbs. But its starting point in the way that having resources gives people the means of causing trouble and loss to others (v. 5) is an issue of recurrent importance in the Psalms, and it opens in a manner that suggests a link with prophecy (see v. 4). Its starting point may indicate that its background lies in an actual experience of trouble; Goulder suggests a political version of this understanding, linking the psalm like other Korahite psalms with the worship in Dan.[18] But if it does have a background in an actual experience of being under attack, its stance is more that of a psalm of trust than that of a protest psalm.[19]

14. On this expression, see Olofsson, "Death Shall Be Their Shepherd," 95–101. Pierre Bordreuil ("*Mizzĕbul lô*," in *Ascribe to the Lord* [P. C. Craigie Memorial; ed. Lyle Eslinger and Glen Taylor; JSOTSup 67, Sheffield: JSOT, 1988], 93–98) repoints to translate, "Who is its prince?"

15. EVV have "though," but it is doubtful whether *kî* can mean that. More likely it indicates the way in which death comes in the midst of the confidence expressed by the line—whereas Yhwh rescues the upright. The *kî* thus takes up the two occurrences with this meaning in v. 16. JM 164b sees the *kî* as asseverative.

16. NJPS takes v. 18b as the rich person's words, but the parallelism of content with the first colon suggests rather that they continue the psalmist's observations.

17. *Tābô'* might be second person, "you go," following on from v. 18b, or it might be third person f., "it [the self] goes," following on from v. 18a.

18. *Psalms of the Sons of Korah*, 181–95.

19. Pierre Casetti (*Gibt es ein Leben vor dem Tod: Eine Auslegung von Psalm 49*, OBO 44 [Göttingen: Vandenhoeck & Ruprecht, 1982]) sees the original material in the psalm (vv. 10–14, 20) as characterized by Qoheleth-like pessimism; the hopeful nature of Ps. 49

Verses 1–4 form an introduction, and vv. 12 and 20 are similar and might be described as refrains. But as wholes vv. 5–12 and 13–20 then hint at an abb′a′ structure. Verses 5–9 and 16–20 both begin with a reference to fear and focus on the fact that wealth does not exempt rich people from death. Verses 10–12 and 13–15 speak more about the way death affects everyone, no matter their wealth or wisdom—unless God takes them.

> The leader's. The Korahites'. Composition.

Heading. See glossary.

49:1–4. The opening section thus compares both with Proverbs and with psalmody and also with the Prophets. The summons to pay attention recalls a teacher, though the summons to the world recalls other Psalms (e.g., 47:1 [2]). Talk of insight and understanding recalls a teacher; talk of listening and of the use of music suggests a prophet (2 Kings 3:15). The straightforward parallelism, prosaic language, and rhythmic regularity could give an impression of doggerel verse and recall the use of the externals of poetic form by a teacher rather than the allusive poetry of a prophet or a psalmist, though there are elements of poetic artistry that do heighten the psalm's rhetorical effect.[20]

> ¹Listen to this, all you peoples,
> give ear, all inhabitants of the age,

The psalm begins, then, with a summons especially like that of a teacher, with two balancing imperatives and two balancing vocatives introduced by "all" and with the object "this" applying to both verbs. Yet the second colon then uses a verb and a noun that are more the language of prophet or psalmist than that of teacher. The closing expression complements the phrase "all you peoples" by pointing to chronology rather than simply geography or ethnicity. The picture of us all as people of a passing age (*ḥeled*) gives a hint of where the psalm is going.[21]

> ²Both ordinary people and people of importance,
> rich and needy alike.

---

as we have it results from later expansion. In criticism, see Oswald Loretz, "Ugaritisches und Jüdisches: Weisheit und Tod in Psalm 49," *UF* 17 (1986): 189–212.

20. See Daniel J. Estes, "Poetic Artistry in the Expression of Fear in Psalm 49," *BSac* 161 (2004): 55–71.

21. Cf. Raabe, *Psalm Structures*, 70.

Verse 2 takes that further, if "sons of a human being" (*běnê 'ādām*) and "sons of an individual" (*běnê-'îš*) denote people of status and people of none[22]—and in any case the second colon does make a similar point with its reference to both rich and *needy. The psalm's question is of importance to people all over the world, of whatever social standing and of whatever resources. This aspect of the summons offers another hint at where the psalm is going, for the "alike" will reappear in v. 10. For all their apparently profound differences, all human groups need to pay attention to this message, because all are affected by it. All human groups need to be taught together because they have more in common than they think.[23]

> ³My mouth will speak with great insight,
>   the talk of my heart with much understanding.

The next two lines also go together. First the psalm claims insight and understanding for the teaching that will follow—again like a teacher (e.g., Prov. 2:2; 3:13, 19). The deep structure of the cola is parallel, though they work by pairing a verbal clause with a noun clause of similar meaning. Talk (see on 63:6 [7]) and understanding provide less familiar equivalents to the nouns in the first colon.

> ⁴I will incline my ear to a lesson,
>   resolve my question to the lyre.

The psalm then indicates the basis for this claim to insight and declares that the teaching does not in fact come from a source such as personal discernment or the teaching of older generations. It comes from listening in the present, but listening in the manner of a seer, accompanied by the music of a *lyre. There are no other references to accompanying teaching with music; presumably the psalm refers to the use of music to free one to see a truth or to hear God, though it might be that the listening and the teaching were simultaneous. It is the listening that underlies the claim to attentiveness. I will incline my ear; you must therefore incline yours (cf. the similarity of language with v. 1). What the psalmist will consider and teach is a lesson (*māšāl*) or a question (*ḥîdâ*). A *māšāl* is a poetic saying, typically deep and perhaps puzzling, with the ambiguity and openness of poetry. A *ḥîdâ* is something enigmatic, perhaps of a

22. But Aquinas (*Commentary on the Psalms*, on Ps. 50) and Brueggemann (*Message of the Psalms*, 107) see them as having the reverse meaning, and J. van der Ploeg ("Notes sur le Psaume xlix," *OtSt* 13 [1963]: 137–72 [see 141–42]) sees them as synonyms.
23. Cf. Brueggemann, *Message of the Psalms*, 107.

trivial kind like a riddle,[24] perhaps a profound and puzzling life question such as the one this psalm seeks to grapple with.

49:5–9. The first main section starts from a recurrent experience of honorable people and makes a comment on the particular attitudes and myths treasured by people who cause them trouble.

> [5]Why should I be afraid in times of trouble,
>   when the waywardness of my assailants surrounds me,

Verse 5 immediately makes clear that the psalm's question *Why? is not a mere theoretical one but one that relates to fear. The parallelism works by the first colon mentioning fear and trouble (*bad) and raising the question of what the psalmist fears and what kind of trouble is meant and the second colon making this more specific. Verse 5b also makes even clearer that the psalmist has in mind circumstances like those regularly presupposed by prayer psalms, whether or not the psalm issues from a current experience like that. The psalmist knows that from time to time it is possible to be under pressure on all sides from the *waywardness of "assailants"—here uniquely 'ăqēbîm from the word for "heel." These may be people who try to trip others up and use devious methods to do so, or they may be cheats more generally (see 41:9 [10]).

> [6]People who trust in their resources,
>   who exult themselves in their great wealth?

Verse 6 sharpens the point in parallel abb'a' cola, with both the verb and the noun expression in the second colon taking further those in the first. The reference to trusting in resources or wealth suggests that the point is not that the assailants use these to bring the psalmist down by a means such as bribing a court. It is rather that they press on with their wrongdoing in the confidence that they will always get away with it. The actual peril of their attitude is implied by the psalm's verbs. It talks about their *trust and their exulting (*praise). These are verbs that deserve to have Yhwh as their object (e.g., 22:4–5 [5–6]; 34:2 [3]), but here their object is resources and wealth. The line thus stresses the enormity of their attitude to life and also hints at the danger of the position they put themselves in.

> [7]Huh! It cannot at all redeem a person,
>   give God his ransom.

24. Leo G. Perdue ("The Riddles of Psalm 49," *JBL* 93 [1974]: 533–42) takes this as the key to understanding the psalm.

They are terribly mistaken. The point is first made with emphasis by repeating the verb (lit. "it cannot redeeming redeem"). Talk of *redemption often loses its monetary connotations, but here these are important. The assailants think they can buy their way forward in life and on into a happy old age. To put it in modern terms, they can buy themselves a band of bodyguards and the best health plan available. In Israel, there were circumstances in which the life of a person could be ransomed (Exod. 21:28–32), but this was not invariably possible. It is self-evident that likewise the rich do not always manage to buy themselves long life. The second colon gives the point more precision and explains why. The source of life is God, and it is therefore God to whom the redemption price, the ransom, has to be paid, and God is not committed to letting such a process decide whether people live or die. People do not live by bread alone but by every word that issues from Yhwh's mouth (cf. Deut. 8:3)—one implication of which is that even if you eat all the right things, if God decides your body will stop working, it will stop working. Money can no more buy you life than it can buy you love.

> [8]The redemption price for their life would be costly,
>   it would be permanently insufficient,
> [9]So that he should live on forever,
>   not see the Abyss.

Verses 8–9 explain the point further. The price you would have to pay God for life is very large. Indeed (again the second colon in v. 8 takes the point further), it is infinite. No matter how much money you have, it would never be enough. So there is no prospect of someone paying a price high enough to guarantee life going on as long as one might wish (v. 9) and thus not seeing the *Abyss.

49:10–12. The second section expounds the general facts that lie behind the comments about the rich assailants. These are the facts they ignore. No one can evade death.

> [10a-b]For he can see that the insightful die,
>   foolhardy and idiot perish, alike.

First, it makes no difference how clever you are. The verb picks up from the previous colon (indeed, LXX and Jerome make it part of the same line); I take it that the psalm continues to speak of the person who is bound to "see the Abyss." The repeated verb then carries its force on into the subsequent colon, which adds the stupid to the equation and underlines the fact that death claims both groups "together." The doubling of terms to describe the stupid hints that this category includes the rich person who expects to buy life. The foolhardy (*kĕsîl*) are the kind of people who have confidence when there are no grounds for confidence (cf. v. 13). Yet even this person can surely see the facts about death as it claims everyone; for instance, it claims insightful and stupid alike. Implicitly the psalm thus asks such a person to decide which category applies to them.

> ¹⁰ᶜThey leave their resources to others,
> ¹¹though their inward thought is that their home will be forever,
> [MT]
> [or] people whose grave will be their home forever, [LXX]
> Their dwelling for all generations—
> people who called extensive land their own.

The next two lines belong together and work abb'a'.²⁵ Death means that people leave their resources or strength (the word is picked up from v. 6) to others (v. 10c), and it makes no difference how extensive those resources are (v. 11c). They may have owned vast estates;²⁶ they have to pass them on. The middle two cola then offer parallel descriptions of the home to which they go when their resources are insufficient to keep them here. "Their inward thought" (MT)/"their grave" (LXX) is the subject of both cola, which give parallel content to it or offer parallel descriptions of it. Both "home" and "dwelling" are plural, which makes one reflect on the fact that wealthy people will have more than one residence—in Israel, perhaps a winter home in the Jordan Valley and a summer home in the mountains. But these plurals are no doubt grammatically intensive rather than numerical. They attach mistaken expectations about how long they will live in their fine home, their splendid dwelling (MT); the grave will turn out to be their actual fine home and splendid dwelling, and that will be so forever and for all generations (LXX). There is to be a "forever" about their experience, but it is not the one they are looking for (v. 9).

> ¹²So a human being with prestige does not abide;
> he is like animals that perish.

Verse 12 rounds off this section by summarizing the point. Everyone has to die, and that applies specifically to the wealthy as it applies specifically

25. The parallelism between the cola in v. 11a perhaps suggested to MT that vv. 10 and 11 comprise two tricola, but it is in principle more likely that they form three bicola, and this understanding works with that.

26. Pl. *'ădāmôt* comes only here; this coheres with the idea that the pl. is intensive rather than numerical.

to the wise. The two balancing cola make a point that recurs in Ecclesiastes and contrasts with one in Ps. 8. Yhwh put humanity in a position of splendor in relation to the animal world, almost godlike in the authority exercised over the animal world. But at this crucial point humanity is nothing like God and just like the animals. For all the value of being human, we die just like animals. And it is no good for the wealthy to pretend that things could be otherwise for them. The point applies specifically to human beings with prestige. The word (*yěqār*) picks up the verb "is costly" in v. 8 (*yāqar*) and suggests the status associated with wealth. People of wealth think they can buy life, but even in their wealth they do not abide. There is some irony about the verb (*lûn*), which literally refers to staying the night. Even with wealth a human being can barely stay the night, any more than an animal with no credit card. The reader may be invited to see the point underlined by a further implicit paronomasia, human beings *bîqār*, "with prestige," turning out to be like *bāqār*, "cattle."[27]

49:13–15. From the people with resources who have too great expectations concerning them, the psalm turns back to the fools and implicitly the wise of v. 10.

> ¹³This is the way of the foolhardy,
>   and after them those who like their talk. (Rise) [MT]
>   [or] and the end of those who like their talk. (Rise) [Tg]

Verse 13 thus reintroduces the people whose foolhardiness (*kēsel*) lies in thinking they have wisdom when they have not and thus have confidence about their future when they have no grounds for it (cf. v. 10). It will become clear in v. 14 that their "way" is not the way they behave (as in 1:1) but the way things turn out for them (as in 35:6). In MT "This [is] the way" extends its reach into the second colon; in Tg, only "This [is]" does so. The second group of people may be those who like the talk (lit. "mouth") of the fools, or they may be people who like their own talk. That is then another way of characterizing the self-confident, people who are like the mockers or bigmouths of 1:1, their mouths always open but their ears always closed (cf. Prov. 13:1).

> ¹⁴Like sheep they have headed for Sheol;
>   death shepherds them.
> The upright have dominion over them at morning,
>   and their form is for wasting by Sheol
>   instead of its having a lofty home.

---

27. Cf. Raabe, *Psalm Structures*, 73. Judah Jacob Slotki ("Psalm xlix 13, 21," *VT* 28 [1978]: 361–62) emends to *bāqār*.

Two lines then describe how their "way" will turn out. The opening colon is a little enigmatic: why do they head for Sheol like sheep? The second colon clarifies this. It is because they are being herded or shepherded—by death itself. In Canaanite thinking Death was a deity, and such language would have more literal meaning. In death you come under the authority of Death. Read in the context of the rest of the OT, such language is more a figure of speech. Dying is like leaving the realm where God shepherds you (cf. Ps. 23:1; 28:9) for a realm where Death shepherds you.

In an analogous way, context would decide how people read the tricolon that follows in v. 14b (see on 1:5). In the context of belief in a resurrection day, it would sound like a reference to the upright being in a superior position to the fools when that morning dawns. The dominion might consist in the fact that the upright rise to new life in heaven while the fools rot in *Sheol. Evidently the idea would not be of a resurrection of both upright and fool (contrast Dan. 12:2; Rev. 20:11–15). But within the context of most OT thinking, not least in the Psalms, the line would speak more of a reversal within this life for people who experience trouble and *waywardness (v. 5). The morning is the moment when God acts in this life to deliver (e.g., 30:5 [6]; 90:14), and the upright will experience God's deliverance then. They will have dominion over the fools because they will be vindicated and the fools will take their place, and perhaps because the upright will trample on their graves.[28] Instead of threatening death, they will be threatened by death. It will be their forms that are for wasting, not those of the upright. Instead of continuing to enjoy their impressive homes on earth (cf. vv. 6, 10–11), Sheol will be their home. Instead of being able to ensure that they enjoy a longer life than others, they will enjoy a shorter one.

> **15**Yet God will redeem my life from the power of Sheol,
>   for he will take me. (Rise)

Verse 15 will likewise be open to different interpretations in different contexts. Interpreted in light of the conviction that there is to be a positive afterlife, it suggests that the psalmist expects to be one of those whom Yhwh "takes" from Sheol to heaven—the verb is used of Enoch and Elijah when Yhwh "took" them from their earthly families and friends (Gen. 5:24; 2 Kings 2:3, 5, 9, 10).[29] In light of broader OT usage,

---

28. Cf. Raabe, *Psalm Structures*, 74–76; he also discusses possible emendations of the line such as those presupposed by NRSV.

29. See E. Podechard, "Psaume xlix," *RB* 31 (1922): 5–19; Paul Volz, "Psalm 49," *ZAW* 55 (1937): 235–64; van der Ploeg, "Notes sur le Psaume xlix," 162–72; Markus Witte, "'Aber Gott wird meine Seele erlösen,'" *VT* 50 (2000): 540–60. See also M. J. Mulder's discussion,

this "taking" will be a rescuing from this-worldly trouble (cf. Ps. 18:16 [17]; Ezek. 36:24; 37:21), a rescuing from the threat of Sheol or from the way death can get its clutches on us in life (cf. 16:10; 18:5 [6]; 30:3 [4]).[30] The language of v. 15a especially parallels Hos. 13:14. Like other psalms, this one expresses a strong conviction that God is involved in the this-worldly lives of people, bringing them healing and rescue from persecution. Either way, the *redemption that the rich think their wealth can buy for them (v. 7) is something for which we are actually dependent on God. Here suddenly and for the only time is God the subject of the psalm, in the realm where the rich thought they were in control but are not. It is now more explicit that the rich are also the fools, as the wise are also the upright.

49:16–20. The closing section returns to the theme of the first (main) section (see v. 5). It comprises five internally parallel lines.

> ¹⁶Do not be afraid when someone becomes rich,
>   when the honor of his house increases,

The implication is that the psalmist will not be the only one who might be tempted to be afraid when rich and wicked people are thriving—indeed, it perhaps implies that the psalmist does not really feel this temptation but is concerned for people who do. The verb applies to both cola, which then offer two descriptions of people who are doing well. In general, they are getting rich; specifically, their homes become more stylish.

> ¹⁷For at his death he cannot take it all;
>   his honor does not go down after him.

But all that is temporary, as the psalm has kept underlining. The two cola correspond to those in v. 16. People cannot take all their riches with them—the colon perhaps deliberately understates the matter, aware that actually they cannot take any of it.[31] Their *honor (the word recurs from v. 16b) does not go down after them like an entourage.

> ¹⁸When he blesses himself while he is alive,
>   and they praise you when you do well for yourself,

"Psalm 49:15 en 16," in *Loven en geloven* (N. H. Ridderbos Festschrift; ed. M. H. van Es et al.; Amsterdam: Ton Bolland, 1975), 117–34.

30. Indeed, as Christian exegetes Diodore (*Psalms 1–51*, 158) and Theodore (*Psalms 1–81*, 644–45) take it this way.

31. If the obj. were simple *kōl*, we could translate "any of it," but the presence of the article may make this difficult (see BDB 482a; but contrast JM 160k).

There, then, are the rich congratulating themselves on their achievements, and other people are doing the same. But perhaps "blessing oneself" involves tempting providence; only here do people thus congratulate themselves (contrast 62:4 [5]), though v. 6 uses related verbs for the unwise. And perhaps having everyone speak well of you also tempts providence.

> ¹⁹He goes to the company of his ancestors,
>   who to the end will not see light.

For while they are doing that, they find themselves making a journey they had not planned. In principle joining one's ancestors is a fine way to end one's life, but one wants to live out one's threescore years and ten before doing so. It is a grim fate to do well for oneself and then find oneself suddenly in one's ancestors' company without having had a chance to enjoy one's achievements. The second colon underlines the grimness of this fact. This is a one-way journey (cf. 2 Sam. 12:23). Once your family closes the door on the family tomb again, you are in the dark. You will never see the light again (to ignore those momentary further occasions when the tomb opens again to welcome another new occupant). Further, here as elsewhere *light will also be a figure for blessing and fullness of life. All that is over. There is no possibility of seeing it again.

> ²⁰A human being is with prestige but does not understand;
>   he is like animals that perish.

To close, it would have been entirely appropriate to repeat v. 12, but the psalm again prefers its repetition to have variation. We have been thinking about human beings with prestige and about the fact that they may not abide as they think they will (*bal-yālîn*, v. 12), but arguably it is even sadder that they do not face the fact—they do not understand (*lō' yābîn*). Apparently, the psalmist is an exception to this rule (contrast v. 3).[32]

Theological Implications

How can we face the threat of death with its unfairnesses and inequalities? The opening of the psalm already recognizes that this is not a question that can be solved by thinking hard. When it comes to facing death, the intellectual has no advantage over the simple. The psalm's

32. Cf. Fokkelman, *Major Poems*, 3:85.

stress on openness to God (v. 4) implies not that it will produce an amazing new insight but that this question is one that can only be handled on the basis of trust in God. The body of the psalm then initially affirms that this is not a question that can be resolved on the basis of power. But the psalm's main stress is that neither is it a question that money can solve.[33] The best security system may not keep one safe; the best insurance plan may not keep one healthy. "Use your mind," "Might is right," and "Money talks" are blind alleys.[34] Death is "the philosophic scale for measuring what endures on this side of the grave."[35]

So how can we face the threat of death before our time? Christian commentators routinely suggest that v. 15 implies a "bold grasping after" the idea of an afterlife. It does not do so, and this is fortunate, because this would not be brave but cowardly, an easy way out. The idea of an afterlife (beyond the boring one lived in Sheol) is a nice idea, but until Jesus died and rose again, it was an idea that lacked a basis. In a context where many peoples did believe in an afterlife without much basis for doing so, the OT's boldness lies in declining to do the same (pending God's providing the idea with a basis). And in taking the stance it does, the psalm insists on locating the redeeming activity of God not in some other realm that we cannot see and for which it did not yet have any evidence, but in the realm of this life. God is one who really exists, really does deliver from death, and really does put down the wicked. When things look otherwise, the psalm commits itself to still trusting God to do that. The NT passage that best resonates with the psalm is thus not a passage about resurrection but Luke 12:16–21. Things do not always work out that way—sometimes the righteous suffer, and the wicked sin with impunity—but the Psalms know that this is not reason to give up on the conviction, because they know that there are good grounds for it.

33. Cf. Markus Grimm, "Menschen mit und ohne Geld," *BN* 96 (1999): 38–55.
34. Cf. Goldingay, *Songs from a Strange Land*, 141–44.
35. J. David Pleins, "Death and Endurance," *JSOT* 69 (1996): 19–27 (see 27).

Psalm 50

Worship and Life

Translation

Composition. Asaph's

[1]El, God,[1] Yhwh has spoken,
    called to the earth from the rising of the sun to its setting.
[2]From Zion, perfect in beauty, God has shone forth—
    [3]our God comes and cannot be silent![2]
Fire consumes before him,
    around him it has whirled powerfully.
[4]He calls to the heavens above
    and to the earth, for the making of a decision about his people.
[5]"Gather for me the people committed to me,
    who sealed[3] a covenant with me over sacrifice."
[6]And the heavens have proclaimed his faithfulness,
    for God—he is exercising authority. (Rise)

[7]Listen, my people, and I will speak,
    Israel, and I will charge you;
    I am God, your God.

---

1. LXX translates "the God of gods," but there is no parallel for *'ēl 'ĕlōhîm* having this meaning.

2. In the context the negative *'al* suggests that this is a declaration about what cannot happen rather than a jussive (GKC 109f).

3. Craigie (*Psalms 1–50*, 365) urges a present translation of this ptc. as referring to the people reaffirming the covenant in the liturgy that he connects with the psalm, but there are no other instances of this verb being used for the periodic reaffirming of an existent covenant rather than the sealing of a new one.

⁸Not concerning your sacrifices do I rebuke you,
    or your whole-offerings that are before me regularly.⁴
⁹I would not take a bull from your house
    or goats from your folds.
¹⁰For to me belongs every animal⁵ in the forest,
    the cattle on a thousand mountains.⁶
¹¹I acknowledge every bird in the mountains [MT]/heavens [LXX],
    and the creature of the wild is with me.
¹²If I get hungry, I shall not tell you,
    for to me belong the world and what fills it.
¹³Do I eat the flesh of buffalo
    or drink the blood of goats?
¹⁴Sacrifice a thank-offering to God
    and fulfill your promises to the Most High.
¹⁵Call me on the day of trouble;
    I will rescue you, and you will honor me.

¹⁶But to the faithless God has said,
    What are you doing in proclaiming my statutes,
    taking my covenant on your lips,⁷
¹⁷When you are one who is against my instruction,
    who has thrown my words behind you?
¹⁸If you have seen a thief, you have accepted him [MT]/run with him
    [LXX]⁸
    and cast your lot with adulterers.⁹
¹⁹You have given your mouth to evil,
    with your tongue you frame deceit.
²⁰You sit speaking¹⁰ against your brother,
    ascribe failings to your mother's child.
²¹Since you have done these things, if I were silent,¹¹

4. NRSV understands the second colon as an independent sentence, "Your whole-offerings are before me regularly," but poetically it is more likely that the second colon picks up from the first.

5. *Ḥaytô* has an idiosyncratic additional *w* on the const. ending (see JM 93r; GKC 90k, o); cf. 79:2.

6. Lit. "on the mountains of a thousand," odd in Hebrew as in English. LXX takes this *ēlep* as meaning "cattle," not "thousand."

7. The yiqtol clause continues the infinitival construction (*TTH* 118).

8. MT has the unusual construction *rāṣâ 'im*, but this is paralleled in Job 34:9 in a similar context. LXX implies *wattārāṣ* for MT *wattireṣ*.

9. Lit. "Your share [*ḥēleq*] is with adulterers," perhaps implying that they share their life with them or that they associate with them in business. Marina Mannati ("Les accusations de Psaume L 18–20," *VT* 25 [1975]: 659–69) takes this and the other accusations to refer to religious unfaithfulness, but this seems forced.

10. On the asyndeton, see *TTH* 163.

11. There are other ways of construing the colon (e.g., *TTH* 119 and GKC 112cc see the weqatal as indicating a question), but the sense is hardly affected. LXX and Jerome take the

you would think that I was just[12] like you;
I rebuke you and lay it out before your eyes.

[22]Do consider this, you people who put God out of mind,
lest I tear you and there is no one to save you.
[23]The person who sacrifices a thank-offering honors me;
to the person who directs his way
I will show God's deliverance.

Interpretation

Like Ps. 49, the psalm addresses Israel rather than addressing God, though the claims in vv. 1–6 make one inclined to call it a prophecy rather than a homily.[13] If Ps. 49 came anywhere else than in the Psalter, it might be Proverbs; if Ps. 50 came anywhere else, it would be one of the prophetic books. But even as a prophecy or quasi-prophecy, it might have been part of a liturgy, such as one celebrating the covenant, if there was such a regular celebration, or it might have been one delivered by a prophet on some occasion and then preserved for use on other appropriate occasions when (for instance) the priests thought it was needed. It does not give any indication of a date of composition.[14]

It comprises a substantial introduction describing Yhwh's coming (vv. 1–6), an address to the people as a whole about their worship (vv. 7–15), a challenge to individual faithless people about their lives (vv. 16–21), and a conclusion summing up the implications (vv. 22–23).[15]

Composition. Asaph's

Heading. See glossary. Asaph was known as a Levitical music leader and seer in David's day (1 Chron. 15:17, 19; 16:4–7; 2 Chron. 29:30), while his descendants were music leaders in the Second Temple. The other Asaph psalms are Pss. 73–83; perhaps this psalm in isolation from

colon as a simple statement, "You did these things, and I was silent," but this less idiomatic understanding seems to attribute something to God that God is rather denying.

12. "Just" reflects the fact that the verb *hāyâ* is repeated; lit. "that in being I was like you"; on the use of the inf. const. rather than abs., see GKC 113x.

13. Cf. Stephen Breck Reid, "Psalm 50: Prophetic Speech and God's Performative Utterances," in *Prophets and Paradigms* (Gene M. Tucker Festschrift; ed. Stephen Breck Reid; JSOTSup 229; Sheffield: Sheffield Academic Press, 1996), 217–30. Contrast Gerstenberger, *Psalms*, 1:210.

14. N. H. Ridderbos ("Die Theophanie in Ps. 1 1–6," *OtSt* 15 [1969]: 213–26) argues for a link with Josiah.

15. L. C. Allen ("Structure and Meaning in Psalm 50," *Vox evangelica* 14 [1984]: 17–37 [see 20–21]) finds a stepped structure in the psalm.

those was given a link with Asaph because of his being a seer. It is the kind of prophecy he might have uttered, and he is the kind of person who might have uttered such a prophecy.

50:1–6. So the prophet professes to have heard Yhwh setting under way a process whereby to issue an authoritative verdict on Israel's life. The psalm does not imply that there has been anything for the congregation to see by way of representation of Yhwh's appearing to it. It is the prophet who gives testimony to having sensed or seen Yhwh speaking and appearing, as prophets such as Isaiah and Ezekiel did, to give the message that will follow in vv. 7–23.

> ¹El, God, Yhwh has spoken,
>> called to the earth from the rising of the sun to its setting.

The psalm begins with a particularly fulsome and solemn naming of God, more so than any other in the Psalter. "El" designates God as the great creator, sovereign among the heavenly beings (cf. Jerome's *fortis*). It is a title that links Israelite faith with the faith of other peoples around. "God" designates God as deity over against humanity. "Yhwh" designates God by the name revealed to Israel as the one especially active in Israel's story. This threefold designation of God carries over as also the subject of the second colon, which itself focuses on spelling out the implications of "spoken." To what end has God spoken? To summon the whole earth to listen. Why, we do not yet know, and we will not know until v. 4, or rather v. 7, or rather v. 16.

> ²From Zion, perfect in beauty, God has shone forth—
>> ³ᵃour God comes and cannot be silent!

First, vv. 2–3a clarify another question: from where did Yhwh speak? The answer is, from Mount Zion.[16] The taken-for-granted emphasis on Zion makes a link behind Ps. 49 to Ps. 48. The description of Zion as "perfect in beauty" parallels the description there as "the most beautiful height, the greatest joy in all the earth" (48:2 [3]), and like those descriptions it speaks religiously and theologically rather than in terms of physical geography. Lamentations 2:15 refers back to (virtually) these precise words, as it does to Ps. 48:2 [3], with grievous irony—or the psalm refers back to Lamentations in light of the restoration of temple and city after the exile. Either way, at this point there is no need for irony. At this point there is no doubt that Yhwh dwells on Mount Zion, and

---

16. But Michael D. Goulder (*The Psalms of Asaph and the Pentateuch*, JSOTSup 233 [Sheffield: Sheffield Academic Press, 1996], 38–40) sees this as an addition to turn a northern psalm into a Jerusalem psalm.

Yhwh has shone forth from there in the prophet's awareness. But that latter statement changes the agenda, or pushes it in a new direction. "Shining forth" is what Yhwh does when coming to act, not coming to speak (e.g., 80:1–2 [2–3]; 94:1–2). The prophet will not merely be sharing words but announcing action. The second colon then pushes the line in yet another direction, rhetorically if not substantially. The prophet intervenes to affirm the necessity that Yhwh indeed come and not be silent. That verb superficially refers merely to speech, but it suggests speech that implies or commissions action (e.g., 35:22)—a silence about matters such as the spilt blood of God's servants (Rashi). The prophet also adds another title for God, "our God," which people could naturally take as pointing toward the nature of the action that people would look for (as in 80:1–2 [2–3]; 94:1–2), action that brings the downfall of Israel's enemies and thus the deliverance of Israel. (In reality, things will be more complicated.)

> ³ᵇFire consumes before him,
>   around him it has whirled powerfully.

Verse 3b–c coheres with that as it describes the nature of God's appearing or coming (cf. 18:7–15 [8–16]). The original location from which Yhwh spoke was Sinai, and the line applies to Zion the imagery associated with that original speaking (cf. 18:7–15 [8–16]). Yhwh's appearing or coming brings fire that consumes Yhwh's enemies and thus Israel's enemies. The second colon uses a much less familiar verb, $śā'ar$, to add that this fire not only precedes Yhwh, as if you could relax once Yhwh passes, but whirls around on all sides. There is no safety zone.

> ⁴He calls to the heavens above
>   and to the earth, for the making of a decision about his people.

In v. 4 we start again; Yhwh once more "calls." This time initially Yhwh calls to the heavens, though then not unexpectedly again calls to the earth. In light of what we have heard in the meantime, we might expect that Yhwh is calling heaven and earth to court with the intention of acting in judgment against them and on behalf of Israel. Or they might be summoned to be present in court like a jury to agree that such action against Israel's enemies is appropriate and/or to witness to Yhwh's declaration of intent (cf. Deut. 4:26; Isa. 1:2). The last words of the line are compatible with that. The EVV assume that Yhwh summons them "that he may judge his people," but that translation resolves an ambiguity about the word.[17] It

---

17. Cf. Johanna W. H. Bos, "Oh When the Saints," *JSOT* 24 (1982): 65–77 (see 67).

is the context that must determine whether the verb means *deciding *for*
someone or deciding *against* them. The context will have given the hearers
the impression that it is the first, but the expression itself is ambiguous.

> [5]"Gather for me the people committed to me,
>   who sealed a covenant with me over sacrifice."

Yhwh also has that people summoned to court—who Yhwh addresses
is not specified (it is presumably not the heavens and earth), but we
might speculate that it is heavenly aides. The verb applies to both cola,
which describe the people in two parallel ways. First, they are "my *committed ones." Samuel Terrien suggests that this word "implies that not
every member of the chosen people is noted for fidelity to the terms and
conditions of the covenant,"[18] but the context suggests the opposite—the
very definition of the covenant people as a whole lies here.[19] They are
a people committed to Yhwh (there can be an irony about that, as will
eventually emerge). How did they come to be Yhwh's committed ones?
This happened through their sealing of their commitment to a covenant
with Yhwh—literally to "my covenant," one that Yhwh laid down; they
simply agree to be bound by it. That took place through the solemn rite
of sacrifice, perhaps with the implication suggested by the verb translated "seal" (*kārat*). The verb literally means "cut," apparently alluding
to a rite associated with sealing a covenant: see Gen. 15:7–21. As one
cuts up the animal, one wishes such a fate on oneself if failing to keep
one's commitment.

> [6]And the heavens have proclaimed his faithfulness,
>   for God—he is exercising authority. (Rise)

The introduction closes with a reference to the heavens that pairs with
the appeal to the earth in v. 1. The heavens have declared that Yhwh
has indeed been *faithful. Yhwh is indeed exercising *authority. This
clarifies that ambiguity in v. 4 about why the heavens and the earth are
summoned. As the jury in this court, the heavens and the earth agree
with the case put forward by Yhwh, the plaintiff.

50:7–15. Listening to the psalm, the spirits of Yhwh's people will
have kept rising through vv. 1–6. Surely its implication is that Yhwh is
coming to act in decisive faithfulness on their behalf against their foes?
They are to have a rude awakening. Verses 1–6 have set them up to be

---

18. *Psalms*, 397.
19. Cf. Hartmut Gese, "Psalm 50 und das alttestamentliche Gesetzesverständnis," in
Rechtfertigung (E. Käsemann Festschrift; ed. Johannes Friedrich et al.; Tübingen: Mohr,
1976), 57–77 (see 65).

confronted, and v. 7 announces that. Yet the real confrontation does not come in vv. 7–15. Yhwh does not, for instance, say that there is something wrong with their attitude to sacrifice or their understanding of it, though the lines do safeguard against such misunderstanding. Verses 7–15 constitute more of a huge raising of suspense.

> 7Listen, my people, and I will speak,
>   Israel, and I will charge you;
>   I am God, your God.

Even in v. 7, only the second colon brings their disabusing over who are the objects of Yhwh's concern. In the first colon they are exhorted to listen, the verb carrying over into the second colon. But then the verb "charge" makes more specific the kind of speaking Yhwh has in mind. Yhwh intends to utter a solemn admonition (ʿûd), like the solemn admonitions Yhwh issued at Sinai (ʿēdût; see 19:7 [8]).[20] The unexpected third colon then itself constitutes a solemn self-declaration, like the description with which the psalm opened. This adds to the soberness established by the talk of charging the people. All the authority of Yhwh as the people's God lies behind the charge. The seriousness of who Yhwh their God is relates to the substance of the charge as this will unfold through vv. 7–15, as well as providing reason why it should be taken seriously as a charge from this God. It will be about this God and not merely from this God.

> 8Not concerning your sacrifices do I rebuke you,
>   or your whole-offerings that are before me regularly.

Verse 8 then initiates the raising of suspense as it begins to speak of what Yhwh does not rebuke the people for. The first colon raises a question ("Why does Yhwh not rebuke them concerning offerings?") that the second answers ("Because the offerings are there before Yhwh"—they are scrupulous in making them). To make the poetry work, the two kinds of offerings are separated—prosaically put, "I do not rebuke you for your sacrifices or whole-offerings because they are regularly before me." The two terms cover two main set forms of offering, sacrifices that were shared by offerer and Yhwh, and *whole-offerings that were totally given over to Yhwh (see Lev. 1; 3). "Regularly" (tāmîd) recalls the application of this term to the "regular" whole-offering, sacrificed night and morning, and thus this word strictly applies only to the whole-offerings and not to the shared sacrifices.

20. NRSV translates "testify against you," which implies accusation, but Yhwh does not testify against Israel in vv. 7–15, and even in vv. 16–22 Yhwh does not testify against Israel as a whole. But ʿûd also denotes the solemn declaration of something (e.g., 81:8 [9]).

> ⁹I would not take a bull from your house
>   or goats from your folds.

Even if this were not so, Yhwh would have no need to take extra animals from the people's herds and flocks. The NRSV has Yhwh not "accepting" such animals, but the verb is *lāqaḥ*, and for "accept" one would expect *rāṣâ* (e.g., 51:16 [18]; 119:108; Amos 5:22; Mic. 6:7). That verb indeed comes in v. 18; further, v. 14 will imply that Yhwh does accept offerings.

> ¹⁰For to me belongs every animal in the forest,
>   the cattle on a thousand mountains.
> ¹¹I acknowledge every bird in the mountains, [MT]/heavens, [LXX]
>   and the creature of the wild is with me.

Verses 10–12 add another consideration. Read in light of v. 8, the point about v. 9 would be that the people's scrupulousness makes it unnecessary for Yhwh to come and take animals from them. But it is vv. 10–12 that give the actual reason why Yhwh has no need to do that. Even if Yhwh wanted further animals, there would be no need for Yhwh to come and appropriate them from people's herds and flocks, because Yhwh owns all the creatures[21] of the wild.

> ¹²If I get hungry, I shall not tell you,
>   for to me belong the world and what fills it.

After the two parallel lines of parallel cola making this point, v. 12 notes the implication—there will be no need to tell Israel if Yhwh does get hungry, given that all those animals are available to Yhwh. With irony, Yhwh speaks as if this were a real possibility ("if" is *'im*, not *lû*).[22]

> ¹³Do I eat the flesh of buffalo
>   or drink the blood of goats?

Those acerbic comments could clearly be misunderstood, but v. 13 safeguards against their possible implications. At one level the presupposition of sacrifice is indeed that one offers something to eat whose smell, at least, Yhwh savors (Gen. 8:21). Yhwh shares in sacrifices and receives whole-offerings in their entirety. No doubt Israelites sometimes understood this process literalistically, but they also knew that Yhwh

21. On *zîz*, see 80:13 [14].
22. See GKC 159m, r.

115

was not the kind of person who ate and drank, and v. 13 reminds them of that. Yhwh neither eats the animals of the wild that vv. 10–12 has spoken of[23] nor the domestic animals mentioned in v. 9, which were offered in sacrifice.

> [14]Sacrifice a thank-offering to God
>   and fulfill your promises to the Most High.

So what is the point? Verse 14 begins to explain. When people make an offering in response to God's having done something for them, they are expressing their gratitude in a tangible way. There is more than one circumstance in which they may do that (again, see Lev. 3); the second colon specifies one such circumstance: some thank-offerings are made in fulfillment of a *promise made when praying for the *Most High so to act. The NRSV's "offer to God a sacrifice of thanksgiving" could imply that the psalm looks for the offering of a prayer of thanksgiving rather than an actual sacrifice, while Tg turns the sacrifice into the offering of a life of obedience (cf. Rom. 12:1), but it is hard to take the Hebrew (translated more literally above) that way. Further, it is then harder to make sense of the second colon, which implies something more concrete than a mere prayer. Indeed, it would be odd for the psalm to abandon the idea of concrete offerings, because both the offerers and Yhwh would surely be glad to have such concrete tangible expressions of gratitude (as Leviticus assumes). It would be a step backward in a relationship with God to abandon them. The worshippers have bodies and not merely spirits, so a material offering is apposite for them and therefore welcome to Yhwh, for what it says about their gratefulness, not because it will satisfy Yhwh's appetite. There is certainly nothing new about this declaration by the prophet. They know it, and the psalm does not indicate that they have forgotten; Yhwh is simply reminding them of it.[24]

> [15]Call me on the day of trouble;
>   I will rescue you, and you will honor me.

In light of that, the final verse of this section sums up the dynamic of a relationship with Yhwh. People pray, Yhwh acts, they honor Yhwh. The point about sacrifice is that it is a way of honoring Yhwh for acting in response to prayer. "Call me" is a little peremptory (see 89:16 [17]).

23. Verse 13a refers to the *'abbîr*, a term for powerful human beings or animals and referring to a wild animal such as buffalo or bison, not the *par*, the farm animal, as in v. 9.

24. See Raymond Pautrel, "Immola Deo sacrificium laudis," in *Mélanges bibliques* (A. Robert Festschrift; Paris: Bloud & Gay, 1957), 234–40.

50:16–21. We have now had two sections of raising suspense. First there was the summons to gather Israel for what seemed likely to be a declaration about taking action on their behalf. Then there were the words suggesting that actually Yhwh was about to charge Israel with wrongdoing, but all Yhwh did was tell them that there was nothing wrong with their sacrifices. They have been twice set up; vv. 16–21 therefore bring the real message with force.

> 16But to the faithless God has said,
>   What are you doing in proclaiming my statutes,
>   taking my covenant on your lips,

Like vv. 7–15, the final major section begins with a 3-3-3 tricolon. Yet again, suspense is tightened through an ambiguity about v. 16. Who is the *faithless? The word is singular, as "people" and "you" were through vv. 7–15, so it would be natural to understand Yhwh to be charging the people as a whole with being faithless. The further two cola in v. 16 (with the question applying to both cola and the two verbal expressions paralleling each other) would cohere with this. To be faithless is appalling, but further, there is an outrageous tension between being faithless and having the effrontery still to appear in Yhwh's presence and join together in proclaiming the covenantal statutes you are ignoring.

> 17When you are one who is against my instruction,
>   who has thrown my words behind you?

In turn, another pair of parallel cola in v. 17 begin to spell out the nature of the faithlessness that the psalm condemns. It involves being *against and repudiating Yhwh's "instruction," pushing it away and excluding it from one's life. The word (*mûsār*) is most common in Proverbs (e.g., 1:2–8), where it can mean both teaching and chastisement; here the second colon clarifies that it refers to teaching, putting the point more vividly. This opposition to Yhwh's instruction involves throwing Yhwh's words over one's shoulder as one goes along, so that they lie behind us and we cannot see them making demands on us or accusing us. What words are these?

> 18If you have seen a thief, you have accepted him [MT]/run with him
>   [LXX]
>   and cast your lot with adulterers.

Verse 18 begins to suggest a particular focus on the Ten Words. It also starts making more and more clear that it is the individual faithless person within the community who is being confronted, not the people as a whole, and presumably that indicates that this was also the case in vv. 16–17. Further, the psalm gives more precision to the nature of the faithlessness it confronts. First, these two parallel cola show that the psalm is not directly concerned with people who are themselves thieves or adulterers (it would then simply condemn them as thieves and adulterers) but with the kind of person who accepts and associates with such people, perhaps getting a vicarious thrill from this. It is such an attitude of acceptance that stands in tension with appearing in worship and affirming Yhwh's statutes and covenantal requirements that exclude such behavior (e.g., in the Ten Words, Exod. 20:14–15 [13], where the verbs related to "thief" and "adulterer" come). Israelites are expected to oppose and repudiate theft and adultery, and also thieves and adulterers (Scripture does not speak in terms of hating the sin and loving the sinner, because the sin is embodied in the person). Instead of opposing and repudiating, the faithless accept such people.

> [19]You have given your mouth to evil,
>   with your tongue you frame deceit.

Likewise, they are not directly involved in evil deeds—they do not go around killing people—but they are indirectly involved in this. They give (lit. "send") their mouth to do evil (*bad). The second colon makes more specific how that comes about, by their being involved in the talk that formulates ways of deceiving people. The verb in the second colon (*ṣāmad*) is a rarer one, the only occurrence of the hiphil; literally, they "bind" deceit, devise a plan that is bound to come to fruition.

> [20]You sit speaking against your brother,
>   ascribe failings to your mother's child.

Further, they behave in such ways toward members of their own family. The "brother" might mean simply that they are laying actions against other members of the household of Israel, but the parallel reference to the mother's child suggests the psalm has in mind people acting thus toward members of their immediate family. They sit in the gathering of the court at the city gate and make such accusations, perhaps because that is the way to gain a bigger share of the family's own land and possessions. Again the second colon introduces a hapax, which perhaps suggests that accusing one's brother of a nonexistent "failing" (*dŏpî*) is an act of unparalleled heinousness. In light of the link with two of the Ten Words in v. 18, one could reckon that vv. 19–20 relate to the prohibition on false witness and making wrong use of Yhwh's name (in swearing to tell the truth).

> [21]Since you have done these things, if I were silent,
>   you would think that I was just like you;
>   I rebuke you and lay it out before your eyes.

God must confront the person who acts thus. A tricolon closes off the section, as one began it. The rationale for this confrontation implies a repetition or addition to the critique. Part of the failure of these individuals lies in their accepting wrongdoers and failing to speak up about wrongdoing (see esp. v. 18). Yhwh will not be like that. Silence (*ḥāraš* hiphil) often implies inaction (cf. NJPS), and v. 22 will refer to action, but first the unexpected third colon affirms that Yhwh will speak rather than be silent. We knew from the beginning that Yhwh was not going to stay silent, and we had associated ourselves with that (v. 3); here is the payoff line. Yhwh does not rebuke the people regarding their worship (v. 8) but does rebuke these individuals about their lives. Yhwh lays it out—the verb (*'ārak* hiphil) can be a term for laying out a legal case (e.g., Job 23:4)—before their eyes, in a way they therefore cannot escape.

50:22–23. The transition to plural imperative in v. 22 buttresses the tricolon in v. 21 in signaling a transition to two closing lines that drive the point home. They do so by summarizing the implication of the two major sections, though in reverse order.

> [22]Do consider this, you people who put God out of mind,
>   lest I tear you and there is no one to save you.

Although v. 22 thus drives home the point in vv. 16–21, realistically it makes this transition to a plural—there is, after all, more than one such person in the community, and the plural reduces the opportunity for any particular individual to reckon that Yhwh is speaking to someone else. What Yhwh wants is for such people to *think*. That desire has also applied to the community as a whole in its attitude to sacrifice, but the description of the addressees as people who put God out of mind (*ig-nore) makes clear that they are more the people addressed individually in vv. 16–21. If they continue thus, they will find God acting and not merely speaking (see on v. 21). Yhwh will tear at them like a lion. The implication may be that the punishment fits the crime, for that is what the addressees are doing in their subtle way (cf. 7:2 [3]; 17:12; 22:13 [14]). The punishment will also fit the crime in that the only one who saves people from trouble is Yhwh (e.g., 7:1 [2]; 22:20 [21]; 33:16), and Yhwh is on the wrong side.

> ²³The person who sacrifices a thank-offering honors me;
>   to the person who directs his way
>   I will show God's deliverance.

Finally, in another tricolon Yhwh returns to the theme of vv. 7–15, though with an elaboration that takes vv. 16–21 into account. Here the movement between speaking of an individual and of a group is reversed. Verses 7–15 referred to the people as a whole; v. 23 refers to the individual person. The first and last colon restate the second colon in v. 15, in reverse order. The regular relationship of an individual to God involves regularly experiencing God's deliverance and regularly honoring God with a thank-offering as a response to that. But who is it who sees God's deliverance? The middle colon describes such a person as one who "directs [śîm] his way."[25] The prophet challenges individuals to accept responsibility for their way of life (see just now 49:13 [14]; also, e.g., 1:6; 37:14) in light of the challenges in vv. 16–21.

Theological Implications

Cassiodorus imagines the entire psalm addressed to the Jewish people by the Christian church.[26] That is a procedure of great spiritual danger. Augustine is wiser to urge us to see ourselves addressed by Scripture: "Let each one then examine his heart."[27]

The psalm sets before us three possibilities for Christian worship. First, we might expect that God will appear to our prophets in spectacular ways and that they will come to worship with a revelation for us about the way God looks at our worship and our lives. Second, we might need to look at what our worship implies regarding our assumptions about God. For instance, does God want all the effusive declarations of love that we make, given that worship in Scripture does not involve these? Are these made just for our own sake? On the other hand, is something wrong with our worship if it is only a matter of words and feelings and not a matter of concrete and material offerings that cost us something and reflect the fact that God made us concrete and material beings? Third, we might

25. It is an elliptical phrase (the more so since the noun actually lacks the suffix "his," though that can be inferred from the suffix on the verb in the last colon), but the meaning is clear enough.

26. *Psalms*, 1:479–92.

27. *Psalms*, 180–81.

expect that God will confront us in our worship about the way we collude with wrongdoing or involve ourselves subtly in wrongdoing, in the three areas that vv. 16–21 focus on. The normal life of believers revolves around three elements—our directing our way, our experiencing God delivering us from trouble, and our making thank-offerings to God.

Psalm 51

Sin, Cleansing, Renewal

Translation

> The leader's. Composition. David's. When Nathan the prophet came
> to him as he had come to Bathsheba.

> [1]Be gracious[1] to me, God, in accordance with your commitment;
>> in accordance with the abundance of your compassion wipe away
>> my rebellions.
> [2]Wash me abundantly[2] from my waywardness,
>> from my failure purify me.

> [3]For my rebellions I do acknowledge,
>> my failure is before me continually.
> [4]You, you alone are the one I have failed,
>> I have done what is evil in your eyes,
> So that[3] you are faithful in your speaking,
>> right in your decision.[4]

1. Not "be merciful" (LXX): the verb is *ḥānan*, not (e.g.) *ḥûs* (which Tg uses).
2. K has *hrbh*, either imper., "manifest abundance [as you] wash," or inf. abs. functioning as an adverb, "abundantly wash," the more frequent construction. Q has *hereb*, shortened impv.
3. *Lĕma'an* here signifies result rather than purpose; see JM 169g; N. H. Ridderbos, "Psalm 51:5–6," in *Studia biblica et semitica* (T. C. Vriezen Festschrift; ed. M. A. Beek; Wageningen: Veenman & Zonen, 1966), 299–312; H. A. Brongers, "Die Partikel *lĕma'an* in der biblisch-hebräischen Sprache," *OtSt* 18 [1973]: 84–96 [see 88–89]); against Goldingay, *Songs from a Strange Land*, 156. Alternatively the line might involve an ellipsis, implicitly beginning, "[I make this confession] so that you are faithful . . ." (e.g., Edward R. Dalglish, *Psalm Fifty-One* [Leiden: Brill, 1962], 109–12; cf. Luther, *First Lectures*, 1:235–43).
4. In the first colon the parallelism of the two cola perhaps generates the unique qal inf. of *dābar*, rhyming with the subsequent form from *šāpaṭ*. The parallelism also makes it likely that the second colon, like the first, is a statement (so TNIV) not a plea (so NRSV).

⁵Yes, I was born in waywardness,
  my mother conceived me in failure.
⁶Yes, you like truthfulness in hidden places,
  in the secret place you make me acknowledge insight.⁵

⁷Will you remove my failure with hyssop so that I may be pure,
  Will you wash me so that I may be whiter than snow,
⁸Will you make me hear of joy and gladness,⁶
  May the bones you crushed rejoice.
⁹Hide your face from my failures
  and wipe away all my wayward acts.

¹⁰Create a pure heart for me, God,
  make a new, steadfast spirit within me.
¹¹Do not dismiss me from your presence,
  do not take your holy spirit from me.
¹²Do return⁷ to me the joy of your deliverance,
  uphold me with a wholehearted spirit.

¹³I will teach rebels your ways,
  failures will turn to you.
¹⁴Rescue me from death, God,
  my God who delivers.
May my tongue resound your faithfulness;⁸
    ¹⁵my Lord, will you open my lips,
    may my mouth tell your praise.

¹⁶For you would not like a sacrifice, were I to give it;⁹
  you would not accept a whole-offering.
¹⁷The godly sacrifice¹⁰ is a broken spirit,
  a broken, crushed heart, God, you would not despise.
¹⁸Do good to Zion in your acceptance of it;
  may you build up Jerusalem's walls.
¹⁹Then you will like true sacrifices,

5. The use of the yiqtol and the clash with v. 5 make it unlikely that v. 6 refers to the way God formed the person morally (against Dalglish, *Psalm Fifty-One*, 121–27).

6. Syr has the nice misreading "make me full" (satisfy me) for "make me hear" (implying *taśbîʿēnî* for *tašmîʿēnî*).

7. The impv. takes the lengthened form *hāšîbâ*.

8. Preceded by a cohortative and an impv. and followed by an appeal in the yiqtol and then by a jussive, the verb looks more like a jussive than a yiqtol.

9. GKC 108d–f gives three possible significances for a cohortative dependent on another verb. It can express intention, "so that I should give it"; *TTH* 64 and DG 87 take the clause thus. It can constitute the apodosis of a conditional clause (the condition may be only implicit): "else I would give it"; this is GKC's own understanding. Or it can constitute the protasis of a conditional clause. This seems the most natural.

10. Lit. "the sacrifices of God" or "the sacrifices for God."

burnt offering and whole-offering;
then people will take up bulls[11] onto your altar.

Interpretation

With Ps. 38 this is one of only two psalms that focus on confessing sin. It begins with appeals for cleansing in vv. 1–2, which are taken further in vv. 7–9; meanwhile, vv. 3–6 form the psalm's acknowledgment of the nature of wrongdoing. Verses 1–9 thus form a stepped structure, outlined further in the introduction to vv. 7–9 below. Verses 10–12 then add appeal for inner renewal, vv. 13–15 for the opportunity to testify to God's deliverance, and vv. 16–19 for the restoration of the city and thus for sacrifice to regain its proper place. This outline shows how even Ps. 51 might not seem very penitential, since it concentrates more on urging God to deal with the consequences of the suppliant's sin than on expressing penitence for it or owning the nature of it or even seeking forgiveness for it. It thus contrasts with penitential prayers such as those in Ezra 9, Neh. 9, and Dan. 9, though it parallels them in expressing a general sense of sinfulness and loss rather than referring to a specific sin or a specific experience of chastisement. When it speaks of suffering and loss, it does so in general terms (vv. 8, 17), and it speaks of rebellions, failures, and wayward acts in the plural as well as in the singular and of failure that characterizes the whole of the suppliant's life rather than being expressed in a concrete act. No doubt that is the nature of a prayer included in the Psalter for general use. And Aquinas comments that of the Penitential Psalms, "this one is more often repeated in Church because it alone beseeches mercy and thus it obtains favour."[12]

The psalm makes much use of repetition:[13] abundance/abundantly (vv. 1, 2); wipe away (vv. 1, 9); wash (vv. 2, 7); rebellion(s)/rebels (vv. 1, 3, 13); waywardness/wayward acts (vv. 2, 5, 9); failure/fail (vv. 2, 3, 4, 5, 7, 9, 13); purify, be pure (vv. 2, 7), acknowledge (vv. 3, 6); faithful/faithfulness (vv. 4, 14); like (vv. 6, 16, 19), crush (vv. 8, 17), joy (vv. 8, 12), heart and spirit (vv. 10, 17), spirit (vv. 10, 11, 12), deliver/deliverance (vv. 12, 14), sacrifice (vv. 16, 17, 19), whole-offering (vv. 16, 19), accept/acceptance (vv. 16, 18), truth/true (vv. 6, 19); cf. also the repetition of "come" in the heading. It

---

11. Or "then bulls will go up." Dalglish (*Psalm Fifty-One*, 201) takes the verbs in v. 19 as jussive, following on v. 18.

12. *Commentary on the Psalms*, on Ps. 50 (= 51 in EVV).

13. Cf. Pierre Auffret, "Notes sur la structure littéraire de Ps li 1–19," *VT* 26 (1976): 241–49; Jean Magne, "Répétitions de mots et exégèse dans quelques Psaumes et le Pater," *Bib* 39 (1958): 177–97 (see 179–86).

has been dated in the time of David,[14] Josiah,[15] the exile,[16] and after the exile.[17] The closing verses' appeal to God to build up the walls of Jerusalem need not imply that the walls are broken down and thus that the plea belongs to the exile or afterward. Nor need their comments about sacrifice indicate a different attitude from that expressed in v. 17, with the same implication.[18] On the other hand, the closing lines do suggest that the psalm does not originally relate to the sin of a private individual but to that of a leader such as the king or of the people as a whole.[19] This also fits with the plea that God's holy spirit should not be withdrawn, since the OT connects Yhwh's spirit more with the king or the people as a whole than with ordinary individuals. The appropriateness of the psalm as an expression of corporate confession is further suggested by the way its opening appeals to the characteristics of God and of sin in terms quite similar to those which appear in connection with Yhwh's attitude to Israel's sin in the classic self-description in Exod. 34:6–7.[20] The recurrence of reference to sacrifices in vv. 16–19 may explain the psalm's location here as an appropriate response to Ps. 50.

> The leader's. Composition. David's. When Nathan the prophet came to him as he had come to Bathsheba.

Heading. See glossary. By comparing the two comings, using the same verb and the particle *ka'ăšer* (contrast EVV), the heading suggests that there is a significant correspondence between David's action and Nathan's action; the former invokes the latter.[21] In general terms, the prayer would be very appropriate to David, and the words of the story in 2 Samuel resonate with some words from the psalm. With the hope that God may be gracious and the acknowledgment of having done evil in God's eyes (2 Sam. 12:9, 22), compare vv. 3 and 6. The words "I have failed Yhwh" (2 Sam. 12:13) recall "I have failed you alone" (v. 4), though the difference is crucial; it may seem

---

14. E.g., Goulder, *Prayers of David*, 51–69.

15. So Dalglish, *Psalm Fifty-One*.

16. E.g., Diodore, *Psalms 1–51*, 165.

17. E.g., Gerstenberger, *Psalms*, 1:215.

18. So, e.g., Gurdon C. Oxtoby, "Conscience and Confession," *Int* 3 (1949): 415–26 (see 423).

19. Cf. Diodore, *Psalms 1–51*, 166; Theodore, *Psalms 1–81*, 666–69, noting that Paul's quotation from v. 4 (Rom. 3:4) supports this understanding; Jacques Vermeylen, "Une prière pour le renouveau de Jérusalem," *ETL* 68 (1992): 257–73. Contrast Werner H. Schmidt, "Individuelle Eschatologie im Gebet," in *Neue Wege*, ed. Seybold and Zenger, 344–60. Ernst Würthwein ("Bemerkungen zu Psalm 51," in the same volume, 381–88 [see 381]) therefore deletes "holy."

20. Cf. McCann, "Psalms," 885.

21. Cf. Dahood, *Psalms*, 2:2.

questionable whether David could get away with saying that he had sinned against God alone. So more likely the psalm was not designed specifically for David to utter on that occasion, though the links just noted may be the reason for making an imaginative link with David's situation.[22]

51:1–2. The psalm begins with an appeal for cleansing in two parallel lines that are also internally parallel. Both work abb′a′. They are also bound together by the recurrence of "abundance" (*rōb*) and "make abundance" (*rābâ* hiphil). Abundance of compassion opens up the possibility of abundance of cleansing.

> ¹Be gracious to me, God, in accordance with your commitment;
>> in accordance with the abundance of your compassion wipe away my rebellions.
>
> ²Wash me abundantly from my waywardness,
>> from my failure purify me.

Between them the two lines speak in three ways about the attitude or nature of God as this relates to such cleansing, in three ways about the nature of the psalmist's sin, and in three images about the nature of the cleansing that the psalm seeks. These three threefold motifs appear in a way that provides a different structure for the two lines from the formal one expressed in their parallelism. With some theological wisdom, the appeals to God's attitude or nature come first and occupy the bulk of v. 1. They refer to God's *grace, *commitment, and compassion, "three of Yahweh's 'canonical' characteristics,"[23] in a way matching Yhwh's self-description at Sinai (see Exod. 34:6). The psalm is asking God to act in accordance with that self-revelation. The rest of v. 1 and v. 2 then speak about sin as *rebellion, *waywardness, and *failure.

They appeal for restoration in three parallel ways. One might have expected that the psalm would ask for rebellion to be pardoned, waywardness to be carried, and failure to be forgiven, but in fact each appeal works within a single broad metaphor as it speaks of wiping away, washing, and cleansing. This suggests a close link with sacramental ways of thinking (v. 7 is even more explicit about this). Dealing with sin requires more than merely acting in the space between the two parties, acting in the relationship. It requires something outward. The effect of sin is comparable to the effect of contact with death or of using false objects of worship or of eating strange creatures. Such acts defile a person, conveying an invisible stain, and sacramental

22. In the introduction to this commentary (in vol. 1), see the comments on "David and the Psalms."

23. Hossfeld and Zenger, *Psalms 2*, 19.

washing is one element in removing such defilement.[24] So the psalm asks first for the wiping away (*māḥâ*) of rebellions. Elsewhere that might refer to wiping away a record of rebellions from the divine archives (cf. 109:14), but here there is no reference to the record book, and the context rather suggests that this first appeal is already working with the sacramental metaphor. The second verb (*kābas*) is also an everyday word, not for washing the person but for washing clothes. Literally it denotes "treading," as when one does laundry, a vigorous and thorough exercise presupposing serious dirt (cf. Jer. 2:22). But in the OT it more often refers to a washing that links with sacramental cleansing (e.g., many occurrences in Lev. 15). The third verb (*ṭāhar*) refers more intrinsically to a sacramental cleansing that makes something defiling into something pure. The implication of the focus on these images for restoration is that when God's people sin, this conveys to them a defilement that makes God as hesitant to have contact with them as a human being is to have contact with something defiling. They need God to remove this defilement in order for it to be possible for God to have contact with them. Indeed, they need God to remove it in order for it to be possible for other human beings to have contact with them. The psalm does not give any hint as to how God would do that. Perhaps one is to imagine that God can do this "magically," as when God takes away Nathan's leprosy and thus his defilement (2 Kings 5).

51:3–6. The "for" introduces not so much a further basis for the appeal for cleansing (as if the confession was a basis for the appeal) as an explanation of why the cleansing is necessary. Five internally parallel lines open and close with references to *acknowledgment. Acknowledgment of sin pairs with acknowledgment of insight, qatal with yiqtol, qal with hiphil, the suppliant as subject and God as subject. At the same time, vv. 3 and 4a belong together as confessions of sinfulness, while vv. 5 and 6 belong together in the way they begin. Verse 4b thus stands at the center of a stepped structure, the heart of the confession of sin being a confession that God was in the right in the guilty verdict that the psalm presupposes. Once again the psalm uses a number of images to describe what it speaks of and, in particular, this time speaks of sin in four ways. In vv. 3–6 the terms "*rebellion," "*failure" (twice the noun, once the verb), and "*waywardness" recur; v. 4 adds "evil (*bad)." Thus the suppliant's sin is characterized as deliberate defiance, coming short of expectations, walking the wrong way, and acting in a way that God finds distasteful.

> ³For my rebellions I do acknowledge,
>   my failure is before me continually.

---

24. Theodoret comments that forgiveness is not enough; purging is also needed to remove the "awful stench of sin" (*Psalms*, 1:295).

Like praise psalms and thanksgiving psalms, then, the suppliant follows the initial address to God with a "for." Praise, thanksgiving, and confession are logical exercises and ones with definable content, not merely acknowledgment that focuses on the psalmist's feelings but acknowledgment that has reasons behind it. But this is a very different kind of "for" from the one that appears in praise psalms or thanksgivings. It involves confession, not of our faith or of what God has done for us, but confession of what we have done. The psalm emphasizes the personal nature of the recognition by including the pronoun "I," and it uses the yiqtol of *yāda*ʿ; the qatal would have sufficed, but the yiqtol makes explicit that this acknowledgment is more than a past event or a onetime recognition. The second colon underlines the point further. Instead of the suppliant's offerings being continually before God (50:8), the suppliant's shortcomings are continually before the suppliant's own eyes.

> [4]You, you alone are the one I have failed,
> 　I have done what is evil in your eyes,
> So that you are faithful in your speaking,
> 　right in your decision.

Verse 4a makes the nature of this shortcoming slightly more specific, though not more concrete. We can fail all sorts of people (e.g., 2 Kings 18:14), and doing wrong against other people also involves failing God, for a variety of reasons (e.g., Gen. 39:9; Prov. 14:31). David failed Bathsheba and Uriah, and Israel failed its covenant partners (e.g., when it rebelled against Babylon). If this were a psalm for David to pray after that failure, one can only assume that Nathan or someone followed it with a mighty rebuke. Although David had failed Yhwh, he could not say he had failed Yhwh alone (perhaps he had failed Yhwh most of all, but that is not what the psalm says, and even that may be questionable).[25] The psalm might more plausibly use the expression in the context of Israel's breaking faith with its covenant partners, if it was felt that Israel really owed them nothing. But failure in relation to Yhwh mostly suggests worship of other deities. It might be possible to do right by other people and not do right by Yhwh, the opposite to David's habit, since the OT portrays him as always faithful to Yhwh even though he often failed his fellow human beings.

The further acknowledgment in v. 4b presupposes a judgment God has uttered; one could again imagine David making this acknowledg-

---

25. See further J. Coppens's discussion, "Le péché offense de Dieu ou de prochain?" in *Le notion biblique de Dieu*, BETL 41 (Gembloux: Duculot, 1976), 163–67. Perhaps the heading assumes that we might render the colon "against you, the only one," which is hardly exegetically natural in itself but might be possible in such a context.

ment or see it as a response to the confrontation in Ps. 50. There was nothing faithless about God's word of condemnation; it was entirely deserved. God was being *faithful. The second colon makes explicit that the "word" God has uttered was an *authoritative word of judgment, a decision as to what has been done wrong and what shall happen now.[26] But evidently the suppliant assumes that it may be possible to get the judge to have mercy. When God declares that wrongdoing must be punished, one need never assume that this is a final word, because God is always having to decide whether this is a moment for justice or mercy and might be prevailed on to have a change of mind on the matter. The suppliant does not dispute the fairness of God's verdict but can still ask for mercy. Relationships with God are not like experiences in a law court, where the judge has to do what the law says.

> [5]Yes, I was born in waywardness,
>   my mother conceived me in failure.

Verse 5 returns to confession and makes the earlier confession more radical. Prayer psalms commonly claim a life of commitment to God. This psalm goes to the other extreme. *Waywardness and *failure go back to the very beginning of the suppliant's life, whether one identifies that as birth (the first colon) or conception (the second colon). One can see how this declaration would apply to Israel as a whole, whose sinfulness goes back to the moment when its relationship with Yhwh was sealed at Sinai (and cf. Ezek. 16), and one can then apply it to the church, which is sinful through and through and always in need of reformation. The line has been used as a proof text for original sin, and it is compatible with the idea that since the first human beings' disobedience, sin is as natural to humanity as breathing, though it does not imply that this sinfulness somehow links with sex,[27] and it is striking that the line does not refer to uncleanness associated with birth.[28] Nor does it imply that this sinfulness is transmitted genetically (rather than, e.g., environmentally, by the effect of parents on the children they bring up). But the point of the line is to make another personal statement about the suppliant's particular life, and it is not clear that this personal statement is assumed to apply to everyone. Nor does the rest of the OT think of humanity as

26. John S. Kselman ("A Note on Ps 51:6," *CBQ* 39 [1977]: 251–53) notes that "speak" and "decision" elsewhere form a set phrase (e.g., Deut. 17:9).

27. Cf. Hans Joachim Stoebe, *Gott, sei mir Sünder gnädig* (Neukirchen: Neukirchener Verlag, 1958), 64–65. Contrary to his image, even Augustine makes this point (*Psalms*, 193), while Theodoret notes that Eve's sin antedates her having sexual relations with Adam (*Psalms*, 1:297).

28. But see J. K. Zink, "Uncleanness and Sin," *VT* 17 (1967): 354–61.

thoroughly sinful in this way. It does assume that we are all affected by sin (e.g., 130:3; 143:2; Prov. 20:9; Eccles. 7:20), as do other Middle Eastern peoples.[29] Likewise, the idea that sinfulness was brought about by the wrongdoing of the first human beings is not in conflict with the OT and may be implied by it (cf. Gen. 8:21 in the context of Gen. 1–11).

> [6]Yes, you like truthfulness in hidden places,
>   in the secret place you make me acknowledge insight.

In isolation, v. 6 is obscure, but seeing it in association with v. 3, the opening line of the stepped structure with its earlier reference to acknowledging the truth, enables us to be more precise about its meaning. The opening "Yes" (*hēn*) in v. 6 also makes a link and a contrast with what immediately precedes. Whereas verse 5 acknowledges how radically sin has characterized the suppliant's entire life, v. 6 notes how radically God looks for *truthfulness or trustworthiness and wisdom, as God has now enabled the suppliant to recognize. The places that are hidden or secret may be the location of the sins on which vv. 3–6 as a whole focus. As well as standing in front of the suppliant (v. 3) and of God (v. 4a) and being a reality through the suppliant's entire life (v. 5), sin characterizes the suppliant's private life; God is concerned for truthfulness and insight in the way people talk and behave behind closed doors. That covers both private religion (in their homes people might be secretly praying to other deities) and secret plotting (wrongdoing starts behind closed doors, with people planning individually and/or discussing possibilities together).[30]

51:7–9. Three internally parallel lines return to pleas for cleansing and restoration, indicating that vv. 1–9 as a whole form a stepped structure:[31]

Wipe away (v. 1)
  Wash me (v. 2a)
    Purify (v. 2b)
      I acknowledge (v. 3)
        I have failed (v. 4a)
          You are faithful (v. 4b)
        In failure (v. 5)

---

29. Cf. Dalglish, *Psalm Fifty-One,* 127–30; Dalglish offers comparisons and contrasts with the psalm as a whole.

30. The expressions for hidden places (*ṭuḥôt*) and secret place (*sātum*) are both used uniquely here in the OT, but in later Hebrew *ṭûaḥ* refers to plastering something over and *satam* to closing the door (see *DTT*).

31. Cf. Terrien, *Psalms,* 402–3.

> Make me acknowledge (v. 6)
> So that I may be pure (v. 7a)
> Wash me (v. 7b)
> Wipe away (v. 9)

Two opening lines of appeal (vv. 1–2) and three later lines of appeal (vv. 7–9) thus bracket five lines of confession.

> [7]Will you remove my failure with hyssop so that I may be pure,
> Will you wash me so that I may be whiter than snow,

Verse 7, then, restates the prayer in v. 2 (though vv. 7–8a use the yiqtol rather than the imperative; hence the translation "Will you . . ."), taking up the language of purification and washing, though reversing the words over against the order in v. 2 in a way that contributes to the stepped arrangement of the lines. With some subtlety the first colon also takes up the root *ḥāṭā'* from v. 2b in using the piel privative of the verb, which more literally means "de-fail me." The line also goes beyond v. 2 in specifying the means of the purifying or de-failing, the use of hyssop. There is nothing special about hyssop in itself; it is a convenient plant for the sacramental sprinkling of blood or water in a variety of connections. Here the parallelism with washing suggests sprinkling with water rather than with blood and thus points to a similarity to the rite for cleansing a tent where someone has died, where the piel privative form of the verb also occurs (Num. 19:14–19).[32] The supplicant here uses the term metaphorically. The failure of which the psalm speaks has left a stain that needs cleansing. The supplicant asks God to act like the friend who sprinkles the people who live in that tent (and the tent itself and its furnishings) so that people and tent become pure again and able to live their ordinary lives. In the second colon there is some irony about wanting to be whiter than snow, since it is often people with skin disease who are whiter than snow (e.g., 2 Kings 5:27) and are in a state of impurity such as the one the supplicant seeks to escape. But it is also a natural image for true cleansing, because whiteness contrasts either with bloodiness (Isa. 1:18) or with the dark clothing and dirty appearance taken on by people mourning their sin (e.g., Neh. 9:1).

> [8]Will you make me hear of joy and gladness,
> May the bones you crushed rejoice.

The result will be joy. The first colon appeals for God to speak a word that will convey joy and gladness. When we acknowledge to someone

---

32. Cf. Tg. The parallelism works against Goulder's suggestion (*Prayers of David*, 56–57) that the colon refers to a purgative drink containing hyssop.

that we have let them down in some way, we wait anxiously for the response, hoping it will assure us that things are all right. In an analogous way the suppliant hopes for a response from God, perhaps an assurance regarding God's acceptance via a priest. Nathan's "Yhwh has remitted your sin [*'ābar* hiphil]; you will not die" could be an example of such a word, though its qualification ("the son who is to be born to you will definitely die") takes the edge off this good news and prohibits its being a word that brings joy and gladness (2 Sam. 12:13–14). The second colon makes the notion of joy and gladness more concrete. The crushing that David is about to experience after Yhwh's response to his confession is one the suppliant has already experienced (cf. 38:8 [9], that earlier penitential psalm; also 44:19 [20]). Thus part of the psalm's background may be an experience of physical trouble, as is often the case in prayer psalms. The bones stand for the person as a whole with particular reference to the physical state (cf. 6:2 [3]; 38:3 [4]). The difference from most prayer psalms is that usually physical suffering has nothing to do with sin. Here the implication is that the suppliant has felt the results of sin in the body.

> [9]Hide your face from my failures
>   and wipe away all my wayward acts.

Failures and waywardness reappear once more (cf. v. 2), but momentarily the first colon puts the matter a very different way. So far the psalm has been concerned for the removal of what causes stain, and that is again the aim of the second colon, which also takes up its verb from v. 1. If that happens, there will be no need for the averting of God's *face; there will be nothing for God to find distasteful. The appeal to hide the face rather recalls the more abstract expressions that opened the psalm; it would be an expression of grace, commitment, and compassion. It is a unique application of a common image. Everywhere else the psalms plead for God's face *not* to be hidden; they want God's attention. The suppliant needs to avoid that attention momentarily, needs the averting of the face in order meanwhile to have something done about what makes God not want to look at this person, like a mother averting her face from the smell of her baby even while she takes action to clean it up.

51:10–12. The further three internally parallel lines begin by speaking once more about purity, but this marks a transition to speaking of inner renewal in language that suggests fulfillment of the kind of promises that appear in (e.g.) Ezek. 36:26.[33]

33. Cf. Lloyd Neve, "Realized Eschatology in Psalm 51," *ExpT* 80 (1968–69): 264–66; R. Press, "Die eschatologische Ausrichtung des 51. Psalms," *TZ* 11 (1955): 241–49.

> ¹⁰Create a pure heart for me, God,
>   make a new, steadfast spirit within me.

The new plea presupposes that the person needs not only cleansing but also renewing. It will be v. 17 that makes more explicit why that is. The fact that the spirit is broken, the heart crushed, actually clears the way for renewing. Only something that is broken can be made new. Being broken is not a sufficient condition for being renewed, but it is a necessary one. It opens up the space for God to do that new work. "Create" (*bārāʾ*) is a rare verb, suggesting the sovereign power God exercises in doing something seemingly impossible (the verb does not have a particular association with the work of "creation" that set the world going). The earlier plea has presupposed that it is indispensable that God should purify the outward person; if God merely purified the heart, the person who was still stained would still not be able to stand before God or before the community or before the self. But it is also indispensable for the inner person to be pure. In part that is for similar reasons; the community may not be able to see the stain there, but God and the suppliant can. The psalm's language also suggests a further reason. In effect, the suppliant is asking God to do a transformative work in the inner person that deals not only with the stain that results from past wrongdoing but also with the dynamics that will continue to produce wrongdoing (cf. Jer. 17:9). The psalm has noted that God looks for truth and wisdom in our private lives and behind closed doors (v. 6). The plea corresponds to that. Because of the person's brokenness, God needs to do a creative work. Because of the inclination to sin that has caused that brokenness, this creative work needs to issue in a heart that is pure and stays pure.

The second colon thus restates the point.[34] The verb "make a new" *ḥādaš* (piel) often means repair or restore, and that would fit with the idea that the suppliant's spirit is broken, though there is another sense in which that spirit was never in good order (see esp. v. 5). In keeping with the parallelism, then, v. 10b asks God totally to transform and not merely to repair something old. The NJPS indeed translates the verb "create" (it had "fashion" for *bārāʾ*). "Spirit" thus restates "heart" but goes beyond it, because "spirit" draws attention to the dynamism of the inner springs of a person's being, a dynamism that reflects the fact that God is spirit and is the one who breathes spirit into the person. Paradoxically, perhaps,

34. The word order is similar in both cola: the noun first, then the adj., then the verb, then the pronominal expression, with the invocation "God" standing at the center of the abcdaʹbʹcʹ line. Perhaps it is for a related reason that f. *rûaḥ* is defined by a m. adj. *nākôn* (steadfast), since the latter then rhymes with the parallel adj. *ṭāhôr* (pure).

the suppliant then asks that this spirit that God creates should be a "steadfast" one; it should combine stability with dynamism. A steadfast spirit will lack the weaknesses the psalm has implied, the susceptibility to rebelliousness, waywardness, and failure. It will be firm and reliable, determined and committed, prepared and set to go God's way (cf. 57:7 [8]; 78:37; 112:7; 1 Sam. 7:3; Ezra 7:10; Job 11:13).[35]

> [11]Do not dismiss me from your presence,
> do not take your holy spirit from me.

An appeal about spirit recurs, but first the suppliant asks not to be thrown out of God's presence (*pānîm*), the place where it is possible to see God's *face and thus appeal to God: not to be thrown out like a petitioner coming before the king in unseemly clothes. This might especially suggest being unable to come to worship. Although the suppliant is in a state of sin, the very fact of praying shows that this has not meant being separated from God. By God's grace, sin does not separate from God. But in due course it will do so, unless the sinner repents and unless God takes the kind of action the psalm has been pleading for. The second colon then makes the point in an opposite way. If the first prayer was "Do not cast me away from you," the second is, "Do not take yourself away from me." As the previous line balanced heart and spirit, this line balances face and spirit. The phrase "holy spirit" comes in the OT only here and in Isa. 63:10–11; in the NT it becomes a technical term that starts to crowd out other expressions with similar meaning. Arguably "holy spirit" is a tautology, as both "holy" and "spirit" refer to the distinctive godness of God. In this context, however, it underlines the paradox of the fact that the spirit of God or God's awesome transcendent deity resides in a human being, as the psalm asks that the dynamic supernatural one may not withdraw from the suppliant even though the latter is a failure.

> [12]Do return to me the joy of your deliverance,
> uphold me with a wholehearted spirit.

An appeal about spirit recurs a third time, but again something else comes first, in this case a restating of the appeal in v. 8a. Formally the expression "the joy of your *deliverance" parallels the expression "the God of your deliverance," which one would translate more idiomatically "your delivering God," "your God who delivers." Joy does indeed deliver, but in this expression the genitive is subjective rather than adjectival. The psalm asks God to deliver and thus to restore joy. The second colon

35. Cf. Goldingay, *Songs from a Strange Land*, 167.

makes more explicit how God goes about that deliverance, while also introducing the further reference to spirit. The three references to the spirit of God involved with the human spirit thus occur in parallelism in the second colon in each of these three verses (10–12). Each second colon begins *wĕrûa*, follows that with its qualifier, then with a verb of appeal (an imperative or yiqtol), and closes with a first-person suffix. In this third verse, the appeal to make new (v. 10) and not to remove (v. 11) is succeeded by an appeal to uphold. Elsewhere "uphold" usually implies that the person is standing and that God ensures that this continues to be the case (cf. 3:5 [6]; 37:17, 24), but the present context implies that the supplicant has fallen over (cf. 145:14?), so that "upholding" could imply lifting up. The agent or means of this is a "wholehearted" spirit (*nādîb*). The adjective usually refers to a social category, to "nobles" (47:9 [10]), and LXX here takes it to refer to God's authoritative spirit. But other words from this root usually refer to the enthusiasm of human giving (e.g., 54:6 [8]). They can also refer to God's generosity (Hos. 14:4 [5]),[36] but here the context suggests that the word offers another way of characterizing the spirit that God needs to create within the supplicant, a spirit that will in the future maintain its enthusiastic commitment to God. But the possibility of reading this as a reference to God's spirit draws attention to an ambiguity that runs through these three parallel second cola. One could ask each time, is this God's spirit or the supplicant's? And each time it may be that we should think of the activity of the divine spirit on the human spirit.

51:13–15. The topic changes. The MT structures these as three parallel lines, each including a first-person verb referring to the supplicant's speaking about God, about God's ways (v. 13), God's faithfulness (v. 14), and God's praise (v. 15). More likely the tricolon comes last and closes the section.[37] It is still thus the promise to give testimony to God's act of deliverance that often appears in a prayer psalm, though it puts an emphasis on the need for God to make that possible. Psalm 32 might be seen as a fulfillment of this kind of commitment.[38]

> **13**I will teach rebels your ways,
>   failures will turn to you.

*Rebellion and *failure again come in parallelism (cf. v. 3), but now the rebellion and failure are those of other people to whom the supplicant expects to teach God's ways. The supplicant is hardly now withdrawing

36. DG 3 indeed translates "your generous spirit," carrying over the suffix from the first colon.
37. So Fokkelman, *Major Poems*, 2:167.
38. Cf. Kirkpatrick, *Psalms*, 293.

the acknowledgment of rebellion and failure but hopes to be about to experience God's restoration and therefore to be in a position to teach other people about that aspect of God's "ways." "God's ways" can be the ways God expects of people, but it would be rather presumptuous to speak of teaching these until they are better embodied in the suppliant's own life.[39] Rather, the suppliant hopes soon to get some very real experience of the generous ways God acts toward people such as rebellious failures (cf. 103:7; 145:17) and thus to be in a position to "teach" about these in the way one does in a testimony (cf. 34:11 [12]). The verb is cohortative: almost "I commit myself to teaching." That will then have the intended effect of such a testimony, that its hearers respond by taking the same stance in relation to God that the suppliant has taken. In this case, they, too, will "turn" to God (cf. Rashi). This is a rarer expression in the psalms than one might have expected (but see 7:12 [13]; 22:27 [28]). The presupposition is that at present the direction of their lives is different; they have recourse to other deities, or they put their trust in other political resources. They will turn from that to Yhwh.

> [14a–b]Rescue me from death, God,
>   my God who delivers.

A renewed plea follows on this promise to give testimony. The EVV have "rescue me from bloodguilt" (*bloodshed), which would be an odd plea if it referred to the consequences of sins already committed; we might have expected "cleanse me from bloodguilt" (cf. Isa. 4:4), in keeping with the psalm's earlier imagery. The verb suggests, rather, the idea of rescue from having one's own blood shed. One might be killed as an act of retribution for having shed blood (in which case there would indeed be little difference in meaning)[40] or as a punishment for (e.g.) worshipping other deities. While the Torah prescribes the death penalty in both cases and specifically rules out ransoming a murderer (Num. 35:31–32), the OT does not indicate that the death penalty was actually applied to people who committed acts for which the Torah prescribed this penalty. The nature of penalties perhaps varied, and such rescue is thus a possible hope. But in the context the psalm's language more closely recalls the way Ezekiel speaks of the fatal consequences of failing to tell people how to escape from the danger they are in if they fail

39. Though Karl Barth (*Dogmatics* 4/1 [Edinburgh: Clark, 1956], 580) sees here a powerful illustration of a proper confidence in God's grace and forgiveness.

40. Which we might think of David as liable to (cf. Tg), though interestingly the heading to the psalm refers not to David's having Uriah killed but only to his affair with Bathsheba (cf. Gerstenberger, *Psalms*, 1:212).

to turn to Yhwh for restoration (cf. Ezek. 33:1–9).[41] The suppliant is acknowledging the obligation to pass on this message and asking to be preserved from the consequences of not doing so. The appeal to act like the God who *delivers takes up the language of v. 12.

> 14cMay my tongue resound your faithfulness;
>   15my Lord, will you open my lips,
>   may my mouth tell your praise.

Verses 14c–15 support this understanding as the suppliant returns to explicit appeal concerning the opportunity to give that testimony, which will *resound with God's faithfulness. By cleansing and renewing, "my *Lord" will open the suppliant's lips to tell God's praise. God will thus have put a new song in the suppliant's mouth (40:2–3 [3–4]). Each of the three cola refers to a part of the body associated with speech.[42] It is an edifying idea that opening our lips is a separate act whereby God makes it possible to speak when otherwise the suppliant would be silent, but the context suggests that the factor that opens the lips is the act of restoration itself.[43]

51:16–19. The previous line would have made a natural strong ending for the psalm; the final four lines form a coda, subdividing into two pairs. The theme of sacrifice runs through the whole.

> 16For you would not like a sacrifice, were I to give it;
>   you would not accept a whole-offering.

The coda starts with two parallel cola expressing a recognition that the making of offerings, like other forms of worship and prayer, is inappropriate where a person has done something morally wrong or acted in a way that ignores God's will. Fellowship sacrifices and *whole-offerings (the two regular forms of sacrifice in 50:8) were not designed to gain one cleansing from sin or to make compensation for wrongdoing but were expressions of fellowship and commitment. As a wrongdoer the suppliant cannot just behave normally and offer such worship, the worship that one would regularly offer. This is not a revolutionary statement questioning the general appropriateness of sacrifice. Its idea is a common Middle Eastern one: the Egyptian Instruction for King Meri-ka-Re, for

41. Cf. John Goldingay, "Psalm 51:16a," *CBQ* 40 (1978): 388–90.
42. The first and last have parallel jussives referring to the giving of testimony, with their objects (*faithfulness, *praise) also parallel.
43. It is also an edifying reapplication of the words when traditional Christian liturgy makes the prayer in this verse the very opening of worship, suggesting that it is only as God opens our lips that we can praise God at all.

instance, declares, "More acceptable is the character of one upright of heart than the ox of the evildoer."[44] The psalm may likewise imply "not this without that" rather than "not this at all but only that."[45]

> [17]The godly sacrifice is a broken spirit,
>   a broken, crushed heart, God, you would not despise.

But neither is the answer some other sort of offering. For instance, the answer is not to bring a purification offering or reparation offering instead of a fellowship offering or a burnt offering. The former were designed to deal with certain forms of failure but not with acts of rebellion or moral shortcoming, certainly not where such acts were deliberate. In that circumstance the Torah has no sacrifice to prescribe. All one could do is turn from rebellion and shortcoming and cast oneself in repentance on God's mercy. Metaphorically one could offer God one's spirit and heart that have been broken and crushed by the kind of chastisement v. 8 has implied. This inner person might be more likely now to direct the person in the right way, though the psalm does not quite make that explicit (EVV's "contrite" is an interpretation of the word, which literally means "crushed," its meaning in v. 8). More likely its point is that when we offer to God an objective brokenness of body and spirit, God has a hard time resisting this offering.[46] The person that has been broken provides the evidence that God's chastisement has been implemented.[47]

> [18]Do good to Zion in your acceptance of it;
>   may you build up Jerusalem's walls.

Verse 18 then gives us a more concrete indication of what the restoration that the psalm looks for would look like.[48] The individual or the leader or the community that has spoken individually through the psalm needs to have their city restored. They need God's acceptance (*rāṣôn*) of the city that has forfeited God's acceptance through its rebellion, and they need

44. See Dalglish, *Psalm Fifty-One*, 196–97.
45. Cf. Kidner, *Psalms*, 1:193.
46. Cf. André Caquot, "Purification et expiation selon le Psaume li," *Revue d'histoire des religions* 169 (1966): 133–54 (see 152).
47. The line is parallel in substance, though formally varied. Verbal clause complements noun clause; the first colon speaks of God, the second addresses God; a negatived verb complements a positive verb; "broken, crushed heart" complements "broken spirit." The reference to spirit and heart complements those in v. 10.
48. But Rudolf Mosis understands the plea more metaphorically in relation to the city's restoration ("Die Mauern Jerusalems," in *Gesammelte Aufsätze zum Alten Testament* [Würzburg: Echter, 1999], 295–316).

God to do *good to it instead of letting it be defeated and destroyed. The second colon makes more specific what "doing good" would look like. In the OT the first reference to building up Jerusalem's walls relates to Solomon, who apparently inherited from David a wall that needed completing, a wall with a "breach" (1 Kings 3:1; 9:15; 11:27).[49] That building up might be seen as an answer to a prayer of David's such as this. After the walls' destruction in 587, they would need building up again, and NRSV's "rebuild" assumes the prayer refers to such a rebuilding.

> [19]Then you will like true sacrifices,
>   burnt offering and whole-offering;
>   then people will take up bulls onto your altar.

The tricolon closing off the psalm looks to that future situation when the relationship between God and the people has been renewed, when they have turned to God and God has restored them. Then their worship can once again take its normal form, and they can offer "true sacrifices" (see 4:5 [6]). God "will like sacrifices of truth" as God "likes truth in hidden places" (v. 6). The line again pairs the main regular forms of offering mentioned in 50:8. In addition, a complex network of connections links the cola. The first and second form a pair as the second adds the two words for *whole-offering that complement the word for sacrifices. The first and last stand in parallelism in content, though they differ in structure. The second and third belong together as one gives the names of the offering, and the other vividly describes what they involve and how costly they are. Like Ps. 50, the psalm thus closes by recognizing that worship that (allegedly) expresses the depths of what lies in us is incomplete unless it is complemented by worship that makes our reaching out to God something concrete and visible and not merely something inward.[50]

Theological Implications

"A knowledge of this psalm is necessary and useful in many ways. It contains instruction about the chief parts of our religion, about repentance, sin, grace, and justification, as well as about the worship we ought to render to God. These are divine and heavenly doctrines. Unless they are taught by the great Spirit, they cannot enter the heart of man."[51]

49. Cf. Goulder, *Prayers of David*, 67.
50. Cf. Kathryn L. Roberts, "My Tongue Will Sing Aloud of Your Deliverance," in *Psalms and Practice*, ed. Reid, 99–110 (see 107).
51. Luther, *Selected Psalms*, 1:305.

The psalm begins from the reality of divine *grace, *commitment, and compassion, a powerful trinity of divine qualities; God is not fundamentally a judge figure but a parent figure. "Our whole life is enclosed and established in the bosom of the mercy of God."[52] It is against the background of such an understanding of God that we can face the nature of our sin[53] as *rebellion, *waywardness, *failure. We are not people who always do our best or people who are not really responsible for who we are because we are shaped by our background, but we are people who are responsible for ourselves. We may be people who are committed to Yhwh, but that fact may coexist with a proper awareness of being moral and religious failures. Sometimes we are in the right, but sometimes we are in the wrong and God is in the right. We thus need our sins wiped away, and we ourselves need washing and purifying; the psalm does not ask for forgiveness but for a word from Yhwh that will produce the cleansing of the stain that makes our beings objectionable to God, to other people, and to ourselves. The psalm holds together what must be held together,[54] including specifically the relational and the sacramental, as Jesus does (cf. John 13).[55] But in addition, we need something done about the way sin characterizes our entire being, otherwise cleansing will only lead to our acquiring more stain, so the psalm also asks for a renewing of the inner spirit through the action of the divine spirit. That is both necessitated and facilitated by the way God has crushed the spirit and the body. If Yhwh will cleanse and renew, the suppliant will be able to witness in words to Yhwh's faithfulness and deliverance. And if Yhwh will bless Zion, people will be able likewise to honor Yhwh with their gifts.

Words for sin come twelve times in vv. 1–9 and twice in vv. 10–19; God is named once in vv. 1–9 and six times in vv. 10–19. Sin gives way to God; with confession, sin gives way to God's presence. "The poet literally and literarily is emptied of sin and filled with grace."[56]

---

52. Ibid., 1:320. On Luther's interpretation of the psalm, see Jack E. Brush, *Gotteserkenntnis und Selbsterkenntnis: Luthers Verständnis des 51. Psalms* (Tübingen: Mohr, 1997).

53. Cf. Seizo Sekine, "Psalm 51," in *Transcendency and Symbols in the Old Testament*, BZAW 275 (Berlin: de Gruyter, 1999), 157–214 (see 213).

54. Cf. Mays, *Psalms*, 204.

55. Cf. Brueggemann, *Message of the Psalms*, 100.

56. Schaefer, *Psalms*, 129. Cf. Claire Vonk Brooks, "Psalm 51," *Int* 49 (1995): 62–66.

Psalm 52

Divine and Human Commitment

Translation

> The leader's. Instruction. David's. When Doeg the Edomite went and told Saul, "David has gone to Ahimelech's house."
>
> ¹Why do you exult yourself in evil, warrior?—
>   God's commitment holds every day.[1]
>
> ²You plan destruction with your tongue,[2]
>   like a sharpened razor, you doer of deceit.[3]
> ³You dedicate yourself to evil rather than good,
>   to falsehood rather than speaking faithfulness. (Rise)
> ⁴You dedicate yourself to all-consuming words,
>   to a deceitful tongue.[4]

1. Lit. "God's commitment [is] every [or all] day"; the noun clause is elliptical, though not much more so than (e.g.) 7:11 [12]; 37:26; 44:15 [16]. NRSV links "every day" to v. 2 and on the basis of Syr emends *ḥesed 'ēl* to *'el-ḥāsid*, but the resultant text is still jumpy. TNIV takes the noun as the rare *ḥesed* II (cf. Claus Schedl, "'*ḥesed 'ēl*' in Psalm 52 [51],3," *BZ* 5 [1961]: 259–60; he also repoints the word), but it is doubtful if readers could be expected to understand it thus. LXX implies *ḥāmās* for *ḥesed*, which provides good parallelism with *rā'â*, but LXX then has to ignore *'ēl*. For support of MT, see Walter Beyerlin, *Der 52. Psalm* (Stuttgart: Kohlhammer, 1980), 50–53.
2. Or "your tongue plans destruction" (LXX, Jerome). But Meir Lubetski ("The Utterance from the East," *Religion* 20 [1990]: 217–32) suggests that *hwt* means not destruction but a word, thought, or incantation.
3. I take the last phrase to describe the warrior (NRSV, TNIV) rather than the tongue itself (NJPS).
4. Or this phrase might be vocative (NRSV, TNIV), like the last phrase in v. 2.

⁵God himself⁵ will break you up forever,
  snatch you up and pull you from your tent,
  uproot you from the land of the living. (Rise)
⁶The faithful will see and revere,
  and will laugh at him:
⁷"There is the man
  who does not make God his stronghold.
But has trusted in the abundance of his wealth;
  he finds strength in his destruction."

⁸But I am like a flourishing olive tree
  in God's house.
I have put my trust in God's commitment
  forever and ever.
⁹I will confess you forever,
  because you acted.
I will look to your name because it is good,
  in the presence of people committed to you.

Interpretation

The psalm begins by addressing a human being rather than God; thus far one might think of it as a quasi-prophetic psalm like Ps. 50 or a wisdom psalm.⁶ But it eventually turns out to be a variant on a psalm of trust. We do not know anything about its date, and opinions vary from the time of David to the postexilic period. Even if it had its origin in the confrontation of a particular individual, presumably it appears in the Psalter because it could be applied to other comparable situations where powerful people used deceitful means to threaten the lives of others.

The leader's. Instruction. David's. When Doeg the Edomite went and told Saul, "David has gone to Ahimelech's house."

Heading. See glossary, and for this event, 1 Sam. 21–22. The heading virtually quotes 1 Sam. 22:9, but there is no very close link between the psalm and the story as a whole; Doeg does not commit deceit though he does commit huge destruction. It is thus difficult to imagine the psalm

5. BDB gives *gam* its usual meaning "also," but the line does not seem to emphasize the correspondence of God's act and the strong man's act. *HALOT* gives it the adversative meaning "but" (cf. Jerome), but this seems a bit colorless. LXX has "therefore," but it is doubtful if *gam* can have this meaning. I take it to convey emphasis (the heading to *HALOT*'s reference to this occurrence). LXX takes the verbs in v. 5 as jussive, but vv. 6–7 rather implies they are indicative.

6. Cf. Beyerlin, *Der 52. Psalm*; Hossfeld and Zenger, *Psalms 2*, 28–33.

being written with that incident in David's life in mind, but presumably the heading indicates that it was brought into connection with that story. One might more naturally imagine it being used in connection with Absalom's rebellion.[7] On the other hand, the parallel with the heading in Ps. 51 might make one wonder whether the warrior whom the psalm indicts is David himself.[8]

52:1. The first line states the theme of the psalm as a whole. Verses 2–4 will expand on the warrior's exulting in evil; vv. 5–7 will expand on the "Why?" and vv. 8–9 will expand on the comment concerning God's commitment.

> [1]Why do you exult yourself in evil, warrior?—
> God's commitment holds every day.

The rhetorical *Why? introduces a question that constitutes a disguised statement of conviction, suggesting "It is going to get you into trouble," and thus "So it's stupid to do it" (cf. lāmmâ in 2:1). The problem about "exulting yourself in evil" is the link of verb and noun. "Exulting oneself" (*praise) is a verb whose object needs to be Yhwh (34:2 [3]; 63:11 [12]; 64:10 [11]; contrast 49:6 [7]). Exulting in evil (*bad) is thus a frightening expression. The temptation that comes from being a warrior or person of strength (gibbôr) is that one can use one's strength in dishonorable ways and can trust in these. Warriors or people of strength do not necessarily do that (cf. 19:5 [6]; 45:3 [4]; 89:19 [20]), but that is their temptation. The stupidity of it lies in the reminder in the second colon, which has several possible implications. It might imply that the only thing worthy even of a warrior's trust is God's *commitment. It might imply that the guarantee of that commitment to people who belong to God means that this exulting will turn out to be unwise. It might imply that this is the warrior's own conviction, in connection with his own life; he thinks it applies to him, but his wickedness means it does not.

52:2–4. Three parallel lines give the background to the warrior's exulting himself in evil; each of the first cola are parallel, as are each of the second cola. The weapons of the warrior turn out to be words. Does this cast the description of him as a warrior in ironic light? If he had real strength, he would be able to act openly, but in fact he does everything by deception. He is rather pathetic, really. Yet for his victims, deception is no joke.

> [2]You plan destruction with your tongue,
> like a sharpened razor, you doer of deceit.

7. See Goulder, Psalms of David, 75.
8. So Samuel A. Meier, "The Heading of Psalm 52," HAR 14 (1994): 143–58.

The point is made straightaway. His tongue is the means of planning destruction.[9] The second colon underlines the point, giving the line an abb'a' structure (warrior-tongue-tongue-warrior). This tongue is thus actually as dangerous as a razor. And if there is any doubt, we are talking about a razor that has just been sharpened. It can be thus dangerous because its owner is doing deceit with it (see on 32:2). There can no doubt be harmless deceit, but the psalms know well that death can come from the deceit that (for instance) tells lies in court in the manner of Jezebel's false witnesses against Naboth.

> ³You dedicate yourself to evil rather than good,
>   to falsehood rather than speaking faithfulness. (Rise)

Verse 3 looks deeper at the significance of the warrior's deceitful planning of destruction. The implication of a commitment to destructiveness is that the warrior is *dedicated to the *bad rather than the *good. He has made a basic choice about the orientation of his life. The second colon spells this out again and re-expresses v. 2b, adding *falsehood and making explicit its antithesis, *faithfulness, the most basic requirement of an Israelite.

> ⁴You dedicate yourself to all-consuming words,
>   to a deceitful tongue.

"Dedicate yourself" reappears, this time with words as its object; but they are "consuming" words, words capable of swallowing someone up and thus totally destroying them (cf. 21:9 [10]; 35:25). The second colon restates the way words consume, using sister expressions to ones in v. 2 and closing with another reference to the tongue as an inclusion for the section.

52:5–7. That description in vv. 2–4 sounds very threatening and would be very threatening were it not for God's involvement, which will give the faithful something to be astonished at in vv. 5–7. In fact, more space is given to the astonishment than to the reversal itself.

> ⁵God himself will break you up forever,
>   snatch you up and pull you from your tent,
>   uproot you from the land of the living. (Rise)

Whereas the Psalms sometimes see trouble as the "natural" outworking of wrongdoing, here v. 5 speaks of God's active involvement in this process. And whereas the warrior's action involves words and takes place behind

9. See on 5:9 [10].

closed doors, God's action involves forceful, vigorous, and public deeds. And whereas vv. 2–4 kept using variations on the same way of describing the warrior's actions, extended over three lines, v. 5 generates a sequence of vigorous verbs—contradictory if taken literally—to describe God's actions, all within one line. The line is admittedly a tricolon, but that also means that our sense of breathlessness at the end of the second colon is given no respite as the psalm plunges straight into another colon. First, then, the warrior is like a building or a city, and God is breaking him up, or he is like teeth that God is smashing (cf. 58:6 [7]); and God is doing so forever, in such a way that he can never be reconstructed, like Jericho when Joshua destroyed it. Or the warrior is like hot coal, but this does not stop God snatching him up (the verb *ḥātâ* is otherwise only used with coals as its object).[10] Or more literally, he is a man securely established in his home,[11] but this does not stop God bursting in like the FBI and hauling him out (the verb *nāsaḥ*; cf. Deut. 28:63; Prov. 2:22); there turned out to be no security. Or he is like a plant that seems firmly rooted in the land, but he will find himself unceremoniously uprooted (cf. Job 31:8, 12) from the land of the living: that is, he will be dead (see Ps. 27:13).

> [6]The faithful will see and revere,
> and will laugh at him:

So the *faithful have something to be astonished at. Faithfulness is thus set over against the strength that exults in and dedicates oneself to evil, deceitfulness, and falsehood. The sequence of verbs is noteworthy. First, "see" and "*revere" are very similar (*yirĕʾû, yîrāʾû*). Proper sight naturally issues in revering. But then both issue in laughter, another collocation one would not have predicted yet one that makes sense. Laughter is first a divine prerogative (2:4; 37:13; 59:8 [9]) and then therefore a human possibility. By implication God will laugh at the pretensions of the warrior as the background to the acts in v. 5.

> [7]"There is the man
> who does not make God his stronghold.
> But has trusted in the abundance of his wealth;
> he finds strength in his destruction."

---

10. Aq, Jerome, and Tg take the verb as a form of *ḥātat* ("dismay, shatter") or take *ḥātâ* as a by-form of *ḥātat*, which also fits in the context.

11. Lit. his "tent." This word can be used for a dwelling (e.g., 84:10 [11]; 132:3), but it might pick up the address to the "warrior," who will be in a tent (so Goulder, *Psalms of David*, 72–73). Reference to Yhwh's tent (Weiser, *Psalms*, 413) would surely need some pointer.

The explicit basis for the laughter of the faithful comes in v. 7. The warrior is a man of faith as he is a man of love or dedication (vv. 3–4), but his faith is as misdirected as his love and dedication. We know that God is the only object for *trust, but the warrior has other things to trust in. We think we know what is the object of his trust, for in effect vv. 1–4 have told us. In this verse, the point is summarized by the eventual description of him as trusting in his capacity for destruction. The Hebrew word translated "destruction" is picked up from the beginning of v. 2; in the Hebrew text, it is actually the first word in vv. 2–4 and the last word in vv. 5–7. We know that God is the only *stronghold, the only one in whom to find strength, but the warrior thinks there is strength somewhere else. But before then, we are slightly surprised by the reference to his trusting in his wealth—surprised rhetorically, because vv. 1–6 have not mentioned wealth, though hardly surprised substantially, for wealth gives strong people extra capacity for wrongdoing.[12] Money and power are a formidable combination unless God stands up on the other side. It is hard for the faithful to laugh at this combination when it is going strong, but they will laugh in due course, when the *gibbôr* (warrior [v. 1]) becomes a mere *geber* (man [v. 7]).

52:8–9. Whereas vv. 5–7 have been looking in faith to the future, vv. 8–9 tell us the stance the psalmist takes in the present, in the meantime, before there is actually anything to laugh at. The sequence of "I" statements contrasts with the sequence of "you" statements in vv. 1–4, a contrast made possible by the "God" statement in vv. 5–7.

> [8]But I am like a flourishing olive tree
>   in God's house.
> I have put my trust in God's commitment
>   forever and ever.

The warrior is destined to be uprooted, but the psalmist is like a tree that is not so destined. The olive is a tree of fabled longevity and wondrous fruitfulness and a figure for flourishing and security (Jer. 11:16; Hos. 14:6 [7]). There were such trees on the grounds of the temple and tree images on its walls; these come together as in imagination the psalmist is an olive tree in the temple, flourishing like a well-watered tree rather than one withered by lack of water.

The secret is that the psalmist knows where to put *trust; contrast v. 7b. The divine *commitment that is the object of trust is the commitment v. 1b spoke of, which thus reappears in this last section, following on the reworking of *gibbôr* as *geber* and the reappearance of "destruc-

---

12. Tg and Syr provide a word for "riches" to parallel "wealth" in the final colon, but this is surely not an indication of a different text (against NRSV).

tion."[13] Further, the trust that is "forever and ever" corresponds to the commitment that holds "every day" (v. 1).

> [9]I will confess you forever,
>   because you acted.
> I will look to your name because it is good,
>   in the presence of people committed to you.

Verse 9a sounds like the promise of praise that often appears in a prayer psalm, which underlines the overlap between protest psalms and trust psalms.[14] We might then more pedantically translate the second verb "you will have acted"; that is, the praise the psalmist will offer is praise for the act of reversal that God will perform. Covertly this psalm is a plea to God to vindicate the trust of which it speaks. Lasting *confession stands alongside lasting trust as an aspect of the believer's relationship with God.

Meanwhile v. 9b likewise expresses the commitment to trust under pressure that characterizes a prayer psalm. It makes more explicit that the psalmist is one who feels under pressure from the powerful of whom the psalm has spoken, though it does not quite say that the psalmist is personally under attack. The looking could be a looking for God to intervene on behalf of other members of the faithful in whose presence the psalmist stands. Looking to God's *name is a unique expression, though it is perhaps understandable as comparable to looking for God's word (e.g., 119:74, 81, 114, 147); the name or the word is then the basis for waiting (so NIVI).[15] Or it might simply be equivalent to looking for God. That might be supported by the fact that the designation of God's name as *good is also unusual (though cf. 54:6 [8]), but designating God as good is common enough. The occurrence of this word makes for another pairing with the opening line. The warrior exults in evil; the psalmist looks to God's name because it is good. The completed pairing of evil and good then accompanies the pairing in v. 3. The waiting of which the psalm speaks is done in the temple, the place of security and flourishing, in the presence of the faithful, the people under pressure, the people committed to God. The last word thus makes another link with v. 1b: "God's commitment holds every day"; God's people can therefore take the risk of staying *committed to God.

---

13. Cf. Fokkelman, *Major Poems*, 2:169.

14. In light of vv. 1–8, it seems artificial to infer that the line refers to present praise based on an act that has already taken place (against Kraus, *Psalms 1–59*, 509–10).

15. NRSV emends *'ăqawweh* to *'ăhawweh*, "I will proclaim your name," which is an easier text; but see Beyerlin, *Der 52. Psalm*, 41–46. This meaning can also be obtained by hypothesizing a verb *qāwâ* III (see *TLOT* 3:1126).

Theological Implications

The psalm concerns the objects of our exulting and our trust. On one side there is trust in power and wealth, which combined with deceit seem to make all things possible. The psalm overtly challenges people who think that way, but covertly it addresses people who lack power and wealth and are the victims of that deceit. They are invited to keep trusting in God's commitment and to let their membership in the community of the committed (cf. 50:5) be one without irony. Living in the company of God and of God's people means they can thrive.

Psalm 53

Is God There?

Translation

The leader's. On Sickness/Entreaty/Adornment/Dancing/Pipe.
Instruction. David's.

¹The crass person says in his heart,
    "God is not here.
People act corruptly and loathsomely in wickedness;[1]
    there is no one who does good.
²God looks out from the heavens
    at human beings
To see if there is someone sensible,
    someone seeking guidance from God.
³Every one of them turns back,
    altogether they are foul.
There is no one who does good,
    there is not even one.
⁴Do they not acknowledge,
    those who do harm,
Those who eat up my people as they eat food—
    do they not call God?"

1. In 14:1 [2] *'ălîlâ* is the direct obj. of the two verbs, but here *'āwel* can hardly be so (wickedness is inherently corrupt and loathsome, so cannot be rendered so) and must rather be adverbial acc. (cf. **LXX**), the two hiphil verbs being declarative.

⁵There, they are overwhelmed by terror,
    where there is no terror.
For God scatters the bones of your besieger;²
    you are shamed,³ because God rejects them.

⁶Who will bring from Zion
    the deliverance⁴ of Israel?
When God brings a restoration of his people,
    Jacob will rejoice, Israel will be glad.

Interpretation

Rather oddly, one might think, Ps. 53 is a variant on Ps. 14 (or vice versa).⁵ This more likely reflects the way the Psalter accumulated through the bringing together of groups of psalms than suggesting that the psalm was of distinctive importance to Israel.⁶ But the presence of both versions in the Psalter invites us to treat them independently, though we will learn from comparing them.⁷ Here Ps. 53 stands in contrast with the preceding psalm. Psalm 52 confronted powerful, wicked people and constituted a declaration of faith in God's commitment, which makes wrongdoing certain to meet its reward. Psalm 53 confronts people who do not believe this. Psalm 52 indicted people who dedicate themselves to evil rather than good. Psalm 53 laments the fact that there is no one doing good.⁸ Verses 1–4 describe the fool's attitude; it is a kind of lament, each second colon having only two beats. The fool expresses this lament in qatal verbs, suggesting the way people have been acting and continue to act. Verse 5 brings a response to this lament, also in the qatal and thus in the form of a declaration that God has acted (i.e., is committed to acting and will act).⁹ Verse 6 then expresses a reaction to that word. We do not know when the psalm was written, but the invasion and defeat of Sennacherib (see 2 Kings 18–19) provide a setting against which to imagine it.¹⁰

2. NRSV emends *ḥōnāk* to *ḥānēp*, "the ungodly."
3. LXX and Jerome's third-person verb looks like a simplifying reading. I take MT's hiphil as declarative rather than causative (against NJPS), since it is difficult then to see who is the "you."
4. *Yĕšuʿ ôt*, more likely a dialectical form of the sg. than an intensive pl.?
5. A northern variant? So Dahood, *Psalms*, 2:19; Rendsburg, *Linguistic Evidence*, 61–62.
6. Against Hossfeld and Zenger, *Psalms 2*, 44.
7. See the commentary on Ps. 14. The comparison illustrates the way Ps. 42–83 generally prefer the word "God" over the name Yhwh.
8. Cf. Beyerlin, *Der 52. Psalm*, 121–22.
9. See the comments in Hossfeld and Zenger, *Psalms 2*, 39, on the qatals in vv. 1–5.
10. Cf. Theodore, *Psalms 1–81*, 692–93.

The leader's. On Sickness/Entreaty/Adornment/Dancing/Pipe.
Instruction. David's.

Heading. See glossary. For the second expression, there are three roots *ḥālâ* from which *maḥălat* might derive, while Sym, Aq link it with *ḥûl*, "whirl, dance," and one Tg MS links it with the root *ḥālal*, suggesting "pipe";[11] presumably the word denotes a tune or a way of singing. Midrash Tehillim suggests the significance of the psalm's link with David as it identifies the stupid person of v. 1 (*nābāl*) as Nabal,[12] whose scene in David's story comes between that of Doeg (see Ps. 52) and the Ziphites (see Ps. 54) in 1 Sam. 22–26.[13] The word *maśkîl* (here "Instruction") reappears within the psalm itself in v. 2.

53:1–4. The main part of the psalm gives us the fool's perspective on how the world is. These opening eight lines come in four pairs.

> ¹The crass person says in his heart,
>   "God is not here.
> People act corruptly and loathsomely in wickedness;
>   there is no one who does good.

In this person's heart (not in words that ever get uttered, because they would count as blasphemy) is a stupid conviction. The second colon reveals its nature. It parallels the stupidity Job warns his wife about when she objects to the way God is acting in the world (Job 2:10) and the stupidity Yhwh attributes to Job's friends who had not spoken the truth about Yhwh as Job had (42:8). Or perhaps it is the opposite of theirs. They were convinced they knew how God acted in the world; this fool cannot see God acting in the world and does not think God is doing so. The expression in the second colon is conventionally rendered "There is no God," but in the cultural and literary context it will not be a declaration of metaphysical atheism. It rather declares that God is not present in the world as the speaker experiences it. In 37:10 *ʾên* (there is no) refers to the faithless vanishing, in 39:13 [14] to the suppliant disappearing, in Gen. 5:24; 37:30 to the fact that Enoch and Joseph have disappeared. The Tg renders, "There is no God punishing him"; NJPS, "God does not care." In light of the way the psalm unfolds, it seems that the crass person (*nābāl*) is an individualization or personification of Israel as a whole.

There is much evidence for the truth of the crass person's declaration (v. 1b). Indeed, it corresponds to one Yhwh is also capable of making

---

11. Cf. Stec, *Targum of Psalms*, 109.
12. *Midrash on Psalms*, 1:484–86. Cf. the comment on the heading to Ps. 14.
13. Kidner, *Psalms*, 1:196.

(Jer. 5:1–5). The plural verbs suggest that the line is not a description of the (singular) fool but constitutes the fool's assessment of everyone else. The declaration that people act corruptly parallels Judges' generalization regarding people in its day (Judg. 2:19) and Isaiah's description of the nation as a whole in his day (Isa. 1:4), while the declaration that they act loathsomely similarly parallels Ezekiel's description of the nation as a whole (Ezek. 16:52). Both terms might more immediately suggest religious wrongdoing, and thus "[in] *wickedness" clarifies that the fool's concern is people's behavior toward one another rather than their stance toward God. The second colon neatly parallels the second colon in v. 1a; there is no one doing *good, and there is no God doing anything about it.

> ²God looks out from the heavens
>   at human beings
> To see if there is someone sensible,
>   someone seeking guidance from God.

Verse 2a anticipates Ps. 102:19–20 [20–21], where God looks out from the heavens, sees what is going on, and does something to deliver people in prison and doomed to die. The fool agrees that God looks out from the heavens to see what is going on and sees its corruption, loathsomeness, and meanness, but the fool makes no reference to God's then doing something about it. That has been anticipatorily excluded by the conclusion that "there is no God [active here]."

What God is looking for is someone sensible, a *maśkîl*; the word came in the heading as *Instruction. Good sense is thus set in antithesis to being corrupt, loathsome, and mean. These are actually stupid. But in this line itself, the second colon answers the implied question "What does it take to be sensible?" Whereas having nothing to do with God is stupid as well as loathsome and corrupt, *seeking guidance from God and following it is the sensible principle on which to structure one's life.

> ³Every one of them turns back,
>   altogether they are foul.
> There is no one who does good,
>   there is not even one.

Ironically, the conclusion of the fool is that there is no one in the category of "sensible"; obviously this conclusion rebounds on the fool. Everyone turns away from God instead of having recourse to God for guidance, like a human being abandoning a friendship relationship (Jer. 38:22). The second colon restates the point in v. 1b. People in general are as unpleasant as milk that has gone bad.[14] Verse 3b first repeats the conclusion in v. 1b, and then adds to it an even more definitive affirmation of the point. "There is not even one." The conclusion recalls Yhwh's assessment of things when the great creation experiment has gone totally wrong (Gen. 6:5, 11–12).

> [4]Do they not acknowledge,
>   those who do harm,
> Those who eat up my people as they eat food—
>   do they not call on God?"

Verse 4 makes more explicit that link between being people of insight and submitting oneself to God. In isolation, the opening words "Do they not know/acknowledge" are difficult, since the verb expects an object (the absolute use of *yāda'* to mean "understand" is very rare). We have to read on to the end of the verse to discover the verb's object. As all these opening lines in vv. 1–4 form pairs, they operate somewhat like the two cola in a regular line, and one of the poetic possibilities of such lines is to let words in one colon apply also in the other. Here the two lines work abb'a', the opening and closing cola (v. 4a–d) forming a pair, and the two middle cola (v. 4b–c) forming a pair. The interrogative at the beginning then applies also to the verb in the last colon, and the implicit object of the opening verb is the same as the explicit object of the closing verb. The lines concern acknowledging God and calling God. Both have similar meaning to seeking guidance from God (v. 2). Real wisdom or knowledge, then, involves acknowledgment of God. Knowledge that leaves God out of account is not real knowledge. But in addition, knowledge that stops short of acknowledgment is not the real thing. Like Ps. 52, this psalm uses a rhetorical question to express the extraordinary nature of the wicked person's stance, though it is yet another kind of rhetorical question. The truth is, these people do not acknowledge God, but it seems so unbelievable that anyone should not acknowledge God that the psalm puts the matter as a question in the opening colon and again in the closing one.

The middle two cola (v. 4b–c) begin by describing these people who do not acknowledge or call on God as people who harm others. How do they do that? (v. 4b). They are totally cold-blooded (v. 4c). They eat up their own people, in the manner of foreign invaders who consume the lands, assets, and lives of the people they attack (e.g., Jer. 10:25). And as they do that they heartlessly carry on eating their fill. Indeed, their doing so will be made possible by consuming their fellow countrymen's

14. See BDB on *'ālah*.

belongings. Once again refusal to acknowledge God and callousness in relation to other people go together. Indeed, this would be a good description of the Assyrians when they invaded Judah, according to the account in the OT story, so that the fool's comments may relate to other peoples and not to Judah, to a foreign nation that eats up "my people" and despises Yhwh.

53:5. Verse 5 has no formal mark of a change of speaker, but the content marks this further pair of lines as a response to the fool's words.

> ⁵There, they are overwhelmed by terror,
>   where there is no terror.
> For God scatters the bones of your besieger;
>   you are shamed, because God rejects them.

There is no empirical way of responding to the stupid person's assessment of the situation in the world. The only possible response is one that comes from the awareness that God has as good as acted. The psalmist knows that terror will overwhelm the people who are consuming the Israelites. It is so certain, it can be spoken of as if it had already happened. The terrifying nature of this terror is underlined by the idiom in the first colon, which involves linking a verb (*pāḥad*) with its cognate noun (*paḥad*) so as to talk of being "terrified [with] terror," and then stressed by the contrast the second colon notes. Things had been fine; suddenly they are horrific.

In the second line the psalm suggests a more concrete picture, and the singular suffix for the addressee indicates that here it directly addresses the fool in respect of the foolish words in vv. 1–4. The fool is entitled to be anxious, being indeed someone under siege. The siege has not come because of being a fool; it is the siege that has brought the folly to the surface as it has found expression in the gloomy words in vv. 1–4. The problem with those words was not that they were untrue, but that they were not the whole truth. God has actually rejected these people the fool rightly protests at. The second colon thus explains the inevitable fact that lies behind the inevitable bringing down of the fool's own besieger. But the fool's stance as vv. 1–4 have described it, with its commitment to only half the truth, means that paradoxically the act of deliverance will also be an act of shaming. The fool's conviction that God could possibly leave things as they are is an insult to God, and the fool will be exposed as one who has so insulted God.

It is in v. 5 that the major difference from Ps. 14 appears, substantially changing the tone of the psalm.[15]

---

15. Fokkelman, *Major Poems*, 3:92.

53:6. The pleading question suggests that in at least the first of this last pair of lines the fool once more speaks.

> 6Who will bring from Zion
>   the deliverance of Israel?
> When God brings a restoration of his people,
>   Jacob will rejoice, Israel will be glad.

The EVV take the "Who?" question as a wish, "O that deliverance for Israel would come from Zion," but a literal translation is as appropriate. Either way the line may express the fool's longing that the promise in v. 5 should indeed come true, or it may express the fool's doubt as to whether this is possible. In different words 52:8–9 [10–11] has implied that Zion is the place from which blessing comes; the fool lacks the conviction the psalmist expressed there.

On the other hand, v. 6b is a declaration of conviction, which therefore presumably constitutes the psalmist's final response. There is nothing else that can be said to prove to the fool that the events promised in v. 5 will take place. All that remains is for the events themselves to demonstrate the truth of those promises. "Brings a restoration" (*šûb šĕbût*) usually refers to the restoration of the community after the exile; indeed, LXX, Jerome, and Tg have "brings back the captivity." This presupposes the natural assumption that *šĕbût* comes from the verb *šābâ* "take captive" (cf. BDB). But this does not fit all occurrences of the phrase (esp. Ezek. 16:53; Job 42:10), and more likely *šĕbût* comes from *šûb* itself, so that the phrase means "turn a turning" (cf. *HALOT*) and can have broader meaning. It need not refer to the exile.[16]

Theological Implications

When it seems that wrongdoing pervades the whole of experience, it is tempting to doubt whether God is really involved in events. Like Pss. 37; 49; and 73, this psalm is designed to express and build up conviction that God is indeed involved. Although God is not acting now, God will act. The psalm thus does face facts. It does not suggest that the crass person is reading humanity (including God's people) in a more gloomy way than it deserves. Yes, all have sinned. Some years ago, the people of Haiti exalted an ordinary Christian minister to its presidency, but in the week in which I write, he has just been deposed, having become

---

16. See John M. Bracke, "*Šûb šebût*," *ZAW* 97 (1985): 233–44. On the other hand, the Q *šĕbît* at (e.g.) 85:1 [2] looks more like a noun from *šābâ*, and the variants suggest some confusion between the two possibilities in MT. See *HALOT*.

as implicated in violence as those he replaced. Christians act corruptly and loathsomely in the way they relate to money, sex, and power, like other people.

The psalm faces such realities but then declares the intention to live by faith and hope. The psalmist knows that the fact that God is not acting is no indication that God will not act. Indeed, God's act is so certain it can be spoken of as if it had already happened. The psalm offers no evidence for that. Perhaps the evidence is contained within the very word "God." Perhaps the fool's conclusion deconstructs and drives us back to look at the logic that led to it. The word "God" cannot denote a being who is uninvolved in the world, or if it denotes such a being, it has redefined the notion of "God" beyond anything Israel could recognize. To put it another way, if "God is not here," then the meaning of that statement has come to be "there is no God" in any worthwhile meaning of the word "God." "God is not here" can only be an interim statement, and the psalmist affirms that this interim will come to an end. Therefore the wish implied or expressed in v. 6a is appropriate, as is the anticipation expressed in v. 6b.

Psalm 54

The Name That Rescues

Translation

The leader's. With strings. Instruction. David's. When the Ziphites
came and said to Saul, "David is hiding with us!"[1]

[1]God, by your name deliver me,
   by your might will you decide for me.
[2]God, listen to my plea,
   give ear to the words of my mouth.
[3]For strangers [MT]/willful people [Tg][2] have risen against me,
   terrifying people have sought my life,
   people who have not kept God before them. (Rise)

[4]There—God is a helper for me,
   my Lord is the very sustainer of my life.[3]
[5]He will return evil to my watchful foes [Q]/

1. Lit. "Is David not hiding with us?" The interrogative is used to introduce a surprising
statement to affirm that it really is true (GKC 150e).
2. MT has *zārîm* (cf. 109:11), and Tg implies *zēdîm* (cf. 86:14), the reading of some
later MSS; for this variation, cf. 19:13 [14].
3. In other contexts, one might render "among the sustainers of my life" (cf. KJV,
though it has "with"), but this seems an unlikely description of God. GKC 119i suggests
that the expression ascribes to Yhwh a similar character as people who sustain. More
likely both the *b* of identity (*IBHS* 11.2.5e) and the intensive pl. indicate emphasis; cf.
118:7; Judg. 11:35 (JM 133c; 136f).

May evil return to my watchful foes [K];[4]
in your truthfulness wipe them out.

[6]For your munificence I will sacrifice to you;
  I will confess your name, Yhwh, for it is good,
[7]Because it has rescued me from all trouble,
  and my eye has looked at my enemies.[5]

Interpretation

This classic prayer psalm begins with a lengthy plea to God to listen
and act on my behalf (vv. 1–2), then goes on to a rather brief "lament"
explaining why this is needed (v. 3). At the center is an expression of
trust in God's ongoing relationship with the suppliant, which leads into
a further plea (vv. 4–5). The closing lines promise to bring a public expression of praise, both tangible and verbal, when God has acted (vv.
6–7). Every line incorporates parallelism, in each case involving possible
word pairs.[6] There are no concrete indications of a date or of the kind of
person for whom the psalm was designed. We could imagine it on the
lips of a Naboth or a Nehemiah; following on Ps. 53, which he associates with the story in 2 Kings 18–19, Theodore sees this as Hezekiah's
prayer on that occasion.[7]

The leader's. With strings. Instruction. David's. When the Ziphites
came and said to Saul, "David is hiding with us!"

Heading. See glossary, and for the story, 1 Sam. 23:14–29 and 26:1–25;
"with us" appears only in the first passage, but see the comments on the
Ps. 53 heading for the significance of the order of Pss. 52–54.[8]
The psalm's reference to people "seeking my life" (v. 3) may have suggested the linking of psalm and story (cf. 1 Sam. 23:15); on the second of

4. For the alternative K *yšwb* and Q *yāšîb* readings, see also Prov. 12:14. Q has the
more common idiom (e.g., Gen. 50:15), and it fits the context in that it keeps Yhwh as
the subj. But K can be translated as jussive, which improves the parallelism. Jerome has
"May he return the evil," which both fits the context and improves the parallelism, but
one would expect *yāšēb* to give this meaning.
5. On the verb, see 22:17 [18] for the meaning "feast the eyes on."
6. See Watson, *Classical Hebrew Poetry*, 137–38.
7. See *Psalms 1–81*, 696–97.
8. But Beyerlin (*Der 52. Psalm*, 120–23) argues from the similarity between v. 6b and
52:9 and the sequencing in the headings that Ps. 54 was deliberately placed to follow Ps.
52; in which case, Ps. 53 was subsequently added in between. See further, Auffret, *Voyez
de vos yeux*, 17–18.

these occasions, David also "looked at his enemy" (cf. v. 7) in spectacular fashion. David also had Absalom "seeking his life" after he "rose against him" (2 Sam. 16:11; 18:31–32).[9]

54:1–3. Although it has the classic features of a prayer psalm, this example is unusual in leaping straight into a plea, and although the appeals to act and to hear are to be expected, we might have expected them to come in the reverse order. It coheres with this that only after the double appeal do we get the reasoning that makes it necessary. In other words, we might have expected the verses to come in the order 3, 2, 1. The actual order expresses urgency rather than logic.

> ¹God, by your name deliver me,
>   by your might will you decide for me.

In issuing an imperative appeal for deliverance in its first colon, then, the plea is a very direct way to begin; contrast the next psalm (but cf. Pss. 12; 16; 26; 35).[10] "Your *might" makes explicit one aspect of "your *name," or nature, that is relevant to the suppliant's need. "Decide for me" (*dîn*, a synonym of *šāpaṭ*; *authority) indicates the stance God needs to take in order to act to *deliver. The suppliant needs God to determine that the enemy is in the wrong and then act accordingly.

> ²God, listen to my plea,
>   give ear to the words of my mouth.

The logically prior *plea takes a similar shape.[11] In keeping with the nonlogical nature of the sequence, the second noun expression is more general than the first; all pleas involve the words of my mouth, but not all words of my mouth are pleas.

> ³For strangers [MT]/willful people [Tg] have risen against me,
>   terrifying people have sought my life,
>   people who have not kept God before them. (Rise)

9. Cf. Goulder, *Prayers of David*, 94.

10. The 3-2 rhythm reflects the fact that the opening appeal to "God" applies to the second colon as well as the first; otherwise, the cola are neatly parallel. Each comprises a *b* expression with a second-person singular suffix (one m. noun, one f.) and a second-person singular verb with first-person singular suffix (one hiphil impv., one qal yiqtol).

11. An invocation applying to both cola leads into an impv. (one qal, one hiphil; the first very familiar, the second more unusual), then an obj. with a first-person suffix (the first a one-word singular direct obj., the second a plural compound expression prefixed by *l*).

At last then come the reasons, the factors that make this plea so urgent.[12] Designating the attackers as strangers (MT) may suggest that they have no reason to be attacking. These are not neighbors who might have a case against the suppliant (it is harder to love your neighbors than people far off). Or it may eventually be clarified in the third colon, which could suggest these are people estranged from God. Meanwhile, designating them as "terrifying" or ruthless (the common English translation) indicates why people who are merely "strangers" come to be a reason for such a prayer. After these further neat two parallel cola, we are surprised to find a further colon, which gives the reasoning or lament more content and makes the section come to an end with a tricolon. While we can take it as a self-standing clause, the line reads more dynamically if we take it as a relative clause, but either way it further qualifies those terrifying strangers and further explains why they are so terrifying. No sense that God is there holds them back from ruthless deeds. Yes, the suppliant needs God's help.

54:4–5. The plea and lament give way to a double declaration of confidence in God's ongoing nature (two participles) before returning to the plea. In K that return comes in the first colon of v. 5, while Q has a continuing declaration of confidence in v. 5a and a return to plea only in v. 5b.

> [4]There—God is a helper for me,
>   my Lord is the very sustainer of my life.

So the psalm makes two positive declarations about God in a pattern following that of vv. 1–2.[13] "Sustainer of my life" answers to "sought my life" (*nepeš*, *person*; v. 3). If there is one who sustains the suppliant's life, it is easier to live with the threat constituted by having someone seek one's life.

> [5]He will return evil to my watchful foes [Q]/
> May evil return to my watchful foes [K];
>   in your truthfulness wipe them out.

The wish (K) or declaration of confidence in what God will do (Q) follows from that. The implicit assumption is that once evil (*bad*) is let

---

12. Once again the opening word ("for") applies (initially) to two cola, and the rest of these two cola are then closely parallel. First, there are two m. pl. nouns, each coming in emphatic position at the beginning of its clause. Then come two third-person qatal verbs (one qal, one piel). Objects for these verbs again complete the lines, one prepositional, one direct. These two predicates come in logical order: the attackers arose against me, with the specific obj. stated by the second predicate.

13. The opening word again applies to both cola, which are otherwise structurally parallel as "my *Lord*" parallels "God," then "sustainer" parallels "*helper*," and "of my life" parallels "for me."

loose, it either must or can find a resting place somewhere. The suppliant expects or prays that it may find this resting place in the perpetrators of the evil, the *watchful foes, rather than in the person for whom they undeservedly intended it. It is either them or me. In the second colon a further direct plea complements the declaration or wish, making explicit what it will look like when evil returns to the foes. The two cola offer complementary accounts of the linkage between wrongdoing and trouble. Events come about both through the working out of the inherent dynamic lying in acts and through purposeful divine action. Both ways of looking at the matter are needed.[14] *Truthfulness sums up the implication of v. 4, while "wipe them out" sums up the implication of v. 5a.

54:6–7. Finally the suppliant looks beyond the crisis and the deliverance to the worship in which it will issue, in two further internally parallel lines.

> [6]For your munificence I will sacrifice to you;
> I will confess your name, Yhwh, for it is good,

As is often the case, v. 6 combines worship in symbol with worship in word, two complementary expressions of a personal gratefulness for Yhwh's act of deliverance. The suppliant promises to bring Yhwh an offering as a sign of gratitude for the favor the psalm asks for. Yhwh's "munificence" (*nĕdābâ*) is the willing generosity Yhwh will have shown in acting in love (for the application of the word to Yhwh, cf. Hos. 14:4 [5]; and cf. Ps. 51:12 [14]).[15] Parallel to "I will sacrifice" (qal cohortative with indirect object) is "I will *confess" (hiphil yiqtol with direct object), while "your *name" parallels and provides the suffix for "[your] munificence." The second colon then becomes rather longer than the first through the invocation (which will apply to both cola) and the subordinate clause. Given the point the line makes, it is especially appropriate that the actual name "Yhwh" should appear, though it is rare in this part of the Psalter.

> [7]Because it has rescued me from all trouble,
> and my eye has looked at my enemies.

Why is Yhwh's name good (contrast the "bad" of v. 5)? The very first colon of the psalm, its opening plea, has implied the answer. By way of inclusion, at the psalm's close it returns to the saving efficacy of Yhwh's name, formally in a qatal statement rather than a plea, though the qatal

14. Cf. Tate, *Psalms 51–100*, 48.
15. Cf. Dahood, *Psalms*, 2:26–27. EVV take *nĕdābâ* to denote the sacrifice of a freewill offering, its common meaning, but as the colon is *promising* an offering, this may be illogical. Such an offering would not be a freewill offering but one made in fulfillment of a promise.

statement is certainly one still made in hope. The closing line explaining why Yhwh's name is good thus anticipates the declaration that will be possible when Yhwh has acted. Because Yhwh's name stands for Yhwh in person, the *name can be the subject of verbs such as *save or protect (20:1 [2]).[16] The psalm closes with the suppliant imagining looking with satisfaction or relief at the fallen foes (cf. this verb in 22:17 [18]).[17]

Theological Implications

Noting that the Church of England Book of Common Prayer sets this psalm for Good Friday, John Eaton comments that its compilers were not unaware that on that day Jesus prayed for his enemies' forgiveness.[18] The psalm anticipates the NT idea that God's sorting out of human destiny has a negative side as well as a positive one and that it is all right for the victims of persecution to look for their enemies to be put down as well as for their own rescue (see Rev. 6:9–11). Both OT and NT thus express both a desire for enemies to come to Yhwh and a desire for them to be punished. The psalm's particular focus is to look for an "aggressive engagement" of Yhwh on behalf of what is right.[19] It offers to the NT the awareness that this is Yhwh's business; it is not our business to avenge ourselves. It may be that honestly expressing our desire for enemies to be punished, in the conviction that God really exists and is active in our world (a desire that may coexist with a desire for their coming to acknowledge Yhwh) is our enemies' best insurance against being the victims of our desire to punish them. The David of the Psalms models the point[20] even if the David of Israel's narratives is more of a fighter.

It is Yhwh's *name that is the means of deliverance and rescue. A name such as Yhwh or Jesus sums up who the bearer of the name is. It thus points to the might of God (v. 1) and the generosity of God (v. 6). Appeal to Yhwh's name is at the center of prayer (v. 1) and at the heart of hope (v. 6). The psalmist flees "to the saints' last asylum."[21]

---

16. NRSV has "he has delivered me," but there is no direct antecedent for the "he."

17. Formally the two cola are parallel (lit. "for from all trouble it has rescued me and at my enemies has looked my eye": thus abcb′c′d, with concrete "enemies" complementing abstract "trouble"). In content, they are also parallel, though the words used to make the point are rather different.

18. *Psalms*, 145–46; cf. *BCP* 17. Contrast Weiser's comments on the suppliant's self-will and low instincts that make the prayer "subject to the judgment of the New Testament" (*Psalms*, 416–17).

19. Keel, *Symbolism*, 207–8.

20. Cf. Hilary, "Psalms," 243.

21. Calvin, *Psalms*, 2:322.

Psalm 55

How to Throw Things at Yhwh

Translation

The leader's. On strings. Instruction. David's.

[1]Give ear to my plea, God;
    do not hide from my prayer for grace.
[2]Pay heed to me, answer me;
    I am restless in my lament and agitated,
[3]At the noise of the enemy,
    in the face of the pressure of the faithless.
For they make harm fall down upon me
    and in anger rage against me.
[4]My heart whirls within me
    as deathly terrors have fallen on me.
[5]Fear and trembling enters me;
    shuddering has enveloped me.
[6]I said, "O that[1] I had wings:
    like a pigeon I would fly and rest.
[7]There, I would flee far away,
    I would lodge in the wilderness, (Rise)
[8]I would hurry to a shelter for myself
    from the raging wind, from the tempest."

[9]Lord, swallow up, divide their speech,
    because I see violence and contention in the city.

---

1. Lit. "who will give" (see GKC 151a–b; JM 163a).

¹⁰Day and night
    they go around it, on its walls.
Harm and troublemaking are within it,
    ¹¹destruction² is within it.
Injury and deceit
    do not leave its square.
¹²For it is not an enemy who taunts me, which I could bear;
    it is not someone who was against me who has acted big over me,
        from whom I could hide,³
¹³But you, one of my kind,
    my acquaintance, someone I knew.
¹⁴Together we would enjoy fellowship;
    in the house of God we would walk in the throng.

¹⁵"Great desolation will be upon them, [K]/Death will beguile them, [Q]⁴
    they will go down to Sheol alive,
    because there is great evil in their sojourning place, in their midst."

¹⁶I—I call out to God,
    and Yhwh—he will deliver me. [MT]/hear me. [LXX]⁵
¹⁷Evening, morning, and noon
    I lament and am agitated.
But he has listened to my voice;
    ¹⁸he has redeemed my life safe and sound
From the encounter with me,⁶
    for many indeed⁷ have been with me.
¹⁹God will listen so as to put them down—
    the one who sits enthroned of old, (Rise)
In whom there are no changes—
    whereas they do not revere God.
²⁰He has reached out his hands against his partners;⁸
    he has violated his covenant.

2. *Hawwôt*; most occurrences are pl., suggesting that this is an abstract noun (*IBHS* 7.4.2).

3. LXX apparently reads the double *lō'* (not) in v. 12 as *lu'* (if).

4. K has the one word *yšymwt* (intensive pl.); Q reads as two words *yaššî māwet*.

5. For MT's *yôšî'ēnî*, LXX implies *yišmā'ēnî*.

6. I take *qărob* as a form of the noun *qĕrob*, though it might equally be the inf. const. of *qārab*, "from [their] encountering me."

7. I take the prep. on *bĕrabbîm* as emphatic. JM 133c suggests that it "adds practically nothing." *IBHS* 11.2.14b sees it as governing the clause.

8. *Šĕlōmāyw*, the pl. of *šālôm* with a suffix, is a unique expression here, though it presumably has a meaning similar to expressions such as *šĕlômîm* (69:22 [23]), *'îš šĕlômî* (41:9 [10]), *'ănî-šālôm* (120:7), and *šôlĕmî* (7:4 [5]). The pl. is unexpected and might be intensive ("someone totally at peace with him"), but since the psalm alternates between sg. and pl. with regard to the enemies, it might also do so with regard to the objects of their action. LXX "in doing retribution" implies a form of the verb *šālēm* piel.

²¹The curds in his mouth were smooth,⁹
    but he had encounter in his mind.¹⁰
His words were softer than oil,
    but they—they were drawn swords.¹¹

²²"Throw onto Yhwh what is given you,
    and he—he will sustain you.
He will never allow
    the faithful person to fall down."¹²
²³So you, God, will cause them to go down
    to the deepest pit.
The people who seek to kill by fraudulence—
    they will not have half their days;
    but I will trust in you.

Interpretation

Verses 1–8 and 9–14 of this prayer psalm alternate between pleas for
God to listen and act and protests at the pressure that makes this plea
necessary. The pleas are brief, and they disappear in vv. 15–23. There the
protest also becomes less prominent; these verses begin and end with
declarations of hope (vv. 15, 22) that make statements of hope possible
(vv. 16–19, 23). As we noted in connection with Pss. 42–43, while its
swings might reflect its being a kind of journal of someone's feelings, it
is more likely a form of composition, though no doubt one designed to
reflect the fact that people's prayers often involve such swings.

It thus can be outlined as follows:

Plea and protest (vv. 1–8)
    Plea for God to listen (vv. 1–2a)
    Protest focusing on the suppliant's need (vv. 2b–8)
Plea and protest (vv. 9–14)
    Plea for God to act (v. 9a)
    Protest focusing on the friends' wrongdoing (vv. 9b–14)

9. Tg, Sym, and Jerome imply *mēḥămā'ôt* (than curds) for MT's hapax *maḥmā'ōt*,
suggesting "his mouth was smoother than curds," but the pl. verb is then odd.

10. Lit. "His mind was encounter" (cf. *TTH* 189.2).

11. Lit. "They were openings/open things," i.e., unsheathings/unsheathed things; cf.
37:14.

12. The word order suggests "He will never allow" rather than "He will not allow
. . . to fall down forever," though the meaning may be no different if "fall down" suggests
tumbling to death.

Declaration of hope and response (vv. 15–21)

Declaration that action will follow because of the attackers' wrong-doing (v. 15)

Response of hope (vv. 16–19)

Protest at the friend's wrongdoing (vv. 20–21)

Declaration of hope and response (vv. 22–23)

Declaration that action will follow because of the suppliant's need (v. 22)

Response of hope (v. 23)

The attacker is singular in vv. 3a, 12–13, 20–21, and plural in vv. 3b, 9, 10 (?), 15, 18, 23 (cf. movement between sg. and pl. in 56:1–2 [2–3]). Perhaps the singular individualizes the group, or perhaps the suppliant thinks of one main opponent with many allies. One can imagine the psalm being used by an ordinary individual under pressure or a king or governor speaking as leader of the people. There are also particular parallels between the psalm and Jeremiah. He also whirls, and his heart moans (Jer. 4:19; cf. vv. 2, 4). Jeremiah or Yhwh also wishes to get away from the city to the wilderness and to find lodging there (Jer. 9:2 [1]; cf. vv. 7–8). Jeremiah also sees people as talking *shalom* but doing so deceitfully (Jer. 9:8 [7]; cf. v. 20). Jeremiah also wishes such people to live out only half their days (Jer. 17:11; cf. v. 23). The parallels may mean that Jeremiah reflects the language of this particular psalm or may mean that both independently use common figures. One MS of Jerome's translation calls this "the voice of Christ against the Jewish leaders and the traitor Judas,"[13] reflecting awareness of the story of Jesus being betrayed and disowned by his own people and perhaps of the particular overlap of language when he protests at how long he has to "endure" them (Matt. 17:17).[14]

The leader's. On strings. Instruction. David's.

Heading. See glossary. One could imagine the psalm on the lips of David while he was pursued by Saul, or during Absalom's revolt, with the enemy as Ahitophel.[15] But the talk of desolation (v. 15, K) might also invite us wistfully to imagine the psalm as a gift of David to his desolate daughter (2 Sam. 13:20), for her to use as the "lament of a woman who has been raped."[16]

13. So Kirkpatrick, *Psalms*, 308.

14. See Terrien, *Psalms*, 428.

15. See Calvin, *Psalms*, 2:328; *Midrash on Psalms*, 1:491–95. Tg names Ahitophel in v. 13.

16. Cf. Ulrike Bail, "Die Psalmen," in *Kompendium feministische Bibelauslegung*, ed. Luise Schottroff and Marie-Theres Wacker (Gütersloh: Kaiser, 1998), 180–91 (see 186–88). See the comments under "Theological Implications" for this psalm.

55:1–8. The first section naturally begins with a plea to God to listen (vv. 1–2a), explained by a description of the suppliant's feelings (vv. 2b–3b), explained by the action of the enemy (v. 3c–d). Verses 4–5 elaborate on the suppliant's feelings, and vv. 6–8 describe the suppliant's consequent impossible longings.

> ¹Give ear to my plea, God;
> do not hide from my prayer for grace.

The opening appeal comprises two parallel clauses, a positive and a negative verb, a direct and indirect object referring to the suppliant's prayer (*plea and prayer for *grace), and the invocation (the only one in the section) that makes the first colon longer than the second but applies to both. Tellingly, the second verb (*'ālam* hitpael) usually refers to hiding from other people in need instead of acting to help them (Deut. 22:1–4; Isa. 58:7).

> ²Pay heed to me, answer me;
> I am restless in my lament and agitated.

The second line first renews the appeal for a hearing and then underlines it by a second verb making explicit that the suppliant wants not just a hearing but a response. The second colon then begins to give the background to the appeal. It, too, is internally parallel as it expresses the suppliant's distress by means of two similar verbs, both first-person declarative hiphil.[17] The first verb implies a restlessness like Esau's in relation to Jacob, or Israel's in relation to Yhwh (Gen. 27:40; Jer. 2:31), these being the only other occurrences of the verb *rûd*, but it will also recall the more familiar *yārad* (go down), which will come later (vv. 15, 23). The paronomasia hints here at "I am going down," plunging, in free fall.[18] In due course Yhwh will respond to that fear (v. 22b). The second verb (*hûm*) similarly suggests wandering about in confusion, though following on the noun "lament" (*śîaḥ*) in turn it may also carry resonances from *hāmâ* (roar).[19] The verb is cohortative, suggesting the suppliant's self-giving to the lament and thus a pressing of the issues on God.[20] The suppliant is agitating as well as agitated.

17. So BDB, though it notes the possibility of taking the second verb as qal from *hîm* rather than hiphil from *hûm*. Either way, both verbs have the *î* vowel in the second syllable, as does the intervening nominal expression "in my lament," *běśîḥî*.

18. Sym has *katēnechthēn*; Jerome, *humiliatus sum*.

19. LXX and Jerome have words for "troubled"; Aq, "sounded" (cf. NJPS, "moaning").

20. Unless the cohortative has lost its meaning (so GKC 108g; DG 68).

> ³At the noise of the enemy,
>> in the face of the pressure of the faithless.
> For they make harm fall down upon me
>> and in anger rage against me.

Two cola then explain in parallel *min*-phrases the reasons for this agitation. Subsequent lines will show that the "noise" is people's talk about the suppliant, which is characterized by deceit and taunting (see vv. 9–12, 21). This naturally puts "pressure" on the suppliant. Two further words describe the people responsible for the noise and the pressure. They are enemies and *faithless. Again, subsequent lines in the psalm will explain the link between these two words. They are people who committed themselves to faithfulness (vv. 12–14, 20); how scandalous and hurtful that they should have turned into enemies.

But that is how it is (v. 3c–d). After the opening "for," at either end of the line stand parallel yiqtol verbs, inside them stand prepositional expressions, and at the center is the sinister word *harm. Friends are people who would want to keep harm firmly away from us, but these are people who push it to the edge of the roof so that it *falls down on us as we stand below (the verb is *mûṭ* hiphil, which in the qal usually refers to slipping or faltering; see v. 22).[21] Friends are people characterized by love, but these are people characterized by anger and harassment. The second colon thus looks behind the action to the inexplicable feelings that lead to it.

> ⁴My heart whirls within me
>> as deathly terrors have fallen on me.

Verse 4 begins a two-line elaboration of v. 2b.[22] The first colon elaborates v. 2b: inside, the suppliant is all in a whirl, travailing like a woman giving birth (*ḥûl*). What kind of whirl is this? The second colon explains. "Deathly terrors" (lit. "terrors of death") might be objectively terrifying realities that threaten death or savor of the realm of death or might be a subjective feeling of terror in that connection. Here the parallelism would suggest the latter. But the OT does not regularly associate fear with death, and the psalm may merely use "deathly" as a form of superlative.[23] The reference to terror explains the whirling of heart; the whirling of heart

21. Mitchell Dahood ("'A Sea of Troubles,'" *CBQ* 41 [1979]: 604–7) suggests that *yāmîṭû* rather represents a word from *nāṭâ*.

22. Syr abbreviates vv. 4–5 as a whole: "Terror has fallen on me, deathly shadows have covered me."

23. See *IBHS* 14.5b.

clarifies the meaning of the terror. There is some irony in talk of such terror "falling" (*nāpal*, a more prosaic equivalent to *mût* in the previous line). Terror falling on them was what happened to Israel's enemies (Exod. 15:16; Josh. 2:9). It should not be happening to an Israelite at the hands of fellow Israelites or of other people.

> ⁵Fear and trembling enters me;
> shuddering has enveloped me.

The elaboration continues, speaking again in terms of how things are inside and outside the suppliant. That feeling of terror is something that comes on the suppliant from outside because the objective cause of terror does so. Fear and trembling "comes into me" (the hendiadys is marked by the singular verb).[24] It does not arise from inside me, as if I were a fearful person, but it ends up inside me and makes me tremble. "Trembling" is another noun that is supposed to apply to Israel's enemies, not to an Israelite (see Exod. 15:15, the only other occurrence). To put it another way, shuddering—a more violent convulsion than trembling—covers over me like clothing or like an overwhelming flood. These feelings thus occupy me inside and out, like an army that simultaneously occupies and surrounds a city.

> ⁶I said, "O that I had wings:
> like a pigeon I would fly and rest.

The experience makes the suppliant long to be able to flee. The first colon contains an implicit answer to the question "What are these wings for?" but the second colon makes it explicit. An Israelite would be used to seeing pigeons flitting to safety from danger: how often does a pigeon get caught? It can dart up to the security of a crevice in (for instance) the temple wall (cf. Song 2:14) and sit cooing while its real or imagined attacker can only look on.

> ⁷There, I would flee far away,
> I would lodge in the wilderness, (Rise)

The suppliant thinks not of metaphorical or literal safety in the temple but of literal safety in the wilderness, with its many caves and clefts that make it almost impossible to find a person. In theory the city is a place of safety and the wilderness a place of danger, but the two places' profiles are reversed in a context such as the one the psalm presupposes.[25] As

---

24. Watson, *Classical Hebrew Poetry*, 326.
25. Cf. Hossfeld and Zenger, *Psalms 2*, 53.

the parallelism confirms, the image of flying like a bird is all but abandoned in v. 7 (but see 11:1). The line has in mind human flight, on legs, so that one cannot merely rest like a bird but needs to find lodgings like a human being.

> [8]I would hurry to a shelter for myself
>   from the raging wind, from the tempest."

Verse 8 states the point again. In one sense the literal nature of the imagery is even clearer; the suppliant is talking about a human being finding refuge. But the second colon offers another image for the danger that makes shelter necessary. The image for danger is not now the town over against the wilderness but storm over against shelter. The terrifying reality is now wind and tempest; "raging" is a guess for *sō'â*, which comes only here, perhaps as an onomatopoeic invention of the psalmist to provide a word that makes for paronomasia with *sā'ar* (tempest). "One way or another, if only I could find refuge."

55:9–14. The psalm returns to plea, but the plea moves logically from an appeal for God to listen (vv. 1–2a) to an appeal for God to act (v. 9a). Once again the appeal is buttressed by reasons, this time a more substantial lament at the troublemaking within the city that is designed to put the suppliant down (vv. 9b–11), which is especially outrageous because of who its perpetrators are (vv. 12–14).

> [9]Lord, swallow up, divide their speech,
>   because I see violence and contention in the city.

"Swallowing up" is a frequent and powerful image for the destructive action of the faithless (e.g., 35:25). Here it is reversed; the suppliant asks the sovereign *Lord to do what the faithless are trying to do (cf. 21:9 [10]). The TNIV takes the implicit object of the verb to be the people themselves, but "swallow up" and thus confound can be what Yhwh does to plans (Isa. 19:3, to which Tg assimilates the text here), and more likely the implicit object of the verb is "their speech" (lit. "their tongue"), not the people themselves. Their hostile attempt at swallowing is effected by words (cf. 52:4 [6]), so the appeal is to reverse the situation by swallowing the enemies' speech by dividing it.[26] The two halves of the first colon are parallel, with two rhyming piel imperatives.[27] The second colon is

---

26. John S. Kselman and Michael L. Barré ("Psalm 55," *CBQ* 60 [1998]: 440–62 [see 448–49]) suggest that *pallag lěšônām* is a const. expression suggesting "the discord of their tongue" (they repoint *peleg*), following E. Podechard, *Le Psautier 1A* (Lyon: Facultés catholiques, 1949), 218.

27. To rhyme with *balla'*, *pallag* replaces the expected *pallēg* (GKC 52n).

internally parallel in an analogous way, being structurally similar, with the nouns playing the part of the parallel verbs in the first colon. "Speech" might suggest curses, and *violence might suggest physical attacks, but "contention" (*rîb*) suggests that the attacks on innocent people take more direct form than cursing and more subtle form than physical attack. The enemies' weapon is the tongue with which they make outrageously false accusations. Dividing their speech may imply dividing them against each other and thereby relieving the pressure.[28]

> 10a-bDay and night
> they go around it, on its walls.

So "they" are continuously going around the city making such accusations. In light of what precedes, we might see the "they" as taking up the "their" of v. 9, though that pronoun had no recent antecedent (the "they" in v. 3 had no antecedent at all). But the subjects of the next two clauses are "harm and troublemaking" and "injury and deceit," so we might plausibly see "violence and contention" as the subject in v. 10a. These abstract nouns and the people who embody them are at work all over the city; again the subsequent lines will spell out further how that is ("its walls, . . . within it, . . . within it, . . . its square"). Perhaps the lines imply that the threats the suppliant experiences are but a personal experience of social disorder characterizing the life of the city as a whole, of the kind that OT prophets describe. Initially the plotters are walking about the walls, a natural place for a stroll then as now (especially for people who want to do some plotting?). These abstracts are the negative equivalents to the light and truthfulness that a suppliant in a comparable psalm (43:3) beseeches Yhwh to send out. They might then correspond not to ordinary people out for a stroll but to the lookouts that protect the city. But these lookouts undermine it.

> 10cHarm and troublemaking are within it,
> 11destruction is within it.
> Injury and deceit
> do not leave its square.

The next lines look at the insides of the city, bounded by those walls. First they find the presence of *harm, troublemaking, and destruction throughout it (*bĕqirbāh* is repeated). Then they look at the city square, the place that counts most, the most public place in the sense that here

---

28. Commentators often make a link with the confusion of tongues at the Tower of Babel (e.g., Weiser, *Psalms*, 420), but there is little by way of verbal or substantial link with the story.

accusations are tested, and deception brings devastation on the successful accusers' victims. The city's walls, which are supposed to be its people's protection, have become their danger, and the city itself is under attack from its internal enemies.[29]

> [12]For it is not an enemy who taunts me, which I could bear;
>   it is not someone who was against me who has acted big over me,
>   from whom I could hide,

The second half of the lament occupies vv. 12–14. The three lines are all internally parallel, the repetition serving to underline the enormity and the pain of their content.[30] There was no history of conflict between suppliant and attacker. The suppliant had never done wrong by this attacker, and the attacker had never been someone who was *against the suppliant before. There was no history of bad relations to make the suppliant wary.

> [13]But you, one of my kind,
>   my acquaintance, someone I knew.

These two cola lead into two companion contrasting positive statements. Far from being an enemy, this attacker was a friend. It was "one of my kind," literally "a person according to my order," perhaps one who belonged to my class or group, perhaps one whom I classified as an equal.[31] The significance of that is explained further by the synonyms in the second colon: this was someone I thought I knew. The piling up of synonyms further emphasizes the enormity of the act. The suppliant's assumptions about this person have been shattered, and that may imperil many of the suppliant's other assumptions about people and about life. Is anything certain?

> [14]Together we would enjoy fellowship;
>   in the house of God we would walk in the throng.

Verse 14 further underlines the enormity of the situation. I had reason to think I knew this person. We were not casual acquaintances. We would "enjoy fellowship" (*sôd*). The second colon underlines the terrible nature

29. Ulrike Bail, "'O God, Hear My Prayer': Psalm 55 and Violence against Women," in *Wisdom and Psalms*, ed. Brenner, 242–63 (see 249).

30. After the *kî*, in v. 12 in each clause there is the negative *lō'*, then a participial expression (one qal, one piel and explicitly suffixed), then a third-person verb (one piel yiqtol with a suffix, one hiphil qatal with an indirect obj.) in an unmarked relative clause, then a simple *w*-yiqtol verb (one qal, one niphal with a prepositional expression).

31. On the comparative formula, see translation note on 58:4 [5].

of it all by noting that this was not merely a matter of sharing everyday life but of enjoying such friendship in the very setting of God's house where we stood shoulder to shoulder in great occasions of worship. How could such a friend have turned against me?

55:15. The EVV take v. 15 as a prayer, which then pairs with the prayer in v. 9 and forms an inclusion with it. But the change of tone in v. 15 is very marked and suggests a change of speaker, and the change from singular to plural in referring to the enemy supports that.[32] A person such as a priest may therefore speak here (cf. 12:5 [6]), or this might constitute the suppliant's self-addressed reassurance (cf. 42:5, 11 [6, 12]; 43:5). Either way, the tricolon constitutes a response to the protest and prayer in the psalm as a whole so far, the verbs being yiqtols rather than jussives.

> [15]"Great desolation will be upon them, [K]/Death will beguile them, [Q]
>   they will go down to Sheol alive,
>   because there is great evil in their sojourning place, in their midst."

Both K and Q express the promise vividly in the first colon, K by the starkness of its noun clause, Q by the image of death "beguiling" people, creeping upon them unexpectedly, deceptively, and unavoidably. The second, parallel colon restates that elliptically: death will come upon them so suddenly that it is as if they are still alive as they descend to Sheol. The story in Num. 16 provides a vivid picture of what this looks like. The unexpected third colon then provides the rationale for the promise. There is great evil wherever they sojourn and in the midst of them wherever they are, and Yhwh will not let their grotesque behavior stand unpunished.

55:16–21. The promise makes for a transition in the psalm. While the first half of this third section focuses on plea, it takes a different form from the pleas that opened vv. 1–8 and 9–14. Indeed, there is no actual plea in vv. 16–21.[33] The suppliant speaks of calling out to God but does not actually do so (v. 16a), then expresses the conviction that God will deliver (v. 16b). In the next line the suppliant again speaks of lamenting but does not actually do so (v. 17a), then expresses the conviction that God has heard this plea and has redeemed (vv. 17b–18). Both these parallel statements constitute a response to the promise in v. 15, partly in the qatal (in the conviction that God has heard and thereby initiated deliverance), partly in the yiqtol

---

32. Cf. Mandolfo, *God in the Dock*, 75–82. The context gives fewer pointers to the same being true of v. 20, as Mandolfo suggests.

33. Buttenwieser (*Psalms*, 711) sees v. 18 as precative qatal, but the context gives no hint of this, and seeing vv. 17b–18 as referring to an answer to prayer makes better sense of the verb forms as a whole.

(because the actual deliverance still lies in the future). Yet the psalm does then once again protest at the behavior of the betrayer of friendship (vv. 20–21). Paradoxically there is thus no movement in the description of "them" and "him," but there is movement in the suppliant's stance from plea for a hearing (vv. 1–8) to plea for action (vv. 9–14) to conviction that Yhwh has heard and has as good as acted (vv. 16–21).

> [16]I—I call out to God,
>   and Yhwh—he will deliver me [MT]/hear me [LXX].

The first element in the response comprises a neatly parallel bicolon affirming the respective roles of the suppliant and Yhwh in life. The formal parallelism, with the subject preceding the yiqtol verb in each colon and with the pairing of "God" and "Yhwh," highlights the contrasting complementarity of these roles. It is my job to call out; it is Yhwh's job to *deliver. The contrastive element in the parallelism thus includes the fact that "I" am the emphatic subject in the first, and "Yhwh" is the emphatic subject in the second, while "to God" is the indirect object in the first and "me" the object in the second.[34]

> [17a–b]Evening, morning, and noon
>   I lament and am agitated.

The point about calling on God is made again in v. 17a–b, which parallels and expands on v. 16a. The reference to lamenting and agitation picks up from v. 2b, with both verbs now cohortative. But in the first colon the specifying of the all-day nature of the suppliant's lamenting and agitation (or agitating) constitutes the more marked new nuance over against what has preceded (cf. the use of the more prosaic expression "all day long" to refer to people's attacks in 56:1–2 [2–3]).

> [17c]But he has listened to my voice;
>   [18]he has redeemed my life safe and sound
> From the encounter with me,
>   for many indeed have been with me.

I then take v. 17c as the beginning of a new pair of lines.[35] These in turn parallel v. 16b yet contrast with it because their verbs are now

---

34. This parallelism might suggest that we understand the tenses of the two cola in a similar way (so TNIV) rather than taking the second as future (so NRSV, NJPS); Calvin (*Psalms*, 2:338) takes both as future.

35. I follow *BHS*'s analysis of vv. 17–18 but presuppose a removing of the maqqeph from *miqqěrob-lî* so that the phrase has two stresses. For the last verb in v. 17, Syr im-

wayyiqtol and qatal. Temporally Yhwh's act of redemption remains
future, but its concrete actuality and/or its certainty in Yhwh's purpose
means it can be spoken of using the qatal, the "perfect of certainty" that
sometimes appears in psalms to refer to a response to prayer and an
act of deliverance that the suppliant knows is coming.[36] "*Redeemed
my life" (*nepeš*, *person; v. 18a) constitutes a restatement of "deliver"
(v. 16), and "safe and sound" (*well-being) gives more precision to
the result of that. The enjambment in the succeeding line (v. 18b–c)
explains further what the suppliant needed deliverance from, and its
second colon then takes the point further. Why did the suppliant need
such deliverance from an "encounter" (like that English word, *qĕrob*
and related words can refer to a hostile encounter as well as a friendly
or neutral one)? Because there were many "with me": in the context,
many fighting with me.[37]

> ¹⁹God will listen so as to put them down—
>   the one who sits enthroned of old, (Rise)
> In whom there are no changes—
>   whereas they do not revere God.

Verse 19 then constitutes another pair of linked lines, arranged
abb'a' (NJPS and TNIV translate them bb'aa', NRSV and NIVI bab'a').
In v. 19a the suppliant returns to describing Yhwh's ongoing character
and activity, using a yiqtol verb like those in vv. 16–17a. The necessary concomitant of Yhwh's delivering the suppliant is Yhwh's putting
down the suppliant's attackers. At the moment the suppliant belongs
to the weak (*'ānî/'ānāw*), and the line asks that Yhwh may reverse this,
using the verb *'ānâ* (III, piel), "put down." The putting down reverses
the process whereby people have "acted big" (v. 12). The verb also
recalls the other verb *'ānâ* (I), "answer," the subject of appeal in vv.
1–2. Yhwh *'ānâ* in both senses.[38] How can Yhwh so act? The second
colon explains that this is possible because Yhwh is "the one who
sits [enthroned] of old." The third colon expands on this explanation.
Yhwh is thus also one who does not change or disappear or pass on
(cf. 102:26–27 [27–28]), like an image (Isa. 2:18) or a human life (Job

plies *wĕ'ašmîa'* ("and I make [my voice] heard"), which makes better sense with MT
versification.
  36. Cf. NRSV (though it moves to present for v. 18b); contrast TNIV, NJPS.
  37. See BDB 767b for this nuance. In other contexts, "with me" would mean "supporting me," but all the other references in the psalm to other people are to opponents, and
the psalms usually attribute redemption not to the support of many other human beings
but to the support of God (thus Tg makes God the subject).
  38. Briggs (*Psalms*, 2:29) assumes that a form of *'ānâ* I was original (cf. Tg), but MT's
verb with its third-person suffix must be *'ānâ* III.

9:25–26).[39] The fourth colon completes the abb′a′ sequence both by explaining why Yhwh must put the faithless down and by offering a contrast with the middle two cola. Fancy people not *revering God when those things are true of God!

> **20**He has reached out his hands against his partners;
>   he has violated his covenant.

There follows another sudden transition from the plural to a singular focus on the suppliant's individual betrayer, which will continue through v. 21 in three 3-2 lines that are internally parallel and parallel with each other. These cumulatively underline once more the suppliant's pain and outrage and thus seek to get God to take action against them (cf. vv. 12–14), implicitly in keeping with the reassurances or convictions that have been expressed in vv. 15–19. Thus here there is no plea following the lament, perhaps because the suppliant knows the plea has been answered.

The scandal in the first colon is that it was against "his *shaloms*" that the supposed friend acted, against people who were at peace with him. The suppliant is perhaps generalizing from personal experience and seeing the friend's action as part of a pattern. In doing so, this person has violated his covenant, a very strong comment in the parallel colon. Talk in terms of covenant might imply a formal partnership between people or might be a metaphor for a relationship that involved mutual commitment. Either way, talk of violation implies there was something sacred here. The things that one violates (*ḥālal* piel) are places or things that are holy. This expression is yet another way to stress the enormity of the person's action, to which God must therefore respond.

> **21**The curds in his mouth were smooth,
>   but he had encounter in his mind.
> His words were softer than oil,
>   but they—they were drawn swords.

The violation involved duplicity (cf. v. 11) rather than open attack, which is easier to combat. The speaker's words are as pleasant as a refreshing bowl of leben or yogurt or as soothing as oil applied to a wound. But the person speaking in friendly fashion was planning a

---

39. Tg understands *ḥălîpôt* to refer to the wicked not "changing their ways," and *lāmô* does usually refer to "them." But there is no parallel for *ḥālap* or its derivatives having that meaning, and *lāmô* can refer to "him" (see GKC 103f with note 3). The immediate antecedent of the opening *'ăšer* is God, not the enemies, which prepares the reader for the less usual meaning of *lāmô*.

hostile "encounter" (cf. v. 18), and in their deceptiveness those words were actually capable of bringing harm or death, not healing or life. In Hebrew one opens or unsheathes swords as one opens or unsheathes one's mouth or lips in speaking, and in the case of the words of the wicked, the little opening of the mouth is a metaphorical unsheathing of a sword (cf. 109:2).

55:22–23. The closing four lines constitute declarations that Yhwh will answer the prayer. They begin with two parallel lines addressed to the person under pressure, then two parallel lines and a final statement of trust addressed to God (there is no parallelism within any of these lines). The encouragement in v. 22 speaks to an individual "you,"[40] suggesting that it addresses the suppliant and is a response to the preceding protest (not, for instance, an exhortation by the suppliant to other people), though one could again not exclude the possibility that it involves self-address by the suppliant, and this is how subsequent readers would often use it. Verse 23 is then in turn the suppliant's final declaration of trust in that word and in the God to whom the psalm as a whole has appealed.

> [22]"Throw onto Yhwh what is given you,
>   and he—he will sustain you.
> He will never allow
>   the faithful person to fall down."

The opening line expresses an invitation to reliance on Yhwh and does so in a suggestive way. The experience of attack is something "given you." In later Hebrew this noun means "burden,"[41] but its apparent link with a verb meaning "give" hints at an unusual statement of Yhwh's responsibility for the ills that other people do to us (in ignorance of this noun, unique here in the OT, one would translate "throw onto Yhwh what he gave you").[42] By virtue of the fact that Yhwh allows these, they can boldly be described as something God gives. We can then be invited to give them back, indeed to throw them back, like a hot potato we do not wish to catch. Presumably what that literally involves is what the psalm has been doing through vv. 1–21, which has been one long exercise in throwing onto Yhwh (cf. 2 Kings 23:6) or throwing at Yhwh (cf. Nah. 3:6). The way Yhwh "sustains" us through our lives after we are thrown onto him at birth (Ps. 22:10 [11]) encourages us to believe he will do so when we throw our experiences onto him. This verb (*kûl* pilpel) most commonly means "nourish," though suggestively it can also mean "en-

---

40. Tg adds "David" to make this explicit.
41. See *DTT*; also *CP* 56. The ancient versions are not sure what to make of the word.
42. See the comments in GKC 117x.

dure" (Mal. 3:2). If a person such as a priest speaks these lines, then this speaker is encouraging the suppliant to keep believing that the throwing of oneself that has characterized the psalm will see its fruit.

The parallel line goes on to explicate what the sustaining will mean. Yhwh promises protection. The third line from the psalm's beginning spoke of the faithless making it possible for trouble to fall down on people (v. 3); the third line from the end promises that Yhwh will never make it possible for the faithful themselves to *fall down (v. 22). The verb might refer either to faltering in their own faithfulness under this pressure or to their being convicted or otherwise overwhelmed by calamity through the attacker's plotting and thus falling down into Sheol (cf. v. 23).

> [23]So you, God, will cause them to go down
>   to the deepest pit.
> The people who seek to kill by fraudulence—
>   they will not have half their days;
>   but I will trust in you.

The closing lines then form the suppliant's response of trust in Yhwh to those promises. Although Yhwh will not let the faithful stumble, the faithless will fall straight down, to the abode of the dead. That will be the way Yhwh fulfills the promise in v. 22. These people cannot then carry on their murderous activity. The lines also and more specifically constitute a further response to the promise in v. 15. They take up the idea there of the attackers going straight down to Sheol and specifically take up the verb "go down." The abode of the dead is now termed (lit.) "the pit of *abyss"; two words of similar meaning are put together. In the context of later Jewish thinking, this would suggest divisions within Sheol,[43] but there is little indication of such thinking within the OT, and here the expression is rather a way of emphasizing how deeply and thus inescapably they are cast physically into the grave and metaphysically into Sheol.

The last line in turn restates Yhwh's earlier rationale for taking the attackers down to Sheol. It is an act undertaken in light of their being "people of *bloodshed and fraudulence" (see 5:6 [7]). In both respects their actions are mirrored in their fate. The punishment fits the criminal. They are people who seek to bring about the death of others, so they will lose their lives; and they do that by guile, so they will find themselves having a nasty surprise (cf. v. 15b). The content of v. 15, though not the actual words, reappears yet again in the second colon, as "not have half their days" restates "go down to Sheol alive." In the midst of

---

43. Thus it is referred to as Gehenna in *Midrash on Psalms*, 495.

life they will find themselves in death. The psalm's final colon makes a statement of *trust that more directly responds to the content of the promise in v. 22.

Theological Implications

We have grieved at the horrific story of the Rwandan genocide and grieve at stories of how in some parts of the world churches are violently harassed. Presciently, the *One Year Bible*[44] sets Ps. 55 for reading each September 11, along with Isa. 8:1–9:21 and Prov. 23:4–5 with its reference to the wisdom to show restraint. Psalm 55 encourages people of prayer

- to throw onto God what God or other people throw onto us.
- to do this on behalf of churches in other parts of the world if we do not experience such attacks, as we enter into the trouble and harassment that they experience.
- to be open to God with the inner turmoil of our hearts and the outer turmoil that causes this.
- to be open with God about the way we could long to be away to the safety of some other place where we would not be subject to such experiences.
- to urge God to act directly to frustrate the plans of people who attack us and our sister churches.
- to draw God's attention to ways in which such malice characterizes the places where we live.
- to grieve before God at the way people who were members of our communities or our churches are the people who are now attacking us.
- to ask for God to punish our attackers rather than taking matters into our own hands.
- to trust God to do that and to protect us.

The invitation may especially "give space to the specific experience of violence suffered by women," which takes its most radical and painful form in rape, fundamentally not a sexual act but an act of violence that seeks to break and put down.[45] As was the case with Tamar, this often involves someone the woman knows well, even someone within

44. Wheaton, IL: Tyndale, repr. 1988.
45. Bail, "'O God, Hear My Prayer,'" 243.

179

the family, and it often robs the woman of her speech (2 Sam. 13:20). The psalm can thus give her speech back, both in protest and in a statement of trust in God that brings into being a "counter-discourse" that "enables the powerless object of violence to rediscover herself as a subject possessing her own identity" and to find that "God is on the side of the praying woman who uses this psalm to articulate her experience of rape."[46] This potential extends also to women subjected to other forms of sexual abuse, whom the psalm might help to express their pain and anger and to reach out to God for justice and healing.[47]

46. Bail, "'O God, Hear My Prayer,'" 257, 263; she suggests Gen. 19 and Judg. 19 as intertexts for the psalm.
47. Andrea Bieler, "Psalmengottesdienste als Klageräume für Überlebende sexueller Gewalt," *EvT* 60 (2000): 117–30 (see 123–26).

Psalm 56

Fear of Humanity, Trust in God

Translation

The leader's. On the silent[1] pigeon of far-off ones. David's. Inscription. When the Philistines seized him at Gath.

[1]Be gracious to me, God, because someone hounds me;
    all day long a fighter oppresses me.
[2]All day long my watchful foes hound me,
    because many are the people fighting against me on high.
[3]On the day when I am afraid,
    I do trust[2] in you.
[4]In God, whose word I praise—
    in God I have trusted.
I am not afraid:
    what can flesh do to me?

[5]All day long, in words about me they harass me; [MT]/shame me;
    [LXX]/make plans against me; [Syr, Sym][3]
    all their thoughts are against me, to bring trouble.
[6]They stir up strife, [MT]/band together, [LXX, Jerome, Tg][4] they hide,[5]

1. MT's *'ēlem* is presumably a noun from the root *'ālam* (cf. Jerome). LXX may imply *'ēlîm* (gods/mighty ones), which could also be taken as from *'ayil* ("terebinths"; so NRSV). One of these plurals is easier with the pl. "far off."

2. "I do trust" represents the turn of phrase in which the pronoun is expressed.

3. For MT's *yĕ'aṣṣēbû* (*'āṣab* I) LXX implies *yĕtā'ăbû*, Syr and Sym *yiwwā'ăṣû* (cf. *BHS*). *'Āṣab* II means "shape," but one can hardly infer the translation "twist" (against Rogerson and McKay, *Psalms 51–100*, 39).

4. For MT's *yāgûrû*, LXX, Jerome, and Tg imply a form such as *yāgôddû* (cf. 94:21).

5. For Q's *yiṣpônû* (Qal), K implies *yaṣpînû* (declarative hiphil); the meaning is not affected.

these people watch my steps,
 as they look for my life.
[7]For their harmfulness[6] carry them off,[7]
 in anger put the peoples down, God.
[8]May you yourself have recorded[8] my lamenting;[9]
 put my tears into your flask—
 yes, they are in your record.[10]
[9]Then my enemies will turn back
 on the day when I call;
 I know this, because God is mine.
[10]In God whose word I praise,
 in Yhwh whose word I praise,
[11]In God I have trusted;
 I am not afraid:
 what can human beings do to me?

[12]My promises to you are binding on me, God;
 I will fulfill my thank-offerings to you.
[13]For you have saved my life from death,
 yes, my feet from being tripped,[11]
So as to walk before God
 in the light of life.

Interpretation

Like Ps. 55, in this prayer psalm fearful protest wrestles with confident trust and in parallel sections increases in conviction before coming to a brief confident close. Here vv. 1–4 and 5–11 form the parallel expressions of this struggle, comprising pleas, laments, and protests, and eventually

6. For MT's *'āwen*, LXX and Jerome imply a form of *'ayin* (nothing/there is not); cf. NIVI, "on no account."

7. Lit. "carrying off for them"; i.e., *pallet* is inf. const. NRSV emends to *pallēs* (weigh to them), which it then translates "repay them," but this is somewhat elliptical. Turning the colon into a question (e.g., Hossfeld and Zenger, *Psalms 2*, 59–60, 64) seems arbitrary.

8. The impv. on either side and the parallelism in v. 8a–b suggest taking the qatal as precative (cf. DG 60c; TNIV).

9. Tg has "wandering," which fits the more common meaning of the root *nôd*, but the word can also refer to the bodily movement (e.g., shaking) associated with grief; cf. NRSV "tossing."

10. On *hălō'* as a strong affirmative, cf. GKC 150e; also Auffret, *Voyez de vos yeux*, 42–43. Both here and in v. 13 the expression may introduce an explanatory comment or alternative reading (cf. Barthélemy, *Psaumes*, 356).

11. The verb *dāḥâ* means "thrust at/overthrow/knock over" (cf. 35:5; 36:12 [13]; 62:3 [4]), so it is likely that *dĕḥî* refers to the enemies causing the suppliant to fall rather than to the suppliant simply stumbling.

statements of confidence and trust expressed in overlapping terms. Verses 12–13 then form a closing statement of commitment and confidence. Once again the alternating between lament and confidence likely reflects the fact that the attacks of other people and the trustworthiness of God are both realities that a supplicant is called to acknowledge, rather than suggesting the transcript of a psychological alternation between lament and trust. Since the bulk of the psalm speaks of the oppression as present, it seems more likely that the psalm presupposes a situation of attack and looks forward to deliverance than that it looks back on a situation of attack and presupposes that deliverance has happened.[12] As usual, we do not know when the psalm was written, but we can imagine it on the lips of a preexilic king or a postexilic governor (for whom the plural "peoples" would be especially appropriate) or on the lips of a private individual in any period.

> The leader's. On the silent pigeon of far-off ones. David's. Inscription.
> When the Philistines seized him at Gath.

Heading. See glossary. The second phrase may designate a tune; "pigeon" makes a concrete link with Ps. 55.[13] There are two stories of David and Gath, in 1 Sam. 21:10 [11]–22:1 and 27:1–29:11, though neither says that David was seized. Although Ps. 34 has already made a link with the first story, it is with this that Ps. 56 also has a number of verbal points of contact: David's fear (the only occasion fear is attributed to him), the use of the verb *hālal* (v. 4), *yôm* (day [v. 6]), the double *hălō'* (is it not?/yes [vv. 8, 13]). The Tg makes this specific by adding reference to Ishbi in v. 1. If understood to mean "wandering," the word *nôd* (v. 8) might also suggest a link with these stories. The heading thus presents the psalm as suggesting how one might pray in a situation like David's.

56:1–4. The first section of the psalm thus comprises a plea (v. 1aα), a protest giving the background to the appeal (vv. 1aβ–2), and a declaration of trust (vv. 3–4). Already the balance of the prayer is noteworthy. Little prominence is given to an actual request; the bulk maintains an almost equal balance between protest and trust, which give expression to the recognition that the supplicant needs resolutely to face two sets of facts.

> **1**Be gracious to me, God, because someone hounds me;
>   all day long a fighter oppresses me.

---

12. Against Weiser, *Psalms*, 422.

13. Christopher Begg ("'Dove' and 'God[s]' in Ps 56,1," *ETL* 64 [1988]: 393–96) suggests a link with the Middle Eastern motif of the dove messenger that carries people's laments to the gods. Cf. Urs Winter, "Die Taube der Fernen Götter in Ps. 56,1," in *Vögel als Boten*, ed. Othmar Keel, OBO 14 (Göttingen: Vandenhoeck & Ruprecht, 1977), 37–78.

The opening plea for *grace repeats that in Pss. 4 and 51; it will reappear in the next psalm. The four succeeding clauses in vv. 1aβ, 1b, 2a, and 2b all then stand parallel as backings for this opening appeal. It is as victim that the suppliant appeals for grace. First, someone (*'ĕnôš*) "hounds me." That translation[14] bridges the meaning of the two verbs *šā'ap/šûp*. In theory one might distinguish these as denoting "lust after" and "trample on," but the meaning of the one can leak into the meaning of the other. Here the next line and the next section (see v. 6) suggest "lust after" (cf. also 57:3–4 [4–5]), but the immediate parallel with "oppress" suggests "trample." The second colon thus explicates the nature of what is happening to the suppliant in terms (more literally) of someone "putting the squeeze on me" as one squeezes an orange. It also complements the earlier qatal verb with a yiqtol and adds that this is an all-day-long, continuous business, in which there is no let up. Further, here the person becomes specifically a fighter, someone engaging in warfare; the word (*lōḥēm*) is similar to the verb "oppress" (*lāḥaṣ*), so that the two words reinforce each other in sound as well as in meaning.

> ²All day long my watchful foes hound me,
>> because many are the people fighting against me on high.

Verse 2 underlines the basis for that opening appeal partly through repetition from v. 1: "all day long," "hound(s)," "fighter/fighting." But now plurals complement the singulars of v. 1; there are "many" of them, indeed. *Watchful foes suggests that the lines do work with both meanings of *šā'ap/šûp*. The adversaries are looking for an opportunity to fulfill their desire to swallow up the suppliant and do so from "on high," a good place from which to trample on someone.[15]

> ³On the day when I am afraid,
>> I do trust in you.

The opening two verses of plea and protest give way to two verses of trust. Indeed this central line in the section holds its two features in balance, fear (v. 3a) and trust (v. 3b). Again there is repetition, as "on the day when" takes up from the double "all day long" (*yôm* is often simply a way of saying "when," but in this context it picks up those earlier occurrences). Again there is some parallelism between the lines, though here none between the cola within each line. Fear is a natural

---

14. From Dahood, *Psalms*, 2:40.
15. Jerome and Aq take *mārôm* as an invocation, "O Most High" (cf. Tg), but there is no parallel for such usage. For "[on] high," cf. 10:5; 73:8. See further Hossfeld and Zenger, *Psalms 2*, 59.

response to the experience described in vv. 1–2. Apparently the suppliant then tells God that *trust and fear coexist, perhaps because the point about trust is its object, not the quality of it as a subjective feeling or attitude. Trust does not bring an end to fear, but it makes it possible to live with fear.

> ⁴In God, whose word I praise—
>> in God I have trusted.
> I am not afraid:
>> what can flesh do to me?

The two lines in v. 4 then take up the two cola in v. 3, in abb′a′ order. In v. 4a–b the second colon takes up the affirmation of *trust in v. 3b, though using a qatal verb. This might just be for variety, or it might be looking back to the past. It precedes this with another affirmation that elaborates it: trust goes along with or is expressed in or is based on the fact of praising God's word. The reference to God's word comes at the center of an abcb′a′ sequence in vv. 3–4 (fear-trust-word-trust-fear),[16] implying the key importance of this "word" to the move between fear and trust. In the context the word will likely be God's word of promise (see 33:4), the kind of promise expressed in the previous psalm in response to the suppliant's lament and protest (55:22 [23]). It is enthusiasm for God's promising word that makes trust possible. Only in this psalm is God's word the object of praise.[17]

In v. 4c–d the first colon takes up the verb from v. 3a and negatives it, thereby suggesting a further contradiction: "I am afraid, I do trust, I am not afraid." All are true and coexist. The basis for being afraid is what human beings can do to me (vv. 1–2), but the basis for not being afraid is what human beings cannot do to me. Their capacity to lust after me and watch for me and trample on me and fight against me and oppress me has set against it God's word of promise, in light of which mere human beings can do nothing. The human beings are, after all, only flesh (*bāśār*; see Isa. 31:3). Their real though limited capacity to do harm has set against it God's unlimited capacity to restrain them. All that is needed is for God actually to be gracious (v. 1).

56:5–11. But a believer's life is often lived with a tension between the reasons for fear and the reasons for trust, and the psalm goes back to its beginning and works through the logic of vv. 1–4 once more, at greater length. The lament in vv. 5–6 re-expresses the content of vv. 1–2. The plea in vv. 7–8 makes explicit the implications of the plea in v. 1aα, and

16. Cf. Schaefer, *Psalms*, 139.
17. LXX implies *dĕbāray*, "[with] my words," assimilating to v. 5; Syr lacks the "word" phrase.

the declaration of confidence in v. 9 follows from that. The statement of trust in vv. 10–11 then restates that in vv. 3–4.

> [5]All day long, in words about me they harass me; [MT]/shame me;
>   [LXX]/make plans against me; [Syr, Sym]
> all their thoughts are against me, to bring trouble.

So the suppliant reverts to the "all day long" of vv. 1–2 and speaks of "words about me," taking up the reference to God's word in v. 4.[18] The second colon explains the nature of these words and the way they cause trouble. Alongside "all day" is "all their thoughts," all directed to cause trouble (*bad).

> [6]They stir up strife, [MT]/band together, [LXX, Jerome, Tg] they hide,
>   these people watch my steps,
>   as they look for my life.

Four verbs explain that further, all explicating what those "thoughts" involve, what vv. 1–2 spoke of as watchful foes lusting after the suppliant. To stir up strife they hide (*ṣāpan*; perhaps there is some overlap with *ṣāpâ*, "keep watch"). The parallel colon makes explicit that they do "watch my steps," literally "my heels"; that is, they follow after me, seeking opportunity to trip me up or ambush me. They "look for my life" (*nepeš*, *person), that is, for my death (NJPS). The verb is a familiar one, usually with a positive meaning, here used in a chillingly different connection.

> [7]For their harmfulness carry them off,
>   in anger put the peoples down, God.

The suppliant's plea begins. *"Harmfulness" sums up vv. 1–2 and 5–6. "Carry off" (*pālaṭ*) is a snide word, since it usually suggests "carry off to safety," meaning *rescue, but it can denote carrying off to safety from the viewpoint of the carrier, such as a lion carrying off its prey (Isa. 5:29). The second colon clarifies that it is this sort of carrying off that the psalm has in mind. The suppliant wants God to act with the energy of anger to put down "peoples." The horizon of the psalm has thus broadened from that of one individual to a group of foes and fighters, even to whole nations. The suppliant does not ask for these foes to be forgiven; that

---

18. Thus it is less likely that *dĕbāray* refers to "my affairs" (EVV). But the expression is difficult in the context (hence Syr's omission of it?); I take MT as objective genitive (so Raabe, *Psalm Structures*, 94; cf. GKC 128h; 135m). *BHS* suggests *dābār* (dittog.), "a word," which one might (e.g.) see as the direct obj. of *'āṣab* II: "They frame a word."

would be to ignore the demands of moral and social order and encourage the triumph of wrong over right. It is necessary that they be put down for the sake of the fulfillment of God's right purpose in the world.[19] But it is by a prayer that the suppliant seeks to bring this about, not by an action or even by a curse.

> [8]May you yourself have recorded my lamenting;
> put my tears into your flask—
> yes, they are in your record.

The plea now focuses on the suppliant. The psalm imagines the existence of record books at the heavenly court analogous to those at an earthly court and asks God to make sure that these include "my lamenting," more literally the visible shaking or tossing that were the outward expression of anguish, and thus (by implication) that they include the people responsible for it. The second colon thus constitutes a parallel appeal to God to take note of another physical manifestation of anguish. An imperative balances a precative (both ending -$â$), and "my tears" balances "my shaking"; while "shaking" is $nôd$, "flask" is $nō'd$. A flask is a regular container for (e.g.) water; we know nothing of a practice of collecting one's tears in OT times, so this is presumably a metaphor for keeping the tears so as to keep them in mind. The third colon returns to the image of the first. The assumption of the prayer is not that the tears somehow establish a credit balance with God, but that they appeal to God's compassion and therefore push God to take action against the attackers.

> [9]Then my enemies will turn back
> on the day when I call;
> I know this, because God is mine.

The declaration of confidence presupposes God's response to that plea. The language of "turning back" corresponds to the plea for God to put down "peoples." It is the terminology of warfare (cf. 9:3 [4]; 35:4; 40:14 [15]; 44:10 [11]; 70:2 [3]). "On the day" takes up once more the language of vv. 1–3, but especially of v. 3. "The day when I am afraid" has suggestively become "the day when I call." It is this that transforms fear into confidence; or rather, this and the fact that God is one who responds to

19. Gerstenberger (*Psalms*, 1:228) suggests that *'ammîm* can mean "people/persons" and thus that the words can be those of an ordinary individual, but his only example of such use of the pl. is 57:9 [10], which does not convince. But perhaps an ordinary person might use this word to appeal to the principle that Yhwh puts down the peoples and ask for that to be applied in the putting down of particular enemies.

such a call, which expresses the fact that "God is mine." The EVV's more literal "God is for me" is an overtranslation (*lĕ* means "belonging to" and does not quite mean "committed to") but not by much. The great thing that the psalmist knows is not that "you are God" but that "you are my God," one who helps us and one to whom we are not strangers.[20]

> ¹⁰In God whose word I praise,
>   in Yhwh whose word I praise,
> ¹¹In God I have trusted;
>   I am not afraid:
>   what can human beings do to me?

A restated declaration of trust in Yhwh follows. The first colon corresponds to v. 4a, except that "word" lacks a suffix. The second repeats the first, except for substituting "Yhwh" for "God." The third and fourth cola repeat v. 4b–c. The fifth repeats v. 4d, except for substituting "human beings" (*'ādām*) for "flesh" (*bāśār*); it is the term that appears in the parallelism in Isa. 31:3. The repetitions, the extra colon, and the variations all serve to underline the declaration.

56:12–13. Like Ps. 55, the prayer closes with a declaration of confidence and commitment, and like Ps. 54, it also looks forward to bringing an offering to mark what Yhwh has done and speaks as if that act is already a reality, which in a sense is so, if Yhwh has determined to act. The two verses thus stand in the present between a future that will see promises fulfilled (v. 12) and a past in which Yhwh has answered prayer (v. 13), though the very fact that the promises are still future indicates that the answer is also still future from the point of view of the suppliant's experience. Indeed, vv. 12–13 presuppose more than one event that we have not been told of. On one hand, v. 12 presupposes that the suppliant has made promises to come back with thank-offerings if and when Yhwh answers the plea expressed in the psalm. On the other, v. 13 presupposes that Yhwh has heard the prayer and made a commitment to answering it and that the suppliant knows that this is so. We do not know how the suppliant would have made the promises or how Yhwh would have signified this response.

> ¹²My promises to you are binding on me, God;
>   I will fulfill my thank-offerings to you.

The suppliant declares (lit.), "Your promises are upon me." These *promises might imply "the promises you expect" and not simply "the promises made to you" (the genitive might be subjective not objective);

---

20. Augustine, *Psalms*, 223.

that is, someone bringing a plea of this kind might be expected to make a commitment to return with a sacrifice when Yhwh has answered their prayer. But the parallel second colon (a verbal clause accompanies the noun clause) puts the emphasis on the suppliant's commitment.

> ¹³For you have saved my life from death,
>   yes, my feet from being tripped,
> So as to walk before God
>   in the light of life.

Verse 13 then states the reason for fulfilling these promises. We might translate "for you will have saved," seeing the verb as past from the point of view of the moment when the offerings will be made, but this might undermine the assumptions of the verse. The suppliant speaks by faith, as if the act of deliverance has already happened, because in God's purpose it has happened. The first line speaks in two parallel cola about the actual act of deliverance. The enemies were waiting for the suppliant's life (v. 6), but Yhwh "has saved my life" (again *nepeš*, *person). More concretely, Yhwh has thus rescued the suppliant's feet from being tripped: the expression is different from ones that appeared earlier, but the reality is the same (see vv. 1–2, 6).

The result of Yhwh's rescue is to restore the suppliant to the proper experience of an Israelite, of which the two cola in v. 13b again offer parallel pictures. Other psalms speak of the light of Yhwh's face (e.g., 4:6 [7]; 44:3 [4]); this line divides up those two nouns. The suppliant will be able to walk "to the face of Yhwh," to live in the realm where Yhwh's *face shines on people. To put it another way, it is to walk "in the light of life," to walk where Yhwh's *light shines on people and gives them fullness of life.

Theological Implications

The psalm works with two related polarities, trust over against fear and God over against humanity,[21] though "each occurrence of the word 'afraid' . . . is accompanied by the word 'trust.'"[22] It is the word of God that makes possible the move from fear of human beings to trust in God. Elsewhere the word that God often utters is the exhortation backed by a promise: "Do not be afraid; I am with you" (e.g., Isa. 41:10, 13, 14; 43:1–5). The psalm hints at the recognition that fear and trust may coexist. The life of faith is then one in which we live in trust even if we

21. Mays, *Psalms*, 208.
22. McCann, "Psalms," 902.

also know fear. Perhaps, indeed, trust only exists in the presence of fear. The psalmist

> makes no pretension to that lofty heroism which contemns danger. . . . The true proof of faith consists in this, that when we feel the solicitations of natural fear, we can resist them, and prevent them from obtaining an undue ascendancy. Fear and hope may seem opposite and incompatible affections, yet . . . the latter never comes into full sway unless there exists some measure of the former. In a tranquil state of the mind, there is no scope for the exercise of hope.[23]

23. Calvin, *Psalms*, 2:349–50.

Psalm 57

Simultaneously Expecting
and Possessing

Translation

The leader's. Do not destroy. David's. Inscription. When he fled from
Saul into the cave.

[1]Be gracious to me, God, be gracious to me,
   because I have taken refuge with you for my life.
In the shadow of your wings I will take refuge
   until destruction[1] passes.
[2]I call on God Most High,
   on God who brings it to an end for me.
[3]He must send from heaven and deliver me:
   he must have rebuked[2] the one who hounds me; (Rise)
God must send his commitment
   and his truthfulness [and deliver] my life.
[4]I will lie down among lions, [MT]/dogs, [Syr]
   human beings devouring,
Their teeth a spear and arrows,
   their tongue a sharp sword.

1. See on 55:11 [12].
2. NJPS with "My persecutor reviles" takes *ḥērēp* as a regular qatal, but the translation produces a jerky, asyndetic effect. More likely LXX and Jerome are right that God
continues to be the subj. of the verb, which generates good parallelism; the jussives on
either side point to the qatal being precative. Only here is Yhwh the subj. of this verb, but
Yhwh is often the subj. of similar verbs (e.g., *gāʿar*).

⁵Be on high over the heavens, God,
 over all the earth your honor.

⁶They are setting a net for my feet;
 my life is bowing down. [MT]/they are bowing down my life. [LXX]³
They are digging a pit before me;
 they are falling right into it. (Rise)
⁷My heart is set, God,
 my heart is set.
I will sing and make music;
 ⁸awake, my soul.⁴
Awake, harp and lyre;
 I will wake the dawn.⁵
⁹I will confess you among the peoples, my Lord;
 I will make music for you among the countries.⁶
¹⁰For your commitment is as great as the heavens,
 your truthfulness as the skies.
¹¹Be on high over the heavens, God,
 over all the earth your honor.

Interpretation

This prayer psalm presupposes a context in which the suppliant is under attack (vv. 1, 4, 6), but its dominant feature is a declaration of trust and confidence that God will deliver. The psalm is a "prayer of petition with a strongly emphasized confession of trust."⁷ It thus stands between a psalm of protest or lament (in which trust may be more muted) and a psalm of trust (where it may be difficult to be clear whether the suppliant is under pressure or to be clear what that pressure is). While we could not take for granted that a repeated line (vv. 5, 11) marks the end of a section in the manner of a refrain, in this case that makes sense. The two halves of the psalm, comprising eight lines each, then both begin from the situation of attack (vv. 1, 6) and go on to declare confidence

3. I.e., LXX implies *kāpĕpû* for *kāpap*, which is elsewhere transitive. Barthélemy suggests that the net is the subj. of the verb (*Psaumes*, 362), but the m. verb after f. subj. is harsh.

4. Hardly "awake my honor"—i.e., my honored one, Yhwh—since the psalm does not treat Yhwh as asleep, like some other psalms. *Kābôd* (usually *kābēd*) sometimes refers to the "liver," that is, the inner person (cf., e.g., 16:9).

5. "I will awake at dawn" (LXX) requires a doubly idiomatic usage, taking the hiphil as declarative in order for it to have the same meaning as the qal in the previous two cola, and *šāḥar* to be adverbial. This seems too much to expect readers to pick up.

6. As at 44:14 [15], L misdivides *ballĕ'ummîm* as *bal-'ummîm*.

7. Hossfeld and Zenger, *Psalms 2*, 69 (italicized in the original).

in God. But only the first includes an actual plea (v. 1), unless we count vv. 5 and 11, while only the second makes a commitment to praise and confession (vv. 7–10). Like Pss. 55 and 56, between its sections the psalm combines repetition with movement toward greater confidence. Indeed, in isolation vv. 1–5 might seem to be a prayer and vv. 6–11 a thanksgiving. The collocation of the two parts suggests another prayer that is confident of an answer, so confident it can speak as if the answer has already come, like Ps. 56.

Psalm 57 indeed has a number of links with Ps. 56. The heading presupposes a similar setting, and it begins with the same plea. In v. 3 it goes on to use the uncommon verb *šā'ap* ("hound"; cf. 56:1–2 [2–3]) and in v. 5 to urge God to be "on high," where attackers currently locate themselves (56:2 [3]). Repetition of words is also a feature of the psalm ("be gracious," v. 1; "take refuge," v. 1; "my life," vv. 1, 3, 6; "must send," v. 3; "commitment and truthfulness," vv. 3, 10; "heaven/the heavens," vv. 3, 5, 10, 11; "honor/soul" [*kābôd*], vv. 5, 8, 11; "set/setting," vv. 6–7; "my heart is set," v. 7; "make music," vv. 7, 9; "awake/wake," v. 8; and the whole of vv. 5 and 11). In addition seven of the sixteen lines involve a word doing double duty (that is, occurring in one colon but applying to both). Four are invocations, all in the middle of the line and applying to both cola (vv. 5, 7a–b, 9, 11). Two are verbs, one at the beginning of a line, one in the middle (vv. 1, 3). One is an adjective, at the beginning of a line (v. 10).

The psalm would be suitable for an ordinary person or a leader under attack, before or after the exile. Verses 7–11 reappear in a slightly different form as Ps. 108:1–5.

The leader's. Do not destroy. David's. Inscription. When he fled from Saul into the cave.

Heading. See glossary. It is again the story in 1 Sam. 21:10 [11]–22:1 that refers to David "fleeing" from Saul and hiding in a "cave" (cf. Ps. 56). But 1 Sam. 24 also refers to David's being in a "cave," where he cuts off Saul's *kānāp* (the corner of his garment); compare *kĕnāpêkā* (your wings) in v. 1 here.[8]

57:1–5. The first section, then, begins with the psalm's only explicit plea, but plea is in the background in one sense or another through vv. 1–5.

---

¹Be gracious to me, God, be gracious to me,
   because I have taken refuge with you for my life.

---

8. Cf. Slomovic, "Historical Titles," 372–73.

In the shadow of your wings I will take refuge
until destruction passes.

The opening appeal for *grace corresponds to that in Ps. 56 though here the colon is completed by a repetition of the verb rather than by the reason for the appeal. The reason comes in the second colon, literally "My *person takes refuge with you."

The second line picks up the verb (but changes to yiqtol), but first, in telling us where the suppliant takes *refuge, makes clear that it does utilize the image of taking refuge in some safe place; it is not a dead metaphor for reliance, as is often the case (contrast LXX). As usual, the image of God's wings may link with the wings in the temple, though it becomes a metaphor for a protectiveness that extends to life in the world. It is then only in the second colon, the last colon in the two opening lines, that we find an indication why this is necessary. Destruction is on the prowl or hurtling around, like a raging epidemic or a violent wind or a rampaging army. But none of these threatens forever. The object of attack simply needs somewhere safe to sit out the crisis, and the suppliant has such a place.

²I call on God Most High,
on God who brings it to an end for me.

The psalm makes a transition to talking about God rather than to God. The verb applies to both cola; it is yiqtol rather than cohortative, so this is probably not the suppliant's self-exhortation, though it is not clear whom the suppliant is addressing. The fact that overt protest is not prominent in the psalm may make it unlikely that the psalm is addressing the enemies. Perhaps the line begins the process of confessing God before other people (cf. v. 9). Or perhaps the transition from speech addressing God is purely formal; God is still the implicit addressee even if God now "overhears" the suppliant speaking about God, hopefully with the extra attention involved in overhearing. The suppliant issues a reminder, then, either to the self, or to the foes, or to other people, or to God, regarding who God is. On one hand, God is the *Most High, the exalted and powerful one who can protect from hostile forces. In the second colon the common noun for God, 'ĕlōhîm, is complemented by the rarer proper noun 'ēl, which also suggests God's might, while "Most High" is complemented by the almost unique description of God as the one who brings things to an end for me (gāmar; cf. 138:8). The verb's implied object is the destruction of which the previous line spoke.⁹

9. In isolation the verb might suggest that Yhwh completes a purpose for me (cf. Aramaic gĕmar in Ezra 7:12), but the verb's other (intransitive) occurrences (7:9 [10]; 12:1 [2]; 77:8 [9]) denote coming to an end. So, in the context, it more likely means that Yhwh

> ³He must send from heaven and deliver me:
>   he must have rebuked the one who hounds me; (Rise)
> God must send his commitment
>   and his truthfulness [and deliver] my life.

The two parallel lines fit with that; again the psalm speaks *of* God but perhaps intends to be overheard. The supplicant needs God not to be confined to the heavens but to become involved in events here on earth, like the king intervening in events in the city when there is trouble. The one who threatens destruction is one who hounds the supplicant (see on 56:1–2 [2–3]), but a responsive taunt or rebuke from God is all that is needed to sort out matters.[10] It is thus God who needs to do some sending, and what God must send is quasi-aides such as 43:3 appealed for. God's *commitment and *truthfulness are personified as if they were members of God's cabinet, and therefore God is indirectly urged to send them on this important mission. There is no need to ask God to come in person (God may have other things to do); God's commitment and truthfulness will be quite enough. They will mean deliverance.[11]

> ⁴I will lie down among lions, [MT]/dogs, [Syr]
>   human beings devouring,
> Their teeth a spear and arrows,
>   their tongue a sharp sword.

The two lines amplify the nature of the destruction that threatens the supplicant, though the verb is cohortative and the cola apparently constitute a statement of faith or determination. The verb "lie down" thus compares with that in 3:5 [6]; 4:8 [9]; it suggests lying down to sleep in a relaxed way, notwithstanding the dangers that surround (cf. v. 1).[12]

---

brings destruction to an end. Here and at 138:8, LXX and Jerome translate *gāmar* as if it were *gāmal* (cf. *HALOT*; *DCH*).

10. In the first line, the verb again applies to both cola; the second colon spells out the negative side to such deliverance, with the precative verb paralleling the jussives. The parallel line then repeats the first jussive verb, provides it with the subj. and obj. that it lacked, and provides the second jussive verb with its subj. and another obj. I thus follow LXX in assuming that "my life," which MT takes as the beginning of v. 4, is actually another obj. for "deliver." There is no need to add a verb to the text; "deliver" in the first colon is presupposed in the last colon, in keeping with the psalm's liking for double-duty words.

11. Understanding the verbs as jussive rather than indicative fits the context with its reference to prayer; they tell us what the content of the prayer is (cf. Auffret, *Voyez de vos yeux*, 61; against Raabe, *Psalm Structures*, 115).

12. It thus seems unnecessary to infer that the cohortative has simply lost its meaning (but cf. GKC 108g; DG 68; JM 114c; *IBHS* 34.5.3). *TTH* 52 takes it to suggest "despondent resignation."

The first line thus begins by describing the danger figuratively, while its second colon explains the figure.[13] The parallel line then provides specificity to both preceding cola. How are the attackers like lions or dogs? In that their teeth are extremely dangerous, like the weapons in the hands of human attackers. But as human beings, their more literal weapon is their tongue, with the dangerous potential of a sword (cf. 59:7 [8]; 64:3 [4]), a sharp sword like the tongue of a seducer or a prophet (cf. Prov. 5:3–4; Isa. 49:2). It is the means whereby the human beings go about their devouring. A culture that assumed the existence of demons might describe demons in such terms or might use the psalm with such meaning, but we have little explicit indications of such beliefs in Israel, so it would be unwise to take this as what the imagery originally refers to in the psalm.[14] Notwithstanding whatever attackers, the suppliant will lie down and sleep, perhaps having taken refuge in the temple, perhaps besieged in a city or a military camp.

> [5]Be on high over the heavens, God,
>   over all the earth your honor.

In the line that closes the first half of the psalm, the suppliant again directly addresses God, having allowed God to overhear the previous three lines. As is the case with the closing line of Ps. 21 (the only other occurrence of this imperative), one might initially reckon that the suppliant is urging God to act in a way that reflects and manifests the divine majesty. But the verb more often denotes exaltation in the eyes of people, and this connotation fits the context (cf. 18:46 [47]). It also fits the talk in terms of exaltation *over* the heavens (contrast *from* heaven, v. 3) and the earth. Indirectly the psalm indeed urges God to act, but directly it looks back to the consequences that will follow. The result of the act that v. 3 has bidden will be that God sits on high—very high, indeed, high above the heavens—in the estimate of the world. It will be then (the parallel asyndetic colon asserts) that God's *honor shines over all the earth. This double bidding is thus another way of expressing confidence: "I know you are going to act, and that is both what enables me to sleep and what enables me to look forward to your exaltation in people's eyes."

13. The verb *lāhaṭ* usually means "burn" (cf. NRSV mg), but this rather complicates the verse with a further passing metaphor. I follow *HALOT* in seeing the word as from *lāhaṭ* II, "devour." In isolation, one would then take "human beings" as its obj., but in light of the last colon in the verse, I rather take it as subj. MT and LXX divide the line differently. Both the verb and the prep. apply to both cola.

14. Against Rogerson and McKay, *Psalms*, 2:43. But see the comment on 59:7 [8]; 72:9.

57:6–11. The second half of the psalm goes through its sequence of elements again, though as usual in a different configuration and balance. The suppliant protests at the current situation but expresses the conviction that God has as good as acted (v. 6), makes a commitment to confess God's act (vv. 7–9), and again urges God to be on high (v. 10).

> ⁶They are setting a net for my feet;
>   my life is bowing down. [MT]/they are bowing down my life. [LXX]
> They are digging a pit before me;
>   they are falling right into it. (Rise)

Qatal verbs run through these two lines, so that while they continue the description of the suppliant's predicament that occupied v. 4, they give v. 5 a quite different significance (and remove any reason to wonder whether v. 5 is an interpolation disturbing the psalm's natural flow). If the four qatals have a consistent significance, that can hardly be to refer to something that has actually happened, which does not fit the psalm as a whole.[15] I take them all as instantaneous qatals, describing something that is in the midst of happening. The first three indeed refer to something that can be seen happening, while the last refers to something the suppliant knows is about to happen, has as good as happened.[16] The metaphor with which the psalm describes the attackers' actions changes again. Now they are not lions but hunters, and their resources are thus not plots but metaphorical nets (cf. 9:15 [16]; 10:9; 35:7–8) placed over pits (cf. 7:15 [16]; 9:15 [16]). The result is that the suppliant's life is falling down into the net and thus into the pit. In the context, it makes sense to give the verb "bow down" (*kāpap*) its literal physical meaning rather than referring it to an inner depression, which is also hard to reconcile with the rest of the psalm. All the first three cola are thus parallel.[17] The two words of the asyndetic last colon then land with a thump, literally "they-fell in-its-midst."[18] Further, "they are falling" contrasts with "my life is bowing down." The suppliant is in the midst of falling but will not; it is they who will end right in the pit they dug.

15. Contrast Beat Weber, "Formgeschichtliche und sprachliche Beobachtungen zu Psalm 57," *SJOT* 42 (2001): 295–305.

16. JM 112k takes it as precative, but there is no hint of this in the context.

17. Prosaically put, "They dug a pit in front of me and set [over it] a net for my feet, and I fell into it." LXX's reading makes them even more parallel than MT's.

18. The parallel in 7:15–16 [16–17] mixes qatals and yiqtols and thus supports the assumption that such expressions refer to an event that has not literally happened yet, but can be spoken of as if it has, though I take 9:15 [16] to refer to such an event that has actually happened (contrast Prov. 26:27).

> ^{7a–b}My heart is set, God,
>   my heart is set.

"My heart is set" in turn forms a contrast with the foes' "setting" a trap. There are two forms of determination here, and the suppliant is convinced about which one will win. The line also makes for another contrast with the acknowledgment that "my life is bowing down/they are bowing down my life" (v. 6). The point is underlined by the rare exact repetition in the second colon; the invocation again applies to both cola. The participle is a strong one; the suppliant's heart is set firm in the manner of David's throne or God's throne (e.g., 93:2; 2 Sam. 7:16). There is a degree of self-commitment involved in seeking guidance or help from God or in studying the Torah (e.g., 2 Chron. 19:3; Ezra 7:10), and it is that kind of self-commitment that the suppliant here claims.

> ^{7c}I will sing and make music;
>   ⁸awake, my soul.
> Awake, harp and lyre;
>   I will wake the dawn.

Four lines now indicate that in the suppliant's case this is a commitment to confess what God will have done.[19] Admittedly there will be a moment before it becomes explicit that the commitment is to confession. In these two lines, all we learn is that the suppliant is committed to singing and making *music and waking the dawn, and stirs up the soul and the musical instruments to that end. In the first and last cola, waking the dawn is a vivid image to parallel singing and making music; it suggests that the suppliant will be so eager to begin praise as to be impatient for the breaking of dawn, which marks the time for morning worship, and will be keen to hurry it up. Contrary to the usual arrangement, "David said: 'I will awake the dawn, the dawn shall not awake me.'"[20] In the two middle cola, the implication of stirring up the soul is that such worship does not necessarily happen naturally but that neither are we helpless with regard to whether it happens. We can stir up our inner beings, indulge in conversation with them (cf. 42:5, 11 [6, 12]; 43:5) to the end that they come alive, like a parent waking a child. A psalm that is less confident

19. I thus take vv. 7–8 as three bicola, a more usual arrangement than MT's two tricola. Verses 7c–8 work abb′a′, on the outside a pair of declarations in the cohortative; in between, a pair of imperatives. Taking vv. 7–8 as two tricola, Beat Weber ("'Fest ist mein Herz, o Gott,'" *ZAW* 107 [1995]: 294–95) takes the two cohortatives as performatives, fulfilling the intentions stated in vv. 7a–b and 8a–b: "Right now I hereby sing and wake the dawn."
20. *Midrash on Psalms*, 1:501–2.

that God is about to act can focus on waking God (7:6 [7]; 44:23 [24]; 59:4 [5]), but a psalm that is confident of that can focus on the response of confession that God's act will justify. The companion colon of exhortation wakes up the instruments, *harp and *lyre, that will make the music and accompany the singing. Alongside the two lines' abb'a' structure is the fact that the verb "awake" recurs in each colon of v. 8, reflected in MT's verse division. So the worship the psalm is concerned for requires the awaking of the inner being and the musical instruments, which will justify the suppliant in waking the dawn itself.

> ⁹I will confess you among the peoples, my Lord;
> I will make music for you among the countries.

It is the companion two internally parallel lines in vv. 9–10 that make explicit that the object of this worship is to confess what God has done: that is, will have done.²¹ In other contexts, a commitment to *confession could refer to confession that will begin when God has acted. But here the psalm puts such emphasis on this confession, referring not to an actual act but to God's characteristic qualities of *commitment and *truthfulness, that the lines more likely refer to confession the suppliant is prepared to make now in the conviction that God is going to act. The reference to confession/making music among the peoples/countries makes the lines especially appropriate to a king or governor, and that in turn adds significance to the confession of God as my *Lord; the ruler acknowledges dependence on and subordination to a higher authority. The reference to peoples/countries also fits the cosmos-wide reach of God's commitment and truthfulness and the cosmos-wide manifestation of God's splendor (vv. 10–11).²²

> ¹⁰For your commitment is as great as the heavens,
> your truthfulness as the skies.

To give reasons for the confession, two nouns are picked up from v. 3.²³ It is the fact of Yhwh's commitment that makes possible the move

21. The abca'b' cola in v. 9 are neatly parallel: first-person singular yiqtol verb (one hiphil, one piel) with second-person singular suffix, the prep. *b*, m. plural noun (the second being a less common synonym), with "my Lord" occupying middle place in the line and applying to both cola.

22. This in itself makes questionable Weiser's arbitrary limitation of these peoples/nations to dispersed Israel (*Psalms*, 428).

23. These abcb'c' cola are also neatly parallel, though here the element that applies to both is the initial expression "for is great." After that, each colon comprises the prep. *'ad*, a m. pl. word for heavens/skies (the less common word again comes second), and a m. sg. segholate noun for *commitment/*truthfulness with a second-person sg. suffix.

from lament to confidence in the psalm.[24] The expression "is great as far as the heavens/skies" is unusual (but cf. 36:5 [6]). It may be a kind of superlative, but it is significant that the psalm is confessing that God's greatness extends to that realm from which v. 3 asked God to deliver.

> [11]Be on high over the heavens, God,
>   over all the earth your honor.

Perhaps that expression is there because it leads neatly into this repeated urging. This manifests one slight variation from the first urging in v. 5; "heavens" now does not have the article in the Hebrew. For all the confidence in God that the psalm exhibits, the suppliant does want to see God act in deliverance and thus find exaltation in the world's eyes, in a way demonstrating the honor that is obscured when this servant of God is under pressure. And perhaps the new context means that nearly identical words have different meaning: "at the end of the song . . . the same imperative is a hymnic reinforcement of God's greatness."[25]

Theological Implications

The suppliant stands before God as "one who simultaneously possesses and yet expects."[26] The suppliant stands before God, before the people of God, before the world, before opposition, and before himself or herself as someone under pressure, threatened by destruction, hounded, threatened with being devoured, attacked physically and/or verbally, aware of invisible traps lying ahead and of the possibility of falling into these. Yet the psalm does not focus on these perils. It is aware of a refuge, of being able to rest confident in God's protection and confident that God will answer the plea to show grace and to deliver, to send agents of the divine commitment and truthfulness to rebuke the attackers, and thus to manifest the divine splendor before the world. It can thus speak of God's deliverance in the same tense as it speaks of the attackers' plotting. The certainty of God's act means a kind of collapse of chronology. Events that are literally future cease to be purely future because they are actual in the life of God. And because they are actual in the life of God, they are actual in the life of the suppliant. They mean that the suppliant's heart can be ready even now to glorify God before the people of God, the world, and the attackers.

---

24. See Sung-Hun Lee, "Lament and the Joy of Salvation in Lament Psalms," in *Book of Psalms*, ed. Flint and Miller, 224–47.
25. Fokkelman, *Major Poems*, 3:96.
26. Weiser, *Psalms*, 428 (in italics in the original).

Psalm 58

The Gods Must and Will Fulfill
Their Responsibility

Translation

The leader's. Do not destroy. David's. Inscription.

¹Do you really speak faithfully, gods,[1]
　　do you make decisions for human beings uprightly?
²No, with your mind you devise [acts of] wickedness;
　　on the earth[2] with your hands you mete out[3] violence.

³Faithless people go astray from the womb,
　　people who speak falsely drift from birth.

1. MT has *'ēlem* (cf. Ps. 56 heading). Tg and Aq take this as a noun from *'ālam* I, meaning "[in] silence," but this makes poor sense, though it stimulates R. Isaac (*Midrash on Psalms*, 1:503) to edifying comments on the wisdom of staying silent in time of conflict; see Peter Krawczack, *"Es gibt einen Gott, der Richter ist auf Erden!" (Ps 58, 12b)* (Berlin: Philo, 2001), 177–94. Seybold (*Psalmen*, 231) keeps MT. Sym with "clan/nation" rather links the noun with *'ālam* II (bind), but such a noun is otherwise unknown and also does not fit very well. LXX and Jerome imply *'ulām*, "but"; this again does not fit well, and further, it should come at the beginning of the clause. I accept the common emendation to *'ēlim*, which might have been altered to avoid the impression that the psalm made polytheistic assumptions. Watson (*Classical Hebrew Poetry*, 268) apparently accepts this emendation but assumes that the word is from *'ayil* ("ram," a term for leaders). Christopher Begg ("Psalm 58,2a," *ETL* 64 [1988]: 397–404) emends to *'ĕlōhîm* and takes the question as a doubter's address to God.

2. Or "in the land"; either way, the focus will be on the land of Israel.

3. The precise meaning and associations of *pālas* are uncertain; contrast *HALOT* with BDB.

⁴They have poison like a snake's poison,⁴
    like that of a deaf viper that stops⁵ its ear,
⁵So that it does not listen to the voice of charmers,
    the expert weaver of spells.

⁶God, tear out the teeth in their mouth;
    break the lions'⁶ fangs, Yhwh.

⁷They must vanish, as waters that go away;
    he must direct his arrow[s],⁷ so must they dry up.
⁸As a snail that vanishes as it goes,
    or a woman's⁸ stillbirth, they must not see the sun.
⁹Before your pots sense the thorn,
    as someone living, so must fury whirl him off.

¹⁰The faithful one will rejoice when he sees redress,
    will bathe his feet in the blood of the faithless.
¹¹A person will say, "Yes, there is fruit for the faithful;
    yes, there are gods making decisions⁹ on earth."

Interpretation

At the center of the psalm stands a plea (v. 6) for Yhwh to take action in relation to wrongdoing in the world (vv. 3–5), the prayer being expanded in jussive declarations or curses (vv. 7–9). This lament, plea, and curse are set in a distinctive framework. First the psalm confronts the supernatural agents who are behind the wrongdoing in the world (vv. 1–2). In content it thus compares with Pss. 52 and 82, though in the former the psalm confronts a human being. But in form, this confrontation compares with the protest addressed to God that often begins a psalm. The closing anticipation of the rejoicing that will follow from

4. Ernst Jenni ("Pleonastische Ausdrücke für Vergleichbarkeit," in *Neue Wege*, ed. Seybold and Zenger, 201–6) sees this as simply a pleonastic comparative formula. He also construes the sentence differently: "The poison they have is like a snake's poison."

5. On the jussive-like form of *ya'ṭēm*, see DG 62.

6. NEB assumes the meaning "apostates" (see 34:10 [11]), but "fangs" rather suggests "lions."

7. K can be read as sg. (cf. LXX, Jerome); Q has pl. (cf. Tg, Syr). The expression involves a metonymy; strictly one directs (lit. "treads/bends") one's bow (cf. 7:12 [13]).

8. On the question whether this is a const., see C. Steyl, "The Construct Noun, *ešet* [*sic*] in Ps. 58.9," *JNSL* 11 (1983): 133–34.

9. LXX and Jerome assume that *'ĕlōhîm* refers to God and that *šōpĕṭîm* is pl. only to agree formally with it, but this usage is very rare, and Sym is more likely right in the context that the phrase is pl. and refers to gods, subordinate heavenly beings distinguishable from God (cf. v. 1).

God's act (vv. 10–11) also compares with the statement of confidence that can close a psalm, though it has a parallel distinctive motif in its anticipation that the gods at whom the initial protest were addressed will have at last fulfilled their vocation. There are a number of detailed correspondences and complementarities between vv. 1–2 and 10–11.[10]

The psalm contains a number of unusual expressions, and these have stimulated many proposals for emendation. Some of the unusual expressions may point to a northern origin (see, e.g., v. 2a),[11] but they go along with the way the psalm presents "a plethora of drastic pictures in a very original, robust language"[12] and long lines (4-4, 4-3, and 3-4). We do not know what kind of person speaks or in what kind of context the psalm would be used or who wrote it or when.[13]

> The leader's. Do not destroy. David's. Inscription.

Heading. See glossary.

58:1–2. The psalm begins, then, by confronting the gods in the way that God does in Ps. 82. There it is explicit that God speaks (as in Ps. 50); here the rest of the psalm suggests that the speaker is a prophet or an ordinary person. For "gods" or "sons of gods/sons of God" as divine beings subordinate to the one true God, see also (e.g.) 138:1; Exod. 15:11; Job 1:6. The OT makes clear that Israelites often worshipped many gods, and outside the OT a psalm such as this might presuppose such polytheism. But in the context of the OT these are heavenly beings subordinate to Yhwh, brought into being by Yhwh, due to serve Yhwh in the world by overseeing what happens to humanity, and liable to death if they do not do so. Perhaps we are to see the psalmist as a prophet admitted to Yhwh's council, in whose meeting they are present.

> [1]Do you really speak faithfully, gods,
>   do you make decisions for human beings uprightly?

The rhetorical question implies the negative answer that v. 2 makes explicit. In the two parallel cola, the opening interrogative and the invocation apply to the second colon as well as the first, while each colon incorporates a noun used adverbially: "with faithfulness/uprightness." The second noun must be so used; it is the parallelism that suggests that

---

10. See Auffret, *Voyez de vos yeux*, 86–88. For this structure, cf. also Krawczack, *"Es gibt einen Gott,"* 327.

11. So Rendsburg, *Linguistic Evidence*, 63–67.

12. Kraus, *Psalms 1–59*, 536.

13. Klaus Seybold ("Psalm lviii," *VT* 30 [1980]: 53–66) suggests that it originally comprised vv. 1–2, 4, 7–9, 11, with the other verses being later additions.

the same is true of the first noun. While *faithfulness suggests behavior that takes due account of who people are, uprightness suggests behavior that takes due account of objective standards of right and wrong. Each colon also incorporates a verb; "make *decisions" clarifies what sort of speaking the psalmist has been referring to. In the court of heaven the gods are speaking faithlessly and procuring wrongful decisions, and apparently God is doing nothing about this.

> ²No, with your mind you devise [acts of] wickedness;
>   on the earth with your hands you mete out violence.

Two cola indicate the way they act instead of exercising their power faithfully and uprightly.[14] "With your mind" and "[with] your hands" complement each other.[15] The first denotes where the wrongdoing starts, the second how it is implemented. "Devise" and "mete out" also parallel each other.[16] The first suggests how the wrong is initiated, the second how it is implemented. "[Acts of] wickedness" and "violence" then parallel each other,[17] one general and one more specific. The line refers to acts of *wickedness that involve *violence.

58:3–5. There is a sharp transition from vv. 1–2 as the psalm stops addressing the gods and now describes the way human beings act. It is not explicit what is the relationship of the critique in vv. 1–2 and that in vv. 3–5. Are these the results of the gods' devising and dealing? Or are they the earthly realities that the gods collude with rather than confronting? Or are the descriptions simply parallel, indicating that things are wrong in heaven and on earth? Certainly the gods' failure does not remove responsibility from the human agents of faithlessness.[18]

> ³Faithless people go astray from the womb,
>   people who speak falsely drift from birth.

14. Again, the particle "no" (more literally "indeed"), the prep. *b*, the expression "on earth," and the "your" in the second colon apply to both cola.

15. The parallelism (with one sg., one pl.) suggests that the prep. on one and the suffix on the other apply to both. Thus "your hands" is not the subj. of the second verb: see Sym against LXX; contrast also MT's const. *ḥămas*.

16. Both are second pl. yiqtol (one qal, one piel), with energic nun. See GKC 47m. This form commonly comes at the end of a sentence and thus in pause; it thus suggests that "on earth" is the beginning of the second colon here, which matches the content, since the plans are made in heaven but implemented on earth.

17. One f. and one m., and again one pl. and one sg. But one would expect *ʿăwālôt* and not *ʿōlōt* as the pl. of *ʿawlâ*, and *ʿōlōt* may rather be a northern form of the sg. noun (cf. Dahood, *Psalms*, 2:58). Syr and Tg have sg.

18. Cf. Weiser, *Psalms*, 431.

The two cola are neatly parallel. "Faithless people" are "people who speak falsely," which makes them much like the gods of vv. 1–2. The reference to false speech gives specificity to *faithless and suggests how they go about their faithlessness. "Go astray" is more literally "act strangely," act as a stranger (*zûr*); "drift" or "wander about" (*tāʿâ*) then puts the point more familiarly: the verb means literally to wander but also to do so ethically. "From the womb" is then paralleled by (more lit.) "from the insides" (*beṭen*): that is, the first word refers to the womb in particular, the second to a person's insides more generally. The psalm's lament concerns people characterized by dishonest acts and words from the very beginning of their lives and throughout.[19]

> ⁴They have poison like a snake's poison,
>   like that of a deaf viper that stops its ear,
> ⁵So that it does not listen to the voice of charmers,
>   the expert weaver of spells.

And they are lethal. Their tongues have an effect like that of poison; they have fatal consequences for their victims. The second colon elaborates the point by describing the snake in question as one that will not listen to attempts to get it to stop its work. The cola thus work abcdec′e′fgh, with overlapping elements and elements that apply to both cola:

They have poison	like	the poison of a	snake,	
	like	a deaf	viper	that stops its ears.

The second colon explains what kind of snake the psalm has in mind, and why it is especially lethal: it will not listen to anyone.

Verse 5 in turn explains what sort of listening the psalm has in mind. In this further overlapping parallel line, "so that it does not listen to the voice of" applies to the second colon as well as the first, giving space in the second colon to expand considerably on "charmers." No matter how expert the spell-weavers, they cannot halt this viper. In the same way, the false speech of the faithless cannot be stopped or rendered ineffective. It insists on doing its lethal work. (Although there no doubt were charmers in Israel, in the context of this simile it would be allegorical to ask who the literal equivalents of the charmers are: they are there to emphasize the mortal danger the snakes and the faithless bring.)

---

19. The fact that the line describes only the faithless means that it does not relate to the question of the original sin of all humanity.

58:6. A prayer[20] issues logically from the confrontation in vv. 1–2 and the lament in vv. 3–5.

> ⁶God, tear out the teeth in their mouth;
>   break the lions' fangs, Yhwh.

Humanly speaking, nothing can be done about the wickedness in the world, and the gods are also colluding with it rather than doing something about it. The only thing to do is pray for the violent action that is needed if the victims of the faithless are to be rescued. Again the cola are parallel. Forming a bracket around the line, the proper name "Yhwh" complements "God" (unusual in Pss. 42–83). This parallelism reinforces the fact that "God" is here *'ĕlōhîm*, not *'ēlim*, the word hypothesized in v. 1; the psalm now addresses God rather than the gods. Two words for "tear/break down" also complement each other. Neither specifically means "break" in the simple sense; both rather suggest disabling dangerous weapons. The line emphasizes the weapons' danger by adding the word "fangs" to "teeth" and by adding a new word to describe these people: they have the danger of a lion as well as that of a snake. The psalm urges Yhwh to act to remove the danger.

58:7–9. The urging of action is reinforced by jussives. In isolation we might see these as curses, but in the context they re-express the aim of the prayer in a series of figures.[21]

> ⁷They must vanish, as waters that go away;
>   he must direct his arrow[s], so must they dry up.
> ⁸As a snail that vanishes as it goes,
>   or a woman's stillbirth, they must not see the sun.

The suppliant thus states the desired result of Yhwh's action in similes suggesting that the faithless simply cease to exist, vanishing or melting

---

20. But LXX has aorist statements, a declaration of confidence about what Yhwh has in effect already done.

21. The expression *kĕmô* appears five times. It is an equivalent to *k* or *ka'ăšer* and is here used in broadly similar ways in each line. In the first line, the first two are equivalent to *k* ... *k* ... meaning "as ... so ... ," introducing verbal clauses, irregularly for *k* but not for *ka'ăšer*; and *kĕmô* can be equivalent to either. In the middle line, a second *kĕmô* is implicit before the closing verb, but like the English equivalent it can be omitted. In the third line, the double *kĕmô* comes wholly in the second colon, where it is only formally equivalent to *k* ... *k* ... and is used before nouns. The importance of analogy in Ps. 58 comes to a climax here: see David P. Wright, "Blown Away Like a Bramble," *RB* 103 (1996): 213–36. For v. 9b, cf. *sicut* ... *sic* ... in some Vulgate MSS (see R. Althann, "Psalm 58,10 in the Light of Ebla," *Bib* 64 [1983]: 122–24 [see 123]).

away,[22] and both compare this vanishing with something that "goes [away]."[23] The first colon imagines them vanishing in the way that water vanishes when it soaks into the ground. In the second, the opening phrase states more literally the action that will be required to effect that, and the closing phrase parallels the one in the previous colon.[24] Verse 8 then adds two further images. The first may assume the idea that a snail's slimy trail represents its dissolving as it goes. The second is a particularly powerful image for the transition from apparent liveliness to lifelessness, which the psalm reworks. Other passages speak of stillborn children that do not see the sun or the light (Job 3:16; Eccles. 6:3–5); here the psalmist apparently urges more directly that the faithless themselves should not do so. The line works aba'c, with the final phrase linking back to the first phrase in v. 7. Thus "They must vanish" and "They must not see the sun" form a bracket around the intervening similes.[25]

> [9]Before your pots sense the thorn,
>   as someone living, so must fury whirl him off.

Their vanishing is willed again, though the imagery is unclear to us, perhaps because of the denseness with which it combines further images. The psalm now addresses the faithless of whom it has spoken in the third person through vv. 3–8. The simile in the first colon may refer to the speedy way thorns can make their presence felt when they blaze under a cooking pot (cf. Eccles. 7:6).[26] This provides a picture for the speed with which the psalm asks that Yhwh's fury would "whirl off" the faithless person. It is a regular image for such destruction, though it usually involves the faithless being swept off like chaff.[27] The psalm asks that wrath may do that instantly, as it were, while the faithless person is still alive (cf. 55:15 [16]).

22. The form in v. 7 comes from *māʾas*, a by-form of *māsas*, which at least suggests a paronomasia with the regular *māʾas* I, suggesting "be rejected" (cf. Marina Mannati, "Psaume lviii 8," *VT* 28 [1978]: 477–80).

23. The verbs at the end of vv. 7a and 8a are both forms of *hālak*, hitpael and qal.

24. The line thus works abcb', with hitpael "dry up" paralleling hitpael "go away." I thus take it that the subj. of *yitmōlālû* is again the waters and that the verb comes from BDB's *mālal* III, not its *mālal* IV (cf. LXX and Jerome; *HALOT*; contrast BDB itself). Although *mālal* is not elsewhere used of a liquid, the more common synonym *yābēš* is so used.

25. The verb is pl., so the subj. can hardly be the stillbirth (against NRSV), and it fits the context to understand the qatal as precative. But if one took the first word to mean an aborted embryo (see *HALOT*), the pl. might apply to the two nouns in v. 8.

26. Or perhaps to the speedy way thorns can grow up, if we take the first noun as *sîr* II (so NRSV, TNIV) not *sîr* I (so LXX, Jerome, NJPS).

27. NRSV takes *ḥārôn* to refer to the burning of the thorns, but elsewhere the word always refers to (Yhwh's) burning wrath.

58:10–11. The final two 4-4 lines close the prayer with an equivalent to the statement of confidence that often closes a psalm.

> ¹⁰The faithful one will rejoice when he sees redress,
>   will bathe his feet in the blood of the faithless.

The *faithful one is the subject of both parallel cola. The faithful one might be the psalmist, might be someone the psalmist cares about whose experience provided the impetus for the psalm, or might just be an individualized representative of the people. The two predicates are then parallel, a more abstract expression being complemented by a chillingly concrete one that explains what the first will look like. For the hyperbolic metaphor of bathing one's feet in something, compare and contrast Job 29:6.[28] The metaphor suggests total and irreversible deliverance from danger as God or the gods at last take action against those who are currently spilling the blood of faithful people. The latter *see* the redress, but they do not take it, for that is God's business (see 94:1; Deut. 32:35).[29] For *nāqām* EVV have words such as "vengeance" but this gives a misleading impression. The word indeed implies acting with conviction, even passion, yet it does not refer to the taking of personal revenge but to God's putting things right by seeing that people in the wrong are punished.[30] The faithless were overturning the proper God-given order of the world, and the faithful look forward to seeing that order vindicated.

> ¹¹A person will say, "Yes, there is fruit for the faithful;
>   yes, there are gods making decisions on earth."

Why would the faithful so rejoice? Two further parallel cola explain. The word pair *faithfulness and making *decisions recurs from v. 1, thus "constitutes the frame for this poem, and indicates the greatest worry of the poet: these two concepts are lacking in the land, and only God can remedy the situation."[31] The present situation is one in which the world is characterized by moral anarchy, and the heavenly beings who have responsibility for doing something about that are doing nothing. When God, or rather the gods as God's agents, act to put down the faithless and deliver the faithful, this reassures the faithful that God does run the world on the basis of right and wrong, not on the basis of power. It

28. A. Anderson, *Psalms*, 1:434.
29. Cf. John N. Day's comments on this psalm, *Crying for Justice* (Grand Rapids: Kregel, 2005), 55 (though he sees "gods" in the psalm as a term for human rulers).
30. See (e.g.) *NIDOTTE*.
31. Fokkelman, *Major Poems*, 3:98.

reassures the faithful that God's commitment to justice is not a merely theoretical one. Their commitment to faithfulness will be fruitful as the faithless ones' commitment to wrongdoing will receive its reward (cf. Isa. 3:10–11). The designated agents of God's will in the world take action for the sake of justice.

Theological Implications

"The lack of justice in the world is not some impersonal natural inevitable condition of human life. It is the intended work of the hearts and hands of responsible powers."[32] But "our struggle is not with flesh and blood, but with the rulers, with the authorities, with the world powers of this darkness, with the wicked spiritual entities in the heavens." We therefore need to be people who are "with every prayer and plea praying at every moment in the Spirit, and to this end keeping alert with all persistence in pleading for all the saints" (Eph. 6:12, 18). Psalm 58 shows us how to engage in that struggle in prayer on behalf of the saints as we confront the powers that fail to operate in the world in accordance with their divine commission; it shows us how to urge God to act against these powers and their earthly agents.

We have noted that modern Christians living in reasonable comfort do not like the violence of the way the Scriptures talk about these matters. This is so even though we profess ourselves concerned about (e.g.) the oppression that prosperous peoples in the Western world bring to poor peoples elsewhere and in our own countries (without ceasing to collude with it and profit from it). Erich Zenger notes that expositors such as Augustine were not so "squeamish" and that the problem seems to lie with questions of taste in our culture.[33] If we do not like the way the psalm expresses the matter, it challenges us to formulate another way of expressing it. But we could recall that the language of the psalm is evocative, "challenging the reader to identify with oppressed and suffering people, even though the reader may be quite comfortable"; it "evokes in us an awareness of the terrible wickedness that is in the world."[34] It challenges us to look for the terminating of that wickedness with passion, not (e.g.) to be unfeeling about the necessity for evil to be put down.

In praying this psalm, Christ would pray it on behalf of the oppressed.[35] Others who read this commentary probably have to see themselves as the

32. Mays, *Psalms*, 211.
33. *A God of Vengeance?* 34–36.
34. Tate, *Psalms 51–100*, 89.
35. Cf. Augustine, *Nine Sermons of Saint Augustine on the Psalms* (London: Longmans, 1958), 111, as quoted by Tate, *Psalms 51–100*, 89.

psalm's victims, for we ourselves are among the briars due for burning, and we need to let the prayer make us turn to Christ, who both prays the prayer and undergoes the burning.[36] "Only if you are thought worthy by the Master of the vineyard to destroy the briars in His vineyard, may you, the righteous, rejoice in their destruction."[37]

But as a speech act, it also functions perlocutively in relation to God.[38] While only v. 6 directly addresses God, the rest of the psalm indirectly does so. The whole is designed to move Yhwh to action, by drawing attention to the failure of Yhwh's aides (vv. 1–2), the unstoppable wickedness of the faithless (vv. 3–5), the way action against them needs to work out (vv. 7–9), and the effect this will have on the faithful (vv. 10–11). But the psalm also functions perlocutively in relation to the victims of the faithless, the "human beings" (*běnê ʾādām*) of the first line on whose lips individually (*ʾādām*) the last line puts a confession belying that declaration in the first line. It encourages them to believe that God is the kind of heavenly authority who hears people crying out in the context of oppression and responds by acting against their oppressors (Luke 18:8). For fortunately, Isa. 24:21 promises that "on that day Yhwh will attend on high to the army on high, and on earth to the kings of the earth."

---

36. Cf. Dietrich Bonhoeffer, "Sermon on a Psalm of Vengeance," *ThTo* 38 (1981–82): 466–71.

37. *Midrash on Psalms*, 1:507.

38. Cf. Krawczack, *"Es gibt einen Gott,"* 329–33.

Psalm 59

How to Pray in Terror

Translation

The leader's. Do not destroy. David's. Inscription. When Saul sent and
they kept watch on his house to kill him.

¹Save me from my enemies, my God,
  will you set me on high above those who rise against me.
²Save me from people who do harm,
  deliver me from people seeking bloodshed.
³Because there, they lie in wait for my life,
  they stir up strife [MT]/band together [Jerome, Tg]¹ against me,
    strong people.
Not because of my rebellion and not my shortcoming, Yhwh,
  ⁴nor my waywardness, do they rush to organize themselves.

Get up to meet with me, look, ⁵yes, you,²
  Yhwh, God, Armies, God of Israel.
Wake up to attend to all the nations;
  do not show grace to any harmful betrayers. (Rise)
⁶Again and again³ they growl like a dog in the evening
  as they go around the city.

---

1. See on 56:6 [7].

2. MT makes *wĕ'attâ* the beginning of v. 5. I follow Dahood (*Psalms*, 2:68) in linking it with v. 4b, which generates a neat 4-4 line. The "yes" renders the initial *w*, which
(even as the opening of v. 5) makes it less likely that the colon is a statement, "You are
Yhwh . . ." (so NRSV).

3. *Šûb* followed asyndetically by another verb denotes repeated action (GKC 120g).
John S. Kselman takes it to refer to turning away from Israel, as traitors ("Double Entendre
in Psalm 59," in *Book of Psalms*, ed. Flint and Miller, 184–89).

⁷There, they bellow with their mouths,
  swords on their lips,
   because who is listening?

⁸But you, Yhwh, are amused at them,
  you laugh at all the nations.
⁹My strength,⁴ I will watch for you,
  because God is my haven.
¹⁰The God who is committed to me⁵ will come to meet me;
  God will enable me to look at my watchful foes.

¹¹Do not slay them, lest my people put them out of mind;
  make them stumble about, by your might,
And put them down, my Lord our shield,
   ¹²through the shortcoming of their mouth, the word on their lips,
So that they are caught by their majesty
  and through the oath and the lie that they proclaim.
¹³Put an end to them in wrath,
  put an end to them so that they are no more,
So that people may acknowledge that God rules over Jacob,
  to the ends of the earth. (Rise)
¹⁴So again and again they growl like a dog in the evening
  as they go around the city.
¹⁵These—they stumble about for food
  if they do not have plenty and stay the night.

¹⁶But I—I will sing of your strength,
  I will resound in the morning at your commitment,
Because you will have been a haven for me,
  a refuge at the time when I was in trouble.
¹⁷My strength, for you I will make music,
  because God is my haven, the God who is committed to me.

Interpretation

The psalm is a particularly intense prayer for rescue from attackers. Its forcefulness develops through the psalm, though interwoven with the strength of feeling is a developing strength of conviction that Yhwh will answer.

4. MT has ʿuzzô, but LXX, Jerome, and Tg plausibly imply ʿuzzî. MT's third person perhaps links with the third-person expressions in the companion colon. Cf. also K's third-person suffix on ḥsdw in v. 10a.
5. Lit. "the God of my commitment" (ḥasdî); so Q. K's ḥsdw (his commitment) is harder to make sense of; LXX implies ʾĕlōhay ḥasdô, "my God [with] his commitment."

Verses 1–4a constitute quite a moderate and regular plea for rescue in light of people's attacks and the fact that the suppliant has not deserved these. Verses 4b–7 intensify the prayer with a more confrontational plea presupposing that Yhwh is asleep and asking for Yhwh not to show grace, with more concrete description of Yhwh as one who can answer such a plea and of the attackers as comparable to scavenging dogs. Verses 8–10 add a new element and further affect by means of a statement of confidence in what Yhwh will do. Verses 11–15 intensify the prayer yet further with more concrete shocking pleas and a partial repetition of the reasoning from vv. 4b–7, though that also begins to express confidence. Verses 16–17 parallel vv. 8–10, though they constitute not merely a statement of confidence but also a commitment to give testimony to Yhwh's protection when the crisis is over.

"With an artistic mixture of imagery and factual statement, the psalm sketches a positively eerie scenario of hostile intimidation and contrasts it with impressive images of YHWH as the protector and savior of those under deadly threat."[6] Alongside the developing intensity of the psalm is a liking for repetition of words, phrases, and lines, and for paronomasia.[7] Like previous psalms, Ps. 59 stresses the murderous capacity of words (v. 7; cf. 52:2 [4]; 57:4 [5]; also 64:3 [4]).[8]

The reference to the nations suggests that a ruler such as a king or governor speaks. One can imagine the psalm on the lips of someone such as Hezekiah or Nehemiah when their city is under pressure from an imperial power or from other local peoples. This is supported by references to God as "God of Israel" (v. 5) and as "our shield" (v. 11), to "my people" (v. 11), and to Yhwh's ruling over Jacob (v. 13), with the implication that in answering the prayer, Yhwh is so ruling. The link with Ps. 2 (see v. 8) might suggest that the king speaks.

> The leader's. Do not destroy. David's. Inscription. When Saul sent and they kept watch on his house to kill him.

Heading. See glossary. The last phrase refers to 1 Sam. 19:11, with the plan to kill David "in the morning" (cf. v. 16) after keeping watch overnight; the reference to "watching" makes for an interesting link with v. 9. Other links are Jonathan's claim for David's innocence and his warning about shedding blood (1 Sam. 19:4–5; cf. vv. 2–4); the fact that it was Michal through whom David escaped provokes the Midrash

6. Hossfeld and Zenger, *Psalms 2*, 85 (with the word "images" italicized in the original).

7. Auffret (*Voyez de vos yeux*, 95–116) systematically works out the implications of these for a reading of the psalm's structure.

8. For other links see Goulder, *Prayers of David*, 130.

213

into a series of comments on the value of a good wife.[9] In general the content of the psalm does not match David's situation at this moment, so that the psalm further illustrates the way the headings overlap verbally with the content of the psalm and suggest a possible context in which a person such as David might use it, rather than making a point about its actual origin.

59:1–4a. The psalm begins, then, with an appeal for action against the suppliant's attackers (vv. 1–2), supported by further description of them (v. 3a–b) and an appeal to the suppliant's own innocence (vv. 3c–4a).

> [1]Save me from my enemies, my God,
>   will you set me on high above those who rise against me.

The plea for deliverance is conventional, though also initially abrupt, so that the psalm's eventual development of forcefulness does cohere with this curt beginning. The intensity also emerges in the fact that every one of the five words has a first-person suffix: save *me* from *my* enemies, *my* God, lift *me* up above those who rise against *me*. The suppliant is entirely self-focused. The rest of the psalm will show why, though it will also see the suppliant moving away somewhat from that focus (see esp. vv. 16–17). The line is neatly parallel, in stepped abcb'a' order, with "save" (*nāṣal* hiphil) given more precision by "set me on high" (*śāgab* piel), whose yiqtol form offsets the abruptness of the opening imperative.[10] The second colon suggests that as the attackers are lifting themselves on high, the suppliant asks to be lifted up higher; the root *śāgab* will be taken up in the noun *miśgāb* in vv. 9 and 17.

> [2]Save me from people who do harm,
>   deliver me from people seeking bloodshed.

Intensification begins with a line that parallels v. 1, is internally parallel, and comprises verbs and construct phrases in abb'a' order. It begins by repeating the opening verb, this time paralleling it by the more familiar "*deliver." The enemies become compound expressions, people who do *harm and people of *bloodshed. Thus through the two lines the description of the enemies grows more worrying, but in both lines the verbs about deliverance surround and circumscribe the activity of the enemies.[11]

9. *Midrash on Psalms*, 1:508–12.
10. Further, "those who rise against me" (*qûm* polel) is a less common word than "my enemies" (the standard *'āyab*).
11. Cf. McCann, "Psalms," 912.

> ³ᵃ⁻ᵇBecause there, they lie in wait for my life,
>   they stir up strife [MT]/band together [Jerome, Tg] against me,
>   strong people.

Verbal clauses expand further on those two construct expressions. "Because there" and "strong people" come at either end of the line and apply to both cola, and "lie in wait for my life" and "stir up strife against me" parallel each other, so that the line works abcc′b′d. That gives some emphasis to the unexpected and worrying further description of the attackers with which the line closes. The deictic particle "there" (*hinnēh*) invites the addressee (God) to look at the reality to which the suppliant points, to the "strong people" (*ʿazzîm*) who come at the end of the line as an unexpected subject for the whole. The word's only other occurrence in the Psalms is 18:17 [18]; otherwise in the Psalms, strength is usually an attribute of God (e.g., 28:7–8). Attributing strength to attackers therefore again intensifies the plea. The suppliant is in serious trouble. These people lie in wait like a lion, and they stir up strife (MT; *gûr* is also a noun for a lion cub), working together as a pack (Jerome, Tg).

> ³ᶜNot because of my rebellion and not my shortcoming, Yhwh,
>   ⁴ᵃnor my waywardness, do they rush to organize themselves.

And they have no reason for doing so. The suppliant is not guilty of positive *rebellion nor negatively of *failing to meet obligations. In the parallel colon, *waywardness is the third of the OT's three dominant images for wrongdoing, so that the line makes a comprehensive claim about blamelessness. The terms might refer to offenses against the attackers or to offenses against God, of which the attackers might accuse the suppliant or which might make God decline to respond to the prayer. The double verbal expression also offers another way of conceptualizing their action, or two ways of doing so. They are people in a hurry, thus bringing extra pressure to the suppliant, and they are well organized. They establish themselves or sort themselves out for their project (*kûn hitpol*). The invocation stands at the center of the line somewhat like that in the first (though the rhythm means that this one belongs more unequivocally to the first colon), "Yhwh" thus pairing with "my God" as the first section of the psalm comes to an end.

59:4b–7. The reversion to imperative marks v. 4b as the beginning of a new section (against MT); it then becomes clear that vv. 4b–5 are two parallel lines of plea that correspond to vv. 1–2, followed by two parallel lines of background for it that correspond to vv. 3–4. This second four-line section is thus broadly parallel to the first, though it expresses itself much more strongly.

> ⁴ᵇGet up to meet with me, look, ⁵yes, you,
>   Yhwh, God, Armies, God of Israel.

Opening the first line, the imperative "get up" is familiar from 7:6 [7] and 44:23 [24] (also 35:23 in the hiphil), where it presupposes that Yhwh is at the moment seated in inactivity; it challenges Yhwh to stand up to act instead of sitting uninvolved. "To meet with me" has an ironic touch: that expression usually denotes a hostile encounter, but here it denotes joining with the suppliant to deliver, not to attack. But the first thing needed is for Yhwh to look. If the suppliant can thus get Yhwh's attention, action will surely follow. The invocation occupying the whole second colon backs up that. After all, the one addressed has the power as Yhwh *Armies and the commitment as Israel's God that make action both a possibility and a responsibility.

> ⁵ᵇWake up to attend to all the nations;
>   do not show grace to any harmful betrayers. (Rise)

One could see this second line as especially parallel to and expanding on v. 4b. "Wake up" is even straighter in its implications about what God is doing (or not doing) at the moment. God is apparently asleep and needs to wake up (cf. the parallelism in 35:23; 44:23 [24]: see the comment there). "Get up to meet (with me)" is thus paralleled by "Wake up to attend (to the attackers)." "Attend" (*pāqad*) also reverses the irony of "meet," since elsewhere in the Psalms it denotes an attentiveness with positive implications (8:4 [5]; 17:3; 65:9 [10]; 80:14 [15]; 106:4). Here the usage follows that more characteristic of the prophets, where "attending" is a euphemism for "punishing" (cf. Ps. 89:32 [33]). The second colon takes further the process of expanding on v. 4b, spelling out the implications of "attend" in negative terms in a plea as chilling as any in the Psalter. What more terrifying prayer could there be than to ask for Yhwh not to show *grace? It contrasts with the appeal for grace in other psalms (e.g., the redoubled one just now in 57:1 [2]), but it recalls Yhwh's commitment not to show grace to Israel itself because of its failure of response to God (Isa. 27:11). Like that threat it underlines the fact that there is indeed no cheap grace, no easygoing forgiveness for the persistent willfulness of the people of God, or of those who attack them (cf. Isa. 26:10, where the verb "show grace" recurs). People can only expect to experience Yhwh's grace if they turn from letting others down and seeking their *harm. (Although God often shows grace when we do not so turn, we cannot *expect* that.)

> ⁶Again and again they growl like a dog in the evening
>   as they go around the city.
> ⁷There, they bellow with their mouths,
>   swords on their lips,
>   because who is listening?

Verses 6–7 draw Yhwh's attention more specifically to the conduct that provokes such a terrible prayer. In v. 6, it is not clear why enemies should be focusing their activity in the evening. Perhaps that motif is part of the simile with which the first colon closes; dusk is the time when scavenging animals appear (Hab. 1:8; Zeph. 3:3). Going around the city could imply going about it inside the walls or going around its outside. If one thinks of a foreign army besieging the city, the latter is appropriate; but if one thinks of the kind of trouble Nehemiah refers to, the former might also apply. The implications of growling (*hāmâ*; cf. 46:3, 6 [4, 7]) and bellowing with metaphorical swords on their lips are illustrated in the speeches of the Rabshakeh in Hezekiah's day (2 Kings 18–19) or the taunts and plots of his detractors in Nehemiah's day (Neh. 4; 6). The question whether anyone is listening to their taunts and blasphemies also arises in these stories (see 2 Kings 19:16, 20; Neh. 4:4). The suppliant will echo it: Is Yhwh listening? At the same time, unpleasant creatures such as wild dogs might be seen as embodiments of demonic forces, like wild goats; Keel comments that "if in any psalm the adversaries of the suppliant bear demonic features," it is here.[12]

59:8–10. A new element following on the second section of plea and lament is this declaration of confidence in Yhwh as the one who will indeed protect the suppliant.

> ⁸But you, Yhwh, are amused at them,
>   you laugh at all the nations.

The opening affirmation corresponds to the one in Ps. 2:4, using the same two verbs in parallelism and in the same order, though addressed to Yhwh rather than stated in the third person. As well as thus making a confession, it implicitly claims an undertaking that Yhwh has made and challenges Yhwh to keep it. It is in keeping with this that the psalm refers to "all the nations" (cf. 2:1, 8). The psalm looks at the suppliant's present need in light of that general undertaking by Yhwh.[13] Theodoret adds a telling reference to Isa. 40:15.[14]

12. *Symbolism of the Biblical World*, 87.
13. One might, indeed, translate the verbs as impv., like the one in v. 1b, but the context in vv. 8–10 (and perhaps the link with Ps. 2) make a statement of confidence more likely. "But you are Yhwh; you are amused . . ." is also possible.
14. *Psalms*, 1:339.

217

> 9My strength, I will watch for you,
>   because God is my haven.

The invocation of Yhwh as "my *strength" is more distinctive; the last line of this psalm is the only other place where this expression comes as an invocation, though there are many places where Israelites confess Yhwh in such terms. Exodus 15:2 is tellingly the first of these (also Ps. 28:7–8; 46:1 [2]). Here the psalm acknowledges Yhwh's strength in light of the pressure from "strong people" (v. 3). Yhwh's strength is an attribute that enables Yhwh to take action against threats such as the one the psalm describes and makes it possible to "watch" for Yhwh like the lookout "watching" for the morning (130:6).[15] Although Saul's men watched David in hostile fashion (see the heading), the suppliant watches for Yhwh in expectant and hopeful fashion. The second colon is not formally parallel to the first, but is so in substance, since the idea of Yhwh as *haven (the root takes up the verb in v. 1b) links with that of Yhwh's strength. "Haven" and "strength" come together again in vv. 16–17 (cf. 46:1, 7, 11 [2, 8, 12]; 62:6–7 [7–8]). Yhwh is somewhere to hide in safety.

> 10The God who is committed to me will come to meet me;
>   God will enable me to look at my watchful foes.

The section closes with a further statement of confidence in parallel cola, in the third person rather than the first.[16] Here the metaphor of Yhwh as impersonal haven to which I go gives way to the metaphor of Yhwh as personal agent coming near to me. Like "watching" and the earlier "meeting," "come to meet" is often a negative image, suggesting attack (e.g., 18:5, 18 [6, 19]), not least when used of Yhwh (17:13). The verb thus hints that in a situation when people are approaching the suppliant with hostile intent, Yhwh will come near with more friendly implications (cf. 21:3 [4]). The result will be that the suppliant can "look at" the *watchful foes, presumably with relief or satisfaction, though "gloat" (NJPS, TNIV) is an overtranslation.[17]

59:11–13. The third section of plea again takes the psalm's logic forward. It had begun with a prayer for deliverance *from* attackers, moved to pray *against* them but in general terms, and now goes on to a series of eyebrow-raising and perhaps contradictory pleas, backed up by descrip-

15. Syr's *'šbḥ*, "I will sing," implies *'āšîrâ* for *'ešmōrâ*, assimilating to v. 16.
16. Hossfeld and Zenger (*Psalms 2*, 84, 85, 91) take the verbs as jussive and thus attach v. 11 to what follows.
17. For the verb, see 54:7 [9].

tions similar to those in vv. 6–7. While MT implicitly takes vv. 11–12 as two tricola, I have taken them as three bicola, broadly following NJPS, but there are many ways of analyzing them (see *BHS*; TNIV; NRSV for further possibilities).

> ¹¹ᵃ⁻ᵇDo not slay them, lest my people put them out of mind;
> make them stumble about, by your might,

The section begins with the eyebrow-raising plea for the attackers to be treated a little like the Canaanites, not annihilated but kept alive for the spiritual benefit of Israel (cf. Judg. 2:20–23; also Exod. 9:16). In asking for a relatively positive alternative to slaughter, the parallel colon uses a vivid verb (*nûaʿ*) that suggests people stumbling about because they are drunk or blind (Lam. 4:14) or perhaps wandering about because they have no home (Lam. 4:15).

> ¹¹ᶜAnd put them down, my Lord our shield,
> ¹²ᵃthrough the shortcoming of their mouth, the word on their lips,

The suppliant restates the fate desired for the attackers. If they are not to be slain, their being put down (*yārad* hiphil) might have to have a different meaning from that in 55:23 [24], perhaps suggesting their removal from a position of power so that they can no longer be a threat (cf. 56:7 [8]). The invocation of the *Lord as a shield expresses by means of another image the notion of the sovereign and powerful God's being a protection and a haven (vv. 1, 9); the combination of the singular and plural pronouns coheres with the idea that the suppliant prays as a leader of the community. The two parallel phrases in the second colon restate v. 7. They lack a preposition, and EVV take them to refer to the basis for the appeal ("for the shortcoming"). More likely they are implicitly governed by the "by" (*bĕ*) on either side or the "through" (*min*) in the parallel clause in v. 12c and indicate the means of the people being put down as well as the reason for it. They can make whatever plots they wish and utter whatever threats they wish; these will be their downfall.

> ¹²ᵇSo that they are caught by their majesty
> and through the oath and the lie that they proclaim.

In the statement of the aim of that putting down,[18] "caught" continues the military image, and the idea of being captured "by their majesty," as if it were a trap they have laid for themselves (cf. 9:15 [16]), also suggests a continuation of thinking. It is from their posi-

18. EVV take v. 12b as a jussive, but the *w* suggests a purpose clause.

tion of power and influence that the suppliant longs to see the attackers "put down," and it is by their power and influence, which traps them into making their attack, that they will be caught. They say, "Who is listening?" (v. 7), and their downfall lies in that statement of confidence arising out of their position. The first colon (v. 12b) thus parallels the first colon in the previous line (v. 11c), and v. 12c in turn parallels v. 12a in speaking of the attackers' use of words as the basis for their being put down. Here the words are oaths, which are worrying because they put pressure on the oath-makers to do what they have sworn and because they bid to harness the power of heaven to implement the oaths. And they are lies, which perhaps implies false accusations that might imperil the suppliant at the hands of people who believe them. But the oath and lie might also link with or imply curses. The fact that the verb "proclaim" (*sāpar* piel) suggests a public declaration fits with all that. It is ironic that the verb usually refers to the proclamation of Yhwh's deeds (e.g., 26:7; 40:5 [6]; 44:1 [2]; 48:13 [14]), and to the proclamation of Yhwh in 2:7, which links with Yhwh's laughing at the nations (see v. 8).

> [13]Put an end to them in wrath,
>   put an end to them so that they are no more,
> So that people may acknowledge that God rules over Jacob,
>   to the ends of the earth. (Rise)

The further plea to put an end to them is surprising after v. 11a. We can make a logical story out of vv. 11–13: the attackers are not to be instantly slain like Sennacherib's army but to be put down in such a way that they stumble and stagger toward Sheol before the eyes of Israel, or "put an end to them" might mean bring to an end their status as a sovereign people. But we could equally take v. 13a at its face value on the basis of the awareness that "burning indignation [or abject terror] does not study logical consistency."[19] The verb, repeated for emphasis, is first qualified by a statement of how or why Yhwh will act (if the act is undertaken in wrath, the job will be done properly) and then further qualified by a statement of its consequent result.

The people whom the suppliant hopes will learn from what happens are presumably not the attackers themselves, who are now dead (unless we are again not to press for too much logic in this anxious prayer). Neither are they "my people," the explicit subject in v. 11a; at least, they are not only people in Israel. The second colon indicates that they are the peoples of the world in general; the phrase forms another link with

19. Kirkpatrick, *Psalms*, 336.

the promise in Ps. 2 (see 2:8).[20] The content of the confession to which they are to be drawn implies that they understand Yhwh's rule over Jacob to be a beneficent one. Yhwh's making decisions for Jacob means that its attackers are put down, but people in general have nothing to fear from that.[21]

59:14–15. A renewed lament at the attackers' actions follows.

> [14]So again and again they growl like a dog in the evening
>   as they go around the city.
> [15]These—they stumble about for food
>   if they do not have plenty and stay the night.

After the repetition of v. 6 (except for the added *w* at the beginning), the lament takes off in a different direction from v. 7. With further irony, the attackers are described—within the comparison with scavenging animals—as already lurching or wandering about (cf. v. 11) in their quest for food, instead of bellowing for it and expecting to find it. So v. 15 might continue to describe the way they cause trouble, but more likely makes a transition to describing in different terms yet again the fate that will overtake them: not death and destruction but frustration because they will not fulfill their aims. I have taken the final verb as *lûn* I used in its usual way, not least on the basis of links between vv. 15–16 and 30:5 [6]. The colon then suggests either that the "dogs" have to spend the night scavenging (cf. Tg), or—if the negative carries its force into the second clause—that because they do not have food they cannot settle down for the night (cf. Syr). Either way, the line continues to describe the pressure the attackers put on the suppliant, though it also implies that they do not succeed in their attacks. The LXX and Jerome, however, take this as a unique qal use of *lûn* II, "moan," which underlines their failure and also suggests yet another irony. "Moaning" (*lûn* niphal or hiphil) is elsewhere Israel's activity, especially on the way to the promised land (e.g., Num. 14:2, 36). So these attackers will find themselves in the position Israel reckoned it occupied during its wanderings (the verb for "wander," *nûaʿ*, comes in Num. 32:13), always looking for something to eat and not finding it. Even when Israel did stumble about and complain, Yhwh did fill them with plenty (*śābaʿ*; Ps. 105:40; 107:9; with more equivo-

---

20. That link makes it unlikely that the psalm refers to Israelites spread through the world who hear of this deliverance or Israelites throughout the land. See also Keel, *Symbolism*, 42.

21. But Qimchi refers this to the nations seeing God's judgment on wicked Israelites, comparing Amos 3:2.

cal connotations, 78:29; Exod. 16:8, 12). That will not be the destiny of these scavengers.[22]

59:16–17. The last two verses correspond to vv. 8–10 in expressing confidence in God but take the actual form of a promise to give testimony to Yhwh's deliverance.

> ¹⁶But I—I will sing of your strength,
>   I will resound in the morning at your commitment,
> Because you will have been a haven for me,
>   a refuge at the time when I was in trouble.

The promise follows on directly from vv. 14–15, linked by *w*, suggesting a contrast between the words of the attackers and the words of the suppliant. Whereas the former are reduced from bellowing expectantly to stumbling about (and perhaps complaining) because they do not have what they have expected, the suppliant will have something to sing about. The unnecessary "I" over against the unnecessary "these" in v. 15 underlines the contrast. The parallelism works abcb′dc′. *Resound thus corresponds to sing; the former suggests volume, the latter implies words with content. *Commitment in turn corresponds to *strength, the two together suggesting two sides to Yhwh's character (see esp. 62:11–12 [12–13]); both pick up the earlier declaration of confidence (see vv. 9–10). The reference to morning, a time of deliverance and/or praise (e.g., 5:3 [4]; 46:5 [6]; 49:14 [15]), also makes for a contrast with the earlier reference to evening as a time of scavenging, disappointment, and complaint. The line suggests a fuller comparison with 30:5 [6], where the verb *lûn* (v. 15 here) recurs in the course of making a contrast between grief at the experience of people's attacks at "evening" and "resounding" that comes with "morning."

The rationale for that praise again picks up from vv. 9–10 with their reference to Yhwh as a haven. The equivalent word in the parallel colon, *mānôs* (refuge), makes a different link with the earlier part of the psalm, since its root verb, *nûs*, makes a nice contrast with the twice-repeated verb *nûaʿ* (vv. 11, 15; even though one could hardly press the point that these two roots come next to one another in BDB!). Having Yhwh as refuge contrasts with stumbling about because Yhwh has acted.

> ¹⁷My strength, for you I will make music,
>   because God is my haven, the God who is committed to me.

---

22. LXX and Jerome (and EVV) further have to assume that as well as being a unique use of *lûn*, *wayyālînû* is wayyiqtol in the apodosis of a conditional clause, a very rare construction (DG 79; GKC 111t). Josef Tropper ("Sie knurrten wie Hunde," *ZAW* 106 [1994]: 87–95) argues for *lîn*.

The final line repeats vv. 9–10a, with variations, like those of vv. 14–15 in relation to vv. 6–7. "I will make music" is an especially subtle change from "I will watch," involving only one consonant (*zāmar* for *šāmar* in v. 10). Watching is what the suppliant has to do now; making *music will be possible then. Verse 17 also parallels the two lines that precede, comprising a declaration of intent about testimony and some reasons in a *kî* clause. The new verb parallels "sing" and "resound" but points rather to melody and rhythm.

Theological Implications

Psalm 59 prays with particular urgency out of a sense of grave danger. It shows that when people are helpless, they can pray in extreme ways. There is little that is moderate or balanced about the psalm. It describes the enemies in immoderate ways, and its petitions are immoderate. Christians are usually hesitant to address God with the freedom that the psalms use. Christians behave as if God is more like a judge or headmaster than a father; the OT assumes that we are rather like children in relation to parents in our freedom to address God and can speak as freely as children do to parents.

Most of the readers of this commentary will never find themselves in the dire situation presupposed by the psalm, but countless people in the world (many of them Jews or Christians) are in this situation. Today, I think of American, British, and Iraqi people in Iraq and of Israelis and Palestinians. The psalm invites people who cannot or must not attack their attackers and specifically invites their leaders (who are particularly exposed to danger) to bring their terror to God and to articulate to God their desire for their attackers to be put down.

Psalm 60

How to Claim God's Past Word

Translation

The leader's. On Lily.[1] Testimony. Inscription. David's. For teaching. When he fought against Aram-naharaim and Aram-zobah, and Joab returned and hit Edom in the Valley of Salt, twelve thousand of them.

[1]God, you have spurned us, broken out upon us, been angry:
   will you turn to us.[2]
[2]You have shaken the land and torn it open;
   mend its cracks, because it has collapsed.
[3]You have made your people see hardship,
   you have made us drink wine that made us reel.[3]
[4]You have given[4] those who revere you a banner
   to flee to because of the bow.[5] (Rise)
[5]So that your beloved may be rescued,
   deliver with your right hand and answer us [K]/me [Q].[6]

1. Only this heading uses the word in the sg. The MT accent takes it as const., but the form can also be abs., and the other occurrences (of the pl.) are all abs.
2. The yiqtol is less confrontational than an impv.
3. Lit. "wine, reeling."
4. NJPS and DG 60c take this as a precative qatal (which would then form a third way of bidding God to act, after the yiqtol and the impv.), but the preceding qatals are all indicatives, and indicative makes sense here.
5. Unusually, not *qešet* but *qōšeṭ*, which could mean "truth" (Tg), but that makes poor sense here (see BDB).
6. K has *w'nnw*, Q *wa'ănēnî*; so also LXX, Jerome, and Tg. K fits what precedes; Q's first sg. may assimilate to what follows and to Ps. 108:6 [7].

[6]God spoke by his holiness:
I will exultantly allocate Shechem
   and measure out the Vale of Succot.
[7]Gilead will be mine,
   Manasseh will be mine,
Ephraim will be my helmet,
   Judah my scepter.
[8]Moab will be my washbasin,[7]
   at Edom I will throw my shoe;
   raise a shout against me,[8] Philistia.
[9]Who will bring me to the fortified city,
   who might lead[9] me to Edom?

[10]Have you yourself not spurned us, God?—
   and you do not go out among our armies, God.
[11]Give us your help against the foe,[10]
   given that[11] human deliverance is empty.
[12]Through God we will act with might;
   he himself will trample down our foes.

Interpretation

This congregational psalm opens with a protest, such as appears in many prayer psalms (cf. esp. Ps. 44) at the way God has abandoned the people, and with prayer for deliverance (vv. 1–5). Much more unusually, it then quotes a word from God (vv. 6–9). This word does not directly address the preceding protest and in a sense implicitly continues it: the fact that God long ago made this declaration underlines the oddness of the experience the psalm laments. Verses 10–12 thus renew the protest and the prayer and express confidence that God will make deliverance possible. The way the protest leads into the recollection of the oracle,

7. LXX's "my hope basin" reflects the meaning of a second root *rāḥaṣ* in Aramaic. Luther infers that the psalm refers to a cooking pot, comments that "we must deal with the mystery of cooking," and goes on to do so (*First Lectures*, 2:286–92).

8. NJPS has "acclaim me," but the *'al* is then odd. Syr assimilates to the different text in 108:9 [10]; cf. NRSV, TNIV.

9. Gunkel reads *mî yanḥēnî* for MT's *mî nāḥanî* (haplog.; *Psalmen*, 259), but the qatal can be used in doubtful questions (see *TTH* 19). Barthélemy (*Psaumes*, 393) suggests that the *y* on *mî* does double duty; it also functions as a preformative *y* on the verb, which is thus yiqtol.

10. LXX takes *miṣṣār* as from *ṣar*, meaning "adversity" (cf. 4:1 [2]), but it has to mean "foe" in v. 12b.

11. The *w* marks this as something more like a circumstantial clause than a causal one (see *TTH* 159, against GKC 158a; JM 170c).

and that into the renewed protest, puts a question mark by the view that sees the psalm as a liturgy.[12]

Although the psalm seems to presuppose a particular historical context and makes concrete geographical allusions, as usual it lacks the kind of concreteness that would enable us to adjudicate between the many proposals for a date, which include the time of David,[13] the divided monarchy, the eve or the experience of exile,[14] the Persian period, and the Maccabean period. Fortunately the *kind* of context it presupposes is clear, so that lack of certain historical knowledge does not much affect an understanding of the psalm. It presupposes a situation in which people have experienced reversal but have a word from God to claim, and it would prove useful in the many times of conflict with Edom before, during, and after the exile.

A variant of vv. 5–12 reappears as part of Ps. 108.

The leader's. On Lily. Testimony. Inscription. David's. For teaching. When he fought against Aram-naharaim and Aram-zobah, and Joab returned and hit Edom in the Valley of Salt, twelve thousand of them.

Heading. See glossary. "For teaching" comes only here in the headings, but it recalls 2 Sam. 1:18. For the incident the heading alludes to, see 2 Sam. 8, which refers to Moab and Philistia as well as Edom (cf. v. 8); also 2 Sam 10:6–19.[15] Second Samuel 8:13 has "eighteen thousand" rather than "twelve thousand," presumably reflecting variant text forms. Second Samuel 8:2 also twice uses the verb "measure out" (cf. v. 6). The reference to Aram-naharaim may relate to the journey to the Euphrates mentioned there, or it may derive from the psalm's possible allusion to Jacob's journey back from northern Mesopotamia in v. 6. If one reads the psalm in light of the heading, the national reverses in vv. 1–5, 10–11 will be the ones that antedated David's own reign.[16]

60:1–5. The opening five lines combine protest and accusation (vv. 1a, 2a, 3–4) with plea for action to reverse God's bringing trouble (v. 1b, 2b, 5).[17] Verse 1 focuses on God's attitude, v. 2 on the needs of the land, and vv. 3–5 on the needs of the people.

---

12. So John W. Hilber, *Cultic Prophecy in the Psalms*, BZAW 352 (Berlin: de Gruyter, 2005), 198–202.

13. E.g., Broyles, *Conflict of Faith and Experience*, 145.

14. E.g., Ulrich Kellermann, "Erwägungen zum historischen Ort von Psalm lx," *VT* 28 (1978): 56–65; Ernst A. Knauf, "Psalm lx und Psalm cviii," *VT* 50 (2000): 55–65. Graham S. Ogden ("Psalm 60," *JSOT* 31 [1985]: 83–94) then sees Isa. 63:1–6 as a response to the psalm.

15. Raymond J. Tournay discusses the "Davidic rereading" of this psalm in "Psaumes 57, 60 et 108," *RB* 96 (1989): 5–26.

16. Cf. Calvin, *Psalms*, 2:398.

17. Cf. Auffret, *Voyez de vos yeux*, 71.

> [1]God, you have spurned us, broken out upon us, been angry:
> will you turn to us.

Against MT I take v. 1 as 4-2, understanding the accusation to occupy the whole first colon and the brief plea to occupy the second. Either way, after the opening invocation the three asyndetic verbs powerfully pile up the psalm's protest. On "spurned," see on 44:9 [10]. "Break" (*pāraṣ*) is a more concrete, vivid, and complex expression; it might suggest breaking the people down, breaking them up, or breaking out upon them. The verbs on either side refer to God's attitude and thus suggest the last meaning, though the way this attitude expresses itself and the clue that tells people that this is God's attitude is in the experience of being broken down or broken up. Similar considerations apply to the declaration that God is angry, which is another way of saying that the people have experienced God acting in the way someone acts when they are angry. Over against those three asyndetic verbs is then the brief plea for a change in attitude on God's part, a turning back on the part of the one who has turned away.[18]

> [2]You have shaken the land and torn it open;
> mend its cracks, because it has collapsed.

In moving to the needs of the land, again the first colon protests at what God has done, portraying the land as the victim of something like a landslide caused by a violent storm, which God has brought about. And again the second colon comprises a plea to reverse what the first colon has described. "Mend" is *rāpâ'*, the verb meaning "heal," and the affective connotations of that verb may carry over into this usage. The EVV have the land "collapsing," but the qatal verb rather implies it has actually collapsed.

> [3]You have made your people see hardship,
> you have made us drink wine that made us reel.

The third protest and plea will go on for three times as long as the first two, implying that the psalm's most pressing agenda lies here. The fact that the psalm now becomes more expansive gives it the scope to use parallelism, and here two second-person hiphil verbs introduce parallel descriptions of what God has done. One is more abstract, and one more concrete but metaphorical. The first is tough: hardship (*qāšâ*) was the

---

18. Cf. Tg and LXX. EVV have "restore us," but *lānû* is then odd, and after the preceding three verbs, a verb that denotes a movement on God's part fits better. For the intransitive use of *šûb* pol, see BDB and *HALOT*.

people's experience in Egypt (Exod. 1:14; 6:9; Deut. 26:6). But the second goes beyond it: the experience involves not merely hard work but also deathly danger. God's making the people see hardship has meant giving them a poisoned cup to drink, in the manner of an assassin at a Middle Eastern banquet. Both hardship and drinking poison are terms used to describe the exile (Isa. 14:3; 51:17, 22): it is an experience like the exile that the people have had. And it is "your people" you have done this to. In light of the second colon, the verb *rāʾâ* (see) might be reckoned to remind people of *rāwâ*, "drink deeply."[19]

> [4]You have given those who revere you a banner
>   to flee to because of the bow. (Rise)

Further, they are people who *revere you. Although the psalm does not include an explicit "declaration of innocence" like that in Ps. 44, this implies one. The people God has treated in this way are worshippers and servants of God. Whereas the Midrash suggests that God has spurned the people because they have spurned God (cf. Hos. 8:3),[20] the psalm does not see matters this way. There is also a snide implication to the sentence. The first colon speaks of God giving a gift, and Tg assumes that the banner is a good gift. After a triumphant deliverance following the exodus, Moses declared that Yhwh *was* the people's banner (Exod. 17:15). Prophets speak of a banner for the gathering of exiles to return to Jerusalem (e.g., Isa. 11:12). But the second colon goes on to indicate that this is a banner with negative implications, a banner for people to flee to as they run from a hail of arrows directed at them, perhaps a banner that summons people to take refuge in the city (cf. Jer. 4:6).[21] The words *nēs* and *hitnôsēs* (banner, flee to) comprise a paronomasia,[22] the aural similarity belying the contrast; banners are ideally designed for soldiers setting out for victory, not for fleeing to. Verse 4 also completes a triple paronomasia between *qāšâ* (hardship), *hišqîtānû* (you have made us drink), and *qešeṭ* (bow); the bow is the means of bringing the hardship for which being made to drink poison is a metaphor.

> [5]So that your beloved may be rescued,
>   deliver with your right hand and answer us. [K]/me. [Q]

19. Cf. G. R. Driver, "Notes on the Psalms," *JTS* 36 (1935): 147–56 (see 151–53).
20. *Midrash on Psalms*, 1:514.
21. It thus makes rhetorical sense to divide the line 3-3, not 4-2 with MT.
22. Goulder, *Psalms of David*, 146. Tg and Aq indeed take *hitnôsēs* as a denominative from *nēs* (to raise/rally to) rather than a form from *nûs* ("to flee to"; so LXX, Jerome). The idea is still that the people are overwhelmed by the enemy.

After the two lines of protest at the way God has treated the people, these lines make their plea arising from that. Unusually, it begins with a statement of the purpose of the act it seeks; this first colon also includes a third description of the people designed to motivate God. As well as being "your people" and "those who revere you," they are "your beloved" (yĕdîdêkā), a strong term of endearment (cf. Isa. 5:1), recalling the name of David himself (from a by-form of this root) and the name Yhwh gave Solomon, Yedidiah (2 Sam. 12:25). Surely God accepts the desirability of rescuing these beloved from the attacks they are experiencing. (The term is used with an opposite irony in Jer. 11:15.) The second colon then brings vv. 1–5 to a climax with verbs denoting the action God needs to take to that end. It is not enough that verbs relating to rescue should appear in the passive (as happens in the first colon); they need a subject. The hand that has been raised in striking the people needs to be raised to deliver them. The line then closes with an appeal to "answer" or "respond," reflecting the fact that the psalms' understanding of answers to prayer has in mind actions, not just words.

60:6–9. A word from God follows, an unusual feature in a psalm. One might have expected it to be a word of response, but it seems not to be that. The word that follows goes behind the present crisis to the basis of the nation's life, the divine will with regard to the land as a whole and its environs. This constitutes, then, not a word God now utters, but a word the psalm recalls for the sake of the one who uttered it and of the people who need to be able to keep claiming it. The NRSV and TNIV take verses 6–8 as three tricola, but this would be a very unusual arrangement, and the actual oracle can as naturally be taken as a series of bicola (except for v. 8), with v. 6a as an extrametrical introduction. I infer the time reference of the noun clauses in vv. 7–8 from the verbal clauses in the lines on either side.

> [6]God spoke by his holiness:
> I will exultantly allocate Shechem
>   and measure out the Vale of Succot.

This speaking, then, is a speaking that occurred when Yhwh arrived at the land with the Israelites, according to the story as now told in Joshua. It constitutes a very solemn asseveration. In 150:1 bĕqodšô means "in his sanctuary," and Jerome and Tg take it thus here (LXX and Syr are ambiguous, like the Hebrew). But in connection with oaths it means "by his holiness" (Amos 4:2; cf. Ps. 89:35 [36]). If the statement that follows were one made in response to this prayer, "in his sanctuary" would be plausible, but if the statement is one Yhwh made long ago, its location seems less relevant than its seriousness. Yhwh made a solemn personal commitment to the declaration that follows. The statement is a kind of restatement of Yhwh's promise to Abraham or of a principle that underlies that promise. Yhwh claims ownership of the land that is to be described, and therefore claims the right to allocate it to people. The implied setting of the statement is the moment when Israel has achieved its occupation of the land, which Joshua describes as coming to its completion at Shechem (Josh. 8:30–35; cf. Deut. 27:11–13), the implicit location of the distribution of the land in Josh. 13–22 (and cf. Josh. 24:1). Perhaps tradition preserved the poetic declaration by Yhwh about this allocation that follows, or perhaps it is a contemporary summary of what Deuteronomy and Joshua describe Yhwh as assuming back then.[23] It does not have a close relationship to the promise in 2 Sam. 7, nor need it presuppose that Ephraim has already fallen.[24]

Only here does God "exult":[25] it is a very human term for uninhibited rejoicing, a striking testimony to God's impassioned nature. God really enjoys the idea of (for instance) "allocating" Shechem. The EVV translate *ḥālaq* as "divide," but Shechem is a city to be allocated to a clan (namely, Ephraim), not one to be divided.[26] "Measure out" likely has similar implications, since God will not measure out allocations within the Vale of Succot (in Gilead, across the Jordan) but will allocate it to one of the clans (namely, Gad; see Josh. 13:24, 27). These two places thus stand for the land west and east of the Jordan, perhaps chosen because they recapitulate Jacob's journey in Gen. 33:17–18.

> [7]Gilead will be mine,
>   Manasseh will be mine,
> Ephraim will be my helmet,
>   Judah my scepter.

Verse 7a–b (2-2) then parallels that (in abb′a′ order) and generalizes it, with its reference to the area to which Succot belongs and then to Manasseh, Ephraim's twin clan (perhaps the psalm refers to the part of Manasseh east of the Jordan, so that the whole line denotes that area as a whole).

23. NJPS takes the lines that follow as indirect speech, the speaker presumably being David. But there is no *kî*, the speakers in the psalm so far have been pl., and it is not clear why David would give such attention to (e.g.) allocating Shechem or measuring out Succot (*pace* Goulder, *Psalms of David*, 147–48).

24. Seybold (*Psalmen*, 237) dates it in the time of Josiah.

25. Christopher R. North ("*'e'lōzâ 'ăhallĕqâ šĕkem,*" *VT* 17 [1967]: 242–43) therefore argues for reading the last syllable as enclitic *zeh*.

26. Even if Shechem stands for Samaria, Yhwh does not divide it up but leaves that to the clan.

The psalm then moves even further away to look at the big picture of God's claims. Here Ephraim is explicitly mentioned, but the parallelism with Judah suggests that it refers to the northern kingdom as a whole, as Judah will refer to the southern kingdom as a whole. But the line relates to peoples and not just territories. It constitutes a claim not only to be sovereign over these territories but also to use these peoples as a means of exercising sovereignty. God is the warrior who invades them in order to take control of them, but God acts as warrior by means of these two peoples. So Ephraim is like the headgear that the warrior wears for protection, and Judah is like the commander's staff that the warrior wields. The two terms thus complement each other, one protective, one aggressive. The latter term recurs from Gen. 49:10, where it applies to Judah (see also Num. 21:18). Literally, it is simply a commander (*mĕḥōqēq*; cf. LXX, Jerome), apparently a metonymy rather like the English word "staff" applied to people.

> [8]Moab will be my washbasin,
>   at Edom I will throw my shoe;
>   raise a shout against me, Philistia.

The position of surrounding peoples is quite different. Whereas Ephraim and Judah are honorable parts of the warrior's equipment, Moab is simply the basin in which he washes his mucky feet. The term recalls the foul-smelling Moabite water, the Dead Sea. It is the second colon that makes explicit that the basin is for washing feet[27] as it adds that Edom is where the warrior throws his shoes as he does so. An obscure passage in Ruth indicates that removing a shoe could be associated with some questions about ownership of land (Ruth 4:7), but the parallel with the warrior throwing his shoe at something is not close. The notion of ownership does not seem relevant in v. 8, though both passages might suggest a gesture of contempt. Yhwh does claim ownership of the land of Israel but does not in the same sense claim ownership of Moab, Edom, and Philistia. Yhwh is certainly ultimately sovereign over them, as the line presupposes and as the exodus story specifically notes (cf. Exod. 15:14–15),[28] and Yhwh does allocate these lands to their peoples, but they are not part of Yhwh's land. Indeed, the line makes almost a contrary point. Moab and Edom are just places where the warrior washes his feet and throws his dirty shoes at the end of the day. In light of that (the unexpected third colon snidely adds), Philistia is welcome to raise the battle shout against Yhwh. While Yhwh does not claim a special relation-

27. Cf. Dahood, *Psalms*, 2:80.
28. Cf. McCann, "Psalms," 917.

ship to any of these territories, an implication of v. 8 would be that one would not expect Moab, Edom, or Philistia to be causing trouble to the people who are God's helmet and staff. The line thus implies a contrast with the experience to which vv. 1–5 testify. On the other hand, 2 Sam. 8 (the story the heading refers to) seems to prove the truth of v. 8, since that chapter records a series of aggressive victories rather than a series of occasions when these peoples put David under pressure.

> 9Who will bring me to the fortified city,
>   who might lead me to Edom?

The "I" continues in these two parallel cola, so presumably God continues to speak.[29] It is admittedly unique for God to talk in terms of being brought or led; God is elsewhere the subject of these verbs (e.g., 23:3; 27:11; Jer. 31:9).[30] But the picture of God as commander in chief asking where the scouts are to show the way to a city is no more anthropomorphic than the images of vv. 6–8, such as the picture of God needing some protective headgear (v. 7; cf. also 35:2 and the looking around in Isa. 59:15–16 where this language also recurs). In v. 9, then, God seeks to call the people who are God's weaponry or army to be about their work. The question is not a despairing one but a challenging one. We do not know what is "the fortified city" or whether the second colon defines it as a city in Edom, whether God rather has two projects in mind, or whether the first term stands for cities in general and the second makes it more concrete. Reference to Edom might suggest that this summary of God's intentions reflected the time of David noted by the heading or the time after the exile when Judah would have wished to regain land occupied by Edom. The Midrash interestingly applies the two cola to the Roman and Byzantine Empires.[31]

60:10–12. The invocation shows that the psalm marks a change of speaker to that of the first section and reverts to its concern, which is now reinforced by the recollection in vv. 6–9. The solemn declaration has not been fulfilled. Will God now do something about it?

> 10Have you yourself not spurned us, God?—
>   and you do not go out among our armies, God.

---

29. Commentators usually assume that someone else—perhaps the king—speaks, but there is no indication of such a transition here; contrast the reversion to pl. verbs in v. 10. Cf. Fokkelman, *Major Poems*, 3:105; but contrast Hossfeld and Zenger, *Psalms 2*, 97.

30. In isolation, the first colon might be read as "who will bring me the besieged city [as an offering]?" which would suit Yhwh being the speaker, but the parallel second colon provides the prep. "to" and makes the first unambiguous.

31. *Midrash on Psalms*, 1:516.

The opening pronoun thus responds to vv. 6–9, though it does so in a subtle way. Initially we might translate the opening words "Is it not you, God?" (cf. LXX, Jerome) and take them as a statement of confidence, but the rest of the line undoes that understanding. Rather, it suggests that whereas God has looked for someone to show the way to the city that needs taking, for the community it feels as if they are doing their part but God is not acting: "You are asking who will show the way, but *you* are the problem." The accusation of spurning takes up that in v. 1. The parallel colon indicates once more where the evidence of spurning lies. That past act is inferred from the present experience that the one who talks about taking the city is actually missing when the army advances. Spurning is regularly the implication of this. Their defeat indicates that they do not just *feel* abandoned. The presence of God and abandonment are empirical realities not feelings. The evidence of abandonment is clear. "God" stands at the center of each colon, but "God" is surrounded by accusation of abandonment and letdown.

> [11]Give us your help against the foe,
>   given that human deliverance is empty.

As happened through vv. 1–5, the protest leads into a plea. Verse 4 had spoken about one form of giving; v. 11 asks for a new form (though the verb is now the rarer *yāhab*), the giving of *help. The second colon buttresses the plea with a new consideration, though the language is not so new. The protests and pleas in vv. 1–5 had concluded with a plea for God to deliver by using the right hand that is so powerful; vv. 10–11 conclude their protests and pleas with the correlative acknowledgment that "human *deliverance is empty" (on this word, see the comments on 89:47 [48]).

> [12]Through God we will act with might;
>   he himself will trample down our foes.

The psalm closes on a note of confidence. In a sense this is unexpected, though it is a common feature of prayer psalms. The two cola interestingly complement each other. The first declares a confidence about our action, action undertaken "through God," but *our* action. For *b* the EVV have "with," but "through" more clearly expresses the point, which is not that God accompanies the people but that God is the means of their acting. "Might" spells out the point, following as it does the affirmation about God's might in 59:11 [12]. Leading on from v. 11, the colon's declaration also bears comparison with 33:16–17. But how does this work? How do we act with might through God? The second colon does not answer that

233

question, but perhaps underlines it with its complementary formulation. Here God is the subject of the verb. It will be the Israelite forces that directly trample down their foes; but behind their action will be God's. And the order perhaps implies that it is the second that is decisive. The "he himself" (*hû'*) balances the "you yourself" at the beginning of this final section, while the confident statement about "foes" balances the protest about the "foe" in v. 11.

Theological Implications

The distinctive feature of Ps. 60 is the word of Yhwh from the past that it incorporates. The content of that word indicates that God does claim ownership of the land of Israel, the area on either side of the Jordan that forms the traditional allocation of the twelve clans and also claims sovereignty over the peoples around who might dispute occupation of that land. (This does not provide a shortcut to the resolution of political questions in the Middle East today.) When the people of God find themselves not experiencing life in a way that coheres with that word, the psalm embodies four appropriate reactions. One is a protest to God for abandoning them. A second is a plea to return to them and restore them. A third is reminding God and ourselves of the word under which we live our lives and which obligates God. A fourth is confidence that God will do that and confidence about acting in light of it. "Faith is never happier than when it can fall back upon the promise of God."[32]

32. Spurgeon, *Treasury of David*, 3:30.

Psalm 61

How Prayer Suspends
the Distantness

Translation

The leader's. With a stringed instrument.[1] David's.

[1]Listen to my voice, God,
    attend to my plea.
[2]From the end of the earth I will call to you
    when my heart flags.
Will you lead me to a crag that rises high above me,[2]
    [3]for you have been a refuge to me,
    a strong tower before the enemy.

[4]I shall stay in your tent forever;
    I shall find refuge in the shelter of your wings. (Rise)
[5]For you yourself, God, will have listened to my promises;
    you will have given their allocation to the people who revere your
        name.

1. This heading alone has *'al nĕgînat* (a dialectical sg. abs. form, not a const.; see GKC 80f). LXX and Jerome assimilate to the more usual *binĕgînōt*.
2. Not merely "that is higher than I" (NRSV, TNIV), which is not saying much, nor "that is too high for me"; if that were the meaning, we would expect a verb for "lift" rather than "lead" (and see next note).

235

⁶May you add days to the days of the king,
  his years, like one generation after another.³
⁷May he live⁴ forever before God;
  appoint commitment and truthfulness to guard him.

⁸Thus I shall make music to your name evermore
  in fulfilling⁵ my promises day by day.

Interpretation

The psalm is usually seen as a prayer, but it has also been reckoned
to be a thanksgiving.⁶ I take it as something that stands between these,
a psalm of trust or confidence.⁷ It presupposes the need to call on God
in prayer, but it incorporates no statement of urgent need such as often
appears in a prayer psalm, and v. 3 indeed looks back to an experience
of God's deliverance. But after a plea (vv. 1–3) it soon moves on to declarations of confidence in God (vv. 4–5). A concern with the king then
suddenly comes into focus (vv. 6–7) and as quickly disappears while the
psalm ends with a promise of praise (v. 8).⁸ Although one might read the
whole psalm as an ordinary person's prayer incorporating a prayer for
the king, if we see the psalm as a whole as a king's prayer, that fits some
of the imagery earlier in the psalm. For those two lines, then, the king
moves from praying directly for himself to praying for the king in the
third person.⁹ I take it to imply a time when Israel has a king and thus
to be preexilic, but there is no basis for further precision.¹⁰

The leader's. With a stringed instrument. David's.

Heading. See glossary.

3. Lit. "like a generation and a generation": perhaps implying (to put it prosaically),
"May he reign through the time of one generation and through the next."
4. BDB takes *yāšab* to mean "sit enthroned," but this is not a common usage, and
the rest of the line rather points to the more regular meaning.
5. Perhaps the common inf. of purpose or perhaps simply circumstantial (cf. GKC
114o).
6. So Weiser, *Psalms*, 443.
7. Cf. Gerstenberger, *Psalms*, 2:6 (though he takes it as a congregational psalm, dating it in the exile or afterward).
8. See further Pierre Auffret, "Essai sur la structure littéraire du Psaume 61," *JANESCU*
14 (1982): 1–10; W. H. Bellinger, *A Hermeneutic of Curiosity* (Macon, GA: Mercer University
Press, 1995), 25–38.
9. If vv. 6–7 are a later addition (so Gunkel, *Psalmen*, 261), this still leaves us to
consider how the psalm as we have it functions.
10. Beat Weber ("Psalm lxi," *VT* 43 [1993]: 265–68) argues for the time of Hezekiah.

61:1–3. The first three lines constitute the personal plea in the psalm, but the psalm is noticeably lacking in any description of a predicament and instead seems to be a general prayer for God to be attentive (v. 1) when times of need come (v. 2a–b) and to act as in the past (vv. 2c–3).

> ¹Listen to my voice, God,
>   attend to my plea.

The parallelism compares with that in 17:1. Both the imperatives have the slightly deferential -*â* sufformative, the second verb heightening the first. The first noun (more literally "*resounding noise/sound*," suggesting something loud and urgent) is then given more precision by the second.

> ²ᵃ⁻ᵇFrom the end of the earth I will call to you
>   when my heart flags.

I take the second line as a description of the circumstances in which the suppliant from time to time calls on God. Both prepositional phrases qualify the verbal phrase at the center, which applies to each of them. They thus describe two different aspects of the kind of situation out of which the suppliant prays, or two different situations. One involves being far away from the presence of God in Jerusalem; the king would have reason to be far away when battle required this. "The end of the 'ereṣ" usually means the end of the earth (a campaign in a country such as Moab could count as that), but the expression could denote the end of the land (as the context shows it must in Jer. 12:12). The king could use it in connection with either context.[11] The other aspect of the situation involves one's heart flagging. The verb ('āṭap) suggests becoming exhausted through pressures and demands, which might also point to a situation when the king is on campaign. The phrase suggests a person's whole being running out of energy; it is not merely a statement about how one feels inside (contrast EVV "my heart faints").

> ²ᶜWill you lead me to a crag that rises high above me,
>   ³for you have been a refuge to me,
>   a strong tower before the enemy.

11. "The brink of the underworld" (Dahood, *Psalms*, 2:84) requires an unusual meaning for both words.

The plea comes to a climax with a tricolon.[12] The NJPS understands it as a statement ("You lead me . . ."), but this leaves going nowhere the plea to which vv. 1–2b have referred. Rather vv. 2c–3 *are* that plea (cf. NRSV, TNIV). "Lead" picks up the verb in 60:9 [11]. Following on the two ways of describing the suppliant's need in v. 2a–b, the geographical and the physiological, the tricolon introduce a third, a natural/military image with several variants. The suppliant is someone such as David, whose life is threatened by pursuing enemies and who needs to find a place of hiding where they cannot reach him. In v. 2c it is not yet clear what the image denotes. It might simply be a metaphor for whatever means of deliverance Yhwh provides in a particular situation, or it might refer to the city of Jerusalem, the crag city (cf. Jer. 21:13), to which the king looks forward to returning from "the end of the earth."[13] But the two succeeding cola in v. 3 suggest that rather it is God in person who *is* the crag (cf. the exposition of this imagery in 27:4–6). The middle colon makes it specific that the point about a crag is to be a *refuge. The last colon reworks the image in speaking in terms of a tower of *strength, for a tower is a humanly made construction to provide people with a refuge within a city, one that has a fair chance of protecting them and even of giving them opportunity to dispose of their enemies (e.g., Judg. 9:50–53). While the imagery thus makes the three cola parallel, the difference in tenses reflects the fact that v. 2c looks to the future and v. 3 provides the backing for that in recollecting past experience.[14] The line bases its plea for God to be a refuge on the fact that God has been a refuge in the past. The dynamic is again that of 27:4–6.

61:4–5. A statement of confidence follows the plea, one line looking to the future, one stating the basis for that looking to the future with confidence.

> [4]I shall stay in your tent forever;
>   I shall find refuge in the shelter of your wings. (Rise)

In the two parallel cola, the first verb is explicitly cohortative in form, while the second comes from a final *h* verb, which as such does not have a distinctive cohortative form[15] but which I take to be implicitly cohortative. The cohortative might then be a statement of confidence

---

12. MT's verse division perhaps presupposes the same understanding as Jerome, that the *b* expression in v. 2c is a further description of a predicament from which the suppliant needs rescue. But "crag" is regularly an image for a resource, not for an obstacle.

13. Cf. *Midrash on Psalms*, 1:518.

14. NRSV has "You are my refuge," but if that is the psalm's point, one wonders why it uses a verbal clause rather than a noun clause.

15. See GKC 75l.

or a prayer ("May I . . ."); the next line suggests it is the former. The first verb (*gûr*) is the one that refers to a person who lives somewhere as a resident alien, a status that conveys some security but not the same security as that of a citizen. Whether the term suggests real or limited security depends on the context (contrast 15:1 and the use of the noun *gēr* in 39:12 [13]). Here the context suggests real security, and the parallel verb in the second colon also makes that explicit. Next come two parallel *b* expressions that once more take up images in 27:4–6, "tent" (again, cf. also 15:1) and "shelter." These might refer literally to the temple but likely have a broader reference as images for protection. The temple as God's tent is a place to find shelter, but being away from the temple does not mean that one is no longer in that tent or place of shelter. Specifically, the image of God's wings recalls the wings of the cherubim and thus appeals to that figure for protection, but it does not imply that God's protection is known only there (cf. 17:8; 36:7 [8]; 57:1 [2]). The "forever" that closes the first colon, and thus stands at the center of the abca'b' arrangement, applies to both.

> ⁵For you yourself, God, will have listened to my promises;
>   you will have given their allocation to the people who revere your
>   name.

The further *kî* clause formally parallels that in vv. 2c–3 but likely has different reference.[16] Verses 2c–3 refer back to what has preceded this present prayer and is the basis for it; v. 5 projects forward to a time when this plea will have been answered. Thus "listened" takes up the verb from v. 1, now used to describe a fact rather than a plea, though its object is the *promises that would accompany a plea (cf. v. 8), the promise to bring an offering and give testimony to what God has done (see 22:25 [26]; 50:14; 56:12 [13]). The assumption is that God will be motivated to act by the fact that answering the suppliant's prayer will lead to the proclamation of God's power and love in doing so. The second colon then describes the act that issues from the listening. "Given their allocation" is language that belongs to the story of Israel's occupation of the land (Deut. 2:5, 9, 12, 19; Josh. 12:6–7).[17] The pressures of history will often imperil possession of their land by Israel, the people who *revere God's *name. It is the king's responsibility, under God, to see that does not happen. Here he imagines being in a position to tes-

---

16. DG 60c takes the verbs as precative, which would be plausible if one took v. 4 as a prayer (it would then make the whole of vv. 1–7 a prayer), but the *kî* works against it.

17. NJPS's "request" takes *yĕruššâ* as not an instance of the word for possession, the obj. of "give" in most of its occurrences, but as a by-form of *'ăreššet*, itself a hapax. This seems hazardous.

239

tify to the fact that God has indeed granted him that possession on the people's behalf, or more likely (cf. LXX, Jerome) that God has granted the people themselves their possession, when it was in danger of being taken over by their enemies.

61:6–7. While vv. 6–7a might be a further statement of confidence in what God *will* do, the imperative in v. 7b suggests that vv. 6–7a are jussives and that the two lines are a prayer. But why this transition to a prayer for the king? Does it indicate that an ordinary suppliant prays for the king? Although the king is of considerable importance to ordinary Israelites, that is hardly enough to explain such a sharp transition. It is hard to find other texts that suggest an ordinary individual would pray thus for the king in the midst of a personal prayer (84:9 [10] is the nearest example).[18] Is the king the messiah?[19] The transition is still very sharp, and we would expect some indication of the kind that Tg's gloss provides, that the prayer refers to a king who does not yet exist rather than to a king who does exist. Does it indicate that the suppliant is the king and that the king here prays for himself? While this seems the right general assumption, the reason for the transition is again not clear.[20] Most likely the transition indicates that the actual king who speaks elsewhere in this psalm prays not merely for himself but also for kings in general, for the generic king. This will have implications for himself, but its reach will not be confined to him. That also adds to the significance of the prayer for long life. It will not exclude the desire that the present king may live his full life and not have it cut short (see 21:4 [5]), but it may also imply a prayer for the monarchy as a whole to continue in existence "forever." Such a plea would fit with the nature of God's promise to David and David's responsive prayer (2 Sam. 7:16, 29).

> [6]May you add days to the days of the king,
>   his years, like one generation after another.

This prayer for long life is expressed in two parallel cola. The EVV take these as a verbal clause followed by a noun clause, but LXX more plausibly assumes that the verb at the end of the first colon applies to both (like "forever" in v. 4). The nouns "days" and "years" correspond, and each colon has a repeated word ("days" and "generations").

> [7]May he live forever before God;
>   appoint commitment and truthfulness to guard him.

18. Kraus (*Psalms 60–150*, 9–10) points to two Mesopotamian examples.
19. So Tg; cf. *Midrash on Psalms*, 1:518.
20. Dahood (*Psalms*, 2:84) quotes a fifth-century Phoenician parallel.

The bulk of the first colon restates v. 6 once more, but the last phrase, "before God," adds something that is then developed in the second colon and points to the burden of the line as a whole, a burden that coheres with the psalm as a whole. To live before God is to live in the sphere of God's love, blessing, and protection (see on 56:13 [14]), to live where God sees and notes all that we do and reaches out to us in need. Passages such as the classic Gen. 17:1 may also imply that living before God implies transparency and the awareness of a solemn side to God's seeing and noting all that we do, and it will be good if the king keeps this in mind. But here the second colon implies that the stress lies on the encouraging aspect to living before God. The parallelism's alternative way to express the idea is once more to take up the idea of God's sending quasi-aides to protect us (cf. 43:3; 57:3 [4]), figures that embody God's *commitment and *truthfulness (cf. 2 Sam. 7:15, 28, in God's conversation with David).

61:8. The psalm closes with a commitment to give the testimony that will fulfill the *promises referred to in v. 5.

> ⁸Thus I shall make music to your name evermore
>   in fulfilling my promises day by day.

The "thus" makes the suppliant king's personal link with vv. 6–7. If he is permitted to live "forever"—that is, to enjoy a human life of its proper length, not one that is cut short—then he will see that this life is characterized by praise that lasts "evermore" (a different but synonymous expression), praise of God's *name. This line's two time expressions, "evermore" and "day by day," balance each other with their reference to persistence and regularity. The first (cohortative) verb refers to making *music as the manner of the praise; the second (infinitival) verb identifies the object of that praise. The music is at least as integral to the fulfillment of the promise as the offering, which is not explicitly mentioned. Perhaps that is because the actual offering in its muteness and thus its ambiguity "did not do justice to the uniquely personal nature of the deliverance to which the thank offering was a response."[21] This does not take away from the indispensability of the offering, which makes clear that gratitude is more than mere feelings and words. If we may take literally the notion of daily fulfillment of promises, that note also suggests that it is the king who prays this psalm, for no ordinary person makes daily offerings.[22]

21. Keel, *Symbolism*, 325.
22. Ibid., 279.

Theological Implications

Calvin notes that Ps. 61 manifests no sense that God is not accessible to prayer because one is not in the temple,[23] and Werner R. Mayer adds that "prayer suspends the distantness between the supplicant and the deity."[24] Like 1 Kings 8, the psalm presupposes that Yhwh has made a special commitment to be accessible in the Jerusalem temple, but this by no means implies that Yhwh is not accessible elsewhere. Perhaps a suppliant would face Jerusalem and address Yhwh as the one who was known to have taken up residence there, even when the temple had been destroyed (cf. also Dan. 6:10). The psalm further makes clear that prayer does not have to be confined to crises, neither does thanksgiving, and neither does the experience of God being a refuge. The suppliant has known what it was like to pray in a crisis and expects to have that experience again, but here stays in touch with Yhwh in the meantime and expects to be acknowledging God's faithfulness every day, not forgetting experiences of it when they are some time past. Further, there is an experience of God providing us with a refuge when we are under particular pressure, and there is an ongoing experience of God providing us with a refuge that is our security day by day.

23. *Psalms*, 2:411.
24. "'Ich rufe dich von ferne, höre mich von nahe,'" in *Werden und Wirken des Alten Testaments* (Claus Westermann Festschrift; ed. Rainer Albertz et al.; Göttingen: Vandenhoeck & Ruprecht, 1980), 302–17; as summarized by Tate, *Psalms 51–100*, 116.

Psalm 62

The Heart of Old Testament Theology

Translation

The leader's. On Jeduthun. Composition. David's.

¹Yes, toward God my spirit is silent;
  from him is my deliverance.
²Yes, he is my crag and my deliverance,
  my haven: I shall not fall down for long.
³How long will you attack a person,
  commit murder, all of you?[1]

Like a wall bent over, a fence thrown down:[2]
  ⁴yes, from his exalted position they plan to throw him down.[3]
They delight in[4] deceit;

---

1. Following LXX, which implies piel *tĕraṣṣĕḥû* (also the Ben Naphtali reading according to [e.g.] Gunkel, *Psalmen*, 264). L has pual *tĕrāṣĕḥû* ("You will be murdered, all of you"), but such a warning is odd at this point, and *rāṣaḥ* does usually refer to murder, illegal slaying (except Num. 35:27, 30). EVV reduce the meaning to (e.g.) "crush," but there are no other examples, and it would be especially odd to use the piel thus.

2. EVV have active participles, but the Hebrew has qal passive. One would expect *gĕdērâ dĕḥûyâ*, not *gādēr haddĕḥûyâ*, but see DG 112.

3. For MT's *miśśĕʾētô*, Jerome implies *maśʾētô*, and LXX has *maśʾētî* (. . . to pull down his/my exaltation).

4. For MT's *yirṣû*, LXX implies *yāruṣû* (they run [in] deceit).

243

with their mouth[5] they bless but with their heart they slight. (Rise)
[5]Yes, be silent for God, my spirit,
    for from him is my hope.
[6]Yes, he is my crag and my deliverance,
    my haven: I shall not fall down.
[7]On God rests my deliverance and my honor;
    my strong crag, my refuge is God himself.

[8]Trust in him at all times, people; [MT]
[or, Trust in him all you congregation of the people; (LXX)][6]
    pour out your heart before him, God our refuge. (Rise)
[9]Yes, human beings are a breath;
    mortals are deceit.
Going up on scales,[7]
    they are less than a breath, altogether.
[10]Do not trust in extortion, do not become worthless through robbery;
    when resources blossom,[8] do not give them your heart.

[11]One thing God has spoken,
    two things that I have heard,[9]
That God has strength,
    [12]and that you, my Lord, have commitment,
    for you recompense a person according to their deeds.

Interpretation

Another psalm of trust follows. Psalm 62 does not address God until the last line. It has four different addressees: some attackers (v. 3), the suppliant's own self (v. 5), the people in general (v. 8), and finally, but briefly, God (v. 12). We might infer that formally vv. 1–3b address the attackers, vv. 3c–7 the suppliant's heart, vv. 8–11 the people, and v. 12 God, but the division between vv. 11 and 12 is artificial, and this raises the question whether that inference as a whole is too schematic. Perhaps the psalm as a whole implicitly speaks to all four of these addressees. In speaking to the attackers, it constitutes a kind of prophecy, like (e.g.) Ps. 50, yet one whose concern is the suppliant's own vulnerability. In speak-

5. Lit. "with his mouth"; see GKC 145m for this distributive usage.
6. MT has *běkol-ʿēt ʿām*; LXX implies *kol ʿēdat ʿām*.
7. I take this as a circumstantial inf. (cf. GKC 114o; *IBHS* 36.2.3e) rather than as an alternative to the finite verb (see *TTH* 204).
8. Lit. "resources: when they blossom"; the extraposition corresponds to that in casuistic laws (DG 121, remark 3).
9. A. M. Honeyman ("ʾiḏ, ḏū and Psalm lxii 12," *VT* 11 [1961]: 348–50) argues from the *zû* that the meaning is "once, twice."

ing to the self, it constitutes a kind of meditation or self-exhortation, like (for instance) Pss. 42–43. In speaking to the people, it constitutes a kind of testimony or homily, but one given in the midst of danger rather than after an experience of deliverance. In speaking to God, it is a declaration of confidence of the kind that appears in a protest psalm. "Gunkel's important observation that the genre of the psalm of confidence grew out of the song of lament means not least that the psalms of confidence represent an effort to *endure* the crisis complained of, precisely when and because it is ongoing."[10]

It manifests a number of further rhetorical features. The particle *'ak* opens vv. 1, 2, 4, 5, 6, 9. Verses 1–2 are reworked and expanded in vv. 5–7. There are instances of paronomasia in vv. 3b and 4b, vv. 3c and 4a, and vv. 9 and 10a, and a number of repetitions of words and images. A number of elliptical expressions tax readers and drive them to work hard to stay with the poet (vv. 1a, 3b–4a, v. 7).[11] There are no indications of a date.

> The leader's. On Jeduthun. Composition. David's.

Heading. See glossary. Jeduthun was one of the three temple music leaders in David and Solomon's day, with Asaph and Heman (1 Chron. 16:41–42; 2 Chron. 5:12); another Jeduthun was a seer in Josiah's day (2 Chron. 35:15). The preposition *'al* suggests a way of singing associated with Jeduthun.

62:1–3b. The first section of the psalm begins with two occurrences of the particle *'ak*, which can be restrictive ("only") or asseverative ("truly"). Given the psalm's liking for paronomasia, there need be no presumption that it has the same meaning throughout. The NIVI and NJPS mix their renderings, while NRSV always takes it restrictively, and TNIV always takes it asseveratively. To signal the rhetorical point, I have opted for consistency and have reckoned that the asseverative is the more plausible consistent rendering.

> [1]Yes, toward God my spirit is silent;
> from him is my deliverance.

The logic as well as the construction[12] of v. 1 is taxing. The conviction that God is the source of deliverance is a commonplace one, but

10. Hossfeld and Zenger, *Psalms 2*, 112; referring to Gunkel, *Psalmen*, 262–63.
11. For approaches to the psalm as a stepped structure, see Auffret, *Voyez de vos yeux*, 117–27. David Bland ("Exegesis of Psalm 62," *ResQ* 23 [1980]: 82–95) sees it as a royal psalm.
12. It begins (lit.) "my spirit [is in] silence." *HALOT* repoints *dûmîyâ* to the f. ptc. *dômîyâ*, but that is not an option in 39:2 [3], where the construction is hardly harsher.

the usual response to that awareness is to make a loud noise to God, not to be silent (see on 39:1–2 [2–3]). Yet the psalm as a whole bears out this opening claim, for the suppliant is silent toward God throughout the psalm until the statement of faith in the last line. In Ps. 39 silence is motivated by an un-Israelite hesitation about saying something offensive; here the second colon indicates that the reason for silence is confidence in God's deliverance. Being silent to God is a novel way of declaring trust.[13] Thus LXX's "is submitted" (Sym translates more literally) and Rashi and Qimchi's "hope" are not so far out.

> ²Yes, he is my crag and my deliverance,
>   my haven: I shall not fall down for long.

Verse 2 expands on the second colon. Its own two cola are parallel, and each might be seen as a hendiadys. God is the crag that delivers me, or is my crag and thus the one who delivers me; to put it another way, God is my haven and thus the one who ensures that I do not *fall down, at least not "for long."[14] The terms recall previous psalms, *crag (cf. 61:2 [3]), *deliverance (cf. 60:11 [13], though the word is *těšû'â* there), *haven (cf. 59:9, 16, 17 [10, 17, 18]), and "fall down" (60:2 [4]).

> ³ᵃ⁻ᵇHow long will you attack a person,
>   commit murder, all of you?

It becomes explicit whom the psalm is addressing and why it has been making the declarations in vv. 1–2. The four other occurrences of *'ad-'ānâ* in the Psalter all address God (13:1–2 [2–3]),[15] so that this usage illustrates the way the psalm is silent to God but noisy to human beings. The second, parallel colon goes beyond the first in speaking of murder and not just attack and/or in clarifying the meaning of that first verb,[16] and in introducing the subject with its "all." Retrospectively, the line suggests that the suppliant "doth protest too much"[17] in v. 1, or perhaps that the silence it mentions is other than we might have thought. The psalm does not imply that the psalmist's spirit is calm or restful or characterized by inner stillness. Casting oneself on God and saying nothing, as the psalm

13. Cf. Gerstenberger, *Psalms*, 2:9.

14. For *rabbâ*, "greatly" (KJV) is rather bathetic (contrast John Ellington, "Psalm 62:2," *BT* 50 [1999]: 243–46), while "ever" (EVV) gives good sense but is hard to justify. I have translated in light of the use of *rabbat* in 120:6; 123:4; 129:1, 2.

15. Something similar is true of other words for "how long?" such as *'ad-mātāy* (as in 6:3 [4]).

16. *Těhôtětû*, from *hût* or *hātat*, is a hapax of unknown origin; the meaning is inferred from the context.

17. William Shakespeare, *Hamlet*, act 3, scene 2.

clearly states, can coexist with deep anxiety. Still less does it suggest that the psalmist has come through a period of struggle to a stillness of soul.[18] Reliance and disquiet are not mutually exclusive.

62:3c–7. The psalm ceases to address the attackers (as v. 4 makes clear) and instead addresses the psalmist's own self (as v. 5 makes clear) in the manner of Pss. 42–43. Thus the content of the section parallels that of vv. 1–3b, though the sections work abb'a': that is, vv. 3c–4 re-express v. 3a–b, while vv. 5–7 re-express vv. 1–2.

> ³ᶜLike a wall bent over, a fence thrown down:
> ⁴ᵃyes, from his exalted position they plan to throw him down.

I thus take vv. 3c–4a as the next line.[19] The MT's linking v. 3c with what precedes makes the "yes" in the subsequent colon the beginning of the line, as it is elsewhere in the psalm, and follows well from the MT reading "You will be murdered" in v. 3a–b. But linking v. 3c with what follows makes for a sequence of bicola through vv. 1–7, with some parallelism between the two cola in this line and with the repetition of forms of the same verb at the end of each of them. Whereas v. 3a–b spoke of attack and murder and spoke literally, the psalm now speaks of pulling down and begins with a simile. Further, we can now take the image of a collapsing wall/fence more naturally, as an image for vulnerability rather than for being a threat (as the MT reading implies).[20] So the line begins by describing the intended result of the attackers' action, then goes on to the process whereby they will achieve their work. They have a plan. But is it realistic? The second colon hints that this is not so. At present the psalmist stands in an exalted position (*śĕ'ēt* from *nāśā'*), a position of dignity and significance. The context suggests that this is because of the considerations described in vv. 2 and 6–7. The attackers are wrong in their assessment because they do not take God into account.

> ⁴ᵇThey delight in deceit;
> with their mouth they bless but with their heart they slight. (Rise)

Three two-word clauses offer more description of the process whereby they intend to do their work. As usual, the assailants do not indulge in their murderous assault by frontal attack but by deceit. The second and third of these brisk clauses make the contrast between their public words and their private acts, which might be plots to pervert the cause of justice. The talk of blessing and "cursing" (as EVV have it) would rather

18. Against (e.g.) Weiser, *Psalms*, 446–47.
19. Cf. Hauge, *Between Sheol and Temple*, 247.
20. Cf. Rashi; Kirkpatrick, *Psalms*, 349.

suggest prayers and curses. But the second verb is not *'ālâ*, the word that most explicitly denotes "curse" in the sense of calling down trouble on someone, but *qālal* (piel), which means "curse" in the sense of disparage or treat with dishonor or treat as contemptible (e.g., 37:22; Gen. 12:3; Lev. 20:9). (Admittedly the practical result of insult as opposed to curse might not be so different; the person is being cut down in significance in relation to the community and thereby risks losing their place in it.) As the converse of slighting, blessing implies "honoring thankfully," recognizing someone as an embodiment of blessing and/or praying for them to be that.[21]

> ⁵Yes, be silent for God, my spirit,
>   for from him is my hope.

The psalm returns to the theme of v. 1, which provides the basis for the conviction that the attackers will fail, but it now addresses the psalmist's own spirit or self (*nepeš*, *person). It constitutes an exhortation to a confident silence, not a declaration of such silence, and thus rather suggests a growth in anxiety, a reduction in confidence. The basis for the exhortation is that *hope comes from God, the hoped-for deliverance of which the equivalent colon in v. 1 spoke.

> ⁶Yes, he is my crag and my deliverance,
>   my haven: I shall not fall down.

In turn v. 6 reworks v. 2, the only difference being the omission of "for long." That has the opposite effect to the change from statement to exhortation. The psalmist declares that there will be no fall at all, not even a temporary fall.

> ⁷On God rests my deliverance and my honor;
>   my strong crag, my refuge is God himself.

Verse 7 first reinstates the *deliverance displaced from v. 5b (though this time *yešaʿ*) and then adds *honor, which also takes up the theme of v. 4a. The expression is again a kind of hendiadys, "my deliverance from dishonor." The attackers want to displace the psalmist from a position of prestige in the community; God will see that it does not happen. In this context *kābôd* thus refers to the psalmist's position of honor in the community (cf. 3:3 [4], which also refers to the lifting up of the psalmist's head). The second colon continues the restatement of v. 6, though adding interest by the new word *refuge and by the addition of the qualifier

21. Cf. *TLOT* 271.

"strong" (lit. "the crag of my *strength"). The two parallel cola are both elliptical noun clauses:[22] literally, "on God my deliverance and my honor, my strong crag and my refuge in God." "Structurally and theologically, the reality of God encompasses the psalmist."[23]

62:8–10. The addressees change again, now to the people of God in general. The section forms an abb'a' pattern, with two outside lines about where to put your trust and give your heart and where not to do so and two inside lines that indicate the reasons.

> [8]Trust in him at all times, people; [MT]
> [or, Trust in him all you congregation of the people; (LXX)]
>   pour out your heart before him, God our refuge. (Rise)

*Trust is the attitude the psalm has expressed (vv. 1–3a) and has urged on the self (vv. 3b–7), without using the word. Now it urges this attitude on the people as a whole ('am).[24] The time reference perhaps takes up the fact that for anyone there are times when it is tempting not to trust, and these are the moments when it is most important to do so; that is how things are at this moment for the psalmist. Any fool can trust when there is no pressure. The verb in the second colon makes for an interesting parallel to the first. The implication of vv. 1–7 is that trust implies silence, though the eight lines that say so rather contradict themselves. Arguably they have constituted a pouring out of the psalmist's *heart before God (though not to God), and this is what the psalm now commends as an expression of trust. Expressions such as "pour out the heart" are actually rather rare (see 42:4 [5]; 1 Sam. 1:15; Lam. 2:19). The verb much more often has "anger" as its object, which puts us on the track of its implications, as does the fact that it also appears in connection with pouring out a complaint (cf. Pss. 102 heading; 142:2 [3]). The psalm is encouraging the community to an act of faith that pours out its resentment, grief, and fear before God, the act that psalms are often modeling. The colon then adds to the line as a whole a twofold qualifier of the "him" in the prepositional expressions in each line. It is worth pouring out one's heart to God as our *refuge—an image that sums up the implications of vv. 2, 6–7—and/or it is especially appropriate to do so when we particularly need God as our refuge and God is not functioning as such.

22. Each comprises a prep., the word "God," and two noun expressions with first-person suffix, in abcc'b'a' order.
23. McCann, "Psalms," 923.
24. We might see the cola as each dividing into two, 2-2 and 2-2, and as working aba'c. The first comprises a verbal expression followed by the temporal phase and an invocation, the second a verbal expression and a double qualifier for its suffix.

⁹ᵃ⁻ᵇYes, human beings are a breath;
   mortals are deceit.

Taken out of context, the statements about humanity would look in conflict with the OT's positive understanding of humanity as made in God's image, but parallel passages make clear that describing humanity as a breath is a comment on the shortness and vulnerability of human life (see on 39:4–7 [5–8]). That helps us to see how this generalization relates to the context. The pressure of other people's attacks can make a person fear being put down forever. It is difficult to imagine the situation changing. The psalm reminds the community that situations do change. People in power today are gone tomorrow. They cannot escape the fact about human experience that this line describes. In the parallelism, the terms for "human beings" and "mortals" may not be synonymous but contrasting, "the children of humanity" being ordinary people, "the children of a person" people of some status.²⁵ That would heighten the point here. The first colon acknowledges that ordinary people's lives are vulnerable; the second points out that actually the same is true of people in power. The other nouns in the parallelism perhaps increase this possibility: the children of humanity are indeed a breath, but the children of a person are deceit. The line picks up this word from v. 4. There is no intrinsic link between being a breath and being deceit, but the line draws attention to another aspect of the deceitfulness of these particular people. They think, talk, and behave as if they will be in power forever, and they get ordinary people to collude with them. The community as a whole needs to stop doing so and to see that these other people, too, are a breath.

⁹ᶜGoing up on scales,
   they are less than a breath, altogether.

A vivid metaphor expands on the point. Imagine trying to weigh a breath. The pan with this item of nonsubstance in it shoots into the air as the pan with the weights in it bangs down on the other side of the balance. That is how much substance (actually, less than that) attaches to humanity in general and/or to important people in particular, if they are all weighed at once. Again, this is not to deny the significance that Scripture elsewhere attaches to humanity, but further to develop the significance of the shortness of human life, especially the lives of important people, who look less evanescent than ordinary people but are just

25. See on 49:2 [3].

as short-lived and vulnerable. The background to the metaphor may be the idea that death is the moment when we are "weighed."[26]

> [10]Do not trust in extortion, do not become worthless through robbery;
> when resources blossom, do not give them your heart.

The section closes by accompanying the exhortation to put *trust in the right place, with an exhortation not to put it in the wrong place, but it jumps a stage in an argument. It does not urge the people to avoid trusting in human beings, and particularly in powerful human beings, as opposed to God. It urges them not to trust the same things as those powerful people who are attacking the psalmist. The first colon itself comprises two neatly balanced parallel clauses: (lit.) "do not trust in extortion, do not become empty in robbery."[27] The first noun is more concrete, the second more general, calling a spade a spade. The second verb adds significantly to the first by picking up the root *hebel* (breath), as the first colon picked up the verb *bāṭaḥ* (trust). The EVV take the verb *hābal* to mean "put empty hopes," which is an implication, but the denominative verb itself does not make explicit the idea of hope; nor is the idea of hope intrinsic to the other occurrences of the verb (2 Kings 17:15; Jer. 2:5; 23:16; Job 27:12). Rather, the idea is that trusting in extortion and thus in robbery will hasten people to that moment when they become breath, rather than putting off that moment. The people are therefore urged not to come to share in and live by the worldview of the psalmist's attackers. It does not pay. The second half of the line spells out the implications. If you are not to trust, you are not to give your heart, or (more idiomatically) to pay attention. It is both a means of not trusting and a result of not trusting. "Resources" (*ḥayil*) can be military or financial; the context here suggests the latter (against NJPS). Whose resources are blossoming? The TNIV assumes they are those of the people themselves, and the idea that we need not to get overattached to our own wealth is an edifying one but not one that fits the context. More likely the people are not to fall into the trap of the attackers, who see other people prospering and start working out how to defraud them. The psalm warns against that process.

62:11–12. There is nothing to mark the beginning of a new section, but by the time we come to v. 12, the psalmist has a fourth addressee, God, and vv. 11–12 belong together, even though v. 11 refers to God in the third person.

---

26. Cf. Keel, *Symbolism*, 240–41.

27. Each comprises the negative *'al*, a second-person plural qal yiqtol verb, the prep. *b*, and a noun, the two clauses being arranged abb'a'.

> ¹¹ᵃ⁻ᵇOne thing God has spoken,
> two things that I have heard,

Verse 11a–b (3-2) forms the introduction to a statement. One might have thought that "God has spoken" would introduce a prophecy, but the "one . . . two . . ." form is that of a numerical saying belonging to wisdom writing (e.g., Prov. 6:16–19; 30:15–31),[28] and the statement in vv. 11c–12 is not a prophetic word but the kind of summative theological statement that one would associate more with wisdom than with prophecy.

> ¹¹ᶜThat God has strength,
> ¹²and that you, my Lord, have commitment,
> for you recompense a person according to their deeds.

The statement constitutes a tricolon to round off the psalm.[29] The noun clauses comprising the first two, shorter cola balance two forms (third and second person), the two terms "God" and "my *Lord," and most significantly two attributes of God, *strength[30] and *commitment. The first term picks up from v. 7b. God has power in the world. The question is, What does God do with it? The parallel colon sets *commitment alongside power. God exercises power in such a way as to work out commitment to people, not, for instance, merely for divine self-aggrandizement or arbitrarily. Conversely, God manifests commitment in a way that involves the exercise of power. In numerical sayings, the emphasis often lies on the last in the series, and here the point would be that God is one characterized not merely by power but also by commitment (unlike the attackers).

That works itself out in the way described in the closing colon. Recompensing a person according to their deeds is not the first principle of the way God relates to people in the OT. God made promises to Abraham and Sarah that had no basis in anything they had done, and God chose Israel in a way that also had no such basis, as Moses points out (Deut. 7:7–8; 9:4–8). But Moses goes on to note that Israel's subsequent life involves an interaction between God's commitment and people's re-

28. But see more generally Watson, *Classical Hebrew Poetry*, 144–49. It can also denote "repeatedly" (e.g., Job 33:14), but this seems less relevant here, and the one-two statements are surely the ones itemized in vv. 11c–12a.

29. Unless we count the *kî* as extrametrical and see the line as 4-4. In contrast, Hossfeld and Zenger (*Psalms 2*, 110–11) divide v. 12b into two and thus take vv. 11–12 as three bicola.

30. Kraus (*Psalms 60–150*, 12) takes this as one of the passages where *ʿōz* means protection; contrast *HALOT*. "Strength" fits better in the context, though the connotations of the other root may also attach to the word.

sponsiveness (Deut. 7:9–10). In the absence of such responsiveness, God "recompenses" them; the verb (*šālam* piel) in Deut. 7:10 is the same as comes here in the psalm. One might thus infer that the psalm refers to the punishment of people such as the attackers to whom it has referred. But they have been referred to in the plural, whereas the individual "person" mentioned previously (v. 3) was the psalmist. Since the verb "recompense" can have positive meaning as well as negative, it seems likely that both meanings apply here. God's powerful commitment is expressed in making things work out for the individual, for blessing or trouble as they deserve. That is the conviction that has underlain the psalm as a whole. The effect of the transition to address of God in v. 12 is to make it a closing declaration of confidence addressed to God.

Theological Implications

The psalm's concern with silence has made it seem an appropriate text to encourage contemplative prayer,[31] yet this "is not the silence of contemplative piety but the silence after storm,"[32] or rather, in the midst of storm. It finally suggests that if there is a way to live through the storm, it is in light of some basic truths about God. Indeed, "the number of things to be learnt about God is very small and may be reduced to just two."[33] They summarize the central contents of the OT's understanding of relationships between God and humanity.[34] "In these two things are contained nearly all the Scriptures."[35] They are "the two pillars on which we rest, and may defy the surges of temptation."[36]

---

31. E.g., Dietrich Bonhoeffer, *Meditating on the Word* (Cambridge, MA: Crowley, 1986), 58–63.

32. Westermann, *Living Psalms*, 152.

33. Rogerson and McKay, *Psalms*, 2:63 (with "learnt" italicized because it is a quotation from the psalm).

34. So Georg Fohrer, *Theologische Grundstrukturen des Alten Testaments* (Berlin: de Gruyter, 1972), 99.

35. Augustine, *Psalms*, 256.

36. Calvin, *Psalms*, 2:431.

Psalm 63

A Threefold Dynamic for Life

Translation

Composition. David's. When he was in the Wilderness of Judah.

[1]God, you are my God, I search for you;[1]
  my whole person thirsts for you.
My body aches for you,
  in a land that is dry and faint, without water.
[2]So I have seen you[2] in the sanctuary,
  beholding[3] your power and honor.
[3]For your commitment is better than life;
  my lips glorify you.
[4]So I will worship you throughout my life;
  in your name I will lift my hands.

[5]As with a rich feast my whole person is full,
  and with resounding lips my mouth gives praise.
[6]When I have been mindful of you on my bed,
  in the night watches I talk about you.
[7]For you have been my help;
  in the shade of your wings I resound.
[8]My whole person has stuck to you;
  your right hand has upheld me.

1. Or "God, my God, you—I search for you" (cf. LXX; Kraus, *Psalms 60–150*, 17, 18).
2. Jerome implies a niphal verb, as MT at 42:2 [3]; cf. Theodoret, *Psalms*, 1:358.
3. Circumstantial inf. (GKC 114o).

⁹But they, the people who seek to destroy my life, [MT]
[or, But they, the people who seek my life in vain, (LXX)]⁴
    go to the depths of the earth.
¹⁰The ones who pour him down by the power of the sword
    are prey for jackals.
¹¹But the king—he rejoices in God,
    all who swear by him exult,
    for the mouth of people who speak falsehood is stopped up.

Interpretation

In contrast to Ps. 62, the whole of Ps. 63 addresses God, except perhaps the very last line, which makes for an even tighter contrast with Ps. 62. In English, the opening verb of the psalm can give the impression that it is a lament; the suppliant is one who is at the moment seeking but is not able to reach God, from a situation that is literally or metaphorically dry.⁵ But it is a yiqtol, like the verbs in vv. 3b, 4, 5, 6b, 7b, 8b, and 9–11. More likely that verb and at least some of those later ones describe aspects of the ongoing dynamic of the suppliant's life with God, and v. 1 refers not to a onetime present searching that has not reached what it is looking for but to an aspect of an ongoing pattern of life with God. That life involves searching, thirsting, fainting, bringing to mind, muttering, and cleaving. But it also involves looking, seeing, being filled, being supported, being delivered. And further, it therefore also involves glorifying, worshipping, lifting hands, resounding, praising, rejoicing, and exulting. That combination of motifs could suggest that the psalm is a thanksgiving, but if so, one would expect more reference to the past experience that is the basis for thanksgiving. Rather, it is a psalm of trust that presupposes experiences of God's deliverance but does not issue from one such experience.

The psalm does not divide into sharply defined sections, but for convenience we may distinguish vv. 1–4, 5–8, and 9–11 as three sections of deepening urgency.⁶ The last recalls Ps. 61 and suggests that it is designed for the king to use. There is no indication of a particular date within the monarchic period. F. Asensio sees Pss. 61; 62; and 63 as a triptych,⁷ while P. Auffret stresses the links between Pss. 63; 64; and 65.⁸

4. MT has *lĕšô'â*; LXX implies *laššāw'*.
5. Thus Lindström (*Suffering and Sin*, 405) describes the psalm as "to be used in a situation of acute danger."
6. Cf. Anthony R. Ceresko, "A Note on Psalm 63," *ZAW* 92 (1980): 435–36; also Calvin, *Psalms*, 2:432–43. See also the discussion in Auffret, *La sagesse a bâti sa maison*, 267–83.
7. "Teología bíblica de un tríptico," *EstBib* 21 (1962): 111–25.
8. *Voyez de vos yeux*, 135–36.

Composition. David's. When he was in the Wilderness of Judah.

Heading. See glossary. The last phrase alludes to the narrative in 2 Sam. 15–17, where one can indeed imagine David in a dry and thirsty land recalling how he had seen Yhwh in the sanctuary and had celebrated Yhwh's acts there and looking for Yhwh to put down his enemies again. The reference to David and his supporters being "faint" (2 Sam. 16:14) may have especially suggested the link. These parallels imply that the passage alludes to those narratives rather than 1 Sam. 22–25.[9]

63:1–4. Verses 1–4 begin to describe the dynamics of the king's life with God.

> ¹God, you are my God, I search for you;
>   my whole person thirsts for you.
> My body aches for you,
>   in a land that is dry and faint, without water.

In the opening noun clause, the second "God" is *'ēl* (cf. Jerome's *fortitudo*), so the confession is less repetitive than it looks in English, though it would not be surprising if the clause originally read "Yhwh, you are my God." "Search for" is the vivid denominative *šāhar* from the noun *šahar*, the word for daybreak, which can thus suggest acting with the effort and commitment we show when we get up early to do something. Luther has "I keep watch."[10] Verse 6 may indicate that we should take the verb more literally than usual, so that it offers some justification for the Orthodox Church's designating this a morning psalm.[11] The parallel colon as a whole then develops the implications of the single word "I-search-for-you" at the end of the first colon. "Thirst" (see on 42:2 [3], the only other occurrence of the metaphor of thirst for God in the Psalms)[12] makes the same point as the earlier verb in a complementary and metaphorical way; "my whole *person" spells out the preformative "I," and "for you" gives separate expression to the suffix "you."

The second line then elaborates the matter in a way that makes v. 1 as a whole work abb'c in its description of the king's recurrent seeking of God. Thus the first colon forms a straight parallel to v. 1b as "my

9. Cf. Hossfeld and Zenger, *Psalms 2*, 123.

10. *First Lectures*, 1:302.

11. See (e.g.) Fan Stylian Noli, compiler, *The Eastern Orthodox Prayer Book* (Boston: Albanian Orthodox Church in America, 1949), 28.

12. Psalm 143:6 does refer to a person who is like faint earth.

body aches for you" re-expresses "my whole person thirsts for you."[13] The colon does not refer to the body over against the soul; the OT does not see body or flesh (*bāśār*) and spirit or soul or person (*nepeš*) as a pair of complementary aspects to the human being in the way that body and soul are in English. In the Psalms, only in 16:9–10 and 84:2 [3] do *bāśār* and *nepeš* come together as they do here; *nepeš* refers to me as a whole being, and specifically a being with longings (in this context it might more precisely suggest desire; cf., for instance, 27:12),[14] while *bāśār* refers to me as a physical being (without the negative implications that attach to *sarx* in the NT). The final colon in the verse then provides background to what has preceded, though only in metaphorical terms.[15] It is certainly in a dry land that one would thirst and ache. To add another level to the metaphor, even the land itself there faints with thirst because it has no water.

> [2]So I have seen you in the sanctuary,
>   beholding your power and honor.

With v. 2 we receive some literal description of the way the king has gone about the search and satisfied the thirst and presumably how he does so on a regular basis. In due course vv. 9–11 will give us some idea of the pressures that stimulate the search and the longing to which v. 1 referred; the way he handled this pressure was to take it to the sanctuary (cf. the story in 2 Kings 19). There he was able to see God. Perhaps he did so in some metaphorical sense (see again on 42:2 [3]; also 27:4 in its context), or perhaps the expression refers to seeing symbols that suggested God's presence, such as the covenant chest (Qimchi). Many kings could have seen images of Yhwh in the temple, but that would not be the reference of this expression for the compilers of the Psalter who knew that Yhwh forbad such images. The parallel colon spells out the implications of seeing God and how it relates to those pressures. What the king actually saw was God's power and *honor (perhaps a hendiadys, God's splendid power). That was proclaimed in the recounting of God's acts toward Israel, made visible in the splendor of worship with its sacrifices, processions, and rituals, and symbolized by the chest. All this brought home God's power and honor and thus reinforced the convictions that vv. 9–11 will express. Longing and thirst are thus satisfied.

13. The sound is similar, reflecting the sense: *ṣām'â lĕkā napšî*, then *kāmah lĕkā bĕśārî*—hence perhaps the choice of the hapax *kāmah*.
14. The parallelism and the verb indicate that *nepeš* does not merely mean "soul" here. Luther has "How many ways my flesh thirsts for Thee" (*First Lectures*, 1:302).
15. Cf. the interpretive "as" in Syr and Sym.

³For your commitment is better than life;
　　my lips glorify you.

Verse 3 brings a transition to the third of the recurrent attitudes expressed in the psalm: longing for God (v. 1), experience of God (vv. 2–3a), and worship of God (vv. 3b–4). The opening declaration that God's commitment is better than life is puzzling. The way and the context in which people would experience God's commitment are in the gift of life, and what the suppliant is seeking is the sustaining of life. Perhaps the expression takes up v. 1 and refers to life within its metaphor; one might compare the use of *ḥayyîm* to mean something like "sustenance" (Prov. 27:27), like the related *miḥyâ*. The point, then, is that the commitment God has shown Israel over the centuries, from the exodus onward, is better than the ordinary sustaining of life that the literally thirsty person seeks and finds.[16] The suppliant therefore glorifies God, the second colon continues.

⁴So I will worship you throughout my life;
　　in your name I will lift my hands.

Verse 4 elaborates on that with another verb, *worship, and a different use of the word for "life" (on any theory of the earlier meaning of that word). The second colon is parallel in substance, as "in your *name I will lift my hands" corresponds to "I will worship you" (with an implicit parallelism between "hands" and "knee," the noun from which the word "worship" is formed).[17]

63:5–8. Verses 5–8 go over similar ground to vv. 1–4. The psalm again speaks of God's meeting the suppliant's needs on an ongoing basis (vv. 5a, 8), of particular experiences of God's reaching out in the past (vv. 6–7a), and of the suppliant's responsive worship (vv. 5b, 7b).[18]

---

16. Theodore (*Psalms 1–81*, 814–15) has "better than lives," presumably a misunderstanding of the Hebrew pl. *ḥayyîm*, which prompts the observation that it is better than living many times, because even these are going to come to an end.

17. It is also parallel in an additional formal sense, as the first colon ends with a *b* expression and the second opens with one.

18. I have reckoned it likely that the four yiqtol clauses that form the four second cola all have parallel reference to that ongoing relationship. With LXX, I have thus taken these four lines as separate and parallel sentences. In vv. 6–8 the three opening cola all have qatal verbs; the middle one, *hāyîtā* (v. 7a), seems to refer to the past, since "you are my help" would require no verb (cf. NRSV against NJPS, TNIV), and I have reckoned that all three are likely to be parallel, like the subsequent yiqtols. All three refer to a past act whose significance continues into the present.

> [5]As with a rich feast my whole person is full,
> and with resounding lips my mouth gives praise.

Thus v. 5 returns to the psalm's opening image to describe the other side of the coin, the way God on an ongoing basis more than meets the suppliant's needs. Coming to God with the pressing needs of someone in a position of responsibility who is recurrently confronted by foes, the suppliant finds that God abounds in meeting the needs of the whole *person (cf. v. 1; *nepeš* might again mean more specifically "desire"). The image is that of a rich meaty feast abounding in (lit.) suet and fat. Perhaps the nature of a festal banquet suggests the imagery, and perhaps the fact that passages such as Lev. 3:16–17 do not allow worshippers to eat suet heightens the sense of how rich this meal is. The companion colon articulates the response. Thus if the first colon corresponds to v. 1, the second with its reference to *resounding corresponds to vv. 3b–4.[19]

> [6]When I have been mindful of you on my bed,
> in the night watches I talk about you.

In turn v. 6 is not a pair of parallel subordinate clauses with the "when" applying to the second as well as the first and the whole line dependent on v. 5 (so EVV); rather, it is another self-contained sentence.[20] Being *mindful of God is comparable to seeing God (v. 2); it will involve recalling what God has done in the past (see also v. 7a). Where is the bed on which the king is so mindful? The context with its references to the sanctuary (v. 2, and implicitly the parallel colon, v. 6b) may suggest that as suppliant the king stayed overnight in the sanctuary, perhaps rising at appointed hours for prayer and praise, though we have no explicit reference to such a practice in Israel, and this may involve too much inference. The king might engage in such recollection in the palace, perhaps anxious about the pressures he has to face, like any ordinary mortal. Or he might engage in such recollection while on a campaign. Whatever is the case, the second colon indicates that the recollection issues in praise. The parallelism between the lines, that is, suggests that this talking is the kind that appears in (e.g.) 35:28 and also in 77:11–12 [12–13] and 143:5, where the verb is again parallel with "been mindful,"

---

19. The idea that the praise of the second colon issues in the sense of fullness to which the first colon refers (Lindström, *Suffering and Sin*, 410) is suggestive, but the order of the cola rather suggests the more usual idea that Yhwh's filling the suppliant leads to praise.

20. So *TTH* 138i (though taking the sentence as a hypothetical).

though it is the kind of quiet talking within oneself that one does in the night on one's bed.

> [7]For you have been my help;
>   in the shade of your wings I resound.

Verse 7 makes explicit the subject of the mindfulness and the talking, the fact that God has been a *help to the king. He has known God's deliverance in previous crises. That again makes his voice *resound as he dwells in the *shade of God's wings. This might once more suggest an allusion to the sanctuary; perhaps the king is there, or perhaps he appeals to the imagery suggested by the cherubim in order to describe Yhwh's protection in everyday life.

> [8]My whole person has stuck to you;
>   your right hand has upheld me.

The king restates his past but habitual turning to God by using the image of sticking or adhering.[21] When used metaphorically, elsewhere the verb denotes people's adherence to Yhwh rather than other gods (e.g., Deut. 11:22; Josh. 22:5; 2 Kings 18:6), and that makes sense here. The whole psalm indeed constitutes a claim to treat God as the king's sole resource in crises. The reappearance yet again of *nepeš* (*person) makes for an inclusion with v. 5. Since v. 8 rounds off vv. 1–8, it also makes an inclusion with v. 1a, which indeed this line once more restates. With his whole being the king has relied on God. The other side of the relationship ("You are our God, we are your people") is that God has ever held the king up (see 41:12 [13]). God has never let him be put down by enemies or let him collapse through his own tiredness. The similarity between "stuck" and "upheld" (*dābĕqâ, tāmĕkâ*)[22] reflects the interlinking asserted by the line. The mutuality of this commitment is reflected in the fact that the suffix *-kā* (you/your) comes fifteen times in the psalm, the suffix *-î* (I/me/my) fourteen times.[23]

63:9–11. After the metaphorical lyricism of the opening verses, the concreteness and directness of the last section surprises, but in its way it constitutes the climax to which the psalm has been working, the point of it. The NJPS takes the whole as a jussive prayer, but there are no distinguishable jussives, and the context offers no pointers to such a change in the significance of the yiqtols. Indeed, the *w* with which the

21. In other contexts, one could take *dābĕqâ* as stative, but the parallelism between the lines suggests it is here fientive.

22. Terrien, *Psalms*, 463.

23. Schaefer, *Psalms*, 153.

section opens suggests that the verbs have similar significance to the ones that have preceded. The section thus forms a third statement of confidence in God's ongoing provision and upholding. It also thus makes more explicit that the psalm is not concerned merely for a sense of God's presence, merely for an essentially spiritual or religious experience (nor does it thus follow that these last verses are therefore "on a lower level").[24] The God of the Psalms is not one who is merely involved in people's inner lives, as readers whose outer lives are quite comfortable may be inclined to infer.

> [9]But they, the people who seek to destroy my life, [MT]
> [or, But they, the people who seek my life in vain, (LXX)]
>   go to the depths of the earth.

Verse 9 thus introduces a group of people who have not been mentioned before, but who turn out to have been invisibly present. They are people who (lit.) "seek my *person/life for devastation."[25] Once again the king speaks of his *nepeš*, suggesting a contrast with the thirsting for God, sticking with God, and finding full satisfaction, of which he has spoken earlier. The background to those experiences is the fact that there are indeed people who from time to time seek the destruction of his person, and because of that he thirsts and sticks. His being satisfied lies in the fact that God frustrates that purpose. His statement of confidence is that he knows that the fate they seek for him is the one that overcomes them. He has seen it happen before, and he will see it again. They end up in Sheol.[26] The LXX's alternative reading in the first colon anticipates their failure.

> [10]The ones who pour him down by the power of the sword
>   are prey for jackals.

In this parallel statement, the first colon comprises another description of the attackers' action.[27] The pouring down (*nāgar* hiphil; cf. Jer. 18:21)

24. So Kirkpatrick, *Psalms*, 352.
25. *Šô'â*, the modern Hebrew word for the holocaust (cf. 35:8).
26. For *taḥtîyôt hā'āreṣ* KJV has "the lower parts of the earth," which is fine if it implies simply the underside of the earth, but it could imply the later idea of there being several gradations in Sheol, as is more the case with KJV's "the lowest parts of the earth" for the same expression at 139:15.
27. The EVV's "they are poured down" takes the verb as impersonal, but the pl. verb is not usual (see GKC 144g), and the sg. suffix is odd; thus Kraus (*Psalms 60–100*, 18) emends it to pl. It is easier to reckon that the attackers continue to be the subj. of the verb and that the line now speaks of the suppliant in the third person (cf. Johnson, *Cultic Prophet and Israel's Psalmody*, 281).

perhaps refers to the idiom in 2 Sam. 14:14. The attackers are likened to people who pour water onto the ground, which then disappears into it, or the reference to the sword may suggest it is blood they are pouring.[28] Instead, the parallel colon declares that they will meet with death themselves, a death in battle that will mean the body not receiving proper burial but becoming prey for jackals and never reaching its proper rest, even in those depths of Sheol.

> [11]But the king—he rejoices in God,
>   all who swear by him exult,
>   for the mouth of people who speak falsehood is stopped up.

The psalm closes with another contrasting final tricolon. As in Ps. 61 the king speaks about himself in the third person because he speaks not merely about himself but about kings generically.[29] The notion of joy has been implicit in the talk about praise in vv. 1–8, but it now becomes explicit. In parallelism with the reference to the rejoicing of the king is a reference to the exulting of the people as a whole; the verb is the hitpael of *hālal* (*praise), so that it takes up from v. 5. The middle colon defines these people as those who swear by "him." Elsewhere the actual phrase "swear by him" always refers to God, but people do swear by the king (e.g., 1 Sam. 17:55; 2 Sam. 15:21), and that meaning makes sense here; the "in God" of the first colon carries over into the second to indicate the object of the exulting. The third colon then explains that people will so exult because they see the vindication and deliverance of the one by whom they swear. The attackers are now defined as people who speak *falsehood, in the manner of Sennacherib and his staff in 2 Kings 18–19, or of people within Israel who doubt the king's competence and speak for policies other than one that involves trusting in Yhwh. The victories God grants the king make clear that his attitude of trust in Yhwh is the right one and have the effect of shutting the mouths of those other people. "Stopped up" (*sākar*) is a vivid verb to suggest this; the only other occurrence of the niphal refers to damming the springs of the deep (Gen. 8:2).[30] It makes for an effective inclusion for the psalm: God's response when the suppliant searches (*šāḥar*) is to stop up (*sākar*). Mouths that speak falsehood (*šāqer*) are stopped up; mouths that praise are opened (v. 5).[31]

---

28. But NRSV takes the idiom as signifying being given over *to* the power of the sword. Tg with "terrify him" apparently takes *nāgar* as a by-form of *gûr*.
29. Gunkel (*Psalmen*, 266) again sees the reference to the king as a later addition.
30. Cf. BDB for cognates with similar meaning.
31. McCann, "Psalms," 928.

Theological Implications

Although the psalm appears here as a king's statement of confidence, its dynamics are such that might be shared by others who share in the Davidic covenant (see Isa. 55:3–5). They too may live their lives in light of its threefold dynamic. As one experiences ongoing pressure from other people, this involves ongoing searching, thirsting, aching, being upheld, and thus being more than satisfied. As part of that, it involves bringing to mind, sticking, seeing, beholding, and being helped. And as a result it involves glorifying, worshipping, lifting hands, resounding, praising, rejoicing, and exulting.

Psalm 64

The Power of Language and the Power of Recollection

Translation

The leader's. Composition. David's.

[1]Listen to my voice, God, with my lament;
    from the terror of the enemy may you guard my life.
[2]May you hide me from the company[1] of evil people,
    from the crowd of people who do harm,
[3]People who whet their tongue like a sword,
    who direct[2] their bitter word like an arrow.
[4]Shooting[3] from[4] hiding at the virtuous person,
    they shoot at him suddenly and do not fear.
[5]They take hold of an evil word for themselves,[5]
    they proclaim it, hiding traps.[6]

1. While *sôd* can also mean "plans," *rigšâ* has to mean "crowd," and this retrospectively establishes the meaning of *sôd* as "company" (cf. BDB and NJPS against NRSV and TNIV).
2. See on 58:7 [8]. To avoid the metonymy, J. A. Emerton suggests an ellipse: "They have strung [their bows]—their arrows are bitter words" ("The Translation of Psalm lxiv.4," *JTS*, n.s., 27 [1976]: 391–92).
3. LXX and Jerome take v. 4a as a further clause dependent on v. 2 (cf. EVV), but this makes for rather a long enjambment with a heavy break at the end of the colon before the asyndetic second colon. I rather take v. 4a as a circumstantial inf. leading into v. 4b.
4. Lit. "in."
5. The use of *ḥāzaq* piel is unique (cf. BDB), but in general the piel of *ḥāzaq* can have the same variety of meanings as the hiphil, and I take it here to have the well-established hiphil meaning "grasp." For "encourage each other in evil plans" (TNIV), one would expect a direct personal obj. and an impersonal prepositional expression instead of the opposite.
6. I take the "evil word" to carry over its force into the second colon as obj. of "proclaim" and understand the inf. as circumstantial. EVV's "They talk about hiding" (cf. LXX, but contrast Jerome) requires a unique use of *l* (though *'el* is so used: see 2:7).

They say, "Who will see them?"
 ⁶as they plot [acts of] wickedness.[7]
"We have perfected a well-plotted plot;
 yes, the human heart and mind are deep."

⁷But God has shot them with an arrow;
 suddenly their blows came.
⁸They made it tumble on themselves with their tongue;[8]
 all who see them would shake their head/flee.
⁹Everyone was in awe;
 they have proclaimed God's act,
 taught about his deed.[9]

¹⁰The faithful person rejoices in Yhwh,
 and takes refuge in him,
 and all the upright of heart exult.[10]

Interpretation

"While Psalm 63 was focused on God, with the enemy on the edges of the picture, here the composition is reversed, although the outcome is the same."[11] Verses 1–6 form a plea to God for protection from people who are plotting trouble in such a way as to imperil the suppliant's life. Despite the reference to "lament" (v. 1), the prayer presupposes a threatening situation rather than one in which calamity has actually fallen. It is thus a "protective psalm,"[12] with an anxiety about it that prevents us calling it a psalm of trust. Verses 7–9 then comprise a sequence of wayyiqtol and qatal statements, which I take to refer to past experience of God's deliverance or to the proclamation of such acts in worship, which builds up faith. Either way they lead to the affirmation in v. 10, which constitutes an answer to the opening lines and echoes the end of Ps. 63.

7. See 58:2 [3].
8. Or "They made their tongue tumble against themselves" (cf. Barthélemy, *Psaumes*, 413, following Qimchi); "their tongue" is then explicative of the verb's suffix. For possible emendations, see Michael Barré, "A Proposal on the Crux of Psalm lxiv 9a," *VT* 46 (1996): 115–19.
9. *śākal* hiphil; given the parallelism, "understand" (Jerome) or "ponder" (NRSV, TNIV) are less likely, as is "his deed which they perceived" (NJPS).
10. JM 119k argues that this weyiqtol form indicates that this and the opening verb are jussive; but coordinating *w* is quite possible if the two verbs are understood to have the same time reference.
11. Kidner, *Psalms*, 2:227.
12. Mowinckel, *Psalms*, 1:220.

265

The psalm contains a number of paronomasias, a number of calculated repetitions and reuses of words, and thus some ironies. It also contains several expressions difficult to construe. All these have generated proposals for emending the text, though the difficulties of interpretation may issue from the psalm's elusive and allusive poetic nature. We do not know when it was written; we can imagine it on the lips of leaders or of ordinary people before or after the exile. The Midrash sets it on the lips of Daniel (see Dan. 6).[13]

> The leader's. Composition. David's.

Heading. See glossary. A. Strobel argues for a setting in Absalom's revolt.[14]

64:1–6. The bulk of the psalm, then, concerns the activity of people plotting against the suppliant. It begins with two lines of plea (vv. 1–2), but the section is dominated by a lament at these people's secretive activity, which makes it more threatening than open hostility (vv. 3–6). The lines might refer to political plotting or to the use of magic and curses.

> **¹**Listen to my voice, God, with my lament;
>   from the terror of the enemy may you guard my life.

The opening line comprises a standard two-part plea, for God to listen and to act. The LXX translates "as I make request" and Jerome "as I speak," but *śîaḥ* implies something more affective than that (cf. 55:2 [3]). The psalm moves quickly from the first request to the second; usually the second colon would re-express the request for a hearing (e.g., 61:1 [2]). This speedy transition suggests a sense of urgency.[15] The reason for it, even if nothing has yet happened, begins to be expressed in the second colon and is elaborated in the lines that follow. Yet despite the terrifying nature of the threat, the action the psalm looks for is not the putting down or killing of the enemy but simply protection. As is often the case, the "terror" from which the psalm seeks protection is not the subjective feeling of dread but the objective dreadfulness of the threat that confronts the suppliant.

> **²**May you hide me from the company of evil people,
>   from the crowd of people who do harm,

---

13. *Midrash on the Psalms*, 1:526–29.
14. "Le psaume lxiv," *RB* 57 (1950): 161–73.
15. So Gerstenberger, *Psalms*, 2:17.

In elaborating that second colon, v. 2 re-expresses this point. While the opening verb thus restates "guard my life," the subsequent prepositional phrase takes the description of peril in a slightly different direction. The parallel colon in turn restates that description. Both cola make clear that the singular "enemy" is not to be taken to imply that merely one person threatens the suppliant. The psalm is talking about a company or a crowd of *bad people who do *harm. The verbs cognate with "company" and "crowd" come together in 2:1–2 and perhaps reflect the psalm's concern with the pressure on a leader.

> ³People who whet their tongue like a sword,
>   who direct their bitter word like an arrow.

Verse 3 expands on the wrongfulness, in two further parallel cola arranged abcdb′c′d′e. There are two third-person qatal verbs; the preposition on "sword" carries over to "arrow" (cf. Syr), and the suffix on "tongue" carries over to "word." As is commonly the case in the psalms, the people's weapons are their words. Their tongue is like the sword they sharpen in order to make sure it does its work; their word is like the arrow that they aim at its target. They thus intend their word to be bitter; the adjective closes off the line. The expression thus probably involves a metonymy or metalepsis: the word is bitter because it issues in bitterness, and/or the arrow is bitter because it is dipped in poison (cf. Tg). "Word" will reappear in v. 5 and "arrow" and "tongue" in vv. 7–8, where it will transpire that God is also an archer, and that the assailants' tongues are their own downfall rather than that of the suppliant.

> ⁴Shooting from hiding at the virtuous person,
>   they shoot at him suddenly and do not fear.

Verse 4 itself involves a sequence of such repetitions and paronomasias. Every word in the line resonates with other verses. "Shoot" (*yārâ*) comes in both cola and will recur in v. 7: at the moment the enemies are doing the shooting, and that fearlessly, but they would be advised to recall who has done shooting before. "Hiding" is a noun related to the verb in v. 2: in light of the fact that they are in hiding, the suppliant has already asked to be given a place of hiding. They shoot at a person who is virtuous or perfect (*tām*), in the conviction that they have perfected (*tāmam*) a plan to put this person down (v. 6). They shoot suddenly, but so does God (v. 7; the only two uses of *pit'ōm* in the Psalms). "Fear" (or is it *revere?) is *yārē'*, following on the two occurrences of *yārâ*; shooting and fearing/revering should go together but do not.[16] These people do not fear/revere, but the rest of humanity will turn out to be wiser (v. 9).

> [5a-b]They take hold of an evil word for themselves,
>   they proclaim it, hiding traps.

In light of these paronomasias, the opening of v. 5a–b suggests an irony. It will eventually transpire that the plotters are taking hold of an evil word for themselves in a different sense from the one they think. Likewise the parallel colon has them making proclamation about their plan to each other and perhaps to other people, boasting about it confidently,[17] but they are going to find their proclamation giving way to another (v. 9). The new verb for "hide," *ṭāman*, will generate another paronomasia with "perfect" (*tāmam*) in v. 6.

> [5c]They say, "Who will see them?"
>   [6]as they plot [acts of] wickedness.
> "We have perfected a well-plotted plot;
>   yes, the human heart and mind are deep."

I take vv. 5c–6a as a further bicolon.[18] The plotters' misguided confidence (v. 5c) regarding their *wickedness explains the misguided openness of their talk (v. 5a–b). As is often the case, "see" (*rā'â*) makes for another paronomasia with "fear/revere" (*yārē'*), while "plot" will reappear twice in the next colon. The irony will be extended when "see" reappears in v. 8.

In v. 6b–c the two further forms from *ḥāpaś* perhaps convey a sense of bathos; these people are all plotting, plotting, plotting. Meanwhile the opening verb takes up the root *tāmam* (and/or *ṭāman*).[19] They have perfected (and/or hidden) a well-plotted plot. So they think. The second colon sounds like a proverbial saying (cf. Prov. 18:4; 20:5; Eccles. 7:24). In the context it continues the plotters' statement from the first colon and thus carries further irony. They are so confident, so sure of their plans on the basis of their wisdom. They are such deep thinkers; their minds are so sharp. So they think.

64:7–9. The psalm now sets another consideration against all that. Jerome and EVV take these wayyiqtols and qatals as perfects of certainty

---

16. The similarity of *rā'â*, *yārē'*, and *yārâ* can cause confusion; Syr takes the last verb in v. 4 to be *rā'â* (see).

17. EVV assume that *sāpar* piel has a watered-down sense (cf. BDB), but it can retain its usual meaning, albeit with this irony.

18. Cf. Gunkel, *Psalmen*, 269.

19. See *BHS*; also NJPS's note.

that refer to the future,[20] but there is no parallel for such a long sequence of these, and their content does not correspond to that of the plea. If one may imagine the parts of a psalm belonging to different stages in the suppliant's experience, vv. 7–9 might offer testimony to an act of deliverance that responded to the prayer in vv. 1–6, but the evidence is that in such circumstances people used a thanksgiving/testimony psalm. A sequence of qatals might be precative, but this sequence is dominated by wayyiqtols, making this even less plausible a solution than usual. More likely the psalm is speaking of something that is literally past. This might be the suppliant's own past experience of God's deliverance, a motif in Ps. 61. More likely (in light of v. 9) it is God's activity in the people's life, which was celebrated in worship in a way that gives the suppliant personal confidence in a time of personal peril, as in Ps. 63.

> [7]But God has shot them with an arrow;
>   suddenly their blows came.

Thus v. 7 recalls the way God has shot arrows at people like this in the past; the verb and the noun are taken up from vv. 3–4.[21] In the parallel colon, "suddenly"[22] likewise picks up from v. 4. In contrast, "blows" comes only here in the Psalms but elsewhere often describes God's acts against Israel's foes (e.g., Josh. 10:10; Judg. 11:33; 1 Sam. 4:8, 10).

> [8]They made it tumble on themselves with their tongue;
>   all who see them would shake their head/flee.

Verse 8 puts the foes' downfall another way. Actually v. 7 had already put it two ways, as God's act (v. 7a) and as something that simply happened (v. 7b). Verse 8a now describes it as something they brought on themselves, in keeping with the irony and paronomasia that has characterized the psalm. They have been expecting to make people collapse; actually they have made things collapse on themselves. Their tongue was their weapon (v. 3); their tongue has become the cause of their self-inflicted disaster. The second colon continues this analysis. They had assumed that no one would see their traps (before falling into them); now people see what has happened to the trappers themselves, and they shake their head in satisfaction or horror (*nûd* hitpolel; so LXX) and/or flee (*nādad* hitpol; so Jerome). There is yet another irony there. The foes might have been looking for a victory that horrified people or

---

20. Cf. DG 82c; *TTH* 82; GKC 111w.
21. But LXX and Syr take *wayyōrēm* as from *rûm*, "be on high."
22. MT associates this with the first colon, but linking it with the second makes for a 3-3 line and a parallel with its place in v. 4b.

made them flee in fear, but they have actually experienced a defeat that had that effect.

> [9]Everyone was in awe;
>> they have proclaimed God's act,
>> taught about his deed.

There was thus indeed a sense in which people responded with fear or *reverence, but it was a different sense from the one the plotters had in mind, and this wise fear or reverence on everyone's part (e.g., 33:8; 40:3 [4]; 52:6 [8]; 67:7 [8]) contrasts with the plotters' senseless lack of it (v. 4). On the other hand, this reaction of reverence or fear (*yārē'*) linked logically with the seeing (*rā'â*) that the end of v. 8 spoke of (Sym pardonably repeats a form of *rā'â* here at the beginning of v. 9). This reverence/fear thus issued in a proclamation that likewise differed from that of the plotters (v. 5). They are people doing harm (*pō'ălê 'āwen*, v. 2); this deed of God's (*pō'al*) reverses that. The third, parallel colon in this tricolon advertises that we are coming to the end of a section. Yes, wise people have both issued and listened to this proclamation and teaching, but the action of the plotters indicates that they have ignored it. And a speech act with positive significance replaces all the speech acts designed to have malicious effect.[23]

64:10. A further tricolon in v. 10 (3-2-2) closes off the psalm with the lesson that the suppliant especially needs to hear.

> [10]The faithful person rejoices in Yhwh,
>> and takes refuge in him,
>> and all the upright of heart exult.

If this verse is true, is complaint (v. 1) possible? The first two cola are parallel in form though temporally sequential. "The faithful person" is the subject of both cola; a qatal verb then balances a yiqtol verb, and "in him" balances "in Yhwh." The order of the verbs is suggestive. The faithful person begins by rejoicing in the story of what Yhwh has done, then responds (*w*-consecutive) by taking refuge, finding in Yhwh the refuge that vv. 1–2 asked for. The final colon is in turn parallel to the first in content, generalizing its point, as it takes up the hitpael of *hālal* from 63:11 [12]. The plotters have made a point about the heart (v. 6; the word *lēb*, translated "mind" there). The psalm's final irony lies in the fact that they thought they were deep, but actually they were both shallow and crooked. They thought they could make the upright collapse, but upright people can know they do not collapse.

23. Cf. Schaefer, *Psalms*, 155.

Theological Implications

Two marks of the psalm suggest theological reflections. One concerns language. The psalm's systematic use of paronomasia, repetition, irony, metonymy, and metaphor presupposes a sense of the unity of reality that is grounded in God. Everything connects. The law of reality is the law of correspondence, because one God's being lies behind it. We can look for connections even where things look unconnected or conflicted and can believe there is meaning and coherence even where things look meaningless and fragmented.

The other concerns worship. One of its key features is the recollection of what God has done in the past. Worship appropriately gives opportunity to express our experience, our laments, and our longings, but if we stop at that, we have hardly moved forward. Worship makes it possible to express our fears and longings because it provides a context in which we can also be reminded of what God has done and therefore can be expected to do again. That is what can make it possible to leave worship in a different place from the one we occupied when we arrived.

Psalm 65

Politics and Harvest, Israel and the World

Translation

The leader's. Composition. David's. Song.

¹To you silence is praise,[1]
   God in Zion,
And to you a promise is fulfilled,
   ²one who listens to prayer;
All flesh can come right to you,
   ³with their wayward deeds.[2]
Whereas[3] our rebellions are too mighty for me, [MT]/us, [LXX]
   you are the one who expiates them.

⁴The good fortune of the one you choose
   and bring near to dwell in your courtyards!
We shall be filled with the goodness of your house,
   your holy palace.[4]

1. LXX and Syr have "Praise is fitting," a true and good (though less striking) point that requires considerable stretching of the meaning of the root from which they are deriving the word, which usually means "resemble." That root has been taken to be *dāmâ*, and this has been taken to imply the pointing *dōmîyâ* rather than *dumîyâ* (from *dûm*); so (e.g.) *DCH*. But there is sufficient overlap between the various roots *dûm*, *dāmâ*, and *dāmam* to make this repointing unnecessary; *dumîyâ* could presuppose *dûm* as a by-form of *dāmâ*.
2. For the const. phrase, see BDB 183b, and for this idiom elsewhere, see 105:27; 145:5.
3. In the asyndetic line, the first colon is subordinate to the second.
4. On the const., see on 46:4 [5].

⁵You answer us with awesome deeds in faithfulness,
God who delivers us.

An object of trust for all the farthest points of the earth
and the distant sea,⁵
⁶Establisher of the mountains by his vigor,
girded with might,
⁷Stiller of the seas' roar,
the roar of their waves, yes, the tumult of the countries,
⁸The people who live at the farthest points are in awe at your signs;⁶
you make the entrances of morning and evening resound.

⁹You have attended to the earth and watered it;⁷
you greatly enrich it.
God's stream is full of water;
you prepare their grain⁸ because thus you prepare it,⁹
¹⁰Saturating its furrows, smoothing its grooves,¹⁰
you soften it with rains,¹¹ you bless its growth.
¹¹You have crowned the year of your goodness;
your cart tracks flow with richness.¹²
¹²Wilderness pastures flow,
hills gird on joy,
¹³Meadows put on flocks,
vales wrap on wheat,¹³
they shout, yes they sing.

Interpretation

This psalm of praise reverts to the focus on address to God that characterized Ps. 63. Verses 1–3 acknowledge Yhwh as the object of trust and praise, the one who answers prayer, and the one who pardons wrongdoing. Verses 4–5a then begin a celebration of God's good gifts and God's acts of deliverance toward the people who worship on Zion. Verses 5b–8 elaborate

5. Tg's reference to the distant "islands" (cf. *BHS*) assimilates to Isa. 66:19.

6. Perhaps "so that . . ." (so GKC 111l; *IBHS* 33.3.5b).

7. The form *těšōqěqehā* comes from *šûq*, which I take to be a by-form of *šāqâ* (so *HALOT*; cf. Vrs) rather than a different verb meaning "be abundant" (so BDB).

8. Presumably "people's grain," but there is no antecedent for the suffix.

9. The f. suffix refers back to *'ereṣ*; the first, second, and fourth cola in v. 9 all end with this suffix.

10. Not "ridges" (EVV)—see BDB and *HALOT*; *gědûd* comes from *gādad* (cut) and parallels *telem* rather than contrasting with it.

11. Not merely "showers," as the etymology of *rěbîbîm* hints.

12. Lit. "fat" (cf. 63:5 [6]).

13. Not "corn" in the American sense; *bar* and *dāgān* (v. 9) have similar meanings.

273

on the second of these themes, spelling out the worldwide significance of God's beneficent power. Verses 9–13 elaborate the first aspect in commemorating God's generosity with the rain that makes the crops grow.

It has been suggested that vv. 1–8 and 9–13 are of independent origin, though the distinctiveness of vv. 5b–8 over vv. 1–5a is also marked, and vv. 9–13 do spell out the nature of God's "goodness" (vv. 4, 11). Whether the parts are of separate origin or not, part of the psalm's interest lies in the collocation of its different themes. The whole psalm would fit the celebration of Passover/Unleavened Bread or Pentecost or Sukkot, seasons when Israel looks forward to or celebrates the harvest, makes pilgrimage to the sanctuary, and commemorates God's acts in its own life.[14] When the Day of Atonement happened just before Sukkot, this would heighten the significance of the collocation of sin with praise for the harvest. The movement between singular and plural in vv. 3–5 suggests that the psalm could be used by an ordinary worshipper aware of being a member of the people as a whole, or a king or governor, or most likely by a priest.

The leader's. Composition. David's. Song.

Heading. See glossary. Psalms 65–68 are all "songs."[15] Some LXX MSS add, "of Jeremiah and Ezekiel, from the decree of the sojourning when they were about to set forth" (or some variation on that). That would apparently connect the psalm with the moment when people were being taken off into exile and suggest linking the promises of v. 1c with prayer for restoration from exile.[16]

65:1–3. The opening section of the psalm focuses on God in Zion (where presumably this praise is offered), one to whom people fulfill promises and to whom they come despite their sin. I take the three verses as four 3-2 lines.

1a–bTo you silence is praise,
God in Zion,

An opening acknowledgment, recalling that in Ps. 62, declares that silence is praise:[17] that is, once again that silence can be a novel way of

---

14. The links with a situation such as that described in 1 Kings 8:35–36 (e.g., A. Anderson, *Psalms*, 1:464) seem less obvious.

15. On their links, see Hossfeld and Zenger, *Psalms 2*, 141, 167–68.

16. Cf. Qimchi; Theodoret, *Psalms*, 1:364. Cassiodorus makes the link with the people's actual *return* (in which presumably the two prophets did not share), by taking "they" to refer to people in general, not the prophets (*Psalms*, 2:96).

17. See further Eduard Thurneysen, "Das Wunder des Gottesdienstes," *EvT* 12 (1956): 529–33.

recognizing God, insofar as it implies a trustful rest in God. Although Ps. 65 does not then follow the formal structure of a praise hymn in which a comment about praise is followed by the reasons for praise, it reflects its substance, beginning in the second colon. Restful silence is possible in connection with God in Zion, the one in whose presence the worshippers stand; the psalm will go on to elaborate on that.

> ¹ᶜAnd to you a promise is fulfilled,
> ²ᵃone who listens to prayer;

The second line of acknowledgment (vv. 1c–2a) again begins *lĕkā*: to this God, promises are appropriately fulfilled. This time the reasons follow more concretely in the second colon. God is one who listens to prayer in such a way as to answer it. The rest of the psalm will imply a particular reference to prayers for rain and for a good harvest (cf. Ps. 67), alongside which is the commitment to bring offerings to God when these prayers have been answered. Perhaps this repeated "to you" links with the evidence from elsewhere in the OT that Israelites often saw Baal rather than Yhwh as the deity who made the crops grow. No—to you, to you, says the psalm.[18] Certainly other prayers were also naturally accompanied by promises: e.g., 1 Sam. 1:10–11, set in the context of "the festival" at Shiloh. That story suggests that a festival pilgrimage to the sanctuary was also the natural occasion for individual prayers with their associated promises and that a subsequent visit would be the occasion for keeping those promises.

> ²ᵇAll flesh can come right to you,
> ³ᵃwith their wayward deeds.

The third line again follows the structure of the first two, with the opening colon another statement about God as object of worship. In the immediate context "all flesh" suggests all Israelite humanity, the whole nation that comes to Yhwh on Zion as they make their pilgrimage for the festival, but vv. 5b–8 will open up the possibility of a broader meaning, a reference to all the world. The second colon then brings a surprise. The worshippers come to Zion not only "with" praise and offerings but also "with" sins.[19] It transpires that the joy of the festival does not exclude an awareness that people come as those whose lives are *wayward. Can they do that? The distinctive opening preposition highlights the question but also implies the answer, for it already declares that people come not merely "to you" but "right to you," *'ad* not just *lĕ*.

18. Cf. Cassiodorus, *Psalms*, 2:97; Brueggemann, *Message of the Psalms*, 135.
19. The construction involving the verb *bô'*, but with a word for "with," recurs in 66:13; cf. GKC 119n.

> 3b-cWhereas our rebellions are too mighty for me, [MT]/us, [LXX]
> you are the one who expiates them.

Verse 3b–c begins with the suppliant personally acknowledging that there is indeed a problem here. That is now articulated in terms of the people's *rebellion, which is quite overwhelming for the suppliant. If one thinks of the "I" as that of an ordinary member of the community, this suggests that it means the rebellion places an obstacle between humanity and God that we cannot overcome. We cannot come into God's presence as if our lives were in order. How can rebels come before the king? Yet this is possible because God overcomes what would be overwhelming, because the Great King covers or erases the record of rebellions. But the move in MT between "me" and "our" recalls Isaiah's move between his own stained lips and those of the people as a whole (Isa. 6:5). This raises the question whether the "I" is rather that of some representative person such as a priest or king aware that the people's rebellion is overwhelming because he cannot do anything to overcome its implications. It is just as well that God is the one who does so. This is then underlined by the use of the verb *kipper*. The verb probably means either "cover" or "wipe off," though we do not know which of these. Nor are we sure of its background and connotations, except that the effect of this action is to deal with something that would be an obstacle or problem between humanity and God; hence the translation "expiate."[20] What is striking about this occurrence of the verb is that God is its subject. The verb is most common in Exodus, Leviticus, and Numbers, where it refers to action taken by human beings to cover stains or shortcomings or to wipe them away, though it is doubtful whether it is possible to do that in respect of deliberate waywardness or rebellion. But this further act of praise that brings vv. 1–3 to a climax acknowledges that God does what the suppliant cannot do. We can be overwhelmed by our people's wrongdoing; God is not.

65:4–5a. "The *good fortune of . . ." often begins a psalm or a section of a psalm, and these three lines (all again 3-2) will turn out to set an agenda for the remainder of it. Verse 4a sums up the opening lines and introduces what follows. Verses 5b–8 will expand on v. 5a, relating more to God's awesome deeds, while vv. 9–13 will expand on the good things of God's house (v. 4b). Verse 4a resumes the singular of v. 3a (MT); verses 4b–5a in turn resume the plural "our" of v. 3b.

> 4The good fortune of the one you choose
> and bring near to dwell in your courtyards!

20. For discussion, see (e.g.) *NIDOTTE*.

> We shall be filled with the goodness of your house,
> your holy palace.

The reference to "the one"[21] fits with the singular expressions that run through vv. 1–3. Like the NT, when the OT talks about God choosing, this does not usually relate to ordinary individuals except insofar as they are members of the chosen people or insofar as God chooses individuals in special connections. So this verb suggests that the psalm belongs to someone who is thus specially chosen, such as a king or a priest (e.g., Num. 16–17; Deut. 17:14–20; 18:1–5; 1 Sam. 16:1–13; 1 Chron. 28:1–6; Hag. 2:20–23). A priest in particular is indeed one "brought near" to God by virtue of his role in the temple (e.g., Exod. 40:12, 14, 32; Lev. 7:35; 9:7–8; Num. 16:5, 10; Ezek. 40:46; 44:15–16). The king is not spoken of in these terms, and only exceptionally is the language applied to the coming "prince" (Jer. 30:21).[22] Likewise, while Ps. 15:1 does speak of an ordinary person "dwelling" in the temple (*šākan*), it would be a priest who most literally "dwells" in the temple courtyards, the environs that surround God's own dwelling at the center of the palace complex.[23]

If v. 4a applies in particular to a priest, v. 4b then significantly generalizes its statements. The entire people will enjoy the good things that issue from this house/sanctuary/palace: it is a dwelling, it is a holy place, it is a place of splendor. A cohortative appropriately follows the enthusiastic declaration in v. 4a, though it is a cohortative of assurance.[24] The festival the people are celebrating is the evidence that v. 4b is true. The *goodness or good things there will immediately be the fine food and drink that people enjoyed at the festival. Coming to the temple on such an occasion is like coming to the royal *palace for a banquet, but these good things will be symbols of something broader. The festival celebrates the goodness of God that gave people the land and gives them this year's harvest. It is the God who dwells in this house who is key to their staying in the land. If God ever abandons this house, they would find themselves losing the land itself (as the exile showed). It is God's presence in this holy place that makes it possible for them to come and

---

21. It is actually *yiškōn* (lit. "[so that] he may dwell") that eventually establishes that the line refers to an individual.

22. Ahaz's "drawing near" a Damascene altar (2 Kings 16:12), if anything, underlines the unacceptability of a king's "drawing near."

23. On the nature of these courtyards at various periods, see Keel, *Symbolism*, 128–44.

24. NJPS renders "may we be sated" and translates the yiqtol in v. 5 with an impv. (so also LXX there, matching its impv. in v. 2a; cf. Jerome in vv. 10–11), but this seems to introduce an alien note into the ethos of praise in the psalm. Contrast Dahood (*Psalms*, 2:109), who sees the whole as a prayer psalm.

ask God to give good things to them each year (e.g., Ps. 67). It is from God's presence there that good things flow out.

> ⁵ᵃYou answer us with awesome deeds in faithfulness,
> God who delivers us.

Verse 5a speaks of the other side to "good fortune." Whereas "goodness" suggests the year-by-year blessings of the harvest, awesome deeds suggests the more occasional acts that make people bow in *reverence before God. While people did pray for the harvest and God did "answer" such prayers, actual references to God's "answering" relate rather consistently to prayers for God to act amid crises (e.g., 3:4 [5]; 4:1 [2]; 20:1, 6, [2, 7]; 60:5 [7]). Likewise *faithfulness would be expressed in the harvest and in such awesome deeds, but the latter dominate the use of the word (e.g., 7:17 [18]; 9:4, 8 [5, 9]; 35:24, 28; contrast 85:10–13 [11–14]). God's *delivering, too, relates to such acts.

65:5b–8. Verses 5b–8 might be a long enjambment dependent on v. 5a, but I rather see it as a long extraposition leading into v. 8.²⁵ Either way, in substance it follows on from v. 5a as it describes the being of the God who answers and delivers. In doing so, however, it broadens the description in typical even if unexpected directions. First, the one who so acts is not a mere local God of Israel but the God of all the earth. Second, that makes this God not merely (e.g.) an object of fear but also an object of *trust for all the earth. God's acts on Israel's behalf invite all the earth into trust in this God. Third, the implication or the basis of these "awesome deeds" is this God's power over the whole creation. The four lines work abb′a′; the two inside lines describe God's acts, the two outside lines describe people's reaction.

> ⁵ᵇAn object of trust for all the farthest points of the earth
> and the distant sea,

Thus v. 5b first describes God, astonishingly, as an [object of] *trust for the whole world. There is no indication that in its reach it means less than it says (e.g., that it has in mind only Israelites all over the world), though I assume it means that this is what Israel's God *can* be, rather than indicating that the whole world are "anonymous Israelites" who trust in Yhwh without realizing it. The reference to the ends of the earth and the distant seas implies a merism. Israel's God is the trust of such faraway places and also the trust of all nearer areas. There is a further abb′a′ neatness about the construction of the parallel noun phrases,

---

25. Seybold (*Psalmen*, 252–54) sees v. 5b as the beginning of a hymnic fragment, linking with what follows.

which read "the farthest points of the earth and the sea of the distant ones": the phrases work plural-singular then singular-plural.

> [6]Establisher of the mountains by his vigor,
>   girded with might,

Verse 6 makes that astonishing statement easier to understand. The God of whom the psalm speaks is not only one whose activity on Israel's behalf implies good news for other peoples but also one who makes the whole world secure and thus makes the lives of all those other peoples secure. The psalm refers to God's being creator, but it does so with two distinctive slants on that. First, the moment when God established the mountains was long ago, but as usual the participles (continuing in v. 7) deconstruct the distinction between an act at the beginning and an ongoing activity in the world. God *is* and not merely *was* the establisher of the mountains. God still keeps the world firm on its foundations. Second, the nature of God's creative work is not merely a matter of bringing it into being. Declarations about creation such as these do not answer the question "Where did the world come from?" but the question "Is the world secure?" It is the firmly established nature of God's world that makes God trustworthy. God has the vigor to make sure that the world is secure. The parallel colon supports that. This God is one who girds on *might. God's might in overcoming sin in a way that is beyond human beings (v. 3, *gābar*) thus stands in continuity with the might shown in creation (*gĕbûrâ*). Both the verb "gird" and this noun suggest a military image; a warrior is a *gibbôr* who girds on armor. God is not merely an efficient contractor (v. 6a) but also a powerful fighter.

> [7]Stiller of the seas' roar,
>   the roar of their waves, yes, the tumult of the countries,

Verse 7 follows on from that and indicates why it needs to be so. Stilling the seas' roar was an aspect of the work God did at the Beginning (see Pss. 29 and 46). There were tumultuous dynamic forces of which God needed to gain control before creating the world as a safe and secure place. But those forces continue to assert themselves (as Pss. 29 and 46 recognize; in light of v. 6 here, note especially the latter's reference to the possibility of the mountains falling into the sea). Again we see the good news in the psalm's participles. God's stilling is not merely a past event, and it had better not be so, because we can see for ourselves the tumultuous dynamic of nature, and we need someone who constrains and harnesses it rather than leaving it to wreak out-of-control havoc. That is the more true when we see this tumultuousness of reality also expressed in the turbulence of the nations (the great powers). So the parallelism in the line has the participle governing three parallel objects. First there is the seas' roar. Then there is the roar of their waves, which simply underlines the point. It is those gigantic waves that awesomely embody the sea's tumult. But then there is also the tumult of the countries. This third phrase is unexpected. The line would be quite complete without it, and the extra clause makes this an attention-drawing long bicolon or tricolon. It also brings us up short by the novelty of its content over against the first two phrases. Indeed, in light of vv. 5a and 5b we might even reckon that this last phrase in the line explicates what has preceded. It is especially in the tumult of the nations that the turbulent dynamic of the seas finds expression, and the reason why God's acts in Israel are good news for the world as a whole is that these acts provide evidence that Israel's God has the tumultuous forces of international politics under control.[26]

> ⁸The people who live at the farthest points are in awe at your signs;
> you make the entrances of morning and evening resound.

In turn v. 8 rounds off the section and coheres with that understanding. "Farthest points" picks up from v. 5b.[27] The peoples' awed *revering of God restates the trust of v. 5b. Again this is no doubt a vision of what is possible for them rather than a description of how things yet are. The "signs" that provoke this awe will again be God's extraordinary acts in delivering Israel from Egypt (e.g., 78:43; 105:27; 135:9), which (among other things) demonstrate for the sake of smaller peoples like Israel that the nations, great powers such as Egypt (or Assyria, Babylon, Persia, or Greece), will not dominate the world forever. The second colon restates the first, complementing the clause in which the far-off peoples are the subjects with one in which they are the objects. Their awe is a response to what God does in making them thus *resound. The "entrances of morning and evening" are the directions from which morning and evening arrive, the east and the west, a novel and allusive parallel to "farthest points." It is another way of saying that the whole world responds to God's acts.

65:9–13. From God's involvement in politics, the last section turns back to God's involvement in nature, developing the implications of v. 4b as the previous section developed the implications of v. 5a. It provides lingering, intense, sensuous portraits of two stages in that involvement.

---

26. LXX's understanding generates a quite different interpretation of vv. 7b–8 as a whole: "The nations will be in tumult, and the people who live at the farthest points will be in fear. . . ."

27. Though the word is now the f. *qěṣôt* instead of the anomalous m. const. *qaṣwê*.

The first half (vv. 9–10) revels in a portrait of God making it rain in the fall and winter, for whether the rains come is the key factor in whether the crops grow and thus whether people eat or die. God is the subject of all ten verbs (the exception is the one in v. 9c, but that proves the rule). There is no doubt that it is God who makes the harvest possible, not Baal or some force within nature (though see the comment on "blessing" in v. 10).[28] The second half (vv. 11–13) revels in a portrait of God in the spring and summer making the crops abound, though here the clauses move away quickly from God's acts to the acts of nature, not in making the crops grow, but in rejoicing in what God does in it. While the section opens with a qatal and a wayyiqtol (cf. also v. 11a), most of its verbs are yiqtol, and I take the whole to describe God's year-by-year activity.

> ⁹You have attended to the earth and watered it;
> 　you greatly enrich it.
> God's stream is full of water;
> 　you prepare their grain because thus you prepare it,

First, God attends. Elsewhere, God's attending to the earth might be bad news (59:5 [6]), but here it is good news because it issues not in calamity but in watering it, like a farmer caringly watering his animals. God thus enriches the land and makes it abundant.

God is able to do that on the basis of possessing a fine irrigation system, with a stream or channel delivering water in a controlled way from God's storehouses or dams in the heavens to the places where it is needed on earth. The move from threatening seas to a beneficent stream parallels that in Ps. 46. The statement is an extraordinarily hopeful one given the precariousness of the rains as Israel experienced it. There is no hint that God might not have carved out this channel so effectively or that someone might have dynamited it. On the contrary, v. 9d declares, the result of God's having this channel is that grain indeed grows well. God prepares and provides grain through having thus prepared and provided the land that grows it.

> ¹⁰Saturating its furrows, smoothing its grooves,
> 　you soften it with rains, you bless its growth.

Enough has been said (we might think), but the psalmist cannot resist saying it some more. Verse 10 adds nothing in content but further enhances the affect of the description. In two parallel infinitival phrases

---

28. Silvia Schroer compares this psalm with a prayer to Baal for rain ("Psalm 65," *UF* 22 [1990]: 285–301).

(continuing the finite verbs)[29] within v. 10a, arranged abb'a', the psalm twice focuses its camera over the furrows and grooves that the plow has dug and the rains have smoothed. Then in two parallel yiqtol clauses within v. 10b it pulls the camera back somewhat and pans over the earth again. First we watch God soften it by means of the autumn rains; then we watch God make its growth flourish by means of the winter rains. God's blessing is what makes for fruitfulness; usually God only blesses living things, so that there is an implicit personification of the earth and/or the crops here. God makes them capable of generating life as happened in making the animal and human creation generate life (Gen. 1:22, 28).

> [11]You have crowned the year of your goodness;
> your cart tracks flow with richness.

That prepares the way for the transition to talk about the harvest. Suddenly the film has fast-forwarded to early summer, the time of the crucial grain harvest. The EVV's "You crown the year with your goodness" may be misleading. We should perhaps think not of a gold crown that sits on top of someone's head but of a wreath around their shoulders; and the expression is "year of your goodness," the year characterized by good things that come from God, perhaps "your good year." The word "*goodness" picks up from v. 4b: it is in the harvest that we experience the goodness that issues from God's presence. The second colon expresses that more concretely and vividly. It is as if God the farmer is driving home with his cart so full of rich grain that it is overflowing from the cart and thus from its tracks.[30]

> [12]Wilderness pastures flow,
> hills gird on joy,
> [13]Meadows put on flocks,
> vales wrap on wheat,
> they shout, yes they sing.

It is not only cultivated crops that thus abound. The first four cola in the final two lines follow an aba'b' pattern. The rains make the pastures in the wilderness flourish with natural growth of grass (v. 12a). The reference is not to actual desert but to areas without settled human habitation because they have only low rainfall, though they are thus sporadically able to sustain small-scale crops. But now it is as if they,

---

29. Cf. GKC 113z.

30. This seems more likely than that the cart is a carriage from which God makes rain flow, both because we have left behind that stage in the drama and because a cart is an odd vehicle to use in this connection.

too, are overflowing (the verb repeats from the previous colon). That flourishing would be a huge blessing for the community's flocks (v. 13a). If the wilderness pastures flourish, then their meadows can support such numerous flocks that it will look as if they are clothed in them. The pastures/meadows thus form one half of the picture of flourishing in vv. 12–13a. The hills/vales form the other half of the picture (vv. 12b and 13b), returning to the picture of abundant grain. It is as if the hills and vales wrap themselves in wheat as the meadows clothe themselves in flocks. Each is completely covered. The result of that is that these hills and vales also gird themselves (yet again the same image of clothing) in joy. Although this might be a metonymy (it is the human beings, the harvesters of the grain, who so rejoice), it parallels the picture of trees clapping their hands (e.g., Isa. 55:12). It more likely sees nature itself as joining in worship, by virtue of the fact that it possesses the vital requirements for worship such as hands to wave or clap. So the picture perhaps points to the way grain sways and waves in the breeze in the manner of a congregation of worshippers swaying and waving their hands. The imagery also suggests that the earth's fruitfulness is itself its act of praise. It is through its fruitfulness that it glorifies God.[31] This link between its fruitfulness and its praise extends the link between the earth and humanity, since there is a sense in which the fruitfulness of our lives of faithfulness is an aspect of our worship.

Formally, these four cola in vv. 12–13b would be complete in themselves, but they are actually completed by a further colon that turns v. 13 into a final closing tricolon. As the hills rejoice, so the vales shout and sing as the ears of grain whistle in the wind (Qimchi). In retrospect, the lines need that final colon, which pairs with v. 12b and brings the two lines and the psalm as a whole to a glorious close. It is the hills and vales that shout and sing for joy, but they do invite the human worshippers to join in.

Theological Implications

Psalm 65 holds together a series of pairs of realities that may not seem to belong together or may drift apart. It begins by hinting that a proper response to God involves trust as a form of praise, prayers, and associated promises that we do keep, and it also involves recognition of our wrongdoing. The last of these stimulates the observation that a

31. Cf. Howard N. Wallace, *"Jubilate Deo omnis terra:* God and Earth in Psalm 65," in *The Earth Story in the Psalms and the Prophets*, ed., Norman C. Habel (Sheffield: Sheffield Academic Press, 2001), 51–64 (see 59).

scene in which a leader acknowledges sinfulness "is nearly unthinkable in our public life."[32] As I write in the aftermath of the invasion of Iraq, there have been many reasons why leaders might so acknowledge failure, but no such acknowledgments have so far been forthcoming. In the psalm, admittedly, it seems likely that the leader who makes this acknowledgment is a person such as a priest rather than a king. The psalm therefore suggests the further reflection that it is the task of pastors to lead the church in public acknowledgment of the nation's waywardness and rebelliousness, not standing superior in relation to it, but identifying with it.

Second, it holds together God's relationship with the whole world and God's relationship with Israel. The dynamic of God's relationship with both involves the assumption that the world is drawn to acknowledge God through what it sees happening in the lives of the people of God. When this does not happen, it is easy for the people of God to feel that this is their fault, and that may often be so, though the psalm invites at least as much an opposite inference. It is God who must make such things happen, and the psalm invites us to urge God to act in the lives of the people of God so that the world does come to recognize God.

Third, the psalm holds together politics and harvest. It may have been easy for Israel to let those drift apart. They knew that Yhwh was sovereign in history, but they often turned to Baal for help with the harvest. The psalm assumes that one God is lord of the whole of reality and thus of these two aspects of it. God is sovereign in the onetime events and the recurrent cycle of nature, in deliverance and in blessing. And the earth, which we are inclined to view as inanimate, is one with humanity in having the capacity to worship and glorify God.[33]

---

32. Brueggemann, *Message of the Psalms*, 135.
33. Cf. Howard N. Wallace, *"Jubilate Deo omnis terra,"* in *Earth Story* (ed. Habel), 51–64.

Psalm 66

Praise and Thanksgiving,
Community and Individual,
Israel and the World

Translation

The leader's. Song. Composition.

¹Shout to God, all the earth,
  ²make music for the honor of his name,
  make his praise honored,
³Say to God, "How awesome in your deeds;[1]
  at the greatness of your strength your enemies wither[2] before you.
⁴All the earth bows low to you,
  makes music to you, makes music to your name." (Rise)

⁵Come and see God's deeds,
  awesome in his assertive action[3] upon[4] humanity.

1. EVV have "awesome are your deeds," but "awesome" is sg., "deeds" pl. Hebrew can tolerate such nonagreement (cf. GKC 145r), but JM 149b emphasizes how rarely a predicative adj. disagrees with its noun. I take it that the asyndetic exclamation forms an extraposition leading into the parallel colon. Cf. v. 5.
2. For *kāḥaš*, EVV have "cower"; but see John H. Eaton, "Some Questions of Philology and Exegesis in the Psalms," *JTS*, n.s., 19 (1968): 603–9 (see 603–4), and cf. BDB.
3. *'ălîlâ* usually implies wanton or arbitrary deeds, and I assume that a positive form of such a meaning attaches to the word here (cf. 9:11 [12]). Vrs imply pl. *'ălîlôt*.
4. *'Al*: hardly "for" (TNIV) or even merely "among" (NRSV).

⁶When he turned sea into dry land,
  they crossed over⁵ the river on foot.
There we rejoiced in him,
  ⁷one who rules forever by his vigor.
His eyes watch the nations;
  the rebellious—they cannot stand tall. (Rise)

⁸Worship our God,⁶ peoples,
  make heard the voicing of his praise,
⁹The one who places us⁷ in life⁸
  and has not given our foot to faltering.
¹⁰For you have tested us, God,
  you have smelted us as silver is smelted,
¹¹You have brought us into a net,
  you have put a constraint on our hips,
¹²You have let people ride at our head,⁹
  we have come into fire and water,
  but¹⁰ you have brought us out into flourishing.

¹³I will come into your house with whole-offerings,
  I will discharge to you my promises,
¹⁴Those which my lips uttered
  and my mouth spoke in my trouble.
¹⁵As whole-offerings I will send up fatlings to you,
  with the aroma of rams;
  I will make ready¹¹ bulls and goats. (Rise)

¹⁶Come and listen, and I will tell, all who revere God,
  what he has done for me.¹²
¹⁷To him I called with my mouth,
  and he was extolled on my tongue.
¹⁸If I could have seen¹³ harm in my heart,
  my Lord would not listen.

5. In the context, the yiqtol verb seems likely to have straightforward past reference; v. 6b will support this.

6. Tg and Syr have simply "God."

7. *Napšēnû*, lit. "our *person."

8. The parallelism supports this understanding rather than "among the living."

9. EVV have "ride over our head," but this would require *'al*; see (e.g.) 18:43 [44] for the regular use of *lĕ* with *rō'š*. In light of referring vv. 9–12 to the exodus, Erik Haglund takes *'ĕnôš* to denote Moses (*Historical Motifs in the Psalms* [Lund: CWK Gleerup, 1984], 48). But the premise is unpersuasive.

10. Not "and" (so LXX).

11. Cf. NEB; the verb *'āśâ* (do, make) can mean "prepare" or "provide" and is often used thus in connection with sacrifices.

12. *Napšî*, "for me in *person"?

13. To spell out the meaning of *rā'îtî*, NRSV and TNIV have "had cherished," seen with approval, while NJPS has "had in mind," envisaged.

> [19]But in fact[14] God listened,
>   paid heed to the sound of my plea.
> [20]God be worshipped,
>   the one who did not turn away my plea,
>   or his commitment from me.

Interpretation

The psalm begins in vv. 1–12 like a hymn, alternating challenges to worship with recollections of the acts of God through which the people came to be in the land and were sustained in their life there, but vv. 13–20 then constitute an individual's thanksgiving for an act of deliverance, accompanying the fulfilling of a promise to bring an offering.[15] These two parts might be of separate origin, like (e.g.) the different parts of Ps. 108, though neither could quite stand on its own. Whether this is so or not, the combination of elements in the psalm as we have it illustrates the intrinsic link between praise and thanksgiving, between God's acts in the past and in the present.

The offerings in vv. 13–20 are much greater than an ordinary single individual would offer. The language can hardly be merely hyperbolic, but possibly an ordinary person might speak as sharing in the worship of the people as a whole, as when we make our confession or declare our faith in worship but speak as "I" (cf. 50:8–10; Isa. 1:11). More likely the scale of the offerings indicates that a leader such as a king or governor speaks, and if we read the psalm that way, it forms a more coherent whole in which both parts relate to the destiny of the entire people. We do not know what particular answer to prayer might have inspired the psalm.

The hymn in vv. 1–12 divides into three sections, a summons to shout (vv. 1–4), a summons to come and consider what God once did (vv. 5–7), and a summons to worship in light of what God has done (vv. 8–12). In this sequence summons is more prominent nearer the beginning, reasons for praise more prominent nearer the end, and a heightening appears as the sections comprise three lines, then four, then five. The testimony in vv. 13–20 divides into two parts (vv. 13–15 and vv. 16–20); the second with its "come and listen" echoes the "come and see" in the second section from the beginning (v. 5). In the hymn there is movement between address to people and ad-

---

14. *'Ākēn*; not "therefore" (LXX, Jerome).
15. On this, see Julia M. O'Brien, "Because God Heard My Voice," in *The Listening Heart* (Roland E. Murphy Festschrift; ed. Kenneth G. Hoglund et al.; JSOTSup 58; Sheffield: Sheffield Academic Press, 1987), 281–98.

dress to God; in the testimony, there is the same movement but in the reverse direction.[16]

In its celebration of God's awesomeness, with the implications of this for the whole world as well as for Israel, Ps. 66 follows well on Ps. 65.[17]

The leader's. Song. Composition.

Heading. See glossary. Some LXX MSS add "Of the resurrection," suggesting that Christians used (part of) the psalm at Easter.

66:1–4. The opening section focuses on challenging the whole world to acknowledge God. Unusually, it begins with a tricolon, underlining the force of its challenge. Verses 3–4 then spell out the content of this acknowledgment, first in terms of the deeds that warrant it, then by describing the acknowledgment as actually happening. All three are long lines, conveying the weight of the challenge.

> ¹Shout to God, all the earth,
> ²make music for the honor of his name,
> make his praise honored,

The first thus begins by paralleling *shout with make *music, indicating both noise and melody, gusto and beauty. It likewise parallels "God" and "the honor of his name," a phrase suggesting why God should be praised. Reference to God's *name implies a concealed allusion to the name Yhwh, which might have been present in a pre-Elohistic version of the psalm, e.g., in vv. 1 and 3, and which sums up God's majestic character. Between the opening two cola and applying to both is the object of the exhortation, "all the earth." Like Ps. 65, this psalm assumes that the deliverance God granted Israel at the beginning of its story (vv. 5–12) and in recent events (vv. 13–20) gives not only Israel but also the whole world good reason to worship Israel's God. Unexpectedly, there then follows the third colon, which pairs especially with the second, so that it is the second that holds the line together as it pairs with both the first and the third. Like the second, the third colon comprises an imperative verb, then the word "*honor," then another noun with a third-person suffix.[18] The *praise needs to match the person: the person is majestic (v. 2a); the praise also needs to be so.

16. On the psalm's rhetorical patterns, see Pierre Auffret, "Voyez les oeuvres de Dieu," *VT* 53 (2003): 431–44.

17. See (e.g.) Schaefer, *Psalms*, 160; Hossfeld and Zenger, *Psalms 2*, 147–48.

18. Lit. it reads, "Make his praise honor." Syr and Tg imply *kĕbôd tĕhillātô*, "the honor of his praise," assimilating to the previous colon.

> ³Say to God, "How awesome in your deeds;
>   at the greatness of your strength your enemies wither before you.

The second line starts in a way that suggests a parallel exhortation to vv. 1–2; its opening colon pairs with v. 1, beginning with an imperative and the expression "to God." It then goes on to give content to the recognition that the first line urged. The way the earth is to make God's praise majestic is by declaring how awesome is God in the deeds done on Israel's behalf; that word also picks up from the previous psalm (see Ps. 65:5 [6]). In turn its second colon spells out why those deeds so make people *revere God. God's *strength contrasts with the enemies' responsive withering.[19] The enemies are particular people who oppose Israel and thus oppose God's purpose. They are not identical with the world that is urged to acknowledge God (there is no parallelism here). It is because the enemies wither before God that the world as a whole is urged to recognize God.

> ⁴All the earth bows low to you,
>   makes music to you, makes music to your name." (Rise)

The world continues its words of acknowledgment, actually doing what the first line urged;[20] the expressions "all the earth" and "makes music" and the reference to God's *name recur (cf. vv. 1–2). The addition is the verb "*bows low." As shouting and making music complemented each other in vv. 1–2, so here bowing low and making music complement each other. As it is a little odd to think of shouting and making music at the same time, so also it is difficult to bow low and make music at the same time; but here one verb suggests an appropriate bodily and visible acknowledgment of God's majesty, and the other an appropriate auditory and aesthetic recognition of it. The entire statement is one made by faith. The whole earth does not bow down to God. But the awesomeness of God's deeds means this is so certain that in an act of worship one can envisage it as already happening, for the nature of worship is to collapse the distinction between visible reality and true reality.

19. *IBHS* 31.4g sees this yiqtol as describing what the enemies should do, but in the context it seems to state the basis for the world's acknowledging Yhwh and thus to indicate what they actually do.

20. Since the line continues to address God, it likely continues the words put on the lips of the peoples in v. 3 (against Gerstenberger, *Psalms*, 2:26). The suppliant addresses the nations in vv. 1–2, the opening of v. 3, and vv. 5–9; the transition to the suppliant's address to God is marked by an invocation there.

66:5–7. A second summons invites people to "come and see" but gives most space to the content of what people see, the reasons for the kind of worship vv. 1–4 have urged.

> ⁵Come and see God's deeds,
>   awesome in his assertive action upon humanity.

The section begins with another long line. On the invitation to "come and see God's deeds," see on 46:8 [9].²¹ The world is invited to come and behold the people whose existence issues from God's act. The second colon spells out the reasons for this looking, again taking up the description of God as awesome in deeds (cf. v. 3).²²

> ⁶ᵃ⁻ᵇWhen he turned sea into dry land,
>   they crossed over the river on foot.

Verse 6a–b goes on to explicate the nature of that assertive action. What people can see now is the result of God's ongoing action in the people's life, but this stands in continuity with great acts that go back to the beginning of Israel's story. I take the first asyndetic clause as subordinate to the second; the two cola briefly summarize the Red Sea story. This "sea" can be spoken of as a "river" under the influence of language from Ugaritic texts, where both words can refer to waters that embody threatening and assertive cosmic forces such as were indeed embodied in the Red Sea.²³ Here the parallelism thus makes it likely that both words refer to the Red Sea. But the word "river" might also suggest reference to the Jordan;²⁴ sea and Jordan stand in parallelism in Ps. 114:3, 5. Worshippers might hold both crossings in their minds, particularly if they were celebrated together liturgically.²⁵

> ⁶ᶜThere we rejoiced in him,
>   ⁷ᵃone who rules forever by his vigor.

Verses 6c–7a continue with the reaction of the people on that occasion, with which the present generation identifies ("we") in the manner

21. The verb there is *ḥāzâ* rather than *rāʾâ*, but the meaning is similar.
22. Again I take it that God is the subj. of the phrase (cf. NJPS, NRSV), which is here an enjambment rather than an exposition. The alternatives ("awesome is his assertive action" or "his awesome assertive action"; cf. NIVI, TNIV) require another disagreement, this time m. ptc. preceding f. noun.
23. Cf. Dahood, *Psalms*, 2:120–21.
24. Tg makes that explicit.
25. Cf. Hans-Joachim Kraus, "Gilgal," in *Reconsidering Israel and Judah*, ed. Gary N. Knoppers and J. Gordon McConville (Winona Lake, IN: Eisenbrauns, 2000), 163–78.

of (e.g.) Deut. 26:5–9.[26] The song in Exod. 15:1–18 ends with the declaration that Yhwh "will reign forever and ever" and has other verbal links with the psalm: for instance, it too describes Yhwh as "awesome" and uses the yiqtol of the verb for "cross over" (Exod. 15:11, 16). On the other hand, the closing reference to God's *might makes another link with Ps. 65 (see v. 6 [7]).

> [7b-c]His eyes watch the nations;
> the rebellious—they cannot stand tall. (Rise)

That ruling means God keeps watch on the nations, on great powers such as the Egyptians, who attacked the Israelites. Therefore, they had better not become rebellious or stubborn (*sārar*), resisting God's rule. Another result of the Red Sea event was that Israel exalted God (*rûm* polel); woe betide anyone like Pharaoh who stands there exalted[27] and thus demands to be put down.

66:8–12. A third summons begins with yet another exhortation and supports it with four lines of reasons. There are no verbal links here with the story of Israel's beginnings, either the Red Sea or the journey to the land. The fact that this section continues the psalm of praise also suggests that it does not relate to a particular more recent event, such as the one of which vv. 13–20 will eventually speak. More likely it comprises a summary of God's ongoing dealings with Israel and prepares the way for that specific testimony in vv. 13–20.

> [8]Worship our God, peoples,
> make heard the voicing of his praise,
> [9]The one who places us in life
> and has not given our foot to faltering.

The exhortation comprises two parallel cola and also parallels the opening line of the psalm as a whole.[28] The basis for this worship is

---

26. Tate, *Psalms 51–100*, 149. The verb is cohortative and thus invites the translation "Let us rejoice," which might imply that "there" presupposes a celebration near the Jordan (see previous note), where people could indeed "come and see" (v. 5) what God did, but this requires quite a lot of reading into the text. I have rather assumed that the verb is a "pseudo-cohortative" with past reference; see *IBHS* 34.5.3; GKC 108g; DG 68. The meaning of *šām* can hardly be reduced to "come" (TNIV) or "therefore" (NJPS), but it does link with the idea that the worshippers are identifying with the exodus generation and their experience; cf. "Were you there when they crucified my Lord?" (cf. Harry P. Nasuti, "Historical Narrative and Identity in the Psalms," *HBT* 23 [2001]: 132–53 [see 137–38]).

27. *Rûm* qal (Q)/intransitive hiphil (K); cf. GKC 53de; JM 54d.

28. "Peoples" parallels "all the earth" there; "*worship" and "make heard" parallel "shout" and "make music"; "our God" parallels "God"; "the sound/voicing of his *praise" parallels "his praise."

then expressed initially in participial clauses.[29] Even if the line referred to a once-for-all event in the past, a participle would imply that God continues to be one who puts the people in life and does not let their feet falter. But it is likely that the line refers directly to God's ongoing activity. While in isolation the first expression would make one think of God's giving people their life in the land, the land of life or the land of the living (27:13; 52:5 [7]), the parallelism in the line points in the other direction. In these parallel cola,[30] being in life and not faltering will be not sequential experiences but two ways of describing the same experience, as they are in 56:13 [14]. Both describe the way God continually gives people their life in the land (cf. KJV, "holdeth our soul in life") and ensures that they do not falter or *fall down there so that their lives come to an end. God has long been doing that in the people's experience.

> **10**For you have tested us, God,
>   you have smelted us as silver is smelted,

But v. 10 begins to acknowledge that this experience is not as straightforward as it initially sounded. Like v. 9 this describes an ongoing experience, something that has characterized the nation's life. The people do fall down, even if not "for long" (30:6–7 [7–8]; 60:1 [3]). When that happens, it is a kind of test (see 17:3; 26:2). People may be faithful to God and faithful to one another, but who knows how deep that faithfulness goes? Reversals expose people for what they really are. The second colon re-expresses the point in a more uncomfortable concrete way. Although smelting can imply refining away dross (e.g., Isa. 1:25), it is more often a vivid way of portraying a test. The smelting establishes that this is real silver and not dross (again, see 17:3; 26:2, where the two verbs stand in parallelism).

> **11**You have brought us into a net,
>   you have put a constraint on our hips,

Verse 11 begins to describe the nature of the testing, though it does so metaphorically. The people are familiar with an experience like the one that comes to an animal when it is hunted, a common image for people's attempts to bring about the downfall of others. It can apply to Yhwh's capturing the king to take him off into exile (Ezek. 12:13). The parallel colon repeats the point in less familiar words, so much so

29. Only "who puts/places" is actually a ptc. (v. 9a), but a participial construction regularly continues with a finite verb (GKC 116x), and this happens in v. 9b.

30. They comprise two verbs of similar meaning, two prepositional expressions, and two nouns for parts or aspects of the person, with third-person pronominal suffixes.

that the word for "constraint" (*mûʿāqâ*) is otherwise unknown and of uncertain meaning, but it has the advantage that it rather resembles the word for "net" (*mĕṣûdâ*).

> ¹²You have let people ride at our head,
>   we have come into fire and water,
>   but you have brought us out into flourishing.

Things are put more literally. The people have been defeated by other nations and put under the authority of foreign kings. Or in another image, they have been like people trying to escape from fires engulfing a city (something that happens when it is besieged and taken, but also at other times) or like people overwhelmed by flash floods (in Isa. 43:2, Yhwh promises to take the exiles out of the other side of such experiences). At last, a third colon brings the people out from these experiences, so that the section comes to a close with a tricolon. All those six cola in vv. 10–12b are but the background to this further statement about God's positive action toward Israel over the centuries. No, God has not given their foot to faltering. What looked like such an experience was indeed a testing, for God as well as for them. But they came through it, and so did Yhwh. If the language in vv. 10–12b reflects that used to describe the exile, then this closing colon suggests that Yhwh has indeed brought about a new exodus.[31] As Yhwh brought them out from Egypt and into the promised land, so Yhwh has kept on bringing them out of experiences of constraint and affliction into flourishing or fullness or satiation (*rĕwāyâ*; see Ps. 23:5, the only other occurrence).[32]

66:13–15. The move between "we" and "I" occurs elsewhere (e.g., Ps. 118), but the reference to fulfilling promises advertises that these verses also signify a move from a celebration of God's deeds in general to a celebration of a recent event, a move from praise to thanksgiving or testimony. Like vv. 1–7, vv. 13–20 are subdivided into two subsections by the renewed invitation in v. 16, paralleling that in v. 5; "Rise" comes at both points. The tricolon points to v. 15 being a closing line and marks a change from addressing God in thanksgiving to addressing other people in testimony; vv. 13–15 focus on offerings, vv. 16–20 on testimony. Within vv. 13–15, v. 13 makes a general statement of which v. 14 gives more detail on the second part and v. 15 more detail on the first part.

---

31. So Mays, *Psalms*, 223. Rashi and Theodoret (*Psalms*, 1:371) assume the psalm refers to the exile.

32. LXX, Syr, and Tg might suggest *rĕwāḥâ* (space, respite, relief) for *rĕwāyâ* (drinking one's fill), or the use of the two words may overlap or merge.

> ¹³I will come into your house with whole-offerings,
> I will discharge to you my promises,

Typically, the thanksgiving begins by declaring the intention to come and offer worship, though presumably the suppliant is already in the temple and in this sense has already "come." If there were any doubt as to the reason for coming with *whole-offerings, then the second colon makes clear the reason. The suppliant had prayed and had promised to come back with an offering in gratitude when God answered this prayer, and the suppliant is now doing so. Thank-offerings were usually shared by offerer and God; the promise of whole-offerings perhaps suggests a particularly pressing crisis, a particularly urgent prayer, and a particularly grateful fulfillment of promises.

> ¹⁴Those which my lips uttered
> and my mouth spoke in my trouble.

That second colon is spelled out in v. 14. It first underlines the acceptance of responsibility for the promises. They are ones that the suppliant's own lips uttered; the verb *pāṣâ* suggests opening the lips wide and speaking out loud (cf. "I opened my big mouth"). Compared with that, the second colon's reference to the mouth speaking is more colorless, but the point about the second colon lies in its last phrase, "in my trouble," which indeed is the point about the line as a whole. It was the pressure of trouble that generated the prayer and the promise. It is the psalm's only indication of the problem that the suppliant had to bring to God, though maybe we are to infer its nature further from the general statements in vv. 8–12. It has been a recurrence of that kind of experience.

> ¹⁵As whole-offerings I will send up fatlings to you,
> with the aroma of rams;
> I will make ready bulls and goats. (Rise)

Verse 15 in turn spells out v. 13a. It signals this by the opening repetition of the word *whole-offerings and underlines it with its root verb *ʿālâ*: (lit.) "I will cause to go up to you offerings that go up." Beyond that, what each of the three cola does is indicate the concrete nature of the offerings and thereby further stress their costliness, the "sacrifice" involved in them, and thus the suppliant's sense of indebtedness to God for the act of deliverance. First they are fatlings, calves that are raised and fed well in order to make a fine feast. It is indeed a sacrifice, a "waste," to burn the whole of such an animal as an act of appreciation to God. The second colon speaks of rams, also a gift of significant value because they are valued for their wool and for food, but the emphasis lies on the aroma of their meat barbequing. The third colon closes off the section by summarizing the first two, though using a different verb and different nouns.

66:16–20. The offerings would be incomplete without the words that give glory to God for answering prayer, words that are addressed to the community as the offerings were given to God. This final section forms a stepped structure as it tells its story by moving between present and past:

> In the present: the suppliant's testimony (v. 16)
> > In the past: the suppliant's prayer (v. 17)
> > > Behind that: the suppliant's integrity (v. 18)
> > In the past: God's response (v. 19)
> In the present: the suppliant's testimony (v. 20)

> ¹⁶Come and listen, and I will tell, all who revere God,
>   what he has done for me.

The final invitation begins with a sequence of verbs running through the first colon, which raises suspense: come for what, listen to what, tell of what? The vocative then lengthens the line and increases suspense by focusing on the addressees, the entire community of Israel as the people who revere God. The section thus contrasts with the exhortations to praise in vv. 1–12, which addressed the world as a whole. Then in the second colon comes the answer to the question "What?" Its prosaic wording belies its significance.

> ¹⁷To him I called with my mouth,
>   and he was extolled on my tongue.

Verse 17 begins the process of going behind that. The mouth that had made the promises (v. 14) was doing so in connection with calling on God for help. As the OT sees it, calling on God when one is in need is a form of praise. It indicates a recognition that God is the one to look to for help, not (e.g.) other deities or foreign allies. By the prayer God was therefore extolled on the suppliant's tongue (lit. "under the tongue"; cf. 140:3 [4]; Song 4:11).³³

33. Or were the words of praise under the tongue ready for uttering when God would answer the prayer—on the tip of the suppliant's tongue or under the suppliant's breath? They

295

> 18If I could have seen harm in my heart,
>   my Lord would not listen.

Verse 18 makes a converse point. The psalms regularly express awareness of a condition that needs meeting if a prayer is to have a claim on
God. Only a person committed to God can expect God to respond to
prayer (in grace God may respond even if someone is a wrongdoer, but
one has no right to *expect* that: see on 59:5 [6]). Thus in a prayer psalm
the suppliants often cover their bases by making an assertion about
their faithfulness (e.g., 44:17–22 [18–23]). Here the suppliant recalls that
necessity. Looking inside, the suppliant might have had to acknowledge
planning, plotting, or praying for *harm, like the "people who do harm"
who often appear in the Psalms. The trouble that came would then be
quite deserved. The *Lord (who could have known about such plans
or plots or spiritual acts) would then not listen to the prayer for help.
Chrysostom comments elsewhere that a suppliant might have feared that
one could not call on God the way David does because we are not David
but just ordinary persons, whereas actually it is not who you are (in this
sense) that decides whether God listens to your prayer. "Rather, in every
instance he gives close scrutiny to our behaviour. If yours is such as to
plead in your favour, you will be heard in every respect. If not, even if
you were David you would not succeed in winning God over."[34]

> 19But in fact God listened,
>   paid heed to the sound of my plea.

The fact that God did listen to the *plea shows that there was no
such harm in the suppliant's heart. The basis for our making heard the
voicing of God's praise (v. 8) is the fact that he has heard the voicing of
our prayer.

> 20God be worshipped,
>   the one who did not turn away my plea,
>   or his commitment from me.

Thus the psalm closes with another tricolon. While the exhortation
to worship God often comes as a summons at the beginning of a psalm
(and cf. v. 8), the participial expression "God be *worshipped" more often
comes nearer the end as a response to a testimony or a declaration of

---

would then form a nice contrast with the harm that sits under some other people's tongues
(10:7; cf. Job 20:12). But that may be reading too much into the prep.
   34. *Psalms*, 1:45.

confidence in God's faithfulness (e.g., 18:46 [47]; 28:6; 31:21 [22]). Thus here its basis lies in that fact that God did answer prayer. The point is made in a unique expression as the psalm speaks of God not "turning away" the prayer (*sûr* hiphil), like people pushing away or abandoning their gods (Josh. 24:14) or a husband pushing away his wife (Isa. 49:21), or a judge turning away a suppliant's *plea. Neither (the third colon adds) did God push away or abandon *commitment to the suppliant.

Theological Implications

In worship, praise and thanksgiving belong together. When we give praise for God's great deeds, that praise is given extra force by our awareness of the way God has acted in our lives. When God does so act, that inspires praise going beyond acknowledgment of this particular new act; it reinforces conviction concerning the foundational great acts.

In worship, leaders and community belong together. In a modern context people become leaders because they volunteer to do so, but in a traditional society they often become leaders because they belong to the "wrong" family or clan. They do not choose to go into the kitchen, and they do not have the opportunity to get out of the kitchen if they do not like the heat. It is with extra feeling that leaders therefore take a lead in worship and testimony with their people, expressing their gratitude for God's protection as they play the role they never sought, and their people are appropriately appreciative to God and to them.

In worship, world and people of God belong together. The world is called into worship of God in respect of God's extraordinary acts on behalf of God's people, because those acts are undertaken for the sake of the whole world, not just for the sake of one people. People often speak as if the God of the OT was only concerned for Israel, but "never is Your concern reserved only for the people of one nation; You are the God of all."[35]

35. Jerome, *Homilies*, 1:45. Cf. Spurgeon, *Treasury of David*, 3:109.

Psalm 67

Blessed for the Sake of the World

Translation

The leader's. On strings. Composition. Song.

[1]May God be gracious to us and bless us;
    may he shine his face with us, (Rise)
[2]So that your way is acknowledged on the earth,
    your deliverance among all nations.[1]

[3]May peoples confess you, God,
    may peoples confess you, all of them,
    [4]may countries rejoice and resound.
For you decide for peoples with uprightness;
    the countries on the earth—you lead them. (Rise)
[5]May peoples confess you, God,
    peoples confess you, all of them.

[6]As earth has given its produce,
    may God, our God, bless us.
[7]May God bless us,
    so that all the ends of earth revere him.

1. The "rise" at the end of v. 1 perhaps implies the view that v. 2 begins a new sentence leading into v. 3, which fits the change in person in v. 3 (cf. Tate, *Psalms 51—100*, 153–54). But it would be more usual for such an inf. (beginning v. 2) to depend on the preceding verb, and this makes for the kind of balance in the psalm's structure outlined in the introduction to the psalm.

Interpretation

Psalm 67 is a prayer for God's blessing to be known in the nation's life in such a way that the world as a whole comes to acknowledge God. The interrelationship of these two ideas thus continues from Pss. 65 and 66. It follows a stepped structure:[2]

Prayer for blessing and thus for the world's recognition of God (vv. 1–2)
> Prayer for the peoples to confess God (vv. 3–4a)
>> The basis in God's sovereignty among the peoples (v. 4b–c)
> Prayer for the peoples to confess God (v. 5)
Prayer for blessing and thus for the world's recognition of God (vv. 6–7)

Admittedly it is unclear how much of the psalm is a prayer. The whole is expressed in the third person, with no imperatives and perhaps no forms in which the jussive is different from the yiqtol (but see on v. 1b). But translations have always implied the view that the psalm is less likely to be simply a declaration of what God will do and more likely one that asked for what God might do, and thus have read at least the opening verbs, vv. 1–2, as jussives. The similarity with the Aaronic blessing (Num. 6:24–26) presumably supports this conclusion. I have reckoned that NJPS is then right that when similar expressions recur in the closing lines, vv. 6–7, they are likely to have the same significance; contrast TNIV (NRSV has indicative in v. 6, jussive in v. 7). For vv. 3–5, NJPS has indicative, but I have reckoned it more likely that jussives also continue through vv. 3–5 (cf. TNIV, NRSV).

We do not know the date of the psalm.[3] Given that it speaks both of God's acts of deliverance (v. 2) and of the harvest (v. 6),[4] it is possible that it was especially used at a festive occasion that combined these concerns. The suggestion that it belongs specifically to Sukkot issues from v. 6a translated with a past tense,[5] but that understanding may be wrong (see

2. Cf. W. Beyerlin, *Im Licht der Traditionen*, VTSup 45 (Leiden: Brill, 1992), 11–13; Beat Weber, "Psalm lxvii," *VT* 43 (1993): 559–66.
3. It would help if we knew the date of the Aaronic blessing (see v. 1) and were sure that the psalm follows it or builds on it (or shares with it a common background in traditions), but we know none of these things. Helen G. Jefferson ("The Date of Psalm lxvii," *VT* 12 [1962]: 201–5) argues for a First Temple date, Qimchi sees it as another exilic psalm, and Harald-Martin Wahl ("Psalm 67," *Bib* 73 [1992]: 240–47) supports a Second Temple date. Beyerlin (*Im Licht der Traditionen*, 1–50) argues for a redactional development of the psalm.
4. See Eep Talstra and Carl J. Bosma, "Psalm 67," *CTJ* 36 (2001): 290–313.
5. Cf. Weiser, *Psalms*, 472.

comment), and this one verb is too little to build such a theory on.[6] The rest of the psalm suggests that it more likely belongs to an occasion when people were looking forward to the harvest, not one when the harvest was over; thus it more likely belongs to Passover/Unleavened Bread (or possibly Pentecost); see the introduction to Ps. 65.

> The leader's. On strings. Composition. Song.

Heading. See glossary. Some LXX MSS add "David's," which draws attention to the fact that like the previous psalm, Ps. 67 MT has no reference to a specific king or worship leader.

67:1–2. The opening prayer starts off from the terms of Aaron's blessing.

> [1]May God be gracious to us and bless us;
>   may he shine his face with us, (Rise)

The fact that this wish is expressed as a prayer for "us" rather than a declaration for "you" need not preclude its being pronounced by a priest, as Christian ministers sometimes use "us" forms of prayers and blessings.[7] Each of the jussive verbs recurs from Aaron's blessing, though in a different order and in slightly variant forms. The subject of the verbs is here "God" rather than "Yhwh," and God's face shines "with us" (perhaps something more relational, like speaking "with" someone)[8] rather than "to us" (and thus external in its relationship). The collocation of *graciousness and blessing already brings together two themes that often appear separately (see on 24:5), as the psalm presupposes God's involvement in once-for-all historical events and in the ongoing cycles of nature and of human life. Both issue from the shining[9] of God's *face, God's life-giving smile. Both grace and blessing are not merely spiritual matters but realities that bring deliverance in life's crises and fullness of life in the outward aspects of human experience such as family life, food, and health. Augustine comments that people who have "blessed" God (according to the traditional rendering of *bārûk* in the last verse of Ps. 66) may go on to ask for God to "bless" them; there is an ongoing mutual relationship between these two blessings.[10]

---

6. See the discussion in Hossfeld and Zenger, *Psalms 2*, 150–53, though they do not see the psalm as looking forward to the harvest either.

7. Gerstenberger, *Psalms*, 2:32.

8. Cf. *IBHS* 11.2.4a.

9. It is this verb (*yā'ēr* rather than *yā'îr*) that is the nearest to an unequivocal jussive (cf. *DCH*, but contrast BDB and *HALOT*).

10. *Psalms*, 281.

> ²So that your way is acknowledged on the earth,
>   your deliverance among all nations.

Verse 2 then gives this prayer a wholly distinctive slant over against the Aaronic blessing, but one that continues the emphasis of Pss. 65–66. While the Aaronic blessing is located in the broad context of Yhwh's purpose that the whole world should seek blessing like Israel's, that context and purpose receive no mention in the blessing itself. It focuses simply on Israel. In contrast, here the aim of God's being gracious to "us" and blessing "us" (that is, the aim both of God's involvement in Israel's historical or political life and of God's involvement in nature) is that the world as a whole should come to *acknowledge God. The opening verb applies to both cola, which thus work abcb'c'. In each, after the verb comes a *b* expression referring to the world, then a noun for God's activity, with the suffix -*kā*. Thus "among all nations" prevents us from thinking that the first *b* expression means merely "in the land [of Israel]," and "your deliverance" explicates the nature of God's "way." It is God's way to act in *deliverance (as the story in Numbers presupposes), but this is significant not merely for Israel but also for the whole world, and not even just for some nations apart from Israel but indeed for all the nations. This is so because Yhwh's way involves the kind of activity v. 4b will describe. Admittedly, throughout the psalm the concern is not merely with the needs of these nations but also with the God whom the nations acknowledge and confess, not so much with the gift as with the giver. That point is also emphasized by the fact that in v. 2 the psalm turns to address God, as it will through vv. 3–5.[11]

67:3–5. The central section develops that point in v. 2. Perhaps it makes little difference whether we translate these yiqtols as jussive or as indicative. Either way they refer to events that will issue from the jussives in v. 1.

> ³May peoples confess you, God,
>   may peoples confess you, all of them,
> ⁴ᵃmay countries rejoice and resound.

In the first two parallel cola, the peoples doing the *confessing are the nations of v. 2, with the last phrase emphasizing that all of them are involved, as v. 2b stressed. I take the further clause in v. 4a as again parallel to those two and thus as completing a tricolon, which works

---

11. Weiser, *Psalms*, 475.

abc, abd, a'a"b'.[12] The peoples (*'ammîm*), who were the nations in v. 2 (*gôyîm*), are now the "countries" (*lĕ'ummîm*), a much rarer third word. The meaning of these words is not sharply distinct; the collocation of the different terms rather underlines in a further way how the whole world is involved in the acknowledgment and confession of God. Indeed, they are not merely confessing and realistically acknowledging how things are but rejoicing and resounding: that is, resounding with joy. They know that it is indeed true that God's blessing and delivering of Israel is also good news for them.

> 4b-cFor you decide for peoples with uprightness;
> the countries on the earth—you lead them. (Rise)

Why that is so, v. 4b–c makes explicit in two more parallel cola, abcb'da', in which "peoples" and "countries" reappear. The line forms the center of the psalm. The good news is that God *decides for the peoples. The link with v. 4a provides another indicator that the conventional English translation of *šāpaṭ* as "judge" (NRSV) obscures the point. This action of God's is one to rejoice in. Admittedly even God's making decisions for the nations might not be reason for rejoicing. Sometimes authorities make decisions that are not good news for the people over whom they exercise power. So the psalm adds that God decides for people with uprightness, fairness, or equity. God's upright dealings with Israel are a paradigm for God's dealings with the world, rather than being an activity that ignores the needs of other peoples. The verb in the second colon puts the point vividly. "Leading" (*nāḥâ*) describes the way shepherds care for their flocks, and it is a natural verb to apply to God's relationship with Israel (e.g., 77:20 [21]; 78:14, 53, 72). How strikingly, then, that it here applies to the nations. They, too, are God's flocks.

> 5May peoples confess you, God,
> peoples confess you, all of them.

As the psalm then begins its return journey through its stepped structure, v. 5 simply repeats v. 3, but with extra strength after that statement in v. 4b. Yes, the peoples may well confess God.

67:6–7. The psalm returns to its beginning, though whereas v. 5 simply repeated v. 3, these final lines vary the expressions of vv. 1–2 in several ways.

---

12. But the Sinaiticus MS of LXX suggests, "For you decide for the world with faithfulness; you decide for the peoples with uprightness," which makes three bicola of vv. 3–4. The extra words could have been omitted by homoioarcton.

> 6As earth has given its produce,
>   may God, our God, bless us.

First, the opening verb is the only qatal in the psalm. The LXX thus translates as aorist, but an isolated aorist would be odd. Following Sym, the NIVI has "Then the land will yield its harvest," which fits the context better, but the qatal is an odd way to express that conviction. The NRSV translates as perfect, which also fits the context by pointing to a past act with implications for the present; Tate similarly translates by a present tense to designate an action that is repeated in experience.[13] The NJPS has "May the earth yield its produce," in the context plausibly assuming that the qatal is precative.[14] I have tried to leave the translation ambiguous, allowing both for the perfect/present and precative understanding. The second colon spells out the implication of God's causing the earth to give its produce. The expression "God, our God" expresses "the program of the Elohistic Psalter's theology," which involves "a folding together of the universal and the particular."[15]

> 7May God bless us,
>   so that all the ends of earth revere him.

The closing line first repeats words from v. 6b, hastening on to the longer second colon, which one might alternatively render simply as a parallel jussive ("and may all . . ."). The colon again stresses that God's activity benefits the whole world, not just some nations beyond Israel, underlining that point with the reference to the *ends* of the earth. This brings to a novel climax the sequence of such terms through the psalm (the earth, all nations, peoples, peoples all of them, countries, peoples, countries in the earth, peoples, peoples all of them, earth, all the ends of earth). And to their acknowledgment, confession, rejoicing, and resounding is added *revering. The closing line thus brings together the opening line's concern with Israel (v. 7) and the central line's concern with the world as a whole (v. 4b–c).

Theological Implications

Key aspects of the significance of Ps. 67 emerge when we set it alongside the Aaronic blessing:

13. *Psalms 51–100*, 154.
14. So DG 60c.
15. Hossfeld and Zenger, *Psalms 2*, 149.

303

Yhwh bless you and guard you.
Yhwh shine his face to you and be gracious to you.
Yhwh lift his face to you and set well-being on you. (Num.
6:24–26)

That is a blessing for the Aaronide priests to utter; when priests are not present, outside the Jerusalem temple, the psalm makes it possible for the congregation to bless one another. That is a blessing that never lifts its eyes beyond Israel; the psalm sees Israel's blessing as designed to benefit the whole world, and the omission of a prayer for Israel's well-being further highlights the point. That is a blessing emphasizing Yhwh's name. In pronouncing the blessing (Yhwh adds), the priests set Yhwh's name on the people (Num. 6:27); the psalm never mentions Yhwh's name, and again thereby it draws attention to the universality of God's involvement with the world.

The psalm comes at the end of Sabbath worship in the synagogue, suggesting the way it holds together a relationship with God and an involvement of God in the reality of everyday life, to which one returns after worship. In the Church of England's Book of Common Prayer, it features in two interesting connections. It can be used any day to follow the NT lesson at Evening Prayer as an alternative to the Nunc Dimittis, sharing with it a focus on the fact that God's deliverance of Israel also brings light to the nations; and it can be used in the Marriage Service. In the Episcopal Church in the United States it can also be used on the Sunday before Ascension Day, the beginning of Rogationtide.[16]

16. See (e.g.) *The Book of Common Prayer . . . according to the Use of the Episcopal Church* ([New York]: Seabury, 1979), 916.

Psalm 68

God Then and Now

Translation

The leader's. David's. Composition. Song.

[1]When God arises, [MT]/May God arise, [LXX, Jerome][1] his enemies
> scatter,
> those who are against him flee from before him.
[2]You disperse them as smoke disperses,[2]
> as wax melts before fire.
Faithless people perish from before God,
> [3]but the faithful—they are glad.
They exult before God,
> they rejoice with gladness.

[4]Sing to God,
> make music to his name.
Lift it up to the one who rides on the clouds/through the steppes,
> whose name is—Yah;[3] exult before him.

---

1. In Num. 10:35, the subsequent verb has a *w*. In the psalm in MT, the construction is asyndetic, suggesting that the first verb is dependent on the second and that the emphasis in v. 1 as a whole lies on the result of God's arising rather than on the arising in itself. This fits v. 2 (which has no equivalent in Num. 10).

2. I take *hindōp* as a composite form, combining the consonants of niphal *hinnādēp* and the vowels of qal *nĕdōp* (GKC 51k).

3. The dash represents the *bĕ* on *bĕyāh*, which I take as emphatic (see on 54:4 [6]; and C. F. Whitley, "Some Functions of the Hebrew Particles *beth* and *lamedh*," *JQR* 62 [1971–72]: 199–206 [see 204–5]).

[5]God in his holy dwelling
   is father for orphans, governor for widows.[4]
[6]God—he[5] enables the desolate to live at home,
   brings out the captives, in fetters,[6]
   but rebels live in dry land.

[7]God,[7] when you went out before your people,[8]
   when you marched through the wilderness, (Rise)
[8]Earth shook, yes heavens poured,[9]
   from before God, the one of Sinai,
From before God, the God of Israel;
   [9]you shed very generous rain,[10] God.
Your possession, and it languishing[11]—you yourself have provided for
      it;[12]
      [10]your dwelling[13]—they have lived in it,
   you who provide for the weak with your goodness, God.

[11]The Lord gives a word;
   the women who pass on the news being a great army,[14]
[12]the kings of armies flee, flee,[15]

4. The cola come in the opposite order in the Hebrew, because the subj. comes in its regular position after the predicate.

5. Conversely (see previous note), here the subj. comes first and thus has some emphasis.

6. *Kûšārôt* is a hapax. The root *kāšar* usually refers to what is fitting, skillful, or successful, and the expression might indicate that God brings the captives out with success. More suggestive are links with Ugaritic terms related to music, suggesting "with songs" (see *HALOT*). But A. van Selms argues that etymologically *kāšar* cannot be linked with the Ugaritic words and points to Akkadian support for KJV's "bound with chains" ("The Root *k-ṯ-r* and Its Derivatives in Ugaritic Literature," *UF* 11 [1979]: 739–44).

7. Judg. 5:4 has "Yhwh"; so also "God" occurs twice in the next verse where Judges has Yhwh.

8. NJPS has "army"; cf. *TDOT*, 11:176.

9. *Nāṭap* means more than "drip" (BDB; *HALOT*); cf. Tate, *Psalms 51–100*, 163.

10. Lit. "rain of generosity," with generosity (*nĕdābôt*) being pl.; I take it as intensive. There are a number of such plurals in the psalm; some may be examples of the Phoenician-type alternative form of the f. sg. (cf. Dahood, *Psalms*, 2:148).

11. Taking *nil'â* as a ptc. (cf. DG 37); for the qatal one would expect *nil'ĕtâ*.

12. For the meaning of *kûn* in this context (polel), see 65:9 [10].

13. *Ḥayyâ* usually means a single living thing; LXX and Jerome take it as a collective referring to animals, while BDB takes it to mean a group or company. I rather see it as a variant on *ḥawwâ* ("tent-village"; so *HALOT*; *DCH*).

14. I again take the asyndeton as idiomatic (see on v. 1a).

15. Translations take this colon (and perhaps the rest of vv. 12–13) as the words of the messengers, but elsewhere the verb *bāśar* requires a verb such as *'āmar* to introduce the message itself (e.g., Isa. 40:9). Further, in v. 12a one would expect the women to use qatals or participles rather than yiqtols. Kraus (*Psalms 60–150*, 44), indeed, makes v. 11b the beginning of the Lord's word.

While the young girls[16] of the house share the spoil
  [13]though they stay among the enclosures,
The wings of a dove covered in silver,
  its pinions in pale gold.
[14]When Shaddai scatters kings there,[17]
  it snows[18] on Salmon.

[15]Mount Bashan is a majestic mountain,
  Mount Bashan is a craggy[19] mountain.
[16]Why do you keep watch, craggy mountains,
  on the mountain God desired as his dwelling?—
  yes, Yhwh will live there forever.
[17]God's chariotry were[20] myriads,[21] doubled thousands,
  the Lord among them at Sinai in holiness.[22]
[18]You went up to the height, you took captives,
  you received gifts among people,[23]
  and yes, rebels—to live as Yah God.[24]

[19]The Lord be worshipped day by day;
  God, our deliverer, carries us. (Rise)
[20]God is for us a God who does deliver;
  the departure to death[25] belongs to Yhwh the Lord.
[21]Yes, God smashes the head of his enemies,
  the hairy crown of the one who goes about in his great guilt.
[22]The Lord said, "From Bashan[26] I will bring them back,

16. LXX and Jerome take *nāwâ* as from *nā'â*, so that it would suggest "beauty" or "beauties"; BDB views it as from *nāwâ* and thus as meaning "dwelling." Either way, it refers to the same people.

17. Lit. "in/on it." The expression has no antecedent and might refer anticipatively to Salmon.

18. On the quasi-jussive form, see GKC 109k.

19. Lit. "mountain of crags" and in the next line "mountains, crags" (see GKC 131c; JM 131c; *TTH* 188.1).

20. The time reference of v. 17 derives from v. 18.

21. The ending is more likely adverbial than the sign of a dual (JM 100o).

22. While *qōdeš* can mean "holy place" (e.g., 20:2 [3]), its more usual meaning fits here (cf. 60:6 [8]).

23. Or perhaps "consisting of people," in the way the Levites were offered to God (e.g., Num. 18:6–7), which thus need not mean they would be sacrificed (contrast Goulder, *Prayers of David*, 203).

24. Or "rebels at Yah God's living [there]."

25. Cf. Tg. EVV have "escape from death," but *tôṣā'ôt* nowhere else means escape, while the prep. is *lĕ*, and it is preferable to avoid reckoning that *lĕ* can mean "from" (so *HALOT* on *tôṣā'ôt*; cf. *CP* 176–77). Martin R. Hauge ("'The City Facing Death,'" *SJOT* 1 [1988]: 1–29) sees the phrase as reflecting the fact that the sanctuary is a place of life, the world outside a place of death.

26. Among others, James H. Charlesworth takes this as an instance of *HALOT*'s *bāšān* II, meaning a mythical dragon-snake ("Bashan, Symbology, Haplography, and Theology in Psalm 68," in *David and Zion* [J. J. M. Roberts Festschrift; ed. Bernard F. Batto and

bring them back from the depths of the sea,
²³So that your foot may smash in blood,
your dogs' tongue, too—its share²⁷ is from your enemies."

²⁴People saw your journeying,²⁸ God,
the journeying of my God, my king, in holiness.²⁹
²⁵Singers came first, strings behind,
in the midst of girls playing tambourines.
²⁶In the great congregation³⁰ worship God,
Yhwh—you from the fountain of Israel.
²⁷There was little Benjamin, ruling them,³¹
the officials of Judah, their noisy throng,³²
the officials of Zebulun, the officials of Naphtali.

²⁸May your God have commanded your strength;
be strong, God.
You who acted for us ²⁹from your palace—
up to Jerusalem kings are to bring you tribute.
³⁰Blast³³ the creature³⁴ in the reeds,
the assembly of the strong among the bullocks, the peoples.³⁵
Trampling on those who love³⁶ silver,
May you have scattered the peoples who delight in encounters.
³¹Bronze/red cloth/blue cloth/envoys/Hashmonites³⁷ are to come
from Egypt,
Sudan is to hasten with its hands to God.

Kathryn L. Roberts; Winona Lake, IN: Eisenbrauns, 2004], 351–72), though this also requires emendation in the context to make sense.

27. *Minnēhû* from the hapax *mēn*, a synonym of *mānâ*.

28. Once again the pl. is intensive or abstract in this colon and the next.

29. LXX takes *qōdeš* to denote the holy place, but more likely the meaning is the same as in v. 17.

30. The hapax *maqhēlâ* (but cf. *qāhal*); yet again intensive pl.

31. Syr "in silence" (and LXX, "in ecstasy"?) implies *bĕdôm* for *rōdēm*.

32. Understanding the hapax *rigmâ* in light of Akk. *rigmu* (noise). Jerome's "in their purple" perhaps assumes a variant on *rĕqāmâ* (cf. 45:14 [15]), for which there is support in the Tg tradition (see Stec, *Targum of Psalms*, 133).

33. See on 9:5 [6].

34. If *ḥayyâ* can mean "community" (see on v. 10), that would fit the context here; cf. the parallelism. Tg has "camp."

35. Epexegetical genitive (Johnson, *Sacral Kingship*, 76, comparing GKC 128f).

36. I read *rōṣê* for *raṣṣê*, a hapax of uncertain meaning. It is conventionally translated "pieces" (see BDB): the colon would then speak of "humbling itself [cf. *rāpas* hitpael in Prov. 6:3] with pieces of silver," which the assembly brings as an offering (cf. NJPS, TNIV). But in this new line and with the parallelism, one would expect the sg. ptc. *mitrappēs* to be a description of God.

37. *Ḥašmannîm* is another hapax. "Envoys" follows Vrs; "bronze" assumes this is the Egyptian word *ḥsmn*; "red cloth" and "blue cloth" interpret in light of Ugaritic (see *HALOT*; Dahood, *Psalms*, 2:150); for Hashmonites, see Num. 33:29–30.

³²Kingdoms of the earth, sing to God,
    make music to the Lord, (Rise)
³³To the one who rides through the primeval highest heavens—
    there, he gives out his voice, his strong voice.
³⁴Give strength to God,
    whose majesty is over Israel, his strength in the skies.
³⁵You are awesome, God, from your sanctuary,[38]
    the one who is God of Israel,
Who gives strength and great might[39] to the people;
    God be worshipped.

Interpretation

Psalms usually begin either by addressing God or by exhorting worshippers to join in acknowledging Yhwh and giving the reasons for that. Psalm 68:4–6 issues such an exhortation, with reasons for the praise in the form of a description of God's activity. Although there is no *kî* to introduce the reasons, otherwise this is a fairly straightforward example of such exhortations to worship. But they normally come at the very beginning of a psalm, whereas Ps. 68:1–3 is a confession of faith in God's activity (MT) or a third-person plea (Vrs). The former is an uncommon opening for a psalm (but see, e.g., Pss. 27; 46; and 48), the latter a very uncommon one (Ps. 20 and 21 are the nearest parallels). After this unusual beginning the psalm issues the kind of exhortation to worship that usually opens a praise psalm. The psalm closes (vv. 32–35) with a further exhortation to worship (somewhat in the manner of Pss. 96; 98; 135). Just before that closing praise it turns to plea (vv. 28–31), as Deborah's song closes with a prayer in what is basically a praise psalm (see Judg. 5:31).[40] In the ancient versions, this closing prayer pairs with the opening third-person plea in vv. 1–3, so that in their translation plea/prayer and exhortation to praise form a bracket around the whole. In between the opening and closing elements, the major part of the material (vv. 7–23) is dominated by a series of declarations about God's activity, mostly in narrative form, which in the context constitute the reasons for praise and thus the content of the praise. Some of this material addresses God, some addresses no one in particular, some is rhetorically addressed elsewhere.[41] After that, vv. 24–27 describe and react to a worship procession, a description that seems to be another form of praise.

38. Pl. of amplification.
39. Intensive pl. once more.
40. Cf. Gerstenberger, *Psalms*, 2:42.
41. See further J. P. Fokkelman, "The Structure of Psalm lxviii," *OtSt* 26 (1990): 72–83 (see 75–76). Pierre Auffret surveys approaches to the psalm's structure in *Merveilles à nos yeux*, BZAW 235 (Berlin: de Gruyter, 1995), 1–30.

As a whole, then, Ps. 68 (MT) is a praise psalm, introduced by a confessional prologue that anticipatorily makes declarations about God's activity in the world and is supplemented by a plea for that activity to be known now. Although the psalm thus bears partial comparison with other praise and prayer psalms, it is quite distinctive over against them. It bears as much comparison with praise psalms and prayers outside the Psalter in Exod. 15; Num. 10; Deut. 33; Judg. 5; and Hab. 3.

The narrative praise in the psalm has been construed in a number of ways. The Tg sees it as incorporating reference to Moses's climbing Sinai, while Eph. 4:7–10 infers christological significance from it. It has been understood to refer particularly to incidents in the time of David, either the transfer of the covenant chest to Jerusalem or David's triumph over Absalom, or to the deliverance from Sennacherib, and to hoped-for acts of God in the future.

One factor that makes possible this variety in interpretation emerges when one compares Ps. 68 with those other passages, especially Judg. 5, which refers to specific places (Seir, Edom, Taanach, the Kishon) and specific people (Shamgar, Jael, Deborah, Barak). Psalm 68 refers to Sinai and to Jerusalem, and eventually to Egypt and Sudan, but beyond that only incidentally to Bashan and enigmatically to Salmon. Judges 5 is distinctively concrete; Ps. 68 is distinctively unspecific. This supports the suggestion that it is "not based upon any particular historical victory, but upon the victories of Yahweh in the long history of Israel"[42] or that it arose from a particular event but speaks in general terms. As is characteristic of psalms as opposed to similar material outside the Psalter, Ps. 68 is designed for use in many different contexts, and its lack of concrete historical references facilitates that. We cannot surely infer that this is the reason for its taking this form, though it might be the reason for its being retained and incorporated in the Psalter. We can usefully imagine its being used (e.g.) in connection with celebrating the taking of the covenant chest to Jerusalem, but it is unwise to make any specific historical occasion the key to the psalm's interpretation.

A further factor making possible that variety in interpretation is the interweaving of qatal and yiqtol verbs in the psalm. The fact that yiqtol verbs can refer to past events[43] makes it possible to reckon that some such verbs in the psalm refer (e.g.) to events such as the exodus and Israel's journey to the promised land. The fact that such verbs can refer to future events makes it possible to reckon that some of these verbs refer to what God will yet do. Conversely, it is conventional sometimes to translate qatals by present tense verbs (e.g., if they are functioning like statives,

---

42. Briggs, *Psalms*, 2:94.
43. See Ps. 18 for examples.

or are equivalent to gnomic aorists) or by future-tense verbs (if they are describing future events as if they have already happened).[44] Further, there is the possibility that verbs formed like yiqtols are jussive and that verbs formed like qatals are precative. So both yiqtol and qatal verbs can be interpreted in varying ways, affecting understandings of the psalm as a whole. In principle I have taken the combination of qatal and yiqtol as a sign that the psalm systematically mediates between God's acts in the past and God's analogous or related ongoing activity in the people's life, without assuming that every qatal refers to a historical event and every yiqtol to that ongoing activity. The psalm keeps moving between these two, within sections or between sections.

As is the case with other psalms, the awareness that the psalm seems distanced from particular historical contexts has led to attempts to see the concrete events it refers to as liturgical ones rather than historical ones. This, too, leads to varied results, and it can be based on a fallacy. It can be the nature of a lyric to refer to liturgical events and to the historical events that the liturgy celebrates ("O come all ye faithful, . . . come ye to Bethlehem . . ."), but one cannot infer the liturgy from the lyric. It is a lyric, not a liturgy. Psalm 68 does refer to liturgical events such as processions, but one cannot infer that it was used in a liturgy that can be constructed from it. In itself, it is a celebration of God's acts in Israel's life that is designed to build up faith and stimulate prayer for those acts to continue. It was presumably used in worship, but it does not offer any concrete indication of a regular worship occasion when it was used. Nor do we have any evidence from outside the Psalter regarding its use, though the synagogue uses it at Pentecost. As with a historical interpretation, it does no harm to imagine it used on a regular occasion such as Pentecost or Sukkot, but it is unwise to make such possible use the key to its interpretation.

In part as a result of such features as we have been considering, "Psalm 68 has always been considered with justice as the most difficult of all the Psalms."[45] Admittedly "always" broadly means "since the dawning of modernity." While Augustine describes it as "difficultly understood,"[46] Theodoret's editor, Robert C. Hill, notes that Theodoret "admits no difficulty with it,"[47] and Cassiodorus calls it a "spacious psalm" that "has run on like those great rivers which bring more abundant fertility to the fields as they lay hold of more land."[48] Medieval Jewish exegetes, such

---

44. Though see Max Rogland, *Alleged Non-past Uses of* Qatal *in Classical Hebrew* (Assen: Van Gorcum, 2003).

45. William F. Albright, "A Catalogue of Early Hebrew Lyric Poems," *HUCA* 23 (1950): 1–39 (see 7).

46. *Psalms*, 299.

47. *Psalms*, 1:380.

48. *Psalms*, 2:140.

as Rashi and Ibn Ezra, and Reformation commentators, such as Luther and Calvin, do not feel any more difficulty with this psalm than with others.[49] It seems to have become difficult soon after Calvin's day, for Simeon de Muis, who died in 1644, called it "the torture of critics and the reproach of commentators."[50] It is difficult to interpret as a whole and also in many of its details. Sometimes (as in v. 13b–c) the words in a line may be clear, but we are not sure how to relate them to a context. Sometimes we do not recognize the words (the psalm includes a high number of hapaxes), or we cannot see how they relate to their sentences, and thus many proposals have been made for emending the text, though as usual, I have generally sought to interpret MT and ancient versions that might witness to other Hebrew traditions.

Likewise, "every conceivable occasion and date have been suggested for this Psalm, from the age of Joshua to that of the Maccabees."[51] The century that has elapsed since those words were written has not clarified the question.[52] Possibly the psalm developed over the centuries and belongs to many periods.[53] Its concrete links with those other praise psalms and prayers outside the Psalter do not help resolve this question, since we also do not know their date nor the direction of their relationship with Ps. 68, though this does not take away from the possibility of illumining the psalm by comparing it with these passages that have some similar features.

The leader's. David's. Composition. Song.

Heading. See glossary.

68:1–3. This "prologue" or "preface"[54] to the psalm introduces its theme, the fact that God consistently acts to put down opponents and give the faithful reason to rejoice. In LXX and Jerome, phrases that appear in Num. 10:35 as a prayer or exhortation to God, "Arise, Yhwh," become in the psalm a wish, "May God arise," which fits with other psalms' frequent urging of God to arise (*qûm*) to fight against enemies (e.g., 3:7 [8]; 7:6 [7]).[55] The LXX and Jerome also take the subsequent

49. See Luther, *First Lectures*, 1:324–50; Calvin, *Psalms*, 3:4–44 (contrast his editor, James Anderson, who adds many more and longer footnotes to his translation of Calvin's work on this psalm than he does elsewhere).

50. As quoted by Anderson (see previous note), 5.

51. Kirkpatrick, *Psalms*, 375.

52. E.g., Johannes C. de Moor has recently again argued for the time of Joshua, in *The Rise of Yahwism*, rev. ed. (Louvain: Peeters, 1997), 171–91.

53. See (e.g.) Gerstenberger, *Psalms*, 2:34–45.

54. Respectively, Gerstenberger, *Psalms*, 2:35; and Calvin, *Psalms*, 3:6 (on v. 1).

55. Oddly, according to the English translation, Jerome begins his homily on Ps. 68 with "God arises; his enemies are scattered" (*Homilies*, 1:50), but Patrologia latina, vol. 26, col. 1012, has the same version as his translation.

verbs in vv. 1–3 as jussive. In MT, however, the form of the opening verb is yiqtol,[56] and it is natural also to take the subsequent verbs as yiqtols, so that the whole opening section constitutes a declaration rather than a prayer or wish. A further question concerns whether we read the lines as statements about God's characteristic activity or declarations about what God will do in the future. In previous psalms we have taken such yiqtols in the former sense, and that would be the natural assumption here; the subsequent statements concerning God's characteristic nature and activity will support this understanding. They thus declare that Moses's prayer is certainly answered in Israel's experience, and they set the agenda for the psalm as a whole. Yet while in MT vv. 1–3 are thus not a prayer, LXX and Jerome may bring out their subtext, a concern that MT will acknowledge before we get to the end (see vv. 28–31). That is, at least part of the psalm's agenda does lie in a concern to prevail upon God once again to act in this way. I take vv. 2–3 as three bicola rather than two tricola (MT). As well as being intrinsically the more likely arrangement, this leaves the double simile in v. 2a–b as one matching bicolon, vv. 2c–3a as one contrasting bicolon joined by *w* (avoiding what would otherwise be an asyndeton in v. 2), and v. 3b–c as a further bicolon with parallel clauses.

> ¹When God arises, [MT]/May God arise, [LXX, Jerome] his enemies scatter,
> those who are against him flee from before him.

The three opening verbs are the same as those in Num. 10:35.[57] As elsewhere, the implication of God's arising is that God fights against enemies, specifically God's enemies, but we may suspect that they are the suppliants' enemies, too, and this will eventually become explicit. Perhaps the enemies scatter simply because God arises. God will not necessarily need to do anything. The second colon then spells out the point in speaking of those who are *against God fleeing "from before him," which paints a picture of their running away at the sight of God's arising. While this description of God's arising might have in mind a liturgical representation of the event, with Yhwh's return to the sanctuary

---

56. That is, *yāqûm* rather than *yāqōm* (GKC 72f) or *yāqum*, with the accent on the second syllable (Gen. 27:31). Forms such as the latter, which is "only orthographically different from *yāqûm*" (GKC 72t), would make it possible to take *yāqûm* as jussive if the context required it, but here it does not, and the orthographic difference makes the difference. Thus Albright ("Catalogue," 17) repoints the verb (and the following verbs) in order to make it jussive.

57. Though as well as the first verb in Num. 10:35 being impv. and followed by a *w*, the second and third verbs there have defective middle vowels, and the verse refers to Yhwh, not God.

symbolized by that of the covenant chest, there is no concrete indication of this (contrast Ps. 132). The fact that Num. 10 explicitly refers to the covenant chest, while the psalm does not do so, would be odd if the psalm links with a procession involving the chest.[58] There is no particular reason to take these verbs to refer to a liturgical event rather than a political one. This preface is a theological statement about God's characteristic activity.

> [2a–b]You disperse them as smoke disperses,
>   as wax melts before fire.

Over against the description of enemies scattering and fleeing, v. 2a–b makes the complementary point that while this is their action, it issues from proactive dispersing on God's part, even if all God has to do to make that happen is arise. The nature of the dispersing is expressed in two similes. It will resemble the way smoke disperses, blown away by the wind. More chillingly, it will resemble the way wax melts when held before fire.

> [2c]Faithless people perish from before God,
>   [3]but the faithful—they are glad.
> They exult before God,
>   they rejoice with gladness.

The opening colon sums up the point in more literal terms. Its summarizing relationship to what precedes perhaps explains MT's placing the verse division after this colon. God's enemies are the *faithless, and God's arising means they perish, again "from before" God. The second colon draws a contrast between faithless and *faithful (who come in emphatic position before the verb) and between perishing and rejoicing. The joy will be based on the fact that God's enemies are the oppressors of the faithful, so that their perishing is what means the deliverance of the faithful.

Verse 3b–c in turn expands on that second colon with two parallel verbs and a reappearance of the root "be glad" from v. 3a in the form of the noun "gladness." The expression "before God" also reappears, applying to both cola. The faithful exult not merely in the event itself or in its consequences or in their winning the battle (if they are involved in the fighting). They also exult in the giver of the victory. In vv. 1 and 2 people fled and perished "from before God," but exulting and rejoicing happen simply "before God." There is no need to run. God's presence is the cause of the flight and death of the faithless, but it is the location of the rejoicing of the faithful.

58. Cf. Dahood, *Psalms*, 2:134.

68:4–6. The second section moves explicitly to address people, to urge them to praise God on the basis of what they know to be true about God's characteristic activity. It thus corresponds broadly to the opening exhortations in a praise psalm. Implicitly it reconfigures the statements about God's activity in vv. 1–3, which anticipatorily also provide reasons for this praise.

> ⁴Sing to God,
>   make music to his name.
> Lift it up to the one who rides on the clouds/through the steppes,
>   whose name is—Yah; exult before him.

The opening brief exhortation to praise in v. 4a–b comprises two parallel plural imperatives, one qal and one piel, one drawing attention to the words of the song, the other to the *music of this praise. Parallel nouns follow, identifying the object of the praise, with the *lĕ* on the first noun applying to both. The second indirectly specifies who this God is, for the God's unstated *name is Yhwh, or Yah (to use the form that will come in the next line).

The next line as a whole parallels that as well as being once more internally parallel. Again each colon has a plural imperative, though the second (taking up a verb from v. 3; see below) comes near the end of the line, giving the line an abb′a′ shape that makes it self-contained and hints that vv. 5–6 will go in a different direction. The preposition *lĕ* this time follows both verbs. After the first it does so rather oddly because "extol" (*sālal*) usually governs a direct object, but the result is to continue the form of expression from v. 4a–b. Here the construction involves the ellipse of the grammatical object, a word for a song or voice.[59] After the second verb the preposition appears in the composite expression *lipnê*, "before," which completes a fourfold sequence running through vv. 1–4 and further underlines the contrast between flight and death, on the one hand, and rejoicing and exulting, on the other. The verb also almost resumes from v. 3, though the form is *ʿālaz* rather than *ʿālaṣ*.

The object of the praise is again twice identified, in interesting ways. First, God is either "the one who rides through the steppes" (so Jerome; that idea will be taken further in v. 7) or "the one who rides on the clouds," in a heavenly limousine (that idea will be taken up in v. 33).[60] That descrip-

---

59. Cf. Tg; the construction parallels that with *nāśāʾ* in Isa. 42:11. This parallel and the parallel with references to praise on either side make it less likely that the ellipse involves a word for a highway (so LXX, Jerome), though the latter fits with Jerome's understanding *ʿărābôt* to mean "steppes" (cf. Stec, *Targum of Psalms*, 129).

60. *ʿĂrābôt* usually means "steppes," but in PBH can mean "heaven." Yhwh does elsewhere ride on clouds, like Baal, and here *ʿărābôt* could be equivalent to *ʿărāpôt* from the root *ʿrp*. The LXX has "west," taking the word as *ʿereb*, "sunset, evening."

tion is a standard one applied to Baal in Ugaritic literature, and similar expressions are applied to Yhwh elsewhere (Deut. 33:26; Isa. 19:1). It is a compressed version of the picture in 18:7–15 [8–16] of God coming to act, transported yet also concealed by dark and frightening thunderclouds.[61] The OT thinking would assume that Yhwh, not Baal, is the *real* deity who rides on the clouds, and the point here may be polemical, though the context does not particularly suggest that. The designation is a reason for singing because it is always linked to the idea of the faithless being put down and the faithful being delivered.[62] Second, God's *name is Yah (cf. v. 18), as in Exod. 15:2 (also Exod. 17:16; Isa. 12:2; 26:4; 38:11; Ps. 118:14; Song 8:6 mg). This variant on Yhwh appears in names such as Elijah and in expressions such as *halĕlû-yāh*. We do not know whether Yah is a shortened form of Yhwh or Yhwh is a lengthened form of Yah or whether the two names have separate origins. Yah is more of a bare name identifying God over against other gods, rather than a name with a significance such as Exod. 3:13–15 explains. In particular it makes explicit that the "rider" is indeed Yah, not Baal.[63]

> [5]God in his holy dwelling
>   is father for orphans, governor for widows.

Verse 5 works out some implications of v. 4. The one who rides on the steppes or clouds does so as the one whose holy dwelling is in the heavens; the clouds bring Yah to earth. And Yah comes to earth to act there, as one who cares for vulnerable people such as orphans and widows. The combination of the two terms suggests that the orphans are the young people who have lost their father, and the widow is their mother. Through losing the male head of the family, they have lost their security and their place in the community. Orphans are people who need a father to see that they are looked after, and widows are people who need a "champion" (NJPS) or "defender" (TNIV) to act on their behalf. The orphans need not be little children; the orphan in Job 24:3 has a donkey, as the widow has an ox, but it is harder for a family that has lost its male head to survive economically and harder for it to avoid having these appropriated by someone, so that it ends up in even tougher straits. "Governor" is *dayyān*, conventionally a judge (cf. NRSV). Like *šōpēṭ*, it denotes someone in a position of authority who uses their authority to defend the rights of the vulnerable. In Middle Eastern thinking, that is central to the task of

61. See esp. 18:10 [11].

62. See Umberto Cassuto, "Psalm lxviii," *Biblical and Oriental Studies* (Jerusalem: Magnes, 1973), 1:241–84 (see 245).

63. Cf. Bill T. Arnold and Brent A. Strawn, "*Bᵉyāh šᵉmô* in Psalm 68,5," *ZAW* 115 (2003): 428–32.

people in authority such as kings. This expectation is undergirded by the fact that it is central to the activity of the deity. The description is the other side of that in vv. 1–2. It is as God puts down the faithless that orphans and widows find they have a champion (cf. the sequence in vv. 19–23). The God who lives in a heavenly dwelling does not stay there all the time but acts in the world in this way.

> [6]God—he enables the desolate to live at home,
>   brings out the captives, in fetters,
>   but rebels live in dry land.

The desolate people who need to be taken home could include orphans and widows but might include others: for instance, people who lose their homes through debt or had to move elsewhere during time of famine. In parallel with them are people who are taken captive in war.[64] As usual, the third colon is then unexpected and advertises that we come to the end of a section. In content there is a contrasting parallelism between the first two cola and the last, and the contrast in content is heightened by a contrast in expression. The people concerned are the subject rather than the object, they are described by means of a participle rather than a regular noun, the verb is a qatal rather than a participle, and the adverbial expression "in dry land" lacks a modifier equivalent to the sufformative on "at home" or the preposition on "songs." If the rebels are the people who cause either the homelessness or the captivity, they might be either Israelites or foreigners. But in 66:7 the rebels were foreigners, as they are in v. 18 (below), and that fits here. Dry land will be the fate that makes them homeless or exiles, the fate they had imposed on others. The talk of rebels may indicate that the image of God as father runs through vv. 5–6 as a whole.[65] It is the responsibility of the head of the (extended) family to see that orphans and widows are looked after and that homeless and captives are brought back home (cf. Gen. 14) but also to see that rebels are disciplined (cf. Deut. 21:18–21; Isa. 30:1).

68:7–10. Another new section sees a move from addressing worshippers to addressing God and a move from general statements to a more narrative-like account of what God has done and does, which implicitly provides parallels to the statements in vv. 1–3 and vv. 4–6.[66] Verses 7–8 have a closeness to Deborah and Barak's words in Judg. 5:4–5 similar to

---

64. The two cola follow abcdb'c'd' order: "God" is the subj. of both clauses, then there follow two hiphil participles, two m. pl. nouns as objects, and two adverbial expressions beginning *b* (though one is the word *bayit*, the other the prep. *b*).

65. Cf. Tate, *Psalms 51–100*, 176.

66. I have redivided the lines. The sequence of cola is difficult; E. Vogt reorders them ("'Regen in Fülle,'" *Bib* 46 [1965]: 359–61).

that of v. 1 to Moses's words in Num. 10, but we have noted one striking difference: the concrete geographical references to Seir and Edom do not appear.[67] That coheres with a second feature. In its concreteness Judg. 5 resembles a testimony psalm, and in keeping with that, it begins with a declaration of intent to praise Yhwh. We have seen that vv. 4–6 more resemble the introduction to a praise psalm, and the general nature of the content of vv. 7–10 and what follows is in keeping with this. That includes (third) that rain appears in vv. 9–10 not merely as a spectacular sign of God's presence on one occasion but also as a gift that makes the crops grow. It is difficult not to read vv. 7–8 as describing Yhwh's original journey to the land of Canaan with the people, but when vv. 9–10 declare that God's rain renews the languishing land and that God provides for the weak (using yiqtol verbs as well as qatals), that sounds more like a description of God's ongoing activity. The one leads to the other. Comparison with Hab. 3 is also illuminating. There, Yhwh's original journey through the wilderness to the land is the pattern for a coming act in history in which Yhwh asserts authority in the world. Here, that original journey links with God's ongoing provision for land and people. There was no particular reason to reckon that vv. 4–6 referred to the people as a whole (though Tg sees v. 6b–c as referring to the exodus), but the grounds for those prayers and statements lie in God's activity in relation to that people, of which this section now speaks. God's primary relationship is with the people (Israel, the church), which is designed to be God's bridgehead in the world and provides the context in which we as individuals find our place in God's purpose and relate to God.

> [7]God, when you went out before your people,
>   when you marched through the wilderness, (Rise)

Verse 7 begins with the moment when God "went out" (*yāṣāʾ*) before the people. "Bring out," the hiphil of this verb, came in v. 6b, a conventional theological usage. It is much rarer to speak of God "going out." This usage follows that applied to a human king who "goes out" at the head of the army (1 Sam. 8:20; cf. Judg. 4:14; 5:4; 2 Sam. 5:24; Hab. 3:13). The parallel colon likewise speaks of God marching as a warrior (*ṣāʿad*; cf. Judg. 5:4; 2 Sam. 5:24; Hab. 3:12). The language is not exodus language, as those parallels also indicate; the verb is never used of Yhwh's going out from Egypt with Israel.[68] And the second colon pictures God as located in the wilderness rather than going into the wilderness.

---

67. See further Raymond Tournay, "Le Psaume lxviii et le livre des juges," *RB* 66 (1959): 358–68; Édward Lipiński, "Juges 5,4–5 et Psaume 68,8–11," *Bib* 48 (1967): 185–206.

68. Exod. 11:4 refers to Yhwh's going out to kill Egyptians. Exod. 13:21–22 uses other terms to refer to God's going out before the people.

While it will doubtless presuppose that God once went out from Egypt, it does not refer to this but rather presupposes that the wilderness is God's abode, from where (we are perhaps to infer) God first went into Egypt on a rescue mission. The next line will make explicit where this abode is in the wilderness.

> [8a–b]Earth shook, yes heavens poured,
> from before God, the one of Sinai,

The scene begins to move on. God marches before the people toward the land, and the result or evidence is a mighty storm; thunder makes the ground shake, and rain pours from the skies. There is no mention of rain in Deut. 33, though rain does feature in Hab. 3:10, in Judg. 5:4–5, and then (by implication) in Judg. 5:20–21 as they describe the river Kishon sweeping the enemy away. Here, too, rain features not merely because a thunderstorm forms a spectacular indication of God's presence but also because rain fulfills a function; here its significance is that rain is indispensable to Canaan itself, not on a onetime but on an ongoing basis. The storm forms a response to the presence of "God, the one of Sinai."[69] Sinai, then, is God's mountain, as Exod. 3:1 describes Horeb. That might be a prospective description (the mountain would become holy through God's appearing to Israel there), but in light of Ps. 68 it might be understood to declare something that was already so. Yhwh was already the God of Horeb, which is the portal of heaven. The journey through the wilderness (v. 7) is a journey from Sinai to the land, undertaken by the God who dwells at Sinai. Once again there is a contrast between God's going "before" the people (v. 7) and the storm issuing "from before" God, though a less sinister contrast than that in vv. 1–4.

> [8c]From before God, the God of Israel;
> [9a]you shed very generous rain, God.

This God is first further identified as "God, the God of Israel." That makes an important statement complementing the preceding one. The God of Sinai is the God of Israel; the God of Israel is the God of Sinai. On one hand, God is independent of Israel. God is not naturally bound up with this people. God has an independent existence, located (as far

---

69. Cf. Sym; see *HALOT* on *zeh*; *IBHS* 19.5d; *CP*, 114. On the basis of regular usage, it would be easier to translate "this Sinai" with LXX (cf. *IBHS* 17.4.1) or "this is Sinai" and to take the phrase as a clarification. But either way it then obscures more than clarifies. It seems to make Sinai the setting of the storm, but the storm language is then difficult; though the OT story refers to thunder as an accompaniment of God's appearing at Sinai, it does not otherwise refer to rain there (not surprisingly).

as earth is concerned) in this remote place that would never be under Israel's control. A symbol of this is Elijah's journey there to meet with the God of Sinai. It is a symbol partly because it is the only account of such an event. On the other hand, this God *is* the God of Israel. The God of Sinai entered into association with this people ("your people," v. 7) and with this land (vv. 9b–10). There is no natural link between this God, this people, and this land, but there is now as inexorable and indissoluble a link as that between a patriarch and his family or a shepherd and his flock or a king and his country. Further, the God of Sinai is God, and the God of Israel is God. If "God" has here replaced "Yhwh,"[70] then a result is to make a further explicit theological statement. The God of Israel who is the God of Sinai is not merely a deity associated with a particular geographical location or with a particular people, and thus one whose being stands alongside other deities associated with different locations and peoples, as some Israelites will sometimes have assumed. This God is—God. Hence earth shook and heavens poured when God appeared, as Canaanite religion reckoned happened when Baal appeared. The second colon begins to make explicit that the storm is not merely an audiovisual accompaniment to God's appearing. As in Ps. 65 and implicitly in Ps. 67, rain is the key to life. If there is rain, there is life; if there is no rain, there is death. A paradox is thus implicit in the fact that the God who chooses to live in the wilderness is the one who gives the gift of rain, even if it is somewhere else that God does so. And God does give this gift, in abundance. It is rain of great generosity, as generous as the love of God (Hos. 14:4 [5]) and an expression of that love. Only in these two passages is *nĕdābâ* applied to God; it usually refers to human generosity, especially as expressed in "freewill offerings" (though see also Ps. 51:12 [14]). Words such as "shower" (TNIV, NRSV) are hardly appropriate to the verb *nûp* (v. 9) any more than to *nāṭap* (v. 8).[71] We are talking serious rain here, rain that drenches, douses, soaks, and saturates. Thus v. 9a pairs with v. 8a as v. 8c pairs with v. 8b, so that vv. 8–9a take abb′a′ form.

> [9b]Your possession, and it languishing—you yourself have provided for it;
> [10]your dwelling—they have lived in it,
> you who provide for the weak with your goodness, God.

The tricolon closing the section begins by noting the vital significance of this gift. Without it, the land languishes, and therefore the people do.

---

70. See "The History behind the Psalter" in the introduction to volume 1 of this commentary and the introduction to Pss. 42–43.

71. *Nûp* literally means "swing" and makes one think of the kind of rain that drives almost horizontally and veers with the wind.

But by means of this copious rain, God provides what the land needs to enable it to grow crops. Here for the first time in the Psalter the land is God's "possession" (*naḥălâ*; Israel was God's possession in 28:9, while the land was Israel's possession in 47:4 [5]). "The one of Sinai" has decided to make this land a personal possession. It is therefore open to being lent to the people who also belong to this God. The third colon further identifies the one who thus provides; the verb recurs from the first colon, though now hiphil rather than polel. It also further identifies the people who are provided for: the *weak, here a designation of the people as a whole. Unless God does so welcome the people to live in this possession and dwelling, they will be landless, and unless God does then provide this land with rain, they will starve. The section thus comes to an end at a point quite similar to that which vv. 4–6 reached. In the context, the goodness with which God provides for the people will be not simply the goodness of God's character (though that is presupposed) but also the good things that this good God gives, the things that make life possible, the rains and the crops that they make grow.

68:11–14. The theme changes abruptly from God's ongoing provision of rain for the land to God's ongoing victories over kings, yet this is the other side to two issues that dominate Israel's life: will the crops grow and will it be able to maintain itself over against other peoples? The section uses the yiqtol throughout and declares that on a continuing basis God is sovereign and active in the political world as well as in the natural world, speaking as Lord and acting as Shaddai (vv. 11, 14). I follow NRSV rather than MT in understanding the versification.

> [11]The Lord gives a word;
>   the women who pass on the news being a great army,
> [12a]the kings of armies flee, flee,

So it begins with a tricolon. The *Lord speaks the word that decides the result of a battle.[72] Dramatically, the psalm then holds back from telling us directly the nature of this event or the result of the uttering of this word. Instead, it turns to the people who herald the event, announcing the news around the city or the country, a great women's army that recalls Miriam and her company (Exod. 15:20–21; see also 1 Sam. 18:6–7).[73] The unexpected third colon then makes an ironic contrast

72. The LXX and Jerome apparently take the verb to govern two accusatives, as if it signified "gives the women . . . a word"—that is, commissions them to proclaim. This would make good sense, but the usage is hard to parallel (see GKC 117ff).

73. Albright comments, "The less said about the 'female bearers of good tidings' the better" ("Catalogue," 21); they can be eliminated by treating this noun as a Phoenician-type (collective) f. sg. (cf. Dahood, *Psalms*, 2:140–41). But since the OT does give women this

with the kings of the "real" armies, who are in headlong flight. This is the result of God's speaking that was held back.

> 12bWhile the young girls of the house share the spoil
> 13though they stay among the enclosures,
> The wings of a dove covered in silver,
> its pinions in pale gold.

Another group of women appear. We imagine the army having returned home with its spoil, and this other group of women sharing in it or sharing it out. Judges 5:29–30 incorporates this motif, but with irony; there is no irony here. The second colon manifests another link and contrast with Judg. 5. Not having actually taken part in the battle is no bar to sharing in the spoil. Looking after the home or the sheep[74] plays as vital a role as fighting when the community is at war. So the words overlap with Judg. 5:16 but with contrast in significance as well as in wording; there is no critique here.

Verse 13b–c is obscure; perhaps it refers to some item of spoil such as an army emblem or a winged helmet, plated in silver and gold, perhaps something that a woman could wear as an ornament.[75]

> 14When Shaddai scatters kings there,
> it snows on Salmon.

Verse 14 is likewise obscure, though we may guess that it summarizes this section. If so, the scattering of the kings takes up the opening line, and the snow might be items left behind by the fleeing army or their bones bleached white by the sun. There is a hill called Salmon near Shechem (Judg. 9:48), and this would imply that the line expresses astonishment at a wonder. It is a proverbial saying; the Shechem area does not experience serious snow, so that the victory is almost as extraordinary as snow in Los Angeles.[76] Etymologically, *ṣalmôn* may link with a word for

---

role, that seems unnecessary. The Tg refers v. 10a to the giving of the Torah, and v. 10b to Moses's and Aaron's passing it on to the people.

74. In Ezek. 40:43, the only other occurrence, *šĕpattayim* (here translated "enclosures") means something like "pegs" or "hooks" or "shelves," but that does not fit here. Etymology and context would allow it to denote human habitations or sheepfolds (see BDB and *HALOT*) or saddlebags (*HALOT* on the similar word *mišpĕtayim*, Gen. 49:14; Judg. 5:16).

75. For further possibilities, see Tate, *Psalms 51–100*, 178–79; Othmar Keel, *Vögel als Boten*, OBO 14 (Göttingen: Vandenhoeck & Ruprecht, 1977), 28–35.

76. Commentators refer to the possibility that Salmon was a mountain east of the Jordan, which would lead well into the mention of Bashan in the next line. The only evidence for this is the reported occurrence of Asalmanos in one reading of a passage in Ptolemy's *Geography*, book 5, chap. 14 (see, e.g., Eerdmans, "Essays on Masoretic Psalms," 292; Goulder, *Prayers of David*, 258). But in the edition of this work available

"dark" and/or could remind readers of that word,[77] and the reference to snow might connect with this: Dark Mountain is covered in white. The title "Shaddai" appears in the Psalter only here and at 91:1. We do not know its etymology, and generally it seems to be simply a name, like Yah, perhaps with an archaic ring to it. There is one occasion when the OT sees significance in the name, emerging from its similarity to a verb meaning "destroy" (*šādad*), which suggests that it designates God as Destroyer (Isa. 13:6). This connotation would fit here.

68:15–18. Rhetorically this further section moves in a new direction as it addresses Mount Bashan, and in content it makes for another form of link between past and present, the reality of God's dwelling.

> [15]Mount Bashan is a majestic mountain,
>   Mount Bashan is a craggy mountain.

It begins by looking across from the mountain chain running through the heartland of Ephraim and Judah to the higher and more impressive mountains on the other side of the Jordan, running south from Mount Hermon through the Golan and Gilead. Mount Hermon in particular is indeed a mighty or majestic mountain, literally, a "mountain of God."[78] It towers into the heavens and thus suggests the possibility of or the claim to a link between heaven and earth. Perhaps a sanctuary was there, and in this sense it was indeed a "mountain of God." The parallel colon adds the fact that this mountain chain includes a number of impressive peaks, beginning with the several peaks of Hermon itself.

> [16]Why do you keep watch, craggy mountains,
>   on the mountain God desired as his dwelling?—
>   yes, Yhwh will live there forever.

---

to me (Claudius Ptolemy, *The Geography*, trans. and ed. Edward Luther Stevenson [repr., New York: Dover, 1991], 126), the name is Alsadamus. The uncertainty of this reading, in a Greek work from hundreds of years later than the psalm and in a MS two thousand years later than the psalm, makes this a hazardous basis for an argument. Partly on the basis of Syr, Severin Grill suggests that Salmon stands for Mount Gerizim as a rival place of worship to Zion; cf. the succeeding reference to Mount Hermon ("Der Berg Salmon," *TZ* 17 [1961]: 432–34).

77. Cf. *HALOT*; Tg; and *Midrash on Psalms*, 1:542. If Salmon does refer to a mountain east of the Jordan, this link might also be the point of the reference.

78. J. A. Emerton emphasizes that not least in a context such as the present one, it is unlikely that *'ĕlōhîm* is merely a way of expressing the superlative ("The 'Mountain of God' in Psalm 68:16," in *History and Traditions of Early Israel* [Eduard Nielsen Festschrift; ed. André Lemaire and Benedikyt Otzen; VTSup 50; Leiden: Brill, 1993], 24–37 [see 29–30]).

What is the look in its eyes? The other uses of the word for "keep watch" (*rāṣad*), one in Hebrew and one in Aramaic, involve watching wisdom furtively but ambitiously in order to get hold of wisdom or watching someone furtively in order to rob them;[79] hence LXX, Jerome, and NJPS find hostility (cf. Rashi), while NRSV and TNIV find envy. At which mountain might one imagine the towering peaks of Hermon looking (without wanting to be seen staring) with hostility and/or puzzled astonishment because God had chosen to locate a sanctuary there? That mountain might be the mountain range as a whole that forms the heart of the land of Canaan, and thus the land itself, which is Yhwh's own land (cf. vv. 9–10; and Exod. 15:17). Dan, on its nearby but insignificant hillock, would be a more specific candidate. So would Tabor, between Zebulun and Naphtali, where there may have been a sanctuary (cf. 89:12 [13]),[80] though Tg treats it along with Carmel as one of the rejected mountains symbolized by Bashan. So certainly would Zion (cf. v. 29), an unimpressive little spur of the Judean mountain chain, surrounded by higher mountains even in the immediate vicinity, so that Mount Hermon would regard it as particularly pathetic. In the immediate context (v. 17) so would Sinai, a place with which the psalm presupposes Yhwh had been associated (vv. 7–8). Whichever mountain Bashan eyes in resentful astonishment, it does so as itself a mountain that is in its way as mighty and majestic as God. Surely it would therefore be the mountain where God chose to dwell! But it knows that God has unaccountably actually viewed this other mountain as desirable and precious (*ḥāmad*), like gold. For God, this is the desirable residence, one indeed where God intends to stay forever. The point is added in an unexpected third colon that suggests an end to a subsection. That closing word "forever" may make more explicit that the mountain in the previous colon is indeed Zion, the place God did make a commitment to forever (e.g., 48:8 [9]). But this "forever" is not the usual expression *lěʿôlām* or *ʿad-ʿôlām* but *lāneṣaḥ*, which is more inclined to have negative connotations (e.g., 13:1 [2]; 44:23 [24]). Perhaps this "forever" has Mount Hermon's horrified perspective in mind.

> [17]God's chariotry were myriads, doubled thousands,
> the Lord among them at Sinai in holiness.

79. See BDB; *HALOT*; and *DTT*.

80. See (e.g.) Hans-Joachim Kraus, "Die Kulttraditionen des Berges Thabor," in *Basileia*, 2nd ed. (Walter Freytag Festschrift; ed. Jan Hermelink and Hans Jochen Margull; Stuttgart: Evangelische Missionsverlag, 1961), 177–84; J. Gray, "A Cantata of the Autumn Festival," *JSS* 22 (1977): 2–26.

The answer to the rhetorical question *Why? begins here. Whether or not there was anything impressive about the mountain God chose, there was something highly impressive about the forces God had available in the process of establishing a dwelling there, and the craggy mountains across the Jordan know that. They are a little like Balaam's donkey, who can see the invisible things that human beings miss (Num. 22:22–34), or like Elisha, who can see chariotry filling the mountains around him, ready to protect him (2 Kings 6:16–17). The OT references to chariotry that have more direct significance again come in the story of the Red Sea deliverance and the story of Deborah. The Hebrew text of Exod. 14–15 refers ten times to Pharaoh's chariotry, while the Hebrew of Judg. 4–5 refers seven times to Sisera's chariotry. Both turn out to be spectacularly useless when Yhwh decides to act. They ignore the reality of another chariotry in whose midst (the second colon adds) was its commander, the *Lord. The subsequent words in that second colon are rather terse, there being no "at." I follow the ancient versions in assuming that here Sinai is the place where God *was*, in holiness, in contrast to Deut. 33:2, which speaks of Yhwh coming *from* Sinai, to which vv. 7–8 have referred.[81]

> [18]You went up to the height, you took captives,
>   you received gifts among people,
>   and yes, rebels—to live as Yah God.

So gathered with these forces, Yah went up to the height. "The height" usually refers to Yhwh's location in the heavens (e.g., 7:7 [8]; 18:16 [17]), but it can also refer to a height on earth (e.g., Jer. 31:12; Ezek. 34:14). This fits the present context, though the "height" might have various references. The Tg refers it to Mount Sinai, which fits the context, but in Tg it is Moses who does the climbing, fitting the story in Exodus, where Yhwh comes down on Sinai rather than going up on it. Yah did go up to enter into possession of the mountain country of Canaan (cf. Exod. 33:3, 5) and then to enter into possession of Zion and take up residence there.[82] Both the broader and the narrower event (the taking of Canaan and of Zion) involved taking peoples captive. The parallel colon adds that Yah in the process received gifts from human beings, tribute that recognized that Yah is indeed the victorious king.[83] Then a

81. NRSV and TNIV ("the Lord came from Sinai") assimilate to Deut. 33:2 by changing *bām sînay* to *bāʾ missînay*. NJPS has "as in Sinai," which requires considerable inference, though the implication that the colon makes a comparison with God's subsequent dwelling on Zion is true enough to the context.

82. See on 47:5, 9 [6, 10].

83. The Tg continues to refer the line to Moses and has him *giving* gifts (that is, the Torah; cf. Syr; also *Midrash on Psalms*, 1:545). This perhaps involves a paronomasia,

third colon turns the line into a tricolon that once more closes off the section. It hails back to the taking of captives, noting that these givers of tribute did not do so willingly but under compulsion. The colon thus adds to the description of the event as a demonstration of Yah's power, one that astonishes and troubles the mountains of Bashan (and the peoples whom they symbolize?). These "rebels" (cf. v. 6) did not welcome Yah to come and dwell in their land or their city, as Rahab did. But that did not hold Yah back from continuing the journey from Sinai to Canaan to Zion.

68:19–23. Verses 19–23 revert to talk about God's ongoing activity, in a way that follows from vv. 15–18, and to talk about God rather than to God.

> ¹⁹The Lord be worshipped day by day;
>   God, our deliverer, carries us. (Rise)

The opening declaration[84] that the Lord should be *worshipped compares with Ps. 66 (see 66:20), as well as with v. 35 (below). "Day by day" or "every day" or "day after day" are common terms to characterize worship (e.g., 61:8 [9]; 72:15; 96:2; 145:2; Isa. 58:2). The second colon provides the basis for expectation. Such ongoing worship is the appropriate response to God's ongoing activity as one who *delivers and carries. The other passage where Yhwh "carries" Israel is Isa. 46:1–3, which makes a telling contrast between peoples who have to carry their gods and the people who are carried by their God. In a crisis, then, God delivers us by carrying us.

> ²⁰God is for us a God who does deliver;
>   the departure to death belongs to Yhwh the Lord.

Verse 20 makes a parallel declaration restating that. The first colon differs only verbally from v. 19b. Noteworthy is the hapax *môṣāʾâ* in the intensive plural. The second colon makes the converse point. God's *delivering us involves dealing with our attackers and thus imposing an exit on them (*tôṣāʾôt*, another intensive or abstract plural).[85]

---

reading *lāqaḥ* as *ḥālaq*. That rewriting of the line lies behind the quotation in Eph. 4:8, on which see the introduction in vol. 1 of this commentary under "The Psalms and the New Testament."

84. MT points to understanding v. 19 as 2-3-2, but one would expect something more like 4-3 in this psalm, and this fits the usage of the expression "day by day."

85. There is another neat rhetorical pattern about the line. In the first colon, the second and fourth words begin with the prep. *l*; in the second line, the first and third words do so.

> ²¹Yes, God smashes the head of his enemies,
>   the hairy crown of the one who goes about in his great guilt.

Once more v. 21 elaborates on what precedes.[86] Imposing an exit on the enemies that threaten Israel with death involves disposing of God's own enemies. Either God treats Israel's enemies as God's own, or God's enemies become the people's enemies because of Israel's association with God. The subject and verb in the first colon also apply to the second, which consequently has four words to spell out the two nouns in the first colon. The head becomes the hairy crown, perhaps more likely a reference to the barbarian or demonic appearance of the warriors[87] than a reference to Nazirite-type vows taken by them (cf. Judg. 5:2). And "his enemies" becomes "the one who goes about in his great guilt."[88] The phrase suggests another way of seeing why the nations have become God's enemies. They have offended by their opposition to God's purpose. In fact, they are faithless rebels (vv. 2, 6, 18).

> ²²The Lord said, "From Bashan I will bring them back,
>   bring them back from the depths of the sea,

The Tg takes this as a promise that God will bring back the faithful, but in the context yet again v. 22 elaborates the previous line, declaring that God will not let the guilty escape. In an image like that in Amos 9:1–4, God's enemies are imagined fleeing to the far east and the far west, the far heights and the far depths. Bashan reappears as an image not only for the heights but also for the east; the second colon clarifies that this is implied by the reference, since "the sea" (the Mediterranean) stands more regularly for the west. There even the depths of the sea will provide no refuge (cf. Amos 9:3), the reference to depth taking up that other significance in the reference to Bashan as a high mountain area (cf. vv. 15–16). As in v. 21, the opening subject and verb in the first colon also apply to the second, while the verb "I will bring them back" recurs at the center of the line, which works abcddc'.

> ²³So that your foot may smash in blood,
>   your dogs' tongue, too—its share is from your enemies."

86. Thus *'ak* here is asseverative/emphatic ("yes"; cf. TNIV) rather than restrictive/adversative ("but"; against LXX, Jerome, NRSV).

87. Cf. Gunkel, *Psalmen*, 285.

88. Here alone is *'āšām* pl., and I again take it as intensive. Strictly the colon perhaps involves a metonymy, "the hairy crown going about in its great guilt" (but see GKC 128c).

Verse 23 enlarges yet more on the point. These deliverances will not be theoretical or uncertain, as if the enemies might have disappeared but may reappear again. It is God who does the killing, but the people will witness the consequences. Or rather, they will be in physical contact with it, as will their animals, with enthusiasm ("share" suggests a choice delicacy). The verb and prepositional phrase in the first colon also apply in the second: that is, the dogs (the scavengers who feed off abandoned corpses) "smash" their tongues in the blood as the people "smash" their feet in it. The verb *māḥaṣ* is repeated from v. 21 in a distinctive usage that emphasizes the people's (and the dogs') association with God's act. This is not an act of judgment that happens at a distance, in such a way that enables the people to isolate themselves from it. They share in its implications, if not in its actual execution.[89]

68:24–27. Once again the psalm goes back to the once-for-all events that brought God to the divine dwelling on earth (vv. 24–25, 27), while also calling for celebration in the present (v. 26).

> [24]People saw your journeying, God,
> the journeying of my God, my king, in holiness.

For a moment the first colon again addresses God, as it imagines people seeing God go up to Zion at the beginning. Following on vv. 20–23 the watchers will be the enemies, the inhabitants of Canaan and of Zion, who see Yhwh take over their land and their city. They are the people for whom Mount Bashan stands as it "watches" incredulously (but it is the ordinary verb *rā'â* here). For the speakers, the individualized members of the present congregation, "my God" on that occasion proved to be "my king," a sovereign active on my behalf, though also one whose authority I am committed to recognizing. The awesome holiness that characterized the God of Sinai continued to characterize this God in coming to Zion.

> [25]Singers came first, strings behind,
> in the midst of girls playing tambourines.

Verse 25 offers more detail on the picture of that journey, which involved another army, of singers and string-players (the words are masculine) surrounded or preceded and followed by girls dancing and playing tambourines. The detail suggests that vv. 24–25 have in mind

---

89. The distinctiveness of the usage makes it usual to read *tirḥaṣ* (bathe) for *timḥaṣ*, assimilating to 58:10 [11]; so, e.g., NRSV, which claims the support of Vrs. But while the latter are inclined to paraphrase the line, they do not use the verb "bathe."

specifically the ceremonial move of Yhwh to Zion (2 Sam. 6), though it will doubtless reflect some form of regular practice.[90]

> [26]In the great congregation worship God,
>   Yhwh—you from the fountain of Israel.

The psalm turns to address the current generation themselves, urging them to join in the *worship still ongoing at the place that constituted the destination of God's journeying and/or in the procession that re-enacts that journeying. The command corresponds to one repeated in Deborah's song (Judg. 5:2, 9), suggesting that the worship of the present congregation relates to the past events the psalm relates. The verb in the first colon applies to both cola, with the two terms for God as its parallel objects, and the two prepositional expressions applying to both. Thus the worshippers form the great present congregation assembled for that celebration, and the second colon identifies these addressees as people who are "from the fountain of Israel." That is presumably a description of Yhwh (see 36:9 [10]), the fountain from which Israel sprang. The story the psalm celebrates tells of the origins of Israel as God's people; the present generation are the people sprung from those beginnings.

> [27]There was little Benjamin, ruling them,
>   the officials of Judah, their noisy throng,
>   the officials of Zebulun, the officials of Naphtali.

Once again the viewpoint changes. The psalmist now speaks like someone watching the procession and pointing out its features. First there is Benjamin, the little brother, with an importance out of propor-tion to its size because it saw the beginning of Israel's occupation of the land, and because it is the clan from which Israel's first king came, and because Israel's capital is located in its area. Then there is Judah, the dominant southern clan, from which the subsequent line of David came. Then there are two northern clans, not Ephraim and Manasseh but two numerically smaller clans from further north. While these two will represent the northern clans in general, it is significant that (with Asher) they are the two farthest away. They are not distinctively promi-nent in Deborah's song, despite the northern background of the event it commemorates, but they are the two that are named in Isa. 9:1 [8:23] in connection with their being the first victims of Assyrian invasion (cf. 2 Kings 15:29) because of their location to the far north and east of the

---

90. On the women's role in liturgical processions, see Keel, *Symbolism*, 339–41. The Tg takes these to be Miriam and her friends and thus takes v. 24 to refer to the crossing of the Red Sea.

land. All this suggests that the line again relates not directly to the worship that takes place in the present but to the journeying that brought Yhwh to the land and to Zion at the beginning. Once again the section closes with a tricolon.

68:28–31. As the psalm nears its end, the penultimate section turns to exhort God to act in accordance with the pattern that the psalm has celebrated. Urgings alternate with and lead into jussives or yiqtols in vv. 28–29 and 30–31. Either way, these jussives or yiqtols issue from the urgings.

> [28a–b]May your God have commanded your strength;
> be strong, God.

The plea begins with a third-person precative qatal[91] and a direct exhortation in the parallel colon.[92] The latter implies a synergy. God's commanding Israel's strength rather implies that God endows the people with this gift (the concern with Israel's strength will recur in the psalm's last line). Yet the psalm's presupposition is not that God gives this gift and then stays in the sanctuary, leaving Israel to go out to fight. God goes out and gets involved in the battle, giving the gift in its midst as the people fight and discover that they achieve more than they could have dreamed because God is acting for/with them. So "be strong" or "act with strength" parallels "command your strength."

> [28c]You who acted for us [29]from your palace—
> up to Jerusalem kings are to bring you tribute.

I take vv. 28c–29 as the next line since v. 29 as a unit is hard to construe.[93] Here it seems likely that the first colon does not look back from the present to what God did in the past but looks back from the moment when the prayer has been answered as God again acts from the divine *palace in the heavens (cf. 18:6 [7]). The response to this new demonstration of God's strength will be the kings of the nations bringing tribute to the one who has manifested the power that identifies the real king.

> [30a–b]Blast the creature in the reeds,
> the assembly of the strong among the bullocks, the peoples.

---

91. Indicative "commanded" makes poor sense here, and the impv. in the context encourages the reader to take the qatal as precative (LXX has impv.).

92. NJPS's "the strength, O God, which you displayed for us" requires us to posit a hapax *'uzzâ* as an alternative to *'ōz* in the previous colon.

93. The pausal form of *mēhêkālekā* suggests that one Masoretic tradition divided the lines thus (cf. Kirkpatrick, *Psalms*, 394).

Verse 30a–b repeats the exhortation to demonstrate strength, putting the point more concretely and vividly. The creature in the reeds is the hippopotamus or water buffalo (cf. Job 40:21). In Job 40:15–24 this creature, like Leviathan, the sea dragon, is a symbol for dynamic disorderly power asserting itself against humanity and against God's purpose in the world, and that fits the context here. It is such power that is embodied in the earthly powers that assert themselves against Israel. So the psalm urges God to put them down. The parallel colon goes halfway to making that more explicit, since an "assembly" (ʿēdâ) suggests a gathering of human beings, an "assembly of wrongdoers" like that of 22:16 [17]. There as here the expression for a human assembly is accompanied by references to dangerous animals. "Strong" ones also appear in 22:12 [13], referring to animals that stand for human beings and (e.g.) in 76:5 [6]) referring directly to human beings. "Bullocks" is then an unequivocally animal term (EVV "calves" gives a misleading impression of lovable creatures gamboling in the meadow), yet these are "bullocks of the peoples." The demonic creature that embodies disorder expresses itself through human peoples acting with the frightening strength of powerful animals.

> 30cTrampling on those who love silver,
> May you have scattered the peoples who delight in encounters.

To put it more straightforwardly, they are peoples who love silver and delight in military "encounters" (see 55:18, 21 [19, 22]). They like making war because they like what they gain from it. While nations customarily gloss their wars with other rationales, appropriating the resources of other peoples is usually a significant factor in deciding to make war.[94]

> 31Bronze/red cloth/blue cloth/envoys/Hashmonites are to come from Egypt,
> Sudan is to hasten with its hands to God.

Again jussives or yiqtols follow on from the imperative. We do not know the meaning of the noun in the first colon, though the general meaning is clear, and the reference to Egypt gives precision to the symbolism of v. 30. "Sudan" represents kûš, the area south of Egypt ("Ethiopia" [NRSV] is further south and east); it appears as a makeweight for Egypt (cf. Isa. 20:3–5; 43:3; 45:14; Ezek. 30:4, 9; Nah. 3:9). There need be no implication that Egypt is Israel's current enemy, though sometimes it would be

---

94. In the two parallel expressions for the enemies, a yiqtol balances a ptc., and the word "peoples" in the second colon applies also to the first. To balance the parallel expressions for the enemies are parallel verbs to describe God's action—one a hitpael ptc., one a piel that I take as another precative (LXX, Syr, and Jerome have impv.).

that; it is the old enemy from the beginning of Israel's story, and in light of those other passages, it also features as a source of tribute. The parallel verbal expression is a vivid one, "hastening" going beyond merely "coming," as if the peoples cannot get to Jerusalem quickly enough to hold out their hands with their tribute for God.

68:32–35. The psalm closes with a final exhortation to the world to acknowledge Yhwh, paralleling vv. 4–6 but now explicitly addressed to the nations. The passage compares with Deut. 33:26–27 with its description of God as the "primeval" one who "rides the heavens/skies . . . in his majesty."

> ³²Kingdoms of the earth, sing to God,
>   make music to the Lord, (Rise)
> ³³To the one who rides through the primeval highest heavens—
>   there, he gives out his voice, his strong voice.

The nations are addressed as kingdoms (*mamlĕkôt*), an unusual alternative word for nations (cf. 46:6 [7]). As subject they carry over into the second colon, where "make *music" parallels "sing" (as in v. 4) and "the *Lord" parallels "God."

Verse 33 extends the parallelism as the whole line forms an expansion on God/the Lord, so that vv. 32–33 work abcb′c′c″c‴. Thus initially the potential worshippers are prominent in the two lines, then the nature of their worship, but eventually all attention attaches to its object. This God is the one who rides in "the heavens of heavens of old," an impressive construct chain re-expressing the description in v. 4. The description of God as riding in the highest heavens glorifies God, as does the description of the heavens as stretching back in time as well as up in space. If they extend back to times of old, so does God, only more so. The second colon parallels the participle with a verbal clause speaking further of God's lordship in creation. In those heavens that extend far into space and time, God speaks, and speaks loudly, in the thunder and makes things happen.

> ³⁴Give strength to God,
>   whose majesty is over Israel, his strength in the skies.

The first colon adds to the nature of the acknowledgment of God. It is also a matter of giving strength to God, which might mean simply acknowledging that God has strength but might also imply yielding up one's own strength to God.[95] In two parallel phrases, the second colon amplifies further the nature of the one to be acknowledged in light of that

95. See 29:1.

new command. On one hand, Yhwh's majesty is over Israel, so kingdoms must not pretend to a majesty of their own in the way people have been doing so far in the Psalter (10:2; 31:18, 23 [19, 24]; 36:11 [12]; 46:3 [4]). On the other, Yhwh is one who indeed possesses strength, and that in the skies, evidenced in the way the divine voice sounds forth there and implements heaven's purpose.

> [35]You are awesome, God, from your sanctuary,
>   the one who is God of Israel,
> Who gives strength and great might to the people;
>   God be worshipped.

Almost finally, the psalm turns back to God not merely to command worship but also to offer it. First it acknowledges the awesomeness of this God (*revere) who rides, acts, and speaks in and from the heavens, where (it now adds) God's "sanctuary" stands. The word is now *miqdāš*, but it takes up the reference to "his holy abode" (*mě'ôn qodšô*) in v. 5. But then the parallel colon adds the astonishing fact that this God is also the God of Israel (cf. on vv. 8c–9a). The two cola sum up one key conviction of the psalm.

The final line completes an abb'a' pattern in this closing verse. As the God of Israel, God gives the people strength (that word again; cf. vv. 28, 33, 34); but to underline it the psalm adds another hapax, though from a familiar root. The second colon repeats the expression from v. 19 (and cf. v. 26). It means that the psalm does not end with actual worship, but it does end with God.

Theological Implications

A key to understanding the significance of this complex psalm is the interrelationship between what Yah has done in the past and what Yah continues to do, both of which Israel celebrated in its worship. Israel knows from its story of its past that Yah, who had a palace in the heavens and had established another dwelling on a mountain in Sinai, marched through the wilderness ahead of Israel. It knows that Yah then ascended another mountain in order to establish a new home in the mountain country of Canaan and specifically on Mount Zion, accompanied by the clans Yah had led to the land. That meant defeating forces opposing this intent and thus winning their acknowledgment.

In the process Yah the God of Sinai became the God of Zion. The collocation of Sinai and Zion is significant given the stress in the Sinai story on Yhwh's expectations of Israel and the stress in the Zion tradition on Yhwh's grace and promises to Zion, though in this connection the order of events is interesting. The story in the Torah declares that Yhwh's commitment to Israel came first and that Israel's commitment to Yhwh is a response to that. The further addition of the Zion tradition points up the fact that Yhwh's grace and promises continue to stand in dialectical relationship with Israel's commitment. There is no once-for-all move from promise to obedience.

That past move is not merely a onetime event in the past. It offers indications regarding Yah's ongoing activity. It is regularly the case that when God arises, enemies scatter, and the faithful heave a sigh of relief. By nature, God is one who acts on behalf of orphans, widows, the desolate, and captives; by nature God is a deliverer, one who carries us.[96] God regularly provides the rain for this land that God took possession of and thus provides good things for the powerless people who live as God's guests there. God continues to scatter the powerful there, to refuse to let the guilty get away with their wrongdoing, and to require their recognition. God intends to live there permanently, even though a home on some place like Mount Hermon would be more impressive.

There are two natural responses to that. One is worship and celebration, which is strikingly something in which the whole world can join. The fact that God puts down opponents is good news for the world, not just for Israel. The other is prayer, because it is not to be assumed that all this works automatically. Sometimes it happens on God's own initiative, but sometimes God waits to be aroused.

96. On the importance to African Americans of the description of God as "father to the fatherless," see Cheryl Townsend Gilkes, "'Mother to the Motherless, Father to the Fatherless,'" *Semeia* 47 (1989): 57–85.

Psalm 69

When People Mock Zeal for Yhwh's House

Translation

The Leader's. On lilies. David's.

¹Deliver me, God,
   because waters have reached to my life.[1]
²I have sunk in a deep flood[2]
   where is no foothold.
I have come into watery torrents;
   a deluge has engulfed me.
³I have become weary with calling;
   my throat has become dry.
My eyes have failed,
   waiting for my God.[3]
⁴More than the hairs on my head
   are the people who are against me for nothing.

1. The suffix can be assumed from that on the first verb, though suffixes can be omitted from *nepeš* as from words for parts of the body (e.g., 17:9; Ruth 4:15). EVV have "coming up to my neck," which may be what the waters do, but it is doubtful whether *nepeš* itself (*person) ever means "neck," for which Hebrew has other words (see esp. Isa. 8:8; also v. 3). Cf. *TDOT* 9:505.

2. *Yāwēn* occurs only here and in 40:2 [3]; it is usually translated "mud," but "flood" makes better sense.

3. "Waiting" (*měyaḥēl*) depends on the suffix of "my eyes" (cf. the construction in, e.g., Gen. 3:8). The Erfurt Codex (see *BHS*) has "from waiting" (*mîyaḥēl*)—"ingeniously," *TTH* 161 comments; cf. LXX, Tg, Jerome, Aq, and Sym agree with MT.

Many are the people who are putting an end to me,
    my enemies, falsely.
What I did not steal,
    now I am to restore.[4]
[5]God, you are the one who knows of[5] my stupidity;
    my guilty deeds are not hidden from you.

[6]The people who look for you must not be shamed because of me,
    Lord Yhwh Armies.
The people who seek help from you must not be dishonored because
        of me,
    God of Israel.

[7]Because it is on account of you that I have borne reviling,
    that dishonor has covered my face.
[8]I have become a stranger to my relatives,
    an alien to my mother's offspring.
[9]Because it is passion for your house that has destroyed me;
    the reviling of people who revile you has fallen on me.
[10]When I wept and fasted,
    it turned into reviling for me.
[11]When I made sackcloth my clothing,
    I became a byword to them.
[12]People who sit at the gate mumble about me—
    and drinkers sing about me.[6]

[13]As for me, my plea to you, Yhwh,
    is a time of acceptance.
God, with your great commitment answer me,
    with your truthfulness that delivers.
[14]Rescue me from the mud, may I not sink;
    may I be rescued from the people who are against me, yes, from
        the watery torrents.
[15]May the watery deluge not engulf me,
    may the flood not swallow me,
    may the pit not close its mouth over me.
[16]Answer me, Yhwh, because your commitment is good;[7]

4. EVV translate as a question, but there is no marker of that.

5. The *l* marking the direct obj. may be an Aramaism (see *IBHS* 10.2.1d, also discussion in *IBHS* 10.4; JM 125k).

6. I follow 4QPs[a] *ngnw* (cf. LXX, Jerome, Sym, Syr)—more literally, "play"—for MT *ûněgînôt* (cf. Aq). 4QPs[a] also has the *bî* in the second colon rather than the first, but either way it will apply in both cola. In MT, the verbless second colon ("the songs of drinkers") may be a second predicate for "became" in v. 11 or a second subj. for "mumble."

7. For MT *kî-ṭôb*, 4QPs[a] has *kṭwb* (in accordance with the goodness [of your commitment]), assimilating to the second colon.

in accordance with the greatness of your compassion, turn your
   face to me.
[17]Do not hide your face from your servant,
   because I am in distress; answer me quickly.[8]
[18]Come near to me, restore me;[9]
   because of my enemies, redeem me.

[19]You yourself know my reviling,
   my shame, and my dishonor.
All my foes are before you;
   [20]reviling has broken my spirit, and I am ailing.
I looked for someone to show grief, but there was no one,
   for comforters, but I have not found them.
[21]People have put bitterness in my food,
   and for my thirst they give me vinegar to drink.

[22]May their table become a trap before them,
   and for their partners[10] a snare.
[23]May their eyes grow dark so that they cannot see;
   make their loins shudder continually.
[24]Pour out your wrath on them;
   may your angry burning overtake them.
[25]May their encampment become desolate,
   may no one live in their tents.
[26]Because you—the people you hit, they have pursued;
   the suffering of people you struck, they have proclaimed.[11]
[27]Give them punishment upon their punishment;
   may they not come to your faithfulness.
[28]May they be erased from the scroll of the living,
   not be written with the faithful.
[29]When I am weak and suffering,
   may your deliverance, God, set me on high.

[30]I will praise the name of God with a song,
   I will exalt him with thanksgiving,
[31]And it will please Yhwh more than an ox,
   a bull having horns and divided hoofs.
[32]When the weak see, they will be glad;

---

8. NRSV takes *mahēr* as an impv., "make haste," but in other contexts (e.g., 79:8) we have to take it as an inf. used adverbially, and so probably it is here (TNIV, NJPS).

9. Lit. "Come near to my *person [perhaps 'right near'], restore it."

10. For *wĕlišĕlômîm*, cf. 55:20 [21]. LXX, Jerome, Aq, Th, Sym, Syr imply *ûlĕšillûmîm*, "and for [their] recompense." Tg implies *ûšĕlāmîm*, "and [their] fellowship offerings." The suffix from the first colon carries over to the second.

11. For *yĕsappērû*, see on 2:7. LXX and Syr imply a verb such as *yôsîpû*, "they added to." Jerome, Sym, Aq follow MT.

you who seek help from God—yes, your spirit will revive.[12]
[33]Because Yhwh is one who listens to the needy
  and does not despise his captives.
[34]Heaven and earth must praise him,
  the seas and everything that moves in them.
[35]Because God will deliver Zion,
  build up the cities of Judah.
People will live there and possess it,
  [36]the offspring of his servants will own it;
  the people dedicated to his name will dwell in it.

Interpretation

Psalm 69 is a psalm of protest and plea (some pleas being imperative, many jussive), closing with a declaration of trust based on the conviction that God does hear such prayer. The earlier part of the psalm alternates between plea and protest.

Plea (v. 1a)	Protest (vv. 1b–5)
Plea (v. 6)	Protest (vv. 7–12)
Plea (vv. 13–18)	Protest (vv. 19–21)
Plea (vv. 22–29)	Confession of trust (vv. 30–36)

In vv. 1–5 one might reckon that the suppliant is a private individual speaking of the acts of other elements within the community, in the manner of many psalms. But vv. 7–12 suggest someone with a distinctive religious commitment, suggesting that the attackers are people with other forms of religious commitment, whom God should remove from the community, the psalm urges. Further, v. 6 already suggests that the suppliant is not merely a private individual but someone who in some sense represents a community. The protests and the pleas thus concern the destiny of this community as well as that of this individual, and the confession of trust looks forward to a restoring of Jerusalem and Judah.[13] The circumstances or attitudes reflected in the psalm recall those of Jeremiah, who was literally in danger of sinking in the mud in a cistern and who pleaded for action against his persecutors, as Nehemiah also did.

12. One might take the line as jussive.
13. It has been reckoned that this diversity within the psalm reflects a redactional process: see (e.g.) Erhard S. Gerstenberger, "Psalm 69," *Covenant Quarterly* 55, nos. 2–3 (1997): 3–19. Contrast L. C. Allen, "Rhetorical Criticism in Psalm 69," *JBL* 105 (1986): 577–98; and further on the psalm's structure, Pierre Auffret, "'Dieu sauvera Sion,'" *VT* 46 (1996): 1–29.

Both were accused and shamed by opponents. As usual we cannot infer the precise nature of an individual suppliant's experience from the details of the language used to describe it, not least its hyperbole. Understood literally, for instance, the lament that the suppliant has no sympathizers (v. 20) looks in tension with the psalm's concern with people who do seem to identify with the suppliant (vv. 6, 32), and similarly v. 8 should hardly make us infer that the suppliant is literally abandoned by immediate family. It is a "richly faceted prayer of lament or petition."[14]

> The Leader's. On lilies. David's.

Heading. See glossary. One might imagine the psalm on the lips of David as someone who experienced opposition and for whom the building of Yhwh's house was an important project.[15] For "on lilies," Tg has "concerning the exiles of the Sanhedrin," recognizing the exilic references in the psalm; it incorporates further exilic references into its translation of vv. 1–3, 14–15 (cf. Qimchi). Theodoret likewise associates it with the exile.[16]

69:1–5. The psalm begins with a brief initial plea (v. 1a) but then focuses on a description of the suppliant's experiences, expressed first metaphorically (vv. 1b–3), then literally (vv. 4–5), but in both cases hyperbolically.[17] While the first and last lines are 2-4 and 4-3, the bulk of the section expresses itself in the characteristic short lines of a lament, each having only two stresses in the second colon: 3-2, 2-2, 2-2, 2-2, 3-2, 2-2, 2-2. The rhythm thus expresses the way life is bringing the suppliant up short, and experience is achieving no closure. After v. 1 the lines come in pairs: v. 2, v. 3, v. 4a–d, and vv. 4e–5.

> ¹Deliver me, God,
>   because waters have reached to my life.

Following on the opening plea for *deliverance, v. 1 introduces the metaphor that will dominate vv. 1–2 and recur in vv. 14–15. The image of overwhelming waters, the embodiment of dynamic forces asserted against God and God's people and an image for death itself, has occurred earlier in the Psalter (18:16 [17]; 29:3; 32:6; 42:7 [8]; 46:3 [4]), but this psalm expounds the metaphor particularly systematically. Its initial summary plaint, indeed, is that these waters are imperiling the suppliant's very life (like the sword in Jer. 4:10).

14. Hossfeld and Zenger, *Psalms 2*, 172, though they emphasize its individual nature.
15. Cf. Goulder, *Prayers of David*, 217–29.
16. *Psalms*, 1:395.
17. Cf. Watson, *Classical Hebrew Poetry*, 319–20.

> ²I have sunk in a deep flood
>   where is no foothold.
> I have come into watery torrents;
>   a deluge has engulfed me.

Verse 2a–b indicates how they are doing so. "Sinking" involves an experience that is a metaphorical equivalent of the literal one that overtook Pharaoh's officers and then Jeremiah (Exod. 15:4; Jer. 38:6) and became Jeremiah's metaphor for what would happen to his king (Jer. 38:22; cf. Ps. 9:15 [16]). The "deep flood" has overlapping resonances, since the "deeps" were also where the Egyptians drowned (Exod. 15:5)[18] and suggest something far deeper than a person is ever going to be able to find a footing in (e.g., 68:22 [23]; 88:6 [7]; Jon. 2:3 [4]). The second colon makes that explicit.

The parallel line adds nothing in content, but the point needs further expressing for the sake of the suppliant and for the sake of the God whom the psalm seeks to move to action.[19] Its abb′a′ arrangement suggests closure; it brings the end of the exposition of this metaphor that was stated in v. 1b and developed through v. 2.

> ³I have become weary with calling;
>   my throat has become dry.
> My eyes have failed,
>   waiting for my God.

Verse 3 moves to more literal (if hyperbolic) description of the suppliant's prayer during this crisis, though it takes the form of a further protest: it is about weariness in calling on God for help rather than merely about the calling itself (cf. 6:6 [7]). Whereas metaphorically the suppliant is overwhelmed by water, literally (the second colon adds) the suppliant's throat is dry like that of a professor who has just given a two-hour lecture.

The parallel line adds eyes to voice. It assumes that when we pray, we then *wait, looking expectantly for God to do something. The suppliant has been doing that, staring intently like a lookout watching for signs of the army returning to a city, but seeing—nothing. Thus as the throat is dry, so the eyes have used up their ability to focus.

18. *Mĕṣôlâ* rather than *mĕṣûlâ*.

19. Even the verb "come" and the noun "water" are repeated from v. 1 (the verb was translated "reach" there). "Torrents" (*maʿămaqqîm*) is another word for "deep" and in the singular would differ by only one letter from "foothold" (*moʿŏmād*). The second colon then adds yet another noun of similar meaning and a verb that begins with *š*, like the noun, suggesting the rush of the waters.

> 4a-dMore than the hairs on my head
>   are the people who are against me for nothing.
> Many are the people who are putting an end to me,
>   my enemies, falsely.

Verse 4 begins to make explicit what the floods represent. They stand for enemies (cf. 18:16–17 [17–18]). The overwhelming nature of the waters corresponds to the numerousness of these people who are *against the suppliant, expressed in another hyperbole. Further, there is no basis for their attacks.

The parallel line could have said they were *trying* to put an end to the suppliant (cf. EVV); what it says is that they are actually doing so.[20] Their enmity involves *falsehood, the manufacturing of charges against the suppliant.

> 4e-fWhat I did not steal,
>   now I am to restore.
> 5God, you are the one who knows of my stupidity;
>   my guilty deeds are not hidden from you.

Verse 4e–f moves on from that. Like Job, all the suppliant has to do is plead guilty and put things "right," then everyone can "move on." But like Job, the suppliant will not do so. That itself would involve a falsehood. The "now" (*'āz*) is not so much temporal as logical; it suggests an ironic "therefore."[21]

The declaration about the suppliant's actual wrongdoing in turn pairs with that line.[22] While the suppliant would acknowledge being a sinner, the point about this statement is hardly to admit to having done serious wrong, which would undermine the psalm's argument and conflict with the kind of claims the rest of the psalm makes. It is a hypothetical statement, or another ironical one.[23] Whatever sin there is in the psalmist's life, God knows about it; the enemies do not. It is then God's business to expose it and do something about it. God is in a position to do so; the "friends" are not. The suppliant does not believe there is any such secret sin to be exposed.[24] Wrongdoing is characterized first as singular stupid-

---

20. It adds a less common word for "be many" and a less common way to describe the enemy. The second colon parallels the second colon in v. 4a–b, so that v. 4a–d works aba'b'.

21. Cf. BDB.

22. Verse 5 takes abcdd'b'c' form. "You [are the one who]" corresponds to "from you." The positive qal "know" corresponds to negatived niphal "are not hidden."

23. Calvin, *Psalms*, 3:50.

24. Cf. Lindström, *Suffering and Sin*, 341–43.

ity (see 38:5 [6]). It does not pay (as the enemies' reaction would soon prove). It is then characterized as plural guilty acts (the feminine form of the word in 68:21 [22]); it offends God. To put the two expressions together, it does not pay, because it turns out to offend God. The line's opening invocation of God applies to both cola and acts as an inclusion around vv. 1–5. In addition, it means that vv. 1–5 speak of suffering in the three classic directions, as what *I* experience, as what *they* are doing, and also as something in which *you* are involved. This last is understated, but the line's implication is that God knows exactly what is going on, knows that the suppliant is not characterized by stupidity or guilty deeds, and is therefore complicit with the enemies' unwarranted attacks.

69:6. The address to God reverts to prayer, in the third person and less briefly than in v. 1a, though less expansively than will be the case later in the psalm. The verse comprises another pair of parallel lines.

> ⁶The people who look for you must not be shamed because of me,
>   Lord Yhwh Armies.
> The people who seek help from you must not be dishonored because
>   of me,
>   God of Israel.

The shaming of people because of the suppliant can hardly refer simply to the discouragement of their faith. It implies that they themselves are identified with the suppliant, most likely because he is their leader; he is someone such as a king or a governor. Their destiny is tied up with his. Thus they look for Yhwh as he waits for Yhwh (v. 3). The plea to *Lord Yhwh *Armies underlines the fact that Yhwh has the ability to act in response to this prayer. If Yhwh does not do so, the people will not be the only ones who are shamed.

The second line parallels the first.[25] It is the invocation of God that most differs: v. 6b focused on God's power; this invocation focuses in a complementary way on God's relationship with Israel. That means Yhwh has the reason and obligation as well as the capacity to answer the prayer. The prayer leaves Yhwh with no way out.

69:7–12. The psalm segues into its most substantial section of protest, with address to God continuing, so that it begins with another implicit accusation toward God ("you"). That remains muted, yet it runs through the section, surfacing in vv. 7, 9, 10, and 11. Formally, however, the section is dominated by how things are for the suppliant ("I"), and it closes with

25. Thus v. 6c–d comprises another negated third-person yiqtol verb (though now niphal rather than qal), another *bî* (because of me), another pl. ptc. with second-person singular suffix (though now piel ["*seek help from"] rather than qal), and another invocation of God. The two lines work abcdefa′bc′d′e′.

the attitude of other people ("they"). It comprises 3-3 lines (except vv. 9 and 12, which are 3-4 and 4-3), which gives a more poised or assertive tone to it. The concreteness of its description of the background to the suppliant's suffering is a distinctive feature of the psalm, combined as it is with the more traditional description in vv. 1–4.[26]

> ⁷Because it is on account of you that I have borne reviling,
>   that dishonor has covered my face.

The opening "because [it is] on account of you [that]" applies to both cola and sets the tone for the section. God is indirectly the reason for the suppliant's shame; vv. 9, 10, and 11 will explain the point further. After that opening phrase, the two cola comprise two descriptions of the shame, whose content is closely parallel though their form is different: a verb with "I" as its subject and "reviling" as its object, and a verb with "dishonor" (the word in v. 6) as its subject and "my face" as its object. The implication of "bearing" or "carrying" reviling is similar to that of dishonor "covering my face."

> ⁸I have become a stranger to my relatives,
>   an alien to my mother's offspring.

The shame affects the attitude of the suppliant's family. The line implies more than that the family are horrified at what they see. Rather, the shame affects the family's attitude. They disown the suppliant, like a family disowning someone who has committed a terrible crime or changed their religion. Here the verb applies to both cola, and the other words comprise neatly parallel expressions. "Stranger" parallels "alien"; the former is not the usual qal participle *zār* but a unique hophal participle *mûzār*, perhaps implying one who has been deliberately turned into a stranger. "My mother's offspring" suggests that "relatives" (*'ahîm*) has its more specific meaning, "siblings," even sons of the same mother. It is the closest family, the people with whom the suppliant lives, who have turned away.

> ⁹Because it is passion for your house that has destroyed me;
>   the reviling of people who revile you has fallen on me.

There follows a more specific account of the sense in which God is reason for the shame. The suppliant cares deeply for the temple in the way that people such as Elijah and Jehu cared passionately for the na-

---

26. Cf. Lindström, *Suffering and Sin*, 324–25; he infers a process of redaction for the psalm.

tion's allegiance to Yhwh (1 Kings 19:10, 14; 2 Kings 10:16). One could imagine leaders of the First or Second Temple period who campaigned for worship that was more exclusively devoted to Yhwh and/or insisted on worship that did not use images or pressed for other reforms. The nature of Israel's worship could provoke passionate reactions in Yhwh, and it would not be surprising if it provoked them also in people (e.g., Ezek. 8:3, 5). Such passion has "consumed" the suppliant (cf. 119:139) not merely in the sense of being felt to be very important but in the sense of being "my undoing" (NJPS). Perhaps it is this itself that has led to personal attacks, as commonly happens to someone who campaigns for religious change, though the subsequent lines may suggest that the problem is rather people's misinterpretation of the suppliant's concern, expressed in sadness and penitence about what happens in the temple. The second colon makes that more explicit, picking up the word "reviling" from v. 7. As the suppliant sees it, people's worship involves reviling Yhwh. For instance, it compromises Yhwh's deity (through worshipping Yhwh in the company of other deities), or it compromises Yhwh's nature (because of reckoning that Yhwh can be imaged). But other people do not see it that way, and they attack the suppliant for suggesting that they are attacking Yhwh or because they infer admission of personal sin.

> ¹⁰When I wept and fasted,
>   it turned into reviling for me.

The passion expressed itself in weeping and fasting, and that too brought reviling. In the context, the weeping and fasting are presumably not for personal confession or discipline (though the attackers may have interpreted them thus) but are further expressions of grief and vicarious repentance with regard to what is going on in the temple.[27] The underlying assumption is that such weeping and fasting by one person can affect God's attitude to the people as a whole. But other people naturally saw them as compounding the suppliant's offensiveness.

> ¹¹When I made sackcloth my clothing,
>   I became a byword to them.
> ¹²People who sit at the gate mumble about me—
>   and drinkers sing about me.

27. Thus although grammatically *napšî* could be the obj. of the verb, "I wept with fasting for my self," in the context *napšî* is more likely the subj. of *ṣôm*, "while my self fasted" (cf. Tg) or the delayed second subj. of the first verb ("I myself wept . . .").

Verse 11 re-expresses the point. Wearing clothes of coarse cloth rather than nice apparel is another expression of grief, alongside weeping and fasting, expressing the suppliant's grief at what goes on in the temple and doing so on behalf of the community (cf. 35:13–14). That, too, backfires because it turns the suppliant into a byword (see 44:14 [15]). People infer from the signs of penitence that the suppliant is someone who needs to seek forgiveness for personal sin.

So the suppliant becomes a topic of gossip among people sitting about talking and drinking in the plaza.

69:13–18. The suppliant reverts to plea, the imagery and language taking up those of the protest in vv. 1–4 but now turning it into plea. The section divides into two, with the two usual concerns of a plea that Yhwh should listen and take action with regard to the predicament the plea concerns. But the subsections do not simply relate sequentially to these two concerns; they interweave them:

Plea for an answer (v. 13)	Plea for action (vv. 14–15)
Plea for an answer (vv. 16–17)	Plea for action (v. 18)

> [13]As for me, my plea to you, Yhwh,
>   is a time of acceptance.
> God, with your great commitment answer me,
>   with your truthfulness that delivers.

The psalm makes explicit that it reverts to *plea as it asks for "a time of acceptance." The use of such phrases elsewhere indicates that this denotes not (e.g.) a liturgically right time for prayer but the moment when God accepts a plea (cf. Isa. 58:5) or the moment when God acts in deliverance (cf. Isa. 49:8; 61:2), or perhaps both, because the former issues in the latter.[28]

The next line may support the idea that it could be both, because the two cola cover both. The invocation and the imperative apply to both cola, which then incorporate two balancing *b* expressions. "Your truthfulness that delivers" (lit. "the *truthfulness of your *deliverance") balances and spells out "your great *commitment" and makes explicit the point that an "answer" involves not merely words but action. Christians sometimes say that God answers all prayers but that the answer to some is "No." The Psalms would not regard "No" as an answer.

28. It is thus not clear what would be the meaning of Tg's adverbial understanding of the expression "at a time"; one prays not *at* an acceptable time but *for* an acceptable time. NJPS thus supposes the ellipse of a jussive verb, "may it come." NRSV links the phrase with what follows as part of a redivision of lines.

> ¹⁴Rescue me from the mud, may I not sink;
>   may I be rescued from the people who are against me, yes, from
>   the watery torrents.

The plea then becomes more concrete, though in a way that reverts to the metaphor of vv. 1–2 while also referring to the enemies who are the literal problem. The complex parallelism involves three verbs and three *min* expressions. But the two main verbs are both forms of *nāṣal*, though one is hiphil, one niphal (thus one active, one passive). Although v. 2 spoke of sinking as already a fact, it is evidently not an irreversible or final one. Of the *min* expressions, the middle one ("the people who are *against me") gives the literal interpretation of the other two. The collocation of "mud" and "watery torrents" (the latter taken up from v. 2) reflects the fact that a flood brings mud and mire with it (cf. Isa. 57:20). Indeed, it may well be the mud in the torrent rather than the water that brings death to people.

> ¹⁵May the watery deluge not engulf me,
>   may the flood not swallow me,
>   may the pit not close its mouth over me.

Verse 15 restates the point in jussive terms. The first two cola are straightforwardly parallel, and almost every word is again taken up from v. 2, with the apparent statement of fact turned into a wish that the "fact" may not become a reality. The novelty is the verb "swallow," and that turns out to anticipate the unexpected third colon, which brings the subsection to a close. This third colon introduces a third way of describing the suppliant's danger, one already implicit but now explicit. Being drowned by the flood means being swallowed by the earth, by the grave, by Sheol (106:17; Exod. 15:12; Num. 16:30, 32, 34). It means falling into the pit (cf. 55:23 [24]) and having it close its mouth over us. Death is personified as a monster that threatens to swallow us. "Close" (*'āṭar*) is a hapax, but related expressions suggest that it carries the connotation of "shut tight." When this closing happens, it cannot be opened.

> ¹⁶Answer me, Yhwh, because your commitment is good;
>   in accordance with the greatness of your compassion, turn your
>   face to me.

The second subsection begins by returning to a plea for an answer. The verb form in v. 16a is the same as that in v. 13, and the reasoning takes up the comment about God's *commitment but adds that it is *good. In the context, the connotation of "good" may be that God's commitment is both kind and generous and also welcome to those who receive it. The second colon spells out the nature of this good commitment: it expresses itself in compassion. The second verb likewise spells out the nature of an "answer." When a plea is not answered, it implies Yhwh is looking the other way. When an answer comes, it involves Yhwh's face turning our way. The line thus works abb'a'.

> ¹⁷Do not hide your face from your servant,
>   because I am in distress; answer me quickly.

In turn, it transpires that v. 17 forms an abb'a' pairing with v. 16 as a whole. The plea not to hide the *face expresses in negative terms the plea to turn; "turn the face" is *pānâ*, "face" is *pānîm*. When Yhwh's face turns, that means action: God sees and acts. When Yhwh's face hides, that means nothing happens: God does not see and thus does not act. The second line once more repeats the expression "answer me" that came in v. 16a but underlines this urging with the qualifier "quickly" (for this appeal, cf. 31:2 [3]; 79:8; 102:2 [3]; 143:7).

> ¹⁸Come near to me, restore me;
>   because of my enemies, redeem me.

The section closes with a return to the action this answer needs to bring. The suppliant needs Yhwh to draw near rather than staying distant. The two subsequent verbs make explicit that this implies not merely a sense of God's nearness but also an experience of God acting (cf. Lam. 3:57–58; Mal. 3:5), as is the case negatively when people "come near" (Pss. 27:2; 119:150). The implication of that is then expressed in more theological terms as *restoring and *redeeming.

69:19–21. Once more the psalm reverts to protest or lament, again speaking of God (v. 19), of the self (v. 20), and of other people (v. 21). And once more it reuses expressions that have featured already, especially in vv. 6–10.

> ¹⁹You yourself know my reviling,
>   my shame, and my dishonor.
> All my foes are before you;
>   ^{20a}reviling has broken my spirit, and I am ailing.

The declarations about what God knows are expressed simply as statements of fact. What is their implication? Is it good news that God knows about the reviling, the shame, and the dishonor (the words pick up from vv. 6, 7, and 10)? Does it mean that God is bound to take action? Or does it underline the pain? Is the point that God knows but fails to take action? The line thus makes these unfulfilled promises the prospective basis for the cosmos praising Yhwh (v. 34).

The second line repeats the point, the first colon paralleling v. 19a, the second referring once more to the reviling and adding the affect it has. Literally, it has broken the suppliant's "heart," but that English translation would give a misleading impression (*mind). The description of their affect comes to a climax with a hapax, *nûš*, which I take as a by-form of *'ānaš* and thus to suggest the kind of ailment that seems destined to end in death.

> ²⁰ᵇ⁻ᶜI looked for someone to show grief, but there was no one,
> for comforters, but I have not found them.

The further pair of parallel cola explicates the point further. If life is against us, then having people with us so that we are not alone is something that helps us live through the experience. The suppliant has no such community. There are many people full of enmity and reviling but no friends. As well as looking for God to act (v. 6a), the suppliant looked to other people for support but found none. The verb applies to both cola, then there are two *l*-expressions (one a qal infinitive, one a piel participle) and two negatives that express the frustrating of the looking, one a noun clause, one a verbal clause. The word for showing grief (*nûd*) denotes the outward expression of grief in shaking the head. Comparison with 44:13–14 [14–15] suggests that shaking the head is an expression of grief that recognizes the horror of what has happened. But clearly this suppliant is looking for a shaking of the head that identifies with the person's pain rather than stands superior in relation to it. "Comfort" (*nāḥam* piel) also suggests an identification with the suppliant; in other contexts it suggests the relief of one's own feelings, and here it is the expression of feelings for someone else. But there is no one manifesting a sense of horror, and the suppliant has found no one to show they share the pain.

> ²¹People have put bitterness in my food,
> and for my thirst they give me vinegar to drink.

On the contrary, instead of drawing this person who is overcome by suffering to eat with them (cf. 2 Sam. 3:35; 12:17),²⁹ they take action to ensure that the suppliant's food and drink are unpleasant if not poisonous, so that they make the situation worse rather than better.³⁰ We do not

29. Cf. Kraus, *Psalms 60–150*, 63.
30. In the parallel abcb'a'c' cola, two verbs complement each other, one wayyiqtol qal, one qatal hiphil. Accompanying them are two correlative prepositional expressions with first-person suffixes on the nouns. Completing the cola are two direct objects.

know the exact meaning of *rōʾš*, though it apparently refers to something bitter, but "vinegar," sour wine (*ḥōmeṣ*), speaks for itself.

69:22–29. An extraordinarily powerful prayer follows. It alternates wish, in the third person (vv. 22, 23a, 24b, 25, 27b, 28); and plea, in the second person (vv. 23b, 24a, 27a, 29); and gives one line to the reasoning that lies behind it (v. 26). At the same time the catastrophe for which the psalm asks increases in intensity as the lines unfold.

> [22]May their table become a trap before them,
>   and for their partners a snare.

The wish starts from where the preceding section left off.[31] People have made the suppliant's table a place of bitterness rather than sustenance, and the line asks for the punishment to fit the crime. It contains one or two other possible implications. A festive meal would be likely to be a festal meal, and Tg assumes that this table will be a sacrificial meal. Further, the precise nature of the reversal for which the line asks recalls a frequent motif in the Psalms. Enemies are frequently setting traps and snares, and they plot together to do so. Their table would be a natural place to undertake such planning, and the line asks that their plotting may rebound on them. Indeed, perhaps it imagines a table in the form of a mat laid on the ground, like a picnic table, which could thus actually cover a trap, with its food as the bait.[32]

> [23]May their eyes grow dark so that they cannot see;
>   make their loins shudder continually.

Worse, for them in their own being, is the wish for their physical affliction. The two cola complement each other in the way they articulate this, not least in the move from a wish to an actual plea; the psalm now asks directly for divine action. The affliction will again link with their wrongdoing and its implications for the suppliant, since another feature of plotting is that it takes place in the dark (Isa. 29:15); darkness also suggests confusion with regard to what would otherwise be wisdom (Job 38:2). Further, if the attackers can see, they can take action against the suppliant; if they lose their sight, they cannot do so. The story of Elisha asking for his Aramean would-be captors to lose their sight provides a nice illustration and also a nice contrast (2 Kings 6). Instead of making

31. Both the subj. and the verb in the line apply to both cola; "snare" complements "trap," and "before them" is extended to "for their partners" (both being *l* expressions).

32. Cf. Keel, *Symbolism*, 91. See also E. Vogt, "'Ihr Tisch werde zur Falle' (Ps 69,23)," *Bib* 43 (1962): 79–82.

their table a snare or simply striking them down as the king assumes he would wish to do (not unreasonably, given Elisha's conduct on other occasions), Elisha requires the king to set a feast before them. Similarly the loins are a symbol of strength and the place on which one girds one's weapons (e.g., Ezek. 29:7; Job 40:16), so that disabling the loins means disabling the warrior (e.g., Deut. 33:11; Isa. 45:1). If the loins shudder, the person cannot fight.

> [24]Pour out your wrath on them;
>   may your angry burning overtake them.

The direct urging becomes much more forceful. Pouring out wrath is a theme that occurs only twice in the Psalms (cf. 79:6; also Jeremiah's prayer in Jer. 10:25). It is more commonly a description of something God threatens to do to Israel (e.g., Jer. 6:11; Hos. 5:10), sometimes holds back from doing (Ezek. 20:8, 13, 21), but in due course actually does (Lam. 2:4; 4:11; Ezek. 22:31). God also threatens to pour out wrath on Israel's enemies (e.g., Ezek. 21:31 [36]; 30:15; Zeph. 3:8) but is never said to do so. So the psalm asks for God to act toward the suppliant's attackers in accordance with such undertakings and actions expressed in the Prophets. The second colon expresses the point in a more novel way, taking up the literal experience of seeking to escape but failing (e.g., Jer. 39:5; cf. 42:16). Although talk of wrath and angry burning presumably indicates that God is expected to be truly indignant at the way human beings treat one another—God is not cold and dispassionate, like a judge—talk in such terms also suggests the fearful heat of what the objects of this wrath experience.

> [25]May their encampment become desolate,
>   may no one live in their tents.

That is implicit in the lines that follow, which speak in more down-to-earth terms of the impact of that wrath on people. Admittedly the terms are still figurative as the psalm quaintly speaks in the two parallel cola of encampment and tents. It is as if the psalmist envisages a nomadic people. But the quaintness is accompanied by a devastating substance. Again the prayer uses language that in the Psalms appears otherwise only in Ps. 79:7 but corresponds to Yhwh's threats with regard to Israel (e.g., Lev. 26:22; Ezek. 33:28) and its attackers (e.g., Isa. 42:15; Ezek. 30:7) and God's actions toward Israel (e.g., Jer. 33:10; Lam. 1:4). The encampment becoming desolate might simply imply that the settlement is being flattened, but the verb (šāmam), like the English equivalent, is also inclined to imply its being empty. The second colon makes this explicit.

The tents are empty rather than devastated, because their inhabitants have all been killed.

> ²⁶Because you—the people you hit, they have pursued;
> the suffering of people you struck, they have proclaimed.

Verse 26 stands out in the section because it alone provides a rationale for this terrible prayer, in two parallel cola. En passant it slips in a key observation about the experience of the suppliant and of people who go through similar experiences. They are people whom God hit and struck. The psalm relates to the experience of someone like Job or the servant in Isa. 53, whom God has hit or made to suffer or struck (all three words come in Isa. 53:3–5). Instead of supporting such people (cf. vv. 19–21), the attackers have made their situation worse. In the manner of Job's friends or of the people who give their testimony in Isa. 53, they have pursued them and added to their troubles (LXX), or (more specifically) have talked about them in such a way as to further their shame (MT; cf. v. 12). It certainly would be easy to justify such action. If people are under God's judgment, surely it is our task to identify with God, isn't it? But that can be self-serving—it makes us feel better—and the psalm (like Job and Isa. 53) assumes that there are times when we have to discern that God's bringing suffering does not imply the guilt of those to whom it comes. Indeed, the line perhaps implies that hitting people is always God's business, not ours, which would fit with the fact that its response to other people's attacks is prayer rather than retaliation.

> ²⁷Give them punishment upon their punishment;
> may they not come to your faithfulness.

The prayer continues to be a terrifying response. In the two parallel cola it asks that the attackers may be punished forever, now suggesting a contrast with Isa. 53:6. In the Psalms, ʿāwōn usually means *waywardness, but elsewhere its meaning flows over into its consequences as guilt and punishment, and here alone in the Psalms the word requires such a translation (against KJV). The OT often speaks of people carrying their ʿāwōn (e.g., Gen. 4:13) or of Yhwh carrying it (e.g., Ps. 32:5). Either they have to accept responsibility for their ʿāwōn and live with the consequences, or Yhwh remits this responsibility and absorbs the consequences. The psalm asks that far from doing the latter, Yhwh may not even simply leave the attackers carrying their ʿāwōn but add to the burden it constitutes and keep doing that. The doubling of punishment corresponds to what God did in the exile (Isa. 40:2). The second colon makes the same point in another way, asking that they may not come to be the beneficiaries of

Yhwh's instinct to be faithful rather than to punish. All this "presumes that the wicked remain happily unrepentant in their wrongdoing."[33]

> [28]May they be erased from the scroll of the living,
>   not be written with the faithful.

Verse 28 returns to the prayer of v. 25 and re-expresses the point in parallel cola.[34] The prayer again corresponds to declarations of intent that Yhwh has uttered (e.g., Gen. 6:7; Exod. 32:33) and implemented (Gen. 7:23). While it involves a metaphor, the metaphor is close to reality. The people would have lists of who belonged to the community, to the faithful, but it is death that means one no longer belongs on that list. It would be monstrously inappropriate for such people to have an ongoing place in the community.

> [29]When I am weak and suffering,
>   may your deliverance, God, set me on high.

I have reckoned that while v. 28 brings to an end the plea for the attackers' punishment, v. 29 brings the entire section to an end with another plea for the suppliant's own protection.[35] The suppliant's initial self-description takes up the reference to suffering (v. 26) but prefaces it with the recognition of *weakness. It then sets over against it the power of Yhwh's *deliverance, for which the psalm asked at the beginning (v. 1; cf. v. 13), which can lift a suppliant into security above what imperils it, in the manner of a *haven.

69:30–36. The psalm comes to a marked change, analogous to what appears elsewhere (e.g., Ps. 22) but distinctive. In MT it does not involve an actual declaration that God has answered the prayer,[36] but it implies one in its declarations that God does do so (vv. 29, 33) and in the response it expects.

> [30]I will praise the name of God with a song,
>   I will exalt him with thanksgiving,

33. A. Anderson, *Psalms*, 1:508.

34. Two third-person plural niphal verbs and two prepositional expressions come in abb'a' order, such as perhaps advertises that the section is coming to an end.

35. In other words, I take the verb as jussive (NRSV, TNIV) rather than indicative (LXX, NJPS), partly because v. 30 looks like a new beginning. But perhaps v. 29 is Janus-faced (cf. Fokkelman, *Major Poems*, 3:129).

36. In v. 33a, LXX and Jerome imply *sāmaʿ* (Yhwh listened) for MT *šōmēaʿ*, and they naturally then translate the qatal verb in v. 33b as past rather than as continuing the participial construction.

The appropriate response to an experience of deliverance is to *praise God's *name for it. The first colon focuses on sound (*hālal*, *šîr*), the second on significance: the thanksgiving or testimony or *confession functions to magnify Yhwh in people's eyes.[37]

> ³¹And it will please Yhwh more than an ox,
>   a bull having horns and divided hoofs.

Perhaps that is why the psalm goes on to the unusual comment that while praise and offerings are both necessary, the former is more important than the latter. While the former can be just words and the offerings provide evidence that worshippers mean what they say, offerings are mute while thanksgiving makes clear the reasons that should draw other people into trust and praise. Thus a *šîr* (song) is better than a *šôr* (the two words come at the end of each first colon in vv. 30 and 31), even a full-grown and doubtless well-fattened ox, with horns and divided hoofs and therefore acceptable for sacrifice (e.g., Lev. 11:3). But it would be odd for someone so passionate about the temple and about outward religious observances (vv. 9–11) to be unenthusiastic about sacrifices, and the last lines of the psalm could imply another reason for the logic here. They suggest that the psalm presupposes a time when Jerusalem and Judah need deliverance and building up, and at such a time the offering of sacrifices would be impossible. Alternatively, the suppliant may have no access to the worship of the temple, perhaps because it is under the control of the attackers. The psalm therefore rejoices that this does not make it impossible to give Yhwh a proper and pleasing response when prayers are answered (cf. 51:16–19 [18–21]).

> ³²When the weak see, they will be glad;
>   you who seek help from God—yes, your spirit will revive.

But what counts is seeing the event of which the testimony speaks. The *weak (cf. v. 29) are people who have no alternative to *seeking help from God. They are also people who may lack the resources for splendid offerings, another reason for emphasizing their lesser importance.[38] The line works aba'b', with a twist at the end. When they see what God does, they will be glad and their spirits will come back to life from their

---

37. The parallel cola include two first-person verbs (one cohortative, and one yiqtol with a suffix), an obj. in the first colon resumed in the second, and two *b* expressions; the whole works abca'c'.

38. Cf. Alphonso Groenewald, "Cult-Critical Motif in Psalm 69.32," in *Psalms and Liturgy*, ed. Dirk J. Human and Cas J. A. Vos, JSOTSup 410 (London: Continuum, 2004), 62–72.

broken state (v. 20); or rather, *your* spirit will do so. People will not yet
have seen their own relief, but hearing the testimony of one who has
seen such relief will make possible that move to joy and renewal.

> ³³Because Yhwh is one who listens to the needy
> and does not despise his captives.

The basis for this is a conviction about who Yhwh is, which the testimony has reinforced.³⁹ The suppliant has proved that Yhwh does listen
(a common plea in psalms, though not one that has featured in this one)
to the *needy (who have also not appeared; but the word is a close relative of "weak"). Declaring that Yhwh has not "despised" the suppliant
puts the same point in a less usual way (but cf. 22:24 [25]; 51:17 [19]);
to despise is to treat as not worth paying attention to. Likewise "captives" picks up from 68:6 [7] and prepares the way for the last lines of
the psalm.

> ³⁴Heaven and earth must praise him,
> the seas and everything that moves in them.

First the psalm extends the circle of *praise to embrace heaven and
earth. It is hardly enough that merely the suppliant should give the response of praise (v. 30) nor even that other needy people should rejoice.
This is the first time in the Psalter that the heavens and earth are involved
in praise (cf. 96:11). Other mentions of the earth such as 66:1, 4 refer to
its human inhabitants, whereas here the second colon makes explicit
that the psalm calls on the inanimate world. Psalm 148 constitutes a
vast expansion on this line.

> ³⁵ᵃ⁻ᵇBecause God will deliver Zion,
> build up the cities of Judah.

And the reason for this circle of praise? God's action toward Jerusalem
and Judah. That is reason for praise not merely within Jerusalem and
Judah itself, among its neighbors (the opponents the psalm bewails?),
and among all the world's peoples, but also through the whole cosmos.
The line thus elaborates on the reference to Yhwh's captives (v. 33).⁴⁰
*Deliverance is expressed in building up (again, cf. 51:18 [20] and other
links with Ps. 51). God's concern is both with Zion and with the land as

39. "Yhwh" stands at the center of the line, applying to both cola. A ptc. pairs with a
finite verb, a positive with a negative, and two pl. nouns complement each other.
40. The opening words apply to both lines, then two verbs and two objects complement each other.

a whole. The affirmation corresponds to the promises about Judah and Jerusalem that appear in Jer. 30–33 and in Isa. 40–66 (e.g., Isa. 44:26; 61:4; Jer. 33:7).

> 35cPeople will live there and possess it,
>   36the offspring of his servants will own it;
>   the people dedicated to his name will dwell in it.

The closing tricolon rejoices in what will follow from that. Talk of dwelling in, possessing, and owning the land recalls the language used of its original occupation. In the exile this land came to be controlled by Babylon and much of it occupied by peoples such as Edomites, but God will enable the Judeans to enter into possession of it again, live there again, own it again (e.g., Isa. 49:8; 54:3; 57:13; Jer. 30:3; 31:24). Talk of God's "servants" (plural), which has come only once in the Psalter (34:22 [23]), again recalls the prophets' promises about the restoration of Judah and Jerusalem (e.g., Isa. 54:17; 65:8–9, 13–15; and the reference to "offspring" in, e.g., 54:3). The first two cola thus pair with each other, with the subject of the second implicitly the subject of the first (cf. Syr) and the two cola making those unfulfilled promises the prospective basis for the praise of the cosmos. The third colon is then distinctive in its expressions as well as in its place. The idea of being *dedicated to God's *name is a distinctive one (cf. only 5:11 [12]; 119:132), as is the idea of "dwelling" in Zion or in the land ($š\bar{a}kan$); it is usually God who does that (e.g., 1 Kings 6:13; 8:12; but see Isa. 65:9). So the psalm closes with a distinctive promise that is a further basis for praise though also an implicit challenge to be people dedicated to Yhwh's name.

Theological Implications

Midrash Tehillim has little to say about Ps. 69;[41] indeed, whereas all but three of the psalms in Books I and II of the Psalter are shorter than this psalm, there is only one of them (Ps. 66) about which it has less to say. Were Jewish commentators embarrassed by the prayers for punishment? Certainly modern Christian commentators are thus embarrassed.[42] Or were Jewish commentators inhibited by the enthusiasm of early Christians for the psalm, especially as the Christians used it against Jews?[43] In contrast, the NT especially values Ps. 69, especially the prayers for

41. *Midrash on the Psalms*, 1:550–51.
42. See, e.g., Weiser, *Psalms*, 495.
43. See, e.g., Augustine, *Psalms*, 308–9; Cassiodorus, *Psalms*, 1:153–56; and Rosenberg, *Psalms*, 2:257.

punishment. Jesus sees the psalm embodied in his experience (John 15:25; cf. v. 4). It helped the early Christians understand his violent act in driving people out of the temple with a whip (John 2:17; cf. v. 9a) and understand people's attacks on him and on them (Rom. 15:3; cf. v. 9b). They saw him being treated as the suppliant was in being given vinegar to drink (John 19:28–29; cf. v. 21). Paul saw his own people experiencing the fulfillment of the prayers for retribution and blindness (Rom. 11:9–10; cf. vv. 22–23). Revelation echoes the prayer for the pouring out of God's wrath in describing this outpouring as now happening (Rev. 16:1; cf. v. 24). Acts takes up the prayer for the encampment to become a desolation and sees it fulfilled in Judas (Acts 1:16, 20; cf. v. 25). Revelation echoes the prayer for people to be erased from the scroll of the living, for instance in its promise that people whose names are written there will not be in the new Jerusalem (Rev. 21:27; cf. v. 28).

There is no NT reference to the declaration of intent in vv. 30–36, though the NT might have imagined it on the lips of Jesus in connection with God's deliverance of him in raising him from death as it did the equivalent closing section of Ps. 22.[44]

There is some irony in the fact that the point where the NT concentrates most of its use of the psalm is where commentators see it as unworthy of the NT.[45] Apparently it was fine for the suppliant to pray the prayers in vv. 22–29.[46] The NT implies that they fit into God's purpose that wrongdoing should receive its reward and that people who are unjustly attacked should be delivered. We who write commentaries on the Psalms are more likely to belong to the oppressors than to the oppressed, so that our perspective on the psalm is likely to be different from that of oppressed people. "The attitude of great poets is to cheer up slaves and horrify despots" (Walt Whitman).[47] We are wise to be scared of the psalm's prayer and to be keen to make sure no one prays it. Luther points out that the words about the table (v. 22) can apply to people who come to the Lord's Table.[48]

---

44. Cf. Richard B. Hays, "Reading Scripture in Light of the Resurrection," in *The Art of Reading Scripture*, ed. Ellen F. Davis and Richard B. Hays (Grand Rapids: Eerdmans, 2003), 216–38 (see 221–24).

45. See (e.g.) Kidner, *Psalms*, 1:248.

46. Theodoret assumes so, independently of any christological application of it (*Psalms*, 1:399–402).

47. *Leaves of Grass*, as quoted in *The New York Times Magazine*, July 11, 2004, 20.

48. *First Lectures*, 1:376.

Psalm 70

A Plea for Haste

Translation

The leader's. David's. For commemoration.

¹God, to save me,
    Yhwh, to my help, hurry.
²May they be shamed and reviled,
    the people who seek my life.
May they turn around and be dishonored,
    the people who want trouble for me.
³May they turn back because of their shameful deceit,
    the people who say "Hey, hey."
⁴But may they rejoice and be glad in you,
    all the people who seek help from you.
May they say continually, "God be great,"
    the people dedicated to your deliverance.
⁵As I am weak and needy,
    God, hurry to me.
You are my help and my rescuer;
    Yhwh, do not delay.

Interpretation

In contrast to other psalms, Ps. 70 is almost pure plea. Every line includes at least one imperative or jussive, with the imperatives in vv. 1

and 5 forming a frame around the jussives in vv. 2–4. The jussives divide into appeals for attackers to be shamed (vv. 2–3) and for people who look to Yhwh to have reason to rejoice (v. 4). The psalm as a whole thus manifests the following structure:

Imperative: Hurry to help and rescue (1 line; v. 1)
    Jussive: May attackers be shamed (3 lines; vv. 2–3)
    Jussive: May people who turn to Yhwh rejoice (2 lines; v. 4)
Imperative: Hurry to help and rescue (2 lines; v. 5)

Both vv. 1–3 and vv. 4–5 thus comprise four lines, though within these sections the subdivision is unequal, with the first half putting more stress on the shaming of the attackers and the second putting more emphasis on direct address to God. After v. 1 there are no internally parallel lines, but every line as a whole is parallel to one that follows and/or precedes.

Psalm 70 links closely with Ps. 69. That preceding psalm expressed concern that the suppliant and the community should not be shamed, reviled, and dishonored (69:6–10, 19–20 [7–11, 20–21]), though perhaps oddly did not ask that this fate should overcome the people causing shame, reviling, and dishonor. Psalm 70 thus complements its plea. The urgent prayer for "rescue" (v. 1) also picks up from the preceding psalm (69:14 [15]), while the "hurry" in vv. 1, 5 (*ḥûš*) recalls the "hasten" in 69:17 [18] (*māhar*). The "people who seek help from you" (*mĕbaqqĕšêkā*) appear here (v. 4; for the verb, see also v. 2) as there (69:6 [7]). This psalm pleads for them to have reason to rejoice (v. 4), as that psalm did (69:32 [33]). This psalm prays for people who are dedicated to Yhwh's deliverance (v. 4); that psalm prayed for people who are dedicated to Yhwh's name (69:36 [37]; both times *'ōhăbê*). This suppliant is among the weak and needy (v. 5), as was the earlier suppliant (69:29, 32, 33 [30, 33, 34]). Psalm 70 thus re-expresses and adds to the plea that precedes. Presumably for this reason it appears here as well as within Ps. 40 (in 40:13–17, for instance, the balance between imperative and jussive is more precise), though opinions differ as to which is the earlier version. Psalm 70 also has phrases in common with Ps. 71. When we read Ps. 70 in light of Pss. 69 and 71, we might hear it on the lips of a leader, but the psalm itself contains no concrete pointers in that direction.

The leader's. David's. For commemoration.

Heading. See glossary, and compare the heading to Ps. 38. The psalm has other phrases in common with Ps. 38 in vv. 1b and 2a–b (cf. 38:12, 22 [13, 23]).

> ¹God, to save me,
>   Yhwh, to my help, hurry.

70:1. The opening line has a distinctive jerky tone. The two invocations are parallel, as are the two *l* expressions with first-person singular suffixes, one with an infinitive verb appealing for rescue and one with a noun appealing for *help, but only with the last word do we find the imperative verb that governs the line as a whole. The line thus contrasts with the neater and more conventional 40:13 [14], which begins with an imperative and repeats the name Yhwh, so that it works abcbc′a′. But why does the suppliant need rescue and help?

> ²May they be shamed and reviled,
>   the people who seek my life.
> May they turn around and be dishonored,
>   the people who want trouble for me.

70:2. In beginning to explicate that, the psalm turns to the jussive plea that picks up the terms of Ps. 69, though it takes them in a new direction. It focuses not on any actual or possible shaming of the suppliant or the suppliant's community but on the desired shaming of their troublers, people who "seek my life" (cf. 35:4; 38:12 [13]; 54:3 [5]; 63:9 [10]). It constitutes a four-word shorter equivalent to the six-word line 40:14a–b [15a–b].

The following line parallels that and exactly corresponds to 40:14c–d [15c–d]. The first colon comprises a further pair of jussive plural verbs linked by simple *w*, the first of these (*sûg*) being the one verb of the four that does not appear in Ps. 69 (but see 35:4, which verse as a whole uses almost the same words as v. 2 here). "Turning around" is what one does instead of pushing on with an attack; it is the verb used of Jonathan's bow not "turning around" (2 Sam. 1:22). Parallel to "seek my life" is "want trouble [*bad] for me."

> ³May they turn back because of their shameful deceit,
>   the people who say "Hey, hey."

70:3. Once again v. 3 parallels the preceding lines. At the moment the attackers are people who can be free with their "Hey!" as a taunt or expression of confidence; the second colon parallels the previous second colon, adding their speech to their action (v. 2b) and their desire (v. 2d).[1] In the first colon the single verb *yāšûbû* parallels the meaning

---

1. Cf. Schaefer, *Psalms*, 168.

of the one in v. 2c rather than corresponding to the one in 40:15 [16], *yāšōmmû*. The attackers will find that their deceitful attacks issue only in shame.[2] They will see Yhwh's act of deliverance (v. 1) and know they are as good as defeated.

> [4]But may they rejoice and be glad in you,
>   all the people who seek help from you.
> May they say continually, "God be great,"
>   the people dedicated to your deliverance.

70:4. There follows the first of two lines that correspond to 40:16 [17][3] and continue the formal structure of vv. 2–3 but reverse the significance. Here the subject is people who are seeking, as in v. 2b, but they are seeking something quite different. There are again two verbs to describe the experience the psalm asks for, but they are a very different pair of verbs from the pairs in v. 2a and v. 2c.

Likewise v. 4c–d speaks of people with very different desires from the people in v. 2d. They are *dedicated to Yhwh's *deliverance, resting themselves on that hope. And when they experience that, they will be able to make the declaration in the first colon with renewed conviction. They will "say" something quite different from what the attackers are currently "saying." Thus v. 4 as a whole points to a very different set of desires, words, and actions over against those of vv. 2c–3.

> [5]As I am weak and needy,
>   God, hurry to me.
> You are my help and my rescuer;
>   Yhwh, do not delay.

70:5. We return to imperative[4] for the two lines that round off the psalm. I take the first colon as a circumstantial clause (the subject coming first suggests this) whose appeal to being *weak and *needy leads into the second colon, with its repeat of the appeal for haste (cf. v. 1). Thus in this line, as in every line in the psalm, it is the plea that has the emphasis, even though here the reason for the plea comes first instead of second in the manner of the previous five lines. The content of the plea itself contrasts with the one in 40:17 [18], which asks for God to "take thought" (*ḥāšab*, not *ḥûš* as here). It generates parallelism with

---

2. For the understanding of *'ēqeb*, see Dahood, *Psalms*, 2:168, though I see no need to repoint the word.

3. Ps. 70 here has "God" rather than "Yhwh" and the more common *yěšû'â* for *těšû'â*.

4. Contrast 40:17 [18]. The two terms for God in v. 5 make for an interesting contrast with 40:17 [18].

the second colon and makes the double appeal for speedy action (v. 1) a distinctive feature of this version over against that in Ps. 40.

The last line parallels the one that precedes. The noun clause compares and contrasts with v. 5a. It has the regular word order and is a self-standing clause, unlike v. 5a, but "You" answers to "I," while "*help" and "rescuer" answer to "weak" and "needy." The plea not to delay in turn restates v. 5b. The appeal for help also makes for an inclusion with v. 1, as do the two designations for God, which contrast with those in Ps. 40.

Theological Implications

The structure of the psalm and a comparison with the version in Ps. 40 suggest two theological observations. First, in isolation jussives such as those that dominate the psalm might be merely wishes or curses that did not really involve God, but the structure of the psalm sets them in the context of prayer, so that they spell out the visible effect of the acts that the psalm directly asks from God. Conversely, in isolation the imperatives might imply that God must act in direct interventionist fashion, while the jussives allow for the fact that God works through "natural" processes. Second, it is sometimes said that God answers prayer with "Yes," "No," or "Wait." We have noted that the Psalms would not take "No" for an answer (see on 69:13 [14]). Nor are they very keen on "Wait." They assume we can press God about timing as well as about the matter itself. Admittedly this is because their prayers generally look more urgent than ours; when the ax is about to fall, there is no time for "Wait." Edmund Hill thus comments that this is elemental prayer at its crudest. It is "How to Pray: Lesson 1."

> Point 1 of lesson 1: Prayer is yelling out "Help!" to God when you are in a jam. . . . Point 2: You don't have to be full of noble sentiments in order to pray. . . . A longing [to get your own back] is more easily turned into prayer than is the noble effort to be magnanimous and forebearing. . . . Point 3: However, it is desirable that your primitive emotions should not be wholly *self*-centred . . . and that you should associate others with what you desire for yourself. . . . Point 4: The one absolutely necessary predisposition for prayer—to recognise and admit your abjectness before God. . . . To realise—that is to make real to yourself—that you need God.[5]

There is then something paradoxical about the fact that v. 1 was one of the opening prayers in daily worship in the Western church from

5. *Prayer, Praise and Politics*, 11–13.

the early Christian centuries until it was abandoned in the course of twentieth-century liturgical revision.[6] The fifth-century monk Cassian reports some advice from an Egyptian abbot, Isaac:

> For keeping up continual recollection of God[7] this pious formula is to be ever set before you. "O God, make speed to save me: O Lord, make haste to help me," for this verse has not unreasonably been picked out from the whole of Scripture for this purpose. For it embraces all the feelings which can be implanted in human nature, and can be fitly and satisfactorily adapted to every condition, and all assaults. Since it contains an invocation of God against every danger, it contains humble and pious confession, it contains the watchfulness of anxiety and continual fear, it contains the thought of one's own weakness, confidence in the answer, and the assurance of a present and ever ready help. For one who is constantly calling on his protector, is certain that He is always at hand. It contains the glow of love and charity, it contains a view of the plots, and a dread of the enemies, from which one, who sees himself day and night hemmed in by them, confesses that he cannot be set free without the aid of his defender. This verse is an impregnable wall for all who are labouring under the attacks of demons, as well as impenetrable coat of mail and a strong shield. It does not suffer those who are in a state of moroseness and anxiety of mind, or depressed by sadness or all kinds of thoughts to despair of saving remedies, as it shows that He, who is invoked, is ever looking on at our struggles and is not far from His suppliants. It warns us whose lot is spiritual success and delight of heart that we ought not to be at all elated or puffed up by our happy condition, which it assures us cannot last without God as our protector, while it implores Him not only always but even speedily to help us. This verse, I say, will be found helpful and useful to every one of us in whatever condition we may be. For one who always and in all matters wants to be helped, shows that he needs the assistance of God not only in sorrowful or hard matters but also equally in prosperous and happy ones, that he may be delivered from the one and also made to continue in the other, as he knows that in both of them human weakness is unable to endure without His assistance.[8]

It would be good if we meant it as often as we prayed it, Luther comments.[9]

---

6. See, e.g., Cassiodorus, *Psalms*, 2:162; *BCP*, 43; contrast (e.g.) *The Book of Common Prayer . . . according to the Use of the Episcopal Church* ([New York]: Seabury, 1979), 42, 80. Hill (*Prayer, Praise and Politics*, 12) wonders whether its Christian monastic use goes back to Jewish monastic use (e.g.) at Qumran, which might explain the separation of Ps. 70 from Ps. 40.

7. The phrase picks up the expression in the heading.

8. Cassian, "Conferences," book 10, chap. 10 (*NPNF*[2] 11:405–6).

9. *First Lectures*, 1:385, 391.

Psalm 71

The God of Past, Present, and Future

Translation

David's. Of the sons of Jonadab and the first exiles. [LXX]

¹I rely on you, Yhwh;
    may I never be shamed.
²In your faithfulness may you save me, rescue me;
    incline your ear to me, deliver me.
³Be a crag for me,
    an abode to which I can always come.
May you have commanded my deliverance,[1]
    because you are my cliff, my fastness.
⁴My God, rescue me from the hand of the faithless,
    from the grasp of the wicked and the robber,[2]
⁵Because you have been my hope, my Lord Yhwh,
    my trust from my youth.
⁶On you I have been upheld from birth,
    from my mother's womb.
You are my support;
    of you is my praise[3] always.

1. In the context, between the impv. in vv. 3a and 4a, I take the qatal verb as a precative. But a reader could construe the clause to mean "[which] you have commanded as my deliverance."

2. I understand the hapax *ḥômēṣ* in light of Akkadian *ḥamaṣu* (cf. Dahood, *Psalms*, 2:172).

3. Sym implies *tōḥaltî* (my hope) for MT *tĕhillātî*.

⁷I have been a real sign⁴ to many,
    as you have been my strong refuge.⁵
⁸My mouth will be full of your praise,
    of your glory all day.

⁹Do not cast me off for my old age;
    when my strength wastes away, do not abandon me.
¹⁰Because my enemies have said of me,
    and the people who watch for my life have planned together,
¹¹Saying, "God has abandoned him;
    chase him and seize him, because there is no one to rescue him."
¹²God, do not be far from me;
    my God, hurry⁶ to my help.
¹³May they be shamed and waste away,
    the people who attack my life.
May they wrap on reviling and dishonor,
    the people who seek trouble for me.
¹⁴But I—I will hope always
    and add to all your praise.
¹⁵My mouth will proclaim your faithfulness,
    your deliverance all day.
Because⁷ I do not know the art of writing,⁸
    ¹⁶I will come with the mighty acts of my Lord Yhwh,
    I will commemorate your faithfulness alone.

¹⁷God, you have taught me from my youth,
    and until now I proclaim your wonders.
¹⁸So even until old age with its gray hair,
    God, do not abandon me,
Until I proclaim your strength to a generation,
    your might to every one who will come,
    ¹⁹and your faithfulness, God, on high.
You who have done great things:
    God, who is like you?
²⁰You who have let me see calamities,
    many and hard,
You will revive me again,
    and from the depths of the earth raise me again.⁹

4. "Real" takes up the *k* on *kĕmôpēt* (cf. *IBHS* 11.2.9; GKC 118x).
5. Lit. "my refuge as to strength" (*IBHS* 10.2.2e; GKC 131r).
6. Q has *ḥûšâ*; K implies *ḥîšâ* as if the verb were *ḥîš*.
7. EVV have "(al)though," but it is doubtful if *kî* can mean that.
8. *Sĕpōrōt* comes only here; the root can suggest counting or writing. Sym and Tg suggest the former (cf. BDB), but "counting" is an odd word here, and the lack of a suffix is a problem. I rather follow LXX and Jerome (cf. *HALOT*).
9. K has pl. suffixes ("us" not "me") in v. 20a and 20c, but not in v. 20d or v. 21; some of the Vrs support one or other of the readings. Perhaps these issued from the reference

²¹You will grant me much greatness
   and turn around to comfort me.
²²Yes, I—I will confess you with the harp,¹⁰
   [confess] your truthfulness, my God.
I will make music for you with the lyre,
   Holy One of Israel.
²³My lips will resound when I make music for you,
   my whole being, which you have redeemed.
²⁴Yes, my tongue will talk of your faithfulness all day,
   because they have been shamed, because they have been reviled,
   the people who seek trouble for me.

Interpretation

Psalm 71 is a prayer psalm in which a suppliant comes to God with pleas and declarations of trust relating to the different stages of life: youth, middle age, and old age.

In MT it has no heading (in L it even lacks a number). It is the first psalm lacking a heading since Ps. 33 except for Ps. 43, which in some sense forms a unit with Ps. 42. Psalms 70 and 71 also link, though not as closely as Pss. 42 and 43 with their common structure and refrain. Nor do Pss. 70 and 71 constitute as close a unity as Pss. 9 and 10, which together form an alphabetical psalm.¹¹ They do have a number of verbal links. Verse 12 (Q) bids Yhwh to "hurry to my help" in the same unusual word order as 70:1 [2]. In bidding Yhwh to deliver, v. 2 uses not only the common *nāṣal* (hiphil) but also the uncommon *pālaṭ* (piel), like 70:1, 5 [2, 6]. The words for shame, reviling, and dishonor in v. 13 (cf. also vv. 1, 24) recur from 70:2 [3]. Hebrew participial descriptions of the attackers as people who (for instance) "seek trouble for me" recur in vv. 13, 24; cf. 70:2 [3].

In contrast to Pss. 42–43, while thus having wording in common, Pss. 70 and 71 are formally rather distinct. Psalm 70 has a very neat formal structure and manifests a resolute focus on plea. Psalm 71 is looser in structure and more diverse in content. Its pleas are less urgent, being set in the context of affirmations of trust and hope that almost make this a psalm of trust rather than a prayer psalm. I have taken the threefold prospect of praise as a clue to its structure and thus divided it into three sections, vv. 1–8, 9–16, and 17–24. These are slightly more uneven in

to national experience in vv. 17–19. Reference to national reversals here seems to disturb the flow, though they might again indicate that it is the king who speaks.
   10. Lit. "the instrument [of] the harp"; cf. 1 Chron. 16:5.
   11. Contrast Jean-Marie Auwers, "Les Psaumes 70–72," *RB* 101 (1994): 242–57.

length than this verse division implies, since a number of verses include more than one line.

Plea		1–4	9, 12–13	17–19a
Lament/protest			10–11	
Expression of trust and hope	5–7			19b–21
Anticipation of praise		8	14–16	22–24

Each of the sections could thus almost stand on its own. The second is more urgent than the first, and perhaps it is this that releases the last section into the most extensive expression of trust and anticipation. The plea about greatness (v. 21) suggests that the speaker is not just an ordinary individual but a leader such as a king or an "I" representing the whole people.

A distinctive feature of the psalm is its close relationship with lines from other psalms as well as Ps. 70, such as Pss. 22; 31; and 38.[12] A number of these are noted in the comments. This does not amount to the near-precise repetition that features when, for instance, Ps. 70 as a whole reappears within Ps. 40. Rather, lines, phrases, and words recur in new forms or new orders or new combinations, as in a collage or filigree,[13] suggesting the psalmist is someone who is well familiar with these other psalms in oral usage and takes up and adapts their phrases or that the authors of these other psalms used Ps. 71 thus.

Acquaintance with this tradition becomes the means of working out concerns that focus on the way, in one's life with God and with people, one stands on a line from youth or young adulthood through middle age to old age.[14]

David's. Of the sons of Jonadab and the first exiles. [LXX]

Heading. The first element in this LXX heading invites readers to imagine David as the person who is using this psalm as an old man or a man looking forward to old age. In the OT story David does not actually become an old man until he is about to die and be succeeded by Solomon (see 1 Kings 1; 1 Chron. 23:1), but in that story Absalom's revolt comes not long before the account of his old age (see 2 Sam. 13–19). Readers could thus imagine David praying the psalm in the context of Absalom's revolt and looking forward to old age. The reference to Jonadab points

12. See (e.g.) Toni Craven, "Psalm 71," *Int* 58 (2004): 56–58.
13. Cf. Crenshaw, *Psalms*, 153.
14. Though Theodore (*Psalms 1–81*, 926–29) assumes that the psalm refers to the youth and old age of Israel as a people.

the imagination in a second direction. The link with exiles suggests that this is not David's nephew Jonadab (2 Sam. 13) but Rechab's son Jonadab (2 Kings 10:15, 23) whose "sons" appear in Jer. 35, just before the exile, or that the heading sets up a link between these two people with the same name. The heading thus makes a connection with the exile, identifies that as the calamity of which the psalm speaks, and invites us to imagine faithful people such as the Rechabites praying this prayer in exile.

71:1–8. The opening section introduces the psalm's two distinctive features: its relationship with the wording of the preceding psalm and with other psalms and its theme of youth and old age. Verses 1–6 take the suppliant from past and present experience of God to praise; vv. 7–8 then go through this sequence again more briefly. Verses 1–3 correspond closely to 31:1–3a [2–4a]; the ancient versions assimilate it further at a number of points. The theme of shame also makes an immediate link with Pss. 69 and 70 (see 69:6, 19 [7, 20]; 70:2, 3 [3, 4]), as does the rare word for "rescue" (*pālaṭ*; see 70:5 [6]). In the form the lines appear here, vv. 1, 2, 3a–b, and 3c–d follow an abb′a′ order. The middle two lines are internally parallel and also parallel to each other; all their verbs are imperative or volitive yiqtol. The outside two lines manifest no internal parallelism but are broadly parallel to each other; each comprises a plea and a reason. These themselves come in abb′a′ order, suggesting an abcc′b′a′ order for the whole:

Confession of dependence (verbal clause; v. 1a)
   Plea (cohortative, negative; v. 1b)
      Plea for what Yhwh should do—spelling out v. 1 (v. 2)
      Plea for what Yhwh should be—anticipatorily spelling out v. 3c–d (v. 3a–b)
   Plea (precative, positive; v. 3c)
Confession of dependence (noun clause; v. 3d)

Verses 4–8 then begin anew with an invocation and a repetition of the unusual verb that came in v. 2, which this psalm also has in common with Pss. 31 and 70. More broadly, vv. 4–8 recall 22:3–10 [4–11]. The wording varies from Ps. 22 more than that of vv. 1–3 in its relationship with Ps. 31, but certain expressions—rescue, trust, on you I have been upheld from birth, from my mother's womb, you are my support, praise—all occur or have equivalents in Ps. 22.[15]

---

15. In 22:9 [10] the striking *gōḥî* is equivalent to the enigmatic *gôzî* in 71:6; in 22:10 [11] *hošlaktî* is equivalent to *nismaktî* in 71:6.

> ¹I rely on you, Yhwh;
>   may I never be shamed.

The psalm opens with a brief declaration of its bottom-line concerns, both of them suggesting vulnerability. The suppliant is someone who *relies on Yhwh on one hand, and on the other is exposed to the shame of the community. Verses 1–3 will explicate further the nature of this dependency; the rest of the psalm will explicate more of the exposure. The two clauses stand in asyndetic relationship, but the lines that follow suggest that in substance the first is subordinate to the second (as is explicitly the case in, for instance, 16:1; and cf. the *kî* clause in 71:3b). Plea is the focus in vv. 1–3.

> ²In your faithfulness may you save me, rescue me;
>   incline your ear to me, deliver me.

In the meantime, v. 2 spells out what "never be shamed" implies.[16] Save, *rescue, and *deliver all have similar meaning. They underline the need to which they refer without explicating what peril the suppliant needs to escape from, though we know it will imply shame. The plea to listen is more vividly expressed as inclining the ear, like someone listening carefully, rather than paying little attention to this plea that is just one among many that come to these ears. With some illogic this plea to listen comes only after two of the verbs relating to the need to escape. It slows the pace and gives more emphasis to the final verb, the most common and the most technical of the verbs for this need. It most distinctively denotes something that God alone can do.

> ³Be a crag for me,
>   an abode to which I can always come.
> May you have commanded my deliverance,
>   because you are my cliff, my fastness.

The first line makes the same point in a different way in parallel cola. Strictly, the parallelism appears only in the two nouns; the opening verbal expression also applies to the second colon, and the closing subordinate clause also applies to the first. Unlike v. 2, this exhortation does not ask God to do anything, just to be there. A crag or an abode does not have to do anything to deliver us; it simply has to be available at the moment we need it. In v. 2, God needs to take the action; in light of v. 3a–b, the suppliant will be the person who does so. Here, on one

16. Each line includes two verbs, the first pair both yiqtol, the second pair both impv.; each pair is linked by *w*, though the first *w* is explicative.

hand Yhwh will be a *crag, a high cliff on which the suppliant will be secure like a bird or a hunted animal. Going beyond that, Yhwh will be a place to live (mā'ôn, an interesting difference from mā'ôz, "stronghold," in 31:2 [3]; cf. 90:1; 91:9). Most often that word refers to Yhwh's abode in heaven or on Zion (e.g., 26:8; Deut. 26:15), but this line uses it more metaphorically: Yhwh *is* an abode.

Lest we should have inferred too much about there being no need for Yhwh actually to do anything, v. 3c–d makes explicit that there is such need, though it pictures Yhwh's involvement in yet another way. It is a matter of commanding resources as well as acting and being available (cf. 44:4 [5]). Presumably Yhwh does this by commanding the divine *ḥesed* (42:8 [9]) or the divine aides (91:11) to take action to *deliver, perhaps by bringing the suppliant to the safety of that crag-abode (cf. 43:3). The second colon provides two further descriptions of this crag, as cliff and fastness, so that the three similar nouns parallel the three similar verbs in v. 2. This repetition thus complements that one and undergirds it. Because Yhwh *is* the threefold security, the threefold plea is the more plausible.

> ⁴My God, rescue me from the hand of the faithless,
>   from the grasp of the wicked and the robber,
> ⁵Because you have been my hope, my Lord Yhwh,
>   my trust from my youth.

*Rescue me picks up from v. 2, though the verb is now imperative.[17] While the *faithless often appear in the Psalms, the *wicked come much less often and "robber" only here. Rhetorically the line thus increases in intensity.

The invocation of my *Lord Yhwh at the center of v. 5 again applies to both two-stress phrases on either side, as does "because you [have been]," and perhaps "from my youth," which announces the theme that will recur through the psalm. Balancing each other are then the near synonyms "my hope" and "my trust." Both words suggest that the suppliant could live in the conviction that the threats and sufferings of the present would not have the last word. *Hope suggests more the event one looks for, and *trust indicates the person one looks to.

> ⁶On you I have been upheld from birth,
>   from my mother's womb.
> You are my support;
>   of you is my praise always.

---

17. Verb and invocation apply to both cola, with the two "from" clauses as parallel expressions.

Verse 6a–b spells out the point.[18] Again the prepositional expression and the verb apply to both cola, with each parallel *min* expression emphasizing how lifelong has been Yhwh's upholding. Hope and trust have not been based merely on Yhwh's character but also on experience of Yhwh's upholding.

I have taken the first colon in v. 6c–d as repeating that point, though we do not know the meaning of the word translated "support."[19] But in general we can see why vv. 5–6c would provide the reasons for v. 6d.

> [7]I have been a real sign to many,
>   as you have been my strong refuge.

Verse 7 then opens a restatement of vv. 4–6 with a unique declaration. A sign (*môpēt*) is an extraordinary act of God, usually associated with a national event such as the exodus (e.g., 78:43; 105:5, 27). Only here is the idea applied to God's dealings with an individual, which supports the idea that the psalm belongs to a leader such as a king. The NEB has "a solemn warning," which is often the word's implication in connection with the exodus; Yhwh's wonders there constituted a warning sign for Pharaoh. Here too it is not the suppliant's affliction that constitutes the solemn sign (there are no parallels for such a usage)[20] but the suppliant's deliverance by Yhwh. I treat the noun clause in the second colon as subordinate to the main clause in the first; it is the way Yhwh has been a *refuge that has made the suppliant a sign. The plea in vv. 1–4 has been well-met in the past.

> [8]My mouth will be full of your praise,
>   of your glory all day.

The talk of future praise suggests the end of a section (cf. vv. 14–16, 22–24). The suppliant is confident that there will be reason for *praise in the future as there has been in the past—indeed, not merely reason to utter praise but also reason to be full of praise.[21]

18. I take v. 6 as a double bicolon; MT has a 3-4-3 tricolon, with the last colon looking structurally unrelated to the line as a whole.

19. I follow Vrs in translating *gôzî* thus, though we do not know the basis for their translation. Etymologically, the word should mean "cutter," but this makes poor sense, even joined to what precedes as it is in MT: "Who cut me from my mother's womb" sounds more like a C-section than the cutting of the umbilical cord.

20. A. Anderson (*Psalms*, 1:513) refers to 31:11 [12] (which does not use this word) and Deut. 28:46 (whose usage is a unique ironic one, and the word is applied to curses, not to events or people).

21. Once again the two suffixed nouns are parallel (in rhyming position at the end of the cola, with the second a rarer word than the first), and the subject, verb, and adverb apply to both cola.

71:9–16. In the second section, vv. 9 and 12–13 are a plea in imperative and jussive form, embracing a protest in vv. 10–11 that gives the
basis for the plea. They then lead into a declaration of confidence and a
promise of praise (vv. 14–16). The talk of abandonment and of the lack
of a rescuer continues to recall Ps. 22, as does v. 12, though its actual
wording is closer to 38:21 [22]. The language of vv. 14–16 also recalls
Ps. 38 (hope, deliverance [the rare *tĕšûʿâ*], commemorate).

> ⁹Do not cast me off for my old age;
> when my strength wastes away, do not abandon me.

But v. 9 is not a wholly new beginning. It has no invocation, and it
takes up a motif from vv. 5–6. Looking back to the past, the suppliant can
see a life characterized by God's upholding. But will the future continue
to be like that? Verse 9 need not imply that the psalm is designed only
for someone who is already a senior.[22] Indeed, the wording rather goes
against that, and v. 18 will more directly suggest that old age lies in the
future. But the psalm does embrace a life as a whole, from birth to old
age, asking about God's involvement in this whole. The line works abb′a′,
book-ended by two second-person yiqtol verbs with a first-person suffix
and the negative ʾal; the first asks for God not to push me away, the second for God not to go away. Inside these bookends are two prepositional
phrases. The first is in itself purely chronological. "Old age" carries no
inherently negative connotations; indeed, a person's senior years are
when they have most respect and may be most valued in the community. The second thus spells out the implications in this context. These
are the years in which a person no longer has the physical strength to
fight the kind of attacks about which the psalm has already spoken and
is about to say more.

> ¹⁰Because my enemies have said of me,
> and the people who watch for my life have planned together,

Thus v. 10 introduces these attackers' words in another abb′a′ line
whose second colon systematically heightens the first. They not only
"say" (speech in itself is not very worrying) but "plan" (they are intending to do something). Indeed, they plan "together," which reinforces the
point further. Thus they are not merely enemies in a general sense but
also people who "watch for my life." In other contexts that expression
would be a positive one, suggesting that people are looking after me

22. Bill Blackburn ("Psalm 71," *RevExp* 88 [1991]: 241–45) expounds the whole psalm
from this perspective.

(e.g., 97:10). If these are people who once were doing this in a positive
sense, they now are doing it in a negative sense.[23]

> **11**Saying, "God has abandoned him;
>   chase him and seize him, because there is no one to rescue him."

Their actual words come in v. 11. Here the suppliant is the uncomfortable suffix to the first verb and the third (and implicitly to the second,
and to the closing participle). *God's* alleged abandonment (implying that
the suppliant is a great sinner) means *they* can take action, convinced
that the closing noun clause speaks the truth. But if the suppliant can
forestall the first bit of calculation, as the prayer in v. 9b has attempted
to do, then this will also forestall the noun clause and cause the whole
line to abort.

> **12**God, do not be far from me;
>   my God, hurry to my help.

The invocation marks the fact that the suppliant is resuming the
plea from v. 9 after the explanation in vv. 10–11.[24] The line reworks
38:21b–22a [22b–23a] (cf. also 22:19 [20]; 35:2, 22) but also makes a
link with 70:1 [2]. Being far away and helping are true antitheses: to
be far away is to decline to help; to help means drawing near. Thus the
second colon systematically intensifies the first. The addressee is not
merely "God" but also "my God." The noun "*help" makes explicit the
point implicit in "do not be far from me." And "hurry" adds to the force
of the challenge.

> **13**May they be shamed and waste away,
>   the people who attack my life.
> May they wrap on reviling and dishonor,
>   the people who seek trouble for me.

The link with Ps. 70 continues (see 70:2 [3]).[25] Once again it parallels a looser relationship with Ps. 22, and the suppliant combines these
links with distinctive expressions. The adversaries are people who are
attacking (*śāṭan*), perhaps by accusing; the psalm asks that they put on
(*'āṭâ*) reviling and dishonor, like clothes. The first pair of nouns makes

23. Cf. Gerstenberger, *Psalms*, 2:62.
24. The line comprises parallel clauses, each involving an invocation and a verbal
expression—one negative and thus yiqtol, one positive impv.
25. The two lines are formally parallel, with jussive expressions (including doubled
verbs then doubled nouns) in the opening cola and participial ones in the second cola.

a link with v. 9b as well as with 70:2 [3], asking that they may have the experience that the suppliant fears.[26]

> ¹⁴But I—I will hope always
>   and add to all your praise.
> ^{15a–b}My mouth will proclaim your faithfulness,
>   your deliverance all day.

With v. 14 comes a transition to the further confession of trust and promise of *praise. The expression of hope (*wait) is unusual here. Perhaps it issues from the recollection of Ps. 38 and thus generates the suggestive combination of hope and promise of praise. As well as complementing hope with praise, the second colon complements "always" with the verb "add" and the adjective "all." The three expressions combine to make a powerful assertion of the continuous nature of the ongoing trust and praise that the suppliant promises. The pronoun "I" and the suffix "your" make a neat inclusion for the line.

That note continues in the "all day" of v. 15a–b.[27] *Faithfulness implies *deliverance; deliverance expresses faithfulness.

> ^{15c}Because I do not know the art of writing,
>   ¹⁶I will come with the mighty acts of my Lord Yhwh,
>   I will commemorate your faithfulness alone.

Verse 15c is puzzling,[28] but it links as easily with v. 16 as with v. 15a–b, and it is at the end of the section that one would expect the tricolon. Indeed, the cola of vv. 15–16 work abcb′a′, so that we might see this central common element as linking with both vv. 15 and 16. Perhaps the profession in v. 15c links with the psalm's distinctive points of connection with other psalms; the psalmist is not confident about composing a prayer from scratch. But the more explicit point is that this perceived lack of skill leads the suppliant to focus on giving oral testimony to Yhwh's acts of *might and *faithfulness; the parallel nouns (plural and singular) take up the overlapping pair in v. 15a–b. Thus the suppliant comes to worship in the temple with those mighty acts as the subject for praise, thereby commemorating Yhwh's faithfulness. Like the two nouns,

---

26. Syr *wnḥprwn* assimilates more closely to 70:2 [3].

27. In the abcdc′ line, this expression at the beginning of the second colon, along with the subject and verb at the beginning of the first, applies to both cola, with the two objects of the verb (both f. nouns with second-person suffixes) standing in parallelism.

28. Raymond J. Tournay ("Notules sur les Psaumes," in *Alttestamentliche Studien* [Friedrich Nötscher Festschrift; ed. Hubert Junker and Johannes Botterweck; Bonn: Hanstein, 1950], 271–80 [see 274–79]) cuts the Gordian knot by analyzing it as the comment of a scribe who could not read the MS he was working on.

the two verbs stand in parallelism, the second going beyond the first in explaining the object of the coming. Finally, "of you alone" underlines "of my *Lord Yhwh."

71:17–24. The invocation and the reversion to qatal suggest another new beginning, and this is confirmed by the reversion to plea. But hopefulness characterizes this last section, which closes with a further four-line promise of praise based on the conviction that the prayer will be answered.

> [17]God, you have taught me from my youth,
>   and until now I proclaim your wonders.

Once again the supplicant looks back over the years from youth to the present. The line is a neatly parallel one.[29] Psalm 25:4 asks to be taught Yhwh's "ways" or "paths," which include the wonders Yhwh does. Those who know of them are then called to "declare" these (e.g., 64:9 [10]; 145:4). The Tg implies that Yhwh "teaches" by giving experience of "wonders," but it is doubtful whether "teach" (*lāmad* piel) can have that meaning. Rather, the *wonders are the great acts that Yhwh has done in Israel's history, of which the supplicant has always been learning, and thus learning to live by, and also always proclaiming.

> [18]So even until old age with its gray hair,
>   God, do not abandon me,
> Until I proclaim your strength to a generation,
>   your might to every one who will come,
> [19a]and your faithfulness, God, on high.

The plea issuing from this experience is that the pattern of those wonders should continue through the rest of the supplicant's life. The line repeats the plea and some of the words from v. 9. Old age means weakness and vulnerability, and "the idea of being abandoned by one's deity at this vulnerable time seems more than anyone can bear," but God's ways are not always fathomable, and people do seem to be abandoned.[30]

The implicit motivation for God to stay faithful that the supplicant offers to God (vv. 18c–19a) is that the pattern of the supplicant's proclamation will then also continue. I take the verb in v. 18c, which repeats from v. 17, to apply to all these three cola and thus to govern three parallel nouns of overlapping meaning, each with a second-person suffix. The line as

---

29. The two verbs complement one another in their reference to being taught (qatal) and then proclaiming (yiqtol), and the two temporal expressions do the same. The opening invocation then applies to both cola, and the closing noun is the obj. of both verbs.

30. Crenshaw, *Psalms*, 144.

a whole then recalls 22:30b–31a [31b–32a]. The three nouns form more abstract equivalents to the "wonders" of v. 17 (though "your strength" is more literally "your arm," so it is more concrete than the other two). Verse 18c–d works abcc′b′, with the two *l*-expressions together at the center. They actually comprise a compound expression ("to everyone in the generation to come") divided between the two cola to make the parallelism work, though as is often the case this introduces potential for misunderstanding. Thus LXX infers that the compound expression refers to a proclamation of Yhwh's *might to every generation, but Syr more plausibly refers the expression to a proclamation to the entire generation that will live and come to worship between now and the suppliant's death. The unexpected third colon not only adds reference to God's *faithfulness, a quality allied to strength and might, but appends the qualifier "on high," which applies to the whole line. Yhwh's strength, might, and faithfulness operate in the heavens as well as on earth.

> 19b–cYou who have done great things:
>   God, who is like you?

Verse 19b–c further describes the content of that proclamation. The "great things" that God has done parallel the "wonders" of v. 17 and refer to the deliverance from Egypt (cf. 106:21). They are the basis for the rhetorical question in the second colon, the question that arose from the great wonder that brought to its climax Yhwh's initial series of wonders (Exod. 15:11). That parallel further explicates the preceding reference to Yhwh's strength, might, and faithfulness "on high," for that line in Moses's Song affirmed that the Red Sea event demonstrated that there was no one like Yhwh "among the gods."

> 20You who have let me see calamities,
>   many and hard,
> You will revive me again,
>   and from the depths of the earth raise me again.

Admittedly, there is still the problem that the suppliant's current experience clashes with that. The point is underlined by the similarity in the structure of vv. 19b–c and 20; both begin with *ʾăšer* ([you] who). On one hand, Yhwh is one who has done great things. On the other, Yhwh is one who has let the suppliant see disasters. The point is underlined by the addition of "many and hard" to "calamities," as a parallel colon. The characterization of Yhwh as one who brings disasters thus takes a whole line, not just a colon like the characterization of Yhwh as one who does great things.

But v. 20c–d reverses all that. It gives another whole line to a further positive characterization of God, a statement of conviction about how God will surely act again in strength, might, and faithfulness. At either end of the line is a verbal expression introduced by *šûb* with its meaning "do again," and in between is an adverbial expression. The second colon as a whole explicates the first. Yhwh's wonder at the Red Sea took Pharaoh to the depths: the depths of the sea in a physical sense but the depths of the earth in the metaphysical sense, the depths under the earth, the depths of Sheol. Calamities have put the suppliant into those same depths, but restoration to life will mean being lifted up from this out-of-due-time experience of life in Sheol.

> ²¹You will grant me much greatness
> and turn around to comfort me.

Indeed, the further parallel line declares, it will mean being lifted up to renewed greatness, even to more marked greatness than the suppliant knew before, as Yhwh turns around to bring comfort instead of trouble. In 69:20 [21] the verb *nāḥam* (piel) was used to mean "comfort" in the English sense of consoling someone (cf. the niphal in 77:2 [3]), but here it is used to denote not an expression of sympathy that leaves the situation unchanged but action that changes the situation and thus leaves the person more grounds for feeling comfort (cf. 86:17).

> ²²Yes, I—I will confess you with the harp,
> [confess] your truthfulness, my God.
> I will make music for you with the lyre,
> Holy One of Israel.

That will make new praise possible. Verse 22a–b brings a transition to looking forward to such praise, an anticipation that will run through the remaining four lines of the psalm. "Yes, I—I will *confess" (the pronoun is expressed) applies to both cola. The suffix "you" is then spelled out in the second line as "your *truthfulness," which now applies not only to God's acts in the past but also to these new acts to which the suppliant looks forward.

Verse 22c–d parallels and restates that line, though there is no parallelism within it. The parallelism all lies with what preceded. So "make *music" complements "confess," the sound over against the significance. *Lyre complements *harp. And "Holy One of Israel" defines "God," one of the three occurrences in the Psalms (cf. 78:41; 89:18 [19]) of God's characteristic title in Isaiah. In the context it underlines the earlier emphasis on Yhwh's incomparability. Yhwh is *the* holy one. "Who is like you, majestic in holiness?" (Exod. 15:11).

> ²³My lips will resound when I make music for you,
>   my whole being, which you have redeemed.
> ²⁴Yes, my tongue will talk of your faithfulness all day,
>   because they have been shamed, because they have been reviled,
>   the people who seek trouble for me.

Yet again the suppliant restates this commitment to praise. Here the first colon combines reference to the *resounding that comes from the lips and the *music that comes from the instruments. The second colon goes beyond that. It is the whole *person that will be involved in this worship, because it is the whole person that God has *redeemed.

The closing line in turn parallels v. 23 rather than manifesting internal parallelism. First, however, it picks up the "Yes" (*gam*) that opened v. 22, the first line in this promise of praise. Then "tongue" complements "lips," while "talk" complements "resound" and again suggests reference to the content as well as to the sound of the suppliant's praise. The content is then defined again in terms of an experience of God's *faithfulness. In addition, "talk" usually refers to something quiet rather than out loud (cf. 1:2), so that the verb points to a quiet praise that occupies the worshipper's lips even when no one is present. If there is an element of parallelism within the line, it comes in the spelling out of that faithfulness in the second colon. The people who seek trouble for me (v. 13) reappear, but the plea regarding them has been answered. Thus the psalm closes with another reminiscence of 70:2 [3]. And the reference to the troublers' shaming forms an inclusion with the plea that the suppliant not be shamed (v. 1).

Theological Implications

Psalm 71 has four distinctive features. First is its close verbal relationship with the tradition of Israel's prayers, with which one might compare the way scriptural phraseology features in Christian worship. While there are prayers and praises in the Psalter that gain their effectiveness through their individuality, there are other prayers and praises that gain their effectiveness through the use of familiar forms and wording. The psalm gives expression to what the psalmist wants to say to God by taking up familiar and hallowed phrases and creating a new composition from them. This language thus sets the psalmist firmly within the established framework of the relationship between God and Israel and enables this familiar prayer language to become the means of expressing the psalmist's distinctive concerns. Such a way of praying reminds us when we pray that we are not alone. We join a community of prayer that has been in dialogue with God for three millennia. We pray within the framework of that proved relationship.

Second, Ps. 71 makes more mention of God's *faithfulness than any other passage in the OT; ṣĕdāqâ is the psalm's "dominant *theologoumenon.*"[31] God's faithfulness is initially the basis for an appeal for deliverance (v. 2). But it appears predominantly as the subject of testimony, when that prayer is answered (vv. 15–16, 19, 24). God is centrally defined as one who is faithful, who does the right thing by Israel. This is a people God entered into a relationship with, and God will be faithful to that commitment. "The whole of the psalm lauds with the greatest concentration the Lord's grace freely given."[32]

Third, the psalm expounds that theme in the context of looking over a life as a whole: birth and youth, middle age and old age. It looks back to a life upheld by God from youth, indeed from its very beginning, from birth (vv. 5–6). It has been a life of learning about God's awesome deeds and a life of proclaiming them (v. 17). As a middle-aged person, the suppliant stands between youth and old age. Will life continue to be like that into old age, when one lacks the strength to defend oneself (v. 9)? Will God continue to be faithful so the suppliant can continue to proclaim God's acts (v. 18a–b)? The psalm looks forward to making a difference even after one's life is over (v. 18c–19a).

Fourth, there is also no psalm that makes more use of the word "always" (tāmîd). The suppliant asks "always" to be able to come to God for protection (v. 3). That will mean that Yhwh will "always" be the topic of the suppliant's praise (v. 6), all day (v. 8). Yhwh will "always" be the suppliant's hope (v. 14a): and the suppliant will keep adding to "all" Yhwh's praise (v. 14b). Yhwh's deliverance will be the topic of praise "all day" (v. 15; cf. v. 24). Yes, throughout this life that the psalm looks back on and forward to, surely God will be faithful and the suppliant will live in hope and praise.

31. Seybold, *Psalmen*, 274.
32. Cassiodorus, *Psalms*, 2:178.

Psalm 72

A Vision for Government

Translation

Solomon's.

¹God, give your decisions to the king,
  your faithfulness to the king's son.
²He will give judgment for your people with faithfulness,
  for your weak ones with decisiveness.
³Mountains will bear well-being for the people,
  and the hills, through faithfulness.
⁴He will decide for the weak among the people,
  deliver the needy,
  crush the extortioner.
⁵People will reverence you[1] when the sun shines[2]
  and before the moon,
  generation after generation.[3]
⁶He will come down like rain on mowing,
  like heavy rains, an overflowing [on][4] the earth.

1. For *yîrā'ûkā*, LXX implies *ya'ărîk* (he will live on), but this causes difficulty with the last phrase in v. 5 ("generation after generation"). LXX has to take that as another temporal expression instead of the subject of the verb, whereas in this usage elsewhere the expression has a prep. (e.g., 10:6; 33:11; 45:17 [18]; 49:11 [12]).
2. Lit. "with the sun." Shalom M. Paul points to a Ugaritic parallel for *'im* meaning "like" ("Psalm 72:5," *JNES* 31 [1972]: 351–55 [see 352]). M. Dietrich and O. Loretz suggest Ugaritic parallels for *'m* meaning "before" ("Von hebräisch *'m/lpny* (Ps 72:5) zu ugaritisch *'m* 'vor,'" in *Ascribe to the Lord* (P. C. Craigie Memorial; ed. Lyle Eslinger and Glen Taylor; JSOTSup 67; Sheffield: JSOT Press, 1988), 109–16.
3. Lit. "generation of generations."
4. The prep. *'al* in v. 6a applies also to this parallel noun.

⁷In his time the faithful person⁵ will flourish,
and abundance of well-being, till the moon is no more.

⁸So may he dominate people from sea to sea,
from the river to the ends of the earth.
⁹Before him wildcats⁶ will kneel,
his enemies lick the dust.
¹⁰Kings of Tarshish and foreign coasts
will bring him offerings.
Kings of Sheba and Seba
will present gifts.
¹¹So all kings will bow low to him,
all nations serve him,
¹²Because he rescues the needy when they cry for help⁷
and the weak who have no helper.
¹³He pities⁸ the poor and needy
and delivers the lives of the needy.
¹⁴From viciousness, from violence he restores their lives;
their blood is important in his eyes.

¹⁵So may he flourish, and may he be given⁹
gold from Sheba.
May pleas for him be said always,
all day may blessings be invoked for him.
¹⁶May he be [like] an abundance of grain in the land,
on the top of the mountains.
May his fruit shake like Lebanon,
may they thrive from the city like the herbage in the land.
¹⁷May his name be forever;
before the sun may his name have offspring.¹⁰
So may people pray to be blessed like him,
may all nations count him fortunate.

5. Or "faithfulness," *ṣedeq* for *ṣaddîq* (so LXX, Jerome, Syr; contrast Aq, Sym).

6. Barthélemy understands "sailors" (*Psaumes*, 504–8); see on 74:14.

7. For *mĕšawwēaʿ*, the LXX, Syr, and Jerome imply *miššôaʿ*, "from a powerful person" (see BDB 447b).

8. As a form from *ḥûs*, the verb *yāḥōs* looks like another jussive (for the yiqtol one would expect *yāḥûs*); cf. *TTH* 58. But this is hard in the context, and BDB sees it as a yiqtol; cf. GKC 109k; DG 62b and remark 2. JM 80k solves the problem by hypothesizing a by-form *ḥāsas*.

9. Lit. "may one give to him." The impersonal construction continues through the verse. Hossfeld and Zenger (*Psalms 2*, 203–4) translate "May he [the king] give him [the poor person] . . ." But the poor were pl. in vv. 13b–14, and it would thus be hard for readers to pick up the magnificently novel idea of the king giving Sheba's gold to the poor person, praying for him, and blessing him.

10. *Yinnôn* (Q, niphal) and *ynyn* (K, hiphil or qal) are forms from *nûn* or *nîn*, a hapax presumably related to *nîn*, "offspring." LXX, Jerome, Tg, and one later Hebrew MS read the more familiar *yikkôn*, "endure."

Interpretation

Unlike Ps. 20, this psalm does begin as an actual prayer for the king, though it makes an immediate transition to third-person verbs like those in Ps. 20. I see it as having three themes and three sections, each section interweaving two of the themes:

The king's commitment to the weak and the flourishing of the crops (vv. 1–7)

The nations' acknowledgment of the king and his commitment to the weak (vv. 8–14)

The nations' acknowledgment of the king and his flourishing (vv. 15–17)

Each section begins with an explicit volitive: an imperative in v. 1, jussives in vv. 8 and 15. Verses 8 and 15, further, begin with *wĕ*; the only other lines beginning thus are v. 11 (marking the transition between two subsections) and v. 17c–d (marking the end of the entire psalm).[11] Of the remaining verbs, one or two are distinctively yiqtol (e.g., v. 4, "deliver") or distinctively jussive (e.g., v. 16, "be"), but most could be either, and translations vary in how they take them. Fortunately it makes little difference because the verbs that follow each of those volitives in vv. 1, 8, and 15 are implicitly dependent on the volitives, whether they take the form of yiqtols or jussives.

The psalm as a whole is a prayer for the king and a promise regarding what will issue from the answering of the prayer,[12] apparently a prayer from the time of the monarchy when Israel had kings and needed this kind of prayer to be answered. More indirectly the psalm sets up prospects and warnings for kings and criteria for assessing them, and it functions as a piece of teaching that informs Israel on how to pray for its kings.

Its requests parallel the prayers of other Middle Eastern peoples for their kings.[13] Like these, the psalm prays that the king may know heaven's

11. Patrick W. Skehan takes these as lines that close sections ("Strophic Structure in Psalm 72 [71]," *Bib* 40 [1959]: 302–8; cf. also John S. Kselman, "Psalm 72," *BASOR* 220 [1975]: 77–81)—less plausibly, as the subject changes with these lines.

12. B. Renaud ("De la bénédiction du roi à la bénédiction de Dieu [Ps 72]," *Bib* 70 [1989]: 305–26) sees the idea of blessing as the key to the psalm, holding together as it does prayer and oracle.

13. See Roland E. Murphy, *A Study of Psalm 72 (71)* (Washington, DC: Catholic University of America, 1948), 45–54, though Murphy doubts the relevance of these parallels, and while Israel made a point of having kings like other nations (1 Sam. 8:5), there is no need to think that Israel directly "imitated" these forms from foreign sources (ibid., 63). See also Kraus, *Psalms 60–150*, 78; more generally Keel, *Symbolism*, 280–90; Martin

blessing, may live long, may rule justly in a way that protects the needy, may have wide dominion, and may have offspring.[14] The reference to the "king's son" may suggest that it was used at the coronation of a new king, when the father with whom he would initially share the kingship might still be alive. It would have particular point at a king's coronation, but we have no direct information on when it was used.

Solomon's.

Heading. The heading *lišĕlōmōh* is almost unique (cf. only Ps. 127). The Tg assumes that it means "by Solomon," expanding the heading to declare, "By means of Solomon it was said in prophecy." This sets the stage for a messianic understanding of the psalm,[15] which could alternatively link with the conviction that it comes from a period when Israel had no king. It then expresses convictions about the king that Israel will one day have again. But that makes it a prayer for God's blessing on a nonexistent king, which seems phony. Psalms of Solomon 17:21–43 (from just before the time of Christ) is a prayer for God to raise up a king who will rule Israel, put down oppressors, and purge Jerusalem;[16] it makes explicit that it is a prayer concerning a king to come, and it shows us what such a prayer looks like. Comparison with the Prophets also indicates that Ps. 72 is not about a future king; prophecy takes up the psalm's themes and turns expressions of hope concerning present kings into expressions of hope concerning that future king. It is not quoted in the NT, though subsequent Christian interpreters saw it as applying to Jesus. Calvin warns interpreters about pushing that understanding when the psalm does not explicitly point in this direction.[17]

Arneth, "Psalm 72 in seinen altorientalischen Kontexten," in *"Mein Sohn bist du,"* ed. Otto and Zenger, 135–72.

14. Murphy (*Study of Psalm 72*, 47) quotes a Babylonian example (see also the section on "Psalmody before the Psalms" of the introduction in volume 1 of this commentary).

15. See (e.g.) P. Veugelers, "Le Psaume lxxii," *ETL* 41 (1965): 317–43; J.-M. Carrière, "Le Ps 72 est-il un Psaume messianique?" *Bib* 72 (1991): 49–69; Loretz, *Psalmstudien*, 171–213; Erich Zenger, "'So betete David für seinen Sohn Salomo und für den König Messias,'" in *Jahrbuch für biblische Theologie* 8 (1993): 57–72. That has been seen as a "canonical reading" of the psalm, a reading implied not by its content but by its place in the Psalter as a whole (e.g., Gerald H. Wilson, "The Use of Royal Psalms at the 'Seams' of the Hebrew Psalter," *JSOT* 35 [1986]: 85–94; also Knut M. Heim, "The Perfect King of Psalm 72," in *The Lord's Anointed*, ed. Philip E. Satterthwaite et al. (Carlisle, UK: Paternoster, 1995), 223–48. But there is no explicit indication that this is *a* or *the* reading implied either by the text or by this arrangement.

16. Cf. Gunkel, *Die Psalmen*, 305–8.

17. *Psalms*, 3:100; Theodore (*Psalms 1–81*, 938–39) scorns people who apply some verses to Solomon and some to Christ. On echoes of the psalm in the NT and elsewhere, see Craig C. Broyles, "The Redeeming King: Psalm 72's Contribution to the Messianic

The LXX translates "to Solomon," a unique expression perhaps reflecting the fact that the Coda to Pss. 42–72 (see below) implies that Ps. 72 is one of the prayers of David; it is a father's prayer for his son. It is a suggestive introduction for the psalm in light of its contents. At the beginning of his reign Solomon recalled the way his father had walked in faithfulness, and he recognized that he needed God's equipping if he was to exercise authority in Israel (1 Kings 3:6, 9; cf. Ps. 72:1–2). His reign was one that saw great prosperity and saw people eating and drinking and being happy, a time when he "dominated" the nations on this side of the River and a time of "well-being" for his people (1 Kings 4:20, 24 [5:4]; cf. vv. 7–8). During his reign nations from the Euphrates to Egypt brought him "presents" and "served" him (1 Kings 4:21 [5:1]; cf. vv. 10–11), declared him fortunate, and brought him their gold from Sheba (1 Kings 10:1–10; cf. vv. 15, 17). On the other hand, "his famous wisdom . . . is, curiously, not mentioned" in the psalm.[18] As usual, then, there is overlap but not identity between the content of the psalm and that of the heading, reflecting the fact that the heading was added to the psalm in light of this overlap rather than that the psalm was created in the context suggested by the heading.

There is also some irony about the heading, because further features of Solomon's reign were Yhwh's raising up adversaries from the peoples around because of the king's unfaithfulness and his provoking of rebellion against his successor among people who were the victims of his forced labor policies. Here were laid the foundations for the oppressions against which prophets would protest. This prayer was not answered for Solomon.

72:1–7. The first section, then, interweaves concern with the king's faithful exercise of authority and with the broader well-being of the people. In the introduction to this psalm we have noted that many of the verb forms could be understood either as jussive or as yiqtol. In vv. 2–7 the opening verb *yādîn*, "He will give judgment," is unequivocally yiqtol (the jussive would be *yāden*). So is *yôšîaʿ*, "He will deliver," in v. 4 (the jussive would be *yôšaʿ*; cf. Prov. 20:22).[19] I have reckoned that this signals that vv. 2–7 as a whole should be taken as a statement (cf. Jerome, who extends that through the psalm; LXX is more mixed). But these yiqtols do follow on from the imperative in v. 1 and are thus virtual prayers, describing the events that the suppliant longs to see issue from God's answering the prayer in v. 1. The LXX makes that explicit by making v. 2 a purpose clause, and NJPS does that to both vv. 2 and 7.[20] There is no

---

Ideal," in *Eschatology, Messianism, and the Dead Sea Scrolls*, ed. Craig A. Evans and Peter W. Flint (Grand Rapids: Eerdmans, 1997), 23–40.

18. Gerstenberger, *Psalms*, 2:65.

19. Contrast NRSV and NJPS, which translate as jussive in v. 4.

20. And cf. GKC 107n.

marker of such a link in the Hebrew, but the psalm does imply that this will be the purpose and result of God's answering these prayers. Verses 2–7 thus all work out the implications of v. 1.

> ^{1}God, give your decisions to the king,
>   your faithfulness to the king's son.

So the psalm begins with its only unequivocal prayer, that is, the only request put directly to God, containing the only invocation and the only imperative in the psalm. Thus the words "God, give," which in the prosody of the line apply to both cola, in substance apply to the whole psalm. The rest of the cola stands in parallelism. "The king" and "the king's son" are two ways of describing one person; the second may draw attention to the legitimacy of this king as the son of his predecessor. "Your *decisions" and "your *faithfulness" suggest the two values that form the classic hendiadys of the OT's vision for Israel.[21] God's faithful decisions, authoritative policy decisions that embody community faithfulness, might be decisions the king will make and promulgate with God's guidance as need arises or might be a body of decisions like the *mišpāṭîm* in Exodus–Deuteronomy; compare the body of material Samuel writes up (1 Sam. 10:25).

> ^{2}He will give judgment for your people with faithfulness,
>   for your weak ones with decisiveness.

Verse 2 begins to spell out the implications of that. "Give judgment" (*dîn*) is a less common synonym of *decide (*šāpaṭ*), the verb underlying "decisions," but it refers more consistently to judicial decision-making and thus makes that point more explicit. It again governs both cola. The parallel *b*-expressions make for an abb'a' pattern in vv. 1–2, with *faithfulness this time being *ṣedeq* instead of *ṣĕdāqâ*, while *decisiveness or authority is the singular *mišpāṭ* instead of plural. The new expressions in the line are "your people" and "your weak ones." So the people are not the king's people but God's people, which implies a challenge of the kind that Solomon and most other kings failed. The point is underlined by "your *weak ones." Verse 4 will make clear that its implication is not that Israel as a whole is by its nature a company of weak people (though there would be a sense in which that was true). Rather, its point is that within any people there are bound to be the powerful and the weak, the haves and the have-nots, the rich and the poor and that God has a special concern for the weak, the have-nots, and the poor. The way God

21. They more commonly appear together as two sg. nouns; LXX, Jerome, and Syr assimilate to this usage.

then seeks to implement this concern is by commissioning people in authority to care for the weak through acting with decisive faithfulness or the faithful exercise of authority. It was not an idea that worked, but things were no better in the days before Israel had kings, nor are they necessarily so under democratic governments.

> ³Mountains will bear well-being for the people,
>   and the hills, through faithfulness.

I take it that v. 3 again indicates what will follow from the previous line. Once more the verb applies to both cola, as does "for the people," so that in the parallelism "mountains" and "hills" go together, as do *well-being and *faithfulness,²² this latter word appearing once again, as if the psalmist knows well that this prayer is wildly unrealistic. Mountains and hills are a standard pair. They may seem an odd pair of geographical entities to be bearing crops or fruit, but in Israel this is not so. "Mountains and hills" is not far from being a description of the land as a whole, at least as actually occupied by Israel. The slopes of the hill country are often where cereal crops grow, and the slopes of mountains and hills are the sites of olives and vines. In Joel 3:18 [4:18] the mountains flow with wine and the hills with milk (cf. also Ps. 65:12 [13]). The line implies that there is a moral connection between the way the society organizes itself (vv. 1–2) and its experience of prosperity. There are many ways of understanding that link, and the psalm does not discuss these. It simply assumes that there *is* a link.

> ⁴He will decide for the weak among the people,
>   deliver the needy,
>   crush the extortioner.

The link is presupposed again in the reversion to talk about the way the king exercises authority. He is to do so on behalf of the *weak as v. 2 said. The second, parallel colon underlines the point. The parallelism of the verbs underscores the significance of the verb šāpaṭ, "*decide." To put it another way, the manner in which the king exercises authority is by using it for the *deliverance of people. The weak are in turn re-described as the *needy, because neediness follows from powerlessness. The powerful in a society do not go short; the weak do. The third parallel clause makes the correlative negative point. Decisive action designed to deliver the weak and needy implies putting down the people who take advantage of the weakness of other members of the society by robbing

22. Some LXX MSS, Jerome, and Syr omit "through" before "faithfulness," which makes for an easier reading.

them of what belongs to them. They might do this (for instance) by using the courts to foreclose on loans so as to deprive poor people of their land and/or their freedom. It is not enough merely to rescue the weak and needy. The crooks who prey on them need to be put down, both because that restores the proper structures of right and wrong in the world and because it removes the possibility of these particular oppressors acting in the same way again. The verb (*dākā'* piel) thus, on one hand, implies that the king must treat these sharp operators the way they have treated others (cf. 94:5) and, on the other, that he must render them totally incapable of acting that way again, as God once did Rahab (89:10 [11]). The king is to act forcefully like God.

> ⁵ People will reverence you when the sun shines
>   and before the moon,
>   generation after generation.

That will bring God glory. It will make crooks and their victims revere God, in different ways. The opening verb applies to the whole line, as does the closing phrase "generation after generation," which is the verb's delayed subject (there is no word for "people" in the Hebrew of v. 5). The verb is then modified by the two parallel time expressions that come in between. These may suggest that this reverence will last as long as the cosmos itself or, more likely, that it will be expressed by day and by night (Tg; cf. 2 Sam. 12:11–12).

> ⁶He will come down like rain on mowing,
>   like heavy rains, an overflowing [on] the earth.

The king is again the subject, but the results of God's answering prayer for him are now expressed figuratively. The king will be like rain falling on the land. Rain falling on mowing implies an ellipse: either the rain falls on the grass so as to make it grow and make it ready for mowing, or it falls on the fields after they have been mown to prepare them for the next crop, or it falls on grass that has been ravaged, to restore it (so Tg). Once again the verb applies to both cola, and the parallel expression in the second colon intensifies the first. The king is not merely like regular rain but like heavy rains (*rĕbîbîm*, from *rābab*). To add to that, the line adds the hapax *zarzîp*, which in related languages means overflowing or outpouring.²³ The line takes up the theme of v. 3. The king's concern for fairness in society will mean the land also flourishes.

---

23. See *HALOT*; *DCH*'s "sprinkling" is misleading. LXX and Jerome may imply a verbal form such as *zirzîp* (cf. *DTT*), which would make for a good parallel colon, "like heavy rains, he overflows the earth."

> ⁷In his time the faithful person will flourish,
>   and abundance of well-being, till the moon is no more.

Verse 7 in turn reverts to the theme of v. 2, closing off vv. 2–7. God's answering that opening prayer will mean the *faithful will flourish even as the land does; "flourish" (*pāraḥ*) is an agricultural image. The verb applies to both cola, with "abundance of well-being" as a second subject for it and "till the moon is no more" a second temporal expression to parallel "in his days" and going well beyond it. The structure is thus abcb'c'. The promise of that latter expression is that the king's commitment to standing by the faithful will have an effect far beyond his own day.

72:8–14. The beginning of a new section is marked by the first explicit jussive, paralleling the imperative in v. 1, and by a change of subject. But the rhetoric of the section is worked in the opposite direction to that of the first section. Five lines express the wish for worldwide acknowledgment of the king. Then three lines indicate the basis for that, the key factor being the same as the key factor in relation to internal prosperity in vv. 1–7. Within the first five lines, the jussive states the general point, and the succeeding four lines spell it out (as happened in vv. 1–7) in abb'a' fashion. In vv. 12–14, too, the first line states the point, and the following two with their four cola expand on it in abb'a' fashion. But the *w* (so) opening v. 11 compares with the *w* opening to vv. 8 and 15 and suggests that v. 11 marks the beginning of a subsection, resuming from v. 8 and summarizing vv. 8–10 before stating the background to it in vv. 12–14.[24]

> ⁸So may he dominate people from sea to sea,
>   from the river to the ends of the earth.

The jussive is another verb that governs parallel phrases in both cola, paired *min* and *ʿad* expressions ("from . . . to"). The verb *rādâ* suggests something more forceful than mere rule (e.g., 110:2), in keeping with the picture in vv. 1–7. The psalm wants this king to be in a position to exercise forceful leadership in the world as a whole. At the moment this will seem to play into the hands of an ambitious king, but vv. 12–14 will deconstruct that. For the moment, the verb *yērēd*, the first word in v. 6, and the verb *yērĕd*, the first word in v. 8, stand alongside each other in some tension. Is the king like rain for his own people but like an oppressor for others? Or is the implication that this forcefulness in relation to other peoples needs to have the same focus as the forceful behavior

---

24. JM 177l argues that in vv. 8 and 15 the *w* is present solely to mark the jussive more clearly and also sees this *w* in v. 11 as having that significance.

in v. 4, not aiming at self-aggrandizement but at the deliverance of the needy?[25] In the terms of down-to-earth geography, the line longs for his dominion to be exercised in all four directions—perhaps from the Red Sea to the Mediterranean and from the Euphrates to Spain. In more symbolic geography, its vision extends from one side of the earth's land mass, where it meets the sea, to the other side, where it meets it again, and (to put the same point another way) from the river on one side of the land mass to the ends of the land mass.

> [9]Before him wildcats will kneel,
>   his enemies lick the dust.

The wildcats perhaps bring out the more supernatural side to v. 8. The *ṣîyîm* are not merely ordinary desert-dwellers (NJPS, TNIV; LXX and Jerome have "Ethiopians"). They are scary creatures of the desolate wilds that can suggest the presence of the demonic. In 74:14 they feed on the remains of Leviathan, and in Isa. 13:21–22; 34:13–14 they keep company with entities such as *śĕʿîrîm* (NRSV, "goat-demons"), *tannîm* (NRSV, "jackals," but *tannin* refers to the sea monster), and Lilith. It is these who will kneel "before him"; that phrase applies to both cola. In more down-to-earth terms, the king's enemies will "lick the dust," a vivid alternative way of describing their kneeling, because proper prostration involves putting one's head right down to the ground. The line is speaking of genuine submission.

> [10]Kings of Tarshish and foreign coasts
>   will bring him offerings.
> Kings of Sheba and Seba
>   will present gifts.

Their tribute is another sign of the genuineness of their submission. In one sense the bodily public self-humbling of vv. 9 and 11 is more costly to the leaders of other peoples; in another sense the tribute is more costly. The two lines are parallel to one another rather than internally so, each comprising a double subject referring to two peoples in the first colon and a predicate in the second, in the order abca'b'c'. Like preceding lines these refer to rather far-off exotic nations. There is no mention of peoples such as Philistia, Edom, Egypt, or Assyria. Rather, the first line refers to the kings of Tartessus in Spain at the far western edge of the known world (or to Tarsus or Carthage or Sardinia)[26] and to the coasts

---

25. Cf. Alter, *Art of Biblical Poetry*, 132.

26. Or other places: see André Lemaire, "Tarshish-*Tarsisi*," in *Studies in Historical Geography and Biblical Historiography Presented to Zecharia Kallai*, ed. Gershon Galil and Moshe Weinfeld, VTSup 81 (Leiden: Brill, 2000), 44–62.

around the Mediterranean in general (not merely the "islands" [EVV]). The second refers to Arabian kings, perhaps to places on either side of the Red Sea, in Arabia and Ethiopia. The term "offerings" underlines the relative status of the foreign kings and the Israelite kings, as the word *minḥâ* is a term for a gift from an inferior to a superior, most often a gift to God. "Present" (*qārab* hiphil) has similar implications, being most often a term for presenting something to God.

> ¹¹So all kings will bow low to him,
>   all nations serve him,

Verse 11 returns to the generalization of v. 9. Of the two parallel clauses, the first more explicitly parallels v. 9 with its reference to physical prostration. *Bow low is another word that often refers to a posture before God, but it can also refer to prostration before a human being (it does not imply worship). "Serve" will imply doing whatever the king wants.

> ¹²Because he rescues the needy when they cry for help
>   and the weak who have no helper.

Then v. 12 begins to explain the rationale for vv. 8–11 and to undermine any inference that this is merely a matter of one people or king dominating another. The basis for the acknowledgment of other nations and kings is the same as the basis for the nation's internal prosperity. Roland E. Murphy comments, "But one cannot expect even a poet to allege a reason so naive as this; kingdoms are not won by good example."[27] Yet he goes on to note that this is the implication of Job 29:12, and its assumption underlies the picture of the nations waiting for the teaching of God's servant (Isa. 42:4). The naive poet reckons that nations might respond to a king who cares for the needy. The two preceding psalms, like many others, have spoken of God as the great rescuer (70:1 [2]; 71:2), but that is designed to provide powerful human beings with an example. God is by nature a rescuer; so must a king be. Once again the verb applies to both cola, and once again the *needy and the *weak appear as its objects. The first colon is completed by the comment on the needy crying for help. The fact that the verb also regularly applies to a cry addressed to God gives the powerful human being no excuse for declining to listen to the cry; on the contrary, it calls on such a person to be like God in his listening and then in his acting. In turn, the second colon is completed by the note recognizing that often the weak have no *helper. Once more the fact that God is the great helper (e.g., 10:14; 30:10 [11])

---

27. *Study of Psalm 72*, 33.

is reason for the powerful to follow God rather than to leave it to God. The word for crying for help (*šāwaʿ* piel) is neatly similar to the word for deliver (*yāšaʿ*), which comes in the next line. People are calling out with a particular aim, to obtain that deliverance.

> ¹³He pities the poor and needy
>   and delivers the lives of the needy.

Verse 13 parallels v. 12 but goes behind its declaration about action. The action is an expression of pity. The king shares God's pity for Nineveh, which Jonah did not share (Jon. 4:10–11). Pity is a motivation for action, for God and for powerful human beings. A king is not heartless but acts out of identification with the poor and needy and out of grief over them. That is why he *delivers their lives. "Poor" (*dal*) describes the social position of people, a little like the terms "peasant" or "underclass." They would characteristically be people who have lost their land. *Needy describes the consequence of being poor and having no resources.

> ¹⁴From viciousness, from violence he restores their lives;
>   their blood is important in his eyes.

The psalm restates the point once again, in more direct abb'a' parallelism with v. 13. Why are people needy (the word repeated in both cola in v. 13)? The answer comes in the form of a restatement of the reference to violence in v. 4. It is because they are the victims of viciousness, that is, *violence. The latter word restates the former by means of a more familiar term, *ḥāmās* (the *w* is explicative); or we might see the two words as a hendiadys, "lawless violence."[28] The king's action therefore *restores their lives to what they should be. The application to the king of this verb from family relationships suggests that the king has obligations to his people like those of a well-to-do or otherwise powerful member of a family, who is committed to using his resources and energy to restore to normality the situation of people reduced to poverty or servitude. Given that God is the great *restorer (e.g., Isa. 41:14), this is another expectation that the king will be like God. The second colon takes us back into the king's mind, into the attitudes that generate action. For a king, what is important, and what has value? The term is an economic one, and one expects an economic answer, but the psalmist introduces this economic category in order to turn its significance upside down. It is bloodshed that matters to the king, the shedding of the blood of the

28. So Dahood, *Psalms*, 2:183.

needy. That is what determines the kind of policies he pursues. It is this attitude and practice that lie behind the wish that the king may enjoy worldwide dominion. It is such a worldwide ruler that the world needs. Perhaps the idea is that only then would God dare to risk fulfilling that wish, as well as that because the king is known to be that kind of ruler, peoples will willingly bow down to him.

72:15–17. The closing section of the psalm brings together the two themes of fruitfulness from vv. 1–7 and of the king's worldwide recognition from vv. 8–14, but gives both a new twist. The fruitfulness is now the king's own, for which the fruitfulness of the land is a figure, and the recognition issues in seeking the blessing he enjoys. I have reckoned that it makes sense to translate the entire section as jussive, though only vv. 15a, 16a, and 17a are unequivocally so. Whereas earlier the ambiguous verbs could be seen as declaring the consequences of the opening prayer/wish, here that is not so. They all seem to be wishes in themselves.

> **15**So may he flourish, and may he be given
>   gold from Sheba.
> May pleas for him be said always,
>   all day may blessings be invoked for him.

So v. 15a–b[29] again begins with a resumptive *w*, like v. 8 at the opening of the middle section. It declares the standard wish for a king, associated with his accession to the throne: literally, "May he live" (e.g., 1 Kings 1:34, 39). The second verb spells out the implication of this flourishing that has been expressed in vv. 8–11.

Then the psalm turns in on itself in the sense that it asks for its own burden to be taken up continuously, which will be a recognition on the part of the praying people that the king is the key to their destiny. The psalm as a whole has already indicated the content of the desired prayer. The parallel cola work abb'a'. The two impersonal third-person singular jussive expressions for prayer, *plea, and blessing, interpret each other. On one hand, it is blessing that the people are pleading for. On the other, the link with pleading suggests that blessing involves more than merely congratulating the king for what he has and is, nor is it a matter of merely uttering a conventional blessing formula such as one uses in greeting someone. It involves calling down blessing on the king, perhaps both because the king has been a blessing and because they long for him to continue to be so. Inside these two verbal expressions come the mutually reinforcing hyperbolic "always" and "all day."

29. Given that v. 15c–d looks like a bicolon, I take v. 15a–b as a line in its own right.

> ¹⁶May he be [like] an abundance of grain in the land,
>   on the top of the mountains.
> May his fruit shake like Lebanon,
>   may they thrive from the city like the herbage in the land.

Verse 16a–b talks once more about flourishing crops, but it will eventually emerge in the next line that these are now a figure for human fruitfulness, which also implies that "blessing" has its common meaning.[30] The meaning of *pissâ*, translated "abundance," is actually quite uncertain,[31] though the subsequent line has the effect of clarifying its implications. The verb and the construct expression in v. 16a apply also to v. 16b, where "on the top of the mountains" (where there would be less likelihood of abundance than in more sheltered spots?) constitutes a second *b*-expression paralleling "in the land" and giving precision to it.

Verse 16c–d explains why the psalm has returned to talk about crops and explains what these crops are. The line broadly parallels v. 16a–b, though it is also internally parallel. Each colon begins with a jussive verb (one singular, one plural, "fruit" being treated once as singular, once as plural) and includes a *k*-expression, the order being abca′db′. Metaphor thus becomes simile, or the explicit simile retrospectively establishes that v. 16a–b was actually a metaphor. The subject becomes no longer the king but "his fruit" in the sense of his offspring (cf. esp. 132:11), and the line offers two more standards for his fruitfulness. One is Lebanon; it would be quite something for fruit to flourish like the trees in forests of Lebanon shaking (it is an odd verb to use). More down to earth but even more remarkable is the further comparison with the "herbage in the land."

> ¹⁷May his name be forever;
>   before the sun may his name have offspring.
> So may people pray to be blessed like him,
>   may all nations count him fortunate.

Verse 17a–b re-expresses the point in parallel cola, abcc′a′b. The subject "his *name" thus repeats, while the verb changes from the familiar and repeated "may it be" to the hapax "may it have offspring," and the temporal expression changes from the familiar "forever" to "before the sun."[32]

30. Cf. André Caquot, "Psaume lxxii 16," *VT* 38 (1988): 214–20.
31. For this usual understanding, see *HALOT*; Caquot, "Psaume lxxii 16," offers alternative suggestions for the line.
32. The parallelism suggests that the latter expression implies "as long as the sun shines" and thus may have different implications from "before the moon" in v. 5.

Then v. 17c–d rounds off the psalm in two parallel cola, beginning with another resumptive *w*. "May people pray to be blessed like him" (*bārak* hitpael, followed by *b*) parallels the promise to Israel's ancestors (Gen. 22:18; 26:4; also Jer. 4:2), where the subject is "all the nations of the earth"; here "all nations" comes in the parallel colon. The wish thus asks that the king may be an embodiment of the fulfillment of that promise. His blessing will be such that the whole world may pray for it. That is a measure of the magnitude of his blessing, but it is also an indication of what God purposes to do for the world through him. The parallel verb *'āšar* (piel; "*good fortune") is more distinctive to this psalm (though see Gen. 30:13; Mal. 3:12).

Theological Implications

At the end of Book II, Psalm 72 in an act of intercession brings together a remarkable constellation of words and ideas: *authority, *faithfulness, care for the poor, *deliverance and restoration of the *weak and *needy, *well-being, *reverence for God, recognition by the nations, intercession, fruitfulness, renown. Such a prayer might be worryingly ideological or wonderfully devious. It could work in the favor of the government (the psalm talks in terms of kings, but the issues it raises apply to presidents, prime ministers, and governments in general). It undergirds the government's claim to authority and recognition and encourages it to enjoy the perks of its position. But at the same time it presupposes that the basis for its expectation of enjoying well-being is that it gives priority to faithfulness to its people, and specifically that it gives itself to the needs of the weak. In this sense, Ps. 72 offers "a vision of the kingdom of God,"[33] or "a political fairy tale" in which the poor are always in the right, and the king effortlessly does the proper thing and gets the fair reward.[34] It "reflects the . . . tension between the experience of hurt and the grand dream."[35] "The introduction of the kingship marks the deepest cleft in the religious and social history of early Israel."[36] But "what would the world look like, the psalmist implicitly asks, if we imagine a ruler governing not by coercion but by compassion and unswerving equity, who did not exploit the weak but championed them?"[37]

33. Patrick D. Miller, "Power, Justice, and Peace: An Exegesis of Psalm 72," *Faith and Mission* 4, no. 1 (1986): 65–70 (see 65).

34. Hill, *Prayer, Praise, and Politics*, 140–44.

35. Brueggemann, *Israel's Praise*, 68.

36. Bernd Janowski, *Stellvertretung* (Stuttgart: KBW, 1997), 41; cf. Hossfeld and Zenger, *Psalms 2*, 204.

37. Alter, *Art of Biblical Poetry*, 133.

The idea that the king's concern for the poor is what entitles him to reign over the world as well as over Israel could thus function to undergird the king's rule if he can claim to do that. But one gathers the impression from the OT that this was only occasionally so. Consequently the doctrine of the legitimacy of the monarchy in Ps. 72 has the potential to undermine itself.[38] The king can hardly object to this prayer, but one imagines it might make him feel uncomfortable, especially as it proceeds. In vv. 1–7 the relationship between those words and ideas (authority, well-being, concern for the poor, etc.) is unstated. Commitment to the needy is simply "part of a permanent, inevitable system," along with prosperity and permanence. But in the middle section of the psalm it becomes "a condition for the working of the rest of the system."[39] The king's commitment to the poor becomes the "motor" of the system the psalm presupposes, even if there remains a "moral contradiction between praying that the king may protect the poor from oppression and that he may receive tribute from the nations" because the burden of tribute falls on the poor of those nations.[40]

Further, the relationship between divine commitment to the king and his commitment to the poor is never resolved. This is hardly surprising. It is a particular example of the built-in, irresolvable tension between divine commitment and human obligation. The psalm implicitly makes promises and issues demands, all in the form of a prayer that the subject of the prayer is invited to reflect on, in the manner of the prayers Paul tells his congregations he is praying for them (e.g., Phil. 1:9–11). But it knows that the promises do not make commitment unnecessary, nor does the strength of our commitment to God and God's priorities become the decisive factor in the relationship between us and God. Both are integral to life with God, with the mutuality that applies in human relationships.

38. Walter Houston, "The King's Preferential Option for the Poor," *BibInt* 7 (1999): 341–67.

39. David Jobling, "Deconstruction and the Political Analysis of Biblical Texts," *Semeia* 59 (1992): 95–127 (see 103).

40. Houston, "King's Preferential Option," 350.

Psalm 72:18–20
Coda to Book II

Translation

[18]Yhwh God be worshipped, the God of Israel,
  doer of wonders alone.
[19]His honorable name be worshipped forever;
  may the whole earth be full of his honor.[1]
Yes, yes!

[20]The pleas of David ben Jesse are concluded.

Interpretation

[72:18–20]. Although these lines have verse numbers that presuppose their attachment to Ps. 72, they are actually a coda to Book II of the Psalms, comparable to those that follow Pss. 41; 89; and 106.

[18]Yhwh God be worshipped, the God of Israel,
  doer of wonders alone.
[19]His honorable name be worshipped forever;
  may the whole earth be full of his honor.
Yes, yes!

---

1. The context suggests that the verb is jussive rather than yiqtol. *'Et* here seems to mark the subject (DG 95a).

This is the most expansive of the codas. Yhwh is explicitly God—that is, the only God. The declaration that Yhwh is God fits with a feature of Pss. 42–72, the preference for the invocation "God" rather than the name "Yhwh," which makes clear that Yhwh is not merely a private local God of a particular people but *the* God. The declaration that this God is one who does *wonders coheres with that: it is the truly sovereign God who can do such wonders. This God "alone" can do so. The more extravagant description naturally issues in a more extravagant call for the *worship of this God. Thus to the call that Yhwh's *name be worshipped forever is added a call for Yhwh's *honor to be recognized everywhere. "Yes, yes!" (*'āmēn, 'āmēn*) is an appropriate response to this bidding, suggesting that v. 19 in origin might be a liturgical exchange. "'Amen' became more and more a speech-act of trust and hope in God."[2]

> [20]The pleas of David ben Jesse are concluded.

Actually they are not, or at least only for a while;[3] indeed, *IBHS* 25.2 understands the pual to mean "are to be concluded."[4] Psalms 3–41 and 51–72 have been David psalms; Pss. 86 and 138–145 will be further David psalms. Indeed, neither are the David psalms merely "pleas"; LXX calls them *hymnoi*, which is more accurate (*hymnos* can describe lament as well as praise). Presumably this note belongs to the end of the David collection comprising Pss. 51–72, which would have already existed as a collection before it was incorporated into the Psalter. That may indicate that the coda belonged to this collection and that the development of the subsequent praise codas began from such an already-existing praise coda rather than that the coda was subsequently inserted before this footnote.[5]

Theological Implications

The coda invites readers to treat all the prayers and praises of Pss. 42–72 as reason for praise.

---

2. Hossfeld and Zenger, *Psalms 2*, 218.
3. Ibid., 209, comparing Job 31:40.
4. Might *kollû* be a composite reading that blends qal *kālû* and pual *kullû*? But GKC 52q takes it as simply unusual.
5. Cf. Goulder, *Prayers of David*, 243–44. For other possibilities, see D. C. Mitchell, *The Message of the Psalter*, JSOTSup 252 (Sheffield: Sheffield Academic Press, 1997), 66–69.

Psalm 73
Yes, God Will Restore Me

Translation

Composition. Asaph's.

[1]Yes, God is good to Israel,[1]
   to the pure of heart.

[2]But I was almost turned aside in my footsteps [K]/
But I—my footsteps all but turned aside [Q],
   my steps were nearly made to slip,[2]
[3]Because I was jealous of the exultant people,
   of the well-being of the faithless, which I beheld.[3]

---

1. For *lĕyiśrā'ēl*, the NRSV presupposes the repointing *layyāšār 'ēl*, "[God is good] to the upright, God [is good] to the pure of heart," which generates good parallelism but is simply a conjecture. R. Tournay ("Le Psaume lxxiii," *RB* 92 [1985]: 187–99 [see 187–91]) sees *lĕyiśrā'ēl* as an aspect of a collective rereading of the original version of the psalm.

2. K has f. sg. *špkh* (*šuppĕkâ*); see DG 26. Q has the grammatically more correct pl. *šuppĕkû*.

3. NRSV and NJPS take the line as two parallel clauses, which they then take to be asyndetic (more likely the second would be subordinate to the first, "when I beheld the well-being of the faithless"; cf. LXX, Jerome, Syr, TNIV; Briggs, *Psalms*, 2:143). But the word order rather suggests that "well-being" is a second obj. of "was jealous of," with the closing verb an asyndetic relative clause. The verb *qānā'* (be jealous) can take an indirect or a direct obj., though one could assume that the *b* on *bahôlĕlîm* carries over to *šĕlôm*.

⁴Because there are no pressures for them threatening their death;⁴
  their belly is stout.
⁵In the burdens of human beings they have no part;
  they are not afflicted with other people.
⁶Thus prestige has bedecked them⁵
  while⁶ a garment of violence wraps around them.
⁷Their eye⁷ has bulged from callousness,
  the schemings of their heart have overflowed.
⁸They mock and speak of trouble,⁸
  from their eminence they speak of extortion.
⁹They have set their mouth in the heavens,
  and their tongue ranges in the earth.
¹⁰Thus blows come repeatedly⁹ to his people,
  and abundant water¹⁰ is drained by them.
¹¹And they say,¹¹ "How would God care?
  Is there recognition with the Most High?"
¹²There—these are the faithless,
  and forever carefree,¹² they have amassed wealth.

¹³Yes, in vain I have kept my heart clean,
  washed my hands in innocence.
¹⁴I have come to be afflicted¹³ continuously,
  and my reproof is each morning.

¹⁵If I had said I would speak out like that—
  there, I would have betrayed the company of your children.
¹⁶So I thought to understand this,

4. Lit. "There are no fetters for their death." Reworking *lĕmôtām* as *lāmô tām* produces the easier "There are no fetters for them; their body is whole and hearty" (cf. KJV). M. Mannati ("Les adorateurs de Môt dans le Psaume lxxiii," *VT* 22 [1972]: 420–25) sees this as a reference to the Canaanite god Death.

5. More lit. "has necked them."

6. I take the asyndeton and the move from qatal to yiqtol to indicate that the second colon provides the background to the first.

7. For *'ênēmô*, the LXX implies *'ăwōnāmô* (their waywardness), which makes good sense.

8. LXX and Jerome take the *b* as instrumental, but *dibber* can be followed by *b* of the obj. (cf. BDB 181b). The two verbs are linked by coordinating *w*.

9. Lit. "return," following Q *yāšûb* (qal) rather than K *yāšîb* (hiphil).

10. Lit. "waters of full"; see GKC 128w; DG 42 remark 4. LXX implies *wîmê* (and days of) for *ûmê* (and waters of).

11. The *w* consecutive follows on the frequentative yiqtol (*TTH* 113.4).

12. Lit. "carefree of eternity."

13. The expression combines the verb *hāyâ* and the niphal ptc. rather than simply using the niphal verb; it thus underlines the ongoing nature of the affliction (*TTH* 135.5). The *w* consecutive follows on v. 13 rather paradoxically as it makes a contrast with what preceded (*TTH* 74).

> which was[14] the burden in my eyes,
> [17]As[15] I went to God's sanctuary,[16]
> where I would consider[17] their end.
> [18]Yes, you will set them among deceptions;[18]
> you are making them fall to lies.[19]
> [19]How they are coming to destruction in a moment,
> coming to a complete end through horrors.
> [20]Like a dream, after you awake, my Lord,
> when you arise,[20] you will despise their shadow.[21]
>
> [21]When my heart is embittered,
> and my spirit—I am pierced through,
> [22]Then I am stupid and I have no sense;
> I became a monster with you.
> [23]But I have always been with you;
> you have held my right hand.
> [24]In your purpose you will lead me;
> after, you will take me to honor.
> [25]Whom do I have in the heavens?—
> and with you, I have not wanted anyone on the earth.
> [26]Although my flesh and my heart have come to an end,
> God is the crag of my heart and my allocation, forever.
> [27]For now: people who are far from you perish;
> you are terminating everyone who is unfaithful to you.
> [28]But for me—nearness to God is good for me;
> I have made my Lord Yhwh my refuge,
> so as to speak out about all your acts.

14. For the demonstrative functioning as copula, Q has m. *hû'*, K f. *hî'*. The two cola are asyndetic; I take the second as a relative clause rather than seeing the first as subordinate to the second (NRSV, TNIV) or seeing both as parallel (NJPS).

15. *'Ad* usually means "until," but see BDB for this meaning, which makes more sense here; BDB also notes that the yiqtol can be used after *'ad*.

16. On the pl. (for which cf. 68:35 [36]), see GKC 124.

17. The cohortative might suggest the deliberation of the act (*TTH* 54; GKC 108h; DG 68) or may be an archaism, the form being used without its traditional meaning (*JM* 114c).

18. For *ḥălāqôt*, the EVV have "slippery places," but elsewhere the word has the metaphorical meaning of "slippery words" (as usually do other words from this root). This makes sense here, and the parallelism confirms it. Cf. LXX, though it sees this as referring to the deceptions of the faithless themselves.

19. *Maššû'ôt* from *nāšā'*; but readers could also connect it with *šw'* and understand it to suggest "desolations" (cf. NRSV, TNIV). This leads well into v. 19 and is the meaning required in 74:3.

20. Taking *bā'îr* as equivalent to *běhā'îr* (from *'ûr*) rather than as meaning "in the city" (LXX), which gives poor sense.

21. BDB takes *ṣalmām* as an odd instance of the word *ṣelem* meaning an image, but more likely it is a homonym from *ṣālam* II (cf. discussion in *HALOT*).

Interpretation

Like many others, this psalm speaks on behalf of someone living among a people oppressed by the faithless and personally experiencing that oppression. Yet it focuses not so much on the suffering this brings (which appears only in vv. 10 and 14) as on the questions raised by the fact that the faithless are able to get away with such behavior. The suppliant has felt tempted to accept their cynical view of life and of God but has regained faith that God's involvement in the world will provide protection and deliverance and bring about their downfall. The psalm begins with a timeless declaration about God, and in this respect and in its concern with "the problem of suffering" and with understanding, it resembles a wisdom psalm,[22] though it is not didactic in tone. It tells a story that makes it resemble a thanksgiving or testimony psalm, though it does not indicate that God has acted. It speaks of people's continuing attacks, and in this respect it resembles a lament, though it presupposes that the suppliant has gained an assurance that God will deliver; agonizing lies in the past. It thus expresses confidence in God, and in this respect it resembles a psalm of trust. The speaker seems to be a leader of the community, and in this respect it resembles a royal psalm.[23]

It opens with its conclusion (v. 1). It then offers its narrative account of what has happened: the way the suppliant was demoralized (vv. 2–3, 13–14), the success and the oppression of the faithless that generated this (vv. 4–12), and the way the suppliant came to see things differently (vv. 15–20). It then expounds the suppliant's renewed conviction (vv. 21–26) and closes with a summary of its negative and positive implications (vv. 27–28).

The contrast between "Israel" and the people described in vv. 3–10 suggests the context of a preexilic community assailed by attackers such as Assyria or Babylon or the Second Temple community surrounded by and intermingled with other communities such as those mentioned in Ezra–Nehemiah. This could cohere with the fact that a number of communal laments will follow among Pss. 74–89.[24] The speaker will then be the king or a leader such as Nehemiah with opponents such as Sanballat and his colleagues. The psalm includes words better known

---

22. Cf., e.g., J. Luyten, "Psalm 73 and Wisdom," in *La sagesse de l'Ancien Testament* (ed. M. Gilbert; BETL 51; Louvain: Leuven University Press, 1979), 59–81; James F. Ross, "Psalm 73," in *Israelite Wisdom* (Samuel Terrien Festschrift; ed. John G. Gammie et al.; Missoula, MT: Scholars Press, 1978), 161–75.

23. Cf., e.g., Ernst Würthwein, "Erwägungen zu Ps 73," in *Wort und Existenz* (Göttingen: Vandenhoeck & Ruprecht, 1970), 161–78; John H. Eaton, *Kingship and the Psalms* (London: SCM, 1976), 75–78.

24. McCann, "Psalms," 968.

from Aramaic[25] and other unusual words and forms,[26] and its Hebrew may be a northern dialect.[27]

> Composition. Asaph's.

Heading. See glossary.

73:1. In the manner of a testimony psalm, it begins with its conclusion, with a "yes" introducing the affirmation the suppliant is now able to make in light of the process the psalm will recount. The opening line reflects the fact that in its nature as testimony, a thanksgiving exists for the sake of the community; it exists to build up the community's faith. "I am going to tell you a story; I am going to tell you what happened to me," the psalmist implies, "but the thing I want to leave with you is just this: the goodness of God."[28]

> ¹Yes, God is good to Israel,
>   to the pure of heart.

Formally, "God is good to Israel" is a commonplace affirmation (perhaps even an aphorism). To say God is *good can be a routine statement about the way God brings blessing on the lives of the people (Jer. 33:11; cf. Pss. 25:8; 100:5) or protects them (Nah.1:7; cf. Ps. 34:8 [9]) or delivers them from crises (Lam. 3:25; cf. Ps. 86:5). Such a statement of "orientation" can be one made in untested, rather unthinking, and shallow faith. But in this context it is more than routine. The conviction is one that has been sharply tested by what the suppliant can see going on in the community. Here it is uttered as a statement of "renewed orientation" after an experience of "disorientation" such as the one the psalm will recount, and it thus gains a new depth. With spiritual bravery, the Midrash goes as far as to count the afflictions of which the psalm speaks as themselves gifts of God's goodness. They are good because they contribute to the purifying of the heart.[29]

The implication of the parallelism is then that by definition Israel is pure of heart, which is certainly its vocation. At the same time, the line sets up a tension that the rest of the psalm will explore. The faithless are people whose hearts are full of schemings (v. 7), which stands in contrast with purity of heart, and the suppliant has had to battle to remain someone with the first characteristic of heart rather than the

---

25. *Mûq*, v. 8; *śāgâ*, v. 12.
26. E.g., *ḥarṣubbôt* (v. 4); *'ûlām* (v. 4); *maśkîyôt* (v. 7); *tihălak* (v. 9); *hălōm* (v. 10).
27. Cf. Rendsburg, *Linguistic Evidence*, 73–81.
28. D. Martyn Lloyd-Jones, *Faith on Trial* (repr., London: Inter-Varsity, 1974), 13.
29. *Midrash on Psalms*, 2:1.

second. Purity of heart means that the inner attitude coheres with the outward word. The words of the faithless may be fine, but inside they are planning wrongdoing; their hearts are the opposite of their words. The psalm will thus go on to rejoice in the fact that Yhwh will make them drink their own medicine (v. 18). The suppliant has had to face the temptation to become a person like them (vv. 2, 13) and begins by affirming the realization that this would forfeit Yhwh's goodness, which in the long run the pure of heart will experience. The implication is that when Israel fails to be pure of heart, it cannot complain if Yhwh ceases to be good to it. Yet at the same time, Yhwh's commitment is one made to Israel as Israel actually was; it was not based on Israel's purity of heart (Deut. 9:6–7). And the further implication is that when Israel fails to be pure of heart, Yhwh cannot simply abandon it as if the relationship were a contract rather than a covenant.[30]

73:2–3. Now the psalm looks back to the experience that made that affirmation deconstruct. It thus works backward, starting with the attitude the psalmist had come to take to life, which almost derailed that life.

> [2]But I was almost turned aside in my footsteps [K]/
> But I—my footsteps all but turned aside [Q],
>   my steps were nearly made to slip,

The line takes up the image of life with God as involving walking along the right path (e.g., Ps. 1). The right path is not the only path one can take; paths often diverge, and it is possible to choose the wrong one and turn aside, to go in the wrong direction. Travelers have to keep their wits about them. Further, the right path is a narrow one, like a narrow path along a Judean hillside. One has to be careful not to lose one's footing. The Q reading suggestively combines a qal perfect and a pual verb.[31] Going astray involves personal responsibility: it is my feet that turn aside. But it also involves yielding to pressure or temptation that causes me to lose my footing. (The second verb literally refers to being "poured out"; my steps were nearly poured out like water from a jug.) The image of the path suggests that the psalmist refers not merely to going astray in attitude to God but also to going astray in behavior, following that of the faithless, whose life seems to "work."

The "but I" contains some emphasis. Structurally, it stands outside the neat parallelism of the rest of the line, which works abcdb'c'd'.[32] In substance, it makes a contrast with what precedes, first with the "Yes,"

30. Cf. Brueggemann's comments, *Message of the Psalms*, 116, 195.
31. K has passive ptc. *ntwy* (*nāṭûy*), Q the easier *nāṭāyû*.
32. "Almost" and "nearly" are parallel *k* expressions, with the second taking the first further, "like a little" and "like nothing." The verb forms are parallel (more closely so in

because the "but I" implies a "No" that the suppliant had been uttering inside. Then it contrasts with "God" as the subject of the previous
verse ("God is . . . , but I was . . .) and with Israel/the pure in heart. The
psalmist had all but become someone of embittered heart (v. 21) and/or
of scheming heart (v. 7) rather than of pure heart. That would imperil
a person's place in Israel.

> ³Because I was jealous of the exultant people,
>   of the well-being of the faithless, which I beheld.

It was a natural jealousy that almost brought the suppliant's downfall.
While the OT usually sees it as appropriate for Yhwh to feel jealousy (e.g.,
78:58; contrast 79:5), it tends to see human jealousy as sinful or stupid
(e.g., 37:1; 106:16) unless exercised for Yhwh's sake (e.g., 69:9 [10]; 119:139
is more ambivalent). It likely has some sympathy for marital jealousy
(e.g., Prov. 6:34; 27:4), which provides the analogy for Yhwh's jealousy
over Israel's unfaithfulness, but no sympathy for jealousy toward people
who do well in life through dishonesty. Such jealousy has the capacity
to draw us into emulating them (e.g., Prov. 3:31; 23:17; 24:1, 19), and it
rots the bones (Prov. 14:30). The psalm gives testimony to both of these.
It has already acknowledged how jealousy could have taken the worshipper off the straight and narrow way. It will soon acknowledge the way
jealousy rotted the worshipper's heart (vv. 21–22). The objects of jealousy
are people who are *hôlĕlîm*, which could mean confident and/or boastful
and/or stupid and/or mad (cf. 75:4 [5]).[33] The parallel "*faithless" could
then generalize any of these. When overcome by jealousy, the psalmist
saw only the confident exulting of the faithless and saw the basis for their
attitude in the *well-being they enjoyed as a result of their wrongdoing.
The confident talk of Sennacherib's general or of Sanballat (2 Kings 18–19;
Neh. 4) illustrates the phenomenon. The closing verb is doubly suggestive.
It is the eyes that are the problem (cf. Gen. 3:6). In parallelism with "be
jealous," the verb likely suggests deliberately looking rather than merely
seeing accidentally. And the verb is yiqtol; the psalmist kept looking at
them or could not avoid continually seeing them.

73:4–12. Continuing to move backward, the psalm goes on to detail
the way life worked out for faithless people, which almost derailed the
psalmist.

Q), with the pual adding emphasis to the qal. Then "my footsteps" (lit. "my feet") is followed by "my steps."

33. There is likely more than one verb *hālal*. It is most frequent in the piel, meaning
"praise"; the idea of "exult/boast" is related to that. But sometimes it suggests "be stupid/
mad," sometimes "shine." As at 5:5 [6], Tg has "mock," while LXX and Jerome paraphrase
on the basis of the context.

⁴Because there are no pressures for them threatening their death;
  their belly is stout.

In spelling out their well-being, the first colon is obscurely expressed,
but the second clarifies it. The faithless experience no pressures that
threaten their deaths or make death arrive before it should, as ought
to happen to such people if Yhwh is making life work out the way it is
supposed to. On the contrary, physically they are the picture of health
and prosperity. The preexilic community under siege or the Second
Temple community with its economic hardship would contrast with the
flourishing attackers or rivals.

⁵In the burdens of human beings they have no part;
  they are not afflicted with other people.

The nature of their well-being is explicated further in two negatives.[34]
In isolation the line implies a rather gloomy general view of human experience as characterized by trouble and affliction. The picture of human
life as dominated by burdens (*'āmāl*) would fit Ecclesiastes (e.g., 1:3).
But "burdens" can denote the suffering that comes to some people but
not others (e.g., Ps. 25:18), and the second colon's reference to being afflicted or hit (*nāga'*) makes that point more specific. The faithless are not
liable to the debilitating and life-threatening difficulties that Israelites
are experiencing (e.g., 2 Chron. 26:20; and the noun *nega'*, Ps. 91:10).
Verse 5b thus forms a negative counterpart to v. 4b.

⁶Thus prestige has bedecked them
  while a garment of violence wraps around them.

Translations take *ga'ăwâ* to mean pride in a negative sense (cf. 31:18,
23 [19, 24]), but it often means prestige or majesty (e.g., 68:34 [35]), and
this makes sense here. Because the faithless are successful and people
are inclined to assume that they must have deserved it or to think that
they had better keep in favor with them, they have a prominent and
honored place in the world. Their prestige hangs around their necks
like a garland honoring someone; indeed, they may literally wear victory garlands. And that is so despite the other garments they wear.
The colon's word order works with some subtlety as the line reads

---

34. Structurally the cola are not very parallel, but they have parallel prepositions ("in"
and "with"), parallel words for humanity ("a human being" and "other people"), parallel
negative particles ("they have no part" and "not"), and parallel expressions for suffering
(the noun "burden" and the verb "afflict").

"There wraps a garment—violence for them." Thus initially we think that the garment and the wrapping have positive significance parallel to that of the prestige and the bedecking, but the word *ḥāmās* (lawless violence) turns everything upside down. Never mind the prestige that hangs around their necks as decorative garlands; *ḥāmās* is their actual clothing.

> ⁷Their eye has bulged from callousness,
>   the schemings of their heart have overflowed.

Again the first colon is obscurely expressed: (lit.) "Their eye has gone out from fat." In the OT, reference to human "fat" is generally pejorative, as in English. It usually implies resistance to God; a fat heart is like a hard heart (e.g., 17:10; 119:70). The eye, in turn, expresses what is inside the person, for instance, arrogance or humility or scorn or niggardliness or generosity or pity or desire.[35] So the eye coming out because of fat suggests looks and thus actions that express a person's willfulness. The second colon then parallels this, with its specific reference to the *heart and its scheming.

> ⁸They mock and speak of trouble,
>   from their eminence they speak of extortion.

The faithless people are able to mock the faithful in the sense that they are confident that they can plan *bad things for them and can succeed in implementing these plans. The second colon explains their confidence: they make their plans from their lofty and powerful position (lit. "from on high"). It also explains the nature of the trouble they are planning: oppression, or more specifically extortion, the heavy financial burdens they can place on their victims (*'ōšeq*; cf. 62:10 [11]; 72:4).[36]

> ⁹They have set their mouth in the heavens,
>   and their tongue ranges in the earth.

The high-low metaphor continues. The EVV reckon that the line reworks it; the faithless are not merely looking down on the faithful to speak against them but also looking up to heaven to speak against God with the same confident arrogance. They indeed do that in v. 11, but the second colon does not fit that understanding here. "Heaven and earth"

---

35. See BDB 744b.

36. The parallelism thus works abcc'a'b: "from their eminence" parallels "mock," "extortion" parallels "trouble" (the *b* perhaps carries over), and (unusually) the verb "speak" is exactly repeated.

suggests the world as a whole, and v. 9 rather restates and heightens v. 8 in a fine hyperbole. From their position of eminence and to enforce their will, the faithless can speak words that resound far and wide through the heavens, and they can let their tongues loose in a way that has implications for the whole earth.[37] The words will be the words planning financial oppression of which v. 8 spoke.[38]

> **¹⁰**Thus blows come repeatedly to his people,
> and abundant water is drained by them.

There are two ways of reading the line. For the first colon Jerome has "thus his people turn here [*hălōm*, given its usual meaning]";[39] that is, they are inclined to follow the faithless. The "abundant water" of the second colon would then suggest their enjoying provision and prosperity (cf., e.g., 65:9 [10]; Isa. 66:11–12). But the psalm does not otherwise speak of the people in these negative terms. Further, "abundant water" is more commonly a negative image for overwhelming dangers and distresses (e.g., Pss. 18:16 [17]; 32:6; 46:3 [4]; 66:12; 69:1, 2, 14, 15 [2, 3, 15, 16]), and this understanding seems more likely here, though the verb takes the image in a different direction. These waters do not overflow the people; rather, the people drink them to the dregs. Similar expressions will recur in 75:8 [9] (cf. Isa. 51:17; Ezek. 23:34). The opening of the psalm has declared that God is good to Israel, but what actually happens to "his people" looks quite different.[40] In the first colon, it fits with this to follow Tg in taking *hălōm* as a hapax from *hālam* (smash), which comes in 74:6. "Blows return to his people" is then paralleled by "Abundant water is drained by them."[41]

> **¹¹** And they say, "How would God care?
> Is there recognition with the Most High?"

---

37. Cf. P. A. H. de Boer, "The Meaning of Psalm lxxiii 9," *VT* 18 (1968): 260–64.

38. The parallelism thus again works abcc′a′b′: "range" parallels "set" (but the second verb is third sg. f. yiqtol piel rather than third pl. m. qatal qal), "in the earth" parallels "in the heavens," and "their tongue" parallels "their mouth" (but it is subj. rather than obj.). The suggestion that "mouth" and "tongue" are devouring heaven and earth (Helmer Ringgren, "Einige Bemerkungen zu lxxiii. Psalm," *VT* 3 [1953]: 265–72 [see 267–69]) does not fit the context very well, and while it fits the reference to the mouth, in the OT the tongue is a means of speaking, not of eating.

39. Similarly LXX, though it implies *'ammî* (my people); cf. Syr.

40. B. Renaud ("Le Psaume 73," *RHPR* 59 [1979]: 541–50) sees v. 10 as an aspect of the turning of an individual psalm into one about the community (see the textual comment on v. 1 and the note on v. 15).

41. The prep. is *l*, which could also apply to *'ammô*.

The fact that the faithless are able to get away with their violence and scoffing provokes this conviction. God lives in heaven and/or in the temple and is not involved in everyday life in the world or in the city. The faithless might grant that God "knows," that there is "knowledge" with the Most High (cf. EVV), but *yāda'* and *da'at* more likely indicate that God does not take any notice of what goes on (cf. NEB). The point is underlined by the terms for God, *'ēl* and *'elyôn*. Both suggest the might and power of God: surely this exalted deity does not bother with ordinary this-worldly affairs. But such a view deconstructs. The might of God means that God can and will not only know but also do something about it.

> 12There—these are the faithless,
>   and forever carefree, they have amassed wealth.

"There" is a marker indicating that the section is coming to a close, announcing that the line will be a summary of the nature and experience of the *faithless. But there is then a sharp disjunction between the two cola. The first simply issues its pointer; the second explicates how scandalous all this is. These are people who are always *šālēw*: the word combines the notions of prosperity and freedom from care. The verbal expression then takes up the first nuance.

73:13–14. The facts about the wicked provoked this logical conclusion about the psalmist's experience.

> 13Yes, in vain I have kept my heart clean,
>   washed my hands in innocence.

The "Yes" parallels the "Yes" that opened the psalm, but it introduces a statement of conviction clashing with the earlier one.[42] Once again the psalmist refers to a heart that is unsullied, here speaking of having made sure that this was so (using the verb *zākâ* rather than the adjective *bar*). The second colon parallels that claim with another verb for "cleansing" and with a claim to purity of behavior and not merely purity of heart. Paradoxically, cleansing one's hands presupposes that actually they are clean in the sense that they do not have blood on them, like the hands of the faithless (cf. Isa. 1:15–16), though they might be affected by blood that had come through actions other than one's own (Deut. 21:1–9). The psalmist can claim such innocence: not sinlessness, of course, but the innocence of a relatively righteous person of honorable life. The person who is to ascend Yhwh's mountain needs to have innocent hands and a

42. LXX spells this out by beginning "And I said . . ."

pure heart, and such a person can expect to carry away Yhwh's blessing and faithfulness (Ps. 24:3–5). This has not proved true. The claim to a clean heart and innocent hands stands under the sign of the "in vain" that followed the opening "Yes." That righteous life was pointless. It led nowhere.

> [14]I have come to be afflicted continuously,
> and my reproof is each morning.

While a member of "his people" affected by the blows and the unpleasant drought of v. 10, only now does the psalmist tell us about being personally affected by the wrongdoing of the faithless. The problem of evil is one thing when it is an intellectual problem about the way God treats other people. It is another thing when we are personally affected. Whereas the faithless are not "afflicted" (v. 5) but rather are "ever" carefree (v. 12), affliction is the psalmist's continuous experience. The second colon parallels "continuously" (lit. "all the day") by "each morning," and the verb "afflict" by the noun "reproof."[43] The sequence recalls the way foes such as the Rabshakeh or Sanballat combined action with insult but also the common experience reflected in the Psalms and in Job, that the individual sufferer's affliction was compounded by the fact that people added to it their rebuke for the wrongdoing that the psalmist was assumed to be guilty of.

73:15–20. We know from the psalm's opening that vv. 13–14 cannot have been the psalmist's final conclusion. Now we learn the process that led from this interim suspicion to that declaration of conviction.

> [15]If I had said I would speak out like that—
> there, I would have betrayed the company of your children.

The psalmist has given us the impression of having indeed said this, but evidently the words had been uttered only in the heart. They were never uttered outwardly as a public declaration (*sāpar* piel). That would have been an act of unfaithfulness. One might have thought it would be an act of betrayal in relation to God (cf. 78:57), but the line focuses on its implications for the psalmist's relationship with the community (cf. 25:3; 59:5 [6]); "company" (*dôr*) is another expression paralleling Ps. 24:3–6.[44]

---

43. EVV have "punishment," but *tôkaḥat* and the verb *yākaḥ* almost invariably refer to something verbal (cf. LXX and Jerome).

44. J. Clinton McCann ("Psalm 73," in *The Listening Heart* [Roland E. Murphy Festschrift; ed. Kenneth G. Hoglund et al.; JSOTSup 58; Sheffield: JSOT, 1987], 247–57 [see 250]) sees v. 15 as the center of the psalm, reflecting the fact that the psalm as a whole is community oriented.

They are God's children. It would mean letting them down. They need people to stand firm in faith when under pressure as a testimony to the truth of the faith even in those circumstances and as an inspiration. In particular, they need their leader to do that.

> 16So I thought to understand this,
>   which was the burden in my eyes,

It is the combination of suffering and unintelligibility that is hard to live with (unintelligible blessing is fine; intelligible suffering—for instance, when we do wrong and suffer—we can live with). Generally, suppliants in the Psalms want the suffering removed, but Ps. 73 wants the unintelligibility removed; hence its appeal to academic readers of the Psalms. The psalmist longs for understanding, for knowledge (*da'at*). The psalm has spoken of God's supposed lack of knowledge (v. 11). Have the faithless spoken for the fear in the psalmist's own heart? Is there anything to know? The second colon in turn picks up "trouble/burden" from v. 5, as v. 14 picked up "afflicted."[45] The psalmist needs to understand the burdened nature of Israel's experience.

> 17As I went to God's sanctuary,
>   where I would consider their end.

In what connection did the psalmist go into the sanctuary, and how did that make the difference? Perhaps the psalm refers to an occasion of worship such as one of the great festivals. It is a standard function of such worship to enable us to reframe the way we see things, usually by reaffirming the truths we know, not by our seeing wholly new things. When Israelites worship, they reaffirm that Yhwh is the king of kings and lord of lords. Looking at Yhwh in the sanctuary means gaining a new awareness of Yhwh's power and honor (63:2 [3]). That is indeed not a new truth, but it is something that everyday life can seem to belie. When people have seen its truth once more, this sends them out from worship able to live their everyday lives in light of the knowledge that it really is true. In a similar way, the psalmist knew that the faithless were on their way to getting their comeuppance, but everyday experience seemed to belie it. Going into the sanctuary made it possible to reflect on that truth and generated a new conviction about it. For *bîn* (consider), NRSV has "perceived," TNIV "understood," but that implies that the psalmist gained new insight, whereas the "solution" the psalm

---

45. EVV take the "trouble" to lie in the task of understanding, but there are no parallels for this usage of *'āmāl*, and the link with v. 5 also makes it more likely that the word keeps its usual meaning.

goes on to share is more a reaffirmation of regular Israelite insight, as in NJPS's "reflected on."

But going into the sanctuary need not imply an act of worship. The psalmist might just have sat there and meditated or talked with a priest. Indeed, reading this psalm in light of the one that follows would suggest it was the ruined sanctuary that the psalmist went to[46] and that it was the enormity of what the faithless had done there that made it certain that Yhwh would bring about their downfall. But one way or another, in the sanctuary the psalmist gained a new conviction about the "end" or destiny the faithless were on their way to.

> [18]Yes, you will set them among deceptions;
>   you are making them fall to lies.

Verses 18–20 explain the nature of that end, beginning with another "Yes" (cf. vv. 1, 13).[47] They first focus on how this end will come about. It implies some poetic justice. The faithless have their way through the "schemings" (v. 7) whereby they engineer trouble for people in the manner of Sanballat. They will fall to similar devices, as often happens in circles where deception becomes the stock in trade (cf. the sardonic account of Second Temple history in Dan. 11). And/or, in another poetic justice, they will find themselves devastated, like the sanctuary itself (74:3).[48]

> [19]How they are coming to destruction in a moment,
>   coming to a complete end through horrors.

Their fall will be sudden and complete (again the picture compares with Dan. 11; also Isa. 41:11–12). It will happen—indeed it has as good as happened—with a suddenness and a thoroughness unexpected both by the faithless themselves and by their victims (cf. Ps. 6:10 [11]).[49] Thus there is an appalling horror about it. "Horrors" (*ballāhôt*) often suggests coming to a dreadful end in sudden death (e.g., Ezek. 26:21) as one falls into the hands of the king of horrors (Job 18:14).

46. Cf. Cole, *Shape and Message of Book III*, 22–23.
47. After that, the cola are closely parallel. "You are making them fall" (instantaneous qatal) balances but takes further (in tense and meaning) "You will set them" (yiqtol), and the prepositional expression "to lies" balances "among deceptions."
48. Cole, *Shape and Message of Book III*, 25.
49. Again, after the introductory "how" the cola are closely parallel. "They are coming to a complete end" (more lit. "They are coming to an end, they are ceasing") balances but adds emphasis to "They are coming to destruction" (both expressions are instantaneous qatal), and the prepositional expression "through horrors" balances and takes further "in a moment." EVV's "are swept away" apparently nuances the meaning of *sûp* (come to an end) in light of the noun *sûpâ* (storm wind).

> [20]Like a dream, after you awake, my Lord,
> when you arise, you will despise their shadow.

The imagery further underlines Yhwh's involvement in what will happen (v. 18) and the complete nature of the destruction (v. 19), though again the line is difficult to construe.[50] I understand it to work abcb'da': on awaking or arising, the *Lord will despise the faithless as a mere dream, a mere shadow. Whereas v. 19 spoke simply about what will happen to the faithless, v. 20 returns to Yhwh's involvement in this (cf. v. 18), going behind Yhwh's actual action to the stirring that leads to action. At the moment nothing is happening; Yhwh is sitting inactive in the face of wrongdoing as if asleep (cf., e.g., 44:23–26 [24–27]). But going to the sanctuary has reinforced in the psalmist the assurance that Yhwh *will* stir and *will* arise. When that happens, the menace of these faithless people will be no more than the menace of a bad dream, which may be terrifying when it happens but is nothing when one wakes up, or the menace of a dark shadow that can seem threatening but actually has no corresponding reality. Yhwh (and their victims) can despise or dismiss the faithless as that. The Tg applies the verse to the final judgment; the psalm itself reckons that God is involved in present experience.

73:21–26. Verses 18–20 concern the facts of what will happen; vv. 21–26 turn to the worshipper's consequent attitude in a series of reversals of the attitude expressed earlier in the psalm.[51]

> [21]When my heart is embittered,
> and my spirit—I am pierced through,

The EVV have past tenses through vv. 21–22, but the first three verbs are yiqtol, so more likely the psalm generalizes its point. Being under attack from people and having Yhwh sit and do nothing can have a devastating effect on the heart or spirit (lit. "kidneys"; cf. 7:9 [10]; 16:7; 26:2; 139:13).[52] The psalm uses two rare and vivid verbs. "Is embittered" links with words for sourdough and vinegar (cf. 69:22). "I am pierced through" comes from *šānan* "sharpen," an unusual verb used in

50. Lit. "Like a dream from waking, Lord, in arising you will despise their shadow." The line thus does not make explicit who is the subject of the two gerunds. Translations take the first two words as a simile making a comparison with a human being awaking from a dream, but the parallelism suggests that the whole line more likely refers to Yhwh.

51. Cf. Leslie C. Allen, "Psalm 73: An Analysis," *Tyndale Bulletin* 33 (1982): 93–118 (see 104).

52. The line works abcc'b': after the opening "for," the two verbs are parallel (hitpael and hitpolel), as are "my heart" and "my kidneys." But the second verb, the last word in the line, is a surprising first person.

a number of metaphorical and/or idiomatic ways that will also bring to mind the much more common word *šēn*, "tooth" (also *šĕnînâ*, "cutting word/taunt"). The verbs express the paradox that our embitteredness and pain is both something that comes upon us and also something we are responsible for. And it is something we can find a way out from, the psalm testifies.

> ²²Then I am stupid and I have no sense;
>   I became a monster with you.

The psalm acknowledges the devastating further results of letting oneself become embittered and hurt. It makes a person behave in a dim and foolish fashion, like someone who knows nothing. In what sense? The second colon explains. First, it picks up an ambiguity in the word for "stupid," *ba'ar*, which links etymologically with words such as *bĕ'îr*, "animal." Thus "stupid" is capable of suggesting that one has no more intelligence than a donkey. In the second colon the suppliant confesses to having been a *bĕhēmôt*: the word is the plural of the word for cattle, but in the plural it suggests a monster, concretely a hippopotamus or crocodile, yet also a monster that embodies resistance to God's purpose (Job 40:15).[53] So the psalm confesses that bitterness and hurt generate an attitude to God that has the stupid, pretentious, clumsy aggressiveness of a demonic monster. "With you" is slightly odd in this context, but the expression will be picked up in vv. 23 and 25 and by anticipation suggests the enormity of that attitude when all along the worshipper had actually been "with you."[54]

> ²³But I have always been with you;
>   you have held my right hand.

The opening *wa'ănî* compares and contrasts with the one that opened v. 22, and the subsequent "with you" also compares and contrasts with the one that closed v. 22 (cf. also v. 25). I was with you in a really bad sense (v. 22), but I came to realize that I was with you in a really good sense (v. 23) and that this is all I need (v. 25). The qatal verbs also contrast with the yiqtols in vv. 21–22a (TNIV and NRSV largely reverse the tenses). The psalmist thus moves from the generalizations in the present in vv. 21–22 to a realization concerning the past, that the awareness of abandonment was actually misleading. The fact that Yhwh was doing nothing meant a form of abandonment, but in another sense it

53. On the honorific or intensive pl., see on 45:9 [10]; 49:3 [4]; 53:6 [7].
54. Cf. M. Mannati, "Sur le quadruple *avec toi* de Ps. lxxiii 21–26," *VT* 21 (1971): 59–67 (he adds another "with you" in v. 25a).

did not mean that. The psalmist has still been in Yhwh's presence. In what sense has that been so? In modern parlance this would imply something about our inner sense of God's presence, "in communion with God,"[55] but in clarifying the question, the second colon points in a different direction. I have been with God in the sense that God has been holding my right hand: that is, actually God has been active, supporting me not merely emotionally but also practically. After all, the attacks of the faithless could have overcome me or killed me, but they have not. I remain standing. Yhwh's taking the suppliant's right hand re-expresses, complements, and makes more concrete the idea of the suppliant being with Yhwh. When a powerful person stands at the right hand of the weak or needy (109:31; 121:5), it means they will be protected or rescued. When Yhwh actually takes the right hand of someone, it indicates identification with them and gives them divine recognition and support, as God does to Israel (Isa. 41:13). If not a king (cf. Isa. 45:1), the psalmist has been treated like one.

> [24]In your purpose you will lead me;
> after, you will take me to honor.

The psalm returns to yiqtol verbs, and it makes sense to refer these to what Yhwh is doing now and will be doing.[56] The EVV's "You will guide me with your counsel" makes it sound as if Yhwh is giving advice in order to guide the psalmist's decision-making, but it makes better sense to take ʿēṣâ here to suggest Yhwh's wise and effective purpose or plan or intention (cf. 14:6; 20:4 [5]; 33:10–11).[57] Likewise "leading" implies more than merely pointing the way: Yhwh actually takes the psalmist to the fulfillment of that intention (cf. 5:8 [9]; 31:3 [4]; 43:3; 67:4 [5]; 107:30; 139:10). The second colon explicates this, though the parallelism means that in isolation it is somewhat elliptical; prosaically put, the line declares, "Afterward, in your purpose you will lead me and take me to honor."[58] Whatever is the reason for Yhwh's not acting now but rather leaving the faithless in power, this will not be the end of the story. Yhwh is still committed to working out that purpose. Thus "after" (i.e., afterward, in due course) things will change. At the moment the psalmist is mocked and reproved (vv. 8, 14), but Yhwh will bring about a restoration to honor

55. Briggs, *Psalms*, 2:147.
56. Contrast NJPS, which oddly has past tense verbs.
57. Cf. Cassiodorus, *Explanation of the Psalms*, 2:206.
58. Or, if the prep. and suffix on ʿēṣâ apply also to kābôd, "afterward, in your purpose you will lead me, and in your honor you will take me." But "take" is then rather elliptical (in, e.g., 18:16 [17]; 49:15 [16], the context gives more indication of whence or whither God takes the speaker).

instead of shame. The psalmist's "after" (*'aḥar*) thereby contrasts with the "end" (*'aḥărît*) of the faithless (v. 17). Thus Tg's "After the honor that you said you would bring upon me is complete" explicates the point well;[59] Theodoret refers it to the return from the exile (the oppressors in the psalm being the Babylonians).[60] In contrast the Midrash assumes that the psalm solves its problem by appeal to a future life.[61] But there is no specific reason to take "after" to mean "after this life" nor to understand the common verb "take" to refer to "taking to heaven," nor is there any parallel for understanding *honor (*kābôd*) to refer to heavenly glory.[62] Rather, this is the honor that Yhwh gives to a person such as David and his successors (1 Chron. 17:18; 29:12), the kind of honor the similar Ps. 49 spoke of (see Ps. 49:16–17 [17–18]) and/or the kind of honor in the community whose loss Ps. 7:5 [6] protested.[63]

> [25]Whom do I have in the heavens?—
> and with you, I have not wanted anyone on the earth.

Prosaically put, "Whom do I have in the heavens or on the earth?" (humanly speaking, the answer is "No one"). "But with you I have not wanted [anyone]." The faithless speak in a way that resounds through the heavens and through the earth (v. 9), assuming the possession of power on earth and perhaps implicitly dismissing the idea that anyone exercises power in or from the heavens (cf. v. 11). The rhetorical question in v. 25 is then one with positive implications. There is indeed someone in the heavens, and this is someone who, in a real sense, belongs to the psalmist, who has gained a new assurance of having God's support there. Further, contrary to the implicit view of the faithless (the second colon adds), this makes a difference on earth. While the psalmist has now received spiritual and emotional reassurance from God, this is not all God promises. The psalmist has no need to look for anyone on earth apart from the God of the heavens, who is active here, or no need to desire to look for some other god because Yhwh does not come through.

59. But MT's disjunctive accent on *'aḥar* shows that it took this as the conjunction "afterward," not the prep. "after."

60. *Commentary on the Psalms*, 2:8.

61. *Midrash on Psalms*, 2:1.

62. Though in the NT, compare 1 Tim. 3:16 (Gunkel, *Psalmen*, 319). Markus Witte, "Auf dem Weg in ein Leben nach dem Tod," *TZ* 58 (2002): 15–30, sees vv. 24–26 as a later addition to the psalm to give it this meaning. S. Jellicoe suggests that *kābôd* means "theophany" ("The Interpretation of Psalm lxxiii. 24," *ExpT* 67 [1955–56]: 209–10). For *kābôd* (without a prep.) used to mean "to honor," cf. Prov. 29:23.

63. Cf. Harris Birkeland, "The Chief Problems of Ps 73 17ff," *ZAW* 67 (1955): 99–103 (see 102).

> ²⁶Although my flesh and my heart have come to an end,
>   God is the crag of my heart and my allocation, forever.

"I am done for, I am finished, I am as good as dead" (cf. Prov. 5:11). That is true of the psalmist's outer person and of the inner, as v. 21 has made clear. Yet that situation can be transformed through Yhwh's being involved and through the renewed realization that Yhwh is involved even when it does not look like it. The line works abcc'b'de. First, "Forever, God is" stands against "have come to an end." The psalmist's physical and spiritual resources really have come to an end, but that is not all that has to be said. Against the limitations of "I" are set the limitlessness of "God," and against the limitations of "have come to an end" are set the limitlessness of "forever"—in other words, to the end of my life (for this meaning of *lĕʿôlām*, see, e.g., 44:8 [9]; 45:2 [3]; 52:9 [11]; 61:4, 7 [5, 8]). The "forever" balances the one in v. 12 and also, by being the last word in the longest line in the psalm thus far, makes the line threaten to last forever.[64]

Specifically, against "my flesh" is set "my allocation." My flesh coming to an end may suggest that the faithless have torn it all off and consumed it (cf. Mic. 3:2–3). But the word is *šĕʾēr*, not the more usual *bāśār*. This could suggest "my kin" (e.g., Num. 27:11), which would add resonance to Yhwh's being the psalmist's allocation, because the exhausting of "my kin" would imply that the family's allocation of land would fall into abeyance and would have to be taken over by someone else. Either way, the psalmist's coming to the end of resources would not be the end, because Yhwh is the psalmist's metaphorical allocation as Yhwh was for the priests who had no land (Num. 18:20; cf. Pss. 119:57; 142:5 [6]; Lam. 3:24). Then, "the crag of my heart" corresponds to "my heart." When the inner person is in a state of collapse, this too need not be the end. In its metaphorical usage, a crag is usually a place where a person climbs to take refuge (e.g., 61:2 [3]; 71:3), which makes poor sense here. Perhaps the crag is here a source of resource and refreshment (e.g., 78:15, 20; 81:16 [17]).

73:27–28. The last two lines sum up the psalmist's renewed conviction.

> ²⁷For now: people who are far from you perish;
>   you are terminating everyone who is unfaithful to you.

---

64. The word order (crag-of-my-heart and-my-allocation God forever) makes it hard to take v. 26 as a tricolon (against Fokkelman, *Major Poems*, 2:193; cf. TNIV); MT thus makes it a four-stress colon.

The "now" confronts the "now" introducing the interim false conclusion in v. 12, that the faithless are always carefree and prosperous. After the opening "for now," the line works abb'a'. If the faithless in vv. 3–12 are other peoples, presumably it is not they who appear here as people who are far from Yhwh and unfaithful to Yhwh. These are rather people the psalmist could have been tempted to join, Israelites who give up their adherence to Yhwh and have recourse to other gods. Being far from Yhwh does not denote having a feeling of being distanced from God when we might like to feel near. It is to have chosen to move away from Yhwh (cf. 119:150), moving away in order to approach another deity (cf. Jer. 2:5; Ezek. 44:10). The second colon makes that point more explicit in using the verb *zānâ*, which denotes forbidden sexual activity, including unfaithfulness to one's spouse, and thus metaphorically the worship of other gods (e.g., Jer. 3:1; Ezek 23; Ps. 106:39); appropriately, one is literally unfaithful *from* Yhwh. The natural result of moving away from the source of life is to lose one's life. The second colon makes more explicit how that happens. It is not merely the natural result by a process intrinsic to the act. It is something Yhwh deliberately brings about; the psalm uses quite a violent and frightening verb (cf., e.g., 54:5 [7]; 69:4 [5]; 94:23). The second colon underlines the point further by making explicit that this applies to "everyone" and by using the instantaneous perfect instead of the yiqtol.

---

²⁸But for me—nearness to God is good for me;
  I have made my Lord Yhwh my refuge,
  so as to speak out about all your acts.

A tricolon closes off the psalm. As the "now" of v. 27 picked up v. 12, the "but for me" (lit. "but I") picks up vv. 2, 22, 23, introducing a declaration that will contrast with vv. 2 and 22 and reaffirm v. 23. As distance from God is more than merely an inward matter, so also is nearness to God; it reworks the idea of being "with God" (v. 25). The psalmist is now aware of being close to God even when it does not look (or feel) like it. Further, the psalmist is aware of a commitment to coming near to Yhwh to worship and seek Yhwh's help (cf. 65:4 [5]; 119:169; 148:14) rather than moving away from Yhwh to approach other deities or to look to other resources so as to fix things for oneself. That will be "good for me" because it will prove itself to be the means of Yhwh being good to me, acting on my behalf, delivering me. The word "good" in turn picks up v. 1.

The second colon re-expresses the point. Being near God means making my *Lord Yhwh my *refuge, the one who is committed to being the place of safety where I hide and thus find that deliverance. It is not that the psalmist is now satisfied with a spiritual nearness to God and therefore can live with people's attacks. The psalm's duality is present-future, not inner-outer or earthly-heavenly. The psalmist is now once more convinced that God comes through for people and does act to put down wrongdoers. Whereas the faithless set their mouth in the heavens, God will set them among deceptions, and therefore the psalmist can set or make God as refuge: the verb is again *šît*. The collocation of God (*'ĕlōhîm*), my Lord, and Yhwh near the close of the psalm in the confession of a psalmist who stands for Israel parallels and confronts the collocation of God (*'ēl*) and the Most High in the dismissive question of the faithless in v. 11.

Like the psalm's opening, its final colon corresponds to a standard element in a testimony psalm, though it makes the point in a distinctive way, in an infinitival clause appended to the declaration in v. 28a–b.[65] The verb picks up from v. 15: there has been a speaking out that the worshipper has resisted, but the closing colon looks forward to another very different speaking out. Recounting *all* Yhwh's acts suggests that the psalm leaps over the prospect of giving praise for the act of deliverance that the psalm looks for to giving praise for the broader range of Yhwh's acts of deliverance that go back to the exodus. This particular act will take its place in that sequence and make it possible to celebrate them with new conviction. Yhwh's acts of deliverance in the past are a true guide to what we may expect from Yhwh now.

Theological Implications

Psalm 72 prayed that God would act through the king so as to grant well-being and freedom from violence and extortion forever (vv. 3, 4, 14, 17). But often, all one can see is the well-being of the faithless and their exercise of violence and oppression forever (73:3, 6, 8, 12).[66] At the beginning of Book III of the Psalter, Ps. 73 restates the convictions of Pss. 1–2 but does so in light of the realism that has characterized the rest of Books I and II.[67] "Initially the psalmist was on slippery ground (vv. 1–3), while the wicked seemed secure (vv. 4–12). In the end the reverse is true; the wicked are slipping (vv. 18–20) and the psalmist is stable (vv. 21–28)";

---

65. Dahood (*Psalms*, 2:196) sees the inf. as circumstantial, but whereas the previous clause refers to the past, the telling of Yhwh's acts must be future, when Yhwh has again acted; the inf. is thus of purpose. LXX adds "in the gates of Maiden Zion," which makes a good double bicolon rather than MT's closing tricolon.

66. Cole, *Shape and Message of Book III*, 15–16.

67. McCann, "Psalms," 967–68; cf. Walter Brueggemann, "Bounded by Obedience and Praise," *JSOT* 50 (1991): 63–92; Walter Brueggemann and Patrick D. Miller, "Psalm 73 as a Canonical Marker," *JSOT* 72 (1996): 45–56.

likewise, initially the wicked seem to be doing well "forever" whereas the psalmist is perpetually afflicted, but in the end the wicked come to a complete end in a moment, whereas actually God was continually with the psalmist and was the psalmist's allocation "forever."[68] The psalm brings out a feature that characterizes many psalms. The change that comes over the psalmist issued not from Yhwh's having acted but from the psalmist having gained a conviction that Yhwh will act. The psalm thus expresses a renewed orientation toward the wicked (vv. 18–20), toward the self (vv. 21–22), and toward God (vv. 23–26).[69] After being the subject of the opening declaration (v. 1), God totally disappears through vv. 2–14, crowded out by "I" (with a focus on the psalmist's feelings) and "they" (with a focus on the activity of the faithless). Verse 11 is the exception that proves the rule; there God appears, only to be dismissed. Then things change, though only gradually. First, Yhwh is the reference of the "your" in v. 15, and v. 17 refers to God's sanctuary. In vv. 18 and 20 God is addressed and becomes the subject of the verbs and in v. 20 is at last invoked ("my Lord"). The address continues in the interwoven confession and testimony that dominate vv. 22–28, where in each line God is the addressee or the subject.[70]

Thus the psalmist's heart has changed. In light of the recurrence of reference to the heart (vv. 1, 7, 13, 21, 26a, 26b), Martin Buber comments that in Ps. 73 "the heart determines."[71] Faithfulness needs to be a matter of the heart and thus the actions of the hands, not merely a matter of our words, for it is the heart that generates schemes against other people. Likewise the heart needs to be the locus of trust within us, otherwise we become embittered. These are demanding expectations, and the pressures of life may mean that we come to the end of our hearts' resources; but even this need not be a catastrophe, because when our hearts come to an end, God is still its place of refuge.

The declarations in Pss. 1–2 that the faithful flourish and the faithless perish and that God rules the world through the anointed king of Israel have been severely tested in the psalms that follow. Indeed, Ps. 2 itself began from an experience that seemed to conflict with Ps. 1 but declared that it would not always be so, and Ps. 73 does the same, reaffirming the truth of these declarations but (like Ps. 2) acknowledging that they are made by faith rather than by sight.[72] Psalm 2's closing reference to

68. Schaefer, *Psalms*, 178.

69. Tate, *Psalms 51–100*, 238–39.

70. See Pierre Auffret, "Et moi sans cesse avec toi," *SJOT* 9 (1995): 241–76 (see 273–74).

71. *Right and Wrong* (London: SCM, 1952), 34 = *Good and Evil* (New York: Scribner's, 1952), 31.

72. Cole, *Shape and Message of Book III*, 26.

Yhwh's being a refuge also tacitly acknowledged the facts about life that have since become prominent; it presupposed that people would be under pressure and would need a refuge. Here v. 28 reaffirms this in light of the explicitly owned reality of such pressure. More specifically, it begins from the problem as Pss. 37 and 49 acknowledge it (though it feels the problem more acutely)[73] and affirms the same solution.[74] Succeeding psalms will continue to reflect the fact that life does not work out in accordance with the theory, like the laments that follow Pss. 1–2.

Psalm 73 is a highpoint in the Psalter. Often it has been so described in the conviction that it looks forward to heaven and/or because it focuses on an inner relationship with God in the present.[75] Actually it does neither of these. Like Job it courageously and spiritually insists on maintaining faith in a God who is active in the present, not just in an afterlife, and a God who is active in the visible world, not just in an invisible inner life. When Paul affirms that God delivers not only from wrath in the future (1 Thess. 1:10) but also from this-worldly perils (2 Cor. 1:10), he follows the convictions of the psalm that God is more than a presence in the individual's afterlife and an inner presence.[76]

The psalm's expectation is thus like that in the book of Job (whom God does deliver) and unlike that in Ecclesiastes (which focuses on the fact that often God does not deliver). It also parallels Mal. 3:13–4:3 [3:13–21],[77] and the convictions expressed there show how this expectation need not relate merely to the experience of an individual. The fulfillment of its vision could come in the life of the community when Yhwh's day arrives.

73. Cf. Crenshaw, *Psalms*, 114–15.
74. Cf. Dahood, *Psalms*, 2:188.
75. See, e.g., Hossfeld and Zenger, *Psalms 2*, 238.
76. Cf. Leslie C. Allen, "Psalm 73: Pilgrimage from Doubt to Faith," *BBR* 7 (1997): 1–9 (see 9).
77. Gerstenberger, *Psalms*, 2:72.

Psalm 74

What Is Permanent?

Translation

Instruction. Asaph's.

¹Why have you spurned permanently, God?
 Why does your anger smoke at the flock you pasture?
²Be mindful of your assembly, which you acquired of old,
 which you restored as your very own tribe,
Mount Zion, where you settled:
  ³direct your steps to the permanent ruins,[1]
  all the wrong the enemy brought about in the sanctuary.[2]

⁴Your attackers roared in the midst of the place of assembly;
 they treat their signs as signs.
⁵It would look[3] like someone bringing up
 axes against a forest thicket,

---

1. See the note on 73:18.
2. The three cola in vv. 2c–3 relate rather loosely to each other. Initially one would understand "Mount Zion" as a further obj. of "be mindful," though in light of v. 3 one might rather take it as an extraposed obj. of the verb in v. 3a. In turn, v. 3b hangs rather loosely onto v. 3a. Perhaps the *l* on *lĕmaššu'ôt* also applies to *kol*, though that is itself presumably the obj. of the succeeding verb (lit. "everything [that] the enemy did wrongly/calamitously in the sanctuary"); cf. the use of *rā'a'* hiphil in Mic. 3:4. Alternatively, the use of the verb in (e.g.) Num. 16:15 to mean "hurt" (a person) might justify "everything [that] the enemy harmed."
3. Cf. Barthélemy, *Psaumes*, 536; lit. "It would make itself known." But *yiwwāda'* is difficult; LXX links it with the previous line, adding a negative. For possible emendations of vv. 4–5, see J. A. Emerton, "Notes on Three Passages in Psalms Book III," *JTS*, n.s., 14 (1963): 374–81 (see 374–77); P. R. Ackroyd, "Some Notes on the Psalms," *JTS*, n.s., 17

[6]And now[4] its engravings[5] altogether
    they would smash with hatchet and cleavers.
[7]They gave over your sanctuary to fire, down to the ground;[6]
    they violated the place where your name had settled.
[8]They said in their heart, "We will put them down[7] altogether";
    they burned all God's places of assembly in the land.
[9]We have not seen our signs,
    there have no longer been prophets,
    there has been no one with us who knew how long.

[10]How long shall the foe scoff, God—
    shall the enemy revile your name permanently?
[11]Why do you turn back your hand,
    yes,[8] withholding[9] your right hand from the midst of your
        garments?[10]

[12]But God, my king of old,
    bringer of deliverance[11] in the midst of the earth,[12]
[13]You were the one who parted the sea[13] by your might,
    shattered the heads of the dragons on the waters.

(1966): 392–99 (see 392–93); A. Robinson, "A Possible Solution to the Problem of Psalm 74 5," *ZAW* 89 (1977): 120–21.

4. Instead of *'attā*, K may imply *'ēt* (time), which is difficult to construe ("and the time [when] its engravings . . ."?); but it may simply be a spelling variant.

5. LXX and Sym imply the easier *pĕtāḥêhā* (its doors) for MT *pittûḥêhā*.

6. MT less naturally links "to the ground" with what follows ("they profaned to the ground").

7. LXX, Tg, and Jerome take *nînām* to mean "your offspring," but this is harder to make sense of.

8. MT links "yes, your right hand" with the first colon, but the parallelism makes it more likely that it belongs to the second (cf. LXX, Vg). The *w* is explanatory (DG 37).

9. Tg takes *kallēh* straightforwardly as piel impv. from *kālâ*, but this requires a jerky understanding of the line (". . . yes, your right hand from the midst of your garments—destroy"). LXX and Jerome with "forever" perhaps take the word as inf. abs. used adverbially. With Eaton (*Psalms*, 189), I rather take it as piel inf. abs. from *kālā'*; cf. *yikleh* from this verb (Gen. 23:6; and see GKC 75qq). This spelling makes a link with 73:26 (see Cole, *Shape and Message of Book III*, 30). One could emend to produce a more regular form of *kālā'* (see, e.g., Kraus, *Psalms 60–150*, 96). The prep. makes the expression elliptical, "withholding your right hand [so that it does not come out] from the midst of your garments."

10. K implies *ḥôq* (statute) for Q *ḥēq* ("bosom" or the fold in one's garments there).

11. Pl., suggesting "acts of deliverance."

12. To take this as a statement, "Yet God my king is from of old . . . ," fits less well, since the lines on either side are addressed to God, and vv. 1–3, 10–11, and 18–23 all address God in their first line.

13. Jonas C. Greenfield hypothesizes another verb *pārar* and translates "made the sea flee" ("*'Attā pōrartā bĕ'ozkā yam*," in *Language, Theology, and the Bible* [James Barr Festschrift; ed. Samuel E. Balentine and John Barton; Oxford: Oxford University Press, 1994], 113–19).

[14]You were the one who crushed the heads of Leviathan;
   you would make it food for a company of wildcats.[14]
[15]You were the one who split spring and stream;
   you were the one who dried up perennial rivers.[15]
[16]Day is yours, night also is yours;
   you were the one who established the light, yes, the sun.
[17]You were the one who set all the bounds of the earth;
   summer and autumn, you were the one who shaped them.

[18]Be mindful of this; the enemy has taunted, Yhwh,[16]
   a crass people has reviled your name.
[19]Do not give the life of your dove[17] to an animal;[18]
   do not permanently ignore the life[19] of your weak people.
[20]Have regard for the covenant,
   for pastures of violence fill the dark places in the land.[20]
[21]The broken must not turn back[21] disgraced;
   the weak and needy must praise your name.
[22]Arise, God, defend your cause,
   be mindful of your taunting by a crass people all the time.
[23]Do not ignore the voice of your watchful foes,
   the uproar of those who arise against you, going up continually.

Interpretation

The psalm presupposes a similar situation to Ps. 73, and verbal links (notably the only other occurrence of the word translated "ruins" in v. 3;

14. Lit. "for a people, for wildcats." NJPS takes the *ṣîyîm* to be sailors (from *ṣî* I rather than *ṣî* II), but sailors eating Leviathan's heads seems a rather bizarre picture. On *BHS*'s emendation *lĕʾamlĕṣê yām* (to the sharks of the sea), see CP 236–37; see also Mitchell Dahood, "Vocative *Lamedh* in Psalm 74,14," *Bib* 59 (1978): 262–63; Theodor H. Gaster, "Psalm lxxiv.14," *ExpT* 68 (1956–57): 382.

15. Lit. "rivers of perennial" or "rivers of perennial-ness" (see GKC 128w; BDB 450b).

16. LXX implies "the enemy has taunted Yhwh," but more likely the construction follows that in v. 10, and "your name" is also the implicit obj. of "taunt."

17. For MT *tôrekā*, LXX implies *tôdekā*, "the one who confesses you." But Christopher T. Begg ("The Covenantal Dove in Psalm lxxiv 19–20," *VT* 37 [1987]: 78–81) suggests that "dove" does have covenantal implications.

18. *Ḥayyat* is apparently a dialectical alternative to *ḥayyâ*. LXX and Jerome have pl. "animals," perhaps implying *ḥayyōt*; Syr implies *hawwōt* (destruction).

19. *Ḥayyat* recurs as a const., meaning "life," which was the meaning of *nepeš* in the first colon. Thus the line uses *ḥayyat* in two different ways and uses two different words for "life."

20. LXX and Aq imply "The dark places in the land are full of pastures of violence"; *mālēʾ* can mean "be full of" or "fill."

21. Syr implies *yēšēb* (dwell) for MT *yāšōb*.

cf. 73:18) suggest that it was deliberately placed to follow Ps. 73. But its drive lies elsewhere, and placed here it thus builds on Ps. 73. The fact that Yhwh is going to put down the faithless (Ps. 73) provides the basis for urging Yhwh to do so (Ps. 74). The two psalms complement each other. In Ps. 73 the thinking of an individual was prominent, though the individual spoke as a member of the community, and this poked through at one or two points. In Ps. 74 the community has the prominence, though conversely the individuality of a representative pokes through in v. 12 (but it is noteworthy that only in vv. 9 and 12 do first-person verbs or suffixes appear at all).[22] The psalm is thus a community prayer. Verses 1–3 comprise an opening questioning and plea, ending with a tricolon. Verses 4–9 protest the desolation the enemy wrought, again ending with a tricolon, after which vv. 10–11 return to questioning. Verses 12–17 then speak about a different kind of past, when Yhwh acted in power; this contrasts with Yhwh's present inaction and suggests a different basis for urging Yhwh to act. The psalm then closes in vv. 18–23 with a further plea; every verse there has an imperative, an imperatival yiqtol, or a jussive.[23]

We do not know what was the event that brought about the devastation of Yhwh's sanctuary and indicated Yhwh's rejection of the people, though the fall of Jerusalem in 587 is the obvious candidate.[24] In the years immediately after that event, an inquiry as to the reason for it might have met with a snorting reply from Yhwh. Lamentations recognizes that the reason is obvious. But the psalm starts from a sense of permanent rejection,[25] and after two or three decades people who were too young to bear responsibility for the events that led to the city's fall might be asking how long abandonment is to persist. The situation and the questions then correspond to those in Lam. 5. It might also be significant that the psalm does not claim that Yhwh's rejection was undeserved and protest Yhwh's injustice (contrast Ps. 44) but focuses on the effect of events on Yhwh's honor and on Yhwh's kingship.[26] One can

22. Cf. Gerstenberger, *Psalms*, 2:77.

23. On the psalm's structure, see further Graeme E. Sharrock, "Psalm 74," *AUSS* 21 (1983): 211–23; Pierre Auffret, "Essai sur la structure littéraire du Psaume lxxiv," *VT* 33 (1983): 129–48; J. P. M. van der Ploeg, "Psalm 74 and Its Structure," in *Travels in the World of the Old Testament* (M. A. Beek Festschrift; ed. M. S. H. G. Heerma van Voss et al.; Assen: Van Gorcum, 1974), 204–10; Meir Weiss, "Die Methode der 'Total-Interpretation,'" in *Congress Volume: Uppsala 1971*, VTSup 22 (Leiden: Brill, 1972), 88–112 (see 96–106).

24. Raija Sollamo ("The Simile in Ps. 74:5," *SEÅ* 54 [1989]: 178–87 [see 182–85]) suggests that v. 5 refers to Nebuchadnezzar as one who cut down forests and assailed the temple woodwork.

25. But the sense of permanency is a subjective one, an expression of how complete the destruction was; in itself it does not indicate that the psalm must date from long after the temple's destruction (Hossfeld and Zenger, *Psalms 2*, 240).

26. Cf. Mays, *Psalms*, 247.

imagine the psalm being used on an occasion of fasting such as those referred to in Zech. 7–8.

The Tg understands the "crass one" in v. 22 to be a king, perhaps Antiochus Epiphanes.[27] His oppression might seem to have been much shorter than the one implied by Ps. 74, but three years can seem to last forever. It has been suggested that an origin in the Maccabean period is too late for the psalm to have gained a place in the Psalter,[28] but the speedy inclusion of Daniel in the Scriptures makes that an unconvincing argument. Indeed, the swift answering of such a prayer in that context might have led to its speedy inclusion, as the swift vindication of the visions in Daniel likely led to its inclusion.

Either occasion enables us to imagine the use of the psalm.[29] Alternatively, it might link with some other, unknown invasion of Jerusalem between the sixth and second century.[30] Goulder sees it as a lament for the fate of Bethel, adapted in v. 2 for use in Jerusalem;[31] George Wesley Buchanan relates it to the fall of Jerusalem in AD 70.[32] Or perhaps it was written for a recurrent worship occasion rather than issuing from a particular historical event.[33] Similarities with Mesopotamian city laments may suggest that apparent references to destruction belong to the convention of such laments and are not to be pressed into a connection with an actual destruction of the city.[34]

Instruction. Asaph's.

Heading. See glossary.

74:1–3. The psalm begins with questions and pleas, rather more extensive than the pleas that usually begin a protest psalm.

> [1]Why have you spurned permanently, God?
> Why does your anger smoke at the flock you pasture?

27. Stec, *Targum of Psalms*, 146. Cf. Herbert Donner, "Argumente zur Datierung des 74. Psalms," in *Wort, Lied und Gottesspruch: Beiträge zu Psalmen und Propheten* (Joseph Ziegler Festschrift; ed. Josef Schreiner; Würzburg: Echter, 1972), 41–50.

28. So, e.g., Dahood, *Psalms*, 2:199.

29. Cf. Calvin, *Psalms*, 3:160–61.

30. So, e.g., Gunkel, *Psalmen*, 322.

31. *The Psalms of Asaph*, 63.

32. "The Fall of Jerusalem and the Reconsideration of Some Dates," *RevQ* 14 (1989): 31–48 (see 38–48).

33. So Folker Willesen, "The Cultic Situation of Psalm lxxiv," *VT* 2 (1952): 289–306.

34. So Walter C. Bouzard, *We Have Heard with Our Ears, O God*, SBLDS 159 (Atlanta: Scholars Press, 1997), esp. 174–85.

The *Why? makes an abrupt beginning (cf. Ps. 13 and contrast Ps. 22), "a hasty opening that ignores etiquette."[35] The starting point for the psalm's questions lies in a past event with present implications (v. 1a) and in a present reality (v. 1b).[36] Long ago the shepherd had rejected the flock. Rejected is an action: it implies leaving it to its own devices, unprovided for and unprotected from wild animals (contrast the shepherd's role as described in Ps. 23). How could a shepherd do that (cf. John 10:11–15)? But the question relates not merely to the original event of rejection, whose rationale the flock might be prepared to accept (it was caused by their going astray). It relates to the permanence of this rejection (cf. Pss. 44:23 [24]; 77:8 [9]; 79:5; 89:46 [47]). "The Lord does not reject forever," Lam. 3:31 declares; well, it sure looks like it, Lam. 5:20 responds. The evidence of the past act of permanent rejection lies in the continuing reality of which the second colon speaks. The TNIV has God's anger simply "smoldering," which would suggestively imply that Yhwh's anger is not blazing as it once was; it has cooled down somewhat, even if it is still there. But other such references to smoke do not suggest this hopeful idea (e.g., 18:8 [9]; 80:4 [5]). Rather, Yhwh's anger seems as real as ever (cf. Tg, "Why is your anger strong?"). That is evidenced by what the psalm will go on to describe. The Psalms regularly infer God's anger from the nature of what happens to Israel. The evidence of God's anger remains incontrovertible.

> 2a–bBe mindful of your assembly, which you acquired of old,
> which you restored as your very own tribe,

As the psalm sees it, Yhwh will have to grant that there is no reasonable answer to the questions in v. 1. Implicit plea can thus give way to explicit plea; in a sense v. 2 thus restates v. 1. "Be *mindful" is a key exhortation in the psalm (cf. vv. 18, 22); uniquely, this psalm issues the exhortation three times. First, Yhwh is urged to be mindful of the people. They were just described as the flock Yhwh pastures. Now they are described as Yhwh's assembly or congregation or community (ʿēdâ), a company that gathers to hear Yhwh's word and make decisions. The parallel description sees them as "the tribe of your possession." The expression recurs in Jer. 10:16 = 51:19, and Israel is often described as Yhwh's possession (naḥălâ;

35. Gerstenberger, *Psalms*, 2:78.
36. The qatal verb is thus complemented by a yiqtol verb. "Why, God, permanently?" applies to the second colon as well as the first. "The flock you pasture" (lit. "the flock of your pasture") may also be the implicit obj. of the first verb as well as the second, notwithstanding the prep. *b*, but *zānaḥ* is elsewhere used absolutely (e.g., 44:23 [24]; 77:7 [8]); yet this hardly suggests that its meaning should be reduced to "be angry" (so Reuven Yaron, "The Meaning of *Zanaḥ*," *VT* 13 [1963]: 237–39).

e.g., Pss. 68:9 [10]; 78:62, 71), but Israel is not otherwise described as a tribe (*šēbeṭ*); the word regularly applies to the twelve tribes or clans that make up Israel as a whole (thus Tg has the plural here). This second, unusual expression heightens the pressure on Yhwh, who has a special relationship to this people as if they were Yhwh's own clan. The two verbs add to the pressure. Both of them parallel the act of praise at the Red Sea (Exod. 15:13, 16). Yhwh had made a point of acquiring this people (*qānâ*; cf. 78:54) and *restoring them (*gāʾal*; cf. 77:15 [16]). Both verbs often imply spending money (e.g., Ruth 4:1–10), and in combination this connotation likely does attach to them here. The assembly or tribe were like people for whom Yhwh accepted a family obligation and therefore expended resources to enable them to gain their freedom (from Egypt). Yhwh thereby reaffirmed a relationship with them. Thus whereas "acquiring" implies reference to their becoming Yhwh's people, "restoring" implies action that issued from that status. Both acquiring and restoring happened "of old" (cf. v. 12; 44:1 [2]; 77:5, 11 [6, 12]), in the days of the exodus and the Red Sea deliverance. Yhwh needs to act now consistently with those events.

> ²ᶜMount Zion, where you settled:
>   ³direct your steps to the permanent ruins,
>   all the wrong the enemy brought about in the sanctuary.

The last colon of v. 2 changes the focus to a place rather than a people, and v. 3 continues this focus. I thus take vv. 2c–3 as a tricolon closing off the section. It is not only the people, Yhwh's special possession, that needs to be taken note of but also the place where Yhwh "settled" (*šākan*). The people had come to settle in the land "long ago" (cf. 78:55), and Yhwh had likewise settled on Mount Zion (cf. 68:18 [19]; 135:21). The further two cola explain the need to pay attention to it. Indeed, they urge that Yhwh not merely pay attention (for instance, by looking down from the heavens) but also pay a visit, "lifting up steps to the permanent ruins." At this stage in the psalm and in the setting of vv. 2a and 3b, this expression suggests coming to look rather than coming to take action.[37] Micah 1:3 uses a different expression for Yhwh's striding out to act; but this coming will surely lead to action. If the psalm were used on a fasting occasion in the ruined temple, one can imagine the suppliants pointing God to these ruins. The third colon expands on the last phrase in the second. The ruins are a wrong (or a calamity—something *bad) brought about by a foe. It is the very sanctuary that has been treated thus, the

---

37. The expression comes only here, though Gen. 41:44 refers to "lifting up hands or feet"; the context there, too, does not suggest that it means "run" (BDB) or "bestir yourself" (NJPS).

place that is holy because Yhwh dwells there. The last colon thus pairs with the first. Prosaically put, the line comprises one verbal expression ("direct your steps"), two descriptions of the place in its theological significance ("Mount Zion, where you settled, the sanctuary"), and two descriptions of what has happened to it (turned into a permanent ruin by the enemy's wrongful/calamitous action).

74:4–9. After the opening plea, the psalm focuses on the reason for it, elaborating on vv. 2c–3. Of the three directions for a lament, here the focus lies on "they" ("we" appears in v. 9; "you" does not appear, but it has been the focus of vv. 1–3). The verbs are qatal in vv. 4 and 7–9, which is what one would expect in light of the implication in vv. 1–3 that the destruction is long past, but the verbs in vv. 5–6 are yiqtol (see on 77:13–20 [14–21]). The opening and closing lines with their references to signs form a pair (vv. 4, 9); vv. 5–6 form a pair describing the destruction; vv. 7–8 form a pair describing the burning of the sanctuary.

> ⁴Your attackers roared in the midst of the place of assembly;
>   they treated their signs as signs.

The psalm looks back, then, to the actual time of attack and destruction. The attackers roared like a lion in the place where the people regularly assembled for worship (*môʿēd*; cf. *ʿēdâ* in v. 2).[38] Shouts of exultation were regularly to be heard there, but these were very different shouts of exultation, by the people's foes (cf. Lam. 2:7). In what sense are these people Yhwh's attackers? Are they people who attack Yhwh? Or (as their coming reflects Yhwh's rejection of the people), are they attackers that Yhwh sends? Their signs might be their ensigns or standards, tokens of their victory, which they erected in the temple; Num. 2:2 refers to such [en]signs belonging to the twelve clans, though we have no reference to their being located in the temple. But v. 9 will refer to signs in the more usual sense, and more likely this clarifies the meaning in v. 4. The attackers had signs from their gods, encouraging them to go about their destructive work, and/or signs from Yhwh (cf. Isa. 36:10), and their success gave them reason to treat these as true signs.

> ⁵It would look like someone bringing up
>   axes against a forest thicket,
> ⁶And now its engravings altogether
>   they would smash with hatchet and cleavers.

---

38. LXX takes *môʿēd* to mean the worship itself (cf. Lam. 2:6; BDB), but it must mean the place in v. 8.

The simile conveys the horror of the event. Men were hacking about with axes, hatchets, and cleavers; all these words have similar meaning, so the effect is to convey an impression of workmen wielding a panoply of weapons. It is as if they were making a clearing in a wood, when actually they are in the temple. They are not hacking trees but smashing the woodwork that beautifies the temple. The simile would be enhanced by the fact that this woodwork was carved with representations of trees (1 Kings 6:29). The agents of destruction were indeed hacking down a quasi-forest.

> ⁷They gave over your sanctuary to fire, down to the ground;
>   they violated the place where your name had settled.
> ⁸They said in their heart, "We will put them down altogether";
>   they burned all God's places of assembly in the land.

It would naturally follow to set the smashed woodwork on fire. But this is no ordinary woodwork. It is the woodwork of "your sanctuary" (cf. v. 3).³⁹ The parallel second colon underlines the point. This place was a sanctuary, a holy place, because it was the place where Yhwh's *name had settled (cf. v. 2c): Yhwh was there in person. Yhwh's name was proclaimed there regularly as the one whose presence and activity were well-known in Israel, so that the declaring of the name brought home the reality and presence of its owner. The action involved not just demolition but also desecration. The holy was treated as something ordinary.

"They said in their *heart" implies "They made up their mind." Their actions were not thoughtless or accidental; they did not issue from the heat of the moment. They had formulated a plan. The recurrence of "altogether" (cf. v. 6) underlines the point. So the first colon describes the formulating of a plan, the second its implementation.⁴⁰ The place of assembly in Jerusalem was by no means the only such place set on fire.⁴¹

> ⁹We have not seen our signs,
>   there have no longer been prophets,
>   there has been no one with us who knew how long.

39. Though there the word was *qōdeš*, here *miqdāš*.

40. "Them" in the first colon is explained by the noun in the second; "all" corresponds to "altogether."

41. Unless we translate "the whole of God's place of assembly" (pl. of amplification; cf. A. Anderson, *Psalms*, 2:541; and see further A. Gelston, "A Note on Psalm lxxiv 8," *VT* 34 [1984]: 82–87). It is less likely that the psalm would be concerned about the fate of "all God's places of assembly in the earth," especially in the context; nor is there basis for the translation "synagogues" (Aq, Sym).

A tricolon closes off the section; the line pairs with v. 4. The foes saw signs; they were given direction by their gods or by Yhwh, or so they said. But the Israelites have seen no signs. They have heard from no prophets who could tell them how long the devastation would last.[42] The first colon thus leads into the second, and the second into the third. While in themselves the noun clauses in v. 9b–c would make good sense if they referred to the present, the past tense verb in the first colon likely determines their time reference, though their point would carry on into the present. The verse may imply some irony. Before and immediately after 587, at least, Jeremiah was prophesying and offering signs in Jerusalem and declaring how long, but he was taken off elsewhere soon after the city's fall. The book of Jeremiah also shows how there were many other prophets in the city in the years running up to its fall, but they would all have been silenced by the event itself. Having promised that it would not happen, they might have nothing to say when it did. Thus Lam. 2:9 portrays prophecy as gone from the community.

74:10–11. In light of the lament, the psalm reverts to questioning followed by overt plea, following the pattern of vv. 1–3. "Why?" and "God" and "permanently" recur.[43]

> **10**How long shall the foe scoff, God—
> shall the enemy revile your name permanently?

Initially, the question is now no longer "Why?" but the also familiar "How long?" (e.g., 80:4 [5]; another Hebrew expression in 79:5; 89:46 [47]). This might sound more like a request for information to which an answer such as "seventy years" might then be a satisfactory response, but in reality that would not be so. The implication is that the situation has continued for quite long enough, and the question is again a disguised plea for action *now*. The content of the two parallel verbal clauses makes clear why this is the case.[44] It goes beyond what has been explicit in vv. 1–9, though it works out its implications: the enemies' action counts as scoffing and reviling of Yhwh's name ("your name" is the object of the first verb as well as the second), such as the Assyrian authorities went in for (Isa. 36–37). In reality, surely five minutes is long enough for that. Permanent reviling is even less thinkable than permanent rejection and permanent desolation (vv. 1, 3).

42. Oswald Loretz argues for a reference to divination: see *Leberschau, Sündenbock, Asasel in Ugarit und Israel* (Altenberge: CIS, 1985), 81–107. See also J. J. M. Roberts, "Of Signs, Prophets and Time Limits," *CBQ* 39 (1977): 474–81.

43. Cf. Auffret, "Essai," *VT* 33 (1983): 134.

44. "Foe" and "enemy" parallel each other, as do "scoff" and "revile"; so in a way do "How long?" and "permanently," and "God" and "your name."

> [11]Why do you turn back your hand,
> yes, withholding your right hand from the midst of your garments?

But then the "Why?" returns. What Israel needs is that Yhwh's hand should be wielded (e.g., 10:12; 37:24; 44:2 [3]; 73:23). Why then does that hand turn away or turn back (cf. Lam. 2:3)? The second colon gives precision to the question. It is Yhwh's right hand that is restrained, the hand that has most power, and instead of being wielded, it sits there in Yhwh's pocket, withheld. The verb closes the line to bring the little section to a close; the line thus works abcc'db'.

74:12–17. The subsequent description of Yhwh's activity forms not so much a declaration of trust as a further set of reasons why Yhwh should act, in six neatly parallel lines. The explicit "you" ("you are the one who") comes seven times. Yhwh's inactivity does not cohere with the activity that originally characterized Yhwh. The psalm has already appealed to God's acts at the exodus and Red Sea (v. 2), and here that appeal is extended and brought into association with God's acts at creation. The language used suggests that the section would make people think of both creation and the Red Sea event, not mainly or exclusively the former[45] nor mainly or exclusively the latter.[46] The language is able to do that because its own focus lies on the fact of Yhwh's asserting kingship (cf. v. 12), which happened both in creation and at the Red Sea. Israel uses creation and the Red Sea event as prisms through each of which it looks at the other: Yhwh acted with might and delivered and established kingly authority at creation and at the Red Sea. The Red Sea deliverance was Yhwh's great creative act; the creation was Yhwh's first act of deliverance. Further, the imagery for making these assertions parallels that used by contemporary peoples in stories about a deity asserting kingship (see also the comment on v. 22, below).

> [12]But God, my king of old,
> bringer of deliverance in the midst of the earth,

The "but" (*w*) introduces the contrast between Yhwh's action (or rather, inaction) and Yhwh's historical characteristics, first expressed as appellatives. In MT God is not merely "king" (so Syr, Tg) nor "our king" (LXX) but "my king" (cf. 44:4 [5]; 68:24 [25]; 84:3 [4]). The "my" contrasts with the first-person plurals of v. 9 and the other plurals in the psalm; perhaps Israel here speaks as "I" and appeals to the King personally committed to

---

45. So, e.g., Seybold, *Psalmen*, 289.
46. So, e.g., Elmer B. Smick, "Mythopoetic Language in the Psalms," *WTJ* 44 (1982): 88–98 (see 90).

Israel, or perhaps a leader speaks throughout the psalm and here appeals to Yhwh's particular commitment to a leader. "Of old" (cf. 44:1 [2]; 55:19 [20]; 68:33 [34]; 77:5, 11 [6, 12]; 78:2) further sets the agenda for vv. 12–17 because the suppliant will here note how Yhwh acted way back at the Red Sea and at the very creation. It was there that Yhwh brought *deliverance "in the midst of the earth," in the public arena as a demonstration of worldwide power (cf. Gen. 48:16; Isa. 19:24; 24:13).[47] As Ps. 72 made clear, deliverance is the task of a king. In the parallelism of the line, deliverance thus works out the implications of being king, while "in the midst of the earth" is a spatial note to complement the temporal "of old."

> [13]You were the one who parted the sea by your might,
> shattered the heads of the dragons on the waters.

The references to Yhwh's kingship, might, deliverance, and parting of the sea would initially suggest reference to the Red Sea event. There Israel experienced Yhwh's might (Exod. 15:2, 13) and deliverance (14:13, 30; 15:2) and declared that Yhwh would always reign as king (15:18).[48] The shattering of the dragons in the waters would then refer to the slaughter of the Egyptian army in the Red Sea (so Tg).[49]

> [14]You were the one who crushed the heads of Leviathan;
> you would make it food for a company of wildcats.

The Red Sea event was thus the moment when Yhwh crushed the heads of the Egyptian Leviathan and left its soldiers on the shore to be eaten by desert creatures (cf. Tg; also Ezek. 29:3–5).[50] But through vv. 13–14 the language becomes less and less like language used of the Red Sea event and more like language used elsewhere in connection with the conquest of resistant supernatural powers of old. Other Middle Eastern stories spoke of a deity's victory over turbulent waters, the embodiment of anarchic dynamic force. These could then be personified as a sea monster with its seven heads; in the Ugaritic story of Baal and Anat, Leviathan/Lotan has seven heads, which corresponds to the sevenfold "you are the one who . . ." in vv. 13–17 (cf. also Rev. 12:3; 17:3).[51] These

47. While *běqereb hāʾāreṣ* could mean "in the midst of the *land*" (NJPS; cf. Isa. 5:8; 6:12; 7:22), the succeeding verses suggest the broader meaning. Exod. 8:22 [18]; Isa. 10:23 are more ambiguous.

48. Buchanan ("The Fall of Jerusalem," 32–36) calls the psalm a midrash on Exod. 15.

49. Cf. BDB. But DG 20; *IBHS* 7.4.3a; and JM 136f take the plural as intensive.

50. On the yiqtol in v. 14b, see on 77:13–20 [14–21].

51. So Dahood, *Psalms*, 2:205; cf. *ANET* 138, also the figure in Keel, *Symbolism*, 54.

other Middle Eastern stories do not essentially link such victories with creation but rather with the assertion of the deity's sovereignty, but the OT is more inclined to utilize their imagery to convey the significance of Yhwh's act of creation, and vv. 15–17 will speak more unambiguously about creation. Here the movement through vv. 13–14 parallels that in Isa. 51:9, as will vv. 14–17. Both the Red Sea deliverance and the original creation appear in vv. 13–14; we need not worry about how to separate them.

> 15You were the one who split spring and stream;
> you were the one who dried up perennial rivers.

The two verbs can again suggest the Red Sea event (e.g., Exod. 14:16, 21–22; Neh. 9:11), but they are also familiar from Gen. 1–11 (1:9–10; 7:11; 8:7, 14). "Spring" likewise recalls Gen. 1–11 (7:11; 8:2), while "rivers" can be a term for the Red Sea (Ps. 66:6). Once more, then, these two parallel cola speak of Yhwh's action in terms that could recall both creation and the Red Sea. On both occasions Yhwh parted waters so dry land would appear.[52]

> 16Day is yours, night also is yours;
> you were the one who established the light, yes, the sun.

The second colon would unequivocally suggest creation; the unusual word for "light" ($mā'ôr$) comes in Gen. 1:14–16. Likewise the fact that God names day and night (Gen. 1:5) is a sign that they belong to God.[53]

> 17You were the one who set all the bounds of the earth;
> summer and autumn, you were the one who shaped them.

"Bounds" would usually denote the boundaries of different nations; this would imply that God set the bounds of Philistia, Moab, Egypt, and so on. Yet the OT does not otherwise see these boundaries as established by God long ago but, rather, recognizes that such boundaries are not fixed once and for all and pictures God moving peoples around. Psalm 104:9 speaks of God at creation setting a boundary for the deep so that it could not again overwhelm the earth, and that makes sense for boundaries

52. Tg takes $bāqa'$ to imply cutting open the ground to release the waters and refers it to Yhwh's provision for the Israelites on their journey; the second colon then refers to the drying up of the Arnon, the Jabbok, and the Jordan to enable the Israelites to get to the land. But for the creation reference, see J. A. Emerton, "'Spring and Torrent' in Psalm lxxiv 15," in *Volume du Congrès: Genève 1965*, VTSup 15 (Leiden: Brill, 1966), 122–33.

53. "The light, yes, the sun" (v. 16) parallels "your hand, yes, your right hand" (v. 11). Sym and some LXX MSS have "moon" for "light."

here, though the verse expresses it as setting the boundaries of the earth, the point where the land is secure from being overwhelmed by the sea. Likewise, the parallel colon adds, God shaped summer and autumn, the dry, hot months from May to September, and the rainy season that follows. The EVV have "summer and winter," which could be misleading; *ḥōrep* suggests the rainy season rather than the cold depths of winter.[54] The reality of bounds here is again important; the hot summer is good for the ripening fruit, but to enable people to start next year's plowing, the transition to autumn rains is vital. Thus the new year comes at the end of the dry season and the hoped-for beginning of the rainy season. The final colon reverses the regular order of verb and objects (which are extraposed) to mark the end of the section (as happened in v. 11), with "the bounds of the earth" forming an inclusion with "the midst of the earth."

74:18–23. One final time the psalm reverts to plea, this time without rhetorical questions.

> ¹⁸Be mindful of this; the enemy has taunted, Yhwh,
>   a crass people has reviled your name.

The psalm reverts to its first imperative (v. 2) and then takes up the protest in v. 10, though the verbs are now qatal. "This" might refer to what precedes, as some LXX witnesses make explicit,[55] or might refer to what follows, or might not need to be tied down too precisely; perhaps the psalm simply wants to get Yhwh's attention. Here it goes on to express a concern for Yhwh's honor rather than for the community Yhwh acquired. The new elements in the line are the actual name "Yhwh," which is appropriate given the coming reference to "your name," and the description of the enemy as a people that is crass or stupid (*nābāl*), one that behaves as if God is not involved in the world (53:1).[56]

> ¹⁹Do not give the life of your dove to an animal;
>   do not permanently ignore the life of your weak people.

The psalm then goes on to appeal to Yhwh's concern for the people, but it does so in terms of the people's neediness rather than Yhwh's personal interests. Here only is the people a dove, the onomatopoeic *tôr*; all a dove can do is coo helplessly.[57] The second colon restates the

---

54. Contrast Terrien, *Psalms*, 536, 541.

55. Some also take "Be mindful of this" as a separate, self-contained colon; see Rahlfs's edition.

56. The parallel cola work abcdb'c'e.

57. "Pigeon" (*yônâ*) is more common as a metaphor, sometimes with similar implications (e.g., Jer 48:28; Hos. 7:11; 11:11).

point, this time picking up the word "permanently" from the protest in v. 10 and paralleling "be mindful" (v. 18) with "*ignore." The reference to *weak ones makes explicit the point about being a dove. The people might seem to face even greater peril than a dove, because they cannot fly to some cleft in the rock; or rather, they have sought to fly to their crag, to Yhwh, but this has not worked.

> 20Have regard for the covenant,
>   for pastures of violence fill the dark places in the land.

This is the only appeal to the covenant in the Psalms (though cf. 89:39 [40]), but it would be encouraged by Yhwh's commitment to be mindful of the covenant (e.g., 111:5, 9). The suppliant wants Yhwh not only to turn the mind (v. 18) but also to turn the eyes. Which covenant does the psalm appeal to? The parallel with Ps. 89 might suggest the covenant with David, and the context of the exile might require appeal to that covenant with its stress on Yhwh's commitment and on the impossibility of Yhwh's ever abandoning David. In the exile, appeal to the Mosaic covenant would backfire. The appeal to the covenant gains emphasis from the uneven structure of the line, two words in the first colon and six (five stresses in MT) in the second, which explains why the suppliant needs Yhwh to have regard. In doing so, it further broadens the psalm's horizon, from the city to the land as a whole. Dark places can be places to hide (139:11–12?—cf. BDB), but the image is more often a negative one; darkness suggests distress, dread, mourning, perplexity, and confusion (18:28 [29]; 35:6; 107:10, 14). The whole land is characterized by a deep gloom because it has been taken over by lawless *violence. The striking expression "pastures of violence" offers a contrast to "pastures of peace" (Jer. 25:37), "pastures of grass" (Ps. 23:2), and "pastures of God" (83:12 [13]), which suggest what the land is supposed to be. "Pastures of violence" is what it has become, a land dominated by violence. The clause is proleptic; more literally, "pastures of violence fill the land so that it has become a land of dark places."

> 21The broken must not turn back disgraced;
>   the weak and needy must praise your name.

The victims of violence are the broken, the *weak, and the *needy; the line piles up terms for them. They are broken by the attacks of people who are in a position to take advantage of them (cf. 9:9 [10]; 10:18; also the related verb in 44:19 [20]). They are the weak over against the people with great power, and the needy over against people who have limitless resources. Here the terms describe the people as a whole over against invaders such as the Assyrians, the Babylonians, or the Syrians, people who have the power and resources to crush Israel. In a jussive avowal, the psalm declares what must be done for the broken, weak, and needy, first negatively, then positively. They must not have to turn back before their foes in shame (cf. 6:10 [11]; 70:3 [4]), as they have long been doing (Lam. 1:8).[58] Rather, they must have reason to begin to praise God for delivering them.

> [22]Arise, God, defend your cause,
> be mindful of your taunting by a crass people all the time.

The psalm reverts to direct imperatives, with a characteristic exhortation to stop sitting and doing nothing and to get up to take action, expressed more straightly as the psalm draws near its end (cf. 44:26 [27]). "Defend your cause" gives precision to the first imperative and does so more innovatively. Other psalms ask Yhwh to defend "my" cause (35:1; 43:1; 119:154). This psalm's argument arises from the effect of the enemy's attacks on Yhwh's reputation as well as on the people's lives. The second colon explains this, taking up the exhortation to be mindful of the crass people's taunting from v. 18,[59] forming a triple inclusion around the section. The exhortation to be mindful acts also as an inclusion around the psalm as a whole. The cause is Yhwh's and not merely theirs because the enemies' taunting affects not merely the people (so Tg; cf. 44:13 [14]; 79:4, 12) but also God, and it goes on all the time. As well as the taunting by earthly enemies described in Isa. 36–37, people using the psalm might recall Middle Eastern stories about the attacks of junior gods on a senior god, reflected in Isa. 14:12–15.[60]

> [23]Do not ignore the voice of your watchful foes,
> the uproar of those who arise against you, going up continually.

The psalm ends on the same note: surely Yhwh's own honor is the most powerful thing to appeal to, isn't it? Again it bids Yhwh not to *ignore what is going on (cf. v. 19), but here it refers to the way this affects Yhwh. The taunting voice that people can hear is the voice of Yhwh's *watchful foes. It is as if they are plotting against Yhwh; these foes recur from v. 4. The second colon expands on that idea. Yhwh has been urged to arise in order to act, and the background is the fact that

---

58. It is hard to parallel the idea that the colon refers to turning back empty-handed from one's prayer.

59. Though here there is no word for "people," facilitating Tg's application of the term to a king.

60. See, e.g., Tate, *Psalms 51–100*, 250.

these people have already so arisen. It is as if one can hear their warrior shout as they attack Yhwh. Its sound is going up all the time; the expression is different from that in v. 22, but it repeats the point, and the word *šāʾôn* recalls the verb *šāʾag* in v. 4. The actual close of the psalm is very abrupt, like that of Ps. 88. The psalm stops rather than finishes. Its rhetoric thus reflects the situation it presupposes. It achieves no closure, as the people's experience has achieved no closure.[61]

Theological Implications

The word "permanence" (*neṣaḥ*) runs through the psalm. Has God rejected Israel permanently (v. 1), given that Zion's desolation seems permanent (v. 3)? Is the enemy to revile Yhwh's name permanently (v. 10)? Will Yhwh permanently put the life of this weak people out of mind (v. 19)?[62] The four references to permanence are paralleled by four references to Yhwh's name (vv. 7, 10, 18, 21). Zion is its dwelling place (v. 7). But it is doubly blasphemed (vv. 10, 18). Yet this surely must produce a response that will lead to its being praised (v. 21).

When the people of God finds itself thus abandoned by God, as it is in much of the West as the church is in decline, the appropriate response is not to pretend that this has not happened or to turn away from God or to try to fix things ourselves but to turn to God in protest. We then direct God's attention to our sorry state, to its implications for God, who is also discredited by this situation, and to God's covenant commitment to us. We thus urge God, "Defend your cause." One basis on which we do that is that God has already won the decisive victory over resistant powers. God did that at creation, did it at the Red Sea, and did it at the cross and resurrection. It is therefore weird of God to let forces that dismiss God look as if they have won the victory now. It is not in our interests for God to do that, but more profoundly, it is not in God's interests.

Christians often speak in cliché terms about the "now" and the "not yet." The fact that God's purpose will be consummated at the End but that God has already done the decisive thing in Christ means that even now we sometimes experience the fullness of the End: people get healed, raised from the dead, filled with the Spirit. The OT's perspective comple-

61. Hossfeld and Zenger (*Psalms 2*, 242) thus contrast with the related Psalms 79 and 80.

62. D. Winton Thomas argues that in passages such as this [*lĕ*]*neṣaḥ* means "utterly" rather than "permanently" ("The Use of נצח as a Superlative in Hebrew," *JSS* 1 [1956]: 106–9; cf. Peter R. Ackroyd ("נצח—εἰς τέλος," *ExpT* 80 [1968–69]: 126), but the latter meaning is required in v. 10, and it seems more likely that the expression has the same meaning on all four occasions in the psalm.

ments that. It is more inclined to look at the overlap between now and the Beginning, at the implications of the Beginning for present experience. God won a great victory at the Beginning in putting down opposing foes. For the OT, this fact also means we can experience God's victory now, experience the fullness of God's creation purpose.

Churches outside the West have less reason to use this psalm for themselves; perhaps they can use it for us. Assuming that Asaph wrote the psalm long before the destruction it refers to, Cassiodorus comments on the depth of love implied in this grieving over an event that will come after his day.[63] Those who use the psalm long after the desolation of Jerusalem are similarly invited into a loving grief for a city that continues to be populated by the broken and riven by uproar.[64]

63. *Psalms*, 2:223–24.
64. Luther's tropological, allegorical, and anagogical (not to say anti-Jewish) exposition of the psalm is particularly sustained: see *First Lectures*, 1:431–54.

Psalm 75

In Your Way and in Your Time

Translation

The leader's. Do not destroy. Composition. Asaph's. Song.

¹We have confessed you, God,
 we have confessed and your name was near;¹
 people have declared your wonders.²

²Yes, for I seize the appointed time;
 I myself decide with uprightness.
³Whereas earth and all its inhabitants are trembling,³
 I am the one who ordered its pillars. (Rise)
⁴I have said to the exultant, "Do not exult,"
 to the faithless, "Do not lift up a horn."
⁵Do not lift up your horn on high,
 or speak with forward neck."⁴

⁶Yes, for not from the east or the west
 and not from the pasturage of the mountains:

1. For *wĕqārôb šĕmekā*, LXX implies *wĕqārô' bišmekā* (and called on your name), a more conventional idea.
2. KJV takes "your wonders" as the subj. of the verb, but elsewhere it is always the obj., and that understanding works here.
3. See on 46:6 [7]. Here the contrast with "order" or "establish" supports the translation "tremble" rather than "melt." On the construction, see GKC 116w.
4. For MT *bĕṣawwā'r*, LXX with "against God" perhaps implies *baṣṣûr* (against the Rock), assimilating to 1 Sam. 2:2. LXX's paraphrase shows that the expression is awkward here (Kidner, *Psalms*, 2:272). Sym implies "speak forward [arrogant] things with your neck [i.e., your pride]"; cf. the other occurrences of *'ātāq* (31:18 [19]; 94:4; 1 Sam. 2:3).

[7]Yes, for God is the one who decides;
    he puts down one person and lifts up another.
[8]Yes, for there is a chalice in Yhwh's hand,
    with fermented wine, full of spices.
He is pouring from this; they will indeed drain its dregs;
    all the faithless on the earth will drink.
[9]And I myself will proclaim[5] forever,
    I will make music to Jacob's God.
[10]And I will cut all the horns of the faithless;
    the horns of the faithful will be lifted up.

Interpretation

The psalm does not follow the form of any of the common genres (psalms of praise, protest, trust, and thanksgiving). A "we" (v. 1), a divine "I" (v. 3), and a human "I" (v. 9) speak, which would justify describing the psalm as a liturgy involving a congregation, a leader such as a king, and someone who speaks for God. But it is not always clear which verses belong to which speaker.[6] It is certain enough that the congregation speaks in v. 1, though the leader could be expressing its words. God speaks in vv. 2–3, but how far do God's words extend? Does the *"Rise" suggest a change of speaker at v. 4? Do the leader's words begin there ("I [have] said" usually introduces the psalmist's own words)?[7] But readers would more likely assume that God's "I" continues through vv. 4–5. They might even continue through vv. 6–8; God can self-refer in the third person. But the change in person hints at a change of speaker, and v. 6 begins with *kî*, like v. 2, when the speaker changed.[8] Conversely, the absence of any indication that the speaker changes in v. 10 suggests that this "I" continues to be the leader's; the content of v. 10 might then mark this as a royal psalm. So I analyze it as follows:

The congregation's testimony (qatal verbs; v. 1)

Yhwh's words providing the rationale for that testimony (vv. 2–5)

The leader's confession responding to Yhwh's words (yiqtol verbs; vv. 6–10)

The threefold division of the psalm then suggests an answer to the question about form. Reference to past testimony belongs in protest psalms

5. LXX implies *'āgîl* (I will rejoice) for MT *'aggîd*.
6. Seybold (*Psalmen*, 291) posits a redactional process to explain this opacity.
7. Cf. Gerstenberger, *Psalms*, 2:82.
8. Cf. Dahood, *Psalms*, 2:211–12.

lamenting the fact that Yhwh is not acting now in the way the people have known in the past (cf. Ps. 44:1 [2]). The quoting of a word from Yhwh and of the response to that word belongs in the same context (cf. Ps. 60). So this psalm recalls the testimony that the congregation has given in the past (v. 1), which by implication it cannot give now. Yhwh responds by claiming once again to be the kind of God that this testimony acknowledged (vv. 2–5). And the leader responds to that claim with a declaration of faith and commitment (vv. 6–10). We do not know what historical or liturgical context the psalm may link with, though one can imagine it being used in connection with the Assyrian invasion (so LXX of Ps. 76) or with the exile or with the Maccabean wars.[9]

The psalm's theme and language overlap with those of Hannah's song in 1 Sam. 2:1–10. Hannah begins by declaring that her horn has lifted up through Yhwh (contrast v. 5). She warns about "forwardness" (cf. v. 5). She describes Yhwh as one who puts down and lifts up (cf. v. 7). She refers to Yhwh's having set in place the columns that support the earth (cf. v. 3, though the language is different). She refers to Yhwh's making decisions in the world (cf. vv. 2, 7, though the verb is different). Comparison of the two highlights how Hannah's song is simply her song of praise, whereas the psalm is a liturgy. Hannah's song stands between the birth of her son and the event it will bring about, the anointing of Israel's kings; the former is a promise of the latter. The psalm implies a different relationship between past and future. Past wonders are not continued in present acts of God, but God promises they will be, and thus the psalm's closing praise resembles Hannah's but offers it on the basis of Yhwh's word rather than on the basis of having yet seen Yhwh act. Hannah's song closes with a promise of Yhwh's involvement with the anointed king; the psalm closes with such a leader speaking confidently of being able to fulfill the king's role in putting down the faithless. One might thus see the psalm as taking up the issues raised in Hannah's song and reformulating them in a different and more ambiguous context. It declares that Hannah will be proved right and that the leader will act in that conviction.

Further, as Ps. 74 entered into conversation with Ps. 73, here Ps. 75 does so with both, reaffirming that Yhwh is involved when it looks as if the opposite is the case. The key word *mô'ēd* reappears (v. 2; cf. 74:4, 8), though now it refers to an appointed time rather than an appointed meeting.[10] The exultant faithless (73:3) also reappear; vv. 5 and 7 now confront them with the fact that they will be put down.[11]

9. And for different liturgical possibilities, see Kraus, *Psalms 60–150*, 104; Gerstenberger, *Psalms*, 2:84.

10. Sym does give *mô'ēd* the meaning "assembly"; *lāqaḥ* (seize) could then have the same significance as in 73:24 (cf. Goulder, *Psalms of Asaph*, 83).

11. See further Cole, *Shape and Message of Book III*, 37–45.

> The leader's. Do not destroy. Composition. Asaph's. Song.

Heading. See glossary.

75:1. The psalm begins, then, with a tricolon recalling the praise the congregation has offered in the past.

> ¹We have confessed you, God,
>   we have confessed and your name was near;
>   people have declared your wonders.

The LXX and Jerome translate the verbs as future, EVV as present, and *yādâ* hiphil is very frequent in the yiqtol with future or present reference, but these two occurrences are qatal, the only instances. The change to *sāpar* piel for the third colon points us toward the reason for using the qatal, since this verb is used to refer to actual past declarations in 44:1 [2]; 78:3.[12] The congregation is recalling the confession and declaration it has made in the past. The content of that confession and declaration appears in two parallel expressions in the second and third cola. First, the congregation has experienced Yhwh's *name come near to it.[13] Yhwh's name stands for Yhwh in person acting on the people's behalf to deliver them (44:5 [6]; 54:1 [3]; 124:8), and the nearness of the name or the person means that Yhwh is indeed so present to act on their behalf when they are in trouble (34:18 [19]; cf. 85:9 [10]; 145:18). "The name of Yhwh came from afar" to take action against invading Assyria (Isa. 30:27). The parallel reference to Yhwh's *wonders restates that. From the beginning the people's history has been marked by such wonders (see esp. 78:4, 11, 12, 32). But is this still so? Can the congregation still declare them (as in Ps. 78) or do so only as a feature of past history (as in Ps. 44)?[14]

75:2–5. Verse 3 makes clear who is the "I" in v. 2. Yhwh speaks to confirm the testimony to which v. 1 refers.

> ²Yes, for I seize the appointed time;
>   I myself decide with uprightness.

---

12. Cf. Rashi, who then takes the noun clause to refer to God's name being near on our lips; also Weiser (*Psalms*, 520–22), who refers it to a preceding moment in the liturgy.

13. The verbal clauses indicate the time reference of this noun clause, and the *w* introduces a causal clause (cf. GKC 158a).

14. The parallelism in the line works in intricate ways (roughly abaca'c'). The first verb recurs in the second colon; then the verb changes root, stem, and person for the third colon. The indirect obj. in the first colon applies also to the second, and the appellative in the first applies to the second and third. The topics of the confession are expressed in diverse ways in the second and third cola.

Jerome and EVV take the opening *kî* as forward-looking: "When I seize . . ."[15] The transition from v. 1 is then doubly jerky, as the speaker changes, and there is also no verbal link. I rather take the *kî* as asseverative but reckon that it also keeps its characteristic logical force and thus indicates some continuity; hence the double translation "Yes, for." It is almost as if Yhwh is interrupting the declaration in v. 1 to confirm it. Or perhaps this is indeed a carefully constructed liturgy in which the priest's lines carry on from the congregation's. One might then translate the yiqtol verbs as future, but the logic is better if we translate them as present. The basis for the community's confession is the fact that Yhwh does make decisions about what goes on in the world. The fact that Yhwh *will* make such decisions would be a basis for hope but not so much for confession or declaration, and these verbs refer to things that can be pointed to. Yhwh is claiming to be one who does determine that certain things will happen and also when they will happen (cf. 102:13 [14]; Dan. 8:19; 11:27, 29, 35). The emphasis on the timing hints at the psalm's agenda and the way it might respond to Ps. 74.[16] That psalm wanted to know whether God had abandoned the people forever, how long God was going to let the situation continue, why Yhwh was not acting, and when God would act. Psalm 75 responds by declaring that Yhwh has the times under control. In itself this is no consolation; indeed, Ps. 74 was assuming this rather than doubting it. The question is, How does Yhwh exercise this control? What sort of times does Yhwh choose? What sort of events does Yhwh determine?

Initially the second colon suggests that it will decline to answer such questions; the extra pronoun "I" increases the emphasis on the divine sovereignty exercised in such decision-making and threatens simply to tell the psalmist to shut up in the manner of God addressing Job. But the next word reverses that implication and means that this parallel second colon does clarify the first as it adds the key word "[with] uprightness" to describe the manner of Yhwh's *deciding. In this assertion giving content to the confession in v. 1, Ps. 75 challenges people who say Ps. 74 (i.e., "Why have you spurned us?" etc.) and urges them to keep believing that Yhwh's sovereignty over the nature and the timing of events has that quality.[17]

15. *TTH* 136β and DG 121c take it as a conditional clause. LXX renders similarly but construes the lines as a whole differently.

16. A paronomasia underlines the point: "How long" (74:9) is *'ad-mâ*; "appointed time" is *mô'ēd* (Cole, *Shape and Message of Book III*, 39).

17. There is no indication that the colon refers to an eschatological judgment (so Gunkel, *Psalmen*, 328), though "Yhwh's coming is always something 'final,' 'conclusive'" (Kraus, *Psalms 60–150*, 104–5). Thus Angel González Núñez sees it as eschatological in the sense

> ³Whereas earth and all its inhabitants are trembling,
> I am the one who ordered its pillars. (Rise)

When Yhwh does act with uprightness and thus speaks or reaches out, earth trembles (46:6 [7]; Amos 9:5), and so do people (Exod. 15:15; Josh. 2:24). For Yhwh's own people, that trembling is good news. Yet it might cause disquiet, and the second colon thus reminds Israel of the basis for its remaining calm. Again EVV have a present tense verb, but the qatal suggests that Yhwh refers rather to the putting of the earth's pillars in good order at the Beginning; compare the common use of *kûn* (e.g., Ps. 74:16). The "I" who acts now (v. 2) is the "I" who so acted then. That original act means that the present trembling is not one to worry about. In 11:3 earth's "foundations" seems to refer to its moral order, and that may also be the reference here (cf. also 82:5).

> ⁴I have said to the exultant, "Do not exult,"
> to the faithless, "Do not lift up a horn."

One might translate "I [hereby] say," but in the context v. 4 more likely looks behind vv. 2–3 and gives us the exhortation Yhwh issued before taking the action that vv. 2–3 presuppose. For the exultant faithless, see on 73:3. We know from the modern world and the church that it is almost impossible for powerful people not to exult in their power, and that is why nations and leaders fall. Yhwh recalls warning them about their danger, but the warning goes unheeded, and so they end up trembling as their world shakes. Lifting its horn is the means by which an animal expresses its will and its power, of which its horn is thus a symbol, and the image becomes a metaphor for the assertion of human power—not necessarily in a sinful sense (cf. 89:17, 24 [18, 25]).

> ⁵"Do not lift up your horn on high,
> or speak with forward neck."

The line continues in staircase parallelism as it repeats words from the end of v. 4 with some variation: the verb is qualified by "on high," and the noun now has a suffix. "On high" points toward God's realm (7:7 [8]; 10:5; 18:16 [17]; 68:18 [19]; 92:8 [9]; 93:4) and almost suggests "toward the one who is on high."[18] By its nature, the possession and

---

of envisaging the coming of a definitive new order ("El Salmo 75 y el juicio escatológico," *EstBib* 21 [1962]: 5–22).

18. But translating *lammārôm* as "against the Most High" (cf. TNIV) makes this too explicit. Elsewhere the expression simply means "on high" (see on 56:2 [3]), and for "against" one would expect *'al* rather than *l*.

exercise of power puts someone into a riskily godlike position; it is very hard not to behave as if one *is* God or to look as if one is doing that. The second colon completes an abb′a′ parallelism in vv. 4–5 as "speak with forward neck" balances "exult." "Forward" (*'ātāq*) appears elsewhere as here in the company of references to exulting and speaking with insolence (31:18 [19]; 94:4; 1 Sam. 2:3; *'ātaq* means "go forward"). But these other passages do not refer to the neck. Here the reference to the neck accompanies and parallels the reference to the horn. In an animal such as an ox, the neck is a locus of strength, and it suggests the capacity to decide the direction one will take or to walk head high. Thus having a yoke on one's neck harnesses one's strength and controls one's direction and actions (e.g., Gen. 27:40; Deut. 28:48; Job 41:22 [14]; Mic. 2:3). So Yhwh's warning concerns the impudent stance expressed in the words of the faithless.[19]

75:6–10. A human leader in turn affirms God's word.

> [6]Yes, for not from the east or the west
>   and not from the pasturage of the mountains:
> [7]Yes, for God is the one who decides;
>   he puts down one person and lifts up another.

The opening *kî* again marks a change of speaker; the psalm declares recognition of the truth of what Yhwh has said. Verse 6 begins a statement that one would expect to continue with words such as "come decisions about putting down and lifting up," but v. 7 abandons that construction and jumps straight to a positive declaration. In itself, then, v. 6 leaves the reader to provide its conclusion, a common Hebrew device (e.g., 27:13; 84:10 [11]) that also occurs in English ("If you touch that . . .").[20] The verse does the same with the points of the compass. After east and west we might expect north and south, but instead we find another expression for areas where someone might go to look hard for something.[21]

---

19. There are other words for being *stiff*-necked (cf. KJV), though no doubt the line implies that these people are stiff-necked: they will not turn to listen and pay heed to Yhwh.

20. Technically, aposiopesis: see GKC 167a.

21. "The pasturage of the mountains" might denote Sinai and/or the area between Sinai and Canaan and thus suggest the south; the reader then has to supply only "nor from the north." Kirkpatrick (*Psalms*, 452) suggests that the north is unmentioned because it is from this direction that the trouble comes. Tg obtains four directions by understanding "and not from the pasturage [or] the mountains," which it takes to mean north and south; cf. also Mitchell Dahood, "The Four Cardinal Points in Psalm 75,7 and Joel 2,20," *Bib* 52 (1971): 397. But "the pasturage of the mountains" is not an obvious way to refer to the south; neither are "pasturage" and "mountains" obvious ways to refer to north and south, as is suggested by the fact that other interpreters (e.g., Hill, *Prayer, Praise and Politics*, 105) reverse their meaning from that implied by Tg.

"Mountains" (*hārîm*) is spelled the same as a word for "lifting up," which makes for a nice paronomasia linking vv. 4, 5, 6, and 7.[22]

Verse 7 then begins with a further, resumptive *kî* introducing the positive declaration. The exultant, faithless people live their lives on the assumption that they *decide what happens in the world, but this is not so. The second colon makes explicit what sort of decisions we are talking about. God can make the decision about someone losing power (cf. 18:27 [28]; 147:6 for this verb, but also the recurrence in Isa. 2:11–17; 5:15; 10:33; 13:11; 25:11–12; 26:5). God can also make the decision about someone gaining power. As "decides" picks up from v. 2, "lifts up" (*rûm* hiphil) picks up from vv. 4–5 and thus takes up the warning to the faithless about their assumption that they can lift themselves up, that they are in control. It is not so. The combination of putting down and lifting up recurs in 1 Sam. 2:7 and in different words in Isa. 2:11–17; 5:15, testimonies to the way these realities were illustrated in Israel's experience. We should perhaps not infer that Yhwh is always the power behind (for instance) the election or non-reelection of a president. In a general sense that will indeed be so, since nothing happens without Yhwh allowing it, but the psalm likely refers to the fact that from time to time Yhwh takes particular, deliberate action to bring someone to power or to remove them.

> [8]Yes, for there is a chalice in Yhwh's hand,
>   with fermented wine, full of spices.
> He is pouring from this; they will indeed drain its dregs;
>   all the faithless on the earth will drink.

Yet another resumptive *kî* explains how it is that Yhwh "puts down." It may be that Yhwh simply makes people drink too much, or perhaps the drink is a trial (cf. Num. 5:11–31). But the background to the picture may be the work of an assassin at a Middle Eastern banquet (cf. 60:3 [5]), posing as a cupbearer such as Nehemiah. First, like a vintner or a bar steward, Yhwh mixes the drinks. Their basis is (lit.) "wine that has fermented" and has thus gained in alcoholic potency (cf. Tg "strong wine");[23] it is not "new wine" that has not yet had a chance to do that. Further, it is (lit.) "full of mixture," wine combined with herbs and spices (and spirits?) in the manner of a drink such as sangria, except that this mixture may be no ordinary blend (thus Tg makes it "a chalice with a curse . . . full of a bitter mixture").

Like a wine waiter, Yhwh brings a chalice of this concoction to the banqueting table and pours from it. It is as if Yhwh's action happens

22. Indeed, Rashi and Qimchi take *hārîm* as this hiphil inf. from *rûm*, for *midbar* reading *midbār* (so also many later Hebrew MSS, and cf. EVV).

23. Cf. *Midrash on Psalms*, 2:10. "Foaming wine" makes less sense.

before the psalmist's eyes.[24] Yhwh's aim is that the guests drink every drop, encouraged by the fine taste of this blended drink. All the *faithless in the earth thus drink. We are left to imagine the result.

> [9]And I myself will proclaim forever,
>   I will make music to Jacob's God.

The undertaking to proclaim and make *music, in two parallel cola, takes up the theme of v. 1, though it uses different verbs, and they are now yiqtol rather than qatal. It is classic for a lament to speak of such confession in the past (it is more difficult in the present because Yhwh is not so acting now). It is also classic for a lament eventually to make a commitment to such proclamation in the future, when *Jacob's God has again so acted in putting down the faithless.

> [10]And I will cut all the horns of the faithless;
>   the horns of the faithful will be lifted up.

"The horns" reappear from v. 5, "the faithless" from v. 8, "lifting up" from v. 7. Making the faithless drink the concoction is the way their horns are cut off so that the *faithful can be restored to their proper position. There is no indication of a change of speaker in v. 10, so presumably the king or other leader continues to speak; once again we recall that it is the vocation of the king to see that the faithless are put down and the faithful thus exalted (cf. also 101:8). At one level it is Yhwh who puts the faithless down (v. 8); but the one through whom Yhwh does so is the king or leader of Israel, who is inspired and encouraged to do so by the knowledge that this is Yhwh's intention.[25]

Theological Implications

A 1970s song by Graham Kendrick declared the assurance that things will always work out in our lives "in your way and in your time." My prayers may at the moment seem unanswered, but God never comes too quickly or too late. I can wait patiently and be sure I will not regret it

---

24. I take this as an instantaneous qatal. MT links the last verb, "they drink," with the preceding colon, but it is then hard to make sense of the prosody of the line; we would probably need to take it as a tricolon. For possible emendations of the verse, see E. Weisenberg, "A Note on מזה in Ps lxxv 9," *VT* 4 (1954): 434–39; R. Tournay, "Notes sur les Psaumes," *RB* 79 (1972): 39–58 (see 43–50); Meindert Dijkstra, "He Pours the Sweet Wine Off, Only the Dregs Are for the Wicked," *ZAW* 107 (1995): 296–300.

25. RSV implies *yĕgaddēaʿ* (he will cut) for MT *ʾăgaddēaʿ*, making God the one who acts.

because I know that God will make things work out. The psalm declares that this applies not only to individuals but also to communities such as persecuted churches and churches that God has abandoned.

Can we be sure? In reassuring us, the psalm offers three striking metaphors.[26] First, God is like a builder who has made the world's foundations secure. When the world shakes physically, militarily, morally, or socially, this is not an indication that it might be about to fall apart. God remains the one who secured it. Second, human beings are nevertheless like animals raising their horns, asserting themselves against God and against one another. (Yet that means, among other things, that if we are the horn-raisers, we may not be able to claim that earlier reassurance. We will be the ones God has to put down.) Third, the assertive people will not succeed, because God is also like an assassin mixing a lethal potion, a victor making people drink so much that it will make them incapable of action, or a city elder supervising a trial by ordeal. (How bold the Scriptures are in their images!)

In light of that, we may look forward to rejoicing when we see God put down the assertive and may accept our responsibility to act against the assertive ourselves.

26. Cf. Tate, *Psalms 51–100*, 259–60.

Psalm 76

Revere or Fear

Translation

The leader's. With strings. Composition. Asaph's. Song.

¹God is known in Judah;
  in Israel his name is great.
²His shelter came to be in Salem,
  his dwelling in Zion.
³There he broke the bow's flames,
  shield and sword and war. (Rise)

⁴You are resplendent,¹
  majestic from the mountains full of prey.²
⁵The stouthearted let themselves be spoiled,³ they fell into deep
    sleep;⁴
  none of the brave men lifted their hands.
⁶At your blast, God of Jacob,
  both chariot and horse lay stunned.

⁷You—you are to be revered;
  who can stand before you in⁵ the time of your anger?

1. Th implies *nôrā'* ("to be revered"; cf. v. 7) for the less familiar *nā'ôr*, while Tg has a double translation suggesting both words.

2. Lit. "mountains of prey." LXX's "eternal mountains" simplifies the difficult expression, perhaps on the basis of the fact that a synonym of *ṭerep* is *'ad*, and that *'ad* can mean "perpetuity" as well as "prey."

3. One would expect *hištôlĕlû*; the preformative on *'eštôlĕlû* is an Aramaism (GKC 54a).

4. Lit. "They slumbered their sleep."

5. Lit. "from."

⁸From the heavens you made your decision heard;
　earth revered and was still,
⁹When God rose to exercise authority,⁶
　to deliver all the weak in the earth. (Rise)

¹⁰Yes, for human fury confesses you;⁷
　you bind⁸ the leftovers of great fury.⁹
¹¹Make promises and fulfill them to Yhwh your God;
　all those around him bring tribute to the one who is to be
　　revered.¹⁰
¹²He curbs¹¹ the spirit of leaders,
　one to be revered by earth's kings.

Interpretation

Three times the psalm describes who Yhwh is by means of a niphal participle, and then it indicates by means of qatal verbs how this links with Yhwh's acts (vv. 1–3, 4–6, 7–9). After these three three-line sections, a closing three-line section describes and urges the appropriate human response (vv. 10–12).¹² Broadly, the first and last sections speak about God, the middle ones address God.

Psalm 76 has a number of links with Pss. 46–48, though its placing here reflects the way it takes up motifs from Pss. 72–75.¹³ Like Ps. 46, it focuses on Yhwh's acts in the manner of a testimony psalm, but the acts are the great events of the nation's story, going back to the time when Yhwh came to reside in Jerusalem.¹⁴ It is thus a praise psalm rather than a testimony psalm, though like Ps. 46 it lacks the introductory exhorta-

6. "When you rose to exercise authority, God" (cf. TNIV) keeps the address to God of vv. 4–8 and 10, but the lack of a suffix on the inf. makes this hard—contrast v. 6—and the unannounced transition to a third-person reference recurs in v. 11.

7. J. A. Emerton ("A Neglected Solution of a Problem in Psalm lxxvi 11," *VT* 24 [1974]: 136–46) emends *tôdĕkā* to *tādôk* from *dākak* or *tādûk*, from *dûk*, producing the more intelligible expression "You crush human fury."

8. For this mainly PBH meaning of *ḥāgar*, cf. Rashi, followed by KJV, and *DTT*. For *taḥgōr*, LXX implies *tĕḥoggekā*: "The remains of great fury celebrate you."

9. "Great fury" translates the pl. (of amplification) *ḥēmōt*, though this might be an alternative form of the sg. (see on 68:9 [10]).

10. Lit. "to the [object of] reverence" (cf. Isa. 8:12–13).

11. Or "tests" (cf. Dahood, *Psalms*, 2:220); see *bāṣar* II (*DCH*), IV (*HALOT*).

12. Cf. Jörg Jeremias's comments, "Lade und Zion," in *Probleme biblischer Theologie* (G. von Rad Festschrift; ed. Hans Walter Wolff; Munich: Kaiser, 1971), 183–98 (see 190).

13. See Cole (*Shape and Message of Book III*, 46–53); also Pierre Auffret, "C'est Dieu qui juge," *ZAW* 109 (1997): 385–94 (see 392–93).

14. Thus Pierre Buis ("Psaume 76," *ETR* 55 [1980]: 412–15 [see 415]) sees it as generalizing the point of Pss. 46 and 48.

tion to worship that commonly appears in both praise and testimony psalms. Both have been described as "Zion songs,"[15] though both focus more on Yhwh than on Zion (see on Ps. 48). Like Pss. 46–48, it also recalls the Assyrian crisis (in particular, compare v. 3 with 46:9 [10]). But in having been interpreted historically, liturgically, and eschatologically, it compares with Ps. 47,[16] though each of these interpretations requires much reading into the text. It has been connected historically with the time of David[17] as well as with the Assyrian crisis,[18] but it also looks behind these to the Red Sea event (see esp. vv. 6–7). Thus if it links with one event, it sets that in an act of praise for the whole story of God's deliverance of Israel. Liturgically, it has been connected with an annual celebration of Yhwh's acts of deliverance,[19] and it may plausibly be seen as belonging to a worship event in Jerusalem. But we have no direct data on the nature of such an event.

Jerome translated the qatal verbs as future, and Qimchi referred the psalm to the last great battle with Gog and Magog, but its overt focus in vv. 1–9 is on what the people know God has already done. Nevertheless, it no doubt implies the conviction that God will so act in the future; the verbs in vv. 10–12 are yiqtol, and we might understand them to make this reference explicit. So the psalm reflects events in Israel's story, but it does not encourage us to tie it to particular events; this story will have been celebrated in worship, but we do not know how; the psalm celebrates the fact that Yhwh will so act again, but the term "eschatological" confuses rather than clarifies.

> The leader's. With strings. Composition. Asaph's. Song.

Heading. See glossary. LXX adds "to the Assyrian," which makes explicit one of the contexts to which the psalm relates.

76:1–3. So the psalm begins by celebrating how Yhwh is made known in Jerusalem and by declaring the acts whereby that has come about.

> [1]God is known in Judah;
>   in Israel his name is great.

"Is known" may turn out to be an understatement; in light of vv. 4 and 7, perhaps we should understand the niphal participle to suggest "is

---

15. Gunkel, *Psalmen*, 199, 330.
16. Cf. Weiser, *Psalms*, 525.
17. Cf. Otto Eissfeldt ("Psalm 76," *TLZ* 82 [1957]: 801–8), who connects it specifically with the victory narrated in 2 Sam. 5:17–25.
18. So, e.g., Rashi.
19. So Mowinckel, *Psalms in Israel's Worship*, 1:140–54.

one who makes himself known" or "is to be *acknowledged." In the two
parallel cola, the reference to Israel over against Judah indicates that
the line presupposes Yhwh's lordship over the whole of the twelve-clan
nation. The pairing of Judah and Israel usually suggests the southern
and the northern kingdoms, but in this context "Israel" might denote
the whole people over against the clan where Yhwh's tent was located
(v. 2). Either way, the line raises the question "How is God made known
there, or why is God to be acknowledged there, and what makes God's
name great?"

> ²His shelter came to be in Salem,
>   his dwelling in Zion.

Part of the answer lies in the fact that Yhwh took up residence in
Jerusalem.[20] In these two parallel cola, "shelter" and "dwelling" both
suggest rather temporary places to live, and rather unimpressive ones.
Both words can refer to an animal's lair, though the context does not
suggest that resonance here (as it does in 10:9; 104:22, with specific references to lions).[21] Their point rather is to stress the temporary nature
of the kind of dwelling Yhwh once had, which contrasts with the situation that obtained after David's day. Yhwh had been long on the move,
residing in a portable sanctuary that changed its location (Gilgal, Shiloh,
Gibeon . . .) even after the people itself came to settle in the land at the
end of their wanderings. Then David brought Yhwh's tent to Jerusalem.
The name Salem otherwise occurs only in Gen. 14:18 and the allusion
to this incident in Heb. 7:1–2.[22]

> ³There he broke the bow's flames,
>   shield and sword and war. (Rise)

The further answer to that question about how Yhwh is known in
Judah complicates the historical picture suggested by the psalm. The
capture of Jerusalem and Yhwh's move there did not involve a great deal

20. Syntactically, the *w* consecutive could continue the ptc. (cf. GKC 116x; TNIV?).
But the explicit use of the verb *hāyâ* suggests rather that the line is making a point about
an event.

21. Contrast W. A. M. Beuken's emphasis, "God's Presence in Salem," in *Loven en
geloven* (N. H. Ridderbos Festschrift; ed. M. H. van Es et al.; Amsterdam: Ton Bolland,
1975), 135–50.

22. Goulder (*Psalms of Asaph*, 85–88) suggests that it originally referred to a location
in Ephraim (cf. Salim in John 3:23), and Terrien (*Psalms*, 549) sees here a chronological
sequence: first Salem in the north, then Zion in Judah. But see J. A. Emerton, "The Site
of Salem," in *Studies in the Pentateuch*, ed. J. A. Emerton, VTSup 41 (Leiden: Brill, 1990),
45–71.

of battle. The description in vv. 3–6 suggests more the Red Sea event, the conquest of the land, and later events such as the defeat of the Assyrian invasion. It is thus the first indication that the psalm celebrates great acts such as that defeat, setting it into connection with the whole story of Yhwh's acts. In turn, these events are seen as manifestations of the world's rulers' recurrent attempts to resist Yhwh's lordship there (e.g., Pss. 2; 46; 48; 110). While "flames" might be simply a vivid term for flashing arrows, burning arrows were much more dangerous than regular arrows, particularly in a siege, because of their capacity to set a city on fire (cf. Isa. 50:11). Either way, "breaking" is an odd thing to do to arrows (contrast Ezek. 39:3) but a natural thing to do to bows (cf. Ps. 46:9 [10]), so perhaps the expression involves a metonymy, which continues in the description of Yhwh's breaking shield, sword, and [weapon of] war. The line as a whole concerns not directly the abolition of war but also the defeat of people making war on Jerusalem. It brings *šālôm* to *šālēm*.[23]

76:4–6. A second sequence restates the point.

> ⁴You are resplendent,
>   majestic from the mountains full of prey.

The further niphal begins this second section in a way paralleling the first, but then the pronoun indicates that Yhwh is now addressed. Yhwh shines out with bright light like the sun. In 93:4 Yhwh is more majestic than the sea with its dynamic force; here a comparison with the mountains in their impressiveness and strength could make a similar point (cf. KJV). But the reference to prey hardly fits with that. Rather, the mountains around Jerusalem are full of prey as a result of the victory described in the verses on either side; the prey is the bodies of defeated attackers (cf. 124:6; Nah. 2:12–13 [13–14]), in a spectacular reversal of what had been threatened (Isa. 5:29; 31:4). Yhwh's majesty is reflected in the splendor of the victory this evidences.

> ⁵The stouthearted let themselves be spoiled, they fell into deep sleep;
>   none of the brave men lifted their hands.

The section again makes a transition to qatal, explicating how Yhwh's majesty was made manifest. It is typical of Israel's experience to be attacked by people who are bold and confident of their capacity to win victory, people such as the Egyptians at the Red Sea or Sennacherib's Assyrians. The reversal of their expectations is described with some irony

23. Cf. Kraus, *Psalms 60–150*, 110.

as the psalm uses the verb "spoil" in the hitpolel, which suggests "let themselves be spoiled" rather than merely "were spoiled." Superpowers showed up expecting to take spoil; that was in part the way their missions were financed, the way their armies were paid (e.g., Exod. 15:9; Isa. 8:1–4; 10:6). But these stouthearted warriors simply gave up the fight, lay down to sleep, found themselves incapable of raising a hand so as to wield a weapon in attack or even in defense, and thus let themselves be spoiled. Faced with the majestic one (*'addîr*, v. 4), the people who were stout (*'abbîr*) of heart ceased to be so. Yet at this point the psalm does not imply that there was anything supernatural about their falling deep asleep (nor of this being the sleep of death, though that will follow); it does not speak of their being overcome by *tardēmâ*, the supernatural sleep by which God overwhelms people (e.g., 1 Sam. 26:12). They just gave in to indolent slumber, in contrast to what one would expect of people such as the Assyrians (Isa. 5:27). The parallel colon makes the point with further irony: literally "all the men of ability/strength/valor did not find their hands." These top-notch warriors lay there wondering where their hands were in order to lay them on their bows, shields, and swords (v. 3) so as to defend themselves, but they never found them.

> ⁶At your blast, God of Jacob,
>   both chariot and horse lay stunned.

Whereas v. 5 thus spoke of something mysterious yet human and empirical, v. 6 goes on to look behind this mystery to discern Yhwh's activity. The strange event issued from the blast of the hot breath of *Jacob's God, something with the force of an explosion such as knocks people over.[24] It was this that meant not only that people fell asleep (v. 5) but also that chariot[25] and horse lay stunned; here the psalm does use the verb *rādam*, the root of *tardēmâ*, suggesting a supernatural deep sleep. The line as a whole recalls the Red Sea deliverance (106:9; Exod. 14:21–28; 15:1, 21).

76:7–9. A third time the psalm states the point.

> ⁷You—you are to be revered;
>   who can stand before you in the time of your anger?

Once again the opening of the section parallels that of the previous ones but goes on to offer some variation. This time the niphal participle

---

24. *Ga'ărâ* is more than a rebuke (see *NIDOTTE*).

25. Chariots are thus personalized; they, too, lie in a state of collapse. EVV's "rider and horse" presupposes that *rekeb* can also mean "charioteer" or that it should be repointed (e.g.) as *rōkēb* (cf. Exod. 15:1, 21); and cf. LXX.

453

is preceded by "you," making clear that address to Yhwh continues; the pronoun is then repeated after the participle. From the viewpoint of the victims of Yhwh's blast and of Yhwh's anger, Yhwh is to be feared, but from Israel's viewpoint Yhwh's blast and anger are the means of Yhwh's deliverance being put into effect, so *yārē'* likely has its common meaning of *revere. The paronomasia between *nôrā'* here and *nā'ôr* in v. 4 suggests a link between the two ideas. It is as one to be revered that Yhwh is resplendent; Yhwh's splendor finds expression in being one who is revered. The idea that no one can stand before the angry Yhwh continues the thought of the previous line. If you stand in front of a powerful person when they are angry, the blast of their anger knocks you down. One word from them, and you are done. That is good news for little Israel, reason to bow down in reverent awe: see, for instance, the reference to Yhwh's snorting anger (*'appayim*) at the Red Sea, which makes Yhwh "to be revered" to Israel (Exod. 15:8, 11) but certainly "fearful" to Israel's attackers.

> ⁸From the heavens you made your decision heard;
>   earth revered and was still,

Once again the niphal participle gives way to qatal verbs that provide its basis; first comes a verb that looks behind Yhwh's actions to the decision-making that lay behind it. The earthly event had its background in a decision in the heavens that issued in action on earth. The God who dwells on Zion is also the one who dwells in the heavens and who thus thunders from there. In the second colon the earth where the decision is received complements the heavens where it is made, and the *revering, amazed silence with which it is received complements the audibility of its proclamation. The world as a whole thus looks on with awe as Yhwh's decision about the destiny of Israel's attackers is announced. The next verse will make clear that once again this *yir'â* is amazed awe rather than fear.

> ⁹When God rose to exercise authority,
>   to deliver all the weak in the earth. (Rise)

The first colon perhaps repeats the previous line—*mišpāṭ* is a synonym of *dîn*—and refers to Yhwh's standing up in the heavenly cabinet to declare with authority the decision v. 8 referred to (cf. Isa. 3:13). But rising to exercise authority could also denote standing to take action, and certainly the second colon refers to the action that follows from Yhwh's decision-making. In other contexts, one might reckon that *'ereṣ* refers to the land rather than the earth, but here it more likely has the same meaning as in v. 8. Thus, typically, it makes clear that Yhwh's action on Israel's behalf at a moment such as the Red Sea deliverance, the victories of David, or the defeat of Assyria is undertaken not merely for the benefit of Israel but also for the benefit of the whole world. All the *weak peoples gain from the putting down of a superpower.

76:10–12. The final three-line section draws inferences from the first three, making a statement of confidence concerning the way Yhwh habitually acts or a statement of expectation about how Yhwh will act in the future.

> [10]Yes, for human fury confesses you;
>   you bind the leftovers of great fury.

Although the *kî* could suggest that v. 10 belongs with what precedes, the transition to yiqtol verbs distinguishes this verse and rather suggests it as the first line of a final further three-line section. I take the *kî* to be asseverative but also to keep the connotation of "for" (cf. 75:2, 6–8 [3, 7–9]).[26] "Human fury confesses you" is an elliptical assertion that when Yhwh acts in the way vv. 1–9 has described, human powers such as Egypt and Assyria that have summoned up their fury to act against Yhwh find themselves having to acknowledge Yhwh. The fury of the second colon is presumably that same fury, and "leftovers" (*šě'ērît*) suggests another link with the story of the Assyrian crisis. There such calamity comes to Judah that only "leftovers" seem to remain (Isa. 37:4). Here the psalm declares either that Yhwh will similarly reduce Israel's furious foes to leftovers (cf. Isa. 14:30) and then bind them, or more likely that in a positive sense Yhwh will bind the people of Judah who are left over from those furious attackers (cf. Isa. 37:32).[27]

> [11]Make promises and fulfill them to Yhwh your God;
>   all those around him bring tribute to the one who is to be revered.

Although such an exhortation might appropriately have been addressed to the earth as a whole that benefits from Yhwh's acts, the phrase "Yhwh your God" indicates that attention reverts to Israel, the direct beneficiary of Yhwh's exercise of authority over the superpower and of Yhwh's promise to bind Judah's leftovers. Further, whereas the psalm referred to God's name in v. 1, only here does it actually utter the name

26. Linking v. 10 to what precedes could also suggest that this fury is Yhwh's fury against humanity (objective rather than subjective genitive); cf. Tg. But that makes the difficult line even more difficult.

27. John Day ("Shear-Jashub [Isaiah vii 3] and 'The Remnant of Wrath' [Psalm lxxvi 11]," *VT* 31 [1981]: 76–78) links the phrase with the name of Isaiah's son, taking it as a reference to Assyrian leftovers.

Yhwh, "in a sort of climax."[28] If we understand the psalm historically, the time for making *promises could be the time of crisis before the deliverance the psalm focuses on. The likely implication of the first line is then "You made promises: now fulfill them."[29] But more likely vv. 10–12 are making the psalms' typical transition to a statement about the worshippers' ongoing life in the future (cf. 50:22–23). Who, then, are "all those around him" who bring tribute? The term can denote Yhwh's aides (e.g., 89:7 [8]), but they hardly bring tribute. It is not a term to describe earthly peoples in general as beneficiaries of Yhwh's acts. Most often it denotes attackers (e.g., 44:13 [14]; 79:4), and this suggests that v. 11b restates v. 10a. The people who have set themselves against Yhwh are now to offer submissive tribute to the one who they now acknowledge is to be *revered. The use of that last word, in a context where it has denoted a positive revering rather than a negative fearing, suggests that the line offers hope even to enemies such as Egypt and Assyria. Their defeat draws them toward recognition of Yhwh, too. It is they who decide whether for them the word has positive or negative connotations. But either way, the emphasis lies on their glorifying of Yhwh.

> [12]He curbs the spirit of leaders,
>   one to be revered by earth's kings.

The first colon is ambiguous. The verb *bāṣar* can refer to cutting off grape clusters, then to cutting off a city. So the colon could suggest cutting off the spirit of people, that is, their lives. But presumably the kings of the second colon are the same people as the leaders of the first, and this suggests a less negative vision for these leaders/kings in keeping with vv. 10–11. They are being cut down to size and put in their place in such a way as to drive them to acknowledge Yhwh as the one who is to be revered. The last colon thus incorporates yet another niphal participle, such as have characterized the psalm (one in each of the four sections, including the opening and closing cola) and yet another part of the root *yārē'* (four in the psalm as a whole: vv. 7, 8, 11, 12). The God who is known in Zion is to be revered throughout the world.

Theological Implications

The psalm is thus suggestive about revering or fearing and about the choice a superpower makes in that connection. To a superpower,

28. Gerstenberger, *Psalms*, 2:85.
29. An extension of the idiom noted in GKC 110f.

the power of Yhwh is a threat. It imperils the superpower's own power and prestige. The latter's power and prestige threaten to look as if they rival Yhwh's, and therefore they need to be put down. Yhwh is therefore someone fearful. Conversely, for little peoples it is good news that the superpower's power and prestige make a challenge to Yhwh and invite its being put down. That fact means Yhwh is someone to be revered (acknowledged and trusted) rather than feared. The Jonah story shows that, fortunately, it is possible for a superpower to turn to Yhwh, bow down before Yhwh, and change its ways, though this does not happen very often. The psalm's expectation is that, rather, it is through being put down that the superpower will come to acknowledge Yhwh. One way or another, though, this will come about, and it will also bring about an acknowledgment of Yhwh by the rest of the world's leaders. The psalm thus moves from a self-revelation of God in Zion to an acknowledgment of God throughout the world.[30]

30. Cole, *Shape and Message of Book III*, 46.

Psalm 77

The Pain and the Hope
of Recollection

Translation

The leader's. On Jeduthun. Asaph's. Composition.

¹Aloud to God, yes, I shall cry out,[1]
　　aloud to God, so that he may give ear to me.[2]
²In my time of distress I have sought help from my Lord;
　　my hand by night has reached out and does not grow numb.
My heart has refused to be comforted;
　　³I shall call God to mind and complain,
　　I shall murmur as my spirit faints. (Rise)

⁴You have grasped the guards on my eyes;
　　I have been constrained[3] and I cannot speak.
⁵I have thought about former days,
　　years of long ago.
⁶I shall call to mind[4] my song at night;
　　with myself I shall murmur,
　　and my spirit has sought hard.

⁷Is it forever that my Lord will spurn?
　　Will he never again delight?

1. Lit. "[with] my voice to God and I will cry out." The opening adverbial expression (cf. GKC 144m) is extraposed and followed by *w* apodosis (cf. JM 156l; GKC 143d).
2. Presumably not *w* plus inf. const., despite the form, but *w*-qatal; see GKC 63o. On *w*-qatal to indicate purpose, see JM 119m; GKC 112p.
3. For *pā'am*, EVV have "troubled," but "thrust" or "impel" (BDB) is the more basic meaning (cf. Judg. 13:25).
4. LXX, Sym, and Syr make this the last word in v. 5, which makes that a neater bicolon. It is then necessary to emend *něgînātî* (my song) to a verb such as *hāgîtî* ("I have talked"; cf. LXX) or *niggantî* ("I have sung"; Barthélemy, *Psaumes*, 567).

⁸Has his commitment permanently ceased to exist,
    his word failed for all time?
⁹Has God put showing grace out of mind,
    or has he shut off his compassion in anger? (Rise)

¹⁰And I have said, That is what has hurt me:
    the years of the right hand of the Most High.
¹¹I will make mention of[5] the deeds of Yah,
    yes, for I shall call to mind your wonders of old.
¹²I shall talk of all your work,
    I shall murmur of your deeds.

¹³God, your way was with holiness:
    who was a god as great as God?
¹⁴You were the God who does wonders;
    you made known your might among the peoples.
¹⁵You restored your people with your arm,[6]
    the descendants of Jacob and Joseph. (Rise)
¹⁶Waters saw you, God,
    waters saw you, they would convulse;
    yes, deeps would tremble.
¹⁷Clouds poured down water,
    skies gave sound;
    yes, your arrows would fly about.
¹⁸The sound of your thunder in the whirlwind,
    your flashes of lightning lit up the world;
    the earth trembled and shook.
¹⁹Your way was in the sea
    and your paths[7] in mighty waters,
    but your steps were not acknowledged.
²⁰You led your people like a flock
    by means of Moses and Aaron.

Interpretation

In a distinctive way, the psalm combines lament at trouble and declaration of God's past acts. It moves from lament and questioning (vv. 1–3, 4–6, 7–9) to reflection and recollection (vv. 10–12, 13–20) and never

5. I take it that Q's *'ezkôr* has assimilated K's hiphil *'zkyr* to the other qals of this verb in the psalm.
6. *Zĕrôaʿ* has no suffix, but body parts need not have a suffix when the verb makes clear to whom they belong (e.g., Gen. 38:28; 1 Kings 11:26; Job 21:25), especially in references to God restoring "with outstretched arm" (e.g., Exod. 6:6); contrast Exod. 15:16, where the context requires the suffix.
7. Q has sg., but Vrs as well as K have pl.

moves back again. It thus compares and contrasts with Pss. 44 and 89, whose movement is the opposite, from declaration of God's acts to lament, and with Ps. 74, which moves from lament to declaration and back again.[8] Indeed, vv. 13–20 could stand alone as a declaration concerning God's acts (like Pss. 44:1–8 [2–9]; 74:12–17; and 89:1–37 [2–38]) and may once have done so. But if so, links between the two parts indicate that vv. 1–12 were composed with vv. 13–20 in mind; the psalm does not bring together two separate compositions. Among the words it repeats are the suppliant's threefold declaration of intent to "call to mind" (zākar; vv. 3, 6, 11) and its accompanying threefold "I shall murmur" ('āśîḥâ; vv. 3, 6, 12). These signal the psalm's agenda and bind the first part to the second. The recurrence of varying forms of staircase parallelism in both parts—in vv. 1, 3, 6; and in 11, 16–19—also has this effect, as do links in both parts with Exod. 15 (where staircase parallelism also recurs, in 15:6, 11).[9]

In the context of the opening lines, vv. 13–20 do not represent a move from gloom to confidence, from protest to praise, as if the suppliant's questions are resolved by the recollection of the Red Sea story.[10] Rather, their distinctive effect is to leave God and suppliant with the acts of the past that contrast with the present. They leave the suppliant with the hurt of that contrast but also with the potential hope, and they leave God with the challenge of it.[11] In a sense, then, vv. 13–20 function in the place of the actual plea in the psalm, which is otherwise missing.[12] The recollection is both a pained recounting of how things were once different, and an implicit exhortation to Yhwh to make things different again. It is not simply praise that resolves the protest of the earlier verses, though it does constitute the counterargument with which one side of the suppliant's being seeks to encourage the other side.

The LXX translates vv. 1–5 with aorist verbs (v. 6 with imperfects). The effect is to make the whole psalm look back on an experience of prayer and its answer.[13] Since yiqtol verbs can refer to the past, this is a possible understanding for many of the lines. But it makes the dynamic of the psalm difficult to understand, since it constitutes a recollection of a crisis

8. Cole (*Shape and Message of Book III*, 54–62) details links with Ps. 74.

9. Cf. John S. Kselman, "Psalm 77 and the Book of Exodus," *JANESCU* 15 (1983): 51–58; P. Auffret, "La droite du Très-Haut," *SJOT* 6 (1992): 92–122 (see 114–20); Beat Weber, *Psalm 77* (Weinheim: Beltz, 1995), 207–12; Meir Weiss, "פעלך בכל והגיתי,'" in *Texts, Temples, and Traditions* (M. Haran Festschrift; ed. Michael V. Fox et al.; Winona Lake, IN: Eisenbrauns, 1996), *47–*58, 408.

10. So, e.g., Artur Weiser, "Psalm 77," *TLZ* 72 (1947): 133–40. See the commentary below on vv. 10–11.

11. Cf. Pat Graham, "Psalm 77," *ResQ* 18 (1975): 151–58.

12. Mays, *Psalms*, 253.

13. Cf. Theodoret, *Psalms*, 2:18–28; Cassiodorus, *Psalms*, 2:238–50; NEB.

that is evidently now over; yet it gives no account of Yhwh's response in word or deed,[14] since vv. 13–20 refer to acts of old that Yhwh undertook, not to acts for the suppliant. Further, it seems perverse to take the parallel sequences of cohortatives in vv. 3 and 6 as having mere past reference.[15] Rather, then, the yiqtols refer to the suppliant's ongoing prayer, and the qatals to the past prayer that continues into the present.

From vv. 1–6 we might infer that the suppliant is speaking of personal trouble, and even in vv. 7–20 there is nothing explicit to indicate that the suppliant is a leader rather than an ordinary person. The implication would then be that the psalm illustrates the way an individual may find resources in time of difficulty by reflecting on what God has done for the people as a whole.[16] But the appeal to God's great acts for the people as a whole in the past makes it more likely that the difficulty is communal rather than individual. Perhaps, then, the suppliant is an individual troubled by the way God has been acting.[17] Or perhaps the talk in terms of "my trouble" means that a person such as a king or governor speaks; the closing reference to Israel's leaders would fit with that. The psalm would then compare with Ps. 73, and also contrast with it, because here there is no resolution. Or perhaps the "I" is the "I" of each member of the congregation, so that the psalm would compare with Lamentations. Its setting might be the exile and the prayer of the whole community in that context, though the reference to Joseph (v. 15) might mark it as a northern psalm.[18]

The leader's. On Jeduthun.[19] Asaph's. Composition.

Heading. See glossary and (for Jeduthun) the heading to Ps. 62.

77:1–3. The psalm describes the suppliant's prayer and reflection in the first of two parallel three-line sections: each middle line (vv. 2a–b, 5) recollects the way the suppliant has been praying and thinking, and each third line (vv. 2c–3, 6) is a tricolon dominated by cohortatives but closing with a reference to lamenting and to the suppliant's spirit.

14. Syr may provide one in v. 2 by reading "his hand" instead of "my hand," but even that expression may refer to Yhwh's hand being heavy on the suppliant.

15. So GKC 108g; *TTH* 52; DG 68 (in contrast, DG 63b sees the yiqtol in v. 1 as implicitly cohortative). Note especially the form *wĕˀehĕmāyâ* in v. 3; final *h* verbs do not usually have a distinct cohortative form (JM 79o; GKC 75l).

16. So Gregory M. Stevenson, "Communal Imagery and the Individual Lament," *ResQ* 39 (1997): 215–29.

17. So William-A. Goy, "Dieu a-t-il change," in *Hommage à Wilhelm Vischer* (Montpellier: Causse, Graille, Castelnau, 1960), 56–62.

18. For these and other possibilities, see Weber, *Psalm 77*, 248–64.

19. K has the rarer form Jedithun (cf. the heading to Ps. 39 K; Neh. 11:17 K; 1 Chron. 16:38).

> ¹Aloud to God, yes, I shall cry out,
>   aloud to God, so that he may give ear to me.

The psalm opens with a subtly parallel line. Formally, "aloud to God" is repeated, each time followed by a verb prefixed by *w*, one cohortative, one qatal. But the verbal expression in the first colon also applies to the second, and the line involves staircase parallelism[20] as the second colon repeats the opening phrase and then takes the matter further in going on to tell us the object of the crying out. "Crying out" (*ṣāʿaq*) is typically what Israel does under pressure, such as that of oppression in Egypt (Exod. 3:7, 9; Deut. 26:7) and what individuals do in terrible need or anguish (Deut. 22:27; 2 Kings 4:1; 6:26). "Aloud" is literally "[with] my voice," a strictly unnecessary expression (with what else can one cry out?) that heightens the statement and underlines its out-loud nature. This heightening becomes clearer when we compare with 3:4 [5], which also begins "aloud with my voice." Here the verb is "cry out," not the blander "call" (*qārāʾ*). It is cohortative not yiqtol, and it is preceded by the *w* (translated "yes"). Likewise "give ear" is a more vivid and less usual verb than "listen" to express the suppliant's first need, but both verbs express the recognition that if it is possible to get Yhwh's attention, then everything else will surely follow. The recurrence of the preposition *ʾel* (to) expresses the two-sided nature of prayer: I cry out to God; God gives ear to me. Except that God is not doing so.

> ²ᵃ⁻ᵇIn my time of distress I have sought help from my Lord;
>   my hand by night has reached out and does not grow numb.

The change to qatal verbs suggests that the suppliant has been thus crying out for some time; the declaration of intent in v. 1 did not imply beginning something new. The psalm never indicates the nature of the suppliant's distress or trouble; its focus is rather on the fact that Yhwh does not respond to the pleas that issue from this experience. The suppliant has been doing what one is supposed to do in trouble, *seeking help from the *Lord. Doing so by night heightens the point. The suppliant has stayed awake to pray at night in the way one will stay awake through the night for some important project (cf. v. 6; 6:6 [7]; 119:62; 134:1; Lam. 2:19). The psalms more commonly refer to day and night (e.g., 22:2 [3]; 42:3, 8 [4, 9]); here the second colon gives specificity to the first, as when one colon refers to the hand and the second to the right hand (74:11). The rest of the second colon also re-expresses the

20. See Watson, *Classical Hebrew Poetry*, 150–56.

first, though in slightly puzzling terms. Associated with seeking help from someone is reaching out one's hand (cf. 28:2; 143:6, though there the hands are plural, as in LXX here; for the singular, cf. Prov. 1:24). But the verb for "reach out" strictly means "flow," like the eye with tears (Lam. 3:49; the expression also came in 75:8 [9]).[21] On the other hand, one can see the appropriateness of the verb "grow numb," for raised arms will tire like that. The suppliant persists, not giving in to such numbness.

> ²ᶜMy heart has refused to be comforted;
> ³I shall call God to mind and complain,
> I shall murmur as my spirit faints. (Rise)

The MT makes a tricolon of v. 2, but v. 2c links as well with v. 3, and more likely the tricolon closes off the section. To let one's heart (*person) be comforted is to accept things that cannot be changed (such as someone's death; Gen 24:67; 2 Sam. 13:39) or things that are right even though painful (Ezek. 14:22) or things that have now been put right or are going to be put right (Jer. 31:15–16; Ezek 32:31). But there are times when Yhwh does not so accept things (Isa. 57:6), and the suppliant does not intend to accept them, and thus to give up praying, until Yhwh has actually acted. Acceptance or comfort will follow on that (Pss. 71:21; 86:17). In the meantime, then, the suppliant makes a series of commitments (the verbs in v. 3 are all cohortative; the dominance of the verbs in the two cola is noteworthy).[22] The first is to keep calling God to mind, to keep being *mindful, rather than giving in to the temptation to put God out of mind, to stop envisaging the possibility of God acting. The second is thus to keep making a noise. For *hāmâ*, EVV have groan or moan, but the word often means something more tumultuous and aggressive (46:3, 6 [4, 7], "rage"; cf. also 42:5, 11 [6, 12]; 43:5; 55:17 [18]; 59:6, 14 [7, 15]; 83:2 [3]). On the other hand, "murmur" (*śîaḥ*) implies something more turned in on the self, which fits the closing phrase about the spirit fainting.

77:4–6. A further three-line section parallels the first in recollecting the way the suppliant has been thinking (v. 5) and in closing with a tricolon that refers to murmuring and to the suppliant's spirit (v. 6). What is new is the direction in which the verses speak. Verses 1–3 talk about God; vv. 4–6 address God. They are thus confrontational and not merely wistful.

21. For *niggĕrâ* from the rare verb *nāgar*, LXX and Syr imply easier readings from *neged*, "before him" (*negdô*) or "before me" (*negdî*), while Tg eases the construction by reading "my eye," with Lam. 3:49.
22. Weber, *Psalm 77*, 57.

> ⁴You have grasped the guards on my eyes;
>   I have been constrained and I cannot speak.

The guards on one's eyes are presumably one's eyelids (cf. Tg).²³ The EVV then take the first colon to mean "you have kept me awake," but the previous lines have indicated that actually the suppliant has anyway been determined to stay awake, so talk of God's compelling this would be odd.²⁴ Rather, the first colon means that God's action (or inaction) has been keeping the suppliant's eyes shut²⁵ in the sense of giving these eyes nothing to see, no act of deliverance (contrast 37:35–36; 48:8 [9]; 54:7 [9]). The parallel reference to not speaking supports this understanding: Yhwh has likewise obliged the suppliant to be someone with nothing to say by way of uttering praise for God's acts, because there are no such acts to speak about. The rest of the psalm shows that the psalmist is not refraining from speaking about the trouble of the present situation; this is not the failed silence of Ps. 39. The prayer, "Open my lips" so that I can declare your praise (51:15 [17]), has not been granted (contrast 40:5 [6]; 66:16; 145:11, 21).

> ⁵I have thought about former days,
>   years of long ago.

That comment in v. 4b introduces the theme that will occupy the rest of the psalm, the contrast between this present experience and the way things were in the past. Then there were things to see and talk about. Verses 13–20 will make specific that the psalmist refers not to personal experiences earlier in life but to God's great deeds in Israel's past. Within vv. 4–6, this initial reflection parallels v. 2a–b. Alongside the seeking of help from Yhwh was the thinking about this contrast.

> ⁶I shall call to mind my song at night;
>   with myself I shall murmur,
>   and my spirit has sought hard.

Again the development of vv. 4–6 parallels that in vv. 1–3 as the section comes to an end with a tricolon dominated by cohortatives,

---

23. Cf. *šomrâ*, a guard on my mouth, in 141:3. Weber (*Psalm 77*, 64–66) renders "You have grasped my eyes [in the night] watches," which makes good sense but requires more reading into the line.

24. Thus for *'āḥaztâ*, Jerome and Sym imply *'āḥaztî*, making the suppliant the one who keeps the eyes open, while LXX and Syr have a pl. verb, implying that the eyes kept their eyelids open (LXX^B then has "my enemies" for "my eyes," implying "my enemies set watches against me").

25. Cf. Rashi.

repeating the commitment to being *mindful and murmuring and including another reference to the suppliant's spirit. It is the context that has to determine what kind of songs (*strings) the psalm refers to. In 69:12 [13] MT they were mocking songs, but here the context does not point to that, and the parallel with v. 3 rather suggests they are praise songs. With distress the psalmist is calling Yhwh to mind (v. 3) and calling to mind past praise of Yhwh (v. 6); the combination parallels 42:6–8 [7–9], which also refers to singing at night. The description in the second and third cola of the psalmist's murmuring "with myself" (lit. "with my *heart") and of "my spirit searching out" also recalls the inner argument related in Pss. 42:5, 11 [6, 12]; 43:5. The recollection of how things were contrasts with the reflection on how things are. The absolute use of ḥāpaś piel (search hard) is odd.[26] The verb usually refers to literal searches, but it can denote searching for insight (Prov. 2:4), and here it could suggest a search for understanding or for the right attitude. Or it may be a heightened synonym for dāraš (v. 2) and refer to the way the psalmist sought help from God. The third colon will then be parallel with the first, with this seeking paralleling the singing referred to there.

77:7–9. Another three-line section further indicates the content of the cry, the complaint, and the murmur. The Tg highlights the unthinkable nature of these questions by undertranslating them, beginning each verse "Is it possible that . . . ?"

> [7]Is it forever that my Lord will spurn?
> Will he never again delight?

A question about the *Lord spurning or pushing away also arose in Pss. 42–43, but there it was a "Why?" question (cf. also 44:9, 23 [10, 24]; 60:1, 10 [3, 12]; 88:14 [15]; 89:38 [39]); both forms of question came in 74:1. Lamentations 3:31 reckons the answer to this question is "No," but the psalmist is not yet sure, or is no longer sure (cf. Lam. 5:19–22). The parallel colon re-expresses the point as a negative: for delight or accept (rāṣā), see also 44:3 [4]; 85:1 [2].[27]

> [8]Has his commitment permanently ceased to exist,
> his word failed for all time?

---

26. Jerome, Sym, Th, and Syr thus imply a first-person verb: "I have searched my spirit."

27. The line works abcb′a′: interrogative prefixed to adverbial expression for time, yiqtol verb, subject (also applying to the second colon), yiqtol verb (compound and negatived), adverbial expression for time.

The line re-expresses v. 7, using qatal verbs and formulating the point perhaps even more paradoxically. *Commitment is by definition something that does not fail. The declaration that Yhwh's commitment lasts forever is the refrain in Ps. 136 and recurs elsewhere (e.g., 89:2 [3]; 100:5). Nowhere else does a psalm ask whether Yhwh's commitment has ceased. Its question is an unthinkably earth-shattering one, literally (33:5); even heaven-shattering (36:5 [6]; 57:10 [11]). The verb ('āpēs) is also a strong one; a related noun ('epes) means "nothing, zero." "Permanently," the key word in Ps. 74, underlines the point yet further. The second colon again repeats the point.[28] It seems that God's word could not be relied on, and not just temporarily but for all time. It would make sense if this is a king's prayer and thus the colon refers to God's promise to David. Psalm 18:30 [31] declared that Yhwh's word was proved. It now looks disproved. "Yhwh has said this" ('āmar), 2 Sam. 7:5, 8 declared. There is no doubt that this "saying" ('ōmer) has failed to come true, and the only question is whether it has failed for all time. The verb (gāmar) is another that suggests coming to nothing. It is a rare verb, suggesting some irony: in 57:2 [3]; 138:8 it denotes Yhwh's bringing things to completion in a positive way. Calvin compares the lament in 74:9.[29]

> [9]Has God put showing grace out of mind,
>   or has he shut off his compassion in anger? (Rise)

Once again, the further restatement of the question seems unthinkable, as *grace and compassion feature alongside commitment in Yhwh's fundamental self-definition (Exod. 34:6), but the question is pressed by events. Like the expressions "showing grace" and "compassion," the line's verbs take the preceding line further once more. It is not merely that grace and compassion have ceased or failed. It is also that God seems to have deliberately put them out of mind (*ignore). That frightening but familiar verb is then complemented by a frightening but less familiar one. God seems to have shut off his compassion in the way Israelites were forbidden to shut off their hand from the needy (Deut. 15:7). In this case, that implies not miserliness but anger; "anger" and "compassion" stand next to each other in harsh tension. And it is anger without obvious explanation, another contravention of Exod. 34:6; God was supposed to be slow to anger, even when there was good reason for it.[30]

28. The line works abca'c'b': interrogative prefixed to qatal verb, *l* expression for time, subject, qatal verb, subject (the prefix carrying over from the first noun), *l* expression for time.

29. *Psalms*, 3:212.

30. The parallelism in the line works abcda'b'ec': there are two different interrogatives, two different verbs, two different objects (one a gerund, one a noun). Then the

77:10–12. Yet another three-line section follows. As vv. 7–9 explicate the cry of vv. 1–3, vv. 10–12 explicate the actual address to God in vv. 4–6 and the reflection to which vv. 4–6 referred (verbs from v. 6 recur in vv. 11–12). The section moves from qatal to yiqtol and cohortative as vv. 4–6 moved from qatal to cohortative, both looking back to the way the suppliant has been thinking and declaring the thoughts of the present.

> ¹⁰And I have said, That is what has hurt me:
> the years of the right hand of the Most High.

So the section begins by recalling once more the words that express what the suppliant continues to say inside, the pain that characterizes the suppliant's current experience.[31] The pain lies in that recollection of the "years of long ago" (v. 5).[32] Both "right hand" and "Most High" suggest might and power, but the present action of the Most High's right hand is rather inaction. That contrasts with what has been true in the past, which is about to be expounded. This exposition will suggest a specific resonance for the reference to God's "right hand": see Exod. 15:6, 12.

> ¹¹I will make mention of the deeds of Yah,
> yes, for I shall call to mind your wonders of old.
> ¹²I shall talk of all your work,
> I shall murmur of your deeds.

So v. 11 twice takes up the verb from v. 6. In other contexts the first verb (*zākar* hiphil) could refer to something more like "commemorat-

---

subject "God" at the center of the line applies to both cola, as perhaps does the qualifier "in anger."

31. The MT accent marks *ḥallôtî* as first-person qatal from *ḥālal*. LXX takes it as from *ḥālal* II (begin), but this is difficult to fit in the context. I rather take it as piel inf. const. (with suffix) from *ḥālâ* I (be weak, sick) or *ḥālâ* IV (distress [in *DCH*'s enumeration]), with Jerome, Aq, Tg, and perhaps Th (unless it links the verb to *ḥûl* or a by-form). NJPS apparently understands "my weakness" to imply "my fault" (cf. Weiser, *Psalms*, 531–32; also, on the psalm in general, Luther, *First Lectures*, 2:19), but that requires considerable reading between the lines, and there are no other pointers in the context to such an inference. *Midrash on Psalms*, 2:20, allows for linking the word with *ḥālal* I (profane), while Sym links it with *ḥālal* III (pierce). Tg^B (Stec, *Targum of Psalms*, 150) adds an alternative translation, "this is my entreaty," taking the word as from *ḥālâ* II, "entreat" (cf. TNIV), but the psalm does not actually make these years the subject of entreaty, and the ellipse of *pānîm* (face) as obj. of this verb for entreat would be unparalleled (J. A. Emerton, "The Text of Psalm lxxvii 11," *VT* 44 [1994]: 183–94 [see 185]). The same difficulty attaches to Weber's suggestion (*Psalm 77*, 95–111) that the expression refers to what has appeased the suppliant. Seybold (*Psalmen*, 299) renders "resolution," but this is hard to justify.

32. Most Vrs and EVV take *šĕnôt* as inf. of *šānâ*, "the change in the right hand . . . ," but Tg^B (cf. TNIV) takes it as pl. from *šēnâ*. This was the meaning of the word in v. 5, and this psalm likes to repeat words, with the same meaning, rather than with paronomasia.

ing," but it can also denote less celebratory talk (e.g., 1 Sam. 4:18; Ezek. 29:16), and in this context the talk of Yah's deeds is indeed wistful. The second colon systematically takes further the first, as is initially advertised by the *kî* (yes, for). Yiqtol verb is succeeded by cohortative, the second colon moves to direct address of God, and deeds are succeeded by *wonders (adding "of old," which perhaps implicitly applies to both cola), the word that describes God's acts in Egypt and at the Red Sea (cf. 78:12; Exod. 15:11). The name Yah comes in Exod. 15:2.

Two further parallel cola, continuing to address God, then repeat the point; here a *w*-qatal verb is similarly succeeded by a cohortative. "Talk" (*hāgâ*; cf. 1:2; 63:6 [7]) suggests something quiet and meditative rather than loud, and this is confirmed by the parallel verb "murmur" (cf. vv. 3, 6). The suppliant is referring not to out-loud praise, which would normally be the way one recalled Yhwh's deeds, but to quiet, rather pensive reflection.[33]

77:13–20. The content of the pensive recollection, focusing on the Red Sea deliverance, occupies the rest of the psalm. The section is framed by four bicola (vv. 13–15, 20), but these enfold four tricola with staircase parallelism (vv. 16–19), which might themselves be of independent, earlier origin.[34] The first three (vv. 16–18) use more metaphorical storm language and work in totally asyndetic fashion. The use of yiqtol verbs to describe past events (marked in the translation by the modal expression "would") is characteristic both of the Red Sea song in Exod. 15 (where tricola also recur) and of other accounts of Yhwh acting in stormlike fashion (e.g., Ps. 18:7–15 [8–16]; Hab. 3:10–15);[35] cf. also Pss. 78; 44:2 [3]; 74:5–6, 14. For people for whom this was not regular usage, it might convey vividness. In Exod. 15 and here the poems superimpose onto the exodus story the imagery of a divine victory over forces of disorder, embodied in and symbolized by the sea. Thus the sea takes over much of the place of the Egyptian army. The imagery and the syntax of the final tricolon (v. 19) are such as to make a transition to a more regular reference to the Red Sea event.

> [13]God, your way was with holiness:
>   who was a god as great as God?

---

33. Contrast Weber, *Psalm 77*, 60, who argues that both "make mention" and "murmur" have meanings in vv. 11–12 that differ from vv. 3 and 6.

34. Cf. Helen G. Jefferson, "Psalm lxvii," *VT* 13 (1963): 87–91; Oswald Loretz, *Ugarit-Texte und Thronbesteigungspsalmen* (Münster: Ugarit, 1988), 384–94. Contrast W. van der Meer, "Psalm 77,17–19," *ETL* 70 (1994): 105–11, who sees the lines as a new actualization of these motifs.

35. See Weber, *Psalm 77*, 217–20.

The EVV translate the noun clauses in vv. 13–14a with present-tense verbs, but vv. 10–12 have made us expect reference to God's past activity, and vv. 14b–20 confirm that. So the noun clauses more likely refer to the way God has acted in the past. This first line of recollection well instances the way *'ĕlōhîm* suggests reference to Yhwh in Pss. 42–83; "Yhwh, your way was with holiness: who was a god as great as Yhwh?" would be the more familiar OT way of making the point.[36] Those implicit references to Yhwh as God bracket the line. The two cola then each contain a more general reference to deity. First, God's way of acting was once characterized by holiness, that is, by the supernatural, dynamic power that belongs to God (cf. 98:1; Exod. 15:11); the moral connotations of holiness are not in mind here. Then, to put it another way, that action was the work of a god (*'ēl*) far greater than any other.[37] That point is made by a rhetorical question with very different implications from those in vv. 7–9. Both the statement and the rhetorical question express both the pain and the hope.

> [14]You were the God who does wonders;
> you made known your might among the peoples.

"The God" is *hā'ēl*, the word just translated "god" but now with the article, and the description of God as one who "does *wonders" exactly corresponds to the Red Sea description of God in Exod. 15:11. That was also the occasion when God acted so that the Egyptians would know/acknowledge who was God (Exod. 14:4, 18; and for the hiphil, Ps. 98:2). It was the occasion when Yhwh's might was thus manifested (Exod. 15:2, 13), an event that the peoples would hear about and tremble (Exod. 15:14).

> [15]You restored your people with your arm,
> the descendants of Jacob and Joseph. (Rise)

Talk of *restoring the people with your arm also recalls the Red Sea event (Exod. 15:13, 16), though there the people are "the descendants of Israel" (e.g., Exod. 14:29; 15:1) rather than of Jacob or Joseph. "Household of Jacob" has similar meaning to "descendants of Jacob" (e.g., Ps. 114:1) and "household of Joseph" can appear alongside it (Obad. 18). "Descendants/household of Jacob" naturally refers to the whole people, but it is doubtful if "descendants/household of Joseph" is simply a synonym (any more than "descendants/household of Judah" would be), even

---

36. Cf. "our God" for the last word in the line in LXX, Syr, and "the God of Israel" in Tg.

37. On the use of these terms for god/God, see further on 82:1.

469

though the Joseph clans, Ephraim and Manasseh, were originally the biggest in the people as a whole. "Joseph" would more naturally suggest the northern clans in particular. This is not to imply that Judah's descendants did not take part in the exodus (though this has been suggested) but rather that there is reason for drawing attention to the fact that among the clans were the descendants of Joseph. The reason would be that the psalm was composed for the northern clans. But there would be a sense in which Judeans could identify with Joseph as a key figure in the story of Israel as a whole and thus could see themselves as among Joseph's people.

> [16]Waters saw you, God,
>   waters saw you, they would convulse;
>   yes, deeps would tremble.

The language continues to recall the Red Sea event, when the "waters" might be reckoned to have seen Yhwh and convulsed, the "deeps" froze, and the whole event made peoples "tremble" (Exod. 15:8, 14).[38] On the other hand, the talk of waters convulsing and deeps trembling suggests a metonymy, as it is usually earth that convulses and trembles, as in Ps. 97:4, where it is also earth that "sees."[39] In other words, the whole description in v. 16 is one that more naturally applies to "earth" than to "waters/deep"; it is the Red Sea reference that causes the transfer of epithets. Further, the language thus moves toward the semantic field of the metaphorical description of God's coming to act in the world that appears in (e.g.) Ps. 18:7–15 [8–16], which derives its expressions from the phenomena of a storm.

> [17]Clouds poured down water,
>   skies gave sound;
>   yes, your arrows would fly about.

"Water" comes again, but it has now lost its reference to sea and refers instead to rain, as Red Sea language disappears and storm language becomes more overt; the three cola speak of rain, thunder, and lightning. The powerful, convulsive, and frightening nature of a thunderstorm provides imagery to describe the powerful, convulsive, and frightening implications of God's action in the world, putting down nations that exercise power over weak peoples. When God speaks and acts in the world to overturn things, the experience is like that of a terrible storm that can sweep people away with its torrents (as the Red Sea also did),

38. The staircase parallelism works abcabded'b'.
39. Thus Tg assumes the "they" is people.

shake the earth by its noise, and frighten by its flashes of lightning dart-
ing about in unpredictable fashion. The psalm thus continues to refer
to the Red Sea event, because this was what happened there, but it does
so by means of quite different language and imagery.

> ¹⁸The sound of your thunder in the whirlwind,
>   your flashes of lightning lit up the world;
>   the earth trembled and shook.

The description in terms of storm continues in the three cola. The first
refers more explicitly to the noise of thunder (God's thunder) and the
violent wind that accompanies it.⁴⁰ The second refers more explicitly to
the lightning whose flashes counteract the darkening effect of the clouds
obscuring the sun.⁴¹ The third describes the storm's quaking and shaking
effect on the earth. Here it is the earth that "trembles," as it does more
literally than the waters do.

> ¹⁹Your way was in the sea
>   and your paths in mighty waters,
>   but your steps were not acknowledged.

Talk of the sea and the waters, and the more prosaic syntax (there is
no asyndeton), suggest a transition away from the picture in vv. 16–18.
Yet as another tricolon, v. 19 links with what precedes, and the opening
two noun clauses parallel v. 18a. The further description of the sea as
"mighty waters" also suggests a continuity with language about God's
intervention in the world that appears elsewhere (e.g., Ps. 18:16 [17];
32:6; 144:7). Conversely, Exod. 15 does not refer to Yhwh's way (*derek*);
the expression referring to God's activity in the world picks up from v. 13
(but cf. 18:30 [31]). While Israel walks through the sea, Exod. 15 has no
direct reference to Yhwh doing so. Further, reference to Yhwh's path
(*šĕbîl*) or steps (*ʿāqēb*) comes only here. So the first two cola recall the
fact that God was present and active in characteristic fashion at the Red
Sea as Israel went through the experience of almost being overwhelmed
by the power of Egypt. Yhwh waded or rode through those deep waters.
The object of that was that Yhwh should be "acknowledged" (Exod. 14:4,
18; cf. v. 14). But this did not actually happen.⁴²

40. On the assumption that this is the meaning of *galgal* (from *gālal*, "roll"), though
it usually means "wheel," and Tg may understand it to refer to the round horizon (cf. LXX,
Jerome, KJV?; Stec, *Targum of Psalms*, 150).
41. The "your" in the first colon applies here too; cf. LXX, Syr, Jerome, and 97:4,
where the suffix is present because there is no equivalent parallel noun.
42. The last colon is usually taken to denote that people could not see Yhwh's footsteps,
which might have the down-to-earth implication that the return of the waters conceals

> ²⁰You led your people like a flock
>   by means of Moses and Aaron.

The language of leading corresponds to Exod. 15:13. The image of flock compares rather with Ps. 78:52; 80:1 [2], and yet it also recalls the fact that Exod. 15:13 relates how the people were led to Yhwh's *nāweh*, often a term for a sheepfold (e.g., 2 Sam. 7:8; Isa. 65:10). The image of leading fits with that of way and path. In the Red Sea story, Yhwh gave Moses instructions as to where Israel needed to go, and Moses passed them on (Exod. 14:1–4, 15–18). Aaron does not appear alongside Moses in the Red Sea story, but "by means of Moses and Aaron" corresponds to Num. 33:1 (cf. also 1 Sam. 12:6; Mic. 6:4; and earlier in Exodus, e.g., 11:10; 12:50).

The psalm stops abruptly, as psalms sometimes do, but its closing colon might have special point if the suppliant is the people's leader. If Yhwh then led the people by means of these leaders, can Yhwh not do so now?

Theological Implications

The psalm points the way to avoid two mistakes. "In my time of distress I have sought help from my Lord," it says, and Jerome comments: "It is not always easy to do that. When we are in trouble we are dejected and think of nothing but our trouble; yet the best course in time of affliction is to pray earnestly to God."[43] Admittedly, much of the lament, questioning, and reflection in the psalm addresses not God but the self or the congregation, and that might be dangerous. Verses 1–10 could encourage inordinate self-pity were it not for the fact that they are followed by the turning to recall God's acts in vv. 11–20, which pulls us out of it.[44] The shift halfway through the psalm is a shift from "I" to "you," from self to God.[45] It is not a total transition from despair to hope,[46] but it is a transition from hopelessness to possibility. The psalmist lives with both vv. 1–10 and vv. 11–20.[47]

---

them but also stimulates suggestive reflection on the mystery of the event: when a wonder happens, no one sees Yhwh act, but we see only the result, not the act itself. A comparison can also be made with Exod. 33:18–23 (Weber, *Psalm 77*, 162), but the more concrete link with the use of *yāda'* in v. 14 and in Exod. 14:4, 18 points in this other direction.

43. *Homilies*, 1:68; cf. Augustine, *Psalms*, 360, who compares Ps. 14:4.

44. So Peterson, *Where Your Treasure Is*, 99–109.

45. Walter Brueggemann, "Psalm 77," *Journal for Preachers* 6, no. 2 (1983): 8–14; cf. *Israel's Praise* (Philadelphia: Fortress, 1988), 138.

46. So McCann, "Psalms," 984.

47. As McCann also comments, "Psalms," 985.

On the other hand, whereas Amy Carmichael used to say, "In acceptance lieth peace,"[48] the psalm says that peace is not always the most important thing. Refuse to be comforted; do not give in to acceptance too soon. In the context of distress, as your spirit faints, cry out aloud, seek help from your God, seek hard, keep your hands stretched out in appeal like the woman in Jesus' parable (Luke 18:1–8), complain, murmur. Think about God, about the days when you enjoyed God's blessing, about the praise you used to be able to offer. Face tough questions, and face the hurt. Remind yourself and remind God of the great things that God did in delivering us as his people at the beginning. Only if you do that can you look to God to give ear to you.

48. http://www.4himnet.com/bnyberg/where_lieth_peace.html.

Psalm 78

The Story That Needs Passing On

Translation

Instruction. Asaph's.

¹Give ear, my people, to my teaching;
    turn your ear to the words of my mouth.
²I shall open my mouth with a parable,
    pour out mysteries of old.
³Things that[1] we have heard and acknowledged,
    and our ancestors have told us,
⁴We will not hide[2] from their descendants,
    telling the coming generation:
The praises of Yhwh and his might,
    his wonders that he did.
⁵He set up a declaration in Jacob,
    put teaching in Israel,
Which he commanded our ancestors
    to get their descendants to acknowledge,
⁶So that the coming generation might acknowledge,
    descendants who are to be born,
Might rise up and tell their descendants,
    ⁷so that they might put their confidence in God,
And not ignore God's deeds
    but observe his commands,

1. The *'ăšer* introduces an independent relative clause preceding the verb of which it is the obj. (cf. 69:4 [5]; see GKC 138e).
2. EVV add "them" as a direct obj., but see previous note.

8And not become like their ancestors,
   a rebellious and defiant generation,
A generation that did not make its heart firm,[3]
   whose spirit was not true to God.

9The Ephraimites, equipped as archers,
   turned back on the day of engagement.
10They did not keep God's covenant
   but refused to walk by his teaching.
11They ignored his acts,
   his wonders that he showed them.

12Before their ancestors he did wondrous deeds,
   in the land of Egypt, the region of Zoan.
13He split the sea and enabled them to pass through it,
   he made the water stand up like a heap.
14He led them with a cloud by day,
   and all night with a fiery light.
15He would split open[4] crags in the wilderness,
   and he gave them to drink like the deeps, abundantly.[5]
16He brought out streams from the cliff,
   and he made water descend like rivers.

17But they continued to fail him
   and to defy the Most High in the desert.
18They deliberately tested God
   in asking food for themselves.[6]
19They spoke against God, they said,
   Can God spread a table in the wilderness?
20Yes, he hit a crag and water ran,
   torrents overflowed.
Can he also give bread
   or supply meat for his people?

21Therefore Yhwh listened and raged,
   and fire broke out against Jacob,
Yes, anger arose against Israel,

---

3. EVV have "a generation whose heart was not steadfast," taking *hēkîn* as declarative hiphil. This gives good parallelism, but elsewhere when this noun and the hiphil verb come together, the noun is the obj. (e.g., 10:17), and when this noun is the subj., the niphal is used (see v. 37).

4. The piel draws attention to the result of the action; contrast the qal in v. 13 (*IBHS* 22.2a).

5. In isolation, one might take *tĕhōmôt* as sg. (intensive pl. form; see on 68:9 [10]) and thus translate "abundant deep" (so *IBHS* 6.3.2b), but *tĕhōmôt* is pl. in 77:16 [17] and in Exod. 15 (as in 15:8), with which Ps. 78 has many links.

6. Or perhaps "for their appetite" (*person).

²²because they did not have faith in God,
    they did not trust his deliverance.
²³He commanded the skies above,
    opened the doors of the heavens.
²⁴And he rained manna on them to eat,
    gave them grain from the heavens.
²⁵People ate the bread of heroes;
    he sent them provisions⁷ to fill them.
²⁶He would set going the east wind in the heavens,
    he drove the south wind by his might.
²⁷He rained meat on them like dust,
    winged birds like the sand at the seas.
²⁸He made them fall inside his camp,
    around his dwelling.
²⁹They ate and were very full,
    he brought them their desire.
³⁰They had not turned aside from their desire,
    their food still in their mouth,
³¹And God's anger arose against them,
    and he slew some of their sturdiest,
    put down Israel's youth.

³²Despite all this they still failed him
    and did not have faith despite his wonders.
³³He made their days end in emptiness,
    their years in terror.
³⁴When he slew them they would seek help from him,
    turn and search for God.⁸
³⁵They were mindful that God was their crag,
    God Most High their restorer.
³⁶But they enticed him with their mouth,
    with their tongue they would lie to him.
³⁷Their heart was not firm with him;
    they were not true to his covenant.

³⁸Because he was compassionate,
    he would expiate waywardness and not destroy.
Again and again he turned his anger,
    would not stir any of his wrath.

7. Words from the root *ṣûd* commonly refer to hunting and game, but most occurrences of *ṣēdâ* and some other words from the root need to refer to provisions; BDB takes them as from a different root. Verses 27–28 do refer to game, but here in v. 25b the parallelism suggests that the word refers to the manna.

8. *Šûb* followed by another verb can denote to do something again, as in v. 41 (see GKC 120d), but in this context it more likely has its common reference to turning back to God.

476

³⁹He was mindful that they were flesh,
a wind that is passing and does not return.

⁴⁰How much they would defy him in the wilderness,
grieve him in the wasteland.
⁴¹Repeatedly they tested God,
vexed the Holy One of Israel.
⁴²They were not mindful of his hand,
the day when he redeemed them from the foe,
⁴³When[9] he put his signs in Egypt,
his portents in the region of Zoan.

⁴⁴He turned their rivers[10] to blood;
they could not drink from their streams.
⁴⁵He would send against them swarms and they devoured them,
frogs and they devastated them.
⁴⁶He gave their produce to the caterpillar,
their labor to the locust.
⁴⁷He slew their vines with hail,
their sycamore figs with flood.
⁴⁸He gave over their livestock to hail,
their cattle to lightning flashes.
⁴⁹He would send against them his angry fury,
wrath, rage, distress,
A commission of aides bringing trouble[11]
⁵⁰that would clear[12] a path for his anger.
He did not spare their lives from death
but gave them over to epidemic.
⁵¹He hit every firstborn in Egypt,
the first issue of vigor in the tents of Ham.
⁵²He set his people on the move like sheep
and drove them like a flock in the wilderness.
⁵³He led them in safety[13] and they were not afraid,
but their enemies—the sea covered them.
⁵⁴He brought them to his holy territory,[14]
the mountain that his right hand acquired.

9. I take the *'ăšer* to resume the *'ăšer* in v. 42, though in isolation one might take it as meaning "the one who" and leading into vv. 44–55 (cf. LXX, Syr, Jerome).

10. Lit. "their Niles," perhaps pl. of amplification, "their great river" (see GKC 124e), perhaps the Nile and its different branches and canals.

11. Lit. "aides of troubles" (see JM 141f).

12. The m. verb had f. subject, but this was some way away and was spelled out in m. pl. words, so it is not particularly odd, though one might translate, "By a commission of aides bringing trouble, he would clear . . ."

13. In the context, one might render *lābeṭaḥ* as "to safety," but elsewhere it regularly means "in safety."

14. Lit. "border," or perhaps "mountain" (cf. LXX); see *CP* 248.

⁵⁵He drove out nations before them,
>   allotted them as a share to possess,¹⁵
>   settled Israel's clans in their tents.

⁵⁶But they tested and defied God Most High
>   and did not keep his declarations.
⁵⁷They went away and were disloyal like their ancestors;
>   they turned like a treacherous bow.
⁵⁸They vexed him with their high places;
>   with their images they aroused him.

⁵⁹God listened and raged,
>   and utterly¹⁶ rejected Israel.
⁶⁰He abandoned the dwelling at Shiloh,
>   the tent he settled among people.
⁶¹He let his might go into captivity,
>   his glory into the hand of the foe.
⁶²He gave his people over to the sword,
>   he raged at his possession.
⁶³Fire consumed its young men,
>   and its girls were not lamented.¹⁷
⁶⁴Its priests fell by the sword,
>   and its widows would not weep.

⁶⁵But the Lord awoke like someone asleep,
>   like a warrior making a noise because of wine.
⁶⁶He beat back his foes,
>   gave them permanent reviling.
⁶⁷But he rejected the tent of Joseph,
>   did not choose the clan of Ephraim.
⁶⁸He chose the clan of Judah,
>   Mount Zion, to which he dedicated himself.
⁶⁹He built his sanctuary like the heights,
>   like the earth which he founded as a permanency.
⁷⁰He chose David his servant
>   and took him from the sheep pens,
>   ⁷¹brought him from following the ewes

15. Lit. "as the share of [their] possession." LXX and Jerome have "as a possession by the line," but MT accents more plausibly take this as a const. phrase as in 105:11; Deut. 32:9; 1 Chron. 16:18. In such contexts *ḥebel* refers to the share allocated by the measuring line (cf. also Josh. 17:5, 14; 19:9). The *b* is then predicative (*b* essentiae) as in Josh. 13:6, 7; 23:4 (JM 133c).

16. David Noel Freedman ("God Almighty in Psalm 78,59," *Bib* 54 [1973]: 268) sees *mĕ'ōd* here as an instance of a title for God, "Almighty" (cf. *DCH*).

17. It fits the context to derive *hûllālû* from *yālal* (cf. LXX, Jerome) rather than from *hālal* (cf. Tg, Aq, Th, Sym), which would be a rather elliptical way of saying they "were not celebrated" (in marriage).

>   To shepherd Jacob his people,
>   Israel his possession.
> 72He shepherded them in accordance with the integrity of his heart,
>   and he would lead them with the great skillfulness of his hands.

Interpretation

"There are many things that could be said, and the psalm is endless,"[18] its length inducing "weariness."[19] Like (e.g.) Ps. 49, this "formidable" composition,[20] the longest in the Psalter except for Ps. 119, is not really a psalm at all, insofar as none of it addresses God. To put it another way, it reflects the fact that the word "psalm" covers liturgical texts in general. These are mostly addressed to God, but some are addressed to the congregation or to individuals.

This example is dominated by narrative accounts of aspects of God's relationship with Israel from Egypt through to the time of David. Such a narrative might have a number of functions. It could fulfill an apologetic or political purpose, buttressing the position of Judah, Jerusalem, and David. It could be an expression of praise; the analogous poetic accounts of God's deeds in Pss. 105–7 are introduced as subjects for praise. Either of these purposes may be in the background of the psalm; that is, at an earlier stage the material might have been used thus. But the psalm itself introduces the narrative by an exhortation to listen and a reminder about the need to learn from the story of the ancestors a lesson about faithfulness. It is designed not merely to record the past but to change people for the future.[21] The psalm is an exhortation in poetic form, like Deut. 32. In this respect it parallels Pss. 49 and 50, but in contrast to them its exhortation takes this narrative form. To be more precise, its opening exhortation is filled out by extensive narrative elements. But it also compares with the gargantuan prose narrative from Exodus to 2 Samuel, which tells its stories much more fully. Perhaps that prose narrative implies an exhortation not to behave as your ancestors did; the psalm makes this explicit. On one hand, it closes down the openness of the prose narrative; there are other insights that might be derived from the latter, as well as that hortatory one. On the other, it does make one point explicit and inescapable: the vital importance of faithfulness and obedience rather than rebellion and defiance.

18. Jerome, *Homilies*, 1:88.
19. Cassiodorus, *Psalms*, 2:250.
20. Fokkelman, *Major Poems*, 2:210.
21. Cf. Edward L. Greenstein, "Mixing Memory and Design: Reading Psalm 78," *Prooftexts* 10 (1990): 197–218; Westermann, *Praise and Lament*, 235–42.

In this emphasis it also compares with Paul's appeal to these events in 1 Cor. 10:1–11, though it does not manifest Paul's passion and urgency in confronting the Corinthians with their problems. This would fit with the idea that its concern with people's disobedience and rebellion is a matter of principle or theory rather than a present problem (cf. Pss. 81; 95). The psalm then has its background in the need always to remind God's people of the danger of disobedience and rebellion, and it is designed for regular liturgical use to this end. It compares with the liturgical exhortations to repentance in the service of Morning Prayer and the Commination service in the Church of England Book of Common Prayer. This fits with the way the speaker moves between "I" and "we" in vv. 1–4 (cf. Josh. 24:14–24).

I take the clues to the psalm's structure as follows. The opening exhortation in vv. 1–8 stands out from the whole as a statement of the psalm's purpose, in general terms. In contrast, vv. 9–11 focus on Ephraim and its failure in relation to God, and vv. 67–72 at the end of the psalm match this focus on Ephraim and on Judah, which now becomes the object of God's choice. Inside the bracket formed by these two sections are two sections reviewing Israel's story in ways that parallel the biblical narrative, looking at the wilderness period (vv. 12–31) and at the broader canvas of the period from Egypt to the monarchy (vv. 44–66); the order of the psalm is more logical than chronological.[22] Each of these narrative sections follows the same sequence, relating marvels of grace that God did, acts of rebellion and testing on Israel's part, and a response of wrath and chastisement on God's part. At the center of the psalm stands a more general comment on Israel's story as a whole and on the themes of failure and grace (vv. 32–43), which in content pairs with the introduction. At this point, too, the psalm's order is rhetorical and logical rather than chronological, so that here we find "the heart of the matter right in the middle, where it belongs."[23]

The psalm thus manifests the following structure:

Statement of purpose: to get people to listen and submit to God (vv. 1–8)
  Ephraim's failure (vv. 9–11)
    God and Israel in the wilderness (vv. 12–31):
      God's wondrous deeds (vv. 12–16)

---

22. Anthony F. Campbell, "Psalm 78," *CBQ* 41 (1979): 51–79 (see 54).

23. Marjo C. A. Korpel and Johannes C. de Moor, "Fundamentals of Ugaritic and Hebrew Poetry," *UF* 18 (1986): 173–212 (see 208); cf. also Beat Weber, "Psalm 78," *TZ* 56 (2000): 193–214 (see 195). Auffret (*Voyez de vos yeux*, 175–236) notes many more detailed verbal phenomena.

Israel's defiance and testing (vv. 17–20)

God's rage (vv. 21–31)

The characteristic dynamics of that relationship (vv. 32–43):

Israel's failure (vv. 32–37)

God's compassion (vv. 38–39)

Israel's defiance and testing (vv. 40–43)

God and Israel from Egypt to Shiloh (vv. 44–64):

God's great acts (vv. 44–55)

Israel's testing and defiance (vv. 56–58)

God's fury (vv. 59–64)

Ephraim's rejection and God's choice of David (vv. 65–72)

The psalm's ending with God's choice of Judah, Jerusalem, and David might have various implications regarding its date. It might suggest that it comes from David or Solomon's day.[24] It might come from the period after the split between Ephraim and Judah, when Ephraim was usually the stronger of the two, and it might thus buttress Judah's position.[25] It might come from shortly after the fall of Ephraim and respond to that.[26] It might come from the later preexilic period, when Judean kings such as Josiah again sought to exercise authority in the north.[27] It might come from the exilic or Second Temple period with its rivalry between Judah and Samaria, when (we know from Chronicles) the election of David remained very important to the community.[28] It might come from a messianically inclined Second Temple community.[29] The question is complicated by the possibility that the psalm might have developed in stages to the form that we have.[30] In particular, while the bulk of the

24. See, e.g., Otto Eissfeldt, *Das Lied Moses Deuteronomium 32, 1–43 und das Lehrgedicht Asaphs Psalm 78* (Berlin: Akademie, 1958), 26–43.

25. See, e.g., John Day, "Pre-Deuteronomic Allusions to the Covenant in Hosea and Psalm lxxviii," *VT* 36 (1986): 1–12.

26. See, e.g., R. J. Clifford, "In Zion and David a New Beginning," in *Traditions in Transformation* (Frank Moore Cross Festschrift; ed. Baruch Halpern and Jon D. Levenson; Winona Lake, IN: Eisenbrauns, 1981), 121–41 (see 138–41); Archie C. C. Lee, "The Context and Function of the Plagues Tradition in Psalm 78," *JSOT* 48 (1990): 83–89; Philip Stern, "The Eighth Century Dating of Psalm 78 Re-argued," *HUCA* 66 (1995): 41–65.

27. So, e.g., H. Junker, "Die Entstehungszeit des Ps. 78 und des Deuteronomiums," *Bib* 34 (1953): 487–500.

28. See, e.g., Gunkel, *Psalmen*, 342; R. P. Carroll, "Psalm lxxviii," *VT* 21 (1971): 133–50.

29. See Notker Füglister, "Psalm lxxxviii [sic]," in *Congress Volume: Leuven 1989* (Leiden: Brill, 1991), 264–97 (see 296).

30. See, e.g., Whybray, *Reading the Psalms as a Book*, 48–49.

psalm relates to the people as a whole, the verses near the beginning and near the end that specifically refer to Ephraim and Judah have been seen as marking the adaptation of the psalm to Judean interests.

Fortunately, we do not need to know the psalm's date in order to understand it, because vv. 1–8 make its purpose explicit, whatever its date. In any of these periods someone might have urged the lesson to which vv. 1–8 refers. On the assumption that the presence of this exhortation in the Psalter implies that it was used on some regular worship occasion, the speaker might be a prophet,[31] a priest,[32] a Levitical teacher or preacher,[33] or a king.[34]

The psalm has many links with other material in the Scriptures.[35] Its beginning parallels Ps. 49 but goes on to recall Deuteronomy with its stress on passing on the story of Yhwh's deeds from one generation to another; the "rebellious and defiant" generation of v. 8 recalls the "rebellious and defiant son" of Deut. 21:18.[36] Its attitude to Ephraim recalls Hosea, where Yhwh's rejection of Ephraim is a major motif. Hosea 7:16 describes Ephraim as "like a treacherous/slack bow"; cf. v. 57. Hosea 10:14 talks about a disaster to the northern kingdom on a "day of battle"; cf. v. 9.[37]

In its account of events in Egypt, in the wilderness, and in the land, the psalm overlaps with Exodus–Joshua but does not exactly correspond to it in the order of events or in the wording. The accounts of Israel's provocations in the wilderness, and of the plagues in Egypt in particular, manifest many detailed parallels in wording with Exodus and Numbers but at the same time (for instance) mingle expressions that parallel the narrative of events before and after Sinai.[38] A feature of the parallelism here is that the first cola often tell the story in similar terms to Exodus and Numbers, while the second cola re-express the point in more novel ways (e.g., vv. 15, 16, 19). If we knew (for instance) when the Exodus–Joshua narrative was written and which was the direction of the relationship between the narrative and the psalm, this would help us in dating the psalm. But opinions again differ on both these questions. Perhaps the

31. Cf. Johnson, *The Cultic Prophet and Israel's Psalmody*, 47.

32. Cf. Weiser, *Psalms*, 539.

33. Cf. Gerhard von Rad, *The Problem of the Hexateuch and Other Essays* (Edinburgh: Oliver & Boyd: McGraw-Hill, 1966), 267–80.

34. Cf. Goulder, *Psalms of Asaph*, 108.

35. See Haglund, *Historical Motifs in the Psalms*, 89–101.

36. Nasuti (*Tradition History and the Psalms of Asaph*, 81–93) notes the Deuteronomic features of the psalm as a whole.

37. Stern ("The Eighth Century Dating of Psalm 78," 49–51) adds other examples from Amos that seem to me less compelling.

38. Tate (*Psalms 51–100*, 292) includes a table comparing vv. 44–51 with the exodus narrative and its possible forms in J, E, and P, and with Ps. 105.

psalm is dependent on that narrative as we know it (or, for instance, on the J version of the narrative of the plagues)[39] and expands on it with the help of other traditions or Scriptures or simply the author's creativity, in midrashic fashion. Or perhaps the narrative is later than the psalm and expands on it.[40] The detailed nature of the verbal links makes it less likely that the two are independent versions of the story.[41] But we do not know how far the psalm's distinctive motifs reflect independent traditions and how far they come from the writer's imagination, nor do we know when Exodus–Joshua was written or the nature and date of the sources it used. Fortunately, our uncertainty about such questions does not hinder comparison of the two versions of the story, which helps us identify the psalm's distinctive features.

The poetry is characterized by rather straightforward parallelism and likes to repeat words, which signal its preoccupations. These include human acknowledging, being mindful, being true (or not); human ignoring, defying, testing/trying, failing; and God doing wonders, being mindful, raging, and slaying. Other repetitions involve paronomasia (see vv. 9, 30, 33, 66). The narrative sections of the psalm make substantial use of yiqtol verbs as a narrative tense (see on 77:13–20 [14–21]; to signal them, I mostly translate with "would").

The psalm follows on from the previous one. Psalm 77:11 [12] turned from lament to declare, "I will make mention of the deeds of Yah, yes, for I shall call to mind your wonders of old," which are expressions of God's "might" (77:14 [15]). In Psalm 78 an "I" again speaks, focusing on not ignoring God's deeds (v. 7), the wonders God did (v. 4) of old (v. 2), which are expressions of God's might (v. 4). These deeds are once again the acts involved in the Red Sea deliverance (77:16–19 [17–20]; cf. 78:13, 53), when God "restored" Israel (77:15 [16]; cf. 78:35) and "led" them "like a flock" (77:20 [21]; cf. 78:52–53). God is again "Most High" (77:10 [11]; 78:17, 35, 56). But the "I" speaks to a different end.[42]

Instruction. Asaph's.

Heading. See glossary.

---

39. Cf. Johannes Schildenberger, "Psalm 78 (77) und die Pentateuchquellen," in *Lex tua veritas* (Hubert Junker Festschrift; ed. Heinrich Gross and Franz Mussner; Trier: Paulinus, 1961), 230–56.

40. So Goulder, *Psalms of Asaph*, 114–15.

41. As George W. Coats argues, *Rebellion in the Wilderness* (Nashville: Abingdon, 1968), 199–224. On the literary considerations in both versions, see William T. Koopmans, "Psalm 78, Canto D," *UF* 20 (1988): 121–23.

42. See further Cole, *Shape and Message of Book III*, 62–72.

78:1–8. While the opening exhortation recalls the language of a prophet or teacher, the subsequent stress on the passing on of Israel's story from one generation to another recalls Deut. 6. There are some long, complex sentences occupying two or more lines (see vv. 3–4, 5–8), and the particle *'ăšer* appears in vv. 4 and 5, neither of which are regular features of the poetry of the Psalms.

> ¹Give ear, my people, to my teaching;
>   turn your ear to the words of my mouth.

In the Psalms, "give ear" and "turn your ear" are usually exhortations addressed to God (see esp. 80:1 [2]), and "the words of my mouth" can also be addressed to God (19:14 [15]; 54:2 [4]), but here the verbs address a human audience, as in 45:10 [11]; 49:1 [2]. In contrast to Pss. 45 and 49, however, this psalm explicitly addresses Israel, not an individual person or humanity in general. The question it raises concerns the community, not just the individual, and concerns the distinctive relationship between Yhwh and Israel, not nations in general. The exhortations thus further parallel those of a prophet or of Yhwh through a prophet (e.g., Isa. 1:10; 28:23; 55:3). "My people" can also be a prophet's term (e.g., Isa. 3:12; 5:13; 10:2; though it is difficult to be sure when this "my" refers rather to Yhwh). In turn, "the words of my mouth" are elsewhere Moses's or God's or Ms. Wisdom's (e.g., Deut. 32:1; Prov. 8:8; Hos. 6:5), while "my teaching" is more the phrase of a wisdom teacher, not offering mere information but urging listeners to the right kind of life (e.g., Prov. 3:1; 4:2). Both thus suggest something authoritative. The author indeed speaks both as a prophet and as a teacher and begins by seeking to open up the audience to the sort of attentiveness and responsiveness it should give to either. The parallel with Deut. 32 is especially instructive as that exhortation also urges Israel to learn lessons from its own story. The Midrash infers that the Psalms, like the Prophets and Proverbs, *are* Torah.[43]

> ²I shall open my mouth with a parable,
>   pour out mysteries of old.

Once again "opening the mouth" and "pouring out" can denote praise or prayer to God but can also refer to the speech of a prophet or a wisdom teacher (e.g., Job 33:2; Prov. 1:23; 31:26; Ezek. 3:2, 27; 33:22). They suggest something more than mere regular human speech, something that comes from depths inside. A parable (*māšāl*) is likewise

43. *Midrash on Psalms*, 2:22.

the business of a prophet and a wisdom teacher (e.g., Num. 23:7, 18; Job 27:1; 29:1; Ezek. 17:2; and cf. Ps. 49:4 [5]). It suggests something intense, weighty, and profound—not in this context a mere aphorism or "proverb" but "a story with a meaning" (NEB). Matthew takes up these words to apply to Jesus's parables (Matt. 13:34–35). "Mysteries" (ḥîdôt) makes it more explicit that the psalm will deal with deep questions (again, cf. 49:4 [5]; Prov. 1:6; Ezek. 17:2). Elsewhere the word can denote "riddles," but again, in this context these are something more profound than that. If the speaker can gain the audience's attention, it will hear something wise and deep. They are mysteries that the people's story "of old" reveals.

> ³Things that we have heard and acknowledged,
>   and our ancestors have told us,
> ⁴We will not hide from their descendants,
>   telling the coming generation:
> The praises of Yhwh and his might,
>   his wonders that he did.

Israel knew that wisdom more often lies in what has been passed down through the generations than in the latest theory or research finding, which will soon be outdated. So like a wisdom teacher, this psalmist is taking a place in a chain. There are things that the ancestors passed down to the current generation, and it is the current generation's task to pass them on to the next. (This generation's "parents" directly passed on the story, but 'ābôt here will include ancestors more generally, going back to those who were involved in the events the psalm will relate.) The process of learning has three stages to it. First, the ancestors tell their story (and the story they have received). In this context, that telling is the story of what they saw and heard as God acted and as they made their mistakes. Second, their descendants listen to this story rather than ignoring the outdated old fogies. Third, they *acknowledge its truth, heed it, respond to it. The language in v. 3 recalls 44:1 [2], though (as with the links with Ps. 77) the point is different. There the recollection leads into confronting Yhwh with the disparity between past acts and present experience. Here it leads into confronting the community with the disparity between God's acts and its habitual response.

Verse 4a goes on to the further stage in the process just referred to. It is vital that the present generation plays its role as the link between the past generation and the next generation. Without this, the chain of learning will be broken.

The *praises of Yhwh are more precisely Yhwh's "praiseworthy deeds" (TNIV). "His might" begins to explicate what it is that is praiseworthy

485

about Yhwh, and "the *wonders that he did" takes that further. The line as a whole stands in apposition to v. 3 and explicates it.

> 5He set up a declaration in Jacob,
>   put teaching in Israel,
> Which he commanded our ancestors
>   to get their descendants to acknowledge,
> 6So that the coming generation might acknowledge,
>   descendants who are to be born,
> Might rise up and tell their descendants,
>   7so that they might put their confidence in God,
> And not ignore God's deeds
>   but observe his commands,
> 8And not become like their ancestors,
>   a rebellious and defiant generation,
> A generation that did not make its heart firm,
>   whose spirit was not true to God.

An extraordinarily long sentence follows, reminiscent in length as well as in content to the exhortations in Deuteronomy. Yhwh's *declaration concerns Yhwh's expectations of the people (cf. 'ēdâ in v. 56). "Teaching" (tôrâ) will then have similar meaning. The expectation in this declaration and teaching may have the general reference implied in the bulk of the psalm: obedience, trust, reliance, faithfulness to their covenant obligations. Or it may refer specifically to the requirement to teach and pass on the account of Yhwh's deeds and expectations (e.g., Deut. 4:9–14; 6:20–25). Or it may refer specifically to the establishment of a regular occasion for this celebration and teaching (cf. Deut. 31:9–13; and the use of 'ēdût in Ps. 81:5 [6]).

Certainly the second line assumes that the passing on to which vv. 1–4 refer is not merely a cultural tradition but especially a divine obligation. They are surely to pass on this teaching in such a way that it is not just known but also *acknowledged.

Verses 6–7 are more likely three bicola than the two tricola implied by MT.[44] Verse 6a–b continues to restate the point about that process involving three generations (past, present, and future), but then vv. 6c–7a goes beyond that to the fourth generation. Perhaps it is significant that three or four generations are (ideally) the constituents of a family living together. There is a negative side to that (Exod. 34:7) but also a positive side. The verbs in vv. 6c–7a take up from v. 5a. Yhwh set up and put (qûm hiphil, śîm) declaration/teaching; it will be the coming generation's task to respond by rising up (qûm qal) and putting (śîm) their confidence in

---

44. Cf. Gunkel, Psalmen, 337.

the right place. "Confidence" (*kesel*) announces a theme for the psalm. Fools (*kĕsîlîm*; 49:10 [11]; 92:6 [7]; 94:8) are people who put their confidence elsewhere (49:13 [14]). The trouble is that the Israelites have often shown themselves to be fools.

Not *ignoring God's deeds (v. 7b–c) is the more specific basis for the people's confidence. The line puts together the two elements in the covenant relationship: God's acts and their obedience to God. The starting point in the relationship is God's acts, but the relationship becomes effective only when the people keep these acts in mind. The second colon makes explicit how they do that. "I am Yhwh your God who brought you out of the land of Egypt: you are to have no other gods . . ." (Exod. 20:2–3). Yhwh does not simply act in grace and then go no further; instead, Yhwh feels free to issue commands on the basis of those acts. The people's job is to observe these commands.

Verse 8 acknowledges a solemn alternative, the alternative that will be explored in the psalm. The line nuances what we have been told about the people's ancestors. They have passed on accounts of what Yhwh has done and about the expectations Yhwh laid on them, and evidently they told their own story "warts and all" (as the OT narrative also shows). These "ancestors" or "parents" (*'ābôt*) acknowledge that they had behaved as if they were children, a generation of children who were rebellious and defiant in relation to their own parents (the words recur in Deut. 21:18, 20).

The second line in v. 8 explains the nature of this rebellious defiance. There was something wrong with their *heart or spirit, the dynamic center of their being. They had not made their heart firm. The notion is a striking one. We might have assumed that our heart provided us with our stability or firmness, but the psalm assumes that we do the firming of our heart. The result of the people's failure to do so was that their spirit was not *true to God. This is the tendency the psalm will illustrate.

78:9–11. The sudden reference to the Ephraimites is surprising, and v. 9 has been seen as a later addition. If it were not here, the psalm would move seamlessly from vv. 1–8 to vv. 10–11, and the main bulk of the psalm that follows does not relate to Ephraim in particular. But the closing verses do so, describing how God did not choose Ephraim but did choose Judah as the place for God's sanctuary and did choose David as the people's leader. While the bulk of the psalm thus concerns God's dealings with the people as a whole, this opening and closing bracket around its story has that other agenda, and vv. 9–11 provide implicit background to vv. 67–72.

> [9]The Ephraimites, equipped as archers,
>   turned back on the day of engagement.

"This is surely a dark verse."[45] The opening critique of Ephraim might link with the relatively negative account of the northern clans' occupation of their land (and specifically Ephraim's) in Judg. 1, which contrasts with the positive account of Judah's occupation of its land. First Chronicles 7:20–24 tells of another Ephraimite defeat with which this critique might link; Tg has a long midrashic addition to the psalm relating the Ephraimite action to events while people were still in Egypt. Judges 12:2 refers to yet another occasion when the Ephraimites allegedly failed to play their part in a military engagement. The psalm's later focus on events centering on Shiloh in Ephraim (vv. 56–67) might point in a different direction; Israelite forces indeed fled on that occasion (1 Sam. 4:10), as they also did when the Philistines defeated Israel at Mount Gilboa and killed Saul (1 Sam. 31:1, 7), opening up the way for David to become king. But we have noted that Hos. 10:14 refers to a "day of battle" in the northern kingdom, which may mean that the verse refers to events related to the fall of Ephraim to Assyria. The phrase "equipped as archers" is literally "handlers of shooters of the bow," an odd expression[46] that draws attention to itself and raises questions such as will be clarified only when we get to v. 57. There the verb "turn back" will recur, while the phrase "faulty bow," literally "bow of deceit" (*qešet rĕmîyâ*), resembles "shooters of the bow" (*rômê-qešet*) here.[47] Whatever the event, on this occasion the Ephraimites were equipped for battle all right, but their bows were treacherous. There was nothing actually wrong with the bows, but something lacking in the people who wielded them. But for the moment, v. 9 teases the hearer; the clarifying of its opaqueness will come only later.

> [10]They did not keep God's covenant
> but refused to walk by his teaching.
> [11]They ignored his acts,
> his wonders that he showed them.

Although these two lines would be applicable to the people as a whole, in the context they refer specifically to Ephraim, and it is also natural to continue to take "Ephraim" to refer to the northern clans in general,

45. Luther, *First Lectures*, 2:40. He therefore goes on to offer a series of allegorical interpretations.

46. It combines two expressions for archers, "handlers of the bow" (e.g., 1 Chron. 12:2) and "shooters of the bow" (Jer. 4:29). Eissfeldt takes the const. as indicating a superlative (cf. 45:12 [13]; GKC 133h; *IBHS* 14.5b), "the best equipped of the shooters of the bow" (*Das Lied Moses*, 27). GKC 130e rather sees the two constructs as in apposition; "shooters" might then be an explanatory gloss on "equipped" (we are actually unsure of the meaning of the verb *nāšaq*). Or the text may combine two readings.

47. Cf. Kidner, *Psalms*, 2:282. Fokkelman (*Major Poems*, 2:216) notes the chiastic order of the paronomasia.

who were often described by the name of their central and dominant clan. Ephraim's declaring independence from Jerusalem and the Davidic line could be described as a turning away from Yhwh. But the psalm's language more parallels the summary closing judgment on Ephraim's story in 2 Kings 17, with its references to the way they had walked, their not keeping Yhwh's teaching, and their ignoring God's covenant and the way God had brought them out of Egypt (e.g., vv. 7, 15, 22, 37–38).

Talk in terms of "keeping" God's covenant indicates that "covenant" here refers not to God's commitment to them nor to the mutual relationship between Israel and God but rather to covenant as the commitment or obligation God lays on them. It is thus another way of speaking of Yhwh's "declaration," the expression that was in parallelism with "teaching" in v. 5 as "covenant" is here. "Refusing" to walk by that teaching puts more sharply the point about "not keeping"; it more resembles Jeremiah's language as he surveys the life of both Ephraim and Judah (e.g., Jer 11:10; but see also Isa. 1:20; Hos. 11:5).

The second line then goes behind their deeds to the attitude that underlay them. In substance though not in words, it presupposes covenantal thinking in one of those other senses. The covenant relationship was based on the principle that God took the initiative in acting on Israel's behalf and that Israel responded by (for instance) treating Yhwh alone as God and not worshipping by means of images. Failing so to respond involved ignoring the acts that both demanded Israel's response as an obligation and encouraged it as an expression of gratitude. Again, the second colon puts the point more sharply: these acts were *wonders, which Yhwh took the initiative in showing them. The Ephraimites failed to live by the principles declared in vv. 1–8 (see esp. vv. 4, 7); the psalm's (Judean?) audience had better not follow their example.

78:12–16. God and Israel in the wilderness (a): God's wondrous deeds.

The psalm segues into a description that relates to the people as a whole. It speaks of events leading up to the exodus (v. 12), the Red Sea deliverance (v. 13), God's leading on the subsequent journey (v. 14), and God's provision on that journey (vv. 15–16). There can be various reasons for thus reviewing the nation's story: it can (for instance) be an expression of praise or the backdrop to confession. Verses 9–11 have already hinted at what vv. 17–22 will make explicit, that here the point of the review is to introduce a contrast between the might Yhwh has exercised on Israel's behalf and the people's lack of response to that.

> 12Before their ancestors he did wondrous deeds,
>   in the land of Egypt, the region of Zoan.

The ancestors reappear, the people who told the story of what Yhwh had done and had received the command to pass on Yhwh's declaration but then failed to live by it (vv. 3, 5, 8). The end of that sequence of statements has its sad background in the fact that these were people who had seen Yhwh's *wonders. Although this word for wonders (*pele'*) elsewhere refers to the Red Sea deliverance (Ps. 77:11, 14 [12, 15]; Exod. 15:11), here the second colon makes explicit that it refers to the wonders that began in Egypt (Exod. 3:20; there the word was *niplā'ôt*, from the same root as just now in v. 11). "Zoan" makes the point more specific. It is the name of the store city in the Nile Delta that the Israelites worked on (cf. Num. 13:22; Isa. 19:11, 13; 30:4; Ezek. 30:14), often called Tanis (cf. LXX, Jerome, Tg) or Avaris but apparently called Raamses in Exod. 1:11.

> ¹³He split the sea and enabled them to pass through it,
>   he made the water stand up like a heap.

The exodus was followed by the Red Sea deliverance, described as it often is in terms of God's act on the sea rather than God's defeat of the Egyptians. In Canaanite stories the Sea asserted itself in all its dynamic power and threatened to overwhelm order and stability in the heavenly world, and thus in the earthly world. The Red Sea was not tumultuous and did not threaten to take the initiative in overwhelming Israel, yet it was a devastating threat because (following Yhwh's directions!) Israel had allowed itself to be boxed in by it as the Egyptian army followed it. But Yhwh split it in two. The verb comes in Exod. 14:16, 21, though there it is Moses who divides the sea. This verb also recalls another Middle Eastern story, about the conflict between Marduk, the Babylonian god, and Tiamat, the dragon of the deep. Marduk split Tiamat, tore her apart, disposed of the threat that she constituted, and thus earned recognition as the top god. Yhwh similarly split the Red Sea and thus established sovereign authority in the world (cf. Exod. 15:18). The sea ceased to be a threat. Israel could pass through it. The parallel description of the waters standing up like a heap follows Exod. 15:8.[48] It is another figure of speech, since standing up like a heap is more what happens to a river if it is halted (cf. Josh. 3:13, 16).

> ¹⁴He led them with a cloud by day,
>   and all night with a fiery light.

The language of leading, cloud by day and fire by night, in turn most closely follows Exod. 13:21–22. This leading thus came between Egypt

---

48. LXX, Syr, Tg have them standing "as [in] a bottle," implying *nōd* for *nēd*.

and the Red Sea, though the Red Sea story itself refers separately to the cloud and fire and to Yhwh's leading the people (Exod. 14:19–24; 15:13). The sequence in vv. 13–14 (splitting the sea and guiding by cloud and fire) also corresponds to the prayer in Neh. 9:11–12.

> ¹⁵He would split open crags in the wilderness,
>   and he gave them to drink like the deeps, abundantly.
> ¹⁶He brought out streams from the cliff,
>   and he made water descend like rivers.

The provision of water is a recurrent motif in the story of Israel's journey through the wilderness from Egypt to Canaan. This begins immediately after the Red Sea event (see Exod. 15:22–27), though such provision from a *crag recalls the next such occasion (Exod. 17:6; cf. Deut. 8:15; Ps. 105:41; 114:8). "Splitting open" reuses the verb from v. 13 in a novel way; this verb is not otherwise used in the Torah in this connection (though see Isa. 35:6, niphal; 48:21, qal).[49] Verse 15b makes explicit the object of this rock-splitting and emphasizes the quantity of water in a marked hyperbole. The language of splitting the great deep was used in a quite different connection in Gen. 7:11; we might also compare the references to the deeps in Exod. 15:5, 8. Here it has become a symbol for extravagant provision. God can split waters and make them like a cliff or split a cliff and make it produce waters; it is all the same to God.[50]

Verse 16 parallels v. 15. The first colon restates v. 15a. Again, streams have become good news: contrast Exod. 15:8, but compare Isa. 48:21. The cliff (*sela'*) is the noun in Num. 20:8–11 (cf. Neh. 9:15). The second colon again takes the first further in emphasizing the magnificence of God's provision and the reversal of the significance of water, since elsewhere the "rivers" can be those threatening floodwaters (e.g., Ps. 74:15; 93:3).

78:17–20. God and Israel in the wilderness (b): Israel's defiance and testing.

> ¹⁷But they continued to fail him
>   and to defy the Most High in the desert.
> ¹⁸They deliberately tested God
>   in asking food for themselves.

If vv. 9–11 allude to the later faithlessness of Ephraim, "continued" probably does not take up from vv. 9–11 but rather implies reference to

49. I take the piel in the psalm as resultative.
50. Cf. Schaefer, *Psalms*, 192.

*failures and defiance interwoven with those first wonders in vv. 12–16, in Egypt, on the shores of the Red Sea, and on the subsequent journey (e.g., Exod. 6:9; 14:10–12; 15:22–27). The psalm apparently assumes that the audience will know about this aspect of their history. The stance people took there continued through the wilderness journey. The Torah does not use the expressions "failure" and "defiance" of those earlier events, though it does of later events in the wilderness (e.g., Num. 20:10; 21:7).

The Torah's first reference to the people "testing" Yhwh comes in connection with the story about provision of water in Exod. 17:2 at the place to be called "Testing," but Num. 14:22 sees such testing as characteristic of the people's time in the wilderness ("these ten times"). Here the psalm connects testing with asking for food, which suggests the stories in Exod. 16 and/or Num. 11. For the people to be testing Yhwh reverses the proper order of relationship: see Exod. 15:25; 16:4. We might think that God has no reason to test us, because God can look into our hearts, know what we are capable of, and know how we would respond to different pressures, whereas it is understandable for us to need to test God, because we cannot know what God will do. The OT sees this the other way around. Israel knows enough about God from God's acts such as those described in vv. 12–17 to make it reasonable to know what God can do and to trust God to look after them. To test God is to presuppose that we do not know enough about what God can and will do. God, too, bases assessments of us on the basis of our acts, so that events that test us make public what we are. In this case, the people's testing of God was deliberate or was an expression of who they really were. Literally, "They tested God in their heart": that expression does not mean that there was a contrast between the inner and the outer person, but that there was consistency between them. The people's crying out for food was not just a onetime weakness or aberration but an indication of an inner lack of trust that expressed itself in this testing.

> ¹⁹They spoke against God, they said,
>   Can God spread a table in the wilderness?
> ²⁰Yes, he hit a crag and water ran,
>   torrents overflowed.
> Can he also give bread
>   or supply meat for his people?

The Torah puts the emphasis on the way people spoke against Moses and Aaron (e.g., Exod. 16:2–3), but Yhwh is the real object of their complaint and attack (e.g., Exod. 16:7–8; 17:7). The fact that they overtly attack Moses and Aaron means they never verbalize the convictions in vv. 19–20. The second colon is very long (five words), which underlines the enormity of their question. "Spread a table in the wilderness" expresses very vividly the point in Exod. 16:32 in emphasizing the marvelous nature of what will be needed if they are to eat well on the journey. "Table" may etymologically imply "hide" (cf. BDB) and thus suggest something spread on the ground, around which people would sit for a banquet.

"Hit a crag" (cf. v. 15) again suggests Exod. 17:1–7; in the order of the Torah narrative, it was the marvelous healing of the waters in Exod. 15:22–27 that stood in the background to Exod. 16, where God indeed provides both bread and meat. "Torrents" and "overflowed" once more imply the reversing of the significance of such words, which usually suggest something threatening (e.g., 69:2 [3]; 74:15).

The parallel questions in the last line re-express the one in v. 19b, but they make it frighteningly more concrete. The narrative presupposes that experiences of God acting to deliver and provide should increase our conviction that God will so act again, and the Psalms presuppose this in the way they relate the testimonies of people who have seen God act. But the people deny this logic: it just does not follow that the God who provided water can also provide bread and meat.

78:21–31. God and Israel in the wilderness (c): God's rage.

The report of God's reaction to the people's defiance and testing begins with a general description of God's rage (vv. 21–22). It goes on to an account of how God responded to the people's skeptical words (vv. 23–29), and at first one might read this as simply an expression of God's graciousness; they said that God cannot do it, but with a smile God does it. But it then becomes clear that the rage has not abated (vv. 30–31). We have noted links between vv. 12–16, 17–20 and the story of Israel in Egypt, at the Red Sea, and in the wilderness. These last links now become more dominant; in commenting on individual verses, I note the close verbal links with Exod. 16–17; Num. 11; and Num. 14. What is also noticeable is that (like vv. 12–20) the lines use these chapters' phraseology in quite independent configurations, bringing together phrases from different stories.

> ²¹Therefore Yhwh listened and raged,
> and fire broke out against Jacob.
> Yes, anger arose against Israel,
> ²²because they did not have faith in God,
> they did not trust his deliverance.

The five cola work aba'cc'; MT sees v. 21 as a tricolon beginning the section, but I see vv. 21c–22 as a tricolon closing off the subsection. The language in v. 21 now suggests the incident related in Num. 11:1–3 (Yhwh listened, fire, anger), where the reason for the people's complaining was not explicit. The words suggest the fierceness of Yhwh's reaction to the people's questions. By asking for food in the terms that vv. 18–20 described, the people were testing God's patience; they will soon discover they are testing it beyond where it will go.

The indictment of the people's lack of faith (be *true) in turn parallels the explicit note in Num. 14:11, though it also suggests a contrast with the faith the people had once come to (Exod. 14:31). There they had had faith in Yhwh's deliverance, which they had just experienced (Exod. 14:13). *Trust makes the parallelism work by means of a word with more background in the Psalms. The object of trust is usually a person, and v. 22b implies that they did not trust in Yhwh as deliverer: they did not maintain trust in the one who had "become my deliverance" (Exod. 15:2).

> ²³He commanded the skies above,
>   opened the doors of the heavens.

The EVV begin v. 23 with "yet," but an unassuming *w*-consecutive leads straight on from v. 22. There is nothing about v. 23 that explicitly suggests good news. While "commanding the skies above" and "opening the doors of the heavens" is implicitly what Yhwh does in providing for the people in Exod. 16 and Num. 11, the language is different, and the second expression is familiar in a different connection. The heavens can be opened to bring blessing (Mal. 3:10), so this expression suggests good news, but it can also suggest bad news, since the shutting of the heavens means the restraining of its overwhelming floods (Gen. 7:11; Isa. 24:18). (KJV's "though he had commanded" reflects the awareness that vv. 23–29 refer to events before Num. 11 and 14.)

> ²⁴And he rained manna on them to eat,
>   gave them grain from the heavens.

It is thus by no means to be taken for granted that something descending from the open heavens is a blessing rather than a curse. Nor is it to be taken for granted that a sentence beginning "he rained" will convey good news: see Gen. 7:4 (when those floods are let loose); 19:24; and Exod. 9:23. But here the raining is indeed good news, as in Exod. 16:4, so it is in v. 24 that we might translate the *w*-consecutive with a "but." What falls from the open heavens is not a destructive flood but the gift of manna, "a fine, flaky substance" left behind by the morning dew (Exod. 16:14). It was as if grain fell from the sky. The verse thus begins to imply an extraordinary contrast between vv. 21–22 and 23–29, though it will eventually become clear that there is continuity and not merely contrast. The "gift" of food will introduce a further act of chastisement (vv. 30–31), as happens in Num. 11.

> 25People ate the bread of heroes;
>   he sent them provisions to fill them.

But meanwhile, human beings eat "bread from the heavens" (Exod. 16:4). Israel had doubted whether God could provide them with bread (v. 20); now God has done so. "Heroes" (*'abbîrîm*) are usually impressive human figures (e.g., Lam. 1:15; and cf. Ps. 76:5 [6]) or bulls (68:30 [31]), but here the link with v. 24 suggests that bread from the heavens is the food of the impressive beings who live in the heavens (cf. LXX, Syr, Tg).[51] Ordinary people[52] now eat this (does this itself presage trouble?). The second colon underlines the wonder of God's provision in a different way, by emphasizing how substantial it was ("to fill them," lit. "to fullness," is the expression in Exod. 16:3, 8).

> 26He would set going the east wind in the heavens,
>   he drove the south wind by his might.

Yet again there is some ambiguity about the description. The hot and/or violent east wind off the desert is usually bad news (e.g., Gen. 41:6; Exod. 10:13; Ps. 48:7 [8]; Jer. 18:17), though it had been good news for Israel at the Red Sea (Exod. 14:21). The same can be true of the south wind (Zech. 9:14). (Perhaps the expressions for south and east in parallelism refer to a southeast wind.) But the picture of Yhwh's setting the wind off on a journey (*nāsaʿ* hiphil) takes up the language of Num. 11:31—bad news for the quails but good news for the Israelites. Again, Yhwh "drove" the east wind to bring a locust plague in Exod. 10:13, though "his might" was on their side at the Red Sea (Exod. 15:2, 13).

> 27He rained meat on them like dust,
>   winged birds like the sand at the seas.
> 28He made them fall inside his camp,
>   around his dwelling.

Once more, the verb "he rained" need not resolve the ambiguity in v. 26, but it then becomes clear that for the moment all this forcefulness works in Israel's favor. Yet the addition of reference to meat after the reference

51. Cf. *gibbōrê kōaḥ* in 103:20, also the divine title *'ăbîr yaʿăqōb* (e.g., 132:2, 5).
52. That is, over against heavenly beings, *'îš* here denotes "human beings" (again cf. Tg), not "each individual" (though that would also be true), which is the point in Exod. 16:16, 18, 21.

to bread makes clear that God is also responding to the people's terrible question about what God could or could not do (v. 20). There is thus a certain aggressiveness about the way it becomes clear how God can do what they doubted: God does this on a vaster scale than they could have imagined. The second colon makes explicit the nature of the meat and also adds a second simile; the two similes are both common, especially in connection with promises of many descendants, though they do not otherwise appear together. Contrary to the people's expectations, the extravagance of God's supply of water (vv. 16, 20a–b) is here matched by the extravagance of God's supply of food. For the details, see Num. 11:31–32.

The birds' falling in the camp recalls Exod. 16:13; Num. 11:31; the parallel colon adds a point that could be inferred from that account.[53]

> ²⁹They ate and were very full,
>   he brought them their desire.

The first colon returns to the language of Exod. 16:8, 12, while the second makes a link with Num. 11:4, 34–35. The verses continue to emphasize the extravagance of God's provision. "Desire" (*ta'ăwâ*) is morally neutral (see on one hand Gen. 3:6, on the other Ps. 21:2 [3]), but of course it was desire that had led to the people's testing God. In itself the provision of abundant grain and meat from the heavens would look to be an act of pure grace, but it is about to turn out to be preliminary to a further act of chastisement for the testing that issued from desire. It is as if fulfilling their desire exposes its disgusting nature. When people challenge Jesus to do something like this (John 6:31), that therefore carries some irony. They are reflecting their own unbelief and risking a gift that brings trouble.[54] But Yhwh's provision is also an indication that God is "slow to anger." Acts of grace following on rebellion do give people a chance to turn.

> ³⁰They had not turned aside from their desire,
>   their food still in their mouth,
> ³¹And God's anger arose against them,
>   and he slew some of their sturdiest,
>   put down Israel's youth.

---

53. On the pl. *miškĕnōt*, see 43:3.

54. On the use of the passage in John, see Georg Geiger, "Aufruf an Rückkehrende," *Bib* 65 (1984): 449–64; M. J. J. Menken, "The Provenance and Meaning of the Old Testament Quotation in John 6:31," *NovT* 30 (1988): 39–56; Diana M. Swancutt, "Hungers Assuaged by the Bread from Heaven," in *Early Christian Interpretation of the Scriptures of Israel*, ed. Craig A. Evans and James A. Sanders (Sheffield: Sheffield Academic Press, 1997), 218–51.

The psalm parallels the distinctive thrust of Num. 11:20, 33. The fact that they had not "turned aside" (*zārû*) again does not imply there was anything wrong about their desire, but it is an unusual expression that reflects Yhwh's warning that the food would become something disgusting (*zārā*ʾ; Num. 11:20).[55] But the second colon restates how they were simply continuing to enjoy this apparently fine and plentiful food—then everything went wrong. There is a deceptiveness lying behind their relationship with God (cf. v. 36), but v. 30 already "catches the people in the act: while they are still stuffing themselves death strikes," and God "reciprocates their double-heartedness with his own trick," because the food turns out to be a punishment.[56] Once more the reference to God's "anger" arising "against" them corresponds to Num. 11:33, though the verb here is less vivid if more devastating. There, the story speaks of Yhwh hitting the people with a very severe blow (*nākâ* hiphil, *makkâ*), resulting in many deaths. Here, the second colon heightens the description by speaking of God "slaying" some of the people (*hārag*).[57] Thus the place came to be called "The Graves of Desire" (Num. 11:34). The description of God's victims as "sturdy," from *šāmēn*, parallels language used of people after they have entered the land (e.g., Deut. 32:15; Neh. 9:25). That might draw the attention of people hearing the psalm to the peril they were in, as people in the land who seemed in a strong position, compared with the Ephraimites, whom Yhwh had cast off. The further parallel with the description of Yhwh's bringing Nebuchadnezzar to Jerusalem so that he "slew their youth" (2 Chron. 36:17) might hint at a similar warning.

78:32–37. The characteristic dynamics of Israel's relationship with God (a): Israel's failure.

Whereas vv. 17–31 have manifested a series of detailed parallels with Exod. 16–17; Num. 11; and Num. 14, now vv. 32–37 revert to the more general parallelism with Exodus and Numbers that characterized vv. 12–16. They thus express themselves in more independent fashion, though they also reflect language that appears elsewhere in the Scriptures. It is this that gives an impression of standing back a little from the particularities of the wilderness period and making comments on the characteristic dynamics of that relationship between Israel and God.

---

55. BDB gives *zûr* I the meaning "be a stranger," and its most familiar form is indeed *zār* (stranger), but its own meaning is more likely "turn aside" (see *HALOT*, also *DCH*). There seem to be three roots *zûr*, none of them common except in the form of that ptc. *zār*. The psalm utilizes the homonymy (or does not distinguish) between *zûr* I (turn aside) and *zûr* II (be disgusting).

56. Fokkelman, *Major Poems*, 2:218.

57. The prep. *b* suggests "some of" (BDB; cf. Tg).

³²Despite all this they still failed him
and did not have faith despite his wonders.

One might have thought that the experience of God's rage would jolt people to their senses, but a series of stories in Exodus and Numbers indicate that this never happened. Prophets explicitly marvel that in their own day "despite all this" the people have not turned from their faithlessness (Jer. 3:10; Hos. 7:10); once again the language hints at the stories' significance for people who listen to the psalm. Isaiah 5:25; 9:12, 17, 21 [11, 16, 20]; and 10:4 likewise note how Yhwh keeps acting against them and "despite all this" does not give up doing so. The parallel colon makes specific the way the people continue to *fail, by not having faith ("be *true"; cf. v. 22) in or despite his *wonders (cf. vv. 4, 11).⁵⁸ This lack of faith was illustrated in the way they declined to make one experience of God's marvelous provision the basis for believing that God would take them through their next crisis.

³³He made their days end in emptiness,
their years in terror.

The verb *kālâ* could introduce a Wisdom idea, that people's days were "consumed" by emptiness as they passed (Job 7:16; Eccles. 6:12; 7:15; 9:9), but here the verb more likely continues to describe the way God "terminated" their days as a mere breath (*hebel*). Terror (the similar word *behālâ;* cf. Lev. 26:16; Jer. 15:8) thus overtook them in the way v. 31 has described. The link with the people's not having faith in Yhwh (v. 32), which otherwise comes in the Pentateuch only in Num. 14:11, suggests that vv. 32–33 refer to the way the whole wilderness generation died out as a result of Yhwh's response to the events in Num. 13–14.

³⁴When he slew them they would seek help from him,
turn and search for God.
³⁵They were mindful that God was their crag,
God Most High their restorer.

Notwithstanding the declaration in v. 32, they did sometimes respond to their chastisement. In the stories in Exodus and Numbers, there are no examples of Israel responding to chastisement by *seeking help from Yhwh or by turning to Yhwh, still less by searching for Yhwh,⁵⁹ and it is

58. In isolation, one would render *b* "in," but in the abb'a' line the meaning of *b* in the parallel colon likely carries over (cf. Johnson, *Cultic Prophet and Israel's Psalmody*, 54).
59. On this verb, see 63:1 [2].

also hard to find indications of a response expressed in any other words. It is Chronicles that most often describes Israel as "seeking help" from Yhwh, but even there this is not a response to chastisement. In Judges the people do "cry out" to Yhwh in their suffering, though they do not "turn" to Yhwh, and never in the OT do they "search for" God. Perhaps, in midrashic fashion, the psalm simply infers that they did so after their different chastisements on the journey from Egypt to Canaan in order to make the point it wishes to make (rather in the way Heb. 11 assumes that the people it refers to acted by faith).

Likewise, the stories do not have Israel recognizing that God *Most High is their *crag, as some psalms do (e.g., 71:3; 73:26), or as their *restorer (but for this verb, cf. 74:2; 77:15 [16]). Any *mindfulness they show is of a less constructive kind (Num. 11:5; contrast Ps. 77:3, 6, 11 [4, 7, 12]).

> ³⁶But they enticed him with their mouth,
>   with their tongue they would lie to him.

Because the stories about the wilderness period do not explicitly refer to the people's turning to Yhwh, they also do not comment on the deceptiveness of any such turning. "Entice" is a striking verb to use. When it appears in a religious context, it almost always refers to Yhwh's deceptiveness (e.g., 1 Kings 22:20–22; Jer. 20:7), but elsewhere it can suggest a man deceiving a woman, or a woman a man (e.g., Judg. 14:15; 16:5; Job 31:9), or other forms of deceptiveness (e.g., Prov. 1:10; 16:29; 24:28). The parallel root is also used of lies told between men and women (Judg. 16:10, 13) but more commonly of deceptive lying in court and in other settings. In general, the OT certainly presupposes that people come to Yhwh with expressions of devotion that cannot be trusted.

> ³⁷Their heart was not firm with him;
>   they were not true to his covenant.

The reference to the *heart once more points to the way the people's outer inconstancy reflected the inner person (cf. v. 18), while the description of their heart as not firm picks up from v. 8. It noted that they had not taken responsibility for their heart's firmness and added that their spirit was thus not true to God. Here the equivalent declaration is that they were not true to God's covenant—that is, to the covenant obligation God laid on them (cf. v. 10). What Yhwh looked for was that they should treat Yhwh as their God; that was what they failed to do in not consistently seeking help from Yhwh or turning to Yhwh or searching for Yhwh. There is a semantic and a substantial link between this failure to be *true to God (*'āman* niphal, vv. 8, 37) and their failure to have faith in God and God's wonders (*'āman* hiphil, vv. 22, 32). The line summarizes the nature of Israel's relationship with God as 1 and 2 Kings and the Prophets describe it.

78:38–39. The characteristic dynamics of Israel's relationship with God (b): God's compassion.

> 38Because he was compassionate,
>   he would expiate waywardness and not destroy.
> Again and again he turned his anger,
>   would not stir any of his wrath.

Neither do the stories in Exodus and Numbers refer to God's compassion, but they stand under the sign of Yhwh's self-description as compassionate and Yhwh's declaration of intent to show compassion with sovereign generosity (Exod. 33:19; 34:6). Here that compassion expresses itself in an instance of the remarkable use of the verb *kipper* with God as subject (see on 65:3 [4]), which is equivalent to the reference to Yhwh's carrying waywardness (the verb *nāśā'*) in Exod. 34:6–7. God's compassion expresses itself in taking the initiative to solve the problem caused by people's *waywardness. The Masoretic marginal note in *BHS* identifies this as the middle verse in the Psalter, as does the Talmud, which also tells us that this line was one of the verses recited to someone who was receiving the forty-lash punishment of Deut. 25:3.[60]

The second line re-expresses the point, taking up another aspect of Exod. 34:6–7, its description of Yhwh as "slow to anger." God's "turning" or diverting this anger (where did it go?) compares with their "turning" to God (v. 34), except that in the meantime they have given up turning to God. One might have expected God to give up turning this anger, but God has not. The second colon complements "anger" (*'ap*) by the stronger word "wrath" (*ḥēmâ*), which suggests the furious heat of anger, and also gives a complementary description of one's relationship with one's anger or wrath. In the first colon anger is something that arises from inside us unbidden, and the question is what we do with it. In the second colon wrath is something that we deliberately stir up in order to be able to utilize its energy in undertaking some violent act. God has vast reservoirs of wrath to call on to this end ("any of his wrath," lit. "all his wrath") but kept declining to do so at all, despite people's deservingness. The EVV have God not stirring up "all his wrath," implying that he did stir up some of it, and in the context of the psalm as a whole that makes sense. But vv. 38–39 look more gracious, and more likely here the expression

60. *b. Qiddušin* 30a; *b. Makkot* 22b.

500

denotes that on many occasions God's slowness to anger meant that Israel was not on the receiving end of God's wrath at all.

> ³⁹He was mindful that they were flesh,
>   a wind that is passing and does not return.

Why should that be so? The consideration that elicited God's compassion and made God expiate the people's waywardness was an awareness about the people. God's *mindfulness once more recalls the people's mindfulness (v. 35), except that the people gave up their mindfulness. They ignored God's strength, exercised on their behalf; God did not ignore their weakness. In a Pauline context the reference to their flesh would suggest that God was taking into account their moral weakness, but *bāśār* is morally neutral, like "body" in Paul. On the other hand, "flesh" can suggest weakness over against God's strength, something short-lived over against God's eternity (e.g., 56:4 [5]; Isa. 31:3), and the second colon makes clear that connotation here. The Israelites are not like the heavenly beings we will read of in Ps. 82, who have power and the capacity to live on unless God takes it away. The Israelites are feeble and short-lived, but precisely because of this God has mercy on them. In one sense they are not at all like *rûaḥ* (Isa. 31:3), but in another sense they are only too like *rûaḥ* (the word for "wind" here).

78:40–43. The characteristic dynamics of Israel's relationship with God (c): Israel's defiance and testing.

> ⁴⁰How much they would defy him in the wilderness,
>   grieve him in the wasteland.
> ⁴¹Repeatedly they tested God,
>   vexed the Holy One of Israel.

Over against Yhwh's "again and again" and "any" stands the people's "How often?" (*kammâ*, lit. "How much?"). Yhwh's aim had been to counteract their defiance (v. 8), but they insisted on it through the years in the wilderness, the wasteland (the rarer word parallels the more familiar one). To put it another way, they grieved God (*'āṣab*). Perhaps the verb suggests "vexed" in the sense of "annoyed," but it is noteworthy that this root characteristically refers to pain and hurt (e.g., 16:4; 127:2; 147:3).

While vv. 40 and 41 are internally parallel, v. 41 as a whole is also parallel to v. 40 as a whole. First, "repeatedly" (lit. "they repeated and") takes up "How often?" Their testing God (see v. 18) was not just a onetime act; their grieving him also involved vexing.⁶¹ And the object of that is

---

61. *Tāwâ* and associated nouns otherwise mean "mark," and KJV thus infers here the meaning "set a limit to." BDB and *HALOT* more plausibly infer a second verb occurring

the powerful God (*'ēl*), who is also "the Holy One of Israel" (see 71:22). That title for God emphasizes the enormity of the people's action; it also recalls the way Yhwh "showed himself holy" when Moses and Aaron failed to do so—at "Holy Place" (*qādēš*; Num. 20:1, 12–13).[62]

> [42]They were not mindful of his hand,
>   the day when he redeemed them from the foe,
> [43]When he put his signs in Egypt,
>   his portents in the region of Zoan.

Two further lines expound the nature of that defying, grieving, testing, and vexing. The opening colon takes up from vv. 35 and 39. The mindfulness of v. 35 indeed did not last. Here the object of the verb is Yhwh's hand, so often referred to in Exod. 3–15 as undertaking the activity vv. 44–55 will go on to recall. That story and v. 35 see this as the way Yhwh "restored" the people (*gā'al*), but here the psalm rather speaks of it as the way Yhwh *redeemed them (*pādâ*). For Yhwh, Israel was like a family member who has fallen into enslavement; Yhwh thus acted like a *gō'ēl* in actually paying the price to restore this family member (cf. Deut. 7:8; 9:26).

Yhwh did that by means of signs or portents: the two words come together especially in Deuteronomy (e.g., 4:34; 6:22; 7:19). A sign (*'ôt*) can be something ordinary that receives special significance (like a ring) or something inherently extraordinary that is also specially significant in some connection. A portent (*môpēt*) is something inherently extraordinary (though it may nevertheless be something "natural," such as a person—but an extraordinary person) that points to something else, perhaps something in the future. These signs and portents happened in Egypt and specifically in the area of Zoan (see v. 12). There Yhwh "put" or set these signs and portents (cf. 105:27; Jer 32:20), put them down with some firmness.

78:44–55. God and Israel from Egypt to Shiloh (a): God's great acts. After that central general description of the dynamics of Israel's relationship with God, vv. 44–66 as a whole revert to a more concrete description. In this respect vv. 44–66 parallel vv. 12–31, but whereas vv. 12–31 focus on the wilderness period, vv. 44–66 offer a more broad-canvas account of that relationship, from the time of Moses to the time of Samuel. On the other hand, vv. 44–66 follow the same sequence, God's acts on Israel's behalf, the faithlessness of Israel's response, and God's reactive wrath.

---

only here in the OT but known in PBH, Aramaic, and Syriac (see *DTT*), which can denote the arousing of strong negative feelings in various senses. Its precise meaning here is uncertain; LXX and Jerome have "provoke," Tg "disgust," BDB "pain," *HALOT* "hurt."

62. Cf. Goulder, *Psalms of Asaph*, 119.

First, then, vv. 44–55 elaborate on the story of those signs and portents in Egypt (vv. 44–51) and then go on more briefly to summarize the way Yhwh took Israel from Egypt to Canaan (vv. 52–55). Like vv. 17–31, the section has detailed verbal links with the scriptural story, though it uses the same words in independent configurations.

> ⁴⁴He turned their rivers to blood;
>   they could not drink from their streams.
> ⁴⁵He would send against them swarms and they devoured them,
>   frogs and they devastated them.
> ⁴⁶He gave their produce to the caterpillar,
>   their labor to the locust.
> ⁴⁷He slew their vines with hail,
>   their sycamore figs with flood.
> ⁴⁸He gave over their livestock to hail,
>   their cattle to lightning flashes.

The lines summarize the story, mostly in terms from Exodus; the reader has to work out that "their" refers to Egypt (v. 43). For v. 44, see Exod. 7:17–19, though "streams" is a novelty over against the narrative (rather cf. v. 16). For "swarms" in v. 45a, see Exod. 8:21, 24 [17, 20]; and for "frogs" in v. 45b, see Exod. 8:2, 6 [7:27; 8:2]. For the locusts, see Exod. 10, though the rest of v. 46 is the psalm's distinctive formulation. "Send" (*šālaḥ* piel) is a very common verb in Exod. 3–14, but its occurrence here makes for an irony, as there it often refers to the pharaoh's sending off the Israelites (EVV, "letting them go," as in Exod. 3:20; 14:5). The pharaoh's unwillingness to send off Israel leads to Yhwh's sending off these swarms.

For the hail decimating the cattle in vv. 47–48, see Exod. 9. The "flood" and the "lightning flashes" link with the reference to heavy rain there.[63] Likewise the narrative refers to plants and trees as the victims of the hail and lightning (Exod. 9:25); the psalm makes this more concrete in referring to vines and sycamore figs, which also reflect the way disasters such as these would be experienced in Canaan (e.g., Joel 1:7). The verb "slay," which applied to the Egyptians in Exod. 4:23; 13:15 but is here oddly applied to vines and trees, is picked up from vv. 31, 34.

> ⁴⁹He would send against them his angry fury,
>   wrath, rage, distress,
> A commission of aides bringing trouble
>   ⁵⁰ᵃthat would clear a path for his anger.

---

63. But *ḥănāmal* is a hapax in the OT; while *HALOT* has "flood," LXX and Aq have "frost," and Th and Tg have another word for "locust."

The verb "send" recurs (cf. v. 45), but here "he would send his fury" corresponds to "you would send your fury" in Exod. 15:7; the word for anger (*'ap*) then appears in the plural as the word for nostrils in Exod. 15:8. In the parallel colon, the three further words for hostility powerfully underline the violent force of Yhwh's action against Egypt. If "anger" suggests snorting, "fury" (*ḥārôn*) suggests something that blazes (*ḥārâ*), and "wrath" (*'ebrâ*) something that bursts out and overwhelms (*'ābar*).[64] The last two words are trickier. The word for "rage" (*za'am*) may suggest an attitude such as "indignation"[65] or may denote its outworking as "curse."[66] The latter would lead well into *ṣārâ* if that does have its usual meaning "distress," but *ṣārâ* might imply hostility[67] or might link with *ṣîr* and suggest emissary (see the next line).[68] That does in any case draw our attention to the fact that the point of the words resides less in the feelings that lie behind God's action as in the harshness of the experience that comes to the Egyptians (rather as when we speak of a raging fire or a furious battle), as the preceding and succeeding verses suggest. And further, the effect of the words comes from the heaping up of synonyms rather than from precision as to their individual meaning.[69]

I take vv. 49–50 as three bicola rather than a random pair of tricola.[70] In v. 49c, the word for the "commission" (*mišlaḥat*) of supernatural aides again takes up the root for "send." In Exod. 12:23 the destruction of Egypt's firstborn is the responsibility of "the Destroyer" (*hammašḥît*; cf. also 2 Sam. 24:17; 1 Chron. 21:15; and 1 Cor. 10:10; Heb. 11:28). The only passage that speaks of such figures in the plural is Ezek. 9, which also illustrates how it is usually the people of God whom such figures attack. Here these aides do the work that makes it possible for God's anger to find full expression. Again, the idea will be that the destructive work is thoroughly done rather than that the feelings are fully expressed. The KJV strikingly describes them as "evil angels," but evidently these angels are under Yhwh's control and sovereignty. Their work is not bad in Yhwh's eyes but bad in the experience of their victims; they are "calamitous angels." Indeed, they may simply be personifications of God's fury, wrath, rage, and distress, as elsewhere (for instance) God's light,

---

64. For people using the word, this could still be so, even if *'ebrâ* comes from a different root *'ābar* (cf. *HALOT*).

65. So in PBH; see *DTT*.

66. So at Qumran.

67. See BDB's *ṣārâ* II.

68. Mitchell Dahood ("*ṣîr* 'Emissary' in Psalm 78,49," *Bib* 59 [1978]: 264) repoints *wĕṣārâ* as *wĕṣîrēhû* ("yes, his emissary") in this connection.

69. See *TDOT* on *'ānap*.

70. The word order suggests that vv. 49c–50a depends on v. 49a–b with v. 50a as a relative clause (cf. Tate, *Psalms 51–100*, 279) rather than vv. 49c–50a being an independent sentence.

truthfulness, and commitment are agents of the comfort that God sends
(e.g., 43:3; 57:3 [4]).

> **50b–c**He did not spare their lives from death
>   but gave them[71] over to epidemic.
> **51**He hit every firstborn in Egypt,
>   the first issue of vigor in the tents of Ham.

In Exod. 9:15, "epidemic" presumably refers to the deadly hail, but
presumably v. 50b–c continues to describe the killing of the firstborn,
doing so in the psalm's own terms: "give over" (*sāgar* hiphil) recurs (cf.
vv. 48, 62).

Again, in Exodus the verb "hit" (*nākâ* hiphil) applied both to the deaths
through the hail and to the deaths of the firstborn (e.g., Exod. 9:25; 12:29).
"First issue of vigor" parallels and explicates "firstborn," as in Gen. 49:3;
Deut. 21:17; Ps. 105:36. The expression underlines the poignancy and
grievousness of the loss of the firstborn from the perspective of their
fathers. Their firstborn sons are the firstfruits of their own manliness;
the loss of them means a loss of their manliness. "The tents of Ham"
similarly spells out "Egypt," Ham being its ancestor (Gen. 10:6); "tents
of" will simply mean "dwellings of" (cf. Jer. 30:18; Zech. 12:7).

> **52**He set his people on the move like sheep
>   and drove them like a flock in the wilderness.
> **53**He led them in safety and they were not afraid,
>   but their enemies—the sea covered them.

Two further lines relate God's taking the people from Egypt to the other
side of the Red Sea. After the death of the firstborn, Exodus describes the
Israelites as getting on the move (*nāsaʿ*) from Egypt onward and then
through the Red Sea and onward (e.g., Exod. 12:37; 13:20; 14:15; 16:1;
17:1). On the other hand, in Exodus only Moses is getting the people
moving (the hiphil form of the verb, which appears here in the psalm
and in Exod. 15:22; and cf. Ps. 80:8 [9]). Likewise, only in poetry such
as the Psalms is God the shepherd driving the flock on this journey (see
77:20 [21]; 80:1 [2]).

Thus Yhwh "led" the people (cf. Exod. 13:17, 21; 15:13) in safety to
the other side of the Red Sea. The reference to their not being afraid
(*pāḥad*) adds interestingly to the comments about fearing and revering
in Exod. 14:10, 13, 31; 15:11 (*yārēʾ*); 15:16 (*paḥad*). Exodus also uses the
same language as the psalm to spell out the explanation in terms of the
sea "covering" (Exod. 14:28; 15:5, 10) their "enemies" (Exod. 15:6, 9).

---

71. *Ḥayyātām*, lit. "their life"—or "their animals" (Tg).

> ⁵⁴He brought them to his holy territory,
> the mountain that his right hand acquired.

Like Exod. 15, the psalm moves straight from the Red Sea to the people's arrival in Canaan. So Yhwh "brought them" (cf. Exod. 15:17) to "his holy territory" (cf. "your holy dwelling" in Exod. 15:13). That expression is spelled out as his "mountain," the mountain country of Canaan (not Zion in particular; again cf. Exod. 15:17), which his "right hand" (Exod. 15:6, 12—there with reference to the Red Sea) "acquired" (*qānâ*; Exod. 15:16—there with reference to the people). Psalm 74:2 already used this verb (also with reference to the people), probably implying "acquired by purchase," but here the context does not suggest a monetary transaction (cf. rather Gen 14:19, 22).

> ⁵⁵He drove out nations before them,
> allotted them as a share to possess,
> settled Israel's clans in their tents.

The fact that Yhwh is the undisputed owner of this land makes it possible for Yhwh to give it to Israel, as v. 55 describes in a closing tricolon explicating how God brought Israel into the land. First, God dispossessed its previous occupants. "Drive out" (*gāraš*) is again a word that comes in Exodus to describe the Pharaoh's driving out the Israelites, Yhwh's undertaking to drive out people such as the Canaanites, and the Israelites' own doing so; it also comes in Joshua in that connection (Exod. 6:1; 11:1; 12:39; 23:28–31; 33:2; 34:11; Josh. 24:12, 18). The Pentateuch argues that Yhwh is thus implementing just judgment on these peoples; the psalm rather sees Yhwh as having an owner's rights to introduce or remove inhabitants of the land.

Second, having dispossessed those previous occupants, Yhwh allotted the nations (that is, by metonymy, their land) to the different Israelite clans.[72] The term "allot" (lit. "cause to fall") corresponds to Josh. 17:5 and suggests an allocation by drawing lots, in which case the colon affirms that this "chance" method of dividing up the land is one that leaves matters to God's sovereignty. It is Yhwh who decides where the lot falls (cf. Prov. 16:33). The point is underlined by the word "share" (*ḥebel*), another metonymy. Literally the word refers to the line people would stretch out in dividing up the land (cf. Zech. 2:1 [5]), not for the allocation of land to the clans but for its smaller-scale division among

---

72. KJV takes the suffix on *wayyappîlēm* to refer to the Israelites as the indirect obj. ("he allotted [to] them a share"), but for Yhwh's giving the nations as a possession, cf. Josh. 23:4; Ps. 2:8.

the families in a village. That becomes an image for Yhwh's dividing up the land between the clans, thus declaring that Yhwh was involved in all the detail of the allocation. "A share to possess" (*naḥălâ*) could then refer either to the entire land as Yhwh's possession (cf. Exod. 15:17) or to the tracts of land that individual clans and families possessed (the more common usage in Joshua).

Either way, the end result (the third colon adds) is that Yhwh thus settled the clans there in their tents. Once more the psalm moves to its own way of putting things. Settling Israel (*šākan* hiphil) suggests making it possible for them to dwell securely (cf. Num. 14:30); the verb is more often used of Yhwh's settling among the people (cf. v. 60). "Tents" again simply means "dwellings," though Josh. 22:4–8 makes the association with the people's entering into possession of the land (and may indicate that the psalm refers to their own dwellings rather than the dwellings of the people they dispossess).

78:56–58. God and Israel from Egypt to Shiloh (b): Israel's testing and defiance.

Earlier critiques of Israel related to the time between Egypt and the land. Now, having spoken of Yhwh's giving people the land, the psalm speaks of the same failures after that event.

> [56]But they tested and defied God Most High
>   and did not keep his declarations.
> [57]They went away and were disloyal like their ancestors;
>   they turned like a treacherous bow.

The psalm underlines the consistency of the people's behavior by repeating verbs used earlier. They tested God (cf. vv. 18, 41); the verb is not elsewhere used of Israel's acts in the land, though it is the subject of a prohibition (Deut. 6:16) and of an implicit warning (Ps. 95:9). They defied God (cf. v. 17, where God is also "Most High"; also vv. 8, 40); this is a verb that the prophets use (e.g., Ezek. 20:8, 13, 21) and that characterizes Judah's self-description (Lam. 1:18, 20; 3:42). They did not "keep" his "declarations" (cf. the verb in v. 10 and the sg. *'ēdût* in v. 5).

Verse 57 makes that consistency explicit, first in terms that are new for the psalm but familiar from other critiques of the people. They have moved away from their commitment to Yhwh (cf. Pss. 53:3 [4]; 80:18 [19]). In other words, they have been disloyal or unfaithful by turning to other deities or scorning Yhwh (cf. Jer. 3:20; 5:11). The second colon makes the point vividly though once more metonymically: the idea is that they swerved and missed the target like an arrow shot from a bow that did not shoot straight and thus let down the person who used it. The word *rĕmîyâ* can mean both treachery or deceptiveness and slackness,

and both meanings may apply in this context: a slack bow is one that lets
the archer down. The phrase makes a link with v. 9; see the comment.

> ⁵⁸They vexed him with their high places;
>   with their images they aroused him.

The verbs in the neat abb'a' closing line of this section describe the
results of the people's action, and the two *b* expressions give more precision to their treachery. Both verbs suggest the strength of feelings the
people arouse in Yhwh. The first (*kā'as* hiphil) usually denotes provoking
someone to anger, but it may also hint at the pain that people's hostility
can cause, and in this context that would fit with the way the psalm has
used similar words. The second likewise suggests the arousing of strong
feelings such as the violent passion someone feels when their loved one
has been unfaithful. The high places and the images involved in Israel's
worship have that effect. People could go to the traditional local sanctuaries in the land and worship the images of other gods, or they could go
there and worship Yhwh by means of images. The interweaving of terms
in the first two commandments (Exod. 20:3–6) suggests that in the end
the OT sees little difference in effect between these. Worshipping Yhwh
in the way people worshipped other gods at the traditional sanctuaries
was, in effect, worshipping a different god. It cannot be Yhwh that is
worshipped that way.

78:59–64. God and Israel from Egypt to Shiloh (c): God's fury.

While one might reckon that vv. 56–58 describe the kind of events we
read of in Judges, the chastisement the psalm goes on to describe relates
more specifically to events recorded in 1 Samuel.

> ⁵⁹God listened and raged,
>   and utterly rejected Israel.

The first colon repeats the declaration in v. 21, underlining how events
in the land repeat the pattern set in the wilderness. Perhaps, then, we
should not press the question of what Yhwh now heard, or perhaps we
should imagine Yhwh listening to the prayers people prayed in the local
sanctuaries and before their images of Yhwh. Normally a declaration
that Yhwh had listened to the people's prayers would be very good news
(e.g., 6:8–9 [9–10]; 28:6; 66:19), but here Yhwh's hearing is bad news, as
in v. 21. Or perhaps (in light of v. 60) we should picture Yhwh hearing of
what has been happening in a sanctuary such as Shiloh (hearing reports
of it in the heavenly cabinet?). Whereas Eli heard of events there and
did nothing (1 Sam. 2:22–25; 3:13), Yhwh heard of it and acted. The
people have rejected Yhwh, pushed Yhwh out of their lives (cf. Num.

11:20; 1 Sam. 8:7); therefore they find themselves rejected, pushed out of Yhwh's life or realizing that Yhwh has walked out on them (cf. Ps. 53:5 [6]; Lam. 5:22).

> **60**He abandoned the dwelling at Shiloh,
> the tent he settled among people.

The psalm has not so far referred to the fact that through the people's journey in the wilderness, they knew God's presence among them as God dwelt in their midst in a tent. The people's arriving in the land meant that Yhwh caused the tent ('*ōhel*) or dwelling (*miškān*)[73] to dwell or settle (*šākan*) there. The expressions parallel Josh. 18:1, though there the Israelites are the subject of the verb.[74] Thus the very presence of Yhwh is settled or made to dwell in the very midst of ordinary human beings ('*ādām*).[75] The comment recalls Solomon's incredulous question in 1 Kings 8:27. How grievous, then, is the opening verb of the line.

> **61**He let his might go into captivity,
> his glory into the hand of the foe.

Although the OT may imply that the sanctuary was located at various places between the time of Joshua and Samuel, in 1 Samuel it again stands at Shiloh, as in Joshua's day. The outworking of God's abandonment of it (v. 60) is described in 1 Sam. 4. Israel took the covenant chest from Shiloh to the battle near Aphek, but that failed to stop the Philistines from defeating Israel, and the chest was captured. "Splendor has gone into exile from Israel," the priest's daughter-in-law exclaimed. The two cola of the verse express the same point. In other contexts "his glory" might denote "his glorious one," meaning his glorious people (e.g., Isa. 46:13), but here the parallelism suggests that Yhwh in divine glory (e.g., Isa. 60:19) goes into the power of the Philistines through their capture

---

73. Exodus uses the term '*ōhel* both of the tent of Exod. 33:7–11 and of the more elaborate tent of Exod. 25–31; 35–40; it uses the term *miškān* (dwelling) only of the latter. First Samuel describes the sanctuary at Shiloh only as a tent and a palace (*hêkāl*). We have already noted that "tent" can simply mean "dwelling" (see vv. 51, 55), though, in connection with Yhwh's sanctuary, it might refer to the incorporation of the earlier mobile dwelling within a building (see the discussion in Keel, *Symbolism*, 162–63). Usually Exod. 25–31 and 35–40 are regarded as coming from the exile or afterward, which might suggest a late date for the psalm, though the use of the two words in parallelism here corresponds to 2 Sam. 7:6.

74. Thus we should hardly follow LXX and Tg, which imply qal *šākan* ([where] he dwelt) for MT *šikkēn* (he caused to dwell/settled).

75. Or perhaps "at Adam," though in Josh. 3:16 this was simply where the water heaped up.

of the chest. For "his might," LXX with "their might" and Syr with "his people" offer readings that highlight the scandal of MT. The risk God accepted in coming to dwell among the people in a visible and tangible way is that the fate of the visible and tangible tent and chest (cf. Ps. 132:8) is the fate of the one who dwells there, as the fate of an image suggests the fate of the one it represents.

> [62]He gave his people over to the sword,
>   he raged at his possession.
> [63]Fire consumed its young men,
>   and its girls were not lamented.
> [64]Its priests fell by the sword,
>   and its widows would not weep.

The psalm turns to the effect of God's rage (the verb recurs from v. 59) on the people themselves, Yhwh's *possession; here that term refers to Israel (cf. v. 71) rather than to the land (cf. v. 55). For the sword, see 1 Sam. 4:2, 10. That narrative makes no direct comment on Yhwh's involvement; it leaves the reader to make the theological inference. The psalm knows that it was Yhwh who caused Israel's defeat, and it says so.

The narrative makes no reference to fire, but that is a regular result of the siege and capture of a city, and Jer. 7, at least, implies that Shiloh was destroyed in the course of these events. But the reference to fire may reflect the influence of Num. 11:1–3 and denote a supernatural and/or metaphorical fire rather than a regular one.

On the other hand, only too literally did its priests fall by the sword in fulfillment of Yhwh's word (1 Sam. 4:11). And at least one of their widows could not lament her husband because she herself died in childbirth soon after hearing of her husband's death (1 Sam. 4:19–22).[76] But the expression recurs in Job 27:15 and likely suggests that the calamity is so great that there is no opportunity to undertake the proper mourning processes or so overwhelming that it overtakes such processes (cf. Jer. 24:1–9).

78:65–72. In accordance with the pattern that runs through Israel's story, Yhwh's rage eventually subsides and Yhwh acts in mercy.

> [65]But the Lord awoke like someone asleep,
>   like a warrior making a noise because of wine.

The Philistines soon discovered that they could not mess with Yhwh (1 Sam. 5–6), and Tg links vv. 65–66 with that experience: it includes reference to their being afflicted with hemorrhoids (cf. 1 Sam. 5:6). But

---

76. Tg[B] makes this link (cf. Stec, *Targum of Psalms*, 154).

vv. 67–72 imply a longer time frame. For decades the Philistines remained dominant in the land, but after seeming to be long asleep, the *Lord awoke, as elsewhere suppliants beg the Lord to do (Pss. 35:23; 44:23 [24]; 59:5 [6]); cf. 73:20.[77] Here the psalm recognizes that technically the Lord awakes from inactivity rather than from sleep, "like" someone asleep rather than from actual sleep. But Yhwh has been sitting there in heaven, doing nothing, and the effect is the same for Israel. Yet the problem lies in Yhwh's unwillingness to act rather than in an inability to do something, like the incapable Baals. As usual, Yhwh has been living with the tension between the necessity to be faithful to Israel and the necessity to chastise Israel, and for decades he has given priority to the latter; but at last Yhwh decided that enough was enough. And when that happens, it has revolutionary results. Instead of being totally inactive, Yhwh is vigorously active (there are no half measures with Yhwh). In the first colon Yhwh resembles a man who had fallen asleep; now in an even more daring image Yhwh resembles a warrior who has been drinking too much and arises to roar his battle cry with great energy. Yhwh will indeed be a dangerous person to mess with.

> **66**He beat back his foes,
> gave them permanent reviling.

One might not have thought that drunkenness made for efficient war-making; there are limits to that simile. Yhwh is alert enough to be in a position to handle enemies with violent efficiency. Once again a pattern is repeating itself, but here it is a pattern in Yhwh's positive action, repeating the verb *nākâ* (hiphil). As Yhwh once struck the Egyptians (v. 51), so Yhwh now strikes the Philistines and Ammonites. The period of inaction had been a period of Israel's disgrace, but now Yhwh takes away this disgrace (1 Sam. 11:2; 17:26) and gives it to their foes. And the story of Yhwh's defeat of Ammon and Philistia indeed ever resounds to their disgrace.

> **67**But he rejected the tent of Joseph,
> did not choose the clan of Ephraim.

A further surprise follows, though one presaged by vv. 9–11. In v. 59 God rejected Israel as a whole, but the fact that Shiloh lay in Ephraim and that God never went back there could suggest that God in particular rejected the northern clans. That is now explicit. Once Israel's center of gravity had lain there. While Joseph was one of Jacob's younger sons, he

---

77. These verses instance the more common *qîṣ*; this psalm's form implies the by-form *yāqaṣ*.

had become their leader, and his sons gave their names to the two biggest clans. Joshua was an Ephraimite, and the main route of the clans' occupation of the land took them via Jericho and Ai to Shechem, in the heart of the Josephites' territory, where Joshua proclaimed Moses's teaching to the assembled people (Josh. 8:30–35; see also Josh. 24). The tent and the covenant chest were evidently settled at Shiloh in Ephraim in 1 Sam. 1–4. One might have thought that the return of the covenant chest would mean the rebuilding of the sanctuary at Shiloh, as the return of the vessels from the Jerusalem temple would later mean the rebuilding of that temple. But the covenant chest never got back to Shiloh. For decades it was stuck at Kiriath-Jearim, between the location of its exile and the sanctuary whence it had been taken. In the meantime, the leadership and center of gravity in Israel moved away from the north, where Saul came from, and from the great Joseph clans, specifically Ephraim, at its center. First and Second Samuel say nothing about God rejecting/not choosing them, but the psalm infers as much from the positive choice God did make. The point will be made even more sharply if we translate "the rod/scepter of Ephraim": cf. *šēbeṭ* in Gen. 49:10, with its enigmatic reference to Shiloh (?).[78] God's rejecting the line of kings in Ephraim then links with God's choice of the Davidic line (v. 70).

> [68]He chose the clan of Judah,
>   Mount Zion, to which he dedicated himself.

Specifically, the center of gravity moved from Ephraim to Judah, where David came from, for when David formed the plan to move the chest to the state capital, this meant Jerusalem, not a city in the north. The narrative does not associate God's initiative with this, though in connection with his plan to move the covenant chest to Jerusalem David declares that God had chosen Judah and his territory (1 Chron. 28:4), notwithstanding his forfeiture of any honorable position among Jacob's sons (Gen. 38). Solomon later declares that God chose Jerusalem (1 Kings 8:16, 44, 48), and eventually God agrees (e.g., 1 Kings 11:13, 32, 36), as does the narrator in Chronicles (2 Chron. 12:13). Psalm 132:13 adds that God chose Zion, and Ps. 87:2 that Yhwh was dedicated to Zion's gates. The parallel verbs "chose" and "*dedicated himself" indicate that the psalm is talking about not merely a feeling on Yhwh's part but also a practical commitment.

> [69]He built his sanctuary like the heights,
>   like the earth which he founded as a permanency.

---

78. Cf. Stern, "Eighth Century Dating of Psalm 78," 58.

The psalm goes even further in attributing to God the actions of people such as David and Solomon. In the narrative, Yhwh builds their household, but they build Yhwh's house or sanctuary (the term in, e.g., 1 Chron. 22:19); here Yhwh builds the sanctuary. But the emphasis lies on the impressiveness of Yhwh's building. The heights will be the heights of the heavens.[79] The second colon clarifies the likeness between the sanctuary and the heavens. The heavens are surely something that Yhwh has established as a permanency. The psalm assumes that the earth is likewise something that will last because God founded it (cf. 24:2; 89:11 [12]; 104:5). It is not like a building whose superstructure lacks solid foundations. Yet there is an irony sitting here; despite their secure foundations, Yhwh can decide that earth and heavens pass away (102:25–26 [26–27]).

> [70]He chose David his servant
>   and took him from the sheep pens,
> [71]brought him from following the ewes,
> To shepherd Jacob his people,
>   Israel his possession.

Verses 70–71 work abb′cc′, and I take vv. 70–71a as a tricolon (cf. Vg, Jerome), marking the move to this important reference to David in the last three verses of the psalm. Alongside the talk of Zion and the sanctuary is talk of Yhwh's choice of David (cf. the combination in Ps. 132). First Samuel itself does talk about God originally choosing Saul and then rejecting him (e.g., 1 Sam. 10:24; 15:23, 26) and then choosing David from among his more impressive brothers (1 Sam. 16). As servant, David is in a position of special responsibility to God, but also he has a special commitment on God's part to him. "My servant" is Yhwh's own description of David in making such a commitment to him and recalling how "I took you from the fold, from following the sheep" (2 Sam. 7:8). This was what Yhwh had done on that occasion in 1 Sam. 16, when none of his brothers proved to be the one Yhwh had "chosen" and he was fetched from his task of looking after the sheep. Yhwh's choice of David was as unpredictable as Yhwh's choice of Mount Zion.

So the shepherd boy became the shepherd king. As shepherd it was David's job to fight off the flock's attackers (1 Sam. 16:18; 17:34–37), and as king it became David's job likewise to protect God's people. Yhwh had "raged at his possession" (v. 62) but is now seeing that it gets cared for.

> [72]He shepherded them in accordance with the integrity of his heart,
>   and he would lead them with the great skillfulness of his hands.

79. With the ptc. *rāmîm*, cf. the noun *měrômîm* in Job 31:2.

David's victory over Goliath showed that he had both the conviction about Yhwh and the guts and skill to do that (1 Sam. 17:34–37). On one hand, David was a person with integrity (cf. 1 Kings 9:4). This was not so with regard to his personal life as years went past, but there was no doubt that he was always committed to Yhwh rather than to other gods, and this is the basis on which he is set up as a model (e.g., 1 Kings 11:4, 6; 15:3, 5). On the other hand, David was also a person with the gifts to shepherd Israel. In speaking of his "leading" the people, the psalm reverses its previous practice of using human verbs to describe God's activity. "Leading" Israel is God's task (vv. 14, 53); it now becomes David's, in leading the people through dangers (cf. v. 53) like a shepherd guiding his flock. "Skillfulness" is not elsewhere an attribute of David, though it is of Solomon (1 Kings 4:29 [5:9]), and of Yhwh in making the cosmos (Ps. 136:5).

Theological Implications

The psalm recognizes the crucial connection between the past, the present, and the future generation. Only because it listens to previous generations does the present generation know who it is and how to live in light of the reality of its God. Wisdom books assume this because they assume that wisdom is passed on from one generation to another; every generation does not have to start from scratch. The psalm makes a more specific point. God has been involved with Israel's life from its beginnings, so it would be foolish not to heed the lessons of that story. But further, the present generation has a responsibility to make it possible for coming generations also to heed those lessons. Psalms thus not only express the emotions that lie inside us; they also pass on to us information that needs to affect us.[80]

Once written Scriptures exist, does this necessity cease? Actually oral communication (preaching, teaching) continues to be a key means whereby the story of God's dealings is passed on. We have a hard time understanding the writings of peoples who could not also pass them on orally (for instance, material from Ugarit or Qumran). This suggests that their being passed on by a living community plays an important role in enabling succeeding generations to understand them. It also underlines the importance of the way we do pass them on. There is great power in the way preachers and teachers do so. For better and for worse, the way they tell the story influences people more than the written version of the stories does. For the people of God, deciding to remember is then the key to faithfulness; deciding to forget is the key to failure.

80. So Phillip McMillion, "Psalm 78," *ResQ* 43 (2001): 219–28 (see 228).

The psalm announces that it will relate "mysteries" (v. 2). In what sense does it do so? Any of a series of motifs in the story might evoke wonder at the extraordinary things it relates. The psalm offers a quite different model for understanding the nation's history from that of Deut. 26:5–9.[81] But here, too, God's marvelous acts by their extraordinary nature evoke wonder. By their unpredictability (for instance, the rejection of Shiloh and the choice of Zion) they evoke wonder. The provocative rebelliousness of God's people evokes wonder. God's persistent turning from chastisement to mercy evokes wonder. The way this convoluted story ends with God's marvelous choice of David evokes wonder. The psalm highlights the wonder of its story by the way it puts the focus on God. Here it is Yhwh who divides the Red Sea, not Moses. It is Yhwh whom the people attack, not Moses and Aaron, but it is Yhwh who expiates their wrongdoing, not the people themselves. It is Yhwh who sets them going toward the land, not Moses. It is Yhwh who settles the sanctuary in Canaan, not Joshua. It is Yhwh who gives the people to the sword, not the Philistines. It is Yhwh who builds the temple, not Solomon. Generally speaking, Israel's story is one that could be portrayed as a this-worldly event, like the story of any nation, even if it is a remarkable story. The psalm knows that it is not merely that.

Yet the advantage and the disadvantage of a narrative such as that of the psalm is that it does not make totalizing claims. The psalm does not declare that God's people always respond to God's acts with rebellion, that disaster always means the people have rebelled, that God always casts people off when they rebel, or that God always turns back to them in due course. Rather, it sets before the people the fact that this pattern has been there in Israel's story and that people need to take account of it. This challenge is heightened by the open way the narrative ends and by the fact that the psalm actually refrains from declaring a rationale for the rejection of Ephraim and the choice of David, despite the comment in vv. 9–11 (a long time ago in this monumentally long psalm). The psalm's openness, its declining to connect the dots, reminds us that we cannot always know the rationale for what God has done nor can we ever second-guess what God will do.

The opening of the psalm also forestalls any inclination on the part of the listeners to congratulate themselves on being the chosen people. The way it speaks of the failure of Ephraim and the choice of Zion might encourage Judah to do so. Indeed, the main part of the psalm might have been composed to give ideological buttressing to Judah's position. But if it were, it deconstructs, and the opening of the psalm makes sure

81. Cf. Dietmar Mathias, *Die Geschichtstheologie der Geschichtssummarien in den Psalmen* (Frankfurt: Lang, 1989), 110.

we do not miss the fact. Verses 9–11 at least raise the possibility that it was because of its failure that Ephraim was rejected; therefore Judah needs to take heed lest it falls. Jeremiah 7 and 26 make explicit how Jerusalem cannot ignore the lesson of Shiloh's story.[82] The psalm thus speaks to the supersessionist instinct in Christian faith, which sees God as having rejected Israel and sees the church as having taken Israel's place. Given the failures of the church, it would require Christians who take that view to expect that God has also cast off the church, or will do so. Thus Jerome urges Christian readers not to stand superior in relation to Jews or heretics and to remember Paul's exhortation not to boast against the olive whose natural branches have been cut off (Rom. 11:17–18), because we could go the same way.[83] Luther likewise, having interpreted the psalm in light of the Jews' rejection of Christ, adds that "we wretched, most evil Christians" need to hear it.[84]

82. Jeremiah thus coheres with the psalm rather than being a "critical treatment" of its "ideological claim" (so Walter Brueggemann, *Abiding Astonishment* [Louisville: Westminster John Knox, 1991], 44).

83. *Homilies*, 1:89.

84. *First Lectures*, 2:44.

Psalm 79

When Nations Attack Us
and Scorn God

Translation

Composition. Asaph's.

[1]God, the nations came into your possession,
    they defiled your holy palace,
    they turned Jerusalem into ruins.
[2]They gave your servants' corpses
    as food for the birds of the heavens,
    the flesh of people committed to you for the creatures[1] of the
        earth.
[3]They poured out their blood like water
    around Jerusalem,
    with no one to bury them.
[4]We became an object of reviling to our neighbors,
    of derision and scorn to people around us.

[5]Until when, Yhwh?—will you be angry forever?
    Will your passion burn like fire?
[6]Pour out your fury on the nations that have not acknowledged you,
    upon kingdoms that have not called on your name,
[7]Because they have consumed Jacob,
    desolated his abode.

1. On the form *ḥaytô,* see on 50:10.

8Do not bear in mind against us the wayward acts of an earlier
    generation;
  may your compassion meet us quickly,[2]
  because we are very low.
9Help us, God our deliverer,
  for the sake of the honor of your name.
Rescue us and expiate our shortcomings,
  for your name's sake.
10Why should the nations say,
  "Where is their God?"

May the redress for the blood of your servants that was poured out
  be acknowledged among the nations before our eyes.
11May the groan of the captive come before you;
  in accordance with the greatness of your strength preserve[3] the
    people doomed to death.
12Give back to our neighbors sevenfold into their bosom
  their reviling with which they have reviled you, Lord.

13And we as your people, the flock you shepherd,
  will confess you forever;
  from generation to generation we will declare your praise.

Interpretation

This community prayer psalm begins with four lines of protest at what has happened to Judah and Jerusalem (vv. 1–4), the focus being on the activity of the nations that brought that about. A rhetorical question marks a transition to petition (vv. 5–12). Unusually, petition occupies the bulk of the psalm, though as sometimes happens in the psalms, it works through its agenda three times (vv. 5–7, 8–10a, 10b–12). Each time the suppliant urges God to punish the nations or deliver the people, basing this both on the suffering of the people and on the nations' despising of God. The psalm closes with the common promise to declare Yhwh's praise for the answering of this prayer (v. 13).

In its possible background and its language, it parallels Ps. 74. Again it speaks of the community as "the flock you pasture," speaks of "reviling," of divine anger that seems to last "forever," of the despising of Yhwh's "name," and looks forward to being able to "declare" Yhwh's praise. It

---

2. Lit. "[in] hurrying may your compassion meet us"; the inf. functions as an adverb.

3. Syr and Tg with *šry* imply *hattēr* (free) from *nātar* (cf. Ps. 105:20), for MT's *hôtēr* from *yātar*.

also has verbal links with the psalms on either side. But more striking are the many expressions or whole lines that correspond to ones in other psalms: see on vv. 4, 5, 6–7, 8c, 10a, 11.[4] The detailed nature of the links suggests a direct connection rather than a common dependence on a tradition,[5] and their numerousness suggests that Ps. 79 is dependent on these various others rather than their being separately dependent on it, though it might be that the psalm is sometimes the source. Either way, the extent of the parallels marks out this psalm over against most others. Like the author of Ps. 71, the psalmist is someone soaked in the Psalms and/or the traditions that underlie psalmody. This hardly implies holding a copy of a Psalter and copying phrases but rather that the author has assimilated its contents. It is then also striking that the psalm is one that expresses particularly strong feelings of offense, loss, grief, anguish, horror, shame, fear, desire, and yearning. Evidently the use of familiar expressions already validated by the community facilitates the expression of the strong feelings that appear in the psalm.

The context presupposed by the psalm is clear enough. The land has been invaded, Jerusalem has been taken, and the temple has been defiled. Like Lamentations, the psalm gives no direct indication of which such occasion gave rise to it, but the only such major occasion the OT reports is the catastrophe of 587.[6] These events, then, at least indicate the kind of occasion against which to imagine the psalm (though it does not explicitly refer to the temple being destroyed, as happened in 587).[7] And its lack of specificity means it invites suppliants in other contexts to use it. These might be people who experienced some other attack on the city; we can imagine it being used in the context of the assault of Antiochus Epiphanes in the mid-160s,[8] and we know it was applied to a subsequent event in 162 BC (1 Macc. 7:17).[9] Or they might be people who lived some time after 587, still grieving the desolation those events brought. The question in v. 5 and the appeal in v. 8 suggest that the trouble

4. Hossfeld and Zenger (*Psalms 2*, 305) also note links with Jeremiah and Joel.

5. Contrast Gerstenberger, *Psalms*, 2:101.

6. Beat Weber ("Zur Datierung der Asaph-Psalmen 74 und 79," *Bib* 81 [2000]: 521–32) sees it as an exilic psalm that has taken Ps. 74 as its model. Leslie J. Hoppe also sees it as an exilic adaptation of earlier material ("Vengeance and Forgiveness," in *Imagery and Imagination in Biblical Literature* [Aloysius Fitzgerald Festschrift; ed. Lawrence Boadt and Mark S. Smith; CBQMS 32; Washington, DC: CBA, 2001], 1–22). But see the comment on the similarity to Mesopotamian city laments in the treatment of Ps. 74 above.

7. Thus Gunkel (*Psalmen*, 349–50), for instance, connects it with some otherwise unknown event in succeeding centuries.

8. So, e.g., Theodoret, *Psalms*, 2:41 (assuming that it was written prophetically for that event by Asaph); and Cassiodorus, *Psalms*, 2:275–76 (assuming it was so written by David).

9. Cf. Theodore, *Psalms 1–81*, 1084–85.

happened some time ago and that the prayer reflects the experience of living with its consequences over a period (cf. Lam. 5; Isa. 63:7–64:12 [11]). The psalm would then fit the occasions of fasting referred to in Zech. 7–8. The Talmud refers to its use annually on the fast of the Ninth of Ab, which memorializes the various occasions when Jerusalem fell (along with Ps. 137 and—in some congregations—Lamentations),[10] and nineteenth-century visitors to Jerusalem report the way it was used at the "Wailing Wall" of the Second Temple each Friday afternoon.[11]

Composition. Asaph's.

Heading. See glossary.
79:1–4. The first four lines comprise a protest at the action of the major powers that caused terrible affliction to Judah and Jerusalem. The point is underlined by the fact the first three lines are all tricola.

> ¹God, the nations came into your possession,
>   they defiled your holy palace,
>   they turned Jerusalem into ruins.

The notably "terse" invocation of God[12] gives the psalm's beginning a sense of urgency. The Midrash bids us look at this opening verse in light of Lam. 4:12. Who would have believed this could happen, not least in light of the miracles of deliverance in Jerusalem's story?[13] In the Prophets, "the nations" can denote the superpower of the day (e.g., Isa. 5:26; 14:26), and it makes sense to understand the expression in this way here (Israel's neighbor nations appear in v. 3). If we wish to put flesh on the expression, then we may think of the Babylonian forces in the 580s. From the beginning, the psalm seeks to motivate God by drawing attention to the way God is affected by the nations' actions. So first, they have invaded Yhwh's *possession, the land of Canaan (cf. 68:9 [10]).[14] Surely Yhwh must be concerned about that.

Perhaps worse, they naturally made straight for the *palace where the King lived. This is no ordinary palace, but a holy one, and their foreign feet have defiled it (cf. 74:4; Isa. 52:1; Lam. 1:10; Joel 3:17 [4:17]). It is not that the mere presence of foreigners is defiling; if foreigners came

10. See minor tractate *Soferim* 18.3.
11. http://www.bibleplaces.com/wailingwall1800s.htm.
12. Gerstenberger, *Psalms*, 2:100.
13. *Midrash on Psalms*, 2:42–44.
14. In 78:62, 71 Israel itself was Yhwh's "possession" (cf. 74:2), but here the immediate context in v. 1 suggests reference to the place rather than the people, and the verb also points in that direction. BDB takes the word to denote the temple, but this is hard to parallel.

into the temple to worship Yhwh and respected Yhwh's instructions about such worship, their feet would hardly defile it (see, for instance, the invitation in Ps. 100, a psalm whose language is reflected in v. 13). But these are no worshippers of Yhwh, and on an occasion such as the destruction in 587, they went straight for the temple's holiest precincts in a way no Israelite would, not even a priest, not even the high priest except once a year, and trashed (or dragged off) the holiest of its accoutrements such as the covenant chest.

Third, they devastated the city itself. Talk of the city as turned into "ruins" (*'îyîm*) might seem risky, since this description of Jerusalem comes elsewhere only in Mic. 3:12 and when Micah's words are quoted in Jer. 26:18 (otherwise the word comes only in Mic. 1:6, applied to Samaria). Taking up Micah's words hints that what happened was no chance but a fulfillment of prophecy. It was God's deliberate act to punish the city. But in this line the unexpected third colon at the same time reflects the reality that was most pressing for later suppliants. The invaders are long gone (and the temple was rebuilt in 520–516), but it was a considerable time before the city was rebuilt and hardly to its former glory.

> ²They gave your servants' corpses
>   as food for the birds of the heavens,
>   the flesh of people committed to you for the creatures of the earth.

Whereas v. 1 refers to the land, the city, and the temple, vv. 2–4 moves on to speak of the people affected by this invasion. Initially they leap beyond the fact that the invasion inevitably brought the deaths of many people to the fact that dying in battle means people receive no proper burial. In some ways this is worse than death itself. It means that people do not go to join their ancestors and rest in the family tomb and that their surviving family members have no opportunity properly to mourn them. When someone is killed and their family cannot see the body, mourn over it, and bury it, they find it very hard to achieve "closure." The body matters to the person and to the survivors; it is the visible form of the person. Once again the first two cola would make a satisfactory bicolon, but an unexpected third colon underlines the point.[15] Here the scandal of the event is that the people who are so treated are God's servants, people *committed to God. Continuing v. 1, that is not a comment on their personal devotion so much as on their status as people belonging to Yhwh. By definition, Israelites are servants of Yhwh, people

---

15. It generates complex parallelism in the line as a whole, abc, def, b'c'e'f'. The first two cola complement each other without parallelism, with the second colon simply completing the construction begun in the first. The third then parallels both the first two, presupposing the verb in the first and the opening noun in the second.

committed to Yhwh (cf. 50:5). So their enemies' treatment of them is an insult to their master.

> ³They poured out their blood like water
>   around Jerusalem,
>   with no one to bury them.

Although we could understand v. 3 as a bicolon with the second line longer than the first, the fact that vv. 1–2 were tricola suggests that we should find another here. Verse 3 first goes behind v. 2 to the actual deaths of people. In the country around the city where battles were fought and/or throughout the city itself (*sĕbîbôt* could have either meaning), the invaders poured out blood as if it were water. The image points both to their heartlessness and to the quantity of blood shed, the number of people who were killed. Then in the last phrase the psalm comes back to the fact that death in battle means scavengers consuming corpses before the dead people's families can come to collect them for burial.

> ⁴We became an object of reviling to our neighbors,
>   of derision and scorn to the people around us.

Reversing the more common pattern, the first section of the psalm comes to an end with a bicolon, neatly parallel, abcb′b″c′. The shame involved in defeat is a recurrent theme in the OT. After the opening verb, the words correspond exactly to 44:13 [14], where see the comment; cf. also Lam. 5:1. The words suggest that other local peoples have laughed at the Judeans for believing that they could resist the attacks of their enemies when they could not, and for trusting in a God who did not save them. The taunts in Isa. 36–37 and the warnings of prophets (e.g., Jer. 24:9; 29:18; Ezek. 5:14–15; 22:4–5) have come true (cf. vv. 10, 12; also Isa. 54:4). And as years pass, their neighbors continue to laugh (cf. Neh. 1:3; 2:17; Dan. 9:18). The situation thus contrasts with that presupposed by Ps. 78:66.

79:5–7. A rhetorical question marks a transition to the first petition, expressed in terms paralleled by 89:46 [47] and Jer. 10:25.

> ⁵Until when, Yhwh?—will you be angry forever?
>   Will your passion burn like fire?

This particular interrogative expression "Until when?" occurs elsewhere only in 89:46 [47], where also it is followed by "forever" and then by the question about whether Yhwh's fury will "burn like fire." As in 13:1 [2] the first colon comprises a pregnant question, "Until when, Yhwh?"

(cf. 6:3 [4]; 90:13), followed by a complete question, "Will you be angry forever?" which makes explicit its frightening possible answer.[16] At the same time, the pregnant expression implicitly urges, "Make it be not for long; set a date now," so that the complete question then stands in tension with it. Thus the second and third questions are like the first in being rhetorical ones, but they are a different form of rhetorical question. There is a sense in which the first question is seeking information, though it also implies what sort of reply it looks for. The second and third look like requests for information, but they are nothing of the sort. They look for denial. At the same time they are also scarcely disguised petitions, appropriate for beginning the petition section. They implicitly urge, "Do not be angry forever—in fact, stop now; your passion must not burn like fire." "Like fire" balances "forever," because fire carries on burning until it has consumed everything.[17] Over against other pleas concerning Yhwh's anger, the reference to passion or jealousy (*qinʾâ*) marks out this one, though it recalls the declaration about the burning, fiery nature of passion in Song 8:6–7. But it also recalls the warning about Yhwh's anger and passion burning against the person who turns away from Yhwh (Deut. 29:20 [19]) and Ezekiel's warnings about Yhwh's passion being expressed on the people as a whole, specifically on the city and the temple (e.g., 5:13; 8:3, 5). Yhwh is, after all, a consuming fire, a jealously passionate God, inclined like a cuckolded husband to blazing anger when people are unfaithful (see Deut. 4:23–24; 5:8–9; 6:14–15); see also the use of the related verb in Ps. 78:58. Again, the expression of Yhwh's passion against Judah, not in its favor, contrasts with the promises in (e.g.) Isa. 9:7 [6]; 37:32; 42:13; 63:15.

> [6]Pour out your fury on the nations that have not acknowledged you,
> upon kingdoms that have not called on your name,

Verses 6–7 as a whole take up Jer. 10:25.[18] But in this context, "your fury" picks up the other word from 89:46b [47b]; it also came in 78:38. Then the verb "pour out," introducing the psalm's overt petition, is itself taken up from v. 3, and it thus implicitly provides some backing for the petition. The fact that the nations poured out blood means it is appropriate for Yhwh to pour out fury. Pouring out is often what one does with

16. It seems less likely that the colon comprises one paradoxical question, "Until when, Yhwh, will you be angry forever?" (cf. NJPS).

17. Or perhaps the "until when" also applies to the second colon: "Until when will your passion burn like fire?"

18. Jeremiah 10:25 has *ʿal* instead of *ʾel* in the first colon; *mišpāḥôt* (families) for *mamlākôt* (kingdoms); pl. *ʾākĕlû* for the odd sg. *ʾākal*; and an extra phrase before the end: "They have devoured him and consumed him."

anger: one does not merely let it drip out gently but lets it overflow and overwhelm or drown its object, as if one were opening a dam. Thus the psalm's petition is not that Yhwh's fury should simply turn away from Jerusalem and the holy mountain (cf. Dan. 9:16) or dissipate and die its natural death, as fury eventually does (e.g., Gen. 27:44; Esther 7:10). That would not put things right. Also, the psalm's overt argument is not that the nations' punishment should fit the crime. It is rather that these are nations and kingdoms that have not *acknowledged Yhwh and have declined to call on Yhwh. That story in Isa. 36–37 shows this to be an understatement; the psalm, too, assumes that the superpower had opportunity to call on Yhwh in recognition and submission, but it did not do so. It did not merely mock Judah; it also mocked Yhwh (e.g., Isa. 37:23). Isaiah therefore declared that Yhwh would demonstrate who is really in control of world events. The psalm asks for Yhwh to fulfill these undertakings.[19]

> [7]Because they have consumed Jacob,
>   desolated his abode.

The first petition comes to a close with a different motivation. Indeed, this is more explicitly a motivation ("because"). There is a second reason why Yhwh ought to take action against the nations. As well as the wrong they have done to Yhwh, there is the wrong they have done to Israel. The image of "consuming" Jacob—it is the ordinary word for eating—provides an alternative, frightening image to that of "pouring out" their blood. The verb can be used of people, crops, herds, and buildings (e.g., Jer. 5:17; 17:27). Perhaps the image of fire continues: their fire has consumed Jacob (Jer. 5:14; 17:27). "Desolated his abode" is an alternative way of expressing the point. Zechariah 1:15 suggests that the nations went beyond earning Yhwh's wrath.

79:8–10b. The second petition again appeals to the people's suffering and to Yhwh's honor, but it focuses on another motivation, or rather a possible counterargument.

> [8]Do not bear in mind against us the wayward acts of an earlier
>   generation;
>   may your compassion meet us quickly,
>   because we are very low.

---

19. The verb and noun apply to both cola, the rest of the cola being then neatly parallel: two complementary prepositions, two complementary nouns (one with the article, one without), two relative particles, two negatives, and two complementary verbal expressions with a second-person suffix.

Another tricolon introduces the new section. The psalm hints further at a link with the fall of Jerusalem in 587 by its reference to the *wayward acts that have characterized the community's life in the past,[20] which contrasts with the appeal to the community's commitment in other psalms (e.g., Ps. 44). The hope of the psalm is that although the community might have to grant the appropriateness of Yhwh punishing it for its waywardness, surely there comes a time when enough is enough (cf. Lam. 5, where v. 7 also refers to the present generation continuing to pay for the sins of past generations). Surely Yhwh does not need to be *mindful of that waywardness forever (cf. Ps. 25:7). Implicitly the community does thus claim that it prays as a people committed to Yhwh, one that does not (now) decline to acknowledge Yhwh and call on Yhwh (see v. 6). On that basis it asks for Yhwh to turn from punishment. The second colon can be read in light of the first and/or the third. That is, Yhwh's compassion may be the basis on which the community asks Yhwh to put its sins out of mind (e.g., 51:1 [3]) and/or the basis on which it asks Yhwh to take account of its suffering (e.g., 77:9 [10]). Once again Yhwh's compassion is personified, as if it were an agent that is semi-independent of Yhwh, like one of Yhwh's aides sent out to meet with the community in order to see what needs to be done for it on Yhwh's behalf in the context of its crisis (cf. 43:3; 57:3 [4]). The picture compares and contrasts with 59:10 [11], where "the God of my commitment" (as the expression literally has it) is expected to come to take that action. The urging that God's compassion should come quickly (lit. "hurry"; cf. 69:17 [18]) links with the question "Until when?" and with the appeal that Yhwh's anger should not burn forever (v. 5). The community wants to see compassion now, not ongoing anger. The point is underlined by the verb "meet" (*qādam* piel), which suggests anticipating someone's coming and going out to meet them. In a literal sense it is too late for that, but Yhwh can still behave in that urgent way. All this also links with the final colon, which takes up one of the motivations for Yhwh to act. When things go well, we hold our head high; when we suffer, our head bows down. Victors stand high over the people they have put down. This community is very low. It desperately and urgently needs God to act on its behalf. The colon corresponds to Ps. 142:6 [7] (except that there the verb is singular).

> [9]Help us, God our deliverer,
> > for the sake of the honor of your name.
> Rescue us and expiate our shortcomings,
> > for your name's sake.

---

20. NJPS takes the *'ăwōnōt ri'šōnîm* to be the "former wayward acts" of this community rather than "the wayward acts of the former people." But for *ri'šōnîm* used thus, cf., e.g., Lev. 26:45.

Two parallel lines explicate the nature of the action the community looks for and restate the motivation for the petition. The two opening verbs plead for *help and rescue. "Help" is implicitly spelled out in the description of God as (lit.) "the God of our *deliverance," and both terms suggest dealing with the "low" state of the community, restoring it to its former glory. "Rescue" has the same implication, but in turn it is implicitly spelled out in a different sense in the phrase that follows (cf. the use of this verb in 39:8 [9]; 51:14 [16]).[21] Here the community acknowledges that it is in the present mess because of its own shortcomings or *failures, so that before restoring it, God must get past those. In v. 8 it might have been trying to evade responsibility in blaming past generations. Here it is either owning that its own life has also fallen short or acknowledging its oneness in responsibility with that earlier generation (cf. Neh. 1:5–11). In v. 8 it asked God not to be mindful of wrongdoings; here it urges God to "expiate" them, as in 78:38 (and see 65:3 [4]). The fact that this psalm uses the imperative makes this urging the more direct (the other examples use the yiqtol; Deut. 21:8 is the only other OT passage that uses this imperative toward God). Only if God is prepared to expiate their shortcomings will it be possible for restoration to follow. Isaiah 44:22 indicates God's positive response to such a prayer.

The two parallel second cola take up the second of the motivations for Yhwh to act but also implicitly link these two motivations. The lines refer twice more to Yhwh's name or reputation. The next line will make explicit that the psalm's concern lies with the nations' attitude to Yhwh's name, as in v. 6. The context here suggests an appeal to the fact that Yhwh's name will be vindicated and its *honor restored not only by putting the nations down but also by building the community up when Yhwh has absolved it of its shortcomings. The putting down and the building up are closely related. Historically, it was the putting down of Babylon that made possible the restoration of the community.

> 10a–bWhy should the nations say,
> "Where is their God?"

A further rhetorical question closes off this second section of petition. It further explicates that point about Yhwh's name. It corresponds to Ps. 115:2,[22] though it also compares with 42:3, 10 [4, 11]; Joel 2:17. The

21. In these passages, BDB takes the verb to denote deliverance from sin, but more likely it has its usual meaning, and the appeal refers to rescue from the consequences of sin. LXX and Syr omit the copula on "[and] rescue" and thus make it possible to read the verb with the previous line. The verse as a whole becomes two 3-3, 2-2 lines instead of 3-2, 3-2.

22. The only difference is the enclitic -nā' attached to "where" in 115:2.

reality of God is proved by God doing things, and if God continues to leave Judah desolate and devastated, the nations have good reason to be asking whether God is really God.

79:10c–12. A third sequence follows. Once again the psalm appeals to the needs of the community (here in jussives rather than imperatives) and then appeals to the affront to Yhwh.

> 10c–dMay the redress for the blood of your servants that was poured
> out
>   be acknowledged among the nations before our eyes.

The psalm assumes that the fact that the nations were Yhwh's agents in punishing Judah for its waywardness does not excuse the nations themselves; they were acting for their own reasons, and they themselves deserve to be punished for their actions (cf. Isa. 10:5–19). In v. 6 the psalm raised the question of the nations *acknowledging God, and the motif of acknowledging recurs. The community wants the superpower to acknowledge the truth about itself as well as the truth about God. "Pouring out" also recurs once more as the psalm again points to the way people's blood has been poured out (cf. v. 3), and it also recalls once again that these people were Yhwh's servants (v. 2). Their master is therefore slighted by this action, and the fact that they are Yhwh's servants also means that Yhwh ought to feel some sense of obligation to them. For "redress" (here *nĕqāmâ*), see on 58:10 [11]. There, too, the psalm speaks of *seeing* redress; it wants God's involvement in the worshipper's life to be not merely religious theory but especially something that can be seen in the world. This psalm, too, implies the recognition that such redress is something that God is responsible for; the community itself does not seek vengeance. A difference here is that what the community speaks of seeing is the superpower's acknowledgment of this redress and thus acknowledging the wrong in what it did and the appropriateness of its paying the penalty.

> 11May the groan of the captive come before you;
>   in accordance with the greatness of your strength preserve the
>   people doomed to death.

The prayer continues in two long lines in vv. 11–12.[23] The twofold striking description of the community corresponds to Ps. 102:20 [21]. First, although they are not exiles—it is the people of Jerusalem who

23. In MT, v. 11 is 4-5, v. 12 is 4-4. MT places the athnach accent after "your strength" and hints that we take v. 11 as a tricolon, 4-2-3, but "in the greatness of your strength" seems to link more with what follows.

527

speak—they are captives (cf. also Lam. 3:34). Instead of being a free people, able to control their own destiny, they are subject to the constraint of a superpower. In the latter part of the exile and for some while afterward, moreover, the authority that directly makes decisions about life in Jerusalem is the provincial government in Samaria, the people who are also one of their neighbors who are scorning them (cf. Neh. 2–4). Thus the people groan under their subjection, longing to be free of foreign domination (cf. Ezra 9; Neh. 9). In the parallel colon they describe themselves as (lit.) "children of death." In the present context this might indicate that they feel as if the forces of death have already overwhelmed them. Many of them have been killed, and the survivors feel that they have nothing to live for. But elsewhere similar expressions suggest "doomed to die" or "deserving to die" (1 Sam. 26:16; 2 Sam. 12:5). Fortunately their sense of terminal weakness can be contrasted with God's great strength; the phrase corresponds to Exod. 15:16,[24] so that the psalm is appealing to God to act in accordance with the pattern set at the Red Sea. "Preserve" is another striking expression. The most common, niphal form of the verb *yātar* means "remain over"; *yeter* is one word for "leftovers" or "remnant," and that is what the community is. So the hiphil verb suggests "Keep a remnant in existence," perhaps even "Make it abundant" (Deut. 28:11; 30:9).

> [12]Give back to our neighbors sevenfold into their bosom
> their reviling with which they have reviled you, Lord.

The petition in v. 10b concerned the superpower; this petition concerns those neighbors who (in the sixth and fifth centuries) are the people that dominate Judah's life. But the psalm's overt point here is not that they have reviled Judah (as in v. 4, and in Ps. 89:50–51 [51–52] where similar words recur). It is that they have reviled the *Lord. The psalm's concern is Yhwh's honor. Like the superpower, their own master, the local peoples have derided the idea that Yhwh is a God who needs to be taken seriously. The psalm asks for their derision to rebound on them sevenfold (i.e., infinitely?), and to reach right inside them. People's scorn and shaming does reach right inside us and affect our inner being (cf. 89:50–51 [51–52]). The sevenfold repayment recalls Yhwh's promise to Cain (Gen. 4:15), though the psalm's request merely for their reviling to rebound on them in this way might seem rather mild compared with that promise (and with Lamech's seventy-sevenfold, Gen. 4:24). Yhwh had warned Israel of sevenfold punishment (Lev. 26:18, 21, 24) and arguably has implemented that threat; the psalm asks that other

---

24. Though there the prep. is *b*, here *k*.

peoples should have a little taste of the same treatment. But the psalm contains no plea for revenge for the ruin of the city and the slaughter of its people or even for their own reviling (vv. 1–4). Its concern here is only the reviling of Yhwh.

79:13. The psalm closes, as psalms often do, with the community looking forward to proclaiming what God has done when God has answered this prayer.

> ¹³And we as your people, the flock you shepherd,
>   will confess you forever;
>   from generation to generation we will declare your praise.

The self-description as "your people, the flock you shepherd" corresponds to Ps. 100:3 (except that the prepositions there are third person). Yhwh's restoring the community will instance Yhwh's relating to it as its shepherd, who rescues the flock. And that will give it something to *confess. The first two cola would make a satisfactory complete line in which the second colon completes the sentence begun in the first, like v. 12. But a third colon paralleling the second then completes a tricolon to close off the psalm. While this look forward at the end of a psalm regularly envisages praising God forever, this is particularly appropriate in a psalm such as this that seeks God's permanent restoration of the community.

Theological Implications

A plea for Yhwh to restore Israel and punish the great powers of the day, like that in this psalm, is one to which Yhwh says "Yes" in Zech. 1:12–17 and in the visions that follow. Further, the psalm's plea for requital is milder than the prayer God similarly agrees to answer in Rev. 6:9–11; see also Jesus's warning in Matt. 23:35 and his promise in Luke 18:1–8[25] and the echo of v. 3 in Rev. 16:6. "The psalm, with its appeal to divine wrath, cries out for God's justice as the guaranteeing force of a *world order* and as a court of justice especially for the victims—and does not, as may appear at first sight, call for irrational vengeance."[26]

Yet this prayer for God to punish the great powers of the day causes discomfort to modern Christians who are citizens of the great powers of the day. Mennonite writer Perry B. Yoder notes, "Peace is a middle-class luxury, perhaps even a Western middle-class luxury." In the Phil-

---

25. Cf. Kidner, *Psalms 73–150*, 288.
26. Hossfeld and Zenger, *Psalms 2*, 307.

ippines he discovered that people "saw advocacy for peace as support for their oppression. . . . Talking of peace in this context sounded like the language of oppression used by oppressors to keep the oppressed in their place."[27] Christians in the two-thirds world feel similarly less discomfort than Christians in the West at the psalm's prayer for God to act to restore the fortunes of the oppressed people of God. It is a remarkable act of restraint and trust in God when people who are the victims of oppression by a superpower respond by urging God to do something rather than by acting in violence themselves.

In any case the psalm is equally concerned for restoring the honor of God's name. "The repeated use of the pronoun 'your' shows that God is an interested party; the offense deals with 'your inheritance,' 'your servants,' 'your faithful' (vv. 1–2). God has to act 'for the glory of your name' (v. 9)."[28] Yet this prayer of Israel is not disinterested. "The psalmist believes that there is a convergence of interest, Israel's self-interest, but also the transcendent interest of God. This troubled prayer is the activity of locating and articulating that convergence of interest." Perhaps "it is only when 'the temple' is undone" that one dares pray as this psalm does, "when the core, meaning, and structure of life are undone"; when that is the case, so one must pray.[29]

Christians sometimes also assume that God could not forgive Israel except on the basis of its offering the proper sacrifices, though presumably as long as the temple was defiled, sacrifices could not be offered. Psalm 79 is the one community prayer in the Psalms that acknowledges the community's failures, and it thus shows how the fact that we have failed God need not inhibit our prayer. The need for God to be honored in what happens to us and the need to restore us in our cast-down-ness overwhelm the need to keep punishing us. The psalm assumes that the one who ultimately expiates sins is Yhwh, and Yhwh can do that with or without sacrifices. The basis for its appeal for forgiveness is not something that the community does. It is God's compassion. It is this compassion and not our faithfulness that makes it possible for us to pray. Thus after AD 70 "instead of plunging into despair because there were now no means of cleansing the people's sins, [Israel] turned to its father in heaven and remembered that it is he who forgives sins and he can do so with or without the Temple."[30]

---

27. *Shalom* (repr., Nappanee, IN: Evangel, 2005), 3.
28. Schaefer, *Psalms*, 195; cf. Spurgeon, *Treasury of David*, 3:376.
29. Brueggemann, *Message of the Psalms*, 72–73.
30. Michael Wyschogrod, *The Body of Faith* (San Francisco: Harper, 1989), 17.

Psalm 80

Praying for Joseph

Translation

The leader's. For lilies.[1] Declaration. Asaph's. Composition. Concerning the Assyrian [LXX].

[1]As the one shepherding Israel, give ear,
  as the one driving Joseph like a flock.
As the one sitting on the cherubim, shine
  [2]before Ephraim, Benjamin, and Manasseh.
Stir up your might;
  come to bring deliverance for us.
[3]God, restore us;
  shine your face so that we may be delivered.

[4]Yhwh, God, Armies,
  how long have you fumed at your people's plea?
[5]You have fed them tears as food,
  made them drink many tears, by measure.
[6]You have made us a source of contention to our neighbors;
  our enemies mock at will.[2]
[7]God Armies, restore us;
  shine your face so that we may be delivered.

---

1. The prep. is *'el*, elsewhere *'al* (as in the Ps. 45 heading).
2. *Lāmô*, lit. "for them[selves]"; cf. Sym "unhindered." As at 44:10 [11], LXX, Jerome,
and Syr imply *lānû*, "for us."

⁸You set a vine on the move from Egypt;
    you drove out nations and planted it.
⁹You cleared the way before it,
    and it took deep root[3] and filled the land.
¹⁰Mountains were covered with its shade,
    mighty cedars[4] with its branches.
¹¹It put out its boughs to the sea,
    its shoots to the river.
¹²Why have you broken its walls,
    and all who pass by pluck it?
¹³The boar from the forest[5] tears at it;
    the creature of the wild feeds on it.

¹⁴God Armies, do turn,
    look down from the heavens and see,
    attend to this vine,
¹⁵The stock[6] that your right hand planted,
    and to the son you made strong for yourself.
¹⁶Burned with fire, cut up,
    they perish at the blast from your face.[7]
¹⁷May your hand be upon the one at your right hand,
    upon the man you made strong for yourself.
¹⁸And we will not turn aside from you;
    bring us to life and we will call on your name.
¹⁹Yhwh God Armies, restore us;
    shine your face so that we may be delivered.

Interpretation

This community prayer links well with both preceding psalms. Like much of Ps. 78, it focuses on Ephraim and its rejection by God and in contrast to much of the OT sees the history of the whole people from

3. For hiphil *wattašrēs*, LXX, Jerome, Sym, and Tg have "You made it take root," which makes sense; but in Job 5:3 the verb must mean "take root," and this also makes best sense in the only other occurrence, Isa. 27:6, so it is likely to be the regular meaning and the meaning here.

4. Lit. "cedars of God"; cf. the translation in Aq, Tg, and DG 44.

5. The ayin (ʿ) in *mîyāʿar* is raised, perhaps to mark the center of the Psalter by another calculation than that noted at 78:38 (GKC 5n) or perhaps to reflect the possibility of reading *mîyĕʾōr*, "from the Nile."

6. For the hapax *kannâ*, LXX implies *kônĕnāh*, impv. from *kûn* polel, "[re-]establish it." Hossfeld and Zenger (*Psalms 2*, 310) take this form as impv. from a qal verb *kānan* with the same meaning as *kōnēn* (impv. from *kûn*).

7. Jerome understands the verb as jussive, "may they perish" (so NRSV), but this is a harder transition.

an Ephraimite viewpoint. It is the suffering of Ephraim in particular that seems odd in light of God's acts in bringing Israel out of Egypt into Canaan. But Ps. 78 made no appeal for Ephraim and rather proceeded to Yhwh's turning to Judah. Thus Ps. 80 parallels the Judean prayer in Ps. 79 in appealing for God to restore the community, and it starts where Ps. 79 finished, with reference to Yhwh's shepherding. Further, like Ps. 79 it implies that the calamity that has come over the community lies some time in the past, and the question is how long it will go on; and like Ps. 79, it takes a somewhat ambiguous stance concerning the extent to which the community's own waywardness provides quite enough explanation for its experience. Psalm 80 has some detailed links with Ps. 78 (see 80:1, 2, 8) that raise the question whether Ps. 80 is a kind of response to or protest against the implications of Ps. 78. So Yhwh rejected Joseph. Must that rejection be permanent?[8]

A first clue to the psalm's structure is the way vv. 3, 7, and 19 repeat the same prayer, with some heightening each time as the appellative moves from "God" to "God Armies" to "Yhwh God Armies." A second clue is that vv. 1, 4, and 14 all begin with appellatives. I thus take the psalm to divide into two sections of four lines and two of six, each with some coherence. Verses 1–3 focus on appeal, on describing God. Verses 4–7 focus on protest at the calamity that has overcome the community. Verses 8–13 retell the story of the exodus and occupation of the land and ask how the calamity fits into that; the way this section lacks both appellative and any form of the repeated prayer parallels the way Ps. 46 lacks its "refrain" at a point where we would expect it. Verses 14–19 focus on a petition that takes up the recollection in vv. 8–13.[9] The structure thus provides organization for what are the regular features of a community prayer. It begins with address to God and appeal for God to hear and deliver, and goes on to rhetorical questions that introduce protest at the community's experience. It relates to what you, God, have done (vv. 4–6a, 12a—this has special prominence), to what the enemies have done (vv. 6b, 12b–13), and to how things are for the community itself (v. 16—though there are no first-person verbs). It incorporates recollection of how God has acted in the past with its contrast with the present, further petitions, and a promise to call on God in the future.

H. Heinemann argued that the psalm came from the time of Saul,[10] but it has more often been linked with the last decade of Ephraim's life,

---

8. See further, Thomas Hieke, "Psalm 80 and Its Neighbors in the Psalter," *BN* 86 (1997): 36–43; Cole, *Shape and Message of Book III*, 88–95.

9. It would be natural to take v. 14 as the close of vv. 8–13, given its similarity to the final line of each of the other strophe (cf. N. J. Tromp, "Psalm lxxx," *OtSt* 25 [1989]: 145–55 [see 147]), but this would leave vv. 15–16 syntactically stranded.

10. "The Date of Psalm 80," *JQR* 40 (1949–50): 297–302.

between 732 and 722.[11] Its parallels with Ps. 79 might make us think rather of the life of Ephraim somewhat later, when surviving Ephraimites (perhaps people who had moved to Judah) longed for the restoration of their clans, and Josiah attempted to reassert Davidic authority there.[12] Or one might think of such people praying in this way during the exile[13] and/or after the exile when Samaria controlled Ephraim's territory[14] and/ or in the second century.[15]

> The leader's. For lilies. Declaration. Asaph's. Composition. Concerning the Assyrian [LXX].

Heading. See glossary. LXX's extra expression would fit with one of the eighth- or seventh-century dates noted above.

80:1–3. The first section, then, gives special prominence to descriptions of Yhwh. With EVV, I take vv. 1–2 as three bicola, rather than two tricola as in MT.

> [1a-b]As the one shepherding Israel, give ear,
> as the one driving Joseph like a flock.

The appeal to God to listen to this plea is a natural and standard beginning for a psalm. The appellatives are less usual. In the Psalms, only in 23:1 is God elsewhere described as shepherd (though 28:9 appeals to God to shepherd). But in blessing Joseph, Ephraim, and Manasseh, the ancestor Israel refers to God as the one who has shepherded him all his life (Gen. 48:15). The problem is that the community is not experiencing God as shepherd or as shepherding in the way Ps. 23 or Gen. 48 describe. "Drive" is in general much less common a verb but one that is relatively more often applied to God. It appeared in 78:52, significantly with reference to God's leading the people through the wilderness "like a flock." The EVV translate the word here as "you who lead," but both "shepherd" and "driver" are participles, which as such leave their time reference open. It seems unlikely that the line describes God as one who now leads the people; the people's problem is that God has actually abandoned the flock. It was back on that journey from Egypt to the land that God did act thus, as Ps. 78 notes, and more likely the psalm refers back to that.

---

11. E.g., Otto Eissfeldt, "Psalm 80," in *Kleine Schriften* (Tübingen: Mohr, 1966), 3:221–32.

12. E.g., Nasuti, *Tradition History and the Psalms of Asaph*, 99.

13. Walter Beyerlin dates its final form here ("Schichten im 80. Psalm," in *Das Wort und die Wörter* [Gerhard Friedrich Festschrift; ed. Horst Balz and Siegfried Schulz; Stuttgart: Kohlhammer, 1973], 9–24).

14. E.g., Tate, *Psalms 51–100*, 311–13.

15. So Theodore, *Psalms 1–81*, 1096–97.

Shepherding and driving is God's proper relationship with the community, but God is not behaving as shepherd and driver. The second colon also gives precision to the noun in the first: "Israel" becomes "Joseph." The psalm has a special concern with the northern clans.[16]

> [1c]As the one sitting on the cherubim, shine
>   [2a]before Ephraim, Benjamin, and Manasseh.

The construction continues as the psalm addresses God by means of another participle, "you sitter [on] the cherubim." This description recurs in 99:1; 1 Sam. 4:4; 2 Sam. 6:2; 2 Kings 19:15; 1 Chron. 13:6; Isa. 37:16, where it describes God's permanent position of exaltation. It is both a metaphysical statement and a description of how that statement was represented in the sanctuary, where the cherubim pointed to the enthroned position of the invisible God. Likewise the psalm likely assumes that God is still sitting there. But the parallel with what precedes hints that it continues to describe God in terms that apply more obviously to the past than to the present. Yhwh sits on the cherubim when coming to take action (2 Sam. 22:11; Ps. 18:10 [11]). Joseph's problem is that the God who has sat on the cherubim to come to the assistance of the people in this fashion in the past has not been doing so recently. The imperative verb makes that more explicit. In coming from Sinai, Yhwh "shone from Mount Paran" (Deut. 33:2), and Yhwh has likewise "shone" from Zion (Ps. 50:2). But again, Yhwh has not been shining lately "before Ephraim, Benjamin, and Manasseh." These three offspring of Rachel (two grandsons, one son) come together in Jacob's blessing (Gen. 49:22–27), and as clans they appear together on the west side of the wilderness dwelling (Num. 2:18–24). Here these two dominant northern clans that make up Joseph in the narrow sense embrace little Benjamin, the other Rachel clan. They want to see Yhwh shine again—that is, take action (see on 50:2).

> [2b]Stir up your might;
>   come to bring deliverance for us.

The third line makes that explicit. It is good news if God is not stirred up ('*ûr*) against us in our waywardness (78:38), but we need God's energy to be stirred up on our behalf when oppressors assail us (cf. the qal of this verb in 44:23 [24]; 59:4 [5]). The psalm has no doubt of Yhwh's *might (gĕbûrâ); the problem is getting Yhwh to activate it. Yhwh once did so on Judah's behalf, acting as a *gibbôr* (78:65). Joseph needs Yhwh

16. The line is neatly parallel, abca'db'; verb and simile apply to both cola.

to be more evenhanded in this respect, to bring *deliverance (lit. "come for deliverance for us").

> ³God, restore us;
>> shine your face so that we may be delivered.

The restatement of this plea will turn out to be a refrain in the psalm. "Restore" (*šûb* hiphil) expresses more briefly the action denoted by "bring a restoration" (see 53:6 [7]). The second colon explicates what that will involve. Behind the act that restores will be God's *face smiling rather than frowning. Yhwh will look on the community with favor, and the positive look will generate action on its behalf (cf. 67:1 [2]). And issuing from that action will be *deliverance. The parallelism supports Calvin's view that the prayer refers to the restoration of the nation's fortunes, not its spiritual or inner renewal.[17]

80:4–7. The second section looks behind the community's need to the divine action that has put it into difficulties.

> ⁴Yhwh, God, Armies,
>> how long have you fumed at your people's plea?

It begins with another elaborate invocation of God, one that further emphasizes Yhwh's capacity to act in warrior might (*Armies). The psalm does not necessarily see Yhwh as warring against the community, but neither has Yhwh been warring for it. The psalm accuses Yhwh of fuming with anger against it.[18] The fuming of Yhwh's anger is good news when it operates against people who cause trouble to Israel (cf. the cognate noun Ps. 18:8 [9]). But now Yhwh has been fuming at the people's *plea. Yhwh is supposed to listen to pleas (54:2 [4]), to give ear to them (55:1 [2]; cf. v. 1 here), to attend to them (61:1 [2]); that is Yhwh's nature (65:2 [3]) and often Yhwh's practice (66:19–20). But not lately for Joseph. "How long?" is usually followed by a yiqtol verb (e.g., 74:10; 82:2), sometimes by a participle (1 Kings 18:21). The unusual use with a qatal verb may be an idiomatic way of referring to the future ("How long will you have fumed?"); it may draw attention to how long this has been going on and/or express astonishment at what has been happening.[19]

---

17. *Psalms*, 3:298.

18. Unless we take the verb *ʿāšan* as an Aramaism meaning "be strong" (cf. G. R. Driver, "Textual and Linguistic Problems in the Book of Psalms," *HTR* 29 [1936]: 171–95 [see 186–87]; cf. *DTT*). But it is easier to infer ellipse of a word for anger: cf. 74:1; Deut. 29:20 [19]. Kraus (*Psalms 60–100*, 137) has "in spite of," but *b* means "at" in those two passages.

19. Cf. *TTH* 19; DG 59b.

> [5]You have fed them tears as food,
>   made them drink many tears, by measure.

The neatly parallel line[20] again makes for a contrast with what Yhwh is supposed to do. Psalm 56:8 [9] asks Yhwh to keep the suppliant's tears in mind, and thus respond to them (cf. 39:12 [13]). Instead, the community has been having the same experience as the suppliant in 42:3 [4]. It cannot focus on food or drink; all it can do is grieve. Psalm 80 adds that it is Yhwh who has caused this by bringing disaster on the community and leaving it there. The Tg understands "food of tears" to mean "food dipped in tears" and takes the tears of the second colon likewise to be plentifully mingled with their drink. "By measure" is literally "[by the] third." The "third" is a measure (cf. "quart"), but we do not know of what. Whereas in the context of Isa. 40:12 it suggests something laughably small, here it suggests something horrifically big.

> [6]You have made us a source of contention to our neighbors;
>   our enemies mock at will.
> [7]God Armies, restore us;
>   shine your face so that we may be delivered.

Whence the tears? The first colon begins to explain, though it does so allusively. "You have made us contention/strife [*mādôn*] to our neighbors" might denote "You have made our neighbors fight against us," or "You have made us something that our neighbors fight over." The expression compares and contrasts with Ps. 44:14 [15], where Yhwh makes the people "a reason for shaking the head [*mānôd*]."[21] Mockery could have accompanied that, as in the story in Isa. 36–37; the yiqtol verb suggests that the mockery is ongoing. Perhaps both the fighting and the mocking are continuing realities, so that the line refers to the way hostile neighbors fight and mock in light of the events yet to be described in vv. 12–13 and 16. In the Second Temple period, Ezra–Nehemiah show how this description would well match the activity of the peoples who surrounded Judah and occupied the former territory of Joseph. The contention will then be as much legal or political as military, which fits

---

20. It works abca'c'd. The two verbs are qatal and wayyiqtol, and they also complement each other in meaning. The two occurrences of "tears" are sg. and pl., one direct obj. and the other indirect; the word is collective; and the pl., which occurs only here and at Lam. 2:11, is thus intensive. Then "[as] food" is complemented by "[by the] third."

21. Paul de Lagarde assimilates the text here to that in Ps. 44 (see *Novae Psalterii Graeci editionis specimen* [Göttingen: Dieterich, 1887], as referred to by Gunkel, *Psalmen*, 354).

a word from the root *dîn*, not least the two occurrences of *mādôn* outside Proverbs (see Jer. 15:10; Hab. 1:3).

Verse 7 then repeats v. 3 except for the strengthening of the appellative to God *Armies, which also acts as an inclusion with v. 4.

80:8–13. In due course another rhetorical question leads into another explicit protest, so that vv. 12–13 recall vv. 4–6, but first vv. 8–11 provide essential background. Initially the section thus moves in a quite new direction in recalling the exodus and occupation of Canaan. The recollection parallels (e.g.) 44:1–3 [2–4], though there the recollection begins the psalm, and the protest comes later. Here we already know that this is a psalm of petition and protest; the recollection thus functions to raise suspense.

> **8**You set a vine on the move from Egypt;
>   you drove out nations and planted it.

The lines thus look back to the exodus and occupation of Canaan, yet these are described not as actions of the people who came out of Egypt and occupied the land but as actions of Yhwh, who set them on the move, dispossessed the Canaanites, and brought them into the land. Further, they are not simply described in that straightforward literal fashion. Psalm 44:2 [3] speaks of Yhwh planting the people in the land; here, v. 8 begins a more systematic, original, and creative exposition of a metaphor that will continue through most of the rest of the psalm.[22] With the olive tree and fig tree—also used as metaphors for Israel as a people—the vine is one of the key plants for an Israelite. Grapes were not only eaten in their natural state in the fall and fermented as wine, but they were also turned into grape syrup (honey) and dried fruit, important sources of sugar. At the same time v. 8 mixes the metaphorical with the literal. Obviously one does not literally set a vine on the move. That is what one does with a people or with sheep; the verb is taken up from 78:52. Likewise "drive out" is taken up from 78:55.

> **9**You cleared the way before it,
>   and it took deep root and filled the land.

The line neatly exploits the range of meaning of the opening verb, which suggests clearing things up and removing things out of the way but also clearing away enemies (Zeph. 3:15). In both senses Yhwh cleared the ground, and thus the vine could properly root itself; literally, "it rooted

22. See Thomas Hieke, "Der Exodus in Psalm 80," in *Studies in the Book of Exodus*, ed. Marc Vervenne, BETL 126 (Louvain: Leuven University Press, 1996), 551–58.

its root."[23] And it could therefore flourish and fill the land. In terms of
the OT story, the line sums up the narrative from Joshua to David, in
whose day at last Israel did occupy the whole land.

> [10]Mountains were covered with its shade,
>   mighty cedars with its branches.
> [11]It put out its boughs to the sea,
>   its shoots to the river.

The hyperbole continues, keeping the imagery. It is as if the vine
became a giant plant like Jack's beanstalk. It grew so extensively that
it covered the mountains as cedar trees clothe the mountains so that
none of their slopes are exposed to the sun. Indeed, it towered over the
cedars themselves (!).

And laterally, its boughs and its roots extended from the great sea/river
on one side of the world land mass to that on the other.[24] Or (if the psalm
is being more prosaic), they extended one way to the Mediterranean and
the other to the Euphrates, fulfilling the promise of Deut. 11:24;[25] again
this suggests the flourishing of the Davidic empire.

> [12]Why have you broken its walls,
>   and all who pass by pluck it?
> [13]The boar from the forest tears at it;
>   the creature of the wild feeds on it.

The transition again recalls Ps. 44 (see 44:1–8 [2–9] and 9–16 [10–17]).
All that effort and care, with its fine results, contrasts with what followed.
Once again a second-person verb initially makes the point sharply as
the psalm moves from "you set on the move . . . , you drove out . . . , you
planted . . . , you cleared the way" to "you have broken." Neither the good
events nor the bad events happen purely as a result of natural or economic
or human factors; indeed, the psalm pays no attention to these. Nor does
it attribute the good events to God but the bad events to chance or to
evil powers or to human sinfulness. It knows that Yhwh is the sovereign
Lord, and therefore events can be traced to Yhwh's activity.

And once more that transition leads into an account of the quite
different results of God's action: contrast vv. 9b–11 and 12b–13. Literally what has happened is that enemies have invaded the land, and

---

23. There is a further neat rhetorical flourish. "Cleared the way before it" involves
the piel verb *pānâ* and the more common cognate noun *pānîm*. "Took deep root" involves
the denominative verb *šāraš* and the more common cognate noun *šōreš*.

24. So Keel, *Symbolism*, 21.

25. Thus the parallelism works by dividing the two subjects (one m., one f.) and the
two prepositional phrases (one with *'ad*, one with *'el*) between the two cola.

they have succeeded because Yhwh has declined to protect it. Thus the aspect of viticulture that the psalm takes up at this point is the construction of walls to protect vines from human beings and wild animals. But Yhwh has broken down the walls (cf. Isa. 5:5, where the word for "wall" recurs in the exposition of this same image). Thus every passerby can pluck a bunch of grapes for refreshment. One person doing that would be tolerable; everyone doing it means disaster.[26] The wild boar also does so, with less gentleness than a human being might show; indeed, so do wild creatures in general. Perhaps the boar stands for the superpower, the wild creature for local peoples, Israel's neighbors.[27]

*Why? the psalm asks, characteristically.[28] Again, compare 44:23–24 [24–25]. But it is a risky question, because it might seem that Isa. 5:1–7 makes the answer quite clear (cf. also Jer. 2:21). One can thus imagine a prophet such as Amos or Hosea in Samaria in the 720s offering a quick and tart answer to this question on the lips of a priest such as Amaziah (see Amos 7:10–17). Further, the several comparisons with Ps. 44 then draw attention to a difference; Ps. 80 includes no claim to having lived a committed life, like ones that appear in Ps. 44 and other psalms. Such a claim (if true) would rule out Isaiah's answer to the "Why?" But the absence of such a claim might seem almost tantamount to an admission of guilt. Perhaps, then, one should read Ps. 80 in light of Ps. 79 and reckon that the psalm implicitly recognizes the guilt of the past but wants Yhwh to reckon that enough is now enough. The "Why?" then asks not so much why Yhwh acted in chastisement at all but why Yhwh acted in a way that brought such far-reaching destruction.

80:14–19. It would have been quite appropriate to have the "refrain" close off vv. 8–13, and the opening of v. 14 looks like the beginning of that refrain, but it turns out to be a new invocation introducing a tricolon in v. 14 that marks a new section.

> ¹⁴God Armies, do turn,
>   look down from the heavens and see,
>   attend to this vine,

26. Perhaps the w-qatal is frequentative: cf. the yiqtols in v. 13, and see *TTH* 133. But the yiqtols in vv. 8 and 11 seemed to have simple past reference (cf. DG 62a), and this may suggest that we should not read too much subtlety into vv. 12–13. The w implies result, like English "and."

27. Tg understands *zîz* to refer to the cockerel, Peddi Victor ("Note on Psalm lxxx.13," *ExpT* 76 [1965–66]: 294–95) to the leader boar, and D. Winton Thomas ("The Meaning of זיז in Psalm lxxx.14," *ExpT* 76 [1965–66]: 385) to an insect.

28. Auffret's understanding of the psalm's structure makes him see this "Why?" as the central word in the psalm (*Voyez de vos yeux*, 261).

> [15]The stock that your right hand planted,
>   and to the son you made strong for yourself.

The fact that "turn" is the qal of *šûb*, while "restore" is the hiphil of the same verb, heightens the impression that v. 14a is a variant on the refrain.[29] But "turn" is what a psalm needs Yhwh to do before "restoring" (cf. 90:13). At the moment Yhwh has turned away; the community needs Yhwh to turn back. In light of vv. 12–13 (see the comments) it might seem an exhortation with some chutzpah. Prophets such as Hosea urged Ephraim to "turn" to Yhwh (e.g., Hos. 14:1–2 [2–3]), and Jeremiah also speaks to Ephraim thus, even if only rhetorically (Jer. 3:12). Here Ephraim reverses the bidding. The other two cola in v. 14 then spell out the implications of this turning. First it will mean that Yhwh looks. At the moment Yhwh is behaving like the king in the palace who declines to look over the palace walls to see what is going on in the city so as to do something about it. The psalm appeals to Yhwh to act in accordance with the declaration about looking down from the heavens in 33:13–14; 102:19 [20] and repeats the appeal simply to "see" (e.g., 59:4 [5]). The final verb also involves some risk or chutzpah, since when Yhwh attends to something (*pāqad*), this often implies punishing wrongdoing (again, cf. 59:5 [6]). "I will attend to the altars of Bethel," Yhwh said through Amos (Amos 3:14). But Yhwh also attends in order to bless, deliver, or restore (e.g., Pss. 8:4 [5]; 65:9 [10]; 106:4). The suppliants look Yhwh boldly in the face and urge that kind of attention.

Tellingly, the basis for this urging in v. 15 is indeed not the community's faithfulness but Yhwh's own past action in relation to it. The logic thus overlaps with that of Moses's prayer in Exod. 32:11–13, with its background in image-making at Sinai that anticipatorily paralleled that involved in Jeroboam's setting up the Ephraimite state. The stock that Yhwh has let be ravaged is something planted by Yhwh's own right hand. This is the right hand that Ps. 78:54 spoke of in a more literal connection with the people's taking of the land, and the right hand with which Yhwh won the victory at the Red Sea (Exod. 15:6, 12), but also the right hand that has lately been acting in odd and grievous ways (Ps. 77:10 [11]). The son might likewise be the son that Yhwh took firm hold of in Egypt to bring him out to be Yhwh's servant rather than the pharaoh's, notwithstanding the resistance of the pharaoh who sought to hold onto him (Exod. 4:22–23); surely Yhwh is not giving up on the project this insistence initiated. But the recurrence of this language in v. 17 will sug-

---

29. In 85:4 [5], indeed, *šûb* qal is usually reckoned to have the transitive meaning "restore," but this is a very unusual usage, and more likely the qal here carries a different meaning from the hiphil.

gest that it is rather the son of 2:7; 89:26 [27].[30] The colon then indicates that these Ephraimites recognize that God's commitment to David and his line justifies and requires their commitment to it.

> [16]Burned with fire, cut up,
>   they perish at the blast from your face.

As vv. 8–11 led into vv. 12–13, so vv. 14–15 lead into v. 16 with its reminder of the facts about the vine and the community. The vine has been not merely left unprotected and ravaged but also burnt and cut up. The description can be understood literally of a vine, if we assume that the vine was first cut up and then burned as fuel (cf. Ezek. 15), though the word order is odd, and the expressions suggest a metonymy and/or a metaphor. Burning is what attackers do to a city, and "cut up" (*kāsaḥ*) appears only once elsewhere, in a context similar to the present one (Isa. 33:12); a more general sense of "destroy" (applicable to a city) would make sense in both passages.[31] Isaiah 33:12 also speaks of people being burned and speaks in a way that coheres with the second colon here. The fire that burns up the vine is one that comes from the blast of Yhwh's hot breath. Once again the psalm is taking the risk of describing the fate of the vine in a way that coheres with the language of prophets speaking of Yhwh's punishment for the community's waywardness, the risk of having Yhwh retort, "Yes it is, and rightly too." But it is also taking up language that is supposed to apply to Israel's attackers, not the people itself (Pss. 76:6 [7]; 104:7), and implicitly drawing attention to the oddness of the community's experience.

> [17]May your hand be upon the one at your right hand,
>   upon the man you made strong for yourself.

Presumably the man at God's right hand is the king (cf. 110:1); compare v. 15b, where the *bēn* (son) is described in similar terms to the *ben-ʾādām* (man) here. The expression "Yhwh's hand upon" is obscure, but the implications are clear (see Ezra 7:6, 28; 8:31); when Yhwh's hand is on someone, they succeed in what they do, mysteriously and against the odds. Once Yhwh took hold of David, a mere human being (*ben-ʾādām*—it is the expression often used of Ezekiel to set him over against Lord Yhwh), and made him strong. The psalm again urges God

---

30. Cf. Tg. NRSV omits v. 15b as an anticipatory duplicate of v. 17b; vv. 14a–b and 14c–15a will then be two bicola. Mays sees the addition as designed to establish that the "son" is indeed the people as a whole, not the king, and suggests that v. 17 be read in light of v. 15 rather than vice versa (*Psalms*, 263–64).

31. Cf. also BDB.

to continue in keeping with the project initiated in the past. The possibility that the "man" is the king opens the line—and specifically the term *ben-ʾādām*—to a later messianic interpretation.[32]

> ¹⁸And we will not turn aside from you;
>   bring us to life and we will call on your name.
> ¹⁹Yhwh God Armies, restore us;
>   shine your face so that we may be delivered.

Once more the psalm compares and contrasts with Pss. 44 and 78. There the verb (*sûg*, a rare one, especially in this connection) comes in the niphal, not the qal (which did appear in 53:3 [4]). In Ps. 44 the suppliants affirm that they have not turned aside from Yhwh (44:18 [19]); Ps. 78 declares that Israel did indeed so turn aside (78:57; cf. Zeph. 1:6). The contrast here again hints at an admission that the suppliants cannot make the affirmation in Ps. 44 and would have to accept the judgment in Ps. 78. But once again they are declining to look to the (rather distant?) past and are focusing on a commitment for the future. They long for the community to be brought back to life.[33] In substance, the plea parallels v. 17 and sums up its implications. The final clause then parallels v. 18a, complementing its negative with a positive. Yhwh will be the one they call on in praise and prayer. The expression constitutes the promise of praise that often closes a protest psalm.

The final refrain sums up the psalm's plea, buttressing it with the longest form of an invocation of God in the psalm (cf. v. 4).

Theological Implications

In what circumstances can the people of God cry out, "Why?" The most plausible historical context for this psalm may be the prayer of members of the northern clans living in Judah and worshipping in Jerusalem. In that context, the circumstance is when we have been on the receiving end of God's chastisement and know God's face has been turned away for decades, and when churches need to "mourn their demise."[34] We can continue to be sure that God's people still matter to God, and we can ask whether enough is enough. The situation of the church in Europe suggests a context for the psalm. But as usual the psalm declines to offer

32. Cf. A. Gelston, "A Sidelight on the Son of Man," *SJT* 22 (1969): 189–96; David Hill, "'Son of Man' in Psalm 80 v. 17," *NovT* 15 (1973): 261–69.
33. NJPS has "preserve our life," but the psalm implies that the community is effectively dead, and that would be true of Ephraim, at least in the seventh century.
34. Leonora T. Tisdale, "Psalm 80:1–7," *Int* 47 (1993): 396–99 (see 398).

concrete indication of its background, and we have noted that there are other possibilities. It might come from the lips of Judeans concerned for their northern brothers and sisters, and this reminds us that psalms of lament and protest can be intercessions as well as supplications for ourselves. It might then also belong on the lips of the church in Africa as it prays for the church in Europe. A third possibility is that it comes from the Ephraimites in the 720s. If it does, then one can imagine that God would inspire the kind of response we read in Amos. And we might imagine it on the lips of the church in the United States today, seeking for God's restoration to the great times of the past but destined for more cutting down unless it faces more facts about itself and God.[35]

35. Cf. Luther's comments about the church in his day, in *First Lectures*, 2:100.

Psalm 81

Do Listen!

Translation

The leader's. On/concerning the Gittite. Asaph's.

[1]Resound for God, our strength,
  shout for Jacob's God.
[2]Raise the music, sound[1] the tambourine,
  the lovely[2] lyre with the harp.
[3]Blow the horn at the beginning of the month,
  at the full moon, for our festival day.
[4]For it is a law for Israel,
  a decision for Jacob's God.
[5]A declaration in Joseph[3] that he laid down
  when he went out over the land of Egypt.[4]

---

1. Lit. "give"; cf. the expression "give voice" (Gunkel, *Psalmen*, 359).

2. Or "melodious," if there is a second adjective *nāʿîm* from *nāʿam* II (see, e.g., *DCH*).

3. Here alone the name has the long form *yĕhôsēp*, though the form is common in PBH (Scott C. Layton, "Jehoseph in Ps. 81,6," *Bib* 69 [1988]: 406–11, sees it as a pointer to a late date for the psalm), and such forms occur with other words (cf. GKC 53q). Rendsburg (*Linguistic Evidence*, 48–49) sees it as a northern form. It is thus doubtful if the distinctive spelling is ideologically significant (against P. A. H. de Boer, "Psalm 81:6a," in *In the Shelter of Elyon* [G. W. Ahlström Festschrift; ed. W. Boyd Barrick and John R. Spencer; JSOTSup 31; Sheffield: JSOT, 1984], 67–80 [see 77]).

4. Genesis 41:45 refers to Joseph's "going out over the land of Egypt." The context refers both to his having authority in Egypt and to his going about in the land, and the phrase itself has been read in light of the former (e.g., Tg) or the latter (e.g., Jerome).

I listened to[5] lips[6] I had not acknowledged:[7]
    [6]I turned his shoulder from the burden;
    his hands moved on from the basket.[8]
[7]In distress you called and I rescued you,
    answered you in the secret place of thunder.

I tested you at the waters of Contention. (Rise)
    [8]"Listen, my people, and I will make a declaration to you,
    Israel, if you listen to me. . . .
[9]There is not to be a strange god among you;
    you are not to bow down to an alien god.
[10]I am Yhwh your God,
    the one who brought you up from the land of Egypt:
    open your mouth wide, and I will fill it."

[11]But my people did not listen to my voice;
    Israel was unwilling to listen to me.[9]
[12]So I sent them[10] off by the unyieldingness of their mind;
    they could walk by their own plans.

[13]If only my people were listening to me,
    if only Israel would walk on in my ways,[11]
[14]I would quickly subdue their enemies;
    against their foes I would turn my hand.
[15]Those who are against Yhwh would wither before him,[12]
    and their fate would be forever.
[16]He fed him from the best of wheat,
    from the crag with honey I would fill you.

But in the context of Ps. 81, it makes poor sense to see Joseph as the subj., whether Joseph the individual or Joseph the people, and Exod. 11:4 does also speak of Yhwh "going out in the midst of Egypt." This makes better sense here. In this context, "went out over the land of Egypt" then suggests going about in Egypt. LXX has "from" for "over," assimilating to Exod. 20:2; it is hardly a sign that *'al* can mean "from" or that LXX read *min*.

5. Subsequent lines use the yiqtol to refer to the past, and that makes sense here.

6. Lit. "a lip" (cf. Pss. 12:2 [3]; 22:7 [8]; 120:2; Prov. 12:19; 17:4, 7).

7. LXX and Syr have third-person verbs in this colon and in v. 6a.

8. LXX implies the verb *'ābad* for MT's *'ābar* and then has "in," not "from."

9. Lit. "would not to me." EVV take *'ābâ* to mean "yield" here, but this is hard to parallel. It is usually followed by an inf. or linked in some other way with another verb, often *šāma'*, and on other occasions presupposes such a verb; here the significance of *šāma'* hangs over from the previous colon.

10. Lit. "him" (Israel).

11. NRSV takes this as an unfulfilled wish with no apodosis, but contrast *TTH* 145.

12. See on 66:3. Since Israel was referred to by pl. pronouns in v. 14, and Yhwh has just been referred to, "before him" refers to Yhwh, as in 66:3.

Interpretation

The psalm begins like a praise psalm with an exhortation to worship (vv. 1–3) and then a "for" clause, but the reasons that follow indicate that in this psalm the form is used to make a different point. The reasons (vv. 4–5b) in fact direct the worshippers back to the exhortation, which turns out not merely to introduce the psalm but also to convey its main point. Yhwh requires such worship. The remainder of the psalm explains this as it moves "from hymn to oracle."[13] The speaker now (v. 5c) introduces words from Yhwh, first admitting a failure to acknowledge these words previously. The recollection of these words from Yhwh occupies the rest of the psalm and expands on that obligation to worship Yhwh. Yhwh makes four points. These refer back to the deliverance of Israel from the Egyptians (vv. 6–7b), introduce the expectations that were given to the people in light of that, to listen to Yhwh and rely on Yhwh (vv. 7c–10), note that the people did not respond (vv. 11–12), and point out what the people lose as a result (vv. 13–16).

In its entirety, then, this psalm addresses the people, not God, first with the exhortation to worship, then with the words from God. Like Ps. 50, it might be delivered by a priest, Levite, or prophet,[14] but v. 5c may rather suggest that the congregation speaks throughout, so that the psalm is a self-exhortation. In Ps. 81 the community urges itself to worship Yhwh and rely on no one else. Among hortatory psalms, the exhortation to worship actually gives it more in common with Ps. 95 than with Ps. 50.[15] The focus on worship of Yhwh alone rather than on the moral injunctions of the Ten Words reinforces this comparison and contrast.[16] Passover or Sukkot would be possible occasions for its use (see on vv. 3, 5a–b). The reference to Joseph suggests an origin among members of the northern clans before the fall of Ephraim or later.[17] In this respect, as in its recollection of the exodus, Red Sea, wilderness, and Sinai, it links with preceding psalms, and in stressing Israel's disobedience, it links in particular with Ps. 78. Hossfeld and Zenger speak of its "intense ties" with Ps. 80, to which it responds,[18] and Goulder of "a formidable parallel between Psalm 81 and Deuteronomy 32, especially

13. Terrien, *Psalms*, 581.

14. John W. Hilber (*Cultic Prophecy in the Psalms*, BZAW 352 [Berlin: de Gruyter, 2005], 150–61) stresses its parallels with Assyrian oracles and infers that it is more likely a prophetic oracle than a sermonic imitation of one.

15. Cf. Nasuti, *Tradition History and the Psalms of Asaph*, 102.

16. Cf. Mowinckel, *Psalms in Israel's Worship*, 2:71–72.

17. T. Booij ("The Background of the Oracle in Psalm 81," *Bib* 65 [1984]: 465–75) argues for the late preexilic period.

18. *Psalms 2*, 325–26.

32.12–16,"[19] with its account of Yhwh's relating to Israel in the wilderness, drawing attention to the absence of any strange god there, giving Israel honey from the rock and finest wheat, yet needing to confront the people for their unfaithfulness.

> The leader's. On/concerning the Gittite. Asaph's.

Heading. See glossary. The Gittite (cf. Pss. 8; 84) may be an instrument (Tg) or a melody. It might be named after the "winepress" (*gat*; cf. LXX, Jerome) and thus suggest a link with harvest (cf. vv. 10, 16), or it might be the feminine of the word for a person or thing from Gath. Ibn Ezra connects it with Obed-Edom the Gittite, a Levitical singer (see 1 Chron. 13:13–14; 16:4–5), and it might link with the (annually commemorated?) journey of the covenant chest from his house (2 Sam. 6:11–15).

81:1–5b. So the psalm begins with an exhortation to worship (vv. 1–3) and the reasons for that (vv. 4–5b). The exhortation matches other such exhortations in the psalms, though in light of vv. 4–5b, the subsequent reference to music and tambourine, and calling God our "strength," resonate with the Red Sea story (see Exod. 15). It is an exhortation to celebrate God's act of deliverance.

> [1]Resound for God, our strength,
>   shout for Jacob's God.
> [2]Raise the music, sound the tambourine,
>   the lovely lyre with the harp.
> [3]Blow the horn at the beginning of the month,
>   at the full moon, for our festival day.

So the psalm begins with a standard exhortation to *resound[20] and shout (cf. 47:1 [2]; 66:1) to the God who is our *strength and is *Jacob's God; vv. 6–16 will spell this out. Each of the two opening lines is internally parallel, but they also parallel each other. Verse 2 is distinctive first in issuing an exhortation concerning *music rather than noise. Second, it takes for granted the identity of the object of this praise and, instead of referring to this, details the instruments that will play the music: *lyre, *harp, and tambourine. Women mainly played the tambourine as they danced (e.g., 68:25 [26]; Exod. 15:20).[21] Third, v. 2 thinks in terms of beauty as well as quantity of noise.

The third parallel (and internally parallel) line refers to a further instrument and then to the occasion(s) for the celebration the lines urge.

---

19. *Psalms of Asaph*, 158.
20. Though the hiphil is less common than piel or qal.
21. Cf. Keel, *Symbolism*, 339–40.

Blowing a ram's horn is not in itself part of the act of worship but is a signal to tell people that the moment for worship has come. Such a horn can produce only one or two notes and is thus not really a musical instrument like the trumpet, which appears in 98:6.[22] Blowing a horn much more commonly relates to giving a signal for battle, and the expression comes only here in the psalms,[23] but Num. 10 requires the blowing of silver trumpets at the three annual festivals and at the beginning of the month, as well as to signal the breaking of camp. The parallelism of "at the beginning of the month" (lit. "at the month") and "at the full moon" might mean these are the same time: that is, the (lunar) month begins with the full moon. But it is usually reckoned that the month begins with the new moon.[24] In that case, the two expressions refer to the beginning and midpoint of the month. The reference to the full moon might be present simply as a makeweight, so that we should not build too much on it.[25] But it might be no coincidence that a trumpet blast marks the beginning of the seventh month, the new year, and that on the fifteenth day of that month, Sukkot begins (see Lev. 23:23–43; also more generally, Num. 10:10); this worship occasion might thus be Sukkot.[26] Passover could also work to the same time frame (2 Chron. 30:21–23),[27] and this would fit v. 5a–b. The theme of the psalm fits either festival with its reminder of the exodus and Yhwh's associated requirements regarding worship.

> [4]For it is a law for Israel,
>   a decision for Jacob's God.
> [5a–b]A declaration in Joseph that he laid down
>   when he went out over the land of Egypt.

The expected "for" follows the exhortation to worship, but it has unanticipated implications. The two broadly parallel lines indeed refer to Yhwh's delivering Israel from Egypt, yet the reason for celebration is not that great event but the fact that it was the occasion when Yhwh laid

22. See ibid., 340–44.

23. In 47:1 [2], the verb *tāqaʿ* (here "blow") refers to clapping; the noun *tēqaʿ* (horn) comes in 150:3 (in the company of tambourine, lyre, and harp).

24. See Mowinckel, *Psalms in Israel's Worship*, 2:235–36; further, Oswald Loretz, "Konflikt zwischen Neujahrsfest und Exodus in Psalm 81," in *Mythos im Alten Testament und seiner Umwelt* (H.-P. Müller Festschrift; ed. Armin Lange et al.; BZAW 278; Berlin: de Gruyter, 1999), 127–43 (see 139–40).

25. So Watson, *Classical Hebrew Poetry*, 139.

26. Cf. Mowinckel, *Psalms in Israel's Worship*, 1:121–24. Tractate *b. Sukkah* 55a refers to the psalm's use then, along with Pss. 29; 50; 82; and 94; see further Henry Plantin, "Deuteronomium och lövhyddofestens psalmer i bSukka 55a," *SEÅ* 55 (1990): 7–38 (see 19–23).

27. Haglund, *Historical Motifs*, 15.

down the expectation that people should so worship. Verse 4 comprises two neatly parallel cola, though the formal parallelism is complicated by some differences of substance. The celebration is a law or statute, and it is an authoritative decision. It is a law for Israel in the sense that Yhwh expects Israel to implement it. This is a decision for Yhwh in the sense that Yhwh, *Jacob's God, lays it down. Kidner notes that Christians may think it odd to be expected to rejoice as ordered, but that the psalm assumes that what God has done for Israel makes that possible.[28] Further, in the context the implicit question is not whether or not people are worshipping but whether or not they are worshipping Yhwh or some other deity.[29]

Verse 5 describes the requirement further as a *declaration laid upon Joseph.[30] In the broad parallelism of the two lines, Joseph parallels Israel as elsewhere Judah parallels Israel. It is again doubtful if "Joseph" is simply another way of referring to Israel as a whole (see on 77:15 [16]), any more than "Judah" is in other passages. Rather, the psalm makes explicit that God's statute applies to the northern clans. The psalm was originally composed for them, since passages that parallel "Israel" and "Judah" have Judah particularly in mind. But when "Joseph" is used, as here, Judeans would be able to identify with the words, since they were among the people who had been led by Joseph and on whose behalf Yhwh "went out over the land of Egypt" (cf. Exod. 11:4) to undertake the terrible action that would deliver Israel. On that occasion Yhwh issued the "law" about keeping the "feast" of Passover/Unleavened Bread (Exod. 12:14, 24; 13:6). Soon afterward Yhwh demonstrated "strength" and became the topic of Israel's making "music" with its "tambourines" (Exod. 15:2, 13, 20). Soon after this Yhwh "laid down" a "law" and "decision" for Israel (Exod. 15:25) and issued "decisions" that covered Israel's annual feasts (Exod. 21:1; 23:14–17).[31]

81:5c–12. As happens in (e.g.) Ps. 95, the exhortation to worship gives way to a challenge from God that pushes the worshippers in a different direction. In Ps. 81 Yhwh speaks alternately about Israel to an unidentified audience (vv. 6, 11–16a) and then directly to Israel (vv. 7–10, 16b). Perhaps the unidentified audience is the heavenly court, as Yhwh addresses the heavens in Isa. 1:2–3; Jer. 2:12–13.[32] But the intended indirect

28. *Psalms*, 2:293.

29. Cf. Fokkelman, *Major Poems*, 3:144.

30. Norbert Lohfink ("Noch einmal *ḥōq ûmišpāṭ*," *Bib* 73 [1992]: 253–54) notes that *ʿēdût* in v. 5 is a distinctive addition to the hendiadys *ḥōq ûmišpāṭ* in v. 4.

31. The psalm has been used to support the idea that the Joseph clans alone came out of Egypt (e.g., Goulder, *Psalms of Asaph*), or came out before the other clans, but also to support the historicity of the pentateuchal story (e.g., Samuel E. Loewenstamm, "עדות ביהוסף," *Eretz-Israel* 5 [1958]: 80–82, *88).

32. Cf. Gerstenberger, *Psalms*, 2:111.

audience is still Israel, reached in different ways by direct address and
by being invited to overhear indirect address.

> 5cI listened to lips I had not acknowledged:
> 6I turned his shoulder from the burden;
> his hands moved on from the basket.

As also happens in Ps. 95:7, a monocolon introduces the words from
God. The EVV take *šāpâ* to refer to a previously unknown "language,"
but this makes little sense. Rather, the opening verb "I listened" prepares
us for understanding this as a voice I had not *acknowledged. I was not
listening to it before, but now I am listening.[33] The parallel with Ps.
95 suggests that the speaker is a prophet or a Levite, but the admission
of not having previously acknowledged this voice suggests that the "I"
stands for the people as a whole, even if a priest or prophet voices this
admission. This is supported by the fact that vv. 6–11 refer in the singular
to "him" and "you." Israel speaks here.

The words that Israel now acknowledges begin with a reminder from
Yhwh of the way the people was delivered from its oppression in Egypt.
This was a context in which its life was indeed burdensome. Yhwh delivered the people from the burdens of enslavement (Exod. 1:11; 2:11;
5:4–5; 6:6–7). The "burden" is then further defined as the "basket" that
people had to carry, perhaps containing building materials or bricks.[34]
Ironically, the word for "burden" is not the form used in Exodus (e.g.,
1:11), *siblâ*, but *sēbel*, the form used to describe the burden of enslavement
that Solomon imposed on "Joseph" (1 Kings 11:28—the only other occurrence is Neh. 4:17 [11]). The verb describing Yhwh's action ("I turned") is
then paralleled by one describing the effect on the people ("moved on").
The combination points to the fact that the people's liberation required
Yhwh's action but also required the people's reaction.[35]

> 7a–bIn distress you called and I rescued you,
> answered you in the secret place of thunder.

The second recollection opens in a way that might make us think that
Yhwh continues to describe the exodus event; "rescue" is the vivid *ḥālaṣ*
piel, suggesting, "I pulled you out."[36] But none of the words are ones that

33. Cf. Goulder, *Psalms of Asaph*, 153.
34. Cf. Keel, *Symbolism*, 226–27, 271–72. But *dûd* can also mean "pot," and Tg infers
that the colon refers to their making pots. Rashi sees it as the pots they had to tend in
their domestic servitude to Egyptians.
35. The line (v. 6) works as a neat chiasm: abcc′b′a′.
36. Cf. Fokkelman, *Major Poems*, 3:145.

are used in Exodus of that event, and when we reach talk of "the secret place of thunder," that makes one think more of the Red Sea deliverance. The secret place is the place where Yhwh lives in the heavens, whence thunder comes. While the actual words are again different, they overlap with the images used to describe the Red Sea deliverance in 77:18 [19]. This understanding is confirmed by the third recollection, of Yhwh's testing of the people, which soon followed the Red Sea event.

> ⁷ᶜI tested you at the waters of Contention. (Rise)
> ⁸"Listen, my people, and I will make a declaration to you,
>   Israel, if you listen to me. . . .

Verse 7c, like v. 5c, is a monocolon introducing the words that follow, in this case Yhwh's statement of expectations, an "oracle within an oracle."[37] Yhwh's reference to testing the people suggests a link to the testing that soon followed on the Red Sea deliverance (Exod. 15:25–26, though the verb there is *nāsâ*, not *bāḥan*). There, Yhwh tested the people by laying down a law or a decision or a declaration, and these are the same words as in vv. 4–5; in the last case, "make a declaration" (*'ûd* hiphil; cf. 50:7) takes up the noun "declaration." Neither noun nor verb is inherently confrontational in the sense of suggesting that Israel has done wrong.[38] They indicate the way Yhwh laid the law down and thus tested Israel; their positive reaction will indicate that they are people who do what Yhwh says. The subsequent allusion to the Waters of Contention moves the reference on from Exod. 15 to the occasion when the testing happened in the reverse direction: the people tested Yhwh (Exod. 17:1–7). The combining of motifs from different stories about the wilderness journey recalls Ps. 78.

Verse 8 also reminds the people of the words with which Yhwh tested them. "If you will listen" is the same expression as Yhwh uses in Exod. 15:26 (there Yhwh goes on "to my voice," here simply "to me"). That verb, repeated in the imperative and the yiqtol in v. 8, is also the one v. 5c took up; it will come again in vv. 11 and 13. Yhwh had exhorted the people to listen, but Exod. 15:26 records no acknowledgment of that challenge. Now they have said they have acknowledged it (v. 5c).[39] "My

---

37. Tate, *Psalms 51–100*, 323.

38. EVV understand v. 8a as an indictment and v. 8b as a wish (cf. GKC 151e), but the links with Exod. 15:25–26 suggest that it is an open "if." The passage is recalling what Yhwh said then, not recording what Yhwh said when the people had failed the test. *Lû* (v. 13) is in any case the more common word for "if only."

39. The statement of intent "I will make a declaration to you" may apply to both cola, both to the impv. "Listen, my people" and to the conditional "Israel, if you will listen to me." The line then works abcb′a′, with the c element applying both ways.

people" corresponds well to "our strength, . . . Jacob's God" in v. 1, and it recalls the covenantal pairing of "our God/my people." Thus the look back also recalls Yhwh's subsequent words in Exod. 19:3–8, where Yhwh lays down the terms for being Yhwh's people. As Exodus emphasizes, liberation from the service of Pharaoh did not simply mean freedom but also meant entry into the service of Yhwh.

> [9]There is not to be a strange god among you;
>   you are not to bow down to an alien god.

The content of the declaration or law or decision essentially constitutes a restatement of the first of the Ten Words from Sinai; it thus continues the link with the story that begins at Exod. 15. The verbal expressions parallel Exod. 20:3, 5: "There is not to be . . . . You are not to bow down. . . ." But the actual expression "a strange god" comes only in Ps. 44:20 [21] (also simple "stranger[s]" in, e.g., Deut. 32:16; Isa. 43:12); the parallel "alien god" is more common (e.g., Gen. 35:2, 4; Deut. 32:12; Josh. 24:20, 23). The line constitutes the negative counterpart to the positive exhortation in vv. 1–3.[40]

> [10]I am Yhwh your God,
>   the one who brought you up from the land of Egypt:
>   open your mouth wide, and I will fill it."

The parallel with the Ten Words continues as v. 10a–b exactly repeats words from the preamble in Exod. 20:2, except that the suffixed hiphil verb here comes not in a relative clause with *yāṣā'* but as a participle from *'ālâ*. There these words preceded the command; here they follow the command in v. 9 and underline its significance. Other gods are indeed strange and alien gods, gods the people had not known, gods who contrast with Yhwh, who had brought them out of Egypt: how could they turn to another god? The third colon, closing off the subsection, lacks "from the house of slaves" (Exod. 20:2) and instead contains a command that is also a promise, further underlining the point. Yhwh's provision is not only past but also future. It brings not merely escape from Egypt but also bountiful provision. The people are to open their mouths so that Yhwh—not some other deity—can fill them. "Whence it follows, that the reason why God's blessings drop upon us in a sparing and slender manner is, because our mouth is too narrow"[41] or because we are looking in other directions. The idea

---

40. The line is neatly parallel, with two negatived yiqtol verbs (one third person, one second), two occurrences of *'ēl*, and two parallel adjectives.

41. Calvin, *Psalms*, 3:320.

of opening one's mouth for food appears only here in the Psalms,[42] though Ps. 107:9 speaks of Yhwh filling the hungry, and one can see how the stories about the wilderness journey show Yhwh fulfilling this promise.

Verse 10 completes the "oracle within the oracle," Yhwh's recollection of the challenge issued in the wilderness.

> [11]But my people did not listen to my voice;
>   Israel was unwilling to listen to me.
> [12]So I sent them off by the unyieldingness of their mind;
>   they could walk by their own plans.

The challenge was not met; Israel failed the test. The key verb "listen" recurs, chronologically bridging between the previous occurrences. Yhwh had said "Listen" and "if you will listen" (v. 8), and eventually Israel claims to have listened (v. 5c), but in between it had failed to do so. "My people" and "Israel" are parallel as in v. 8, so that the novelty in the line is the second verb, which underlines the deliberateness of people's declining to listen.[43]

Israel turned away from Yhwh, so Yhwh sends them off. They are tough-minded people; when they have made up their minds, they stick by it. The description is especially characteristic of Jeremiah and refers especially to an insistence on worshiping other deities (e.g., 13:10; 16:11–13), which fits here. The EVV with "I gave them over to their stubborn hearts" paraphrase but do so accurately. Yhwh did let go of Israel and let them follow their own inclinations, living by their own instincts.[44]

81:13–16. The psalm closes with Yhwh's "If only . . ."

> [13]If only my people were listening to me,
>   if only Israel would walk on in my ways,
> [14]I would quickly subdue their enemies;
>   against their foes I would turn my hand.
> [15]Those who are against Yhwh would wither before him,
>   and their fate would be forever.

Verse 13 picks up words from vv. 11–12: "my people," "listen," "Israel," "walk" (but the verb is now piel rather than qal), "by," with the single

---

42. Thus Tate (*Psalms 51–100*, 325) sees God as offering to fill the people's mouths with words of exultation, and Kraus (*Psalms 60–150*, 150) with words of prophecy (on the assumption that v. 10c should be moved to follow v. 5c).

43. In Hebrew the line is neatly parallel: abcb′a′c′.

44. The line is again neatly parallel, two verbs (one first-person piel wayyiqtol, one third-person qal yiqtol) and two *b* expressions.

variation of "ways" for "plans."[45] The verbal parallel contrasts with the dissimilarity in substance between how things are and how Yhwh wishes they were. The line thus introduces "a tone of lament, . . . a reflection of the grief of God because of a wayward people."[46]

Two lines then express how things could be if Yhwh's wishes were not frustrated. Their content is surprising, because we have had no reference to current enemies. On the other hand, Israel's story started with trouble and distress (ṣārâ; vv. 6–7), and vv. 14–15 indicate that insofar as these experiences recur in Israel's life, Yhwh will ensure that the pattern of the beginning recurs as foes (ṣārîm) are put down. There is thus no need to assume that the psalm implies that Israel is currently under pressure. This is a general promise. But if Israel does not call on Yhwh for rescue when it is in that need, it may not experience rescue.

A key truth for Israel is that Yhwh's involvement with them means that their enemies are ipso facto Yhwh's enemies; people who are against them are ipso facto people who are against Yhwh. There is thus a strange security in being under attack. But if they turn from Yhwh, they turn from that security. "Their fate" is literally "their time"; 'ēt can sometimes denote the time when your destiny comes upon you, a "time" that turns out to have been fixed ahead of its coming (e.g., 1 Chron. 29:30; Job 24:1; Ps. 31:15 [16]; Eccles. 9:12; Ezek. 30:3).[47]

> ¹⁶He fed him from the best of wheat,
>   from the crag with honey I would fill you.

The move from Yhwh's speaking in the first person (v. 14) to the third person (v. 15) reverses between vv. 16a and 16b.[48] As vv. 14–15 recall the substance of vv. 6–7, this last line recalls the substance of v. 10, though not the actual wording, and confirms that the theory of these last verses is that the experience of the exodus–Red Sea–wilderness period could continue in Israel's life but will not do so if Israel declines to "open its mouth" (v. 10). Indeed, v. 16a declares that this experience has continued in the people's lives, and v. 16b declares that it can

45. Again, the line is thus parallel, with *lû* (if only) applying to both cola, a qal ptc. paired with a piel yiqtol, and two prepositional expressions.

46. Tate, *Psalms 51–100*, 324.

47. But the usage is unusual. Syr has *zw'hwn* (their fear); Tg, *twqphwn* (their strength; Stec, *Targum of Psalms*, 159, "anger"). John H. Eaton ("Some Questions of Philology and Exegesis in the Psalms," *JTS*, n.s., 19 [1968]: 603–9 [see 607–8]) derives 'ēt from 'ānâ III and translates "their submission."

48. The line is again neatly parallel, with two hiphil verbs (but one is third person with a third-person suffix, the other first person with a second-person suffix) bracketing the line, two *min* expressions, and two nouns for the actual foods.

continue.[49] To the promise of ongoing freedom from oppression (vv. 14–15) is added the promise of ongoing plenty. The land Yhwh took the people into was indeed a land with (among other things) "wheat" and "honey" from which they could "feed" and "fill themselves" (Deut. 8:8, 10). Indeed, Yhwh "fed him . . . honey from the cliff" and "the best of wheat" (Deut. 32:13–14).[50] While people might sometimes have gathered wild honey from honeycombs in cliffs, honey from a cliff or crag is a figure of speech, perhaps derived from the idea of water from a cliff or crag.

Deuteronomy 32 speaks prophetically—that is, the provision it speaks of is literally future—but it also, solemnly, goes on to speak about the way Israel would actually abandon Yhwh, despite the warnings that also feature in Deut. 8. Thus there is irony written into the psalm's closing line. It implicitly speaks of provision that has failed to win Israel's on-going adherence to Yhwh. But it also speaks of the possibility that this need not be the end of the story. The last word indicates, too, a reversion to personal address for a final appeal. "I" speaks to "you," recalling the covenantal language of v. 8.

Theological Implications

In titling his study of Ps. 81 "Listen, My People," Pierre Auffret[51] captures its key feature. The psalm is about listening; *šāma'* comes five times. That verb is often translated "hear," but that underplays the intentionality it implies. We can hear and take no notice; if we listen, it implies we heed. Thus *šāma'* often suggests "obey" and not merely "listen."

The psalm notes first that worship involves listening as well as praising. Although Calvin exaggerates in commenting that the use of instrumental music was appropriate under the law but becomes unnecessary in light of the gospel,[52] worship is "not simply music and liturgy" but especially "an occasion when the congregation can become again the listening people of God."[53] It was once the case that Christians could see

---

49. The first verb is wayyiqtol, the second yiqtol. Tg takes the whole line to continue the modal nature of vv. 14–15 (cf. NRSV), but the wayyiqtol is then odd. More plausibly, LXX and Jerome have two past tenses (cf. NJPS). I follow Barthélemy (*Psaumes*, 585–87) in giving the verb forms their common tense significance and thus in referring v. 16a to the past, v. 16b to the potential future.

50. This link surely makes unlikely the translation "from the mountain with wheat," even though this generates excellent parallelism (against, e.g., Loretz, *Psalmstudien*, 231–50).

51. "Écoute, mon peuple!" *SJOT* 7 (1993): 285–302.

52. *Psalms*, 3:312.

53. Mays, *Psalms*, 266.

the first part of a worship service as a not-very-necessary preliminary to the real business of the service, listening to the sermon, and that was unbalanced. The psalm sees the praise as something that God enjoined on the people, because it is a liturgical expression of a commitment truly to acknowledge Yhwh as the one God. It is now more often the case that Christians take the opposite view, that the sermon is a not-very-necessary postlude to the real business of worship, singing praise songs. That, too, is unbalanced.

The acknowledgment of God expressed in praise is not designed to make us feel good but to be an expression of that commitment, which then needs to affect life outside the church building as well as inside it. The question Yhwh had put before the people is, Will they truly listen (v. 8)? The test of that will be whether they look to Yhwh as the one who fills their mouths. The answer is that they did not listen to Yhwh (v. 11). They devised their own ways of seeking to ensure that their needs were met, turning in other directions than to Yhwh. So Yhwh gave them over to these other ways. It is a terrible punishment when God lets us do what our inclinations suggest (cf. Rom. 1:24–32). While the church's defeat sometimes happens despite its faithfulness, it sometimes happens because it has been faithless and because God has given it up.

But that is not the end. Even though giving them up, Yhwh cannot give up on them. Yhwh keeps thinking, "If only they would listen to me" (v. 13). "Like a man weeping and lamenting," like a saddened father, God cries out at the wretchedness we impose on ourselves.[54] "The essence of Israel's identity as God's people is found in the ability to listen."[55] But Yhwh is dependent on the people exercising that ability, and Fokkelman sees the move through the psalm as suggesting that "God's powerlessness increases to desperate proportions."[56] Yhwh keeps speaking and giving people the chance to start listening again. And eventually, won by this longing persistence, the people (or their leader) testify to having now listened to the lips they had not acknowledged before (v. 5c).

54. Calvin, *Psalms*, 3:323.
55. Schaefer, *Psalms*, 200.
56. *Major Poems*, 3:145.

Psalm 82

God Must Accept Responsibility

Translation

Psalm. Asaph's.

[1]God is standing[1] in the divine assembly,
    in the midst of the gods he exercises authority.
[2]How long will you exercise authority for the wicked[2]
    and elevate the faithless? (Rise)
[3]Exercise authority for the poor and orphan,
    act faithfully for the person who is weak and in want.
[4]Rescue the poor and needy,
    save them from the hand of the faithless.
[5]They have not acknowledged it,
    they do not consider it.
They walk about in darkness;
    all earth's foundations totter.[3]
[6]I myself had said, You are gods,
    offspring of the Most High, all of you.
[7]Yet you will die like a human being,
    fall like one of the leaders.

---

1. I take *niṣṣāb* as a ptc., not a qatal (with JM 113c, against *IBHS* 31.3c).

2. NRSV and NJPS take *ʿāwel* adverbially, "with wickedness," but the parallelism of substance between v. 2a and 2b and the grammatical parallel with v. 3a suggest that *ʿāwel* is the verb's obj. and is abstract for concrete, as in 58:2 [3] (cf. TNIV).

3. Francis I. Andersen ("A Short Note on Psalm 82,5," *Bib* 50 [1969]: 393–94) suggests, "They totter all [of them] [in] the foundations of the earth [i.e., in Sheol]." This provides good parallelism but requires considerable inference.

> [8]Arise, God, exercise authority for the earth,
> because you yourself own[4] all the nations.

Interpretation

Who speaks and who is addressed? It is clear that in the last line a human speaker addresses God, in much the way people commonly do in the Psalms, exhorting God to take action in relation to the situation that previous lines have referred to, a situation where the powerful neglect or take advantage of the weak and needy. This suggests that Ps. 82 is a distinctive form of prayer psalm. Yet its protest and prayer concern not the action or inaction of human oppressors but those of the heavenly powers that had the responsibility of exercising authority on behalf of the weak and needy. The speaker in vv. 1 and 8 might then be either the congregation as a whole or a minister or prophet who speaks on their behalf.

The bulk of the psalm, vv. 2–7, thus speaks to or about these heavenly powers. But who is the speaker in these verses? In light of v. 1, commentators usually reckon that the one who asks the questions, issues the exhortations, makes the observations, and reports the convictions in vv. 2–7 is God, who is speaking in the assembly v. 1 refers to; a prophet might then be reporting the words.[5] But there is no explicit indication that God speaks (contrast, e.g., 81:5c [6c]), and in light of v. 8, I take them as also the words of the human being who speaks in v. 1 and 8. This also fits the fact that v. 6 refers to God in the third person (God can do that, but here it reinforces the absence of any positive indication that God speaks). It also fits the similar dynamic of Ps. 58. As in most psalms, in fact, the whole is spoken by a human suppliant, who laments the way things are in the world and urges God to take action about it. There is no need to import the idea that speakers change from the psalmist to God and then back again in a way that is not explicitly indicated. But like Ps. 58, the psalm does also confront the heavenly powers and implicitly the powerful human beings who might be there in worship when such a psalm is prayed (that is explicit in Ps. 58) and are indirectly advised not to continue to count on the gods' collusion

---

4. KJV translates the yiqtol with a future tense verb, but the logic of the psalm seems to be rather that God can act now because of already owning the nations. G. R. Driver suggests "sift" ("Textual and Linguistic Problems in the Book of Psalms," *HTR* 29 [1936]: 171–95 [see 187]), on the basis of a similar Assyrian word, but this seems unnecessary and unjustified, and it obscures the psalm's logic.

5. See, e.g., Jörg Jeremias, *Kultprophetie und Gerichtsverkündigung in der späten Königszeit Israels*, WMANT 35 (Neukirchen: Neukirchener Verlag, 1970), 120–25.

with their wrongdoing. In this sense it indeed has a prophetic nature.[6] But we do not know what kind of worship context such a psalm belongs in. The reference to the gods and their assembly has been reckoned to suggest a Canaanite background[7] and to point to this being a psalm from the premonarchic or early monarchic period,[8] but it has also been dated in the later monarchic period,[9] in the exile,[10] or in the early postexilic period,[11] while the parallels with Daniel could point in the direction of a much later date. It has also been seen as a composite with a long history of development.[12]

> Psalm. Asaph's.

Heading. See glossary.

82:1. The psalm's first premise is that like any ruler, God exercises authority in the world by means of aides who take part in formulating policies and decisions in the heavenly cabinet where God presides and who are then responsible for implementing them.

> [1]God is standing in the divine assembly,
>   in the midst of the gods he exercises authority.

Such a model for picturing God's relationship with other heavenly powers, based on the nature of human decision-making processes, is common throughout the Middle Eastern world. One hardly needs to assume that its appearance in Israel reflects some distinctive influence by (for instance) Canaanite thinking; it is a commonplace. This assembly (*'ēdâ*) is elsewhere referred to as a council (*sôd*; e.g., Ps. 89:7 [8]); a prophet such as Jeremiah is able to speak of what God intends to do

6. Cf. H. Niehr, "Götten oder Menschen—eine falsche Alternative," *ZAW* 99 (1987): 94–98; Willa Boesak, "Psalm 82," *Journal of Theology for Southern Africa* 64 (1988): 64–68 (see 67).

7. See, e.g., Roger T. O'Callaghan, "A Note on the Canaanite Background of Psalm 82," *CBQ* 15 (1953): 311–14. Oswald Loretz calls it a Canaanite short story ("Psalmenstudien," *UF* 3 [1971]: 101–15 [see 113]), but Franz-Josef Stendebach notes that this underplays its polemical nature ("Glaube und Ethos," in *Freude an der Weisung des Herrn* [H. Gross Festschrift; ed. Ernst Haag and Frank-Lothar Hossfeld; Stuttgart: KBW, 1986], 425–40 [see 437]).

8. E.g., Dahood, *Psalms*, 2:269; Terrien, *Psalms*, 591.

9. E.g., Qimchi.

10. E.g., A. Gonzales, "Le Psaume lxxxii," *VT* 13 (1963): 293–309; Hans-Winfried Jüngling, *Der Tod der Götter* (Stuttgart: KBW, 1969), 78–80.

11. E.g., Zoltán Rokay, "Vom Stadttor zu den Verhöfen," *ZKT* 116 (1994): 457–63; Julian Morgenstern, "The Mythological Background of Psalm 82," *HUCA* 14 (1939): 29–126 (see 119–21).

12. E.g., Loretz, *Psalmstudien*, 268–73.

because he has been admitted to this council and has listened to and taken part in its deliberations (Jer. 23:18). Perhaps the psalmist as a prophet has been admitted to this gathering, though the psalm does not speak in terms of such an experience or of seeing anything or of hearing God speak (contrast 1 Kings 22:19–22; Isa. 6; 40:1; Zech. 3:1–5), and the description in v. 1 may be a statement of conviction that does not require that hypothesis.

While "the divine assembly" is more literally "the assembly of *ʾēl*," "God" and "gods" both translate the word *ʾĕlōhîm*. But at its first occurrence *ʾĕlōhîm* governs a singular verb and clearly refers to God (outside the Elohistic Psalter, a psalm would use the name Yhwh), while at the second "in the midst of *ʾĕlōhîm*" is clearly plural.[13] Confusingly to us, Hebrew can thus refer both to the one God and to the subordinate entities, the other heavenly powers, as *ʾĕlōhîm*. In this respect its use of the word for "god" corresponds to the practice in other Middle Eastern languages. There it can connote "not only major deities but also a wide variety of other phenomena: monstrous cosmic enemies; demons; some living kings; dead kings or the dead more generally; deities' images and standards as well as standing stones; and other cultic items and places"—in fact, anything that is not regular humanity.[14] Here, however, Tg has God standing "in the assembly of the faithful, . . . in the midst of the judges of truth," while Aquila has "the assembly of the powerful."[15] The Midrash quotes Exod. 22:8 [7] as a passage where *ʾĕlōhîm* refers to human judges,[16] but that understanding of the Exodus passage is itself questionable. Indeed, it is doubtful whether the OT ever uses the word *ʾĕlōhîm* to mean human authorities, whereas it certainly uses it to mean lesser heavenly beings (e.g., Pss. 86:8; 95:3; 96:4; 97:7, 9). Thus Syr has "the aides/angels" (*mlʾk*), both for *ʾēl* and for *ʾĕlōhîm* in v. 1b.[17] The

13. "In the midst he judges gods" (LXX, Jerome) would require *baqqereb* for MT's *bĕqereb*.

14. Mark S. Smith, *The Origins of Biblical Monotheism* (New York: Oxford University Press, 2001), 6.

15. The pl. words for "faithful" and "powerful" correspond to LXX's "gods" and Syr's "aides" and might imply *ʾēlîm* for *ʾēl* (see R. B. Salters, "Ps. 82,1 and the Septuagint," *ZAW* 103 [1991]: 225–39). But LXX may simply be assimilating to 89:5 [6] to explain a puzzling expression. Sym and Jerome have sg.

16. *Midrash on Psalms*, 2:59. On the broader midrashic interpretation and on the allusion in John 10, see James S. Ackerman, "The Rabbinic Interpretation of Psalm 82 and the Gospel of John," *HTR* 59 (1966): 186–91; J. A. Emerton, "The Interpretation of Psalm lxxxii in John x," *JTS*, n.s., 11 (1960): 329–34; "Melchizedek and the Gods," *JTS*, n.s., 17 (1966): 399–401; A. T. Hanson, "John's Citation of Psalm lxxxii," *NTS* 11 (1965): 158–62; "John's Citation of Psalm lxxxii Reconsidered," *NTS* 13 (1967): 363–67; Jerome H. Nehrey, "'I Said, You Are Gods,'" *JBL* 108 (1989): 647–63; W. Gary Phillips, "An Apologetic Study of John 10:34–36," *BSac* 146 (1989): 405–19.

17. See the discussion in Jüngling, *Tod der Götter*, 24–69.

psalm will itself go on to indicate that although it uses 'ĕlōhîm both for God and for other heavenly beings, at the same time it presupposes a fundamental difference between them. The latter can die, whereas the one God cannot, which raises the question whether they really deserve to be called by the same word.

As for "the assembly of 'ēl," perhaps we should compare that with an expression such as "cedars of God," "mighty cedars" (cf. 80:10 [11]).[18] Normally the king sits enthroned in such an assembly; it is servants and suppliants there who stand (e.g., Exod. 34:2, which uses the same verb as Ps. 82:1a). The king or God will stand up to take action (cf. v. 8); to stand in the course of the court proceedings is more unusual and more represents the posture of a protagonist (cf. Isa. 3:13; 50:8). It may suggest that God has been aroused and stands to make an emphatic statement or that the president stands to give emphatic judgment, perhaps preliminary to setting off to take action.[19] The second, yiqtol, verb with its reference to exercising *authority thus explains the first, a participle.[20] The word order, with the subject preceding the verb, may suggest that v. 1 is a circumstantial clause providing the background and rationale for the challenge in v. 2: "Given that God is standing in the divine assembly, exercising authority in the midst of the gods . . ."

82:2–5. The psalm turns to upbraid those who exercise authority in the world because they do so in a way that favors the wicked at the expense of the needy.

> [2]How long will you exercise authority for the wicked
> and elevate the faithless? (Rise)

The verbs are plural. The Tg reckons that the addressees are human authorities; the point would be that they had better realize that in heaven

---

18. E. Theodore Mullen (*The Divine Council in Canaanite and Early Hebrew Literature* [HSM 24; Chico, CA: Scholars Press, 1980], 230) sees it as a conventional formula (cf. Tate, *Psalms 51–100*, 329). Otto Eissfeldt ("El and Yahweh," *JSS* 1 [1956]: 25–37 [see 29–30]) sees 'ēl as the president of the assembly and *yhwh* (assumed to have been replaced by 'ĕlōhîm in our text) as a member of the assembly who is criticizing other members. Even if that were the significance of an earlier stage in the material's history, it cannot be the meaning of the psalm in the context of the Psalter (cf. Lowell K. Handy, "One Problem Involved in Translating to Meaning," *SJOT* 10 [1996]: 16–27). Indeed, Gerald Cooke ("The Sons of [the] God[s]," *ZAW* 76 [1964]: 22–47 [see 31]) suggests that v. 7 excludes this understanding in the context of the psalm itself (cf. Weiser, *Psalms*, 558).

19. It would make sense for Yhwh to stand if Yhwh were simply a member of the assembly (cf. Simon B. Parker, "The Beginning of the Reign of God," *RB* 102 [1995]: 532–59), but that is hardly the psalm's assumption (see previous note).

20. The two cola are neatly parallel, abcc'b'; each of vv. 1–4 has such chiastic features.

a judgment court is convening, and they had better change their ways.[21] But vv. 6–7 will explicitly address the gods of v. 1, which suggests that they are also the addressees here. It is this rebuke that explains the declaration in vv. 6–7. On the other hand, the content of the protest in vv. 2–4 does match the expectations of human rulers and other influential people in the community in general, in Israel and elsewhere in the Middle East (e.g., Exod. 22:21–22 [20–21]), as well as matching the nature of Yhwh's own commitment (e.g., Deut. 10:18). In other words, the gods are expected to identify with the principles that Yhwh believes in and expects human beings to live by. The presupposition is that the gods share in responsibility for the proper supervision of life in the world, under God but above earthly authorities (cf. the critique of Keret in "The Legend of King Keret").[22] They are to exercise authority for the faithful and elevate them and to see that earthly authorities do so. "The prime obligation of power is to do justice," and where this is not the attitude of the powerful, demons are at work.[23]

In the Psalms, "How long?" is usually a protest addressed to God (see 74:10), but elsewhere it can be a protest and implicit rebuke uttered by one human being to another (e.g., Exod. 10:7; 1 Sam. 1:14; 2 Sam. 2:26; 1 Kings 18:21) or by God (e.g., Exod. 10:3; Num. 14:27; 1 Sam. 16:1). In the context, either a human or a divine protest is possible, but we have had no indication that God speaks, and "How long?" is not the kind of question that a protagonist or a judge utters in court. I thus take it that the same person speaks in v. 2 as in v. 1,[24] but we may perhaps imagine this happening in the setting of the assembly of which v. 1 spoke, the assembly to which a person such as a prophet is admitted (e.g., 1 Kings 22:19–22). A little like Isaiah, who intervenes in a meeting of the cabinet to volunteer when Yhwh is looking for someone to undertake a commission (Isa. 6:8), the suppliant then intervenes in the meeting of the assembly to confront the gods gathered there. In light of the fact that God is standing to give judgment in the cabinet, the psalmist points out that the gods would be wise to consider their position. Yet the familiarity of "How long?" as a

---

21. Cole (*Shape and Message of Book III*, 103) reckons that this is the implication when Ps. 82 is set in the context of the surrounding psalms, while Peterson (*Where Your Treasure Is*, 134) argues similarly on the basis of the psalm's broader canonical context in Israel's life; cf. also Handy, "One Problem Involved in Translating to Meaning." Luther presents a powerful exposition on this understanding of a psalm that "every prince should have painted on the wall of his chamber, on his bed, over his table, and on his garments" (*Selected Psalms*, 2:39–72 [see 51]). I would call such understandings part of the psalm's reception history rather than a canonical understanding (cf. Peter Höffken, "Werden und Vergehen der Götter," *TZ* 39 [1983]: 129–37 [see 136]).

22. KRT C, column 6; see, e.g., *ANET* 149.

23. Hill, *Prayer, Praise and Politics*, 92.

24. Cf. Calvin, *Psalms*, 3:330.

protest in the Psalms would suggest that this resonance also applies here. This protest suggests both indignation and pain. It is not merely the rebuke of a protagonist in a court but also the rebuke of a prophet.

The first colon goes on to provide a textbook example of the way *šāpaṭ* (exercise *authority) is a power word rather than a value word. It does not inherently suggest the exercise of justice. One can exercise authority in a proper way or an improper way, for the faithful or for the *wicked. Nevertheless the expectation is that authority *ought* to be exercised for the faithful. Conversely, it is the faithful, not the *faithless, who ought to be "elevated." Literally, that expression denotes "raising the face" of the faithless. The idea is that as suppliants, people come to the governing authorities with their faces bowed to the ground, seeking action on their behalf when they are (for instance) falsely accused. When the authorities accept their plea, the suppliants can hold their heads high again. But at the moment it is the faithless whom the authorities vindicate, not the people who are in the right.

> ³Exercise authority for the poor and orphan,
>   act faithfully for the person who is weak and in want.

The psalm goes on to express more straightforwardly the point made by the rhetorical question. In other words, the deep structure of vv. 2 and 3 is the same, as the opening verb itself is the same. The way to exercise authority without wickedness is to exercise it for the poor and the orphan (see 72:13; 68:5 [6]). The second colon then rephrases the point. The poor are people who belong to the underclass and are therefore *weak. They count for nothing in the society, they can be taken advantage of, and their needs can be ignored; so they end up in want. The same applies to orphans, whose problem lies not in lacking a loving relationship with their father (though no doubt that would also be true) but in having no one to provide for them and protect them and in having no pull in society, so that they too end up in want. The two verbs *šāpaṭ* and *ṣādēq* (hiphil) correspond to the pair of nouns *mišpāṭ* and *ṣĕdāqâ*, conventionally translated justice and righteousness, which denote making *decisions that express *faithfulness toward the people with whom we are in relationship, doing right by them. In a court context, that will mean finding in favor of them rather in favor of people who (for example) seek to deprive them of their land or housing or freedom. The force of the descriptions is increased by the fact that the four nouns come together: literally, "Exercise authority for the poor and orphan, to the weak and in want act faithfully."[25] Perhaps we should see each of the three pairs

25. Thus the line works abb′b″b‴a′.

of nouns in vv. 3–4a as a hendiadys—poor orphan, disadvantaged weak person, needy poor person.

> ⁴Rescue the poor and needy,
>   save them from the hand of the faithless.

Once again the psalm spells out the point, continuing to use imperatives but utilizing verbs that give precision to "exercise authority" and "act faithfully." Such action involves *rescuing or *saving. "Rescue" means making it possible for people to escape; "save" typically leads into reference to a plight from which no human agency can deliver. The *poor person reappears from v. 3 (such repetitions for emphasis are common in the poetry of the Psalms)²⁶ while *needy is a synonym of "in want" in v. 3. Repetition and variation thus complement each other. For the poor and needy, there is no way of escaping from the power of the *faithless, no way of being able to resume a life that works. They are helpless. Only if God or God's aides take action can there be deliverance. That is how important the action of the gods is.²⁷

In what sense are the gods exercising authority for the wicked and failing the poor and orphan? The gods do not have responsibility for relationships within the Israelite community; that is Yhwh's business. But Israelites were often suffering because of the attacks of other peoples (see Ps. 83), for which these people's gods could then be held responsible,²⁸ though it is odd to speak of Israel as the poor and orphan and not as the people of Yhwh in general (again, see Ps. 83). Might the psalm be protesting the way the gods collude in or inspire the oppression of the vulnerable within the nations they oversee (cf. the critiques in Amos 1:3–2:3)?

> ⁵They have not acknowledged it,
>   they do not consider it.
> They walk about in darkness;
>   all earth's foundations totter.

A pair of brisk 2-2, 2-3 lines brings to an end the challenge in vv. 2–5. Commentators take it that "they" are the "you" whom vv. 2–4 addressed, but there is no pointer to this change. More likely the "they" are the "they"

---

26. Against Kraus, *Psalms 60–150*, 154; there is thus no reason to emend the word.

27. Here the parallelism works first by v. 4a corresponding to v. 3; again a verb leads into two words to describe the vulnerable. Verse 4b then seems about to follow this sequence once again, and the structure does follow insofar as the verbs book-end the line as they did in v. 3. But here "from the hand of the faithless" replaces a fourth pair of nouns to describe the vulnerable.

28. Cf. Goulder, *Psalms of Asaph*, 163–64.

of the previous line, the faithless people from whom the poor need res-cue.[29] This will be confirmed by v. 6, where the gods are again addressed as "you." Behind the faithlessness of the people who oppress or neglect the poor is a refusal to *acknowledge or think about the facts and their community obligations.[30] They prefer to be in the dark. That could have various implications. In parallelism with the previous two clauses, it likely restates their point. The faithless like to live their lives in the darkness of ignorance (e.g., Eccles. 2:14) regarding the way the society should really be and regarding the nature of their own obligations. But the expression also points to the moral darkness of their wrongdoing (cf. Prov. 2:13). Further, more often than either of these, darkness suggests calamity and distress (e.g., Ps. 107:10, 14), and the clause also thus hints that the distress the faithless cause is one that will overtake them, too. Parallel possibili-ties then apply to the declaration that all earth's foundations shake. That might refer to the earth's moral foundations. Using different words, the metaphor appears in 11:3 and perhaps in 75:3 [4]. When faithless people ignore or oppress the poor and no one does anything to rescue them, the very structure of human existence is imperiled. The whole society may collapse. But that leads into the further possibility that the colon refers to the kind of world calamity that may follow when moral and social order collapses. When the faithless walk about in such darkness, this threatens not only the darkness of calamity for them but also that same darkness of calamity for the whole world as its foundations collapse. The wicked and faithless are "putting at risk life in the entire universe."[31]

82:6–7. The exhortation in v. 4 is perhaps only rhetorical; the psalm-ist knows that the gods are not acting thus. Verses 6–7 declare what therefore must follow.

> [6]I myself had said, You are gods,
>   offspring of the Most High, all of you.

Presumably the same speaker continues. If God speaks through vv. 2–5, then God also speaks here, but if a prophet spoke there, then the prophet is again the "I," continuing to address the gods; the "I myself" gives what follows some extra emphasis.[32] The NRSV renders "I say"

29. The "they" can hardly be the poor and needy of v. 4a (against Kidner, *Psalms*, 2:298). They are too far away in the sentence, and the description does not fit them.

30. These verbs are often used absolutely, as here; they come together thus in Isa. 1:3; 6:9; 44:18.

31. Tércio M. Siqueira, "Psalm 82," in *Reading the Hebrew Bible for a New Millennium*, ed. Wonil Kim et al., vol. 2 (Harrisburg, PA: Trinity, 2000), 243–52 (see 249).

32. Tg has the suppliant addressing people who are "reckoned as like [heavenly] aides and like the angels [the Greek word is transliterated] on high."

and takes the whole of the rest of vv. 6–7 as addressed to the gods in the present.[33] More plausibly NJPS renders "I had taken you for divine beings"; that is, the verb connotes "I had said [to myself]" (cf., e.g., Gen. 20:11; Ruth 4:4).[34] The psalmist had had rather an exalted idea about these gods. They were very offspring of God, the *Most High. Perhaps the psalmist means this literally (as the misapprehension that is now being corrected), as Middle Eastern stories do. But the phrase may be more metaphorical, as when Yhwh addresses the king as "my son" (Ps. 2:7; cf. also the expressions in 49:2 [3]; 62:9 [10]; 79:11; 89:6 [7]).

> [7]Yet you will die like a human being,
>   fall like one of the leaders.

Realizing the morally incompetent way the gods are governing the world has made the suppliant realize that they cannot be offspring of the Most High, and that in two senses. It cannot be so because surely they would then show more of a family resemblance. God does not tolerate the neglect or oppression of the poor, so how can God's offspring collude with it? But also it cannot be so because the suppliant knows that God will take the same action against the gods as God takes against human oppressors. God puts them down. They will lose their lives. And if that is a possibility, this too shows they cannot really be God's offspring. They do not share in God's eternity. The psalm thus compares with the Middle Eastern stories in which gods can both come into being and be killed.[35] In the parallelism, "fall" parallels "die"; "fall" often denotes violent death (e.g., 1 Sam. 4:10; 14:13). For the first analogy, Jerome translates *'ādām* as "Adam," and the gods' fate parallels the one that came on humanity as it was deprived of the eternal life that it could have been given.[36] "One of the leaders" then parallels "a human being." "Leaders" (*śārîm*) is a

33. One might then see the qatal as performative (cf. Jacobson, *"Many Are Saying,"* 113–14), but this requires some reading into vv. 6–7 (e.g., Jacobson translates the noun clause as "You may be gods").

34. Cf. Karl Budde, "Ps. 82 6f," *JBL* 40 (1921): 39–42.

35. See, e.g., Cyrus H. Gordon, "History of Religion in Psalm 82," in *Biblical and Near Eastern Studies* (W. S. LaSor Festschrift; ed. Gary A. Tuttle; Grand Rapids: Eerdmans, 1978), 129–31; Matitiahu Tsevat, "God and the Gods in Assembly," *HUCA* 40–41 (1969–70): 123–37 (see 129–30). Tsevat goes on to point suggestively to the idea that the psalm represents not so much the death of the gods but the death of polytheism: "The poem presents two views of the gods, an earlier one and a later one," the former yielding to the latter and dying. Verse 8 then represents a prayer for God to make that historic theological development happen, and also a statement that helps to make it happen (see 134). The old gods then die. Cf. Werner Schlisske's discussion of demythologizing in Ps. 82 (*Gottessöhne und Gottessohn im Alten Testament* [BWANT 97; Stuttgart: Kohlhammer, 1973], 32–46); also Miller, *Interpreting the Psalms*, 120–24.

36. Cf. *Midrash on Psalms*, 2:60; also Jerome, *Homilies*, 1:106.

general term, usually denoting earthly figures. The point might then be that leaders expect to live longer than ordinary people (they get better food and health care), yet they may not do so, or it might be that they often live shorter lives because they die in battle (again, cf. Ps. 83), or it might be that they are executed for failing in their service of the king (cf. Dan. 1–6). But in Dan. 10 the term refers to heavenly figures, and the suppliant's point might be that the gods are shown to be no more eternal than other created heavenly beings.

82:8. The psalm for the first time addresses God, and perhaps its point comes here. We will see how the first three-quarters of Ps. 89 exists as a preliminary to a challenge to God in the last quarter, and Ps. 82 may work in a similar way.

> [8]Arise, God, exercise authority for the earth,
>   because you yourself own all the nations.

In this case, in the end the psalm is a prayer.[37] Indeed, the implication of vv. 1–7 is that "if God does not respond to the prayer and establish the justice for which the psalmist prays, God will have proven that God has no more right to divinity than the gods."[38] Verse 1 noted the fact that God is standing there in the divine assembly, and vv. 2–7 confronted the other members of the assembly who are supposed to do God's work but are not doing so. If vv. 1–7 presuppose that the psalmist is a prophet who is present in the heavenly court, then presumably that continues to be the scene.[39] Prayer is the prophet taking part in its deliberations, not only issuing a challenge to the gods but also issuing a challenge to God to take the appropriate action. The question is, What is God doing about the gods? God exercises authority in this assembly (v. 1); the gods are failing properly to exercise authority for the earth and specifically for the poor and needy (vv. 2–3). In light of that, when is God in person going to exercise *authority for the earth, acting on its behalf in the way that it needs? This verb is the key word in the psalm.[40] (Once again the idea is not that God will judge the world, but that God will act as the one who holds power in the world and can govern it in the way it needs.) At the moment, God is standing in the assembly (v. 1) but not taking action,

37. Mays, *Psalms*, 269.

38. Jacobson, *"Many Are Saying,"* 114.

39. Contrast Jüngling, *Tod der Götter*, 103, who assumes that the court scene is over.

40. Cf. Kenneth M Craig, "Psalm 82," *Int* 49 (1995): 281–84. For other patterns in wording and structure, see Lowell K. Handy, "Sounds, Words and Meanings in Psalm 82," *JSOT* 47 (1990): 51–66; W. S. Prinsloo, "Psalm 82," *Bib* 76 (1995): 215–28; Watson, *Classical Hebrew Poetry*, 290–93.

so the suppliant urges God to arise in this more active sense (cf., e.g., 44:26 [27]; 74:22), in the way 76:9 [10] describes.

God can do that on the basis of being one who owns (*nāḥal*) not merely Israel or Judah (Exod. 34:9; Zech. 2:12 [16]) but also all the nations. The inclusion with v. 1 suggested by the repetition of "exercise authority" is extended by the verbal construction here, as *nāḥal* is followed by *b*, paralleling the two *b* expressions in v. 1.[41] Yhwh exercises authority among (*b*) the gods, and they rule the nations incompetently, but Yhwh has ownership among (*b*) the nations.[42] The point may link with the reference to "leaders" in v. 7, because Dan. 10 pictures each of the nations as having their own heavenly "leader." There is a supernatural being responsible for Persia, another for Greece, and so on (cf. Deut. 32:8–9, where only Jacob is Yhwh's *naḥălâ*). Yet like any top executive, God can delegate authority to subordinate leaders but cannot delegate responsibility to them. When things go wrong, the CEO has to accept responsibility and take action. This is what the psalm urges in light of the way things are in the world, as the faithless neglect and oppress the poor, and the gods do nothing about it.

Theological Implications

Given the reality of wickedness in the world, how can we reckon God to be both powerful and good? Christians usually seek to solve that problem by risking compromising God's power; the problem lies in human free will and/or in the power of Satan. The OT usually seeks to solve it by risking compromising God's goodness; it affirms that God is in control and attributes to God the bad things that happen as well as the good things. Psalm 82 is a rare example of the OT taking the first route. Yhwh has delegated to subordinate heavenly powers responsibility for affairs in the world, and therefore when people neglect the poor, blame for allowing this rests with these powers. "The charge against the gods is not that they are idols or nonexistent but that they have failed to put down wickedness and bring justice."[43] Yet the psalm knows that one can delegate power but not responsibility. Indeed, in keeping with the OT's usual view, it knows that Yhwh does not give power away in such a way as to be unable to take it back. And it therefore urges Yhwh to

41. Fokkelman, *Major Poems*, 3:148.
42. The use of the prep. is grammatically odd, though it hardly means Yhwh merely has ownership of Israel "among" the nations (so Eerdmans, "Essays on Masoretic Psalms," 118), which would surely undermine the psalm's argument and fits ill with the emphasis on "you."
43. Mays, *Psalms*, 269.

exercise responsibility: not just to stand up in court but also to stand up to take action in the world.

The idea of God exercising judgment on the heavenly powers appears as a promise for the End in Isa. 24:21; here it is an expectation for within history. The NT picks up that idea. The heavenly powers were created in or by Christ and through and for Christ (Col. 1:15–16), and by dying Christ has defeated and dethroned them or divested himself of them, and triumphed over them (Col. 2:15). They are subject to him (1 Pet. 3:22), and they cannot separate us from God's love (Rom. 8:38–39). Yet we still battle against them (Eph. 6:12). Evidently they are still capable of asserting themselves, and we still look forward to God's final judgment on them (1 Cor. 15:24–25). And we still pray for God's authority to be exercised over them in the now (cf. Eph. 6:12, 18), as the psalm does. Without the perspective of the psalm, the world is a Kafka-esque place, "given over to the intermediary beings, with which they play their confused game"; it is as well the psalm adds this perspective of comfort and promise.[44]

"The religion of the gods legitimated a hierarchical social system in which those at the top prospered and those at the bottom suffered," one that emphasized the economic prosperity of the powerful at the expense of the exercise of authority in faithfulness toward the needy.[45] It is such a system that the writer and most users of this commentary profit from and collude with. Psalm 82 therefore stands as one of the most worrying texts in the OT. It is also one of the most "spectacular" for its "definition" of God, "who has tied his divinity to the fate of the poor and dispossessed."[46]

44. Martin Buber, *Right and Wrong* (London: SCM, 1952), 33 = *Good and Evil* (New York: Scribner's, 1952), 30.
45. McCann, "Psalms," 1007–8.
46. Hossfeld and Zenger, *Psalms 2*, 337.

Psalm 83

Confrontation, Shame, Death, Acknowledgment

Translation

Song. Psalm. Asaph's.

¹God, you must not keep silence,[1]
    you must not be mute, you must not be quiet, God.

²Because there: your enemies rage,
    your opponents have reared their head.
³Against your people they devise plans;
    they consult with one another against those you cherish.[2]
⁴They have said, "Come on, we will cut them off as a nation,[3]
    and Israel's name will not be brought to mind any more."

⁵Because they have consulted together,
    against you they have sealed an agreement,

---

1. Lit. "[There] must not [be] silence to you," an idiomatic expression (cf. Isa. 62:6). LXX has the more familiar "Who is like you?" connecting *dŏmî* with *dāmâ* I rather than *dāmâ* II or *dāmam*. This does not fit the context of v. 1, but it provides a neat anticipatory link with the close of the psalm.
2. Aq, Sym, and Jerome imply sg. *ṣĕpûnekā*, "the one you cherish," agreeing with "your people."
3. Lit. "from [being] a nation."

⁶The tents of Edom and the Ishmaelites,
  Moab and the Hagrites,
⁷Gebal, Ammon,[4] and Amalek,
  Philistia with the inhabitants of Tyre.
⁸Assyria, too, has joined with them;
  they have become the strength of the offspring of Lot. (Rise)

⁹Deal with them like Midian, like Sisera, like Jabin,
  at the Wadi Kishon,
¹⁰Who perished at En-dor,
  became manure for the ground.[5]
¹¹Treat them—their nobles like Oreb and Zeeb,
  all their leaders like Zebah and Zalmunna.

¹²The people who have said, "We will possess for ourselves
  God's pastures"—
¹³My God, treat them like a whirl,
  like stubble before the wind.
¹⁴Like a fire that burns a forest,[6]
  like a flame that sets mountains ablaze,
¹⁵So may you pursue them with your tempest,
  terrify them with your storm.

¹⁶Fill their faces with humiliation
  so that they may seek help from your name, Yhwh.
¹⁷May they be shamed and terrified forever,
  may they be disgraced and perish,
¹⁸So that they may acknowledge that you,
  whose name is Yhwh alone,
  are the Most High over all the earth.

Interpretation

The psalm begins with an appeal to God to listen to this prayer (v. 1), then goes on to a lengthy statement of the reason why God should do that, with two subsections (vv. 2–4, 5–8). Unusually, this relates to events that are at present threatened rather than actual: there has been no invasion yet.

4. For *gĕbāl wĕʿammôn*, Syr implies *gĕbul ʿammôn*, "the territory of Ammon."
5. Or "for [the place] Adam"; see Rendsburg, *Linguistic Evidence*, 74, who refers to E. Y. Kutscher, *Hebrew and Aramaic Studies* (Jerusalem: Magnes, 1977).
6. "As a fire burns a forest" (NJPS) presupposes that *k* is used as equivalent to *kaʾăšer*, but that "can hardly be right" (GKC 155g); rather, this is an unmarked relative clause, omitting *ʾăšer*.

The even longer petition divides into three parallel subsections, one pointing God to a model in Israel's history for God to follow (vv. 9–11), one centering on imagery from nature (vv. 12–15) and one focusing on the ultimate aim of the action it looks for (vv. 16–18). The length of the petition is also a unique feature. Usually prayer psalms express their desire quite briefly, but this psalm more closely resembles Christian prayers that spend most of their time saying what we want God actually to do. Conversely, the psalm lacks the conventional statement of trust, protestation of past faithfulness (or confession of sin), and commitment to come back with praise when God has answered.

That in itself links with a further distinctive feature. Although it is implicitly a community prayer, the psalm never shows any overt concern for the people in itself, the people to whom the suppliants belong. There is no "we" or "I" in the psalm (except the "my God" of v. 13 and the "we" of the attackers, v. 4). Israel appears only in the third person. No doubt we may suspect that the suppliants are deeply concerned for their own peril and destiny, but the very fact that they offer none of the usual arguments for Yhwh to pay attention (their trust, their past faithfulness, their promises) suggests that this prayer is not simply hiding its self-serving concern. Its focus lies on the way other people's plans affect God.

The psalm has further distinctive features. The list of peoples in vv. 6–8 is unparalleled. They are members of Israel's extended family (vv. 6–7a), other more properly foreign local powers (v. 7b), and an imperial power (v. 8). The list may point to the particular circumstances that gave rise to the psalm, and the OT refers to several times of conflict with groups of peoples like this. Such conflict happened in the time of David (2 Sam. 8), in the ninth century,[7] the eighth century (that fits the links with Isa. 17:12–14),[8] the seventh century,[9] the exile, the Second Temple period (cf. Neh. 4),[10] and the Maccabean period (see 1 Macc. 5). On the other hand, the psalm does not refer to Jerusalem, and the appeal to events in northern Israel in vv. 9–11 might suggest a northern origin for the psalm. But we do not know of an occasion when Israel or Judah was under attack from precisely these peoples, and in different contexts it would also be odd that the psalm does not mention (for instance) Egypt or Aram or Babylon. The fact that the psalm speaks not of these peoples actually attacking Israel but only of their planning to do so suggests a parallel with Ps. 2 (cf. also Ps. 46).[11] That parallel supports the view that

7. Qimchi makes a link with 2 Chron. 20.
8. Tg adds reference to Sennacherib in v. 8.
9. Cf. Jerome, *Homilies*, 1:114.
10. Cf. Theodoret, *Psalms*, 2:58–61.
11. Cf. Kraus, *Psalms 60–150*, 161. Erich Zenger surveys the psalm's theological links with many other psalms in "Die Gotteszeugenschaft des 83. Psalms," in *Und dennoch ist*

the psalm links not with a specific invasion but with the general situation of Israel's vulnerability to the designs of surrounding peoples and its broader theological awareness that the world's attacks on Israel are attacks on Yhwh's purpose, Yhwh's sovereignty, and Yhwh's reputation. If the psalm had its origin in (for example) the eighth century or the early Second Temple period, its presence in the Psalter suggests that it came to be used to express that broader theological awareness.

Psalms 82 and 83 complement each other, especially if we understand the poor and needy in Ps. 82 as Israel. Both psalms speak of bodies making plans for action in the world, both see powerful forces asserting themselves against Yhwh's purpose, and both see these powerful forces as destined for death. Both urge God (*'ĕlōhîm, 'ēl, 'elyôn*) to take action. But Ps. 82 looks at world affairs from the perspective of the divine council; Ps. 83 looks at them from the perspective of the nations' planning.

Song. Psalm. Asaph's.

Heading. See glossary.

83:1. So the psalm begins with an appeal for God's attention, though this takes distinctive form.

¹God, you must not keep silence,
you must not be mute, you must not be quiet, God.

A prayer psalm commonly begins with a positive appeal to God to listen (e.g., Pss. 55; 61; 64; 80; 86; 88) and/or to act (e.g., Pss. 54; 56; 59; 69; 70), but there are a few other psalms that begin thus negatively with an appeal to God not to be silent or mute (see Pss. 28; 109) or quiet. Here the point is underlined by the use of three synonymous expressions. The opposite of silence, muteness, and quiet is the loud assertive raging of a warrior: see Isa. 42:13–14, where Yhwh acknowledges having been mute (*ḥāraš*) for too long and turns to such shouting and roaring, which will mean the people's deliverance. The threefold appeal here suggests the same circumstances. Like Judeans at the end of the exile, Israel has been experiencing Yhwh keeping peace when it needs Yhwh to holler and yell. The words *'ĕlōhîm* and *'ēl* for God book-end the opening line as they book-end the opening colon in Ps. 82.[12] That parallel may suggest that the context of Yhwh's silence and assertiveness is the meeting of Yhwh's cabinet. Like Ps. 82, the prayer wants Yhwh to initiate action there.

---

von Gott zu Reden (Herbert Vorgrimler Festschrift; ed. Matthias Lutz-Bachmann; Freiburg: Herder, 1994), 11–37 (see 32–35).

12. Watson (*Classical Hebrew Poetry*, 285) notes that the line instances how such "frame-words" are usually not identical.

83:2–4. The reason for the appeal lies in the actions of Yhwh's enemies, who are also Israel's enemies. In v. 1 "you" was very prominent, and in vv. 2–3 the suffix *-kā* "you/your" comes four times, underlining the emphasis on their being Yhwh's enemies. Admittedly the actions have not yet reached the point of actual attack, but they may be expected to do so. Yiqtol and qatal verbs alternate between vv. 2a and 2b and again between vv. 3 and 4, so that the verses combine reference to the ongoing implications of the enemies' acts and the concrete acts that lie behind the present.

> ²Because there: your enemies rage,
>   your opponents have reared their head.

The evidence lies before Yhwh's eyes. Yhwh has only to look down to see it. Initially the psalm points not at all to people's doing wrong by Israel but to their doing wrong by Yhwh. They are acting in a way that exposes the fact that they are Yhwh's enemies and opponents (people who are *against Yhwh). While Yhwh is keeping silence instead of giving voice and raging, these anti-God forces are raging and giving voice instead of being submissive to Yhwh (cf. 46:3, 6, 10 [4, 7, 11]; Isa. 17:12). Rearing the head is the action of someone about to act aggressively; tellingly in light of vv. 9–11, the expression is used of Midian in Judg. 8:28 (cf. also Zech. 1:21 [2:4]).[13]

> ³Against your people they devise plans;
>   they consult with one another against those you cherish.

Behind the raging is some "devising." The verb (*'āram* hiphil) is one that suggests cleverness, and like related words, it can denote both a positive shrewdness or prudence or subtlety and a more dubious craftiness or cunning or guile (e.g., Gen. 3:1; Prov. 1:4; 8:5, 12; 15:5; 19:25). So these people are dangerous because they are not merely people who make plans or plots but people who actually think up clever plans or plots and who do so—the parallel verb points out—in dangerous collusion with one another.[14] The line takes one step toward a concern with the threat to the suppliants themselves. The object of these schemes is now not Yhwh but Yhwh's people, the people through whom Yhwh intends to rule the world. This is a people Yhwh treats like a treasure and hides away to make sure it is safe (*ṣāpan*); compare the use of this word in

13. The line works abcb'c', with "because there" applying to both cola, two parallel participial expressions (one qal, one piel) with second-person suffix, then two parallel verbal expressions (one yiqtol, one qatal).
14. The line works chiastically, abb'a'.

Ezek. 7:22 of the temple Yhwh is now going to allow to be desecrated. That latter description ought surely to mean that Yhwh does defend this people aggressively, but it is not evident that Yhwh is doing so.

> ⁴They have said, "Come on, we will cut them off as a nation,
> and Israel's name will not be brought to mind any more."

The qatal verb introduces a more concrete account of the content of the plans. They involve no half measures. We might wonder whether the psalm is exaggerating the nature of the people's peril, but there have certainly been occasions when people have aimed at a final solution of the Jewish problem, like that of Haman in the book of Esther and like that of Hitler. "The poet portrays the conspiracy to rob God of his people."[15] With some irony the first statement of this aim, "We will cut them off" (*kāḥad* hiphil), is expressed by means of another verb that commonly means "hide" (cf. 69:5 [6]; 78:4), like the last word in v. 3. Yhwh is supposed to hide this people because they are precious; the enemies want to hide them so no one can ever find them. They will cease to exist as a nation, that is, in their entirety. Specifically, the result of this action will be that Israel is totally forgotten, to such an extent that its name is not even mentioned.[16] No one will be *mindful of it. Human beings regularly seek to ensure that they will be remembered, for instance by setting up a memorial to themselves. It is the ultimate in nonexistence that one's *name should never be on anyone's lips (cf. Jer. 11:19; also Job 24:20; Ezek. 21:32 [37]). Significantly, this threat applies elsewhere to Ammon (Ezek. 25:10), one of the plotters named later in this psalm.

83:5–8. In this second subsection introduced by *kî*, the further account of the enemies' action parallels and expands on the one in vv. 2–4.[17] In the manner of parallelism, it heightens the force of the first statement. Verse 5 does that by asserting that "your enemies" are not merely making plans against "your people": they have also sealed an agreement (or covenant) against "you." Verses 5 and 8 underline and expand further on the enemies' planning (v. 3), and vv. 6–8 give concreteness to "your enemies/your opponents." The account again interweaves qatal (vv. 5a, 7) and yiqtol (v. 5b), referring to the concrete acts that lie behind the present and to the ongoing reality, though initially in the opposite order to vv. 2–4.

---

15. Schaefer, *Psalms*, 203.
16. After the introductory "they have said," the two cola make parallel statements, though the second implicitly states the result of the first.
17. On the use of *kî* to introduce units longer than simply a clause and with various types of causal significance, see Elias E. Meyer, "The Particle כִּי," *JNSL* 27 (2001): 39–62 (see 57–58 on this passage).

> ⁵Because they have consulted together,
>   against you they have sealed an agreement,
> ⁶The tents of Edom and the Ishmaelites,
>   Moab and the Hagrites,
> ⁷Gebal, Ammon, and Amalek,
>   Philistia with the inhabitants of Tyre.

The "because" clause parallels the one that opened v. 2, while the content of v. 5 especially takes up the content of v. 3, though the time reference parallels v. 4. The complex expanded expression translated "They have consulted [with their mind] together"[18] reinforces "They consult with one another" (*yāʿaṣ* hitpael) in v. 3, and the parallel phrase "They have sealed an agreement" underlines the seriousness of their action. "Sealed" is literally "cut," which presumably refers to a rite such as that described in Gen. 15:7–21. "Seal an agreement [*běrît*]" is then the expression used in the OT for the solemn making of a covenant. The same phrase is thus used here for the solemn sealing of a contract between human partners. The solemnity of the way these peoples entered into their agreement heightens the threat to Israel, but the psalm's emphasis lies somewhere else. We might be inclined to call this a "secular" agreement, though actually it would be made before their gods, and people would reckon that their gods were involved in its fulfillment. (In differing from an OT covenant between God and people, a human agreement may be made between equals and may be more like a contract in that it is made solely for what people get out of it; there is no irrevocable commitment.) Indeed, the psalm sees this agreement as explicitly involving God: it is made "against you." Only here does the OT speak of making a covenant "against" someone. The peoples might see themselves as making plans against Israel, but the psalm knows they are thereby setting themselves against God and knows that this provides a powerful basis for appealing to God. Gods and peoples are working against Yhwh, as is explicit in (e.g.) Isa. 36–37. The resonances of the technical term "seal a covenant" would then suggest that the alliance is establishing a covenant that purports to counter the *real* covenant that Yhwh has sealed with Israel.[19]

In vv. 6–7 we begin to discover who the enemies are: the peoples who surround Judah on the east, south, west, and northwest, or to put it more simply, the peoples up and down Transjordan to the east and the Mediterranean coast to the west. "The tents of Edom" involves an archaism;

18. For the odd expression *lēb yaḥdāw*, one might expect *lēb ʾeḥād* ("[as] one mind"; cf. Jer. 32:39). *BHS* suggests *lēb yaḥad*, but this is hardly any easier.
19. Cf. Bruna Costacurta, "L'aggressione contro Dio," *Bib* 64 (1983): 518–41 (see 520).

"tents" can simply mean "dwellings" (e.g., Pss. 69:25 [26]; 84:10 [11]; 118:15; 120:5). It also involves a metonymy, as "dwellings" then refers to the people who live in them. So "the tents of Edom" refers to "the Edomites," the people who live southeast of Judah across the Jordan and who, after the exile, also occupy the southern half of the traditional territory of the clan of Judah. They often feature as enemies in the OT narrative, attacked by Israel or by Judah or attacking them. The Ishmaelites, people seen as descendants of Ishmael, are a hazier group within the OT but are referred to in a number of extrabiblical texts from the eighth and seventh centuries.[20] They are perhaps more nomadic and more literally tent-dwellers and are usually reckoned to live in the more desert regions east and southeast of Edom. One might have expected allusion to Midian here (cf. v. 9), but the Ishmaelites and Midianites overlapped in OT thinking (see Gen. 37:25–36; Judg. 8:22–28).

Moab is the region north of Edom and east of Judah, across the Dead Sea; the Moabites, too, often feature as attacking and attacked by Israel or Judah. The Hagrites in turn parallel the Ishmaelites as another tribe living in the desert region on the edge of Moab. Presumably they are thought of as closely related to the Ishmaelites, since Hagar was Ishmael's mother. Within the OT, they are referred to elsewhere only in connection with the time of Saul, though solely in a document that belongs to the Second Temple period and might be reflecting terms from that time (1 Chron. 5:10, 19–22).

The famous Gebal (cf. Ezek. 27:9) is an important city north of modern Beirut, usually known by its Greek name Byblos, and reference to this would pair well with the later reference to Tyre. But another Gebal was a mountainous territory in the area of Edom, south of the Dead Sea. This would link well with Ammon, to the north of Moab, east and northeast of the Dead Sea. The reference to Amalek then takes us to the south of Judah, where the Amalekites were a mainly nomadic tribe involved in conflicts with Israel in the period of the judges and the early monarchy (Judg. 3:13, in alliance with Moab and Ammon; Judg. 6:3, 33; 7:12, in alliance with Midian; 1 Sam. 15; 27:8–9; 30:1–20). In turn, Philistia lies to the southwest and west of Judah, while Tyre takes us to the far northwest. Ammon, Amalek, and Philistia, like Edom and Moab, appear from time to time as attackers or victims of Israel and Judah. David's successes included Edom, Moab, Ammon, Philistia, and Amalek (2 Sam. 8).

> [8]Assyria, too, has joined with them;
>   they have become the strength of the offspring of Lot. (Rise)

---

20. See E. A. Knauf, "Ishmaelites," in *Anchor Bible Dictionary*, ed. David Noel Freedman (New York: Doubleday, 1992), 3:513–20.

Assyria sets the list of foes on a broader canvas and immediately suggests that the context is the century of Assyrian hegemony from the late
eighth to the late seventh century, though we know of no occasion when
Assyria supported an attack by these other peoples. A more plausible
historical possibility is that "Assyria" is used to denote the imperial power
of the fifth century, Persia, as in Ezra 6:22, with Philistia represented by
Ashdod in the time of Ezra and Nehemiah. In this period, Judah might
feel that the peoples around put pressure on it with the connivance of
the imperial power, though Ezra–Nehemiah are inclined rather to picture
Persia as buttressing Judah in its disputes with its neighbors. Assyria
also makes the number of foes a round ten, which might be the point.
But the psalm does not draw attention to that (contrast, e.g., Dan. 7:7;
also numerical sayings such as those in Amos 1–2), and thus it is likely
a coincidence. The psalm refers in quasi-concrete terms to the experience Judah had from time to time of being under pressure from those
peoples and from the imperial power, which has become the "strength"
of these other peoples. The list of peoples thus refers to enemies from
varying periods. Literally their "strength" is their "arm." It is a worrying
image. It is with the arm that people can be delivered (44:3 [4]; 77:15
[16]; 79:11; 89:10, 13, 21 [11, 14, 22]), but this strong arm is working
against them.

The closing description of these local foes as "the offspring of Lot"
applies to Moab and Ammon in particular but draws attention to the
fact that most of the peoples mentioned are part of Israel's extended
family.

83:9–11. The psalm moves from the long lament or protest to an even
longer plea in vv. 9–18, which gives concreteness to the plea with which
the psalm opened. This first subsection closes with some emphasis in a
long line incorporating the names of some of Yhwh's victims.

> 9Deal with them like Midian, like Sisera, like Jabin,
>   at the Wadi Kishon,
> 10Who perished at En-dor,
>   became manure for the ground.
> 11Treat them—their nobles like Oreb and Zeeb,
>   all their leaders like Zebah and Zalmunna.

Israel did battle with Midian in Num. 31, but here the further analo-
gies come from events recorded in Judg. 4–8, so the reference to Midian will rather allude to the story in Judg. 6–8, whose victims included
the men named in v. 11. Judges describes Oreb and Zeeb as "officers"
(*śar*), Zebah and Zalmunna as "kings." Here the victims become "nobles"
(*nādîb*) and "leaders" (*nāsîk*).

579

The story of Sisera and Jabin at the Wadi Kishon comes in Judg. 4–5. En-dor is between the Wadi Kishon and Mount Tabor, where the Israelite forces gathered for the battle and where Zebah and Zalmunna slaughtered people, though the name perhaps comes from the story in 1 Sam. 28 (cf. also Josh. 17:11). After the battle near there, foreign forces were killed and their bodies abandoned; there was no one to bury them, so their corpses simply rotted.

Yhwh gave Israel spectacular victory on these occasions. The verses take these acts of God as a pattern for their prayer, seeking for Yhwh to act in the same way again.

83:12–15. The second subsection of the plea moves from the prosaic language of vv. 9–11 to language that reflects traditional ways of speaking theologically about God's action.

> [12]The people who have said, "We will possess for ourselves
>   God's pastures"—
> [13]My God, treat them like a whirl,
>   like stubble before the wind.

The change in imagery begins in v. 12, which I take as the beginning of this subsection.[21] The enemies are portrayed as aiming to take over the land in the way Israel did at the beginning; *yāraš* (enter into possession) is almost a technical term in this connection (e.g., 44:3 [4]; Deut. 4:1, 5, 14, 22, 26). These are peoples, the OT elsewhere affirms, to whom God allocated their own lands to possess, and God told Israel not to dispossess them (e.g., Deut. 2:1–23). But they now aim to take over not merely Israel's land but also Yhwh's land. As motivation to Yhwh to act, the psalm continues to argue that the people's wrongdoing relates more to Yhwh than to Israel. This land is Yhwh's "possession" (*yěruššâ*), which Yhwh "caused us to possess," Jehoshaphat reminds Yhwh when people from Moab, Ammon, Seir (i.e., Edom), and Aram invade Judah (2 Chron. 20:11). But the psalm puts the point in a distinctive way in referring to this land not as Yhwh's possession but as Yhwh's "pastures."[22] These are the pastures that Yhwh waters (Ps. 65:12 [13]), the grassy pastures where Yhwh rests the sheep (23:2). The foes think these are going to become pastures whose growth they will enjoy.

The psalm sets an alternative prospect before them. These pastures grow hay for animals to eat or wheat for human use. After the harvest

---

21. It is also signaled by the *'ăšer* ("[the people] who") with which v. 12 begins, which is unnecessary in poetry as a straightforward relative.

22. Sym's "abode" suggests linking *ně'ôt* with *nāweh* rather than *nāwâ*; perhaps cf. LXX's "sanctuary" ("altar" in some MSS); Tg's "choice land" and Jerome's "beauty" suggest a link with BDB's *nāwâ*.

the wheat is winnowed to separate the grain from the chaff or stubble, and the latter is allowed to blow away in the wind. That provides a standard image for destruction (e.g., Jer. 13:24). I take "like a whirl, like stubble" as a poetic way of saying "like a whirl of stubble," the expressions being divided between the cola to make the parallelism work (cf. Isa. 17:13).[23] Verse 13 introduces a first-person speaker for the only time in the psalm. The parallel with Ps. 2 might suggest that this is the king or another such leader. Either way, "my God" reflects the suppliant's personal claim on Yhwh.

> [14]Like a fire that burns a forest,
>   like a flame that sets mountains ablaze,
> [15]So may you pursue them with your tempest,
>   terrify them with your storm.

The image becomes more threatening. Like brush, stubble itself is easily combustible and may catch fire accidentally or be set on fire. This adds to its power as a metaphor for divine punishment (e.g., Isa. 5:24). But the psalm jumps to a much more frightening form of fire, the sort that engulfs not merely a meadow but also a huge forest such as covers mountains, like the forests of cedar that cover the mountains of Lebanon.[24]

And it is Yhwh who is directly compared with that flaming fire. Amos warned that Yhwh might come like fire on the household of Joseph and consume Bethel with no one to quench it (Amos 5:6), and when Jerusalem fell, Yhwh indeed "burned against Jacob like a flaming fire, consuming all around" (Lam. 2:3). The psalm asks for this to be the experience of Israel's attackers.

Then once more the imagery changes, from fire to storm. There is again continuity, with the talk of wind in v. 13, but a storming tempest is a much more fearful reality than the wind that (helpfully) blows away stubble. When a hurricane hits the southern or southeastern United States, people sometimes flee before it, hoping to get far enough away to escape its force. The psalm prays for a hurricane that the enemy cannot escape and thus be in a position to regroup and attack once more. In both verses the first colon would be quite enough to convey the psalm's

---

23. Cf. the use of *galgal* (from *gālal*, "roll") to denote a whirling wind in 77:18 [19]. TNIV has "tumbleweed," a "plant forming a globular bush that breaks off in late summer and is rolled about by the wind" (*Concise Oxford Dictionary*, s.v. "tumbleweed"). Rashi takes it to mean "thistledown" (cf. NJPS), which behaves in a similar way.

24. The cola are neatly parallel, abca'b'c': two *k* expressions, two third-person sg. f. yiqtol verbs (one qal, one piel), and two objects for these verbs, with the second clarifying the first (the forest is on the mountains) and the first anticipatorily clarifying the second (it is because they are forested that the mountains can burn).

meaning; the restatement in different words in the second colon adds to the prayer's force.[25] Once again v. 15 recalls Isa. 17:13.

83:16–18. The third subsection of the prayer moves to its aim, which might be a surprise after the pleas in vv. 9–15.[26] Given that it is Yhwh that the enemy has attacked, it is the recognition of Yhwh that the prayer seeks through the pleas in vv. 9–15.

> [16]Fill their faces with humiliation
>   so that they may seek help from your name, Yhwh.

For a moment, however, the attackers' annihilation is out of the picture as v. 16 confronts us with just one paradox, that humiliation is the way to blessing. "Humiliation" (*qālôn*) links with a number of words suggesting "to be slight/trifling," and to be treated as such (*qālal, qālâ*). These thus contrast with words that suggest exaltedness or majesty; EVV often have "pride" for such words (see esp. Isa. 2:6–22). The enemies are people whose attitude, which appears in their faces, is that they are really powerful and impressive, and they are not wrong, except when they see themselves as majestically impressive over against Yhwh. The first colon thus asks for Yhwh to make the truth dawn. They need to see themselves as unimpressive over against Yhwh. But the aim of that is positive. When they see this, it has the potential to open them to *seek help from Yhwh, specifically from Yhwh's *name. This did not happen when enemies were defeated in Judg. 4–8, but the psalm looks beyond their mere defeat to this turning to Yhwh. Such turning will indicate that they have seen the error in their aggressive confrontation of Yhwh. So it is for the truth's sake, for Yhwh's sake, that the psalm looks for this seeking, even if it will also be a blessing for the attackers themselves.

> [17]May they be shamed and terrified forever,
>   may they be disgraced and perish,
> [18]So that they may acknowledge that you,
>   whose name is Yhwh alone,
>   are the Most High over all the earth.

25. Again the powerful effect of the prayer is enhanced by the close parallelism, abcc′b′: after the "so," two second-person singular yiqtol verbs (one qal, one piel, as in v. 14), with third-person m. pl. suffix, form an envelope around two *b* expressions (like the two *k* expressions in v. 14) with second-person m. sg. suffix. The second verb makes explicit the panic involved in fleeing from pursuit.

26. Because of this tension, one might see vv. 16b–17a, 18 as later additions (so, e.g., Seybold, *Psalmen*, 328), but this hardly solves anything—both because if a redactor could live with the tension within vv. 16–18, so could an original author, and because the eventual form of the psalm still invites our understanding.

Verse 17 then expands on v. 16a, and v. 18 expands on v. 16b, both adding emphasis. Shame and disgrace are worse than humiliation. Humiliation suggests having self-importance taken away; shame and disgrace suggest having definite opprobrium and ignominy heaped on them. Humiliation is a corrective; shame and disgrace could be also a punishment, though v. 18 will point in another direction. Alongside "be shamed" and "be disgraced," and going beyond these, is "be terrified forever" and "perish."[27] The first verb picks up from v. 15, and the second spells out its implication once more. In other words, terror is not merely a reaction to shame but also an anticipation of death (cf. 6:2–3 [3–4]; 48:5 [6]; 104:29; Exod. 15:15). The plea linking shame and disgrace with terror and death stands in tension with the preceding plea linking humiliation with seeking help from Yhwh.

A tricolon closes the psalm.[28] Again, it goes beyond what Yhwh brought about in Judg. 4–8. *Acknowledging Yhwh parallels and restates "seeking help from Yhwh's name," as "seeking help from Yhwh" implied the acknowledgment that v. 18 anticipates. The difference is that "seeking help from Yhwh" put the focus on what people hope to gain from acknowledging Yhwh, while "acknowledging Yhwh" puts the focus on the way Yhwh is honored when people turn to Yhwh for help instead of reckoning that they can do fine on their own or with the help of other deities.

The unmarked relative clause that forms the middle colon looks odd to Christian eyes. Of course Yhwh is the only God whose name is Yhwh. But such statements, which are common especially in Isa. 40–55, involve an ellipse. To say "You are Yhwh" is in effect to say "You are God," because Yhwh is the only real God. So to say "Your *name alone is Yhwh" is to say "You, Yhwh, are the only God." The last colon then restates that point. Being Yhwh and thus God alone means being the

---

27. Thus the parallelism in v. 17 is complex. The whole verse is parallel to v. 16a. Then the two cola are parallel, abca′b′ (we should perhaps take the terrible "forever" at the center of the line as applying to both cola). And further, each of the two cola is internally parallel, with each second verb taking further the first verb: not only shame but dismay, not only disgrace but death.

28. GKC 144l takes the middle clause as a noun clause with two subjects, "that you—your name is Yhwh alone" (cf. NJPS), but there are no other examples of a noun clause working thus, and the construction of the whole verse is then jumpy. I rather take the middle clause as an unmarked relative clause (cf. TNIV, NRSV). There is also disagreement about the division into cola in this verse. MT suggests "so that they may acknowledge/that you whose name is Yhwh alone/are the Most High," 1-4-2, which looks implausible. TNIV suggests "so that they may acknowledge that you/whose name is Yhwh/alone are the Most High," 2-2-3; but lĕbad usually follows the word it qualifies (e.g., 51:4 [6]; 71:16; 72:18; 86:10; 148:13). So I follow TNIV for the distinction between the first and second colon, but MT for the distinction between the second and third. *BHS* suggests that "so that they may acknowledge" should be treated as the last word in v. 17; v. 18 then becomes a bicolon.

*Most High, because there is no other Most High. Yhwh is not merely a tin-pot Israelite god, as Israel's attackers might think (see the polemic in the story in Isa. 36–37). Yhwh is on high, and Yhwh's exaltation extends to the entire world. The aim of the action that the psalm seeks is to have this acknowledged as even peoples such as the ones listed in vv. 6–8 in their defeat turn to Yhwh for help and acknowledge Yhwh. Instead of their eliminating Israel's name (v. 4), they will acknowledge Yhwh's name.[29] The twofold occurrence of the actual name in the closing section—both drawing attention to the fact that this is indeed God's *name*—contrasts with the references to *'ĕlōhîm* and *'ēl* in v. 1 (see also vv. 12, 13). They also make for a transition from Pss. 42–83 (where the name Yhwh is infrequent) to the rest of the Psalter (where it resumes its usual prominence).[30]

Theological Implications

Psalm 83 is a reaction to "aggression against God"[31] or resistance to God's rule, of the kind that Ps. 2 also responds to. Thus "in the psalm Israel shouts at God finally to do something for God's own 'survival.'"[32] It works by asking that Yhwh should fulfill the declarations that a prophet such as Isaiah had made (Isa. 17:12–14).

It is this that generates what seems to modern readers a strange tension that is a common feature of the OT. The psalmist wants people (a) to be killed, (b) to be humiliated, (c) to turn to Yhwh. How can this be so? For instance, how can people seek help from or acknowledge Yhwh when they have perished?[33] Are the people who seek help from and acknowledge Yhwh different from the people who are humiliated and killed? They are then people who see that or hear of it and react in an appropriate way. The NIVI assumes this in v. 16b and KJV in v. 18. But the translations of v. 16 and vv. 17–18 must surely be similar, and it is hard to reckon that the subjects of these third-person verbs keep changing through vv. 16–18. This objection also applies to the idea that the people who have

29. Hossfeld and Zenger, *Psalms 2*, 339.
30. Hossfeld and Zenger (ibid., 345–46) emphasize the psalm's significance at the close of the "Elohistic" psalms and of the Asaph psalms.
31. Cf. Costacurta, "L'aggressione contro Dio."
32. Erich Zenger, in *The God of Israel and the Nations*, ed. Norbert Lohfink and Erich Zenger (Collegeville: Liturgical Press, 2000), 150.
33. NRSV and TNIV obscure the tension by translating the opening verb "Let them know," which in English could more easily mean that Yhwh's putting them to death has this effect; it demonstrates that Yhwh is Lord. This surely misrepresents the Hebrew. The construction is the same as v. 16b, which v. 18 parallels, with *w* plus a yiqtol verb, which NRSV and TNIV rightly translate "so that."

recourse/acknowledge are survivors of the annihilation for which the psalm has prayed, which also requires an annihilation that leaves survivors and is thus not an annihilation. Another approach is to reckon that the victims turn to Yhwh in vain as they die; Ps. 18:41 [42] allows that the answer to the seeking in v. 16 might be "No."[34] And indeed the question whether Yhwh will respond is secondary to the importance of the recognition implied in the seeking. Yet this seems to underplay the significance of the expressions in vv. 16b and 18a.

It is best to leave the tension and recognize here that the psalm presupposes that all three aims are desirable, even though they are in tension with each other. Death is desirable because that constitutes proper punishment for the attackers' affront to Yhwh and also means secure deliverance for their victims. Humiliation is desirable because that implies a proper public demonstration of the wrongness in their stance and one that they themselves recognize; death does not necessarily bring that about. And positive acknowledgment of Yhwh is desirable because that constitutes their proper positive recognition of the right basis for conducting their lives, though it also brings blessing to them. But the concern with acknowledgment of Yhwh has Yhwh's honor in mind more than the plotters. They have been declining to acknowledge Yhwh; the suppliant wants them to do so, to bring proper glory to Yhwh. Killing them without that acknowledgment fails to achieve what is necessary. "The ultimate goal of God's terrible judgments . . . is that his enemies, too, will be made ashamed and will seek him, that they will turn to him in penitence and will come to realize that power and glory upon the whole earth belong alone to God."[35] Yhwh may not always be able to achieve all three aims (shame, punishment, and recognition), and on different occasions will have to decide which should have priority.

34. *Midrash on Psalms*, 2:63.
35. Weiser, *Psalms*, 564.

Psalm 84

The Double Good Fortune
of the Trusting Person

Translation

The leader's. On/concerning the Gittite. The Korahites'. Composition.

¹How much loved is your dwelling,¹
    Yhwh Armies!
²My whole being craved, yes exhausted itself,
    for Yhwh's courtyards.
My heart and my body, they resound
    to the living God.
³Yes, a bird: it has found a home,²
    a pigeon [has found] a nest for itself,
Where it has put its young,
    near³ your altars, Yhwh Armies.
My king and my God,
    ⁴the good fortune of people who stay in your house,
    who can again praise you. (Rise)

⁵The good fortune of the person who finds strength in you;
    the highways are in their mind,

---

1. On the pl. "dwelling," see 43:3.
2. I have translated this colon in light of the fact that the subj. comes before the verb.
3. I follow Tg and Syr in taking this as the prep. *'et*, rather than following LXX and Jerome in taking it as the sign of the obj., depending on "found."

[6]the people who pass through Balsam Vale.[4]
They [MT]/he [LXX] will make it a spring[5]—
    yes, the first rain will envelop it with blessings.
[7]They will walk from rampart to rampart;
    he will appear to God [MT]/the God of gods will appear [LXX] in
    Zion.

[8]Yhwh, God Armies,
    listen to my plea;
    give ear, God of Jacob. (Rise)
[9]Look at our shield, God,
    behold the face of your anointed.

[10]Because a day in your courtyards is better than a thousand,
    I chose being at the threshold of my God's house—
[Better] than abiding in faithless tents,
    [11]because Yhwh God is a sun and shield.
Yhwh gives favor and honor;
    he does not withhold good things for people who walk with integrity.
[12]Yhwh Armies,
    the good fortune of the person who trusts in you!

Interpretation

Like Pss. 46; 48; and 76, this has been designated a "Zion song,"[6] though that is not a formal categorization; Ps. 84 is very different in its nature and aim from those other Zion songs. Among other things, it is concerned with the relationship between meeting Yhwh on Zion and knowing Yhwh's presence away from there.[7] Like Pss. 42–43, it is also the first of a sequence of Korahite psalms (Pss. 84–85, 87–88),[8] and like Pss. 42–43 it expresses enthusiasm for the "house" or "dwelling" (plural) of "the living God," with its "altars" (though that was singular in Ps. 43) and with "appearing" there. But again its differences are as striking as its similarity. Whereas Pss. 42–43 represent the prayer of someone unable to get to the temple, Ps. 84 implies worshippers who are in Jerusalem or at least are free to go there for the festivals. That difference is signaled

4. On the const. followed by a prep., see GKC 130a; *IBHS* 9.6b.
5. LXX and Syr imply *māʿôn* (refuge) for MT's *maʿān* (spring).
6. So Gunkel, *Psalmen*, 368.
7. Cf. Terrien, *Psalms*, 598.
8. On its place in the Korahite psalms and in relation to Ps. 85, see, e.g., Hossfeld and Zenger, *Psalms 2*, 356–57; Pierre Auffret, "Qu'elles sont aimables, tes demeures!" *BZ* 38 (1994): 29–43 (see 42–43); and on its links with Ps. 83 and other preceding psalms, see Cole, *Shape and Message of Book III*, 115–25.

by the contrasting ways the psalms begin. Psalm 42 speaks of straining and thirsting for God, using yiqtol verbs. Psalm 84 also speaks of longing, but uses qatal verbs; the longing has been fulfilled. In Pss. 42–43, praise is a reality of the past and the future but not of the present. In Ps. 84 heart and flesh resound to the living God. Here there are no tears, no taunts, no downcastness, no breakers and waves, no enemies. The nearest thing there is to sadness relates to the fact that one cannot stay here forever, though the psalm makes a point of affirming that Yhwh's presence and activity are not confined to the temple. The regret, or the psalm's mixed feelings, and the references to a journey suggest that Ps. 84 expresses the worship of people who make pilgrimage for Passover, Pentecost, or Sukkot; the reference to the first rain (v. 6) would suggest the last. The psalm's not having a place with the pilgrimage psalms, Pss. 120–34, points to its distinctive dynamic, its concern with the relationship between the preciousness of a visit to the temple and the realities of the way one must spend the rest of one's life.

That dynamic suggests one should designate it a psalm of trust rather than a praise psalm, and this is confirmed not only by the prayer the suppliant incorporates (vv. 8–9) but also and more explicitly by the closing line. Although the psalm expresses itself in "I" form, it focuses on a pilgrimage that is essentially communal, and one should likely assume that the whole congregation uses the psalm, as is the case with modern metrical versions of the psalm such as "How Lovely Is Your Dwelling Place."[9]

Verses 1–4 express the pilgrim's present enthusiasm, addressing God. Verses 5–7 look back to the journey and reflect on it, addressing the self or other people. Verses 8–9 address God on behalf of the king. Verses 10–12 revert to present enthusiasm addressed to God. The three praise or trust sections all begin or end with a comment on the "good fortune" of people who praise God, find strength in God, and trust in God. The first, third, and fourth sections all address "Yhwh [God] Armies." The reference to the king suggests that the psalm comes from the monarchic period; since it does not speak as if alluding to a future king, a messiah, it would be odd to imagine this reference being added in the postmonarchic period.[10]

The leader's. On/concerning the Gittite. The Korahites'. Composition.

Heading. See glossary and (for the phrase about the Gittite) the comment on Ps. 81.

84:1–4. The psalm thus begins with six lines of praise about how marvelous it is to be in the temple courts.

9. Cf. Gerstenberger, *Psalms*, 2:123.
10. Against Hossfeld and Zenger, *Psalms 2*, 356.

¹How much loved is your dwelling,
  Yhwh Armies!

The EVV's "lovely" is misleading; *yādîd* refers to something or someone who actually is beloved (e.g., 60:5 [7]). It is a comment on the attitude people take to the temple of Yhwh *Armies, on "how much I love to be in them."[11] It is not a merely objective statement about the temple itself, though it certainly implies one. The psalm will go on to convey the nature and basis of this love.

²My whole being craved, yes exhausted itself,
  for Yhwh's courtyards.
My heart and my body, they resound
  to the living God.

The line stands in parallelism with v. 1 and spells out its significance. The keen longing of the *person expresses the belovedness of the temple in a more overtly subjective way, while the reference to the "courtyards" of the temple complex (see 65:4 [5]) expands on the reference to Yhwh's dwelling. The average home would have a courtyard where people ate and talked and worked; this dwelling with its multiplicity of courtyards is more a palace than an ordinary house.

"Craved" (*kāsap*) is a very rare verb (see 17:12; Gen. 31:30; Job 14:15),[12] while "exhausted itself" (*kālâ*) is much more common (e.g., 69:3 [4]; 71:9; 73:26; 90:7). Both are forceful in meaning, the more so in combination. The first suggests greed or keenness or desperation. The second implies that the person was consumed by this feeling. Together, they suggest that the person was torn apart by the longing.[13] Out of the context, the qatals could be taken to imply a longing and fainting that continue into the present, but it would have been natural to use the yiqtol for that (e.g., 17:12; Job 14:15 for the first; Job 11:20; 17:5 for the second). In the context, it makes sense to take these verbs to refer to the intense, consuming longing that the pilgrim had felt in looking forward to coming to Yhwh's courtyards (see on 65:4 [5]).

The second line once again stands in formal parallelism with the first.[14] "My *heart and my body" spells out the implications of "my whole

11. Qimchi; cf. also Rashi.
12. The qal and niphal seem similar in meaning.
13. Cf. Kraus, *Psalms 60–150*, 168; Robert Benedetto, "Psalm 84," *Int* 51 (1997): 57–61 (see 59).
14. The word order tightens the formal parallelism as in each line the double expression comes first: "craved and also exhausted itself my person for Yhwh's courtyards; my heart and my body resound to the living God."

589

being" (see 63:1 [2]); Jerome notes that it is quite something to have the inner and outer person in perfect harmony.[15] "Living God" (see 42:2 [3]) makes explicit something left implicit in "Yhwh's courtyards": the worshipper was excited at the prospect not merely of being in a place but also of meeting with a person. The fact that ordinary Israelites stood in the courtyards but not in the temple proper did not mean they were not thereby in Yhwh's presence. The courtyard of someone's home is where they would welcome visitors. The most marked and significant contrast in the parallelism lies in the move from qatal to yiqtol verbs as the second line describes how things are in the present.[16] The pilgrim's consuming longing has been fulfilled; now it is possible to *resound, to make a noise, with enthusiasm.

> [3a–d]Yes, a bird: it has found a home,
>   a pigeon [has found] a nest for itself,
> Where it has put its young,
>   near your altars, Yhwh Armies.

The verse as a whole makes yet another parallel statement. It is probably not merely making a general observation about how birds nest in the environs of the temple,[17] though it may presuppose such an observation. Metaphorically, the worshipper *is* a bird (cf. 11:1; 102:7 [8]; 124:7), and this is a statement about that particular "bird." A bird is a small, defenseless creature, yet in its capacity for flight it can escape danger. The word *ṣippôr* does not denote sparrows in particular, as LXX implies here (cf. EVV), but small birds in general (cf. 8:8 [9]; 148:10; Jerome, Aq). It is likely onomatopoeic, suggesting their chirping. In the manner of parallelism, *dĕrôr* then seems to make the bird's identity more specific, as at its only other appearance in the OT (Prov. 26:2), though identifying what bird it refers to is a matter of guesswork. The EVV have "swallow," but as a bird nesting in the trees in the temple grounds or in its walls, "pigeon" (LXX) or "sparrow" (Jerome, Aq) is more likely (Tg has words for pigeon or dove in both cola).[18] "Nest" then also makes "home" more specific.

The second line completes the first, initially by further spelling out the implications of "home" and "nest." It is not clear whether we should

---

15. *Homilies*, 1:120; cf. Cassiodorus, *Psalms*, 2:314–15; Calvin, *Psalms*, 3:354–55. In contrast, Luther is bemused by this line (*First Lectures*, 2:137).

16. Cf. Weiser, *Psalms*, 564; Mowinckel, *Psalms in Israel's Worship*, 1:6. Oddly, LXX has present-tense verbs in v. 2a and an aorist verb in v. 2b.

17. It would then be a gnomic qatal; cf. *TTH* 12; JM 112d.

18. See M. J. Mulder, "Herbert Duifhuis (1531–1581) et l'exégèse du Psaume lxxxiv 4," *OtSt* 15 (1969): 227–50 (*duifhuis* = pigeon house, dovecote).

allegorize the reference to the young, though perhaps the pilgrim speaks as one who has brought family or community there for the festival. Their "nest" is specifically near the temple altars, of which there were normally two, the sacrificial altar and the incense altar.[19] A link between birds and altars suggests to Tg that the birds are there for sacrifice, which makes this not so reassuring a home for them, and in any case the altars were fiery and smoky places such as birds would hardly want to be too near.[20] Perhaps "altars" is a synecdoche, standing for the temple as a whole. But the context may suggest that the psalm has in mind the altar as a place of refuge (e.g., 1 Kings 1:50–51); see on v. 5. The fact that the one who lives at the temple is Yhwh *Armies (cf. v. 1) further underlines the safety of being there.

> ³ᵉMy king and my God,
> ⁴the good fortune of people who stay in your house,
> who can again praise you. (Rise)

A tricolon closes off the first section of the psalm.[21] Once again Yhwh Armies is not merely "a great king over all the earth" (Ps. 47:2, 7 [3, 8]; cf. 48:2 [3]) and not merely "our king" (47:6 [7]; 89:18 [19]) but also "my king" (44:4 [5]; 68:24 [25]; 74:12). While this would fit a worshipper who is himself the king and rejoices (or not) in the fact that there is a king above him, it equally fits the position of an ordinary Israelite who is God's servant and knows that "my king" is committed to protect his servants. Likewise Yhwh is not merely "God" but also "my God," with similar implications (cf. 71:4, 12; 83:13 [14]; 86:2). For the combination "my king and my God" in this connection, see 5:2 [3].

The *good fortune of people who stay in Yhwh's house thus consists in the safety and protection they have that arise from living near their protector. The EVV take these to be people who "live" or "dwell" in Yhwh's house. Since the pilgrim is here in Jerusalem for the festival but then has to go home, these are people such as priests and Levites, who spend considerable time in the temple complex, and/or by extension other people living in Jerusalem who can spend time there every day if they wish. They can thus "still" *praise God; they can do it again

19. See Keel, *Symbolism*, 146–49, though he concludes that the pl. here is honorific.
20. Briggs, *Psalms*, 2:226–27.
21. MT apparently has five cola in v. 3, dividing the verse after the fourth. NRSV takes the five as a tricolon followed by a bicolon, but a tricolon would more often close off the section, and I thus understand the first four cola in v. 3 as two bicola and take the last clause with v. 4. That also makes for a parallel between vv. 3e–4 and v. 12, closing off the entire psalm: each has an address to Yhwh introducing a declaration of blessing.

tomorrow, and the next day, and the day after that.[22] For the moment, then, the worshipper's statement would be rather wistful, though v. 5 will move in another direction. But the verb *yāšab* often means "stay" or "tarry" "for a limited or indeff[inite] time,"[23] which could apply to the pilgrim in Jerusalem for the festival who for a few days can keep coming back there. "Staying" in shelters for a week (Lev. 23:42) did not imply spending every moment there.[24]

84:5–7. The praise continues as the psalm speaks of the more regular experience of someone who does not live in Jerusalem. The tricolon with which vv. 1–4 ends is complemented by another to open vv. 5–7.[25]

> [5]The good fortune of the person who finds strength in you;
>   the highways are in their mind,
>   [6a]the people who pass through Balsam Vale.

If v. 4 was wistful, its wistfulness is qualified if not removed by the acknowledgment that actually Yhwh's protection is not confined to people who live in Jerusalem. Admittedly vv. 5–6a express this allusively. First, while *ʿôz* often means simply *strength, it frequently appears in contexts that refer to finding a "refuge" (NJPS's rendering here). That fits the metaphor of the bird in v. 3, who finds refuge in the temple. In turn, while "highways" is just an ordinary word for a highway or route, either within a city or in the open country, the context suggests that it refers to the route of a journey to Jerusalem or even a special pilgrimage way. Thus NRSV adds the gloss "to Zion" and NJPS "[pilgrim] highways," though TNIV's actual translation "pilgrimage" makes the word more specific than it is.[26] The line begins to suggest a point that will be elaborated: people who keep in their *mind the fact that they will be going to Jerusalem for the festival are thereby reminded not only that Yhwh dwells there but also that the Yhwh who dwells there is the real

---

22. LXX "forever" (cf. EVV) implies *ʿad* but MT has *ʿōd*: cf. 42:5, 11 [6, 12]; 43:5; 74:9; 77:7 [8]; 78:17, 32; 83:4 [5]; 88:5 [6]; and esp. 49:9 [10] where, significantly, an expression meaning "forever" is added to make that point.

23. BDB 442b.

24. Keel takes up another frequent meaning of the verb (*Symbolism*, 314) and translates "who sit in your house," this being a possible posture for spending time in Yhwh's presence there (2 Sam. 7:18); that description, too, could then apply to a pilgrim.

25. I follow Briggs (*Psalms*, 2:227) in linking v. 6a with what precedes.

26. The root *sālal* can mean "lift up [praise]" (68:4 [5]), and G. R. Driver suggests "songs of praise" for the noun here ("Textual and Linguistic Problems of the Book of Psalms," *HTR* 29 [1936]: 171–95 [see 187–88]); cf. Dahood, *Psalms*, 2:281. LXX *anabaseis* hardly suggests *maʿălôt* for *měsillôt* (so, e.g., Seybold, *Psalmen*, 331); for *maʿălôt*, LXX would surely have used *anabathmoi*, as in Pss. 120–34. It more likely reflects an awareness of the root *sālal* (cf. A. Robinson, "Three Suggested Interpretations in Ps. lxxxiv," *VT* 24 [1974]: 378–81 [see 378]). Tg's *rwḥṣnwtʾ* suggests places of security and safety.

God who is also a strength and protection to people who live far away. The fact that Yhwh dwells in Jerusalem does not mean that people who live in Hebron or Lachish are beyond Yhwh's sphere of influence. The journey to Jerusalem to meet with Yhwh there actually reminds people of that. So it is not so bad not to be among the people who actually live in Jerusalem and can worship in the temple all the time.

The people who are "passing through" are presumably the people who are on this journey to Jerusalem, though the prosaic detail continues to be unclear, partly because v. 6a implies a paronomasia.

While EVV simply transliterate *'ēmeq habbākā'* as Baka Vale, *bākā'* is a word for a tree or plant, conventionally the balsam tree, though the identification is uncertain. Further, Balsam Vale is otherwise unknown as a place name, and balsam trees are otherwise mentioned only in 2 Sam. 5:22–24 and 1 Chron. 14:13–16, where they are a noteworthy feature of the Vale of Rephaim, west of Jerusalem on the way to Philistia. If one was to locate the valley geographically, one might then identify it with Rephaim or with a valley near there.[27] But "balsam" (*bākā'*) sounds the same as the verb "weep" (*bākâ*; perhaps the balsam "weeps" its resin). Thus Balsam Vale is also Weeping Vale;[28] hence the expression "Vale of Tears." In 2 Sam. 5:22–24 and 1 Chron. 14:13–16 it was a vale where people likely wept when they were the victims of Philistine raids on their crops. This event might be in the worshipper's mind in using an expression that suggests weeping. Perhaps equally in view were analogous pressures from other peoples from whom the worshippers might need protection and/or anxiety about whether the rains will come as fall approaches.[29]

---

⁶ᵇ⁻ᶜThey [MT]/he [LXX] will make it a spring—
yes, the first rain will envelop it with blessings.

In MT, v. 6b then perhaps suggests the mental attitude that people will take to Balsam Vale: in their minds they will turn this place that suggests weeping into a place that suggests water in a more positive sense. On some identifications of the balsam tree, it is characteristic of dry places, and this would add a further resonance. The second colon makes that more specific. If we may imagine the pilgrims coming to Jerusalem for

27. See David Yallin, "Emek ha-Bakha: Bekhaim," *Journal of the Palestine Oriental Society* 3 (1929): 191–92; R. Tournay, "Le Psaume lxxxiv et le ritual israélite des pèlerinage au temple," *RB* 54 (1947): 521–33 (see 524).

28. LXX, Jerome, Aq, Sym; and also Tg, which thus takes this to refer to Gehenna.

29. Goulder (*Psalms of the Sons of Korah*, 40–41) sees Baka Vale as the valley near the town of Baka in Western Galilee (see Josephus, *Jewish War* 3.3.1); this fits with the theory that Ps. 84 originally related to pilgrimages to Dan.

Sukkot in September–October, then the land they come through would likely be withered and dry. But they come in the hope that Yhwh will soon grant the gift of rain, and the landscape will be transformed (not because anything will grow immediately, but because plowing and sowing will become possible). For what remains of the nations after the last great battle, Zech. 14:16–17 associates the gift of rain with pilgrimage to Jerusalem, and it would not be surprising if that reflects a traditional link for Israel itself. It is as people put pilgrimage, worship, and prayer first that they find this blessing of rain, probably not while they are on the journey or when they are in Jerusalem, but hopefully not too long after they get home. Then rain will wrap or envelop (ʿāṭâ) the vale with blessings. Further, in the context of reference to rain and in parallelism with "spring," in a second paronomasia blessings (bĕrākôt) makes one think of the pools (bĕrēkôt) that will result from the rain. They will not be in themselves any use, at least until their water can be diverted somewhere else, but they will be a promise of blessings to come when the crops grow. "Blessings" also makes one think of Blessing Vale, not so far from Rephaim, which marks the site of a stupendous deliverance from attack by overwhelming Moabite, Ammonite, and other forces (2 Chron. 20:26).

The LXX has Yhwh as the subject of the verbs, which makes another profound theological statement. Then LXX, Jerome, Sym, Syr, and Tg (not Aq) nicely understand *môreh* to mean not "early rain" but "teacher" (either meaning is possible in different contexts).[30]

> ⁷They will walk from rampart to rampart;
>   he will appear to God [MT]/the God of gods will appear [LXX] in Zion.

The psalm moves on to describe the goal of the pilgrims' journey, when they are able to walk around the strong places or ramparts (NJPS) of Jerusalem.[31] The psalm thus recalls the invitation to such a walk in 48:13 [14], which also refers to Jerusalem's "rampart." Such a walk re-

30. Barr comments that by the end of v. 5 the LXX translator has "got himself thoroughly lost" (*CP* 249).

31. The word *ḥayil* can refer both to "might" in an abstract sense (59:11 [12]; 60:12 [14]; 76:5 [6]) and to something embodying might, such as wealth (49:6, 10 [7, 11]; 62:10 [11]; 73:12) or an army (33:16; 136:15); A. Anderson (*Psalms*, 2:605) suggests that the term denotes the swelling of the ranks of pilgrims as they near the city. In light of its understanding of *môreh*, Tg nicely takes the first such "army" as gathered in the temple, whence the faithful go to the second, the house of study; and God sees this labor in the Torah (v. 7b). But *ḥēl* can denote a rampart (48:13 [14]), and this fits well; it may require us to repoint *ḥayil*, but just as *ḥēl* is used with the meaning "army," which attaches to *ḥayil*, it would not be surprising if some occurrences of *ḥayil* had the meaning more characteristic of the rarer *ḥēl*.

minds the walkers of the great deeds of Yhwh in looking after the city and its people.[32]

In the second colon, the third-person singular (cf. TNIV, "each appears") complements the earlier third-person plural, as in v. 5 (but in the reverse order).[33] The second colon actually indicates the ultimate goal of the journey; compare TNIV "till." Appearing before Yhwh is the obligation of all Israelites for the three pilgrimage festivals, according to Exod. 23:17.[34] The LXX and Aq, however, suggest "the God of gods will appear in Zion,"[35] which also makes good sense as a statement of that ultimate goal, to see as well as to be seen. The verb refers to Yhwh's appearing in (e.g.) Lev. 9:4 and 1 Kings 3:5, but the best parallel is Ps. 102:16 [17], where the context suggests not (for instance) a visionary manifestation but some action that manifests God's power and love—again, such as Ps. 48 describes. People who know by faith that Yhwh is their refuge even when they are far away from Jerusalem thus have their conviction reinforced as their pilgrimage brings home to them the way Yhwh has proved to be the city's refuge.[36]

84:8–9. The psalm segues from praise to prayer, specifically prayer for the king, as happens in other psalms (e.g., Ps. 80).[37] Perhaps this was a regular aspect of a pilgrimage festival, and/or perhaps these are the words of the pilgrims on their walk.[38]

> [8]Yhwh, God Armies,
>   listen to my plea;
>   give ear, God of Jacob. (Rise)

---

32. The traditional rendering "they go from strength to strength" (cf. LXX, Jerome) has made that expression familiar, but this familiarity conceals the fact that it is an odd expression without parallels in the OT. For the "from . . . to" expression, Sigrid Loersch compares 144:13; Jer. 9:3 [2] ("'Sie wandern von Kraft zu Kraft,'" in *Sie wandern von Kraft zu Kraft* [Reinhard Lettmann Festschrift; ed. Arnold Angenendt and Herbert Vorgrimler; Kevelaer: Butzon, 1993], 12–27 [see 23]). But the differences in these passages highlight rather than solve the difficulty in the traditional translation.

33. The ancient versions have tidier forms of the text: e.g., Jerome has sg. through v. 5 and pl. through v. 7.

34. There the prepositional expression is 'el-pĕnê (to the face of), here simply 'el. Psalm 42:2 [3] has the same verb form but follows it by the odd pĕnê rather than a prep.

35. This simply implies 'ēl for 'el. See discussion in Carmel McCarthy, *The Tiqqune Sopherim* (OBO 36; Göttingen: Vandenhoeck & Ruprecht, 1981), 202–4.

36. If "to Zion" is a later addition, the psalm could in origin be a psalm relating to pilgrimage to Dan. So, e.g., Seybold, *Psalmen*, 331; cf. the footnote to vv. 5–6 above.

37. Cf. Dahood, *Psalms*, 2:282. This undermines the inference that vv. 8–9 must be a later addition (so, e.g., Gunkel, *Psalmen*, 369). Thijs Booij ("Psalm lxxxiv, a Prayer of the Anointed," *VT* 44 [1994]: 433–41) sees the whole as a royal psalm, with vv. 8–9 as its center (see also "Royal Words in Ps. lxxxiv 11," *VT* 36 [1986]: 117–20). See the discussion in Hauge, *Between Sheol and Temple*, 38–40.

38. So Briggs, *Psalms*, 2:225.

The invocation and the tricolon mark the beginning of a new section. Yet again Yhwh is addressed as Yhwh *Armies (cf. vv. 1, 3, 12), or rather here is addressed with the fuller title Yhwh, God Armies. The title again speaks to the psalm's theme of Yhwh's being the people's powerful protector and refuge. The initial appeal, as is often the case in prayers in the Psalms, is simply that Yhwh should listen to the worshipper's *plea. It implies that we should assume that the first thing we need to do in prayer is get God's attention; God may be giving it somewhere else or may just be resting.

The third colon neatly parallels both the first two, giving the verse as a whole an abb′a′ structure.[39] Rhetorically speaking, the person of Yhwh, whom the verse addresses, embraces the actual prayer and gets more words, five of the eight words in the line.[40] "God of Jacob" emphasizes the personal relationship between Yhwh and Israel, which complements the fact of Yhwh's might as the basis of prayer; "God of Jacob" is a "phrase of endearment."[41] The basis for this individual's plea is thus Yhwh's relationship with the people as a whole, going back to Jacob.

> [9]Look at our shield, God,
>> behold the face of your anointed.

It is not surprising for the appeal to listen to be complemented by an appeal to look.[42] Both again presuppose that prayer is about getting God's attention (cf. 59:4 [5]; 80:14 [15]). Indeed, all the psalm asks for is this attention; when God looks down from the heavens and sees what is happening on the earth, appropriate action will surely follow. The object of the plea may seem unexpected, like the transition to plea itself. It is emphasized by the fact that "our shield" comes first, before its verb, though the metaphorical nature of the expression means we are not quite sure how to read the line until we get to the end. Our "shield" in the Psalms is usually God, as it will be in v. 11, and LXX, Jerome, Aq, Sym take "our shield" here as qualifying "God." But it can also apply to human leaders (cf. 47:9 [10]), and when the more familiar noun "your anointed" appears at the end of the line, this suggests that "our shield" and "your anointed" are parallel and refer to the king.[43] Anoint-

---

39. "Give ear" is a less common verb than "listen"; the second verb is hiphil, the first qal.

40. Fokkelman, *Major Poems*, 2:235.

41. Briggs, *Psalms*, 2:228.

42. Again, a less common hiphil verb follows a more common qal. The line works abcb′a′, with the invocation standing at the center and applying to both cola.

43. Tg does take *māginnēnû* as obj. but takes the word in another metaphorical connection as referring to the good deeds of the ancestors. In Leviticus, "anointed" can refer to the (high) priest, but terms such as "your anointed" refer to the king.

ing involves someone who represents God pouring oil over the head of a person who is to function as king or priest, and doing so in God's name; this somehow suggests a designation made on God's behalf that means this person functions with God's recognition. "Our shield" (the person who protects us) is thus "your anointed" (the person you recognized). Specifically, the psalm asks that Yhwh should behold the face of the anointed. To look at someone's face is to look at them as they are looking to you and thus to look at them with favor as they look with appeal. So the prayer is simply a prayer for Yhwh to be willing to answer the king's prayers, which are vital to the people. Perhaps this prayer for the king relates to the theme of the psalm as a whole: Yhwh is the people's protector and refuge. Yhwh's protecting and rescuing the people often involves enabling the king to be an effective leader. So this prayer for the king is indirectly a prayer for the worshipper.

84:10–12. The MT implies that vv. 10–11 comprise two tricola and then a bicolon, which would be an unusual arrangement. I take them as four bicola that come in two pairs—vv. 10–11a go together (in abb'a' order), and vv. 11b–12 go together.

> ¹⁰Because a day in your courtyards is better than a thousand,
>   I chose being at the threshold of my God's house—
> [Better] than abiding in faithless tents,
>   ¹¹ᵃbecause Yhwh God is a sun and shield.

The "because" can hardly follow from the lines that immediately precede. Perhaps the *kî* is simply asseverative (cf. TNIV, NJPS, which do not translate it). I have rather reckoned that the causal significance of the *kî* is prospective. Thus both *kî* clauses, vv. 10a and 11a, provide explanation for the statement in v. 10b.

A pilgrim can spend only a few days in the temple courtyards in Jerusalem each year compared to the hundreds of days that have to be spent at home, and v. 10a makes that point hyperbolically. The thousand days might be a thousand ordinary days, but the subtle prosody and parallelism of these two lines more likely implies that "in faithless tents" also qualifies "a thousand."[44]

The whole of v. 10b–c in fact parallels v. 10a, as v. 8c paralleled the whole of v. 8a–b. Being at the threshold of my God's house is thus

---

44. Hossfeld and Zenger (*Psalms 2*, 348) suggest another way of explaining the thousand by linking the verb that follows. Thus ". . . than a thousand [that] I chose. Being at the threshold of my God's house [is better] than . . ." Goulder suggests "a thousand [shekels]" (*Psalms of the Sons of Korah*, 47–48). For other possibilities see L. Grollenberg, "Post-biblical חָרוּת in Ps. lxxxiv 11?" *VT* 9 (1959): 311–12; George Wesley Buchanan, "The Courts of the Lord," *VT* 16 (1966): 231–32.

another way to speak of being in Yhwh's courtyards. "Being at the threshold" is a denominative verb formed from the word for "threshold"; it comes only here. While many references to the temple threshold concern the role of the Levites who stand there to make sure (for instance) that no one comes into the temple in a state of impurity or (for example) drunkenness, there is no particular reason to think that this verb refers to the role of such a significant "doorkeeper" (TNIV, NRSV). Nor, on the other hand, does being at the threshold imply a lowly position. Rather, the pilgrim speaks of having chosen to come to Jerusalem for the festival because being here in the temple courtyards means so much.[45] It is prosaic to infer that the psalm must have been used at the threshold of the temple courts as part of a liturgy there, though this might be so.

In turn, then, v. 10c spells out the implications of "than a thousand." As "in faithless tents" in v. 10c also applies to v. 10a, "better" in v. 10a also applies to v. 10c. "Abiding" (*dûr*) is another hapax in MT; its links with the word "generation" (*dôr*) mean it suggests a time reference parallel to those in v. 10a. "Faithless tents" perhaps suggests that the pilgrim lives in an area where there were many non-Israelites. Again one might think of the area to the west of Jerusalem, dominated by the Philistines in David's day and by their descendants in the Second Temple period. Or one might think of the area to the south; the faithless tents might be the tents referred to in 83:6–7 [7–8].[46]

The *kî* clause in v. 11a paralleling v. 10a then spells out once more why the pilgrim so loves being in Jerusalem. There Yhwh is at home as refuge and protection, as sun and shield. It is unusual for "sun" to be a positive image, because the sun is such a lethal force (e.g., 121:6). Further, the fact that there was a Babylonian god called Sun and that in Egypt, too, "sun" was a divine epithet perhaps inhibited Israel from describing Yhwh thus.[47] But the sun god was a judge whose roles included preventing anything from staying hidden,[48] and one of the sun's functions is to expose wickedness (Job 38:12–13). This would fit with the sun's being a shield, an even more impressive one than the people's human ruler (v. 9).[49] Thus LXX's paraphrase "because the Lord

45. For the translation, cf. Barthélemy, *Psaumes*, 594–96; it seems less likely that *bāḥar* is here a quasi-stative with present meaning, "I prefer" (so JM 112a).

46. Cf. Cole, *Shape and Message of Book III*, 115.

47. But see Othmar Keel and Christoph Uehlinger, "Jahwe und die Sonnengottheit von Jerusalem," in *Ein Gott allein?* ed. Walter Dietrich and Martin A. Klopfenstein, OBO 139 (Göttingen: Vandenhoeck & Ruprecht, 1993), 269–306 (see 300).

48. Cf. Keel, *Symbolism*, 207–8.

49. Indeed, Seybold (*Psalmen*, 331) sees *šemeš* itself as a word for a round shield (cf. *HALOT* 1592b).

God loves mercy and truth" is not so far out; Tg has "a high wall" for "sun."[50]

11b-c Yhwh gives favor and honor;
   he does not withhold good things for people who walk with integrity.

Verse 11 continues the declaration, explaining why it is better to be in the temple courts, though implicitly its statement also applies to people who have to live their lives among the faithless. The line works with an interesting abcb′a′d pattern (in the translation, it works abcb′c′d, which is not so different). It opens with the two nouns "favor" and "*honor" (*ḥēn* and *kābôd*). In connection with God, these are most familiar as grace and glory, but here they appear in connection with human beings and suggest the enjoyment of favor and honor with other people. The worshipper is aware of being in a vulnerable position in relation to other people, and this will be especially so when dwelling among the faithless. But God grants these. Parallel to favor and honor is "*good things," which suggests the good gifts of God such as a harvest that will take people through the next year; if the psalm was used at one of Israel's festivals, then all these festivals link with aspects of the harvest.

Inside the nouns come the two verbs, "he gives" and "he does not withhold." Beyond the liking for parallelism and the variation attained by pairing a positive with a negative, what is the significance of "does not withhold"? Is it a litotes, an understated way of affirming that God actually gives generously? Or does it articulate a fear: what will we do if the harvest fails? Or does it have both these effects? At the center of the line then comes "Yhwh," applying to both cola. It is as well that the Yhwh who lives in the temple courts is not confined to operating there. And at the end of the line comes a prepositional expression that also applies to both cola. It might constitute a challenge to or an underlining of the promise, and it thus tests the person using the psalm. If we do come to God as people who walk with integrity rather than identifying with the lives of the faithless among whom we live, that underlines the encouraging nature of the description of Yhwh. The recurrence of the verb "walk" from v. 7 is suggestive. People who walk the pilgrimage need to be people who walk their everyday lives with integrity; people who are to walk their everyday lives with integrity will be strengthened in doing so if they walk the pilgrimage. The two walks support each other. "With integrity" is the adjective *tāmîm*; since the LXX, translations have used negative words such as "blameless," but it is a positive word, not a

---

50. In Isa. 54:12 *šemeš* apparently refers to battlements, perhaps because of the way the sun shines through them; the verse hardly provides a basis for translating *šemeš* as "battlement" and then taking it as a metaphor.

negative one (Aq, Sym have *teleiōtēs*). The psalms know that no one is blameless or sinless (so that Jerome's *perfectio* may be no improvement), but they do reckon that the orientation of the lives of Yhwh's people should be fundamentally whole or sound (the implication of the word's etymology)—not psychologically but morally.

> [12]Yhwh Armies,
> the good fortune of the person who trusts in you!

The last line returns to addressing God as the first line did. It once again acknowledges God as Yhwh *Armies, as the first line did, and it once again comments on the *good fortune of the person who belongs to Yhwh, as v. 5 did (cf. also v. 4, with a plural noun). Here this person is characterized as one who *trusts in Yhwh, which is the attitude the whole psalm has expressed as it has implicitly dealt with questions about the uncertainty of the harvest and the vulnerability of living among the faithless. In effect the last line says, "The good fortune of the person who joins in this psalm and means it!"

Theological Implications

One feature of Ps. 84 is the "stream" of designations for God.[51] God is Yhwh, the God specially committed to Israel. God is Yhwh Armies, the one with almighty forceful power. God is the living God, the one who is involved and active in the world, not inactive and asleep. God is my king, the one who protects and honors me as the king's servant. God is my God, like a personal deity; but this is the God of gods who is involved with me. God is simply God, *the* Deity. God is (in LXX) the God of gods, whose being and power no other heavenly being rivals. God is Yhwh God Armies, to put three of these terms together. God is God of Jacob, one whose relationship with Israel goes back to the beginning of the family's story. God is sun and shield, exposing and protecting from people's threats. Erich Zenger describes the temple, the holy place, as a (mythic) metaphor for the God who works wonders from there.[52] This overstates an important point. The temple is only of significance because there pilgrims meet with this God and have their trust in this God reinforced.

In what it says about God, Ps. 84 deconstructs, in the way that statements about God and us often do. This is not a weakness but a strength.

51. Fokkelman, *Major Poems*, 2:234.
52. "Das mythische in den Psalmen 84 und 85," in *Mythos im Alten Testament und seiner Umwelt* (Hans-Peter Müller Festschrift; ed. Armin Lange et al.; BZAW 278; Berlin: de Gruyter, 1999), 233–51 (see 234–35); cf. Hossfeld and Zenger, *Psalms 2*, 350.

We often have to say two things about God that stand in tension. On one hand, Yhwh dwells in the temple, and that makes the temple the most loved and the safest place on earth and a place where any Israelite therefore delights to make pilgrimage. On the other, it is no use for Yhwh to be present in the temple and therefore irrelevant to the lives of people who live in Hebron or Lachish, without Yhwh's protection and blessing. So talk of Yhwh's presence in the temple raises an implicit question that deepens as vv. 1–4 proceed. They already begin with huge delight in the temple as the place that is so loved, and from there they only keep increasing in their enthusiasm. The psalmist had been consumed by longing to be here and now is full of excitement. With some poignancy the psalm reflects on the good fortune of people who can always be in the temple courts, people who can go there every day. So is life all gloom for people who live in Hebron or Lachish?

The fact that many of the lines in the psalm have short second cola, like a lament (see esp. vv. 1–2, 5), might point in that direction. Yet v. 2 has characterized Yhwh as the "living God," an expression suggesting that Yhwh is living and active, and vv. 5–7 indicate that this psalm is no lament. Indeed, the striking thing about it is the very fact that someone who does not live in Jerusalem is the one who expresses this enthusiasm. "Absence diminishes commonplace passions and increases great ones, as the wind extinguishes candles and kindles fire."[53] Part of the power of the Song of Songs lies in the way absence thus enhances the lover's passions. Absence has an inspiring effect. That is the effect of the "holy lovesickness"[54] of which the psalm speaks.

Thus it is the people living in Hebron or Lachish who find strength in Yhwh because they have the highways in their mind. When they are not in Jerusalem, they know they will be there in a few weeks' time, and this has a transformative effect now, comparable to that described in Isa. 40:28–31. Whatever exactly v. 6 refers to, it testifies to another aspect of this transformation. Likewise the prayer for Yhwh's anointed in vv. 8–9 implies an awareness that the king is of huge significance for the country as a whole. They too need his defense and his faithful exercise of authority.

The poignancy, paradox, and tension is expressed once more in vv. 10–12. On the one hand, one day in Yhwh's courts, the place of protection and blessing, is better than a thousand that have to be lived among Philistines or Edomites. Yet Yhwh's gift of favor and honor and the good things of life is not confined to the area within sight of the temple. Its

53. From the Maxims of François de la Rochefoucauld (*The Oxford Dictionary of Quotations*, ed. Angela Partington, rev. 4th ed. [Oxford, 1996], 410).

54. Spurgeon, *Treasury of David*, 3:433.

application is moral and religious, not geographical. It applies to people who walk with integrity and to people who trust in Yhwh wherever they live. In the absence of that walk and that trust, living within sight of the temple does one no good. And conversely, the walk and the trust having that effect is not open only to people who live in Jerusalem, as if Yhwh could only operate within shouting distance of the temple. The psalm's final reference to "good fortune" thus complements the one in the psalm's opening section, and between them they express the psalm's paradox. "The good fortune of people who live in your house!" (to go with the traditional translation for a moment). Yes! But also "the good fortune of the person who trusts in you." That applies wherever they live. They may live with much more uncertainty about how Yhwh's protection and blessing will work out for them. But that is what makes trust necessary. And their periodic visits to Jerusalem are what make trust possible, because of the reminders these visits give them. They leave Jerusalem with some sadness, no doubt, but also with renewed reassurance that they do not leave the sphere where Yhwh's presence can be made known in protection and blessing.

After Christ and after AD 70, the literal temple made of stone was replaced by the metaphorical temple made of people. Indeed, A. R. Johnson in effect suggests that this picks up a motif implicit in the psalm itself since the idea of the "house of Yhwh" overlaps with the idea of the "household of Yhwh," who belong there.[55] In the NT there are no sanctuaries made of bricks and mortar. The Christian congregation is the temple (1 Cor. 3:17), its members being the living stones of a spiritual house (1 Pet. 2:5). In connection with this metaphorical temple, the same dynamic and tension that the psalm describes applies. On Sunday morning or on Wednesday evening or at some great retreat or camp meeting, believers meet as the living stones of this temple and love being in God's presence. This hour is better than the other hundreds of hours in the week. But their calling is to go back to live in the unbelieving world, which operates on a radically different set of principles. They might like to escape that world and live in the bliss of Christian company all the time, like seminary professors, but that is not their vocation. But when they are not sure whether they will know God's protection and blessing in their actual context, they find strength in looking forward to meeting with God in the company of God's people again. They therefore commit themselves to walking in the world meanwhile in integrity and trust.

---

55. *Cultic Prophet and Israel's Psalmody*, 102.

Psalm 85

God Speaks of Shalom

Translation

The leader's. The Korahites'. Composition.

[1]You delighted in your land, Yhwh;
    you brought a restoration of Jacob.[1]
[2]You carried the waywardness of your people;
    you covered all their shortcoming. (Rise)
[3]You withdrew all your fury;
    you turned from your angry burning.

[4]Restore us, God, our deliverance,[2]
    cancel your vexation with us.
[5]Will you be angry with us forever,
    prolong your anger for all generations?
[6]Will you not again bring us to life,
    so that your people may rejoice in you?
[7]Show us your commitment, Yhwh,
    grant your deliverance to us.

[8]I shall listen for what the God Yhwh will speak,
    because he will speak of well-being
To his people, to his committed ones,
    who must not turn to foolhardiness.[3]

1. The line incorporates a double paronomasia, *rāṣîtā 'arṣekā* and *šabtā šĕbît* (Q)/
šĕbût (K; Bratcher and Reyburn, *Psalms*, 745).
2. Lit. "God of our deliverance."
3. Jerome, Aq, and Sym have "so that they may not . . . ," but this is not a usual
meaning of *wĕ'al*. EVV have "they must not . . . ," but this makes it hard to identify a

⁹Yes, his deliverance is near for people who revere him,
  so that honor may settle in our land.
¹⁰Commitment and truthfulness—they have met,
  faithfulness and well-being—they have kissed.
¹¹Truthfulness from the earth—it will spring up,
  faithfulness from the heavens—it has looked down.
¹²Yes, Yhwh—he will give good things;
  our land—it will give its increase.
¹³Faithfulness—it will walk before him
  as he sets his feet on the path.[4]

Interpretation

The psalm divides into three sections of increasing length, if we may treat v. 8 as transitional; or we may say that it divides into two halves, seven lines for a prayer and seven lines for a response. Verses 1–3 recall how Yhwh had mercy on Israel in the past. Verses 4–7 appeal to Yhwh to do that again. Verse 8 declares an intention to listen for a positive response to that plea. Verses 9–13 then expand on the nature of that positive response. In vv. 1–7 the psalm thus addresses Yhwh. In v. 8 an individual soliloquizes, perhaps to be overheard by the congregation and by Yhwh. In vv. 9–13 "we" likewise soliloquize. It is possible that the whole psalm is said by the "I" of v. 8, but vv. 9–13 seem to be a response to v. 8, so more likely the congregation speaks vv. 1–7, a leader speaks v. 8, and the congregation responds with vv. 9–13. The psalm thus starts as if it is going to be a praise hymn, segues into being a protest psalm, and ends up as a psalm of trust.

A key role in the psalm is played by the verb *šûb* (turn [back]). The reminder in vv. 1–3 almost begins with a recollection of Yhwh's restoring Jacob (lit. "you turned a turning) and closes with a recollection of how this involved Yhwh's turning from anger. Verses 4–7 begin with an appeal to restore (lit. "turn") the people once more and go on to appeal to Yhwh again to revive the people (lit. "turn, revive"). The declaration of intent in v. 8 specifies that the people must not turn to foolhardiness. The LXX neatly adds another occurrence of an equivalent verb in v. 4b

poetic structure in the verse. I follow LXX in seeing v. 8d as another *w* clause parallel to the phrases in v. 8c (though LXX paraphrases as "those who turn their heart to him," perhaps puzzled by the way the colon does go in a new direction); cf. Auffret (*Voyez de vos yeux*, 263). For some reworking of the text, see John S. Kselman, "A Note on Psalm 85:9–10," *CBQ* 46 (1984): 23–27.

4. Or "as it sets his feet on the path" (which comes to the same thing); or "as it makes his footsteps into a path [for people to walk on]" (but this requires more reading in); or "as it sets its feet on the path" (but this seems to add nothing).

to cope with the unusual use of *pārar*, "cancel." There are other words that recur. "Your/his people" comes in each of the first two sections (vv. 2, 6). Deliverance comes twice in the second section, as an inclusion, and then to open the statement of trust (vv. 4, 7, 9). The complementary "your land/our land" form an inclusion around the whole psalm (vv. 1, 12). Well-being, truthfulness, commitment/committed ones, and faithfulness dominate the statement of trust and expectation (vv. 10–11; see also vv. 7, 8, 13).[5]

The situation of the people in the late sixth century would be a suitable one against which to imagine the psalm being used, insofar as then, too, Israel protested at Yhwh's continuing anger: see, e.g., Zech. 1:12; but Zechariah does not think in terms of a restoration from exile followed by a subsequent outburst of anger, the sequence the psalm would require.[6] In this connection, Calvin's connection with Antiochus's persecution is more suggestive.[7] Further, once we reckon that the phrase in v. 1b means "bring a restoration" and not "reverse the exile," there is no particular reason to link the psalm with *the* exile. Indeed, the last part suggests that the crisis concerns the failure of the harvest, a recurrent experience throughout First Temple and Second Temple history. The links with Isa. 40–66 in vv. 8–13 might indicate dependence either way. It seems implausible to see vv. 4–7 as the way Israelites might feel at *any* Festival of Sukkot.[8]

The leader's. The Korahites'. Composition.

Heading. See glossary.

85:1–3. The NJPS takes the first three lines as precative qatals and thus makes vv. 1–7 all plea,[9] but it would be hard for hearers to work this out (if the qatals followed the imperatives, things would be different). The same is true of the interpretation that sees the qatals as expressions of certainty regarding what God is going to do.[10] Rather vv. 1–3 correspond to the beginning of psalms such as Pss. 44 and 126, which begin with a recollection of Yhwh's acts in the past that is designed to motivate Yhwh to act now in keeping with these, in a context when Yhwh is not doing so.

5. On the rhetorical features, see further Auffret, *Sagesse*, 285–300; idem, *Voyez de vos yeux*, 262–78.
6. Cf. Hossfeld and Zenger, *Psalms 2*, 365.
7. *Psalms*, 3:367.
8. So Mowinckel, e.g., *Psalms in Israel's Worship*, 1:223–24.
9. Cf. Dahood, *Psalms*, 2:285–86.
10. E.g., Augustine, *Psalms*, 405; Cassiodorus, *Psalms*, 2:321–22; Gunkel, *Psalmen*, 373.

> ¹You delighted in your land, Yhwh;
>   you brought a restoration of Jacob.

Indeed, the psalm starts with a verb that appeared in 44:3 [4], *rāṣâ*. The EVV have "favor"; we need to note that the verb is an affective one. Here, as in 44:3 [4], it denotes an unexplained if not inexplicable delight that Yhwh feels. The word does not come in Deut. 7:6–8, but it might have done. It is the pleasure and the liking that issue in practical favoring, in acting in a loving way. It is the attitude of a father to his son (Prov. 3:12). Here the object of pleasure is the land (in 44:3 [4] it was the people). Yhwh looks at the land of Israel the way pilgrims do, their hearts rising in their chests as they draw near to it. The parallel second colon[11] thus complements the first in two ways. It refers to the people, not the land, and while the verbal expression "brought a restoration"[12] occasionally refers to a land, it likewise usually refers to a people. In isolation, we might then take v. 1 to refer to two events, Yhwh's original election of land and people and a subsequent act of restoration that put things right for people and land after things had gone wrong. But the rest of vv. 2–3 focuses exclusively on the second of these, which suggests that this is also true of v. 1 as a whole. As 44:1–3 [2–4] as a whole thus clarifies that there "delight" refers to Yhwh's original act in giving the land to the people, here vv. 1–3 as a whole clarifies that in this psalm it refers to a subsequent act of restoration. There was a delight that made God act at the beginning; but when things went wrong, the same delight was also the reason why God did not simply turn the other way. What precisely this restoration looked like, the psalm will in due course indicate.

> ²You carried the waywardness of your people;
>   you covered all their shortcoming. (Rise)

In the meantime, the psalm first spells out other implications of Yhwh's delight. A father's delight means putting up with his children's *waywardness and shortcoming or *failure, and Yhwh's delight has the same implication. They are, after all "your people." Once again the point is expressed in parallel cola. Two verbs express what in English we routinely call forgiveness (both images also come in 32:1). First, forgiveness involves "carrying" people's sin. When we do wrong, we have to accept the consequences of it; we have to carry that sin (e.g., Gen. 4:13; Lev. 5:1; 24:15). But the person we have wronged may decline to let it spoil the relationship and insist on continuing to be on loving terms with us.

11. The cola work abca′c′.
12. See on 53:6 [7].

They then carry the wrong rather than letting us do so. Carrying the waywardness of Israel is one of the things that Yhwh claimed to do at Sinai (Exod. 34:7); the psalm notes that Yhwh has done it.

To put it another way, love covers sins (Prov. 10:12). Psalm 78:53 notes how the sea covered Israel's enemies; it overwhelmed them in such a way as to deprive them of life or power. Like carrying, covering does not pretend that the thing is not there (in Hebrew as in English, "cover up" can have negative connotations). When a man is unfaithful to his wife, it does no good to pretend that this never happened. But what the wife could choose to do is to cover it with love and thus deprive it of life and power. A wife might reasonably reckon to do that just once. Extraordinarily, Yhwh had chosen to cover *all* their shortcoming: covered it again and again or sent a huge flood to cover it.

> ³You withdrew all your fury;
>   you turned from your angry burning.

Again, that wife might reasonably be consumed by angry fury when she learned of her husband's unfaithfulness, and so was Yhwh. Yhwh's relationship with Israel's waywardness is not that of a judge adjudicating wrongdoing that did not affect the judge personally, who is called to do so coolly and unemotionally. Yhwh's relationship with Israel's waywardness is that of a parent whose will has been flouted or a spouse whose faithfulness has been treated as nothing. Such a parent or spouse reacts with the fury that is the corollary of love, and so does Yhwh. The point is emphasized by the words that are used. This is no ordinary anger; at least, the ordinary word for anger (*'ap*) does not appear until the very end of the line. This is an anger that expresses itself in fury and burning. It is a seething, ferocious anger. Fury (*'ebrâ*) suggests something that bursts out and overflows (*'ābar*); "all your fury" at the end of the colon corresponds to "all their shortcoming" at the end of the preceding colon. Burning (*ḥārôn*) suggests a white-hot anger that threatens to consume whatever it touches.

The line takes all that for granted. It is background. Its own point is that, extraordinarily, Yhwh did not hold on to that anger but on the contrary withdrew it and turned from it. Again the cola are neatly parallel. As the barb of "all their shortcoming" is graciously preceded by "you covered," so the barb of "all your fury" is graciously preceded by "you withdrew." It is a striking verb, often used for gathering the harvest and gathering people to their family when they die, but also used for Yhwh's taking back the breath from a person who dies (104:29; also 26:9). It is as if, having expressed (let out) some of that inner fury, Yhwh in due course stopped expressing it and pulled it back inside. All Yhwh's fury was not expressed. Yhwh has the capacity to deal with it when retaining it, as human beings sometimes can. The phraseology parallels the image of Yhwh's carrying the people's wrongdoing. The parallel verb, "turn," picks up the verb *šûb* from v. 1[13] and thus rounds off the first section. More commonly the OT speaks of Yhwh's anger turning (e.g., Isa. 5:25), but the expression here corresponds to Moses's challenge in Exod. 32:12. Perhaps, then, vv. 1–3 work with reverse chronology: Yhwh's carrying and turning at Sinai in response to Moses's challenge were the background to Yhwh's giving Jacob the land. But (given that v. 1 spoke of restoration and not merely of the original gift), more likely vv. 2–3 imply that the attitude that Yhwh took at Sinai has been characteristic of Yhwh's relationship with Israel on subsequent occasions where Israel has been wayward. This final image for Yhwh's forgiveness makes Yhwh's anger something semi-externalized and independent of Yhwh, like a fire Yhwh has lit. Yhwh's turning from it would then deprive it of fuel, so that it dies. Or perhaps the image rather suggests—in contrast to the one in v. 3a—that Yhwh has expressed that angry burning in a way that makes it no longer part of Yhwh's own being; therefore Yhwh can turn away from it, no longer being affected by it.

85:4–7. In vv. 1–3 the controlled neatness of the poetry with its parallelism has already eventually come to contrast with its contents. That contrast continues in the prayer in vv. 4–7. The way Yhwh is now acting does not correspond to the way Yhwh acted in the past, and the people need the past pattern to be repeated. The movement in the psalm provides a small-scale parallel to that in Ps. 44, which contrasted Yhwh's past beneficence and present neglect and urged Yhwh to act in commitment and come to the people's help. On the other hand, there is no lament at concrete reversal or letdown, and the prayer is articulated formulaically, which might point to a generally discouraging situation rather than a concrete crisis.[14]

In form and content the four lines work abb′a′. Verses 4 and 7 are overt pleas, with "deliverance" coming in the first colon and the last. Verses 5 and 6 comprise covert pleas that are actually expressed as rhetorical questions. The form that the expression of Yhwh's anger took is not explicit here; it is vv. 9–13 that will make this clear.

> [4]Restore us, God, our deliverance,
>   cancel your vexation with us.

---

13. But in v. 1, the qal was unusually transitive, while here—paradoxically—the verb is hiphil. "Turn your anger" is a common expression (e.g., 78:38), and here it would then be possible to take the *min* as partitive and translate "turned some of your anger." But that can hardly be right, esp. after the "all" in v. 3a. Rather, the hiphil is declarative (BDB 999b) and thus has the intransitive meaning more usual for the qal.
14. Cf. Gerstenberger, *Psalms 2*, 129, 131.

Verse 4 begins by again taking up the verb from v. 1[15] in order to urge Yhwh as God "our *deliverance" or God "who delivers us" to do again what Yhwh had done for Jacob in the past. What the people need deliverance or restoration from is not explicit, facilitating the psalm's use in different contexts. But the parallel colon makes clear that the people's problem is again Yhwh's anger, here first spoken of as vexation (see 78:58). The verb *pārar* (hiphil) usually refers to the rescinding of a covenant or a vow or a commitment (cf. the hiphil of the homonym *pûr* in 89:33 [34]). Implicitly, the context of the psalm is that Israel has rescinded its covenant obligations and that Yhwh has done the same in response; the psalm asks that Yhwh instead rescind the vexation that issued in that.

> [5]Will you be angry with us forever,
>> prolong your anger for all generations?

Another neat, internally parallel abb'a' line[16] asks questions that make it also parallel as a whole in substance to the line that preceded. Yhwh's "prolonging" relates to commitment in 36:10 [11], so there is an unhappy contrast in the usage of this verb that stands out against the positive contrast in the usage of the verb in v. 4b. Yhwh is prolonging anger rather than prolonging commitment.

> [6]Will you not again bring us to life,
>> so that your people may rejoice in you?

The further rhetorical question is formulated rather differently from v. 5. First, there is only one question, and the implicit appeal is a positive one, which is thus introduced by a negative interrogative. The appeal to bring us back to life restates again the appeal to restore us. Indeed it reuses the verb *šûb*, here as an auxiliary verb signifying to do something again—namely, bring us [back] to life. The appeal presupposes that the community is as good as dead, like 80:18–19 [19–20], where the verb again appeared alongside *šûb* hiphil (cf. also the vivid parable in Ezek. 37:1–14). The second colon completes the first rather than being parallel

---

15. The usage is again odd, as *šûb* qal is an intransitive verb; but it here appears with a suffix. Tg takes the suffix datively, "turn to us" (see JM 125ba; *IBHS* 10.2.1i), while M. Dahood ("Enclitic *mem* and Emphatic *lamedh* in Psalm 85," *Bib* 37 [1956]: 338–40) sees the -*m* as enclitic; or it might be a composite form, combining the qal with the suffixed hiphil (for which cf. 80:3 [4]). There are no other certain instances of *šûb* used transitively except in the expression *šûb šĕbût/šĕbît*, which came in v. 1 (and which elsewhere often incorporates the obj. marker *'et*—so there is no doubt of the construction; *HALOT* 1430b), and I take *šûbēnû* as a compressed version of *šûb šĕbîtēnû*.

16. Lit. "Forever will you be angry with us, prolong your anger for all generations?"

609

to it (it is the only non-parallel second colon in vv. 1–7). It extends the comparison with 80:18 [19], where the argument for Yhwh's bringing the people to life is that then "we will call on your name." There is less doubt here that this motivation marks the act as one that will be to the suppliants' advantage. It is not merely an *ad deum* argument, appealing to Yhwh's selfish interests. The people want to be able to rejoice in Yhwh (though that does imply praise) and in their relationship with Yhwh. The point is underlined by the line's emphasis on "you" (the pronoun in v. 6a is expressed, which is grammatically unnecessary) and "your people" (which comes in emphatic position before the verb in v. 6b). In effect, the line appeals to the covenantal relationship between Yhwh and Israel.

> [7]Show us your commitment, Yhwh,
>   grant your deliverance to us.

The last line of the appeal reverts to explicit plea and to straightforward parallelism (abcc′a′d). If *commitment lay between the lines in vv. 4–5, here it is rhetorically visible; the plea asks that it should not be "canceled" but should be "prolonged" and thus become visible in the people's lives in the gift of *deliverance. In light of the links with the Sinai story in vv. 2–3, readers might recall that commitment was another of the key characteristics that Yhwh claimed in Exod. 34:6–7. The psalm appeals to Yhwh to be the God of Sinai, as had been the case in Israel's experience over the years.

85:8. Verses 1–7 would make a reasonably satisfactory complete psalm, comparable with Ps. 44; vv. 8–13 are rather distinctive. First, an "I" declares an intention.

> [8]I shall listen for what the God Yhwh will speak,
>   because he will speak of well-being
> To his people, to his committed ones,
>   who must not turn to foolhardiness.

The "I" is presumably a priest or Levite or some other worship leader, who responds to the reminder and the prayer by declaring the intention to listen to Yhwh, to discover what "the God Yhwh" has to say. The expression *hāʾēl yhwh* otherwise comes only in Isa. 42:5,[17] the first in a series of links with Isa. 40–66 in vv. 8–13. The statement of intent is itself unique in the Psalter, but it compares with Hab. 2:1.[18] There, however,

---

17. The existence of the parallel means one hardly need consider emending the text (cf. *BHS*). Weiser (*Psalms*, 570) construes "Yhwh" as the extraposed subj. of the next colon.
18. LXX adds "in me," assimilating to Hab. 2:1 (Kirkpatrick, *Psalms*, 512).

Yhwh's response follows. This "I" does not wait for Yhwh to speak or tell us what Yhwh says. No word from God follows. The commitment to listening is purely rhetorical, because the speaker immediately declares what Yhwh will speak of,[19] namely, *well-being for the people, which we know they lack at present. At the same time, that subject is not exactly predictable. What the people immediately need is deliverance (vv. 7, 9), rescue from calamity; well-being is the experience of ordinary life going well, which would follow on deliverance. So the line looks beyond the immediate crisis to Yhwh's ongoing goodness. "Speak of" (*dibbēr*) might suggest command (e.g., Exod. 1:17) or promise, for which Hebrew has no separate word (e.g., Jer. 32:42);[20] a command of well-being would also be a promise.

It is dangerous to be a prophet of well-being. This often means being a false prophet (Jer. 6:14; 8:11; 28:9; Ezek. 13:10, 16). It is also dangerous to assume that one knows how Yhwh will respond to a prayer like that in vv. 1–7 (see, e.g., Jer. 14–15), even where the prayer relates to "his people, . . . his *committed ones." Indeed, one might reckon that an appeal to having this status is especially open to backfiring. This is hinted by the appearance of "his people" and "his committed ones" together in 50:4–5. There, they are present in order to be confronted, which shows that both expressions describe the people's status rather than indicating that they actually *are* committed. If the speaker's words do risk taking for granted how Yhwh will reply to the prayer, Yhwh might reply by pointing out what the words imply, that the people need to behave as Yhwh's people and manifest commitment, and not the kind that dissolves as easily as morning mist (Hos. 6:4).

The point becomes explicit in the further parallel description of the people in v. 8d. Yet again the verb *šûb* recurs, this time as a challenge to the people rather than to Yhwh. If they want Yhwh to turn from wrath and turn to restore the people, they had better make sure they do not turn away from Yhwh into the kind of stupidity (*kesel*) that reckons they can make their own decisions and safeguard their own future (see 49:10, 13 [11, 14]). Perhaps the verse implies that it is this assumption that has put them into the mess they are in; they must not revert to it.

85:9–13. The "Yes" marks a change of speaker; the words express "our" confident expectation in response to the leader's words in v. 8, which continues to the end of the psalm. Again, there is no waiting for Yhwh to speak.

19. The use of the yiqtol makes it less plausible to reckon that this is what Yhwh "is saying."

20. Cf. Tate, *Psalms 51–100*, 365.

611

> 9Yes, his deliverance is near for people who revere him,
>   so that honor may settle in our land.

The people first revert to talk of the *deliverance that will need to pave the way for well-being. The declaration that this deliverance is near corresponds especially closely to Isa. 56:1 (cf. also 51:5). Since we have not been told of any special divine word, it seems to be a declaration that reflects "theo-logic." Given the fact that Yhwh is committed to them and they are Yhwh's committed people, deliverance must follow; indeed, it must be not merely certain but also imminent. Yhwh surely cannot allow calamity to continue. But again, the people's self-description gives a hostage to fortune. "People who *revere him" (more literally "his reverers") parallels "his committed ones," substantially as well as formally. "People who revere Yhwh" is a regular description of Israel; by definition they are a people who worship Yhwh rather than worshipping other deities. But those contexts in the sixth century when Yhwh's action is near (Isa. 51 and 56 say) are ones in which the audience was often tempted to be people who revered Yhwh only in a formal sense but reckoned that they needed to look after their own destiny or even to be a people who revered Babylonian gods or other deities; and so were most other periods in OT history. If the leader's promise and/or the people's response thus reckons to use Yhwh for ideological ends, their words may indeed backfire.

The Syr takes the aim of Yhwh's act as "so that his *honor may settle in our land," and the pronoun could certainly carry over from "his deliverance." In Exod. 24:16 Yhwh's *kābôd* does come to settle on Sinai, but the verb *šākan* is not otherwise used of Yhwh's *kābôd*, and Yhwh normally dwells in the sanctuary or in Zion or among the people, not in the land. More likely, then, *kābôd* refers to the people's success and good reputation (cf. 84:11 [12]) that are presently lost in their calamity.

> 10Commitment and truthfulness—they have met,
>   faithfulness and well-being—they have kissed.
> 11Truthfulness from the earth—it will spring up,
>   faithfulness from the heavens—it has looked down.

The use of tenses in these next two lines expresses an even more marked certainty. Verse 11 helps to interpret v. 10. The *faithfulness that looks down from the heavens is evidently Yhwh's, and we already know that *commitment is the characteristic of Yhwh to which the psalm appeals (v. 7). On the other hand, *truthfulness is something emerging from the earth (*'ereṣ*, not *'ădāmâ*), and *well-being is also (ideally) a

feature of worldly life.[21] So the idea of vv. 10–11 is that Yhwh's commitment and faithfulness come together with the earth's well-being and
truthfulness.[22] In each line the verb comes at the end rather than at the
beginning, their usual position, and the effect is to emphasize them
rather than their subjects, given that they are rather striking. Nowhere
else is the unusual verb for meet (*pāgaš*) used thus metaphorically, nor
the even more remarkable verb "kiss" (*nāšaq*).[23] We might think that
commitment and truthfulness, faithfulness and well-being were close
enough to each other not to have to move much to meet or kiss, but v. 11
then underlines the point of these verbs in revealing that the first noun
in each colon in v. 10 refers to something in the heavens, the second to
something on earth. How extraordinary, then, that they meet and kiss.[24]
The verbs also suggest that these divine qualities are semi-independent
of Yhwh, like divine aides, as in 43:3; 57:3 [4]; 61:7 [8]; the point is underlined by the final verb in v. 11.[25] Only here is the verb "look down"
(*šāqap*) used metaphorically—except for Jer. 6:1, which makes for a
noteworthy contrast.[26]

On the other hand, the declaration that truthfulness "springs up" like
a flourishing tree makes the concrete reality behind the psalm come to
the surface here. In other contexts, truthfulness could denote a human
commitment to doing the right thing,[27] but here the focus rather lies
on the workings of God and nature. The statement indeed indicates
that the psalm is after all referring to something natural. Insofar as

21. The contrast is underlined by the fact that v. 11a has f. nouns and verb, v. 11b
m. nouns and verb (Watson, *Classical Hebrew Poetry*, 118).

22. All this has little to do with "justice" and "peace" and the relationship between
them, as this is discussed in (e.g.) C. René Padilla, "The Fruit of Justice Will Be Peace,"
Transformation 2, no. 1 (1985): 2–4 (see 3); World Council of Churches, "God's Justice—
Promise and Challenge," *Ecumenical Review* 37 (1985): 488–90 (see 490).

23. One would expect the niphal, though that is hardly enough to suggest that the verb
is *nāšaq* II, "fight" (so Jürgen Ebach, "'Gerechtigkeit und Frieden küssen sich,'" in *Gott an
den Rändern*, ed. Ulrike Bail and Renate Jost [Gütersloh: Kaiser, 1996], 42–52 [see 42–43]),
whose meaning or existence itself involves some inference.

24. This has provided an image for the incarnation, reflected in the psalm's use in
Advent (cf. Luther, *First Lectures*, 165; Hill, *Prayer, Praise and Politics*, 125–30). It has
also provided an image for the atonement (cf. the comments in Spurgeon, *Treasury of
David*, 3:453, 459–60), on the assumption that this involved reconciling God's mercy and
justice, though exegetically the difficulty is that in Hebrew there is no tension between
ḥesed and *'ĕmet*.

25. The third-century Gnostic writing *Pistis Sophia* thus hypostatized them: see
C. Trautmann, "La citation du Psaume 85 (84,11–12) et ses commentaries dans la Pistis
Sophia," *RHPR* 59 (1979): 551–57.

26. The verbs also generate some paronomasia—*nipgāšû, nāšāqû, tiṣmāḥ, nišqāp*.

27. Dennis McCarthy ("Psalm 85 and the Way of Peace," *The Way* 22 [1982]: 3–9)
warns against this understanding here, which colludes with our desire to feel we can and
must do it rather than depending on God.

the heavens suggest something coming from God, that points to the distance between God and earth. But the practical way the heavens affect the earth is through the gift of rain, and in this way the marriage of earth and heaven is a quite natural one. Neither rain from the heavens nor fruitfulness from the earth would effect anything without the other, but when they meet and kiss, blessing results. Yhwh keeps the rains in storehouses in the heavens and has also implanted the capacity for fruitfulness in the earth.

The parallel with Isa. 40–66 in v. 9 is matched here by the way the language and imagery, and also the understanding of the relationship between divine action and earthly action, recall Isa. 45:8. As is the case there, the people of God do not have to do anything to make Yhwh's purpose take effect. It comes about through Yhwh's action and through forces in the world that are independent of Israel. A difference lies in the prophet's concern with Yhwh's acts in politics through Cyrus. Here v. 12 suggests that the imagery that points to God's making the earth yield its increase actually does refer to that process in nature, not one in politics. Deliverance (v. 9) thus leads the way to well-being (v. 10). It is these lines that indicate how Yhwh's anger was being expressed.

> **12**Yes, Yhwh—he will give good things;
> our land—it will give its increase.

The further "yes" (though here it is *gam* rather than *'ak*) advertises that vv. 12–13 essentially restate vv. 9–11. In case we thought that nature did work independently of Yhwh, v. 12a makes explicit that Yhwh stands behind the process vv. 10–11 have referred to. The parallelism is noteworthy as "Yhwh" and then "our land" (as in v. 9) are the subject of the same verb (except that the first use is masculine, and the second necessarily feminine); both words precede their verb. "Good things" and "its increase" explain each other, both additionally explaining and being explained by "honor" in v. 9. The reference to *good things also extends the parallel with 84:11 [12].[28]

Here there is a further intertextual link with Isa. 52:7; it, too, speaks of "good things" alongside "well-being" and "deliverance." Leviticus 26:4–6 also speaks of the land giving its increase, using the same words as here though in different verb and noun forms, and in addition speaks of well-being (cf. v. 10 here). So while the speakers might have been taking the risk of pronouncing on what Yhwh will do, without listening first,

28. Although the psalm is concerned with rain, it is doubtful whether we have grounds for reckoning that *ṭôb* itself *means* rain (against Dahood, *Psalms*, 2:286; Oswald Loretz, "Ugaritisch *ṭbn* und hebräisch *ṭwb* 'Regen': Regenrituale beim Neujahrsfest in Kanaan und Israel (Ps 85; 126)," *UF* 21 [1989]: 247–58).

alternatively they might be speaking with a right confidence on the basis of what they know Yhwh has said in the Torah and in the Prophets.

> ¹³Faithfulness—it will walk before him
>   as he sets his feet on the path.

Here the language continues to recall Isa. 52:7–10 with its talk of the aide heralding Yhwh's coming; it also recalls the enigmatic Isa. 41:2, where the prophet describes the conqueror from the east as one whom faithfulness calls to its heel. Once again, then, *faithfulness is one of those divine aides, here functioning as a herald or advance guard before Yhwh. The second colon then confirms that when Yhwh's feet are set on the way, the path they will tread is one that walks the way of faithfulness. It will not be the case that Yhwh's feet are set on a path of wrath, as they have been (vv. 4–7). The Tg's faithfulness "makes his footsteps a good way" thus gets the substance of the point.

Theological Implications

A comparison and contrast between Ps. 85 and Ps. 44, another Korahite psalm, is instructive (Ps. 126 is more like Ps. 85). Psalm 44 begins in a similar way by recalling how things once were. The difference is that Ps. 44 has in mind the way Yhwh brought the people into the land at the beginning, whereas in Ps. 85 the people have in mind their having experienced Yhwh's subsequent restoration from calamity, not merely the original gift of the land. We could think of events related in Judges rather than Joshua, but Ps. 85 will in due course make clear another contrast. Here the problem is not defeat by enemies but the failure of the crops.

Psalm 44 goes on to a statement of faith based on the way Yhwh gave the people the land, which is the preamble to a description of the calamity Yhwh has now brought on the people, neither of which have equivalents in Ps. 85. In a sharper contrast in what follows, Ps. 44 goes on to declare that this calamity has come on the people despite their faithfulness to the covenant, whereas Ps. 85 implicitly owns that its negative experience (whatever that is) issued from its wrongdoing (it owns that explicitly in vv. 1–3, though that directly relates to the past, and the people never explicitly acknowledge that it deserved what came more recently).

Psalm 44 then closes with a prayer whose presupposition is that Yhwh is simply inactive and lacking in concern; it therefore seeks to arouse Yhwh to action, to behave in light of the commitment that allegedly characterizes Yhwh. Psalm 85:1–7 also closes with an appeal to Yhwh's

615

commitment but does so in the course of a prayer that in contrast emphatically declares how it sees Yhwh as positively angry and hostile. It thus seeks a change in Yhwh's way of acting rather than a move from inaction to action.

The recollection, statement of faith, protest, protestation of faithfulness, and plea thus comprise the whole of Ps. 44. In Ps. 85 we are now only at v. 7. There follows a declaration of intent to listen for what Yhwh will say in response to all that and a declaration of what Yhwh in fact does or will say, neither of which have equivalents in Ps. 44. The comparison and the contrast is heightened by the fact that in substance though not in words there is some comparison between this declaration and the declaration of faith in Ps. 44:4–8 [5–9]. That declaration was implicitly placed in question by the protest that followed, and the psalm does not come back to it. In contrast, the declaration here in vv. 8–13 follows on the plea and provides the grounds for conviction that God will act, instead of its being called into question by the fact that God is not acting. Thus Ps. 44 leaves things in medias res, while Ps. 85 reaches closure.

Psalm 44, then, compares with the situation of Lamentations; Ps. 85 compares with that of Isa. 40–66, with which it also has a number of links. The difference is that Isa. 40–66 (or at least Isa. 40–55) relates to a specific context, whereas Ps. 85 does not. And Isa. 40–55, at least, focuses on the historical act of deliverance that the people need, while Ps. 85 focuses more on the fruitfulness that will follow Yhwh's act of deliverance.[29]

Both psalms are in the Psalter; both the psalm and the prophet are in the Scriptures. The people of God have to recognize which they must and can pray and what word Yhwh is speaking now. A prophet is someone who knows what time it is,[30] and so is a person who prays.

29. We should hardly assume that the meaning of Isa. 40–55 determines that of the psalm, as Bernard Renaud implies ("Le psaume 85 et son caractère théophanique," in *Ouvrir les Écritures* [P. Beauchamp Festschrift; ed. Pietro Bovati and Roland Meynet; Paris: Cerf, 1995], 133–49 [see 148]).

30. So Eva Osswald, *Falsche Prophetie im Alten Testament* (Tübingen: Mohr, 1962), 22; cf. J. A. Sanders, "Hermeneutics," in *The Interpreter's Dictionary of the Bible*, supplementary volume, ed. K. Crim (Nashville: Abingdon, 1976), 402–7 (see 407).

Psalm 86

A Servant's Claim on His Master

Translation

Plea. David's.

¹Incline your ear, Yhwh, answer me,
  because I am weak and needy.
²Look after my life, because I am committed;
  deliver your servant: you are my God.
As the one who trusts in you, ³be gracious to me, my Lord,
  because I call to you all day long.
⁴Rejoice the soul of your servant,
  because to you, my Lord, I lift up my soul,
⁵Because you are my Lord, good and forgiving,
  big in commitment to everyone who calls you.
⁶Give ear to my plea, Yhwh,
  attend to the sound of my prayers for grace.
⁷On the day of my trouble I call you,
  because you answer me.

⁸There is no one like you among the gods, my Lord,
  and there is nothing like your deeds.
⁹All the nations, which you made,
  will come and bow low before you, my Lord,
  and honor your name,
¹⁰Because you are great and one who does wonders;
  you are God alone.

¹¹Teach me your way, Yhwh,
    I will walk in your truthfulness;
    unite my heart in reverence for your name.
¹²I will confess you, my Lord, my God, with all my heart,
    and I shall honor your name forever.[1]
¹³Because your commitment is great toward me,
    and you will rescue my life from deepest Sheol.

¹⁴God, willful people have arisen against me,
    a group of terrifying people have sought my life,
    people who have not put you before their eyes.
¹⁵But you are my Lord, the compassionate and gracious God,
    long-tempered and big in commitment and truthfulness.
¹⁶Turn your face to me and be gracious to me,
    give your strength to your servant, deliver the son of your maid.
¹⁷Give me a sign of good things,
    so that the people who are against me may see and be shamed,
    because you, Yhwh, have helped me and comforted me.

Interpretation

This prayer psalm uses many phrases and expressions that appear in other psalms and elsewhere in the OT. It is thus another that takes the form of a prayer soaked in the traditional language of a relationship with Yhwh and representative of the best Israelite piety (cf. Pss. 71; 79). It thereby illustrates how the extent to which a prayer expresses in the suppliant's own words the distinctive intensity of a unique experience is not an indicator of how valid the prayer is. In Israel "there is life from tradition and in tradition."[2] James L. Mays compares the Lord's Prayer as one in which the traditional phrases of Jewish piety and theology come to form a profound new whole.[3] By using ways of speaking to God and of God that have been sanctified by their use over the centuries, individuals are able to articulate what they want to say to God. The psalm's appeal to the language of Exodus (see esp. vv. 5, 8, 15) adds to that effect: this suppliant prays as a member of the exodus people. The psalm represents a "renewed Sinai Theology."[4] In a context of affliction, then, people who pray do not abandon the formulas of the faith; arguably these

1. The first verb is yiqtol, but the second explicitly cohortative.
2. Kraus, *Psalms 60–150*, 183; though Terrien sees the suppliant as writing out of "mortal terror" so that "the composition suffers from highly emotional disturbance" (*Psalms*, 613).
3. *Psalms*, 278.
4. Jürgen Vorndran, *"Alle Völker worden kommen"* (Berlin: Philo, 2002), 209.

become more important. The formulas by their nature as formulas imply a season of orientation, but at least the exodus formulas issued out of a season of disorientation, and they thus affirm that "Yahweh is a God peculiarly pertinent to seasons of disorientation." In the latter context Israel does not try to make up new affirmations of faith out of private experience but falls back on the "tried and true formulations that seem to have special credibility in such times."[5]

Although practically every phrase in the psalm can be linked with some verse in the Psalms, it would be misleading to list these in such a way as to suggest that the psalmist was directly taking phrases from those sources. Its relationship with other psalms is more like that of the Revelation of John with the OT, where hardly a verse would survive without the scriptural phraseology that lies behind it, but the book comes into being because the visionary is soaked in the Scriptures rather than because he is directly sampling them at every point.

The psalm also has the standard elements that appear in a prayer psalm, though in a distinctive configuration. It is dominated by its opening plea for attention and rescue (vv. 1–7), though this does not tell us why the suppliant needs deliverance. It goes on to a declaration of the way the nations will come to honor Yhwh in light of what Yhwh will have done (vv. 8–10), which corresponds to a motif that sometimes comes at the end of a psalm. The same is true of the suppliant's declaration of commitment to honoring Yhwh for the anticipated act of deliverance (vv. 11–13). Only with the last section (vv. 14–17) do we get something like a lament with a brief account of the suppliant's predicament, though even here a plea for God to turn and act dominates the prayer. Thus the suppliant's need dominates the outer sections, but the praise of Yhwh dominates the middle sections.[6]

The prayer's dominant image is of Yhwh as the suppliant's master and the suppliant as Yhwh's servant.[7] The word "my Lord" comes seven times,[8] a number equaled only by Lam. 2, which is much longer[9] ("my God" also comes twice). Conversely, words for servant or maid come four times. The psalm thus works within the framework of the relationship of mutual "commitment" between a master and a servant (vv. 2, 5, 13,

---

5. Brueggemann, *Message of the Psalms*, 61, 62 (part of the first quotation is in italics).

6. Further on the structure, see Pierre Auffret, "Essai sur la structure littéraire du Psaume lxxxvi," *VT* 29 (1979): 385–402.

7. Vorndran calls *'ădōnāy* the psalm's *Leitwort* ("*Alle Völker worden kommen*," 91).

8. For each occurrence there are MSS or ancient versions that omit the word or read "Yhwh," assimilating the psalm to more familiar usage.

9. There are other chapters that use the combined title "[My] Lord Yhwh" more times, esp. in Ezekiel.

15). Slightly ironically, the middle sections (vv. 8–13) also three times concern themselves with the honoring and revering of Yhwh's "name," the name the psalm somewhat avoids using in favor of that description of Yhwh's lordly relationship with the suppliant. Further, the word *nepeš* (*person) comes five times, which is a pointer to the servant's need, since the word presupposes our vulnerability as human beings. The word "because" also keeps recurring in two different ways to reinforce the plea. In each of the first four verses it makes statements about the servant's need and thus overtly introduces the reason why Yhwh should reach out to the suppliant. Five times subsequently—including the last line of every section—it does that more covertly in making a statement of faith that indicates the reason why the suppliant or others reach out to Yhwh (vv. 5, 7, 10, 13, 17) (there are other such statements of faith that might have been so introduced, notably in vv. 8, 15).[10] Mostly in connection with these statements, six times the servant addresses his master with the pronoun "you" (vv. 2, 5, 10a, 10b, 15, 17), which also draws attention to the fact that this psalm is entirely addressed to God;[11] other psalms regularly address other people, the self, and no one in particular (see Pss. 85 and 87 on either side). The suffix -$k\bar{a}$ (you/your) also comes 23 times.

While the psalm could no doubt be used by an ordinary individual, the stress on the servant-master relationship would make it especially open to use by a person such as a governor or a king (singular "servant of Yhwh" in the OT usually denotes such a person) or by the community as Yhwh's servant; either would fit well with the references to the nations in vv. 8–10. The fact that the psalm is so soaked in other Scriptures presumably implies that it is quite a late psalm.

> Plea. David's.

Heading. See glossary. We can only speculate why a David psalm "interrupts" the Korah psalms.[12]

86:1–7. The first section begins in the common fashion of a prayer with a plea for Yhwh to listen and an appeal in general terms for God's deliverance, and it provides arguments for that in terms of the suppliant's need and Yhwh's character. The section works abb′a′: appeal to Yhwh for a hearing (v. 1), appeal as a servant to my God, my Lord, for deliverance (vv. 2–3), renewed appeal as a servant to my Lord, my Lord for deliverance (vv. 4–5), renewed appeal to Yhwh for a hearing (vv. 6–7).

---

10. EVV sometimes do not translate the *kî*.

11. Cf. Schaefer, *Psalms*, 211.

12. For sample guesses, see Cole, *Shape and Message of Book III*, 136–37; Cole also discusses at length the psalm's relationship to its context in the Psalter.

> ¹Incline your ear, Yhwh, answer me,
>   because I am weak and needy.

The psalm's first appeal, then, is for Yhwh to listen and answer on the basis of the suppliant being *weak and *needy. There is a neat paronomasia involved in the use of the verb ʿānâ I, "answer," and the adjective ʿānî, "weak," from ʿānâ III. Answering presupposes strength, yet it sounds as if it is related to weakness. It is the natural response to weakness; for it to ignore weakness would be unnatural.

> ²Look after my life, because I am committed;
>   deliver your servant: you are my God.
> As the one who trusts in you, ³be gracious to me, my Lord,
>   because I call to you all day long.

Verse 2a–b is formally parallel to v. 1,[13] but it moves to the substance of the appeal and begins to introduce the psalm's recurrent trope. The suppliant is a servant, which in the case of a servant of this master also means being a person who is *committed. The two noun clauses "I am a committed person [a ḥāsîd]" and "You are my God" stand over against each other at the end of the two parallel cola (the "because" implicitly applies in the second colon as well as in the first). In the background one can sense the mutual relationship that is the individual equivalent to "You are our God" and "We are your people." There is the same ambiguity about the word ḥāsîd as appeared in 85:8 [9]; it can indicate a status or a way of life. Fortunately for us, the fact that Yhwh made a commitment means Yhwh is unable to get out of being committed, even when human beings fail in their commitment. The verb "*deliver" gives specificity to "look after": whereas we always need our life to be looked after, only in dangerous situations do we need deliverance.

A further parallel line (vv. 2c–3) characterizes the suppliant in one more way, addresses God in one more way, issues one more appeal, and adds another "because" clause.[14] The suppliant is one who *trusts. The other side of the master-servant relationship becomes explicit in the first use of the term "my *Lord." This Lord is urged to be *gracious, the attitude that would issue in listening and delivering. The reasoning is the fact that

---

13. Again there are two verbs (asyndetic), a "because" clause identifying the suppliant in two ways, and a term for God as addressee, though they are slightly differently expressed: in the second line, the pronoun comes first. We might reckon that the suffix on ʿabdĕkā also applies to ḥāsîd: "I am one committed to you" (so Dahood, *Psalms*, 2:293).

14. This supports the linking of the last phrase in v. 2 with what follows, which makes the division into poetic lines work better. Like v. 1, the line is not internally parallel, unless we see the "because" clause as spelling out what "trust" means.

621

the suppliant calls on this Lord. Both trust and calling can be directed in other ways than toward Yhwh: for instance, toward other deities. This servant looks to only one master, as later lines will make explicit; but here, perhaps the stress lies on the consideration at the end of the line. The fact that the suppliant calls all day long (or every day) is an indication of how pressing is the situation out of which this plea comes.

> ⁴Rejoice the soul of your servant,
>   because to you, my Lord, I lift up my soul.
> ⁵Because you are my Lord, good and forgiving,
>   big in commitment to everyone who calls you.

Two further lines parallel vv. 2–3 but go beyond them in their appeal and on its basis. Asking for joy goes beyond the appeals in vv. 2–3. As usual, the word "soul" is not a very satisfactory translation of *nepeš*, which was also the word translated "life" in v. 2. The plea asks for the servant's whole being, the inner and the outer *person, to be given joy, even as the servant's whole person is lifted up to its *Lord. In prayer I lift up my hands and my eyes to my Lord, and that is an outward sign that I am reaching up to appeal to my Lord with my whole being. The TNIV paraphrases "I put my trust," NJPS, "I set my hope." There is an implicit contrast with the possibility of lifting up my soul to another deity (cf. 24:4, in some MSS and ancient versions). "Servant" and "Lord" at last come together in the parallelism of the two cola.[15]

Verse 5 begins with a fifth "because," but this "because" clause is quite different from the preceding four. Each of them occupied a colon or less; this one occupies the whole line. And each of them appealed to who the suppliant is (vv. 1–2) or what the suppliant does (vv. 3–4);[16] this one appeals to who Yhwh is. First, my *Lord is *good. Something of the nature of that goodness is spelled out in what follows, which hints that in itself the word points to God's generosity. First, it means God is forgiving. The word comes from *sālaḥ*, not the word for "carry" that EVV regularly translate "forgive," which came in 85:2 [3], but one suggesting the pardon that a person in authority gives an ordinary person; this further fits the focus on the master-servant relationship in the psalm. It is the verb Moses uses in appealing to Yhwh at Sinai (Exod. 34:9). Significantly, the suppliant then goes on to characterize Yhwh as big in *commitment, which was part of Yhwh's own self-characterization at Sinai (Exod. 34:7). Here, uniquely, "forgiving" is an adjective, *sallāḥ*, suggesting that Yhwh is not merely one who does forgive but one who is

15. Formally, the lines are not parallel at all; v. 4b completes v. 4a (again, cf. v. 1). But "servant" and "Lord" form a pair, and the word "soul" comes in both lines.
16. If there is a covert "because" in v. 2b, this would be different.

forgiving by nature.[17] And "calling" is perhaps more pressing or confident
or bold than "calling to" (v. 3; see on 89:26 [27]).

> [6]Give ear to my plea, Yhwh,
>   attend to the sound of my prayers for grace.
> [7]On the day of my trouble I call you,
>   because you answer me.

The psalm reverts to a plea for Yhwh to listen and answer, bringing vv.
1–7 to a close. In the first two parallel cola[18] "give ear" picks up "your
ear" in v. 1. Then, as well as paralleling *plea, "prayers for *grace" picks
up "be gracious" in v. 3.

Verse 7a implicitly adds to the reasons why Yhwh should respond to the
prayer, in speaking for the first time of trouble or pressure or constraint
(*ṣar*) from which the suppliant needs deliverance. It thus corresponds
to the self-description as weak and needy in v. 1b, though it presses that
further, as well as picking up the "day" and the "calling" of vv. 3 and 5.
Then the further "because" clause explicitly provides a restated reason
for that calling, and in doing so picks up the verb from v. 1a and thus
heightens the way in which vv. 1 and 7 form an inclusion: in v. 1 "answer"
was an imperative; now it comes in a statement of faith.

86:8–10. The description of the servant's Lord that follows expresses the
suppliant's faith and implicitly provides further motivation for the master
to respond, though it also takes further the earlier characterization of the
Lord. Its subject is not merely who Yhwh is personally, but who Yhwh is
over against other gods, the other masters that this servant might call on
but does not: because Yhwh is not merely unique in the way that everyone
is unique but is uniquely powerful in deeds. Implicitly, these are the power
and deeds that the servant needs to see operating. Their demonstration,
then, will solve the suppliant's problem and bring Yhwh glory. In this section, vv. 8 and 10 form an inclusion around v. 9. The inclusion declares
the reasons for the expectation expressed in the tricolon in v. 9. Verse 10a
corresponds to v. 8b and v. 10b to v. 8a, so that the whole works abcb′a′.

> [8]There is no one like you among the gods, my Lord,
>   and there is nothing like your deeds.
> [9]All the nations, which you made,
>   will come and bow low before you, my Lord,
>   and honor your name,

17. Hossfeld and Zenger, *Psalms 2*, 372.
18. They work abca′c′, with the invocation of "Yhwh" applying to both cola, two
rhyming hiphil imperatives, and "the sound of my prayers for grace" (the expanded phrase,
with pl. noun) complementing "my plea."

> [10]Because you are great and one who does wonders;
>   you are God alone.

The declaration that there is no one like Yhwh among the gods comes a number of times in the OT.[19] Among the nearest parallels to this one are Exod. 15:11 (though that is a question, with explicit reference to other gods) and 2 Sam. 7:22; 1 Kings 8:23 (direct statements, like this one). All refer to the locus of Yhwh's uniqueness in Yhwh's deeds, which the second colon here makes specific. And all belong in the context of worship; while the declaration is a kind of doctrinal formulation, it is one that takes the (proper?) doctrinal form of doxology.

In contrast, the description of the nations as made by the *Lord is distinctive to this psalm,[20] but it is apposite: "It ought not to be accounted strange if they . . . should at length acknowledge Him who had created and fashioned them."[21] The essential physical expression of their worship involves a symbolic horizontal bodily movement (come) and a symbolic vertical bodily movement (*bow low). The essential verbal and/or mental and/or practical expression of worship involves "honoring" Yhwh's *name (kābēd piel). Etymologically, the English word "worship" suggests acknowledging God's "worth"; that is not suggested by any of the Hebrew words that EVV translate by the word "worship" (such as hištaḥăwû in v. 9b), but "acknowledging God's worth" is suggested by this verb.

Verse 10 then restates v. 8. The first colon makes explicit what was incomparable about my Lord and my Lord's deeds: this Lord is great, and the evidence of that is the *wonders that the Lord does. The second colon expresses more radically the point in v. 10a. My Lord is so unlike the other gods, it does not really do to use the same word for both. Only my Lord deserves the word 'ĕlōhîm. In light of the Lord's act, the nations will acknowledge that and bow down.

86:11–13. The declaration about the nations' commitment is complemented by a declaration of the servant's own commitment, which also relates to the way Yhwh will act to deliver the suppliant. That deliverance will give the suppliant something to confess, and the suppliant will not fall short on that confession.

> [11]Teach me your way, Yhwh,
>   I will walk in your truthfulness;
>   unite my heart in reverence for your name.

19. On the "gods," see on 82:1.
20. The point is highlighted by the inclusion of the particle 'ăšer, usually omitted in poetry.
21. Calvin, *Psalms*, 3:386.

Verses 8–10 have spoken of Yhwh's way of acting in the world in marvelous deeds, and the suppliant wants to understand that some more, in the sense of seeing it operative in life. While the request has implications for a life that is lived in a godly way, it refers first to a life lived by trust in Yhwh as the God who does act thus. Verse 11b spells that out. In the context, walking in Yhwh's *truthfulness means walking a path that Yhwh's truthfulness protects and surrounds. At the moment the path does not look like this; the suppliant wants to experience it that way. Verse 11c again links with what preceded. If there were lots of gods, it might be reasonable to spread one's *reverence—one's worship and prayers—around them. But if Yhwh is the only real God, as Yhwh's deeds indicate, then the suppliant's heart cannot be divided in that way. Yhwh's singleness needs to be matched by an undivided commitment of the person. Elsewhere the OT emphasizes the fact that Yhwh is one and promises that Yhwh will correlatively give Israel one heart and one way—the word "way" comes in the first colon—in reverence for Yhwh (Deut. 6:5; Jer 32:39).[22] The psalm asks for Yhwh to do that.

> [12]I will confess you, my Lord, my God, with all my heart,
> and I shall honor your name forever.

Verse 12 complements the plea for God's work in the inner person with a commitment to do what one can. Yhwh's action counts for nothing without our action; our action counts for nothing without Yhwh's. In the context of v. 11, the first colon would again recall Deut. 6:5. But the psalm speaks of "confession" (*yādâ* hiphil), which by its nature relates to things Yhwh has actually done; like vv. 8–10, the line therefore looks forward to the time when Yhwh has answered the prayer in vv. 1–7. The suppliant will not keep quiet then. So the suppliant will indeed do what the nations are due eventually to do: honor Yhwh's name (cf. v. 9)—and do so forever. When God acts for us, we do not just give one thank-you. It has such an effect on us that the praise will never stop resounding (cf. 30:11–12 [12–13]).

> [13]Because your commitment is great toward me,
> and you will rescue my life from deepest Sheol.

The "because" again relates to the character and action of Yhwh that will be involved in the suppliant's rescue. On one hand, it is Yhwh's great *commitment, words picked up from vv. 5 and 10. On the other, it is

---

22. "One" is *'eḥād*, "unite" is *yāḥad*, and these are two different roots, but the verb would sound near enough to the word for "one" to suggest this link. LXX and Syr, "May my heart rejoice," imply *yiḥadd* from *ḥādâ* for MT *yaḥēd*.

because of the deed that will express that commitment; here the more down-to-earth term "rescue" (*nāṣal* hiphil) takes the place of the more theological term "deliver" (v. 2). The *w*-qatal verb recognizes the facts of the situation: the rescue has not yet taken place, but it will.[23] Finally, the closing prepositional phrase slips in a description of the extreme trouble the suppliant is in. Such descriptions have become more extreme as the psalm has gone on: compare vv. 1, 7. Now in effect the suppliant is deep in *Sheol, overwhelmed by the forces of death even while continuing to be (nominally) in life (cf. 18:5 [6]; 30:3 [4]). Since the Israelites do not seem to have reckoned that Sheol had different levels, "deepest Sheol" refers to Sheol as by nature a deep place from which no one can climb out (cf. 63:9 [10]).[24] Yet that does not make it inaccessible to Yhwh, who can reach in and rescue. The first colon underlines this as it more literally describes Yhwh's commitment as great "over me," so that the two cola contrast height and depth.[25]

86:14–17. The psalm returns to plea for the last section, beginning with the most specific description of the suppliant's predicament and ending with its most specific prayer. Tricola concerned with the psalmist's adversaries open and close the section (vv. 14, 17), while the Lord and the servant dominate the heart of it (vv. 15–16).

> [14]God, willful people have arisen against me,
>   a group of terrifying people have sought my life,
>   people who have not put you before their eyes.

The description of the suppliant's predicament turns out to express itself in terms that are almost the same as 54:3 [5] (see the comment there), which warns us once again against inferring literal experience from language that is formulaic, like the language of Christian prayer.

23. EVV translate with perfect verbs, but it makes sense to translate the *w*-qatal in the usual way, as future. Reckoning that the act of deliverance has already happened makes it hard to make sense of the psalm as a whole (Dahood, *Psalms*, 2:295–96). If we do translate as past, the reference will still be to an act that is future from the suppliant's perspective but will be past when vv. 11–13 become operative (cf. Kidner, *Psalms*, 2:313).

24. But Augustine, for instance, infers that there was an upper and a lower Sheol, the former a place of rest, the latter a place of torment (*Psalms*, 415–16; cf. Cassiodorus, *Psalms*, 2:333–34). Calvin notes that this passage then gives "the Papists" an argument for purgatory, which would be the upper level of Sheol (cf. http://www.catholiceducation. org/articles/apologetics/ap0091.html), but unfortunately he declares that "this argument is too rotten to stand in need of refutation" (*Psalms*, 3:390) and therefore does not offer one. Luther sees the upper level as the grave for bodies, the lower level as the location of souls, but gives a hostage to theological fortune in also referring to souls being in limbo (*First Lectures*, 2:175).

25. Cf. NEB's "stands high above me," with the comments in Rogerson and McKay, *Psalms*, 2:180.

In the three parallel cola God comes first, but then becomes more and more marginalized as the line unfolds. There is no appeal to God in the second or third cola (though the appeal does apply there, too), and in the third colon God appears only to be ignored. Conversely, the suppliant's attackers get a one-word description in the first colon, a two-word description in the second, and then occupy the whole of the third. And the suppliant is the object of one threatening verb in the first colon, then of a life-threatening verb in the second, after which there could be nothing else to say.[26]

The willful or arrogant or proud or insolent (*zēd*) are people who are confident they can make their own decisions and impose them on others. They acknowledge no need to defer to the authority of others, including God (e.g., Deut. 1:43; 17:12–13; 18:20–22). They make up their own mind about the social and moral standards for their lives. Thus "willful" is spelled out in the third colon.

This attitude expresses itself in the behavior toward other people described in the middle colon. A difference from Ps. 54 here is the additional reference to their being a "group." The word is *'ēdâ*, which most commonly refers to the "assembly" or "congregation" of the Israelite people. It suggests that they are well organized and hints that they are a demonic alternative to the proper *'ēdâ*. Their "arising" might be in attacks of any kind: plotting, making war, or making accusations in court. Whichever it is, this aspect of the first colon is spelled out in the second colon's talk of "seeking my life."

> ¹⁵But you are my Lord, the compassionate and gracious God,
> long-tempered and big in commitment and truthfulness.

It is as well that the psalm can set over against that congregation a description of God's compassion, *graciousness, long-temperedness, *commitment, and *truthfulness. This takes up more systematically Yhwh's self-description at Sinai, alluded to in v. 5. The reference compares (e.g.) with 51:1–2 [3–4]; 77:8–9 [9–10]; 78:38, but here the words exactly correspond to the text of Exod. 34:6, perhaps because the formulation was used in liturgy.[27] A difference is that there, the word before the quoted section is the actual name "Yhwh." The occurrence of "my Lord" in its place here presumably reflects patterns of usage in some communities whereby the congregation replaced the name Yhwh with "my Lord," as eventually became universal Jewish practice.[28] At the

---

26. In other words, the cola work abcb′c′b″.

27. Cf. Hermann Spiekermann, "'Barmherzig und gnädig ist der Herr . . . ,'" *ZAW* 102 (1990): 1–18.

28. See the introduction to Pss. 42–43.

same time, in this psalm it plays into the recurrent appeal to the master-servant relationship.

"Long-tempered" is literally "long of angers." The description stands over against the comments in 85:3, 5 [4, 6]. There are times when Yhwh's anger rages and when people may fear that it may continue to rage for a long time, but in other contexts they recognize that it takes Yhwh a long time to get angry or to be willing to express anger.

> ¹⁶Turn your face to me and be gracious to me,
>   give your strength to your servant, deliver the son of your maid.

This time the appeal to turn the face and be *gracious repeats the appeal in 25:16 (cf. also 69:16 [17]). "Turn the face" is not *šûb*, the verb suggesting "turn back" that recurred in Ps. 85, but *pānâ*, which suggests how looking at someone and seeing their predicament leads to action. Like v. 15, the line comprises two long, parallel cola, each of which divides into two; in v. 16 are two parallel verbal expressions in each colon. Turning the face issues in grace; giving *strength issues in *deliverance. "Strength" may again have overtones of "refuge," as in 84:5 [6], but the fact that the psalm refers to "your strength" suggests this is less prominent. Rather, the plea parallels the main idea in 84:5 [6], that Yhwh somehow imparts strength to the suppliant in a way that makes it possible to stand firm, resist, and win out over against the attackers. Thus the suppliant will find deliverance. Here again the suppliant appeals as servant to Lord (v. 15): it is reasonable for a servant thus to expect the master's support. "Son of your maid" characterizes the servant further in conventional fashion as the son of a servant who herself was a member of the master's household. This underlines the sense of obligation that the master should feel to this person who has always been a member of the master's family (cf. the regulation in Exod. 21:4).

> ¹⁷Give me a sign of good things,
>   so that the people who are against me may see and be shamed,
>   because you, Yhwh, have helped me and comforted me.

As v. 14 made the suppliant's need more specific—at least in a figurative sense—so the closing tricolon makes the suppliant's plea more specific, though again not in a concrete way. The psalm stays accessible and usable to many people through not being too concrete. Literally, the servant asks the master to "do with me a sign," asking that the confession that the Lord is one who "does wonders" (v. 10) may be vindicated in the servant's life. Sometimes a sign is something that will merely promise or symbolize the real thing, the actual deliverance. Here the second colon suggests that this sign is more than that, perhaps like the signs in Egypt.[29] But unlike them (at least, in their implications for Egypt), this is a sign of *good things (cf. 84:11 [12]; 85:12 [13]). It is some expression of the master's commitment that will put in their place the people who are *against the suppliant, showing them to be wrong and exposing them to themselves and to the community as a whole.[30] The psalm closes with a final "because" that again makes that more concrete in speaking of *help and comfort (see on 71:21).

Theological Implications

Whereas EVV are dominated by the image of God as Lord because they replace the name "Yhwh" with the word "LORD," the OT itself does not often speak of Yhwh as "Lord." It has a much less patriarchal cast than EVV imply. Psalm 86 proves the rule. It places great emphasis on the fact that Yhwh is my Lord and I am Yhwh's servant, but it does that in order to claim the support of my Lord. To be another's Lord puts one into a position of responsibility. The relationship means the Lord has the resources and the obligation to support the servant. The psalm thus takes up the commitment Yhwh makes to Israel:

> I said to you, You are my servant,
>> I chose you, I did not reject you.
> Do not be afraid, because I am with you;
>> do not be frightened, because I am your God.
> I will strengthen you, yes, I will help you,
>> yes, I will uphold you with my faithful right hand.
> Now: they will be ashamed and disgraced,
>> all the people who contend with you.
> They will become absolutely nothing, they will perish,
>> the people who strive against you.
> You will search for them and not find them,
>> the people who fight you.
> They will become absolutely nothing, nonexistent,
>> the people who make war against you.

> (Isa. 41:9–12)

By definition servants are people who are weak and needy; they have no power and no resources of their own and have to trust their mas-

29. In the context it is less likely to be a prophetic sign or omen (Mowinckel, *Psalms in Israel's Worship*, 2:66) since this would be less likely to have the result described in v. 17b.

30. Michael L. Barré has noted the political imagery in v. 17a–b ("A Cuneiform Parallel to Ps 86:16–17 and Mic 7:16–17," *JBL* 101 [1982]: 271–75).

ter. They are people who have only one master and serve that master wholeheartedly. But the master is someone with power and resources, and a servant can call on the master and expect to find support and help. The relationship is not a merely contractual one, like those in modern employment. It makes demands on the servant and takes away from the servant's freedom, but it also makes demands on the master and takes away from the master's freedom. It gives the servant something to appeal to. In earthly servant-master relationships, doubtless that often failed to work, and a servant might feel inhibited in appealing to it. Servants of Yhwh need no such hesitation.

We have noted that the psalm takes up phraseology from other psalms and from elsewhere in the OT, in the manner that would in due course be followed by the Revelation to John. Revelation 15:4 does seem to take up Ps. 86:9–10 itself, in portraying the worship of the victors at the End. The psalm reckons that the master-servant relationship is good news now and not merely at a far-off End.[31]

---

31. For the psalm's other intertextual relationships, see Vorndran, *"Alle Völker worden kommen."*

Psalm 87

The Nations as Citizens of Zion

Translation

The Korahites'. Composition. Song.

¹Founded by him among the holy mountains,
    ²Yhwh is dedicated to Zion's gates
    more than all Jacob's settlements.
³Honorable things are spoken in you,[1]
    city of God. (Rise)
⁴I will name Rahab and Babylon to the people who acknowledge me;[2]
    yes, Philistia and Tyre, with Sudan;
    each one was born there.
⁵So to Zion it will be said:
    Each and every one[3] was born in it;
    he himself will establish it on high.
⁶Yhwh will record, in writing down[4] the peoples:
    Each one was born there. (Rise)

1. Lit. "Honorable things [are what] is spoken in you." The ptc. is f. pl. and the verb is not only m. but also sg., so the ptc. can hardly simply be the subj. Rather, the construction is impersonal, and the ptc. is the quasi-obj. of the impersonal verb. Cf. Calvin, *Psalms*, 3:398; *TTH* 120.6; JM 128b (GKC 121d doubts this understanding but offers no alternative; cf. GKC 145u).
2. C has "who acknowledge him" (see *BHS*).
3. Lit. "a person and a person"; see GKC 123c.
4. LXX and Th imply *bikĕtob*, "in the writing/register of," for MT's inf. *bikĕtôb*; Jerome and Aq read as MT.

⁷And they sing as they pipe/dance:⁵
All my founts are in you.⁶

Interpretation

Psalm 87 is a prophetic psalm concerning Yhwh's relationship with Zion and with the nations. Verses 1–3 address Zion itself, declaring that "honorable things" are spoken in it. Verse 4 then relates the word from Yhwh that identifies the nature of the honorable message. In vv. 5–6 the psalmist affirms and restates that message, and finally in v. 7 describes the nations' response. The psalm is "terse, abrupt, enigmatic, like a prophetic oracle"[7]—perhaps because that is what it is.[8] This aspect of the psalm makes it unlikely that it is part of a liturgy for processing the admission of individual foreigners into the temple.[9] It has also made it one of the more emended and rearranged of psalms, but allowing for its enigmatic nature, there are not so many indications of variants in the ancient versions, and no emendations or rearrangement have carried conviction. I seek to understand it as it stands in MT.

It is simultaneously one of the most particularist and one of the most universalist of psalms. It enthuses about Zion more dramatically than any other psalm, yet this celebration focuses on the fact that Zion belongs not just to Israel but also to the world. Although it expresses itself in distinctive fashion, its vision is thus one with prophecies such as Isa. 2:2–4 and Isa. 60–62. In its context in the Psalter, it follows well on 86:8–10, though it also has points of contact and contrast with other psalms about Zion, especially Pss. 46 and 48, and with Ps. 83.[10] Like other psalms, it is subject today as much as ever to a wide range of views

5. I take *ḥōlĕlîm* as a qal ptc. from *ḥālal*, "pipers"; cf. Tg, Sym; *DCH*. Aq and Jerome imply a word for "dancers," and BDB thus takes the word as a polel ptc. from *ḥûl*, lacking its preformative *m*. To get this meaning, more likely we should take it as a qal ptc. from a by-form *ḥālal* that means "dance." But piping is quite in place. LXX "make merry" could represent either verb.

6. For the translation of the line, see T. Booij, "Some Observations on Psalm lxxxvii," *VT* 37 (1987): 16–25 (see 21). LXX associates "They sing" (reading *šārîm* as *śārîm*, "leaders") with v. 6 and associates *kol* (all) with the first half of the line. It then has "The abode is in you," implying a form of *mā'ôn* for MT *ma'yānay* (cf. 84:6 [7]). This fits the context very well and looks like an easier reading.

7. Kirkpatrick, *Psalms*, 518.

8. Booij sees vv. 4 and 6 in particular as reflecting a prophetic-visionary moment ("Some Observations on Psalm lxxxvii," 24).

9. So Gerstenberger, *Psalms*, 2:140.

10. See Erich Zenger, "Zion as Mother of the Nations in Psalm 87," in *The God of Israel and the Nations*, ed. Norbert Lohfink and Erich Zenger (Collegeville: Liturgical Press, 2000), 123–60 (see 147–56); idem, "Psalm 87," in *Reading from Right to Left* (D. J. A. Clines

regarding its origin, from the united monarchy to the eighth century to the late seventh century to the exile to the early Second Temple period to the later Persian period to the Hellenistic period.

The Korahites'. Composition. Song.

Heading. See glossary.

87:1–3. The opening two lines constitute a series of affirmations about Zion. The city is the direct addressee in v. 3, and I take it as the indirect addressee in vv. 1–2, though there spoken of in the third person.

> ¹Founded by him among the holy mountains,
> ²Yhwh is dedicated to Zion's gates
> more than all Jacob's settlements.

The psalm thus begins with a tricolon.[11] To put it prosaically, "Yhwh is *dedicated to the gates of Zion, which was founded by him among the holy mountains . . ." (cf. NJPS). The two phrases in vv. 1–2 offer several characterizations of Jerusalem, though they never actually mention the city by this name (and neither will the rest of the psalm). Zion is the city's religious and theological name, Jerusalem more its political one.

First, Zion is founded.[12] In some contexts that suggests security, but this is usually made explicit by qualifiers such as "forever" (78:69; 119:152). Without that, the description more often indicates a claim to consequent ownership (cf. 24:1–2; 89:11 [12]). "Founding" is thus equivalent to "building," "making," or "creating," which have the same implication. But the verb "found" is especially familiar in connection with the founding of the temple and other buildings, especially after the exile. Naturally, that is regularly portrayed as human work, which it literally was (Ezra 3:6–12; Hag. 2:18; Zech. 4:9; 8:9). The founding of Zion was the work of the Jebusites, taken on by David and subsequent kings. The psalm begins by claiming the founding of Zion as actually Yhwh's work. "With his own hands God set this stone [the rock of Zion] in place."[13] Isaiah 14:32 refers to Yhwh's founding of Zion and does so

---

Festschrift; ed. J. Cheryl Exum and H. G. M. Williamson; London: Sheffield Academic Press, 2003), 450–60 (see 457–59).

11. I take the first clause as extraposed—or, to put it another way, the subj. and the verb in the second colon also apply to the first. NRSV and TNIV rather take v. 1 as an independent noun clause, but this makes the line as a whole jerky. For other examples where MT's versification separates the first colon from the rest of its line, cf. Pss. 18; 23; 66.

12. The dictionaries take *yĕsûdātô* as the sole occurrence of a noun for "foundation," a f. equivalent to the usual *yĕsôd*. It seems more economical to take it as a passive ptc., with suffix denoting the agent (cf. GKC 116l).

13. Keel, *Symbolism*, 181.

in a message intended for the Philistines; the psalm will soon note the significance of Zion's founding for Philistia, making for a tighter link with Isa. 14:32. That passage can be read as offering an invitation to the Philistines to find refuge in Zion, this place of security; the psalm will make that invitation explicit.

Specifically, Zion is founded "among the holy mountains."[14] The plural phrase comes only here, though Ps. 133:3 refers to "the mountains of Zion" and 125:2 to "the mountains around Jerusalem," while in light of v. 5c the "mountains" of Isa. 2:2 = Mic. 4:1 will also become significant for this colon.[15] The psalm can hardly mean that Zion itself comprises a number of mountains; literally speaking, it hardly comprises one mountain. But it would be odd to describe the mountains around Jerusalem as particularly holy. The holy mountains might stand for Yhwh's own abode in the heavens and/or for the mountains that underlie the earth. But the more immediate context suggests earthly mountains. Perhaps the phrase refers to mountains such as Sinai, Tabor, Carmel, Hermon, and Zaphon.[16] Later verses in the psalm will point to a related possibility. The idea that all the nations will come and live in Jerusalem is clearly not capable of literal fulfillment. The psalm's picture then begins to remind us of Ezek. 40–48 with its symbolic reworking of regional geography. Perhaps Zion stands among a much broader range of imaginary mountains belonging to Yhwh, which the actual mountains around Jerusalem symbolize. This compares with the way the land as a whole can be described as mountain country, even as "mountains" (e.g., Isa. 14:25; 65:9; Ezek. 6:2–3), and that reference would make sense here: the holy mountains are the holy land as a whole, at the center of which Zion is founded. This would give a clearer coherence to the tricolon as a whole, as both cola in v. 2 then spell out v. 1. Parallel to "the holy mountains" is "Jacob's settlements," the places where Israel lives all over the land.[17] These settlements are all good (Num. 24:5); Zion stands *among* them, but it is more important than all of them, insofar as this is the place where Yhwh personally chose to settle (Ps. 74:2). Yhwh made a different kind of commitment to Zion (cf. 78:67–68).

Specifically, again, Yhwh made that commitment to Zion's gates. A city's gate can stand for the city itself and thus for its people (e.g., Isa.

14. EVV have "on," but one would then have expected 'al not b.

15. The prep. and these parallels work against the idea that the pl. is intensive, so the word really refers to the one holy mountain. "The psalmist has a taste for the plural": mountains, gates, settlements, honorable things, peoples, singers, dancers/pipers, all concentrated on one God, one city (Schaefer, *Psalms*, 213).

16. *Midrash on Psalms*, 2:76, names the first three.

17. They are Jacob's settlements, not Yhwh's; i.e., the phrase does not denote sanctuaries spread through the land.

14:31, where the next verse refers to Yhwh's founding Zion); here the psalm uses the plural because Zion is a big city with several gates. The gates of a city keep it secure, as long as they are kept shut; that is, they have the capacity to safeguard its security. It will transpire that the allusion to them here is ironical, because this will turn out to be a city that is open to other peoples and to the good things they will bring (Isa. 60:11).

> ³Honorable things are spoken in you,
>   city of God. (Rise)

The second line parallels the first insofar as it continues to characterize Zion, though the psalmist now directly addresses the city. The concealed subject of the further reverential passive is Yhwh. Yhwh founded Zion and made a commitment to it, and Yhwh speaks honorable things here in Zion[18] as the psalm is declaimed. The next line will indicate what those *honorable things are. Meanwhile, the city is characterized once more as God's city (see 46:4), the city that belongs to the God who founded it, settled there, and speaks there.

87:4. Here, then, are the honorable words that Yhwh speaks.

> ⁴I will name Rahab and Babylon to the people who acknowledge me;
>   yes, Philistia and Tyre, with Sudan;
>   each one was born there.

The pronoun at the end of the first colon makes clear that Yhwh now speaks; perhaps the prophet-psalmist overhears Yhwh announcing intentions in the court of heaven.[19] The only other passage where Yhwh is the subject of this verb (*zākar* hiphil) is Exod. 20:24, where it refers to Yhwh's name being pronounced in worship or prayer. But the participle, in particular, is used in a down-to-earth sense to refer to a recorder or registrar, and vv. 5–6 will make clear that the verb has this nuance here. Yhwh's declaration is a performative act analogous to that of a king declaring conquered peoples to be members of his realm.[20]

The first object of this naming is Rahab, which is one of the names for a sea monster who embodied and symbolized dynamic powers asserted against God; Egypt can then be thought of as its incarnation

18. LXX has "about you," but this is again an odd meaning for *b*, though a possible one (cf. 122:8). But the preposition's regular meaning "in" fits (cf. Aq; BDB 181b) and parallels the usage in v. 1.

19. So Kraus, *Psalms 60–150*, 187.

20. See Tate, *Psalms 51–100*, 390, and his references.

(cf. 89:10 [11]; Job 9:13; 26:12; Isa. 30:7; 51:9).[21] It can thus be rather a solemn designation, or it can be used to make fun of Egypt as lacking the dynamic power it pretended to have. Pairing with the old enemy to the south is Babylon as the great oppressor to the north. Philistia and Tyre were then among the peoples conspiring in 83:5–8 [6–9], so the first four peoples might suggest a roster of enemy nations that "has now become a unity of citizenship within Zion."[22] But Sudan is then a slightly odd addition to the list, which makes it questionable whether there is a single rationale for mentioning these peoples. They are not actually a coherent collection of traditional enemies, nor do they represent the points of the compass, nor do they especially point to one historical period. And the description of Egypt as Rahab suggests that the psalm has other agenda than merely listing enemies; the name points to Egypt's pretensions and/or to its feebleness (or it might be just a nickname). The five peoples are just other peoples (cf. Isa. 19:18–25). But all feature in the prophecies about foreign nations in the Prophets, which characteristically speak of calamity to come on them, though they also usually include some elements of hope for these peoples. This is the aspect the psalm will take up.

The EVV have "among those who acknowledge me," but the preposition is *l*, which usually means "to." This gives a quite satisfactory sense: Yhwh is naming these nations to "the people who acknowledge me," a description of what Israel is or is supposed to be (cf. 36:10 [11]), like "people who are committed to Yhwh" or "people who revere Yhwh" in 85:8–9 [9–10]. Yhwh is making a declaration to Israel about these peoples.

The content of the announcement comes in the third colon. It is that each of these nations was born in Zion; the nation is spoken of as if it were an individual. If we take that literally, then Yhwh is referring to people who were born in Jerusalem but now live in places such as Egypt and Babylon, presumably because they were taken there in the exile.[23] The psalm will then be a reminder and reaffirmation that these people really do belong to Jerusalem and that Jerusalem belongs to them. By implication, Yhwh really intends that these people should come home. The psalm thus reiterates the promise that Yhwh will bring the exiles home.

There are a number of difficulties with this understanding. These were not distinctively places where there were exile communities; what they

---

21. This is *rahab*, not *rāḥāb* as in Josh. 2. Jerome appositely translates *superbia*, but in his exposition (like other patristic commentators) assumes it is the Rahab of Josh. 2 (*Homilies*, 1:138)!

22. Cole, *Shape and Message of Book III*, 161.

23. So, e.g., Rashi.

have in common is that they are nations mentioned as foreign nations in the Prophets, not that there were exiles there. The psalm never makes the point that Yhwh will bring these people home; it simply says that they were born in Jerusalem—which would be uncontroversial—and leaves matters there. And the psalm is speaking about communities, not individuals. Further, it would be odd to refer to (e.g.) Judeans in Egypt simply as "Rahab."

More likely, the psalm is indicating that nations such as Egypt and Babylon will come to be counted as people who were born in Jerusalem, a novel image. The use of the verb then fits that in 2:7, where Yhwh says to the king, "You are my son; I have fathered you [*yālad*] today."[24] The declaration is one whereby a man makes someone his son; adoption is spoken of as fathering. In a similar way, Yhwh declares that each of these nations has been fathered or adopted in Jerusalem so that they become the city's true citizens. To the consternation of the Israelite immigration officials, "the sovereign Lord himself is going to cook the documents and record that these aliens, let alone non-patrial passport holders, were born there," declaring that this will actually add to the nation's security, not detract from it; "and what aliens they are!"—mostly enemies and oppressors.[25] Even the dragon people come to worship Yhwh.[26] While the idea fits the Prophets' references to other nations coming to Jerusalem and coming to acknowledge Yhwh, on this understanding the line does make a novel, pointed, and vivid statement in describing the nations as in effect people born in Jerusalem. That may make them full members of the "family," as happens when someone is adopted, or they may have the status of servants born in a household who are thus members of it while still distinguishable from the family in the narrow sense (cf. the *yālîd* of Gen. 14:14; 17:12–13; Jer. 2:14).[27]

87:5–7. The last lines of the psalm constitute a double response to Yhwh's words, one in vv. 5–6, another in v. 7.

> [5]So to Zion it will be said:
>   Each and every one was born in it;
>   he himself will establish it on high.
> [6]Yhwh will record, in writing down the peoples:
>   Each one was born there. (Rise)

First comes the psalmist's response, a twofold affirmation of what Yhwh has said. After the resumptive "so" (*w*), each of the two lines restates

24. Tg indeed thinks the psalm here refers to that anointed king.
25. Hill, *Prayer, Praise and Politics*, 83.
26. Roland B. Allen, "Psalm 87," *BSac* 153 (1996): 131–40 (see 138).
27. Cf. Gerstenberger, *Psalms*, 2:139.

Yhwh's point, each thus being parallel to v. 4. "To Zion" thus parallels "to the people who acknowledge me," "it will be said" re-expresses "I will name," "each and every one" re-expresses and emphasizes "each one," and "was born in it" re-expresses "was born there." The "each and every one" thus refers to each of the nations that has been named. As they stand for all the nations, this will imply all the nations.

In the first colon, LXX has "Mother Zion, a person will say."[28] The variant draws attention to the fact that while Zion is feminine, the MT psalm at no point explicitly describes Zion as mother (or daughter) in the manner of (e.g.) Isa. 40–55. In MT, Zion is a city in which the nations are granted citizenship, not a mother gaining children as in Isa. 54. If the MT psalm represents a reinterpretation of Pss. 46 and 48, "a postexilic new version of the preexilic Zion theology,"[29] the LXX's development of the motif "Zion will be called our mother" takes further the MT psalm's own radical reworking of that theology.[30]

Verse 5c stands in some isolation from its context, and in this it parallels v. 1. Indeed, in content and language these two link as they refer to Zion's founding and establishing; the verbs "found" and "establish" come in parallelism in 24:2 (also Prov. 3:19) with reference to the founding and establishing of the cosmos.[31] It is almost as if v. 1 were waiting for a colon to pair with it and that 5c is that colon.[32] Considering the two cola together suggests that while Zion's founding lies in the past, and thus the city is quite secure, its establishing lies in the future.[33] How could that be? Reference to Yhwh's establishing the city or the temple is actually unusual, but in Isa. 2:2 = Mic. 4:1 Yhwh declares that the mountain where Yhwh's house stands "will be established" as or on the top of the mountains, for nations to stream to it. This suggests the point in this context. The establishing of Zion in the future, which will fulfill

28. While possibly an indication that LXX has (e.g.) *'ēm yō'mar* for *yē'āmar* (e.g., Gunkel, *Psalmen*, 380), suggesting haplography in MT or dittog. in LXX, more likely this is simply an interpretive translation. See further Georg Schmuttermayr, "Um Psalm 87 (86), 5," *BZ* 7 (1963): 104–10; J. A. Emerton, "The Problem of Psalm lxxxvii," *VT* 50 (2000): 183–99 (see 187).

29. Hossfeld and Zenger, *Psalms 2*, 382. See further Zenger, "Zion as Mother," 144–45.

30. Cf. Christl M. Maier, "'Zion wird man Mutter nennen,'" forthcoming in *ZAW* 118 (2006): 582–96; cf. John J. Schmitt, "Psalm 87," in *The Psalms and Other Studies on the Old Testament* (Joseph I. Hunt Festschrift; ed. Jack C. Knight and Lawrence A. Sinclair; Nashotah, WI: Nashotah House, 1990), 34–44 (see 35–36).

31. LXX and Jerome use words from the same root for the two different Hebrew words in vv. 1 and 5.

32. Weiser (*Psalms*, 579) thus moves v. 5c up to join v. 1.

33. Contrast LXX, Jerome, Sym, and Th, which have a past verb in v. 5 (Tg and Aq follow MT). Similarly bemused by the yiqtol, NJPS translates "preserve," which is hard to parallel.

the purpose of its founding, is the act that will make it home for Rahab, Babylon, Philistia, Tyre, and Sudan. This also confirms the understanding of the last word in the colon suggested by the word order, that *'elyôn* refers not to Yhwh as the Most High but to Zion being established as the most high.[34]

Verse 6 then restates how Yhwh will establish the city on high. The first colon tells us that this will be by designating these peoples as citizens of Zion, and the second indicates once more how Yhwh will do that. Yhwh's declaration that these peoples were fathered in Zion is put into writing in a metaphorical citizen list. It is as if Yhwh *is* the registrar, the *mazkîr* (see v. 4). This guarantees the position of these peoples. Unlike (for instance) British people becoming citizens of the United States, they do not give up their former identity and their individuality as Egypt, Babylon, Philistia, Tyre, and Sudan but become peoples of a dual citizenship.

> [7]And they sing as they pipe/dance:
> All my founts are in you.

Verse 7 constitutes an enigmatic ending to a psalm that has had its enigmatic moments. To work from the end of the line, I take it that "you" is Zion rather than Yhwh,[35] because the psalm has focused on the significance of Zion and has previously addressed Zion, not Yhwh. "All my founts are in you" is then a response to Yhwh's word about Zion. The image of "fountains" might be used in a variety of connections (see, e.g., Isa. 12:3; Joel 3:18 [4:18]); the present context suggests it refers to the conception of children. If these peoples were fathered in Zion, then that is where the fountains were that brought them into being (Prov. 5:16; cf. Song 4:12, 15). These words are the words of the people singing and piping or dancing, who represent the nations that are being told that they have a place and a home in Zion, like immigrants rejoicing that they have been granted citizenship in the United States. Singing and piping or dancing around Zion would be features of any celebration, so these people are behaving the way anyone would at a festival (see Ps. 122; 1 Kings 1:40). Perhaps the excitement of the festival stimulated this oracle concerning a festival of much wider import.[36] Certainly these

34. The word order is odd if *'elyôn* qualifies *hû'* at the beginning of the line. The word is used to describe the Davidic king in 89:27 [28], the temple in 1 Kings 9:8 and 2 Chron. 7:21, and the people (in relation to the nations) in Deut. 26:19 and 28:1.

35. Grammatically, the *-āk* ending could be f. or m. in pause. Read as f., "in you" completes an abcba sequence in vv. 3–7 (in you–there–in it–there–in you) (Mark S. Smith, "The Structure of Psalm lxxxvii," *VT* 38 [1988]: 357–58).

36. Cf. Weiser, *Psalms*, 580–82.

pilgrims have their distinctive praise to offer. Thus the verse describes the nations' own response to Yhwh's word in v. 4, which the psalmist affirmed in vv. 5–6. After all, foreign shores have been waiting for such a word (cf. Isa. 42:4), even if they did not recognize it.

Theological Implications

The heart of the psalm is the threefold affirmation, expressed in Yhwh's words and then twice in the psalmist's, in vv. 4–6. It is uttered not for the sake of the nations themselves (who are not hearing the psalm and are not addressed) but for the sake of the people of Jerusalem. We know from prayers in Lamentations, Ezra 9, Neh. 9, and Dan. 9 that they became understandably gloomy and closed in on themselves during the exile and afterward, and we know from Ezra–Nehemiah that they felt the need to separate themselves from other peoples in various ways lest they lose their identity and compromise their commitment to Yhwh. The psalm is concerned to encourage them by reminding them of Yhwh's big purpose for Jerusalem. In its vision it compares with a number of passages in the Prophets, especially in Isaiah. To Isa. 2:2–4 it adds that the nations really belong in Jerusalem; they are its citizens. It compares with Isa. 19:18–25 except that it puts Jerusalem at the center of the picture in portraying Yhwh's relationship with the nations on either side of Israel. To Isa. 44:5 it adds that the initiative in setting up this adoptive relationship lies with Yhwh. It compares with Isa. 60–62 except that those chapters focus more on the way the coming of the nations honors Jerusalem itself.

Yhwh never did what the psalm actually says; it is of course logistically impossible (one might again compare the psalm with the vision of a transformed land in Ezek. 40–48). But over subsequent centuries many people within the nations around Israel came to believe in Yhwh, becoming God-fearers or proselytes. Many of these would make pilgrimage to Jerusalem for one of the festivals (and might then be encouraged by this psalm). Their presence there for a festival stands in the background of Acts 2 (see Acts 2:9–11). The ensuing spread of the message about Christ provided another form of partial fulfillment of the prophecy as Gentiles come to be "citizens with the saints and also members of the household of God" (Eph. 2:19). That is itself the firstfruits of something on a vaster scale (Rev. 7). So Ps. 87 becomes a baptism psalm.[37]

The psalm affirms that it is not only the Jerusalem above that is our mother (Gal. 4:26, likely building on v. 5 LXX). Further, the city of God

37. Johanna W. H. Bos, "Psalm 87," *Int* 47 (1993): 281–85 (see 281).

is not only something that lies ahead of us in heaven, a place "whence we are absent, as long as we are mortal."[38] (The hymn "Glorious Things of Thee Are Spoken" is less clear on what it refers to, but it also has little connection with the psalm's own meaning.) Nor do the proselyte nations of Ps. 87 run away from the city to pursue God in private; they stream into it as a place that God loves.[39] The city of God is a place on earth, the scene on which God intends to fulfill the purpose of drawing the nations.

The church suffers from the same temptation as Jerusalem. It is constitutionally inclined to forget that God's purpose is to make all nations its citizens and so becomes gloomy and closed in on itself.[40] The psalm thus sets God's vision before it.

It is probably a coincidence that among the five nations that the psalm names, there is no European people (unless we may count the Philistines, who originally came from across the Mediterranean), but there is an African one.[41] If so, it is a neat coincidence. The psalm declares that an African nation has its citizenship in the city of God. Sudan was born in Zion. Whereas the embracing of ethnic diversity is at least as much a problem in the church as in the world, it coheres with God's intention for Zion. The psalm offers a promise of an ethnically diverse church.

---

38. So, e.g., Augustine, *Psalms*, 419; when he comes to discuss the city of God in *City of God*, Book 11, this is the first Scripture he refers to.

39. Peterson, *Where Your Treasure Is*, 27.

40. Cf. Calvin's long introduction (*Psalms*, 3:393–96).

41. Cf. Hill, *Prayer, Praise and Politics*, 82–87.

Psalm 88

Abba, Father

Translation

Song. Composition. The Korahites'. The leader's. On Sickness/
Entreaty/Adornment/Dancing/Pipe. For affliction/chanting.
Instruction. Heman the Ezrahite's.

¹Yhwh, my God who delivers,[1]
by day I have cried out,[2] by night before you.
²May my plea come before your face;
incline your ear to the sound I make.
³Because my whole person is full of troubles;
my life has arrived at Sheol.
⁴I have come to count with people who go down to the Pit;
I have become like a man who is without strength,
⁵Among the dead an outcast, like the slain,
lying in the grave,
Those of whom[3] you have not been mindful any more;
they have been cut off from your hand.
⁶You have put me in the deepest Pit,
in great darkness, in the depths.

1. RSV emends to produce an occurrence of the verb *šāwaʿ*, "cry for help," which does come in v. 13.
2. In 56:9 [10] a similar phrase means "on the day when I call," but here the verb is qatal. If *yôm* had the same significance, the phrase would thus mean "on the day when I called," which does not lead naturally into the jussive in v. 2; contrast also 138:3, with *běyôm* and two qatal verbs. Further, here "day" is followed by "night," and it is more natural to relate these to each other.
3. The *ʾăšer* is expressed and thus has some emphasis.

[7]Upon me your fury has pressed;
 with all your breakers you have afflicted me. (Rise)
[8]You have put my friends at a distance from me;
 you have made me a great abomination[4] to them.
Imprisoned so that I cannot leave,[5]
 [9a]my eye has become dim through affliction.

[9b]I have called you, Yhwh, every day;
 I have spread out my hands to you.
[10]Do you do wonders for the dead?
 Do the ghosts rise to confess you? (Rise)
[11]Is your commitment recounted in the grave,
 your truthfulness in Destruction?
[12]Are your wonders acknowledged in the darkness,
 your faithfulness in the land of forgetting?

[13]But I—to you, Yhwh, I have cried for help;
 in the morning my plea comes to meet you.
[14]Why, Yhwh, do you spurn me,
 hide your face from me?
[15]I have been weak and dying[6] since youth;
 I have carried your terrors, I am at a loss.
[16]Your great fury has overwhelmed me;
 your dreadful deeds have destroyed me.
[17]They have encircled me like water all day;
 they have surrounded me altogether.
[18]You have put loved one and neighbor at a distance from me,
 my acquaintances . . . darkness . . .[7]

Interpretation

From the prayer psalms in the Psalter, one can construct a kind of template for prayer as the psalms practice it. It can involve addressing God, asking God to listen, recalling the way God has related to us in the past, lamenting or protesting at our situation in the present, declaring that we have not been involved in the kind of wrongdoing that would have justified this (or confessing that we have), urging God to do something about it, declaring that we still trust in God, affirming that

---

4. Taking pl. "abominations" as intensive, unless this is a Phoenician-type sg. (so Dahood, *Psalms*, 2:305).

5. I take the first colon as extraposed and dependent on the suffix on "my eye."

6. For the unusual *gōwēaʿ*, LXX implies a word from *yāgaʿ*, "be weary."

7. Rather than representing alternative text forms, differences in MSS and ancient versions (see *BHS*) likely suggest attempts to make sense of an elliptical text.

we know God has heard our prayer, and promising that we will come back to testify to God's act when God has delivered us. But this is not a template that psalms closely follow; and Ps. 88 is exceptional in its selectivity in relation to it.[8] After the opening address to God and plea for God to listen, it is simply lament and protest. The other elements in the template—even prayer for God to act, as well as either a declaration of innocence or an expression of penitence—are conspicuous by their absence. "There is no petition that did not move at least one step on the road to praise," Claus Westermann declares.[9] Psalm 88 seems to be an exception. It focuses resolutely on telling God how bad things are and feel. If it has a design in relation to Yhwh, it is that stated in v. 2, to get God to listen. Everything serves that end. Perhaps it reckons that if that can be achieved, then all else will follow.

The clue to the psalm's formal structure is the threefold reference to the suppliant's plea in vv. 1–2, 9b–c, and 13, which lead into threefold laments at having been overwhelmed by death, protests at God's abandonment, and laments at the suppliant's alienation from people, in vv. 3–9a, 10–12, and 14–18. Such structural repetitions are a recurrent feature of the Psalms (e.g., Pss. 42–43; 71; 80), and one may infer that one significance of them is that they give the suppliants opportunity to talk themselves out (in prayer or praise) and thus to reach closure. Yet the abruptness with which Ps. 88 ends reflects the fact that it does not reach closure at all but rather exhaustion, rhetorical and personal.[10]

While the psalm is expressed in the first-person singular, so that it is natural to apply it to an individual, it might be a communal psalm, and it was certainly used thus.[11] But the standard Christian view came to be that it belongs on Christ's lips,[12] and the Church of England's Book of Common Prayer sets it for use on Good Friday, the Episcopal Church's Book of Common Prayer for Holy Saturday. But Calvin (for instance) assumes that it is a prayer for praying by an ordinary individual.[13] As with other psalms, however, we should not simply assume that it is something like an excerpt from a prayer journal describing someone's unique

8. See Robert C. Culley, "Psalm 88 among the Complaints," in *Ascribe to the Lord* (P. C. Craigie Memorial; ed. Lyle Eslinger and Glen Taylor; JSOTSup 67; Sheffield: JSOT, 1988), 289–302.

9. *Praise and Lament*, 154.

10. On its structural and rhetorical features, see Irene Nowell, "Psalm 88," in *Imagery and Imagination in Biblical Literature* (Aloysius Fitzgerald Festschrift; ed. Lawrence Boadt and Mark S. Smith; CBQMS 32; Washington, DC: CBA, 2001), 105–18.

11. Cf., e.g., Theodoret, *Psalms*, 2:81–84; Rashi; Qimchi. Tg incorporates reference to the speaker being in exile.

12. Hence Luther's polemical remarks against the corporate interpretation (*First Lectures*, 2:187).

13. *Psalms*, 3:407.

experience in their own words.[14] It actually tells us nothing concrete and specific about the nature of the suppliant's affliction, even whether or not it involved illness.[15] It focuses more on a wide range of ways of expressing the implications of the affliction, especially abandonment by Yhwh and by other people (though there is no reference to attacks by other people, only by Yhwh). It is the lament of an outsider.[16] Its forms of expression come from those of traditional Israelite prayer as illustrated in other psalms, and it may be a liturgical composition, produced by people such as the Korahites or the leader or Heman for use by people in need. A further implication would be that it was used in the context of ministry overseen by people such as the Levites, who encouraged people in such need to bring their agonized prayer to God, perhaps in the company of their family and friends. It then provided them with words to articulate their experience, rather than their experience generating the description. But this does not change its significance as both issuing from the way people prayed out of desperate need (because the traditional words and images reflect that) and being designed to be used by people praying out of desperate need.

There is no indication of a date.

> Song. Composition. The Korahites'. The leader's. On Sickness/Entreaty/Adornment/Dancing/Pipe. For affliction/chanting. Instruction. Heman the Ezrahite's.

Heading. There is no other psalm with such a long sequence of terms in its heading, which may suggest the importance of this extraordinary psalm to the community. See the glossary and the heading to Ps. 53 (for the fifth term). The sixth expression, *lĕʿannôt*, comes only here. Its form is that of the piel infinitive of *ʿānâ*. This might be *ʿānâ* III, which means to "humble" or "afflict" and might refer to affliction by God (cf. v. 7) or by other people (cf. 89:22 [23]) or to self-affliction (e.g., 35:13), or it might be *ʿānâ* IV, which means "sing out" or "chant."

In 1 Kings 4:31 [5:17], Ethan the Ezrahite and Heman are among a group of famous sages, while in 1 Chron. 2:6, both Ethan and Heman are descendants of Zerah (and are thus Judahites). "Ezrahite" might mean "descendant of Zerah," but the word might alternatively designate him as originally a (Canaanite) native of the land.[17] Elsewhere in Chronicles, Ethan and Heman are Levites involved in the leading of worship; Heman

---

14. Cf. Gerstenberger's comments, *Psalms*, 2:145.

15. Cf. McCann, "Psalms," 1027.

16. Karl-Johan Illman, "Psalm 88," *SJOT* 4 (1991): 112–20.

17. Cf. Tg *yṣybʾ*; LXX, "Israelite," perhaps starts from the same understanding of the word but takes it to mean an Israelite citizen. See BDB under *zāraḥ*.

is a Korahite (1 Chron. 6:16–48 [1–33]; 15:17, 19; cf. also 25:1–7, where Heman is also a seer).

88:1–9a. The psalm begins in vv. 1–2 in a regular way by calling on God and pleading for a hearing, though v. 1b hints at what will follow. Verses 3–7, however, bring a remarkable transition to a focus on death. Nothing more extreme could be said than the way these verses speak about how things are for the suppliant personally. "I" has the prominence in the first three lines (vv. 3–5a), and "you" in the second three lines as the suppliant moves to speak of God's involvement in what has happened (vv. 5b–7). There are no references to "them," to other people attacking the suppliant. "This psalm is between Yhwh and the psalmist."[18] In vv. 8–9a the psalm turns to a more down-to-earth description of one aspect of the suffering; here other people do feature.

> ¹Yhwh, my God who delivers,
>   by day I have cried out, by night before you.

For the appeal to Yhwh as "my God who *delivers," compare 65:5 [6]; 68:19 [20]; 79:9; 85:4 [5]. More literally, each time the title is "the God of my/our deliverance." That the invocation of God should occupy a whole colon is unusual and arresting; usually a prayer psalm moves into the burden of its plea briskly (see, e.g., Pss. 74; 79; 83; 86). That is noteworthy in light of where this psalm will go: in effect, the psalm will be all about whether this declaration is true. Indeed, in the context of this psalm that opening phrase is tellingly allusive. We could spell out the implications of the Hebraism in other ways as "God my deliverer" or "God who delivers me": but does the suppliant believe any of these at the moment?

The second colon sharpens the question. When the psalms refer to crying out to Yhwh, they often go on to note that Yhwh listens to this cry and acts (e.g., 34:17 [18]; 107:6, 28), as happened when Israel cried out in Egypt (e.g., Exod. 3:7, 9). But on other occasions this cry is one the suppliant is still uttering (e.g., 77:1 [2]); it has not been heard. So it is here: day and night, and thus continually.[19] The suppliant utters this cry before Yhwh, perhaps in the sanctuary (unless v. 8c indicates that it was impossible to go there) or perhaps simply because wherever one stands, it is before Yhwh. The question is, Does Yhwh notice?

18. Nowell, "Psalm 88," 111.
19. If we understand v. 1b as one colon, the colon divides into two parallel halves, with the verb and the prepositional expression applying to both, and the expressions "day" and "night" divided between them: i.e., "By day I have cried out [before you], by night [I have cried out] before you." Perhaps we should see the prep. *b* applying to *yôm* as well as to *laylâ*. But the colon might be a verbal clause followed by a noun clause: "By day I have cried out, by night [I have been] before you."

> ²May my plea come before your face;
> incline your ear to the sound I make.

The second line thus asks that this *plea may come before Yhwh.[20] It will transpire that this is the only explicit plea in the entire psalm. The suppliant never manages to reiterate the pleas that are recalled in vv. 9 and 13. All the psalm does is seek a hearing; as we have noted, if Yhwh responds to v. 2, everything else will follow.

There is a sense in which the suppliant and the plea certainly come into Yhwh's presence, given that Yhwh is present in the sanctuary and even a cry from far away can reach Yhwh there.[21] Yet it is possible to be in someone's presence but for them not really to be with you. They are focusing on something else. It is as if you were not there. Perhaps this difference in the ideas of being in someone's presence is suggested by the change in the prepositional expressions, from *negdekā* (before you) in v. 1b to *lĕpānêkā* (lit. "to your face"). The latter expression is the more vivid one, suggesting that someone is looking at us: therefore surely they must actually be focusing on us? Or perhaps the psalm now refers to the cry reaching Yhwh's palace in heaven. "The great power of prayer at its purest is shown here; truthful words are not scattered on the unsubstantial breezes, but they seem to come before the Lord's presence like a spokesman, and discharge their appointed task in the place which our physical persons cannot reach."[22]

Whereas both v. 1b and v. 2a mixed the aural (cry out, plea) and the visual (before you, to your face), v. 2b is consistently aural as it focuses on gaining the attention of Yhwh's ear rather than of Yhwh's eyes. It does so the more by speaking of the *resounding noise the suppliant makes rather than the plea with its rational content or the cry with its pain. Listen to the pain, listen to the argument, listen to the noise, the suppliant begs over vv. 1b–2 as a whole.

> ³Because my whole person is full of troubles;
> my life has arrived at Sheol.

---

20. In some respects, formally the line works abca′c′b′: verb, *l* expression, noun. Substantially, it works abca′b′c′: two verbs (one jussive, one impv.), one noun referring to a part of Yhwh's body (with second-person suffix), and one noun referring to the suppliant's prayer (with first-person suffix).

21. Indeed, one might take v. 2a as a further statement: "My plea comes/will come before your face"; the yiqtol then complements the qatal in v. 1b and indicates that the praying of the past continues in the present. But a statement of confidence would be surprising in this context, and the impv. in v. 2b suggests that the verb in v. 2a is a jussive.

22. Cassiodorus, *Psalms*, 2:343.

Apart from the length of the opening invocation, there was nothing very remarkable about the opening of the psalm. Other suppliants have cried out day and night. This sudden move to reasoning that focuses on Sheol is more remarkable.

The suppliant's self-description starts with a vivid verb. Psalm 63:5 [6] has already spoken in terms of my whole *person being full to overflowing with good things, completely sated, like someone who has eaten a good meal (cf. 65:4 [5]; 78:29; 81:16 [17]). This suppliant is full to bursting, too, but with *bad things (cf. 123:3–4). The second colon explains this. "Arriving at" somewhere (*pāgaʿ* hiphil) implies reaching, but perhaps not entering (e.g., Gen 28:12; Job 20:6). One can therefore picture the suppliant as good as dead, tottering at the gates of *Sheol, awaiting the moment when breath finally leaves the body and it is time to enter Sheol.

> [4]I have come to count with people who are going down to the Pit;
>   I have become like a man who is without strength,

Both cola repeat the point. Anyone who thought about it would reckon that the suppliant was in the same position as other people who are dying. The Pit is at one level another way to speak of a grave (cf. *Abyss). People who did not have a family tomb, hewn in rock, might be buried in a grave pit (the word is the ordinary term for a cistern or storage pit). But like Sheol in relation to the grave, the Pit also suggests the place where people's personalities go when their bodies go to the tomb or grave. Since the body goes down into the grave, the personality also "goes down" to this place; its location can hardly be far distant from its body. The second colon again expresses why that is. "Man" is *geber*, which etymologically suggests a he-man, a man in his machismo (*gābar* means to be strong, *gĕbûrâ* is strength, a *gibbôr* is a strong man). But this is a man who has run out of the strength to live.[23] The grave is a place for people who have become totally incapable of doing anything, and the suppliant is already like that, as good as dead.

> [5a–b]Among the dead an outcast, like the slain,
>   lying in the grave,

Yet again the psalm restates the point. The suppliant is among the dead, but now, to make it worse, these dead are like people who have been

---

23. Strength is *ʾĕyāl*, a hapax but related to other words for strength and strong men or leaders (e.g., Exod. 15:15; cf. also Ps. 22:19 [20]). But the root *ʾwl/ʾyl* is a confusing one, and LXX has "help," though Th has "strength," which fits with the related Hebrew words and the context.

killed in battle or people who have been executed. Initially the corpses of the former lay scattered over the battlefield, unburied, though if they were lucky they might then be buried in some mass grave. To be in such company suggests being an outcast (*ḥopšî*). In the OT the word usually means a bond servant freed after his years of service (e.g., Deut. 15:12–13), which suggests that the word describes the suppliant as freed from the servitude of mortal life. And one can imagine Job reckoning himself a free man when he is allowed to die. But this suppliant is not one who relishes his freedom; he is like a man "let go" by his employers when he wants to carry on working. Job would likewise relish being allowed to "lie" in the grave in peace (cf. Job 3:11–19), but this suppliant was not looking for his eternal rest quite yet. So "a free man" is an unlikely expression here. But cognate words to *ḥopšî* often carry the connotation of someone without social standing, which might also link with the use of *ḥopšît/ḥopšût* to mean something like confinement in 2 Kings 15:5; 2 Chron. 26:21.[24] The idea is then taken up again in v. 8c.

> [5c-d]Those of whom you have not been mindful any more;
> they have been cut off from your hand.

So what is so bad about being dead? The answer comes with a transition from sentences about me to sentences about Yhwh. It is that Yhwh does not become involved with the dead. When you literally and finally die at the end of a good life, the OT can accept this. But it objects to the idea of being "let go" before your time; and in this context, when the suppliant is not actually dead, the problem is indeed that Yhwh is not *mindful of you and therefore does not reach out to you to deliver you. So you are cut off from the area where Yhwh's hand operates. Verses 10–12 will expand on that point.

> [6]You have put me in the deepest Pit,
> in great darkness, in the depths.

In v. 4, the suppliant's being in the Pit, or on the way there, was simply a fact without an explanation. Yhwh could do something about it but was not described as responsible for it; no one was made responsible. This second sentence about Yhwh makes Yhwh the person responsible

---

24. For discussion, see Pierre Grelot, "*Ḥofšî*," *VT* 14 (1964): 256–63; Loretz, *Psalmstudien*, 285–309, and his references; *HALOT*; *DCH*; *TDOT*. For the view that the word refers to having a "bed" in Sheol, see, e.g., Ernst Haag, "Psalm 88," in *Freude an der Weisung des Herrn* (H. Gross Festschrift; ed. Ernst Haag and Frank-Lothar Hossfeld; Stuttgart: KBW, 1986), 149–70 (see 151). Hossfeld and Zenger (*Psalms 2*, 390) argue for something like "outcast."

for that affliction, which both makes deliverance more problematic and more possible. More immediately, it sets the relationship between the suppliant and Yhwh on a more confrontational basis. Previously, one could have imagined Yhwh and the suppliant standing on the same side over against the suppliant's affliction. It is now overt that they stand on opposite sides. It was Yhwh who put the suppliant in the Pit, the very deep Pit from which no one can climb out and into which no one can reach (see 86:13). Presumably this is an inference from the facts and from the suppliant's convictions about God's sovereignty, not least in relation to the realm of death. Further, here the psalm describes the suppliant as not merely at death's door but already overwhelmed by death. The suppliant's life is a living death.

The second colon elaborates on the description in speaking of darkness (*maḥšāk*).[25] One of the gloomy features of a tomb or a grave is its darkness. When the stone on a family tomb's opening is removed from time to time for someone else to be put in, light shines in; but when the stone is in its normal position, all is pitch black. That is what the realm of death is like (cf. vv. 12, 18; Job 10:21–22). Talk of the "depths" (*měṣôlâ*) may then suggest a transition of imagery. Such expressions often refer to the deep waters that are overwhelming a sufferer, and deep waters are a common image for death and Sheol (cf. 69:2, 15 [3, 16]); v. 7 will take up the image again. "In great darkness, in the depths" might be a hendiadys, suggesting "in the darkest depths" (TNIV) or "in the deepest darkness." Etymologically *měṣôlâ* could itself easily suggest darkness (cf. *ṣalmāwet*)[26] and might naturally be understood that way after *maḥšāk*.

> [7]Upon me your fury has pressed;
>   with all your breakers you have afflicted me. (Rise)

For a moment Yhwh in person ceases to be the subject, but in substance nothing changes, because the alternative subject is "your fury," until Yhwh becomes the subject again in the second colon.[27] "Press" (*sāmak*) suggests some irony; it is normally a positive word, with meanings such as sustain or uphold. It most often refers to the laying on of hands in ordination. This is a very different imposition of hands.

Once again the second colon explicates the first; there is no doubt of the presence of flood imagery here. Experiencing the outpouring of Yhwh's fury is like being drowned by Yhwh's huge waves of trouble, which also suggest the deep waters of death. "Afflict" (*ʿānâ* piel) compares with *ʿannôt* ("affliction"?) in the heading.

25. "Great darkness" takes account of the fact that the word is actually pl.
26. Cf. LXX here.
27. The line works abcc′b′.

> 8a–bYou have put my friends at a distance from me;
>   you have made me a great abomination to them.

MT understands vv. 8–9 as two tricola; it is more likely to be three bicola (cf. TNIV). Although other people do not appear as the subject of hostile verbs in the psalm, here other people do feature. Yet Yhwh continues to be behind the suppliant's problems; Yhwh is the subject of both verbs here. At the human level, the friends (lit. "my known ones") seem not to be the original causes of the affliction. It is not (for instance) that they are making false accusations against the suppliant. Nor does the psalm quite say that they have responded to that affliction by assuming that Yhwh has caused it and that this must mean the suppliant is a wrongdoer. Rather, they are simply horrified by it; they cannot cope with it. Perhaps they fear that something of this kind might happen to them. For whatever reason, they avoid the suppliant.

The second colon heightens the point in noting how they thus keep their distance because they view the suppliant as an abomination, something to be avoided because of its disgusting nature. This word, common in Deuteronomy, Proverbs, Jeremiah, and Ezekiel, comes in the Psalms only here. It seems as if God is treating the suppliant as an abomination; people are doing that too.

> 8cImprisoned so that I cannot leave,
>   9amy eye has become dim through affliction.

The participle from *kālā'*, used of Jeremiah in Jer. 32:2, suggests another metaphor for the suppliant's situation or extends the metaphor of the pit out of which no one can climb. It is a prison. The second colon may then suggest that the inner life has gone from the suppliant; the light has gone out. But the Psalms refer to the eyes failing in connection with looking long and fruitlessly to God to answer prayer (69:3 [4]; 119:82, 123). In trouble, one's calling is to keep one's eye looking keenly for Yhwh's act of deliverance. The suppliant's eye has been doing that for too long and has become too tired to continue doing so.[28] "Affliction" (*ŏnî*) picks up the verb in v. 7 and puts it near the word for "my eye" (*ênî*). It is *ŏnî* that causes the trouble for *ênî*.

88:9b–12. After a resumptive recalling of the recollection of the suppliant's plea (v. 9b–c), the protest returns to questions about death (vv. 10–12). They are now literally questions, three of them, though also rhetorically so, and actually variants on one question.

28. Cf. Qimchi.

There might be two sorts of significance to such questions about death. There is a sense in which the suppliant is already among the dead, and from this perspective, they are questions that could imply a further deep hopelessness: both a subjective hopelessness (a feeling that things are hopeless) and an objective hopelessness (actually things are hopeless). That is so if the questions imply that the answer to each of them is no. On the other hand, even as rhetorical questions they might be open to a different answer; that is the nature of a question. They might, then, imply the possibility of a yes. Perhaps the suppliant is not totally hopeless. More plausibly, Yhwh might answer yes even though the suppliant assumes the answer is no. Perhaps the situation is not totally hopeless. Perhaps these questions are as near to pleas as the psalm ever gets.[29]

But there is also an obvious sense in which the suppliant is not dead. Dead people do not pray. The lines then refer to the death that threatens the suppliant, who nears the doors of Sheol but has not yet entered it, and the questions constitute motivation for Yhwh to act to deliver the suppliant before that happens. The last chance to do so is here. If Yhwh does not act now, then it will be too late, because Yhwh's policies do not include interfering in Sheol. It is an observable fact that people who die stay dead. There are no wondrous acts of truthfulness and commitment and faithfulness in the realm of the dead and, therefore, no wonders to acknowledge and confess in the way they can be confessed in this world so as to bring honor to Yhwh. (The suppliant ignores occasional miracles such as those in 1 Kings 17 and 2 Kings 4. Jesus's resurrection will make a more radical difference to that rule; but that resurrection has not yet happened.)

> 9b-cI have called you, Yhwh, every day;
>   I have spread out my hands to you.

In returning to the theme of the opening verse, the suppliant is not uttering a plea but recalling all the pleas that have been uttered, which Yhwh has not responded to. Here the verb is "call" rather than "cry out," which draws more attention to the direction of the calling than to its desperate nature; further, it is "called you" rather than "called to you." Yhwh and not some other god is to be the object of the people's prayer and worship, and the suppliant has lived that way, day in and day out, and has approached Yhwh with boldness, straightness, and confidence (see on 89:26 [27]). Once again the aural and the visible appear in the two parallel cola. Prayer is a matter of words for Yhwh to hear and action for

29. See further Frank Crüsemann, "Rhetorische Fragen!?" *BibInt* 11 (2003): 345–60.

Yhwh to see. Openness of hands demonstrates that the hands are empty
and that the suppliant knows this and opens the self in helplessness.

> [10]Do you do wonders for the dead?
> Do the ghosts rise to confess you? (Rise)

The suppliant thus asks two related questions. First, does Yhwh act in
Sheol? The presupposed answer is no. Israel had no doubt that Yhwh is
sovereign over Sheol in the sense that Yhwh controls who goes there and
who does not. Sheol is "before Yhwh" (Prov. 15:11). Yhwh knows what
goes on there and can reach into there (Ps. 139:8; Amos 9:2). If anyone
could release people from Sheol, it is Yhwh. There is no other being in
control there. Yhwh does not even have a subordinate deity responsible
for matters there, as Yhwh has subordinate deities in charge of nations
such as Moab and Persia. There is no need; there is nothing to supervise
or make decisions about with regard to Sheol. Nothing happens there.
Specifically, Yhwh does no *wonders there. It requires a wonder (for
instance) to restore someone from a long-standing illness such as would
naturally be fatal, and it requires a wonder to restore someone to life
when they have actually died. For Yhwh, the second kind of wonder
would be just as easy as the first, yet Yhwh sometimes chooses to do the
first but hardly ever chooses to do the second.

The parallel colon relates to a consequence.[30] First, it parallels "the
dead" with "ghosts" (*rĕpā'îm*). The word comes only here in the Psalms
(but see, e.g., Prov. 2:18; Isa. 14:9). The LXX has "healers," and NRSV
and NJPS have "shades," but both these rest on dubious etymology.[31]
The TNIV has "their spirits," though we should be wary of thinking of
dead people as disembodied (Samuel is embodied in 1 Sam 28). "What
survives in Sheol is not some immortal soul or spirit, but rather the *whole*
man," in this weakened, lifeless form.[32] The *rĕpā'îm* are simply dead
people in their lifeless state. They are not going to be getting up in the
sense of rising from the dead, and they are not going to be getting up in
the sense of standing up to give praise and testimony for what God has

---

30. In substance the second colon follows on the first, but formally they are more
parallel; the line works abca'b'd. First, there are two different nouns referring to the dead,
each being preceded by a different interrogative, but the first noun is indirect obj., the
second is subj. Then, there are two different verbs, both qal yiqtol, but one second-person
sg., the other third-person pl. Finally, there is a noun in the first colon and another verb
in the second.

31. They link the word with the verb *rāpā'* (heal) or *rāpâ* (sink down, become weak).
But the word more likely comes from yet another root; certainly the use of the word shows
no awareness of either meaning. Vg and Sym take the meaning from the *rĕpā'îm* in (e.g.)
Deut. 2:20–21 (KJV, "giants").

32. A. Anderson, *Psalms*, 2:628.

done. This is not (for example) because they are unclean but because they cannot stand up, the posture for praise, and because there will be nothing to give praise and testimony for. A key aspect of the dynamic of Israel's relationship with Yhwh involves Israel praying in the midst of a crisis, Yhwh acting in response to that prayer, and Israel testifying to Yhwh's action. But this means that if Yhwh holds back from doing wonders in Sheol, there is nothing for people to *confess.

So if the question presupposes that the suppliant is effectively dead and the situation is hopeless, it is always possible for Yhwh to make this one of the exceptional moments. If the question relates to the conviction that the suppliant will soon be dead, it motivates Yhwh to take action now rather than waiting for the situation where Yhwh normally exercises that self-denying ordinance.

> ¹¹Is your commitment recounted in the grave,
>   your truthfulness in Destruction?
> ¹²Are your wonders acknowledged in the darkness,
>   your faithfulness in the land of forgetting?

Two further lines restate the question in v. 10b. The two lines are also internally parallel, so that the psalm emphasizes its point by asking this question five times altogether.[33] The two lines actually begin with their two verbs, which parallel the second verb in v. 10b. There is no recounting and no *acknowledging in Sheol because nothing happens there. No news is boring news.

The four cola then go on to describe the realm of death by four words. Physically, it means being in the grave, which is itself visibly the place of destruction. As a term for Sheol, Destruction, too, comes only here in the Psalms (but see Job 28:22; Prov. 15:11). While NRSV transliterates as Abaddon, in the case of this word its etymology is more certain—it comes from 'ābad "perish, vanish," in the piel "destroy"—and there is some indication that people made the link between the noun and the verb (cf. Job 31:12). When you take the rock off a tomb to put another body there, you can see that death is a place of destruction. The body dissolves. Likewise, we have already noted that the grave is a place of darkness (v. 6). It is also a place of forgetting. The root nāšâ is not the word usually translated "forget," which characteristically denotes *ignoring, a deliberate act of putting out of mind, but one that suggests things slipping out of mind (e.g., Lam. 3:17). Death of course means we can no longer remember anything, about people or about God (cf. 6:5 [6]). But also, we are no longer remembered (by people, in due course, and by God).

---

33. Further, v. 12a is all m., v. 12b all f., which adds emphasis (Watson, *Classical Hebrew Poetry*, 126).

Setting up a headstone at someone's grave is a way of trying to ensure that this does not happen. Perhaps the overtones of "ignore" are there: if Yhwh remains aware of us, this does not issue in action, so in effect we are ignored. Yhwh just leaves us there. Ecclesiastes 9:1–10 expands on the point and solemnly also uses that other word for forgetting.

Over against these four words (for the realm of death), the four cola put in parallel "*commitment," "*truthfulness," "*wonders," and "*faithfulness." They are a series of key words that characterize Yhwh's activity with Israel. It is therefore a devastating declaration to imply that none of these is known in the grave. And it is obviously true. When we die, we just lie there. We are not in pain, but we do not experience any of those realities of God's involvement with us in this life. That is why there is nothing to recount or acknowledge.

88:13–18. Yet again the suppliant recalls the plea uttered to Yhwh but ignored (vv. 13–14), returns one more time to a protest about death (vv. 15–17), then once more to the motif of alienation (v. 18).

> ¹³But I—to you, Yhwh, I have cried for help;
>   in the morning my plea comes to meet you.

The protest picks up once again not with an actual plea but with a recollection of the unanswered pleas the suppliant has been uttering. "Cry for help" is yet another verb to describe the suppliant's prayer; it resembles the word for "deliver" (see on 72:12) and thus begins a process whereby vv. 13–14 take up vv. 1–2. Notwithstanding vv. 10–12, the suppliant has not given up crying for help.

The second colon confirms that by adding a yiqtol verb to the qatal.[34] "Comes to meet" (*qādam* piel) suggests getting there ahead of someone so as to be able to greet them or confront them when they arrive. Each daybreak, the suppliant implies, on getting up Yhwh is confronted by this suppliant's *plea; there is no escape (cf. Luke 11:5–10; 18:1–8). Daybreak is supposed to be the time when God appears to deliver (e.g., 90:14; 143:8), but this does not happen, and thus daybreak is the moment when the suppliant's plea shows up to haunt Yhwh.

> ¹⁴Why, Yhwh, do you spurn me,
>   hide your face from me?

But Yhwh consistently turns the other way, like an official pushing the way into the office and ignoring the line of people begging for attention at the door. Yhwh thus spurns the suppliant (*napšî*, emphasizing

---

34. Hossfeld and Zenger (*Psalms 2*, 390) take it as jussive, but the parallelism and the broader context suggest that this continues to be part of a protest, like v. 9.

the neediness of the *person). Unlike the ones in vv. 10–12, these further rhetorical questions are "*Why?" questions, which are more aggressive and accusatory though also implicitly appealing. The one thing they are not doing is asking for information, and if Yhwh had an answer that could "solve" the "problem of suffering," this would not mean the suppliant could put away his or her pen and go home. The "Why?" is more a challenge to action than an inquiry.

"Why, Yhwh?" also applies to the second colon, which then re-expresses the verb as "hide your face." Like "plea," the word "face" is taken up from v. 2. It transpires that the suppliant's plea is not coming before Yhwh's face. Yhwh will not let it do so. "Hide the face" (cf. 44:24 [25]; 69:17 [18]) is a particularly solemn phrase. In spelling out the implications of "spurning," it suggests that Yhwh is not merely refusing to look in such a way as to show sympathy but also refusing to look in such a way as then to take action.

> [15] I have been weak and dying since youth;
>   I have carried your terrors, I am at a loss.

Death is not merely a prospective reality (I am at the gates of Sheol) and a present reality (I am overwhelmed by death); it is also one that has haunted the suppliant since youth.[35] Certainly we are all dying from youth, and Ecclesiastes points out that we make more of life if we recognize the fact. But the suppliant is presumably declaring that whatever the affliction to which the psalm refers, it has been a reality for years; the prospect of death has therefore been a reality all those years. (And that would be so more often in a premodern society with low life expectancy.) The adjective *weak ($\check{a}n\hat{i}$) is related to the verb "afflict" in vv. 7 and 9 (and perhaps in the heading), but it also leads directly to "I" ($\check{a}n\hat{i}$). The paronomasia suggests that "weakness" totally defines "me."

"Terrors" suggests a special dread that falls on people in anticipation of Yhwh acting to bring calamity (e.g., Exod. 15:16; 23:27).[36] The suppliant's experience has involved living with such fearful calamity through all those years.[37]

---

35. I assume that the noun clause in the first colon takes its time reference from the verb at the beginning of the second colon.

36. Cf. *TDOT* on *'êmâ*.

37. The final verb (*pûn*) comes only here. Its meaning is a matter of guesswork; I follow LXX. 4QPs¹ (earlier reckoned to be part of 4QPsˢ) has *'pwrh* (from *pûr*, a by-form of *pārar*, perhaps meaning "I writhe"; Seybold, *Psalmen*, 343–44; cf. *HALOT*); this verb comes in 89:33 [34]. Indeed, LXX's "I am at a loss" may imply this text (see Flint, *Dead Sea Psalms Scrolls and the Book of Psalms*, 93, 234). The verb form is usually reckoned to be a pseudo-cohortative (see note on 66:6).

¹⁶Your great fury has overwhelmed me;
    your dreadful deeds have destroyed me.

As happened in vv. 10–12, the next two lines explain the preceding colon. The terror the suppliant has experienced is the expression of great fury (lit. "burnings") that has threatened to consume the suppliant. "Dreadful deeds" is another rare expression, with similar meaning to "terrors" in suggesting awe-full deeds that inspire awe-full fear. And "destroy" is yet another uncommon expression. The succession of unusual words mirrors the alien and unintelligible nature of the experiences they speak of. Likewise, if the last verb form, *ṣimmĕtûtunî*, is a "barbarous" one,[38] this need not mean it is anything other than the suppliant wrote.

¹⁷They have encircled me like water all day;
    they have surrounded me altogether.

If v. 16 has suggested that Yhwh's terrors were like consuming fire, v. 17 suggests they are like an overwhelming flood. The two images come in Isa. 43:2. The suppliant's experience has been the opposite of the one the prophet promises, or almost so. The fire has not actually consumed, the water has not actually drowned, but Yhwh needs to take action now if the promise is not to fail. The suppliant is encircled and surrounded by these waters, altogether and all day.[39] The forces referred to in vv. 16–17 are described in quasi-personal terms, in the way that commitment and faithfulness are sometimes described (cf. 78:49). Mowinckel sees them as "demons of illness" sent by Yhwh, noting that these take the place of the human enemies who usually appear in the Psalms.[40]

¹⁸You have put loved one and neighbor at a distance from me,
    my acquaintances . . . darkness . . .

The first colon forms a restatement of v. 8a, with "loved one" (though the Hebrew participle is active) and "neighbor" replacing "acquaintances," who then reappear in the second colon. "Darkness" then also recurs from v. 6, without syntactical relationship to the rest of the line. And after that the psalm simply stops. In one Bible I use, this happens to come at the end of a page, and one turns over the page expecting to find continuance and closure, but there is none. "It is characteristic that the last word is

38. So GKC 55d.
39. The line thus works neatly abca'd'c'.
40. *Psalms in Israel's Worship*, 2:9–10.

darkness."[41] It contrasts sharply with the psalm's opening colon, the antithesis of an inclusion. If the psalm has lost its ending or the psalmist died before writing more, the community evidently felt that the psalm was all right as it stands. Its jerky non-ending truly mirrors the life it speaks of and constitutes an appeal to Yhwh analogous to the appeal to the community issued by the jerky non-ending of Mark's Gospel at Mark 16:8. "Life does not always have happy endings."[42]

Theological Implications

When teaching about the psalms, I always include Ps. 88 because it is such an extreme example of an inherently extreme way of praying. I ask students whether they find it encouraging or depressing, and about half of them answer each way. On one hand, it is disturbing to be faced by the reality of such abandonment by God. On the other, it is encouraging that the psalm faces the reality of such abandonment and witnesses that this does not make prayer impossible. And further, it is really important that the people of God face the reality of death, because we understand life only as we reflect on the reality of the death toward which we are moving.[43]

G. A. F. Knight comments that the psalmist is someone who "has entered the Covenant people, but has never fully understood what that entails. . . . How very telling this psalm has been therefore for countless tortured souls throughout Christian history! For it has taught them at what point they have gone wrong in their relationship to God. . . . This black psalm is a warning to us all."[44] The opposite is the truth. It is an odd fact about OT faith that it rarely involves speaking to God as Father, perhaps because it recognizes that other religions treat God as Father and that it is possible to do that too cheaply. But OT faith certainly has the kind of confidence in speaking to God that a person has in speaking to their father when they know that any words can be said, any pain expressed, any accusations voiced. "The Spirit of God . . . has here furnished us with a form of prayer for encouraging all the afflicted who are, as it were, on the brink of despair to come to himself."[45] Glenn D. Weaver suggests that it resonates with the experience of Alzheimer's

41. Kirkpatrick, *Psalms*, 523.
42. M. E. Tate, "Psalm 88," *RevExp* 87 (1990): 91–95 (see 94).
43. Cf. H. D. Preuss, "Psalm 88 als Beispiel alttestamentlichen Redens vom Tod," in *Der Tod*, ed. August Strobel (Stuttgart: Calwer, 1974), 63–79 (see 72).
44. *Psalms*, vol. 2 (Philadelphia: Westminster, 1983), 76, 77, 78. The way in which Knight reckons the psalmist has gone wrong is in becoming an existentialist.
45. Calvin, *Psalms*, 3:407.

disease in reflecting a life that is collapsing into chaos, which the psalm associates with the relentless progression toward death.[46] Beth LaNeel Tanner puts it alongside Judg. 19 and suggests that it resonates with the experience of abused women, for whom "sometimes the story does not end happily ever after."[47]

It is extraordinary that this person keeps praying at all, and the psalm is an expression of extraordinary faith.[48] "Without an answer from God, Psalm 88 closes, dark and disconsolate. . . . But, as he sinks away, the dying person clings to God. That is the hidden miracle of this prayer song which is overshadowed by the darkness of death."[49] Its remarkable expression of an understanding of the relationship between a suppliant and God makes this psalm central for an understanding of OT theology.[50]

"The truth of this psalm is that Israel lives in a world in which there is no answer. . . . God is not always on call." But this does not mean we stop calling.[51] "Dat is some fine psalm," a lady on a bus says to Stingo just before the end of the novel *Sophie's Choice*, and just before he comments—though he knows it is not true—"Someday I will understand Auschwitz."[52]

46. "Senile Dementia and a Resurrection Theology," *ThTo* 42 (1985–86): 444–56 (see 450).

47. *The Book of Psalms through the Lens of Intertextuality* (New York: Lang, 2001), 159–80.

48. A. Anderson, *Psalms*, 2:623.

49. Kraus, *Psalms 60–150*, 195.

50. Cf. Bernd Janowski, "Die Toten loben JHWH nicht," in *Auferstehung-Resurrection*, ed. Friedrich Avemarie and Hermann Lichtenberger (Tübingen: Mohr, 2001), 3–45 (see 9–10).

51. Brueggemann, *Message of the Psalms*, 78, 79.

52. William Styron, *Sophie's Choice* (repr., London: Picador, 1992), 671, 680. Cf. Brueggemann, *Message of the Psalms*, 81, 191.

Psalm 89

Facing Two Sets of Facts (Again)

Translation

Instruction. Ethan the Ezrahite's.

1I shall sing of Yhwh's acts of commitment forever,
  with my mouth for generation after generation I will make known
    your truthfulness.
2Because I have said, "Your commitment[1] will be built up forever;
  the heavens—you will establish your truthfulness in them."
3I sealed a covenant for my chosen,
  I promised to David my servant:
4I will establish your offspring forever,
  I will build up your throne for generation after generation. (Rise)

5So they confess your wonders in the heavens,[2] Yhwh,
  yes, your truthfulness in the congregation of the holy.
6Because who in the sky[3] can be set alongside Yhwh,
  who compares with Yhwh among the divine beings—

1. I take the suffix on "truthfulness" also to apply to "commitment."
2. The initially obvious understanding is "the heavens confess . . ." (so LXX, Jerome, Tg); the heavens then stand for heavenly beings. But the personification is very strong; there is no other passage where the heavens are the subj. of this verb. More conclusively, can the heavens so confess in the assembly of the holy? More likely, the "in" in v. 5b also applies in v. 5a. This is supported by the parallel *b* clauses in v. 6.
3. Lit. "cloud."

⁷God inspiring awe in the council of the holy, greatly,[4]
    inspiring reverence above all those around him?
⁸Yhwh, God of Armies,
    who is like you, powerful,
    Yah, with your truthfulness around you?
⁹You rule over the rising of the sea;
    when it lifts its waves,[5] you are the one who quiets them.
¹⁰You yourself crushed Rahab, he was like a corpse;
    with your powerful arm you scattered your enemies.
¹¹The heavens are yours,
    yes, the earth is yours.
The world and what fills it—
    you are the one who founded them.
¹²North and south—you are the one who created them;
    Tabor and Hermon—they resound in your name.
¹³You have an arm with strength;
    your hand is powerful, your right hand stands high.
¹⁴Faithfulness and authority are the stability of your throne;
    commitment and truthfulness draw near your face.

¹⁵The good fortune of the people who acknowledge the shout,
    Yhwh, who walk in the light of your face.
¹⁶In your name they rejoice continually,
    and in your faithfulness they stand high.[6]
¹⁷Because you are their powerful glory;
    through your delight our horn stands high.[7]
¹⁸Because our shield belongs to Yhwh,
    our king to the Holy One of Israel.

¹⁹You spoke then in a vision to the people committed to you and said:
    I have put help on a warrior,
    I have enabled one chosen from the people to stand up.
²⁰I found David my servant,
    with my holy oil I anointed him.
²¹My hand will be stable with him,
    yes, my arm will make him strong.

---

4. On adverbial *rabbâ* (cf. 62:2 [3]; 78:15) see *IBHS* 39.3.1b and references; also Barthélemy, *Psaumes*, 617–18. *Rab hû'* ("He is great"; cf. LXX, Syr, Tg) would be easier.

5. EVV have "when its waves lift" (cf. Tg), but *nāśā'* is a transitive verb.

6. TNIV has "exult," which fits the parallelism within the verse, but this meaning for *rûm* is rare, if it occurs at all, and in the context, where the verb appears several times (as in the next line), it has its usual meaning. Mitchell Dahood takes the word as a divine title, "Exalted One" ("The Composite Divine Title in Psalms 89,16–17 and 140,9," *Bib* 61 [1980]: 277–78).

7. So Q *tārûm* (cf. LXX, Syr, Tg); K *trym* implies "You make our horn stand high" (cf. Jerome).

²²No enemy will extort from him,⁸
  no wicked person afflict him.
²³I will crush his foes before him,
  strike down the people who are against him.
²⁴My truthfulness and my commitment will be with him;
  by my name his horn will stand high.
²⁵I will put his hand on the sea,
  his right hand on the rivers.
²⁶This man can call me, "You are my father,
  my God, the crag that delivers me."
²⁷Yes, I myself will make him my firstborn,
  on high in relation to the kings of the earth.

²⁸Forever I will keep my commitment to him,
  and my covenant will be true for him.
²⁹I will set his offspring evermore,
  his throne like the days of the heavens.
³⁰If his descendants abandon my teaching,
  do not walk by my decisions,
³¹If they profane my laws,
  do not keep my commands,
³²I will attend to their rebellion with a stick,
  their waywardness with blows.
³³But my commitment I will not annul from him;
  I will not falsify my truthfulness.
³⁴I will not profane my covenant;
  what has come forth from my lips I will not change.
³⁵One time I have promised by my holiness,
  if I were to lie to David . . .
³⁶His offspring will continue forever,
  his throne like the sun before me,
³⁷Like the moon, which will be stable forever,⁹
  a witness in the sky that is truthful.¹⁰ (Rise)

³⁸But you—you spurned, rejected,
  raged at your anointed.

8. The parallel cola that follow and the prep. *b* suggest that the verb is *nāśā'* I (cf. LXX), not *nāśā'* II, "deceive" (cf. Jerome, Tg, Sym).

9. In isolation, one would render this line "like the moon, it will be stable for ever," but this then implies that the throne is also the subj. in v. 37b, whereas the moon needs to be the subj. there (see next note). LXX, Sym, and Tg take the moon as the subj. here.

10. EVV have "a truthful witness in the sky," but the separation of the ptc. from the noun makes this difficult (cf. Timo Veijola, "The Witness in the Clouds," *JBL* 107 [1988]: 413–17 [see 414]). I take it as an unmarked relative clause parallel to that in the preceding colon; cf. Isa. 49:7 (where the *'ăšer* does appear). On the authenticity and background of the MT text here, see E. Theodore Mullen, "The Divine Witness and the Davidic Royal Grant," *JBL* 102 (1983): 207–18.

[39]You renounced your servant's covenant;
   you profaned his diadem to the ground.
[40]You breached all his walls,
   made his strongholds ruins.
[41]All who passed by plundered him;
   he became the scorn of his neighbors.
[42]You lifted his attackers' right hand;
   you made his enemies rejoice.
[43]Yes, you turn back his sword's blade;
   you did not enable him to rise up[11] in battle.
[44]You brought his purity to an end,
   you hurled his throne to the ground.
[45]You cut short the days of his youth,
   you clothed him with shame. (Rise)

[46]Until when, Yhwh—will you hide forever?
   Will your fury burn like fire?
[47]Be mindful—I, what short life;
   for what emptiness you created all humanity.
[48]Who is the man who can live
   and not see death,
   save himself from the hand of Sheol? (Rise)
[49]Where are your former acts of commitment, my Lord,
   which you promised David by your truthfulness?
[50]Be mindful, my Lord, of the scorning of your servants,[12]
   which I have carried in my bosom, every one,[13] of many peoples,
[51]That with which your enemies have scorned, Yhwh,
   that with which they have scorned the steps of your anointed.

Interpretation

Psalm 89 vies with Ps. 18 for the title of third-longest psalm in the Psalter, after Pss. 119 and 78. At first it might seem that Ps. 89 is the "answer" to Ps. 88, but it eventually becomes clear that actually it has similar implications to Ps. 88; we might also see it as a heightened version of Ps. 44. One receives the first impression from the fact that

11. Cf. Tg. EVV's "support/sustain him" gives a rather abstract meaning to *qûm* hiphil. 4QPs[c] follows it by the prep. *l* rather than *b*, which works in the opposite direction.

12. Syr and some later Hebrew and LXX MSS have sg., assimilating to the context, though R. Tournay ("Note sur le psaume lxxxix,51–52," *RB* 83 [1976]: 380–89) and Saur (*Königspsalmen*, 155) see it as original.

13. MT implies "in my bosom all the many peoples" (cf. Sym), which is hard to make sense of; ". . . all the mighty peoples" is not much better. I have uncoupled the const. phrase and assumed that *kol* (which would become *kōl*) presupposes the word for scorn from v. 50a. LXX simply omits the *kol*; Jerome and Aq render *rabbîm* as "wrongdoing[s]."

it begins with a commitment to singing Yhwh's praise for the sovereignty and faithfulness manifested in creation and in the Davidic covenant. Verses 1–4 introduce this twofold theme, and vv. 5–14 and 15–37 elaborate on each aspect. The distinction between the two is marked in their rhythm. In MT, vv. 1–2 are 4-5, 4-4, while vv. 3–4 are 3-3, 3-3.[14] Verses 5–14 then broadly follow the rhythm of vv. 1–2, while vv. 15–37 broadly follow that of vv. 3–4.[15] This praise thus goes on for a substantial time and certainly gives the impression that Ps. 89 is a praise psalm. But then it resembles Ps. 44 in taking an extraordinary somersault (vv. 38–51) in which it protests that everything that has preceded is impossible to reconcile with the way Yhwh has abandoned the current Davidic king. This does not lead it to question the declarations about Yhwh's relationship to creation and to David; these have been allowed to stand. It is rather that those realities put in question what Yhwh has now done. Like Ps. 88, the psalm thus takes the form of a prayer psalm and turns it inside out, though in a different way. Instead of omitting statements of faith, it emphasizes them in order to let them have their scandalous effect.

In some sense the psalm is a royal psalm: it explicitly focuses on Yhwh's commitment to the king. But it does not seem to be a psalm that the king speaks. There is an "I" in the psalm (vv. 1, 2, 47, 49, 50), but the "I" does not say distinctively kingly things. Conversely, there are many references to the king, but these are in the third person (vv. 18, 38–45, 51). Further, there is also a "we" in the psalm (vv. 17, 18). It might be that the king said the whole psalm or that the third-person references to the king reflect the fact that the person who prays it is a Davidide who cannot be king or that it is a liturgy. But more likely it is an act of communal praise and lament in which the people celebrate Yhwh's commitment to the king, and thus to them, and then protest at the way Yhwh has treated the king and thus has treated them.[16] The "I" and the "we" of the psalm are the voice of the congregation speaking corporately and individually, perhaps in the person of a minister. But all this perhaps makes little difference to the thrust of the psalm, because whoever speaks, it presupposes that the destiny of king and congregation are interwoven.

Formally, then, Ps. 89 is a distinctive combination of praise, divine word, and protest that might not have been composed all at once. One might then reckon that the oldest material is the praise section[17] or the

14. An extra hyphen in v. 1b to produce the reading *lĕdōr-wādōr* (as in v. 4b) would make this a neat 4-4, 4-4, 3-3, 3-3 pattern.

15. But they include a number of lines with short second cola.

16. Cf. Richard J. Clifford, "Psalm 89," *HTR* 73 (1980): 35–47.

17. So Goulder, *Psalms of the Sons of Korah*, 211–38.

recollection of Yhwh's commitment to David.[18] Yet such combinations of form recur in the Psalter (e.g., Pss. 9–10; 12; 27; 60; 81; 95), so the mere fact of the combination of forms here hardly indicates the secondary combination of diverse material.[19] Further, the way the psalm uses key words to make its point works against that inference. "Commitment" and "truthfulness" (or "true") come as a pair six times in vv. 1–37 and then again in v. 49 ("committed ones" also comes in v. 19, truthfulness or "true" a further three times). Other words that significantly recur are "establish" and related words (vv. 2, 4, 14, 21, 37), "stand high" (vv. 13, 16, 17, 19, 24, 42), "promise" (vv. 3, 35, 49), and various expressions for "forever" (vv. 1a, 1b, 2, 4a, 4b, 29, 36, 37, 46). In broader respects the reign of Yhwh and the reign of David are portrayed in similar terms; these sections can hardly have been composed independently.[20] Likewise, the way such motifs recur in the last section indicates that the protest was composed with the praise and the recollection in mind. Thus, whether the psalm was composed all at once or in stages, in their context in the psalm the praise and the recollection function to set Yhwh up.

The document 4QPs[x] (formerly known as 4Q236 and as 4QPs89) has been reckoned one of the oldest Psalms scrolls from Qumran. As well as being written with distinctive orthography, manifesting a number of textual differences, and being much corrected, it comprises excerpts from the psalm in a distinctive order, vv. 19–21, 25, 22, 26a, 27, 30. Opinions differ as to whether it preserves an older version of the psalm or a reworking of verses from the psalm in its MT form.[21]

Psalm 89 has often been reckoned to reflect the fall of Jerusalem in 587,[22] the individual king in the psalm then being Jehoiachin (notwithstanding his having already been exiled in 597). But it has also been read against the earlier background of events in the reigns of Rehoboam, Ahaz, and Hezekiah, or of Josiah's death and the later background of

18. So, e.g., E. Lipiński, *Le poème royal du Psaume lxxxix.1–5, 20–38* (Paris: Gabalda, 1967).

19. James M. Ward argues for the psalm's unity ("The Literary Form and Liturgical Background of Psalm lxxxix," *VT* 11 [1961]: 321–39). He also argues against the suggestion that the psalm refers to an annual ritual affliction of the king at a new year festival. For views on the psalm's structure, see Pierre Auffret, *Merveilles à nos yeux*, BZAW 235 (Berlin: de Gruyter, 1995), 31–55.

20. Cf. Jean-Bernard Dumortier, "Un rituel d'intronisation," *VT* 22 (1972): 176–96.

21. See Flint, *Dead Sea Psalms Scrolls and the Book of Psalms*, 38. For different assessments, see J. T. Milik, "Fragments d'une source du Psautier (4Q Ps 89)," *RB* 73 (1966): 94–106; Patrick W. Skehan, "Gleanings from Psalm Texts from Qumrân," in *Mélanges bibliques et orientaux* (H. Cazelles Festschrift; ed. A Caquot and M. Delcor; Neukirchen: Neukirchener Verlag, 1981), 439–52; J. P. M. van der Ploeg, "Le sens et un problème textuel du Ps lxxxix," in ibid., 471–81; Klaus Koch, "Königspsalmen und ihr ritueller Hintergrund," in *Book of Psalms*, ed. Flint and Miller, 9–52.

22. So, e.g., Michael H. Floyd, "Psalm lxxxix," *VT* 42 (1992): 442–57.

the ongoing suspension of the monarchy after the fall of Babylon or its continuing suspension in the Persian period (let alone the Greek period). The question of background becomes more complicated if one reckons that the psalm came into being by a staged process.

> Instruction. Ethan the Ezrahite's.

Heading. See glossary; and for Ethan the Ezrahite, see the heading to Ps. 88. The Tg understands this in an interestingly different way: Ethan becomes Abraham, and *'ezrāḥî* becomes *mizrāḥî*, "eastern"[23] (cf. *mimmizrāḥ*, "from the east," in Isa. 41:2). Abraham then becomes the chosen one in v. 3.

89:1–4. The psalm begins by declaring the intention to sing Yhwh's praise forever on the basis of Yhwh's twofold commitment written into creation and covenanted to David. The creation and the David covenant (rather than the creation and the exodus covenant) are the twofold basis of the community's security.

> [1]I shall sing of Yhwh's acts of commitment forever,
>> with my mouth for generation after generation I will make known
>>> your truthfulness.

Praise psalms commonly begin with an exhortation to sing and then give the reasons (e.g., Pss. 96; 98), and thanksgiving psalms often involve an individual undertaking to celebrate what God has done. It is a rare pattern in a praise psalm for an individual to make a commitment to give the praise (the verb is cohortative). Indeed, only Ps. 101 also has "I shall sing" as its first verb. There the king speaks, and that might be so here, but in other contexts the "I" that determines to offer praise is the "I" that represents the congregation (e.g., 104:33), and the rest of Ps. 89 will suggest that this is so here. In these opening verses, that ambiguity extends to the question of who is the object of Yhwh's *commitment and *truthfulness, though it does so in a creative way. We might reckon that the first obvious object of Yhwh's acts of commitment is the people as a whole (e.g., 106:7, 45). But v. 2 will associate Yhwh's commitment and truthfulness with creation and thus with Yhwh's sovereignty over the whole world (cf. v. 14). Then vv. 3–4 will focus on Yhwh's covenant with David, and the rest of the psalm will focus on the way Yhwh's commitment and truthfulness are shown to David (vv. 24, 28, 33, 49)—for the people's sake, indeed. The last section of the psalm will raise the question whether Yhwh's commitment and truthfulness really are forever and

---

23. Cf. Stec, *Targum of Psalms*, 167.

thus will also imply a question as to whether the suppliant's song will really last forever or is dependent on circumstances. Or it might raise the question whether the worshipper's cohortative appeal implies, "I would like to sing (if I could),"[24] but the circumstances make it impossible because there is no commitment and faithfulness to celebrate.

The second colon restates the first; "with my mouth [I will make known]" balances "I shall sing" (they are actually the last words in their respective cola), suggesting the celebratory and out-loud nature of the testimony the suppliant would like to give to Yhwh's commitment and truthfulness. Part of the complementariness of the two cola is the way the first speaks of Yhwh in the third person while the second addresses Yhwh, as often happens in OT poetry; LXX assimilates the first to the second.

> ²Because I have said, "Your commitment will be built up forever;
> the heavens—you will establish your truthfulness in them."

After such a beginning, the "because" line is to be expected, but it does not have its usual significance, and it again gains further significance from vv. 38–51. When someone says "I said" and does not tell us the addressee, this is commonly a way of saying "I said to myself," "I thought" (e.g., 30:6 [7]; 39:1 [2]), and that makes sense here. The line indicates the expectation the speaker verbalized inside, which lay behind the declaration in v. 1. The worshipper knows of Yhwh's acts of commitment in the past and affirms that this *commitment will last forever; the singing (v. 1) will thus match it. The LXX and Jerome have "because you said"; Yhwh's saying (for which see vv. 3–4) indeed lies behind the suppliant's saying.[25]

To speak of this commitment being "built [up]" involves a unique usage of the verb *bānâ*; it is not a regular way to say "be established" (NRSV) or "stand firm" (TNIV) or "be confirmed" (NJPS). It is v. 4 that will explain why the verb is used here. Meanwhile, what is the basis for this declaration in v. 2a? The second colon explains. It is the nature of the cosmos that gives this assurance. The further reference to Yhwh's *truthfulness in parallel with Yhwh's commitment affirms not merely that it will be as secure *as* the heavens (NRSV), but also that it will be secure *in* the heavens. In other words, Yhwh will demonstrate commitment and truthfulness in the way the cosmos works. Verses 5–14 will expand on the point.

It is surprising that the verbs to describe the building and establishing are yiqtol, but it is difficult to justify RSV's having past tense in the first

24. Tate, *Psalms 51–100*, 409.
25. Aq, Sym, and Th have "I."

colon and present in the second or TNIV's having the opposite; both seem unprincipled. The NRSV and NJPS translate both as present. I assume the yiqtols declare what Yhwh will carry on doing (which will indeed be in continuity with what Yhwh did in the past and keeps on doing in the present). Yhwh will continue to manifest commitment and truthfulness in the cosmos. In light of where the psalm will go, the yiqtols also draw attention to what is needed in the present, when Yhwh's commitment and truthfulness have apparently collapsed. Like the city and temple in the exile, they need to be built up again (this verb is routinely translated "rebuild" in passages such as 69:35 [36]; Neh. 2:5, 17). Again, v. 4 will implicitly take this point further.

> ³I sealed a covenant for my chosen,
>   I promised to David my servant:

There is no announcement that the speaker changes, but evidently it does. Thus NRSV and TNIV add "you said" to the beginning of v. 3. Yhwh declares the basis upon which vv. 1–2 worked. The commitment Yhwh here refers to is the one 2 Sam. 7 and 1 Chron. 17 relate, though the language and the themes are different. There are no references there to sealing a covenant or to David as Yhwh's chosen. Conversely, although the psalm talks about building in vv. 2 and 4, it makes no reference to the building of a house for Yhwh or for David. Likewise, both the narratives and the psalm make many references to stability and establishing, using the verb *kûn*, but they overlap in their use of it only in connection with reference to David's throne; otherwise they link it with different nouns. The psalm speaks seven times of *'ĕmûnâ* (truthfulness), more than any other chapter in the OT, but the narratives never use the word. The narratives and the psalm use the related verb *'āman*, but only in different connections. The psalm also refers seven times to *ḥesed* (commitment), whereas the narratives use the word once. It thus seems that neither the narratives' version of the story nor the psalm is directly dependent on the other; they may go back to a common liturgical tradition,[26] but a key role is played in both by an author's creativity in shaping a composition that works in its context.

26. Cf. Weiser, *Psalms*, 591. On the relationship between Ps. 89 and 2 Sam. 7, see Nahum M. Sarna, "Psalm 89," in *Biblical and Other Studies*, ed. Alexander Altmann (Cambridge, MA: Harvard University Press, 1963), 29–46; Michael Fishbane, *Biblical Interpretation in Ancient Israel* (Oxford: Oxford University Press, 1985), 466–67. Koch offers a detailed comparison of the psalm (MT and 4QPsˣ) with 2 Sam. 7 and 1 Chron. 17 in "Königspsalmen und ihr ritueller Hintergrund." Hans Ulrich Steymans develops a comparison with Akkadian royal oracles in "'Deinen Thron habe ich unter den grossen Himmeln,'" in *"Mein Sohn bist du,"* ed. Otto and Zenger, 184–251.

Yhwh (lit.) "cut" a *covenant (see on 50:5). It may not be so surprising that human beings "cut" a covenant to provide a solemn guarantee that it will hold, but more surprising that Yhwh does so. The fact that Yhwh makes this covenant "for" David, not "with" him, adds to the force of the point; it does correspond to the thrust of the narratives with their stress on Yhwh's sovereignty, even though not to the wording. Like the covenants "with" Noah and Abraham, this is not a mutual agreement between Yhwh and David. The covenant is Yhwh's, which he gives to or lays upon David. The parallel expression "promised" (EVV "swore") further underlines the point, as a promise or oath also involves a solemn self-curse to come into effect if one breaks one's word. In the parallelism, David is first "my chosen" and then "my servant." These two interpret each other. On one hand, election does convey real privilege, relationship with God that other people do not have, but it does so in association with a summons to service. On the other, being Yhwh's servant means not merely hard work but also a position of privileged support and protection.

> ⁴I will establish your offspring forever,
>   I will build up your throne for generation after generation. (Rise)

The continuation of Yhwh's words takes the matter further in a way that is of special relevance for people who live after David's day, both the king, or the person who would be king, and his people. For all of them it is important that Yhwh's commitment to David explicitly referred to establishing his offspring and building up his throne generation after generation, not just in David's own day.

It also now becomes more evident that the talk of building up and establishing in v. 2 links with the building up and establishing of David's dynasty. The verbs underline the point. As David's offspring are established as his successors, his throne is built up; and as this happens, Yhwh's commitment and truthfulness are established and built up. The verbs come in abb'a' order in vv. 2 and 4, suggesting closure here. David's successors are to be established and built up as securely as Yhwh's commitment and truthfulness are established and built up in the cosmos. Conversely, Yhwh's commitment is established and built up in the heavens (expressed and manifested there) as it is also built up and established (expressed and manifested) in connection with David's throne. In effect, Yhwh thus accepts the force of the analogy between these: the commitment and truthfulness embodied in the heavens and in Yhwh's relationship with David's offspring and throne will mirror each other.

669

But in 597 Yhwh threw out the last properly appointed Davidic king and his "offspring," so that none of them would ever sit on this "throne" (Jer. 22:28–30). Jehoiachin is that king, so this link would be especially telling if he is the king to whom this psalm directly refers. It would also be telling if the psalm relates to his Babylonian-appointed successor, Zedekiah, whose offspring the Babylonians killed (2 Kings 25:7) to make sure they did not sit on this throne. Some building up and establishing of Yhwh's commitment and truthfulness is going to be needed. It is as well that Yhwh will continue to manifest them in the heavens to offer evidence that this is possible.

89:5–14. Verses 1–4 have referred both to the heavens, and thus to the creation, and also to Yhwh's involvement in Israel's own history. Verses 5–14 develop both motifs, without distinguishing clearly between them; this is part of the point. Yhwh's activity in creation and in history are one. As happens in passages such as Isa. 51:9–11, the psalm in particular sees Yhwh's activity at creation and at the Red Sea as mirroring each other. Yhwh's power and truthfulness are acknowledged in the heavens in light of the way they were manifested at creation and at the Red Sea.

> ⁵So they confess your wonders in the heavens, Yhwh,
>   yes, your truthfulness in the congregation of the holy.

In other contexts the verb could mean "may they confess" (cf. 67:3, 5 [4, 6]; and RSV here), but that is not the point in this context. The point is that, as a matter of fact, Yhwh *is* so acknowledged (the verb is impersonal). The *w*-consecutive suggests that the line picks up from what precedes; it becomes clear that it picks up specifically from vv. 1–2, which closed with a reference to Yhwh's *truthfulness evidenced in the heavens. This would imply that Yhwh's *wonders are also wonders in the heavens, and vv. 8–10 will support that. Yet the collocation of Yhwh's truthfulness in the heavens with Yhwh's commitment to David invites us to continue to see these in close association. In the heavens the wonders and truthfulness promised and put into effect for Israel are also recognized. Yet further, *wonders (*pele'*) made their first appearance in Scripture in the Song of Moses (Exod. 15:11), so that it is possible here to think of Yhwh's act at the Red Sea (cf. Pss. 77:11, 14 [12, 15]; 78:12).

Alongside the parallelism of "wonders" and "truthfulness" is that of "the heavens" and "the congregation of the holy,"[27] the latter giving precision to the former. It is the body called "the divine assembly," the assembly of the "gods," in 82:1. Like "gods," "holy ones" is a word that

---

27. On them, see L. Dequeker, "Les qᵉdôšîm du Ps. lxxxix à la lumière des croyances sémitiques," *ETL* 39 (1963): 469–84.

can apply to any heavenly beings (e.g., Job 5:1; 15:15 [where it stands in parallelism with "heavens"]; Dan. 8:13). Only here are they called a congregation (*qāhāl*), a word that often refers to an assembly of Israel gathered for worship (e.g., Pss. 22:22, 25 [23, 26]; 35:18; 40:9, 10 [10, 11]). Although that word is used for various other earthly gatherings (e.g., 26:5; Gen. 28:3), those other psalms cohere with the idea that the assembly of the heavenly beings is here fulfilling the role of a congregation, confessing what Yhwh has done (cf. the worshipping role of the heavenly assembly in Rev. 4–5).

> [6]Because who in the sky can be set alongside Yhwh,
>   who compares with Yhwh among the divine beings—
> [7]God inspiring awe in the council of the holy, greatly,
>   inspiring reverence above all those around him?

Verse 6 marks its continuance of v. 5 by incorporating two more *b* expressions (in the sky, among the divine beings). The members of the heavenly assembly might be inclined to fancy themselves, as happens in Middle Eastern stories (cf. Isa. 14:12–14). When they are being sensible, they make no such mistake. They know that none of them is in the same league as Yhwh. For the question and these two verbs, compare Isa. 40:18, and for "divine beings" (*běnê ʾēlîm*), see Ps. 29:1,[28] but the expression is similar to ones in Ps. 82 (see comment there).

Another parallel *b* expression appears in v. 7a; the *ʿal* (above) in v. 7b then goes beyond that. Further, there is a nice paronomasia in the similarity of "be set alongside" (*ʿārak*) and "inspire awe" (*ʿāraṣ*); it is the incomparability of Yhwh that inspires awe. The verbs for "inspiring awe" and "inspiring reverence" (both niphal participles) can be negative, suggesting terror and fear, but they can also denote a positive worshipful response to Yhwh. For *ʿāraṣ*, see Isa. 8:13; 29:23; *yārēʾ* is more common: e.g., Pss. 60:4 [6]; 61:5 [6]; 66:16; 85:9 [10]. It is another expression that occurs as a description of Yhwh first in Exod. 15:11. These words thus fit with the description of the council of the holy as a "congregation." As a "council" (*sôd*) it is the decision-making body that Yhwh chairs (Jer. 23:18, 22), but there is no doubt who is in charge of this body that stands or sits around Yhwh.

> [8]Yhwh, God of Armies,
>   who is like you, powerful,
>   Yah, with your truthfulness around you?
> [9]You rule over the rising of the sea;
>   when it lifts its waves, you are the one who quiets them.

---

28. On the pl. abs. noun, see GKC124q.

In introducing the restated question and the further two-line statement, describing Yhwh as "Yhwh, God of *Armies" underlines the point in
vv. 6–7, especially as the divine beings are themselves the heavenly army
(e.g., Josh. 5:14–15; 1 Kings 22:19; Neh. 9:6; Isa. 24:21). So throughout
vv. 6–9 the particular point of comparison with other heavenly beings
is the unrivaled power of Yhwh. That is made even more explicit in the
second colon by describing Yah as "powerful" (the Aramaism ḥăsîn; cf.
the related words in Dan. 2:37; 4:30 [27]; and, interestingly, in connection
with "the holy ones," 7:18, 22). In this middle colon, both the name Yah
and the question "Who is like you?" correspond to Exod. 15:2, 11.[29] The
third colon picks up "around you" from the previous line;[30] the rest of
the heavenly assembly also embodies Yhwh's *truthfulness, because they
are the means by which that truthfulness is put into operation.

Verse 9 develops the point, further underlining the incomparability
of Yhwh, like the phrases that follow in Exod. 15:11. On the one side
in this line is the tumultuous "rising" and "lifting" of the sea's waves,
pretending to a majesty such as belongs only to Yhwh (cf. 93:1; and the
related verb in Exod. 15:1, 21). The dynamic surging of the sea is a regular symbol for power asserted against God, but here the sea's dynamic
is understated, and over against it is not a rebuke or a taming, as if the
sea had real power and demanded the expenditure of serious energy by
Yhwh, but simply regular "ruling" and gentle "quieting."

> [10]You yourself crushed Rahab, he was like a corpse;
>   with your powerful arm you scattered your enemies.

The point is given concrete expression with a look back to the moment
when Yhwh put such recalcitrant forces under control. For Rahab, see
on 87:4; Tg adds a reference to Pharaoh. But the name will also have
its original reference to the prehistorical forces of which Egypt was a
later embodiment. Like Middle Eastern stories, the OT can speak both
of the sea itself (v. 9) and of the sea monster in this connection. The
psalm's words particularly recall the Babylonian story about Marduk's
crushing Tiamat, though the OT does not see Yhwh as then recycling
the monster in order to create the world or humanity. Here the stress
again lies on Yhwh's power: the result of Yhwh's action was that Rahab
ended up as merely something like a body slain on the battlefield (cf.

---

29. "Who is like you?" usually comes at the end of a colon (e.g., 35:10; 71:19); it
is not directly qualified by an adjective so as to imply "Who is powerful like you?" Cf.
MT's methegh. MT's accent goes on to imply that "powerful" directly qualifies "Yah," but
"powerful Yah" would require the adjective to follow the noun. So I take it as a self-standing adjective qualifying the preceding "you." LXX has "You are powerful, Lord."

30. Though v. 8 has the f. form sĕbîbôtêkā.

this word "corpse/slain" also in 88:5). The second colon then restates this cosmic victory as the scattering of enemies, again as happens in an earthly battle. Once more the language also applies to Yhwh's victory over Egypt and over Canaan (e.g., 44:3 [4]; 77:14–15 [15–16]; Exod. 15:2, 13; also see Ps. 74:13, where the reference is more ambiguous).

> 11The heavens are yours,
>   yes, the earth is yours.
> The world and what fills it—
>   you are the one who founded them.
> 12North and south—you are the one who created them;
>   Tabor and Hermon—they resound in your name.

Three lines then assert Yhwh's ownership of the cosmos, which also implies Yhwh's authority and power over it. The link is reference to the heavens (v. 11a), which connects back with what precedes but also invites reference in the parallelism to the earth. Verse 11c–d then takes up the reference to the earth but completes the double line with a statement that applies to the heavens and earth as a whole, both of which Yhwh founded (the verb in 87:1).

"Founding" implies providing with security. Verse 12 takes matters further. Yhwh "created" north and south: *ṣāpôn*, the great mountain to the north, and *yāmîn*, the right hand, where south lies as one orientates by facing east. "Create" itself suggests the sovereignty of God's action in bringing the world into being. In the parallel colon, Tg takes Tabor and Hermon to denote west and east,[31] but they more likely appear as two significant mountains. Hermon is much bigger but in the distance, Tabor smaller but rising from amid the land of Israel itself. They may be the locations of shrines, and thus their resounding in Yhwh's name indicates that they recognize no other gods. They acknowledge Yhwh, not Baal. The parallelism of the lines invites us to interweave them. Yhwh is the one who created Tabor and Hermon, as well as north and south; and north and south, as well as Tabor and Hermon, resound in Yhwh's name.[32]

> 13You have an arm with strength;
>   your hand is powerful, your right hand stands high.

31. A. Anderson (*Psalms*, 2:637) takes them as alternative expressions for south and north! Goulder sees the two mountains as indications of the northern origin of this part of the psalm (*Psalms of the Sons of Korah*, 213; cf. Mowinckel, *Psalms in Israel's Worship*, 2:152).

32. As some interpreters assume that we should be able to find the four points of the compass here, so others have sought to find four mountains. Zaphon is indeed a mountain, and *yāmîn* might point to the Amanus, a mountain of unknown location (NEB).

¹⁴Faithfulness and authority are the stability of your throne;
commitment and truthfulness draw near your face.

These further two lines resume what has preceded as this celebration of Yhwh's power in creation and history draws to an end. What has been said in these lines justifies a generalization about Yhwh's arm and power, which reappear (cf. v. 10); the reference is expanded to include Yhwh's strength and hand, which adds to its emphasis, and is then given specificity in referring to Yhwh's right hand (generally the more powerful one), which lifts high, raised in authority and/or strength in relation to any opposition. (The parallelism does not imply that simple "hand" refers to the left hand.)

In turn v. 14 takes us back to the moral qualities expressed in Yhwh's actions, *faithfulness, *authority, *commitment, and *truthfulness. The last two form an inclusion with v. 1 (to stretch a point slightly; truthfulness is now 'ĕmet, not the related synonym 'ĕmûnâ). There at the beginning Yhwh's truthfulness was established in the heavens, and Yhwh promised to establish David's offspring and thus build up his throne; here the faithful exercise of authority is the means whereby Yhwh's own throne is established. By implication, the fact that the faithful exercise of authority is the foundation of Yhwh's throne undergirds the promise that this faithful exercise of authority is the foundation of David's throne. Once more commitment and faithfulness are personalized as like aides serving Yhwh, entities that come into Yhwh's presence to receive their orders (cf. v. 8b), for instance to see to the fulfillment of those promises. These qualities both undergird Yhwh's own position in the cosmos and are thus key to Yhwh's activity in the world.

89:15–18. Four lines provide a bridge between the celebration of Yhwh's power as creator and the commemoration of Yhwh's commitment to David. They thus have something in common with vv. 1–4, which comprised an introduction to both motifs. But in vv. 17–18, at least, "we" speak.

¹⁵The good fortune of the people who acknowledge the shout,
Yhwh, who walk in the light of your face.
¹⁶In your name they rejoice continually,
and in your faithfulness they stand high.

We know from the Psalms that Israel's worship emphasized a celebration of Yhwh's power in creation and at the Red Sea such as vv. 5–14 has proclaimed, and v. 15 declares the *good fortune of the people (Yhwh's people, the people of Israel) who *acknowledge the *shout that expresses that celebration. Verse 15b begins to explicate what that good fortune consists in. Psalm 44:3 [4] speaks of the way "the light of your face" gave Israel the land, along with Yhwh's right hand and Yhwh's arm (cf. v. 13). When they walked, they walked with Yhwh's face smiling on them, and that certainly meant good fortune (cf. also 4:6 [7]; 27:1; Prov. 16:15 for the human experience that provides the image). The worship that celebrates Yhwh's power and the walk that experiences the fruitfulness of that power thus relate to one another.

So people rejoice in worship on both sides of their experience of walking that walk. They worship, they walk, they rejoice some more. In Yhwh's *name they thus rejoice continually (lit. "all day"). Yhwh's right hand lifts high (v. 13), expressing the *faithfulness that stabilizes Yhwh's throne (v. 14); and Yhwh's faithful action means that the people themselves stand high, rather than their enemies doing so (13:2 [3]). Yes, great is their good fortune.

> ¹⁷Because you are their powerful glory;
>   through your delight our horn stands high.

But first, "you are the glory of their power" again picks up from vv. 10b, 13b (for Yhwh's "glory," see 71:8; 78:61; 96:6).[33] The phrase suggests that Yhwh is "their powerful, glorious one," though it might hint at the fact that their good fortune consists in Yhwh's powerful glory becoming theirs as Yhwh acts in their experience to give them victory. On the basis of the first understanding, the second colon indicates a fruit of that; on the basis of the second understanding, the second colon restates it. Added to that power and glory of Yhwh is the fact that Yhwh delights in Israel and therefore makes sure—as Yhwh's hand stands high—that their horn stands high (cf. vv. 13, 16). "Standing high" applies more literally to a horn than it does when applied to Israel itself. The horn is an animal's strong offensive weapon; when a bull holds its head and horns high and charges, only the unwise get in the way (cf. 75:4–5, 10 [5–6, 11]).

> ¹⁸Because our shield belongs to Yhwh,
>   our king to the Holy One of Israel.

Whereas the explanation in vv. 15–17 relates more to what precedes, this final line of explanation makes for explicit transition to what lies ahead. The means by which power is exercised in Israel is the king as commander in chief of the army. Thus the means by which Yhwh's power is expressed on Israel's behalf is the king. Usually Yhwh is the people's

---

33. For "You are the power in which they glory," or "You are their glorious power," one would expect the const. phrase in the opposite order.

shield (e.g., 84:9, 11 [10, 12]),[34] but in 47:9 [10] the world's kings were its shields (see comment there). Fortunately, the king belongs to the Holy One of Israel (see 71:22). Even if in one sense there are many holy ones (vv. 5, 7), in another sense there is only one; and astonishingly, he is committed to Israel and thus to its king.

89:19–27. The psalm goes on to recall Yhwh's promise to David. Two themes dominate the promise: David will be delivered from enemies that attack him, and he will be victorious when he attacks other peoples. Verses 21–23 and 24–25 are the central exposition of these promises. Verses 26 and 27 also likely relate respectively to each of them. The same may be true of vv. 19 and 20: that is, v. 19 may refer more to defense, v. 20 more to offense.

> [19]You spoke then in a vision to the people committed to you and said:
> I have put help on a warrior,
> I have enabled one chosen from the people to stand up.

Verse 19a stands on its own to introduce vv. 19–36.[35] "Then" apparently refers back to vv. 3–4; the speaking in a vision is presumably the event narrated in 2 Sam. 7 and 1 Chron. 17 (which certainly refers to speaking and to a vision),[36] but the further account in the psalm again has only a tangential relationship to those chapters. To begin with, Yhwh there spoke simply to Nathan and via him to David,[37] though Yhwh's promise to David was also indirectly good news for his people, the people *committed to Yhwh; and it is plausible to reckon that Yhwh intended the contents of this promise to come to the people whose descendants speak in this psalm (as it did at least when they heard the story). Or perhaps the committed ones are the likes of Samuel, Gad, and Nathan.

The way Yhwh here formulates that promise is first in terms of bestowing help on a warrior.[38] There is hardly anything more important to the Davidic king than Yhwh's *help or deliverance (e.g., 20:2 [3]; 118:13;

---

34. So, indeed, KJV here, implying emphatic *l* in both cola (*IBHS* 11.2.10i).

35. We might treat it as a bicolon in itself: so TNIV.

36. *Ḥizzāyôn* in 2 Sam. 7:17; *ḥāzôn* in 1 Chron. 17:15 and in the psalm.

37. Which might explain why some late MSS have sg. *laḥăsîdĕkā* ("the one committed to you"; cf. NRSV) for pl. *laḥăsîdêkā*. Some LXX MSS have "your sons," and 4QPs^x has [*lb*]*ḥryk*, "your chosen ones." That might be assimilation to vv. 4 and 19b, or it might be an earlier reading (cf., e.g., Jean Ouellette, "Variantes Qumrâniennes du livre des Psaumes," *Revue de Qumran* 25 [1969]: 105–23 [see 110]).

38. Not bestowing "power" (cf. NJPS, TNIV); the word is *'ēzer*, not *'ōz* as in vv. 10, 17. For the verbal expression, cf. 21:5 [6]. NRSV emends *'ēzer* to *nēzer* (crown). A. S. van der Woude ("Zwei alte cruces im Psalter," in *Studies on Psalms* [OtSt 13; Leiden: Brill, 1963], 131–36) suggests that MT's word is a homonym meaning "young man," identified from Ugaritic, so that the clause means, "I have placed a young man over a warrior."

2 Chron. 18:31; 25:8), even for someone with a reputation as a warrior (see Ps. 33:16). The parallel colon indicates how that help will express itself, picking up words from earlier in the psalm. David is the person "chosen," as in v. 3 (the word does not come in the narratives). But here the psalm adds that he was chosen "from the people," which underlines the fact that in Deuteronomy it was the people who were chosen (Deut. 7:6–7). Further, Yhwh had enabled him to stand up (*rûm* hiphil; cf. vv. 13, 16, 17). The parallelism in the line and those links indicate that Yhwh refers not to elevating David to the throne, as EVV "raised up" or "exalted" imply, but to giving him victory over his enemies. Back at the beginning, then, Yhwh's power was indeed applied to supporting and defending the king.

> ²⁰I found David my servant,
>   with my holy oil I anointed him.

Yhwh then goes back to events behind the promise to David and his victories. Again, the phrase "David my servant" follows v. 3; the narratives do have "my servant David." They do not refer to Yhwh "finding" David, but 1 Sam. 13:14 does refer to "seeking him out" as someone to replace Saul. On the other hand, the OT does elsewhere speak of Yhwh "finding" Israel (Deut. 32:10 MT; Hos. 9:10); thus another motif that elsewhere belongs to the whole people here applies to David in particular. It is then Samuel who anoints David with oil (1 Sam. 16); later Yhwh does refer to anointing him, though in unfortunate circumstances (2 Sam 12:7). "Holy oil" is mentioned only (and incidentally) in connection with the high priest (Num. 35:25). The psalm's statement about Yhwh and David thus considerably heightens the way the OT otherwise speaks of the matter. Yhwh found, Yhwh anointed, Yhwh used holy oil. There is no doubt that this was a special act. In the context the point about the reference to David being Yhwh's anointed is that this anointing marks David as the one through whom Yhwh intends to exercise authority in the world. Thus the rebellion of other nations is a rebellion against Yhwh and his anointed (Ps. 2:2). The fact that David is Yhwh's anointed servant means that Yhwh's intent to exercise authority in the world through him will certainly be achieved.

> ²¹My hand will be stable with him,
>   yes, my arm will make him strong.
> ²²No enemy will extort from him,
>   no wicked person afflict him.
> ²³I will crush his foes before him,
>   strike down the people who are against him.

The lines expand on the outworking of vv. 19–20, especially v. 19 if that refers more to defensive action. Yhwh's hand and arm and the idea of stability (*kûn*) again recur from vv. 13–14. The power expressed in creation and at the Red Sea will be applied to supporting David, with the same consistency as is manifest in the way Yhwh rules in the heavens. In the second colon, the verb "make strong" corresponds to 80:15, 17 [16, 18].[39]

The consequence of that would be that he would not be subject to oppressive treatment from some enemy or *wicked person. Defeat means having to pay heavy tribute, affliction that weakens the people as a whole; he will not have to endure this.

That will be so because Yhwh will personally see that his attackers are crushed (*kātat* is a vivid verb; it is applied, for instance, to the gold calf in Deut. 9:21, and *kātît* refers to olives crushed for oil) and struck down (with the kind of knockout blow that means they do not get up again to have another try).

> [24]My truthfulness and my commitment will be with him;
>   by my name his horn will stand high.
> [25]I will put his hand on the sea,
>   his right hand on the rivers.

Once again Yhwh's *truthfulness and *commitment will be sent out like aides (cf. 43:3) to act in the king's support. They will be there "with him," present and active. To make the same point in another way, Yhwh's *name—and therefore Yhwh's person—will be there when he battles, so that his horn stands high. The expression is taken up from v. 17 but now refers to David in particular, not to the people. Whereas vv. 21–23 thus promised the king protection when under attack, vv. 24–25 promise him success when on the offensive.

The sea and the rivers can have literal geographical implications, referring to the Mediterranean and the Euphrates-Tigris, or more metaphorical reference, referring to the sea and rivers that mark the edge of the earth's land mass; or perhaps the one is a symbol of the other. Either way, they are terms for the wide extent of an empire upon which the king will put his hand on Yhwh's behalf (cf. Ps. 2), and specifically his powerful right hand (again, the parallelism does not imply that v. 25a refers to the left hand). He will exercise a power like Yhwh's (cf. v. 13) because Yhwh is with him. It is "sensational . . . that here the authority over the sea is handed over to David, a mortal"; the point is underlined

39. According to *Discoveries in the Judaean Desert*, vol. 16, the scroll 4QPs[x] interestingly has God promising that *his* [David's] hand will establish *you* [pl.], though the reading is disputed (see Ulrich et al., *Qumran Cave 4*, part 11:166).

by repeating "your [his] hand/your [his] right hand," which referred to Yhwh in v. 13.[40] David's kingship actualizes Yhwh's kingship in the world. It is the agency through which Yhwh's rule is extended from the heavens to the earth.[41]

> [26]This man can call me, "You are my father,
>   my God, the crag that delivers me."
> [27]Yes, I myself will make him my firstborn,
>   on high in relation to the kings of the earth.

These two lines further sum up the principle behind vv. 21–25. On one hand, David will prove that Yhwh is the *crag that *delivers (cf. 95:1). Both expressions, crag and deliverance, suggest being rescued from dangers that come to us. In a crisis, then, David can call Yhwh. The verb is used thus transitively: not call *to* or call *on* Yhwh but simply call Yhwh. In regular usage the transitive expression means "summon" (cf. Isa. 41:9; 42:6); it is rather less deferential than "call on." In the midst of crisis, it is such a calling that Yhwh invites (cf. 50:15; also 53:4 [5]; 86:5, 7; 88:9 [10]). To summon Yhwh to our help is not a peremptory act if it is the summons that Yhwh invites. Further, the way the call expresses itself is by reminding Yhwh, "You are my father." At this point the psalm does make a connection with the narratives, though again the psalm represents a distinctive tweaking of the expression. In 2 Sam. 7:14 and 1 Chron. 17:13 the language reflects the formulas of adoption (as does Ps. 2), but the father-son relationship applies specifically to David's successor, not to David himself, and its implications are spelled out in what follows: it will mean Yhwh chastising this son but not casting him off, like Saul. The psalm presupposes the familial relationship, applies it to David himself, and appeals to a different beneficent aspect to it, that in a crisis one can call out "Father!" and one's father will rush to one's protection and aid. "My father, my God, the crag that delivers me" form a marvelous set of epithets.

Once again the companion line moves to the king's aggressive or positive relationship with the rest of the world, in parallel with Ps. 2. Being someone's firstborn is not merely a position that issues from accident of birth; a father can designate someone his firstborn, the senior son with authority in the family second only to the father and with the right to control the family's resources (cf. Gen. 49:3–4). Yhwh intends so to designate David in relation to other "sons," the kings of the earth, even though David is a relative latecomer on the world stage. He will rule the kings of the earth on Yhwh's behalf. David will be "on high," *‘elyôn*.

---

40. Fokkelman, *Major Poems*, 3:164.
41. Mays, *Psalms*, 286.

It is the most striking of the indications in vv. 19–29 that David has a position in relation to worldly powers analogous to Yhwh's in relation to heavenly powers.[42] Once more it is telling that in Exod. 4:22 Israel is Yhwh's firstborn, and in Deut. 26:19 and 28:1 it is Israel that is on high over the nations.

89:28–37. The original covenant promise in vv. 3–4 related to the permanence of David's throne. Yhwh's word now turns to that. We have alluded to a caveat in the narratives on Yhwh's commitment to David's monarchy, and that caveat now comes into focus before Yhwh once again recalls the lasting nature of that commitment.

> [28]Forever I will keep my commitment to him,
>   and my covenant will be true for him.
> [29]I will set his offspring evermore,
>   his throne like the days of the heavens.

First, lest we have forgotten the threefold "forever" of vv. 1–4 (and the twofold "for generation after generation"), the expression recurs in v. 28 (with another formulation in v. 29). In vv. 1–4 it applied not only to the worshipper's praise and to Yhwh's general commitment as reflected in the heavens but also to Yhwh's establishing of David's offspring, and it is this expression of *commitment that naturally recurs here. In parallel, Yhwh's *covenant recurs (cf. v. 3). Although covenant and commitment might seem a natural pair, this is actually one of the rare verses in Scripture that brings them together. In turn "*true" (*ne'ĕmenet*) is a participle related to "truthfulness" in vv. 1–4, so that v. 28 as a whole restates declarations there.

Verse 29 specifically restates v. 4, making explicit a link between David's monarchy and the heavens that were then so prominent in vv. 5–14. Implicitly, Yhwh's power over the whole cosmos undergirds the capacity to give this throne the same lasting power as the cosmos.

> [30]If his descendants abandon my teaching,
>   do not walk by my decisions,
> [31]If they profane my laws,
>   do not keep my commands,
> [32]I will attend to their rebellion with a stick,
>   their waywardness with blows.

Four parallel cola express the possibility of David's sons going astray (cf. 2 Sam. 7:14; though that version of the promise relates only to David's own son). Yhwh's expectations are expressed as teaching or instruction

---

42. Cf. Tryggve N. D. Mettinger, *King and Messiah* (Lund: Gleerup, 1976), 263.

like that of a teacher (*tôrâ*), as authoritative *decisions about what should and should not be done, as laws or statutes like those of a national polity (*ḥuqqôt*), and as commands like those of a parent (*miṣwōt*). These demand to be accepted, lived by, observed, and obeyed. But suppose the kings fail to do that (as if!). What if they turn their backs on the instruction and formulate their own understanding, make their own decisions about how and where to walk, flout the commands, break the laws? "Profane" (*ḥālal* piel) suggests treating something that requires reverence, requires to be treated as special, as if there is nothing special about it (cf. vv. 34, 39; 55:20 [21]; 74:7).

What will then happen? Yhwh will "attend" to the matter (see on 59:5 [6]). The details of Yhwh's warning provide the psalm's most precise parallels with 2 Sam. 7 (they do not appear in 1 Chron. 17), where the "stick" and the "blows" that come from it[43] are part of the threat in its v. 14; further, that verse speaks of the son being "wayward," and one of the psalm's words is "*waywardness." It is part of the relationship between a father and his sons that their waywardness or *rebellion meets with such chastisement. The very words "waywardness" and "rebellion" hint at the fact that when the OT talks in these terms, it is not thinking of the relationship between parents and small children but of that between parents and teenagers or adults within the household (cf. the more serious situation of rebelliousness pictured in Deut. 21:18–21). It means the father is treating the son the way he might treat a rebellious slave (Exod. 21:20) and that the son is feeling the stick when he should be wielding it (Ps. 2:9) or protected by it (Ps. 23:4). Yhwh speaks metaphorically, as when speaking of Assyria as the stick whereby to chastise Israel (e.g., Isa. 10:5). The fact that the words "rebellion" and "waywardness" are singular (plural in LXX) suggests that they refer to the breaching of the covenant as a single act.[44]

> [33]But my commitment I will not annul from him;
>   I will not falsify my truthfulness.

So much for the bad news, on which it is as well to come clean; but the reason for doing so is to offer reassurance. To speak of annulling[45] one's *commitment from someone involves an ellipse and/or a metonymy. One annuls a covenant with someone (cf. v. 34) and thereby removes one's commitment from that person.[46] The second colon explains this

---

43. Thus "blows" (*negaʿ*), which usually refers to "plagues" (NJPS), here denote the blows from the stick, as in 2 Sam. 7:14 (cf. Deut. 17:8).

44. So A. Anderson, *Psalms*, 2:643.

45. The verb usually appears as *pārar*, but here *ʾāpîr* looks like a form from *pûr*.

46. Thus in 2 Sam. 7:15 and 1 Chron. 17:13 Yhwh more straightforwardly promises not to "remove" (*sûr* hiphil) this commitment.

in a quite original formulation: to annul a commitment is to turn one's
*truthfulness into the opposite. In 2 Sam. 7 and 1 Chron. 17, Yhwh's
change of mind about Saul lies in the background, and so it does here.
Yhwh "does not act falsely and does not have a change of mind, because
he is not a human being to have a change of mind," says Samuel, just
after the declaration that Yhwh has had a change of mind about Saul
(*nāḥam* niphal, 1 Sam. 15:11, 29). The verb "act falsely" (*šāqar* piel in
1 Sam. 15:29) is the same verb as here (there are only three other occurrences), and the form is the same except that here Yhwh uses the first
person. We have Yhwh's word for it, not merely Samuel's. Whatever the
discomfiting implications of the way Yhwh related to Saul, they will not
leave David's successors with reason to lie awake at night. The abcb′a′
structure of the line perhaps underlines its negation.[47]

> **34**I will not profane my covenant;
>   what has come forth from my lips I will not change.

To say it even more pointedly: Suppose people profane Yhwh's laws
(v. 31). Surely that gives Yhwh the right to profane the covenant, to de-
sanctify it, to treat it as something ordinary that can be thrown away,
doesn't it? If so, Yhwh will not exercise that right. The second colon
explains why this is the case. The covenant Yhwh is making with David
requires a wholehearted and whole-life response from its beneficiaries,
but it is not conditional in the sense that Yhwh's making it depends on
its meeting the appropriate response. It issues from Yhwh's sovereign
initiative and depends only on Yhwh, even though it does demand that
response. Yhwh has spoken, and Yhwh's word will stand. What comes
out of Yhwh's mouth happens (cf. Isa. 40:8; and for the wording, 45:23).
Yhwh's change of mind about Saul continues to lie in the background.
Yhwh will not change this promise to David, upon which his successors
can therefore rely.

> **35**One time I have promised by my holiness,
>   if I were to lie to David . . .

Are they convinced? In case they are not, yet another reformulation
follows. Yhwh has said it once, and in light of v. 34 once is enough.
Yhwh has made it the subject of a solemn promise. Yhwh's own personal being undergirds this promise; Yhwh's personal character will be
impugned if Yhwh does not keep it. Yhwh does not merely say it (as in
v. 19), or merely promise it (as in v. 3), or merely promise it "by myself"

---

47. So Watson, *Classical Hebrew Poetry*, 32.

(Isa. 45:23), but promises it "by my holiness," by all that I am in my divinity. Nor is that all, because Yhwh then goes on to the self-curse that follows on such a promise: "If I lie to David . . ." The consequences are left to the imagination. The verb "lie" recalls the other great formulation about Yhwh's not having a change of mind (Num. 23:19): "God is not a human being, so that he should lie, or a mortal, so that he should have a change of mind." Again, the verb for "lie" (*kāzab* piel, which comes only another ten times in the OT), here appears in exactly the same form as there except that here we again have Yhwh's word for the point. Yhwh's commitment to David is as secure as Yhwh's commitment to bless Israel, the topic in Num. 23:19.

> ³⁶His offspring will continue forever,
>   his throne like the sun before me,
> ³⁷Like the moon, which will be stable forever,
>   a witness in the sky that is truthful. (Rise)

Two lines conclude the review of Yhwh's commitment to David formulated in terms that relate to the present matter the psalm wants to talk about. Initially it simply reaffirms again the opening promise in v. 4, already restated in v. 29, though here there is nothing about Yhwh's making the offspring continue; it simply will happen. More attention is given to developing the idea of permanency. In English, "forever" often means rather less than it sounds—for instance, when someone promises to love someone else "forever," more literally they mean (at best!) "as long as we both live." The same is true of Hebrew terms such as *ʿad-ʿôlām* (v. 4), *lāʿad* (v. 29), and *lĕʿôlām*, the expression here (cf. 73:12, 26, and the comment). They can refer to eternity in our sense, but they need not do so. How "ever" is this "forever"? Verse 4 said "for generation after generation." Verse 29 said "like the days of the heavens." Verses 36–37 spell that out, though the way the parallelism works makes their statement slightly elliptical. In the parallelism the terms "before me" and "a reliable/truthful witness" complement each other and both apply to both the sun and the moon. Both sun and moon stand before Yhwh (in the court in heaven) as true witnesses. They do that in two senses. They are witnesses to the undertaking that Yhwh is giving, like the heavens and the earth that Yhwh calls on as witnesses elsewhere. Usually Yhwh appeals to witnesses in an unfriendly way (e.g., Deut. 31:28). Here the witnesses are there to testify in court on behalf of the people Yhwh is making a commitment to. They are also witnesses in the sense that they illustrate the nature of the commitment that Yhwh makes: the permanency of the Davidic monarchy will be the same as the permanency of sun and moon. It, too, will be stable and true, in keeping with the characteristics of Yhwh's own person and the way these are reflected in the cosmos. Terms related to these two words, *yikkôn* (stable) and *ne'ĕmān* (truthful), came in vv. 1, 2, 4, 5, 8, 14a, 14b, 21, 24, 28, 33, so that v. 37 picks up the two most prominent notes in the psalm so far. There can be absolutely no doubt that Yhwh is committed to this dynasty.[48]

89:38–45. In light of everything we have read, and not least vv. 35–37, the transition to the last sections of the psalm and the experiences they reflect are devastating. It is these sections that reveal that against all the odds, Ps. 89 is a prayer psalm, a protest at the way Yhwh has been acting. Yhwh has established the right to chastise the king, but Yhwh's action goes beyond that envisaged in v. 32; otherwise, there would be no basis for the protest. "The failure of the monarchy seems to bespeak the very failure of God."[49] While the section proceeds to look in the standard three directions of a protest psalm, like Ps. 22 it begins by going for the divine jugular, and the focus continues to lie there (third-person verbs come in vv. 41 and 51; one first-person verb comes in v. 50, though also see comments on v. 41b).[50] Like Ps. 88, the suppliant makes no request except for Yhwh to pay attention, to "be mindful" (vv. 47, 50). That will surely issue in action.

> [38]But you—you spurned, rejected,
>   raged at your anointed.

The opening *wĕ'attâ* in itself advertises no transition; it could mean simply "and you (yourself)." The bite in the transition comes in the three words that follow, a trio of confrontational verbs not exceeded in power anywhere in the Psalms. Although the king might be referring to himself in the third person as "your anointed," or a potential successor to the throne might be referring to someone such as Jehoiachin in this way, it is as plausible to see the congregation as protesting about Yhwh's treatment of the one on whom its flourishing depends and to whom Yhwh has made those commitments in a way that is supposed to benefit it. All that vv. 1–37 promised has related to the succession of anointeds that

48. Otto Eissfeldt ("Psalm 80 und Psalm 89," in Eissfeldt, *Kleine Schriften*, vol. 4 [Tübingen: Mohr, 1968], 132–36 [see 134–35]) sees the witness as the rainbow. Paul G. Mosca ("Once Again the Heavenly Witness of Ps 89:38," *JBL* 105 [1986]: 27–37) takes it to be the Davidic throne itself. Timo Veijola argues that Yhwh is the witness ("Davidverheissung und Staatsvertrag," *ZAW* 95 [1983]: 9–31 [see 17–22]). All these seem implausible and unnecessary complications.

49. McCann, "Psalms," 1034.

50. In making a comparison with an Akkadian lament, Hans Ulrich Steymans notes the distinctiveness of this element in Ps. 89 ("Traces of Liturgies in the Psalms," in *Psalms and Liturgy*, ed. Dirk J. Human and Cas J. A. Vos, JSOTSup 410 [London: Continuum, 2004], 168–234 [see 179, 184–85]).

followed David, the original anointed, with all the stress on the truthfulness and stability of those promises that v. 37 has just summed up.

That is the person who has been treated in a way described by these
three verbs. Spurn and reject are near synonyms that reinforce each other,
but the second has special significance because it is the one Samuel used
to Saul (1 Sam. 15:23, 26). The previous section has specifically promised
that David's line will not be treated like that (cf. 2 Sam. 7:14–15; 1 Chron.
17:13). "Raged" heightens the repetition in a different way by pointing
to the strength of feeling implied in the action, even if as usual words
for anger and rage say more about the outworking of the feelings as the
victim experiences them than about the feelings themselves.

> ³⁹You renounced your servant's covenant;
>   you profaned his diadem to the ground.

It is thus these experiences that the psalm goes on to. "Renounced"
(*nāʾar*) comes only here and in Lam. 2:7, though the contexts make the
general sense clear. On the other hand, "profaned" gains its significance
from vv. 31 and 34. Yhwh has behaved more like the kind of wayward
king who would deserve chastisement than someone fulfilling the undertaking expressed there. What about the king's position as covenanted
servant (v. 3)? What about his diadem? The word is *nēzer,* not (for example) *ʿăṭārâ*; it is a symbol of consecration rather than of majesty (cf.
LXX *hagiasma*). It thus picks up the significance of the reference in
the preceding line to the king's being anointed and the anointing with
holy oil in v. 20. His diadem marked the way Yhwh had set him apart;
now Yhwh has just treated it and him as something ordinary and has
in effect trampled this wreath (or headband) underfoot. The statement
thus involves an ellipse: "You have profaned his diadem [by casting it]
to the ground."

> ⁴⁰You breached all his walls,
>   made his strongholds ruins.
> ⁴¹All who passed by plundered him;
>   he became the scorn of his neighbors.

Now Yhwh becomes the subject of a different kind of verb. Yhwh is
the actual attacker of the city, presumably Jerusalem. Yhwh has breached
the city walls (the verb is again parallel to 60:1 [3]) and destroyed the
places that were supposed to provide protection. That opens up the king
to be plundered by peoples around and to suffer their scorning (cf. 44:13
[14]). The king is also the referent of a different kind of suffix. Things
that are happening to the city and the people are spoken of as if they are

685

simply happening to him. He stands for city and people, for better and for worse, for him and for them. Conversely, if the congregation speaks here, its own experience shows through the words. It speaks about his experience, but the words relate to its own. It is its city's walls that have been breached, its strongholds destroyed, its property that has been plundered, its name scorned.

> [42]You lifted his attackers' right hand;
>   you made his enemies rejoice.
> [43]Yes, you turn back his sword's blade;
>   you did not enable him to rise up in battle.

The suffixes continue to function thus, but once again the portrait changes. Yhwh is again the subject of all the verbs, yet now not as the actual warrior but as the invisible supporter and strengthener of the enemy warriors. By Yhwh's action they have a mysterious ability to lift their right hand higher than one might have expected, to keep wielding their weapons longer than one might have reckoned. This is not how things were supposed to be (see vv. 13, 16, 17, 24). They fight like men inspired, and they have reason to be excited at what they achieve. The enemies were not supposed to be the people rejoicing (see v. 16).

Conversely, the king's forces mysteriously fight less successfully than one would have expected, fight as if expecting to be defeated, incapable of taking the kind of assertive action that would bring victory. Perhaps the turning back of their sword means not merely that they fail to fight but that they fight each other. "Blade" is literally crag or rock, which may reflect the time when weapons were made of stone (cf. Josh. 5:2–3), but here it also forms another contrast between vv. 1–37 and 38–51 because Yhwh is supposed to be the crag that delivers the king (v. 26) and the people but is actually being the opposite.[51]

> [44]You brought his purity to an end,
>   you hurled his throne to the ground.
> [45]You cut short the days of his youth,
>   you clothed him with shame. (Rise)

Now the suffixes revert to the king in person. The word for "purity"[52] comes only here, but related words all have to do with purity, and the

---

51. If ṣûr actually comes from ṣārar V and is a by-form of ṣar (cf. Seybold, *Psalmen*, 349; and see BDB), the paronomasia might explain the choice of this form of the word.

52. MT has *miṭṭĕhārô*, presumably *min* plus *ṭĕhārô*, which is hard to construe. Perhaps the dagesh is euphonic (Tate, *Psalms 51–100*, 412, compares Exod. 15:17); a noun *miṭhārô* would be easier. In either case, it is the direct obj.

best guess is that the colon's meaning (and the line's meaning) is similar to that of v. 39b, where "to the ground" also comes. Being anointed would imply a position of purity like that of a priest (Tg takes the colon to refer to the priesthood); Yhwh has terminated that. A king's defeat is likely to mean that he loses his throne and the victors replace him with someone else (as happened in 597) or take over the government (as happened in 587). But the expression might simply mean that his kingship is discredited. Certainly hurling the king's throne down is the opposite to the destiny envisaged in vv. 29 and 36.

If the psalm was designed simply for use by a particular king, v. 45a might indicate that he was literally young and has had to get used to the tough lessons of adulthood, or has lost his throne while still young (as Jehoiachin did), or is threatened by premature death (cf. v. 47). But the expression is poetic, like others in the context, and more likely the whole colon is a metaphor with implications a little like Daniel Moynihan's "We'll laugh again. It's just that we'll never be young again."[53] The second colon then forms a parallel but more usual statement, though this precise noun (*bûšâ*) again comes only here. The unusual nature of the expression corresponds to the extraordinary nature of the statement (contrast, e.g., 71:13 with this verb, and also the verb *bôš*).

89:46–51. In the closing verses, the psalm at last comes explicitly to plead with Yhwh for action.

> ⁴⁶Until when, Yhwh—will you hide forever?
>   Will your fury burn like fire?

See 79:5 and the comment; also 80:4 [5], and 13:1 [2], which asks, "How long will you hide your face?" Only here is Yhwh accused of simply "hiding." It is as if Yhwh has totally gone—except that it is not like that at all, because the community can feel Yhwh's presence in no uncertain terms.

> ⁴⁷Be mindful—I, what short life;
>   for what emptiness you created all humanity.

These two lines pull back from the particulars of royalty to adopt a quite different framework. Perhaps the king speaks as just an ordinary human being in a position like that of many of the suppliants in the Psalms, threatened with premature death (cf. esp. Pss. 88 and 90). More likely the ordinary person who prays this psalm reminds Yhwh of how life is for everyone in the circumstances of Yhwh's abandonment. The

---

53. http://www.arlingtoncemetery.net/dpmoynihan.htm.

protest is expressed in an appropriately spluttering way: literally, "Be mindful, I, what duration."[54] The suppliant wants Yhwh to be *mindful of the short span of human life as people often experience it. In general the OT accepts that it is all right for our days to come to an end after a full life, but the Psalms witness to the fact that in traditional societies most people do not live out their threescore years and ten. The community's and/or the king's awareness of the threat of this makes the psalm now ricochet to another position than acceptance of our mortality, a position reminiscent of Ecclesiastes. Yhwh created us for šāwĕ', emptiness, something that looks as if it has substance but actually has none. Ecclesiastes does not use this word, but the psalm's point is similar to the one Ecclesiastes makes when it talks about everything being *hebel*, something with the insubstantiality of a breath. If most people live such a short life, why did Yhwh bother to "create" them? The appearance of that verb outside Isa. 40–66 and Gen. 1–6 is very unusual; here it picks up from v. 12. Yhwh created the world, and it is a place of splendor; Yhwh created humanity, and the whole thing seems pointless. From yet another angle the psalm thus raises the question whether there is consistency between Yhwh's relationship with the cosmos and with David. Despite all that was said in vv. 19–37, it transpires that king and people are just mortal human beings (cf. 144:3–4 in its context).[55]

> [48]Who is the man who can live
>   and not see death,
>   save himself from the hand of Sheol? (Rise)

Like people in the Western world over against people in the two-thirds world, and middle-class people over against poorer people, kings could expect to live longer than their people. They ate better and their living conditions were better. Like Western people and middle-class people, they might then reckon that they had control of their lives but might find that actually some life experience indicates that this is not so at all. The psalm's reflection here corresponds to that in Ps. 49. Money cannot buy long life. The metaphysical playing field turns out to be level. Like 88:4 [5], for "man" the psalm uses the word *geber*, which hints at the idea of he-man or macho man. There is no strong man strong enough to

---

54. *TTH* 189.2 implies that the construction simply involves a quite natural apposition, "Be mindful [that] I [am of] what short life," but it is still an unusual one. For the construction with *mah*, see BDB on *mah*; DG 8.

55. See Jerome F. D. Creach, "The Mortality of the King in Psalm 89 and Israel's Postexilic Identity," in *Constituting the Community: Studies on the Polity of Ancient Israel in Honor of S. Dean McBride*, ed. John T. Strong and Steven S. Tuell (Winona Lake, IN: Eisenbrauns, 2005), 237–49; he takes the verses as a later addition to the psalm.

defeat death, not even a king. The unexpected third colon, which adds nothing to the content of the question, underlines the point and brings this little reflection to an end.

> ⁴⁹Where are your former acts of commitment, my Lord,
>   which you promised David by your truthfulness?

The psalm reverts to the specifics of Yhwh's *commitment to David. It has used the word "commitment" five times in the singular but now reverts to the plural usage with which it started, which signals the way v. 49 forms an inclusion with vv. 1–4. There the suppliant promised to sing of Yhwh's acts of commitment forever and to make known Yhwh's *truthfulness generation after generation. Now there is a different song to be sung. Is the suppliant failing to keep that promise? Did that promise always presuppose that Yhwh's acts of commitment would continue? Does the psalm presuppose that when Yhwh's acts of commitment resume, so will the praise? Would it be unreal to give praise for Yhwh's acts of commitment when these are suspended? Or would that be an act of faith? Does the asking of these questions constitute singing of them and speaking of Yhwh's truthfulness? Is it significant that the suppliant now speaks to "my *Lord" rather than to Yhwh? Or does the very nature of Yhwh's promise in v. 35a invite the kind of challenge the psalm now issues? "By your truthfulness" has the same place in the phraseology as "by my holiness" in v. 35, with the implication that the divine holiness lies in the divine faithfulness.

> ⁵⁰Be mindful, my Lord, of the scorning of your servants,
>   which I have carried in my bosom, every one, of many peoples,

The imperative recurs from v. 47, the only petition the psalm ever utters, and once again the suppliant appeals to "my *Lord." "Scorning" likewise picks up from v. 41, though notably the psalm now speaks of the scorning of Yhwh's servants—plural (contrast vv. 3, 20, 39). This is presumably the "we" who speak in vv. 17 and 18; Yhwh's servants means Israel as a whole. The appeal in v. 50 makes several assumptions. One is that Yhwh is the reason for the people's being scorned; if it were not for their commitment to Yhwh, it would not be happening (for this motif, cf. 42:10 [11]; 44:13–16 [14–17]; 69:9 [10], 74:10; 79:12). Another is that a master will care about a servant's being dishonored; that is built into the relationship. Yet another is that the dishonoring of a servant also implicates their master, so v. 50a appeals to Yhwh's own honor.

The second colon then complements the plural "servants" by speaking as "I" instead of speaking about "them." The king, or more likely each individual member of the congregation, has had to bear every one of the scornful comments uttered by the many peoples who have observed what has happened to Judah.

> [51]That with which your enemies have scorned, Yhwh,
>   that with which they have scorned the steps of your anointed.

The final line underscores the point. While affecting all Yhwh's servants, this scorning affects the king in particular. And because the king is Yhwh's anointed and thus Yhwh's servant in a special sense, the servant through whom Yhwh intends to govern the nations, the scorning of Yhwh's anointed also affects Yhwh. That is again because Yhwh is indirectly the cause of the scorning, because Yhwh surely cares about this anointed, and because Yhwh is once more implicated in the scorning. When the Assyrians derided Yhwh and people who trusted in Yhwh, Hezekiah wondered whether Yhwh would listen to their scorning of "the living God" and urged Yhwh to do so. Isaiah then sent Yhwh's word for Sennacherib, "Whom have you scorned? . . . By means of your aides you have scorned my Lord" (2 Kings 19:4, 16, 22–23). The suppliant might be a rather less deferential Hezekiah and one more concerned for his own scorning than for Yhwh's, or he might be a prophet like Isaiah. Yet (like David protesting Goliath's scorning of the armies of the living God), the suppliant protests the actions of Yhwh's enemies and their scorn of Yhwh's anointed. Yhwh's reputation is tied up with that of Judah and its king as a result of the commitment Yhwh has made and the commission Yhwh has undertaken. The reference to the anointed's steps coheres with that. People did not recognize Yhwh's footsteps at the Red Sea (77:19 [20]); neither do they recognize the footsteps of Yhwh's anointed as having anything to do with the living God. Like Pss. 44 and 88, Ps. 89 stops rather than closing; that reflects the realities of the situation.

Theological Implications

In volume 1 of this commentary, I described Ps. 22 as insisting on facing two sets of facts. Book II of the Psalms started, in Pss. 42–43, with a prayer that does the same. Psalm 89 also does it. Whereas Ps. 22 resolves this conversation one way, closing with all hopefulness and expectation, and Pss. 42–43 leave the conversation unresolved, Ps. 89 resolves it the other way, closing with a protest at Yhwh's abandonment. The Psalms indicate that God deals with different people in different ways and deals with the community in different ways at different stages of its life. All these responses to God's dealings gained a place in God's book of prayers.

It is astonishing that Book III of the Psalter comes to an end with two psalms that terminate with Yhwh's having abandoned Israel. They recall the books of Kings or the books of Chronicles without their hopeful last paragraphs. It is an extraordinary interim ending for a collection of prayers and praises that began with Pss. 1–2, since Ps. 88 in effect belies Ps. 1 and Ps. 89 in effect belies Ps. 2. Psalm 89 also constitutes a very different ending from that of Book II, in Ps. 72, which is implicitly much more hopeful about the monarchy.[56] Whereas Ps. 72 implies a conviction that the reign of God might be embodied in the reign of the king, Ps. 89 makes clear that God has abandoned the king.[57] Robert L. Cole traces the detailed links between Ps. 89 and Pss. 73–88 and concludes that Ps. 89 "encapsulates and summarizes much of the message of Book III."[58] It is as well that Ps. 89 is not the end of the Psalter. Psalm 97 will reaffirm v. 14, and other psalms in Book IV (beginning with Ps. 90) will also affirm that Yhwh does and/or will reign in the world, notwithstanding the demise of the monarchy.[59] Indeed, Ps. 132 will reaffirm Yhwh's commitment to David and to Zion.[60]

Yet they do not clarify how that will come about. At the end of the psalm, Tg has people mocking the slowness of the steps of the Anointed: in other words, mocking the fact that it takes the Messiah a long time to get here. This highlights the fact that in the psalm itself there is no indication that the understanding of Yhwh's reign is coming to be understood eschatologically or that the understanding of the human king's reign is coming to be understood messianically.[61]

56. Cf. Gerald H. Wilson, "The Use of Royal Psalms at the 'Seams' of the Hebrew Psalter," *JSOT* 35 (1986): 85–94 (see 89–91); idem, *The Editing of the Hebrew Psalter*, SBLDS 76 (Chico, CA: Scholars Press, 1985), 209–14.

57. On the links between Pss. 72 and 89, see Cole, *Shape and Message of Book III*, 178–82, and on the movement between Pss. 2; 72; and 89, see Erich Zenger, "'Es sollten sich niederwerfen vor ihm alle Könige,'" in *"Mein Sohn bist du,"* ed. Otto and Zenger, 66–93.

58. Cole, *Shape and Message of Book III*, 205.

59. Cf. Wilson, *Editing of the Hebrew Psalter*, 214–19; Cole, *Shape and Message of Book III*, 219–23, with particular reference to Ps. 90. For another angle, see Frank-Lothar Hossfeld, "Ps 89 und das vierte Psalmenbuch," in *"Mein Sohn bist du,"* ed. Otto and Zenger, 173–83.

60. I owe this point to Tremper Longman.

61. Contrast Christoph Rösel, *Die messianische Redaktion des Psalters* (Stuttgart: Calwer, 1999), esp. 135–46, where he argues that vv. 20, 38, and 51 evidence this. David C. Mitchell (*The Message of the Psalter* [JSOTSup 252; Sheffield: Sheffield Academic Press, 1997], 253–58) similarly argues that the psalm's place in the Psalter means it would have been understood messianically. But the existence of other approaches to interpreting texts about the king—in this case, not least in Isa. 55:3–5—indicates that in OT times people *could* have interpreted the psalm messianically but need not have done so; it does not give

Outside the Psalter, some of the Prophets do affirm that Ps. 89 is not the end of Yhwh's commitment to David's line (see, e.g., Jer. 23:5–6). In keeping with this, the Church of England's Book of Common Prayer sets this psalm for Christmas Day; the incarnation implements the commitment expressed in the psalm and responds to its plea. On the other hand, more recent lectionaries such as that of the Episcopal Church's Book of Common Prayer use only the first part of the psalm. What does that imply about the last part? Is the church in denial about this aspect of its own experience? This would be a shame. The same question is raised by the way hymns and worship songs take up only the first part of the psalm.[62] "Thus [i.e., as expounded in vv. 1–4] runs the covenant; and when the church declines, it is ours to plead it before the ever faithful God, as the Psalmist does."[63]

Isaiah 55:3–5 also affirms that Ps. 89 is not the end of God's commitment to David but does so in a quite different way from Jer. 23:5–6.[64] "Where are the kind of acts of commitment Yhwh showed to David?" the psalm asks. Isaiah 55 responds directly to that question, though also innovatively. It is a feature of Isa. 40–55 to focus on Yhwh's involvement with and commitment to the people of God as a whole and to omit reference to any reestablishment of the monarchy. This comes to a climax with Yhwh making with the people in general a covenant that will last forever, Yhwh's "truthful acts of commitment to David." The language reflects that of the psalm. We have noted that the psalm itself applies language to the king that applies primarily to the people as a whole: they are Yhwh's chosen, Yhwh's firstborn. The prophet goes back behind the psalm to reaffirm that the people are Yhwh's primary concern. To say that the promise to David will be fulfilled in them is not to go back on that promise but to reaffirm it.

Psalm 88's only prayer is, "May my plea come before your face; incline your ear to the sound I make." In Ps. 89, twice repeated in vv. 47 and 50, the prayer is simply, "Be mindful." It is really the sole prayer that is needed. If Yhwh will only do that, everything else will follow.

---

pointers in that direction (cf. Whybray, *Reading the Psalms as a Book*, 94). Even "protomessianic" (Saur, *Königspsalmen*, 185) seems to me a reading into the text.

62. Cf. Ralph W. Klein, "Let Me Not Sing the Song of Your Love off Key," *Currents in Theology and Mission* 27 (2000): 253–62.

63. Spurgeon, *Treasury of David*, 4:25.

64. Cf. Otto Eissfeldt, "The Promises of Grace to David in Isaiah 55:1–5," in *Israel's Prophetic Heritage* (J. Muilenburg Festschrift; ed. Bernhard W. Anderson and Walter Harrelson; New York: Harper, 1962), 196–207; Bernard Gosse, "Le livre d'Isaïe et le Psautier," *ZAW* 115 (2003): 376–87 (see 376–77).

Psalm 89:52

Coda to Book III

Translation

⁵²Yhwh be worshipped forever. Yes, yes.

Interpretation

[89:52]. The prose line numbered as the last verse in Ps. 89 is a coda to Book III of the Psalter (Pss. 73–89), an act of *worship and a declaration of personal commitment like those that follow Pss. 41; 72; and 106. The double "yes" is a response to the preceding bidding, perhaps suggesting that the coda started off life as a liturgical exchange. But "yes" is *āmēn*, a declaration that in this context gains part of its significance from its being related to one of the recurrent key words in Ps. 89, *ʾĕmûnâ*.

Theological Implications

Kirkpatrick comments that "though it is no part of the original Psalm, it is entirely in harmony with the spirit of it, as an expression of the faith which can bless God even when the visible signs of His love are withdrawn."[1] Actually, the coda's relationship with the psalm is more subtle. It is an expression of the faith from which the psalm starts, and in

1. *Psalms*, 543.

this sense it contradicts the more complex expression of faith with which the psalm ends. In this sense it conflicts with the spirit of the psalm. But it also reminds us of the daring profession of faith that the Psalter as a whole makes. To put it another way, it attempts to turn the psalm's way of resolving the conversation between Yhwh's commitment and Yhwh's abandonment into something more like a continuing conversation, comparable to that in Pss. 22 or 42–43. In this sense it does what Ps. 97 or Jer. 23 or Isa. 55 also do. Each of them has a view about how Yhwh will respond to Ps. 89. This coda has no theory about that, but it still declares that Yhwh is to be praised forever. "Yhwh gave, Yhwh took; Yhwh's name be praised," Job also said (Job 1:21).

Glossary

Abyss (*šaḥat*). A term for the place where dead people are (30:9 [10]; 49:9 [10]; 55:23 [24]), sometimes parallel to *Sheol (16:10). The LXX and Jerome translate with words such as "corruption" as if it came from *šāḥat*, which would be a plausible view if there were not the ordinary noun *šaḥat*, meaning "pit," from *šûaḥ*. Its use for the home of the dead presumably derives from the fact that people were sometimes buried in a grave pit rather than a rock-hewn tomb (cf. *bôr*, 88:4, 6 [5, 7]). But the fact that burial does lead to dissolution of the body might mean that the connotations of *šāḥat* carried over to *šaḥat* when used in connection with death.

Acknowledge (*yāda'*). The verb commonly refers to knowing facts or knowing people, and it is usually so translated in EVV. But it often implies "acknowledging" or "recognizing" with the will and not merely the mind—so that knowing implies taking notice of and committing oneself (9:10, 20 [11, 21]; 14:4; 25:4; 37:18). Yhwh can be the subject of the verb with this meaning (1:6; 31:7 [8]).

Against, be (*śānē'*). The verb is usually rendered in English as "hate," but it refers more to hostile action, opposition, or repudiation than to negative feelings (45:7 [8]; 50:17; 69:4, 14 [5, 15]; 86:17). The participle thus means "foes." The converse of "be *dedicated."

Armies (*ṣĕbā'ôt*). The title Yhwh Armies (*yhwh ṣĕbā'ôt*; 46:7, 11 [8, 12]; 48:8 [9]; 84:1, 3, 12 [2, 4, 13) is puzzling. The LXX translates "Lord of the powers" (cf. Jerome), which suggests taking it as an example of a rare construction whereby a name can govern a construct or can be treated as a common noun.[1] The expression would then presumably have similar implications to the extended version of the title "Yhwh, God of the Armies" (69:6 [7]; 89:8 [9]) and the alternative short version "God of the Armies" (80:7, 14 [8, 15]). Some worshippers might take these armies to be Israel's earthly ones, though the OT is less inclined to associate Yhwh with earthly armies than with the heavenly army, the supernatural forces that Yhwh commands (1 Sam. 17:45 pointedly uses a different word to refer to Israel's forces). The great heavenly army (perhaps the plural is intensive) is one Yhwh created and one that serves Yhwh (33:6; 103:21; 148:2). But elsewhere (e.g., Jer. 3:19) LXX renders the title "Lord All-powerful," which suggests taking the plural as abstract and the compound expression as appositional. This would fit with the use of the alternative extended version "Yhwh God Armies," where "God" is

1. See JM 131o.

in the absolute rather than the construct form (Ps. 59:5 [6]; 80:4, 19 [5, 20]; 84:8 [9]).[2] The title would then imply "Yhwh Great Army" or "Yhwh Great Warrior."

Asaph. Psalms 50 and 73–83 are Asaph Psalms. That might imply the conviction that they were composed by Asaph, a Levitical music leader in David's day in 1 Chron. 15–16; 25, or composed and handed down within the choir that bore his name. They have some features (for instance, references to Joseph) that might suggest a northern background.[3]

Authority (*mišpāṭ*). Leadership and decision-making exercised with power and legitimacy (e.g., 76:9 [10]). The EVV usually translate "justice," and *mišpāṭ* is indeed ideally exercised with justice, but this is not always so; it can be exercised unjustly. In this sense the older translation "judgment" is better, since there can be unjust judgment. This is reflected in the characteristic pairing of *mišpāṭ* with *ṣĕdāqâ* or *ṣedeq* (*faithfulness; e.g., 89:14 [15]). Authority needs to be exercised with *ṣĕdāqâ*, but this does not always happen (see 58:1 [2]; 67:4 [5]; 75:2 [3]; 82:2). The pairing safeguards the quality of the exercise of authority, which involves leaders making decisions or exercising authority in such a way that they do what is right by delivering the needy and putting down the powerful. In turn *mišpāṭ* safeguards the decisiveness of a commitment to faithfulness, which is not merely a matter of intending faithfulness or affirming the importance of faithfulness but also of implementing it. The exercise of *mišpāṭ* is not intrinsically a juridical matter; the word covers the exercise of authority in general. Thus the parent verb *šāpaṭ* can imply "judge" (51:4 [6]; 82:1) but in itself means "decide." It means decide *for* as well as decide *against* (e.g., 43:1; 72:4; 82:3, 8) or simply "rule," and *mišpāṭ* means a decision taken by someone who has authority, such as God (48:11 [12]) or the king (72:1, 2), perhaps a decision about what other people should do (81:4 [5]; 89:30 [31]).

Bad, trouble (*raʿ*). The word *raʿ* covers both the bad experiences that people have (and that Yhwh can bring about) and the bad things that people do (of which Yhwh disapproves). Sometimes the focus lies on the first (49:5 [6]; 54:5 [7]; 70:2 [3]; 71:13, 20, 24; 78:49; 88:3 [4]), sometimes on the second (50:19; 51:4 [6]; 52:1, 3 [3, 5]; 55:15 [16]; 56:5 [6]; 64:5 [6]), sometimes both connotations may apply (e.g., 73:8), and sometimes it is hard to tell which applies.

Bloodshed (*dāmîm*). The word for blood is used in the plural in connection with murderous attacks on other people (e.g., 59:2 [3]); the plural perhaps expresses affective value.[4] But "person of bloods" need not be merely a synonym for "slayer"; it often denotes not people who directly shed blood but people who want or scheme for the death of someone (5:6 [7]; 55:23 [24]).[5]

Bow low (*hištaḥăwâ*). To bow right down or prostrate oneself (29:2; 45:11 [12]; 66:4; 72:11; 81:9 [10]; 86:9). The EVV often render "worship," but it refers to the physical

2. GKC 125h understands this title as a conflate expression issuing from the Elohistic redaction of the Psalms. DG 27 and *IBHS* 9.8c see the *m* on *ʾĕlōhîm* as enclitic. JM 131o sees the abs. form of *ʾĕlōhîm* as following from the apparently appositional linking of *yhwh* with *ṣĕbāʾôt*.

3. See, e.g., Martin J. Buss, "The Psalms of Asaph and Korah," *JBL* 82 (1963): 382–92; Nasuti, *Tradition History*; Michael Goulder, "Asaph's *History of Israel*," *JSOT* 65 (1995): 71–81. Goulder sees them as relating to successive episodes in the history of Israel as understood in the 720s (see further his *Psalms of Asaph*).

4. So *TDOT*.

5. See N. A. van Uchelen, "*ʾNšy dmym* in the Psalms," in *The Priestly Code and Seven Other Studies*, by J. G. Fink et al., OtSt 15 (Leiden: Brill, 1969), 205–12.

act of prostration rather than the attitude that accompanies this act, and it can refer to a proper prostration before a human being. There is disagreement about its parsing: BDB takes it as hitpalel from *šāḥâ*; *HALOT* takes it as eshtafel from *ḥāwâ*.

Committed, commitment (*ḥāsîd, ḥesed*). Commitment implies pledging oneself to someone when one has no prior obligation to do so or keeping such a pledge of commitment no matter what happens—as when the other person does not keep the pledge and thus forfeits any right to such commitment. EVV have "steadfast love" and other words. God's commitment is thus a basis for prayer, trust, and hope in crises, and a topic to talk about (42:8 [9]; 44:26 [27]; 48:9 [10]; 51:1 [3]; 52:1 [3]). The human response to God's goodness to us is to be *ḥāsîd* in relation to God (50:5; 52:9 [11]). A *ḥāsîd* is someone who keeps commitment and lives faithfully, against the odds if necessary. It is the opposite of behaving falsely (43:3; 85:8 [9]). Commitment can link with the idea of covenant, but there is no intrinsic link between the two ideas: "commitment" and "covenant" do not commonly occur in the same context.

Composition (*mizmôr*). The noun appears frequently in psalm headings and is conventionally translated "psalm." But *zāmar* and its derived nouns refer more generally to the making of music. They refer to tune, harmony, and rhythm rather than words (e.g., 47:6, 7 [7, 8]; 66:2; 68:4, 32 [5, 33]), or to singing with instruments rather than a cappella (cf. 71:22). Insofar as they do refer to music with lyrics, the nouns suggest "songs" rather than "psalms" in that they imply no presupposition that the music relates to worship or prayer (cf. *zāmîr* in 2 Sam. 23:1; Isa. 25:5). While the OT uses the verb itself only of worship music, the more general use of the derived noun suggests that *zāmar* would also be the general term for making music.

Confess (*yādâ* hiphil). Giving testimony to the truth of something. This may be the truth about what God has done for the speakers (so that the verb is often translated "give thanks"; 42:5, 11 [6, 12]; 43:4, 5; 44:8 [9]; 75:1 [2]), or it may be the truth about what the speakers have done (confession of sin; 32:5), or it may imply testimony to something about a human being (45:17 [18]; 49:18 [19]). By its nature such confession is a public act. The verb is the one from which the noun *tôdâ* (thanksgiving) comes. In confessing the good things Yhwh has done, one is giving thanks for them and vice versa.

Covenant (*běrît*). Making a covenant implies imposing a solemn obligation on oneself or on someone else. It may refer to a mutual commitment, but it need not do so. Thus it may refer to the covenant Yhwh made to Israel (74:20) or to David (89:3, 28, 34, 39 [4, 29, 35, 40]), or to the covenant expectations Yhwh laid on Israel (44:17 [18]; 50:5, 16; 78:10, 37), or to the covenant commitment one human being has made to another (55:20 [21]; 83:5 [6]).

Crag (*ṣûr*). The EVV render "rock," but the word refers not to a large stone but a high cliff in the mountains where a bird or wild animal can find security (61:2 [3]; 62:2, 6, 7 [3, 7, 8]; 71:3; 73:26; 78:35; 89:26 [27]; cf. 1 Sam. 24:2 [3]).

Decide, decision (*šāpaṭ, mišpāṭ*). See *Authority.

Declaration (*'ēdût*). Although etymologically the word might refer to testimony to what Yhwh has done, in ordinary usage it always refers to Yhwh's declarations that express expectations of the people (so 78:5; 81:5 [6]). But this meaning does not suit the occurrences in the headings to Pss. 60 and 80. There it is preceded by "*lily/lilies," and it might be part of the title of a tune.

Dedicate oneself (*'āhēb*). The EVV render "love," which is sometimes appropriate, but the word commonly indicates an act of the will or a commitment rather than (merely) a feeling (see 52:3–4 [5–6]; 69:36 [37]). The antonym of "be *against" (cf. 45:7 [8]).

Deliver, deliverance, deliverer (*yāsaʿ, yěšûʿâ, yešaʿ, těšûʿâ*). The EVV render "save/salvation," but those words are inclined to suggest an act that delivers people from the wrath of God and gives them eternal life. While the Psalms, like other parts of the OT, are concerned for a living, personal relationship between people and God, they do not speak of that as *yěšû'â*. "Deliverance" denotes action that rescues people from the attack of wicked people or from illness or from trouble (e.g., 44:3, 4, 6, 7 [4, 5, 7, 8]). It is not quite true to say that only God can deliver (see 72:4, 13), but it is nearly true. Deliverance is especially God's business because it connotes rescue that no ordinary resources could bring.

Do not destroy (*'al tašḥēt*). The expression comes at the point in the headings to Pss. 57; 58; 59; and 75 when a phrase often seems to designate a tune or way of singing, but such expressions are preceded by *'al* (see Pss. 53; 56). Further, "Do not destroy" is the bidding David issues to Abishai when he is fleeing from Saul but then has Saul at his mercy (1 Sam. 26:9; other occurrences such as Deut. 9:26; Isa. 65:8 seem less relevant). Thus it might constitute another link with the David story and suggest another story to link with the psalm to which it is attached.[6] But the fact that the term appears in the *Inscriptions of Pss. 57–59 suggests the further possibility that it constitutes an exhortation not to destroy the psalm, which is designed to stand as a written testimony.[7]

Face (*pānîm*). See 42:2, 5, 11 [3, 6, 12]; 44:3 [4]; 67:1 [2]; it is also the word that most often lies behind the word "presence" or "before" in EVV (68:1–8 [2–9]; 95:2, 6). It is the face that turns and looks, that notices and acts in love, commitment, generosity, deliverance, and blessing. The shining of the face implies looking on people with a life-giving smile, with love and generosity, and acting accordingly. If someone can be prevailed on to smile at a suppliant, all else will follow. So seeking God's face means seeking for God to look at us in such a way as to act thus, and seeing God's face means seeing such prayers answered as we experience vindication and deliverance. On the other hand, hiding the face, turning the face from people's oppression and need, means ignoring that need, a terrifying act because it means there will be no deliverance or blessing (44:24 [25]; 69:17 [18]; 80:3, 7, 19 [4, 8, 20]). But it is a comforting act when Yhwh's face is averted from our sin (51:9 [11]) and when Yhwh's face is against wrongdoers (34:16 [17]).

Fail, failure (*ḥāṭā', ḥaṭṭā'*). The expressions are routinely translated "sin." In everyday usage, the verb suggests missing a target (Judg. 20:16) or missing one's way (Prov. 19:2), so that in a religious context it would imply coming short of Yhwh's expectations or failure to live up to them. Such shortcoming or failure does not imply doing one's best and failing but means a reprehensible failure to do what was required, a missing the way for which we are responsible.

Faithful, faithfulness, be faithful (*ṣaddîq, ṣĕdāqâ, ṣedeq, ṣādēq*). Acting in the right way in relation to people with whom one is in a relationship. The EVV's "righteous, just, righteousness" thus lose the relationship connotations of the words, which do not directly refer to individual personal morality or to social justice as we understand that idea. They do not suggest treating everyone in the same, just way but doing the right thing by one's relationships or community. For the verb in 82:3, A. Anderson has "a determination to render effective help to the helpless."[8]

Faithless, faithlessness (*rāšā', reša'*). The antonym of *faithful/faithfulness. The conventional English translation "wicked" is rather general. To be *rāšā'* is to fail to keep your commitments to God and/or to other people.

---

6. Cf. Tg; also *Midrash on Psalms*, 1:504, on Ps. 58.

7. See, e.g., P. D. Miller, *Israelite Religion and Biblical Theology*, JSOTSup 267 (Sheffield: Sheffield Academic Press, 2000), 210–32.

8. *Psalms*, 2:594.

Fall down/falter (*môṭ*). One aspect of the significance of "falling down" appears when it is defined as experiencing adversity (*raʿ*; 10:6) or set against its opposite, which is "doing well" (*šalwâ*; 30:6 [7]) or being firmly established like the very creation (104:5). But *môṭ* is also used to refer to falling down morally or religiously, wavering in one's commitment (17:5).

Falsehood, false (*šeqer*). See 52:3 [5]; 63:11 [12]; 69:4 [5]. Falsehood is what does not correspond to reality. It is testimony that does not correspond to what happened, or an image that corresponds to no reality and thus cannot save, or a promise that does not come true.

Good fortune of (*ʾašrê*). The EVV have "Blessed/happy is/are . . . ," but the Hebrew is a noun exclamation without a verb. This construct plural is the only form in which the word occurs (a similar noun *ʾōšer* comes once, in Gen. 30:13). It is not numerical plural but intensive plural.[9] Further, it does not mean "blessing" in a merely "spiritual" sense, though it would include that; the expression would hardly be applied to godless people merely because they did well in life. But it is a less religious-sounding or liturgical word than the English word "blessed." It suggests that people's whole lives work out well. The contexts of the declaration suggest that it has two aspects. Positively, Yhwh gives all good things (84:11–12 [12–13]; cf. 112:1–3; 128; 144:15). Negatively, Yhwh sees people are delivered from trouble and preserved in crises (32:1–2; 33:12; 34:8 [9]; 40:4 [5]; 41:1 [2]; 65:4 [5]). It "is not a wish and not a promise. . . . It is a joyful cry and a passionate statement."[10]

Good, goodness (*ṭôb, ṭûb*). The words are wide-ranging antonyms of *raʿ*, so they can refer to doing what is good as opposed to what is wicked (52:3 [5]; 53:1, 3 [2, 4]) but also to experiencing what is good as opposed to what is bad—that is, blessing (65:4, 11 [5, 12]; 84:11 [12]; 85:12 [13]), what is welcome or lovely (45:1 [2]; 52:9 [11]; 54:6 [8]; 63:3 [4]); 69:16 [17]; 73:28; 84:10 [11]). Perhaps the two ideas come together in the implication that goodness entails generosity (68:10 [11]). Doing good suggests kindness, doing good to someone rather than doing what is merely objectively right (73:1; 86:5).

Grace, be gracious, prayer for grace (*ḥēn, ḥānan, tĕḥinnâ*). The positive, generous attitude a person shows to someone else when there is no existent relationship or desert that the latter could appeal to. In human relationships, it corresponds to the way we may ask someone else to "do us a favor." The noun "grace" hardly occurs in the Psalter (see 45:2 [3]; 84:11 [12]), but "be gracious" is a frequent plea in prayers (e.g., 51:1 [3]; 56:1 [2]; 57:1 [2]). It appeals to the fundamentals of God's nature; there is nothing further back in God to appeal to than this. A *tĕḥinnâ* (6:9 [10]; 55:1 [2]) is then a plea for grace, an appeal to Yhwh's nature as one who acts with favor and grace toward people irrespective of their deservingness but because that is indeed Yhwh's nature.

Harm, harmfulness (*ʾāwen*). It has been argued that "people who do harm" (*pōʿălê ʾāwen*; 53:4 [5]; 59:2 [3]; 64:2 [3]) are people who use words to cause harm to someone by the manipulation of demonic power, but the Psalms' language is too general to infer this or any other specific and precise connotation for the phrase.[11] It simply denotes causing harm to someone. But the language's generality means that psalms where it appears are open to being used by people under various forms of verbal attack that threaten their well-being and life.

Harp (*nēbel*). See *Lyre.

9. Cf. BDB.
10. Martin Buber, *Good and Evil* (New York: Scribner's, 1952), 53. Waldemar Janzen ("ʾAšrê in the Old Testament," *HTR* 58 [1965]: 215–26) renders it as "enviable."
11. See, e.g., *TDOT* or *NIDOTTE* on *ʾāwen*.

Haven (*miśgāb*). The verb *śāgab* means "to be [inaccessibly] high up" (20:1 [2]; 59:1 [2]; 69:29 [30]). A *miśgāb* is thus a place that is inaccessibly and therefore safely high up (9:9 [10]; 18:2 [3]; 46:7, 11 [8, 12]; 59:9, 16, 17 [10, 17, 18]; 62:2, 6 [3, 7]).

Heart (*lēb, lēbāb*). While anatomically *lēb* and *lēbāb* refer to the heart, metaphorically they then do not usually suggest feeling as opposed to thinking but rather refer to the determinative center of the person, the inner being—almost the whole person (51:10, 17 [12, 19]; 55:4 [5]; 57:7 [8]; 61:2 [3]; 62:8 [9]; 69:20, 32 [21, 33]; 76:5 [6]; 78:8; 84:2 [3]). They thus suggest the aspect of the person that thinks about things, forms attitudes, and makes decisions, so that they are close to English "mind" or "will" (48:13 [14]; 49:3 [4]; 58:2 [3]; 62:10 [11]; 66:18; 74:8; 81:12 [13]). The heart can suggest the (secret) inner attitude as opposed to the outward word or act (44:18, 21 [19, 22]; 53:1 [2]; 55:21 [22]; 64:6, 10 [7, 11]; 78:37). It is a key expression in Ps. 73.

Help (*'āzar, 'ēzer, 'ezrâ*). The context in passages such as 44:26 [27]; 46:1, 5 [2, 6] shows how helping does not denote assisting people who are doing their part but delivering people when they are helpless, people such as the needy and weak, who have no power and no resources (cf. 72:12). "Help" is thus a rather feeble equivalent for *'ēzer*, which suggests a powerful person taking decisive action on behalf of a weak person who is in dire need. In English, without "help" we might manage OK but a little less comfortably; in Hebrew, without *'ēzer* we would often be dead (cf. 33:20; 70:5 [6]; 124:8 in their context).

Honor (*kābôd*). The EVV have "glory." The word suggests the visible splendor of a monarch or some other important person, glorious in their impressive array (24:7–10; 63:2 [3]), and then the visible prosperity and thus honor of ordinary people (62:7 [8]; 73:24; 84:11 [12]; 85:9 [10]). The visible honor is then assumed to be an appropriate outward expression of their intrinsic majesty (66:2; 72:19; 79:9), though this may not always be so (49:16–17 [17–18]).

Hope (*tiqwâ, tôḥelet*). Nouns from *qāwâ*, look to, and *yāḥal*, *wait. They can denote the attitude of hoping or waiting (39:7 [8]) or the object of expectation, the thing hoped for (9:18 [19]; 62:5 [6]; 71:5).

Ignore (*śākaḥ*). The EVV often have "forget," but the verb indicates a deliberate act of putting out of mind (45:10 [11]). The antonym of "be *mindful."

Inscription (*miktām*). "Inscription" is the meaning LXX and Tg ascribe to this word in the headings of Pss. 16; 56–60. It might indicate that the psalm was inscribed in clay in the manner of Babylonian psalms; Keel suggests that such a psalm was inscribed on a stele, as a way of giving permanent expression to the prayer before God.[12] This fits its application to Hezekiah's prayer in Isa. 38:9–20.

Instruction (*maśkîl*). If we assume that this word in headings comes from *śākal* I, then "instruction" (that is, this is a psalm that offers a pattern for prayer or praise) is one possible meaning, fitting Ps. 78, though "contemplative poem" and "skilful poem" are other possibilities.[13] Klaus Koenen suggests that the word rather comes from *śākal* II and means "antiphonal song."[14]

Jacob's God (*'ĕlōhê ya'ăqōb*). Jacob's God was one who answered him on the day of trouble (20:1 [2]; cf. Gen. 35:3), and this connotation carries over into the recurrence

---

12. *Symbolism,* 329. Raymond Tournay suggests "secret prayer" ("Sur quelques rubriques des Psaumes," in *Mélanges bibliques* [A. Robert Festschrift; Paris: Bloud & Gay, 1957], 197–204). See further Craigie, *Psalms 1–50,* 154; Tate, *Psalms 51–100,* 66.
13. See BDB.
14. "*Maâkil-*'Wechselgesang,'" *ZAW* 103 (1991): 109–12.

of the title in the Asaph Psalms (75:9 [10]; 76:6 [7]; 81:1, 4 [2, 5]) and elsewhere (46:7, 11 [8, 12]; 84:8 [9]).

Korahites (*běnê-qōraḥ*). Psalms 42–49; 84–85; and 87–88 are "Korahites' Psalms." These are presumably the Korahites who were among the Levitical singing groups (2 Chron. 20:19). The heading may indicate that these psalms were composed by members of this group and/or formed part of its repertoire. The psalms have some shared features, and Michael D. Goulder sees them as a sequence of festal psalms linked to the sanctuary at Dan.[15]

Lead, leader (*nāṣaḥ, měnaṣṣēaḥ*). Leading describes a musical role in 1 Chron. 15:21, and the "leader" might thus be the music director. "The leader's" (as in Ps. 49's heading) perhaps then refers to a collection of psalms. But the leader might be a king or priest who represented the people in worship.[16]

Light (*'ôr*). When the light shines out from Yhwh's face, that suggests people will experience blessing and deliverance (4:6 [7]; 27:1; 44:3 [4]; 97:10–11). Light is thus associated with material good, yet material good set in the context of a relationship with Yhwh (36:7–9 [8–10]; 43:3; 56:13 [14]; 89:15 [16])—like friends enjoying a magnificent meal but enjoying it because they love each other.

Lily, Lilies (*šûšan, šōšannîm*). These words in the headings to Pss. 45; 60; 69; 80 may denote a tune. Lilies are mentioned in two chief connections in the OT. They recur in the Song of Songs (2:1, 2, 16; 4:5; 5:13; 6:2, 3; 7:2 [3]), which may suggest they have romantic associations (as might the occurrence in Hos. 14:5 [6]). This would fit Ps. 45. Then they were a decorative motif in the temple (1 Kings 7:19, 22, 26), which makes Goulder think that the title denotes where the poem was declaimed.[17]

Lord (*'ădōnāy*). The word looks as if it would mean "my lords," but it usually refers to Yhwh. There are two ways of understanding the ending.[18] The plural may be honorific, a plural of majesty, so that the expression means "my Lord." This fits 44:23 [24]; 51:15 [17]; 54:4 [6]; 57:9 [10]; 59:11 [12]; 62:12 [13]; 66:18; 71:5, 16; 73:28; 77:2, 7 [3, 8]. But Ugaritic had a sufformative similar to this -*āy* with an emphatic or intensifying sense, and this sufformative might function simply to reinforce the meaning of the word; an English equivalent might be "*the* Lord." The Vrs render it simply as "the Lord." This fits (e.g.) 55:9 [10]; 68 (six times); 69:6 [7]; 73:20.

Lyre (*kinnôr*). "An instrument which has its sounding box as a base, from which two side arms rise, to be joined across the top by a crossbar."[19] The strings are fastened from the sound box up to the crossbar. It is plucked with a plectrum or with the hand, one hand striking, the other damping strings. The harp (*nēbel*) is a similar stringed instrument often mentioned alongside the lyre. It seems on average to have had more strings and to have had a lower range. Both are especially mentioned in connection with praise (e.g., 57:8 [9]; 71:22; 81:2 [3]).

Might (*gěbûrâ*). The decisive power and strength of a warrior (*gibbôr*). Yhwh is girded with might like a fighter girded with weaponry (65:6 [7]).

Mindful, be (*zākar*). The EVV have "remember," but *zākar* can apply to thinking about the future as well as about the past, and it suggests a deliberate act, not an accidental one,

---

15. See *Psalms of the Sons of Korah*.
16. For other possible understandings of *měnaṣṣēaḥ*, see Tate, *Psalms 51–100*, 4–5.
17. *Psalms of the Sons of Korah*, 124.
18. See, e.g., *IBHS* 7.4.3ef, which reckons that the second understanding is always correct.
19. J. H. Eaton, "Music's Place in Worship," *OtSt* 23 (1984): 85–107 (see 87).

and an act that thus leads to action. So to ask God to be mindful is to ask God to take account of certain facts and to respond appropriately by acting (e.g., 74:2, 18, 22).

Most High (*'elyôn*). In ordinary usage, the word denotes something high (e.g., Neh. 3:25), and it designates David in 89:27 [28]. It thus designates Yhwh as the exalted one. It could suggest Yhwh's exaltation over the world and over other deities and might point especially to Yhwh's power (cf. 46:4 [5]; 47:2 [3]). It was apparently a title of God as worshipped by the pre-Israelite people of Jerusalem and came to be an honorific title for Yhwh (cf. Gen. 14:18–22; also Num. 24:16).

Music. See *composition.

Name (*šēm*). The name stands for the person. It reminds us of that person; it conjures up their presence. That is all the more so when someone's name has a particular meaning and indicates the nature of their character or vocation. So if someone's name lasts, the person lasts (72:17). Where the name resides is where the person resides (74:7). Praise of or mindfulness of or waiting on or reverence for someone's name signifies such a stance in relation to the person (44:8, 20 [9, 21]; 45:17 [18]; 52:9 [11]; 54:6 [8]; 61:5, 8 [6, 9])—and the opposite (74:10, 18). Victory or deliverance comes through Yhwh's name—that is, through Yhwh in person (44:5 [6]; 54:1 [3]). In all these usages, the word presumably suggests that Yhwh's name is proclaimed or called on in such a way as to declare or claim the presence of the one who bears the name.

Needy (*'ebyôn*). In the Psalms the needy characteristically appear in the company of the *weak (69:33 [34]; 70:5 [6]; 74:21; 86:1). The context often makes clear that the word suggests not so much poverty itself as the vulnerability that issues from poverty. It is then the special responsibility of the king to look after the interests of the needy (72:4, 12, 13).

Palace (*hêkāl*). Both *hêkāl* and *bayit* refer to Yhwh's dwelling, but the first designates it as a palace, the second as a house. Either can refer to Yhwh's dwelling in the heavens (11:4; 18:6 [7]; 29:9; 138:2) or to that on earth (27:4; 48:9 [10]; 65:4; 68:29 [30]; 79:1). The psalmist comes to the earthly temple and bows to the heavenly one. But the standard translation "temple" for either word is misleading. Hebrew does not have a word equivalent to temple (hence the need to call it a *holy* palace), unless it is a word such as *miqdāš* (sanctuary; 73:17). As is the case with other expressions, Hebrew uses ordinary words to refer to religious matters rather than developing a special religious vocabulary. Designating the temple on earth or that in the heavens as a house or a palace draws attention to the fact that both are essentially dwelling places, places where people know Yhwh is present and thus (in the case of the earthly one) can be found.

Person (*nepeš*). The word can refer especially to the inner person (the spirit; e.g. 63:5 [6]) or especially to the outer person (the body; e.g. 57:4 [5]) or to the appetite (78:18) or to the whole person, the whole being (77:2 [3]). In Ps. 42:1–6 [2–7] the whole *nepeš* strains toward God and thirsts for God, the suppliant's *nepeš* is poured out, and the suppliant asks the *nepeš* why it is downcast. The EVV often translate "soul," but the above references show that this is inclined to be misleading.

Plea, plead (*tĕpillâ, pālal* hitpalel). Law-court language that pictures the suppliant as standing before a court and asking for mercy on one's own behalf or on someone else's. Applied to prayer (e.g., 66:19–20; 72:15), it thus suggests an appeal for God to intervene for oneself or for someone else. It implies an appeal to Yhwh's nature as one who treats people in the right way, and it implicitly asks that the suppliant or the person on whose behalf one prays be given their rights. Yet it also implies that a suppliant "does not employ the language of an accuser" but that "the one praying adopt the posture and attitude of a suppliant."[20]

Poor (*dal*). Someone who lacks resources and is thus *needy and *weak (72:13; 82:3–4) and dependent on others taking notice of them (41:1 [2]).

Possession (*naḥălâ*). Etymologically "inheritance," but the word can refer to something belonging to God (68:9 [10]), who does not inherit, or to something that can be given rather than passed on in that way (47:4 [5]), and its emphasis lies on the certainty of possession rather than the means whereby something is obtained. It thus suggests property or domain.

Praise (*hālal* piel and hitpael, *tĕhillâ*). An onomatopoeic word that suggests making a lalalalala sound or ululating. The hitpael, "exult oneself," draws more attention to the implications of the praise for the person doing the praising. The words can be used for praising or exulting in what deserves praise and exultation (44:8 [9]) and in what does not (e.g., wealth or other deities; 49:6 [7]; 52:1 [3]).

Promise (*neder*). Hebrew lacks a word that quite corresponds to the English word "promise." EVV's "promise" commonly represents simply the Hebrew word *dābār* (word). The EVV render *neder* (22:25 [26]; 50:14; 56:12 [13]; 61:5, 8 [6, 9]; 65:1 [2]; 66:13) as "vow," a vow being a promise that is made with due solemnity. To English ears "vow" can suggest something more legal and legalistic than a *neder* need be; hence the translation "promise."

Rebel, rebellion (*pāša', peša'*). See, e.g., 32:1, 5; 51:1, 3, 13 [3, 5, 15]. Traditionally translated "transgress/transgression," but one "rebels" against a person who is in authority (cf. the parallelism in 5:10 [11]).

Redeem (*pādâ*). The verb can refer to paying the price to regain something that is forfeit (cf. 49:7–8 [8–9]), but like the English word "redeem," it comes to emphasize the freedom rather than the price-paying (49:15 [16]; cf. 55:18 [19]; 69:18 [19]; 71:23; 78:42). Although the usage sometimes implies the expenditure of effort, generally it abandons the idea of cost (though see 44:26 [27]) and focuses on the act of deliverance whereby Yhwh takes someone as a personal possession and/or liberates them. Being Yhwh's servants puts us under the protection of a master who acts decisively for us and buys us back if that is needed.

Refuge (*maḥseh*). A shelter where vulnerable animals or vulnerable human beings hide from attack or storm or sun (61:3 [4]; 104:18); poverty may mean a human being has no such shelter (Job 24:8). "Refuge" thus comes to be a figure for Yhwh's relationship with vulnerable people (Pss. 46:1 [2]; 62:7–8 [8–9]).[21] But for "take refuge" (*ḥāsâ b*), see the next entry.

Rely on (*ḥāsâ b*). What a person does in relation to something that provides protection, such as a fortress (31:1–4 [2–5]). Mediating between the natural image of taking refuge and the metaphor of reliance is the fact that the wings of the cherubim dominate the temple's inner sanctuary, while carvings of cherubim appear elsewhere in the temple. While the cherubim function mainly to provide Yhwh with transport, it would not be surprising if they also suggested protection. This verb could then denote taking refuge in the temple, though we should not press the image. None of the occurrences of the verb mention the temple, and all apply the verb directly to Yhwh. If the temple was a place of asylum, then this likely has become a metaphor for finding refuge with Yhwh

20. Chrysostom, *Psalms*, 1:83.

21. On its importance in the Psalms, see J. F. D. Creach, *Yahweh as Refuge and the Editing of the Hebrew Psalter*, JSOTSup 217 (Sheffield: Sheffield Academic Press, 1996).

in a more general sense. Relying on Yhwh is thus similar to *trusting in Yhwh;[22] contrast *ḥāsâ b* with *ḥāsâ bĕṣēl kĕnāpêkā*, "take refuge in the shade of your wings" (17:8; 36:7 [8]; 57:1 [2]; 63:7 [8]), or *ḥāsâ taḥat*, "take refuge under" (91:4).

Rescue (*pālaṭ* piel). The qal verb means "escape," and the related nouns mean "people who escape," "survivors"; they often pair with words meaning "remnant." So the piel verb suggests being enabled to escape and survive something.

Resound, sound (*rānan* piel, *rinnâ*, *rĕnānâ*). An onomatopoeic word suggesting a kind of sound, n-n-n-n-n, an inarticulate noise or cry that can signify (for instance) praise and joy (47:1 [2]; 51:14 [16]; 59:16 [17]; 63:7 [8]; 67:4 [5]; 71:23; 81:1 [2]; 89:12 [13]) but also protest and grief (61:1 [2]; 88:2 [3]). The EVV's "shout for joy" thus spells out something not implicit in the word itself, which emphasizes sound rather than verbal content.

Restore (*gā'al*). A restorer (*gō'ēl*) is the next of kin within a family who takes action or spends resources in order to put things right when a family member is in trouble or has been wronged. Used of God, this verb thus puts us in God's family and implies God's accepting family obligations toward us when we are in trouble (69:18 [19]; 74:2; 77:15 [16]). It also refers to the king's obligation to his people (72:14). "Restore me" thus implies "do your duty by me"[23] by making things right for me.

Revere, reverence (*yārē'*, *yir'â*). These words cover both negative "fear" and positive "reverence," and sometimes it is difficult to know which meaning applies (for instance, both translations have been suggested for 76:7, 8, 11, 12 [8, 9, 12, 13]). The positive meaning is more common in the Psalms. The same double significance attaches to *pāḥad* and *gûr*, which suggest something stronger ("dread" and "be in awe"). The niphal participle *nôrā'* denotes Yhwh as one who deserves awed reverence (e.g., 47:2 [3]). Its feminine plural denotes deeds that draw awed reverence from people who see or hear of them, deeds such as the great acts that brought the people out of Egypt and into the land (66:5).

Rise (*selâ*). Dictionaries usually connect the word *selâ* with the root *sālal*, "rise." It appears at the end of lines in psalms without any consistent patterning. Though it sometimes comes at the close of sections (Ps. 66), it often also comes in the middle of a section or in the middle of a sentence (Pss. 67; 68). It may be a liturgical or musical direction ("raise the voice"?), but we do not know. I understand that David Allan Hubbard advocated the theory that it was what David said when he broke a string, which is the most illuminating theory because there is no logic about when you break a string, and there is no logic about the occurrence of *selâ*.

Save (*nāṣal* niphal, hiphil). Over against *rescue or *deliver, "save" more commonly leads into the preposition "from." It draws attention to the peril or trouble from which God saves. Characteristically this is peril or trouble from which God alone can rescue (50:22; 51:14 [16]; 54:7 [9]; 56:13 [14]; 59:1–2 [2–3]; 69:14 [15]; 70:1 [2]; 71:2, 11; 72:12; 79:9; 82:4; 86:13).

Seek help from (*biqqēš*, *dāraš*). Treating someone or something as a resource of guidance and strength. Looking to Yhwh in this way is a marker of being seriously committed to Yhwh (69:32 [33]; 78:34); rather than looking to the traditional gods of the land, one looks to Yhwh (77:2 [3]). "Seek" Yhwh (EVV) gives a misleading impression. The Tg sometimes translates "seek instruction."

Shade of your wings (*ṣēl kĕnāpêkā*). See 17:8; 36:7 [8]; 57:1 [2]; 63:7 [8]. The image may have at least three backgrounds: the wings of a mother bird sheltering a baby bird, the

---

22. Cf. BDB 90b. Tg has "hope."
23. Rogerson and McKay, *Psalms*, 2:97.

cherubim in the temple, and the picture of the heavens as wings, specifically as the sun with wings (cf. Mal. 4:2 [3:20]).[24] But the first of these is the one that most clearly relates to providing shade or protection.[25]

Sheol (*šĕʾôl*). The place where dead people are, a nonphysical equivalent to the grave or the tomb. It is not a place of punishment, unless people are taken there before their time because of their wrongdoing (49:14–15 [15–16]; 55:15 [16]), but just a place where people exist—as bodies do in their graves—rather than really live. God does not intervene there, and therefore there is nothing to praise God for there (88:3–12 [4–13]). If the name originally had a meaning related to (for instance) the verb *šāʾal* (ask), there is no indication that this now influences the meaning of the name; it is simply a place name. It can be used metaphorically to refer to death itself, and insofar as death comes to overwhelm us in life (for instance, if we are seriously ill), then it is as if we are already overwhelmed by Sheol and need to be delivered from it (86:13).

Shout (*rûaʿ, tĕrûʿâ*). Perhaps onomatopoeic words, they refer to a loud shout like that which acclaims a human king or expresses a sense of triumph (cf. 60:8 [10]). Such a shout is a feature of the acclamation of Yhwh in worship (47:1, 5 [2, 6]; 66:1; 81:1 [2]; 89:15 [16]). The EVV make it a "shout of joy," but the word can refer to various kinds of shout and in itself simply refers to the noise.

Strength (*ʿôz*). The word is likely related to *ʿāzaz* "be strong," and in 62:11 [12]; 63:2 [3]; 66:3; 68:28, 33–35 [29, 34–36]; 74:13; 77:14 [15]; 78:26, 61; 81:1; 86:16; 89:10, 17 [11, 18] it simply suggests strength. The notion of Yhwh's strength is important in the Psalms, where nearly half the word's occurrences come. But people could also make a connection with *ʿûz*, "take refuge," and in a number of passages that connotation is also appropriate: see 46:1 [2]; 59:9, 16, 17 [10, 17, 18]; 61:3 [4]; 62:7 [8]; 71:7; 84:5 [6]. Yhwh is a strong refuge.

Strings (*nĕgînōt*). The word comes in the headings to Pss. 54; 55; 61 (sg.); 67; 76, presumably referring to stringed instruments, and as a word for songs (presumably accompanied by strings) in 69:12 [13]; 77:6 [7].

Stronghold (*māʿôz*). A refuge from danger or attack, such as a high rock (cf. 28:8; 31:2, 4 [3, 5]; 37:39; also 43:2 in the context of Yhwh's sending "light" to bring me back home). Readers might link *māʿôz* with *ʿāzaz* (be strong) or *ʿûz* (take refuge), though the collocation of *māʿôz* and *ʿāzaz* in 52:7 [9] suggests the former. Modern opinions also differ as to the word's etymology, but both connotations are apposite.

Trust (*bāṭaḥ b, mibṭaḥ*). The question about trust is where we put it. The question it raises is not whether we trust or doubt or mistrust or fear; ideally trust is the antonym of fear, but the two can coexist (see 56:3–4 [4–5]). It is what we put our trust in, whether in Yhwh (52:8 [10]; 56:4, 11 [5, 12]) or in something such as armaments (44:6 [7]) or wealth (52:7–8 [9–10]; 62:8–10 [9–11]). The noun *mibṭaḥ* denotes the object of trust (40:4 [5]; 65:5 [6]; 71:5). Suggestively, LXX commonly renders "hope" (e.g., 84:12 [13]; 86:2).

Truth, truthfulness, be true (*ʾĕmet, ʾĕmûnâ, ʾāman*). The words suggest a consistency between what someone says, means, and does, and a steadfastness, faithfulness, and reliability in doing what we say (e.g., of God: 57:3, 10 [4, 11]; 89:49 [50]; and of people: 51:6 [8]; 78:8, 22, 32, 37). Thus Yhwh's truthfulness is a special subject of thanksgiving/testimony (71:22; 88:11 [12]; 89:1 [2]).

Violence (*ḥāmās*). The word can refer to more general lawlessness or outrage (e.g., Gen. 6:11, 13), but the references in the Psalms all make sense on the basis of the assump-

24. Cf. Keel, *Symbolism*, 27–30.
25. Cf. Silvia Schroer, "'Under the Shadow of Your Wings,'" in *Wisdom and Psalms*, ed. Brenner and Fontaine, 264–82.

tion that the word denotes violence that is lawless and outrageous, often because it is exercised by means of the law (55:9 [10]; 58:2 [3]; 72:14; 73:6; 74:20).

Wait (*yāḥal* piel). Like *qāwâ*, the verb suggests an attitude of expectancy or waiting, looking for something to happen; see 31:24 [25]; 33:18, 22; 38:15 [16]; 42:5, 11 [6, 12]; 43:5; 69:3 [4]; 71:14. See also *hope. The verbs refer to waiting *for* God rather than waiting *on* God.

Watchful foe (*šōrēr*). The translation follows NJPS and combines two possible understandings of *šōrēr* (5:8 [9]; 27:11; 54:5 [7]; 56:2 [3]; 59:10 [11]). Jerome assumes it relates to the verb *šûr* and thus suggests people who watch for me (with hostile intent). LXX renders "enemies," which rather suggests a link with Akkadian *šâru*.[26]

Waywardness (*ʿāwōn*). See 51:2, 5, 9 [4, 7, 11]. There are two roots *ʿāwâ*, one meaning "twist," one meaning "go astray," not in the sense of accidentally losing one's way but of deliberately choosing the wrong road. A passage such as Jer. 3:21 suggests that people could be aware of the latter connotation of *ʿāwōn*. Sin involves skewing one's way.[27] But *ʿāwōn* might also suggest the first idea, the idea of perversity. People are twisted or crooked in their ways.

Weak (*ʿānî, ʿānāw*). Someone who is vulnerable and powerless, often as a result of circumstances such as having no surviving family. Such people are thus open to being victimized and hounded by the contrivances of others in the community who feel no obligation to its weaker members and rather use their weakness to their own advantage. The EVV sometimes translate "humble" or "lowly," but the words do not denote an inner humility, nor do they point to a group or party within the community as a whole.[28] "Weak" is a way Israel characterizes itself over against other peoples when it wants to call on or glorify Yhwh's help (68:10 [11]; 74:18–23; 149:4). The broader idea of the weakness and vulnerability of the individual and of Yhwh's commitment to punishing anyone who sheds the blood of such a person has become a figure that characterizes the attitude of strong, oppressive nations toward a weak, vulnerable one and Yhwh's involvement in this situation. The weak individual, too, is one who lacks power or resources, rather than someone who is either poor or humble.

Well-being (*šālôm*). A wide-ranging term that covers peace in the sense of freedom from war and a condition of safety, friendship, blessing, and prosperity (55:18, 20 [19, 21]; 69:22 [23]; 72:3, 7; 85:8, 10 [9, 11]).

Whole-offering (*ʿôlâ, kālîl*). The two words point to the nature of these offerings. They are sacrifices that go up (*ʿālâ*) to God in their totality (*kol*): the whole animal is burnt, so the offerer gets no benefit from the offering at all. The former is more common than the latter; both come in 51:19 [21].

Why? (*lāmmâ, lāmâ*). In the Psalms, "Why?" introduces a rhetorical question, as in 49:5 [6]; 68:16 [17]; also *mah* (lit. "What?") in 42:5, 11 [6, 12]; 43:5; 52:1 [3]. Addressed to the self or to other people, such a "Why?" often implies the answer "There is no reason" or "It's pointless" or "It's going to get you into trouble," and thus "So it's stupid to do it." It is thus a disguised statement of conviction. Generally a "Why?" beginning a psalm addresses God and reflects the experience of things not working out properly for the psalmist. "Why?" is then a plea in disguise (42:9 [10]; 43:2; 44:23, 24 [24, 25]; 74:1, 11; 80:12 [13]; 88:14 [15]). If Yhwh gave a straight answer to these questions ("It is for the following reasons . . ."), this would not satisfy the suppliant; it would misunderstand their point. "Why?" is a plea for action that contrasts with the action (or inaction)

26. See BDB and *HALOT* respectively.
27. See *TLOT* 862–66.
28. See Kraus, *Psalms 1–59*, 93–95.

the question refers to and also an accusation. The rhetoric of such questions works by presupposing something that the addressee might want to dispute (that Yhwh is guilty of spurning) and asking a question ("Why?") that takes for granted that possibly disputable point. To answer the question is thus to admit guilt.[29]

Wicked, wickedness (*'awwāl, 'āwel, 'awlâ, 'ôlâ*). An attitude toward other people involving hostility, the opposite of faithfulness (43:1; 53:1 [2]; 58:2 [3]; 64:6 [7]; 71:4; 82:2; 89:22 [23]).

Wonders (*niplā'ôt, pele'*). Extraordinary events that witness to the reality and power of Yhwh (71:17; 72:18; 86:10). The context indicates that sg. *pele'* is commonly a collective, with similar meaning to the plural niphal participle (77:11, 14 [12, 15]; 78:12; 88:10, 12 [11, 13]; 89:5 [6]).

Worship (*bārak*, qal passive participle and piel). When Yhwh is subject, the verb means to "bless" (45:2 [3]; 67:1, 6, 7 [2, 7, 8]), to impart fullness of life and fertility, but this meaning seems odd when Yhwh is the object. Rather the verb then links with *berek* (knee) and implies bowing the knee before Yhwh (66:8, 20; 68:19, 26, 35 [20, 27, 36]; 72:18, 19).

---

29. See A. Jepsen, "Warum?" in *Das ferne und nahe Wort* (L. Rost Festschrift; ed. F. Maass; BZAW 105; Berlin: Töpelmann, 1967), 106–13.

Bibliography

For any work that relates to a particular psalm, the footnotes contain bibliographical detail; a later reference to the same work in the treatment of the same psalm uses a short title. This bibliography comprises more general works, which are always referred to by a short title in the footnotes. I refer to the commentaries of Ibn Ezra, David Qimchi, and Rashi simply by their names, the reference being to their treatment of the passage under discussion as it appears in editions of the Rabbinic Bible, *Miqrā'ôt Gĕdôlôt*. I refer to the translation of Thomas Aquinas's commentary without page reference because it is published only on the Internet.

Allen, Leslie C. *Psalms 101–150*. Rev. ed. Word Biblical Commentary. Nashville: Nelson, 2002.

Alter, Robert. *The Art of Biblical Poetry*. New York: Basic Books, 1985.

Anderson, Arnold A. *Psalms*. 2 vols. New Century Bible. London: Oliphants, 1972.

Anderson, Bernhard W. *Out of the Depths*. Rev. ed. Philadelphia: Westminster, 1983.

Aquinas. *See* Thomas Aquinas

Athanasius, Archbishop of Alexandria. *Letter to Marcellinus concerning the Psalms*. http://www.kensmen.com/catholic/psalmsathanasiusletter.html.

Auffret, Pierre. *Voyez de vos yeux*. Vetus Testamentum Supplements 48. Leiden: Brill, 1993.

———. *La sagesse a bâti sa maison*. Orbis biblicus et orientalis 49. Göttingen: Vandenhoeck & Ruprecht, 1982.

Augustine of Hippo. *Expositions on the Book of Psalms*. In vol. 8 of *The Nicene and Post-Nicene Fathers*, series 1. Edited by Philip Schaff. Edinburgh: T&T Clark, 1886–89; repr., Grand Rapids: Eerdmans, 1989. Also http://www.ccel.org/fathers2/NPNF1-08/TOC.htm.

Barthélemy, Dominique, et al., eds. *Critique textuelle de l'Ancien Testament: Tome 4. Psaumes*. Orbis biblicus et orientalis 50.4. Göttingen: Vandenhoeck & Ruprecht, 2005.

Bratcher, Robert G., and William D. Reyburn. *A Handbook on Psalms*. New York: United Bible Societies, 1991.

Brenner, Athalya, and Carole Fontaine, eds. *Wisdom and Psalms*. Feminist Companion to the Bible, second series, 2. Sheffield: Sheffield Academic Press, 1998.

Briggs, Charles A., and Emilie Grace Briggs. *A Critical and Exegetical Commentary on the Book of Psalms*. 2 vols. International Critical Commentary. Repr., Edinburgh: T&T Clark, 1986–87.

Broyles, Craig C. *The Conflict of Faith and Experience in the Psalms*. Journal for the Study of the Old Testament: Supplement Series 52. Sheffield: JSOT, 1989.

Brueggemann, Walter. *Israel's Praise*. Philadelphia: Fortress, 1988.

———. *The Message of the Psalms*. Minneapolis: Augsburg, 1984.

———. *The Psalms and the Life of Faith*. Minneapolis: Fortress, 1995.

Buttenwieser, Moses. *The Psalms*. Repr., New York: Ktav, 1969.

Calvin, John. *Commentary on the Book of Psalms*. 5 vols. Repr., Grand Rapids: Eerdmans, 1948–49.

Cassiodorus, Senator. *Explanation of the Psalms*. 3 vols. Mahwah, NJ: Paulist Press, 1990–91.

Chrysostom, John. *Commentary on the Psalms*. 2 vols. Brookline, MA: Holy Cross Orthodox Press, 1998.

Cole, Robert. *The Shape and Message of Book III (Psalms 73–89)*. Journal for the Study of the Old Testament: Supplement Series 307. Sheffield: Sheffield Academic Press, 2000.

Craigie, Peter C. *Psalms 1–50*. 2nd ed. With supplement by Marvin E. Tate and W. Dennis Tucker. Word Biblical Commentary. Nashville: Nelson, 2004.

Crenshaw, James L. *The Psalms*. Grand Rapids: Eerdmans, 2001.

Dahood, M. *Psalms*. 3 vols. Anchor Bible. Garden City, NY: Doubleday, 1966–70.

Diodore of Tarsus. *Commentary on Psalms 1–51*. Atlanta: Society of Biblical Literature, 2005.

Eaton, John. *Psalms*. Torch Bible Commentaries. London: SCM, 1967.

Eerdmans, B. D. "Essays on Masoretic Psalms." *Oudtestamentische Studiën* 1 (1942): 105–296.

Flint, Peter W. *The Dead Sea Psalms Scrolls and the Book of Psalms*. Leiden: Brill, 1997.

Flint, Peter W., and Patrick D. Miller, eds. *The Book of Psalms*. Vetus Testamentum Supplements 99. Leiden: Brill, 2005.

Fokkelman, J. P. *Major Poems of the Hebrew Bible*. Vols. 2–3. Assen: Van Gorcum, 2000–3.

Gerstenberger, Erhard S. *Psalms*. 2 vols. The Forms of the Old Testament Literature 14–15. Grand Rapids: Eerdmans, 1988–2001.

Goldingay, John. *Songs from a Strange Land*. Leicester, UK: Inter-Varsity; Downers Grove, IL: InterVarsity, 1978.

Goulder, Michael D. *The Prayers of David*. Journal for the Study of the Old Testament: Supplement Series 102. Sheffield: JSOT, 1990.

———. *The Psalms of Asaph and the Pentateuch*. Journal for the Study of the Old Testament: Supplement Series 233. Sheffield: Sheffield Academic Press, 1996.

———. *The Psalms of the Sons of Korah*. Journal for the Study of the Old Testament: Supplement Series 20. Sheffield: JSOT, 1982.

Gunkel, Hermann. *Die Psalmen*. 5th ed. Göttingen: Vandenhoeck & Ruprecht, 1968.

———. *The Psalms*. Philadelphia: Fortress, 1967.

Gunkel, Hermann, and Joachim Begrich. *Introduction to Psalms*. Macon, GA: Mercer University Press, 1998.

Habel, Norman C., ed. *The Earth Story in the Psalms and the Prophets*. Sheffield: Sheffield Academic Press, 2001.

Haglund, Erik. *Historical Motifs in the Psalms*. Coniectanea biblica: Old Testament Series 23. [Lund]: Gleerup, 1984.

Hauge, Martin R. *Between Sheol and Temple*. Journal for the Study of the Old Testament: Supplement Series 178. Sheffield: Sheffield Academic Press, 1995.

Hilary of Poitiers. *Homilies on the Psalms*. Pages 236–48 in vol. 9 of *The Nicene and Post-Nicene Fathers*, series 2. Edinburgh: T&T Clark. Repr., Grand Rapids: Eerdmans, 1989. Also at www.ccel.org/fathers2/NPNF2-09/Npnf2-09-20.htm.

Hill, Edmund. *Prayer, Praise and Politics*. London: Sheed & Ward, 1973.

Hossfeld, Frank-Lothar, and Erich Zenger. *Psalms 2: A Commentary on Psalms 51–100*. Hermeneia. Minneapolis: Fortress, 2005.

Ibn Ezra. *Těhillîm*. In *Miqrā'ôt Gědôlôt*. Repr., with partial English translation in A. J. Rosenberg, *Psalms*. 3 vols. New York: Judaica, 1991.

Jacobson, Rolf A. *"Many Are Saying."* Journal for the Study of the Old Testament: Supplement Series 397. London: T&T Clark, 2004.

Jerome [Eusebius Hieronymus]. *The Homilies of Saint Jerome*. Vol. 1, *1–59 on the Psalms*. Fathers of the Church 48. Washington, DC: Catholic University of America, 1964.

Johnson, Aubrey R. *The Cultic Prophet and Israel's Psalmody*. Cardiff: University of Wales, 1979.

———. *Sacral Kingship in Ancient Israel*. Cardiff: University of Wales, 1955.

Keel, Othmar. *The Symbolism of the Biblical World*. New York: Seabury, 1978.

Kidner, Derek. *Psalms*. 2 vols. Tyndale Old Testament Commentary. London: Inter-Varsity, 1973.

Kirkpatrick, A. F. *The Book of Psalms*. Cambridge Bible for Schools and Colleges. Repr., Cambridge: Cambridge University Press, 1910.

Kraus, Hans-Joachim. *Psalms 1–59*. Minneapolis: Augsburg, 1988.

———. *Psalms 60–150*. Minneapolis: Augsburg, 1989.

Lindström, Fredrik. *Suffering and Sin*. Stockholm: Almqvist, 1994.

Loretz, Oswald. *Psalmstudien*. Beihefte zur Zeitschrift für die alttestamentliche Wissenschaft 309. Berlin: de Gruyter, 2002.

———. *Ugarit-Texte und Thronbesteigungspsalmen*. Münster: Ugarit, 1988.

Luther, Martin. *First Lectures on the Psalms*. 2 vols. In *Luther's Works*, vols. 10–11. St. Louis: Concordia, 1974–76.

———. *Selected Psalms*. 3 vols. In *Luther's Works*, vols. 12–14. St. Louis: Concordia, 1955–58.

Mandolfo, Carleen. *God in the Dock*. Journal for the Study of the Old Testament: Supplement Series 357. London: Sheffield Academic Press, 2002.

Mays, James L. *Psalms*. Interpretation. Louisville: Knox, 1994.

McCann, J. Clinton, Jr. "The Book of Psalms." In *The New Interpreter's Bible*. Edited by Leander E. Keck. Vol. 4, pages 639–1280. Nashville: Abingdon, 1996.

———, ed. *The Shape and Shaping of the Psalter*. Journal for the Study of the Old Testament: Supplement Series 159. Sheffield: JSOT Press, 1993.

Midrash on Psalms, The. 2 vols. New Haven: Yale University Press, 1959.

Miller, Patrick D. *Interpreting the Psalms.* Philadelphia: Fortress, 1986.

Mowinckel, Sigmund. *The Psalms in Israel's Worship.* 2 vols. Oxford: Blackwell, 1967.

Nasuti, Harry P. *Tradition History and the Psalms of Asaph.* Society of Biblical Literature Dissertation Series 88. Atlanta: Scholars Press, 1988.

Otto, Eckart, and Erich Zenger, eds. *"Mein Sohn bist du"(Ps 2,7): Studien zu den Königspsalmen.* Stuttgarter Bibelstudien 192. Stuttgart: Verlag Katholisches Bibelwerk, 2002.

Peterson, Eugene. *Answering God.* Repr., San Francisco: Harper, 1991.

———. *Where Your Treasure Is: Psalms That Summon You from Self to Community.* Grand Rapids: Eerdmans, 1993.

Qimchi, David. *Těhillîm.* In *Miqrā'ôt Gědôlôt.* Repr., with partial English translation in A. J. Rosenberg, *Psalms.* 3 vols. New York: Judaica, 1991.

Raabe, Paul R. *Psalm Structures.* Journal for the Study of the Old Testament: Supplement Series 104. Sheffield: JSOT, 1990.

Rashi. *Těhillîm.* In *Miqrā'ôt Gědôlôt.* Repr., with English translation in A. J. Rosenberg, *Psalms.* 3 vols. New York: Judaica, 1991.

Reid, Stephen Breck, ed. *Psalms and Practice.* Collegeville, MN: Liturgical Press, 2001.

Rendsburg, Gary A. *Linguistic Evidence for the Northern Origin of Selected Psalms.* Atlanta: Scholars Press, 1990.

Ridderbos, N. H. *Die Psalmen.* Beihefte zur Zeitschrift für die alttestamentliche Wissenschaft 117. Berlin: de Gruyter, 1972.

Rienstra, Marchienne Vroon. *Swallow's Nest: A Feminine Reading of the Psalms.* Grand Rapids: Eerdmans, 1992.

Rogerson, J. W., and J. W. McKay. *Psalms.* 3 vols. Cambridge Bible Commentary, New English Bible. Cambridge: Cambridge University Press, 1977.

Rosenberg, A. J. *Psalms.* 3 vols. New York: Judaica, 1991.

Saur, Markus. *Die Königspsalmen.* Beihefte zur Zeitschrift für die alttestamentliche Wissenschaft 340. Berlin: de Gruyter, 2004.

Schaefer, Konrad. *Psalms.* Berit Olam. Collegeville, MN: Liturgical Press, 2001.

Seybold, Klaus. *Introducing the Psalms.* Edinburgh: T&T Clark, 1990.

———. *Die Psalmen.* Tübingen: Mohr, 1996.

Seybold, Klaus, and Erich Zenger, eds. *Neue Wege der Psalmenforschung: Für Walter Beyerlin.* 2nd ed. Freiburg: Herder, 1994.

Slomovic, Elieser. "Toward an Understanding of the Formation of Historical Titles in the Book of Psalms." *Zeitschrift für die alttestamentliche Wissenschaft* 91 (1979): 350–80.

Soggin, J. Alberto. *Old Testament and Oriental Studies.* Rome: Biblical Institute Press, 1975.

Spurgeon, C. H. *The Treasury of David.* 6 vols. Repr., London: Marshall, 1963.

Stec, David M. *Targum of Psalms.* Collegeville, MN: Liturgical Press, 2004.

Tate, Marvin E. *Psalms 51–100.* Word Biblical Commentary. Dallas: Word, 1990.

Terrien, Samuel. *The Psalms.* Grand Rapids: Eerdmans, 2002.

Theodore of Mopsuestia. *Commentary on Psalms 1–81.* Translated with an introduction by Robert C. Hill. Atlanta: Scholars Press, 2006.

Theodoret of Cyrus. *Commentary on the Psalms.* 2 vols. Washington, DC: Catholic University of America, 2000–2001.

Thomas Aquinas. *Commentary on the Psalms*. http://www4.desales.edu/~philtheo/loughlin /ATP/.

Trudiger, Peter L. *The Psalms of the Tamid Service*. Vetus Testamentum Supplements 98. Leiden and Boston: Brill, 2004.

Ulrich, Eugene, et al. *Qumran Cave 4*. Part 11, *Psalms to Chronicles*. Discoveries in the Judaean Desert 16. Oxford: Clarendon, 2000.

Watson, Wilfred G. E. *Classical Hebrew Poetry*. 2nd ed. Journal for the Study of the Old Testament: Supplement 26. Sheffield: JSOT, 1986.

Weiser, Artur. *The Psalms*. London: SCM; Philadelphia: Westminster, 1962.

Westermann, Claus. *The Living Psalms*. Grand Rapids: Eerdmans, 1989.

———. *The Praise of God in the Psalms*. Richmond: Knox, 1965. Enlarged ed. titled *Praise and Lament in the Psalms*. Atlanta: Knox, 1981.

Whybray, R. Norman. *Reading the Psalms as a Book*. Journal for the Study of the Old Testament: Supplement Series 222. Sheffield: Sheffield Academic Press, 1996.

Zenger, Erich. *A God of Vengeance?* Louisville: Westminster John Knox, 1996.

Subject Index

abandonment 233–34, 658
Abyss 101, 178, 695
acknowledge 72, 301, 695
adoption 637, 679
afterlife 104–5, 107, 419,
  648, 653–54
against, be 695
angel/angels 504, 561
anger 249. *See also* God:
  anger of
anointing 596–97, 677
anxiety 247–48, 362
armies 536, 695–96
Asaph 110, 696
Assyria 65, 77, 579
authority 57, 385, 564,
  696

bad/trouble 696
Babel, Tower of 171
bitter/bitterness/embit-
  tered 267, 403
blessing 247–48, 300–301,
  594
bloodshed 214, 390, 696
bow low 389, 696–97
Byzantine Empire 232

Canaan 80, 88, 319
celebration 548
ceremonies 59
Christians 93, 120–21

cleansing 126, 131,
  137–38
committed/commitment
  32, 147, 188–89, 195,
  199, 466, 612, 621–22,
  625, 666–68, 697
composition 198, 241,
  556, 697
confess/confession 124,
  128, 697
covenant 113, 176, 434,
  487, 489, 577, 666, 669,
  680, 697
crag 697
creation 153, 666
cursing 247–48
Cyrus 614

Dan 66, 68–69, 71
David 125–26, 218, 238,
  240, 366–67, 396,
  513–14, 666, 669, 689
deaf/deafness 205
death/the dead 27–28, 98,
  104–5, 168, 251, 646,
  652, 654
death penalty 136
Decalogue. *See* Ten Words
deception 220, 499
decide/decision. *See*
  authority
declaration 697
dedicate oneself 697
deeds 252–53, 275

deliver/deliverance/de-
  liverer 120, 174, 200,
  301–2, 334, 551, 612,
  646, 697–98
demon/demons 196, 217
diversity 641
"do not destroy" 698

Edom/Edomites 578
enemies 29, 30, 162, 168,
  214–15, 314
Ephraim 230–31, 532–33
eschatology 66
Esther 576
exile 228, 355, 367, 434
exodus 66, 69, 319, 482,
  503
expiation 276

fail/failure 698
faith 189–90
faithful/faithfulness/be
  faithful 57–59, 168,
  204, 378, 418, 698
faithless/faithlessness
  117–18, 205, 566, 698
fall down/falter 699
falsehood/false 45, 699
family 118
fasting 344–45, 426, 520
fat 405
fear 67–68, 167–69, 185,
  189–90, 266

fool 103–5, 150–52, 154, 249, 487
foreigners 520–21, 632
forgiveness 140, 185–86, 216, 530, 606–7
friend/friends 168, 172–73

gender roles 60, 63
God
    acts of 24, 76, 155–56, 227–28, 442, 502, 515, 625
    anger of 227, 425, 523–24, 536, 607–8, 628
    arm of 39
    beloved of 229
    changing the mind of 682
    character of (see God: nature of)
    city of 86
    compassion of 187, 466, 500, 525
    as creator 279–80
    dwelling of 319, 589–90
    face of 23, 39, 347, 698 (see also God: presence of)
    as father 223, 658, 679
    fear of 454, 456
    gifts of 599
    hand of 90–91
    images of 257, 344
    justice of 129, 209, 529
    kingship of/sovereignty of 77, 539, 650
    knowledge of 46, 47, 153
    life-giving nature of 23, 31
    location of 24
    as lord 619–20
    mercy of 129
    name of 90, 111, 147, 161, 194, 316, 582–84, 600
    nature of 156, 222
    power of 252, 569
    praise of 90
    presence of 233, 237, 314, 589–90

    promises of (see God: word of)
    protection of 592
    reign of 76, 80–81, 291
    reliability of 175
    responsibility of 50
    shelter of 25
    as shepherd 529, 534
    sleeping/asleep 47, 48, 50, 216, 511
    strength of 67, 218
    as stronghold 31
    thirsting for 33
    titles of (see God: name of)
    trustworthiness of 183
    uniqueness of 623–24
    war and 71–73
    ways of 136
    wings of 194, 239, 260
    word of 185, 188–89
    wrath of 207n27, 220, 350, 356, 500, 529
gods, other 202–4, 208, 559–62
good/goodness 161, 401, 569, 622, 699
good fortune of 699
good works. See deeds
grace/be gracious/prayer for grace 194, 216, 466, 699

Hannah 440
harm/harmfulness 699
harp. See lyre
harvest 282–83
haven 70, 218–19, 700
heart 401–2, 700
heavenly cabinet/heavenly council 195, 203, 454, 562–63, 568
help 700
Hitler 576
holiness 469, 683
honor 414, 700
hope 369–70, 700
horn 549

ignore 700
incarnation 613n24

inscription 700
instruction 700
integrity 49
intercession 393
Ishmael/Ishaelites 578
Israel
    God's delight in 39
    God's possession of 321
    God's relationship to 484, 497, 500–501
    land of 354–55
    modern state of 93
    as a vine 539, 542

Jacob's God 700–701
jealousy 403
Jeremiah 340, 429
Jerusalem 71, 139, 451, 525
Job 84, 151, 176, 341, 351, 408
joy 86n15
justice 209. See also God: justice of

king/kings/kingship 59, 240
kiss 613–14
knowledge 153
Korahites 701

laughter 145–46
lead/leader 701
Leviathan 431
light 701
lily/lilies 701
liturgy 479, 627
Lord 701
love 607
lyre 701

marriage 54
Messiah/messianic interpretation 54, 240, 382, 543, 691
might 701
mindful, be 701–2
Moses 66, 541, 670
Most High 702
murmur 463, 465
music. See composition
Muslims 93

name 702
nations 70–73, 217,
    432–33, 527, 569
needy 702

oath 220
offering 114, 241, 353. *See
    also* whole-offering
orphan 316–17, 564–65

palace 702
path 402
peace 473
persecution 162
person 257, 702
pilgrimage 588, 592
plea/plead 165, 702–3
politics 76, 87, 136, 234,
    280, 301, 314, 633
polytheism 203, 567n35
poor 390, 564–65, 703
possession 703
power 443–45
praise 241, 315, 353, 370,
    557, 703
prayer 296, 345, 361, 383,
    462, 596, 626, 643–44.
    See also intercession
promise 677, 689, 703. *See
    also* God: word of
prophet/prophets/pro-
    phetic 568, 611, 616,
    632
prosperity 385, 404
protest 38, 65, 84, 180,
    182–83, 436
Psalms 42–43
    composition of 21
    connection between 21
    enemies and 29–30, 31
    geography of 27
    lament and 21
    structure of 21–22
    temple and 21
    theological implications
        33–34
    translation of 19–21
    verses 42:1–5 22–26
    verses 42:6–11 26–30
    verses 43:1–5 30–33

water and 22–23, 27–28,
    30
Psalm 44
    occasion of 37
    structure of 38
    theological implications
        49–51
    translation of 35–37
    verses 1–3 38–40
    verses 4–8 40–41
    verses 9–16 41–44
    verses 17–22 44–47
    verses 23–26 47–49
    war and 40–41
Psalm 45
    fruitfulness and 57–59
    Ruth and 60
    structure of 55, 60
    theological implications
        of 63
    translation of 52–54
    truthfulness and 57–59
    verse 1 55–56
    verses 2–9 56–60
    verses 10–13a 60–61
    verses 13b–16 61–62
Psalm 46
    eschatology and 66
    exodus, the, and 66
    setting of 65–66
    theological implications
        of 73
    translation of 64–65
    verses 1–3 67–68
    verses 4–7 68–70
    verses 8–11 71–72
Psalm 47
    structure of 75
    theological implications
        of 81
    translation of 74–75
    verses 1–5 77–79
    verses 6–9 79–81
Psalm 48
    structure of 83–84
    theological implications
        of 92–94
    translation of 82–83
    use of 85
    verses 1–2 85–87
    verses 3–6 87–88

verses 7–8 88–90
verses 9–11 90–91
verses 12–14 91–92
Psalm 49
    background of 97
    form of 98
    structure of 98
    theological implications
        106–7
    translation of 95–97
    verses 1–4 98–100
    verses 5–9 100–101
    verses 10–12 101–3
    verses 13–15 103–5
    verses 16–20 105–6
Psalm 50
    form of 110
    structure of 110
    theological implications
        120–21
    translation of 108–10
    verses 1–6 111–13
    verses 7–15 113–16
    verses 16–21 117–19
    verses 22–23 119–20
Psalm 51
    date of 125
    structure of 124
    theological implications
        of 139–40
    translation of 122–24
    verses 1–2 126–27
    verses 3–6 127–30
    verses 7–9 130–32
    verses 10–12 132–35
    verses 13–15 135–37
    verses 16–19 137–39
Psalm 52
    date of 142
    theological implications
        148
    translation of 141–42
    verse 1 143
    verses 2–4 143–44
    verses 5–7 144–46
    verses 8–9 146–47
Psalm 53
    comparison to Psalm
        52 150
    context of 150
    structure of 150

theological implications
of 155–56
translation of 149–50
verses 1–4 151–54
verse 5 154
verse 6 155
Psalm 54
date of 158
structure of 158, 159n10
theological implications
of 162
translation of 157–58
verses 1–3 159–60
verses 4–5 160–61
verses 6–7 161–62
Psalm 55
context of 166
Jeremiah and 166
plea and 165, 167, 170
structure of 165–66
theological implications
of 179–80
translation of 163–65
verses 1–8 167–70
verses 9–14 170–73
verse 15 173
verses 16–21 173–77
verses 22–23 177–79
Psalm 56
enemies and 184
structure of 182–83
theological implications
of 189–90
translation of 181–82
verses 1–4 183–85
verses 5–11 185–88
verses 12–13 188–89
Psalm 57
protest of 194
structure of 192–93
theological implications
of 200
translation of 191–92
verses 1–5 193–96
verses 6–11 197–200
Psalm 58
context of 203
polytheism and 203
structure of 202–3, 205
theological implications
of 209–10

translation of 201–2
verses 1–2 203–4
verses 3–5 204–6
verse 6 206
verses 7–9 206–7
verses 10–11 208–9
Psalm 59
structure of 213
theme of 212
theological implications
of 223
translation of 211–12
verses 1–4a 214–15
verses 4b–7 215–17
verses 8–10 217–18
verses 11–13 218–21
verses 14–15 221–22
verses 16–17 222–23
Psalm 60
context of 226, 230
hardship and 228
structure of 225
theological implications
of 234
translation of 224–25
verses 1–5 226–29
verses 6–9 229–32
verses 10–12 232–34
Psalm 61
context of 237
structure of 236
theological implications
of 242
translation of 235–36
verses 1–3 237–38
verses 4–5 238–40
verses 6–7 240–41
verse 8 241
Psalm 62
structure of 244–45
theological implications
of 253
translation of 243–44
use of 253
verses 1–3b 245–47
verses 3c–7 247–49
verses 8–10 249–51
verses 11–12 251–53
Psalm 63
structure of 255

theological implications
of 263
translation of 254–55
verses 1–4 256–58
verses 5–8 258–60
verses 9–11 260–62
Psalm 64
structure of 265
theological implications
of 271
translation of 264–65
verses 1–6 266–68
verses 7–9 268–70
verse 10 270
Psalm 65
context of 274
structure of 273–74
theological implications
of 283–84
translation of 272–73
verses 1–3 274–76
verses 4–5a 276–78
verses 5b–8 278–80
verses 9–13 280–83
Psalm 66
structure of 287–88, 295
theological implications
of 297
translation of 285–87
verses 1–4 288–89
verses 5–7 290–91
verses 8–12 291–93
verses 13–15 293–95
verses 16–20 295–97
Psalm 67
Aaronic blessing and
299
date of 299
liturgy and 304
structure of 299
theological implications
of 303–4
translation of 298
verses 1–2 300–301
verses 3–5 301–2
verses 6–7 302–3
Psalm 68
context of 310
date of 312
liturgy and 311, 314
structure of 309

theological implications
  of 333–34
translation of 305–9
verses 1–3 312–14
verses 4–6 315–17
verses 7–10 317–21
verses 11–14 321–23
verses 15–18 323–26
verses 19–23 326–28
verses 24–27 328–30
verses 28–31 330–32
verses 32–35 332–33
Psalm 69
  structure of 338
  theological implications
    of 355–56
  translation of 335–38
  verses 1–5 339–42
  verse 6 342
  verses 7–12 342–45
  verses 13–18 345–47
  verses 19–21 347–49
  verses 22–29 349–52
  verses 30–36 352–55
Psalm 70
  structure of 358
  theological implications
    of 361–62
  translation of 357
  verse 1 359
  verse 2 359
  verse 3 359
  verse 4 360
  verse 5 360–61
Psalm 71
  context of 366–67
  structure of 366–67
  theological implications
    of 377–78
  translation of 363–65
  verses 1–8 367–70
  verses 9–16 371–74
  verses 17–24 374–77
Psalm 72
  context of 383
  structure of 381
  theological implications
    of 393–94
  translation of 379–80
  verses 1–7 383–87
  verses 8–14 387–91

verses 15–17 391–93
verses 18–20. See Psalm
  72:18–20 coda
Psalm 72:18–20 coda
  theological implications
    of 396
  translation 395
  verses 18–20 395–96
Psalm 73
  context of 400–401
  structure of 400
  theological implications
    of 417–19
  translation of 397–99
  verse 1 401–2
  verses 2–3 402–3
  verses 4–12 403–7
  verses 13–14 407–8
  verses 15–20 408–11
  verses 21–26 411–15
  verses 27–28 415–17
Psalm 74
  context of 423–24
  structure of 423
  theological implications
    of 436–37
  translation 420–22
  verses 1–3 424–27
  verses 4–9 427–29
  verses 10–11 429–30
  verses 12–17 430–33
  verses 18–23 433–36
Psalm 75
  structure of 439
  theological implications
    of 446–47
  translation of 438–39
  verse 1 441
  verses 2–5 441–44
  verses 6–10 444–46
Psalm 76
  context of 450
  structure of 449
  theological implications
    of 456–57
  translation of 448–49
  verses 1–3 450–52
  verses 4–6 452–53
  verses 7–9 453–55
  verses 10–12 455–56
Psalm 77

structure 459–60
theological implications
  of 472–73
translation of 458–59
verses 1–3 461–63
verses 4–6 463–65
verses 7–9 465–66
verses 10–12 467–68
verses 13–20 468–72
Psalm 78
  date of 481
  narrative and 479
  structure of 480–81
  theological implications
    of 514–16
  translation of 474–79
  verses 1–8 484–87
  verses 9–11 487–89
  verses 12–16 489–91
  verses 17–20 491–93
  verses 21–31 493–97
  verses 32–37 497–500
  verses 38–39 500–501
  verses 40–43 501–2
  verses 44–55 502–7
  verses 56–58 507–8
  verses 59–64 508–10
  verses 65–72 510–14
Psalm 79
  context of 519
  structure of 518
  theological implications
    of 529–30
  translation of 517–18
  verses 1–4 520–22
  verses 5–7 522–24
  verses 8–10b 524–27
  verses 10c–12 527–29
  verse 13 529
Psalm 80
  context of 533–34
  structure of 533
  theological implications
    of 543–44
  translation of 531–32
  verses 1–3 534–36
  verses 4–7 536–38
  verses 8–13 538–40
  verses 14–19 540–43
Psalm 81
  addressee of 547

structure of 547
theological implications
of 556–57
translation of 545–46
use of 547
verses 1–5b 548–50
verses 5c–12 550–54
verses 13–16 554–56
Psalm 82
speaker and 559
theological implications
of 569–70
translation of 558–59
verse 1 560–62
verses 2–5 562–66
verses 6–7 566–68
verse 8 568–69
Psalm 83
context of 573–74
structure of 572–73
theological implications
of 584–85
translation of 571–72
verse 1 574
verses 2–4 575–76
verses 5–8 576–79
verses 9–11 579–80
verses 12–15 580–82
verses 16–18 582–84
Psalm 84
pilgrimage and 588, 592
structure of 588
theological implications
of 600–602
translation of 586–87
verses 1–4 588–92
verses 5–7 592–95
verses 8–9 595–97
verses 10–12 597–600
Psalm 85
context of 605
structure of 604–5
theological implications
of 615–16
translation of 603–4
verses 1–3 605–8
verses 4–7 608–10
verse 8 610–11
verses 9–13 611–15
Psalm 86
date of 620

structure of 619–20
theological implications
of 629–30
translation of 617–18
verses 1–7 620–23
verses 8–10 623–24
verses 11–13 624–26
verses 14–17 626–29
Psalm 87
structure of 632
theological implications
of 640–41
translation of 631–32
verses 1–3 633–35
verse 4 635–37
verses 5–7 637–40
Psalm 88
date of 645
liturgical use of 644
structure of 644
theological implications
of 658–59
translation of 642–43
verses 1–9a 646–51
verses 9b–12 651–55
verses 13–18 655–58
Psalm 89
date of 665
kingship and 664
liturgical use of 692
structure of 664–65
theological implications
of 690–92
translation of 660–63
verses 1–4 666–70
verses 5–14 670–74
verses 15–18 674–76
verses 19–27 676–80
verses 28–37 680–84
verses 38–45 684–87
verses 46–51 687–90
verse 52. See Psalm 89:52
coda
Psalm 89:52 coda
context of 693
theological implications
of 693–94
translation of 693
Psalms, books of 11,
395–96, 693–94

punishment 119, 216, 543,
581
purity 133, 401–2, 686–87

Rahab 635, 672
rain 319, 594
rebel/rebellion 276, 703
redeem 703
Red Sea 88–93, 453, 490
refuge 194, 703
rejection 425, 684
rely on 703–4
rescue 704
resound/sound 704
restore 704
resurrection 652
revenge. See vengeance
revere/reverence 704
rise 704
river/rivers. See water
Roman Empire 232

sacrifice 114–16, 137–38,
294–95
Saul 218
save 704
seek help from 704
servant 629–30
shade of your wings 704–5
shame 343
Shechem 230
Sheol 173, 178, 626, 648,
652–53, 705
shout 79, 705
silence 246, 274–75, 574
sin 118, 124, 126, 129,
134, 140, 215, 283–84,
341, 600, 607
sin, original 205
Sinai 333
sing/singing 198, 222
Solomon 60, 139, 382–83,
509
song 90–92
soul 23, 25, 33, 49
body and 33
dark night of the 33
spirit 133–35
strength 215, 238, 705
strings 705
stronghold 705

suffering 177, 179, 409
Sukkot, Feast of 25, 274, 549, 594

tears 187, 537, 593
temple 194, 239, 277–78, 589, 598, 600–602
Ten Words 117, 553
terror 168–69
testing 492, 494, 507–8, 552
thanksgiving 294
theodicy 569
thirst 256, 348
throne 53n6, 58–59, 81, 198, 391, 669–70
tradition 12, 366, 618
trust 107, 185, 189–90, 246, 369–70, 705

truth/truthfulness/be true 32, 57–59, 195, 199, 666–68, 705

uprightness 204

vengeance 208, 527, 529
violence 66, 73, 705–6

wait 706
war 331. *See also* God: war and
washing 131
watchful foe 706
water 27, 28, 68–69, 339, 341, 678
waywardness 706
weak 706
wealth 100–107, 146

well-being 706
whole-offering 706
why 706–7
wicked/wickedness 707
widow 316–17
wisdom 268, 485
women 166, 179–80, 321n73, 329n90, 548
wonders 374, 707
worship 76, 120–21, 271, 289, 547, 590, 624, 707

Yhwh. *See* God

Zaphon 86–87, 89
Zion 84, 111, 156, 333–34, 512, 632

Author Index

Ackerman, James S.
561n16
Ackroyd, Peter R. 420n3,
436n62
Albright, William F.
311n45, 313n56,
321n73
Allen, Leslie C. 53n6,
110n15, 338n13,
411n51, 419n76
Allen, Roland B. 637n26
Alter, Robert 88n22,
388n25, 393n37
Althann, R. 206n21
Andersen, Francis I.
558n3
Anderson, A. 208n28,
274n14, 352n33,
370n20, 428n41,
594n31, 653n32,
659n48, 673n31,
681n44, 698
Anderson, James
312nn49–50
Aquinas, Thomas. See
Thomas Aquinas
Arneth, Martin 381n13
Arnold, Bill T. 316n63
Asensio, F. 255
Athanasius of Alexandria
9
Auffret, Pierre 124n13,
158n52, 182n10,

195n11, 203n10, 213n7,
226n17, 236n8, 245n11,
255, 255n6, 288n16,
309n41, 338n13,
418n70, 423n23,
429n43, 449n13, 460n9,
480n23, 540n28, 556,
587n8, 603n3, 605n5,
619n6, 665n19
Augustine of Hippo
49n27, 70n18, 73,
77n11, 120, 129n27,
188n20, 209, 209n35,
253n35, 300, 311,
355n43, 472n43,
605n10, 626n24,
641n38
Auwers, Jean-Marie
365n11

Bach, Robert 72n19
Bail, Ulrike 166n16,
172n29, 179n45,
180n46
Barré, Michael L. 85n12,
170n26, 265n8, 629n30
Barth, Karl 136n39
Barthélemy, Dominique
20n2, 36n3, 52n3,
182n10, 192n3, 225n9,
265n8, 380n6, 420n3,
458n4, 556n49, 598n45,
661n4

Begg, Christopher T.
183n13, 201n1, 422n17
Bellinger, W. H. 236n8
Benedetto, Robert 589n13
Berlin, Adele 45n20
Beuken, W. A. M. 76n8,
451n21
Beutler, Johannes 26n14
Beyerlin, Walter 42n16,
141n1, 142n6, 147n15,
150n8, 158n8, 299n2,
534n13
Bieler, Andrea 180n47
Birkeland, Harris 414n63
Blackburn, Bill 371n22
Bland, David 245n11
Blumenthal, David R.
50n32
Bodner, Keith 80n20
Boer, P. A. H. de 406n37,
545n3
Boesak, Willa 560n6
Bonhoeffer, Dietrich
210n36, 253n31
Booij, Thijs 547n17,
595n37, 632n6, 632n8
Bordreuil, Pierre 97n14
Bos, Johanna W. H.
112n17, 640n37
Bosma, Carl J. 299n4
Bouzard, Walter C.
424n34
Bracke, John M. 155n16

Bratcher, Robert G. 603n1
Briggs, Charles A. 310n42,
 397n3, 413n55, 591n20,
 592n25, 595n38,
 596n41
Briggs, Emilie Grace
 310n42, 397n3, 413n55,
 591n20, 592n25,
 595n38, 596n41
Brongers, H. A. 122n3
Brooks, Claire Vonk
 140n56
Broyles, Craig C. 50n29,
 226n13, 382n17
Brueggemann, Walter
 99nn22–23, 140n55,
 275n18, 284n32,
 393n35, 402n30,
 417n67, 472n45,
 516n82, 530n29, 619n5,
 659nn51–52
Brush, Jack E. 140n52
Buber, Martin 418,
 570n44, 699n10
Buchanan, George Wesley
 424, 431n48, 597n44
Budde, Karl 567n34
Buis, Pierre 449n14
Buss, Martin J. 696n3
Buttenwieser, Moses
 173n33

Calvin, John 37n11,
 88n24, 162n21, 166n15,
 174n34, 190n23,
 226n16, 242, 253n36,
 255n6, 312n49, 312n54,
 341n23, 382, 424n29,
 466, 536, 553n41,
 556, 557n54, 563n24,
 590n15, 605, 624n21,
 626n24, 631n1, 641n40,
 644, 658n45
Campbell, Anthony F.
 480n22
Caquot, André 76n7,
 138n46, 392n30
Carmichael, Amy 473
Carr, G. Lloyd 55n17
Carrière, J.-M. 382n15
Carroll, R. P. 481n28

Casetti, Pierre 97n19
Cassiodorus, Senator
 48n24, 77n11, 120,
 274n16, 275n18, 311,
 355n43, 362n6, 378n32,
 413n57, 437, 460n13,
 479n19, 519n8, 590n15,
 605n10, 626n24,
 647n22
Cassuto, Umberto 316n62
Ceresko, Anthony R.
 255n6
Charlesworth, James H.
 307n26
Chrysostom, John 37n11,
 77n11, 296, 703n20
Clifford, R. J. 481n26,
 664n16
Coats, George W. 483n41
Cole, Robert 410n46,
 410n48, 417n66,
 418n72, 421n9, 440n11,
 442n16, 449n13,
 457n30, 460n8, 483n42,
 533n8, 563n21, 587n8,
 598n46, 620n12,
 636n22, 691nn57–59
Collins, C. John 96n11
Cooke, Gerald 562n18
Coppens, J. 128n25
Costacurta, Bruna
 577n19, 584n31
Couffignal, Robert 55n16
Couroyer, B. 53n6
Craig, Kenneth M. 568n40
Craigie, Peter C. 53n8,
 76n8, 87n18, 108n3,
 700n12
Craven, Toni 366n12
Creach, Jerome F. D.
 688n55, 703n21
Crenshaw, James L.
 366n13, 374n30,
 419n73
Crüsemann, Frank 652n29
Culley, Robert C. 644n8

Dahood, M. 33n27, 52n5,
 58n22, 86n14, 95n1,
 125n21, 150n5, 161n15,
 168n21, 184n14,

204n17, 211n2, 231n27,
 237n11, 240n20,
 277n24, 290n23,
 306n10, 308n37,
 314n58, 321n73, 360n2,
 363n2, 390n28, 417n65,
 419n74, 422n14,
 424n28, 431n51, 439n8,
 444n21, 449n11,
 504n68, 560n8, 592n26,
 595n37, 605n9, 609n15,
 614n28, 621n13,
 626n23, 643n4, 661n6
Dalglish, Edward R.
 122n3, 123n5, 124n11,
 125n15, 130n29,
 138n44
Day, John 455n27, 481n25
Day, John N. 208n29
de Boer, P. A. H. See Boer,
 P. A. H. de
Dequeker, L. 670n27
Dietrich, M. 379n2
Dijkstra, Meindert 446n24
Diodore of Tarsus 37n11,
 56n20, 105n30, 125n16,
 125n19
Donner, Herbert 424n27
Driver, G. R. 228n19,
 536n18, 559n4, 592n26
Dumortier, Jean-Bernard
 665n20

Eaton, John H. 285n2,
 400n23, 421n9, 555n47,
 701n19
Ebach, Jürgen 613n23
Eerdmans, B. D. 322n76,
 569n42
Eissfeldt, Otto 65n6,
 450n17, 481n24,
 488n46, 534n11,
 562n18, 684n48,
 692n64
Ellington, John 246n14
Emerton, J. A. 53n6,
 264n2, 323n78, 420n3,
 432n52, 449n7, 451n22,
 467n31, 561n16,
 638n28
Estes, Daniel J. 98n20

Fishbane, Michael 668n26
Flint, Peter W. 11n1,
  656n37, 665n21
Floyd, Michael H. 665n22
Fohrer, Georg 253n34
Fokkelman, J. P. 27n17,
  35n1, 68n12, 106n32,
  135n37, 147n13,
  154n15, 200n25,
  208n31, 232n29,
  309n41, 352n35,
  415n64, 479n20,
  488n47, 497n56,
  550n29, 551n36, 557,
  569n41, 596n40,
  600n51, 679n40
Freed, Edwin D. 26n14
Freedman, David Noel
  478n16
Füglister, Notker 481n29

Gaster, Theodor H. 55n16,
  422n14
Geiger, Georg 496n54
Gelston, A. 428n41,
  543n32
Gerstenberger, Erhard S.
  38n12, 55n17, 77n10,
  110n13, 125n17,
  136n40, 187n19, 236n7,
  246n13, 266n15,
  289n20, 300n7, 309n40,
  312nn53–54, 338n13,
  372n23, 383n18,
  419n77, 423n22,
  425n35, 439n7, 440n9,
  456n28, 519n5, 520n12,
  550n32, 588n9, 608n14,
  632n9, 637n27, 645n14
Gese, Hartmut 113n19
Gilkes, Cheryl Townsend
  334n96
Goldingay, John 78n14,
  107n34, 122n3, 126n22,
  134n35, 137n41,
  320n70
Gonzalez, A. 560n10
Gordon, Cyrus H. 89n25,
  567n35
Gordon, Robert P. 85n10
Gosse, Bernard 692n64

Goulder, Michael D.
  27n16, 37n10, 41n15,
  54n13, 55n19, 86n16,
  97, 111n16, 125n14,
  131n32, 139n49, 143n7,
  145n11, 159n9, 213n8,
  228n22, 230n23,
  307n23, 322n76,
  339n15, 396n5, 424,
  440n10, 451n22,
  482n34, 483n40,
  502n62, 547, 551n33,
  565n28, 593n29,
  597n40, 664n17,
  673n31, 696n3, 701n15,
  701n17
Goy, William-A. 461n17
Graham, Pat 460n11
Gray, J. 324n80
Greenfield, Jonas C.
  421n13
Greenstein, Edward L.
  479n21
Grelot, Pierre 649n24
Grill, Severin 322n76
Grimm, Markus 107n33
Groenewald, Alphonso
  353n38
Grollenberg, L. 597n44
Gross, Heinrich 95n3
Grünbeck, Elisabeth 53n6
Gunkel, Hermann 66n8,
  83n6, 86n14, 225n9,
  236n9, 243n1, 245n10,
  262n29, 268n18,
  327n87, 382n16,
  414n62, 424n30,
  442n17, 450n15,
  481n28, 486n44, 519n7,
  537n21, 545n1, 587n6,
  595n37, 605n10,
  638n28

Haag, Ernst 649n24
Haglund, Erik 286n9,
  482n35, 549n27
Handy, Lowell K. 562n18,
  563n21, 568n40
Hanson, A. T. 561n16
Harman, Allan M. 53n6

Hauge, Martin R. 247n19,
  307n25, 595n37
Hays, Richard B. 356n44
Heim, Knut M. 382n15
Heinemann, H. 533
Heschel, Abraham J.
  50n32
Hieke, Thomas 533n8,
  538n22
Hilary of Poitiers 162n20
Hilber, John W. 226n12,
  547n14
Hill, David 543n32
Hill, Edmund 94, 361,
  362n6, 393n34, 444n21,
  563n23, 613n24,
  637n25, 641n41
Hill, Robert C. 33n27,
  56n20, 311
Höffken, Peter 563n21
Honeyman, A. M. 244n9
Hoppe, Leslie J. 519n6
Hossfeld, Frank-Lothar
  11n1, 126n23, 142n6,
  150n6, 150n9, 169n25,
  182n7, 184n15, 192n7,
  213n6, 218n16, 232n29,
  245n10, 252n29, 256n9,
  274n15, 288n17, 300n6,
  303n15, 339n14, 380n9,
  393n36, 396n2, 419n75,
  423n25, 436n61, 519n4,
  529n26, 532n6, 547,
  570n46, 584nn29–30,
  587n8, 588n10, 597n44,
  600n52, 605n6, 623n17,
  638n29, 649n24,
  655n34, 691n59
Houston, Walter 394n38,
  394n40

Ibn Ezra, Abraham 20n2,
  53n6, 312, 548
Illman, Karl-Johan
  645n16

Jacobson, Rolf A. 567n33,
  568n38
Janowski, Bernd 393n36,
  659n50
Janzen, Waldemar 699n10

Jefferson, Helen G. 299n3, 468n34
Jellicoe, S. 414n62
Jenni, Ernst 202n4
Jepsen, A. 707n29
Jeremias, Jörg 449n12, 559n5
Jerome 297n35, 312n55, 472, 472n43, 479n18, 516, 516n83, 567n36, 573n9, 590, 590n15, 636n21
Jobling, David 394n39
Joffe, Laura 22n7
Johnson, Aubrey R. 90n27, 261n27, 308n35, 482n31, 498n58, 602
Jüngling, Hans-Winfried 560n10, 561n17, 568n39
Junker, H. 66n7, 481n27

Keel, Othmar 32n26, 162n19, 217, 221n20, 241nn21–22, 251n26, 277n23, 322n75, 329n90, 349n32, 381n13, 431n51, 509n73, 539n24, 548n21, 549n22, 551n34, 591n19, 592n24, 598nn47–48, 633n13, 700, 705n24
Kellermann, Ulrich 226n14
Kelly, Sidney 68n13
Kidner, Derek 50n31, 61n27, 138n45, 151n13, 265n11, 356n45, 438n4, 488n47, 529n25, 550, 566n29, 626n23
Kirkpatrick, A. F. 135n38, 166n13, 220n19, 247n20, 261n24, 312n51, 330n93, 444n21, 610n18, 632n7, 658n41, 693
Kline, Ralph W. 692n62
Klingbeil, Martin 73
Knauf, Ernst A. 226n14, 578n20

Knight, G. A. F. 658
Köbert, R. 37n11
Koch, Klaus 665n21, 668n26
Koenen, Klaus 700
Koopmans, William T. 483n41
Korpel, Marjo C. A. 480n23
Kraus, Hans-Joachim 49n28, 89n26, 147n14, 203n12, 240n18, 252n30, 254n1, 261n27, 290n25, 306n15, 324n80, 348n29, 381n13, 421n9, 440n9, 442n17, 452n23, 536n18, 554n42, 565n26, 573n11, 589n13, 618n2, 635n19, 659n49, 706n28
Krawczack, Peter 201n1, 203n10, 210n38
Krinetzki, Leo 84n8
Kselman, John S. 129n26, 170n26, 211n3, 381n11, 460n9, 603n3
Kutscher, E. Y. 572n5

Lagarde, Paul de 537n21
La Rochefoucauld, François de. See Rochefoucald, François de la
Layton, Scott C. 545n3
Lee, Archie C. C. 481n26
Lee, Sung-Hun 200n24
Lemaire, André 388n26
Lindström, Fredrik 255n5, 259n19, 341n24, 343n26
Lipiński, Edouard/Edward 80n19, 318n67, 665n18
Lloyd-Jones, D. Martyn 401n28
Loersch, Sigrid 595n32
Loewenstamm, Samuel E. 550n31
Lohfink, Norbert 550n30
Longman, Tremper 691n60

Loretz, Oswald 54n15, 97n19, 379n2, 382n15, 429n42, 468n34, 549n24, 556n50, 560n7, 560n12, 614n28, 649n24
Lubetski, Meir 141n2
Luther, Martin 122n3, 139n51, 140n52, 225n7, 256, 257n14, 312n49, 356, 362, 437n64, 467n31, 488n45, 516, 544n35, 563n21, 590n15, 613n24, 626n24, 644n12
Luyten, J. 400n22

Magne, Jean 124n13
Maier, Christl M. 638n30
Mandolfo, Carleen 173n32
Mannati, Marina 109n9, 207n22, 398n4, 412n54
Mathias, Dietmar 515n81
Mayer, Werner R. 242
Mays, James L. 50n33, 87n20, 93n29, 140n54, 189n21, 209n32, 293n31, 423n26, 460n12, 542n30, 556n53, 568n37, 569n43, 618, 679n41
McCann, J. Clinton 11n1, 50n33, 125n20, 189n22, 214n11, 231n28, 249n23, 262n31, 400n24, 408n44, 417n67, 472nn46–47, 570n45, 645n15, 684n49
McCarthy, Carmel 23n9, 595n35
McCarthy, Dennis 613n27
McGrath, Brendan 54n14
McKay, J. W. 50n33, 92n28, 181n3, 196n14, 253n33, 626n25, 704n23
McMillion, Phillip 514n80
Meer, W. van der 468n34
Meier, Samuel A. 143n8
Menken, M. J. J. 496n54

Mettinger, Tryggve N. D.
680n42
Meyer, Elias E. 576n17
Milik, J. T. 665n21
Miller, Patrick D. 11n1,
393n33, 417n67,
567n35, 698n7
Mitchell, David C. 396n5,
691n61
Moor, Johannes C. de
312n52, 480n23
Morgenstern, Julian 83n7,
560n11
Mosca, Paul G. 684n48
Mosis, Rudolf 138n48
Mowinckel, Sigmund
79n16, 265n12, 450n19,
547n16, 549n24,
549n26, 590n16, 605n8,
629n29, 657, 673n31
Moynihan, Daniel 687
Muilenburg, James 76n7
Muis, Simeon de 312
Mulder, Johannes S. M.
53n6, 54n14
Mulder, M. J. 104n29,
590n18
Mullen, E. Theodore
562n18, 662n10
Murphy, Roland E.
381n13, 382n14, 389

Nasuti, Harry P. 84n9,
291n26, 482n36,
534n12, 547n15, 696n3
Nehrey, Jerome H. 561n16
Neve, Lloyd 65n6, 132n33
Niehr, H. 560n6
Noli, Fan Stylian 256n11
North, C. R. 53n6, 230n25
Nowell, Irene 644n10,
646n18
Núñez, Angel González
442n17

O'Brien, Julia M. 287n15
O'Callaghan, Roger T.
560n7
Ogden, Graham S. 226n14
Olivier, J. P. J. 53n7

Olofsson, Staffan 96n13,
97n14
Osswald, Eva 616n30
Ouellette, Jean 676n37
Oxtoby, Gurdon C. 125n18

Padilla, René 613n22
Palmer, Martin 84n8
Parker, Harold M. 37n11
Parker, Simon B. 562n19
Patterson, Richard D.
53n6
Paul, Shalom M. 379n2
Pautrel, Raymond 116n24
Perdue, Leo G. 80n19,
100n24
Peterson, Eugene 66n9,
73n21, 472n44, 563n21,
641n39
Phillips, W. Gary 561n16
Plantin, Henry 549n26
Pleins, J. David 107n35
Ploeg, J. P. M. van der
99n22, 104n29, 423n23,
665n21
Podechard, E. 104n29,
170n26
Porter, J. R. 53n6
Press, R. 132n33
Preuss, H. D. 658n43
Prinsloo, W. S. 568n40

Qimchi, David 221n21,
246, 257, 265n8,
274n16, 283, 299n3,
339, 445n22, 450,
560n9, 573n7, 589n11,
644n11, 651n28

Raabe, Paul R. 98n21,
103n27, 104n28,
186n18, 195n11
Rad, Gerhard von 482n33
Rashi (Shlomo Yitzhaqi)
53n6, 112, 136, 246,
247n20, 293n31, 312,
324, 441n12, 445n22,
449n8, 450n18, 464n25,
551n34, 581n23,
589n11, 636n23,
644n11

Ratschow, Karl Heinz
75n6
Reid, Stephen Breck
110n13
Renaud, B. 381n12,
406n40, 616n29
Rendsburg, Gary A.
54n14, 60n24, 150n5,
203n11, 401n27, 545n3,
572n5
Reyburn, William D.
603n1
Ridderbos, N. H. 61n30,
110n14, 122n3
Ringgren, Helmer 406n38
Roberts, J. J. M. 76n7,
80n19, 429n42
Roberts, Kathryn L.
139n50
Robinson, A. 87n18,
420n3, 592n26
Rochefoucauld, François de
la 601n53
Rogerson, J. W. 50n33,
92n28, 181n3, 196n14,
253n33, 626n25, 704n23
Rogland, Max 311n44
Rokay, Zoltán 560n11
Rösel, Christoph 691n61
Rosenberg, A. J. 355n43
Ross, James F. 400n22
Rowley, H. H. 28n21

Salters, R. B. 561n15
Sanders, J. A. 616n30
Sarna, Nahum M. 668n26
Saur, Markus 54n15,
663n12, 691n61
Schaefer, Konrad 28n19,
34n28, 87n21, 140n56,
185n16, 260n23,
270n23, 288n17, 359n1,
418n68, 491n50,
530n28, 557n55,
576n15, 620n11,
634n15
Schaper, Joachim 26n14,
76n9
Schedl, Claus 53n6, 141n1
Schildenberger, Johannes
483n39

Schlisske, Werner 567n35
Schmidt, Werner H.
125n19
Schmitt, John J. 638n30
Schmuttermayr, Georg
638n28
Schökel, Luis Alonso
28n18
Schroeder, Christoph
60n26
Schroer, Silvia 281n28,
705n25
Sekine, Seizo 140n53
Selms, A. van 306n6
Seybold, Klaus 201n1,
203n13, 230n24,
278n25, 378n31,
430n45, 439n6, 467n31,
582n26, 592n26,
595n36, 598n49,
656n37, 686n51
Shakespeare, William
246n17
Sharrock, Graeme E.
423n23
Simeon de Muis 312
Siqueira, Tércio 566n31
Skehan, Patrick W.
381n11, 665n21
Slomovic, Elieser 193n8
Slotki, Judah Jacob
103n27
Smick, Elmer B. 430n46
Smith, Mark S. 96n6,
561n14, 639n34
Sollamo, Raija 423n24
Spiekermann, Hermann
627n27
Spurgeon, C. H. 234n32,
297n35, 530n28,
601n54, 613n24,
692n63
Stec, David M. 151n11,
308n32, 315n59,
424n27, 467n31,
471n40, 510n76,
555n47, 666n23
Stendebach, Franz-Josef
560n7
Stern, Philip 481n26,
482n37, 512n78

Stevenson, Gregory M.
461n16
Steyl, C. 202n8
Steymans, Hans Ulrich
668n26, 684n50
Stoebe, Hans Joachim
129n27
Strawn, Brent A. 316n63
Strobel, A. 266
Styron, William 659n52
Swancutt, Diana M.
496n54

Talstra, Eep 299n4
Tanner, Beth LaNeel 659
Tate, Marvin E. 161n14,
209n34, 242n24,
291n26, 298n1, 303,
306n9, 317n65, 322n75,
418n69, 435n60,
447n26, 482n38,
504n70, 534n14,
552n37, 554n42,
555n46, 562n18,
611n20, 635n20,
658n42, 667n24,
686n52, 700n12,
701n16
Terrien, Samuel 113,
130n31, 166n14,
260n22, 433n54,
451n22, 547n13, 560n8,
587n7, 618n2
Theodore of Mopsuestia
25n11, 105n30, 125n19,
150n10, 158, 258n16,
366n14, 382n17, 519n9,
534n15
Theodoret of Cyrus 37n11,
63n31, 127n24, 129n27,
217, 254n2, 274n16,
293n31, 311, 339,
356n46, 414, 460n13,
519n8, 573n10, 644n11
Thomas, D. Winton
436n62, 540n27
Thomas Aquinas 99n22,
124
Thurneysen, Eduard
274n17
Tisdale, Leonora T. 543n34

Tournay, Raymond 54n15,
226n15, 318n67,
373n28, 397n1, 446n24,
593n27, 663n12, 700n12
Trautmann, C. 613n25
Tromp, N. J. 533n9
Tropper, Josef 222n22
Trudiger, Peter L. 85n11
Tsevat, Matitiahu 567n35
Tsumura, David 68n13

Uchelen, N. A. van 696n5
Uehlinger, Christoph
598n47
Ulrich, Eugene 678n39

van der Meer, W. See Meer,
W. van der
van der Ploeg, J. P. M. See
Ploeg, J. P. M. van der
van der Woude, A. S. See
Woude, A. S. van der
van Selms, A. See Selms,
A. van
van Uchelen, N. A. See
Uchelen, N. A. van
Veijola, Timo 662n10,
684n48
Vermeylen, Jacques
125n19
Veugelers, P. 382n15
Victor, Peddi 540n27
Vogt, E. 317n66, 349n32
Volz, Paul 104n29
von Rad, Gerhard. See
Rad, Gerhard von
Vorndran, Jürgen 618n4,
619n7, 630n31

Wahl, Harald-Martin
299n3
Wallace, Howard N.
283n31, 284n33
Ward, James M. 665n19
Watson, Wilfred G. E.
24n10, 36n5, 75n6,
158n6, 169n24, 201n1,
252n28, 339n17,
462n20, 549n25,
568n82, 574n12,

613n21, 654n33,
682n47
Weaver, Glenn D. 658
Weber, Beat 197n15,
198n19, 236n10, 299n2,
460n9, 461n18, 463n22,
464n23, 467n31,
468n33, 468n35,
471n42, 480n23, 519n6
Weisenberg, E. 446n24
Weiser, Artur 21n6,
41n15, 51n34, 55n18,
76, 145n11, 171n28,
183n12, 199n22,
200n26, 204n18, 236n6,
247n18, 299n5, 301n11,
355n42, 441n12,
450n16, 460n10,
467n31, 482n32,
562n18, 585n35,
590n16, 610n17,
638n32, 639n36,
668n26
Weiss, Meir 68n12,
423n23, 460n9

Westermann, Claus
253n32, 479n21, 644
Wharton, James 77n10
Whitley, C. F. 52n4, 305n3
Whitman, Walt 356
Whybray, R. Norman
481n30, 691n61
Willesen, Folker 424n33
Wilson, Gerald H. 382n15,
691n56, 691n59
Winter, Urs 183n13
Witte, Markus 104n29,
414n62
Woude, A. S. van der
60n26, 676n38
Wright, David P. 206n21
Würthwein, Ernst 125n19,
400n23
Wyschogrod, Michael
530n30

Yallin, David 593n27
Yaron, Reuven 42n18,
425n36
Yoder, Perry B. 530n27

Zenger, Erich 11n1,
126n23, 142n6, 150n6,
150n9, 169n25, 182n7,
184n15, 192n7, 209,
213n6, 218n16, 232n29,
245n10, 252n29, 256n9,
274n15, 288n17, 300n6,
303n15, 339n14, 380n9,
382n15, 393n36, 396n2,
419n75, 423n25,
436n61, 519n4, 529n26,
532n6, 547, 570n46,
584nn29–30, 584n32,
587n8, 588n10, 597n44,
600, 605n6, 623n17,
632n10, 638n29,
649n24, 655n34,
691n57
Ziegler, Joseph 69n15
Zink, J. K. 129n28

Index of Scripture and Other Ancient Writings

Old Testament

Genesis

1–6 688
1–11 130, 432
1:5 432
1:9–10 432
1:14–16 432
1:22 282
1:28 282
2 69
2:18–25 60
3:1 575
3:1–6 61
3:6 61, 403, 496
3:8 335n3
3:16 61
4:13 351, 606
4:15 528
4:24 528
5:24 104, 151
6:5 153
6:7 352
6:11–12 153
7:1 494
7:4 494
7:11 432, 491
7:23 352
8:2 262, 432
8:7 432
8:14 432
8:21 115, 130
10:6 505
12:3 248
14 317
14:14 637
14:18 451
14:18–22 702
14:19 506
14:22 506
15:7–21 113, 577
17:1 241
17:12–13 637
19 180n46
19:24 494
20:11 567
22:18 393
24:67 463
26:4 393
27:31 313
27:40 167, 444
27:44 524
28:3 671
28:12 648
30:13 393, 699
31:30 589
33:17–18 230
35:2 553
35:3 700
35:4 553
37:25–26 578
37:30 151
38 512
38:28 459n6
39:9 128
41:6 495
41:44 426n37
41:45 545
48 534
48:15 534
48:16 431
49:3 505
49:3–4 679
49:10 231, 512
49:14 322n74
49:22–27 535
50:15 158n4

Exodus

1:11 490, 551
1:14 228
1:17 611
2:11 551
2:24 48
3–14 503
3–15 502
3:1 319
3:7 48, 462, 646
3:9 492, 646
3:13–15 316
3:20 490, 503
4:22 680
4:22–23 541
4:23 503
5:4–5 551
6:1 506
6:5 48
6:6 459n6
6:6–7 551
6:9 228
7:1 53n6
7:17–19 503
8:2 503
8:6 503
8:21 503
8:22 431n47
8:24 503
9 503
9:15 505
9:16 219
9:23 494
9:25 503, 505
10:3 563
10:7 563
10:13 495
11:1 506
11:4 318n68, 546n4, 550
11:10 472
12:14 550
12:23 504
12:24 550
12:29 505

12:37 505
12:39 506
12:50 472
13:6 550
13:15 503
13:17 505
13:20 505
13:21 505
13:21–22 318n68, 490
14–15 325
14:1–4 472
14:2 86
14:4 469, 471, 471n42
14:5 503
14:9 86
14:10 505
14:10–12 492
14:13 431, 494, 505
14:15 505
14:15–18 472
14:16 432, 490
14:18 469, 471, 472n42
14:19–24 491
14:21 89, 490, 495
14:21–22 432
14:21–28 453
14:25 92
14:27 66, 69
14:28 505
14:29 469
14:30 92, 431
14:31 505
15 90, 310, 431n48, 460, 468, 471, 492, 506, 548, 552, 553
15:1 66, 453, 453n25, 469, 672
15:1–18 291
15:2 66, 218, 316, 431, 468, 469, 494, 495, 550, 672, 673
15:3 90
15:4 340

15:5 340, 491, 505
15:6 91, 460, 467, 505, 506, 541
15:7 66, 504
15:8 66, 454, 470, 475n5, 490, 491, 504
15:9 91, 453, 505
15:10 89, 505
15:11 90, 203, 291, 375, 377, 454, 460, 468, 469, 490, 505, 624, 670, 671, 672
15:12 91, 346, 467, 506, 541,
15:13 66, 426, 431, 469, 472, 491, 495, 505, 506, 550, 673
15:14 469, 470
15:14–15 231
15:14–16 88
15:15 169, 443, 583, 648n23
15:16 88, 169, 291, 426, 459n6, 469, 505, 528, 656
15:17 66, 90, 324, 506, 507, 686n52
15:18 81, 431, 490
15:20 548, 550
15:20–21 321
15:21 453, 453n25, 672
15:22 505
15:22–27 491, 492, 493
15:25 492, 550
15:25–26 552, 552n38
15:26 552
16 493, 494
16–17 493, 497
16:1 505
16:2–3 492
16:3 495
16:4 492, 494, 495
16:7–8 492
16:8 222, 495, 496

16:12 222, 496
16:13 496
16:14 494
16:16 495n52
16:18 495n52
16:21 495n52
16:32 493
17:1 505
17:1–7 493, 552
17:2 492
17:6 491
17:7 492
17:15 228
17:16 316
19:3–8 553
20:2 546n4, 553
20:2–3 487
20:3 553
20:3–6 508
20:5 553
20:14–15 118
20:24 635
21:1 550
21:4 628
21:20 681
21:28–32 101
22:8 561
22:21–22 563
23:14–17 550
23:17 595
23:27 656
23:28–31 506
24:16 612
25–31 509n73
28 62
30 59
32:11–13 541
32:12 608
32:33 352
33:2 506
33:3 325
33:5 325
33:7–11 509n73
33:18–23 472n42
33:19 500
34:2 562
34:6 126, 466, 500, 627
34:6–7 125, 500, 610
34:7 486, 607, 622

34:9 569, 622
34:11 506
35–40 509n73
39 62
40:12 277
40:14 277
40:32 277

Leviticus

1 114
3 114, 115
3:16–17 259
5:1 606
7:35 277
9:4 595
9:7–8 277
11:3 353
15 127
20:9 248
23:23–43 549
23:42 592
24:15 606
26:4–6 614
26:16 498
26:18 528
26:21 528
26:22 350
26:24 528
26:45 525n20

Numbers

2:2 427
2:18–24 535
5:11–31 445
6:24–26 299, 304
6:27 304
10 305n1, 310, 314, 318, 549
10:10 549
10:35 49, 305n1, 312, 313, 313n57
11 492, 492, 494, 497
11:1–3 493, 510
11:4 496
11:5 499
11:20 497, 509
11:31 495, 496
11:31–32 496

11:33 497
11:34 497
11:34–35 496
13–14 498
13:22 490
14 493, 494, 497
14:2 221
14:11 494, 498
14:22 492
14:27 563
14:30 507
14:36 221
16 173
16–17 277
16:5 277
16:10 277
16:15 420n2
16:30 346
16:32 346
16:34 346
18:6–7 307n23
18:20 415
19:14–19 131
20:1 502
20:8–11 491
20:10 492
20:12–13 502
21:7 492
21:18 231
22:2–3 88
22:22–34 325
23:7 485
23:18 485
23:19 683
24:5 634
24:16 702
27:11 415
31 579
32:13 221
33:1 472
33:29–30 308n37
35:25 677
35:27 243n1
35:30 243n1
35:31–32 136

Deuteronomy

1:43 627
2:1–23 580
2:5 239
2:9 239

2:12 239
2:19 239
2:20–21 653n31
4:1 580
4:5 580
4:9–14 486
4:14 580
4:22 580
4:23–24 523
4:26 112, 580
4:34 502
5:8–9 523
6 484
6:5 625
6:14–15 523
6:16 507
6:20–25 38, 486
6:22 502
7:6–7 677
7:6–8 606
7:7–8 252
7:8 502
7:9–10 253
7:10 253
7:19 502
8 556
8:3 101
8:8 556
8:10 556
8:15 491
9:4–8 252
9:6–7 402
9:21 678
9:26 502, 698
10:12 563
11:22 260
11:24 539
13:14 46
15:7 466
15:12–13 649
17:8 681n43
17:9 129n26
17:12–13 627
17:14–20 277
18:1–5 277
18:20–22 627
21:1–9 407
21:8 526
21:17 505
21:18 482, 487
21:18–21 317, 681

21:20 487
22:1–4 167
22:27 462
25:3 500
26:5–9 291, 515
26:6 228
26:7 48, 462
26:15 369
26:19 639n34, 680
27:11–13 230
28:1 639n34, 680
28:11 528
28:46 370n20
28:48 444
28:63 145
29:20 523, 536n18
30:9 528
31:9–13 486
31:11 23n9
31:28 683
32 479, 484, 547, 556
32:1 484
32:8–9 569
32:9 478n15
32:10 677
32:12 553
32:13–14 556
32:15 497
32:16 553
32:35 208
33 310, 319
33:2 325, 325n81, 535
33:11 350
32:12–16 548
33:26 316
33:26–27 332

Joshua

1–12 39, 41
1:2 88
2 636n21
2:9 169
2:24 443
3:13 490
3:16 88, 490, 509n75
4:22 88
5:2–3 686
5:14–15 672

6 79
6:3 91
6:7 91
6:8 88
6:11 91
8:30–35 230, 512
9:2 88
10:10 269
10:29 88
10:31 88
10:34 88
11:5 88
12:6–7 239
13–22 230
13:6 478n15
13:7 478n15
13:24 230
13:27 230
17:5 478n15, 506
17:11 580
17:14 478n15
18:1 509
18:9 88
19:9 478n15
22:4–8 507
22:5 260
23:4 478n15, 506n72
24 512
24:1 230
24:11 88
24:12 506
24:14 297
24:14–24 480
24:17 88
24:18 506
24:20 553
24:23 553

Judges

1 488
2:19 152
2:20–23 219
3:13 578
4–5 325, 580
4–8 579, 582, 583
4:14 318
5 310, 318, 322
5:2 327, 329
5:4 306n7, 318
5:4–5 317, 319

5:9 329
5:16 322, 322n74
5:20–21 319
5:29–30 322
5:31 309
6–8 579
6:3 578
6:33 578
7:12 578
8:22–28 578
8:28 575
9:48 322
9:50–53 238
11:33 269
11:35 157n3
12:2 488
13:25 458n3
14:15 499
16:5 499
16:10 499
16:13 499
18:21 61n29
19 180n46, 659
19:26 66n10
20:16 698

Ruth

1:16–17 63
4:1–10 426
4:4 567
4:7 231
4:15 335n1

1 Samuel

1–4 512
1:10–11 275
1:14 563
1:15 249
2:1–10 439
2:2 438n4
2:3 444
2:7 445
2:22–25 508
3:13 508
4 509
4:2 510
4:4 535
4:8 269
4:10 269, 488, 510,
    567

4:11 510
4:18 468
4:19–22 510
5–6 510
5:6 510
7:3 134
8:5 381n13
8:7 509
8:20 318
10:1 59
10:24 77, 513
10:25 384
11 57, 59
11:2 511
12:6 472
13:14 677
14:13 567
15 578
15:11 682
15:23 513, 685
15:26 513, 685
15:29 682
16 513, 677
16:1 563
16:1–13 277
16:12 56
16:18 57, 513
17:26 511
17:31–47 57
17:34–37 513, 514
17:42 56
17:45 695
17:55 262
18:6–7 321
19:4–5 213
19:11 213
21–22 142
21:10–22:1 183,
    193
22–25 256
22–26 151
22:9 142
23:14–29 158
23:15 158
24 193
24:2 697
26:1–25 158
26:9 698
26:12 453
26:16 528
27:1–29:11 183

27:8–9 578
28 580, 653
30:1–20 578
30:16 25
31:1 488
31:7 488

2 Samuel

1:18 226
1:22 359
2:3 438n4
2:26 563
3:35 348
5:8 20n5
5:17–25 450n17
5:22–24 593
5:24 318
6 329
6:2 79, 535
6:11–15 548
6:12 79
6:15 79
7 230, 668,
    668n26, 676,
    681, 682
7:5 466
7:6 509n73
7:8 466, 472, 513
7:14 679, 680,
    681n43
7:14–15 685
7:15 241, 681n46
7:16 198, 240
7:17 676n36
7:18 592n24
7:22 624
7:23 57
7:28 241
7:29 57, 240
8 226, 232, 573,
    578
8:2 226
8:13 226
10:6–19 226
12:5 528
12:7 59, 677
12:9 125
12:11–12 386
12:13 125
12:13–14 132
12:17 348

12:22 125
12:23 106
12:25 229
13 367
13–19 366
13:20 166, 180
13:39 463
14:14 262
15–17 256
15:10 80
15:21 262
16:11 159
16:14 256
18:31–32 159
22:5 27
22:11 535
23:1 697
24:17 504

1 Kings

1 366
1:11 80
1:34 391
1:39 79, 391
1:40 639
1:50–51 591
3:1 139
3:5 595
3:6 383
3:9 383
4:20 383
4:21 383
4:24 383
4:29 514
4:31 645
6:13 355
6:29 428
7:19 701
7:22 701
7:26 701
8 242
8:12 355
8:16 512
8:23 624
8:27 509
8:35–36 274n14
8:44 512
8:48 512
9:4 514
9:8 639n34
9:15 139

10:1–10 383
10:18 59
11:4 514
11:6 514
11:13 512
11:26 459n6
11:27 139
11:28 551
11:32 512
11:36 512
15:3 514
15:5 514
16:31 61
17 652
18:21 536, 563
18:27 48
19:10 344
19:14 344
22:19 672
22:19–22 561, 563
22:20–22 499
22:30–33 31
22:31 31
22:39 59
22:48 89

2 Kings

2:3 104
2:5 104
2:9 104
2:10 104
3:15 98
4 652
4:1 462
5 127
5:27 131
6 349
6:16–17 325
6:26 462
10:15 367
10:16 344
10:23 367
11:12–13 77
15 37
15:5 649
15:29 329
16:12 277n22
16:18 20n2
17 489
17–18 65
17:15 251

18 37
18–19 150, 158,
   217, 262, 403
18:6 260
18:14 128
18:19 77
19 257
19:4 690
19:15 535
19:16 217, 690
19:20 217
19:22–23 690
19:35 41
23:6 177
23:29 31
25:7 670

1 Chronicles

2:6 645
5:10 578
5:19–22 578
6:16–48 646
7:20–24 488
12:2 488n46
13:6 535
13:13–15 548
14:13–16 593
15–16 696
15:17 110, 646
15:19 110, 646
15:21 701
16:4–5 548
16:4–7 110
16:5 365n10
16:18 478n15
16:38 461n19
16:41–42 245
17 668, 668n26,
   676, 681, 682
17:13 679, 681n46,
   685
17:15 676n36
17:18 414
21:15 504
22:19 513
23:1 366
25 696
25:1–7 646
28:1–6 277
28:4 512
29:12 414

29:23 58
29:30 555

2 Chronicles

5:12 245
7:21 639n34
12:13 512
18:31 677
19:3 198
20 573n7
20:11 580
20:19 701
20:26 594
25:8 677
26:20 404
26:21 649
29:30 110
30:21–23 549
35:15 245
36:17 497

Ezra

3:6–12 633
6:2–3 634
6:22 579
7:6 52n1, 542
7:10 134, 198
7:12 194n9
7:28 542
8:31 542
9 124, 528, 640

Nehemiah

1:3 522
1:5–11 526
2–4 528
2:5 668
2:17 522, 668
3:25 702
4 217, 403, 573
4:4 217
4:17 551
6 217
9 124, 528, 640
9:1 131
9:6 672
9:11 432
9:11–12 491
9:15 491

9:25 497
11:17 461n19
12:27–43 91

Esther

7:10 524

Job

1:6 203
1:21 694
2:10 151
3:11–19 649
3:16 207
5:1 671
5:3 532n3
7:16 498
9:13 636
9:25–26 176
10:21–22 650
11:13 134
11:20 589
14:15 589
15:15 671
17:5 589
18:14 410
20:6 648
20:12 295n33
21:25 459n6
23:4 119
23:8–9 84
24:1 555
24:3 316
24:8 703
24:20 576
26:12 636
27:1 485
27:12 251
27:15 510
28:22 654
29:1 485
29:6 208
29:12 389
31:2 513n79
31:8 145
31:9 499
31:12 145, 654
31:40 396n3
33:2 484
34:9 109n8
38:2 349

38:12–13 598
40:15 412
40:15–24 331
40:16 350
40:21 331
41:22 444
42:8 151
42:10 155

Psalms

1 97, 402, 418, 691
1–2 417, 418, 419, 691
1–41 22
1:1 103
1:2 377, 468
1:3 68
1:5 104
1:6 120, 695
2 58, 63, 88n23, 213, 221, 418, 452, 573, 581, 584, 678, 679, 691, 691n57
2:1 143, 217
2:1–2 267
2:2 88, 88n23, 677
2:4 44, 145, 217
2:5 88
2:7 220, 264n6, 337n11, 542, 567, 637
2:8 217, 221, 506n72
2:9 53n7, 681
2:11 88
3–41 396
3:3 248
3:4 278, 462
3:5 135, 195
3:6 96
3:7 312
4 184
4:1 225n10, 278
4:5 139
4:6 189, 675, 701
4:8 195
5:2 591
5:3 222
5:5 403n33
5:6 178, 696

5:8 413, 706
5:9 144n9
5:10 703
5:11 355
5:13 523
6:2 132
6:2–3 583
6:3 246n15, 523
6:5 654
6:6 340, 462
6:8–9 508
6:9 699
6:10 410, 435
6:11 705
6:13 705
7:1 120
7:2 119
7:4 164n8
7:5 414
7:6 48, 199, 216, 312
7:7 325, 443
7:9 46, 194n9, 411
7:11 141n1
7:12 136, 202n7
7:15 197
7:15–16 197n18
7:17 278
8 103, 548
8:2 44
8:3 523
8:4 216, 541
8:5 523
8:8 590
9 67, 83n6, 365
9–10 21, 665
9:3 187
9:4 278
9:5 308n33
9:8 278
9:9 434, 700
9:10 695
9:11 285n3
9:13 48
9:15 197, 197n18, 219, 340
9:18 700
9:20 96, 695
10 365
10:2 333
10:4 498

10:5 184n15, 443
10:6 379n1, 699
10:7 296n33
10:9 197, 451
10:12 430
10:14 389
10:17 475n3
10:18 434
11:1 170, 590
11:3 443, 566
11:4 702
11:5 46
12 159, 665
12:1 194n9
12:2 546n6
13 425
13:1 48, 324, 522, 687
13:1–2 246
13:2 675
14 150, 150n7, 151n12, 154
14:1 149n1
14:4 472n43, 695
14:6 413
15:1 239, 277
16 159, 700
16:1 368
16:4 501
16:7 411
16:9 192n4
16:9–10 257
16:10 105, 695
17:1 237
17:3 46, 216, 292
17:5 699
17:8 239, 704
17:9 335n11
17:10 405
17:12 119, 589
17:13 218
18 78n14, 310n43, 663
18:2 700
18:3 85n13
18:3–6 42
18:5 105, 218, 626
18:6 330, 425, 702
18:7 67
18:7–15 112, 316, 468, 470

18:8 536
18:10 316n61, 535
18:13 70
18:16 105, 325, 339, 406, 413n58, 443, 471
18:16–17 341
18:17 215
18:18 218
18:27 445
18:28 434
18:30 466, 471
18:35 52n4
18:41 585
18:43 286
18:46 196, 297
18:47 74n2
19:5 143
19:7 114
19:13 157n2
19:14 484
20 309, 381
20:1 70, 162, 278, 700
20:2 307n22, 676
20:4 413
20:6 278
21 196, 309
21:2 496
21:3 218
21:4 240
21:5 676n38
21:9 144, 170
22 34, 256, 352, 366, 367, 371, 372, 425, 684, 690, 694
22:2 462
22:3–10 367
22:4–5 100
22:7 546n6
22:10 177, 367n15
22:12 331
22:13 119
22:15 49
22:16 331
22:17 158n5, 162
22:19 372, 648
22:20 120
22:22 671

22:24 354
22:25 239, 671, 703
22:27 136
22:30–31 375
23 425, 534
23:1 104, 534
23:2 434, 580
23:3 232
23:4 46, 53n7, 681
23:5 293
24 76
24:1–2 633
24:2 68, 513, 638
24:3–5 408
24:3–6 408
24:4 622
24:5 300
24:7–10 700
24:12 39
25:3 408
25:4 374, 695
25:7 525
25:8 401
25:10 32, 45
25:16 628
25:18 48, 404
26 159
26:2 292, 411
26:5 671
26:7 220
26:8 69, 369
26:9 607
27 309, 665
27:1 675, 701
27:2 347
27:4 257, 702
27:4–6 238, 239
27:5–6 25
27:11 232, 706
27:12 257
27:13 145, 292, 444
28 574
28:2 46, 463
28:6 297, 508
28:7–8 215, 218
28:8 705
28:9 104, 321, 534
29 70, 279, 549n26

29:1 74n3, 332n95, 671
29:2 696
29:3 339
29:9 702
30:3 105, 626
30:5 104, 221, 222
30:6 667, 699
30:6–7 292
30:9 695
30:10 389
30:11–12 625
31 366, 367
31:1–3 367
31:1–4 703
31:2 347, 369, 705
31:3 413
31:4 705
31:7 48, 695
31:11 370n20
31:15 555
31:18 333, 404, 438n4, 444
31:21 297
31:23 333, 404
31:24 706
32 135
32:1 606, 703
32:1–2 699
32:2 144
32:5 351, 697, 703
32:6 339, 406, 471
33 365
33:4 185
33:5 466
33:6 695
33:8 270
33:10–11 413
33:11 379n1
33:12 699
33:13–14 541
33:16 120, 594n31, 677
33:16–17 233
33:18 706
33:20 700
33:22 706
34 183
34–42 21
34:2 100, 143
34:8 401, 699

34:10 202n6
34:11 136
34:16 698
34:17 646
34:18 441
34:22 355
35 159
35:1 435
35:2 232, 372
35:4 187, 359
35:5 182n11
35:6 103, 434
35:7–8 197
35:8 261n25
35:10 672n29
35:13 645
35:13–14 345
35:14 25, 49
35:18 671
35:22 112, 372
35:23 48, 48n25, 216, 511
35:24 278
35:25 144, 170
35:26 44
35:28 259, 278
36:5 200, 466
36:7 239, 704
36:7–9 701
36:9 329
36:10 609, 636
36:11 333
36:12 182n11
37 97, 155, 419
37:1 403
37:10 151
37:13 145
37:14 120, 165n11
37:17 135
37:18 695
37:21 57
37:22 248
37:24 135, 430
37:26 57, 141n1
37:35–36 464
37:39 705
38 124, 358, 366, 371, 373
38:1 38
38:3 132
38:5 342

38:6 25, 49
38:8 132
38:12 358, 359
38:15 706
38:21 371
38:21–22 372
38:22 358
39 246, 461n19, 464
39:1 667
39:1–2 246
39:2 245n12
39:4–7 250
39:7 700
39:8 526
39:12 239, 537
39:13 151
40 358, 361, 362n6, 366
40:2 335n2
40:2–3 137
40:3 270
40:4 699, 705
40:5 220, 464
40:9 671
40:10 671
40:10–11 32
40:13 39, 359
40:13–17 358
40:14 187, 359
40:15 360
40:16 360
40:17 360, 360n4
41 395, 693
41:1 699, 703
41:9 100, 164n8
41:12 260
42 21, 30, 365, 588
42–43 19–34, 37, 165, 245, 247, 320n70, 465, 587, 588, 627n28, 644, 690, 694
42–49 701
42–72 396, 383
42–83 22, 150n7, 206, 469, 584
42–89 11
42:1 32, 38
42:1–2 33

42:1–5 22–26
42:1–6 702
42:2 22, 31, 32,
    254n2, 256, 257,
    590, 595n34,
    698
42:3 462, 526, 537
42:4 32, 33, 249
42:5 33, 37, 38, 49,
    173, 198, 463,
    465, 592n22,
    697, 698, 706
42:6 38, 49
42:6–8 465
42:6–11 26–30
42:7 339
42:8 31, 32, 369,
    462, 697
42:9 21, 31, 32, 38,
    48, 706
42:10 38, 526, 689
42:11 20, 21, 22,
    33, 37, 38, 49,
    173, 198, 463,
    465, 592n22,
    697, 698, 706
43 21, 30, 365, 587
43:1 33, 435, 696,
    707
43:1–5 30–33
43:2 21, 32, 37, 38,
    48, 705, 706
43:3 28, 69, 69n14,
    171, 195, 241,
    369, 413,
    496n53, 505,
    525, 586n1, 613,
    678, 697, 701
43:4 22, 697
43:5 20, 22, 33,
    37, 38, 49, 173,
    198, 463, 465,
    592n22, 697,
    706
44 35–51, 89, 225,
    228, 423, 441,
    460, 525, 537,
    539, 540, 543,
    605, 608, 610,
    615, 616, 663,
    664, 690

44–70 21
44:1 89, 92, 220,
    426, 431, 440,
    441, 485
44:1–3 38–40, 538,
    606
44:1–8 460, 539
44:2 430, 468, 538
44:3 189, 465, 579,
    580, 606, 673,
    675, 698, 701
44:4 37, 369, 430,
    591, 698
44:4–8 40–41, 616
44:5 441, 702
44:6 698, 705
44:7 698
44:8 415, 697, 702,
    703
44:9 37, 227, 465
44:9–16 41–44, 539
44:10 187, 531n2
44:13 38, 435, 456,
    522, 685
44:13–14 348
44:13–16 689
44:14 192n6, 345,
    537
44:15 141n1
44:17 697
44:17–22 44–47,
    296
44:18 543, 700
44:19 132, 434
44:20 553, 702
44:21 700
44:23 37, 199,
    216, 324, 425,
    425n36, 465,
    511, 535, 701,
    706
44:23–24 540
44:23–26 47–49,
    411
44:24 38, 656, 698,
    706
44:25 38
44:26 435, 569,
    697, 700, 703
45 52–63, 484,
    531n1, 701

45:1 55, 699
45:2 415, 699, 707
45:2–9 56–59
45:3 143
45:7 695, 697
45:9 412n53
45:10 484, 700
45:10–13 60–61
45:11 696
45:12 488n46
45:13–18 61–62
45:14 308n32
45:17 379n1, 697,
    702
46 30, 64–73, 76,
    83, 83n6, 84,
    279, 281, 309,
    449, 449n14,
    452, 533, 573,
    587, 632, 638
46–48 449, 450
46:1 38, 218, 700,
    703, 705
46:1–3 67–68
46:3 78, 217, 333,
    339, 406, 463,
    575
46:4 86, 272n4,
    635, 702
46:4–7 68–70
46:5 222, 700
46:6 217, 332,
    438n3, 443, 463,
    575
46:7 218, 695, 700,
    701
46:8 290
46:8–11 71–72
46:9 450, 452
46:10 575
46:11 218, 695,
    700, 701
47 74–81, 83, 84,
    450
47:1 38, 98, 548,
    549n23, 704,
    705
47:1–5 77–79
47:2 87, 591, 702,
    704
47:4 321, 703

47:5 325n82, 705
47:6 591, 697
47:6–9 79–81
47:7 591, 697
47:9 135, 325n82,
    596, 676
48 66, 82–94,
    88n23, 93, 111,
    309, 449n14,
    450, 452, 587,
    595, 632, 638
48:1 38, 68
48:1–2 85–87
48:2 111, 591
48:3–8 87–90
48:5 583
48:7 495
48:8 68, 71, 324,
    464, 695
48:9 697, 702
48:9–11 90–91
48:11 696
48:12–14 91–92
48:13 220, 594,
    594n31, 700
49 83n6, 95–107,
    110, 111, 155,
    414, 419, 479,
    482, 484, 688
49:1 484
49:1–4 98–100
49:2 250n25, 567
49:3 412n53, 700
49:4 485
49:5 696, 706
49:5–9 100–101
49:6 143, 594n31,
    703
49:7–8 703
49:9 592n22, 695
49:10 487, 594n31,
    611
49:10–12 101–3
49:11 379n1
49:13 120, 487,
    611
49:13–15 103–5
49:14 222
49:14–15 705
49:15 413n58, 703
49:16–17 414, 700

49:16–20 105–6
49:18 697
50 99, 108–21,
    125, 129, 139,
    142, 203,
    211–23, 244,
    479, 547,
    549n26, 696
50:1–6 111–13
50:2 535
50:4–5 611
50:5 148, 522, 669,
    697
50:7 552
50:7–15 113–16
50:8 128, 137, 139
50:8–10 287
50:10 517n1
50:14 239, 703
50:15 679
50:16 697
50:16–21 117–19
50:17 695
50:19 696
50:22 704
50:22–23 119–20,
    456
51 122–40, 143,
    184, 354
51–72 396
51:1 12, 525, 697,
    699, 703
51:1–2 126–27, 627
51:2 706
51:3 703
51:3–6 127–30
51:4 583n28, 696
51:5 706
51:6 705
51:7–9 130–32
51:9 698, 706
51:10 700
51:10–12 132–35
51:12 161, 320
51:13 703
51:13–15 135–37
51:14 526, 704
51:15 464, 701
51:16 115
51:16–17 39

51:16–19 137–39,
    353
51:17 354, 700
51:18 354
51:19 706
52 141–48, 150,
    153, 202
52–54 158
52:1 143, 696, 697,
    703, 706
52:2 213
52:2–4 143–44
52:3 696, 699
52:3–4 697
52:4 170
52:5 292
52:5–7 144–46
52:6 270
52:7 705
52:7–8 705
52:8 705
52:8–9 146–47, 155
52:9 158n8, 415,
    697, 699, 702
53 22, 149–56,
    158, 158n8, 645,
    698
53:1 433, 699, 700,
    707
53:1–4 151–54
53:3 507, 543, 699
53:4 679, 699
53:5 154, 509
53:6 155, 412n53,
    536, 606n12
54 151, 157–62,
    188, 574, 627,
    705
54:1 441, 702
54:1–3 159–60
54:2 484, 536
54:3 359, 626
54:4 305n3, 701
54:4–5 160–61
54:5 416, 696, 706
54:6 135, 147, 699,
    702
54:6–7 161–62
54:7 218n17, 464,
    704

55 163–80, 182,
    183, 188, 193,
    574, 705
55:1 536
55:1–8 167–70
55:2 266
55:4 700
55:9 701, 706
55:9–14 170–73
55:11 191n1
55:15 173, 207,
    696, 705
55:16–21 173–77
55:17 463
55:18 331, 703,
    706
55:19 431
55:20 337n10, 681,
    697, 706
55:21 331, 700
55:22 185
55:22–23 177–79
55:23 219, 346,
    695, 696
56 181–90, 193,
    194, 201n1, 574,
    698
56–60 700
56:1 699
56:1–2 166, 174,
    193, 195
56:1–4 183–85
56:2 193, 443n18,
    706
56:3–4 705
56:4 501, 705
56:5 696
56:5–11 185–88
56:6 211
56:7 219
56:8 537
56:9 642n2
56:11 705
56:12 239, 703
56:12–13 188–89
56:13 241, 292,
    701, 704
57 191–200, 698
57–59 698
57:1 216, 239, 699,
    704

57:1–5 193–96
57:2 466
57:3 241, 505, 525,
    613, 705
57:3–4 184
57:4 213, 702
57:6–11 197–200
57:7 134, 700
57:8 701
57:9 187n19, 701
57:10 466, 705
58 201–10, 559,
    698
58:1 696
58:1–2 203–4
58:2 265n7, 558n2,
    700, 706, 707
58:3–5 204–5
58:4 172n31
58:6 145, 206
58:7 264n2
58:7–9 206–7
58:10 328n89, 527
58:10–11 208–9
59 211–23, 574,
    698
59:1 700
59:1–2 704
59:1–4 214–15
59:2 696, 699
59:4 199, 535, 541,
    596
59:4–7 215–17
59:5 281, 296, 408,
    511, 541, 681,
    696
59:6 463
59:7 196, 196n14
59:8 44, 145
59:8–10 217–18
59:9 246, 700, 705
59:10 525, 706
59:11 233, 594n31,
    701
59:11–15 218–21
59:14 463
59:14–15 221–22
59:16 246, 700,
    704, 705
59:16–17 222–23

59:17 246, 700, 705
60 224–34, 440, 665, 697, 701
60:1 292, 465, 685
60:1–5 226–29
60:2 246
60:3 445
60:4 671
60:5 278, 589
60:6 307n22
60:6–9 229–32
60:8 705
60:9 238
60:10 465
60:10–12 232–34
60:11 246
60:12 594n31
61 235–42, 255, 262, 269, 574, 705
61:1 266, 536, 704
61:1–3 237–38
61:2 246, 415, 697, 700
61:3 703, 705
61:4 415
61:4–5 238–40
61:5 671, 702, 703
61:6–7 240–41
61:7 415, 613
61:8 241, 326, 702, 703
62 243–53, 255, 274, 461
62:1–3 245–47
62:2 661n4, 697, 700
62:3 182n11
62:3–7 247–49
62:4 106
62:5 700
62:6 697, 700
62:6–7 218
62:7 697, 700, 705
62:7–8 703
62:8 700
62:8–10 249–51, 705
62:9 567

62:10 405, 594n31, 700
62:11 705
62:11–12 222, 251–53
62:12 701
63 254–63, 265, 269, 273
63:1 498n59, 590
63:1–4 256–58
63:2 409, 700, 705
63:3 699
63:5 272n12, 648, 702
63:5–8 258–60
63:6 99, 468
63:7 704
63:9 359, 626
63:9–11 260–62
63:11 143, 270, 699
64 255, 264–71, 574
64:1–6 266–68
64:2 699
64:3 196, 213
64:5 696
64:6 700, 707
64:7–9 268–70
64:9 374
64:10 143, 270, 700
65 255, 272–84, 288, 291, 299, 300, 320
65–66 301
65–68 274
65:1 703
65:1–3 274–76
65:2 536
65:3 500, 526
65:4 64n3, 416, 589, 648, 699, 702
65:4–5 276–78
65:5 289, 646, 705
65:5–8 278–80
65:6 701
65:9 68, 216, 306n12, 406, 541

65:9–13 280–83
65:11 699
65:12 385, 580
66 285–97, 299, 300, 326, 355, 704
66:1 354, 548, 705
66:1–4 288–89
66:2 697, 700
66:3 546n12, 705
66:4 354, 696
66:5 71, 89, 704
66:5–7 290–91
66:6 432, 656
66:7 72, 317
66:8 707
66:8–12 291–93
66:12 406
66:13 703
66:13–15 293–95
66:16 464, 671
66:16–20 295–97
66:18 700, 701
66:19 508
66:19–20 536, 702
66:20 326, 707
67 275, 278, 298–304, 320, 704, 705
67:1 536, 698, 707
67:1–2 300–301
67:3 670
67:3–5 301–2
67:4 413, 696, 704
67:5 670
67:6 707
67:6–7 302–3
67:7 270, 707
68 305–34, 701, 704
68:1–3 312–14
68:1–8 698
68:4 592n26, 697
68:4–6 315–17
68:5 564
68:6 354
68:7–10 317–21
68:9 426, 449n9, 475n5, 520, 703
68:10 699, 706
68:11–14 321–23

68:15–18 323–26
68:16 706
68:18 426, 443
68:19 646, 707
68:19–23 326–28
68:21 342
68:22 340
68:24 430, 591
68:24–27 328–30
68:25 548
68:26 707
68:28 705
68:28–31 330–32
68:29 702
68:30 495
68:32 697
68:32–35 332–33
68:33 70, 431
68:33–35 705
68:34 404
68:35 399n16, 707
69 335–56, 358, 359, 367, 574, 701
69:1 406
69:1–5 339–42
69:2 406, 493, 650
69:3 589, 651, 706
69:4 416, 474n1, 695, 699
69:5 576
69:6 342, 358, 367, 701
69:6–10 358
69:7 695
69:7–12 342–45
69:9 403, 689
69:12 465, 705
69:13 361
69:13–18 345–47
69:14 358, 406, 695, 704
69:15 406, 650
69:16 628, 699
69:17 358, 525, 656, 698
69:18 703, 704
69:19 44, 367
69:19–20 358
69:19–21 347–49
69:20 376, 700

69:22 164n8, 411,
    706
69:22–29 349–52
69:25 578
69:29 358, 700
69:30–36 352–55
69:32 358, 700,
    704
69:33 358, 702
69:35 668
69:36 358, 697
70 357–62, 365,
    366, 367, 372,
    574
70:1 359, 365, 372,
    389, 704
70:2 187, 359, 365,
    367, 372, 373,
    373n26, 377,
    696
70:3 359–60, 367,
    435
70:4 360
70:5 360–61, 365,
    367, 700, 702
71 358, 363–78,
    519, 618, 644
71:1–8 367–70
71:2 389, 704
71:3 368, 415, 499,
    697
71:4 591, 707
71:5 700, 701, 705
71:6 367n15
71:7 705
71:8 675
71:9 589
71:9–16 371–74
71:11 704
71:12 591
71:13 687, 696
71:14 706
71:16 583n28, 701
71:17 707
71:17–24 374–77
71:19 672n29
71:20 696
71:21 463, 629
71:22 502, 676,
    697, 701, 705
71:23 703, 704

71:24 696
72 379–96, 417,
    431, 691,
    691n57, 693
72–75 449
72:1 696
72:1–7 383–87
72:2 696
72:3 706
72:4 405, 696, 698,
    702
72:7 706
72:8–14 387–91
72:9 196n14
72:11 696
72:12 655, 700,
    702, 704
72:13 564, 698,
    702, 703
72:14 704, 706
72:15 326, 702
72:15–17 391–93
72:17 702
72:18 583n28, 707
72:18–20 395–96
72:19 700, 707
73 155, 397–419,
    422, 423, 440,
    461, 700
73–83 110, 696
73–88 691
73–89 693
73:1 401, 699
73:2–3 402–3
73:3 440, 443
73:4–12 403–7
73:6 706
73:8 184n15, 696
73:12 594n31, 683
73:13–14 407–8
73:15–20 408–11
73:17 702
73:18 420n1, 423
73:20 511, 701
73:21–26 411–15
73:23 430
73:24 440n10, 700
73:26 421n9, 499,
    589, 683, 697
73:27–28 415–17
73:28 699, 701

74 420–37, 440,
    442, 460, 460n8,
    466, 518, 519n6,
    646
74–89 400
74:1 465, 536n18,
    706
74:1–3 424–27
74:2 499, 506,
    520n14, 634,
    702, 704
74:3 399n19, 410
74:4 440, 520
74:4–9 427–29
74:5–6 468
74:6 406
74:7 681, 702
74:8 700
74:9 89, 442n16,
    466, 592n22
74:10 536, 563,
    689, 702
74:10–11 429–30
74:11 462, 706
74:12 591
74:12–17 430–33,
    460
74:13 673, 705
74:13–15 68
74:14 43, 380n6,
    388, 468
74:15 491, 493
74:16 443
74:18 702
74:18–23 433–36,
    706
74:20 697, 706
74:21 702
74:22 569, 702
75 438–47, 698
75:1 441, 697
75:2 455, 696
75:2–5 441–44
75:3 566
75:4 403
75:4–5 675
75:6–8 455
75:6–10 444–46
75:8 406, 463
75:9 701
75:10 675

76 84, 440,
    448–57, 587,
    705
76:1–3 450–52
76:4–6 452–53
76:5 331, 495,
    594n31, 700
76:6 542, 701
76:7 704
76:7–9 453–55
76:8 704
76:9 569, 696
76:10–12 455–56
76:11 704
76:12 704
77 458–73, 485
77:1 646
77:1–3 461–63
77:2 376, 701, 702,
    704
77:3 499
77:4–6 463–65
77:5 426, 431
77:6 499, 705
77:7 425n36,
    592n22, 701
77:7–9 465–66
77:8 194n9, 425
77:8–9 627
77:9 525
77:10 483, 541
77:10–12 467–68
77:11 426, 431,
    483, 490, 499,
    670, 707
77:11–12 259
77:13–20 39, 427,
    468–72, 483
77:14 483, 490,
    670, 705, 707
77:14–15 673
77:15 426, 483,
    499, 550, 579,
    704
77:16 475n5
77:16–19 483
77:18 552, 581n23
77:19 690
77:20 302, 483,
    505

78 468, 474–516, 532, 533, 534, 543, 547, 552, 663, 700
78:1–8 484–87
78:2 431
78:3 89, 441
78:4 441, 576
78:5 697
78:8 700, 705
78:9–11 487–89
78:10 697
78:11 441
78:12 441, 468, 670, 707
78:12–16 489–91
78:14 302
78:15 415, 661n4
78:17 592n22
78:17–20 491–93
78:18 702
78:20 415
78:21–31 493–97
78:22 705
78:26 705
78:29 222, 648
78:32 441, 705
78:32–37 497–500
78:34 704
78:35 697
78:37 134, 697, 700, 705
78:38 523, 526, 532n5, 535, 608n13, 627
78:38–39 500–501
78:40–43 501–2
78:41 376
78:42 703
78:43 280, 370
78:44–55 502–7
78:49 657, 696
78:52 472, 534, 538
78:53 302, 607
78:54 426, 541
78:55 426, 538
78:56–58 507–8
78:57 543
78:58 403, 523, 609

78:59–64 508–10
78:61 675, 705
78:62 426, 520n14
78:65 48, 535
78:65–72 510–14
78:66 522
78:67–68 634
78:69 633
78:71 426
78:72 302
79 436n61, 517–30, 533, 534, 540, 618, 646
79:1 702
79:1–4 520–22
79:2 43, 109n5
79:4 44, 435, 456
79:5 403, 425, 429, 687
79:5–7 522–24
79:6 350
79:7 350
79:8 337n8, 347
79:8–10 524–27
79:9 646, 700, 704
79:10 47
79:10–12 527–29
79:11 567, 579
79:12 435, 689
79:13 529
80 436n61, 531–44, 547, 574, 595, 644, 697, 701
80:1 472, 484, 505
80:1–2 112
80:1–3 534–36
80:3 609n15, 698
80:4 425, 429, 687, 696
80:4–7 536–38
80:7 695, 698
80:8 505
80:8–11 35n2
80:8–13 538–40
80:10 562
80:11 68
80:12 706
80:13 115n21

80:14 216, 596, 695
80:14–19 540–43
80:15 678
80:17 678
80:18 507, 610
80:18–19 609
80:19 696, 698
81 480, 545–57, 588, 665
81:1 701, 704, 705
81:1–5 548–50
81:2 701
81:4 696, 701
81:5 486, 559, 697
81:5–12 550–54
81:9 696
81:12 700
81:13–16 554–56
81:16 415, 648
82 202, 203, 501, 549n26, 558–70, 574, 671
82:1 469n37, 560–62, 624n19, 670, 696
82:2 536, 696, 707
82:2–5 562–66
82:3 696, 698
82:3–4 703
82:4 704
82:5 443
82:6–7 566–68
82:8 568–69, 696
83 565, 568, 571–85, 587n8, 632, 646
83:1 574
83:2 463
83:2–4 575–76
83:4 592n22
83:5 697
83:5–8 576–79, 636
83:6–7 598
83:9–11 579–80
83:12 434
83:12–15 580–82
83:13 591
83:16–18 582–84
84 548, 586–602
84–85 587, 701

84:1 695
84:1–3 32
84:1–4 588–92
84:2 23, 257, 700
84:3 430, 695
84:5 628, 705
84:5–7 592–95
84:6 632n6
84:8 696, 701
84:8–9 595–97
84:9 240, 676
84:10 145n11, 444, 578, 699
84:10–12 597–600
84:11 612, 614, 629, 676, 699, 700
84:11–12 699
84:12 695, 705
85 587n8, 603–16, 620, 628
85:1 39, 155n16, 465
85:1–3 605–8
85:2 622
85:3 628
85:4 541n29, 646
85:4–7 608–10
85:5 628
85:8 610–11, 621, 697, 706
85:8–9 636
85:9 441, 671, 700
85:9–13 611–15
85:10 706
85:10–13 278
85:12 629, 699
86 396, 574, 617–30, 646
86:1 702
86:1–3 312–14
86:1–7 620–23
86:2 591, 705
86:5 401, 679, 699
86:7 679
86:8 561
86:8–10 623–24, 632
86:9 696
86:10 583n28, 707
86:11–13 624–26

86:13 650, 704, 705
86:14 157n2
86:14–17 626–29
86:16 705
86:17 376, 463, 695
87 620, 631–41
87–88 587, 701
87:1 673
87:1–3 633–35
87:2 512
87:3 68, 86
87:4 635–37, 672, 688
87:5–7 637–40
88 30, 436, 574, 642–59, 663, 664, 666, 684, 687, 690, 691, 692
88:1–9 646–51
88:2 704
88:3 696
88:3–12 705
88:4 695
88:5 592n22, 673
88:6 340, 695
88:7 27
88:9 679
88:9–12 651–55
88:10 707
88:11 705
88:12 707
88:13–18 655–58
88:14 465, 706
89 30, 395, 434, 460, 568, 660–92, 691n57, 694
89:1 705
89:1–4 666–70
89:1–37 41, 460
89:2 466
89:3 697
89:5 561n15, 707
89:5–14 670–74
89:6 567
89:7 456, 560
89:8 695

89:10 386, 579, 636, 705
89:11 513, 633
89:12 324, 704
89:13 579
89:14 696
89:15–18 674–76, 701, 705
89:16 116
89:17 443, 705
89:18 376, 591
89:19 143
89:19–27 676–80
89:20 59
89:21 579
89:22 645, 707
89:24 443, 697
89:26 542, 623, 652, 697
89:27 639n34, 702
89:28–37 680–84
89:30 696, 697
89:32 216
89:33 609, 656
89:35 229
89:38 465
89:38–45 684–87
89:39 434, 697
89:46 425, 429, 522, 523
89:46–51 687–90
89:47 233
89:49 705
89:50–51 528
89:52 693–94
90 687, 691, 691n59
90:1 369
90:7 589
90:13 523, 541
90:14 104, 655
90:15–16 89
91:1 323
91:4 704
91:9 369
91:10 404
91:11 369
92:6 487
92:8 443
93 76
93:1 672

93:2 81, 198
93:3 491
93:4 443, 452
94 549n26
94:1 208
94:1–2 112
94:4 438n4, 444
94:5 386
94:8 487
94:21 181
94:23 416
95 75, 480, 547, 550, 551, 665
95:1 71, 679
95:2 698
95:3 561
95:6 698
95:7 551
95:9 507
96 309, 666
96–99 76
96:2 326
96:4 85n13, 561
96:6 675
96:11 354
97 691, 694
97:4 470, 471n41
97:7 561
97:9 561
97:10 372
97:10–11 701
98 309, 666
98:1 469
98:2 469
98:6 549
99:1 535
100 75, 521
100:3 529
100:5 401, 466
101 666
101:8 446
102 249
102:2 347
102:7 590
102:13 442
102:16 595
102:19 541
102:19–20 152
102:20 527
102:25–26 513
102:26–27 175

103:7 136
103:21 695
104:5 513, 699
104:7 542
104:9 432
104:18 703
104:22 451
104:29 583, 607
104:33 666
105 482n38
105–7 479
105:5 370
105:11 478n15
105:20 518n3
105:27 272n2, 280, 370, 502
105:36 505
105:40 221
105:41 491
106 395, 693
106:4 216, 541
106:7 666
106:9 453
106:14 61
106:16 403
106:17 346
106:21 375
106:39 416
106:45 666
107:6 646
107:9 221, 554
107:10 434, 566
107:14 434, 566
107:27 25
107:28 646
107:30 413
108 226, 287
108:1–5 193
108:6 224n6
108:9 225n8
109 574
109:2 177
109:14 127
109:29 44
109:31 413
110 452
110:1 542
110:2 387
111:5 434
111:9 434
112:1–3 699

112:7 134
113:3 85n13
114:1 469
114:3 290
114:5 290
114:8 491
115:2 526, 526n22
118 293
118:7 157n3
118:13 676
118:14 316
118:15 578
119 479, 663
119:57 415
119:62 462
119:70 405
119:74 147
119:81 147
119:82 651
119:108 115
119:114 147
119:123 651
119:132 355
119:139 344, 403
119:147 147
119:150 347, 416
119:152 47, 633
119:154 435
119:169 416
120–34 588,
    592n26
120:2 546n6
120:5 578
120:6 246n14
120:7 164n8
121 48
121:4 48
121:5 413
121:6 598
122 639
122:8 635
123:3–4 648
123:4 246n14
124:2 634
124:6 452
124:7 590
124:8 441, 700
126 605, 615
127 382
127:2 501
128 699

129:1 246n14
129:2 246n14
130:3 130
130:6 218
132 314, 513, 691
132:2 495n51
132:3 145n11
132:5 495n51
132:8 510
132:11 392
132:13 512
133:2 59
133:3 634
134:1 462
135 309
135:9 280
135:21 426
136 466
136:5 514
136:15 594n31
137 520
137:3 84
137:8 61n28
138–45 396
138:1 203
138:2 702
138:3 642n2
138:8 194, 195n9,
    466, 653
139:1 46
139:7–12 84
139:10 413
139:11–12 434
139:13 411
139:15 261n26
139:23 46
140:3 295
141:3 464n23
142:2 249
142:5 415
142:6 525
143:2 130
143:5 259
143:6 256n12, 463
143:7 347
143:8 655
144:3–4 688
144:7 471
144:13 595n32
144:15 699
145:2 326

145:3 85n13
145:4 374
145:5 272n2
145:11 464
145:14 135
145:17 136
145:18 441
145:21 464
147:3 501
147:6 445
147:10–11 39
148 354
148:2 695
148:10 590
148:13 583n28
148:14 416
149:4 39, 706
150:1 229
150:3 549n23

Proverbs

1:2–8 117
1:4 575
1:6 485
1:10 499
1:23 484
1:24 463
2:2 99
2:4 465
2:13 566
2:18 653
2:22 145
3:1 484
3:12 606
3:13 99
3:19 99, 638
3:31 403
4:2 484
5:3–4 196
5:11 415
5:16 639
6:3 308n36
6:34 403
7:17 59
8:5 575
8:8 484
8:12 575
10:12 607
12:14 158n4
12:19 546n6
13:1 103

14:30 403
14:31 128
15:5 575
15:11 653, 654
16:4 52n4
16:15 675
16:16–19 252
16:29 499
16:33 506
17:4 546n6
17:7 546n6
18:4 268
19:2 698
19:25 575
20:5 268
20:9 130
20:22 383
22:11 57
22:29 52n1
23:4–5 179
23:17 403
24:1 403
24:19 403
24:28 499
26:2 590
26:25 57
26:27 197n18
27:4 403
27:27 258
29:23 414n62
30:15–31 252
31:26 484

Ecclesiastes

1:3 404
2:14 566
6:3–5 207
6:12 498
7:6 207
7:15 498
7:20 130
7:24 268
9:1–10 655
9:9 498
9:12 555
10:12 57

Song of Songs

1:15 53n6
1:16 56

2:1 701
2:2 701
2:14 169
2:16 701
4:1 53n6
4:5 701
4:11 295
4:12 639
4:14 59
4:15 639
5:12 53n6
5:13 701
6:2 701
6:3 701
7:2 701
8:6 316
8:6–7 523

Isaiah

1:2 112
1:2–3 550
1:3 566n30
1:4 152
1:10 484
1:11 287
1:12 23n9
1:15–16 407
1:18 131
1:20 489
1:25 292
2:2 634, 638
2:2–4 66, 632, 640
2:6–22 582
2:11–17 445
2:18 175
3:10–11 209
3:12 484
3:13 454, 562
4:4 136
5:1 229
5:1–7 540
5:5 540
5:8 431n47
5:13 484
5:15 445
5:24 581
5:25 498, 608
5:26 70, 520
5:27 453
5:29 186, 452
6 561

6:5 276
6:8 563
6:9 566n30
6:12 431n47
7:22 431n47
8:1–4 453
8:1–9:21 179
8:12–13 449n10
8:13 671
9:1 329
9:7 523
9:12 498
9:17 498
9:21 498
10:2 484
10:5 681
10:5–19 527
10:6 453
10:23 431n47
10:33 445
11:12 228
12:2 316
12:3 639
13:4 70
13:6 323
13:11 445
13:21–22 388
14:3 228
14:9 653
14:12–14 671
14:12–15 435
14:25 634
14:26 70, 520
14:30 455
14:31 635
14:32 633, 634
17:12 575
17:12–14 573, 584
17:13 581, 582
19:1 316
19:3 170
19:11 490
19:13 490
19:18–25 636, 640
19:24 431
20:3–5 331
24:13 431
24:18 494
24:21 210, 570, 672
25:5 697

25:11–12 445
26:4 316
26:5 445
26:10 216
27:6 532n3
27:11 216
28:23 484
29:15 349
29:23 671
30:4 490
30:7 636
30:11 317
30:27 441
30:28 70
31:3 185, 188, 501
31:4 452
33:12 542
33:21 69
34:13 46
34:13–14 388
35:6 491
36–37 429, 435, 522, 524, 537, 577, 584
36:10 427
37:4 455
37:16 535
37:23 524
37:32 455, 523
38:9–20 700
38:11 316
38:15 25n12
40–55 44, 583, 616, 616n29, 638, 692
40–66 355, 605, 610, 614, 616, 688
40:1 561
40:2 351
40:8 682
40:9 306n15
40:12 537
40:15 217
40:18 671
40:28–31 601
41:2 615, 666
41:9 679
41:9–12 629
41:10 67, 189
41:11–12 410

41:13 67, 189, 413
41:14 67, 189, 390
42:4 389, 640
42:5 610
42:6 679
42:11 315n59
42:13 48, 48n25, 523
42:13–14 574
42:15 350
43:1–5 189
43:2 293, 657
43:3 331
43:12 46, 553
44:5 640
44:18 566n30
44:22 526
44:26 355
45:1 350, 413
45:8 614
45:14 331
45:23 682, 683
46:1–3 326
46:13 509
47:5 70
48:21 491
49:2 196
49:7 662n10
49:8 345, 355
49:21 297
50:8 562
50:11 452
51 612
51:5 612
51:9 46, 432, 636
51:9–11 670
51:17 228, 406
51:22 228
52:1 520
52:7 81, 614
52:7–10 615
53 351
53:3–5 351
53:6 351
54 638
54:3 355
54:4 522
54:12 599n50
54:17 355
55 692, 694
55:3 484

55:3–5 263,
    691n61, 692
55:12 283
56 612
56:1 612
57:6 463
57:13 355
57:20 346
58:2 326
58:5 345
58:7 167
59:15–16 232
60–62 632, 640
60:11 635
60:19 509
61:2 345
61:4 355
62:6 571n1
63:1–6 226n14
63:7–64:12 520
63:8 45
63:10–11 134
63:15 523
65:8 698
65:8–9 355
65:9 355
65:10 472
65:13–15 355
66:11–12 406
66:18–19 71
66:19 273

Jeremiah

1:10 70
1:15 70
2:5 251, 416
2:12–13 550
2:14 637
2:21 540
2:22 127
2:31 167
3:1 416
3:10 498
3:12 541
3:19 695
3:20 507
3:21 706
4:2 393
4:6 228
4:10 339
4:19 166

4:29 488n46
5:1–5 152
5:11 507
5:14 524
5:17 524
6:1 613
6:11 350
6:14 611
7 510, 516
7:33 43
8:11 611
9:2 166
9:3 595n32
9:8 166
10:16 425
10:25 153, 350,
    522, 523,
    523n18
11:10 489
11:15 229
11:16 146
11:19 576
12:12 237
13:10 554
13:24 581
14–15 611
15:8 498
15:10 538
16:4 43
16:11–13 554
17:9 133
17:11 166
17:27 524
18:16 44
18:17 495
18:21 261
19:7 43
20:7 499
21:13 238
22:28–30 670
23 694
23:5–6 692
23:16 251
23:18 561, 671
23:22 671
24:1–9 510
24:9 522
25:37 434
26 516
26:18 521
28:9 611

29:18 522
30–33 355
30:3 355
30:18 505
30:21 277
31:9 232
31:12 325
31:15–16 463
31:24 355
32:2 651
32:20 502
32:39 577n18, 625
32:42 611
33:7 355
33:10 350
33:11 401
38:6 340
38:22 152, 340
38:24 47
39:5 350
42:16 350
48:28 433n57
51:19 425

Lamentations

1:4 350
1:8 435
1:10 520
1:15 495
1:18 507
1:20 507
2:3 430, 581
2:4 350
2:6 427n38
2:7 427, 685
2:9 429
2:11 537
2:15 86, 93, 111
2:19 249, 462
3:17 654
3:24 415
3:25 401
3:31 425, 465
3:34 528
3:42 507
3:49 463, 463n21
3:57–58 347
4:11 350
4:12 520
4:14 219
4:15 219

5 423, 520, 525
5:1 522
5:19–22 465
5:20 425
5:22 509

Ezekiel

3:2 484
3:27 484
5:14–15 522
7:22 576
8:3 344
8:5 344
9 504
12:13 292
13:10 611
13:16 611
14:22 463
15 542
16 129
16:52 152
16:53 155
17:2 485
20:8 350, 507
20:13 350, 507
20:21 350, 507
21:31 350
21:32 576
22:4–5 522
22:31 350
23 416
23:34 406
23:41 61n29
25:10 576
26:17 85n13
26:21 410
27–28 61
27:9 578
29:3–5 431
29:7 350
29:16 468
30:3 555
30:4 331
30:7 350
30:9 331
30:14 490
30:15 350
32:31 463
33:1–9 137
33:22 484
33:28 350

34:14 325
36:24 105
36:26 132
37:1–14 609
37:21 105
39:3 452
39:14 46
40–48 634, 640
40:43 322n74
40:46 277
44:10 416
44:15–16 277

Daniel

1–6 568
2:37 672
4:27 57
4:30 672
6 266
6:10 242
7:7 579
7:18 672
7:22 672
8:13 671
8:19 442
9 124, 640
9:16 524
9:18 522
10 568, 569
11 410
11:27 442
11:29 442
11:35 442
12:2 104

Hosea

5:10 350
6:4 611
6:5 484
7:10 498
7:11 433n57
7:16 482
8:3 228
9:10 677
10:14 482, 488
11:5 489
11:11 433n57
13:14 105
14:1–2 541
14:4 135, 161, 320

14:5 701
14:6 146

Joel

1 37
1:7 503
1:14 37
1:20 22
2:17 526
3:17 520
3:18 385, 639

Amos

1–2 579
1:3–2:3 565
2:6 43
3:2 221n21
3:14 541
3:15 59
4:2 229
5:6 581
5:22 115
6:4 59
7:10–17 540
9:1–4 327
9:2 653
9:3 327
9:5 443

Obadiah

18 469

Jonah

2:3 27, 340
4:10–11 390

Micah

1:3 426
1:6 521
2:3 444
3:2–3 415
3:4 420n2
3:12 521
4:1 634, 638
6:4 472
6:7 115

Nahum

1:7 401
2:12–13 452
3:6 177
3:9 331

Habakkuk

1:3 538
1:8 217
2:1 610, 610n18
3 310, 318
3:10 319
3:10–15 468
3:12 318
3:13 318

Zephaniah

1:6 543
3:3 217
3:8 350
3:15 538

Haggai

2:18 633
2:20–23 277
2:22 78

Zechariah

1:12 605
1:12–17 529
1:15 524
1:21 575
2:1 506
2:12 569
3:1–5 561
4:9 633
7–8 424, 520
8:9 633
9:9 55n15
9:14 495
12:7 505
14:16–17 594

Malachi

3:2 178
3:5 347
3:10 494

3:12 393
3:13–4:3 419
4:2 705

New Testament

Matthew

5:35 93
13:34–35 485
17:17 166
23:35 529

Mark

1:14–15 81
4:38 50
14:34 26
16:8 658

Luke

11:5–10 655
12:16–21 107
18:1–8 473, 529, 655
18:8 210

John

2:17 356
6:31 496
10:11–15 425
12:27 26
13 140
15:25 356
19:28–29 356

Acts

1:16 356
1:20 356
2 640
2:9–11 640

Romans

1:24–32 557
8:36 47, 50
11:9–10 356
11:17–18 516
12:1 116

743

15:3 356
15:18–32 93

1 Corinthians

1:27–31 94
3:17 602
10:1–11 480
10:10 504
15:24–25 570

2 Corinthians

1:10 419

Galatians

4:25 93
4:26 93, 640

Ephesians

2:19 640
4:7–10 310
4:8 326n83
6:12 209, 570
6:18 209, 570

Philippians

1:9–11 394

Colossians

1:15–16 570
2:15 570

1 Thessalonians

1:10 419

1 Timothy

3:16 414n62

Hebrews

1:8–9 53n6
7:1–2 451

11 499
11:10 93
11:28 504
12:22 93

1 Peter

2:5 602
3:22 570

Revelation

3:12 93
4–5 671
6:9–11 162, 529
7 640
12:3 431
15:4 630
16:1 356
16:6 529
17:3 431
20:11–15 104
21:2 93
21:10 93
21:14 93
21:27 356

Old Testament Apocrypha

1 Maccabees

1–9 37
5 573
7:17 519

Old Testament Pseudepigrapha

Psalms of Solomon

17:21–43 382

Qumran / Dead Sea Scrolls

4Q236

see 4QPs^x

4QPs^a

on Ps. 69
336nn6–7

4QPs^e

on Ps. 89 663n11

4QPs^s

on Ps. 88 656n37

4QPs^t

on Ps. 88 656n37

4QPs^x

on Ps. 89 665,
668n26,
676n37, 678n39

4QPs89

see 4QPs^x

Rabbinic Writings

Babylonian Talmud

Soṭah

48a 48

Qiddušin

30a 500n60

Makkot

22b 500n60

Midrash Tehillim/ Psalms

on Ps. 42 27n15
on Ps. 47 78
on Ps. 53 151
on Ps. 55
166n15, 178n43
on Ps. 57 198n20
on Ps. 58 201n1,
210n37, 698n6
on Ps. 59 213,
214n9
on Ps. 60 228,
228n20, 232,
232n31
on Ps. 61
238n13, 340n19
on Ps. 64 266,
266n13
on Ps. 68
323n77, 325n83
on Ps. 69 355,
355n41
on Ps. 73 401,
401n29, 414,
414n61
on Ps. 75 445n23
on Ps. 77 467n31
on Ps. 78 484,
484n43
on Ps. 79 520,
520n13
on Ps. 82 561,
561n16, 567n36
on Ps. 83 585n34
on Ps. 87 634n16